THE INTERNATIONAL BIBLIOGRAPHY OF SOCIOLOGY

This bibliography, with its sister publications, Anthropology, Economics, and Political Science (known together as the *International Bibliography of the Social Sciences (IBSS)*) is an essential tool for librarians, academics and researchers wishing to keep up to date with the published literature in the social sciences.

The *IBSS* lists journal articles and monographs from all over the world and in over 70 languages, all with English title translations where needed.

From 1991, users already familiar with the bibliography will notice major improvements in contents and currency. There is greater coverage of monographs as well as journals, with continued emphasis on international publications, especially those from the developing world and Eastern Europe. Indexing techniques have been refined: the *IBSS* now offers more specific subject and geographical indexes together with an author index. A subject index in French continues to be provided.

Prepared until 1989 at the *Fondation nationale des sciences politiques* in Paris, the *IBSS* is now compiled and edited by the *British Library of Political and Economic Science* at the *London School of Economics*. The *International Committee for Social Science Information and Documentation* and UNESCO continue to support the publication. The new *International Bibliography* not only maintains its traditional extensive coverage of periodical literature, but considerably extends its coverage of monographic material by incorporating most of that which would previously have been included in the *London Bibliography of the Social Sciences*, publication of which has now been discontinued.

Also available from Routledge

Copies of the *International Bibliography of the Social Sciences* for previous years.

Thematic Lists of Descriptors. Four subject volumes published in 1989, following the classification and index terms of the relevant volume of the *IBSS*.

Copies of the *London Bibliography of the Social Sciences* for previous years are available from Schmidt Periodicals, Dettendorf, D-8201 Bad Feilnbach 2, Germany.

INTERNATIONAL BIBLIOGRAPHY OF THE SOCIAL SCIENCES

BIBLIOGRAPHIE INTERNATIONALE DES SCIENCES SOCIALES

[published annually in four parts / paraissant chaque année en quatre parties: since 1961/jusqu'en 1961: UNESCO, Paris]

International bibliography of sociology / Bibliographie internationale de sociologie [red cover / couverture rouge] Vol.1:1951 (publ. 1952)

International bibliography of political science / Bibliographie internationale de science politique [grey cover / couverture grise] Vol.1:1952 (publ. 1954)

International bibliography of economics / Bibliographie internationale de science économique [yellow cover / couverture jaune] Vol.1:1952 (publ. 1955)

International bibliography of social and cultural anthropology / Bibliographie internationale d'anthropologie sociale et culturelle [green cover / couverture vert] Vol.1:1955 (publ. 1958)

Prepared by

THE BRITISH LIBRARY OF POLITICAL AND ECONOMIC SCIENCE

with the support of the International Committee for Social Science Information and Documentation with the assistance of UNESCO

Editor
Lynne J. Brindley
Librarian, British Library of Political and Economic Science

Editorial Manager
Christopher C.P. Doutney

Assistant Manager
Caroline S. Shaw

Database Design
Robert H. Browne

Editorial Assistants
Claire Chandler
Imogen Daulby
Caroline Hunt
Miranda Hutt
Kate Kilpatrick

INTERNATIONAL BIBLIOGRAPHY OF THE SOCIAL SCIENCES

1993

INTERNATIONAL BIBLIOGRAPHY OF SOCIOLOGY

VOLUME XLIII

BIBLIOGRAPHIE INTERNATIONALE DES SCIENCES SOCIALES

BIBLIOGRAPHIE INTERNATIONALE DE SOCIOLOGIE

Prepared with the support of the International Committee for Social Science Information and Documentation with the financial assistance of UNESCO

Établie avec le concours du Comité international pour l'information et la documentation en sciences sociales avec l'assistance financière de l'UNESCO

London and New York

First published in 1994 by
Routledge
(on behalf of The British Library of Political and Economic Science)
UNESCO subvention 1994-1995, SHS/IDS/53

11 New Fetter Lane
London EC4P 4EE
&
29 West 35th Street
New York, NY 100001

©1994, British Library of Political and Economic Science

Typeset in Great Britain by
Castle Printers, London

Printed in Great Britain by
T.J. Press (Padstow), Padstow, Cornwall

All rights reserved. No part of this book may be reprinted or reproduced or utilized in any form or by any electronic, mechanical, or other means, now known or hereafter invented, including photocopying and recording, or in any information storage or retrieval system, without permission in writing from the publishers.

British Library Cataloguing in Publication Data

A CIP catalogue record for this book is available from the British Library.
ISBN 0-415-11149-8
ISSN 0085-2066

Editorial Correspondence should be sent to:

International Bibliography of the Social Sciences
British Library of Political and Economic Science
London School of Economics
10 Portugal Street
London WC2A 2HD
United Kingdom

Telephone: (U.K.) 071-955-7144
Fax: (U.K.) 071-242-5904
email: ibss@lse.ac.uk

CONTENTS

International Committee for Social Science Information and Documentation	vi
Preface	vii
Selection Criteria	ix
List of periodicals consulted	xi
List of abbreviations	lxvii
Classification scheme	ciii
Bibliography for 1993	1
Author index	367
Geographical index	467
Subject index	475
Index des matières	537

INTERNATIONAL COMMITTEE FOR SOCIAL SCIENCE INFORMATION AND DOCUMENTATION

LE COMITÉ INTERNATIONAL POUR L'INFORMATION ET LA DOCUMENTATION EN SCIENCES SOCIALES

Serge Hurtig, Fondation nationale des sciences politiques, Paris (Chair)

Arnaud Marks, SWIDOC/KNAW, Amsterdam (Secretary General)

ACKNOWLEDGEMENTS

The Editor would like to thank the members of the International Committee, and all those who have contributed to the production of these volumes, particularly: Iris von Essen of Eduskunnan Kirjasto, the Library of Parliament at Helsinki; Dr Katalin Pinter of the Library of the Hungarian Parliament, Budapest; Ekkehart Seusing of the Zentralbibliothek der Wirtschaftswissenschaften, Bibliothek des Instituts für Weltwirtschaft, Kiel; and, Dr Mamoru Yamada of the Japanese Sociological Association.

PREFACE

The **International Bibliography of the Social Sciences** is an annual four volume publication covering Economics, Political Science, Sociology and Social and Cultural Anthropology. It is compiled by the British Library of Political and Economic Science under the auspices of the International Committee for Social Science Information and Documentation. Financial assistance from UNESCO is gratefully acknowledged.

Some 100,000 articles (from over 2,500 journals) and 20,000 books are scanned each year in the process of compiling the **International Bibliography**. Coverage is international with publications in over 70 languages from more than 60 countries. All titles are given in their original language and in English translation.

The selection policy (criteria appear on page ix) is designed to provide a tool for retrospective search rather than current awareness. Each volume represents the most significant new material published in that discipline in a given year.

With the increase in interdisciplinary material published in the social sciences, some items will be listed in more than one of the four volumes. It is nonetheless advisable to check other disciplines in the series to avoid missing relevant items which may for some reason be cited in only one volume.

Production of the **International Bibliography** is computerized. The database from which it is extracted is to be made available on CD-ROM from the end of 1994, providing access to a broader range of material than is cited in these volumes, and updated quarterly.

PRÉFACE

La **Bibliographie internationale des sciences sociales** est un ouvrage annuel en 4 volumes couvrant la science économique, la science politique, la sociologie et l'anthropologie sociale et culturelle. Elle est préparée par la British Library of Political and Economic Science sous les auspices du Comité international pour l'information et la documentation en sciences sociales, et bénéficie de l'assistance financière de l'UNESCO.

Chaque année, quelques 100,000 articles (provenant de 2,500 périodiques) et 20,000 livres sont analysés et indexés en vue de la préparation de la **Bibliographie internationale**. Il s'agit d'une bibliographie véritablement internationale puisqu'elle comprend des publications en plus de 70 langues, provenant de plus de 60 pays. Tous les titres sont présentés dans la langue originale avec une traduction en anglais.

Dans le choix des références, on a davantage cherché à fournir un instrument de recherche retrospective plutôt qu'un service d'information courante. Chaque volume présente les publications les plus significatives parues dans cette discipline au cours d'une année donnée.

Du fait du nombre croissant de publications de nature interdisciplinaire dans les sciences sociales, certains éléments peuvent apparaître dans plus d'un des 4 volumes. Il est cependant conseillé de se reporter aux autres volumes disciplinaires de la série, au cas où des références importantes ne figuraient que dans un seul volume.

La préparation de la **Bibliographie internationale** est informatisée. La base de données dont elle est issue sera disponible sur CD-ROM à partir de la fin 1994. Elle donnera accès à une plus large sélection de publications que celles citées dans ces volumes, et sera mise à jour 4 fois par an.

SELECTION CRITERIA

1. Subject.

Documents relevant to sociology.

2. Nature and form.

Publications of known authorship and lasting significance to sociology, whether in serial or monographic form, typically works with a theoretical component intending to communicate new knowledge, new ideas or making use of new materials.

Previously published materials in all formats are omitted, including most translations. Also excluded are textbooks, materials from newspapers or news magazines, popular or purely informative papers, presentations of predominantly primary data and legislative or judicial texts and items of parochial relevance only.

LIST OF PERIODICALS CONSULTED
LISTE DES PERIODIQUES CONSULTÉS

ABA banking journal. New York, NY.
Aboriginal history. (0314-8769). Canberra.
Academy of management journal. (0001-4273). Ohio.
Acadiensis: Journal of the history of the Atlantic Region. (0004-5851). Fredericton, N.B.
Accounting and business research. (0001-4788). London.
Accounting review. (0001-4826). Sarasota, FL.
Accounting, business and financial history. (0958-5206). London.
Accounting, organizations and society. (0361-3682). Oxford.
Acta asiatica. (0567-7254). Tokyo.
Acta ethnographica. (0001-5628). Budapest.
Acta juridica. (0001592X). Budapest.
Acta juridica hungarica. (0001-592X). Budapest.
Acta oeconomica. (0001-6373). Budapest.
Acta politica. (0001-6810). Meppel.
Acta sociologica. (0001-6993). Oslo.
Acta sumerologica. (0387-8082). Ohsawa.
Acta Universitatis Carolinae: Oeconomica. (0563-038X). Prague.
Acta Universitatis Łódziensis: Folia oeconomica. (0208-6018). Łódz.
Acta Universitatis Łódziensis: Folia sociologica. (0208-600X). Łódz.
Actas de las legislaturas provinciales. Mendoza.
Actualité économique. (0001-771X). Montreal.
Addiction. (0965-2140). Abingdon, Oxfordshire, U.K.
Administration. (0001-8325). Dublin.
Administration and society. (0095-3997). Newbury Park, CA.
Administration for development. (0311-4511). Boroko.
Administrative science quarterly. (0001-8392). Ithaca, NY.
Adoption and fostering. (0308-5759). London.
Advances in public interest accounting. Greenwich, CN.
Affari sociali internazionali. Milan.
Africa. (0001-9720). Manchester.
Africa development = Afrique & developpement. (0850-3907). Dakar.
Africa insight. (0256-2804). Pretoria.
Africa perspective. Witwatersrand.
Africa quarterly. (0001-9828). New Delhi.
Africa today. (0001-9887). Denver, CO.
African affairs. (0001-9909). Oxford.
African arts. (0001-9933). Los Angeles, CA.
African communist. (0001-9976). London.
African development review = Revue africaine de développement. Abidjan.
African economic history. (0145-2258). Boston, MA.

Liste des periodiques consultés

African journal of international and comparative law = Revue africaine de droit international et comparé. (0954-8890). London.
African languages and cultures. (0954-416X). London.
African music. (0065-4019). Grahamstown.
African notes. (0002-0087). Ibadan.
African review. (0856-0056). Dar es Salaam.
African studies. (0002-0184). Witwatersrand.
African studies review. (0002-0206). Atlanta, GA.
African study monographs. (0285-1601). Kyoto.
African study monographs. Supplementary issues. (0286-9667). Kyoto.
African urban quarterly. Nairobi.
Africana. (0871-2336). Porto.
Africana bulletin. (0002-029X). Warsaw.
Africana gandensia. Ghent.
Africana Marburgensia. (0174-5603). Berlin.
Africana research bulletin. Freetown.
Afrika Spectrum. (0002-0397). Hamburg.
Afrique 2000. (1017-0952). Brussels.
Afrique contemporaine. (0002-0478). Paris.
Afrique et l'Asie modernes. (0399-0370). Paris.
Afro-Asian solidarity. Cairo.
Ageing and society. (0144-686X). Cambridge.
Agenda. (1013-0950). Durban.
Agrekon. (0303-1853). Monument Park.
Agricultura y sociedad. (0211-8394). Madrid.
Agricultural history. (0002-1482). Berkeley, CA.
Agriculture and resources quarterly. (1032-9722). Canberra.
Ahfad journal. Omdurman.
Akademika. (0126-5008). Selangor.
Al Muntaka. (0753-9894). France.
Al-Abhath. Beirut.
Al-Qantara. (0211-3589). Madrid.
Albania today. (0044-7072). Tirana.
Állam és jogtudomány. (0002-564X). Budapest.
Allgemeines statistisches Archiv. (0002-6018). Göttingen.
Alternatives. (0304-3754). Boulder.
Amazonia peruana. (0252-886X). Lima.
América indígena. (0002-7081). Mexico City.
American anthropologist. (0002-7294). Washington, DC.
American behavioral scientist. (0002-7642). Newbury Park, CA.
American economic review. (0002-8282). Nashville, TN.
American ethnologist. (0094-0496). Washington, DC.
American historical review. (0002-8702). Washington, DC.
American Jewish history. (0164-0178). Waltham, MA.
American journal of agricultural economics. (0002-9092). Ames, IA.
American journal of comparative law. (0002-919X). Berkeley, CA.
American journal of economics and sociology. (0002-9246). New York, NY.
American journal of international law. (0002-9300). Washington, DC.

List of periodicals consulted

American journal of Islamic social sciences. (0742-6763). Herndon, VA.
American journal of orthopsychiatry. (0002-9432). New York, NY.
American journal of physical anthropology. (0002 9483). New York, NY.
American journal of political science. (0092-5853). Austin, TX.
American journal of primatology. (0275-2565). New York, NY.
American journal of sociology. (0024-9602). Chicago, IL.
American philosophical quarterly. (0003-0481). Bowling Green, OH.
American political science review. (0003-0554). Washington, DC.
American psychologist. (0003-066X). Arlington, VA.
American review of Canadian studies. (0272-2011). Washington, DC.
American sociological review. (0003-1224). Washington, D.C.
American sociologist. (0003-1232). New Brunswick, NJ.
Amerindia. (0221-8852). Paris.
Anadolu/ Anatolia. Ankara.
Anales de ciencias politicas y sociales. Mendoza.
Anales de estudios económicos y empresariales. (0213-7569). Valladolid.
Análise social. (0003-2573). Lisbon.
Analysis. (0003-2638). Oxford.
Anarchist studies. (0967-3393). Cambridge.
Anatolian studies. London.
Ancient Nepal. Kathmandu, Nepal.
Annales æquatoria. (0254-4296). Mbandaka.
Annales d'économie et de statistique. (0769-489X). Paris.
Annales d'études internationales = Annals of international studies. (0066-2135). Brussels.
Annales de droit de Louvain. (0770-6472). Louvain.
Annales de géographie. (0003-4010). Paris.
Annales de l'économie publique sociale et coopérative = Annals of public and cooperative economics. (0770-8548). Brussels.
Annales de l'IFORD. Yaounde, Cameroon.
Annales internationales de criminologie = International annals of criminology = Anales internacionales de criminologia. (0003-4452). Paris.
Annales universitatis Mariae Curie-Skłodowska: Sectio H. Oeconomia. (0459-9586). Lublin.
Annales universitatis scientiatum budapestiensis de Rolando Eötvos nominatae: Sectio iuridica. Budapest.
Annales: Économies, sociétés, civilisations. (0395-2649). Paris.
Annali della fondazione Luigi Einaudi. Turin.
Annali della fondazione Luigi Micheletti. Brescia.
Annali di ca'foscari. Venice.
Annali. Istituto Universitario Orientale. Naples.
Annals of family studies. Tokyo.
Annals of human biology. (0301-4460). London.
Annals of regional science. (0570-1864). Heidelberg.
Annals of the American Academy of Political and Social Science. (0002-7162). Newbury Park, CA.
Annals of the Association of American Geographers. (0004-5608). Washington, DC.
Annals of the Institute of Statistical Mathematics. Tokyo.
Annals of the Institute of Social Science. (0563-8054). Tokyo.
Annals of the South African Museum. (0303-2515). Cape Town.

Liste des periodiques consultés

Année africaine. (0570-1937). Paris.
Année sociale. (0066-2380). Brussels.
Année sociologique. (0066-2399). Paris.
Annuaire de l'Afrique du Nord. (0242-7540). Paris.
Annuaire des pays de l'Ocean indien. (0247-400X). Paris.
Annuaire européen = European yearbook. (0071-3139). Dordrecht.
Annual bulletin. Kobe.
Annual of Institute Kanazawa Economical College. Kanazawa City.
Annual of the Department of Antiquities of Jordan. Amman.
Annual of the Institute of Economic Research Chuo University. Tokyo.
Annual report of studies in humanities and social sciences. Nara City.
Annual report of University of Shizuoka, Hamamatsu College. Shizuoka.
Annual research report of Education Department of Rikkyo University. Tokyo.
Annual review of anthropology. (0084-6570). Palo Alto, CA.
Annual review of energy and the environment. (0362-1626). Palo Alto, CA.
Annual review of information science and technology. (0066-4200). Amsterdam.
Annual review of psychology. (0066-4308). Palo Alto, CA.
Annual review of public health. (0163-7525). Palo Alto, CA.
Annual review of sociology. (0360-0572). Palo Alto, CA.
Anthropological forum. (0066-4677). Nedlands.
Anthropological linguistics. (0003-5483). Bloomington, IN.
Anthropological papers of the American Museum of Natural History. (0065-9452). New York, NY.
Anthropological quarterly. (0003-5491). Washington, DC.
Anthropologie [Paris]. (0003-5521). Paris.
Anthropologie visuelle. Paris.
Anthropology and aesthetics. (0277-1322). Santa Monica, CA.
Anthropology and humanism quarterly. Washington, DC.
Anthropology today. (0307-6776). London.
Anthropos [Athens]. (1105-2155). Athens.
Anthropos [Fribourg]. (0257-9774). Fribourg.
Antipode. (0066-4812). Oxford.
Antiquités africaines. (0066-4871). Paris.
Antiquity. (0003-598X). Oxford.
Antropología. (1131-5814). Madrid.
Antropologia portuguesa. (0870-0990). Coimbra.
Antropologica. (0003-6110). Caracas.
Antropologiska studier. (0003-6129). Stockholm.
Anuario de estudios centroamericanos. (0377-7316). San Jose.
Anuario de eusko folklore. (0210-7732). San Sebastián.
Anuario indigenista. (0185-5441). Colonia Florida.
Anuarul Institutului de Etnografie şi Folclor „Constantin Brăiloiu". (1220-5230). Bucharest.
Apk. ekonomika upravlenie. Moscow.
Applied community studies. (0954-4232). London.
Applied economics. (0003 6846). London.
Applied financial economics. (0960-3107). London.
Appropriate technology. (0305-0920). London.
Apuntes. (0252-1865). Lima.

List of periodicals consulted

Arab affairs. (0950-0731). London.
Arab journal for the humanities. Kuwait.
Arab law quarterly. (0268-0556). London.
Arab studies quarterly. (0271-3519). Belmont, MA.
Arabica. (0570-5398). Leiden.
Archaeology in Oceania. (0003-8121). Sydney.
Archeologia. (0066-605X). Wroclaw.
Archeologia polona. (0066-5924). Wroclaw.
Archeologia polski. (0003-8180). Wroclaw.
Archipel. (0044-8613). Paris.
Archiv des öffentlichen Rechts. (0003-8911). Tübingen.
Archiv des Völkerrechts. (0003-892X). Tübingen.
Archiv für Kommunalwissenschaften. (0003-9209). Stuttgart.
Archiv für Rechts- und Sozialphilosophie = Archives de philosophie du droit et de philosophie sociale = Archives for philosophy of law and social philosophy = Archivo de filosofía jurídica y social. (0001-2343). Stuttgart.
Archiv für Sozialgeschichte. (0066-6505). Bonn.
Archív orientální. (0044-8699). Prague.
Archives européennes de sociologie = European journal of sociology = Europäisches Archiv für Soziologie. (0003-9756). Cambridge.
Archivio di studi urbani e regionali. Milan.
Area. (0004-0894). London.
Argumentation. (0920-427X). Dordrecht.
Armed forces and society. (0095-327X). New Brunswick, NJ.
Arquivo. Maputo.
Artha vijñāna. (0004-3559). Pune.
Artibus asiae. (0004-3648). Ascona.
Artificial intelligence. (0004-3702). Amsterdam.
ASEAN economic bulletin. (0217-4472). Singapore.
Asia and Africa today. (0134-451X). Moscow.
Asia journal of theology. (0218-0812). Singapore.
Asia major. (0004-4482). Princeton, NJ.
Asian and African studies. (0066-8281). Haifa.
Asian and Pacific Migration Journal. (0117-1968). Quezon City.
Asian culture (Asian-Pacific culture) quarterly. (0378-8911). Taipei.
Asian economic journal. Hong Kong.
Asian economic review. (0004-4555). Hyderabad.
Asian economies. (0304-260X). Seoul.
Asian folklore studies. (0385-2342). Nagoya.
Asian journal of public administration. (0259-8272). Hong Kong.
Asian music. (0044-9202). Ithaca, NY.
Asian Pacific communication. (0957-6851). Clevedon, U.K.
Asian perspective [S. Korea]. Seoul.
Asian perspectives [Hawaii]. (0066-8435). Honolulu, HI.
Asian profile. (0304-8675). Hong Kong.
Asian studies review. (0314-7533). Sydney.
Asian survey. (0004-4687). Berkeley, CA.
Asian thought and society. (0361-3968). New York, NY.

Liste des periodiques consultés

Asian-Pacific economic literature. (0818-9935). Guildford.
Asien Afrika Lateinamerika. (0323-3790). Berlin.
Atlal. The journal of Saudi Arabian archaeology. Riyadh.
Aussenpolitik. (0587-3835). Hamburg.
Aussenwirtschaft. (0004-8216). Zürich.
Australian Aboriginal studies. (0729-4352). Canberra.
Australian and New Zealand journal of sociology. (0004-8690). Bundoora.
Australian cultural history. (0728-8433). Kensington, NSW.
Australian economic history review. (0004-8992). Melbourne.
Australian economic papers. (0004-900X). Adelaide.
Australian economic review. (0004-9018). Melbourne.
Australian foreign affairs and trade: The monthly record. (1033-5722). Canberra.
Australian geographer. (0004-9182). Gladesville, NSW.
Australian geographical studies. (0004-9190). Campbell.
Australian Historical Association bulletin. (03212-6986). Canberra.
Australian historical studies. (1031-461X). Carlton.
Australian journal of agricultural economics. (0004-9395). East Melbourne.
Australian journal of Chinese affairs. (0156-7365). Canberra.
Australian journal of international affairs. (0004-9913). Canberra.
Australian journal of linguistics. (0726-8602). Cambridge.
Australian journal of political science. (0032-3268). Canberra.
Australian journal of politics and history. (0004-9522). Queensland.
Australian journal of public administration. (0313-6647). Sydney.
Australian journal of social issues. (0157-6321). Sydney.
Australian journal of statistics. (0004-9581). Canberra.
Australian law journal. (0004-9611). North Ryde, NSW.
Australian National University, Department of Anthropology, occasional papers. Canberra.
Australian quarterly. (0005-0091). Balmain.
Australian studies. (0954-0954). Stirling.
Australian-Canadian studies. (0810-1906). Nathan, Queensland.
Austrian history yearbook. (0667-2378). Minneapolis, MN.
AWR Bulletin. (0014-2492). Vienna.
Awrāq. (0213-6635). Madrid.
Azania. (0067-270X). Nairobi.
Aziia i Afrika segodnia. Moscow.
Baessler-Archiv. (0005-3856). Berlin.
Banaras law journal. Varanasi.
Banca Nazionale del Lavoro quarterly review. (0005-4607). Rome.
Bancaria. (0005-4623). Rome.
Bangladesh development studies. (0304-095X). Dhaka.
Bangladesh journal of political economy. Dhaka.
Bangladesh journal of public administration. Dhaka.
Bank of England quarterly bulletin. (0005-5166). London.
Bank-Archiv. (1015-1516). Vienna.
Banker. (0005-5395). London.
Basler Afrika Bibliographien Nachrichten/ newsletter. (0171-0087). Basle.
BC studies. (0005-2949). Vancouver.
Behavior science research. (0094-3673). New Haven, CT.

List of periodicals consulted

Behavioral and brain sciences. (0140-525X). New York, NY.
Behavioral science. (0005-7940). Baltimore, MD.
Beiträge zur Geschichte der Arbeiterbewegung. (0005-8068). Berlin.
Beiträge zur Japanologie. (0522-6759). Vienna.
Belizean studies. (0250-6831). Belize City.
Benelux. Brussels.
Berkeley journal of sociology. (0067-5830). Berkeley, CA.
Berliner indologische Studien. Reinbek.
Berliner journal für Soziologie. (0863-1808). Berlin.
Bevolking en gezin. Brussels/'s-Gravenhage.
Biblical archaeologist. (0006-0895). Baltimore, MD.
Biblioteka etnografii polskiej. (0067-7655). Warsaw.
BIISS journal. (1010-9356). Dhaka.
Bijdragen tot de taal-, land-en volkenkunde. (0006-2294). Leiden.
Bimestre politico y economico. Buenos Aires.
Bioethics. (0269-9702). Oxford.
Biography. (0162-4962). Honolulu, HI.
Boletim do Museu Paraense Emílio Goeldi: Série antropologia. (0522-7291). Belém.
Boletim informativo e bibliográfico de ciências sociais. Rio de Janeiro.
Boletín de antropología americana. (0252-841X). Mexico City.
Boletin de economicas. Buenos Aires.
Boletín de fuentes para la historia económica de México. (0188-3259). Pedregal de Santa Teresa.
Boletin de la Academia Nacional de la Historia. Buenos Aires.
Boletin de la Asociación Española de Orientalistas. Madrid.
Boletin del Instituto Historico de la Ciudad de Buenos Aires. Buenos Aires.
Boletin. Centro de estudios monetarios latinoamericanos. (0186-7229). Mexico City.
Boletin. IWGIA (International Work Group for Indigenous Affairs). (0107-556X). Copenhagen.
Borneo research bulletin. Williamsburg, VA.
Borneo review. Sabah.
Botswana notes and records. (0525-5059). Gaborone.
Botswana review. Ivoryton, CT.
British journal of addiction. (0952-0481). Abingdon.
British journal of Canadian studies. (0269-9222). London.
British journal of clinical psychology. (0144-6657). Leicester.
British journal of criminology. (0007-0955). London.
British journal of educational studies. (0007-1005). Oxford.
British journal of ethnomusicology. (0968 1221). London.
British journal of industrial relations. (0007-1080). Oxford.
British journal of management. (1045-3172). Chichester.
British journal of political science. (0007-1234). Cambridge.
British journal of psychology. (0007-1269). Leicester.
British journal of social psychology. (0144-6665). Leicester.
British journal of social work. (0045-3102). Oxford.
British journal of sociology. (0007-1315). London.
British review of economic issues. (0141-4739). Stoke-on-Trent.
British review of New Zealand studies. (0951-6204). Edinburgh.

Liste des periodiques consultés

British tax review. (0007-1870). London.
British year book of international law. (0068-2691). Oxford.
Brookings papers on economic activity. (0007-2303). Washington, D.C.
Brookings review. (0745-1253). Washington, DC.
Bulletin d'études indiennes. (0761-3156). Paris.
Bulletin de l'Institut fondamental d'Afrique noire: Série B — Sciences humaines. (0018-9642). Dakar.
Bulletin de la Banque Nationale de Belgique. (0005-5611). Brussels.
Bulletin de la Société d'archéologie copte. Cairo.
Bulletin de la Société des études océaniennes. Papeete.
Bulletin des études africaines de l'INALCO. Paris.
Bulletin du Centre genevois d'anthropologie. Louvain.
Bulletin for international fiscal documentation. (0007-4624). Amsterdam.
Bulletin of Aichi University of Education. Aichi.
Bulletin of concerned Asian scholars. (0007-4810). Boulder, CO.
Bulletin of Czechoslovak law. (0323-2719). Prague.
Bulletin of Eastern Caribbean affairs. (0254-7406). Cave Hill.
Bulletin of economic research. (0307-3378). Oxford.
Bulletin of Education. Tokyo.
Bulletin of graduate studies. Tokyo.
Bulletin of Indonesian economic studies. (0007-4918). Canberra.
Bulletin of Latin American research. (0261-3050). Oxford.
Bulletin of peace proposals. (0007-5035). London.
Bulletin of Tanzanian affairs. (0952-2948). London.
Bulletin of the Akita Prefectural College of Agriculture. Akita City.
Bulletin of the American Schools of Oriental Research. (0003-097X). Baltimore, MD.
Bulletin of the Faculty of Education, Chiba University. Chiba.
Bulletin of the Faculty of General Education of Utsunomiya University. Tochigi.
Bulletin of the Faculty of Humanities of Aichi Gakuin University. Aichi.
Bulletin of the Faculty of Sociology. Kyoto.
Bulletin of the Indian Institute of History of Medicine. (0304-9558). New Delhi.
Bulletin of the Institute of Ethnology, Academia Sinica. (0001-3935). Taipei.
Bulletin of the International Committee on Urgent Anthropological and Ethnological Research. (0538-5865). Vienna.
Bulletin of the Museum of Far Eastern Antiquities. (0081-5691). Stockholm.
Bulletin of the Nanzan Institute for Religion and Culture. (0386-720X). Nagoya.
Bulletin of the School of Oriental and African Studies. (0041-977X). London.
Bulletin of Tibetology. (0007-5159). Gangtok.
Bulletin. Bank of Botswana. Gabarone.
Bulletin. Bank of Finland. (0784-6509). Helsinki.
Bulletin. Committee for Middle East Trade. London.
Bulletin. Kagawa University. Takamatsu.
Bulletin. Oita University, Faculty of Education. Oita City.
Bulletin. Tokyo University, Graduate School. Tokyo.
Bulletin. University of the Ryukyus, College of Law and Letters. Okinawa.
Bulletin. Yokohama City University. Yokohama.
Bungaku-kenkyuka Kiyo (Journal of the Waseda Graduate School). Waseda.
Bungakubu ronshu (Journal of the Aichi Prefectural University). Aichi.

List of periodicals consulted

Business economist. (0306-5049). Watford.
Business history. (0007-6791). London.
Business history review. (0007-6805). Boston, MA.
Business library review. (1045-7798). Reading.
Business quarterly. London, Ont.
By og Bygd. (0084-8212). Oslo.
Cahiers africains d'administration publique = African administrative studies. (0007-9588). Tangiers.
Cahiers d'anthropologie et biométrie humaine. (0758-2714). Paris.
Cahiers d'études africaines. (0008-0055). Paris.
Cahiers d'études arabes. (0985-1909). Paris.
Cahiers d'études sur la méditerranée orientale et le monde turco-iranien. (0764-9878). Paris.
Cahiers d'histoire de l'Institut de recherches marxistes. (0246-9731). Paris.
Cahiers d'outre-mer. (0373-5843). Bordeaux.
Cahiers de l'Asie du Sud-Est. (0399-1652). Paris.
Cahiers de l'homme. (0068-5046). Paris.
Cahiers de l'ISSP. Neuchâtel.
Cahiers de la réconciliation. (0007-9839). Paris.
Cahiers de linguistique asie orientale. (0153-3320). Paris.
Cahiers de Tunisie. (0008-0012). Tunis.
Cahiers des Amériques latines. (0008-0020). Paris.
Cahiers des sciences humaines. (0768-9829). Paris.
Cahiers du CEDAF/ ASDOC-studies. (0250-1619). Brussels.
Cahiers du monde russe et soviétique. (0008-0160). Paris.
Cahiers économiques et monétaires. (0396-4701). Paris.
Cahiers internationaux de sociologie. (0008-0276). Paris.
Cahiers ivoiriens de recherche linguistique. (0252-9386). Abidjan.
California management review. (0008-1256). Berkeley, CA.
Cambridge anthropology. Cambridge.
Cambridge archaeological journal. (0959-7743). Cambridge.
Cambridge journal of economics. (0309-166X). London.
Cambridge law journal. (0008-1973). Cambridge.
Cambridge review of international affairs. (0955-7571). Cambridge.
Canadian Association of African Studies newsletter = Association canadienne des études africaines bulletin. (0228-8397). Ottawa.
Canadian geographer. (0008-3658). Montreal.
Canadian historical review. (0008-3755). Toronto.
Canadian journal of African studies = Revue canadienne des études africaines. (0008-3968). Ottawa.
Canadian journal of agricultural economics = Revue canadienne d'économie rurale. (0008-3976). Ottawa.
Canadian journal of economics = Revue canadienne d'économique. (0008-4085). Downsview.
Canadian journal of philosophy. (0045-5091). Calgary.
Canadian journal of political and social theory. (0380-9420). Montreal.
Canadian journal of political science = Revue canadienne de science politique. (0008-4239). Ottawa.
Canadian journal of sociology = Cahiers canadiens de sociologie. (0318-6431). Edmonton.

Liste des periodiques consultés

Canadian journal of statistics = Revue canadienne de statistiques. (0319-5724). Ottawa.
Canadian public administration = Administration publique du Canada. (0008-4840). Toronto.
Canadian review of sociology and anthropology = Revue canadienne de sociologie et d'anthropologie. (0008-4948). Montreal.
Canadian review of studies in nationalism = Revue canadienne des études sur le nationalisme. (0317-7904). Charlottetown.
Canadian yearbook of international law = Annuaire canadien de droit international. (0069-0058). Vancouver.
Canberra anthropology. (0314-9099). Canberra.
Capital and class. (0309-8786). London.
Capitalism, nature, socialism. (1045-5752). New York, NY.
Caravelle. (0008-0152). Toulouse.
Care in place. (0969-2304). London.
Caribbean quarterly. (0008-6495). Kingston.
Caribbean studies = Estudios del Caribe = Études des Caraïbes. (0008-6533). Puerto Rico.
Caribe contemporáneo. (0185-2426). Mexico City.
Cato journal. (0273-3072). Washington, DC.
Central Asian survey. (0263-4937). Oxford.
Central Asiatic journal. Wiesbaden.
Central banking. (0960-6319). London.
CEPAL review. (0251-2920). Santiago, Chile.
Český lid. (0009-0794). Prague.
Challenge. (0577-5132). Armonk, N.Y.
CHEC journal. London.
Child development. (0009-3920). Chicago, IL.
Child welfare. (0009-4021). Washington, DC.
Children and society. (0951-0605). London.
China business review. (0163-7169). Washington, DC.
China city planning review. (1002-8447). Beijing.
China information. (0920-203X). Leiden.
China law reporter. Chicago, IL.
China newsletter. (0285-7529). Tokyo.
China quarterly. (0009-4439). London.
China reform. Hong Kong.
China report. (0009-4455). New Delhi.
Chinese culture. (0009-4544). Taiwan.
Chinese economic studies. (0009-4552). Armonk, NY.
Chinese sociology and anthropology. (0009-4625). Armonk, NY.
Ching feng. Hong Kong.
Ciências em museus. (0103-2909). Belém.
Ciências sociais hoje. São Paulo.
Cities. (0264-2751). London.
Civilisations. (0009-8140). Brussels.
Civitas. (0009-8191). Rome.
Coastal management. (0892-0753). London.
Coexistence. (0587-5994). Dordrecht.
Cognition. (0010-0277). Amsterdam.
Cognitive linguistics. (0936-5907). Berlin.

List of periodicals consulted

Cognitive science. (0364-0213). Norwood, NJ.
Collection. Purusārtha. (0339-1744). Paris.
Collegium antropologicum. (0350-6134). Zagreb.
Columbia journal of transnational law. (0010-1931). New York, NY.
Columbia journal of world business. (0022-5428). New York, NY.
Columbia law review. (0010-1958). New York, NY.
Commentary. (0010-2601). New York, NY.
Common market law review. (0165-0750). Dordrecht.
Communautés. (0010-3462). Paris.
Communication. (0305-4233). New York, NY.
Communication theory. (1050-3293). New York, NY.
Communisme. (2209-7007). Paris.
Communist and post-communist studies. (0967-067X). Oxford.
Communist economies. (09540113). Abingdon.
Communist economies & economic transformation. (0954-0113). Abingdon.
Community development journal. (0010-3802). Oxford.
Comparative and international law journal of Southern Africa. (0010-4051). Pretoria.
Comparative economic studies. (0888-7233). New York, NY.
Comparative political studies. (0010-4140). Newbury Park, CA.
Comparative politics. (0010-4159). New York, NY.
Comparative social research. (0195-6310). Greenwich, CT.
Comparative studies in society and history. (0010-4175). New York, NY.
Comprehensive urban studies. (0386-3506). Tokyo.
Computational economics. Dordrecht.
Computer science in economics and management. (0921-2736). Dordrecht.
Comunicações do Instituto de Investigação Científica Tropical: Série de ciências etnológicas e etno-museológicas. (0871-178X). Lisbon.
Comunidades y culturas peruanas. Lima.
Comunità internazionale. (0010-5066). Padua.
Conflict quarterly. (0227-1311). New Brunswick.
Conjuntura econômica. (0010-5945). Rio de Janeiro.
Cono sur. (0716-8713). Santiago.
Conservative review. (1047-5990). McLean, VI.
Constitutional political economy. (1043-4062). Fairfax, VA.
Contemporary accounting research. (0823-9150). Toronto.
Contemporary economic policy. (07350007). Huntington Beach, CA.
Contemporary economic problems. (0732 4308). Washington, DC.
Contemporary family therapy. (0892-2764). New York, NY.
Contemporary Pacific. (1043-898X). Honolulu, HI.
Contemporary policy issues. (0735-0007). Huntington Beach, CA.
Contemporary sociology - a journal of reviews. (0094-3061). Washington.
Contemporary Southeast Asia. (0129-797X). Singapore.
Continuity and change. (0268-4160). Cambridge.
Contributions to Indian sociology. (0069-9667). New Delhi.
Contributions to Nepalese studies. Kirtipur.
Contributions to political economy. (0277-5921). London.
Cooperation and conflict. (0010-8367). Oslo.
Corruption and reform. (0169-7528). Dordrecht.

Liste des periodiques consultés

Coyuntura económica. (0120-3576). Bogotá.
Coyuntura social. (0121-2532). Santafé de Bogotá.
Crime and delinquency. (0011-1287). Newbury Park, CA.
Crime and justice. (0192-3234). Chicago, IL.
Crime, law and social change. (0925 4994). Dordrecht.
Criminal law review. (0011-135X). London.
Critica marxista. (0011-152X). Rome.
Critica sociologica. (0011 1546). Rome.
Critical perspectives on accounting. (1045-2354). London.
Critical review. (0891-3811). Chicago.
Critical sociology. (0896-9205). Eugene, OR.
Critique of anthropology. (0308-275X). Amsterdam.
Crossroads. (0741-2037). DeKalb, IL.
Cuadernos americanos. (0185-156X). Mexico City.
Cuadernos de estudios guatemaltecos. (0188-2155). Mexico.
Cuadernos de nuestra América. Havana.
Cuadernos de sección antropologia-etnografia. (0213-0297). San Sebastián.
Cuadernos medico sociales. Rosario.
Cuestiones políticas. Maracaibo.
Cultural anthropology. (0886-7356). Washington, DC.
Cultural studies. (0950-2386). London.
Culture et société. Bujumbura.
Culture, medicine and psychiatry. (0165-005X). Dordrecht.
Curare. (0344-8622). Wiesbaden.
Curator. New York.
Current anthropology. (0111-3204). Washington, DC.
Current history. (0011-3530). Philadelphia, PA.
Current research on peace and violence. (0356-7893). Tampere.
Current sociology. (0011-3921). London.
Current world leaders. (0192-6802). Santa Barbara, CA.
Curriculum journal. (0958-5176). London.
Cyprus journal of economics. (1013-3224). Nicosia.
Cyprus review. (1015-2881). Nicosia.
Czechoslovak and Central European journal. (1056-005X). Flushing, NY.
Czechoslovak economic papers. (0590-5001). Prague.
Dædalus. (0011-5266). Cambridge, MA.
Daigaku ronshu (Bulletin of Hiroshima University). Hiroshima.
Debates de coyuntura económica. (0120-8969). Bogota.
Defence and peace economics. (1043-0717). Yverdon.
Defence economics. (10430717). Reading.
Dekorativnoe iskusstvo SSSR. Moscow.
Delhi law review. Delhi.
Demográfia. (0011-8249). Budapest.
Demografie. (0011-8265). Prague.
Demography. (0070-3370). Washington, DC.
Den'gi i kredit. Moscow.
Derechos humanos. (0327-1846). Buenos Aires.
Desarrollo económico. (0046-001X). Buenos Aires.

List of periodicals consulted

Desarrollo y sociedad. (0120-3584). Bogotá.
Deutschland Archiv: Zeitschrift für das vereinigte Deutschland. (0012-1428). Cologne.
Developing economies. (0012-1533). Tokyo.
Development. (1011-6370). Rome.
Development & socio-economic progress. Cairo.
Development and change. (0012-155X). London.
Development anthropology network. (0756-0488). Binghampton.
Development dialogue. (0345-2328). Uppsala.
Development policy review. (0950-6764). London.
Development Southern Africa. (0376-835X). Halfway House.
Deviant behavior. (0163-9625). London.
Diachronica. (0176-4225). Amsterdam.
Dialectical anthropology. (0304-4092). Dordrecht.
Diplomacy and statecraft. (0959-2296). London.
Dirasat ifriqiyya. Khartoum.
Dirasat: Series A — the humanities. (0255-8033). Amman.
Disasters: Journal of disaster studies and management. (0361-3666). Oxford.
Dissent. (0012-3846). New York, NY.
Documento IWGIA (International Work Group for Indigenous Affairs). (0108-9927). Copenhagen.
Documents. (0151-0827). Paris.
Dokumente. (0012-5172). Bonn.
Dreaming. (1053-0797). New York.
Dreptul. Bucharest.
Droit et pratique du commerce international. Paris.
Droit social. (0012-6438). Paris.
Druzhba narodov. Moscow.
E & S: Économie et statistique. (0336-1451). Paris.
Early China. Berkeley, CA.
East Asian review. Seoul.
East European Jewish affairs. (0038 545X). London.
East European politics and societies. (0888-3254). Berkeley.
East European quarterly. (0012-8449). Boulder, CO.
East-East review. (0861-1667). Sofia, Bulgaria.
Eastern Africa economic review. (0012-866X). Nairobi.
Eastern Africa social science research review. Addis Ababa.
Eastern anthropologist. (0012-8686). Lucknow.
Eastern Buddhist. Kyoto.
Ecological economics. (0921-8009). Amsterdam.
Ecology of food and nutrition. (0367-0244). New York.
Econometric reviews. (0740-4938). New York, NY.
Econometric theory. (0266-4666). New York, NY.
Econometrica. (0012-9682). Evanston, IL.
Economia & lavoro. (0012-978X). Rome.
Economia [Lisbon]. (0870-3531). Lisbon.
Economia [Quito]. (0012-9704). Quito.
Economia e banca. (0393-9243). Trento.
Economia internazionale. (0012-981X). Genova.

Liste des periodiques consultés

Economia y desarrollo. (0252-8584). Havana.
Economic affairs [Calcutta]. (0424-2513). Calcutta.
Economic affairs [London]. (0265-0665). London.
Economic and industrial democracy. (0143-831X). London.
Economic and social history in the Netherlands. (0925-1669). Amsterdam.
Economic and social review. (0012-9984). Dublin.
Economic bulletin. (0013-0036). Athens.
Economic bulletin for Asia and the Pacific. (0378-455X). Bangkok.
Economic bulletin. Banca d'Italia. Rome.
Economic bulletin. National Bank of Egypt. Cairo.
Economic bulletin. Norges bank. (0029-1676). Oslo.
Economic computation and economic cybernetics studies and research. (0424-267X). Bucharest.
Economic development and cultural change. (0013-0079). Chicago, IL.
Economic development quarterly. (0891-2424). Newbury Park, CA.
Economic eye. (0389-0503). Tokyo.
Economic geography. (0013-0095). Worcester, MA.
Economic history review. (0013-0117). Oxford.
Economic inquiry. (0095-2583). Huntington Beach, CA.
Economic journal. (0013-0133). Oxford.
Economic modelling. (0264-9993). Guildford.
Economic notes. (0391-5026). Siena.
Economic papers. [Warsaw]. (0324-864X). Warsaw.
Economic papers. [Australia]. Melbourne.
Economic policy. (0266-4658). Cambridge.
Economic quarterly = Wissenschaftliche Beiträge. (0232-4660). Berlin.
Economic record. (0013-0249). Sydney.
Economic review. (0022-8419). Helsinki.
Economic review. Bank of Israel. (0334-441X). Jerusalem.
Economic review. Federal Reserve Bank of Cleveland. (0013-0281). Cleveland, OH.
Economic review. Federal Reserve Bank of Kansas City. (0161-2387). Kansas City, MO.
Economic studies quarterly. (0557-109X). Tokyo.
Economic systems. (0939-3625). Heidelberg.
Economic systems research. (0953-5314). Abingdon.
Economic theory. (0938-2259). Heidelberg.
Económica. (0013-0419). La Plata.
Economica. (0013-0427). London.
Economics. (0300-4287). Haywards Heath.
Economics and business education. (0969-2509). Hassocks, West Sussex.
Economics and philosophy. (0266-2671). New York, NY.
Economics and politics. (0954-1985). Oxford.
Economics letters. (0165-1765). Amsterdam.
Economics of planning. (0013-0451). Dordrecht.
Économie & finances agricoles. (0070-8798). Paris.
Économie appliquée. (0013-0494). Grenoble.
Économie du centre-est. (0153-4459). Dijon.
Économie internationale. (1240-8093). Paris.
Économie prospective internationale. (0242-7818). Paris.

List of periodicals consulted

Économies et sociétés. (0013-0567). Grenoble.
Economisch en sociaal tijdschrift. (0013-0575). Antwerp.
Economist [Leiden]. (0013-063X). Leiden.
Economy and society. (0308-5147). London.
Ecu. Brussels.
Edinburgh anthropology. (0953-2919). Edinburgh.
Education and urban society. (0013-1245). Newbury Park, CA.
Educational gerontology. (0360-1277). London.
Educational research. (0013-1881). London.
Einheit. (0013-2659). Berlin.
Ekistics. (0013-2942). Athens.
Ekonomický časopis. (0013-3035). Bratislava.
Ekonomika i mat. metody. Moscow.
Ekonomika i org. prom. pr-va. Novosibirsk.
Ekonomika sotrudnichestvo stran-chlenov SEV. Moscow.
Ekonomika sov. ukrainy. Kiev.
Ekonomika str.-va. Moscow.
Ekonomiki nauka. Moscow.
Ekonomisk debatt. (0345-2646). Stockholm.
Ekonomist. (0370-0356). Moscow.
Ekonomski pregled. (0424-7558). Zagreb.
Electoral studies. (0261-3794). Oxford.
Empirica. (0340-8744). Dordrecht.
Employee relations. (0142-5455). Bradford.
Employee responsibilities and rights journal. (0892-7545). New York, NY.
Energy economics. (0140-9883). Oxford.
Energy policy. (0301-4215). Guildford.
English in Africa. (0376-8902). Grahamstown.
English world-wide. (0172-8865). Amsterdam.
Enjeux internationaux travaux et recherches de l'IFRI. (0757-4495). Paris.
Ensayos sobre política económica. (0120-4483). Bogotá.
Entrepreneurship & regional development. (0898-5626). London.
Entrepreneurship, innovation, and change. (1059-0137). New York.
Entrepreneurship: Theory and practice. (1042-2587). Waco, TX.
Environment. (0013-9157). Washington, DC.
Environment and behavior. (0013-9165). Newbury Park, CA.
Environment and planning A: International journal of urban and regional research. (0308-518X). London.
Environment and planning B: Planning and design. (0265-8135). London.
Environment and planning C: Government and policy. (0263 774X). London.
Environment and planning D: Society and space. (0263-7758). London.
Environment and urbanization. (0956-2478). London.
Environmental & resource economics. (0924-6460). Dordrecht.
Environmental law. (0046-2276). Portland.
Environmental politics. (0964-4016). London.
Environmental values. (0963-2719). Cambridge, U.K.
Espace géographique. (0046-2497). Paris.
Espace populations sociétés. (0755-7809). Villeneuve d'Ascq.

Liste des periodiques consultés

Esprit. (0014-0759). Paris.
Estadistica. (0014-1135). Panama.
Estrategia económica y financiera. Bogotá.
Estudios. Asuncion.
Estudios de Asia y Africa. (0185-0164). Mexico City.
Estudios de Economía Aplicada. (1133-3197). Granada.
Estudios demográficos y urbanos. (0186-7210). Mexico City.
Estudios económicos. Mexico City.
Estudios indec. Buenos Aires.
Estudios internacionales. (0716-0240). Santiago.
Estudios migratorios latinoamericanos. Buenos Aires.
Estudios sociológicos. (0185-4186). Pedregal de Santa Teresa.
Estudos de antropologia cultural e social. (0870-4457). Lisbon.
Estudos jurídicos. (0100-2538). São Leopoldo.
Estudos leopoldenses. (0014-1607). São Leopoldo.
Ethics. (0014-1704). Chicago, IL.
Ethnic and racial studies. (0141-9870). London.
Ethnic groups. (0308-6860). New York, NY.
Ethnic studies report. (1010-5832). Kandy.
Ethnographisch archäologische Zeitschrift. (0012-7477). Berlin.
Ethnologia Polona. (0137-4079). Wrocław.
Ethnologica Helvetica. Bern.
Ethnologie française. (0046-2616). Paris.
Ethnology. (0014-1828). Pittsburgh, PA.
Ethnomusicology. (0014-1836). Bloomington, IN.
Ethnos. (0014-1844). Stockholm.
Ethology & sociobiology. (0162-3095). New York, NY.
Etnografia polska. (0071-1861). Wroclaw.
Etnograficheskoe obozrenie. Moscow.
Études Æquatoria. Mbandaka.
Études canadiennes = Canadian studies. (0153-1700). Talence.
Études et documents. (0182-788X). Paris.
Études internationales. (0014-2123). Quebec.
Études maliennes. Bamako.
Études mésoaméricaines. (0378-5726). Mexico.
Études mongoles et sibériennes. (0766-507S). Nanterre.
Études rurales. (0014-2182). Paris.
Études rwandaises: Série lettres et sciences humaines. Butare.
Études sociales. Paris.
Eure: Revista latinoamericana de estudios urbanos regionales. (0250-7161). Santiago.
Euromoney. (0014-2433). London.
Europa Archiv. (0014-2476). Bonn.
Europa ethnica. (0014-2492). Vienna.
Europe-Asia studies. (0038-5859). Abingdon.
European accounting review. (0963-8180). London.
European affairs. (0921-5778). Amsterdam.
European business and economic development. (0966-8004). Bradford.
European economic review. (0014-2921). Amsterdam.

List of periodicals consulted

European history quarterly. (0014-3111). London.
European journal of communication. London.
European journal of operational research. (0377-2217). Amsterdam.
European journal of political economy. (0176-2680). Amsterdam.
European journal of political research. (0304-4130). Dordrecht.
European journal of population = Revue européenne de démographie. (0168-6577). Amsterdam.
European journal of social psychology. (0046-2772). Chichester.
European journal of the history of economic thought. (0967-2567). London.
European journal of women's studies. London.
European journal on criminal policy and research. (0928-1371). Amsterdam.
European research. (0958-9082). Shipley.
European review of agricultural economics. (0165-1587). Berlin.
European review of history = Revue européenne d'histoire. (1350-7486). Abingdon.
European review of Latin American and Caribbean studies = Revista europea de estudios latinoamericanos y del caribe. (0924-0608). Amsterdam.
European sociological review. (0266-7215). Oxford.
Evaluation review. (0193-841X). Newbury Park, CA.
Evolutionary anthropology. (1060-1538). New York, NY.
Explorations in economic history. (0014-4983). Duluth, MN.
Fabula. (0014-6242). Berlin.
Falkland Islands journal. (0256-1824). Stanley.
Families in society. (1044-3894). Milwaukee, WI.
Far Eastern affairs. Moscow.
Federal Reserve bulletin. (0014-9209). Washington, DC.
Federalist. (0393-1358). Pavia.
Feminist legal studies. (0966-3622). Liverpool.
Feminist review. (0141-7789). London.
Feminist studies. (0046-3663). College Park, MD.
Finance & development. (0015-1947). Washington, DC.
Financial analysts journal. (0015-198X). Charlottesville, VA.
Financial management. (0046-3892). Tampa, FL.
Financial news analysis. Dakar.
Finanse. (0430-4896). Warsaw.
Finansy SSSR. (0130-576X). Moscow.
Finanzarchiv. (0015-2218). Tübingen.
Finsk tidskrift. (0015-248X). Turku.
First language. (0142-7237). Chalfont St Giles, Bucks, U.K.
Fiscal studies. (0143-5671). London.
Folia linguistica. (0165-4004). Berlin.
Folia linguistica historia. Berlin.
Folia primatologica. (0015-5713). Basle.
Folk. (0085-0756). Copenhagen.
Folklore [Calcutta]. (0015-5896). Calcutta.
Folklore [London]. (0015-587X). London.
Food and foodways. (0740-9710). New York, NY.
Food policy. (0306-9192). Oxford.
For new sociology. Tokyo, Japan.

Liste des periodiques consultés

Foreign affairs. (0015-7120). New York, NY.
Foreign policy. (0015-7228). Washington, D.C.
Foreign trade review. New Delhi.
Forensic linguistics. (1350-1771). London.
Formation emploi. (0759-6340). Paris.
Foro internacional. (0185-013X). Mexico City.
Forschungen und Berichte. (0863-0739). Berlin.
Forschungsjournal neue soziale Bewegungen. (0933-9361). Marburg.
Forum. Tokyo.
Free associations. (0267-0887). London.
Free China review. (0016-030X). Taipei.
French cultural studies. (0957-1558). Chalfont St Giles, Bucks, U.K.
Games and economic behavior. (0899-8256). Orlando, FL.
Garcia de Orta: série de antropobiologia. (0870-0168). Lisbon.
Gendai no Esupuri. Japan.
Gendai no Shakai Byouri. Japan.
Gendaishakaigaku kenkyu. Sapporo, Japan.
Gender and history. (9053-5233). Oxford.
Gender and society. (0891-2432). Newbury Park, CA.
Genèses. (1135-3219). France.
Geneva papers on risk and insurance theory. (0926-4957). Dordrecht.
Genève-Afrique. (0016-6774). Geneva.
Gentse bijdragen tot de kunstgeschiedenis en oudheidkunde. (0772-7151). Gent.
Genus. (0016-6987). Rome.
Geoforum. (0016-7185). Oxford.
Geografiska annaler: Series B — Human geography. (0435-3676). Uppsala.
Geographia polonica. (0016-7282). Warsaw.
Geographical analysis. (0016-7363). Columbus, OH.
Geographical journal. (0016-7398). London.
Geographical review. (0016-7428). New York, N.Y.
Geographical review of India. (0375-6386). Calcutta.
Geographical review of Japan. (0016 7444). Tokyo.
Geographische Rundschau. (0016-7460). Braunschweig.
Geography. Sheffield.
Geography research forum. (0333-5275). Beer-Sheva.
Geojournal. (0343-2521). Dordrecht.
Geopolitique review. (0752-1693). Paris.
George Washington journal of international law and economics. (0748-4305). Washington, DC.
Georgica. (0232 4490). Konstanz.
German politics. (0964-4008). London.
German yearbook on business history. (0722-2416). New York, NY.
Geschichte und Gesellschaft. (0340-613X). Göttingen.
Gestion 2000: Management et prospective. (0773-0543). Louvain.
Gewerkschaftliche Monatshefte. (0016-9447). Düsseldorf.
Giornale degli economisti e annali di economia. (0017-0097). Milan.
Global environmental change. (0959-3780). Oxford.

List of periodicals consulted

Godishnik na Sofiiskiia universitet "Kliment Okhridski" katedra po politicheska ikonomiia. (0204-9627). Sofia.
Godishnik na Visshiia finansovo- stopanski institut "D. A. Tsenov" - Svishtov. (0323-9470). Varna.
Gospodarka narodowa. (0867-0005). Warsaw.
Gospodarka planowa. (0017-2421). Warsaw.
Gosudarstvo i pravo. (0132-0769). Moscow.
Göteborg studies in educational sciences. (0436-1121). Gothenburg.
Göteborgs etnografiska museum årstryck. (0280-3887). Gothenburg.
Gothenburg studies in social anthropology. (0348-4076). Gothenburg.
Governance. (0952-1895). Oxford.
Government and opposition. (0017-257X). London.
Gradhiva. (0764-8928). Paris.
Grassroots development. (0733-6608). Rosslyn, VA.
Greek economic review. Athens.
Green globe yearbook 1993. (0-0803-9011). Oxford.
Group decision and negotiation. (0926-2644). Dordrecht.
Groupwork. (0951-824X). London.
Hacienda pública española. (0210-1173). Madrid.
Hallinnon tutkimus. Tampere.
Hamburger Jahrbuch für Wirtschafts- und Gesellschaftspolitik. Tübingen.
Harvard business review. (0017-8012). Boston, MA.
Harvard journal of Asiatic studies. (0073-0548). Cambridge, MA.
Harvard law review. (0017-811X). Cambridge, MA.
Health and social work. (0360-7283). Washington DC.
Health care for women international. (0739-9332). London.
Health policy and planning. (0268-1080). Oxford.
Health transition review. (1036-4005). Canberra.
Hebrew annual review. Columbus, OH.
Hemispheres. (0239-8818). Warsaw.
Heritage of Zimbabwe. (0556-9605). Harare.
Hespëris Tamuda. Morocco.
Hessische Blätter für Volks- und Kulturforschung. (1075-3479). Marburg.
High technology law journal. (0885-2715). Berkeley, CA.
Higher education. (0018-1560). Dordrecht.
Himal. (1012-9804). Lalitpur.
Himalayan research bulletin. (0891-4834). New York, NY.
Hispanic American historical review. (0018-2168). Durham, NC.
Historia mexicana: Revista trimestral publicada por el centro de estudios históricos de el Colegio de México. (0185-0172). México.
Historical archaeology. (0440-9213). Tucson, AZ.
Historical journal. (0018-246X). Cambridge.
Historical social research = Historische Sozialforschung. (0172-6404). Cologne.
Historical studies. (0018-2559). Parkville.
History and anthropology. (0275-7206). Reading.
History and technology. (0734-1512). Reading.
History and theory. (0018-2656). Middletown, CT.
History in Africa. (0361-5413). Atlanta, GA.

History of education. (0046760x). London.
History of political economy. (0018-2702). Durham, NC.
History of political thought. (0143-781X). Exeter.
History of psychiatry. (0957-154X). Chalfont St Giles, U.K.
History of religions. (0018-2710). Chicago, IL.
History of the human sciences. (0952-6951). London.
Hitotsubashi journal of commerce and management. (0018-2796). Tokyo.
Hitotsubashi journal of economics. (0018-280X). Tokyo.
Hitotsubashi journal of law and politics. (0073-2796). Tokyo.
Hitotsubashi journal of social studies. (0073-280X). Tokyo.
Hitotsubashi ronso. Tokyo.
Hogaku (Bulletin of Kokugakuin University). Kokugakuin.
Hogaku (Journal. Surugadai University). Surugadai.
Hogaku kenyu. Tokyo.
Hokuriku hogaku. Kanazawa.
Homines. (0252-8908). Hato Rey (Puerto Rico).
Homme. (0439-4216). Paris.
Homme et la société. (0018-4306). Paris.
Hong Kong economic papers. (0018 4578). Hong Kong.
Hong Kong law journal. (0378-0600). Hong Kong.
Hong Kong public administration. (1022-0275). Kowloon.
Hosei Kenkyu. Fukuoka.
Hosogaku Kenkyu. Tokyo.
Housing policy debate. (1051-1482). Washington, D.C.
Howard journal of criminal justice. (0265-5527). Oxford.
Human ethology newsletter. (0739-2036). Amsterdam.
Human nature. (1045-6767). Hawthorne, NY.
Human organization. (0018-7259). Temple Terrace, FL.
Human relations. (0018-7267). New York, N.Y.
Human rights quarterly. (0275-0392). Baltimore, MD.
Human studies. (0163-8548). Dordrecht.
Humor. (0933-1719). Berlin.
ICJ review. (0020-6393). Geneva.
ICSSR newsletter. (0018-9049). New Delhi.
Ideas en ciencias sociales. Buenos Aires.
Identities: global studies in culture and power. (1070-289X). Yverdon.
IDS bulletin. (0265-5012). Brighton.
Ifo-Studien. (0018-9731). Berlin.
Ilmu alam. (0126-7000). Selangor.
Immigrants and minorities. (0261-9288). London.
Impact of science on society. (0019-2872). Paris.
Ind-Africana. Delhi.
Index on censorship. (0306-4220). London.
India quarterly. (0019-4220). New Delhi.
Indian economic and social history review. (0019-4646). New Delhi.
Indian economic journal. Bombay.
Indian economic review. (0019-4671). Delhi.
Indian geographical journal. (0019-4824). Madras.

List of periodicals consulted

Indian journal of agricultural economics. (0019-5014). Bombay.
Indian journal of economics. (0019-5170). Allahabad.
Indian journal of gender studies. (0971-5215). New Delhi.
Indian journal of industrial relations. (0019-5286). New Delhi.
Indian journal of labour economics. Panta.
Indian journal of political science. (0019-5510). Madras.
Indian journal of public administration. (0019-5561). New Delhi.
Indian journal of regional science. (0046-9017). Kharagpur.
Indian journal of social science. New Delhi.
Indian journal of social work. (0019-5634). Bombay.
Indian labour journal. (0019-5723). Shimla.
Indo Asia. (0019-719X). Sachsenheim-Hohenhaslach.
Indo-Iranian journal. (0019-7246). Dordrecht.
Indogermanische Forschungen. (0019-7262). Berlin.
Indonesia circle. (0306-2848). London.
Indonesian quarterly. (0304-2170). Jakarta.
Industria. Bologna.
Industrial & environmental crisis quarterly. (09218106). Lewisburg, U.S.A./ New York.
Industrial and corporate change. (0960-6491). Oxford.
Industrial and labor relations review. (0019-7939). Ithaca, N.Y.
Industrial and social relations. (0258-7181). Bellville.
Industrial archaeology review. (0309-0728). Telford.
Industrial crisis quarterly. (0921-8106). Amsterdam.
Industrial law journal. (0395-9332). Oxford.
Industrial relations. (0019-8676). Oxford.
Industrial relations journal. (0019-8692). Oxford.
Industrial relations journal of South Africa. (02587181). Bellville.
Industry of free China. (0019-946X). Taipei.
Información comercial española. (0019-977X). Madrid.
Information bulletin. (0233-5689). Moscow.
Information economics and policy. (0167-6245). Amsterdam.
Informationen zur Raumentwicklung. (0303-2493). Bonn.
Informations sociales. (0046-9459). Paris.
Informatsionnye soobshcheniia Soveskogo natsional'nogo Tikhookeanskogo komiteta akademii nauk SSSR. Moscow.
Informatsionnyi biulleten' Mezhdunarodnoi assotsiatsii po izucheniiu kul'tur Tsentral'noi Azii. Moscow.
Inquiry. (0020-174X). Oslo.
Institut d'histoire du temps present bulletin. (0247-0101). Paris.
Instructional science. (0020-4277). Dordrecht.
Insurance mathematics & economics. (0167-6687). Amsterdam.
Integración latinoamericana. (0325-1675). Buenos Aires.
Intellectual property law. (0892-2365). New York, NY.
Intelligence and national security. (0268-4527). London.
Interchange. (0826-4805). Dordrecht.
Intercultural communication studies. (1057-7769). San Antonio, TX.
Intereconomics. (0020-5346). Hamburg.
Interfaces. (0092-2102). Providence, RI.

Liste des periodiques consultés

Internasjonal politikk. (0020-577X). Oslo.
International affairs [London]. (0020-5850). London.
International affairs [Moscow]. (0130-9641). Moscow.
International affairs studies. (0867-4493). Warsaw.
International and comparative law quarterly. (0020-5893). London.
International contributions to labour studies. (1052-9187). San Diego.
International currency review. (0020-6490). London.
International economic journal. Seoul.
International economic outlook. Oxford.
International economic review. (0020-6598). Philadelphia, PA.
International interactions. (0305-0629). Reading.
International journal. (0020-7020). Toronto.
International journal for philosophy of religion. (0020-7047). Dordrecht.
International journal for the advancement of counselling. (0165-0653). Dordrecht.
International journal for the semiotics of law = Revue internationale de sémiotique juridique. (0952-8059). Liverpool.
International journal for therapeutic and supportive organizations. (0964-1866). London.
International journal of accounting. (0020-7063). Heidelberg.
International journal of African historical studies. (0361-7882). Boston, MA.
International journal of American linguistics. (0020-7071). Chicago, IL.
International journal of comparative labour law and industrial relations. (0952-617X). Deventer.
International journal of comparative sociology. (0020-7152). Leiden.
International journal of conflict management. (1044-4068). Bowling Green, KY.
International journal of Dravidian linguistics. Trivandrum.
International journal of flexible manufacturing systems. (0920-6299). Dordrecht.
International journal of forecasting. (0169-2070). Amsterdam.
International journal of game theory. (0020-7276). Heidelberg.
International journal of health services. (0020-7314). Amityville, NY.
International journal of human resource management. (0958-5192). London.
International journal of industrial organization. (0167-7187). Amsterdam.
International journal of Kurdish studies. (0885 386X). New York.
International journal of language and the law. London.
International journal of law and the family. (0950-4109). Oxford.
International journal of marine and coastal law. (0927-3522). London.
International journal of Middle East studies. (0020-7438). New York, N.Y.
International journal of moral and social studies. (0267-9655). London.
International journal of offender therapy and comparative criminology. (0306-624X). New York, NY.
International journal of organization analysis. (1055-3185). Bowling Green, KY.
International journal of personal construct psychology. (0893-603X). London.
International journal of philosophical studies. (0967-2559). London.
International journal of politics, culture and society. (0891-4486). New York, NY.
International journal of primatology. (0164-0291). New York, NY.
International journal of psycho-analysis. (0020-7578). London.
International journal of Punjab studies. (0971-5223). New Delhi.
International journal of social economics. (0306-8293). Bradford.
International journal of social psychiatry. (0020-7640). London.

List of periodicals consulted

International journal of the sociology of language. (0165-2516). Berlin.
International journal of the sociology of law. (0194-6595). London.
International journal of therapeutic communities. (0196-1365). London.
International journal of transport economics. (0391-8440). Rome.
International journal of urban and regional research. (0309-1317). Sevenoaks.
International labour review. (0020-7780). Geneva.
International legal materials. (0020-7829). Washington DC.
International migration = Migrations internationales = Migraciones internacionales. (0020-7985). Geneva.
International migration review. (0197-9183). New York, NY.
International minds. (0957-1299). London.
International organization. (0020-8183). Cambridge, MA.
International perspectives. (0381-4874). Ottawa.
International political science review = Revue internationale de science politique. (0192-5121). Guildford.
International public relations review. (0269-0357). London.
International regional science review. (0160-0176). Morgantown, WV.
International relations. (0047-1178). London.
International review of administrative sciences. (0020-8523). London.
International review of applied economics. (0269-2171). Sevenoaks.
International review of education. (0020-8566). Hamburg.
International review of law and economics. (0144-8188). Stoneham, MA.
International review of mission. (0020-8582). Geneva.
International review of psycho-analysis. (0306-2643). London.
International review of retail, distribution and consumer research. (0959-3969). London.
International review of social history. (0020-8590). Amsterdam.
International review of strategic management. (1047-7918). Chichester.
International review of the Red Cross. (0020-8604). Geneva.
International security. (0162-2889). Cambridge, MA.
International small business journal. (0266-2426). Macclesfield.
International social science journal. (0020-8701). Oxford.
International socialism. (0020-8736). London.
International sociology. (0268-5809). London.
International spectator. (0393-2729). Rome.
International studies. (0020-8817). New Delhi.
International studies in the philosophy of science. (0269-8595). Abingdon.
International studies quarterly. (0020-8833). Stoneham, MA.
International tax and public finance. (0927-5940). Dordrecht.
International VAT monitor. (0925-0832). Amsterdam.
Internationales Asienforum. (0020-9449). Cologne.
Interstate. Aberystwyth.
Investigación y gerencia. Caracas.
Investigaciones economicas. (0210-1521). Madrid.
Investigaciones y ensayos. Buenos Aires.
Ipargazdasági szemle. Budapest.
IPW Berichte. (0046-970X). Frankfurt-am-Main.
IPW-Forschungshefte. (0323-3901). Berlin.
IRAL. (0019-042X). Heidelberg.

Liste des periodiques consultés

Iran nameh. Bethesda, MD.
Iranian journal of international affairs. (1016-6130). Tehran.
Iranica antiqua. (0021-0870). Louvain.
Iraq. (0021-0889). London.
Irian. (0304-2189). Jayapura, Irian Jaya.
Irish banking review. (0021-1060). Dublin.
Irish geography. (0075-0778). Dublin.
Irish political studies. (0790-7184). Galway.
Irish studies in international affairs. (0332-1460). Dublin.
Islam. (0021-1818). Berlin.
Islam et sociétés au sud du Sahara. (0984-7685). Paris.
Islamic quarterly. (0021-1842). London.
Israel exploration journal. (0021-2059). Jerusalem.
Israel law review. (0021-2237). Jerusalem.
Israel yearbook on human rights. (0333-5925). Dordrecht.
Issue. (0047-1607). Emory, GA.
Issues & studies. (1013-2511). Taipei.
Issues in reproductive and genetic engineering. (0958-6415). Elmsford, NY.
Istoriia SSSR. Moscow.
Italia contemporanea. (0392-3568). Milan.
Itinerario. Leiden.
IWGIA (International Work Group for Indigenous Affairs) document. (0105-4503). Copenhagen.
IWGIA yearbook (International Work Group for Indigenous Affairs). (0902-6266). Copenhagen.
IWK: Internationale wissenschaftliche Korrespondenz zur Geschichte der deutschen Arbeiterbewegung. (0046-8428). Berlin.
Izvestiia Akademii nauk Azerbaidzhanskoi SSR. Seriia istorii, filosofii i prava. Baku.
Izvestiia Akademii nauk Estonskoi SSR. Seriia obshchestvennye nauki. Moscow.
Izvestiia akademii nauk Gruzinskoi SSR: Seriia istorii, arkheologii, etnografii i istorii iskusstva. Tbilisi.
Izvestiia Akademii nauk Kazakhskoi SSR. Seriia obshchestvennykh nauk. Alma-Ata.
Izvestiia akademii nauk Latviiskoi SSR. Riga.
Izvestiia Akademii nauk Respubliki Kazakhstan: Seriia obshchectvennych nauk. Alma Ata.
Izvestiia Akademii nauk SSSR. Seriia geograficheskaia. Moscow.
Izvestiia Akademii nauk SSSR. Seriia literatury i iazyka. Moscow.
Izvestiia Akademii nauk Turkmenskoi SSR. Seriia obshchestvennykh nauk. Ashkhabad.
Izvestiia akademii timiriaz s.-kh. Moscow.
Izvestiia at. SSSR Seriia Ekonomika. Moscow.
Izvestiia istorii politicheskoi ekonomii v SSSR. Leningrad.
Izvestiia Severo-Kavkazskogo nauchnogo tsentra vysshei shkoly. Seriia obshchestvennykh nauk. Rostov.
Izvestiia Sibirskogo otdeleniia Akademii nauk SSSR. Seriia: istoriia, filologiia i filosofiia. Novosibirsk.
Izvestiia Vseioiuznogo geograficheskogo obshchestva. Leningrad.
Jahrbuch der Wirtschaft Osteuropas = Yearbook of East-European economics. (0449-5225). Heidelberg.
Jahrbuch des öffentlichen Rechts der Gegenwart. (0075-2517). Tübingen.

List of periodicals consulted

Jahrbuch Extremismus & Demokratie. Bonn.
Jahrbuch für Antisemitismusforschung. (0941-8563). Frankfurt.
Jahrbuch für christliche Sozialwissenschaften. (0075-2584). Münster.
Jahrbuch für Geschichte von Staat, Wirtschaft und Gesellschaft Lateinamerikas. (0075-2673). Cologne.
Jahrbuch für Ostrecht. (0075-2746). Munich.
Jahrbuch für Sozialwissenschaft. (0075-2770). Göttingen.
Jahrbuch für Soziologiegeschichte. Leverkusen.
Jahrbuch für Wirtschaftsgeschichte. (0075-2800). Berlin.
Jahrbuch: Asien - Afrika - Lateinamerika. Berlin.
Jahrbücher für Geschichte Osteuropas. (0021-4019). Stuttgart.
Jahrbücher für Nationalökonomie und Statistik. (0021-4027). Stuttgart.
Jamaica journal. (0021-4124). Kingston.
Japan and the world economy. (0922-1425). Amsterdam.
Japan Christian quarterly. (0021-4361). Tokyo.
Japan Christian review. Tokyo.
Japan digest. (0960-1473). Folkestone.
Japan forum. (0955-5803). Oxford.
Japan review of international affairs. (0913-8773). Tokyo.
Japanese annual of international law. (0448-8806). Tokyo.
Japanese journal of religious studies. (0304-1042). Nagoya.
Japanese journalism review. Tokyo.
Japanese religions. (0448-8954). Kyoto City.
Jewish journal of sociology. (0021-6534). London.
Jewish quarterly review. (0021-6682). Philadelphia, PA.
Jewish social studies. (0021-6704). New York, NY.
Jinbun (Journal of Kyoto University). Kyoto.
Jinbun-ronkyu. Nishinomiya.
Jinbungakubu kiyo. Toyama.
Jinko to Kaihatsu. Tokyo.
Jogtudományi közlöny. (0021-7166). Budapest.
Joho To Shakai (Journal of Edogawa University). Nagareyama.
Jokyo. Tokyo.
Josei kukan. Tokyo.
Journal de la Société de Statistique de Paris. (0037-914X). Paris.
Journal de la Société des américanistes. (0037-9174). Paris.
Journal de la Société des océanistes. (0300-953X). Paris.
Journal des Africanistes. (0399-0346). Paris.
Journal du droit international. (0021-8170). Paris.
Journal for the scientific study of religion. (0021-8294). West Lafayette, IN.
Journal for the study of Judaism in the Persian, Hellenistic and Roman periods. (0047-2212). Leiden.
Journal for the theory of social behaviour. (0021-8308). Oxford.
Journal für Entwicklungspolitik. (0258-2384). Vienna.
Journal für Sozialforschung. (0253-3995). Vienna.
Journal of accounting and economics. (0165-4101). Amsterdam.
Journal of accounting and public policy. (0278-4254). New York, NY.
Journal of accounting research. (0021-8456). Chicago, IL.

Liste des periodiques consultés

Journal of African economies. (0963-8024). Oxford.
Journal of African history. (0021-8537). Cambridge.
Journal of African languages and linguistics. (0167-6164). Dordrecht.
Journal of African law. (0221-8553). London.
Journal of African Marxists. (0263-2268). London.
Journal of African religion and philosophy. Kampala.
Journal of agricultural economics. (0021-857X). Oxford.
Journal of agricultural economics research. Washington, NY.
Journal of air law and commerce. (0021-8642). Dallas, TX.
Journal of American studies. (0021-8758). Cambridge.
Journal of analytical psychology. (0021-8774). London.
Journal of anthropological archaeology. (0278-4165). San Diego, CA.
Journal of anthropological research. (0091-7710). Albuquerque, NM.
Journal of applied econometrics. (0883-7252). Chichester.
Journal of applied psychology. (0021-9010). Arlington, VA.
Journal of applied social psychology. (0021-9029). Silver Spring, MD.
Journal of architectural and planning research. Chicago, IL.
Journal of Asian and African affairs. (1044-2979). Washington, DC.
Journal of Asian and African studies [Leiden]. (0021 9096). Leiden.
Journal of Asian history. (0021-910X). Wiesbaden.
Journal of Asian studies. (0021-9118). Ann Arbor, MI.
Journal of Australian political economy. (0156-5826). Sydney.
Journal of Australian studies. Bundoora.
Journal of banking and finance. (0378-4266). Amsterdam.
Journal of BARD. Comilla.
Journal of behavioral education. (1053-0819). New York.
Journal of biogeography. (0305-0270). Oxford.
Journal of biosocial science. (0021-9320). Cambridge.
Journal of British studies. (0021-9371). Chicago.
Journal of business. (0021 9398). Chicago, IL.
Journal of business & economic statistics. (0735-0015). Alexandria, VA.
Journal of business and society. (1012-2591). Nicosia.
Journal of business ethics. (0167-4544). Dordrecht.
Journal of business finance and accounting. (0306-686X). Oxford.
Journal of business law. (0021-9460). London.
Journal of Canadian studies = Revue d'études canadiennes. (0021-9495). Peterborough.
Journal of Caribbean studies. (0190-2008). Lexington, KY.
Journal of child and adolescent group therapy. (1053-0800). New York.
Journal of child and family studies. (1062-1024). New York.
Journal of child psychotherapy. (0075-417X). London.
Journal of Chinese law. (1041-7567). Lincoln, NE.
Journal of Chinese philosophy. Honolulu, HI.
Journal of church and state. (0021-969X). Waco, TX.
Journal of common market studies. (0021-9886). Oxford.
Journal of Commonwealth & comparative politics. (0306-3631). London.
Journal of communication. (0021-9916). New York, N.Y.
Journal of communist studies. (0268-4535). London.
Journal of community and applied social psychology. (1052-9284). Chichester.

List of periodicals consulted

Journal of comparative economics. (0147-5967). Duluth, MN.
Journal of comparative family studies. (0047-2328). Calgary.
Journal of conflict resolution. (0022-0027). Newbury Park, CA.
Journal of constitutional and parliamentary studies. New Delhi.
Journal of consumer affairs. (0022-0078). Madison, WI.
Journal of consumer policy. (0342-5843). Dordrecht.
Journal of contemporary African studies. (0258-9001). Pretoria.
Journal of contemporary Asia. (0047-2336). Manila.
Journal of contemporary history. (0022-0094). London.
Journal of criminal law. (0022-0183). London.
Journal of criminal law and criminology. (0091-4169). Chicago, IL.
Journal of cross-cultural gerontology. (0169-3816). Dordrecht.
Journal of democracy. (1045-5736). Baltimore, MD.
Journal of developing areas. (0022-037X). Macomb, IL.
Journal of developing societies. (0169-796X). Leiden.
Journal of development economics. (0304-3878). Amsterdam.
Journal of development planning. (0085-2392). New York, NY.
Journal of development studies. (0022-0388). London.
Journal of documentation. (0022-0418). London.
Journal of East and West studies. Seoul.
Journal of Eastern African research & development. (0251-0405). Nairobi.
Journal of econometrics. (0304-4076). Amsterdam.
Journal of economic and social measurement. (0747-9662). Amsterdam.
Journal of economic behavior and organization. (0167-2681). Amsterdam.
Journal of economic cooperation among Islamic countries. (0252 953X). Ankara.
Journal of economic dynamics and control. (0165-1889). Amsterdam.
Journal of economic history. (0022-0507). New York, NY.
Journal of economic issues. (0021-3624). Lincoln, NE.
Journal of economic literature. (0022-8515). Nashville, TN.
Journal of economic methodology. (1350-178X). London.
Journal of economic perspectives. (0895-3309). Nashville, TN.
Journal of economic psychology. (0167-4870). Amsterdam.
Journal of economic studies. (0144-3585). Bradford.
Journal of economic surveys. (0950-0804). Oxford.
Journal of economic theory. (0022-0531). Brugge.
Journal of economics & management strategy. (1058-6407). Cambridge, MA.
Journal of economics = Zeitschrift für Nationalökonomie. (0931-8658). Vienna.
Journal of education policy. (0268-0939). London.
Journal of educational sociology. Tokyo.
Journal of environmental economics and management. (0095-0696). Duluth, MN.
Journal of environmental law. (0952-8873). Oxford.
Journal of environmental management. (0301-4797). London.
Journal of environmental planning and management. (0964-0568). Abingdon.
Journal of European economic history. (0391-5115). Rome.
Journal of European public policy. (1350-1763). London.
Journal of European social policy. (0958-9287). Harlow, Essex.
Journal of evolutionary economics. (0936-9937). Berlin.
Journal of experimental child psychology. (0022-0965). Duluth, MN.

Liste des periodiques consultés

Journal of experimental social psychology. (0022-1031). Duluth, MN.
Journal of Family Education Center. Yokohama, Japan.
Journal of family history. (0363-1990). Greenwich, CT.
Journal of family therapy. (0163-4445). Oxford.
Journal of family violence. (0885-7482). New York, N.Y.
Journal of finance. (0022-1082). New York, NY.
Journal of financial and quantitative analysis. (0022-1090). Seattle, WA.
Journal of financial economics. (0304-405X). Amsterdam.
Journal of financial intermediation. (1042-9573). Orlando, FL.
Journal of financial services research. (0920-8550). Dordrecht.
Journal of folklore research. (0737-7037). Bloomington, IN.
Journal of forecasting. (0277-6693). Chichester.
Journal of foreign exchange and international finance. (0970-3632). Pune.
Journal of forensic economics. (0898-5510). Kansas City.
Journal of forensic psychiatry. (0958-5184). London.
Journal of futures markets. (0270-7314). New York, NY.
Journal of gender studies. (0958-9236). Hull.
Journal of health economics. (0167-6296). Amsterdam.
Journal of health politics, policy and law. (0361-6878). Durham, NC.
Journal of historical sociology. (0952-1909). Oxford.
Journal of home economics of Japan. Tokyo.
Journal of housing economics. Cambridge, MA.
Journal of housing research. (1052-7001). Washington, D.C.
Journal of human evolution. (0047-2484). London.
Journal of human resources. (0022-166X). Madison, WI.
Journal of human sciences. Osaka.
Journal of Indian Council of Philosophical Research. (0970-7794). New Dehli.
Journal of Indian philosophy. (0022-1791). Dordrecht.
Journal of Indo-European studies. (0092-2323). Washington, DC.
Journal of industrial economics. (0022-1821). Oxford.
Journal of industrial relations. (0022-1856). Sydney.
Journal of industry and management. Osaka.
Journal of institutional and theoretical economics = Zeitschrift für die gesamte Staatswissenschaft. (0932-4569). Tübingen.
Journal of interamerican studies and world affairs. (0022-1937). Coral Gables, FL.
Journal of interdisciplinary economics. (0260-1079). Bicester.
Journal of interdisciplinary history. (0022-1953). Cambridge, MA.
Journal of interdisciplinary studies: An international journal of interdisciplinary and interfaith dialogue. (0890-0132). Santa Monica, CA.
Journal of international affairs. (0022-197X). New York, NY.
Journal of international and comparative economics. (0940-4821). Heidelberg.
Journal of international business studies. (0047-2506). New Orleans, LA.
Journal of international development. (0954-1748). Chichester.
Journal of international economics. (0022-1996). Amsterdam.
Journal of international financial management and accounting. (0954-1314). Oxford.
Journal of international money and finance. (0261-5606). Guildford.
Journal of international relations. Tokyo.
Journal of Islamic economics. (0128-0066). Selangor.

List of periodicals consulted

Journal of Japanese studies. (0095-6848). Seattle, WA.
Journal of Jewish studies. (0022-2097). Oxford.
Journal of Jewish thought and philosophy. (1053-699X). New York, NY.
Journal of Korean studies. Los Angeles, CA.
Journal of labor economics. (0734-306X). Chicago, IL.
Journal of labor research. (0195-3613). Fairfax, VA.
Journal of language and social psychology. (0261-927X). Clevedon.
Journal of Latin American studies. (0022-216X). Cambridge.
Journal of law and economics. (0022-2186). Chicago, IL.
Journal of law and society. (0263-323X). Oxford.
Journal of law, economics, & organization. (8756-6222). Cary, NC.
Journal of legal pluralism and unoffical law. (0732-9113). Groningen.
Journal of legal studies. (0047-2530). Chicago, IL.
Journal of leisure research. (0022-2216). Alexandria, VA.
Journal of libertarian studies. (0363-2873). Burlingame, CA.
Journal of linguistics. (0022-2267). Cambridge.
Journal of macroeconomics. (0164-0704). Baton Rouge, LA.
Journal of management studies. (0022-2380). Oxford.
Journal of marriage and the family. (0022-2445). Minneapolis, MN.
Journal of mathematical economics. (0304-4068). Amsterdam.
Journal of mathematical sociology. (0022-250X). New York.
Journal of Mauritian studies. Moka.
Journal of medicine and philosophy. (0360-5310). Dordrecht.
Journal of Mediterranean studies. (1016-3476). Msida.
Journal of Micronesian studies. Mangiloa, Guam.
Journal of modern African studies. (0022-278X). Cambridge.
Journal of modern history. (0022-2801). Chicago IL.
Journal of modern Korean studies. Fredericksburg, VA.
Journal of monetary economics. (0304-3932). Amsterdam.
Journal of money, credit and banking. (0022-2879). Columbus, OH.
Journal of multilingual and multicultural development. (0143-4632). Clevedon.
Journal of Natal and Zulu history. Durban.
Journal of Near Eastern studies. (0022-2968). Chicago, IL.
Journal of Northeast Asian studies. (0738-7997). Washington, DC.
Journal of northwest semitic languages. (0259-0131). Stellenbosch.
Journal of occupational psychology. (0305-8107). Leicester.
Journal of occupational rehabilitation. (1053-0487). New York.
Journal of Pacific history. (0022-3344). Canberra.
Journal of Pacific studies. (1011-3029). Suva.
Journal of Palestine studies. (0377-919X). Berkeley, CA.
Journal of parliamentary information. New Delhi.
Journal of peace research. (0022-3433). London.
Journal of peasant studies. (0306-6150). London.
Journal of personality. (0022-3506). Durham, NC.
Journal of personality and social psychology. (0022-3514). Arlington, VA.
Journal of philosophy. (0022-362X). New York, NY.
Journal of phonetics. (0095-4470). London.
Journal of pidgin and creole languages. (0920-9034). Amsterdam.

Liste des periodiques consultés

Journal of planning & environment law. (0307-4870). London.
Journal of planning literature. (0885-4122). Columbus.
Journal of policy analysis and management. (0276-8739). New York, N.Y.
Journal of policy history. (0898-0306). University Park, PA.
Journal of policy modeling. (0161-8938). New York, NY.
Journal of political economy. (0022-3808). Chicago.
Journal of politics. (0022-3816). Austin, TX.
Journal of popular culture. (0022-3840). Bowling Green, OH.
Journal of population economics. (0933-1433). Heidelberg.
Journal of post Keynesian economics. (0160-3477). Armonk, NY.
Journal of pragmatics. (0378-2166). Amsterdam.
Journal of productivity analysis. (0895-562X). Dordrecht.
Journal of psychology. (0022-3980). Washington, DC.
Journal of public economics. (0047-2727). Amsterdam.
Journal of public policy. (0143-814X). Cambridge.
Journal of quantitative anthropology. (0922-2995). Dordrecht.
Journal of real estate finance and economics. (0895-5638). Dordrecht.
Journal of real estate research. (0896-5803). Grand Forks.
Journal of refugee studies. (0951-6328). Oxford.
Journal of regional policy. Naples.
Journal of regulatory economics. (092-680X). Dordrecht.
Journal of religion in Africa. (0022-4200). Leiden.
Journal of research in crime and delinquency. (0022-4278). Newbury Park, CA.
Journal of risk and uncertainty. (0895-5646). Dordrecht.
Journal of ritual studies. (0890-1112). Pittsburgh.
Journal of rural development and administration. (0047-2751). Peshawar.
Journal of rural problem. Tokyo.
Journal of rural studies. (0743-0167). Oxford.
Journal of semantics. (0167-5133). Oxford.
Journal of social and biological structures. (0140 1750). Greenwich, CT.
Journal of social and clinical psychology. (0736-7236). New York, NY.
Journal of social and evolutionary systems. (1061-7361). Greenwich, CT.
Journal of social development in Africa. (1012-1080). Harare.
Journal of social distress and the homeless. (1053-0789). New York.
Journal of social history. (0022-4529). Pittsburgh, PA.
Journal of social issues. (0022-4537). New York, NY.
Journal of social policy. (0047-2794). Cambridge.
Journal of social psychology. (0022-4545). Washington, DC.
Journal of social science. Zomba, Malawi.
Journal of social sciences and humanities. (0023-4044). Seoul.
Journal of social studies. Dhaka.
Journal of social work practice. (0265-0533). Abingdon.
Journal of social, political and economic studies. (0193-5941). Washington, D.C.
Journal of South Asian literature. East Lansing, MI.
Journal of Southeast Asian studies. (0022-4634). Singapore.
Journal of Southern African studies. (0305-7070). Oxford.
Journal of strategic studies. (0140-2390). London.
Journal of structural learning. (0022-4774). New York, NY.

List of periodicals consulted

Journal of the American Oriental Society. (0003-0279). Ann Arbor, MI.
Journal of the American Planning Association. (0194-4363). Chicago, IL.
Journal of the American Statistical Association. (0162-1459). Alexandria, VA.
Journal of the Anthropological Society of Oxford. (0044-8370). Oxford.
Journal of the Asiatic Society. (0368-3303). Calcutta.
Journal of the Asiatic Society of Bangladesh. Dhaka.
Journal of the Assam Research Society. Guwahati.
Journal of the Australian Population Association. (0814-5725). Canberra.
Journal of the Center for Women's Studies. Tokyo.
Journal of the Culture Research Institute. Tokyo.
Journal of the economic and social history of the orient. (0022-4995). Leiden.
Journal of the Gypsy Lore Society. (0017-6087). Cheverly, MD.
Journal of the history of ideas. (0022-5037). Philadelphia, PA.
Journal of the history of philosophy. (0022-5053). St. Louis, MO.
Journal of the history of sexuality. (1043-4070). Chicago.
Journal of the history of the behavioral sciences. (0022-5061). Brandon, VT.
Journal of the Institute of Actuaries. (0020-2681). Oxford.
Journal of the International Phonetic Association. Los Angeles, CA.
Journal of the Japanese and international economies. (0889-1583). Duluth, MN.
Journal of the Madras University: Section A — Humanities. Madras, India.
Journal of the Maharaja Sayajirao University of Baroda. (social science number). Baroda.
Journal of the Malaysian branch of the Royal Asiatic Society. (0126-7353). Kuala Lumpur.
Journal of the Market Research Society. (0025-3618). London.
Journal of the Mysore University: Section A-Arts. Mysore.
Journal of the Oriental Institute. (0030-5324). Baroda.
Journal of the Pacific Society. (0387-4745). Tokyo.
Journal of the Pakistan Historical Society. Karachi.
Journal of the Polynesian Society. (0032-4000). Auckland.
Journal of the Research Society of Pakistan. Lahore.
Journal of the Royal Asiatic Society (Sri Lanka branch). Colombo.
Journal of the Royal Statistical Society: Series A (statistics in society). (0035-9238). London.
Journal of the Royal Statistical Society: Series B (methodological). (0035-9246). London.
Journal of the Royal Statistical Society: Series C — applied statistics. (0035-9254). Oxford.
Journal of the Siam Society. (0857-7099). Bangkok.
Journal of the Walter Roth Museum of Anthropology. (0256-4653). Georgetown.
Journal of theoretical politics. (0951-6928). London.
Journal of time series analysis. (0143-9782). Oxford.
Journal of transport economics and policy. (0022 5258). Bath.
Journal of urban economics. (0094-1190). Duluth, MN.
Journal of urban history. (0096-1442). Newbury Park, CA.
Journal of West African languages. (0022-5401). Dallas, TX.
Journal of world history. (1045-6007). Honolulu, HI.
Journal of world trade. (1011-6702). Geneva.
Journal. Institute of Muslim Minority Affairs. (0266-6952). London.
Journal. Konan University, Faculty of Letters. Kobe.
Journal. Okayama University, School of General Education. Okayama.
Journal. Yamaguchi University, Literary Society. Yamaguchi.

Liste des periodiques consultés

Jurnal antropologi dan sosiologi. (0126-9518). Selangor.
Jurnal ekonomi Malaysia. (0126-1962). Selangor.
Jurnal Pendidikan. (0126-6020). Selangor.
Jurnal pengurusan. (0127-2713). Selangor.
Jurnal psikologi Malaysia. (0127-8029). Selangor.
Kabar seberang. (0314-5786). Townsville.
Kagoshima keizai daigaku shakaigakubu ronshu. Kagoshima.
Kailash. Kathmandu.
Kajian Malaysia. (0127-4082). Penang.
Kansai University review of law and politics. Osaka.
Kansaneläkelaitoksen julkaisuja. (0355-4821). Helsinki.
Kasarinlan. Quezon City.
Kazoku Shakaigaku kenkyu. Tokyo.
Keiei Johogakubu Kiyo (Bulletin of Jobu University). Gumma.
Keio business review. (0453-4557). Tokyo.
Keio economic studies. (0022-9709). Tokyo.
Keizai Ronshu [Journal of Toyama University]. Toyama.
Keizaigaku zasshi [Journal of Osaka Municipal University]. Osaka.
Kenkyu Kiyo [Bulletin of Hyogo Kyoiku University]. Nishiwaki.
Kenkyu kiyo [Journal of Aomori University]. Aomori.
Kenkyu Kiyo [Journal of Kibi Kokusai University]. Takahashi.
Kenkyu Kiyo [Journal. Tamagwa Fukushi University]. Sendai.
Kenkyu-kiyo. Tokyo.
Kenkyu-kiyo [Bulletin of Osaka Kyoiku University]. Osaka.
Kenkyu-liyo. Nagoya.
Kenkyunenpo [Bulletin of Rissho University]. Tokyo.
Kentavr = Centaur. (0320-8907). Moscow.
Kesu Kenkyu. Tokyo.
Khabarskyi vestnik — akademii nauk respubliki Kazakhstan. Alma Ata.
Kigyo-kenkyusho Nenpo. Nagoya.
Kikan Tomorrow. Amagasaki.
Kindai Fudo. Osaka.
Kinki daigaku kyouyou gakuba kenkyu kiyou. Osaka.
Kiswahili. (0856-048X). Dar es Salaam.
Kiyo [Bulletin of Tyukyo University]. Nagoya.
Kiyo [Journal of Seitoku College]. Tokyo.
Kiyo Shakaigakka. Tokyo.
Knowledge and policy. (0897-1986). New Brunswick, NJ.
Kobe economic and business review. (0075-6407). Kobe.
Kokugakuin daigaku nihonbunka kenkyushoho. Tokyo.
Kokumin Seikatsu Kenkyu. Tokyo.
Kölner Zeitschrift für Soziologie und Sozialpsychologie. (0340-0425). Wiesbaden.
Kommunist [Moscow]. Moscow.
Kommunist [Vilnius]. Vil'nius.
Kommunist Azerbaidzhana. Baku.
Konjunkturpolitik. (0023-3498). Berlin.
Korea and world affairs. Seoul.
Korea economic report. Seoul.

List of periodicals consulted

Korea journal. (0023-3900). Seoul.
Korea observer. (0023-3919). Seoul.
Korean culture. (0270-1618). Los Angeles, CA.
Korean financial review. Seoul.
Korean social science journal. Seoul.
Korean studies. (0145-840X). Honolulu, HI.
Közgazdasági szemle. (0023-4346). Budapest.
Kraevedcheskie zapiski. Kuibyshev.
Kratkie soobshcheniia Instituta arkheologii Akademii nauk SSSR. Moscow.
Kredit und Kapital. (0023-4591). Berlin.
Kroeber anthropological society papers. Berkeley, CA.
Krytyka. Warsaw.
Külgazdaság jogi melléklete. (0324-4202). Budapest.
Kunnallistieteellinen aikakauskirja. Finland.
Kwansai Gakuin University Annual Studies. Hyôgo.
Kwansei Gakuin daigaku shakaigakubu kiyo. Hyôgo.
Kwansei Gakuin law review. (0452-9480). Nishinomiya.
Kwartalnik historii kultury materialnej. (0023-5881). Warsaw.
Kyklos. (0023-5962). Basel.
Kyoiku-shakaigaku Kenkyu. Tokyo.
Kyoikugakubu kenkyu hokoku [Bulletin of Yamanashi University]. Kohu.
Kyoto University economic review. (0023-6055). Kyoto.
Kyoyobu kiyo [Bulletin of Rissho University]. Tokyo.
L'annuaire français de droit international. (0066-3085). France.
L.S.E. quarterly. (0269 9710). Oxford.
Labor law journal. (0023-6586). Chicago, IL.
Labour [Canada] = Travail. (0700-3862). St. John's.
Labour [Italy]. (1121-7081). Oxford.
Labour and society. (0378-5408). Geneva.
Labour, capital and society = Travail, capital et société. (0706-1706). Montreal.
Laissez-faire. (0963-6633). London.
Lalit kalā. New Delhi.
Land economics. (0023-7639). Madison, WI.
Language. (0097-8507). Baltimore, MD.
Language & communication. (0271-5309). New York, N.Y.
Language in society. (0047-4045). New York, NY.
Language problems and language planning. (0270-2690). Amsterdam.
Latin American Indian literatures journal. (0888-5613). McKeesport, PA.
Latin American perspectives. (0094-582X). Newbury Park, CA.
Latin American research review. (0023-8791). Albuquerque, NM.
Latinskaia Amerika. Moscow.
Law and contemporary problems. (0023-9186). Durham, NC.
Law and critique. (0957-8536). Liverpool.
Law and philosophy. (0167-5249). Dordrecht.
Law and policy. (0265-8240). Oxford.
Law and society review. (0023-9216). Amherst, MA.
Law quarterly review. London.
LEBA: Estudos de quaternário, pré-história e arqueologia. (08700-0044). Lisbon.

Liste des periodiques consultés

Ledelse og Erhvervsøkonomi. (0902-3704). Copenhagen.
Legislative studies. (0816-9152). Canberra.
Legislative studies quarterly. (0362-9805). Iowa City, IA.
Leiden journal of international law. (0922-1565). Leiden.
Leisure sciences. (01490400). London.
Levante. (0024-1504). Rome.
Leviatán. (0210-6337). Madrid.
Liberian studies journal. (0024-1989). Bloomington, IL.
Libyan studies. (0263-7189). London.
Linguistic inquiry. (0024-3892). Cambridge, MA.
Linguistic review. (0167-6318). Hawthorne, NY.
Linguistics. (0024-3949). Berlin.
Linguistics and philosophy. (0165-0157). Dordrecht.
Linguistics of the Tibeto-Burman area. (0731-3500). Berkeley, CA.
Linguistique africaine. Paris.
Links. (0024-404X). Offenbach.
Literary and linguistic computing. Oxford.
Literatura ludowa. (0024-4708). Wrocław.
Literaturnaia Armeniia. Erevan.
Littérature orale arabo-berbère. (0336-5654). Paris.
Liverpool law review. (0144-923X). Liverpool.
Local economy. (0269-0942). Harlow.
Local government review in Japan. (0288-7622). Tokyo.
Local government studies. (0300-3930). Croydon.
Local population studies. (0143-2974). Matlock.
Lokayan bulletin. (0970-5406). New Delhi.
Lud. (0076-1435). Wroclaw.
Maandschrift economie. (0013-0486). Groningen.
Maghreb machrek monde arabe. (0336-6324). Paris.
Magyar jog. (0025-0147). Budapest.
Magyar Közigazgatás. (0865-736X). Budapest.
Magyar tudomány. (0025-0325). Budapest.
Majalah demografi Indonesia = Indonesian journal of demography. (0126-0251). Jakarta.
Malaysian journal of tropical geography. (0127-1474). Kuala Lumpur.
Man. (0025-1496). London.
Man in India. (0025-1569). Ranchi.
Management accounting research. (1044-5005). London.
Management science. (0025-1909). Providence, RI.
Manchester papers on development. (0260-8235). Manchester.
Manchester School of economic and social studies. (0025-2034). Oxford.
Mankind. (0025-2328). Sydney.
Mankind quarterly. (0025-2344). Washington, DC.
Manusia and Masyarakat. (0126-8678). Kuala Lumpur.
Marine policy. (0308-597X). Guildford.
Marine resource economics. (0738-1360). London.
Marketing letters. (0923-0645). Dordrecht.
Marx-Engels Jahrbuch. (0232-6132). Berlin.
Marxistische Blätter. (0542-7770). Essen.

List of periodicals consulted

Masculinities. (1072-8538). New York.
Mast: Maritime anthropological studies. (0922-1476). Amsterdam.
Mathematical finance. (0960-1627). Oxford.
Mathematical social sciences. (0165 4896). Amsterdam.
Media culture and society. (0163-4437). London.
Medical anthropology. (0145-9740). Reading.
Medical anthropology quarterly. (0745-5194). Washington, D.C.
Medicina y sociedad. Buenos Aires.
Medio ambiente y urbanización. Buenos Aires.
Mediterranean quarterly: A journal of global issues. (1047-4552). Durham, NC.
Medizin Mensch Gesellschaft. (0340-8183). Stuttgart.
Medunarodni problemi. (0025-8555). Belgrade.
Megamot. (0025-8679). Jerusalem.
Meiji daigaku kyouyou ronshuu. Tokyo.
Meiji gakuin ronso. Tokyo.
Melanesian law journal. Papua New Guinea.
Melbourne historical journal. (0076-6232). Melbourne.
Melbourne journal of politics. (0085-3224). Melbourne.
Memoirs. Bukkyo University, Postgraduate Research Institute. Kyoto.
Memoria. Mexico D.F.
Memoriile Comisiei de Folclor. Bucharest.
Mens en maatschappij. (0025-9454). Houten.
Merhavim. Tel Aviv.
Mesoamérica. (0252-9963). Guatemala.
Mesopotamia. (0076-6615). Florence.
Metroeconomica. (0026-1386). Bologna.
Mezhdunarodnye otnosheniia. (0324-1092). Sofia.
Mezinárodní vztahy. (0323-1844). Prague.
Michigan law review. (0026-2234). Ann Arbor, MI.
Middle East business and economic review. Australia.
Middle East journal. (0026-3141). Bloomington, IN.
Middle East papers. Cairo.
Middle East report. (0899-0328). Washington, DC.
Middle East review. Saffron Waldon.
Middle East Studies Association bulletin. (0026-3184). Tucson, AZ.
Middle Eastern studies. (0026-3206). London.
Migracijske teme. (0352-5600). Zagreb.
Milbank quarterly. (0887-378X). New York, NY.
Millennium. (0305-8298). London.
Mind. (0026-4423). Oxford.
Mind and language. (0268 1064). Oxford.
Minerva. (0026-4695). London.
Mirovaia ekonomika i mezhdunarodnye otnosheniia. (0131-2227). Moscow.
MIS quarterly. (0276-7783). U.S.A.
Mitteilungen der Deutschen Orient-Gesellschaft zu Berlin. (0342-118X). Berlin.
Mitteilungen. S.W.A. Wissenschaftliche Gesellschaft = Journal SWA Scientific Society. Windhoek.
Modern Asian studies. (0026-749X). Cambridge.

Liste des periodiques consultés

Modern China. (0097-7004). Newbury Park, CA.
Modern law review. (0026-7961). Oxford.
Mon-khmer studies. (0147-5207). Honolulu, HI.
Monatsberichte der Deutschen Bundesbank. (0012-0006). Frankfurt am Main.
Monatsberichte. Österreichisches Institut für Wirtschaftsforschung. (0029-9898). Vienna.
Monde copte. (0399-905X). Limoges.
Mondes en développement. (0302-3052). Paris/Brussels.
Mondes et cultures. (0221-0436). Paris.
Monetaria. (0185-1136). Mexico City.
Monetary and economic studies. (0288-8432). Tokyo.
Money affairs. (0187-7615). Mexico City.
Mongolian studies. (0190-3667). Bloomington, IN.
Monthly report of the Deutsche Bundesbank. (0418-8292). Frankfurt.
Monthly review. (0027-0520). New York, NY.
Monthly review: State Bank of India, Economic Research Department. (0039-0003). Bombay.
Monumenta Nipponica. (0027-0741). Tokyo.
Monumenta serica. (0254-9948). St. Augustin.
Most: Economic journal on Eastern Europe and the former Soviet Union. Bologna.
Mouvement social. (0027-2671). Paris.
Multilingua. (0167-8507). Berlin.
NACLA report on the Americas. (0149-1598). New York, NY.
Namibiana. (0259-2010). Windhoek.
Narodna tvorchist' ta etnografiia. Kiev.
Národní hospodářství. (0032-0749). Prague.
Narody Azii i Afriki. Moscow.
National Institute economic review. (0027-9501). London.
National interest. (0884-9382). Washington, D.C.
National Museum papers. Manila.
National tax journal. (0028-0283). Columbus, OH.
National Westminster Bank quarterly review. (0028-0399). London.
Nationalities papers. (0090 5992). Omaha, NE.
NATO review. (0255-3813). Brussels.
Natural resources forum. (0165-0203). Guildford.
Natural resources journal. (0028-0739). Albuquerque, NM.
Nature and resources. (0028-0844). Carnforth.
Nauchnye doklady vysshei shkoly. Filosofskie nauki. Moscow.
Nauchnyi kommunizm. Moscow.
Nauka i zhizn'. Moscow.
Negotiation journal. (0748-4526). New York, NY.
NEHA-bulletin. (0920-9875). Amsterdam.
Nenpo Shakaigaku Ronsyu. Tokyo.
Néprajzi Értesítő. (0077-6599). Hungary.
Netherlands international law review. (0165-070X). Dordrecht.
Netherlands yearbook of international law. (0167-6768). Dordrecht.
Netherlands' journal of social sciences/Sociologia Neerlandica. (0038-0172). Assen.
Neue Gesellschaft/ Frankfurter Hefte. (0177-6738). Bonn.
Neue politische literatur. (0028-3320). Frankfurt-am-Main.

List of periodicals consulted

Neue Zeitschrift für Missionswissenschaft = Nouvelle revue de science missionnaire. (0028-3495). Immensee.
New community. (0047-9586). Coventry.
New England economic review. Boston, MA.
New European. (0953-1432). Bradford.
New formations. (0950-2378). London.
New ground. Newtown.
New Hungarian quarterly. (0028-5390). Budapest.
New internationalist. (0305-9529). London.
New left review. (0028-6060). London.
New perspectives on Turkey. (0896-6346). Great Barrington, MA.
New politics. (0028-6494). Brooklyn, NY.
New quest. (0258-0381). Pune.
New technology, work and employment. (0268-1072). Oxford.
New Vico studies. (0733-9542). New York, NY.
New York University journal of international law and politics. (0028-7873). New York, NY.
New York University law review. (0028-7881). New York, N.Y.
New Zealand economic papers. (0077-9954). Wellington.
New Zealand international review. (0110-0262). Wellington.
New Zealand journal of history. (0028-8322). Auckland.
Newsletter. IWGIA (International Work Group for Indigenous Affairs). (0105-6387). Copenhagen.
NFT: Scandinavian insurance quarterly. (Den norske Forsikringsforening/ Försäkringsföreningen i Finland/ Svenska Föräkringsföreningen). Stockholm.
NIAS. (0904-597X). Copenhagen.
Nieuwe West-Indische gids = New West Indian guide. (0028-9930). Dordrecht.
Nigerian field. (0029-0076). Ibadan.
Nigerian forum. (0189-0816). Lagos.
Nigerian journal of economic and social studies. (0029-0092). Ibadan.
Nigerian journal of policy and strategy. Kuru, Nigeria.
Nigerian journal of political science. (0031-8524). Zaria.
Nigerian journal of public administration and local government. Nsukka.
Nihon Keizaiseisaku Gakkai Nenpo. Tokyo.
Ningen Kagaku Kenkyu [Journal of Waseda University]. Tokyo.
Nogyo mondai kenkyu. Tokyo.
Nonprofit and voluntary sector quarterly. (0899-7640). San Francisco, CA.
Nonprofit management and leadership. (1048-6682). San Francisco, CA.
Nord nytt. (0008-1345). Lyngby.
Nordic journal of linguistics. (0332-5865). Oslo.
Norsk økonomisk tidsskrift. (0039-0720). Oslo.
North Korea quarterly. (0340-104X). Hamburg.
Noson Seikatsu Kenkyu. Tsukuba.
Notas mesoamericanas. Puebla.
Notes and records of the Royal Society of London. (0035-9149). London.
Noticario de historia agraria. (1132-1261). Zaragoza, Spain.
Novedades economicas. Buenos Aires.
Nowe drogi. (0029-5388). Warsaw.
Nsukka journal of linguistics and African languages. (0794-6961). Nsukka.

Liste des periodiques consultés

Nueva sociedad. Caracas.
Numen. (0029-5973). Leiden.
Objets et mondes. (0029-7615). Paris.
Observations et diagnostics économiques. (0751-6614). Paris.
Obshchestvennye nauki. Moscow.
Obshchestvennye nauki i sovremennost'. (0869 0499). Moscow.
Obshchestvennye nauki v Uzbekistane. Tashkent.
Obshchestvo i ekonomika. (0207 3676). Moscow.
Ocean development and international law. (0090-8320). London.
Oceania. (0029-8077). Sydney.
Oceanic linguistics. (0029-8115). Honolulu, HI.
Odu. (0029-8522). Ile Ife.
OECD economic studies. (0255-0822). Paris.
OPEC bulletin. (0474-6279). Vienna.
OPEC review. Oxford.
Open economies review. (0923-7992). Dordrecht.
Operations research letters. (0167-6377). Amsterdam.
Option: Izbor. (08611667). Sofia.
Oral history. (0143-0955). Colchester.
Orbis. (0030-4387). Philadelphia, PA.
Ordo. (0048-2129). Stuttgart.
Organization science. (1047-7039). Providence, RI.
Organization studies. (0170-8406). Berlin.
Organizational behavior and human decision processes. (0749-5978). Duluth, MN.
Oriens Extremus. (0030-5197). Wiesbaden.
Orient. (0030-5227). Leverkusen.
Orientalia. (0030-5367). Rome.
Orientalia lovaniensia periodica. Leuvan.
Orissa historical research journal. Orissa.
Orita. (0030-5596). Ibadan.
Osaka daigaku ningenkagakubu kiyō. Osaka.
Osaka economic papers. (0473-4548). Osaka.
Osaka shogyo daigaku ronshu. Osaka.
Osnovnye napravleniia nauchno-tekhnicheskogo progressa v Iaponii. Moscow.
Österreichische Zeitschrift für öffentliches Recht und Völkerrechte. (0378-3073). Vienna.
Österreichische Zeitschrift für Politikwissenschaft. Vienna.
Osteuropa. (0030-6428). Stuttgart.
Osteuropa Wirtschaft. (0030-6460). Stuttgart.
Otechestvennaia istoriia. Moscow.
Otemon economic studies. (0475-0756). Osaka.
Our generation. (0030-686X). Quebec.
Overseas social security news. Tokyo.
Oxford agrarian studies. (0264-5491). Oxford.
Oxford bulletin of economics and statistics. (0305-9049). Oxford.
Oxford economic papers. (0030-7653). Oxford.
Oxford journal of archaeology. (0262-5253). Oxford.
Oxford review of economic policy. (0266-903X). Oxford.
Oyo-shakaigaku Kenkyu [Journal of Rikkyo University]. Tokyo.

List of periodicals consulted

Pacific affairs. (0030-851X). Vancouver.
Pacific economic bulletin. (0817-8038). Canberra.
Pacific historical review. (0030-8684). Berkeley, CA.
Pacific perspective. (0379-626X). Suva.
Pacific review. (0951-2748). Oxford.
Pacific studies. (0275-3596). Laie, HI.
Pacific viewpoint. (0030-8978). Wellington.
Paideuma. (0078-7809). Stuttgart.
Pakistan development review. (0030-9729). Islamabad.
Pakistan economic and social review. Lahore.
Pakistan horizon. (0030-980X). Karachi.
Pakistan journal of history and culture. (1012-7682). Islamabad.
Pamir. Dushaube.
Państwo i prawo. (0031-0980). Warsaw.
Papeles de económia española. (0210-9107). Madrid.
Papers. (0210-2862). Barcelona.
Papers in regional science: Revue d'études canadiennes. (0486-2902). Urbana, IL.
Paradigms. (0951-9750). Canterbury, Kent.
Parliamentarian. (0031-2282). London.
Parliamentary affairs. (0031-2290). Oxford.
Past and present. Oxford.
Patterns of prejudice. (0031-322X). London.
Peasant studies. Salt Lake City, UT.
Penant. (0336-1551). Le Vésinet.
Peninsule. Metz.
Pensamiento iberoamericano. (0212-0208). Madrid.
Pensée. (0031-4773). Paris.
Pensiero politico. (0031-4846). Florence.
Pénzügyi szemle. (0031-496X). Budapest.
Perception & psychophysics. (0031-5117). Austin, TX.
Peripherie. (0173-184X). Berlin.
Perspectiva económica. (0100-039X). São Leopoldo.
Perspectives in energy. London.
Pesquisa e planejamento econômico. (0100-0551). Rio de Janeiro.
Petroleum economist. (0306-395X). London.
Peuples méditerranéens = Mediterranean peoples. (0399-1253). Paris.
Philippine economic journal. Philippines.
Philippine journal of public administration. (0031-7675). Quezon City.
Philippine quarterly of culture and society. (0115-0243). Cebu City.
Philippine studies. (0031-7837). Quezon City.
Philosophie politique. Paris.
Philosophy & public affairs. (0048-3915). Princeton, N.J.
Philosophy & social criticism. London.
Philosophy east and west. (0031-8221). Honolulu, HI.
Philosophy of the social sciences. (0048-3931). Newbury Park, CA.
Planeación y desarrollo. (0034-8686). Colombia.
Planning and administration. (0304-117X). The Hague.
Planning outlook. (0032-0714). Newcastle-upon-Tyne.

Liste des periodiques consultés

Planning practice and research. (0269-7459). London.
Planovoe khoziaistvo. (0370 0356). Moscow.
Policing and society. (1043-9463). New York, N.Y.
Policy and politics. (0305-5736). Bristol.
Policy sciences. (0032-2687). Dordrecht.
Policy studies. (0144-2872). London.
Polin. (0268-1056). Oxford.
Polis [Bologna]. Bologna.
Polis [Moscow]. (03212017). Moscow.
Polis [York]. (0412-257X). York.
Polish perspectives. (0032-2962). Warsaw.
Polish quarterly of international affairs. (1230-4999). Warsaw.
Politica. (0105-0710). Århus.
Politica economica. Bologna.
Politica internazionale. (0032-3101). Rome.
Political communication. (1058-4609). London.
Political economy journal of India. (0971-2097). Chandigarh.
Political geography. (0962-6298). Oxford.
Political geography quarterly. (0260-9827). Guildford.
Political psychology. (0162-895X). New York, NY.
Political quarterly. (0032-3179). Oxford.
Political research quarterly. (1065-9129). Salt Lake City, UT.
Political science. (0032-3187). Wellington.
Political science and politics. (1049-0965). Washington,.
Political science quarterly. (0032-3195). New York, NY.
Political studies. (0032-3217). Oxford.
Political theory. (0090-5917). Newbury Park, CA.
Politička misao. (0032-3241). Zagreb.
Politico. (0032-325X). Milan.
Politics. (0263-3957). London.
Politics and society. (0032-3292). Stoneham, MA.
Politics and society in Germany, Austria and Switzerland. (0954-6030). Nottingham.
Politics and the individual: International journal of political socialization and political psychology. (0939-6071). Hamburg.
Politics and the life sciences. (0730-9384). Dekalb, IL.
Politiikka. Tampere.
Politikon. (0258-9346). Stellenbosch.
Politique africaine. (0244-7827). Paris.
Politique étrangère. (0032-342X). Paris.
Politique internationale. (0221-2781). Paris.
Politiques et management public. (0758-1726). Paris.
Politische Vierteljahresschrift. (0032-3470). Wiesbaden.
Politix. (0295-2319). Paris.
Population. (0032-4663). Paris.
Population and development review. (0098-7921). New York, N.Y.
Population and environment. (0199-0039). New York, N.Y.
Population research and policy review. (0167-5923). Dordrecht.
Population review. (0032-471X). La Jolla, CA.

List of periodicals consulted

Population studies. (0032-4728). London.
Population studies. (0082-805X). New York, NY.
Post-Soviet affairs. (1060-586X). Silver Spring, MD.
Postmodern critical theorising. Adelaide.
Pouvoirs. (0152-0768). Paris.
Praca i zabezpieczenie społeczne. (0032-6186). Warsaw.
Prace etnologiczne. Warsaw.
Practice. (0950-3153). Birmingham.
Pracy i materiały etnograficzne. (0079-4759). Warsaw.
Prague occasional papers in ethnology. Prague.
Praxis international. (0260-8448). Oxford.
Présence africaine. (0032-7638). Paris.
Presidential studies quarterly. (0360-4918). New York, NY.
Primates. Japan.
Priroda. Moscow.
Problèmes d'Amérique latine. (0765-1333). Paris.
Problèmes politiques et sociaux. (0015-9743). Paris.
Problemi spoline trgovine i konjunkture. (0032-938X). Belgrade.
Problems of communism. (0032-941X). Washington, D.C.
Problemy amerikanistiki. Moscow.
Problemy Dal'nego Vostoka. Moscow.
Problemy otechestvenuoi i vseobshchei istorii. Leningrad.
Probus. (0921-4771). Berlin.
Proceedings of the Academy of Political Science. (0065-0684). New York, NY.
Proceedings. American Statistical Association. Alexandria, VA.
Professional geographer. (0033-0124). Washington, D.C.
Progress in human geography. (0309-1325). Sevenoaks.
Progress in planning. (0305-9006). Oxford.
Project appraisal. (0268-8867). Guildford.
Projet. (0033-0884). Paris.
Prokla: Probleme des Klassenkampfs. Berlin.
Przegląd archeologiczny. (0079-7138). Wrocław.
Przeglad orientalistyczny. Warsaw.
Przegląd polonijny. (0137-303X). Wroclaw.
Przegląd socjologiczny. (0033-2356). Łódź.
Przegląd statystyczny. (0033-2372). Warsaw.
Psychoanalytic review. (0033-2836). New York, NY.
Psychological bulletin. (0033-2909). Arlington, VA.
Psychological review. (0033-295X). Arlington, VA.
Psychology and developing societies. New Delhi.
Psychotherapy research. (0894-7597). New York, NY.
Public administration. (0033-3298). Oxford.
Public administration and development. (0271-2075). Chichester.
Public administration review. (0033-3352). Washington, DC.
Public affairs quarterly. (0887-0373). Bowling Green, OH.
Public choice. (0048-5829). Dordrecht.
Public culture. (0899-2363). Philadelphia, PA.
Public enterprise. (0351-3564). Ljubljana.

Liste des periodiques consultés

Public finance = Finances publiques. (0033-3476). Frankfurt am Main.
Public finance quarterly. (0048-5853). Newbury Park, CA.
Public interest. (0033-3557). Washington, DC.
Public law. (0033-3565). London.
Public money and management. (0954-0962). Oxford.
Public opinion quarterly. (0033-362X). Chicago, IL.
Public sector. (0110-5191). Wellington.
Publius: Journal of federalism. (0048-5950). Denton, TX.
Publizistik. (0033-4006). Konstanz.
Quaderni del Dipartimento di studi glottoantropologici. Rome.
Quaderni di sociologia. (0033-4952). Turin.
Quaderni di studi arabi. Venice.
Quadrant. (0033-5002). Melbourne.
Quarterly bulletin. Central Bank of Ireland. (0069-1542). Dublin.
Quarterly economic bulletin. (0952-0724). Liverpool.
Quarterly economic commentary. (0306-7866). Glasgow.
Quarterly economic review. Bank of Korea. Seoul.
Quarterly journal of administration. (0001-8333). Ile-Ife.
Quarterly journal of economics. (0033-5533). Cambridge, MA.
Quarterly journal of the Mythic Society. (0047-8555). Bangalore.
Quarterly review of economics and business. (0033-5797). Champaign, IL.
Quarterly review of economics and finance. (0033-5797). U.S.A.
Quarterly review. Federal Reserve Bank of New York. (0147-6580). New York, NY.
Quarterly review. Sveriges Riksbank. (0346-6583). Stockholm.
Que vous en semble? Bujumbura.
Quest. (1011-226X). Lusaka.
R&D management. (0033-6807). Oxford.
Rabochii klass i sovremennyi mir. (0321-2017). Moscow.
Race and class. (0306-3965). London.
Radical history review. (0163-6545). New York.
Rand journal of economics. (0741-6261). Santa Monica, CA.
Rassegna economica. Naples.
Rassegna italiana di sociologia. (0486 0349). Bologna.
Rassegna parlamentare. Rome.
Rasy i narody. Moscow.
Raven. (0951-4066). London.
Realidad economica. Buenos Aires.
Recherches économiques de Louvain. (0770-4518). Brussels.
Recherches sociographiques. (0034-1282). Québec.
Recherches sociologiques. (0771-677X). Leuven.
Recht der internationalen Wirtschaft. (0340-7926). Heidelberg.
Regards sur l'actualité. (0337-7091). Paris.
Regional politics and policy. (0959-2318). London.
Regional science and urban economics. (0166-0462). Amsterdam.
Regional studies. (0034-3404). Cambridge.
Rekishi to shakai. Tokyo.
Relations internationales. (0335-2013). Paris.
Religion. (0048-721X). London.

List of periodicals consulted

Religion in communist lands. (0307-5974). Keston.
Religion, state and society. (0963-7494). Abingdon.
Renewal. (0968-252X). London.
Res publica [Brusels]. (0486-4700). Brussels.
Res publica [Warsaw]. (0860-4592). Warsaw.
Resarun. Itanagar.
Research bulletin. Meisei University. Tokyo.
Research bulletin. Tokyo University, Graduate School of Sociology. Tokyo.
Research in economic anthropology. (0190-1281). Greenwich, CT.
Research in Melanesia. (0254-0665). Port Moresby.
Research in political economy. (0161-7230). Greenwich, CT.
Research in population economics. (0163-7878). Greenwich, CT.
Research in social movements, conflicts and change. (0163-786X). Greenwich, CT.
Research in social stratification and mobility. (0276-5624). Greenwich, CT.
Research papers in education: Policy and practice. (0267-1522). London.
Research report. National Institute for Educational Research. Tokyo.
Reserve Bank bulletin. (0112-871X). Wellington.
Reserve Bank of India bulletin. (0034 5512). Bombay.
Resources policy. (0301-4207). Oxford.
Response to the victimization of women and children. (0894-7597). New York, NY.
Rethinking Marxism. (0893-5696). New York, NY.
Review. Suva, Fiji.
Review of African political economy. (0305-6244). Sheffield.
Review of Austrian economics. (0889-3047). Dordrecht.
Review of black political economy. (0034-6446). New Brunswick, NJ.
Review of Central and East European law. (0925-9880). Dordrecht.
Review of economic conditions in Italy. (0034-6799). Rome.
Review of economic studies. (0034-6527). Oxford.
Review of economics and statistics. (0034-6535). Amsterdam.
Review of financial studies. (0893-9454). Cary, NC.
Review of income and wealth. (0034-6586). New York, NY.
Review of Indonesian and Malaysian affairs. (0034-6594). Sydney.
Review of industrial organization. (0889-938X). Dordrecht.
Review of international co-operation. (0034-6608). Geneva.
Review of international political economy. (0969-2290). London.
Review of international studies. (0260-2105). Cambridge.
Review of Islamic economics. (0962-2055). Leicester.
Review of Middle East studies. Buckhurst Hill.
Review of political economy. (0953-8259). Sevenoaks.
Review of politics. (0034-6705). Notre-Dame, IN.
Review of quantitative finance and accounting. (0924-865X). Dordrecht.
Review of radical political economics. (0486-6134). Riverside.
Review of rural and urban planning in Southern and Eastern Africa. Harare.
Review of social economy. (0034-6764). DeKalb, IL.
Review of socialist law. (0165-0300). Dordrecht.
Review of the economic situation of Mexico. (0187-3407). Mexico City.
Review of urban and regional development studies. Tokyo.
Review. Federal Reserve Bank of St. Louis. (0014-9187). St. Louis, MO,.

Liste des periodiques consultés

Review. Fernand Braudel Center. (0147-9032). Binghamton, NY.
Reviews in anthropology. (0093 8157). Bedford Hills, NY.
Revista Andina. (0259-9600). Cusco, Peru.
Revista brasileira de ciência política. (0103-3352). Brasilia.
Revista brasileira de ciências sociais. (0102-6909). São Paulo.
Revista brasileira de economia. (0034-7140). Rio de Janeiro.
Revista brasileira de estudos de população. (0102-3098). Brazil.
Revista brasileira de estudos políticos. (0034-7191). Belo Horizonte.
Revista colombiana de antropologia. (0486-6525). Bogota.
Revista de administración pública. (0034-7639). Madrid.
Revista de antropologia. (0120-6613). Bogota.
Revista de ciência política. (0034-8023). Rio de Janeiro.
Revista de ciências sociais. (0041-8862). Ceará.
Revista de ciencias sociales. (0034-7817). Puerto Rico.
Revista de econometria. (0101-7012). Recife.
Revista de economía. Montevideo.
Revista de economia y estadistica. (0034-8066). Córdoba.
Revista de estudios políticos. (0048-7694). Madrid.
Revista de etnografie şi folclor. (0034-8198). Bucharest.
Revista de fomento social. (0015-6043). Madrid.
Revista de historia económica. (0212-6109). Madrid.
Revista de planeación y desarrollo. (0034-8686). Bogotá.
Revista del Banco de la República. (0005-4828). Bogotá.
Revista del Centro de Estudios Constitucionales. (0214-6185). Madrid.
Revista econômica do nordeste. (0100-4956). Fortaleza.
Revista idea. Buenos Aires.
Revista interamericana de planificación. (0037-8593). Guatemala.
Revista mexicana de sociología. (0035-0087). Mexico City.
Revista occidental. Tijuana.
Revista paraguaya de sociología. Asunción.
Revista Universidad EAFIT. (0120-033X). Medellín.
Revue administrative. (0035 0672). Paris.
Revue algérienne des sciences juridiques économiques et politiques. Algiers.
Revue belge de droit international = Belgian review of international law = Belgisch tijdschrift voor internationaal recht. (0035-0788). Brussels.
Revue canadienne d'études de développement = Canadian journal of development studies. (0225-5189). Ottawa.
Revue d'assyriologie et d'archéologie orientale. Paris.
Revue d'économie politique. (0373-2630). Paris.
Revue d'économie régionale et urbaine. (0180-7307). Paris.
Revue d'études comparatives est-ouest. (0338-0599). Paris.
Revue d'études palestiniennes. (0252-8290). Paris.
Revue d'histoire moderne et contemporaine. (0048-8003). Paris.
Revue de Corée. Seoul.
Revue de droit penal et de criminologie. Bruges.
Revue de droit social = Tijdschrift voor sociaal recht. (0035-1113). Brussels.
Revue de l'économie meridionale. (0987-3813). Montpellier.
Revue de l'histoire des religions. (0035-1423). Paris.

List of periodicals consulted

Revue de l'Institut de sociologie. (0770-1055). Brussels.
Revue de l'Institut des bellos-lettres arabes. (0018-862X). Tunis Bab Meuara.
Revue de science criminelle et de droit pénal comparé. (0035-1733). Paris.
Revue des études arméniennes. (0080-2549). Paris.
Revue des études coopératives mutualistes et associatives. (0035-2020). Paris.
Revue des études géorgiennes et caucasiennes. (0373-1537). Louvain.
Revue du droit public: Et de la science politique en France et à l'étranger. (0035-2578). Paris.
Revue du financier. (0223-0143). Vineuil.
Revue du marché commun. (0035-2616). Paris.
Revue du monde musulman et de la Méditerranée. (0997-1327). Aix-en-Provence.
Revue du travail. (0035-2705). Brussels.
Revue économique et sociale. (0035-2772). Lausanne-Dorigny.
Revue européenne de droit public = European review of public law = Europäische Zeitschrift des öffentlichen Rechts = Rivista europea di diritto pubblico. (1105-1590). London.
Revue européenne des sciences sociales: Cahiers Vilfredo Pareto. (0008-0497). Geneva.
Revue fiscalité européenne. (0242-5599). Nice.
Revue française d'administration publique. (0152-7401). Paris.
Revue française d'histoire d'outre-mer. (0300-9513). Paris.
Revue française de science politique. (0035-2950). Paris.
Revue française de sociologie. (0035-2969). Paris.
Revue française des affaires sociales. (0035-2985). Paris.
Revue générale de droit international public. (0035-3094). Paris.
Revue hellénique de droit international. (0035-3256). Athens.
Revue internationale de droit comparé. (0035-3337). Paris.
Revue internationale de droit penal = International review of penal law. (0223-5404). Toulouse.
Revue juridique, politique et économique du Maroc. (0251-4761). Rabat.
Revue politique et parlementaire. (0035-385X). Paris.
Revue québécoise de science politique. (0711-608X). Montreal.
Revue roumaine d'études internationales. (0048-8178). Bucharest.
Revue roumaine des sciences sociales: Série de sociologie. (0080-2646). Bucharest.
Revue roumaine des sciences sociales: Série des sciences économiques. (0035-404X). Bucharest.
Revue roumaine des sciences sociales: Série des sciences juridiques. (0035-4023). Bucharest.
Revue syndicale suisse. (0035-421X). Berne.
Revue Tiers-Monde. (0040-7356). Paris.
Revue trimestrielle de droit commercial et de droit économique. (0244-9358). Paris.
Revue trimestrielle de droit européen. (0035-4317). Paris.
Revue tunisienne de sciences sociales. (0035-4333). Tunis.
Rig. (0035-5267). Stockholm.
Rinrigaku Nenpo. Tokyo.
Riron to hoho = Sociological theory and methods. (0913-1442). Sapporo.
Risparmio. (0035-5615). Milan.
Ritsumeikan review of industrial society. Kyoto.
Rivista di diritto finanziario e scienza delle finanze. (0035-6131). Milan.
Rivista di economia agraria. (0035-6190). Bologna.

Liste des periodiques consultés

Rivista di politica economica. (0391-6170). Rome.
Rivista di storia economica. (0393-3415). Turin.
Rivista di studi politici internazionali. (0035-6611). Florence.
Rivista internazionale di scienze economiche e commerciali. (0035-6751). Milan.
Rivista internazionale di scienze sociali. (0035-676X). Milan.
Rivista italiana di scienza politica. (0048-8402). Bologna.
Rivista storica italiana. (0035-7073). Naples.
Rivista trimestrale di diritto pubblico. (0557-1464). Milan.
Rock art research. (0813-0426). Melbourne.
Roma. Chandigarh.
Ronshu [Bulletin of Tohoku Gakuin University]. Sendai.
Ronshu [Bulletin of Tokyo Women's University]. Tokyo.
Ronshu [Journal of Komatsu College]. Komatsu.
Ronshu [Journal of Matsuyama University]. Matsuyama.
Ronshu [Journal of Matsuyama University]. Matsuyama.
Ronso. Mizunami.
Ronso Shinrigaku Kiyo [Journal of Meiji Gakuin University]. Tokyo.
Rossiiskii ekonomicheskii zhurnal. (0130 9757). Moscow.
Round table. (0035-8533). Abingdon.
Royal Bank of Scotland review. (0267-1190). Edinburgh.
RSA policy review. (1012-764X). Pretoria.
Rural africana. (0085-5839). East Lansing, MI.
Rural development in Nigeria. Ibadan.
Rural history: Economy, society, culture. (0956-7933). Cambridge.
Rural sociology. (0036-0112). College Station, TX.
RWI-Mitteilungen. (0933-0089). Berlin.
Ryukoku Kiyo. Kyoto.
Saeculum. (0080-5319). Freiburg.
SAIS review. (0036-0777). Washington, DC.
SALG newsletter. (0307-1456). London.
Sangeet natak. New Delhi.
Santé mentale au Québec. (0383-6320). Montréal.
Sarawak gazette. Kuching.
Sarawak Museum journal. (0375-3050). Kuching.
Sari. (0127-2721). Selangor.
Sarjana. Kuala Lumpur.
Savanna. (0331-0523). Zaria.
Savings and development. (0393-4551). Milan.
Sbornik Muzeia antropologii i etnografii. Leningrad.
Scandinavian economic history review. (0358-5522). Lund.
Scandinavian housing and planning research. (0281-5737). Stockholm.
Scandinavian journal of development alternatives. (0280-2791). Stockholm.
Scandinavian journal of economics. (0347-0520). Oxford.
Scandinavian journal of the Old Testament. (0901-8328). Aarhus.
Scandinavian political studies. (0080-6757). Oslo.
Schweizerische Versicherungs-Zeitschrift = Revue Suisse d'assurances. (0171-7200). Berne.
Schweizerische Zeitschrift für Volkswirtschaft und Statistik = Revue suisse d'économie politique et de statistique. Bern.

List of periodicals consulted

Science and public policy. (0302-3427). Guildford.
Science and society. (0036-8237). New York, NY.
Science as culture. (0959-5431). London.
Science, technology & development. (0950-0707). London.
Scientific American. (0036-8733). New York, NY.
Scottish journal of political economy. (0036-9292). Oxford.
Searchlight South Africa. (0954-3384). London.
Security dialogue. (0967-0106). London.
Sefarad. (0037-0894). Madrid.
Selected reports in ethnomusicology. Los Angeles, CA.
Semiotica. Berlin.
Senri ethnological studies. Osaka.
Senriyama bungaku-ronshu. Osaka.
Severnye prostory. Moscow.
Shakai bunseki. Tokyo.
Shakai-kagaku tokyu. Tokyo.
Shakai-undo. Tokyo.
Shakaibunka Kenkyu. Hiroshima.
Shakaigaku hyoron. Tokyo.
Shakaigaku kenkyu. Sendai.
Shakaigaku kenkyuka kiyo [Bulletin of Keio-Gijuku Graduate School]. Tokyo.
Shakaigaku nenpō. Sendai.
Shakaigaku Ronko. Tokyo.
Shakaigaku Ronshu. Kariya.
Shakaigaku Ronshu [Bulletin of Momoyama University]. Osaka.
Shakaigaku ronshu [Journal of Nihon University]. Tokyo.
Shakaigaku ronso. Tokyo.
Shakaigaku-nenshi. Tokyo.
Shakaigaku-senko kiyo. Tokyo.
Shakaigaku-zasshi. Kobe.
Shakaigakubu kiyo [Bulletin of Ryukoku University]. Otsu.
Shakaigakubu Kiyo [Journal of Kansai University]. Osaka.
Shakaishinrigaku Kenkyu. Tokyo.
Shinbungaku hyoron. Japan.
Shizen, Ningen, Shakai. Yokohama.
Shnaton. Tel-Aviv.
SIER Bulletin. Kwaluseni.
Signs. (0097-9740). Chicago, IL.
Sikh review. (0037-5123). Calcutta.
Simmei Shakaigaku Kenkyu. Kawasaki.
Simulation and gaming. (0037-5500). Newbury Park, CA.
Singapore economic review. (0217-5908). Singapore.
Singapore journal of tropical geography. (0129-7619). Kent Ridge.
Sino-American relations. Taiwan.
Sino-Western cultural relations journal. (1041-875X). Cedar Rapids.
Siso no Kagaku. Tokyo.
Sistema. (0210-0223). Madrid.
Skandinaviska Enskilda Banken quarterly review. (0349-6694). Stockholm.

Liste des periodiques consultés

Slavic review. (0037-6779). Stanford, CA.
Slavonic and East European review. (0037-6795). London.
Sloan management review. (0019-848X). Cambridge, MA.
Slovo. (0954-6839). London.
Small business economics. (0921-898X). Dordrecht.
Small enterprise development. (0957-1329). London.
Smithsonian contributions to anthropology. (0081-0223). Washington, D.C.
Social action. (0037-7627). New Delhi.
Social action. London.
Social analysis. (0155-977X). Adelaide.
Social and economic studies. (0037-7651). Kingston.
Social anthropology. (0964-0282). Cambridge.
Social attitudes in Northern Ireland. Belfast.
Social behaviour. (0885-6249). Chichester.
Social biology. (0037-766X). New York, NY.
Social choice and welfare. (0176-1714). Berlin.
Social cognition. (0278-616X). New York, NY.
Social compass. (0037-7686). London.
Social dynamics. (0253-3952). Rondebosch.
Social epistemology. (0269-1728). London.
Social forces. (0037-7732). Chapel Hill, NC.
Social history. (0307-1022). London.
Social indicators research. (0303-8300). Dordrecht.
Social justice. (0094-7571). San Francisco, CA.
Social networks. (0378-8733). Amsterdam.
Social philosophy & policy. (0265-0525). Oxford.
Social policy. (0037-7783). New York, NY.
Social policy and administration. (0144-5596). Oxford.
Social problems. (0037-7791). Berkeley, CA.
Social research. (0037-783X). New York, NY.
Social science & medicine. (0277-9536). Exeter.
Social science history. (0145-5532). Durham, NC.
Social science information. (0539-0184). London.
Social science quarterly. (0038-4941). Austin, TX.
Social science research. Tokushima.
Social science teacher. (0309-7544). Liverpool.
Social sciences. (0134-5486). Moscow.
Social sciences in China. (0252-9203). Beijing.
Social scientist. (0970-0293). New Delhi.
Social security journal. (0726-1195). Canberra.
Social service review. (0037-7961). Chicago, IL.
Social services abstracts. (0309-4693). London.
Social studies of science. (0306-3127). London.
Social work and social sciences review. (0953-5225). London.
Social work education. (0261-5479). London.
Socialism and democracy. New York, NY.
Socialisme. (0037-8127). Brussels.
Socialismo y participación. Lima.

List of periodicals consulted

Socialist alternatives. Quebec.
Socialist history. (0969-4331). London.
Socialistische standpunten. Brussels.
Sociétés contemporaines. (1150-1944). Paris.
Society. (0147-2011). New Brunswick, NJ.
Society of Malaŵi journal. (0037-993X). Blantyre.
Socijalizam. (0489 5967). Belgrade.
Socio-economic planning sciences. (0038-0121). Exeter.
Sociolinguistics. (0257-7135). Dordrecht.
Sociologia [Bratislavia] = Sociology. (0049-1225). Bratislava.
Sociologia [Rome]. (0038-0156). Rome.
Sociologia del lavoro. Milan.
Sociologia della comunicazione. Milan.
Sociologia internationalis. (0038-0164). Berlin.
Sociologia ruralis. (0038-0199). Assen.
Sociologia urbana e rurale. Bologna.
Sociologica. Tokyo.
Sociological analysis. (00380210). Washington, DC.
Sociological bulletin. (0038-0229). New Delhi.
Sociological forum. (0854-8971). New York, NY.
Sociological methodology. (0081-1750). Oxford.
Sociological methods and research. (0049 1241). Newbury Park, CA.
Sociological perspectives. (0731-1214). Greenwich, CT.
Sociological quarterly. (0038-0253). Greenwich, CT.
Sociological review. (0038-0261). London.
Sociological review [Kobe]. Kobe.
Sociological theory. (0735-2751). Cambridge, MA.
Sociologie du travail. (0038-0296). Paris.
Sociologische gids. (0038-0334). Meppel.
Sociologos. Tokyo.
Sociologus. (0038-0377). Berlin.
Sociology. (0038-0385). Solihull.
Sociology and social research. (0038-0393). Los Angeles, CA.
Sociology of health and illness. (0141-9889). Oxford.
Sociology of law. Tokyo.
Sociology of religion. (0038-0210). Washington DC.
Sociology of the sciences. Dordrecht.
Sogokagakubu-kiyo. Hiroshima.
Sojourn. (0217-9520). Singapore.
Sophia. Tokyo.
Sophia University studies in sociology. Tokyo.
Soshiolojika. Tokyo.
Soshioroji. Kyoto.
Sots. trudy. Moscow.
Sotsial'no-politicheskii zhurnal. (0868 5797). Moscow.
Sotsiologicheskie issledovaniia (sotsis). (0132-1625). Moscow.
Sou'al. Paris.
South African archaeological bulletin. (0038-1969). Vlaeberg.

Liste des periodiques consultés

South African Archaeological Society: Goodwin series. (0304-3460). Vlaeberg.
South African geographical journal = Suid-Afrikaanse geografiese tydskrif. (0373-6245). Wits.
South African historical journal = Suid-Afrikaanse historiese joernaal. (0258-2473). Pretoria.
South African journal of African languages = Suid-Afrikaanse tydskrif vir Afrikatale. (0257-2117). Pretoria.
South African journal of economic history. Johannesburg.
South African journal of economics = Suid-Afrikaanse tydskrif vir ekonomie. (0038 2280). Pretoria.
South African journal of ethnology = Suid-Afrikaanse tydskrif vir etnologie. (0379-8860). Pretoria.
South African journal of labour relations. (0379-8410). Pretoria.
South African journal of sociology = Suid-Afrikaanse tydskrif vir sosiologie. Pretoria.
South African journal on human rights. (0258-7203). Johannesburg.
South African labour bulletin. Johannesburg.
South African law journal. (0258-2503). Kenwyn.
South African sociological review. (1015-1370). Rondebosch.
South Asia. (0085-6401). Armidale.
South Asia bulletin. (0732-3867). Albany, NY.
South Asia journal. (0970-4868). New Delhi.
South Asia research. (0262-7280). London.
South Asian anthropologist. (0257-7348). Ranchi.
South Asian studies. (0266-6030). London.
South Asian survey. (0971-5231). New Delhi.
South East Asian review. Gaya.
South West African scientific society journal. Windhoek.
Southeast Asia: history and culture. Tokyo.
Southeast Asian affairs. Singapore.
Southeast Asian research materials group newsletter. (0311-290X). Canberra.
Southern Africa record. (0377-5445). Braamfontein.
Southern economic journal. (0038-4038). Chapel Hill, NC.
Sovetskaia arkheologiia. (0038-5034). Moscow.
Sovetskaia etnografiia. (0038-5050). Moscow.
Sovetskaia tiurkologiia. Baku.
Sovetskii muzei. Moscow.
Sovetskoe finno-ugrovedenie. Tallin.
Sovetskoe gosudarstvo i pravo. (0132 0769). Moscow.
Soviet economy. (0882-6994). Silver Spring, MD.
Soviet Jewish affairs. (0038-545X). London.
Soviet studies. (0038-5859). Abingdon.
Soziale Welt. (0038-6073). Göttingen.
Soziologie. (0340-918X). Stuttgart.
Space commerce. (1043-934X). Reading.
Speaking of Japan. (0389-3510). Tokyo.
Spoudai. Piraeus.
Sprawozdania archeologiczne. (0081-3834). Wroclaw.
Sprawy międzynarodowe. (0038-853X). Warsaw.
Sri Lanka journal of social sciences. (0258-9710). Colombo.

List of periodicals consulted

Sri Lanka journal of the humanities. Peradeniya.
St. Andrew's University sociological review. Osaka, Japan.
Staat und Recht. (0038-8858). Berlin.
Staff papers.International Monetary Fund. (0020-8027). Washington, DC.
Statistica. (0039-0380). Bologna.
Statistical papers = Statistische Hefte. (0932-5026). Heidelberg.
Statistician. (0039-0526). Abingdon.
Statistics in transition. Warsaw.
Stato e mercato. Bologna.
Statsvetenskaplig tidskrift. (0039-0747). Lund.
Statute law review. (0144-3593). Oxford.
Storia contemporanea. (0039-1875). Bolonga.
Storia delle relazioni internazionali. (1120-0677). Florence.
Strategic management journal. (0143-2095). Chichester, West Sussex.
Studi bresciani. (1121-6557). Brescia.
Studi storici. (0039-3037). Rome.
Studia demograficzne. (0039-3134). Warsaw.
Studia diplomatica. (0770-2965). Brussels.
Studia Fennica: Folkloristica. (0085-6835). Helsinki.
Studia finansowe. (0511-1307). Warsaw.
Studia i materiały z historii kultury materialnej. (0081-6558). Warsaw.
Studia iranica. (0772-7852). Lésigny.
Studia orientalia. (0039-3282). Helsinki.
Studia prawno-ekonomiczne. (0081-6841). Wrocław.
Studies in American political development. New Haven, CT.
Studies in comparative communism. (0039-3592). Guildford.
Studies in comparative international development. (0039-3606). New Brunswick, NJ.
Studies in conflict and terrorism. (1057-610X). London.
Studies in family planning. (0039-3665). New York, NY.
Studies in history. (0257-6430). New Delhi.
Studies in history and philosophy of science. (0039-3681). Oxford.
Studies in law, politics, and society. London.
Studies in philosophy and education. (0039-3746). Dordrecht.
Studies in political economy. (0707-8552). Ottawa.
Studies in the linguistic sciences. Urbana, IL.
Studies in Third World societies. Williamsburg, VA.
Studies in Western Australian history. Nedlands.
Studies in Zionism. (0334-1771). Tel Aviv.
Studies of broadcasting. Tokyo.
Studies of the Japan Institute of Labour. Tokyo.
Studies. Kwansei Gakuin university, Sociology Department. Hyôgo.
Studii şi comunicări etnologie. (1221-6518). Bucharest.
Study of sociology. Sendai.
Südosteuropa Mitteilungen. (0340-174X). Munich.
Suomalais-Ugrilaisen Seuran Aikakauskirja. (0355-0214). Helsinki.
Survey. (0039-6192). London.
Survey of Jewish affairs. (0741-6571). Oxford.
Survival. (0039-6338). Oxford.

Liste des periodiques consultés

Svobodnaia mysl'. (0131-1212). Moscow.
Syrie & monde arabe. Damascus.
Szigma. (0039-8128). Budapest.
Szociologia. (0133-3461). Budapest.
T'ang studies. Boulder, CO.
Tafsut. Aix-en-Provence.
Tamkang journal of area studies. Taipei.
Tantara. Antananavivo.
Tanzanian economic trends. (0856-3373). Dar es Salaam.
Tareas. (0494-7061). Panama City.
Társadalmi szemle. (0039-971X). Budapest.
Tarsadalomkutatás. (0580-4795). Budapest.
Társadalomtudomanyi kozlemenyek. (0133-0381). Budapest.
Te reo. (0494-8440). Auckland.
Technology and culture. (0040-165X). Chicago, IL.
Technology and development. Tokyo.
Tel Aviv. (0334-4355). Tel Aviv.
Telos. (0090-6514). New York, NY.
Temas de economia mundial. Havana.
Tempo social. (0103-2070). São Paulo.
Temps modernes. (0040-3075). Paris.
Terra Nova. Washington, DC.
Terrain. (0760-5668). Paris.
Terrorism. (0149-0389). London.
Terrorism and political violence. (0954-6553). London.
Text. (0165-4888). Berlin.
Textual practice. (0950-236X). London.
Thai-Yunnan project newsletter. (1032-500X). Canberra.
The journal of communist studies and transition politics. (1352-3279). Ilford.
Theory and decision. (0040-5833). Dordrecht.
Theory and society. (0304-2421). Dordrecht.
Theory culture and society. (0263-2764). London.
Third World planning review. (0142-7849). Liverpool.
Third World quarterly. (0143-6597). London.
Tibet journal. (0970-55368). Dharamshala.
Tibetan review. Delhi.
Tidsskriftet antropologi. (0109-1012). Copenhagen.
Tijdschrift voor economie en management. (0772-7664). Louvain.
Tijdschrift voor economische en sociale geografie = Journal of economic and social geography. (0040-747X). Amsterdam.
Tijdschrift voor sociale geschiedenis. (0303-9935). Utrecht.
Time & society. (0961-463X). London.
Tochi-seido shigaku. Tokyo.
Tohoku daigaku bungakuba nenpo. Sendai.
Tohoku daigaku kyoyobu kiyo. Miyagi.
Tokai law review. Tokyo.
Toshi mondai. Tokyo.
Toshi-mondai Kenkyu. Osaka.

List of periodicals consulted

Town planning review. (0041-0020). Liverpool.
Toyama daigaku keizai ronshu. Toyama City.
TRACE. (0185-6286). Mexico City.
Transactions of the Asiatic Society of Japan. Tokyo.
Transactions of the Institute of British Geographers: New series. London.
Transactions of the Philological Society. (0079-1636). Oxford.
Transafrican journal of history. (0251-0391). Nairobi.
Transformation. (0258-7696). Durban.
Transit. (0938-2062). Frankfurt.
Transit: Europäische Revue. (0938-2062). Frankfurt am Main.
Transition. (1012-8263). Georgetown.
Transportation. (0049-4438). Dordrecht.
Travail et emploi. (0224-4365). Paris.
Trialogue: Information service for East-West-South relations. Berlin.
Tribus. (0082-6413). Stuttgart.
Tricontinental. (0864-1595). Havana.
Trimestre económico. (0041-3011). Mexico City.
Trudy Instituta ethnografii AN SSSR. Moscow.
Trudy Instituta iazyka, literatury i istorii Komi filiala Akademii nauk SSSR. Syktyvkar.
Trudy Nauchno-issledovatel'skogo instituta iazyka, literatury, istorii i ekonomiki Mordovskoi ASSR. Saransk.
Turcica revue d'études turques. Louvain.
Turkish review. Ankara.
Turkish review of Balkan studies. Istanbul.
Turkish review of Middle East studies. Istanbul.
Tuttogiovani notizie. Rome.
Twentieth century British history. (0955-2359). Oxford.
Ufahamu. (0041-5715). Los Angeles, CA.
Ulkopolitiikka. Helsinki.
Unasylva. (0041-6436). Rome.
Unisa Latin American report. (0256-6060). Pretoria.
Uniswa research journal. Kwaluseni.
Unitas. (0041-7130). Helsinki.
Universitas. (0049-5530). Legon.
University of Louisville journal of family law. (0022-1066). Louisville, KY.
University of Western Australia Anthropological Research Museum occasional papers. (0810-8536). Perth.
University studies. Ibaruki-Ken.
Uomo. Rome.
Uomo & cultura. Palermo.
Ural. Sverdlovsk.
Urban affairs annual reviews. (0083-4688). Newbury Park, CA.
Urban affairs quarterly. (0042-0816). Newbury Park, CA.
Urban anthropology. (0894-6019). Brockport, NY.
Urban forum. (1015-3802). Johannesburg.
Urban geography. (0272-3638). Silver Spring, MD.
Urban law and policy. (0165-0068). Amsterdam.
Urban studies. (0042 0980). Abingdon.

Liste des periodiques consultés

Utafiti. (0856-096X). Dar es Salaam.
Utilitas. (0953-8208). Oxford.
Utilities policy. (0957-1787). Oxford.
Valóság. (0324-7228). Budapest.
Verfassung und Recht in Übersee = Law and politics in Africa, Asia and Latin America. (0506-7286). Baden-Baden.
Vestnik Akademii nauk Kazakhskoi SSR. Alma-Ata.
Vestnik Akademii nauk SSSR. Moscow.
Vestnik drevnei istorii. Moscow.
Vestnik Leningradskogo universiteta: Seriia 5 Ekonomika. Leningrad.
Vestnik Leningradskogo universiteta: Seriia 6 Istoriia kpss, nauchnyi kommunizm, filosofiia pravo. (0132 4624). Leningrad.
Vestnik Leningradskogo universtiteta. Seriia. 2 Istoriia, iazykoznamie, literaturovedenne. Leningrad.
Vestnik Moskovskogo universiteta Seriia 13. Vostokovedenie. Moscow.
Vestnik Moskovskogo universiteta. Seriia 10 Zhurnalistika. (0320 8079). Moscow.
Vestnik Moskovskogo universiteta. Seriia 5.Geografiia. Moscow.
Vestnik Moskovskogo universiteta. Seriia 8. Istoriia. Moscow.
Vestnik Moskovskogo universiteta. Seriia 9 Filologiia. (0130 0075). Moscow.
Vestnik Moskovskogo universiteta: Seriia 12 Sotsialno-politicheskie issledovaniia. (0201 7385). Moscow.
Vestnik Moskovskogo universiteta: Seriia 6 Ekonomika. (0201-7385). Moscow.
Vestnik s.-kh. nauki. Moscow.
Vestnik Sankt-Peterburgskogo untverstieta: Seriia 6 Filosofiia, politologiia, sotsiolgiia, psikhologiia, pravo. (0132-4624). St Petersburg.
Vestnik vysshei shkoly. Moscow.
Vestsi Akademii navuk BSSR: Suryia gramadskikh navuk. (0321-1649). Minsk.
Vierteljahresberichte. (0936-451X). Bonn.
Vierteljahrschrift für Sozial- und Wirtschaftsgeschichte. (0340-8728). Stuttgart.
Vierteljahrshefte für Zeitgeschichte. (0042-5702). Munich.
Vierteljahrshefte zur Wirtschaftsforschung. (0340-1707). Berlin.
Viitorul social. Bucharest.
Visual anthropology. (0894-9468). New York, NY.
Vizantiiskii vremennik. Moscow.
Volkskundig bulletin. (0166-0667). Amsterdam.
Volonta. (0392-5013). Milan.
Voprosy antropologii. Moscow.
Voprosy ekonomiki. (0042-8736). Moscow.
Voprosy filosofii. (0042-8744). Moscow.
Voprosy iazykoznaniia. Moscow.
Voprosy istorii. (0042-8779). Moscow.
Voprosy istorii KPSS. (03208907). Moscow.
Voprosy nauchnogo ateizma. (0321-0847). Moscow.
Vostok. Saint Petersburg.
Waseda bulletin of comparative law. (0285-9211). Tokyo.
Waseda business & economic studies. (0388-1008). Tokyo.
Waseda economic papers. (0511-1943). Tokyo.
Waseda Koto Gakuin Kennkyu Nenshi. Tokyo.

List of periodicals consulted

Washington quarterly. (0163-660X). Cambridge, MA.
Weltwirtschaft. (0043-2652). Tübingen.
Weltwirtschaftliches Archiv. (0043-2636). Tübingen.
Werkdocumenten over etnische kunst = Working papers in ethnic art. Ghent.
West African journal of archaeology. (0331-3158). Ibadan.
West European politics. (0140-2382). London.
Western political quarterly. (0043-4078). Salt Lake City, UT.
Wirtschaftsdienst. (0043-6275). Hamburg.
Wirtschaftspolitische Blätter. (0043-6291). Vienna.
Wirtschaftspolitische Mitteilungen. Zürich.
Wirtschaftswissenschaft. (0043-633X). Berlin.
Wisconsin law review. (0043-650X). Madison, WI.
Wissenschaftliche Zeitschrift der Humboldt-Universität zu Berlin: Reihe Gesellschaftswissenschaften. (0863-0623). Berlin.
Without prejudice. (1035-4220). Melbourne.
Women's studies. (0049-7878). Reading.
Women's studies international forum. (0277-5395). Elmsford, NY.
Work and occupations. (0730-8884). Newbury Park, CA.
Work, employment and society. (0950-0170). London.
Working papers in linguistics. Columbus, OH.
World archaeology. (0043-8243). London.
World Bank economic review. (0258-6770). Washington, DC.
World Bank research observer. Washington, DC.
World development. (0305-750X). Oxford.
World economy. (0378-5920). Oxford.
World futures. (0260-4027). New York, NY.
World politics. (0043-8871). Baltimore, MD.
World review. Indooroophilly.
World today. (0043-9134). London.
WSI Mitteilungen. (0342 300X). Cologne.
Wuqûf. (0930-9306). Hamburg.
XXI Secolo. Turin.
Yagl-Ambu. (0254-0681). Papua New Guinea.
Yale law journal. (0044-0094). New Haven, CT.
Yamaguchi daigaku kyoikugakuba ronsoh. Yamaguchi.
Yapi kredi economic review. Levent, Istanbul.
Yearbook of co-operative enterprise. (0952-5556). Oxford.
Yearbook of Finnish foreign policy. (0355-0079). Helsinki.
Yhtyneet kuvalehdet oy. (0355-0303). Helsinki.
York papers in linguistics. (0307-3238). York.
Yugoslav law = Droit yougoslave. (0350-2252). Belgrade.
Zaïre-Afrique. (0049-8513). Kinshasa.
Zambezia. (0379-0622). Harare.
Zambia journal of history. Lusaka.
Zeitschrift für ausländisches öffentliches Recht und Völkerrecht. (0044-2348). Stuttgart.
Zeitschrift für Energie Wirtschaft. (0340-5377). Wiesbaden.
Zeitschrift für Ethnologie. (0044-2666). Berlin.
Zeitschrift für Missionswissenschaft und Religionswissenschaft. (0044-3123). Münster.

Liste des periodiques consultés

Zeitschrift für Parlamentsfragen. (0340-1758). Wiesbaden.
Zeitschrift für Politik. (0044-3360). Cologne.
Zeitschrift für Sexualforschung. (0932-8114). Stuttgart.
Zeitschrift für Soziologie. (0340-1804). Stuttgart.
Zeitschrift für Unternehmensgeschichte. (0342-2852). Stuttgart.
Zeitschrift für vergleichende Rechtswissenschaft. (0044-3638). Heidelberg.
Zeitschrift für Verkehrswissenschaft. (0044-3670). Düsseldorf.
Zeitschrift für Wirtschafts- und Sozialwissenschaften. (0342-1783). Berlin.
Zeitschrift für Wirtschaftspolitik. (0721-3808). Cologne.
Zimbabwe journal of economics. Harare.

LIST OF ABBREVIATIONS USED
LISTE DES ABBREVIATIONS UTILISÉS

A.J.S. American journal of sociology. (0024-9602). University of Chicago Press: Journals Division, P.O. Box 37005, Chicago, IL. 60637, U.S.A.
Acta Hum. Acta humana. (0866-6628).
Acta Oecon. Acta oeconomica. (0001-6373). Akadémiai Kiadó: H-1363 Budapest, P.O. Box 24, Hungary, in association with Hungarian Academy of Sciences.
Acta Sociol. Acta sociologica. (0001-6993). Universitetsforlaget: Journals Department, P.O.Box 2959 Tøyen, 0608-Oslo 6, Norway, in association with Scandinavian Sociological Association.
Acta Univ. Łódz. Acta Universitatis Łódziensis: Folia oeconomica. (0208-6018). Wydawnictwo Uniwersytetu Łódzkiego: ul. Nowotki 143, Łódz, Poland.
Addiction Addiction. (0965-2140). Carfax Publishing Company: PO Box 25, Abingdon, Oxfordshire, OX14 3UE, U.K.
Adm. Sci. Qua. Administrative science quarterly. (0001-8392). Cornell University, Johnson Graduate School of Management: Caldwell Hall, Cornell University, Ithaca, NY 14853, U.S.A.
Admin. Soc. Administration and society. (0095-3997). Sage Publications: 2455 Teller Road, Newbury Park, CA. 91320, U.S.A.
Administration Administration. (0001-8325). Institute of Public Administration of Ireland: 57-61 Lansdowne Road, Dublin 4, Ireland.
Aff. Soc. Int. Affari sociali internazionali. Franco Angeli Editore: viale Monza 106, 20127 Milan, Italy.
Afr. 2000 Afrique 2000. (1017-0952). Institut panafricain de relations internationales: Av. de Fré 265 - 1180, Brussels, Belgium.
Afr. Cont. Afrique contemporaine. (0002-0478). Documentation française: 29-31 Quai Voltaire, 75340 Paris Cedex 07, France.
Afr. Q. Africa quarterly. (0001-9828). Indian Council for Cultural Relations: Azad Bhavan, Indraprastha Estate, New Delhi 110 002, India.
Afr. Stud. African studies. (0002-0184). Witwatersrand University Press: P.O. Wits, 2050 South Africa.
Age. Soc. Ageing and society. (0144-686X). Cambridge University Press: The Edinburgh Building, Shaftesbury Road, Cambridge CB2 2RU, U.K., in association with Centre for Policy on Ageing/ British Society of Gerontology.
Agenda Agenda. (1013-0950). Agenda Collective: P.O. Box 37432, Overport, 4067 Durban, South Africa.
Agr. Soc. Agricultura y sociedad. (0211-8394). Ministerio de Agricultura, Pesca y Alimentacion: Centro de Publicaciones, Paseo de Infanta Isabel 1, 28071 Madrid, Spain.
Am. Anthrop. American anthropologist. (0002-7294). American Anthropological Association: 1703 New Hampshire Avenue N.W., Washington DC 20009, U.S.A.
Am. Behav. Sc. American behavioral scientist. (0002-7642). Sage Publications: 2455 Teller Road, Newbury Park, CA. 91320, U.S.A.

List of abbreviations used

Am. Ethn. American ethnologist. (0094-0496). American Ethnological Society: 1703 New Hampshire Avenue N.W., Washington DC 20009, U.S.A.

Am. Indígena América indígena. (0002-7081). Instituto Indigenista Interamericano: Insurgentes Sur 1690, Colonia Florida, 01030 Mexico, D.F., Mexico.

Am. J. Econ. S. American journal of economics and sociology. (0002-9246). American Journal of Economics and Sociology: 42 East 72 Street, New York, NY 10021, U.S.A.

Am. J. Islam. Soc. Sci. American journal of Islamic social sciences. (0742-6763). Association of Muslim Social Scientists/ International Institute of Islamic Thought: P.O. Box 669, Herndon, VA 22070, U.S.A.

Am. J. Pol. Sc. American journal of political science. (0092-5853). University of Texas Press, Journals Department: 2100 Comal, Austin TX. 78722, U.S.A., in association with Midwest Political Science Association.

Am. Phil. Q. American philosophical quarterly. (0003-0481). Philosophy Documentation Center: Bowling Green State University, Bowling Green, OH. 43403-0189, U.S.A.

Am. Poli. Sci. American political science review. (0003-0554). American Political Science Association: 1527 New Hampshire Avenue, N.W., Washington DC 20036, U.S.A.

Am. Psychol. American psychologist. (0003-066X). American Psychological Association: 1400 North Uhle Street, Arlington, VA. 22201, U.S.A.

Am. Sociol. American sociologist. (0003-1232). Transaction Periodicals Consortium: Rutgers University, New Brunswick, NJ. 08903, U.S.A.

Am. Sociol. R. American sociological review. (0003-1224). American Sociological Association: 1722 N. Street N.W., Washington DC 20036, U.S.A.

An. Est. Cent.Am. Anuario de estudios centroamericanos. (0377-7316). Universidad de Costa Rica, Instituto de Investigaciones Sociales: Apartado 75, 2060 Ciudad Universitaria, Rodrigo Facio, 2050 San Pedro de Montes de Oca, San Jose, Costa Rica.

Anál. Soc. Análise social. (0003-2573). Instituto de Ciências Sociais da Universidade de Lisboa: Avenida das Forças Armadas, Edificio I.S.C.T.E., Ala Sul, 1º andar, 1600 Lisbon, Portugal, in association with Junta Nacional de Investigação Científica e Tecnológia/ Instituto Nacional de Investigação Científica.

Ann. Am. Poli. Annals of the American Academy of Political and Social Science. (0002-7162). Sage Publications: 2455 Teller Road, Newbury Park, CA. 91320, U.S.A., in association with American Academy of Political and Social Science.

Ann. As. Am. G. Annals of the Association of American Geographers. (0004-5608). Association of American Geographers: 1710 Sixteenth Street, N.W., Washington DC 20009, U.S.A.

Ann. Géogr. Annales de géographie. (0003-4010). Armand Colin Éditeur: B.P. 22, 41353 Vineuil, France.

Ann. Inter. Crimin. Annales internationales de criminologie = International annals of criminology = Anales internacionales de criminologia. (0003-4452). Société Internationale de Criminologie = International Society for Criminology = Sociedad Internacional de Criminologia: 4 rue Mondavi, 75001 Paris, France.

Ann. R. Anthr. Annual review of anthropology. (0084-6570). Annual Reviews: 4139 El Camino Way, P.O. Box 10139, Palo Alto, CA. 94303-0897, U.S.A.

Ann. R. Info. Sci. Tech. Annual review of information science and technology. (0066-4200). Elsevier Science Publishers (North-Holland): Sara Burgerhartstraat 25, P.O. Box 211, 1000 AE Amsterdam, The Netherlands, in association with American Society for Information Science: 8720 Georgia Avenue, Suite 501, Silver Spring, MD. 20910-3602, U.S.A.

Liste des abbreviations utilisés

Ann. R. Psych. Annual review of psychology. (0066-4308). Annual Reviews: 4139 El Camino Way, P.O. Box 10139, Palo Alto, CA. 94303-0897, U.S.A.

Ann. R. Soc. Annual review of sociology. (0360-0572). Annual Reviews: 4139 El Camino Way, P.O. Box 10139, Palo Alto, CA. 94303-0899, U.S.A.

Ann. Reg. Sci. Annals of regional science. (0570-1864). Springer-Verlag: Postfach 10 52 80, D-69042 Heidelberg Germany, in association with Western Regional Science Association.

Ann. Soc. Année sociale. (0066-2380). Univeristé libre de Bruxelles, Institut de sociologie: Avenue Jeanne, 44-1050 Brussels, Belgium.

Ann. Sociol. Année sociologique. (0066-2399). Presses Universitaires de France: 108 boulevard Saint-Germain, 75006 Paris, France.

Annales Annales: Économies, sociétés, civilisations. (0395-2649). Armand Colin: 103 boulevard Saint-Michel, 75240 Paris Cedex 05, France, in association with C.N.R.S./ École des hautes études en sciences sociales.

Anthr. Today Anthropology today. (0307-6776). Royal Anthropological Institute of Great Britain and Ireland: 50 Fitzroy Street, London W1P 5HS, U.K.

App. Commun. Stud. Applied community studies. (0954-4232). Whiting & Birch: P.O. Box 872, Forest Hill, London SE23 3HL, U.K., in association with Manchester Polytechnic: Department of Applied Community Studies, 799 Wilmslow Road, Didsbury, Manchester, M20 8RR, U.K.

Arc. Kommunal. Archiv für Kommunalwissenschaften. (0003-9209). Verlag W. Kohlhammer: Heßbrühlstraße 69, Postfach 80 04 30, 7000 Stuttgart 80 (Vaihingen), Germany, in association with Deutsches Institut für Urbanistik: Straße des 17. Juni 112, Postfach 12 62 24, 1000 Berlin 12, Germany.

Arc. Recht. Soz. Archiv für Rechts- und Sozialphilosophie = Archives de philosophie du droit et de philosophie sociale = Archives for philosophy of law and social philosophy = Archivo de filosofía jurídica y social. (0001-2343). Franz Steiner Verlag: Birkenwaldstraße 44, Postfach 10 15 26, D-7000 Stuttgart 1, Germany, in association with Internationale Vereinigung für Rechts- und Sozialphilosophie.

Arch. St. Urb. Region. Archivio di studi urbani e regionali. Franco Angeli editore: Viale Monza 106, 20127 Milan, Italy.

Area Area. (0004-0894). Institute of British Geographers: 1 Kensington Gore, London SW7 2AR, U.K.

Argumentation Argumentation. (0920-427X). Kluwer Academic Publishers: P.O. Box 322, 3300 AH Dordrecht, The Netherlands, in association with European Centre for the Study of Argumentation: Université Libre de Bruxelles, Institut de Philosophie, 143 avenue A.-Buyl, C.P. 188, B-1050 Brussels, Belgium.

Arm. Forces Soc. Armed forces and society. (0095-327X). Transaction Periodicals Consortium: Rutgers University, New Brunswick, NJ. 08903, U.S.A., in association with Inter-University Seminar on Armed Forces and Society: Box 46, 1126 East 59th Street, Chicago, IL. 60637, U.S.A.

Art. Vij. Artha vijñāna. (0004-3559). Gokhale Institute of Politics and Economics: Pune 411004, India.

Asia Bun. Ken. Asia Bunka kenku.

Asia Jiho Asia Jiho.

Asian J. Pub. Admin. Asian journal of public administration. (0259-8272). University of Hong Kong, Department of Political Science: Pokfulam Road, Hong Kong.

List of abbreviations used

Asian Prof. Asian profile. (0304-8675). Asian Research Service: Rm. 704, Federal Building, 369 Lockhart Road, Hong Kong.
Aust. Geogr. Australian geographer. (0004-9182). Geographical Society of New South Wales: P.O. Box 602, Gladesville, NSW 2111, Australia.
Aust. Geogr. Stud. Australian geographical studies. (0004-9190). Institute of Australian Geographers: Department of Geography and Oceanography, University College, University of New South Wales, Australian Defence Force Academy, Campbell, ACT 2600, Australia.
Aust. J. Chin. Aff. Australian journal of Chinese affairs. (0156-7365). Australian National University, Contemporary China Centre: G.P.O. Box 4, Canberra ACT 2601, Australia.
Aust. J. Pol. Sci Australian journal of political science. (0032-3268). Australian Defence Force Academy, Department of Politics: Canberra, ACT 2600, Australia, in association with Australasian Political Studies Association.
Az. Afr. Seg. Aziia i Afrika segodnia.
B. Antropol. Am. Boletín de antropología americana. (0252-841X). Instituto Panamericano de Geografía e Historia: Apartado Postal 18879, 11870 Mexico City, Mexico.
B. Ind. Econ. St. Bulletin of Indonesian economic studies. (0007-4918). Australian National University: Department of Economics, Research School of Pacific Studies, G.P.O. Box 4, Canberra, A.C.T. 2601, Australia.
B. Lat. Am. Res. Bulletin of Latin American research. (0261-3050). Pergamon Press: Headington Hill Hall, Oxford OX3 OBW, U.K., in association with Society for Latin American Studies.
B. Nihon Fuku. Univ. Bulletin of Nihon Fukushi University.
Bang. Dev. Stud. Bangladesh development studies. (0304-095X). Bangladesh Unnayan Gobeshona Protishthan = Bangladesh Institute of Development Studies: G.P.O. Box No.3854, E-17 Agargaon, Sher-e-Bangla Nagar, Dhaka, Bangladesh.
BC. Stud. BC studies. (0005-2949). University of British Columbia: 2029 West Mall, University of British Columbia, Vancouver B.C. V6T 1W5, Canada.
Behav. Brain Sci. Behavioral and brain sciences. (0140-525X). Cambridge University Press: 40 West 20 Street, New York, NY 10011, U.S.A.
Behav. Sci. Behavioral science. (0005-7940). International Society for Systems Sciences/Institute of Management Sciences: P.O. Box 64025, Baltimore, Maryland 21264, U.S.A.
Beliz. St. Belizean studies. (0250-6831).
Berkeley J. Soc. Berkeley journal of sociology. (0067-5830). Berkeley Journal of Sociology: 458A Barrows Hall, Department of Sociology, University of California Berkeley, Berkeley, CA 94720, U.S.A.
Berl. J. Soziol. Berliner journal für Soziologie. (0863-1808). Akademie-Verlag Berlin: Leipziger Str. 3-4, Postfach 1233, O-1086 Berlin, Germany, in association with Institut für Soziologie der Humbodt-Universität zu Berlin: Hans-Loch-Str. 349, O-1136 Berlin, Germany.
Bevolk. Gez. Bevolking en gezin. Centrum voor Bevolkings- en Gezinsstudiën/Nederlands Interdisciplinair Demografisch Instituut: Markiesstrart 1, 1000 Brussels, Belgium/Lange Houtstraat 19, 2511 CV 's-Gravenhage, Postbus 11650, 2502 AR 's-Gravenhage, The Netherlands.
Bioethics Bioethics. (0269-9702). Basil Blackwell: 108 Cowley Road, Oxford OX4 1JF, U.K.
Born. R. Borneo review. Institute for Development Studies (Sabah): Locked Bag 127, 88999 Kota Kinabalu, Sabah, Malaysia.

Liste des abbreviations utilisés

Br. J. Clin. Psycho. British journal of clinical psychology. (0144-6657). British Psychological Society: St. Andrews House, 48 Princess Road East, Leicester LE1 7DR, U.K.
Br. J. Crimin. British journal of criminology. (0007-0955). Oxford University Press: Pinkhill House, Southfield Road, Eynsham, Oxford OX8 1JJ, U.K., in association with Institute for the Study and Treatment of Delinquency.
Br. J. Educ. S. British journal of educational studies. (0007-1005). Basil Blackwell: 108 Cowley Road, Oxford OX4 1JF, U.K.
Br. J. Ind. R. British journal of industrial relations. (0007-1080). Basil Blackwell: 108 Cowley Road, Oxford OX4 1JF, U.K., in association with London School of Economics: Houghton Street, London WC2A 2AE, U.K.
Br. J. Psy. British journal of psychology. (0007-1269). British Psychological Society: St. Andrews House, 48 Princess Road East, Leicester LE1 7DR, U.K.
Br. J. Soc. British journal of sociology. (0007-1315). Routledge: 11 New Fetter Lane, London EC4P 4EE, U.K., in association with London School of Economics and Political Science: Houghton Street, Aldwych, London WC2A 2AE.
Br. J. Soc. P. British journal of social psychology. (0144-6665). British Psychological Society: St. Andrews House, 48 Princess Road East, Leicester LE1 7DR, U.K.
Br. J. Soc. W. British journal of social work. (0045-3102). Oxford University Press: Pinkhill House, Southfield Road, Eynsham, Oxford, OX8 1JJ, U.K., in association with British Association of Social Workers.
Bung. Ron. Bungakubu ronshu (Journal of the Aichi Prefectural University). Aichi Prefectural University.
Bung.-Ken. Kiyo Bungaku-kenkyuka Kiyo (Journal of the Waseda Graduate School). Waseda Graduate School.
C.Asian Sur. Central Asian survey. (0263-4937). Pergamon Press: Headington Hill Hall, Oxford OX3 OBW, U.K., in association with Society for Central Asian Studies: Unit 8, 92 Lots Road, London SW10 4BQ, U.K.
Cah. Afr. Admin. Pub. Cahiers africains d'administration publique = African administrative studies. (0007-9588). Centre Africain de Formation et de Recherche Administratives pour le Développement (CAFRAD): P.O. Box 310, Tangiers, Morocco.
Cah. Amer. Lat. Cahiers des Amériques latines. (0008-0020). Université de la Sorbonne Nouvelle (Paris III), Institut des Hautes Études de l'Amérique latine: 28 rue Saint-Guillaume, 75007 Paris, France.
Cah. CEDAF Cahiers du CEDAF/ ASDOC-studies. (0250-1619). Centre d'étude et de documentation africaines = Afrika Studie-en Documentatiecentrum: 7 Place Royale, B-1000 Brussels, Belgium.
Cah. Ét. Afr. Cahiers d'études africaines. (0008-0055). Éditions de l'École des Hautes Études en Sciences Sociales: 131 boulevard Saint-Michel, 75005 Paris, France.
Cah. Int. Soc. Cahiers internationaux de sociologie. (0008-0276). Presses Universitaires de France: 108 boulevard Saint-Germain, 75006 Paris, France.
Cah. Sci. Hum. Cahiers des sciences humaines. (0768-9829). Editions de l'ORSTOM, Institut français de recherche scientifique pour le developpement en cooperation: Commission des Sciences Sociales, 213 rue la Fayette, 75480 Paris, France.
Cam. Anthrop. Cambridge anthropology. University of Cambridge, Department of Social Anthropology: Free School Lane, Cambridge CB2 3RF, U.K.

List of abbreviations used

Camb. J. Econ. Cambridge journal of economics. (0309-166X). Academic Press: 24-28 Oval Road, London NW1 7DX, U.K., in association with University of Cambridge, Faculty of Economics and Politics: Sidgwick Avenue, Cambridge CB3 9DD, U.K.

Can. J. Afr. St. Canadian journal of African studies = Revue canadienne des études africaines. (0008-3968). Canadian Association of African Studies = Association canadienne des études africaines: Innis College, University of Toronto, 2 Sussex Avenue, Toronto, Ontario M5S IAI, Canada.

Can. J. Phil. Canadian journal of philosophy. (0045-5091). University of Calgary Press: Calgary, Alberta T2N 1N4, Canada.

Can. J. Poli. Canadian journal of political science = Revue canadienne de science politique. (0008-4239). Wilfrid Laurier University Press: 75 University Avenue W., Waterloo, Ontario N2L 3C5, Canada, in association with Canadian Political Science Association = Association canadienne de science politique/ Société québécoise de science politique: Suite 205, 1 Stewart Street, Ottawa, Ontario, Canada K1N 6H7/ Université du Québec à Montréal, Montréal, Québec, Canada H3C 3PN.

Can. J. Soc. Canadian journal of sociology = Cahiers canadiens de sociologie. (0318-6431). University of Alberta, Department of Sociology: Edmonton, Alberta T6G 2H4, Canada.

Can. R. Soc. A. Canadian review of sociology and anthropology = Revue canadienne de sociologie et d'anthropologie. (0008-4948). Canadian Sociology and Anthropology Association: Concordia University, 1455 boulevard de Maisonneuve W., Montreal, Quebec H3G 1M8, Canada.

Caravelle Caravelle. (0008-0152). Presses Universitaires du Mirail: Service des Publications, 56 rue du Taur, 31069 Toulouse Cedex, C.C.P. Toulouse 8620-29 E, France, in association with Institut Pluridisciplinaire d'Études sur l'Amérique Latine à Toulouse: 56 rue du Taur, 31069 Toulouse Cedex, France.

Carib. Stud. Caribbean studies = Estudios del Caribe = Études des Caraïbes. (0008-6533). P.O. Box 23361 University Station, Pío Piedras, Puerto Rico 00931.

CEPAL R. CEPAL review. (0251-2920). United Nations Economic Commission for Latin America and the Caribbean: Casilla 179-D, Santiago, Chile.

Ćeský Lid Ćeský lid. (0009-0794). Academia: Vodickova 40, 112 29 Prague 1, Czech Republic.

Chi. Sogoken. Chiiki Sogokenkyu (Journal of Ryukoku University).

Child Wel. Child welfare. (0009-4021). Child Welfare League of America: 440 First Street NW, Washington DC 20001-2085, U.S.A.

Child. Soc. Children and society. (0951-0605). Whiting and Birch: P.O. Box 872, Forest Hill, London SE23 3HZ, U.K., in association with National Children's Bureau of the United Kingdom.

China City Plan. R. China city planning review. (1002-8447). China Urban Planning Society/ China Academy of Urban Planning and Design: No.9 San Li He Road, Beijing, China.

China Quart. China quarterly. (0009 4439). University of London, School of Oriental and African Studies: Thornhaugh Street, Russell Square, London WC1H 0XG, U.K.

China R. China report. (0009 4455). Sage Publications India: 32 M-Block Market, Greater Kailash I, New Delhi 110 048, India.

Cities Cities. (0264-2751). 88 Kingsway, London WC2 6AB, U.K.

Civilisations Civilisations. (0009-8140). Université Libre de Bruxelles, Institut de Sociologie: 44 avenue Jeanneaterloo, 1050 Brussels, Belgium.

Liste des abbreviations utilisés

Cognition Cognition. (0010-0277). Elsevier Science Publishers: P.O. Box 211, 1000 AE Amsterdam, The Netherlands.
Columb. Law. Columbia law review. (0010-1958). Columbia Law Review Association: 435 West 116th Street, New York, NY 10027, U.S.A.
Comm. Dev. J. Community development journal. (0010-3802). Oxford University Press: Walton Street, Oxford OX2 6DP, U.K.
Commun. Theory Communication theory. (1050-3293). Guilford Publications: 72 Spring Street, New York, NY 10012, U.S.A., in association with International Communication Association: 8140 Burnet Road, P.O. Box 9589, Austin, TX. 78766-9589, U.S.A.
Communication Communication. (0305-4233). Gordon and Breach Science Publishers: 270 8th Avenue, New York, NY 10011, U.S.A.
Comp. Poli. S. Comparative political studies. (0010-4140). Sage Publications: 2455 Teller Road, Newbury Park, CA 91320, U.S.A.
Comp. Polit. Comparative politics. (0010-4159). City University of New York: 33 West 42nd Street, New York, NY 10036, U.S.A.
Comp. Stud. S. Comparative studies in society and history. (0010-4175). Cambridge University Press: 40 West 20th Street, New York, NY 10011, U.S.A., in association with Society for the Comparative Study of Society and History.
Comp. Urban Stud. Comprehensive urban studies. (0386-3506). Tokyo Metropolitan University: 1-1 Minamiousawa, Hachiouji, Tokyo 192-03, Japan.
Confl. Resolut. Journal of conflict resolution. (0022-0027). Sage Publications: 2455 Teller Road, Newbury Park, CA. 91320, U.S.A., in association with Peace Science Society (International).
Contin. Change Continuity and change. (0268-4160). Cambridge University Press: The Edinburgh Building, Shaftesbury Road, Cambridge CB2 2RU, U.K.
Contr. I. Soc. Contributions to Indian sociology. (0069-9667). Sage Publications India: 32 M-Block Market, Greater Kailash 1, New Delhi 110 048, India, in association with Institute of Economic Growth: University of Delhi, Delhi 110007, India.
Contrib. Nepal. Stud. Contributions to Nepalese studies. Centre for Nepal and Asian Studies, in association with Tribhuvan University.
Coy. Soc. Coyuntura social. (0121-2532). Fundacíon para la Educación Superior y el Desarrollo: Calle 78 no. 9-91, Apartado Aéreo 75074, Santafé de Bogotá D.C., Colombia.
Cr. Law Soc. Chan. Crime, law and social change. (0925 4994). Kluwer Academic Publishers: Spuiboulevard 50, P.O. Box 17, 3300 AA Dordrecht, The Netherlands.
Crime Delin. Crime and delinquency. (0011-1287). Sage Publications: 2455 Teller Road, Newbury Park, CA. 91320, U.S.A.
Crit. Anthr. Critique of anthropology. (0308-275X). Critique of Anthropology: P.O. Box 6004, 1005 EA Amsterdam, The Netherlands.
Crit. Persp. Acc. Critical perspectives on accounting. (1045-2354). Academic Press: 24-28 Oval Road, London NW1 7DX, U.K.
Crit. Rev. Critical review. (0891-3811). Critical Review: P.O. Box 14528, Chicago IL. 60614, U.S.A., in association with Center for Independent Thought: 942 Howard Street, Room 109, San Francisco, CA 94103, U.S.A.
Crit. Sociol. Critical sociology. (0896-9205). University of Oregon, Department of Sociology: OR. 97403, U.S.A.
Critica Sociol. Critica sociologica. (0011 1546). S.I.A.R.E.S.: Corso Vittorio Emanuele 24, 00186 Rome, Italy.

List of abbreviations used

Cuad. Am. Cuadernos americanos. (0185-156X). Universidad Nacional Autónoma de México: Ciudad Universitaria, 04510 México, D.F., Apartado Postal 965, México 1.
Cult. Medic. Psych. Culture, medicine and psychiatry. (0165-005X). Kluwer Academic Publishers: P.O. Box 322, 3300 AH Dordrecht, The Netherlands.
Cult. St. Cultural studies. (0950-2386). Routledge: 11 New Fetter Lane, London EC4P 4EE, U.K.
Curr. Hist. Current history. (0011-3530). Current History: Publications Office, 4225 Main Street, Philadelphia, PA. 19127, U.S.A.
Curr. Sociol. Current sociology. (0011-3921). Sage Publications: 6 Bonhill Street, London EC2A 4PU, U.K., in association with International Sociological Association.
Cyprus Rev. Cyprus review. (1015-2881). Intercollege/ University of Indianapolis: P.O. Box 4005, 17 Heroes Avenue, Ayios Andreas, Nicosia, Cyprus/ 1400 Hanna Avenue, Indianapolis, IN. 46227-3687, U.S.A.
Dædalus Dædalus. (0011-5266). American Academy of Arts and Sciences: 136 Irving Street, Cambridge, MA. 02138, U.S.A.
Dai. Ron. Daigaku ronshu (Bulletin of Hiroshima University). Hiroshima University.
Demografie Demografie. (0011-8265). Panorama: Hálkova 1, 120 72 Prague 2, Czechoslovakia, in association with Federální Statistický Úřad.
Demography Demography. (0070-3370). Population Association of America: 1722 N. Street N.W., Washington DC 20036, U.S.A.
Desar. Econ. Desarrollo económico. (0046-001X). Instituto de Desarrollo Económico y Social: Aráoz 2838, 1425 Buenos Aires, Argentina.
Deut. Arch. Deutschland Archiv: Zeitschrift für das vereinigte Deutschland. (0012-1428). Verlag Wissenschaft und Politik: Salierring 14-16, 5000 Cologne, Germany.
Dev. Beh. Deviant behavior. (0163-9625). Taylor & Francis: 4 John Street, London WC1N 2ET, U.K.
Dev. Dialog. Development dialogue. (0345-2328). Dag Hammarskjöld Foundation: Övre Slottsgatan 2, S-75220 Uppsala, Sweden.
Dev. Pol. R. Development policy review. (0950-6764). Sage Publications: 6 Bonhill Street, London EC2A 4PU, U.K., in association with Overseas Development Institute: Regent's College, Inner Circle, Regent's Park, London NW1 4NS, U.K.
Develop. Cha. Development and change. (0012-155X). Sage Publications: 6 Bonhill Street, London EC2A 4PU, U.K.
Dialect. Anthrop. Dialectical Anthropology. (0304-4092). Kluwer Academic Publishers: Spuiboulevard 50, P.O. Box 17, 3300 AA Dordrecht, The Netherlands.
Dreaming Dreaming. (1053-0797). Human Sciences Press: 233 Spring Street, New York, NY 10013-1578, U.S.A.
E & S E & S: Économie et statistique. (0336-1451). Institut national de la statistique et des études économiques: 18 boulevard A. Pinard, 75675 Paris Cedex 14, France.
E. Eur. Quart. East European quarterly. (0012-8449). University of Colorado.
E.Afr. Soc. Sci. Res. R. Eastern Africa social science research review. Organization for Social Science Research in Eastern Africa - OSSREA: P.O. Box 31971, Addis Ababa, Ethiopia.
E.Eur. Jew. Aff. East European Jewish affairs. (0038 545X). Institute of Jewish Affairs: 11 Hertford Street, London, W1Y 7DX, United Kingdom.
E.Eur. Pol. Soc. East European politics and societies. (0888-3254). University of California.

Liste des abbreviations utilisés

East. Anthrop. Eastern anthropologist. (0012-8686). Ethnographic and Folk Culture Society: Post Box No. 209, 7-A, Ram Krishna Marg, Faizabad Road, Lucknow, India.
Ec. Lav. Economia & lavoro. (0012-978X). Marsilio Editori: Marittima — Fabbricato 205, 30135, Venice, Italy, in association with Fondazione Giacomo Brodolini: via Torino 122, 00184 Rome, Italy.
Econ. Dev. Cult. Change Economic development and cultural change. (0013-0079). University of Chicago Press: Journals Division, 5720 S. Woodlawn, Chicago, IL. 60637, U.S.A.
Econ. Devel. Q. Economic development quarterly. (0891-2424). Sage Publications: 2455 Teller Road, Newbury Park, CA. 91320, U.S.A.
Econ. Ind. Dem. Economic and industrial democracy. (0143-831X). Sage Publications: 6 Bonhill Street, London EC2A 4PU, U.K., in association with Arbetslivscentrum (The Swedish Center for Working Life): Box 5606, S-114 86 Stockholm, Sweden.
Econ. Philos. Economics and philosophy. (0266-2671). Cambridge University Press: 40 West 20th Street, New York, NY 10011, U.S.A.
Econ. Plan. Economics of planning. (0013-0451). Kluwer Academic Publishers: P.O. Box 322, 3300 AH Dordrecht, The Netherlands.
Econ. Rec. Economic record. (0013-0249). Economic Society of Australia: c/o A.D. Woodland, Department of Econometrics, Sydney University, Sydney, N.S.W. 2006, Australia.
Econ. Soc. Economy and society. (0308-5147). Routledge: 11 New Fetter Lane, London EC4P 4EE, U.K.
Econ. Soc. R. Economic and social review. (0012-9984).
Educ. Geront. Educational gerontology. (0360-1277). Taylor & Francis: 4 John Street, London WC1N 2ET, U.K.
Educ. Urban. Soc. Education and urban society. (0013-1245). Sage Publications: 2455 Teller Road, Newbury Park, CA. 91320, U.S.A.
Educat. Res. Educational research. (0013-1881). Routledge: 11 New Fetter Lane, London EC4P 4EE, U.K., in association with National Foundation for Educational Research: The Mere, Upton Park, Slough, Berkshire SL1 2DQ, U.K.
Ekon. Preg. Ekonomski pregled. (0424-7558). Savez Ekonimista Hrvatske: Berislaviceva 6, Zagreb, Yugoslavia.
Ekonomist Ekonomist. (0370-0356). Izdatel'stvo Ekonomika: Berezhovskaia naberezhnaia 6, 121864 Moscow, U.S.S.R., in association with Ministerstvo ekonomiki i prognozirovaniia SSR.
Elec. Stud. Electoral studies. (0261-3794). Butterworth-Heinemann: Linacre House, Jordan Hill, Oxford OX2 8DP, U.K.
Eng. Wor.-wide English world-wide. (0172-8865). John Benjamins Publishing: P.O. Box 75577, Amstedldijk 44, 1007 AN Amsterdam, The Netherlands.
Entrepren. Innov. Change Entrepreneurship, innovation, and change. (1059-0137). Plenum Publishing: 233 Spring Street, New York, NY 10013-1578, U.S.A.
Envir. Behav. Environment and behavior. (0013-9165). Sage Publications: 2455 Teller Road, Newbury Park CA. 91320, U.S.A., in association with Environmental Design Research Association.
Envir. Plan. A. Environment and planning A: International journal of urban and regional research. (0308-518X). Pion: 207 Brondesbury Park, London NW2 5JN, U.K.
Envir. Plan. B. Environment and planning B: Planning and design. (0265-8135). Pion: 207 Brondesbury Park, London NW2 5JN, U.K.

List of abbreviations used

Envir. Plan. C. Environment and planning C: Government and policy. (0263 774X). Pion: 207 Brondesbury Park, London NW2 5JN, U.K.
Envir. Plan. D. Environment and planning D: Society and space. (0263-7758). Pion: 207 Brondesbury Park, London NW2 5JN, U.K.
Environ. Urban. Environment and urbanization. (0956-2478). 3 Endsleigh Street, London, WC1H 0DD, U.K.
Environ. Values Environmental values. (0963-2719). White Horse Press: 10 High Street, Knapwell, Cambridge, CB3 8NR, U.K.
Espace Géogr. Espace géographique. (0046-2497). Doin editeurs: 8 place de l'Odéon, 75006 Paris, France.
Espace Pop. Soc. Espace populations sociétés. (0755-7809). Université des Sciences et Techniques de Lille-Flandres-Artois: 59655 Villeneuve d'Ascq Cedex, France.
Esprit Esprit. (0014-0759). Esprit: 212 rue Saint-Martin, 75003 Paris, France.
Est. Demog. Urb. Estudios demográficos y urbanos. (0186-7210). Colégio de México, Centro de Estudios Demográficos y de Desarrollo Urbano: Departamento de Publicaciones, Camino al Ajusco 20, 10740 México D.F., México.
Est. Leop. Estudos leopoldenses. (0014-1607). Universidade do Vale do Rio dos Sinos: 93.000 São Leopoldo RS, Brazil.
Est. Sociol. Estudios sociológicos. (0185-4186). Colegio de México: Camino al Ajusco 20, Pedregal de Santa Teresa, 10740 Mexico, D.F., Mexico.
Ét. Int. Études internationales. (0014-2123). Centre québécois de relations internationales: Faculté des sciences sociales, Université Laval, Québec, G1K 7P4 Canada.
Eth. Groups Ethnic groups. (0308-6860). Gordon and Breach Science Publishers: 270 8th Avenue, New York, NY 10011, U.S.A.
Ethics Ethics. (0014-1704). University of Chicago Press: Journals Division, 5720 S. Woodlawn Avenue, Chicago, IL. 60637, U.S.A.
Ethn. Fr. Ethnologie française. (0046-2616). Armand Colin: 103 boulevard Saint-Michel, 75240 Paris Cedex 05, France.
Ethn. Racial Ethnic and racial studies. (0141-9870). Routledge: 11 New Fetter Lane, London EC4P 4EE, U.K.
Ethnol. Helvet. Ethnologica Helvetica. Schweizerische Ethnologische Gesellschaft = Société Suisse d'Ethnologie = Swiss Ethnological Society: c/o Institut für Ethnologie, Schwanengasse 7, CH-3011 Bern, Switzerland.
Ethnos Ethnos. (0014-1844). Folkens Museum-Etnografiska: S-11527 Stockholm, Sweden.
Ethol. Socio. Ethology & sociobiology. (0162-3095). Elsevier Science Publishing (New York): 655 Avenue of the Americas, New York, NY 10010, U.S.A.
Etnograf. Oboz. Etnograficheskoe obozrenie. Izdatel'stvo Nauka: 90 Profsouuznaya ul., 117864 Moscow, Russia.
Eur. Econ. R. European economic review. (0014-2921). Elsevier Science Publishers: P.O. Box 1991, 1000 BZ Amsterdam, The Netherlands, in association with European Economic Association: 34 Voie du Roman Pays, B-1348 Louvain-la-Neuve, Belgium.
Eur. Ethn. Europa ethnica. (0014-2492). Wilhelm Braumüller: A-1092 Vienna, Servitengasse 5, Austria.
Eur. J. Pol. R. European journal of political research. (0304-4130). Kluwer Academic Publishers: Spuiboulevard 50, P.O. Box 17, 3300 AA Dordrecht, The Netherlands, in association with European Consortium for Political Research: University of Essex, Wivenhoe Park, Colchester CO4 3SQ, U.K.

Liste des abbreviations utilisés

Eur. J. Pop. European journal of population = Revue européenne de démographie. (0168-6577). Elsevier Science Publishers (North Holland): P.O. Box 1991, 1000 BZ Amsterdam, The Netherlands.

Eur. J. Soc. Archives européennes de sociologie = European journal of sociology = Europäisches Archiv für Soziologie. (0003-9756). Cambridge University Press: The Edinburgh Building, Shaftesbury Road, Cambridge CB2 2RU, U.K.

Eur. J. Soc. Psychol. European journal of social psychology. (0046-2772). John Wiley & Sons: Baffins Lane, Chichester, West Sussex PO19 1UD, U.K., in association with European Association of Experimental Social Psychology.

Eur. Sociol. R. European sociological review. (0266-7215). Oxford University Press: Pinkhill House, Southfield Road, Eynsham, Oxford OX8 1JJ, U.K.

Eval. Rev. Evaluation review. (0193-841X). Sage Publications: 2455 Teller Road , Newbury Park, CA. 91320, U.S.A.

Fem. Leg. Stud. Feminist legal studies. (0966-3622). Deborah Charles Publications: 173 Mather Avenue, Liverpool L18 6JZ, U.K., in association with Kent Law School: The University, Canterbury, Kent CT2 7NZ, U.K.

Feminist R. Feminist review. (0141-7789). Routledge: 11 New Fetter Lane, London EC4P 4EE, U.K., in association with Feminist Review: 11 Carleton Gardens, Brecknock Road, London N19 5AQ, U.K.

Folia Ling. Folia linguistica. (0165-4004). Mouton de Gruyter: Postfach 110240, 1000 Berlin 11, Germany, in association with Societas Linguistica Europaea: Olshausenstraße 40-60, DW 2300 Kiel, Germany.

Fors.Jour. Soz. Beweg. Forschungsjournal neue soziale Bewegungen. (0933-9361). Schüren Presseverlag: Deutschhausstr. 31, 3550 Marburg, Germany, in association with Forschungsgruppe Neue Soziale Bewegungen.

Fr. Cult. Stud. French cultural studies. (0957-1558). Alpha Academic: Halfpenny Furze, Mill Lane, Chalfont St Giles, Bucks, HP8 4NR, U.K.

Fst. Lang. First language. (0142-7237). Alpha Academic: Halfpenny Furze, Mill Lane, Chalfont St Giles, Buckinghamshire, HP8 4NR, U.K.

Gend. No Esup. Gendai no Esupuri.

Gend. No Shak. Byo. Gendai no Shakai Byouri. Japan Social Pathological Society.

Gender Soc. Gender and society. (0891-2432). Sage Publications: 2455 Teller Road, Newbury Park, CA. 91320, U.S.A., in association with Sociologists for Women in Society.

Genèses Genèses. (1135-3219). Calman-Lévy: 16, villa Saint-Jacques, 75014 Paris, France.

Genus Genus. (0016-6987). Comitato Italiano per lo Studio dei Problemi della Popolazione: Via Nomentana 41, 00161 Rome, Italy.

Geoforum Geoforum. (0016-7185). Pergamon Press.

Geog.ann. B. Geografiska annaler: Series B — Human geography. (0435-3676). P.O. Box 2959, Tøyen, N-0608 Oslo 6, Norway, in association with Svenska Sällskapet för Antropologi och Geografi = Swedish Society for Anthropology and Geography: University of Uppsala, Department of Physical Geography, Box 554, S-751 22 Uppsala, Sweden.

Geogr. Anal. Geographical analysis. (0016-7363). Ohio State University Press: 1070 Carmack Road, Columbus, OH. 43210, U.S.A.

Geogr. J. Geographical journal. (0016-7398). Royal Geographical Society: 1 Kensington Gore, London SW7 2AR, U.K.

List of abbreviations used

Geogr. Rev. Geographical review. (0016-7428). American Geographical Society: Suite 600, 156 Fifth Avenue, New York, NY 10010, U.S.A.
Geogr. Rund. Geographische Rundschau. (0016-7460). Westermann Schulbuchverlag: Georg-Westermann-Allee 66, 3300 Braunschweig, Germany.
Geojournal Geojournal. (0343-2521). Kluwer Academic Publishers: P.O. Box 17, 3300 AA Dordrecht, Netherlands.
Gesch. Ges. Geschichte und Gesellschaft. (0340-613X). Vandenhoeck und Ruprecht: Postfach 3753, D-3400 Göttingen, Germany.
Gestion Gestion 2000: Management et prospective. (0773-0543). Université Catholique de Louvain, Institut d'administration et de gestion: 16 avenue de l'Espinette, B-1348 Louvain-la-Neuve, Belgium.
Gewerk. Monat. Gewerkschaftliche Monatshefte. (0016-9447). Bund-Verlag: Postfach 900840, 5000 Cologne 90, Germany, in association with Bundesvorstand des DGB: Hans-Böckler-Straße 39, 4000 Düsseldorf 30, Germany.
Gos. Pravo Gosudarstvo i pravo. (0132-0769). Nauka: 121099 Moscow, G-99, Shubinskii per., 6, Russia.
Govt. Oppos. Government and opposition. (0017-257X). Government and Opposition: Houghton Street, London WC2A 2AE, U.K.
Group Decis. Negot. Group decision and negotiation. (0926-2644). Kluwer Academic Publishers: P.O. Box 17, 3300 AA Dordrecht, The Netherlands.
Groupwork Groupwork. (0951-824X). Whiting & Birch: P.O. Box 872, Forest Hill, London SE23 3HL, U.K.
Harv. Law. Rev. Harvard law review. (0017-811X). Harvard Law Review Association: Gannett House, 1511 Massachusetts Avenue, Cambridge, MA. 02138, U.S.A.
Health Care Wom. Int. Health care for women international. (0739-9332). Taylor & Francis: 4 John Street, London WC1N 2ET, U.K.
Health Pol. Plan. Health policy and planning. (0268-1080). Oxford University Press, in association with London School of Hygiene and Tropical Medicine: Keppel (Gower) Street, London WC1E 7HT, U.K.
Health Soc. Work Health and social work. (0360-7283). National Association of Social Workers: 750 First Street, NE. Suite 700, Washington DC 20002-4241, U.S.A.
Health Trans. R. Health transition review. (1036-4005). Health Transition Centre: National Centre for Epidemology and Population Health, Australian National University, GPO Box 4, Canberra ACT 2601, Australia.
Hess. Blät. Volk.Kultur. Hessische Blätter für Volks- und Kulturforschung. (1075-3479). Jonas Verlag für Kunst und Literatur: Weidenhäuser Straße 88, D-3550 Marburg 1, Germany.
High. Educ. Higher education. (0018-1560). Kluwer Academic Publishers: P.O. Box 17, 3300 AA Dordrecht, The Netherlands.
Hist. Anthrop. History and anthropology. (0275-7206). Harwood Academic Publishers: P.O. Box 90, Reading, Berkshire RG1 8JL, U.K.
Hist. Human Sci. History of the human sciences. (0952-6951). Sage: 6 Bonhill Street, London EC2A 4PU, U.K.
Hist. Psychiat. History of psychiatry. (0957-154X). Alpha Academic: Halfpenny Firze, Mill lane, Chalfont St Giles, Bucks, HP8 4NR, U.K.
Hist. Soc. R. Historical social research = Historische Sozialforschung. (0172-6404). Zentrum für Historische Sozialforschung: Zentralarchiv für Empirische Sozialforschung, Universität zu Köln, Bachemerstr. 40, D-5000 Cologne, Germany, in association with

Liste des abbreviations utilisés

Arbeitsgemeinschaft für Quantifizierung und Methoden in der historisch sozialwissenschaftlichen Forschung/ International Commission for the Application of Quantitative Methods in History/ Association for History and Computing: Bachemerstr. 40, D-5000 Cologne 41, Germany/ University of London, Westfield College, Department of History, Kidderpore Avenue, London NW3 7ST, U.K.

Hist. Technol. History and technology. (0734-1512). Harwood Academic Publishers: P.O. Box 90, Reading, Berkshire RG1 8JL, U.K.

Hito. J. Soc. Stud. Hitotsubashi journal of social studies. (0073-280X). Hitotsubashi University, Hitotsubashi Academy: 2-1 Naka, Kunitachi, Tokyo 186, Japan.

Hogaku (J. Suru. Univ.) Hogaku (Journal. Surugadai University). Surugadai University.

Hos. Ken. Hosei Kenkyu.

Hous. Pol. Deb. Housing policy debate. (1051-1482). Office of Housing Policy, Fannie Mae: 3900 Wisconsin Avenue, N.W. Washington DC 20016-2899, U.S.A.

Howard J. Crim. Just. Howard journal of criminal justice. (0265-5527). Basil Blackwell: 108 Cowley Road, Oxford OX4 1JF, U.K., in association with Howard League: 708 Holloway Road, London N19 3NL, U.K.

Hum. Nature Human nature. (1045-6767). Aldine de Gruyter: 200 Saw Mill River Road, Hawthorne, NY 10532, U.S.A.

Hum. Rights Q. Human rights quarterly. (0275-0392). Johns Hopkins University Press: Journals Publishing Division, 701 W. 40th Street, Suite 275, Baltimore, MD. 21211, U.S.A.

Human Relat. Human relations. (0018-7267). Plenum Press: 233 Spring Street, New York, NY 10013-1578, U.S.A.

Human St. Human studies. (0163-8548). Kluwer Academic Publishers: P.O. Box 322, 3300 AH Dordrecht, The Netherlands.

Human. Org. Human organization. (0018-7259). Society for Applied Anthropology: 5205 E.Flowler Avenue, Suite 310, Temple Terrace, FL. 33617, U.S.A.

Humor Humor. (0933-1719). Mouton de Gruyter: Postfach 110240, D-1000 Berlin 11, Germany.

Imm. Minor. Immigrants and minorities. (0261-9288). Frank Cass: Gainsborough House, 11 Gainsborough Road, London E11 1RS, U.K.

Ind. J. Pol. Sci. Indian journal of political science. (0019-5510). Indian Political Science Association: Anna Centre for Public Affairs, University of Madras, Madras 600 005, India.

Ind. J. Reg. Sci. Indian journal of regional science. (0046-9017). Indian Institute of Technology, Regional Science Association: Department of Architecture and Regional Planning, Kharagpur, West Bengal, India.

Ind. J. Soc. Sci. Indian journal of social science. Sage Publications India: 32 M-Block Market, Greater Kailash I, New Delhi 110 048, India, in association with Indian Council of Social Science Research.

Ind. Lab. Rel. Industrial and labor relations review. (0019-7939). Cornell University, New York State School of Industrial and Labor Relations: 207 ILR Research Building, Cornell University, Ithaca, New York 14851-0952, U.S.A.

Ind. Law J. Industrial law journal. (0395-9332). Oxford University Press: Pinkhill House, Southfield Road, Eynsham, Oxford OX8 1JJ, U.K., in association with Industrial Law Society: 28 Boundary Road, Sidcup, Kent DA15 8ST, U.K.

Ind. Rel. J. S.Afr. Industrial relations journal of South Africa. (02587181). University of Stellenbosch Business School: P.O. Box 610, Bellville 7535, South Africa.

List of abbreviations used

Ind. Relat. Industrial relations. (0019-8676). Basil Blackwell: 108 Cowley Road, Oxford OX4 1JF, U.K., in association with University of California, Berkeley, Institute of Industrial Relations: Berkeley CA. 94720, U.S.A.

Ind. Relat. J. Industrial relations journal. (0019-8692). Basil Blackwell: 108 Cowley Road, Oxford, OX4 1JF, U.K.

Ind. Soc. Rel. Industrial and social relations. (0258-7181). University of Stellenbosch Business School: P.O. Box 610, Bellville 7535, South Africa.

Indian J. Publ. Admin. Indian journal of public administration. (0019-5561). Indian Institute of Public Administration: Indraprastha Estate, Ring Road East, New Delhi 110002, India.

Indian J. Soc. W. Indian journal of social work. (0019-5634). Tata Institute of Social Sciences: Deonar, Bombay 400 088, India.

Indust. Corpor. Change Industrial and corporate change. (0960-6491). Oxford University Press: Pinkhill House, Southfield Road, Eynsham, Oxford, OX8 1JJ, U.K., in association with Fondazione ASSI: Piazza Affari 6, 20123, Milan, Italy.

Indust. Environ. Crisis Industrial & environmental crisis quarterly. (09218106). Bucknell University/ Industrial Crisis Institute: Department of management, Lewisburg, PA17837, U.S.A./ New York, U.S.A.

Inf. Raum. Informationen zur Raumentwicklung. (0303-2493). Bundesforschungsanstalt für Landeskunde und Raumordnung: Am Michaelshof 8, Postfach 20 01 30, 5300 Bonn 2, Germany.

Inf. Soc. Informations sociales. (0046-9459). Caisse Nationale des Allocations Familiales: 23 rue Daviel, 75634 Paris Cedex 13, France.

Infor. Com. Esp. Información comercial española. (0019-977X). Secretaría de Estado de Comercio: Paseo de la Castellana 162, piso 16, Madrid 28046, Spain.

Int. J. International journal. (0020-7020). Canadian Institute of International Affairs: 15 Kings College Circle, Toronto, Ontario, Canada M5S 2V9.

Int. J. Advance. Counsel. International journal for the advancement of counselling. (0165-0653). Kluwer Academic Publishers: P.O. Box 322, 3300 AH Dordrecht, The Netherlands.

Int. J. Afr. H. S. International journal of African historical studies. (0361-7882). Boston University, African Studies Center: 270 Bay State Road, Boston, MA. 02215, U.S.A.

Int. J. Comp. L. L. I. R. International journal of comparative labour law and industrial relations. (0952-617X). Kluwer Law and Taxation Publishers: P.O. Box 23, 7400 GA Deventer, Netherlands.

Int. J. Comp. Soc International journal of comparative sociology. (0020-7152). E.J. Brill: P.O. Box 9000, 2300 PA Leiden, The Netherlands.

Int. J. Confl. Manag. International journal of conflict management. (1044-4068). 3-R Executive Systems: 3109 Copperfield Court, Bowling Green, KY. 42104, U.S.A.

Int. J. Health. Ser. International journal of health services. (0020-7314). Baywood Publishing: 26 Austin Avenue, P.O. Box 337, Amityville, NY 11701, U.S.A.

Int. J. Hum. Res. Man. International journal of human resource management. (0958-5192). Routledge: 11 New Fetter Lane, London EC4P 4EE, U.K.

Int. J. Law Fam. International journal of law and the family. (0950-4109). Oxford University Press: Pinkhill House, Southfield Road, Eynsham, Oxford OX8 1JJ, U.K.

Int. J. M.E. Stud. International journal of Middle East studies. (0020-7438). Cambridge University Press: 40 West Street 20th, New York, NY 10011, U.S.A., in association with

Liste des abbreviations utilisés

Middle East Studies Association of North America: University of Arizona, 1232 North Cherry, Tuscon, AZ. 85721, U.S.A.

Int. J. Moral Soc. S. International journal of moral and social studies. (0267-9655). Journals: 1 Harewood Row, London NW1 6SE, U.K.

Int. J. Offen. International journal of offender therapy and comparative criminology. (0306-624X). Guilford Press: 72 Spring Street, New York, NY 10012, U.S.A.

Int. J. Pers. Constr. Psych. International journal of personal construct psychology. (0893-603X). Taylor & Francis: 4 John Street, London WC1N 2ET, U.K.

Int. J. Philos. Relig. International journal for philosophy of religion. (0020-7047). Kluwer Academic Publishers: P.O. Box 322, 3300 AH Dordrecht, The Netherlands.

Int. J. Pol. C. S. International journal of politics, culture and society. (0891-4486). Human Sciences Press: 233 Spring Street, New York, NY. 10013-1578, U.S.A.

Int. J. S. Lang. International journal of the sociology of language. (0165-2516). Mouton de Gruyter: Postfach 110240, D-1000 Berlin 11, Germany.

Int. J. S. Law International journal of the sociology of law. (0194-6595). Academic Press: 24-28 Oval Road, London NW1 7DX, U.K.

Int. J. Soc. E. International journal of social economics. (0306-8293). MCB University Press: 62 Toller Lane, Bradford, West Yorkshire, BD8 9BY, U.K.

Int. J. Therap. Comm. Support. Org. International journal for therapeutic and supportive organizations. (0964-1866). Association of Therapeutic Communities: 14 Charterhouse Square, London EC1M 6AX, U.K.

Int. J. Urban International journal of urban and regional research. (0309-1317). Edward Arnold: Mill Road, Dunton Green, Sevenoaks, Kent TN13 2YA, U.K.

Int. Lab. Rev. International labour review. (0020-7780). International Labour Office (ILO): CH-1211 Geneva 22, Switzerland.

Int. Migr. Rev. International migration review. (0197-9183). Center for Migration Studies: 209 Flagg Place, Staten Island, NY 10304-1199, U.S.A.

Int. Pol. Sci Rev. International political science review = Revue internationale de science politique. (0192-5121). Butterworth-Heinemann: Westbury House, Bury Street, Guildford GU2 5BH, U.K., in association with International Political Science Association.

Int. R. Educat. International review of education. (0020-8566). UNESCO Institute for Education: Feldbrunnenstrasse 58, 2000 Hamburg 13, Germany.

Int. R. Ret. Dist. Res. International review of retail, distribution and consumer research. (0959-3969). Routledge: 11 New Fetter Lane, London EC4P 4EE, U.K.

Int. Reg. Sci. R. International regional science review. (0160-0176). Regional Research Institute: West Virginia University, Morgantown, WV. 26506, U.S.A.

Int. Soc. International socialism. (0020-8736). Socialist Workers Party: PO Box 82, London E3, U.K.

Int. Soc. Sci. J. International social science journal. (0020-8701). Basil Blackwell: 108 Cowley Road, Oxford OX4 1JF, U.K.

Int. Sociol. International sociology. (0268-5809). Sage Publications: 6 Bonhill Street, London EC2A 4PU, U.K., in association with International Sociological Association: Consejo Superior de Investigaciones Cientificas. Pinar 25, 28006 Madrid, Spain.

Inter. Phil. Sci. International studies in the philosophy of science. (0269-8595). Carfax Publishing: P.O. Box 25, Abingdon, Oxfordshire, OX14 3UE, U.K.

Interchange Interchange. (0826-4805). Kluwer Academic Publishers: P.O. Box 322, 3300 AH Dordrecht, The Netherlands.

List of abbreviations used

Interfaces Interfaces. (0092-2102). Institute of Management Sciences and the Operations Research Society of America: 290 Westminster Street, Providence, RI. 02903, U.S.A.

Intern. J. Organiz. Anal. International journal of organization analysis. (1055-3185). 3-R Executive Systems: 3109 Copperfield Court, Bowling Green, KY., 42104, U.S.A.

Iran. J. Int. Aff. Iranian journal of international affairs. (1016-6130). IPIS: P.O. Box 19395-1793, Tajrish, Teheran, Iran.

Iss. Stud. Issues & studies. (1013-2511). National Chengchi University, Institute of International Relations: 64 Wan Shou Road, Mucha, Taipei Taiwan, Republic of China.

J. Air Law Comm. Journal of air law and commerce. (0021-8642). Southern Methodist University, School of Law: Dallas, TX. 75275, U.S.A.

J. Am. Plann. Journal of the American Planning Association. (0194-4363). American Planning Association: 1313 East 60th Street, Chicago, IL 60637-2891, U.S.A.

J. Analyt. Psychol. Journal of analytical psychology. (0021-8774). Routledge: 11 New Fetter Lane, London EC4P 4EE, U.K.

J. Anthr. Res. Journal of anthropological research. (0091-7710). University of New Mexico, Department of Anthropology: Albuquerque, NM. 87131, U.S.A.

J. Appl. Psychol. Journal of applied psychology. (0021-9010). American Psychological Association: 1400 North Uhle Street, Arlington, VA. 22201, U.S.A.

J. Appl. Soc. Psychol. Journal of applied social psychology. (0021-9029). V.H. Winston & Son: 7961 Eastern Avenue, Silver Spring, MD. 20910, U.S.A.

J. Arch. Plan. Res. Journal of architectural and planning research. Locke Science Publishing: P.O. Box 146413, Chicago, IL. 60614, U.S.A.

J. Asian Afr. Aff. Journal of Asian and African affairs. (1044-2979). Journal of Asian and African Affairs: P.O. Box 23099, Washington DC 20026, U.S.A.

J. Asian St. Journal of Asian studies. (0021-9118). 1 Lane Hall, University of Michigan, Ann Arbor, MI. 48109, U.S.A.: University of Wisconsin-Milwaukee, Milwaukee, WI. 53201, U.S.A., in association with Association for Asian Studies.

J. Aust. Pop. Ass. Journal of the Australian Population Association. (0814-5725). Australian Population Association: Division of Demography and Sociology, Research School of Social Sciences, The Australian National University, GPO Box 4, Canberra ACT 2601, Australia.

J. Biosoc. Sc. Journal of biosocial science. (0021-9320). Biosocial Society: Department of Biological Anthropology, Downing Street, Cambridge CB2 3DZ, U.K.

J. Busin. Ethics Journal of business ethics. (0167-4544). Kluwer Academic Publishers Group: P.O. Box 322, 3300 AH Dordrecht, Holland/ P.O. Box 358, Accord Station, Hingham, MA. 02018-0358, U.S.A.

J. Cen. Wom. Stud. Journal of the Center for Women's Studies. Tokyo Gakuen Women's College.

J. Child Adol. Gr. Ther. Journal of child and adolescent group therapy. (1053-0800). Human Sciences Press: 233 Spring Street, New York, NY 10013-1578, U.S.A.

J. Child Fam. Stud. Journal of child and family studies. (1062-1024). Human Sciences Press: 233 Spring Street, New York, NY 10013-1578, U.S.A.

J. Chur. State Journal of church and state. (0021-969X). Baylor University, J.M. Dawson Institute of Church-State Studies: P.O. Box 97308, Waco, TX. 76798-7308, U.S.A.

J. Comm. Journal of communication. (0021-9916). Oxford University Press: 200 Madison Avenue, New York, NY 10016, U.S.A.

J. Comm. App. Soc. Psychol. Journal of community and applied social psychology. (1052-9284). John Wiley & Sons: Baffins Lane, Chichester, West Sussex PO19 1UD, U.K.

Liste des abbreviations utilisés

J. Comm. C. Pol. Journal of Commonwealth & comparative politics. (0306-3631). Frank Cass: Gainsborough House, 11 Gainsborough Road, London E11 1RS, U.K.

J. Comp. Econ. Journal of comparative economics. (0147-5967). Academic Press: 1 East First Street, Duluth, MN. 55802, U.S.A., in association with Association for Comparative Economic Studies.

J. Comp. Fam. Stud. Journal of comparative family studies. (0047-2328). University of Calgary, Department of Sociology: 2500 University Drive, N.W., Calgary, Alberta T2N 1N4, Canada.

J. Consum. Aff. Journal of consumer affairs. (0022-0078). University of Wisconsin Press: 114 N. Murray Street, Madison, WI. 53715, U.S.A., in association with American Council on Consumer Interests.

J. Cont. Asia Journal of contemporary Asia. (0047-2336). Journal of Contemporary Asia Publishers: P.O. Box 592, Manila, 1099 Philippines.

J. Cr-cult. Gerontol. Journal of cross-cultural gerontology. (0169-3816). Kluwer Academic Publishers: P.O. Box 17, 3300 AA Dordrecht, The Netherlands.

J. Crim. Law Criminol. Journal of criminal law and criminology. (0091-4169). Northwestern University School of Law: 357 East Chicago Avenue, Chicago, IL. 60611, U.S.A.

J. Cult. R. Inst. Journal of the Culture Research Institute. Nihon University.

J. Dev. Areas Journal of developing areas. (0022-037X). Western Illinois University: 900 West Adams Street, Macomb, IL. 61455, U.S.A.

J. Dev. Econ. Journal of development economics. (0304-3878). Elsevier Science Publishers (North-Holland).

J. Dev. Soc. Journal of developing societies. (0169-796X). E.J. Brill: P.O.B. 9000, 2300 PA Leiden, The Netherlands.

J. Dev. Stud. Journal of development studies. (0022-0388). Frank Cass: Gainsborough House, 11 Gainsborough Road, London E11 1RS, U.K.

J. E.Afr. Res. Devel. Journal of Eastern African research & development. (0251-0405). Gideon S. Were: P.O. Box 10622, Nairobi, Kenya.

J. Econ. Iss. Journal of economic issues. (0021-3624). Association for Evolutionary Economics: Department of Economics, University of Nebraska-Lincoln, Lincoln, NE. 68588, U.S.A.

J. Econ. Psyc. Journal of economic psychology. (0167-4870). Elsevier Science Publishers (North-Holland): P.O. Box 1991, 1000 BZ Amsterdam, The Netherlands, in association with International Association for Research in Economic Psychology: Egmontstraat 13, 1050 Brussels, Belgium.

J. Econ. Soc. Journal of economic and social measurement. (0747-9662). International Organisations Services: Van Diemenstraat 94, 1013 CN Amsterdam, The Netherlands.

J. Econ. Soc. Geogr. Tijdschrift voor economische en sociale geografie = Journal of economic and social geography. (0040-747X). Royal Dutch Geographical Society = Koninklijk Nederlands Aardrijkskundig Genootschap: Weteringschans 12, 1017 SG Amsterdam, The Netherlands.

J. Educ. Pol. Journal of education policy. (0268-0939). Taylor & Francis: 4 John Street, London WC1N 2ET, U.K.

J. Europe. Soc. Pol. Journal of European social policy. (0958-9287). Longman Group U.K.: Fouth Avenue, Harlow, Essex, CM19 5AA, U.K., in association with Journal of European Social Policy.

List of abbreviations used

J. Exp. S. Psychol. Journal of experimental social psychology. (0022-1031). Academic Press: 1 East First Street, Duluth, MN. 55802, U.S.A.
J. Fam. Law University of Louisville journal of family law. (0022-1066). University of Louisville, School of Law: 2301 South Third Street, Louisville, KY. 40292, U.S.A.
J. Fam. Ther. Journal of family therapy. (0163-4445). Basil Blackwell: 108 Cowley Road, Oxford OX4 1JF, U.K., in association with Association for Family Therapy: 6 Ileol, Seddon, Danescourt, Llandaff, Cardiff CF5 2QX, U.K.
J. Fam. Viol. Journal of family violence. (0885-7482). Plenum Publishing Corporation: 233 Spring Street, New York, NY 10013-1578, U.S.A.
J. Folk. Res. Journal of folklore research. (0737-7037). Indiana University Folklore Institute: 504 North Fess, Bloomington, Indiana 47405, U.S.A.
J. For. Psy. Journal of forensic psychiatry. (0958-5184). Routledge: 11 New Fetter Lane, London EC4P 4EE, U.K.
J. Gender Studies Journal of gender studies. (0958-9236). University of Hull: HU6 7RX, England.
J. Health Econ. Journal of health economics. (0167-6296). Elsevier Science Publishers (North-Holland): P.O. Box 1991, 1000 BZ Amsterdam, The Netherlands.
J. Health Polit. Pol. Law Journal of health politics, policy and law. (0361-6878). Duke University Press: Brightleaf Square, 905 W. Main Street, 18-B, Box 90660, Durham, North Carolina, NC. 27708-0660, U.S.A.
J. Hist. Beh. Sci. Journal of the history of the behavioral sciences. (0022-5061). Clinical Psychology Publishing: 4 Conant Square, Brandon, VT. 05733, U.S.A.
J. Hous. Res. Journal of housing research. (1052-7001). Office of Housing Policy, Fannie Mae: 3900 Wisconsin Avenue, N.W., Washington DC 20016-2899, U.S.A.
J. Hum. Res. Journal of human resources. (0022-166X). University of Wisconsin Press: 4315 Social Science Building, University of Wisconsin, 1180 Observatory Drive, Madison, WI. 53706, U.S.A.
J. Hum. Sci. Journal of human sciences.
J. Ind. Manag. Journal of industry and management.
J. Ind. Relat. Journal of industrial relations. (0022-1856). Journal of Industrial Relations: GPO Box 4479, Sydney, NSW 2001, Australia.
J. Inst. Theo. Ec. Journal of institutional and theoretical economics = Zeitschrift für die gesamte Staatswissenschaft. (0932-4569). J.C.B.Mohr (Paul Siebeck): P.O. Box 2040, D-7400 Tübingen, Germany.
J. Int. Dev. Journal of international development. (0954-1748). John Wiley & Sons: Baffins Lane, Chichester, West Sussex PO19 1UD, U.K., in association with Institute for Development Policy and Management: University of Manchester, Precinct Centre, Oxford Road, Manchester M13 9QS, U.K.
J. Int. Rel. Journal of international relations.
J. Interd. Stud. Journal of interdisciplinary studies: An international journal of interdisciplinary and interfaith dialogue. (0890-0132). Institute for Interdisciplinary Research: 2828 Third Street, Suite 11, Santa Monica, CA. 90405-4150, U.S.A., in association with International Christian Studies Association.
J. Jpn. Stud. Journal of Japanese studies. (0095-6848). Society for Japanese Studies: Thomson Hall DR-05, University of Washington, Seattle, Washington 98195, U.S.A.
J. Labor Ec. Journal of labor economics. (0734-306X). University of Chicago Press: Journals Division, P.O. Box 37005, Chicago, IL 60637, U.S.A., in association with Economics Research Center/NORC.

Liste des abbreviations utilisés

J. Labor Res. Journal of labor research. (0195-3613). George Mason University, Department of Economics: Fairfax, VA. 22030, U.S.A.
J. Lang. Soc. Psychol. Journal of language and social psychology. (0261-927X). Multilingual Matters: Bank House, 8a Hill Road, Clevedon, Avon BS21 7HH, U.K.
J. Law Soc. Journal of law and society. (0263-323X). Basil Blackwell: 108 Cowley Road, Oxford OX4 1JF, U.K.
J. Leg. Stud. Journal of legal studies. (0047-2530). University of Chicago Press: 5720 S. Woodlawn Avenue, Chicago, IL. 60637, U.S.A.
J. Manag. Stu. Journal of management studies. (0022-2380). Basil Blackwell: 108 Cowley Road, Oxford OX4 1JF, U.K.
J. Marriage Fam. Journal of marriage and the family. (0022-2445). National Council on Family Relations: 3989 Central Avenue Northeast, Suite 550, Minneapolis, MN. 55421, U.S.A.
J. Math. Sociol. Journal of mathematical sociology. (0022-250X). Gordon & Breach Science Publishers: P.O. Box 786, Cooper Station, New York, NY 10276, U.S.A.
J. Medic. Philos. Journal of medicine and philosophy. (0360-5310). Kluwer Academic Publishers: P.O. Box 322, 3300 AH Dordrecht, The Netherlands.
J. Mediter. St. Journal of Mediterranean studies. (1016-3476). Mediterranean Institute: University of Malta, Msida, Malta.
J. Micrones. Stud. Journal of Micronesian studies. Unversity of Guam Press: UOG Station, Mangilao, Guam 96923.
J. Mod. Afr. S. Journal of modern African studies. (0022-278X). Cambridge University Press: The Edinburgh Building, Shaftesbury Road, Cambridge CB2 2RU, U.K.
J. Multiling. Journal of multilingual and multicultural development. (0143-4632). Multilingual Matters: Bank House, 8a Hill Road, Clevedon, Avon BS21 7HH, U.K.
J. Occupat. Rehabil. Journal of occupational rehabilitation. (1053-0487). Plenum Publishing Corporation: 233 Spring Street, New York, NY 10013-1578, U.S.A.
J. Pacific Soc. Journal of the Pacific Society. (0387-4745). Pacific Society: 4-1-6 Akasaka, Minato-ku, Tokyo, Japan.
J. Peace Res. Journal of peace research. (0022-3433). Sage Publications: 6 Bonhill Street, London EC2A 4PU, U.K., in association with International Peace Research Institute, Oslo (PRIO): Fuglehauggata 11, 0260 Oslo 2, Norway.
J. Peasant Stud. Journal of peasant studies. (0306-6150). Frank Cass: Gainsborough House, 11 Gainsborough Road, London E11 1RS, U.K.
J. Pers. Soc. Psychol. Journal of personality and social psychology. (0022-3514). American Psychological Association: 1400 North Uhle Street, Arlington, VA. 22201, U.S.A.
J. Personal. Journal of personality. (0022-3506). Duke University Press: Box 6697, College Station, Durham, NC. 27708, U.S.A.
J. Phil. Journal of philosophy. (0022-362X). Journal of Philosophy: 709 Philosophy Hall, Columbia University, New York, NY 10027, U.S.A.
J. Plan. Lit. Journal of planning literature. (0885-4122). Ohio State University Press: 1070 Carmack Road, Columbus, OH. 43210, U.S.A.
J. Policy An. Journal of policy analysis and management. (0276-8739). John Wiley and Sons: 605 Third Avenue, New York, NY 10155, U.S.A., in association with Association for Public Policy Analysis and Management.
J. Polit. Journal of politics. (0022-3816). University of Texas Press, Journals Department: 2100 Comal, Austin TX. 78722, U.S.A.

List of abbreviations used

J. Polit. Ec. Journal of political economy. (0022-3808). University of Chicago Press: 5720 S. Woodlawn Avenue, Chicago, IL. 60637, U.S.A.

J. Pop. Cult. Journal of popular culture. (0022-3840). Popular Press: Bowling Green State University, Bowling Green OH 43402, U.S.A., in association with Modern Language Association of America, Popular Literature Section/ Midwest Modern Language Association, Folklore Section.

J. Pop. Ec. Journal of population economics. (0933-1433). Springer-Verlag: Postfach 10 52 80, D-69042 Heidelberg Germany.

J. Psychol. Journal of psychology. (0022-3980). Heldref Publications: 4000 Albemarle Street, N.W., Washington DC 20016, U.S.A.

J. Refug. S. Journal of refugee studies. (0951-6328). Oxford University Press: Pinkhill House, Southfield Road, Eynsham, Oxford OX8 1JJ, U.K., in association with University of Oxford, Refugee Studies Programme: Queen Elizabeth House, 21 St. Giles, Oxford OX1 3LA, U.K.

J. Reg. Pol. Journal of regional policy. Isveimer: via S. Giacomo, 19 Naples, Italy.

J. Res. Crim. Delin. Journal of research in crime and delinquency. (0022-4278). Sage Publications: 2455 Teller Road, Newbury Park, CA. 91320, U.S.A., in association with National Council on Crime and Delinquency: 685 Market Street, Suite 620, San Francisco, CA. 94105, U.S.A.

J. Roy. Stat. Soc. A. Journal of the Royal Statistical Society: Series A (statistics in society). (0035-9238). Royal Statistical Society: 25 Enford Street, London W1H 2BH, U.K.

J. Rural Prob. Journal of rural problem. Association of regional, agricultural and forestry economics.

J. S.Afr. Stud. Journal of Southern African studies. (0305-7070). Oxford University Press: Pinkhill House, Southfield Road, Eynsham, Oxford OX8 1JJ, U.K.

J. Sci. S. Relig. Journal for the scientific study of religion. (0021-8294). Society for the Scientific Study of Religion: Pierce Hall, Room 193, Purdue University, West Lafayette, IN. 47907, U.S.A.

J. Soc. Clin. Psychol. Journal of social and clinical psychology. (0736-7236). Guilford Publications: 72 Spring Street, New York, NY 10012, U.S.A.

J. Soc. Devel. Afr. Journal of social development in Africa. (1012 1080). School of Social Work: P/ Bag 66022 Kopje, Harare, Zimbabwe.

J. Soc. Distr. Home. Journal of social distress and the homeless. (1053-0789). Human Sciences Press: 233 Spring Street, New York, NY 10013-1578, U.S.A.

J. Soc. Evol. Sys. Journal of social and evolutionary systems. (1061-7361). JAI Press: 55 Old Post Road — No.2, P.O. Box 1678, Greenwich, CT., 06836-1678, U.S.A.

J. Soc. Issues Journal of social issues. (0022-4537). Plenum Publishing: 233 Spring Street, New York, NY 10013-1578, U.S.A., in association with Society for the Psychological Study of Social Issues.

J. Soc. Pol. Journal of social policy. (0047-2794). Cambridge University Press: The Edinburgh Building, Shaftesbury Road, Cambridge CB2 2RU, U.K., in association with Social Policy Association.

J. Soc. Pol. E. Journal of social, political and economic studies. (0193-5941). Council for Social and Economic Studies: Suite C-2, 1133 13th St. N.W., Washington DC 20005-4297, U.S.A.

J. Soc. Work Pol. Israel Journal of social work and policy in Israel. (0334 9977). Bar-Ilan University.

Liste des abbreviations utilisés

J. Soc. Work. Practice Journal of social work practice. (0265-0533). Carfax Publishing Company: P.O Box 25, Abingdon, Oxfordshire OX14 3UE, United Kingdom.
J. Sozialfors. Journal für Sozialforschung. (0253-3995). Europäisches Zentrum für Wohlfarhrtspolitik und Sozialforschung: Berggasse 17, 1090 Vienna, Austria.
J. Struct. Learn. Journal of structural learning. (0022-4774). Gordon and Breach Science Publishers: 270 8th Avenue, New York, NY 10011, U.S.A.
J. Theor. Pol. Journal of theoretical politics. (0951-6928). Sage Publications: 6 Bonhill Street, London EC2A 4PU, U.K.
J. Theory Soc. Behav. Journal for the theory of social behaviour. (0021-8308). Basil Blackwell: 108 Cowley Road, Oxford OX4 1JF, U.K.
J. Urban Ec. Journal of urban economics. (0094-1190). Academic Press: 1 East First Street, Duluth, MN. 55802, U.S.A.
J. Urban Hist. Journal of urban history. (0096-1442). Sage Publications: 2455 Teller Road, Newbury Park, CA 91320, U.S.A.
Jahr. Christ. Sozialwiss. Jahrbuch für christliche Sozialwissenschaften. (0075-2584). Verlag Regensberg: Daimlerweg 58, Postfach 6748-6749, 4400 Münster, Germany, in association with Universität Münster, Institut für Christliche Sozialwissenschaften.
Jahr. Soz.schaft. Jahrbuch für Sozialwissenschaft. (0075-2770). Vandenhoeck & Ruprecht: Theaterstraße 13, P.O. Box 3753, 3400 Göttingen, Germany.
Jahrb. Wirt. Gesch. Jahrbuch für Wirtschaftsgeschichte. (0075-2800). Akademie-Verlag Berlin: Postfach 1233, Leipziger Straße 3-4 1086 Berlin, Germany.
Jap. J. Relig. St. Japanese journal of religious studies. (0304-1042). Nanzan Institute for Religion and Culture: 18 Yamazato-chō, Shōwa-ku, Nagoya 466, Japan.
Jew. J. Socio. Jewish journal of sociology. (0021-6534). Maurice Freedman Research Trust: 187 Gloucester Place, London NW1 6BU, U.K.
Jew. Soc. Stud. Jewish social studies. (0021-6704). Conference on Jewish Social Studies: 2112 Broadway, New York, NY 10023, U.S.A.
Jin. (J. Kyo. Univ.) Jinbun (Journal of Kyoto University).
Jin. Ken. Jinbun kenkyu.
Jin. Kiyo Jinbungakubu kiyo.
Jinbun-ronkyu Jinbun-ronkyu.
Jo. To Shak. Joho To Shakai (Journal of Edogawa University).
Jokyo Jokyo.
Jos. Kuk. Josei kukan.
Jpn. Forum Japan forum. (0955-5803). Oxford University Press: Pinkhill House, Southfield Road, Eynsham, Oxford OX8 1JJ, U.K., in association with British Association for Japanese Studies.
Kaz. Kank. Gaku Kazoku kankeig gaku.
Kaz. Shak. Ken. Kazoku Shakaigaku kenkyu. Japan Society of Family Sociology.
Kei. Jo. Kiyo Keiei Johogakubu Kiyo (Bulletin of Jobu University).
Ken. Kiyo (J. Aomori Univ.) Kenkyu kiyo (Journal of Aomori University). Aomori University.
Kenkyunenpo (B. Ris. Univ.) Kenkyunenpo (Bulletin of Rissho University). Rissho University.
Kiyo Shak. Kiyo Shakaigakka.
Know. Pol. Knowledge and policy. (0897-1986). Transaction Periodicals Consortium: Rutgers University, New Brunswick, NJ 08903.

List of abbreviations used

Kölner Z. Soz. Soz. psy. Kölner Zeitschrift für Soziologie und Sozialpsychologie. (0340-0425). Westdeutscher Verlag: Postfach 5829, D-6200 Wiesbaden 1, Germany.
Korea Obs. Korea observer. (0023-3919). Institute of Korean Studies: C.P.O. Box 3410, Seoul 100-643, Korea.
Korean Soc. Sci. J. Korean social science journal. Korean Social Science Research Council/ Korean National Commission for UNESCO: Box Central 64, Seoul, Korea.
Kyo.-Shak. Ken. Kyoiku-shakaigaku Kenkyu.
Lab. Law J. Labor law journal. (0023-6586). Commerce Clearing House: 4025 W. Peterson Avenue, Chicago, IL. 60646, U.S.A.
Labour [Italy] Labour [Italy]. (1121-7081). Blackwell: 108 Cowley Road, Oxford OX4 1JF, United Kingdom, in association with Fondazione Giacomo Brodolini: Via Torino 122, 00184 Rome, Italy.
Labour Cap. Soc. Labour, capital and society = Travail, capital et société. (0706-1706). McGill University, Centre for Developing Area Studies: 3715 rue Peel, Montréal, Québec H31 1X1, Canada.
Lang. Prob. Lang. Plan. Language problems and language planning. (0270-2690). John Benjamins Publishing: P.O. Box 75577, Amstedldijk 44, 1007 AN Amsterdam, The Netherlands.
Lang. Soc. Language in society. (0047-4045). Cambridge University Press: 40 West 20th Street, New York, NY 10011, U.S.A.
Lat. Am. Pers. Latin American perspectives. (0094-582X). Sage Publishers.
Lat. Am. Res. R. Latin American research review. (0023-8791). Latin American Studies Association: Latin American Institute, 801 Yale NE, University of New Mexico, Albuquerque, NM. 87131-1016, U.S.A.
Law Crit. Law and critique. (0957-8536). Deborah Charles Publications: 173 Mather Avenue, Liverpool L18 6JZ, U.K., in association with Critical Legal Studies Conference of the U.K.
Law Policy Law and policy. (0265-8240). Basil Blackwell: 108 Cowley Road, Oxford OX4 1JF, U.K.
Law Soc. Rev. Law and society review. (0023-9216). Law and Society Association: Hampshire House, University of Massachusetts at Amherst, Amherst MA. 01003, U.S.A.
Leis. Sci. Leisure sciences. (01490400). Taylor & Francis: 4 John Street, London WC1N 2ET, U.K.
Leviatán Leviatán. (0210-6337). Fundación Pablo Iglesias: Monte Esquinza 30, 28010 Madrid, Spain.
Linguistics Linguistics. (0024-3949). Mouton de Gruyter: Postfach 110240, D-1000 Berlin 11, Germany.
Loc. Govt. R. Jpn. Local government review in Japan. (0288-7622). Jichi Sogo Center (General Center for Local Autonomy): 7-1 Nishi-Shimbashi 1-chome, Minato-ku, Tokyo, 105 Japan.
Loc. Govt. St. Local government studies. (0300-3930). Charles Knight Publishing: Tolley House, 2 Addiscombe Road, Croydon, Surrey CR9 5AF, U.K.
Local. Ec. Local economy. (0269-0942). Longman Group: 6th Floor, Westgate House, The High, Harlow, Essex CM20 1YR, U.K., in association with Local Economy Policy Unit: Southbank Polytechnic, Borough Road, London SE1 0AA, U.K.
Local. Pop. S. Local population studies. (0143-2974). Local Population Studies Society: Tawney House, Matlock, Derbyshire, DE4 3BT, U.K.

Liste des abbreviations utilisés

Maan. Econ. Maandschrift economie. (0013-0486). Wolters-Noordhoff: Postbus 58, 9700 MB Groningen, The Netherlands.
Mag. Tud. Magyar tudomány. (0025-0325). Akademiai Kiado, Publishing House of the Hungarian Academy of Sciences: P.O. Box 24, H-1363 Budapest, Hungary, in association with Magyar Tudományos Akadémia: Roosevelt-tér 9, 1051 Budapest, Hungary.
Malay. J. Trop. Geogr. Malaysian journal of tropical geography. (0127-1474).
Man Man. (0025-1496). Royal Anthropological Institute: 50 Fitzroy Street, London W1P 5HS, U.K.
Man India Man in India. (0025-1569). Sudarshan Press: Church Road, Ranchi 834 001 Bihar, India.
Manag. Sci. Management science. (0025-1909). Institute of Management Sciences: 290 Westminster Street, Providence, RI. 02903, U.S.A.
Mankind Q. Mankind quarterly. (0025-2344). Cliveden Press: Suite C-2, 1133 13th Street N.W., Washington DC 20005-4298, U.S.A.
Marx. Blät Marxistische Blätter. (0542-7770). Neue Impulse Verlag: Hoffnungstraße 18, 4300 Essen 1, Germany.
Math. Soc. Sc. Mathematical social sciences. (0165 4896). Elsevier Science Publishers (North-Holland): P.O. Box 1991, 1000 BZ Amsterdam, The Netherlands.
Med. Anthr. Q. Medical anthropology quarterly. (0745-5194). American Anthropological Association: 1703 New Hampshire Avenue N.W., Washington DC 20009, U.S.A., in association with Society for Medical Anthropology.
Media Cult. Soc. Media culture and society. (0163-4437). Sage Publications: 6 Bonhill Street, London EC2A 4PU, U.K.
Mens Maat. Mens en maatschappij. (0025-9454). Bohn Stafleu Van Loghum: Postbus 246, 3990 GA Houten, The Netherlands.
MI. law. R. Michigan law review. (0026-2234). Michigan Law Review: Hutchins Hall, Ann Arbor, MI. 48109-1215, U.S.A.
Middle E. J. Middle East journal. (0026-3141). Indiana University Press: 10th and Morton, Bloomington, IN. 47405, U.S.A., in association with Middle East Institute: 1761 N. Street, N.W., Washington, DC. 20036, U.S.A.
Middle E. Rep. Middle East report. (0899-0328). Middle East Research and Information Project (MERIP): Suite 119, 1500 Massachusetts Avenue, N.W. Washington DC 20005, U.S.A.
Milbank Q. Milbank quarterly. (0887-378X). Cambridge University Press: 40 West 20th Street, New York, NY 10011, U.S.A., in association with Milbank Memorial Fund.
Mind Lang. Mind and language. (0268 1064). Basil Blackwell: 108 Cowley Road, Oxford OX4 1JF, U.K.
Mir. Ek. Mez. Ot. Mirovaia ekonomika i mezhdunarodnye otnosheniia. (0131-2227). Izdatel'stvo Pravda: Ul. Pravdy 24, Moscow 117418, U.S.S.R.
Mir. Ekon. Mezh. Otno. Mirovaia ekonomika i mezhdunarodnye otnosheniia.
Mon. Rev. Monthly review. (0027-0520). Monthly Review Foundation: 122 West 27th Street, New York, NY 10001, U.S.A.
Multilingua Multilingua. (0167-8507). Mouton de Gruyter: Postfach 110240, D-1000 Berlin 30, Germany.
NACLA NACLA report on the Americas. (0149-1598). North American Congress on Latin America (NACLA): 475 Riverside Drive, Suite 454, New York, NY 10115, U.S.A.

List of abbreviations used

Nat. Pap. Nationalities papers. (0090-5992). Association for the Study of Nationalities (U.S.S.R. and East Europe): Department of Sociology, University of Nebraska, Omaha, NE. 68182, U.S.A.
Nav. Tvor. Etn. Narodna tvorchist' ta etnografiia.
Negot. J. Negotiation journal. (0748-4526). Plenum Press: 233 Spring Street, New York, NY 10013-1578, U.S.A.
Nen. Shak. Ron. Nenpo Shakaigaku Ronsyu.
Neth. J. Soc. Sci. Netherlands' journal of social sciences/Sociologia Neerlandica. (0038-0172). Van Gorcum: P.O. Box 43, 4900 AA Assen, The Netherlands, in association with Netherlands' Sociological and Anthropological Society.
New Comm. New community. (0047-9586). University of Warwick, Centre for Research in Ethnic Relations: Coventry CV4 7AL, U.K., in association with Commission for Racial Equality: London, U.K.
New Form. New formations. (0950-2378). Routledge: 11 New Fetter Lane, London EC4P 4EE, U.K.
New Left R. New left review. (0028-6060). New Left Review: 6 Meard Street, London W1V 3HR, U.K.
New Tech. Work. Empl. New technology, work and employment. (0268-1072). Basil Blackwell: 108 Cowley Road, Oxford OX4 1JF, U.K.
Nin. Kag. Ken. Ningen Kagaku Kenkyu (Journal of Waseda University).
Non. Manag. Leader. Nonprofit management and leadership. (1048-6682). Jossey-Bass: 350 Sansome Street, San Francisco, CA. 94104-1310, U.S.A.
Nord. Ny. Nord nytt. (0008-1345). Institute foe Europeaeisk Folkelivsforskning: Brede Alle 69, DK-2800, Lyngby, Denmark.
NY. U. Law. Re. New York University law review. (0028-7881). New York University Law Review: 110 West Third Street, New York, NY 10012, U.S.A.
Obshch. Ekon. Obshchestvo i ekonomika. (0207 3676). Nauka, in association with Rossiiskaia akademiia nauk, Otdelenie ekonomiki.
Obshch. Nauki Sovrem. Obshchestvennye nauki i sovremennost'. (0869 0499). Nauka.
Organ. Stud. Organization studies. (0170-8406). Walter de Gruyter: Genthiner Str. 13, D-1000 Berlin 30, Germany, in association with European Group for Organizational Studies.
Organiz. Sci. Organization science. (1047-7039). Institute of Management Sciences: 290 Westminster Street, Providence, RI., 02903, U.S.A.
Ost. Wirt. Osteuropa Wirtschaft. (0030-6460). Deutsche Verlags-Anstalt: Neckarstraße 121, Postfach 10 60 12, D-7000 Stuttgart 10, Germany, in association with Deutsche Gesellschaft für Osteuropakunde.
Öster. Z. Polit. Österreichische Zeitschrift für Politikwissenschaft. Verlag für Gesellschaftskritik: Kaiserstraße 91, A-1070 Vienna, Austria, in association with Österreichische Gesellschaft für Politikwissenschaft.
Osteuropa Osteuropa. (0030-6428). Deutsche Verlags-Anstalt: Neckarstraße 121, Postfach 1060 12, 7000 Stuttgart 10, Germany, in association with Deutsche Gesellschaft für Osteuropakunde: Schaperstraße 30, 1000 Berlin 15, Germany.
Over. Soc. Sec. News Overseas social security news.
Ox. B. Econ. S. Oxford bulletin of economics and statistics. (0305-9049). Basil Blackwell: 108 Cowley Road, Oxford OX4 1JF, U.K.
Oyo-Shak. Ken. Oyo-shakaigaku Kenkyu (Journal of Rikkyo University).

Liste des abbreviations utilisés

Pac. Aff. Pacific affairs. (0030-851X). University of British Columbia: Vancouver, BC., V6T 1W5 Canada.
Pak. Dev. R. Pakistan development review. (0030-9729). Pakistan Institute of Development Economics: P.O. Box 1091, Islamabad, Pakistan.
Pap. Reg. Sci. Papers in regional science: Revue d'études canadiennes. (0486-2902). Regional Science Association International: University of Illinois at Urbana-Champaign, 1-3 Observatory, 901 South Mathews Avenue, Urbana, IL. 61801-3682, U.S.A.
Papers Papers. (0210-2862). Universitat Autònoma de Barcelona, Departament de Sociologia: Servei de Publicacions, Edifici A, 08193 Barcelona, Spain.
Pensée Pensée. (0031-4773). Institut de recherches marxistes: 64, Boulevard Auguste-Blanqui, 75013 Paris, France.
Peup. Médit. Peuples méditerranéens = Mediterranean peoples. (0399-1253). Institut d'Études Méditerranéenes: B.P. 188-07, 75326 Paris Cedex 07, France.
Phil. Stud. Philippine studies. (0031-7837). Ateneo de Manila University Press: P.O. Box 154, Manila 1099, Philippines.
Philos. Pub. Philosophy & public affairs. (0048-3915). Princeton University Press: 41 William Street, Princeton, NJ. 08540, U.S.A.
Philos. S. Sc. Philosophy of the social sciences. (0048-3931). Sage Publications: 2455 Teller Road, Newbury Park, CA. 91320, U.S.A.
Plan. Desarr. Planeación y desarrollo. (0034-8686). Departamento Nacional de Planeación: Calle 26 No. 13-19 Piso 2º, Santafé de Bogota, Colombia.
Plan. Pract. Res. Planning practice and research. (0269-7459). Pion: 207 Brondesbury Park, London NW2 5JN, U.K.
Pol. Geogr. Political geography. (0962-6298). Butterworth-Heinemann: Linacre House, Jordan Hill, Oxford OX2 8DP, U.K.
Pol. Quart. Political quarterly. (0032-3179). Basil Blackwell: 108 Cowley Road, Oxford OX4 1JF, U.K.
Pol. Res. Q. Political research quarterly. (1065-9129). University of Utah: Salt Lake City, UT. 84112, U.S.A., in association with Western Political Science Association/ Pacific Northwest Political Science Association/ Southern California Political Science Association/ Northern California Political Science Association.
Poli. Sci. Political science. (0032-3187). Victoria University Press: Information and Publications Section, Victoria University of Wellington, Private Bag, Wellington 1, New Zealand, in association with Victoria University of Wellington, School of Political Science and Public Administration: P.O.Box 600, Wellington 1, New Zealand.
Poli. Soc. Policing and society. (1043-9463). Harwood Academic Publishers: 270 8th Avenue, New York, NY.10011, U.S.A.
Policy Pol. Policy and politics. (0305-5736). University of Bristol, School for Advanced Urban Studies: Rodney Lodge, Grange Road, Bristol BS8 4EA, U.K.
Policy Sci. Policy sciences. (0032-2687). Kluwer Academic Publishers: P.O. Box 17, 3300 AA Dordrecht, The Netherlands.
Polis [Moscow] Polis [Moscow]. (03212017). Izdatel'stvo Progress Publishers.
Polit. Indiv. Politics and the individual: International journal of political socialization and political psychology. (0939-6071). Verlag Dr. R. Krämer: Postfach 13 05 84, D-20105 Hamburg, Germany.
Polit. Life Politics and the life sciences. (0730-9384). Association for Politics and the Life Sciences: Northern Illinois University, DeKalb, IL. 60115-2854, U.S.A.

List of abbreviations used

Polit. Psych. Political psychology. (0162-895X). Plenum Publishing: 233 Spring Street, New York, NY 10013-1578, U.S.A., in association with International Society of Political Psychology.
Polit. Soc. Politics and society. (0032-3292). Butterworth-Heinemann: 80 Montvale Avenue, Stoneham, MA. 02180, U.S.A.
Polit. Theory Political theory. (0090-5917). Sage Publications: 2111 West Hillcrest Drive, Newbury Park, CA. 91320, U.S.A.
Politic. Stud. Political studies. (0032-3217). Basil Blackwell: 108 Cowley Road, Oxford OX4 1JF, U.K., in association with Political Studies Association of the United Kingdom: c/o Jack Hayward, Department of Politics, The University, Hull HU6 7RX, U.K.
Politix Politix. (0295-2319). Presses de la Fondation nationale des sciences politiques: 44 rue du Four, 75006 Paris, France.
Pop. Dev. Rev. Population and development review. (0098-7921). Population Council: One Dag Hammarskjold Plaza, New York, NY 10017, U.S.A.
Pop. Res. Pol. R. Population research and policy review. (0167-5923). Kluwer Academic Publishers: P.O. Box 17, 3300 AH Dordrecht, The Netherlands.
Pop. Stud. Population studies. (0032-4728). London School of Economics, Population Investigation Committee: Houghton Street, Aldwych, London WC2A 2AE, U.K.
Popul. R. Population review. (0032-471X). Indian Institute for Population Studies: 8976 Cliffridge Avenue, La Jolla, CA. 92037, U.S.A.
Population Population. (0032-4663). Editions de l'Institut National d'Études Démographiques: 27 rue du Commandeur, 75675 Paris Cedex 14, France, in association with Institut National d'Études Démographiques: 27 rue du Commandeur, 75675 Paris Cedex 14, France.
Pra. Zab. Społ. Praca i zabezpieczenie społeczne. (0032-6186). Państwowe Wydawnictwo Ekonomiczne: Ul. Niecała 4a, Warsaw, Poland.
Practice Practice. (0950-3153). British Association of Social Workers: 16 Kent Street, Birmingham B5 6RD, U.K.
Prague Occ. Pap. Ethn. Prague occasional papers in ethnology. Institute of Ethnology: Prague, Czech Republic.
Prob. Am.Lat. Problèmes d'Amérique latine. (0765-1333). Documentation française: 29/31 quai Voltaire, 75340 Paris Cedex 07, France.
Prof. Geogr. Professional geographer. (0033-0124). Association of American Geographers: 1710 Sixteenth Street, N.W., Washington DC 20009-3198, U.S.A.
Prog. H. Geog. Progress in human geography. (0309-1325). Edward Arnold: Mill Road, Dunton Green, Sevenoaks, Kent TN13 2YA, U.K.
Prog. Plan. Progress in planning. (0305-9006). Pergamon Press: Headington Hill Hall, Oxford OX3 0BW, U.K.
Prokla Prokla: Probleme des Klassenkampfs. Rotbuch Verlag: Potsdamer Str. 98, 1000 Berlin 30, Germany, in association with Vereinigung zur Kritik der politischen Ökonomie.
Prz. Pol. Przegląd polonijny. (0137-303X). Ossolineum, Publishing House of the Polish Academy of Sciences: Rynek 9, 50-106 Wroclaw, Poland, in association with Polska Akademia Nauk, Komitet Badania Polonii.
Prz. Soc. Przegląd socjologiczny. (43, Łódź, Poland). Łódzkie towarzystwo naukowe: ul Rewolucji 1905 roku 41.
Psychoanal. Rev. Psychoanalytic review. (0033-2836). Guilford Publications: 72 Spring Street, New York, NY 10012, U.S.A.

Liste des abbreviations utilisés

Psychol . B. Psychological bulletin. (0033-2909). American Psychological Association.
Psychol. Devel. Soc. Psychology and developing societies. Sage Publications India: 32 M-Block Market, Greater Kailash I, New Delhi 110 048, India.
Psychol. Rev. Psychological review. (0033-295X). American Psychological Association: 1400 North Uhle Street, Arlington, VA. 22201, U.S.A.
Publ. Admin. Public administration. (0033-3298). Basil Blackwell: 108 Cowley Road, Oxford OX4 1JF, U.K., in association with Royal Institute for Public Administration: 3 Birdcage Walk, London SW1H 9JH, U.K.
Publ. Aff. Q. Public affairs quarterly. (0887-0373). Philosophy Documentation Center/ North American Philosophical Publications: Bowling Green State University, Bowling Green, OH. 43403, U.S.A.
Publ. Cult. Public culture. (0899-2363). University of Pennsylvania, University Museum, in association with Center for Transnational Cultural Studies: University Museum, University of Pennsylvania, 33rd and Spruce Streets, Pennsylvania, PA. 19104-6324, U.S.A.
Publ. Finan. Public finance = Finances publiques. (0033-3476). Public Finance/ Finances Publiques: c/- Prof. Dieter Biehl, Institut für Öffentliche Wirtschaft, Geld und Währung, Johann Wolfgang Goethe-Universität, Postfach 111932, D-6000Frankfurt am Main 11, Germany.
Publ. Inter. Public interest. (0033-3557). National Affairs: 1112 16th Street, N.W., Suite 530, Washington, D.C. 20036, U.S.A.
Publ. Opin. Q. Public opinion quarterly. (0033-362X). University of Chicago Press: Journals Division, 5720 S. Woodlawn Avenue, Chicago, IL. 60637, U.S.A., in association with American Association for Public Opinion Research.
Publizistik Publizistik. (0033-4006). Universitätsverlag Konstanz: Postfach 102051, D-7750 Konstanz, Germany, in association with Deutsche Gesellschaft für Publizistik- und Kommunikationswissenschaft/ Österreichische Gesellschaft für Publizistik- und Kommunikationswissenschaft/ Schweizerische Gesellschaft für Kommunikations- und Medienwissenschaft: Martin-Legros-Straße 53, D-5300 Bonn 1, Germany.
Quad. Sociol. Quaderni di sociologia. (0033-4952). Edizioni di Comunità: 20090 Segrate, Milan, Italy.
R. Cen. Est. Consti. Revista del Centro de Estudios Constitucionales. (0214-6185). Centro de Estudios Constitucionales: Plaza de la Marina Española 9, 28071 Madrid, Spain.
R. Ec. Reg. Urb. Revue d'économie régionale et urbaine. (0180-7307). ADICUEER (Association des directeurs d'instituts et des centres universitaires d'études économiques régionales): 4 Rue Michelet, 75006 Paris, France.
R. Econ. Soc. Revue économique et sociale. (0035-2772). Société d'Études Economiques et Sociales: Bâtiment des Facultés des Sciences Humaines (BFSH1), 1015 Lausanne-Dorigny, Switzerland.
R. Et. Coop. Mut. Ass. Revue des études coopératives mutualistes et associatives. (0035-2020). Revue des études coopératives: 255 rue de Vaugirard, 75719 Paris Cedex 15, France.
R. Et. Palest. Revue d'études palestiniennes. (0252-8290). Editions de Minuit: 7 rue Bernard-Palissy, 75006 Paris, France, in association with Institut des Études Palestiniennes / Fondation Diana Tamari Sabbagh.
R. Eur. Lat.am. Caribe European review of Latin American and Caribbean studies = Revista europea de estudios latinoamericanos y del caribe. (0924-0608). CEDLA Edita: Keizersgracht 395-397, 1016 Amsterdam, The Netherlands, in association with CEDLA,

List of abbreviations used

    Interuniversitair Centrum voor Studie en Documentatie van Latijns Amerika/ RILA, Royal Institute of Linguistics and Anthropology: Keizersgracht 395-397, 1016 Amsterdam, The Netherlands.
R. Int. Co-op. Review of international co-operation. (0034-6608). International Cooperative Alliance: Route des Morillons 15, CH-1218 Le Grand Saconnex, Geneva, Switzerland.
R. Mon. Musul. Med. Revue du monde musulman et de la Méditerranée. (0997-1327). Editions ÉDISUD: La Calade,13090 Aix-en-Provence, France, in association with Association pour l'étude des sciences humaines en Afrique du Nord et au Proche-Orient.
R. Soc. Econ. Review of social economy. (0034-6764). Association for Social Economics: c/o Department of Economics, Northern Illinois University, DeKalb, IL. 60115, U.S.A.
R. Soc. Move. Con. Cha. Research in social movements, conflicts and change. (0163-786X). JAI Press: 55 Old Post Road No.2, Greenwich, CT. 066830, U.S.A.
R. Synd. Suisse Revue syndicale suisse. (0035-421X). Revue Syndicale Suisse: Case Postale 64, 3000 Berne 23 , Switzerland.
R. T-Monde Revue Tiers-Monde. (0040-7356). Presses Universitaires de France, in association with Université de Paris, Institut d'étude du développement économique et social: 58 boulevard Arago, 75013 Paris, France.
R. Tun. Sci. Soc. Revue tunisienne de sciences sociales. (0035-4333). Université de Tunis, Centre d'Études et de Recherches Économiques et Sociales: 23 rue d'Espagne, 1000 Tunis, Tunisia.
R. Urban. Region. Dev. S. Review of urban and regional development studies. Tokyo International University, Urban Development Institute: Nakanishi Building 6F, 8-4 Takadanobaba 4-chome, Shinjuku-Ku, Tokyo 169, Japan, in association with Applied Regional Science Conference.
Race Class Race and class. (0306-3965). Institute of Race Relations: 2-6 Leeke Street, King's Cross Road, London WC1X 9HS, U.K.
Rass. It. Soc. Rassegna italiana di sociologia. (0486 0349). Societá Editrice il Mulino: Strada Maggiore 37, 40125 Bologna, Italy.
Raven Raven. (0951-4066). Freedom Press: 84b Whitechapel High Street, London E1 7QX, U.K.
Rech. Soc.graph Recherches sociographiques. (0034-1282). Université Laval, Département de Sociologie: Québec G1K 7P4, Canada.
Recher. Sociolog. Recherches sociologiques. (0771-677X). Collège J. Leclercq: Place Montesquieu 1/10, Leuven, Belgium.
Reg. Sci. Urb. Econ. Regional science and urban economics. (0166-0462). Elsevier Science Publishers (North-Holland): P.O. Box 1991, 1000 BZ Amsterdam, The Netherlands.
Reg. Stud. Regional studies. (0034-3404). Cambridge University Press: The Edinburgh Building, Shaftesbury Road, Cambridge CB2 2RU, U.K., in association with Regional Studies Association.
Regar. Actual. Regards sur l'actualité. (0337-7091). Documentation Française: 29, Quai Voltaire, 75340 Paris Cedex 07, France.
Relig. State Soc. Religion, state and society. (0963-7494). Carfax Publishing Company: P.O. Box 25, Abingdon, Oxfordshire OX14 3UE, U.K., in association with Keston College: 33a Canal Street, Oxford OX2 6BQ, U.K.
Religion Religion. (0048-721X). Academic Press: 1 East First Street, Duluth, MN. 55802, U.S.A.

Liste des abbreviations utilisés

Res. Popul. Econ. Research in population economics. (0163-7878). JAI Press: 55 Old Post Road No.2, Greenwich, CT 06830, U.S.A.
Rev. Afr. Pol. Ec. Review of African political economy. (0305-6244). ROAPE Publications: Regency House, 75-77 St. Mary's Road, Sheffield S2 4AN, U.K.
Rev. Bl. Pol. Ec. Review of black political economy. (0034-6446). Transaction Publishers: Rutgers University, New Brunswick, NJ. 08903, U.S.A., in association with National Economic Association/ Clark Atlanta University, Southern Center for Studies in Public Policy: 240 Brawley Drive, S.W. Atlanta, GA. 30314, U.S.A.
Rev. Bras. Ciên. Soc. Revista brasileira de ciências sociais. (0102-6909). Editora Revista dos Tribunais: Rua Conde do Pinhal 78, 01501 São Paulo, SP. Brazil, in association with Associação Nacional de Pós-Graduação e Pesquisa em Ciências Sociais: Largo de São Francisco, 01-4º andar, s/408 Centro, Rio de Janeiro RJ., Cep 20051, Brazil.
Rev. Brasil. Est. Popul. Revista brasileira de estudos de população. (0102-3098). Associação Brasileira de Estudos Populacionais: NEPO/UNICAMP-CP6166, CEP 13081- Campinas SP, Brazil.
Rev. Cien. Soc. Revista de ciencias sociales. (0034-7817). Universidad de Puerto Rico, Facultad de Ciencias Sociales, Centro de Investigaciones Sociales: Rio Piedras, Puerto Rico 00931.
Rev. Econ. St. Review of economics and statistics. (0034-6535). Elsevier Science Publishers (North-Holland): P.O. Box 1991, 1000 BZ Amsterdam, The Netherlands, in association with Harvard University.
Rev. Ét. Comp. Revue d'études comparatives est-ouest. (0338-0599). Éditions de Centre national de la recherche scientifique: 1 Place Aristide Briand, 92195 Meudon Cedex, France, in association with Institut de recherches juridiques comparatives du C.N.R.S., Centre d'études des pays socialistes/ Économie et techniques de planification des pays de l'est.
Rev. Eur. Sci. Soc. Revue européenne des sciences sociales: Cahiers Vilfredo Pareto. (0008-0497). Librairie DROZ: 11 rue Massot, CH-1211 Geneva, Switzerland.
Rev. F. Braudel. Ctr. Review. Fernand Braudel Center. (0147-9032). State University of New York, Fernand Braudel Center: P.O. Box 6000, Binghamton, NY 13902-6000, U.S.A.
Rev. Fom. Soc. Revista de fomento social. (0015-6043). CESI-JESPRE: Pablo Aranda 3, 28006 Madrid, Spain, in association with INSA-ETEA: Escritor Castilla Aguayo 4, Apartado 439, 14004 Cordoba, Spain.
Rev. Fr. Soc. Revue française de sociologie. (0035-2969). Éditions du Centre National de la Recherche Scientifique: 20-22 rue Saint-Amand, 75015 Paris, France, in association with Institut de recherche sur les sociétés contemporaines: 59-61 rue Pouchet, 75017 Paris, France.
Rev. Int.Am. Plan. Revista interamericana de planificación. (0037-8593). Sociedad Interamericana de Planificación: 3a Avenida Norte No.4, Antigua Guatemala, Guatemala.
Rev. Parag. Sociol. Revista paraguaya de sociología. Centro Paraguayo de Estudios Sociológicos: Eligio Ayala 973, Casilla no.2.157, Asunción, Paraguay.
Rev. Polit. Review of politics. (0034-6705). University of Notre Dame: P.O. Box B, Notre Dame, IN. 46556, U.S.A.
Rev. Sci. Crim. D. P. Revue de science criminelle et de droit pénal comparé. (0035-1733). Éditions Sirey: 22 rue Soufflot, 75005 Paris, France, in association with Université Panthéon-Assas (Paris 2), Institut de Droit Comparé, Section de Science Criminelle.

List of abbreviations used

Rig Rig. (0035-5267). Föreningen för svensk kulturhistoria: Nordiska museet, 11521 Stockholm, Sweden.
Rin. Nenpo Rinrigaku Nenpo.
Rir. to ho. Riron to hoho = Sociological theory and methods. (0913-1442). Japanese Association for Mathematical Sociology: c/o Yukio Shirakura, Hokkaido University, Faculty of Literature, Sapporo 060, Japan.
Riv. It. Sci. Pol. Rivista italiana di scienza politica. (0048-8402). Società Editrice il Mulino: Strada Maggiore 37, 40125 Bologna, Italy, in association with Dipartimento di scienza politica e sociologia politica: via S. Caterina d'Alessandria 3, 50129 Florence, Italy.
Riv. Pol. Ec. Rivista di politica economica. (0391-6170). Servizio Italiano Pubblicazioni Internazionali (SIPI): Viale Pasteur 6, 00144 Rome, Italy.
Ron. (B. Toho. Gak. Univ.) Ronshu (Bulletin of Tohoku Gakuin University).
Rural Sociol. Rural sociology. (0036-0112). Department of Sociology, Wilson Hall, Montana State University, Bozeman, MT. 59715, U.S.A., in association with Rural Sociological Society: Texas A & M University, College Station, U.S.A.
Ryuk. Kiyo Ryukoku Kiyo.
S. Afr. J. Human Rights South African journal on human rights. (0258-7203). Juta: P.O. Box 14373, Kenwyn 7790, South Africa, in association with Centre for Applied Legal Studies: University of the Witwatersrand, Wits 2050, South Africa.
S. Afr. J. Labour Relat. South African journal of labour relations. (0379-8410). University of South Africa, School of Business Leadership: P.O. Box 392, Pretoria 0001, South Africa.
S. Jap. Inst. Lab. Studies of the Japan Institute of Labour.
S.Afr. J. Ethnol. South African journal of ethnology = Suid-Afrikaanse tydskrif vir etnologie. (0379-8860). Bureau for Scientific Publications: P.O. Box 1758, Pretoria 0001, South Africa, in association with Association of Afrikaans Ethnologists = Vereniging van Afrikaanse Volkekundiges.
S.Afr. Sociol. R. South African sociological review. (1015-1370). Association for Sociology in South Africa: Department of Sociology, University of Cape Town, 7700 Rondebosch, South Africa.
S.Asia B. South Asia bulletin. (0732-3867). South Asia Bulletin: c/o Department of History, State University of New York, Albany, NY 12222, U.S.A.
Saeculum Saeculum. (0080-5319). Verlag Karl Alber: Hermann-Herder-Straße 4, 7800 Freiburg im Breisgau, Germany.
SAIS R. SAIS review. (0036-0777). Johns Hopkins University, Paul H. Nitze School of Advanced International Studies: 1619 Massachusetts Avenue N.W., Washington DC 20036, U.S.A.
San. Ment. Qué Santé mentale au Québec. (0383-6320). Revue Santé mentale au Québec: C.P. 548, Succ. Places d'Armes, Montréal, Québec H2Y 3H3, Canada.
Scand. Hous. Plan. R. Scandinavian housing and planning research. (0281-5737). Almqvist & Wiksell International: P.O. Box 638, S-101 28 Stockholm, Sweden, in association with Building Research Institute (Denmark)/ Ministry of Environment (Finland)/ Institute for Urban and Regional Research (Norway)/ Institute for Building Research (Sweden).
Scand. J. Devel. Altern. Scandinavian journal of development alternatives. (0280-2791). Bethany Books: P.O. Box 7444, S-103 91 Stockholm, Sweden.

Liste des abbreviations utilisés

Schw. Z. Volk. Stat. Schweizerische Zeitschrift für Volkswirtschaft und Statistik = Revue suisse d'économie politique et de statistique. Staempfli: Hallerstrasse 7, Postfach 8326, CH-3001 Berne, Switzerland, in association with Schweizerische Gesellschaft für Statistik und Volkswirtschaft/ Société suisse de statistique et d'économie politique: Hallwylstraße 15, CH-3003 Berne, Switzerland.
Sci. Cult. Science as culture. (0959-5431). Free Association Books: 26 Freegrove Road, London N7 9RQ, U.K.
Sci. Soc. Science and society. (0036-8237). Guilford Publications: 72 Spring Street, New York, NY 10012, U.S.A.
Semiotica Semiotica. Walter de Gruyter: Postfach 110240, D-1000 Berlin 11, Germany, in association with International Association for Semiotic Studies.
Shak. Hyor. Shakaigaku hyoron. Nippon Shakai Gakkai = Japanese Sociological Society: Department of Sociology, Faculty of Letters, University of Yokyo, Bunkyo-Ku, Tokyo 113, Japan.
Shak. Ken. Kiyo Shakaigaku kenkyuka kiyo (Bulletin of Keio-Gijuku Graduate School). Keio-Gijuku Graduate School.
Shak. Kenk. Nih. Shak. Gak. Shakaigakushi kenkyu, nihon shakaigakushi gakkai.
Shak. Nen. Shakaigaku nenpō. Tohoku Sociological Society: Sendai, Japan.
Shak. Ronk. Shakaigaku Ronko. Tokyo Metropolitan University.
Shak. Ronso Shakaigaku ronso. Nihon University: Tokyo, Japan.
Shak.-Kag. Tok. Shakai-kagaku tokyu. Institute of Social Science, Waseda University.
Shak.-Sen. Kiyo Shakaigaku-senko kiyo.
Shisō Shisō.
Signs Signs. (0097-9740). University of Chicago Press: 5720 S. Woodlawn, Chicago, IL. 60637, U.S.A.
Simulat. Gam. Simulation and gaming. (0037-5500). Sage Publications: 2455 Teller Road, Newbury Park, CA. 91320, U.S.A.
Slavic R. Slavic review. (0037-6779). American Association for the Advancement of Slavic Studies: 128 Encina Commons, Stanford University, Stanford, CA. 94305, U.S.A.
Slovo Slovo. (0954-6839). University of London: Malet Street, London WC1E 7HU, U.K., in association with School of Slavonic and East European Studies.
Soc. Act. Social action. (0037-7627). Indian Social Institute, Social Action Trust: Lodi Road, New Delhi 130003, India.
Soc. Anal. Social analysis. (0155-977X). University of Adelaide, Department of Anthropology: G.P.O. Box 498, Adelaide 5A 5001, Australia.
Soc. Biol. Social biology. (0037-766X). Society for the Study of Social Biology: c/o Population Council, One Dag Hammarskjold Place, New York, NY 10017, U.S.A.
Soc. Cogn. Social cognition. (0278-616X). Guilford Publications: 72 Spring Street, New York, NY 10012, U.S.A.
Soc. Compass Social compass. (0037-7686). Sage Publications: 6 Bonhill Street, London EC2A 4PU, U.K., in association with International Federation of Institutes for Social and Socio-Religious Research (FERES)/ Centre de Recherches Socio-Religieuses: Université Catholique de Louvain, Belgium.
Soc. Contemp. Sociétés contemporaines. (1150-1944). L'Harmattan: 16 rue des Écoles, 75005 Paris, France, in association with Institut de Recherche sur les Sociétés Contemporaines (IRESCO), CNRS: 59/61 rue Pouchet, 75849 Paris Cedex 17, France.
Soc. Dyn. Social dynamics. (0253-3952). Centre for African Studies, University of Cape Town: Rondebosch 7700, South Africa.

List of abbreviations used

Soc. Epist. Social epistemology. (0269-1728). Taylor & Francis: 4 John Street, London WC1N 2ET, U.K.

Soc. Forc. Social forces. (0037-7732). University of North Carolina Press: P.O. Box 2288, Chapel Hill, NC. 27515, U.S.A., in association with University of North Carolina, Department of Sociology: 168 Hamilton Hall, University of North Carolina, Chapel Hill, NC. 27599-3210, U.S.A.

Soc. Ind. Social indicators research. (0303-8300). Kluwer Academic Publishers: Spuiboulevard 50, P.O. Box 17, 3300 AA Dordrecht, The Netherlands.

Soc. Just. Social justice. (0094-7571). Global Options: P.O. Box 40601, San Francisco, CA. 94140, U.S.A.

Soc. Method. Sociological methodology. (0081-1750). Basil Blackwell: 108 Cowley Road, Oxford OX4 1JF, U.K., in association with American Sociological Association: 1722 N. Street, N.W., Washington, DC. 20036, U.S.A.

Soc. Networks Social networks. (0378-8733). Elsevier Science Publishers (North-Holland): P.O. Box 1991, 1000 BZ Amsterdam, The Netherlands, in association with International Network for Social Network Analysis (INSNA).

Soc. Part. Socialismo y participación. CEDEP (Centro de Estudios para el Desarrollo y la Participación): Ediciones Socialismo y Participación, Av. José Faustino Sánchez Carrión 790, Lima 17, Peru.

Soc. Philos. Pol. Social philosophy & policy. (0265-0525). Basil Blackwell: 108 Cowley Road, Oxford OX4 1JF, U.K., in association with Bowling Green State University, Social Philosophy and Policy Center: Bowling Green, Ohio 43403, U.S.A.

Soc. Pol. Admin. Social policy and administration. (0144-5596). Basil Blackwell: 108 Cowley Road, Oxford OX4 1JF, U.K.

Soc. Prob. Social problems. (0037-7791). University of California Press: 2120 Berkeley Way, Berkeley, CA. 94720, U.S.A., in association with Society for the Study of Social Problems.

Soc. Relig. Sociology of religion. (0038-0210). Association for the Sociology of Religion: Marist Hall, Room 108, Catholic University of America, Washington DC, 20064, U.S.A.

Soc. Sci. China Social sciences in China. (0252-9203). China Social Sciences Publishing House: Jia 158 Gulouxidajie, Beijing 100720, China, in association with Chinese Academy of Social Science.

Soc. Sci. Info. Social science information. (0539-0184). Sage Publications: 6 Bonhill Street, London EC2A 4PU, U.K., in association with Maison des sciences de l'homme/ École des hautes études en science sociales.

Soc. Sci. Med. Social science & medicine. (0277-9536). Pergamon Press: Hennock Road, Marsh Barton, Exeter, Devon EX2 8NE, U.K.

Soc. Sci. Q. Social science quarterly. (0038-4941). University of Texas Press: P.O. Box 7819, Austin, TX. 78713, U.S.A., in association with Southwestern Social Science Association: W.C. Hogg Building, The University of Texas at Austin, Austin, TX. 78713, U.S.A.

Soc. Ser. R. Social service review. (0037-7961). University of Chicago Press: 5720 S. Woodlawn, Chicago, IL. 60637, U.S.A.

Soc. Work Soc. Sci. R. Social work and social sciences review. (0953-5225). Whiting and Birch: 90 Dartmouth Road, London SE23 3HZ, U.K.

Soc. Work. Ed. Social work education. (0261-5479). Whiting and Birch: P.O. Box 872, Forest Hill, London SE23 3HZ, U.K.

Liste des abbreviations utilisés

Social Soc. Res. Sociology and social research. (0038-0393). University of Southern California: Social Science Building, Rooms 168-169, University Park, Los Angeles, CA. 90089-0032, U.S.A.
Social. Int. Sociologia internationalis. (0038-0164). Verlag Duncker & Humblot: Dietrich-Schäfer-Weg 9, 1000 Berlin 41, Germany.
Society Society. (0147-2011). Transaction: Rutgers — The State University, New Brunswick, NJ. 08903, U.S.A.
Socio. Econ. Socio-economic planning sciences. (0038-0121). Pergamon Press: Journals Production Unit, Hennock Road, Marsh Barton, Exeter EX2 8NE, U.K.
Sociol. Bul. Sociological bulletin. (0038-0229). Indian Sociogical Society: Institute of Social Sciences, B-7/18 Safdarjung Enclave, New Delhi 110 029, India.
Sociol. For. Sociological forum. (0854-8971). Plenum Publishing: 233 Spring Street, New York, NY 10013-1578, U.S.A.
Sociol. Gids Sociologische gids. (0038-0334). Boom: Postbus 1058, 7940 KB Meppel, The Netherlands.
Sociol. Lav. Sociologia del lavoro. Franco Angeli Editore: Viale Monza 106, 20127 Milan, Italy, in association with Università di Bologna, Centro Internazionale di Documentazione e Studi Sociologico Sui Problemi del Lavoro: Casella postale 413, 40100 Bologna, Italy.
Sociol. Meth. Sociological methods and research. (0049 1241). Sage Publications: 2455 Teller Road, Newbury Park, CA. 91320, U.S.A.
Sociol. Q. Sociological quarterly. (0038-0253). J.A.I. Press: Old Post Road, No.2, P.O. Box 1678, Greenwich, CT. 06836-1678, U.S.A.
Sociol. Rev. Sociological review. (0038-0261). Routledge: 11 New Fetter Lane, London EC4P 4EE, U.K., in association with University of Keele: Keele, Staffordshire ST5 5BG, U.K.
Sociol. Rur. Sociologia ruralis. (0038-0199). Van Gorcum: P.O. Box 43, 9400 AA, Assen, The Netherlands, in association with European Society for Rural Sociology/Société Européenne de Sociologie Rurale/ Europäischen Gesellschaft für Land- und Agrarsoziologie: c/o Pavel Uttitz (Secretary Treasurer), Forschungsgesellschaft für Agrarpolitik und Agrarsoziologie e.V., Meckenheimer Allee 125, 5300 Bonn 1, Germany.
Sociol. Theory Sociological theory. (0735-2751). Basil Blackwell: 3 Cambridge Center, Cambridge, MA. 02142, U.S.A., in association with American Sociological Association: 1722 N. Street, N.W., Washington DC. 20036, U.S.A.
Sociol. Trav. Sociologie du travail. (0038-0296). Dunod: 15 rue Gossin, 92543 Montrouge Cedex, France.
Sociol. Urb. Rur. Sociologia urbana e rurale. Università di Bologna, Dipartimento di Sociologia, Centro Studi sui problemi della Città e del Territorio (CE.P.CI.T.): via Strada Maggiore 45, 40125 Bologna, Italy.
Sociologia [Rome] Sociologia [Rome]. (0038-0156). Istituto Luigi Sturzo: Via delle Coppelle 35, 00186 Rome, Italy.
Sociologos Sociologos. Sociologos: Tokyo, Japan.
Sociologus Sociologus. (0038-0377). Duncker & Humblot: Postfach 41 03 29, Dietrich-Schäfer-Weg 9, Berlin 41, Germany.
Sociology Sociology. (0038-0385). British Sociological Association: 351 Station Road, Dorridge, Solihull, W. Midlands B93 8EY, U.K.
Sojourn Sojourn. (0217-9520).

List of abbreviations used

Soshiolojika Soshiolojika. Soka University.
Soshioroji Soshioroji. Kyoto, Japan.
Sot. Issle. Sotsiologicheskie issledovaniia (sotsis). (0132-1625). Izdatel'stvo Nauka: Profsoiuznaja ul. 90, Moscow, U.S.S.R., in association with Akademii Nauk SSSR.
Sots.-Pol. Z. Sotsial'no-politicheskii zhurnal. (0868 5797). Gumanitarii.
Soz. Welt. Soziale Welt. (0038-6073). Verlag Otto Schwartz: Annastraße 7, 3400 Göttingen, Germany, in association with Arbeitsgemeinschaft sozialwissenschaftlicher Institute: Universität Bamberg, Feldkirchenstraße 21, 8600 Bamberg, Germany.
Sri Lanka J. Soc. Sci. Sri Lanka journal of social sciences. (0258-9710). Natural Resources, Energy & Science Authority of Sri Lanka: 47/5 Maitland Place, Colombo 7, Sri Lanka.
St. Philos. Educ. Studies in philosophy and education. (0039-3746). Kluwer Academic Publishers: P.O. Box 322, 3300 AH Dordrecht, The Netherlands.
Sta. Mer. Stato e mercato. Società Editrice il Mulino: Strada Maggiore 37, 40125 Bologna, Italy.
Stud. Comp. ID. Studies in comparative international development. (0039-3606). Transaction Periodicals Consortium: Dept. 4010, Rutgers University, New Brunswick, NJ. 08903, U.S.A.
Stud. Demogr. Studia demograficzne. (0039-3134). Panstwowe Wydawnictwo Naukowe: Miodowa 10, 00-251 Warsaw, Poland, in association with Polska Akademia Nauk, Komitet Nauk Demograficznych.
Stud. Pol. Ec. Studies in political economy. (0707-8552). Studies in Political Economy: P.O. Box 4729, Station E, Ottowa, Ontario, Canada K1S 5H9.
Stud. Praw-Ekon. Studia prawno-ekonomiczne. (0081-6841). Zakład Narodowy Imienia Ossolińskich: Wroclaw, Poland, in association with Łódzkie Towarzystwo Naukowe: ul. Piotrkowska 179, 90-447 Łódź, Poland.
Südosteur. Mitteil. Südosteuropa Mitteilungen. (0340-174X). Südosteuropa-Gesellschaft: Widenmayerstraße 49. D-8000 Munich 22, Germany.
Svobod. Mysl' Svobodnaia mysl'. (0131-1212). Izdatel'stvo Pravda: Ul. Pravdy 24, 125047 Moscow, U.S.S.R.
Tex. Prac. Textual practice. (0950-236X). Routledge Journals: 11 New Fetter Lane, London EC4P 4EE, U.K.
Text Text. (0165-4888). Walter de Gruyter: Postfach 110240, D-1000 Berlin 11, Germany.
Theory Cult. Soc. Theory culture and society. (0263-2764). Sage Publications: 6 Bonhill Street, London EC2A 4PU, U.K.
Theory Soc. Theory and society. (0304-2421). Kluwer Academic Publishers: Spuiboulevard 50, P.O. Box 17, 3300 AA Dordrecht, The Netherlands.
Third Wor. P. Third World planning review. (0142-7849). Liverpool University Press: P.O. Box 147, Liverpool L69 3BX, U.K.
Time Soc. Time & society. (0961-463X). SAGE Publications: 6 Bonhill Street, London EC2A 4PU, England.
Tos. Mon. Toshi mondai. Tokyo Institute for Municpal Research: Tokyo, Japan.
Town Plan. R. Town planning review. (0041-0020). Liverpool University Press: P.O. Box 147, Liverpool L69 3BX, U.K., in association with University of Liverpool, Department of Civic Design (Town and Regional Planning).
Urban Aff. Q. Urban affairs quarterly. (0042-0816). Sage Publications: 2455 Teller Road, Newbury Park, CA. 91320, U.S.A.

Liste des abbreviations utilisés

Urban Anthro. Urban anthropology. (0894-6019). The Institute: 56 Centennial Avenue, Brockport, NY 14420, U.S.A.
Urban Geogr. Urban geography. (0272-3638). V.H. Winston & Son: 7961 Eastern Avenue, Silver Spring, MD. 20910, U.S.A.
Urban Stud. Urban studies. (0042 0980). Carfax Publishing Company: P.O.Box 25, Abingdon, Oxfordshire OX14 3UE, U.K., in association with University of Glasgow, Centre for Urban and Regional Research: Adam Smith Building, University of Glasgow, Glasgow G12 8RT, U.K.
Vest. Mosk. Univ. Ser. 10 Zhur. Vestnik Moskovskogo universiteta. Seriia 10 Zhurnalistika. (0320 8079). Moskovskogo universiteta.
Vest. Mosk. Univ. Ser. 5 Geograf. Vestnik Moskovskogo universiteta. Seriia 5.Geografiia. Izdatel'stvo Moskovskogo Universiteta: ul. Gertsena 5/7, 103009 Moscow, Russia.
Vest. Mosk. Univ. Ser. 9 Filol. Vestnik Moskovskogo universiteta. Seriia 9 Filologiia. (0130 0075). Moskovskogo universiteta.
Vis. Anthrop. Visual anthropology. (0894-9468). Harwood Academic Publisher: 270 8th Avenue, New York, NY.10011, U.S.A.
Volks. Bul. Volkskundig bulletin. (0166-0667). Koninklijke Nederlandse Akademie van Wetenschappen, P.J. Meertens Instituut: Keizersgracht 569-571, 1017 DR Amsterdam, The Netherlands.
Vop. Ekon. Voprosy ekonomiki. (0042-8736). Izdatel'stvo Pravda: Ul. Pravdy 24, 125865 Moscow, U.S.S.R., in association with Akademii Nauk SSSR, Institut Ekonomiki.
Wissensch. Z. Humboldt-Univ. Wissenschaftliche Zeitschrift der Humboldt-Universität zu Berlin: Reihe Gesellschaftswissenschaften. (0863-0623). Humboldt-Universität: Mittelstraße 7/8, 1086 Berlin, Germany.
Wom. St. Inter. For. Women's studies international forum. (0277-5395). Pergamon Press: Fairview Park, Elmsford, NY 10523, U.S.A.
Wor. Futur. World futures. (0260-4027). Gordon and Breach Science Publishers: 270 8th Avenue, New York, NY 10011, U.S.A.
Work Occup. Work and occupations. (0730-8884). Sage Publications: 2455 Teller Road, Newbury Park CA. 91320, U.S.A.
World Dev. World development. (0305-750X). Pergamon Press: Headington Hill Hall, Oxford OX3 0BW, U.K.
Yale Law J. Yale law journal. (0044-0094). Yale Law Journal Co.: 401-A Yale Station, New Haven CT 06520, U.S.A.
Z. Ethn. Zeitschrift für Ethnologie. (0044-2666). Dietrich Reimer Verlag: Unter den Eichen 57, 1000 Berlin 45, Federal Republic of Germany, in association with Deutsche Gesellschaft für Völkerkunde/ Berliner Gesellschaft für Anthropologie, Ethnologie und Urgeschichte.
Z. Sexual. Zeitschrift für Sexualforschung. (0932-8114). Ferdinand Enke Verlag: Postfach 10 12 54, D-7000 Stuttgart 10, Germany.
Z. Soziol. Zeitschrift für Soziologie. (0340-1804). Ferdinand Enke Verlag: Postfach 10 12 54, D-7000 Stuttgart 10, Germany.
Zambezia Zambezia the journal of the University of Zimbabwe.

CLASSIFICATION SCHEME
PLAN DE CLASSIFICATION

A. **General studies / Études générales.**

A.1. Sociology and the social sciences / Sociologie et sciences sociales.

A.2. Sociological research / Recherche sociologique.

A.3. Reference works, information services and documents / Ouvrages de référence, services d'information et documents.

B. **Theory and methodology / Théorie et méthodologie.**

B.1. Theory / Théorie.
Epistemology / Epistémologie; Philosophy / Philosophie; Sociological theory / Théorie sociologique.

B.2. Research methods / Méthodes de recherche.
Data analysis / Analyse des données; Data collection / Rassemblement des données.

C. **Individuals. Groups. Organizations / Individus. Groupes. Organisations.**

C.1. Psychology and social psychology / Psychologie et psychologie sociale.

C.2. Individuals / Individus.
Cognition / Cognition; Decision making / Prise de décision; Memory / Mémoire; Personality / Personnalité; Self-concept / Conception de soi.

C.3. Interpersonal relations / Relations interpersonnelles.
Conflict / Conflit; Emotions / Emotions.

C.4. Groups / Groupes.

C.5. Organizations / Organisations.
Management in organizations / Administration des organisations; Organization theory / Théorie de l'organisation.

C.6. Power, leadership and social roles / Pouvoir, leadership et rôles sociaux.

C.7. Opinions and attitudes / Opinions et attitudes.

D. **Culture / Culture.**

Plan de classification

D.1. Culture / Culture.
Postmodernism / Postmodernisme; Social norms, social control and value systems / Normes sociales, régulation sociale et systèmes de valeur; Socialization and alienation / Socialisation et aliénation.

D.2. Everyday culture / Culture quotidienne.

D.3. Ethics and morals / Éthique et morale.

D.4. Law / Loi.

D.5. Magic, mythology and religion / Magie, mythologie et religion.
Christianity / Christianisme; Islam / Islam; Judaism / Judaïsme.

D.6. Science and knowledge / Science et connaissance.

D.7. Language, communication and media / Langage, communication et moyens de communication.
Advertising / Publicité; Information technology and telecommunications / Technologie de l'information et télécommunications; Linguistics / Linguistique; Media / Moyens de communication; Multilingualism / Multilinguisme; Television / Télévision.

D.8. Art / Art.

D.9. Education / Éducation.
Education policy / Politique de l'éducation; Education systems / Systèmes d'enseignement; Primary education / Enseignement primaire; Secondary education / Enseignement secondaire; Tertiary education / Enseignement post-scolaire.

E. Social structure / Structure sociale.

E.1. Social system / Système social.

E.2. Social stratification / Stratification sociale.
Class / Classe.

E.3. Social change / Changement social.

F. Population. Family. Gender. Ethnic group / Population. Famille. Sexe. Groupe ethnique.

F.1. Demography / Démographie.

F.2. Age groups / Groupes d'âges.
Ageing / Vieillissement; Children / Enfants; Youth / Jeunesse.

Classification scheme

F.3. Demographic trends and population policy / Tendances démographiques et politique démographique.
    Family planning / Planification de la famille; Fertility / Fécondité; Morbidity / Morbidité; Mortality / Mortalité; Population ageing / Vieillissement de la population.

F.4. Marriage and family / Mariage et famille.
    Divorce / Divorce; Family law / Droit de la famille; Family structure / Structure de la famille; Marriage and cohabitation / Mariage et cohabitation; Parent-child relations / Relations parents-enfants.

F.5. Gender / Sexe.
    Feminism / Féminisme; Gender differentiation / Différenciation sexuelle; Gender roles / Rôles de sexe; Sex discrimination / Discrimination sexuelle.

F.6. Sexual behaviour / Comportement sexuelle.

F.7. Ethnic groups / Groupes ethniques.
    Ethnicity / Ethnicité; Race relations / Relations raciales; Racial discrimination / Discrimination raciale.

F.8. Migration / Migration.
    Immigrant adaptation / Adaptation des immigrants; Internal migration / Migration interne; International migration / Migration internationale.

G. Environment. Community. Rural. Urban / Environnement. Communauté. Rural. Urbain.

G.1. Ecology. Geography. Human settlements / Écologie. Géographie. Établissements humains.

G.2. Community / Communauté.

G.3. Rural and urban sociology / Sociologie rurale et urbaine.

G.3.1. Rural sociology / Sociologie rurale.
    Peasant studies / Études paysannes; Rural development / Développement rural.

G.3.2. Urban sociology / Sociologie urbaine.
    Housing / Logement; Spatial and social differentiation / Différenciation spatio-sociale; Urban planning and development / Aménagement et développement urbain; Urban poverty / Pauvreté urbaine; Urban transport / Transport urbain; Urbanization / Urbanisation.

H. Economic life / Vie économique.

Plan de classification

H.1. Economic sociology / Sociologie économique.

H.2. Economic systems / Systèmes économiques.

H.3. Economic conditions and living standards / Conditions économiques et niveau de vie.

H.4. Enterprises and production systems / Entreprises et systèmes de production.
   Technology / Technologie.

H.5. Markets and consumption / Marchés et consommation.

H.6. Finance / Finance.

H.7. Economic policy and planning / Politique économique et planification.

I.   **Labour / Travail.**

I.1. Sociology of industry and work / Sociologie de l'industrie et du travail.

I.2. Employment and labour market / Emploi et marché du travail.
   Gender issues / Questions de sexe; Unemployment / Chômage.

I.3. Personnel management and working conditions / Administration du personnel et conditions de travail.
   Job satisfaction / Satisfaction au travail; Personnel management / Gestion du personnel.

I.4. Vocational training, occupations and careers / Formation professionnelle, professions et carrières.
   Managers / Cadres; Professional workers / Travailleurs professionnels; Training / Formation.

I.5. Labour relations / Relations du travail.
   Labour disputes / Conflits du travail; Labour law / Droit du travail; Trade unions / Syndicats; Workers' participation / Participation des travailleurs.

I.6. Leisure / Loisir.

J.   **Politics. State. International relations / Politique. État. Relations internationales.**

J.1. Political sociology / Sociologie politique.

J.2. Political thought / Pensée politique.

Classification scheme

J.3. Political systems / Systèmes politiques.

J.4. Public administration / Administration publique.

J.5. Political parties, pressure groups and political movements / Partis politiques, groupes de pression et mouvements politiques.

J.6. Political behaviour and elections / Comportement politique et élections.

J.7. Armed forces / Forces armées.

J.8. International relations / Relations internationales.

K. **Social problems. Social services. Social work / Problèmes sociaux. Services sociaux. Travail social.**

K.1. Social problems / Problèmes sociaux.
Child abuse / Enfants martyrs; Crime / Délits; Criminal justice / Justice criminelle; Domestic violence / Violence domestique; Homelessness / Sans-abri; Juvenile delinquency / Delinquance juvénile; Poverty / Pauvreté; Substance abuse / Usage des stupéfiants; Suicide / Suicide; Violence / Violence.

K.2. Social security / Sécurité sociale.
Child care / Aide à l'enfance.

K.3. Social work / Travail social.

K.4. Health care / Soins médicaux.
Community care / Garde communautaire; Geriatrics / Gériatrie; Health economics / Économie de la santé; Health policy / Politique sanitaire; Medical ethics / Code déontologique médical; Mental health / Santé mentale.

BIBLIOGRAPHY FOR 1993

BIBLIOGRAPHIE POUR 1993

A: GENERAL STUDIES
ÉTUDES GÉNÉRALES

A.1: Sociology and the social sciences
Sociologie et sciences sociales

1 Africa and the disciplines: the contributions of research in Africa to the social sciences and humanities. V. Y. Mudimbe; Jean O'Barr; Robert Hinrichs Bates [Ed.]. Chicago: University of Chicago Press, 1993. xxiii, 245p. *ISBN: 0226039005, 0226039013. Includes bibliographical references and index.*
2 Buffon and the natural history of man — writing history and the "foundational myth" of anthropology. Claude Blanckaert. **Hist. Human Sci.** 6:1 2:1993 pp.13 - 50.
3 Chaos, Selbstorganisation und Gesellschaft. *[In German]*; [Chaos, self-organization and society]. Klaus Müller [Contrib.]; Raúl Rojas [Contrib.]; Philip Mirowski [Contrib.]; Bernard Gill [Contrib.]; Egon Becker [Contrib.]; Thomas Jahn [Contrib.]; Peter Wehling [Contrib.]. **Prokla** 22:3(88) 9:1992 pp.338 - 450. *Collection of 6 articles.*
4 La democracia ordenada (análisis crítico de la nueva sociología del cono sur latinoamericano). *[In Spanish]*; [Orderly democracy (a critical analysis of the new sociology in the Latin American Cono Sur)]. Jaime Osorio. **Est. Sociol.** XI:31 1-4:1993 pp.111 - 132.
5 Droits de l'homme et sciences de l'homme: pour une ethique anthropologique. *[In French]*; [Human rights and social sciences: towards an anthropological ethic]. Charles Widmer. Geneva: Droz, 1992. 234p. *Bibliogr. and index.*
6 Environmental sociology and the state of the discipline. Shirley Bradway Laska. **Soc. Forc.** 72:1 9:1993 pp.1 - 17.
7 L'esthétisme sceptique et ses limites en histoire de la sociologie. *[In French]*; (Sceptical aestheticism and its limits in the history of sociology.) *[Summary]*; *[Summary in German]*; *[Summary in Spanish]*. François Chazel. **Rev. Fr. Soc.** XXXIV:2 4-6:1993 pp.247 - 269.
8 Explanation and understanding in the human sciences. Gurpreet Mahajan. Delhi: Oxford University Press, 1992. xii, 124p. *ISBN: 0195630084. Includes bibliographical references (p. [103]-119) and index.*
9 Fait et subjectivité. Réflexions sur la possibilité d'une interdisciplinarité droit-sciences humaines. *[In French]*; (Fact and subjectivity. Reflexions on the possibility

A: General studies

of interdisciplinary law/social sciences.) *[Summary]*. Ivan Dechamps. **Recher. Sociolog.** XXIII:3 1992 pp.3 - 26.

10   Forget Baudrillard? Chris Rojek [Ed.]; Bryan Stanley Turner [Ed.]. London, New York: Routledge, 1993. 170p. *ISBN: 0415059887, 0415059895*. Includes bibliographical references and index.

11   Geography, spatial analysis, and social science. Richard Morrill. **Urban Geogr.** 14:5 9-10:1993 pp.442 - 446.

12   Geschichte als Geschlechtergeschichte? Zur Bedeutung des „weiblichen Blicks" für die Wahrnehmung von Geschichte. *[In German]*; [History as gender history? On the implication of the "women's view" for the perception of history]. Ute Frevert. **Saeculum** 43:1 1992 pp.108 - 123.

13   A Gramscian analysis of social science disciplines. Frederick H. Gareau. **Int. Soc. Sci. J.** 136 5:1993 pp.301 - 310.

14   An historian's view of American social science. Dorothy Ross. **J. Hist. Beh. Sci.** XXIX:2 4:1993 pp.99 - 112.

15   Historisierung der Soziologie? Zur Renaissance historischen Interesses unter Soziologen. *[In German]*; [The historization of sociology? On the renaissance of historical interest among sociologists]. Walter M. Sprondel. **Saeculum** 43:1 1992 pp.66 - 77.

16   The human sciences — origins and histories. John Christie. **Hist. Human Sci.** 6:1 2:1993 pp.1 - 12.

17   [An introduction to theoretical sociology - lecture on the history of American sociology]; *[Text in Japanese]*. Shin Ogasawara. Tokyo: Yuhikaku, 1993. 261p.

18   Iskhodnye paradigmy russkoi sotsiologii. *[In Russian]*; (Initial paradigms of the Russian sociology.) N. Novikov. **Svobod. Mysl'** 6 4:1993 pp.55 - 67.

19   Istoriia teoreticheskoi sotsiologii (Vvelenie). *[In Russian]*; (The history of theoretical sociology (introduction).) Iu.N. Davydov. **Sot. Issle.** 5 1993 pp.33 - 50.

20   J. A. Hobson after fifty years: freethinker of the social sciences. John Pheby [Ed.]. Basingstoke, Hants: Macmillan Press, 1993. 283p. *ISBN: 0333464656*.

21   Jürgen Habermas. Michael Pusey. London: Routledge, 1993. 128p. *ISBN: 074580117X*. (*Series:* Key sociologists).

22   Kritik und Engagement: Soziologie als Anwendungswissenschaft : Festschrift für Christian von Ferber zum 65. Geburtstag. *[In German]*; [Criticism and engagement: sociology as a science of application: festschrift in honour of Christian von Ferber's 65th birthday]. Reinhardt P. Nippert [Ed.]; Willi Pöhler [Ed.]; Wolfgang Slesina [Ed.]. München: Oldenbourg, 1991. 578p. *ISBN: 3486558927*.

23   Lehre der Soziologie in Österreich. *[In German]*; [Teaching sociology in Austria]. Max Haller [Ed.]; Rudolf Richter [Ed.]. Vienna: Österreichische Gesellschaft für Soziologie, 1990. 229p. *ISBN: 3901056017*.

24   The mangle of practice: agency and emergence in the sociology of science. Andrew Pickering. **A.J.S.** 99:3 11:1993 pp.559 - 589.

25   Max Weber's comparative-historical sociology. Stephen Kalberg. Cambridge: Polity Press, 1993. 221p. *ISBN: 0745611559*.

26   Novel science — or, how contemporary social science is not well and why literature and semiotic provide a cure. Kenneth Laine Ketner. **Semiotica** 93:1/2 1993 pp.33 - 59.

27   Para una caracterización epistémica y metodológica de las Ciencias Sociales. *[In Spanish]*; [Towards an epistemological and methodological characterization of the

A: Études générales

social sciences] *[Summary]*; *[Summary in Catalan]*. Francesc Quintana. **Papers** 39 1992 pp.101 - 118.
28 The religious roots of American sociology. Cecil E. Greek. New York: Garland Pub, 1992. xii, 269p. *ISBN: 0815303904. Includes bibliographical references (p. 237-269)*. (*Series:* Garland library of sociology. Garland reference library of social science - 786).
29 The sociological imagination in China: comments on the thought of Chin Yao-chi (Ambrose Y.C. King). Thomas A. Metzger. **J. Asian St.** 52:4 11:1993 pp.937 - 958.
30 Sociologies et sciences du politique. *[In French]*; [Sociology and political science] *[Summary]*. Pierre Ansart. **Cah. Int. Soc.** XCIV 1-6:1993 pp.21 - 49.
31 [Sociology and the society today]; *[Text in Japanese]*. Hiroshi Suzuki [Ed.]. Tokyo: Koseisha Koseikaku, 1993. 264p.
32 Sociology in action: applications and opportunities for the 1990s. Geoff Payne [Ed.]; Malcolm Cross [Ed.]. Basingstoke: Macmillan Press, 1993. vii, 248p. *ISBN: 0333542797. Includes index. British Sociological Association.* (*Series:* Explorations in sociology).
33 Stanovlenie sotsiologii v Rossii, osnovnye napravleniia ee razvitiia. *[In Russian]*; [The creation of sociology in Russia, basic management of its development]. V.I. Bochkareva. **Sots.-Pol. Z.** 12 93 pp.38 - 44.
34 "Trivales" Geschichtsbewußtsein oder historische Elemente regionaler Identität? Über den notwendigen Dialog zwischen Geschichts- und Sozialwissenschaften zur Erforschung von Regionalbewußtsein. *[In German]*; ("Trivial" historical awareness or historical elements of regional identity? About the necessary dialogue between history and social sciences for research into regional awareness.) Detlef Briesen. **Inf. Raum.** 11 1993 pp.769 - 780.
35 The unfinished agenda of modernization — trends in European sociology. Helga Nowotny. **Soc. Sci. Info.** 32:1 3:1993 pp.5 - 21.

A.2:   **Sociological research**
            Recherche sociologique

36 "Acting as a switchboard" — Mrs. Ethel Sturges Dummer's role in sociology. Jennifer Platt. **Am. Sociol.** 23:3 Fall:1992 pp.23 - 36.
37 Are we standing at the crossroads — meta analysis of organisational behaviour research in India? Shivganesh Bhargava. **Ind. J. Soc. Sci.** 6:1 1-3:1993 pp.31 - 39.
38 Chaos theory and its implications for social science research. Hal Gregersen; Lee Sailer. **Human Relat.** 46:7 7:1993 pp.777 - 802.
39 Characteristics and recent trends in urban geography. James O. Wheeler. **Urban Geogr.** 14:1 1-2:1993 pp.48 - 56.
40 Education and research in the Czech Republic — burden of the past and hope for the future. Jiří Musil. **E.Eur. Pol. Soc.** 7:1 Winter:1993 pp.59 - 73.
41 Education and research in the social sciences — transition dilemmas in Bulgaria. Atanas Gotchev. **E.Eur. Pol. Soc.** 7:1 Winter:1993 pp.43 - 58.
42 European social science in transition: assessment and outlook. Meinolf Dierkes [Ed.]; Bernd Biervert [Ed.]. Frankfurt am Main; Boulder, Colo: Campus Verlag; Westview Press, 1992. 640p. *ISBN: 3593346885, 0813316294. Includes bibliographical references.*

A: General studies

43 The falsification fallacy. Charles F. Rudder. **St. Philos. Educ.** 12:2-4 1993 pp.179 - 200.
44 A final look back at Soviet sociology. Alexander Filippov. **Int. Sociol.** 8:3 9:1993 pp.355 - 373.
45 L'identità controversa: l'itinerario di Erving Goffman nella sociologia contemporanea. *[In Italian]*; [The controversial identity: the itinerary of Erving Goffman in contemporary sociology]. Rossana Trifiletti. Padua: CEDAM, 1991. vii, 443p. *ISBN: 8813174314. Includes bibliographical references (p. 397-443).*
46 Institutional changes and intellectual trends in some Hungarian social sciences. Rudolf Andorka. **E.Eur. Pol. Soc.** 7:1 Winter:1993 pp.74 - 108.
47 Involvement in research activities — an explanation based on valence, attitude, subjective norm and perceived control. Bansh Gopal Singh. **Psychol. Devel. Soc.** 5:1 1-6:1993 pp.81 - 93.
48 Is there a future for the social sciences in Albania? Fatos Tarifa. **E.Eur. Pol. Soc.** 7:1 Winter:1993 pp.33 - 42.
49 Kontinuitás és diszkontinuitás a 90-es évek magyar társadalomkutatásában. *[In Hungarian]*; (Continuity and discontinuity in the social research in the 1990s.) Pál Tamás. **Mag. Tud.** 38:3 1993 pp.301 - 314.
50 Literatur und soziologie — James T. Farrell und das Chicagoer Department of Sociology. *[In Dutch]*; (Literature and sociology — James T. Farrell and the Department of Sociology at the University of Chicago.) *[Summary]*. Rolf Lindner. **Sociol. Gids** XL:1 1-2:1993 pp.4 - 19.
51 Le longitudinal à travers quantitatif et qualitatif. *[In French]*; (Quantitative and qualitative approach of longitudinal issues.) *[Summary]*. Michèle Ferrand; Françoise Imbert. **Soc. Contemp.** 14/15 6-9:1993 pp.129 - 148.
52 A new agenda for the social sciences. Vesna Pusić. **E.Eur. Pol. Soc.** 7:1 Winter:1993 pp.1 - 13.
53 Orientacje metodologiczne w łódzkim ośrodku socjologicznym. *[In Polish]*; (The methodological orientations in the Lodz Centre of Sociology.) *[Summary]*. Jan Lutyński. **Prz. Soc.** XL 1993 pp.11 - 20.
54 Ownership and authority in the earnings function — nonnested tests of alternative specifications. Charles N. Halaby; David L. Weakliem. **Am. Sociol. R.** 58:1 2:1993 pp.16 - 30.
55 Reflections into the spirit of the Islamic corpus of knowledge and the rise of the new science. Mahmoud Dhaouadi. **Am. J. Islam. Soc. Sci.** 10:2 Summer:1993 pp.153 - 164.
56 Reliability and validity of retrospective behavioral self-report by narcotics addicts. M. Douglas Anglin; Yih-ing Hser; Chih-Ping Chou. **Eval. Rev.** 17:1 2:1993 pp.91 - 108.
57 Relocating cultural studies: developments in theory and research. Valda Blundell [Ed.]; John Shepherd [Ed.]; Ian R. Taylor [Ed.]. London, New York: Routledge, 1993. 236p. *ISBN: 0415075483, 0415075491. Includes bibliographical references and index.* (*Series:* The international library of sociology).
58 Research and "anti-racism" — the case of Peter Foster and his critics. Martyn Hammersley. **Br. J. Soc.** 44:3 9:1993 pp.429 - 448.
59 [Retrospect and perspective in research on research]; *[Text in Japanese]*. Akira Arimoto. **Dai. Ron.** 22 1993 pp.35 - 36.

A: Études générales

60 Le rôle de l'analyse secondaire dans la recherche en sciences sociales. *[In French]*; (The role of secondary analysis in social research.) *[Summary]*. Angela Dale. **Soc. Contemp.** 14/15 6-9:1993 pp.7 - 22.
61 The sociology of British Columbia. Gillian Creese. **BC. Stud.** 100 Winter:1993-1994 pp.21 - 42.
62 Socjologiczne badania nad współczesnością. (Pojęcie, etapy rozwoju i społeczne funkcje). *[In Polish]*; [Sociological research today. (Ideas, the current stage of development and social function). Jan Lutyński. **Prz. Soc.** XLI 1992 pp.167 - 196.
63 Die Soziologie der Genese sozialer Institutionen — Theoretische Perspektiven der "neuen Sozialwissenschaften" in Frankreich. *[In German]*; (The sociology of the genesis of social institutions — theoretical perspectives from the "new French social sciences".) *[Summary]*. Peter Wagner. **Z. Soziol.** 22:6 12:1993 pp.464 - 476.
64 Le travail des catégories statistiques. *[In French]*; (On the framing of statistical categories.) *[Summary]*. Dominique Merllié. **Soc. Contemp.** 14/15 6-9:1993 pp.149 - 164.
65 Trend report — Asian sociologists at work — experiences from family sociology. Stella R. Quah [Contrib.]; Sung-Nam Cho [Contrib.]; Dong-Won Lee [Contrib.]; Chin-Chun Yi [Contrib.]. **Curr. Sociol.** 41:1 Spring:1993 pp.1 - 125. *Collection of 6 articles.*
66 Unconsciousness and society — the sociology of sleep. Brian Taylor. **Int. J. Pol. C. S.** 6:3 Spring:1993 pp.463 - 471.
67 Utiliser un recensement: l'exemple de 1982 pour une étude de la population retraitée. *[In French]*; (The use of the census: a case study of the use of the 1982 census concerning the retired population.) *[Summary]*. Alexandre Kych. **Soc. Contemp.** 14/15 6-9:1993 pp.113 - 128.
68 Women's studies in the 1990s: doing things differently. Joanna de Groot [Ed.]; Mary Maynard [Ed.]. Basingstoke; New York: Macmillan; St. Martin's Press, 1993. 182p. *ISBN: 0312091222. Based on a conference organized by the Goethe-Institut York and the Centre for Women's Studies, University of York, held at the University of York in June 1990. Includes index.*
69 Zum Aufbau der Soziologie in Ostdeutschland. *[In German]*; (The reconstruction of sociology in Eastern Germany.) *[Summary]*. M. Rainer Lepsius. **Kölner Z. Soz. Soz. psy.** 45:2 6:1993 pp.305 - 337.
70 Zwaartepuntvorming in de maatschappijwetenschappen en overheidsbeleid — evaluatie van de TVC-DAS-operatie. *[In Dutch]*; [Public policy and the establishment of Centers of Excellence — results from an evaluation study] *[Summary]*. Chantal Remery; Frans Leeuw; Jos de Haan. **Mens Maat.** 68:1 2:1993 pp.59 - 70.

A.3:   **Reference works, information services and documents**
        Ouvrages de référence, services d'information et documents

71 L'anonymat des données individuelles: études des risques d'identification. *[In French]*; (The anonymity of microdata: a study of disclosure risks.) *[Summary]*. Uwe Blien; Walter Müller; Heike Wirth. **Soc. Contemp.** 14/15 6-9:1993 pp.23 - 42.
72 [The collected papers of D.Hashizume. Vol.1 on bodies]; *[Text in Japanese]*. Daisaburo Hashizume. Tokyo: Keiso Shobo, 1993. 286p.

A: General studies

73 Collins dictionary of sociology. Julia Jary [Comp.]; David Jary [Comp.]. Glasgow: Harper Collins, 1991. xi,750p. *ISBN: 0004343735, 000434359X. Bibliography: p.713-750.*
74 The contemporary thesaurus of social science terms and synonyms: a guide for natural language computer searching. Sara D. Knapp [Comp.]. Phoenix, Ariz: Oryx Press, 1992. xxi, 400p. *ISBN: 0897745957. Includes bibliographical references.*
75 Directory of social research organisations in the United Kingdom. Martin Bulmer [Ed.]; Marleen Schwerzel [Ed.]; Wendy Sykes [Ed.]. London: Cassell & Mansell, 1993. 421p. *ISBN: 0720121655.*
76 L'exploitation statistique des données administratives: l'exemple de la base informatique de l'ofpra. *[In French]*; (The use of an on line data base for scientific purpose: an example.) *[Summary]*. Jean-Paul Grémy; Luc Legoux. **Soc. Contemp.** 14/15 6-9:1993 pp.43 - 58.
77 The globalization of privacy — implications of recent changes in Europe. P.M. Regan. **Am. J. Econ. S.** 52:3 7:1993 pp.257 - 274.
78 Grapevine: the directory of African and Afro-Carribean groups in the UK. Gilbert G. Pennant [Ed.]. London: Community Information Service, 1993. 195p. *ISBN: 1872311059.*
79 [Introduction to sociology: correspondence course of Nihon University]; *[Text in Japanese]*. Motoo Yada [Ed.]. Tokyo: Nihon University, 1993. 365p.
80 (An introductory bibliography for Japanese studies. Vol.1. Part 1. Social sciences 1988-89.); *[Text in more than one language]*. Toho Gakkai. Tokyo: Japan Foundation, 1992. 311p. *ISBN: 4875400063.*
81 Słownik biograficzny działaczy polskiego ruchu robotniczego. T.3. K. *[In Polish]*; [A bibliographical dictionary of the Polish working class]. Alicja Pacholczykowa [Ed.]. Warszawa: Książka i Wiedza, 1992. 619p. *ISBN: 8390041278.*
82 Women in Japanese society: an annotated bibliography of selected English language materials. Kristina Ruth Huber; Kathryn Sparling [Contrib.]. Westport, Conn: Greenwood Press, 1992. xviii, 484p. *ISBN: 0313252963. Includes indexes. (Series: Bibliographies and indexes in women's studies).*

B: THEORY AND METHODOLOGY
THÉORIE ET MÉTHODOLOGIE

B.1: Theory
Théorie

83 Beyond theory — the cumbersome materiality of shock. U. Strohmayer. **Envir. Plan. D.** 11:3 6:1993 pp.323 - 347.
84 Changing sociological perspectives on chance. Mike Smith. **Sociology** 27:3 8:1993 pp.513 - 531.
85 Diversity and agreement in feminist ethnography. Anne Williams. **Sociology** 27:4 11:1993 pp.575 - 589.
86 Durkheim's Montesquieu. W. Watts Miller. **Br. J. Soc.** 44:4 12:1993 pp.693 - 712.
87 Emile Durkheim: sociologist and moralist. Stephen P. Turner [Ed.]. London: Routledge, 1993. 253p. *ISBN: 0415094372*.
88 Fertile obsession — validity after poststructuralism. Patti Lather. **Sociol. Q.** 34:4 11:1993 pp.673 - 693.
89 Foucault on theorizing specificity. M. Hannah. **Envir. Plan. D.** 11:3 6:1993 pp.349 - 363.
90 Harré, Vygotsky, Bakhtin, Vico, Wittgenstein — academic discourses and conversational realities. John Shotter. **J. Theory Soc. Behav.** 23:4 12:1993 pp.459 - 482.
91 Hayek, realism and spontaneous order. Mark S. Peacock. **J. Theory Soc. Behav.** 23:3 9:1993 pp.249 - 264.
92 Die Konstruktionen von Zeit. Zum prekären Verhältnis von akademischer Theorie und lokaler Praxis. *[In German]*; (The constructions of time. On the precarious relationship between academic theory and local practices.) *[Summary]*. Heidrun Friese. **Z. Soziol.** 22:5 10:1993 pp.323 - 337.
93 Marx's embryology of society. Arno Wouters. **Philos. S. Sc.** 23:2 6:1993 pp.149 - 179.
94 Thought experiments and social transformation. Francis Roberts. **J. Theory Soc. Behav.** 23:4 12:1993 pp.399 - 421.
95 [Towards sociology of becoming: view of value and character]; *[Text in Japanese]*. Keiichi Sakuta. Tokyo: Yuhikaku, 1993. 227p.

Epistemology
Epistémologie

96 About the beginning of the hermeneutics of the self — two lectures at Dartmouth. Michel Foucault; Mark Blasius [Ed.]. **Polit. Theory** 21:2 5:1993 pp.198 - 227.
97 Conceptions of text and textuality: critical perspectives in literary theory from structuralism to poststructuralism. Peter Trifonas. **Interchange** 24:4 1993 pp.381 - 396.
98 Conventionalism, scientific discovery and the sociology of knowledge. Angelo M. Petroni. **Inter. Phil. Sci.** 7:3 1993 pp.225 - 240.

B: Theory and methodology

99 A disagreement over agreement and consensus in constructionist sociology. Graham Button; Wes Sharrock. **J. Theory Soc. Behav.** 23:1 3:1993 pp.1 - 25.

100 Dopo Popper: saggio su grandezza e limiti dell'epistemologia popperiana e sul suo superamento. *[In Italian]*; [After Popper: essay on greatness and the limits of Popperian epistemology and on its overtaking]. Costantino Cipolla. Rome: Borla, 1990. 140p. *ISBN: 8826307660.*

101 Epistemologia e sociologia in Karl R. Popper. *[In Italian]*; [Epistemology and sociology in Karl R. Popper's work]. Gianfranco Pecchinenda. Naples: Edizioni Libreria l'Ateneo di G. Pionti, 1991. 114p.

102 Implicit causality as implicit salience. Joseph Kasof; Ju Young Lee. **J. Pers. Soc. Psychol.** 65:5 11:1993 pp.877 - 891.

103 Islamic science — the making of a formal intellectual discipline. Siraj Hussain. **Am. J. Islam. Soc. Sci.** 10:3 Fall:1993 pp.305 - 311.

104 The knowing because experiencing subject — narratives, lives, and autobiography. Liz Stanley. **Wom. St. Inter. For.** 16:3 5-6:1993 pp.205 - 215.

105 Knowledge representation in cognitive systems and science. Markus F. Peschl. **J. Soc. Evol. Sys.** 16:2 1993 pp.181 - 213.

106 Konstruktivismus und Sachhaltigkeit soziologischer Erkenntnis: Wirklichkeit als imaginäre Institution. *[In German]*; (Constructivism and the real world in sociologial knowledge production: reality as an imaginary institution].) Helmut Willke. **Social. Int.** 31:1 1993 pp.83 - 100.

107 Meaning and the "discursive ecology" — further to the debate on ecological perceptual theory. William Noble. **J. Theory Soc. Behav.** 23:4 12:1993 pp.375 - 398.

108 Niektóre z osobliwości sojologii wiedzy. Sugestie badawcze — trudności i perspektywy. *[In Polish]*; (Some peculiarities of sociology of knowledge. Research suggestions — difficulties and perspectives.) *[Summary]*. Mirosław Majewski. **Prz. Soc.** XL 1993 pp.101 - 127.

109 Overestimating causality — attributional effects of confirmatory processing. David M. Sanbonmatsu; Sharon A. Akimoto; Earlene Biggs. **J. Pers. Soc. Psychol.** 65:5 11:1993 pp.892 - 903.

110 The post-modern being in psychology. Yoganand Sinha. **Psychol. Devel. Soc.** 5:1 1-6:1993 pp.31 - 42.

111 Postmodernism and the localities debate — ontological questions and epistemological implications. Barney Warf; John Rennie Short [Comments by]; David Ley [Comments by]; Ben de Pater [Comments by]; Gertjan Dijkink [Comments by]. **J. Econ. Soc. Geogr.** 84:3 1993 pp.162 - 184.

112 Postulat rozumienia i badania surveyowe. *[In Polish]*; (Postulate of understanding and survey research.) Henryk Ogryzko-Wiewiórowski. **Prz. Soc.** XL:2 1993 pp.119 - 128.

113 La relación de conocimiento y el problema de la objetividad de los datos. *[In Spanish]*; [The relationship between knowledge and the problem of data objectivity] *[Summary]*. Hugo Zemelman. **Est. Sociol.** XI:33 9-12:1993 pp.641 - 660.

114 The social imaginary; *[Summary in French]*. Michel Maffesoli [Ed.]; Gilbert Durand [Contrib.]; Patrick Tacussel [Contrib.]; Martine Xiberras [Contrib.]; Brigitte Fourastié [Contrib.]; Philippe Joron [Contrib.]; Patrick Watier [Contrib.]; Philippe-Joseph Salazar [Contrib.]. **Curr. Sociol.** 41:2 Autumn:1993 pp.1 - 85. *Collection of 9 articles.*

115 The street-level epistemology of trust. Russell Hardin. **Polit. Soc.** 21:4 12:1993 pp.505 - 529.

116 Thinking with machines — intelligence augmentation, evolutionary epistemology, and semiotic. Peter Skagestad. **J. Soc. Evol. Sys.** 16:2 1993 pp.157 - 180.

Philosophy
Philosophie

117 After the demise of empiricism: the problem of judging social and educational inquiry. John Kenneth Smith. Norwood, NJ.: Ablex Publishers, 1993. viii,179p. *ISBN: 0893918628. Includes bibliographical references (p. 165-173) and indexes.*
118 Baudrillard, modernism, and postmodernism. Nicholas Zurbrugg. **Econ. Soc.** 22:4 11:1993 pp.482 - 500.
119 Confronting representation(s). N. Duncan; J.P. Sharp. **Envir. Plan. D.** 11:4 8:1993 pp.473 - 486.
120 The discourse of domination: from the Frankfurt School to postmodernism. Ben Agger. Evanston, Ill: Northwestern University Press, 1992. xii, 347p. *ISBN: 0810110040. Includes bibliographical references and index.* (*Series:* Northwestern University studies in phenomenology and existential philosophy).
121 Donagan's Kant. Thomas E. Hill. **Ethics** 104:1 10:1993 pp.22 - 52.
122 Durkheim — sacré et societé. *[In French]*; (Durkheim — the sacred and society.) José A. Prades [Contrib.]; Luigi Tomasi [Contrib.]; Stephano Martelli [Contrib.]; Michel Moffesoli [Contrib.]; Laura Desfor Edles [Contrib.]; Franco Ferrarotti [Contrib.]; Robert Tessier [Contrib.]; Kenneth Thompson [Contrib.]. **Soc. Compass** 40:3 9:1993 pp.363 - 461. *Collection of 8 articles.*
123 Equality and justice in education — Dewey and Rawls. B.A. Weitz. **Human St.** 16:4 1993 pp.421 - 434.
124 The (f)utility of a feminist turn to Foucault. Moya Lloyd. **Econ. Soc.** 22:4 11:1993 pp.437 - 460.
125 How free are you?: the determinism problem. Ted Honderich. Oxford: Oxford University Press, 1993. 145p. *ISBN: 0192831399.*
126 Idealism redux: the class-historical truth of postmodernism. Morton G. Wenger. **Crit. Sociol.** 20:1 1993-1994 pp.53 - 78.
127 James Coleman: social theorist and moral philosopher? Adrian Favell. **A.J.S.** 99:3 11:1993 pp.590 - 613.
128 Justice and difference in the works of Rousseau: bienfaisance and pudeur. Judith Still. New York: Cambridge University Press, 1993. 259p. *ISBN: 0521415853. Includes bibliographical references and index.* (*Series:* Cambridge studies in French).
129 Karl Jaspers as a Kantian psychopathologist, I. The philosophical origins of the concept of form and content. Chris Walker. **Hist. Psychiat.** 4(14) 6:1993 pp.209 - 238.
130 [Karl Mannheim: the thought of an intellectual refugee]; *[Text in Japanese]*. Ritsuro Akimoto. Kyoto: Minerva Shobo, 1993. 239p.
131 Kim jest Walter Benjamin? *[In Polish]*; [Who is Walter Benjamin?]. Kaja Kaźmierska [Tr.]; Tania Rajanti. **Prz. Soc.** XLII 1993 pp.49 - 58.
132 Knowledge, values, and the social order in Hayek's Oeuvre. Gerard Radnitzky. **J. Soc. Evol. Sys.** 16:1 1993 pp.9 - 24.

B: Theory and methodology

133 Lifestyle or Lebensführung? Critical remarks on the mistranslation of Weber's "Class, status, party". Thomas Abel; William C. Cockerham. **Sociol. Q.** 34:3 8:1993 pp.551 - 556.

134 Max Weber, formal rationality, and health lifestyles. William C. Cockerham; Thomas Abel; Günther Lüschen. **Sociol. Q.** 34:3 8:1993 pp.413 - 425.

135 Moralism and cruelty — reflections on Hume and Kant. Annette C. Baier. **Ethics** 103:3 4:1993 pp.436 - 457.

136 On Hegel and the rise of social theory — a critical appreciation of Herbert Marcuse's Reason and Revolution, fifty years later. Kevin Anderson. **Sociol. Theory** 11:3 11:1993 pp.243 - 267.

137 Order without rules — Wittgenstein and the "communicative ethics controversy". David Bogen; Jürgen Habermas [Subject of work]. **Sociol. Theory** 11:1 3:1993 pp.55 - 71.

138 Philosophy of social science: the methods, ideals, and politics of social inquiry. Michael Root. Cambridge, Mass., USA: Blackwell, 1993. 269p. *ISBN: 0631190414, 0631190422. Includes bibliographical references and index.*

139 A piece of lost history — Max Weber and Lowell L. Bennion. Laurie Newman di Padova; Ralph S. Brower. **Am. Sociol.** 23:3 Fall:1992 pp.37 - 56.

140 A pragmatic theory of responsibility for the egalitarian planner. John E. Roemer. **Philos. Pub.** 22:2 Spring:1993 pp.146 - 166.

141 Reconstructing Marxism — South African critiques and a response. Windsor S. Leroke; Yvonne Muthien; Nicoli Nattrass; Philip Nel; Herbert W. Vilakazi; Andrew Levine; Elliott Sober; Erik Olin Wright. **S.Afr. Sociol. R.** 5:(2) 4:1993 pp.65 - 114.

142 Religiöse Ethik und ästhetischer „Rationalismus". Zur Soziologie der Kunst im Werk Max Webers. *[In German]*; [Religious ethics and aesthetic "rationalism". On the sociology of art in the work of Max Weber]. Werner Gephart. **Social. Int.** 31:1 1993 pp.101 - 121.

143 La spiegazione dell'azione sociale in Durkheim. *[In Italian]*; [The explanation of Durkheim's social action]. Paolo Ceri. **Quad. Sociol.** XXXVI:2 1992 pp.55 - 94.

144 Their "own peculiar way" — Karl Mannheim and the rise of women; *[Summary in French]*. David Kettler; Volker Meja. **Int. Sociol.** 8:1 3:1993 pp.5 - 55.

145 Towards a synthetic theory of rationality. Raymond Boudon; Joseph Agassi [Comments by]; Hans Albert [Comments by]; Eliezer Ben-Rafael [Comments by]; Franco Crespi [Comments by]; Stephan Fuchs [Comments by]; Hartmut Kliemt [Comments by]; Paolo Legrenzi [Comments by]; Rino Rumiati [Comments by]; Siegwart Lindenberg [Comments by]; Steven Lukes [Comments by]; Marco Mondadori [Comments by]; Aldo Montesano [Comments by]; Robert Nadeau [Comments by]; Alessandro Pizzorno [Comments by]; Salvino A. Salvaggio [Comments by]; Toon Vandevelde [Comments by]. **Inter. Phil. Sci.** 7:1 1993 pp.5 - 102.

146 Weber symposium — review essays. Thomas Burger [Contrib.]; Alan Sica [Contrib.]; Lawrence A. Scaff [Contrib.]; Harvey Goldman [Contrib.]; Randall Collins [Contrib.]. **Theory Soc.** 22:6 12:1993 pp.813 - 870. *Collection of 5 articles.*

147 Weber, Wagner and thoughts of death. David J. Chalcraft. **Sociology** 27:3 8:1993 pp.433 - 449.

148 Why first language learning is not second language learning — Wittgenstein's rejection of St. Augustine's conception of learning. Christina Erneling. **Interchange** 24:4 1993 pp.341 - 352.

B: Théorie et méthodologie

149 Wittgenstein — mind, body, and society. Theodore R. Schatzki. **J. Theory Soc. Behav.** 23:3 9:1993 pp.285 - 313.

Sociological theory
Théorie sociologique

150 Ainsi va la sociologie aujourd'hui. *[In French]*; [The state of sociology today]. J. Baechler [Contrib.]; A. Petitat [Contrib.]; M. Borlandi [Contrib.]; R. Romano [Contrib.]; R. Lucchini [Contrib.]; J.-B. Grize [Contrib.]; R. Lapointe [Contrib.]; F. Aqueci [Contrib.]; F.Lo Piparo [Contrib.]; G. Busino [Contrib.]; M. Carreras [Contrib.]; J. Freund [Contrib.]; Ch. Widmer [Contrib.]; D. Apothéloz [Contrib.]; M. Micheloni [Contrib.]. **Rev. Eur. Sci. Soc.** XXX:93 1992 pp.5 - 251. *Collection of 18 articles.*
151 Aleksando Bogdanov i teoriia »novogo klassa«. *[In Russian]*; (Bogdanov and the theory of "new class".) Dzh. Biggart. **Sot. Issle.** 7 1993 pp.139 - 150.
152 Analytic induction revisited; *[Summary in French]*. Sheldon Goldenberg. **Can. J. Soc.** 18:2 Spring:1993 pp.161 - 176.
153 Analytical Marxism and historical materialism — the debate on social evolution. Alan Carling. **Sci. Soc.** 57:1 Spring:1993 pp.31 - 65.
154 The body and social theory. Chris Shilling. London: Sage Publications, 1993. 232p. *ISBN: 0803985851.* (*Series:* Theory, culture and society).
155 Caos e ordem na teoria sociológia. *[In Portuguese]*; (Chaos and order in sociological theory.) *[Summary]*; *[Summary in French]*. Franz Josef Brüseke. **Rev. Bras. Ciên. Soc.** 8:22 6:1993 pp.119 - 136.
156 Changing approaches in postmodern sociological thought. Gitta Tulea; Ernest Krausz. **Int. J. Comp. Soc** XXXIV:3-4 9-12:1993 pp.210 - 221.
157 Chaos en organisatie: over de maakbaarheid van de samenleving. *[In Dutch]*; [Chaos and organization: about the making of society]. J.R. Zuidema. **Maan. Econ.** 57:5 10:1993 pp.339 - 362.
158 [Constitution of the theory of form of social science (4)]; *[Text in Japanese]*. Noboru Matsuzaki. **Kei. Jo. Kiyo** 8 1993 pp.77 - 133.
159 Context and prejudice in Max Weber's thought — criticisms of Wilhelm Hennis. Gary A. Abraham; Wilhelm Hennis [Comments by]. **Hist. Human Sci.** 6:3 8:1993 pp.1 - 23.
160 Deconstructing Durkheim: a post-post structuralist critique. Jennifer M. Lehmann. London, New York: Routledge, 1993. 270p. *ISBN: 0415070392.* *Includes bibliographical references and index.*
161 [Development of sociological theory]; *[Text in Japanese]*. Mikio Kodama. Tokyo: Gakubunsha, 1993. 207p.
162 Discourse, ideology, discourse, ideology, discourse, ideógeny... Trevor Purvis; Alan Hunt; Michel Foucault [Subject of work]; Karl Marx [Subject of work]. **Br. J. Soc.** 44:3 9:1993 pp.473 - 499.
163 Dueling structures — the theory of resistance in discourse. Michael Huspek. **Commun. Theory** 3:1 2:1993 pp.1 - 25.
164 Durkheim, language, and history — a pragmatist perspective. Robert Alun Jones; Douglas A. Kibbee. **Sociol. Theory** 11:2 7:1993 pp.152 - 170.

B: Theory and methodology

165 Ecology and carnival — traces of a "green" social theory in the writings of M.M. Bakhtin. Michael Gardiner. **Theory Soc.** 22:6 12:1993 pp.765 - 812.
166 An electronic panopticon? A sociological critique of surveillance theory. David Lyon; Michel Foucault [Subject of work]. **Sociol. Rev.** 41:4 11:1993 pp.653 - 678.
167 Emotion and culture in theories of justice. Mary Douglas. **Econ. Soc.** 22:4 11:1993 pp.501 - 515.
168 The everyday world is problematic — ideology and recursion in Dorothy Smith's micro-sociology. Chris Doran. **Can. J. Soc.** 18:1 Winter:1993 pp.43 - 63.
169 Funktionale Differenzierung und gesellschaftliche Rationalität. Zu Niklas Luhmanns Konzeption des Verhältnisses von Selbstreferenz und Koordination in modernen Gesellschaften. *[In German]*; (Functional differentiation and social rationality. Niklas Luhmann's conception of the relation between self-reference and coordination in modern society.) *[Summary]*. Klaus Bendel. **Z. Soziol.** 22:4 8:1993 pp.261 - 278.
170 Gandhian sociology: an outline. Arun Kumar Sharma. **East. Anthrop.** 46:3 7-9:1993 pp.295 - 316.
171 Georg Simmel: critical assessments. David Frisby [Ed.]. London: Routledge, 1993. *ISBN: 0415060710. 3 vols.*
172 Georg Simmel in Berlin. *[In German]*; (George Simmel in Berlin.) *[Summary]*; *[Summary in French]*. Steffen Sigmund. **Berl. J. Soziol.** 3:2 1993 pp.161 - 181.
173 Gesellschaftstheorie, Kulturphilosophie und Thanatologie. Eine gesellschaftstheoretische Rekonstruktion von Georg Simmels Theorie der Individualität. *[In German]*; [Societal theory, cultural philosophy and thanatology. On reconstructing Georg Simmels theory of individuality]. Armin Nassehi. **Social. Int.** 31:1 1993 pp.1 - 22.
174 Giddens on subjectivity and social order. Gerhard Wagner. **J. Theory Soc. Behav.** 23:2 6:1993 pp.139 - 155.
175 Hard choices — a sociological perspective on value incommensurability. E. Cohen; E. Ben-Ari. **Human St.** 16:3 1993 pp.267 - 297.
176 I "militari" nella riflessione sociologica. *[In Italian]*; ["Militants" in sociological reflections]. Marina Nuciari. **Sociologia [Rome]** XXVII:1-3 1993 pp.299 - 341.
177 Ideia prava v sotsial'noi teorii P.I. Novgorodtseva. *[In Russian]*; (The legal idea in P.I. Novgorodtsev's social theory.) V.I. Shamshurin. **Sot. Issle.** 4 1993 pp.97 - 105.
178 Ideology and the postmodern debate in sociological theory. Mark Gottdiener. **Sociol. Q.** 34:4 11:1993 pp.653 - 671.
179 Institutional conditions for diffusion. David Strang; John W. Meyer. **Theory Soc.** 22:4 8:1993 pp.487 - 511.
180 [M. Weber and theory of modernization]; *[Text in Japanese]*. Masashi Kanno. Tokyo: Koseisha-koseikaku, 1993. 235p.
181 Marx und Luhmann im Cyberspace. Ein Computerprogramm zur Rekonstruktion und zum Formalen Vergleich soziologischer Theorien. *[In German]*; [Marx and Luhmann in cyber space. Computer programmes for the reconstruction and the formal comparison of sociological theories]. Jürgen Klüver. **Social. Int.** 31:2 1993 pp.221 - 236.
182 Max Webers Konzeption des Mikro-Makro-Problems. *[In German]*; (Max Weber's conception of the micro-macro-problem.) *[Summary]*. Thomas Schwinn. **Kölner Z. Soz. Soz. psy.** 45:2 6:1993 pp.220 - 237.
183 Max Webers Staatssoziologie. *[In German]*; (Max Weber's sociology of the state.) *[Summary]*. Stefan Breuer. **Kölner Z. Soz. Soz. psy.** 45:2 6:1993 pp.199 - 219.

184 Die Motive des Gehorsams bei Max Weber — eine Rekonstruktion. *[In German]*; (Max Weber and the motives of obedience — a reconstruction.) *[Summary]*. Peter Baumann. **Z. Soziol.** 22:5 10:1993 pp.355 - 370.
185 [New frontiers in social theory]; *[Text in Japanese]*. Yosuke Koto [Ed.]. Tokyo: University of Tokyo Press, 1993. 216p.
186 Nietzsche, Weber and the affirmative sociology of culture. Georg Stauth. **Eur. J. Soc.** XXXIII:2 1992 pp.219 - 250.
187 Opportunity and structural sociology. David Rubinstein. **J. Theory Soc. Behav.** 23:3 9:1993 pp.265 - 283.
188 Osservare/pensare relazionalmente. *[In Italian]*; [Seeing/thinking in a relational manner]. Pierpaolo Donati. **Sociologia [Rome]** XXVII:1-3 1993 pp.83 - 128.
189 Parsons, Pareto, Habermas: eine Studie zur soziologischen Theoriediskussion. *[In German]*; [Parsons, Pareto, Habermas: a study on the socialogical discussion on theory]. Helge Peukert. Idstein: Schultz-Kirchner Verlag, 1992. 106p. *ISBN: 3824800462. Includes bibliographical references.*
190 The passion of Michel Foucault. James Miller. London: HarperCollins, 1993. 491p. *ISBN: 0002552671.*
191 El pensamiento sociológico español. *[In Spanish]*; [Spanish sociological thought]. Luis Saavedra. Madrid: Taurus, 1991. 237p. *ISBN: 8430601635.*
192 Plaidoyer pour une approche taxinomique en théorie sociale — Talcott Parsons et l'héritage wébérien. *[In French]*; [A plea for a taxonomic approach to social theory — Talcott Parsons and the Weberian heritage]. Ahmed Chakib. **Soc. Sci. Info.** 32:3 1993 pp.447 - 466.
193 Poetic representation, ethnographic presentation and transgressive validity — the case of the skipped line. Laurel W. Richardson. **Sociol. Q.** 34:4 11:1993 pp.695 - 710.
194 Postmodernism and the localities debate — ontological questions and epistemological implications. Barney Warf; John Rennie Short [Comments by]; David Ley [Comments by]; Ben de Pater [Comments by]; Gertjan Dijkink [Comments by]. **J. Econ. Soc. Geogr.** 84:3 1993 pp.162 - 184.
195 The poverty of sociological theory. Nicos Mouzelis. **Sociology** 27:4 11:1993 pp.675 - 695.
196 Pragmatism and social theory. Hans Joas. Chicago: University of Chicago Press, 1993. vi, 272p. *ISBN: 0226400417. Includes bibliographical references and indexes.*
197 Prescience or serendipity? Parallelism in living systems theory and modern sociological theory. Kenneth D. Bailey. **Behav. Sci.** 38:4 10:1993 pp.241 - 254.
198 [The problem of 'Herrschaft' and 'Freiheit' in the theory of Simmel]; *[Text in Japanese]*. Hitoshi Kanno. **Shak. Nen.** 12 1993 pp.1 - 20.
199 Le raisonnement sociologique: l'espace non-poppérien du raisonnement naturel. *[In French]*; [Sociological reasoning: non-Popperian natural reasoning]. Jean-Claude Passeron. Paris: Nathan, 1991. 408p. *ISBN: 2091904120.*
200 Rational choice theory. James S. Coleman [Contrib.]; Jon Elster [Contrib.]; Siegwart Lindenberg [Contrib.]; Bruno S. Frey [Contrib.]; Ole-Jørgen Skog [Contrib.]; Thráinn Eggertsson [Contrib.]; Lars Udéhn [Contrib.]; Geoffrey Evans [Contrib.]. **Acta Sociol.** 36:3 1993 pp.169 - 276. *Collection of 7 articles.*
201 Realismo, fenomenologia e positivismo in Emile Durkheim. *[In Italian]*; [Realism, phenomenology and positivism in Emile Durkheim]. Francesco Boriani. **Sociologia [Rome]** XXVII:1-3 1993 pp.185 - 197.

B: Theory and methodology

202 [The review of Weber at the present day]; *[Text in Japanese]*. Shuzo Kawakami. Tokyo: Keiso Shobo, 1993. 259p.
203 Risk and recreancy — Weber, the division of labor, and the rationality of risk perceptions. William R. Freudenburg. **Soc. Forc.** 71:4 6:1993 pp.909 - 932.
204 Searching for the light: essays on thought and culture. Norman Birnbaum. New York: Oxford University Press, 1993. viii, 252p. *ISBN: 0195068890. Includes bibliographical references and index.*
205 Simmel, Weber und die „verstehende Soziologie". *[In German]*; (Simmel, Weber and cognitive sociology.) *[Summary]*; *[Summary in French]*. Klaus Lichtblau. **Berl. J. Soziol.** 3:2 1993 pp.141 - 151.
206 Social theories of risk. Sheldon Krimsky [Ed.]; Dominic Golding [Ed.]. Westport, Conn: Praeger, 1992. xvii, 412p. *ISBN: 027594168X, 0275943178. Contains revised versions of papers from a workshop, held in Jan. 1991, in Cambridge, Mass. and additional contributions. Includes bibliographical references (p. 366-397) and index.*
207 [Social theory in crisis and renewal]; *[Text in Japanese]*. Yoshiyuki Sato [Ed.]. Tokyo: Marge-sha, 1993. 391p.
208 [The sociological thought of Georges Gurvitch]; *[Text in Japanese]*. Yasushi Naka. Tokyo: Keio Tsushin, 1993. 153p.
209 La sociologie du développement — bilan et perspectives. *[In French]*; [Development sociology — overview and perspectives]. Claude Rivière [Contrib.]; Alain Touraine [Contrib.]; Jacques Lombard [Contrib.]; André Guichaoua [Contrib.]; Roland Waast [Contrib.]; Bernard Schlemmer [Contrib.]; Jean-François Médard [Contrib.]; Yvon le Bot [Contrib.]; Bertrand Badie [Contrib.]; Rita Cordonnier [Contrib.]; Raymond Boudon [Contrib.]. **Ann. Sociol.** 42 1992 pp.25 - 274. *Collection of 10 articles.*
210 La sociologie et les principes de rationalité. *[In French]*; [Sociology and the principles of rationality]. J.-C. Passeron [Contrib.]; J. Freund [Contrib.]; E. Ascher [Contrib.]; G. Busino [Contrib.]; J. Pullen [Contrib.]; J.-B. Grize [Contrib.]; S. Giner [Contrib.]; C. Widmer [Contrib.]; J. Baechler [Contrib.]. **Rev. Eur. Sci. Soc.** XXXI:95 1993 pp.5 - 204. *Collection of 10 articles.*
211 [Sociology of Durkheim]; *[Text in Japanese]*. Kanji Naito. Tokyo: Koseisha-koseikaku, 1993. 251p.
212 Soziale Differenzierung und Individualität. Georg Simmels Gesellschafts- und Zeitdiagnose. *[In German]*; (Social differentiation and individuality. Georg Simmel's diagnosis of society and his time.) *[Summary]*; *[Summary in French]*. Hans-Peter Müller. **Berl. J. Soziol.** 3:2 1993 pp.127 - 139.
213 Soziologie des Risikos. *[In German]*; [Sociology of risk]. Niklas Luhmann. Berlin, New York: W. de Gruyter, 1991. 252p. *ISBN: 311012940X, 3110129396. Includes bibliographical references and index.*
214 The stories told in science fiction and social science — reading "The Thing" and other remakes from two eras. Michael A. Katovich; Patrick A. Kinkade. **Sociol. Q.** 34:4 11:1993 pp.619 - 637.
215 [Structuration theory as critical theory]; *[Text in Japanese]*. Kiyonori Wakasa. **Bung.-Ken. Kiyo** 19 1993 pp.73 - 84.
216 [Structure of theory of social power: a comparison between the theories of Steven Lukes and Niklas Luhmann]; *[Text in Japanese]*. Hideki Tarumoto. **Sociologos** 17 1993 pp.216 - 228.

B: Théorie et méthodologie

217 A symposium — positivism again. Janet Saltzman Chafetz; Charles Camic; James Miley; Charles Smith; Bert N. Adams; David Sciulli; Keith Doubt; Richard Moodey. **Am. Sociol.** 24:2 Summer:1993 pp.59 - 74.
218 System und Akteur. Zum Nutzen zweier soziologischer Paradigmen bei der Erklärung erfolgreichen Scheiterns. *[In German]*; (Some reflections on the benefits of systems and actors theory in explaining successful failure.) *[Summary]*. Johannes Weyer. **Kölner Z. Soz. Soz. psy.** 45:1 1993 pp.1 - 22.
219 Theories of revolution revisited — toward a fourth generation. John Foran. **Sociol. Theory** 11:1 3:1993 pp.1 - 20.
220 Theory-bashing and answer-improving in the study of social movements. John Lofland. **Am. Sociol.** 24:2 Summer:1993 pp.37 - 58.
221 Towards a unified approach to the Shari'ah and social inference. Louay Safi. **Am. J. Islam. Soc. Sci.** 10:4 Winter:1993 pp.464 - 484.
222 The trouble with Anthony Giddens: problems of status and structure in structuration theory. Johann Graaff. **S.Afr. Sociol. R.** 6:1 10:1993 pp.35 - 51.
223 Vital realism in sociology — a metatheoretical grounding in Mead, Ortega, and Schutz. David Lewis; Raymond McLain; Andrew Weigert. **Sociol. Theory** 11:1 3:1993 pp.72 - 95.
224 Was ist der Fall, was steckt dahinter? Die zwei Soziologien und die Gesellschaftstheorie. *[In German]*; (What's the case? and what's behind it? — the two sociologies and the theory of society.) *[Summary]*. Niklas Luhmann. **Z. Soziol.** 22:4 8:1993 pp.245 - 260.
225 Who can accept moral dilemmas? Ragnar Ohlsson. **J. Phil.** XC:8 8:1993 pp.405 - 415.

B.2:   **Research methods**
           Méthodes de recherche

226 Applications of case study research. Robert K. Yin. Newbury Park: Sage Publications, 1993. 131p. *ISBN: 0803951183*. (*Series:* Applied social research methods series).
227 Approaches to social enquiry. Norman Blaikie. Cambridge: Polity Press, 1993. 238p. *ISBN: 0745611729*.
228 Biography and autobiography in sociology. Mary Evans [Contrib.]; Michael Erben [Contrib.]; Dorothy Sheridan [Contrib.]; Liz Stanley [Contrib.]; Judith Aldridge [Contrib.]; Pam Cotterill [Contrib.]; Gayle Letherby [Contrib.]; Janes Ribbens [Contrib.]; Ruth Wilkins [Contrib.]; Barbara Harrison [Contrib.]; E. Stina Lyon [Contrib.]; Michele L. Davies [Contrib.]; Hilary Dickinson [Contrib.]; Nod Miller [Contrib.]; David Morgan [Contrib.]; Anthony Rosie [Contrib.]; Bill Bytheway [Contrib.]; Robin Humphrey [Contrib.]. **Sociology** 27:1 2:1993 pp.5 - 178. *Collection of 15 articles*.
229 The case study in sociology — the contribution of methodological research in the French language; *[Summary in French]*. Jacques Hamel. **Can. R. Soc. A.** 30:4 11:1993 pp.488 - 509.
230 Culture and photography — reading sociology through a lens. Franco Ferrarotti. **Int. J. Pol. C. S.** 7:1 Fall:1993 pp.75 - 95.

B: Theory and methodology

231 Doing research on sensitive topics. Raymond M. Lee. London: Sage Publications, 1993. 248p. *ISBN: 0803988605*.
232 Evaluating social science research: an introduction. Thomas R. Black. London: Sage, 1993. viii, 183p. *ISBN: 0803988524, 0803988532. Includes index.*
233 The function of qualitative research. J.W. Heyink; T.J. Tymstra. **Soc. Ind.** 29:3 7:1993 pp.291 - 305.
234 General social equilibrium — toward theoretical synthesis. Thomas J. Fararo. **Sociol. Theory** 11:3 11:1993 pp.291 - 313.
235 Jednobiegunowa skala kategorii opisowych i jej rozumienie. Eksperyment metodologiczny. *[In Polish]*; (Unipolar scale with descriptive categories and its comprehension. A methodological experiment.) Andrzej Paweł Wejland. **Prz. Soc.** XL:2 1993 pp.129 - 148.
236 Kalejdoskopisk forskning i botkyrka. *[In Swedish]*; (Kaleidoscopic research. The activities at Sweden's immigrant institute and museum.) Annick Sjögren; Oscar Pripp. **Nord. Ny.** 52 1993 pp.55 - 62.
237 Macrocomparative research methods. Kenneth A. Bollen; Barbara Entwisle; Arthur S. Alderson. **Ann. R. Soc.** 19 1993 pp.321 - 353.
238 Mapping it out: expository cartography for the humanities and social sciences. Mark S. Monmonier. Chicago: University of Chicago Press, 1993. xiii, 301p. *ISBN: 0226534162. Includes bibliographical references (p. 267-291) and index. (Series: Chicago guides to writing, editing, and publishing).*
239 The methodology of the Islamic behavioral sciences. Mahmoud Abu-Saud. **Am. J. Islam. Soc. Sci.** 10:3 Fall:1993 pp.382 - 395.
240 Methodology of the national survey of sexual attitudes and lifestyles. J. Wadsworth; J. Field; A.M. Johnson; S. Bradshaw; K. Wellings. **J. Roy. Stat. Soc. A.** 156:3 1993 pp.407 - 422.
241 Metodo storico, antipositivismo e processualità dei fenomeni sociali. *[In Italian]*; [Historical methods, antipositivism and the process of social phenomena]. Luigi Frudà. **Sociologia [Rome]** XXVII:1-3 1993 pp.139 - 176.
242 Narrative methods. Peter Abell [Contrib.]; John Skvoretz [Contrib.]; Kenji Kosaka [Contrib.]; Thomas J. Fararo [Contrib.]; David R. Heise [Contrib.]; David Willer [Contrib.]; Andrew Abbott [Comments by]; Alaina Michaelson-Kanfer [Contrib.]; Guillermina Jasso [Contrib.]. **J. Math. Sociol.** 18:2-3 1993 pp.93 - 266. *Collection of 8 articles.*
243 Narrative's moment and sociology's phenomena — toward a narrative sociology. David R. Maines. **Sociol. Q.** 34:1 Spring:1993 pp.17 - 38.
244 Participatory research — part I. Richard Hall [Ed.]; Randy Stoecker [Ed.]; Edna Bonacich [Ed.]; Budd L. Hall [Contrib.]; Peter Park [Contrib.]; Philip Nyden [Contrib.]; Wim Wiewel [Contrib.]; Thomas Plaut [Contrib.]; Suzanne Landis [Contrib.]; June Trevor [Contrib.]; Darlyne Bailey [Contrib.]; M. Eugenia Sánchez [Contrib.]; G.H. Eduardo Almeida [Contrib.]; Mark Lynd [Contrib.]. **Am. Sociol.** 23:4 Winter:1992 pp.5 - 115. *Collection of 8 articles.*
245 Participatory research — part II. Randy Stoecker [Contrib.]; Edna Bonacich [Contrib.]; Deirdre M. Kelly [Contrib.]; Lynnell J. Simonson [Contrib.]; Virginia A. Bushaw [Contrib.]; Fred Nash [Contrib.]; Pierrette Hondagneu-Sotelo [Contrib.]; Ken Reardon [Contrib.]; John Welsh [Contrib.]; Brian Kreiswirth [Contrib.]; John Forester [Contrib.]; Francesca M. Cancian [Contrib.]; Elizabeth McLean Petras

B: Théorie et méthodologie

[Contrib.]; Douglas V. Porpora [Contrib.]. **Am. Sociol.** 24:1 Spring:1993 pp.5 - 126. *Collection of 8 articles.*
246 Real world research: a resource for social scientists and practitioner-researchers. Colin Robson. Oxford, UK; Cambridge, Mass: Blackwell, 1993. 510p. *ISBN: 0631176888, 0631176896.* Includes bibliographical references and indexes.
247 Recent advances in longitudinal methodology. Trond Petersen. **Ann. R. Soc.** 19 1993 pp.425 - 454.
248 Reflecting on research practice: issues in health and social welfare. Pam Shakespeare [Ed.]; Dorothy Atkinson [Ed.]; Sally French [Ed.]. Buckingham: Open University Press, 1993. x,144p. *ISBN: 0335190391, 0335190383.*
249 Smena paradigm i formirovanie novoi metodologii (popytka obzora diskussii). *[In Russian]*; (Change of paradigms and the shaping of a new methodology (an attempt to review the discussion).) V. Altukhov. **Obshch. Nauki Sovrem.** 1 1993 pp.88 - 100.
250 Social research: philosophy, politics and practice. Martyn Hammersley [Ed.]. London: Sage Pubns, 1993. 242p. *ISBN: 0803988052.*
251 Social science research and the crafting of policy on population resettlement. Michael M. Cernea. **Know. Pol.** 6:3+4 1993-1994 p.176.
252 Some aspects of social science research on development and research institutions in Africa. Cleophas Lado. **J. E.Afr. Res. Devel.** 23 1993 pp.121 - 139.
253 Sotsial'noe poznanie na porpge postindustrial'nogo mira. *[In Russian]*; (Social knowledge of the threshold of the post-industrial world.) V. Bakirov. **Obshch. Nauki Sovrem.** 1 1993 pp.68 - 77.
254 Sotsial'no-kul'turnoe mnogoobrazie v zerkale metodologii. *[In Russian]*; (Socio-cultural diversity in the mirror of methodology.) N. Smirnova. **Obshch. Nauki Sovrem.** 1 1993 pp.78 - 87.
255 Sotsiogenetika: stanovlenie integrirovannoi otrasli znanii. *[In Russian]*; (Sociogenetics: the emergence and development of an integrated field of knowledge.) Iu. Iakovets. **Obshch. Nauki Sovrem.** 4 1993 pp.82 - 88.
256 Techniczne i paradygmatyczne kryteria podziału badań ilościowych i jakościowych w naukach społecznych. *[In Polish]*; (Technical and paradigmatic criteria of dividing quantitative and qualitative studies in social sciences.) Krzysztof Konecki. **Prz. Soc.** XL:2 1993 pp.173 - 178.
257 Telling a story of sudden death. Carolyn Ellis; Sherryl Kleinman [Comments by]. **Sociol. Q.** 34:4 11:1993 pp.711 - 731.
258 Tożsamość społeczna jako rzeczywistość ewokowana w sytuacji wywiadu socjologicznego. *[In Polish]*; (Social identity as a reality evoked in sociological survey situation.) Paweł B. Sztabiński. **Prz. Soc.** XL:2 1993 pp.103 - 118.
259 Wspomnienie jako wycinek autobiografii w kontekście konfliktu społecznego w tradycyjnym zastosowaniu metody biograficznej. *[In Polish]*; (The memoir as a segment of the autobiography in the context of social conflict as far as the traditional biographic method is concerned.) Marek Latoszek. **Prz. Soc.** XL:2 1993 pp.201 - 214.

B: Theory and methodology

Data analysis
Analyse des données

260 Advances in sociology from social network analysis. Stanley Wassermanm [Ed.]; Joseph Galaskiewicz [Ed.]; David Knoke [Contrib.]; Mark S. Mizruchi [Contrib.]; Michael E. Walker [Contrib.]; Barry Wellman [Contrib.]; Martina Morris [Contrib.]; Peter V. Marsden [Contrib.]; Noah E. Friedkin [Contrib.]. **Sociol. Meth.** 22:1 8:1993 pp.3 - 151. *Collection of 6 articles.*

261 Algebraic models for social networks. Philippa Pattison. Cambridge [England], New York, NY: Cambridge University Press, 1993. xxi, 310p. *ISBN: 0521365686. Includes bibliographical references (p. 273-288) and indexes. (Series:* Structural analysis in the social sciences).

262 The aliasing-phenomenon in visual terms. Hermann Singer. **J. Math. Sociol.** 17:1 1992 pp.39 - 50.

263 The analysis of count data — overdispersion and autocorrelation. David N. Barron. **Soc. Method.** 22 1992 pp.179 - 220.

264 Analyzing tabular data: loglinear and logistic models for social researchers. Nigel Gilbert. London: U.C.L. Press, 1993. 186p. *ISBN: 1857280911. (Series:* Social Research Today).

265 Assignment games, chromatic number, and exchange theory. Phillip Bonacich; Elisa Jayne Bienenstock. **J. Math. Sociol.** 17:4 1993 pp.243 - 259.

266 Asymptotic robust inferences in the analysis of mean and covariance structures. Albert Satorra. **Soc. Method.** 22 1992 pp.249 - 278.

267 Can you trust self-report data provided by homeless mentally ill individuals? Robert J. Calsyn; Gary Allen; Gary A. Morse; Ruth Smith; Betty Tempelhoff. **Eval. Rev.** 17:3 6:1993 pp.353 - 366.

268 A combinatorial theory of minimal social situations. Tadeusz Sozański. **J. Math. Sociol.** 17:2-3 1992 pp.105 - 126.

269 Comparing non-nested models for contingency tables. David L. Weakliem. **Soc. Method.** 22 1992 pp.147 - 178.

270 Constrained latent budget analysis. Peter G.M. van der Heijden; Ab Mooijaart; Jan de Leeuw. **Soc. Method.** 22 1992 pp.279 - 320.

271 The covariance structure analysis of ipsative data. Wai Chan; Peter M. Bentler. **Sociol. Meth.** 22:2 11:1993 pp.214 - 247.

272 Critique of the comparative method and the challenges of a transnational world. Ananta Giri. **Contr. I. Soc.** 27:2 7-12:1993 pp.267 - 289.

273 Data analysis for comparative social research: international perspectives. Chikio Hayashi; Tatsuzō Suzuki; Masamichi S. Sasaki. New York; Amsterdam: North-Holland, 1992. xxxiii, 495p. *ISBN: 0444895469. Includes bibliographical references (p. 471-481) and index.*

274 [Data analysis of survey research public opinion poll]; *[Text in Japanese].* Kazufumi Manabe. Tokyo: Keio Tsushin, 1993. 298p.

275 Decomposing longitudinal from cross-unit effects in panel and pooled cross-sectional designs. Robert L. Kaufman. **Sociol. Meth.** 21:4 5:1993 pp.482 - 504.

276 Discourse analytic research: repertoires and readings of texts in action. Erica Burman [Ed.]; Ian Parker [Ed.]. London, New York: Routledge, 1993. 179p. *ISBN: 0415097207, 0415097215. Includes bibliographical references and index.*

B: Théorie et méthodologie

277 Discrete-choice logit models — testing the IIA property. Junsen Zhang; Saul D. Hoffman. **Sociol. Meth.** 22:2 11:1993 pp.193 - 213.
278 Endogenous switching regression models with limited dependent variables. Daniel A. Powers. **Sociol. Meth.** 22:2 11:1993 pp.248 - 273.
279 Estimation of models with correlated measurement errors from panel data. Bradley Palmquist; Donald P. Green. **Soc. Method.** 22 1992 pp.119 - 146.
280 Estimation of the network effects model in a large data set. James B. Duke. **Sociol. Meth.** 21:4 5:1993 pp.465 - 481.
281 The evaluation question approach — a method of measuring attitudes. N.L. van der Sar; B.M.S. van Praag. **J. Econ. Psyc.** 14:1 3:1993 pp.183 - 201.
282 Exchangeability and data analysis. D. Draper; J.S. Hodges; C.L. Mallows; D. Pregibon. **J. Roy. Stat. Soc. A.** 156:1 1993 pp.9 - 37.
283 The FC1 rule of identification for confirmatory factor analysis — a general sufficient condition. Walter R. Davis. **Sociol. Meth.** 21:4 5:1993 pp.403 - 437.
284 Fitting and testing a 'predator-prey' model. Jeffrey Durand; Roger Durand. **J. Math. Sociol.** 17:1 1992 pp.51 - 62.
285 Geen antwoord is ook een antwoord — over de verwaarlozing van "weet niet" — antwoorden in de sociologische analyse. *[In Dutch]*; [No answer is also an answer — on the neglect of "don't know" replies in sociological analysis]. H. van Goor; Joep de Hart [Comments by]; Karin Wittebrood [Comments by]. **Sociol. Gids** 40:5 9-10:1993 pp.408 - 422.
286 Hermeneutisch-klassifikatorische Inhaltsanalyse. Analysemöglichkeiten am Beispiel von Leitfadengesprächen zum Wohlfahrtsstaat. *[In German]*; (Hermeneutic-classificatory content analysis — possible analyses examplified by semi-structured interviews on the welfare state.) *[Summary]*. Edeltraud Roller; Rainer Mathes. **Kölner Z. Soz. Soz. psy.** 45:1 1993 pp.56 - 75.
287 How to analyze the results of linear programs — part 1 — preliminaries. Harvey J. Greenberg. **Interfaces** 23:4 7-8:1993 pp.56 - 67.
288 Interpreting hazard rate models. Jay D. Teachman; Mark D. Hayward. **Sociol. Meth.** 21:3 2:1993 pp.340 - 371.
289 Introducing data analysis for social scientists. David Rose; Oriel Sullivan. Buckingham: Open University Press, 1993. 203p. *ISBN: 0335097081*. Bibliography: *p.199-200*.
290 Lifetime smoking patterns — a transition probability analysis. Frank T. Denton; Byron G. Spencer; Deborah A. Welland. **Socio. Econ.** 27:3 9:1993 pp.181 - 198.
291 Macierz rachunkowości społecznej (SAM) jako baza statystyczna dla analiz makroekonomicznych. *[In Polish]*; (Social accounting matrix (SAM) as a statistical basis for macroeconomic analysis.) Łucja Tomaszewicz. **Stud. Praw-Ekon.** XLVII 1993 pp.99 - 108.
292 The measurement of social well-being. James S. Larson. **Soc. Ind.** 28:3 3:1993 pp.285 - 296.
293 Methodological issues in labour economics — procedures for procedural rationality? Gianni Zappalà. **Labour [Italy]** 7:1 Spring:1993 pp.209 - 231.
294 Multivariate analysis of categorical data. Vol.2. Applications. John P. Van De Geer. Newbury Park: Sage Publications, 1993. 124p. *ISBN: 0803945647*. *(Series: Advanced quantitative techniques in the social sciences)*.

B: Theory and methodology

295 Naukometricheskii analiz struktury sotsiologicheskogo znaniia. *[In Russian]*; (Sciencemetrical analysis of sociological knowledge.) A.V. Kabyshcha; M.R. Tul'chinskii. **Sot. Issle.** 4 1993 pp.38 - 45.
296 A new theory of nested decision processes with memory. Part I — the stochastic framework. Günter Haag; Kathrin Grützmann. **Pap. Reg. Sci.** 72:3 7:1993 pp.313 - 335.
297 A note on idealist models in social science. B. Malmberg. **Geog.ann. B.** 74:2 1992 pp.117 - 123.
298 Notions of position in social network analysis. Stephen P. Borgatti; Martin G. Everett. **Soc. Method.** 22 1992 pp.1 - 35.
299 On the large-sample estimation of regression models with spatial- or network-effects terms — a two-stage least squares approach. Kenneth C. Land; Glenn Deane. **Soc. Method.** 22 1992 pp.221 - 248.
300 On the reliability of meta-analytic reviews — the role of intercoder agreement. William H. Yeaton; Paul M. Wortman. **Eval. Rev.** 17:3 6:1993 pp.292 - 309.
301 The outbreak of cooperation. Natalie S. Glance; Bernardo A. Huberman. **J. Math. Sociol.** 17:4 1993 pp.281 - 302.
302 A permanent etcetera: cross-cultural perspectives on post-war America. Arthur Robert Lee [Ed.]. London: Pluto Press, 1993. viii,199p. *ISBN: 0745306403, 0745306411.* Includes bibliographical references and index.
303 Problema empiricheskogo izmereniia sotsialynoi stratifikatsii i sotsial'noi mobil'nosti. *[In Russian]*; (The problem of empirical measurement of social stratification and social mobility.) V.F. Anurin. **Sot. Issle.** 4 1993 pp.87 - 96.
304 Properties of a latent trait reliability coefficient. David J. Bartholomew; Edward L. Bassin; Karl F. Schuessler. **Sociol. Meth.** 22:2 11:1993 pp.163 - 192.
305 A proportional rewards game — competition among heterogeneous actors. Jeroen Weesie; Albert Verbeek. **J. Math. Sociol.** 17:4 1993 pp.261 - 179.
306 Qualitative data analysis: a user-friendly guide for social scientists. Ian Dey. London, New York, NY: Routledge, 1993. 285p. *ISBN: 0415058511, 041505852X.* Includes bibliographical references and index.
307 Regional subcultures of the United States. Joel Lieske. **J. Polit.** 55:4 11:1993 pp.888 - 913.
308 Regression with dummy variables. Melissa A. Hardy. Newbury Park, Calif: Sage Publications, 1993. vi, 90p. *ISBN: 0803951280, 0803951280.* Includes bibliographical references. (*Series:* Quantitative applications in the social sciences).
309 Review — actual trends or measurement artifacts? A review of three studies of anti-semitism. Tom W. Smith. **Publ. Opin. Q.** 57:3 Fall:1993 pp.380 - 393.
310 Sdvig v tsennostnom izmerenii? *[In Russian]*; (The change in axiological measurement?). A.P. Vardomatskii. **Sot. Issle.** 4 1993 pp.46 - 55.
311 Sinergetika: nachala nelineinogo myshleniia. *[In Russian]*; (Synergetics: principles of non-linear thinking.) E. Kniazeva; S. Kurdiumov. **Obshch. Nauki Sovrem.** 2 1993 pp.38 - 51.
312 Sociologie, classement et quantification. *[In French]*; [Sociology, classification and quantitative analysis] *[Summary]*. Gabriel Gosselin. **Cah. Int. Soc.** XCIII 7-12:1992 pp.321 - 337.
313 Some aspects of qualitative data analysis. G. Herden. **Math. Soc. Sc.** 26:2 9:1993 pp.105 - 138.

314 Spatial and temporal heterogeneity in diffusion. David Strang; Nancy Brandon Tuma. **A.J.S.** 99:3 11:1993 pp.614 - 639.
315 Statistical indicators for the economic & social sciences. Robert Victor Horn. Cambridge, New York: Cambridge University Press, 1993. xii, 227p. *ISBN: 0521413338, 0521413338, 0521423996. Includes bibliographical references (p. 208-219) and index.*
316 "Structure"/"action" contingencies and the model of parallel distributed processing. Loet Leydesdorff. **J. Theory Soc. Behav.** 23:1 3:1993 pp.47 - 77.
317 Suicide attempts and signalling games. R.W. Rosenthal. **Math. Soc. Sc.** 26:1 1993 pp.25 - 33.
318 Two algorithms for computing regular equivalence. Stephen P. Borgatti; Martin G. Everett. **Soc. Networks** 15:4 12:1993 pp.361 - 376.
319 Understanding regression assumptions. William D. Berry. Newbury Park, Calif: Sage Publications, 1993. vii, 90p. *ISBN: 080394263X, 080394263X. Includes bibliographical references. (Series:* Quantitative applications in the social sciences).
320 The use of grade-of-membership techniques to estimate regression relationships. Kenneth G. Manton; Max A. Woodbury; Eric Stallard; Larry S. Corder. **Soc. Method.** 22 1992 pp.321 - 381.
321 Using DEA to evaluate the state of society as measured by multiple social indicators. Akihiro Hashimoto; Hitoshi Ishikawa. **Socio. Econ.** 27:4 1993 pp.257 - 268.
322 Verschiedene Verfahren — verschiedene Ergebnisse? Vergleich der Skalierungsverfahren nach Rasch und Mokken sowie der klassischen Testkonstruktion am Beispiel alltagsästhetischer Schemata. *[In German];* (Different scaling models — different findings? A comparison of the models according to Rasch and Mokken as well as the classical test construction illustrated using the example of aesthetic patterns in everyday life.) *[Summary].* Thomas Müller-Schneider. **Z. Soziol.** 22:5 10:1993 pp.371 - 384.
323 When will they ever learn that first derivatives identify the effects of continuous independent variables, or "officer, you can't give me a ticket, I wasn't speeding for an entire hour". Dennis W. Roncek. **Soc. Forc.** 71:4 6:1993 pp.1067 - 1078.

Data collection
Rassemblement des données

324 Analiza wiarygodności danych ankietowych w perspektywie porównawczej. *[In Polish];* (An analysis of questionnaire data reliability in comparative perspective.) Katarzyna M. Staszyńska. **Prz. Soc.** XL:2 1993 pp.49 - 64.
325 Befragung und Interview. Über soziale und soziologische Situationen der Informationssuche. *[In German];* (Interview and surveys on social and sociological situations of seeking information.) *[Summary].* Heiner Meulemann. **Soz. Welt.** 44:1 1993 pp.98 - 119.
326 Can you trust self-report data provided by homeless mentally ill individuals? Robert J. Calsyn; Gary Allen; Gary A. Morse; Ruth Smith; Betty Tempelhoff. **Eval. Rev.** 17:3 6:1993 pp.353 - 366.
327 Citizen surveys: how to do them, how to use them, what they mean : a special report on designing, conducting, and understanding citizen surveys. Thomas Miller;

B: Theory and methodology

Michelle A. Miller. Washington, D.C: International City Management Association, 1991. ix, 212p. *ISBN: 0873269209. Includes bibliographical references (p. [213]).* (*Series:* Special report / ICMA).

328 Constructing questions for interviews and questionnaires: theory and practice in social research. William Foddy. Cambridge, UK, New York, NY: Cambridge University Press, 1993. xii, 228p. *ISBN: 0521420091. Includes bibliographical references (p. 195-213) and index.*

329 Czy ankieta może zastąpić wywiad? *[In Polish]*; (Can a mailed questionnaire survey replace an interview questionnaire survey?). Franciszek Sztabiński. **Prz. Soc.** XL:2 1993 pp.163 - 172.

330 The discovery of grounded uncertainty — developing standardized questions about strength of fertility motivation. Nora Cate Schaeffer; Elizabeth Thomson. **Soc. Method.** 22 1992 pp.37 - 82.

331 The effect of interviewer characteristics on gatekeeper resistance in surveys of elite populations. Jennifer A. Parsons; Timothy P. Johnson; Richard B. Warnecke; Arnold Kaluzny. **Eval. Rev.** 17:2 4:1993 pp.131 - 143.

332 The effectiveness of using school children in samples and data collection. Chris Tobayiwa. **J. Soc. Devel. Afr.** 8:1 1993 pp.73 - 87.

333 Effects of spouse presence during the interview on survey responses concerning marriage. William S. Aquilino. **Publ. Opin. Q.** 57:3 Fall:1993 pp.358 - 376.

334 Estimating the effect of incentives on mail survey response rates — a meta-analysis. Allan H. Church. **Publ. Opin. Q.** 57:1 Spring:1993 pp.62 - 79.

335 Estimating the effect of nonignorable nonresponse in sample surveys — an application of Rubin's Bayesian method to the estimation of community standards for obscenity. Kenneth C. Land; Patricia L. McCall. **Sociol. Meth.** 21:3 2:1993 pp.291 - 316.

336 Fältarbete, intervju och text. *[In Swedish]*; (Fieldwork, interviews and field notes.) Lena Gerholm. **Nord. Ny.** 52 1993 pp.15 - 19.

337 Field research on human service encounters — diverse solutions to some common problems. J. William Spencer. **Sociol. Meth.** 21:3 2:1993 pp.372 - 393.

338 Homage to Erwin K. Scheuch. Stein Rokkan [Contrib.]; Sidney Verba [Contrib.]; Erwin K. Schcuch [Contrib.]; Alexander Szalai [Contrib.]. **Hist. Soc. R.** 18:66 2:1993 pp.6 - 195. *Collection of 5 articles.*

339 The importance of researcher's gender in the in-depth interview — evidence from two case studies of male nurses. Christine L. Williams; E. Joel Heikes. **Gender Soc.** 7:2 6:1993 pp.280 - 291.

340 Improving organizational surveys — new directions and methods. Paul Rosenfeld [Ed.]; Jack E. Edwards [Ed.]; Marie D. Thomas [Ed.]; Jamshid C. Hosseini [Contrib.]; Robert L. Armacost [Contrib.]; Solomon Dutka [Contrib.]; Lester R. Frankel [Contrib.]; Stephanie Booth-Kewley [Contrib.]; Richard A. Dunnington [Contrib.]; Gary W. Morris [Contrib.]; Mark A. LoVerde [Contrib.]. **Am. Behav. Sc.** 36:4 3-4:1993 pp.414 - 550.

341 Information transmission in the survey interview — number of response categories and the reliability of attitude measurement. Duane F. Alwin. **Soc. Method.** 22 1992 pp.83 - 118.

342 Interviewer gender and gender attitudes. Emily W. Kane; Laura J. Macauley. **Publ. Opin. Q.** 57:1 Spring:1993 pp.1 - 28.

B: Théorie et méthodologie

343 Manufacturing establishments reclassified into new industries — the effect of survey design rules. R.H. McGuckin; S. Peck. **J. Econ. Soc.** 19:2 1993 pp.121 - 139.

344 Metodologiczne problemy badania opinii publicznej w Polsce — społeczna przestrzeń wywiadu kwestionariuszowego. *[In Polish]*; (Methodological problems of studying public opinion in Poland — social context of questionnaire surveys.) Anna Kubiak; Włodzimierz A. Rostocki. **Prz. Soc.** XL:2 1993 pp.81 - 102.

345 No-opinion filters and attitude measurement reliability. McKee J. McClendon; Duane F. Alwin. **Sociol. Meth.** 21:4 5:1993 pp.438 - 464.

346 Osobennosti raboty interv'iuerov pri telefonnykh oprosakh. *[In Russian]*; (The pecularities of interviewer's work during the telephone interrogatories.) T.L. Statsevich. **Sot. Issle.** 7 1993 pp.83 - 88.

347 Polscy respondenci lat osiemdziesiątych. *[In Polish]*; (Polish respondents in the 1980s.) Krystyna Lutyńska. **Prz. Soc.** XL:2 1993 pp.29 - 48.

348 Pytanie i rozmowa. *[In Polish]*; (A question and talk.) Kazimierz Kowalewicz. **Prz. Soc.** XL:2 1993 pp.179 - 186.

349 Questions et réponses: Quelques résultats sur les effets de la formulation des questions dans les sondages. *[In French]*; (Questions and answers: some experiments on the wording of questions in surveys.) *[Summary]*. Jean-Paul Grémy. **Soc. Contemp.** 16 12:1993 pp.165 - 176.

350 Rzetelność wyników badań kwestionariuszowych. Dwa metodologiczne eksperymenty. *[In Polish]*; (Reliability of questionnaire surveys data. Two methodological experiments.) Eugeniusz Śmiłowski; Zbigniew Sawiński. **Prz. Soc.** XL:2 1993 pp.65 - 80.

351 A simple questionnaire survey method for studying migration and residential displacement in informal settlements in South Africa. Owen Crankshaw. **S.Afr. Sociol. R.** 6:1 10:1993 pp.52 - 65.

352 The social relations of intensive interviewing — constellations of strangeness and science. Shirley Harkess; Carol A.B. Warren. **Sociol. Meth.** 21:3 2:1993 pp.317 - 339.

353 Strategies in eliciting sensitive sexual information — the case of gay men. Anthony P.M. Coxon; P.M. Davies; A.J. Hunt; T.J. McManus; C.M. Rees; P. Weatherburn. **Sociol. Rev.** 41:3 8:1993 pp.537 - 555.

354 Tracking and follow-up methods for research on homelessness. Evan H. Cohen; Carol T. Mowbray; Deborah Bybee; Susan Yeich; Kurt Ribisl; Paul P. Freddolino. **Eval. Rev.** 17:3 6:1993 pp.331 - 352.

355 Veränderungen von Zufriedenheitsangaben in Panelbefragungen. Eine Analyse über nicht beabsichtigte Effekte des Längsschnittdesigns. *[In German]*; (Changes in replies to questions about satisfaction in panel surveys. An analysis of non-intentional effects of the longitudinal design.) *[Summary]*. Detlev Landua. **Kölner Z. Soz. Soz. psy.** 45:3 9:1993 pp.553 - 571.

356 Verlust der Repräsentativität durch mangelnde Zentralität — ein Instrumentenexperiment. *[In German]*; (Loss of representativity through insufficient centrality.) *[Summary]*. Peter Atteslander; Udo von Fürstenau; Andrea Maurer. **Soz. Welt.** 44:3 1993 pp.420 - 439.

357 When total randomization is impossible — nested randomized assignment. D. Paul Moberg; Douglas L. Piper; Jiyuan Wu; Ronald C. Serlin. **Eval. Rev.** 17:3 6:1993 pp.271 - 291.

B: Theory and methodology

358 "Who wears the trousers?" Sexual harassment in research settings. Gill Green; Rosaline S. Barbour; Marina Barnard; Jenny Kitzinger. **Wom. St. Inter. For.** 16:6 11-12:1993 pp.627 - 637.
359 Wywiad kwestionariuszowy a logika konwersacji. O pracach Norberta Schwarza. *[In Polish]*; [Interview questionnaires and the logic of conversation. On the research of Norbert Schwarz]. Andrzej P. Wejland. **Prz. Soc.** XLII 1993 pp.31 - 48.
360 Wywiad środowiskowy. Funkcje ukryte, założone i realizowane. *[In Polish]*; (Environmental interview. Hidden, complex and accomplished functions.) Janina Tobera. **Prz. Soc.** XL:2 1993 pp.187 - 200.

C: INDIVIDUALS. GROUPS. ORGANIZATIONS
INDIVIDUS. GROUPES. ORGANISATIONS

C.1: Psychology and social psychology
Psychologie et psychologie sociale

361 Addressing psychology's problems with race. Albert H. Yee; Halford H. Fairchild; Frederic Weizman; Gail E. Wyatt. **Am. Psychol.** 48:11 11:1993 pp.1132 - 1140.

362 Advances in experimental social psychology. Vol.25. Mark P. Zanna [Ed.]. San Diego: Academic Press, 1992. ix, 397p. *ISBN: 0120152258.*

363 Analogue versus clinical depression — a critical reappraisal. Karel Vredenburg; Gordon L. Flett; Lester Krames. **Psychol . B.** 113:2 3:1993 pp.327 - 344.

364 Beyond selecting information — biases in spontaneous questions and resultant conclusions. Holley S. Hodgins; Miron Zuckerman. **J. Exp. S. Psychol.** 29:5 9:1993 pp.387 - 407.

365 Changing behavior and making it stick — the conceptualization and management of conservation behavior. Raymond De Young. **Envir. Behav.** 25:4 7:1993 pp.485 - 505.

366 Cognitive psychology and the rejection of Brentano. John Macnamara. **J. Theory Soc. Behav.** 23:2 6:1993 pp.117 - 137.

367 The cognizer's innards: a psychological and philosophical perspective on the development of thought. Andy Clark; Annette Karmiloff-Smith. **Mind Lang.** 8:4 Winter:1993 pp.487 - 519.

368 The common mind: an essay on psychology, society, and politics. Philip Pettit. New York: Oxford University Press, 1993. xvi, 365p. *ISBN: 0195078187. Includes bibliographical references and index.*

369 Community psychology: theory and practice. Jim Orford. Chichester: John Wiley, 1992. viii, 292p. *ISBN: 047191147X.*

370 Comparative cognition — beginning the second century of the study of animal intelligence. E.A. Wasserman. **Psychol . B.** 113:2 3:1993 pp.211 - 228.

371 Criminal defendants with psychiatric impairment — prevalence, probabilities and rates. Ellen Hochstedler Steury. **J. Crim. Law Criminol.** 84:2 Summer:1993 pp.352 - 376.

372 Cultural psychology: who needs it? Richard A. Shweder; Maria A. Sullivan. **Ann. R. Psych.** 44 1993 pp.497 - 524.

373 Defence and safety — their function in social behaviour and psychopathology. Paul Gilbert. **Br. J. Clin. Psycho.** 32:2 5:1993 pp.131 - 154.

374 Eliminativism. Barbara Hannan; Lynne Rudder Baker; Radu J. Bogdan; Keith Campbell; Paul M. Churchland; Andy Clark; Adrian Cussins; Elizabeth Fricker; Terence Horgan; Frank Jackson; Philip Pettit; Kim Sterelny; Crispin Wright. **Mind Lang.** 8:2 Summer:1993 pp.163 - 326. *Collection of 13 articles.*

375 A field study of social comparison processes in ability evaluation. Margaret Foddy; Ian Crundall. **Br. J. Soc. P.** 32:4 12:1993 pp.287 - 305.

376 Flexible production systems and the social construction of trust. Edward H. Lorenz. **Polit. Soc.** 21:3 9:1993 pp.307 - 324.

377 Freud and Jung — the implications of psychological theory. Alexander Jacob. **Mankind Q.** xxxiii:4 Summer:1993 pp.379 - 408.

C: Individuals. Groups. Organizations

378 From colonial to liberation psychology: the Philippine experience. Virgilio G. Enriquez. Diliman, Quezon City: University of the Philippines Press; University of Hawii Press, 1992. xvi, 169p. *ISBN: 9715420028. Includes bibliographical references (p. 129-150) and index.*

379 Gender issues in clinical psychology. Jane M. Ussher [Ed.]; Paula Nicholson [Ed.]. New York; London: Routledge, 1992. x, 245p. *ISBN: 0415054850. Includes bibliographical references and indexes.*

380 The hegemony of discontent. D. Linger. **Am. Ethn.** 20:1 2:1993 pp.3 - 24.

381 A history of the mind. Nicholas Humphrey. London: Chatto & Windus, 1992. xvii, 230p. *ISBN: 0701139951. Includes index.*

382 Human reasoning: psychology of deduction. Jonathan St.B. T. Evans; Stephen E. Newstead; Ruth M. J. Byrne. Hove, East Sussex: Lawrence Erlbaum, 1993. 310p. *ISBN: 0863773133.*

383 Indigenisation of psychological measurement — parameters and operationalisation. Fakir M. Sahoo. **Psychol. Devel. Soc.** 5:1 1-6:1993 pp.1 - 13.

384 The influence of message framing on intentions to perform health behaviors. Alexander J. Rothman; Peter Salovey; Carol Antone; Kelli Keough; Chloé Drake Martin. **J. Exp. S. Psychol.** 29:5 9:1993 pp.408 - 433.

385 Information processing models: microscopes of the mind. Dominic W. Massaro; Nelson Cowan. **Ann. R. Psych.** 44 1993 pp.383 - 426.

386 The informative functions of research procedures — bias and the logic of conversation. H. Bless; F. Strack; N. Schwarz. **Eur. J. Soc. Psychol.** 23:2 3-4:1993 pp.149 - 165.

387 Integrating knowledge of vertically aligned large-scale spaces. Daniel R. Montello; Herbert L. Pick. **Envir. Behav.** 25:4 7:1993 pp.457 - 484.

388 Intelligence, previous convictions and interrogative suggestibility — a path analysis of alleged false-confession cases. Robert Sharrock; Gisli H. Gudjonsson. **Br. J. Clin. Psycho.** 32:2 5:1993 pp.169 - 175.

389 James Mark Baldwin — a bridge between social and cognitive theories of development. Patricia E. Kahlbaugh. **J. Theory Soc. Behav.** 23:1 3:1993 pp.79 - 103.

390 "Just because I'm paranoid doesn't mean they're not out to get me". David Pimm. **Interchange** 24:4 1993 pp.435 - 442.

391 Measuring locus of control — a critique of general, children's health- and work-related locus of control questionnaires. Adrian Furnham; Howard Steele. **Br. J. Psy.** 84:4 11:1993 pp.443 - 479.

392 The mental simulation of better and worse possible worlds. Keith D. Markman; Igor Gavanski; Steven J. Sherman; Matthew N. McMullen. **J. Exp. S. Psychol.** 29:1 1:1993 pp.87 - 109.

393 Personality and nonverbal social behavior — an ethological perspective of relationship initiation. Jeffry A. Simpson; Steven W. Gangestad; Michael Biek. **J. Exp. S. Psychol.** 29:5 9:1993 pp.434 - 461.

394 Les peurs françaises. *[In French]*; [The fears of the French]. Alain Duhamel. Paris: Flammarion, 1993. 276p. *ISBN: 2080665863.*

395 Pre- and post-impact pain and suffering and mental anguish in aviation accidents. Louisa Ann Collins. **J. Air Law Comm.** 59:2 12-1:1993-1994 pp.403 - 448.

396 Prison group therapy with mentally and emotionally disturbed offenders. Edward M. Scott. **Int. J. Offen.** 37:2 Summer:1993 pp.131 - 145.

397 The problem of religion for constructivist psychology. Bill Warren. **J. Psychol.** 127:5 9:1993 pp.481 - 488.

C: Individus. Groupes. Organisations

398 Psychiatry and ethics — the problematics of respect for religious meanings. Stephen G. Post. **Cult. Medic. Psych.** 17:3 9:1993 pp.363 - 383.

399 Psychological dimensions of aging in India. P.V. Ramamurti; D. Jamuna. **Ind. J. Soc. Sci.** 6:4 10-12:1993 pp.309 - 332.

400 Psychological issues in crisis management. T.C. Pauchant [Contrib.]; C. Dejours [Contrib.]; E.M. Morin [Contrib.]; A.H. Reilly [Contrib.]; P.E. Hodgkinson [Contrib.]; M. Stewart [Contrib.]. **Indust. Environ. Crisis** 7:2 1993 pp.73 - 154. *Collection of 5 articles.*

401 Psychological perspectives on justice: theory and applications. Barbara A. Mellers [Ed.]; Jonathan Baron [Ed.]. Cambridge: Cambridge University Press, 1993. x, 348p. *ISBN: 0521431999. Includes bibliographical references and indexes. (Series:* Cambridge series on judgement and decision making).

402 Psychological research in developing countries — progress, problems and prospects. Mark R. Rosenzweig [Ed.]; Terezinha Nunes [Contrib.]; Jai B.P. Sinha [Contrib.]; Zhong-Ming Wang [Contrib.]; A. Bame Nsamenang [Contrib.]; Graciela Rodriguez Ortega [Contrib.]; Mario E. Rojas Russell [Contrib.]; Çiğdem Kağitçibaşi [Comments by]. **Psychol. Devel. Soc.** 5:2 7-12:1993 pp.123 - 204. *Collection of 5 articles.*

403 Psychological research on the Persian Gulf War. Darrin R. Lehman [Ed.]; Jessica Wolfe [Contrib.]; Pamela J. Brown [Contrib.]; John M. Kelley [Contrib.]; Patricia B. Sutker [Contrib.]; Madeline Uddo [Contrib.]; Kevin Brailey [Contrib.]; Albert N. Allain [Contrib.]; Charles R. Figley [Contrib.]; Julian D. Ford [Contrib.]; David Shaw [Contrib.]; Shirley Sennhauser [Contrib.]; David Greaves [Contrib.]; Barbara Thacker [Contrib.]; Patricia Chandler [Contrib.]; Lawrence Schwartz [Contrib.]; Valerie McClain [Contrib.]; Norman (Noach) Milgram [Contrib.]; James W. Pennebaker [Contrib.]; Kent Harber [Contrib.]; Barbara A. Spellman [Contrib.]; Jodie B. Ullman [Contrib.]; Keith J. Holyoak [Contrib.]; Jon A. Krosnick [Contrib.]; Laura A. Brannon [Contrib.]; Peter Suedfeld [Contrib.]; Michael D. Wallace [Contrib.]; Kimberly L. Thachuk [Contrib.]; David R. Mandel [Contrib.]; Lawrence J. Axelrod [Contrib.]. **J. Soc. Issues** 49:4 1993 pp.1 - 215. *Collection of 11 articles.*

404 La psychologie sociale et ses histoires. *[In French]*; (Social psychology and its histories.) Ian Lubek; Erika Apfelbaum; Henri Paicheler; Serge Moscovici; Mel van Elteren; Eric Haas; Alain Giami; Miho Hotta; Henry L. Minton; Robert Pagès; Odile Vacher; Gregory McGuire; Emmanuel Lazinier; Jacqueline Carroy; Maria Donzelli; Dominique Reynié; José Romay Martinez; Jacqueline Gateaux-Mennecier; Gary Collier; Laurent Lavoie; Gisèle Lavoie; Geneviéve Vermés; Françoise Sellier; Annick Ohayon; Jean-Marie Seca; Gilles Lecocq; Marie-Louise Pellegrin; Ariel Cordier. **Soc. Contemp.** 13 3:1993 pp.13 - 212. *Collection of 22 articles.*

405 Psychology and logic: an evolutionary perspective. Ben Goertzel. **J. Soc. Evol. Sys.** 16:4 1993 pp.439 - 457.

406 Psychology and social action psychological research in the process of social change — a contribution to community development. Hilde van Vlaenderen. **Psychol. Devel. Soc.** 5:1 1-6:1993 pp.95 - 110.

407 Psychology and social issues: a tutorial text. Raymond Cochrane [Ed.]; Douglas Carroll [Ed.]. London: Falmer, 1991. 227p. *ISBN: 1850008353. (Series:* Contemporary psychology series).

C: Individuals. Groups. Organizations

408 The quantitative analysis of social representations. Willem Doise; Alain Clémence; Fabio Lorenzi-Cioldi. New York, London: Harvester-Wheatsheaf, 1993. 165p. *ISBN: 0745013481*. (*Series:* European monographs in social psychology).

409 Radio psychology — a comparison of listeners and non-listeners. A. Raviv. **J. Comm. App. Soc. Psychol.** 3:3 8:1993 pp.197 - 212.

410 Seldom seen, rarely heard: women's place in psychology. Janis S. Bohan [Ed.]. Boulder: Westview Press, 1992. xiv, 459p. *ISBN: 0813313945*. *Includes bibliographical references*. (*Series:* Psychology, gender, and theory).

411 Side effects of chronic lithium therapy in Hong Kong Chinese — an ethnopsychiatric perspective. Sing Lee. **Cult. Medic. Psych.** 17:3 9:1993 pp.301 - 320.

412 Slot rattling from law enforcement to lawbreaking: a personal construct theory exploration of police stress. David A. Winter. **Int. J. Pers. Constr. Psych.** 6:3 1993 pp.253 - 268.

413 The social engagement of social science: a Tavistock anthology. Vol. 2. The socio-technical perspective. Eric Lansdown Trist [Ed.]; Hugh Murray [Ed.]. Philadelphia: Pennsylvania University Press, 1993. 695p. *ISBN: 0812281934*. *Tavistock Institute of Human Relations*.

414 Social facilitation. Bernard Guérin. Cambridge, New York; Paris: Cambridge University Press; Editions de la Maison des sciences de l'homme, 1993. 244p. *ISBN: 052133358X*.

415 Social psychological approaches to health. Derek R. Rutter; Lyn Quine; David J. Chesham. Hemel Hempstead: Harvester Wheatsheaf, 1993. 268p. *ISBN: 0745011845*.

416 Social psychology across cultures: analysis and perspectives. Peter B. Smith; Michael Harris Bond. Hemel Hempstead: Harvester Wheatsheaf, 1993. 274p. *ISBN: 0745011713*.

417 The social psychology of prejudice. J. H. Duckitt. New York: Praeger, 1992. viii, 312p. *ISBN: 0275942414*. *Includes bibliographical references (p. [265]-301) and index*.

418 The societal subject. Niels Engelsted [Ed.]. Aarhus: Aarhus University Press, 1993. 296p. *ISBN. 8772881135*.

419 [Sociology of human suffering]; *[Text in Japanese]*. Katsutoshi Kirino. Kyoto: Sekaishiso-sha, 1993. 222p.

420 The Spanish translation and cultural adaptation of the Diagnostic Interview Schedule for Children (DISC) in Puerto Rico. Milagros Bravo; Michel Woodbury-Farina; Glorisa J. Canino; Maritza Rubio-Stipec. **Cult. Medic. Psych.** 17:3 9:1993 pp.329 - 344.

421 Statistics and the nature of depression. G. Dunn; P.C. Sham; D.J. Hand. **J. Roy. Stat. Soc. A.** 156:1 1993 pp.63 - 87.

422 Structural social psychology and the micro-macro problem. Edward J. Lawler; Cecelia Ridgeway; Barry Markovsky. **Sociol. Theory** 11:3 11:1993 pp.268 - 290.

423 The study of culture, ethnicity, and race in American psychology. Hector Betancourt; Steven Regeser López. **Am. Psychol.** 48:6 6:1993 pp.629 - 637.

424 Symbolic and other cognitive models of temporal reality. Janet L. Jackson; Aladin Akyürek; John A. Michon. **Time Soc.** 2:2 1993 pp.241 - 256.

425 Theory and clinical methods of psychotherapy during the 1991 Gulf War. Moshe Halevi Spero. **J. Soc. Work Pol. Israel** 7-8 1993 pp.57 - 88.

C: Individus. Groupes. Organisations

426 Toward a social psychology of science. Serge Moscovici. **J. Theory Soc. Behav.** 23:4 12:1993 pp.343 - 374.
427 Toward a social theory of psychiatric phenomena. Horacio Fabrega. **Behav. Sci.** 38:2 4:1993 pp.75 - 100.
428 Transforming social representations: a social psychology of common sense and science. Susan Caroline Purkhardt. London, New York: Routledge, 1993. 207p. *ISBN: 0415079608. Includes bibliographical references and index.*
429 The volunteer dilemma. J. Keith Murnighan; Jae Wook Kim; A. Richard Metzger. **Adm. Sci. Qua.** 38:4 12:1993 pp.515 - 538.
430 When warning succeeds — the effect of warning on success in ignoring invalid information. Yaacov Schul. **J. Exp. S. Psychol.** 29:1 1:1993 pp.42 - 62.
431 Working with Jewish ultra-orthodox patients — guidelines for a culturally sensitive therapy. Yoram Bilu; Eliezer Witztum. **Cult. Medic. Psych.** 17:2 6:1993 pp.197 - 233.

C.2: Individuals
Individus

432 An action assembly perspective on social skill. John O. Greene; Deanna Geddes. **Commun. Theory** 3:1 2:1993 pp.26 - 49.
433 Attachment styles, coping strategies, and posttraumatic psychological distress — the impact of the Gulf War in Israel. Mario Mikulincer; Victor Florian; Aron Weller. **J. Pers. Soc. Psychol.** 64:5 5:1993 pp.817 - 826.
434 Autonomic differentiation of temporal components of sexist humor. Mark Winkel. **Humor** 6:1 1993 pp.27 - 42.
435 Being and feeling unique — statistical deviance and psychological marginality. Deborrah E.S. Frable. **J. Personal.** 61:1 3:1993 pp.85 - 110.
436 Confidence — time and emotion in the sociology of action. J.M. Barbalet. **J. Theory Soc. Behav.** 23:3 9:1993 pp.229 - 247.
437 The context of anticipated performance evaluation, self-presentational motivation, and performance effort. Richard J. Palmer; Robert B. Welker; Robert Giacalone. **J. Psychol.** 127:2 3:1993 pp.179 - 193.
438 Convergent and discriminant validation of a children's life satisfaction scale — its relationship to self- and teacher-reported psychological problems and school functioning. E. Scott Huebner; Gary L. Alderman. **Soc. Ind.** 30:1 9:1993 pp.71 - 82.
439 Creative and critical thinking — reflections and applications. Berenice D. Bleedorn [Ed.]; Robert W. Clyde [Ed.]; Richard W. Paul [Contrib.]; David W. Johnson [Contrib.]; Roger T. Johnson [Contrib.]; Mark A. Runco [Contrib.]; Diane Montgomery [Contrib.]; Kay S. Bull [Contrib.]; Lynda Baloche [Contrib.]; Ron Jevning [Contrib.]; Mark C. Biedebach [Contrib.]; Sandra Menssen [Contrib.]; Jin Li [Contrib.]; Howard Gardner [Contrib.]; Thomas F. Morgan [Contrib.]; William M. Ammentorp [Contrib.]; Koos Toren [Contrib.]; Min Basadur [Contrib.]; Susan Robinson [Contrib.]; Luke Novelli [Contrib.]; Sylvester Taylor [Contrib.]; Bertil Johnsson [Contrib.]; Sharon Bailin [Contrib.]. **Am. Behav. Sc.** 37:1 9-10:1993 pp.10 - 164. *Collection of 14 articles.*

C: Individuals. Groups. Organizations

440 Differential fertility and the distribution of traits — the case of IQ. Samuel H. Preston; Cameron Campbell; James S. Coleman [Comments by]; David Lam [Comments by]. **A.J.S.** 98:5 3:1993 pp.997 - 1043.
441 The economic way of looking at behavior. Gary S. Becker. **J. Polit. Ec.** 101:3 6:1993 pp.385 - 409.
442 The effects of problem-solving ability and locus of control on prisoner adjustment. David N. Pugh. **Int. J. Offen.** 37:2 Summer:1993 pp.163 - 176.
443 Effects of the legitimacy of low group of individual status on individual and collective status-enhancement strategies. Naomi Ellemers; Henk Wilke; Ad van Knippenberg. **J. Pers. Soc. Psychol.** 64:5 5:1993 pp.766 - 778.
444 Farsi giustizia da sé: strategie di sopravvivenza e crisi della legalità. *[In Italian]*; (To make one's own justice: survival strategies and legality crisis.) *[Summary]*. Emanuele Sgroi. **Quad. Sociol.** XXXVII:4 1993 pp.4 - 41.
445 Folk concepts, natural language, and psychological constructs — the California psychological inventory and the five-factor model. Robert R. McCrae; Paul T. Costa; Ralph L. Piedmont. **J. Personal.** 61:1 3:1993 pp.1 - 26.
446 From pioneer to freier. The changing models of generalized exchange in Israel. Luis Roniger; Michael Feige. **Eur. J. Soc.** XXXIII:2 1992 pp.280 - 307.
447 From psychological stress to the emotions: a history of changing outlooks. R.S. Lazarus. **Ann. R. Psych.** 44 1993 pp.1 - 22.
448 Gorbachev and Lenin — psychological walls of the Soviet "garrison state". Alexander J. Groth; Stuart Britton. **Polit. Psych.** 14:4 12:1993 pp.627 - 650.
449 The grief process and job loss — a cross-sectional study. John Archer; Valerie Rhodes. **Br. J. Psy.** 84:3 8:1993 pp.395 - 410.
450 Humor and self-concept. Nicholas A. Kuiper; Rod A. Martin. **Humor** 6:3 1993 pp.251 - 270.
451 The humor phenomenon — a theoretical perspective. Micheal J. Lowis; John M. Nieuwoudt. **Mankind Q.** XXXIII:4 Summer:1993 pp.409 - 422.
452 Identity enactment in intellectual discussion. Karen Tracy; Jioanna Carjuzáa. **J. Lang. Soc. Psychol.** 12:3 9:1993 pp.171 - 134.
453 Il contributo di Pareto alla sociologia delle emozioni. *[In Italian]*; (Pareto's contribution to the sociology of emotions.) *[Summary]*. Antonio Mutti. **Rass. It. Soc.** XXXIII:4 12:1992 pp.465 - 488.
454 Il ruolo delle emozioni e dell'umorismo nella ricerca sociologica. Una lettura femminista di Gregory Bateson. *[In Italian]*; (The role of emotions and humour in sociological research.) M. Sclavi. **Critica Sociol.** 105 Spring:1993 pp.40 - 84.
455 Individualism versus collectivism: the concept of collective rights. Marlies Galenkamp. Oslo: Munch Museum, 1993. 249p. *ISBN: 9070116766*. (*Series:* Rotterdamse filosofische studies).
456 Intentional action and unconscious reasons. Fred Vollmer. **J. Theory Soc. Behav.** 23:3 9:1993 pp.315 - 326.
457 Interpersonal dependency and health service utilization in a college student sample. Robert F. Bornstein; Amy B. Krukonis; Kathleen A. Manning; Carla C. Mastrosimone; Stephanie C. Rossner. **J. Soc. Clin. Psychol.** 12:3 Fall:1993 pp.262 - 279.
458 The kingdom of individuals: an essay on self-respect and social obligation. Frederick George Bailey. Ithaca: Cornell University Press, 1993. xiii, 231p. *ISBN:*

C: Individus. Groupes. Organisations

0801428114. Includes bibliographical references (p. [219]-224) and index. (Series: Cornell paperbacks).
459 Laughter in Camus' The Stranger, The Fall, and The Renegade. Anne Greenfeld. **Humor** 6:4 1993 pp.403 - 414.
460 Life satisfaction — a study based on the organization of personal projects. Ünsal Yetoim. **Soc. Ind.** 29:3 7:1993 pp.277 - 289.
461 Logicheskaia kul'tura lichnosti i obshchestva. *[In Russian]*; (The logical culture of the individual and society.) V. Svintsov. **Obshch. Nauki Sovrem.** 4 1993 pp.114 - 125.
462 Loneliness and life satisfaction in Japan and Australia. John F. Schumaker; John D. Shea; Melissa M. Monfries; Gary Groth-Marnat. **J. Psychol.** 127:1 1:1993 pp.65 - 71.
463 Mechanisms of self-regulation: a systems view. Paul Karoly. **Ann. R. Psych.** 44 1993 pp.23 - 52.
464 Minority identity and self-esteem. J.R. Porter; R.E. Washington. **Ann. R. Soc.** 19 1993 pp.139 - 162.
465 The nature of humor appreciation — toward an integration of perception of stimulus properties and affective experience. Willibald Ruch; Sigrid Rath. **Humor** 6:4 1993 pp.363 - 384.
466 Nicht Autonomie, sondern Bastelbiographie. Anmerkungen zur Individualisierungsdiskussion am Beispiel des Aufsatzes von Günter Burkart. *[In German]*; (Not autonomy, but do-it-yourself biography. Notes on the debate on individualization, taking the article by Günter Burkart as an example.) *[Summary]*. Ulrich Beck; Elisabeth Beck-Gernsheim; Günter Burkart [Comments by]. **Z. Soziol.** 22:3 6:1993 pp.178 - 187.
467 On feeling, knowing, and valuing: selected writings. Max Scheler; Harold J. Bershady [Ed.]. Chicago: University of Chicago Press, 1992. vii, 270p. *ISBN: 0226736709, 0226736717. Includes bibliographical references (p. 261-262) and indexes. (Series:* The heritage of sociology).
468 Oral pessimism and depressive symptoms. Christopher Alan Lewis. **J. Psychol.** 127:3 5:1993 pp.335 - 343.
469 Organization and the mother archetype — a Jungian analysis of adult development and self-identity within the organization. Kaaren Hedblom Jacobson. **Admin. Soc.** 25:1 5:1993 pp.60 - 84.
470 Overvaluation of own attributes — mere ownership or subjective frequence? Vera Hoorens; Jozef M. Nuttin. **Soc. Cogn.** 11:2 Summer:1993 pp.177 - 200.
471 Preliminary validation of a multidimensional model of wittiness. Alan Feingold; Ronald Mazzella. **J. Personal.** 61:3 9:1993 pp.439 - 456.
472 The problem of equivalent models in applications of covariance structure analysis. Robert C. MacCallum; Duane T. Wegener; Bert N. Uchino; Leandre R. Fabrigar. **Psychol . B.** 114:1 7:1993 pp.185 - 199.
473 Psychoanalytic theory and loving God concepts — parent referencing versus self-referencing. John R. Buri; Rebecca A. Mueller. **J. Psychol.** 127:1 1:1993 pp.17 - 27.
474 Quality of life, health and happiness. Lennart Nordenfelt. Aldershot: Avebury, 1993. 182p. *ISBN: 1856285537.*
475 Reaction times and intelligence — a comparison of Chinese-American and Anglo-American children. Arthur R. Jensen; Patricia A. Whang. **J. Biosoc. Sc.** 25:3 7:1993 pp.397 - 410.

C: Individuals. Groups. Organizations

476 Reactive effects of concurrent verbalization in person perception tasks. G.H. Mumma; J.G. Draguns; R. Seibel. **Eur. J. Soc. Psychol.** 23:3 5-6:1993 pp.295 - 311.

477 [The relation between individuals and society: a critical comment on Luhmann's system theory]; *[Text in Japanese]*. Hiroshi Kanno. **Shak. Ken. Kiyo** 6 1993 pp.21 - 29.

478 Relationships between overall and life facet satisfaction — a multitrait-multimethod (MTMM) study. Charles E. Lance; Christopher E. Sloan. **Soc. Ind.** 30:1 9:1993 pp.1 - 15.

479 Repetition in canned jokes and spontaneous conversational joking. Neal R. Norrick. **Humor** 6:4 1993 pp.385 - 402.

480 Rethinking imagination: culture and creativity. Gillian Robinson [Ed.]; John F. Rundell [Ed.]. London, New York: Routledge, 1993. 192p. *ISBN: 0415091926, 0415091934. Chiefly papers presented at a conference, held in Melbourne, Australia, Aug. 4-8, 1991. Includes bibliographical references and index.*

481 The rhetoric of self-change — illness experience as narrative. Arthur W. Frank. **Sociol. Q.** 34:1 Spring:1993 pp.39 - 52.

482 Säkularisierung und Selbstthematisierung. Determinanten der biograpischen Selbsreflexion dreißigjäriger ehemaliger Gymnasiasten. *[In German]*; (Secularization and self-reflexion. Determinants of biographical self-evaluation of former German high-school students at the age of 30.) *[Summary]*. Heiner Meulemann; Klaus Birkelbach. **Kölner Z. Soz. Soz. psy.** 45:4 12:1993 pp.644 - 667.

483 Self-efficacy training to speed reemployment — helping people to help themselves. Dov Eden; Arie Aviram. **J. Appl. Psychol.** 78:3 6:1993 pp.352 - 360.

484 Self-identity and specific vulnerability to depressed mood. Britton W. Brewer. **J. Personal.** 61:3 9:1993 pp.343 - 364.

485 Self-monitoring and the regulation of socal experience — a control-process model. Rick H. Hoyle; Bruce A. Sowards. **J. Soc. Clin. Psychol.** 12:3 Fall:1993 pp.280 - 306.

486 Shared intention. Michael E. Bratman. **Ethics** 104:1 10:1993 pp.97 - 113.

487 Situational and personal variations in religious coping. Charles A. Schaefer; Richard L. Gorsuch. **J. Sci. S. Relig.** 32:2 6:1993 pp.136 - 147.

488 Social loafing — a meta-analytic review and theoretical integration. Steven J. Karau; Kipling D. Williams. **J. Pers. Soc. Psychol.** 65:4 10:1993 pp.681 - 706.

489 Sociological perspectives on life transitions. Linda K. George. **Ann. R. Soc.** 19 1993 pp.353 - 379.

490 The stigma of overweight — affective consequences of attributional ambiguity. Jennifer Crocker; Beth Cornwell; Brenda Major. **J. Pers. Soc. Psychol.** 64:1 1:1993 pp.60 - 70.

491 Stress and political leadership. Robert S. Robins; Robert M. Dorn. **Polit. Life** 12:1 2:1993 pp.3 - 17.

492 The "subject" of dreams. Paul Kugler. **Dreaming** 3:2 6:1993 pp.123 - 136.

493 Subjective well-being — the convergence and stability of self-report and non-self-report measures. Ed Sandvik; Ed Diener; Larry Seidlitz. **J. Personal.** 61:3 9:1993 pp.317 - 342.

494 The subjective-objective dimension in the individual-society connection — a duality perspective. Tim J. Juckes; John Barresi. **J. Theory Soc. Behav.** 23:2 6:1993 pp.197 - 216.

C: Individus. Groupes. Organisations

495 Taoism, Confucianism and the Chinese self. B. Morris. **Int. J. Moral Soc. S.** 8:3 Autumn:1993 pp.273 - 296.
496 Toward an empirical verification of the general theory of verbal humor. Willibald Ruch; Salvatore Attardo; Victor Raskin. **Humor** 6:2 1993 pp.123 - 136.
497 Understanding intelligence. Ken Richardson. Milton Keynes: Open University Press, 1991. 154p. *ISBN: 0335093981, 0335093973. Includes bibliographies and index.*
498 Varieties of developmental dyslexia. Ann Castles; et al. **Cognition** 47:2 5:1993 pp.149 - 180.
499 Women and self-help culture: reading between the lines. Wendy Simonds. New Brunswick, N.J: Rutgers University Press, 1992. x, 267p. *ISBN: 0813518334. Includes bibliographical references (p. [245]-257) and index.*
500 Zarys socjopsychologicznej koncepcji rozwoju tożsamości "Ja". Wprowadzenie. *[In Polish]*; [An outline of the socio-psychological and conceptual development of the identity of "I". Introduction.]. Andrzej Kaniowski [Tr.]; Rainer Döbner; Jürgen Habermas; Gertrud Nunner-Winkler. **Prz. Soc.** XLII 1993 pp.9 - 30.

Cognition
Cognition

501 3,2,1... We have cognition. Tom Scutt; Kieron O'Hara. **Mind Lang.** 8:4 Winter:1993 pp.559 - 568.
502 Children's learning difficulties: a cognitive approach. Julie Dockrell; John McShane. Oxford: Blackwell, 1993. 245p. *ISBN: 0631170162.*
503 Cognitive development: an information processing approach. John McShane. Oxford: Blackwell, 1991. ix, 394p. *ISBN: 0631170197. Bibliography: p.345-383. Includes index.*
504 Cognizers' innards and connectionist nets: a holy alliance? Adele Abrahamsen. **Mind Lang.** 8:4 Winter:1993 pp.520 - 530.
505 From rote learning to system building — acquiring verb morphology in children and connectionist nets. Kim Plunkett; Virginia Marchman. **Cognition** 48:1 7:1993 pp.21 - 69.
506 In search of the "hot" cognitions — attributions, appraisals, and their relation to emotion. Craig A. Smith; Kelly N. Haynes; Richard S. Lazarus; Lois K. Pope. **J. Pers. Soc. Psychol.** 65:5 11:1993 pp.916 - 929.
507 Learning and development in neural networks — the importance of starting small. Jeffrey L. Elman. **Cognition** 48:1 7:1993 pp.71 - 99.
508 Learning and labeling. Daniel C. Dennett. **Mind Lang.** 8:4 Winter:1993 pp.540 - 548.
509 Making nets work hard. Kim Plunkett. **Mind Lang.** 8:4 Winter:1993 pp.549 - 558.
510 The mental model theory of conditional reasoning — critical appraisal and revision. Jonathan St. B.T. Evans. **Cognition** 48:1 7:1993 pp.1 - 20.
511 Mood influences on health related judgements — appraisal of own health versus appraisal of unhealthy behaviours. A. Abele; P. Hermer. **Eur. J. Soc. Psychol.** 23:6 11-12:1993 pp.613 - 625.
512 The path beyond first-order connectionism. William Bechtel. **Mind Lang.** 8:4 Winter:1993 pp.531 - 539.

C: Individuals. Groups. Organizations

513 Philosophy and cognitive science. Christopher Hookway [Ed.]; Donald Peterson [Ed.]. Cambridge [Cambridgeshire], New York: Cambridge University Press, 1993. 236p. *ISBN: 0521457637*. *(Series:* Royal Institute of Philosophy lecture supplement).
514 Social causation and cognitive neuroscience. Grant R. Gillett. **J. Theory Soc. Behav.** 23:1 3:1993 pp.27 - 45.
515 Social foundations of cognition. John M. Levine; Lauren B. Resnick; E. Tory Higgins. **Ann. R. Psych.** 44 1993 pp.585 - 612.
516 Social value related response latencies — unobtrusive evidence for individual differences in information processing. F.M.J. Dehue; C.G. McClintock; W.B.G. Liebrand. **Eur. J. Soc. Psychol.** 23:3 5-6:1993 pp.273 - 293.
517 What's special about the development of the human mind/brain? Annette Karmiloff-Smith; Andy Clark. **Mind Lang.** 8:4 Winter:1993 pp.569 - 581.

Decision making
Prise de décision

518 The adaptive decision maker. John W. Payne; James R. Bettman; Eric J. Johnson. Cambridge: Cambridge University Press, 1993. xiii, 330p. *ISBN: 0521415055, 0521425263. Bibliography: p. 279-307. - Includes indexes.*
519 Complainant-respondent differences in procedural choice. Robert S. Peirce; Dean G. Pruitt; Sally J. Czaja. **Int. J. Confl. Manag.** 4:3 7:1993 pp.199 - 222.
520 Directional questions direct self-conceptions. Ziva Kunda; Geoffrey T. Fong; Rasyid Sanitioso; Emily Reber. **J. Exp. S. Psychol.** 29:1 1:1993 pp.63 - 86.
521 Framing, cognitive modes, and image theory — toward an understanding of a glass half full. Kenneth J. Dunegan. **J. Appl. Psychol.** 78:3 6:1993 pp.491 - 503.
522 [Generalization of the social dilemma models: on Umino's classification] *[Summary]; [Text in Japanese]*. Misumi Kazuto. **Rir. to ho.** 8:1 1993 pp.69 - 88.
523 Individual and group decision making: current issues. N. John Castellan [Ed.]. Hillsdale, N.J: L. Erlbaum, 1993. x, 315p. *Based on papers presented at the Science Weekend symposia of the 1990 convention of the American Psychological Association. Includes bibliographical references and index.*
524 Judging risk behaviour and risk preference — the role of the evaluative connotation of risk terms. E.C.M. van Schie; J. van der Pligt; K. van Baaren. **Eur. J. Soc. Psychol.** 23:6 11-12:1993 pp.597 - 611.
525 Making sense of the environment — the role of perceived effectiveness. Donald L. McCabe; Jane E. Dutton. **Human Relat.** 46:5 5:1993 pp.623 - 644.
526 On the evaluation of profability judgments — calibration, resolution and monotonicity. Varda Liberman; Amos Tversky. **Psychol . B.** 114:1 7:1993 pp.162 - 173.
527 Perceived participation in decision-making in a university setting — the impact of gender. Margaret Denton; Işik Urla Zeytinoğlu. **Ind. Lab. Rel.** 46:2 1:1993 pp.320 - 331.

C: Individus. Groupes. Organisations

Memory
Mémoire

528   Autobiographical remembering and self-composing. Craig R. Barclay; Thomas S. Smith. **Int. J. Pers. Constr. Psych.** 6:3 1993 pp.231 - 252.
529   Context, time, and memory retrieval in the interference paradigms of Pavlovian learning. Mark E. Bouton. **Psychol . B.** 114:1 7:1993 pp.80 - 99.
530   Early childhood memories — accuracy and affect. M. Howes; M. Siegel; F. Brown. **Cognition** 47:2 5:1993 pp.95 - 119.
531   Epilepsy and poor memory — who complains and what do they mean? Rhiannon Corcoran; Pamela Thompson. **Br. J. Clin. Psycho.** 32:2 5:1993 pp.199 - 208.
532   Human memory — a basis for better understanding the elusive self-concept. Paula S. Nurius. **Soc. Ser. R.** 67:2 6:1993 pp.261 - 278.
533   Implicit versus explicit impression formation — the differing effects of overt labelling and covert priming on memory and impressions. John J. Skowronski; Donal E. Carlston; Jean T. Isham. **J. Exp. S. Psychol.** 29:1 1:1993 pp.17 - 41.
534   Indirect expression of preference in sketch maps. Pennie S. Seibert; Linda J. Anooshian. **Envir. Behav.** 25:5 9:1993 pp.607 - 624.
535   Knowing and remembering in young children. Robyn Fivush [Ed.]; Judith A. Hudson [Ed.]. Cambridge: Cambridge University Press, 1990. 354p. *ISBN: 0521373255. Conference papers. Includes index. (Series:* Emory symposia in cognition).
536   "My wife knows best" — a comparison of event dating accuracy between the wife, the husband, the couple, and the Belgium population register. Nadia Auriat. **Publ. Opin. Q.** 57:2 Summer:1993 pp.165 - 190.
537   On resolving the enigma of infantile amnesia. Mark L. Howe; Mary L. Courage. **Psychol . B.** 113:2 3:1993 pp.305 - 326.
538   Patterns in the recall of persons in a student community. Devon D. Brewer. **Soc. Networks** 15:4 12:1993 pp.335 - 359.
539   The reality of repressed memories. Elizabeth F. Loftus. **Am. Psychol.** 48:5 5:1993 pp.518 - 537.
540   Rewriting the self: history, memory, narrative. Mark Philip Freeman. London, New York: Routledge, 1992. 249p. *ISBN: 041504197X, 0415041988. Includes bibliographical references and index. (Series:* Critical psychology).
541   Source monitoring. Marcia K. Johnson; Shahin Hashtroudi; D. Stephen Lindsay. **Psychol . B.** 114:1 7:1993 pp.3 - 28.
542   The structure and organization of memory. Larry R. Squire; B. Knowlton; G. Musen. **Ann. R. Psych.** 44 1993 pp.453 - 496.

Personality
Personnalité

543   Aiming at the top? Upward social comparison of abilities after failure. J.F. Ybema; B.P. Buunk. **Eur. J. Soc. Psychol.** 23:6 11-12:1993 pp.627 - 645.
544   Authoritarianism and sexual aggression. William D. Walker; Robert C. Rowe; Vernon L. Quinsey. **J. Pers. Soc. Psychol.** 65:5 11:1993 pp.1036 - 1045.

C: Individuals. Groups. Organizations

545 Authoritarianism, dominance, and social behavior — a perspective from evolutionary personality psychology. Robert D. Smither. **Human Relat.** 46:1 1:1993 pp.23 - 43.

546 Constructing personality tests to meet a structural criterion — application of the interpersonal circumplex. Michael B. Gurtman. **J. Personal.** 61:2 6:1993 pp.237 - 263.

547 Convergence of stranger ratings of personality and intelligence with self-ratings, partner ratings, and measured intelligence. Peter Borkenau; Anette Liebler. **J. Pers. Soc. Psychol.** 65:3 9:1993 pp.546 - 553.

548 Development of a scale measuring genetic variation related to expressive control. Steven W. Gangestad; Jeffry A. Simpson. **J. Personal.** 61:2 6:1993 pp.133 - 158.

549 Ego development and individual differences in personality. P. Michiel Westenberg; Jack Block. **J. Pers. Soc. Psychol.** 65:4 10:1993 pp.792 - 800.

550 An examination of the psychometric properties of measures of negative affect in the PANAS-X scales. Richard P. Bagozzi. **J. Pers. Soc. Psychol.** 65:4 10:1993 pp.836 - 851.

551 The factor structure of the personality research form — a cross-national evaluation. Heinrich Stumpf. **J. Personal.** 61:1 3:1993 pp.27 - 48.

552 A failure of nonshared environmental factors in predicting sibling personality differences. Tammy L. Mann. **J. Psychol.** 127:1 1:1993 pp.79 - 86.

553 Genetic and environmental; effects on openness to experience, agreeableness, and conscientiousness — an adoption/ twin study. C.S. Bergeman; Heather M. Chipuer; Robert Plomin; Nancy L. Pedersen; G.E. McClearn; John R. Nesselroade; Paul T. Costa; Robert R. McCrae. **J. Personal.** 61:2 6:1993 pp.159 - 179.

554 Heritability of interests — a twin study. D.T. Lykken; T.J. Bouchard; M. McGue; A. Tellegen. **J. Appl. Psychol.** 78:4 8:1993 pp.649 - 661.

555 A holistic view of personality: a model revisited. David Magnusson; Bertil Törestad. **Ann. R. Psych.** 44 1993 pp.427 - 452.

556 Individual differences and common dimensions in implicit personality theory. Roos Vonk. **Br. J. Soc. P.** 32:3 9:1993 pp.209 - 226.

557 The influence of personality and demographic variables on ethical decisions related to insider trading. David E. Terpstra; Elizabeth J. Rozell; Robert K. Robinson. **J. Psychol.** 127:4 7:1993 pp.375 - 389.

558 "Judgeable" people — personality, behavior, and competing explanations. C. Randall Colvin. **J. Pers. Soc. Psychol.** 64:5 5:1993 pp.861 - 873.

559 Lay inferences of personality traits — the role of behaviour prototypicality and between-trait differences. B. Wojciszke; R. Pienkowski; A. Maroszek; H. Brycz; M. Ratajczak. **Eur. J. Soc. Psychol.** 23:3 5-6:1993 pp.255 - 272.

560 Narcissism, interpersonal adjustment, and coping in children of Holocaust survivors. Lisa Baron; Marvin Reznikoff; David S. Glenwick. **J. Psychol.** 127:3 5:1993 pp.257 - 269.

561 Optimism, hardiness, and explanatory style as predictors of general well-being among attorneys. Mary E. Sweetman; David C. Munz; Robert J. Wheeler. **Soc. Ind.** 29:2 6:1993 pp.153 - 161.

562 Personality and foreign policy — the case of Stalin. Raymond Birt. **Polit. Psych.** 14:4 12:1993 pp.607 - 625.

563 Personality and self-efficacy as predictors of coping with abortion. Catherine Cozzarelli. **J. Pers. Soc. Psychol.** 65:6 12:1993 pp.1224 - 1236.

C: Individus. Groupes. Organisations

564 Personality and the structure of resource preferences. W. Stangl. **J. Econ. Psyc.** 14:1 3:1993 pp.1 - 15.
565 Power, affiliation, and war — three tests of a motivational model. David G. Winter. **J. Pers. Soc. Psychol.** 65:3 9:1993 pp.532 - 546.
566 Prognostic utility of subcomponents of the borderline personality construct in bulimia nervosa. Howard Steiger; Freedom Leung; Jean Thibaudeau; Lucie Houle. **Br. J. Clin. Psycho.** 32:2 5:1993 pp.187 - 197.
567 Psychometric evaluation of the Singer-Loomis inventory of personality. D.A. MacDonald; C.J. Holland. **J. Analyt. Psychol.** 38:3 7:1993 pp.303 - 320.
568 Relationship of childhood sexual abuse to borderline personality disorder, posttraumatic stress disorder, and multiple personality disorder. John B. Murray. **J. Psychol.** 127:6 11:1993 pp.657 - 676.
569 Repression and dissociation: implications for personality theory, psychopathology, and health. Jerome L. Singer [Ed.]; Sydney J. Blatt; Daniel A. Weinberger; Penelope J. Davis; Gary E. Schwartz; George A. Bonanno. Chicago: University of Chicago Press, 1990. xxiv, 512p. *ISBN: 0226761053. Includes bibliographical references and index. (Series:* The John D. and Catherine T. MacArthur Foundation series on mental health and development).
570 Sex differences in intensity of emotional experience — a social role interpretation. Michele Grossman; Wendy Wood. **J. Pers. Soc. Psychol.** 65:5 11:1993 pp.1010 - 1022.
571 Social phobia and the social egalitarian process. Wouter Gomperts. **Neth. J. Soc. Sci.** 29:1 6:1993 pp.3 - 27.
572 Stability of emotion experiences and their relations to traits of personality. Carroll E. Izard; Deborah Z. Libero; Priscilla Putnam. **J. Pers. Soc. Psychol.** 64:5 5:1993 pp.847 - 860.
573 Viewpoints on personality: consensus, self-other agreement, and accuracy in personality judgment. A.T. Panter; David C. Funder; Stephen G. West; Peter Borkenau; Anette Liebler; Diane S. Berry; Julia L. Finch Wero; Oliver P. John; Richard W. Robins; William F. Chaplin; William Ickes; C. Randall Colvin; Lee Jussim; Karina W. Davidson; Lew Bank; Terry Duncan; G.R. Patterson; John Reid; Alaina Kanfer; J.S. Tanaka; Daniel J. Ozer; Patrick E. Shrout; David A. Kenny. **J. Personal.** 61:4 12:1993 pp.457 - 807. *Collection of 15 articles.*

Self-concept
Conception de soi

574 Analyzing individual status and change with hierarchical linear models — illustration with depression in college students. Richard L. Tate; Jack E. Hokanson. **J. Personal.** 61:2 6:1993 pp.181 - 206.
575 Between a rock and a hard place — self-concept regulating and communicative properties of distancing behaviors. John H. Fleming; Laurie A. Rudman. **J. Pers. Soc. Psychol.** 64:1 1:1993 pp.44 - 59.
576 Birth order, self-concept, and participation in dangerous sports. Monica A. Seff; Viktor Gecas; James H. Frey. **J. Psychol.** 127:2 3:1993 pp.221 - 232.

C: Individuals. Groups. Organizations

577 Caught in the crossfire — depression, self-consistency, self-enhancement, and the response of others. Thomas E. Joiner; Mark S. Alfano; Gerald I. Metalsky. **J. Soc. Clin. Psychol.** 12:2 Summer:1993 pp.113 - 134.

578 Culture and body image — body perception and weight concern in young Asian and Caucasian British women. J. Wardle; R. Bindra; B. Fairclough; A. Westcombe. **J. Comm. App. Soc. Psychol.** 3:3 8:1993 pp.173 - 182.

579 Dependent and self-critical depressive experiences among inner-city adolescents. Suniya S. Luthar; Sidney J. Blatt. **J. Personal.** 61:3 9:1993 pp.365 - 386.

580 The divided self — concurrent and longitudinal effects of psychological adjustment and self-concept differentiation. Eileen M. Donahue; Richard W. Robins; Brent W. Roberts. **J. Pers. Soc. Psychol.** 64:5 5:1993 pp.834 - 846.

581 Effects of self-esteem on vulnerability-denying defensive distortions — further evidence of an anxiety-buffering function of self-esteem. Jeff Greenberg; Tom Pyszczynski; Sheldon Solomon; Elizabeth Pinel; Linda Simon; Krista Jordan. **J. Exp. S. Psychol.** 29:3 5:1993 pp.229 - 251.

582 Effects of social comparison direction, threat, and self-esteem on affect, self-evaluation, and expected success. Lisa G. Aspinwall; Shelley E. Taylor. **J. Pers. Soc. Psychol.** 64:5 5:1993 pp.708 - 722.

583 Enhancement of children's self-esteem through social support training for youth sport coaches. Frank L. Smoll; Ronald E. Smith; Nancy P. Barnett; John J. Everett. **J. Appl. Psychol.** 78:4 8:1993 pp.602 - 610.

584 Gaining and losing weight: identity transformations. Cliff English. **Dev. Beh.** 14:3 1993 pp.227 - 242.

585 Humor, coping with stress, self-concept, and psychological well-being. Rod A. Martin; Nicolas A. Kuiper; L. Joan Olinger; Kathryn A. Dance. **Humor** 6:1 1993 pp.89 - 104.

586 Identity, self, and personality — II. Glimpses through autophotographic eye. Stephen J. Dollinger; Stephanie M. Clancy. **J. Pers. Soc. Psychol.** 64:6 6:1993 pp.1064 - 1071.

587 The idiographic nature of human personality — examples of the idiographic self-concept. Brett W. Pelham. **J. Pers. Soc. Psychol.** 64:4 4:1993 pp.665 - 677.

588 Imaginal dialogues in the self — theory and method. Hubert J. M. Hermans; Trix I. Rijks; Harry J.G. Kempen. **J. Personal.** 61:2 6:1993 pp.207 - 236.

589 Masculinity, femininity, and male scientists' self-esteem and self-acceptance. Vonda O. Long. **J. Psychol.** 127:2 3:1993 pp.213 - 220.

590 Motivational similarity and interpersonal evaluations — the role of ambiguity, self-derogation, and emotion. Avi Assor; Roy Aldor. **J. Personal.** 61:1 3:1993 pp.111 - 1131.

591 Procedural fairness and self-esteem. G. Koper; D.V. Knippenberg; F. Bouhuijs; R. Vermunt; H. Wilke. **Eur. J. Soc. Psychol.** 23:3 5-6:1993 pp.313 - 325.

592 Relations between global and specific domains of self — the importance of individual importance, certainty, and ideals. Herbert W. Marsh. **J. Pers. Soc. Psychol.** 65:5 11:1993 pp.975 - 992.

593 The relationship of gender, self-esteem, and instrumentality to depressive symptomatology. Nancy Felipe Russo; Beth L. Green; George Knight. **J. Soc. Clin. Psychol.** 12:2 Summer:1993 pp.218 - 236.

C: Individus. Groupes. Organisations

594 Salience of rape affects self-esteem — the moderating role of gender and rape myth acceptance. G. Bohner; C. Weisbrod; P. Raymond; A. Barzvi; N. Schwarz. **Eur. J. Soc. Psychol.** 23:6 11-12:1993 pp.561 - 579.
595 Self-awareness, task failure, and disinhibition — how attentional focus affects eating. Todd F. Heatherton; Janet Polivy; C. Peter Herman; Roy F. Baumeister. **J. Personal.** 61:1 3:1993 pp.49 - 61.
596 Self-image resilience and dissonance — the role of affirmational resources. Claude M. Steele; Steven J. Spencer; Michael Lynch. **J. Pers. Soc. Psychol.** 64:6 6:1993 pp.885 - 896.
597 Strategy-dependent effects of reflecting on self and tasks — some implications of optimism and defensive pessimism. Julie K. Norem; K.S. Shaun Illingworth. **J. Pers. Soc. Psychol.** 65:4 10:1993 pp.822 - 835.
598 Using self-portrait photographs to understand self-concepts of Chinese and American university students. Keith Kenney. **Vis. Anthrop.** 5:3-4 1993 pp.245 - 269.
599 The utility of self-concept as a predictor of recidivism among juvenile offenders. Kevin. R. Byrd; Kevin O'Connor; Michael Thackrey; Joseph M. Sacks. **J. Psychol.** 127:2 3:1993 pp.195 - 201.
600 When ego threats lead to self-regulation failure — negative consequences of high self-esteem. Roy F. Baumeister; Todd F. Heatherton; Dianne M. Tice. **J. Pers. Soc. Psychol.** 64:1 1:1993 pp.141 - 156.

C.3: Interpersonal relations
Relations interpersonnelles

601 Adaptation in dyadic interaction — defining and operationalizing patterns of reciprocity and compensation. Judee K. Burgoon; Leesa Dillman; Lesa A. Stern. **Commun. Theory** 3:4 11:1993 pp.295 - 316.
602 Agreements, coercion, and obligation. Margaret Gilbert. **Ethics** 103:4 7:1993 pp.679 - 706.
603 Altruism. Thomas E. Hill [Contrib.]; Christine M. Korsgaard [Contrib.]; David Schmidtz [Contrib.]; Robert Sugden [Contrib.]; Neera Kapur Badhwar [Contrib.]; William A. Galston [Contrib.]; Jean Hampton [Contrib.]; Roderick T. Long [Contrib.]; Douglas J. Den Uyl [Contrib.]; Tyler Cowen [Contrib.]. **Soc. Philos. Pol.** 10:1 Winter:1993 pp.1 - 245. *Collection of 10 articles.*
604 Altruism. Barry Schwartz [Contrib.]; Robert Wuthnow [Contrib.]; Russell Hardin [Contrib.]; Partha Dasgupta [Contrib.]; Richard A. Epstein [Contrib.]; Jerome C. Wakefield [Contrib.]. **Soc. Ser. R.** 67:3 9:1993 pp.314 - 458. *Collection of 6 articles.*
605 Anthropology contra Heidegger part II: the limit of relationship. James F. Weiner. **Crit. Anthr.** 13:3 1993 pp.285 - 301.
606 Attractiveness, attentiveness, and perceived male shortage — their influence on perceptions of other females. Maryann Baenninger; Ronald Baenninger; Deanna Houle. **Ethol. Socio.** 14:5 1993 pp.293 - 303.
607 Attribution in conversational context — effect of mutual knowledge on explanation-giving. B.R. Slugoski; M. Lalljee; R. Lamb; G.P. Ginsburg. **Eur. J. Soc. Psychol.** 23:3 5-6:1993 pp.219 - 238.

C: Individuals. Groups. Organizations

608 Beyond personality impressions — effects of physical and vocal attractiveness on false consensus, social comparison, affiliation, and assumed and perceived similarity. Kunitate Miyake; Miron Zuckerman. **J. Personal.** 61:3 9:1993 pp.411 - 437.
609 Booing — the anatomy of a disaffiliative response. Steven E. Clayman. **Am. Sociol. R.** 58:1 2:1993 pp.110 - 130.
610 La civilité et la politesse — des objets « négligés » de la sociologie politique. *[In French]*; [Civility and courtesy — "neglected" topics in political sociology] *[Summary]*. Claudine Haroche. **Cah. Int. Soc.** XCIV 1-6:1993 pp.97 - 120.
611 A comparative study of relationship structure. Robert A. Hinde; Alison Tamplin; Jane Barrett. **Br. J. Soc. P.** 32:3 9:1993 pp.191 - 207.
612 The construction of social judgments. L.eonard L. Martin [Ed.]; Abraham Tesser [Ed.]. Hillsdale, N.J: Lawrence Erlbaum Associates, 1992. x, 358p. *ISBN: 0805811494. Includes bibliographical references and index.*
613 The contrast effect of physical attractiveness in Japan. Rotem Kowner; Toshiki Ogawa. **J. Psychol.** 127:1 1:1993 pp.51 - 64.
614 Control in dating relationships. Jan E. Stets. **J. Marriage Fam.** 55:3 8:1993 pp.673 - 685.
615 De-constructing concepts of care. Carol Thomas. **Sociology** 27:4 11:1993 pp.649 - 669.
616 Depressive symptoms and perceptions of child behavior. Charlotte Johnston; Kathryn H. Short. **J. Soc. Clin. Psychol.** 12:2 Summer:1993 pp.164 - 181.
617 Detection of deception — a transactional analysis perspective. Eitan Elaad. **J. Psychol.** 127:1 1:1993 pp.5 - 15.
618 Do friends perform better than acquaintances — the interaction of friendship, conflict, and task. Pri Pradham Shah; Karen A. Jehn. **Group Decis. Negot.** 2:2 6:1993 pp.149 - 165.
619 Do people know how others view them? An empirical and theoretical account. David A. Kenny; Bella M. DePaulo. **Psychol . B.** 114:1 7:1993 pp.145 - 161.
620 Do we tell less than we know or hear less than we are told? Exploring the teller-listener extremity effect. Mary L. Inman; Arleigh James Reichle; Robert S. Baron. **J. Exp. S. Psychol.** 29:6 11:1993 pp.528 - 550.
621 Dominance and friendliness — on the interaction of gender and situation. D.S. Moskowitz. **J. Personal.** 61:3 9:1993 pp.387 - 409.
622 The effect of priming causal dimensional categories on social judgments. Christopher W. Williams. **Soc. Cogn.** 11:2 Summer:1993 pp.223 - 242.
623 The effects of relationships and justification in an interdependent allocation task. Jeffrey T. Polzer; Margaret A. Neale; Patrick O. Glenn. **Group Decis. Negot.** 2:2 6:1993 pp.135 - 148.
624 Empirical approaches to social representations. Glynis M. Breakwell [Ed.]; David Canter [Ed.]. Oxford; New York: Clarendon Press; Oxford University Press, 1993. 344p. *ISBN: 0198521812. Includes bibliographical references.*
625 An empirical study of occupational stress transmission in working couples. Fiona Jones; Ben C. Fletcher. **Human Relat.** 46:7 7:1993 pp.881 - 903.
626 An epistemology of trust. T. Govier. **Int. J. Moral Soc. S.** 8:2 Summer:1993 pp.155 - 174.
627 The evolution of human altruism. Philip Kitcher. **J. Phil.** XC:10 10:1993 pp.497 - 516.

C: Individus. Groupes. Organisations

628 Exploring the effects of interacting with survivors of trauma. Gillian Straker. **J. Soc. Devel. Afr.** 8:2 1993 pp.33 - 47.
629 Family of origin influences on late adolescent romantic relationships. Mark J. Benson; Jeffry Larson; Stephan M. Wilson; David H. Demo. **J. Marriage Fam.** 55:3 8:1993 pp.663 - 672.
630 First names and perceptions of physical attractiveness. Philip G. Erwin. **J. Psychol.** 127:6 11:1993 pp.625 - 631.
631 Freundschaft, Alter und Geschlecht. *[In German]*; (Friendship, age, and gender.) *[Summary]*. Yvonne Schütze; Frieder R. Lang. **Z. Soziol.** 22:3 6:1993 pp.209 - 220.
632 From Al-Anon to ACOA — codependence and the reconstruction of caregiving. Janice Haaken. **Signs** 18:2 Winter:1993 pp.321 - 345.
633 Harmless lovers?: gender, theory, and personal relationships. Mike Gane. London, New York: Routledge, 1993. ix, 229p. *ISBN: 0415094488, 0415094496. Includes bibliographical references (p. [213]-222) and index.*
634 How individualists interpret behavior — idiocentrism and spontaneous trait inference. Leonard S. Newman. **Soc. Cogn.** 11:2 Summer:1993 pp.243 - 269.
635 How perceived control and congruent spouse support affect rheumatoid arthritis patients. John W. Reich; Alex J. Zautra; Sharon Manne. **J. Soc. Clin. Psychol.** 12:2 Summer:1993 pp.148 - 163.
636 If lions could speak — investigating the animal-human relationship and the perspectives of nonhuman others. Clinton R. Sanders; Arnold Arluke. **Sociol. Q.** 34:3 8:1993 pp.377 - 390.
637 Interpersonal communication. Peter Hartley. New York; London: Routledge, 1993. 215p. *ISBN: 0415013844, 0415013852. Includes bibliographical references and index.*
638 Interpersonal communication: evolving interpersonal relationships. Pamela J. Kalbfleisch [Ed.]. Hillsdale, NJ: Lawrence Erlbaum, 1993. xix, 302p. *ISBN: 0805812601, 0805812970. Includes bibliographical references and index.*
639 Interpersonal expectations: theory, research, and applications. Peter David Blanck [Ed.]. Cambridge: Cambridge University Press; Editions de la Maison des Sciences de l'Homme, 1993. xviii, 500p. *ISBN: 052141783X, 0521428327. Includes index.* (*Series:* Studies in emotion and social interaction).
640 Interpersonal networks and workplace controls in urban China. Danching Ruan. **Aust. J. Chin. Aff.** 29 1:1993 pp.89 - 105.
641 Interpreting behaviors in mixed-gender encounters — effects of social anxiety and gender. Robin M. Kowalski. **J. Soc. Clin. Psychol.** 12:3 Fall:1993 pp.239 - 247.
642 The jagged line between mediation and couples therapy. Michael Meltsner. **Negot. J.** 9:3 7:1993 pp.261 - 269.
643 The lens of personhood — viewing the self and others in a multicultural society. Daphna Oyserman. **J. Pers. Soc. Psychol.** 65:5 11:1993 pp.993 - 1009.
644 A longitudinal study of the early development of leader-member exchanges. Robert C. Liden; Sandy J. Wayne; Dean Stilwell. **J. Appl. Psychol.** 78:4 8:1993 pp.662 - 674.
645 Loyalty: an essay on the morality of relationships. George P. Fletcher. New York: Oxford University Press, 1993. xii, 211p. *ISBN: 0195070267. Includes bibliographical references (p. 177-202) and index.*
646 The meanings of miscarriage. Gayle Letherby. **Wom. St. Inter. For.** 16:2 3-4:1993 pp.165 - 180.

C: Individuals. Groups. Organizations

647 On human conduct. Michael Oakeshott. Oxford: Clarendon Press, 1991. 329p. *ISBN: 019827758X.*
648 Paternalism and friendship. Ellen L. Fox. **Can. J. Phil.** 23:4 12:1993 pp.575 - 594.
649 Peer evaluation in self-managing work groups. Richard Saavedra; Seog K. Kwun. **J. Appl. Psychol.** 78:3 6:1993 pp.450 - 462.
650 Perceived reciprocity, social support, and stress at work — the role of exchange and communual orientation. Bram P. Buunk; Bert Jan Doosje; Liesbeth G.J.M. Jans; Liliane E.M. Hopstaken. **J. Pers. Soc. Psychol.** 65:4 10:1993 pp.801 - 811.
651 Power and the emergence of commitment behavior in negotiated exchange. Edward J. Lawler; Yoon Jeongkoo. **Am. Sociol. R.** 58:4 8:1993 pp.465 - 481.
652 [The question who am I?: a methodology test of symbolic interactionism]; *[Text in Japanese].* Nobuyuki Takahashi. **Shak. Hyor.** 44(3) 1993 pp.16 - 30.
653 Reactions to individuals who are consistently positive or negative — the impact of differing interaction goals. Isaac Lipkus; Caryl Rusbult. **Human Relat.** 46:4 4:1993 pp.481 - 499.
654 Reciprocal justice and strategies of exchange. Linda D. Molm; Theron M. Quist; Phillip A. Wiseley. **Soc. Forc.** 72:1 9:1993 pp.19 - 44.
655 Relationships as natural categories. Constantine Sedikides; Nils Olsen; Harry T. Reis. **J. Pers. Soc. Psychol.** 64:1 1:1993 pp.71 - 82.
656 Responsibility attributions for men and women giving sane versus crazy explanations for good and bad deeds. Chris L. Kleinke; Michael R. Baldwin. **J. Psychol.** 127:1 1:1993 pp.37 - 50.
657 The role of fairness in negotiation. Cecilia Albin. **Negot. J.** 9:3 7:1993 pp.223 - 244.
658 Seeing virtues in faults — negativity and the transformation of interpersonal narratives in close relationships. Sandra L. Murray; John G. Holmes. **J. Pers. Soc. Psychol.** 65:4 10:1993 pp.707 - 722.
659 Self-directed versus other-directed affect as a consequence of prejudice-related discrepancies. Margo J. Monteith; Patricia G. Devine; Julia R. Zuwerink. **J. Pers. Soc. Psychol.** 64:2 2:1993 pp.198 - 210.
660 Self-disclosure and Asian students' abilities to cope with social difficulties in the United States. Guo-Ming Chen. **J. Psychol.** 127:6 11:1993 pp.603 - 610.
661 Simultaneous talk: parallel talk among Filipino-American students. B.L. Speicher. **J. Multiling.** 14:5 1993 pp.411 - 426.
662 Social cognition and social perception. Susan T. Fiske. **Ann. R. Psych.** 44 1993 pp.155 - 194.
663 [Social differentiation and perception of the other]; *[Text in Japanese].* Masahiro Ogino. **Shak. Hyor.** 44(3) 1993 pp.56 - 71.
664 Social influence sex differences and judgments of beauty — putting the interpersonal back in interpersonal attraction. William G. Graziano; Lauri A. Jensen-Campbell; Laura J. Shebilske; Sharon R. Lundgren. **J. Pers. Soc. Psychol.** 65:3 9:1993 pp.522 - 531.
665 Social skills deficits and psychosocial problems — antecedent, concomitant, or consequent? Chris Segrin. **J. Soc. Clin. Psychol.** 12:3 Fall:1993 pp.336 - 353.
666 Social support network orientation — the role of adult attachment style. John L. Wallace; Alan Vaux. **J. Soc. Clin. Psychol.** 12:3 Fall:1993 pp.354 - 365.
667 Social-cognitive mechanisms in the development of conduct disorder and depression. Kenneth A. Dodge. **Ann. R. Psych.** 44 1993 pp.559 - 584.

C: Individus. Groupes. Organisations

668 Spontaneous humour as an indicator of paradox and ambiguity. Mary Jo Hatch; Sanford B. Ehrlich. **Organ. Stud.** 14:4 1993 pp.505 - 526.
669 Stress and the cognitive-conversational benefits of social interaction. Leslie F. Clark. **J. Soc. Clin. Psychol.** 12:1 Spring:1993 pp.25 - 55.
670 Taking visual disability into account — explaining failure to experts and non-experts. Elke Klein-Allermann; Martin Kumpf. **Argumentation** 7:2 1993 pp.149 - 163.
671 Talk at work: interaction in institutional settings. Paul Drew [Ed.]; John Heritage [Ed.]. Cambridge, New York: Cambridge University Press, 1992. 580p. *ISBN: 0521374898, 0521376335. Includes bibliographical references and indexes. (Series:* Studies in interactional sociolinguistics).
672 A test of the social support deterioration model in the context of natural disaster. Krzysztof Kaniasty; Fran H. Norris. **J. Pers. Soc. Psychol.** 64:3 3:1993 pp.395 - 408.
673 The theory of reasoned action and cooperative behaviour — it takes two to use a condom. Yoshihisa Kashima; Cynthia Gallois; Malcolm McCamish. **Br. J. Soc. P.** 32:3 9:1993 pp.227 - 239.
674 Trust and testimony — nine arguments on testimonial knowledge. T. Govier. **Int. J. Moral Soc. S.** 8:1 Spring:1993 pp.21 - 39.
675 Unmasking pain — detection of deception in facial expressions. Karen E. Galin; Beverly E. Thorn. **J. Soc. Clin. Psychol.** 12:2 Summer:1993 pp.182 - 197.
676 A "user" — designed mediation approach, fostering evolutionary consciousness and competence. Raymond C. Pastorino. **Wor. Futur.** 36:2-4 1993 pp.155 - 164.
677 What do we really want? Mental models of ideal romantic involvement explored through multidimensional scaling. Caryl E. Rusbult; Richard K. Onizuka; Isaac Lipkus. **J. Exp. S. Psychol.** 29:6 11:1993 pp.493 - 527.
678 Women's and men's friendships in comparative perspective. Elke Bruckner; Karin Knaup. **Eur. Sociol. R.** 9:3 12:1993 pp.249 - 266.

Conflict
Conflit

679 Disagreement and concession in disputes — on the context sensitivity of preference structures. Helga Kotthoff. **Lang. Soc.** 22:2 6:1993 pp.193 - 216.
680 The effect of relationship orientation on negotiators' cognitions and tactics. Leonard Greenhalgh; Roderick W. Gilkey. **Group Decis. Negot.** 2:2 6:1993 pp.167 - 183.
681 Exploring conflict resolution styles — a study of Turkish and American university business students. Marcia Lee Agee; Hayat E. Kabasakal. **Int. J. Soc. E.** 20:9 1993 pp.3 - 14.
682 Imagined ideological differences in conflict escalation and resolution. Dacher Keltner; Robert J. Robinson. **Int. J. Confl. Manag.** 4:3 7:1993 pp.249 - 262.
683 Interessenvermittlung und sozialer Konflikt: über Bedingungen und Folgen neokorporatistischer Konfliktregelung. *[In German]*; [Conveying interests and social conflict: conditions and results of neo-corporate conflict resolution]. Michael Nollert. Pfaffenweiler: Centaurus, 1992. 322p. *ISBN: 3890856632.*
684 The intergenerational transmission of disciplinary practices and approaches to conflict. Douglas P. Fry. **Human. Org.** 52:2 Summer:1993 pp.176 - 185.

C: Individuals. Groups. Organizations

685   Mit meinem Vater kann ich darüber nicht reden... Junge türkische Frauen in Deutschland — Lebensrealität und Versuch der Konfliktlösung. *[In German]*; ["I cannot discuss this with my father". Young Turkish women in Germany — the reality of life and attempts at conflict resolution]. Suzan Özkan. **Hess. Blät. Volk.Kultur.** 29 1992 pp.155 - 166.
686   Negotiation in social conflict. Dean G. Pruitt; Peter J. Carnevale. Buckingham: Open University Press, 1993. 251p. *ISBN: 0335098665*. (*Series:* Mapping social psychology).
687   Nonverbal communication and conflict escalation — an attribution-based model. Tricia S. Jones; Martin S. Remland. **Int. J. Confl. Manag.** 4:2 4:1993 pp.119 - 137.
688   Social accounts in conflict situations — using explanations to manage conflict. Sim B. Sitkin; Robert J. Bies. **Human Relat.** 46:3 3:1993 pp.349 - 370.
689   Validation of a category system for arguments in conflict discourse. Manfred Hofer; Birgit Pikowsky. **Argumentation** 7:2 1993 pp.135 - 148.

Emotions
Emotions

690   The adaptive value of humor and laughter. Glenn E. Weisfeld. **Ethol. Socio.** 14:2 1993 pp.141 - 169.
691   Beyond simple pessimism — effects of sadness and anger on social perception. Dacher Keltner; Phoebe C. Ellsworth; Kari Edwards. **J. Pers. Soc. Psychol.** 64:5 5:1993 pp.740 - 752.
692   [The concept of emotion in the sociological theory of action]; *[Text in Japanese]*. Yoshinori Takanhashi. **Jin. (J. Kyo. Univ.)** 39 1993 pp.17 - 36.
693   Control of human aggression — a comparative perspective. Richard K. Lore; Lori A. Schultz. **Am. Psychol.** 48:1 1:1993 pp.16 - 25.
694   Distinguishing the experiences of envy and jealousy. W. Gerrod Parrott; Richard H. Smith. **J. Pers. Soc. Psychol.** 64:6 6:1993 pp.906 - 920.
695   Einsamkeit in Ost- und Westdeutschland. *[In German]*; (Loneliness in East- and West Germany.) *[Summary]*. Nicola Döring, Jürgen Bortz. **Kölner Z. Soz. Soz. psy.** 45:3 9:1993 pp.507 - 527.
696   Emotional communication, culture, and power. Cynthia Gallois [Ed.]; Joseph N. Cappella [Contrib.]; Judee K. Burgoon [Contrib.]; Antonietta Trimboli [Contrib.]; Michael Walker [Contrib.]; Sik Hung Ng [Contrib.]; Ann Weatherall [Contrib.]; Joanna Moody [Contrib.]; Kam Kuen Chan [Contrib.]; Caja Thimm [Contrib.]; Lenelis Kruse [Contrib.]; Mary Anne Fitzpatrick [Contrib.]; Joyce Fey [Contrib.]; Chris Segrin [Contrib.]; Janet L. Schiff [Contrib.]; Patricia Noller [Contrib.]; James Price Dillard [Contrib.]. **J. Lang. Soc. Psychol.** 12:1/2 3/6:1993 pp.3 - 161. *Collection of 9 articles.*
697   Gender differences in sexual jealousy — adaptionist or social learning explanation? Michael W. Wiederman; Elizabeth Rice Allgeier. **Ethol. Socio.** 14:2 1993 pp.115 - 140.
698   Homicidal fantasies. Douglas T. Kenrick; Virgil Sheets. **Ethol. Socio.** 14:4 1993 pp.231 - 246.
699   Humor and pain tolerance. Ofra Nevo; Giora Keinan; Mina Teshimovsky-Arditi. **Humor** 6:1 1993 pp.71 - 88.

C: Individus. Groupes. Organisations

700 Ideological practices and the management of emotions — the case of "wife abusers". John P. McKendy. **Crit. Sociol.** 19:2 1992 pp.61 - 80.

701 [Love as a medium of communication: the semantics of social change]; *[Text in Japanese]*. Gaku Doba. **Shak. Hyor.** 44(3) 1993 pp.72 - 87.

702 Love, hate, anger, and jealousy in close relationships — a prototype and cognitive appraisal analysis. Julie Fitness; Garth J.O. Fletcher. **J. Pers. Soc. Psychol.** 65:5 11:1993 pp.942 - 958.

703 Not all smiles are created equal — the differences between enjoyment and non-enjoyment smiles. Mark G. Frank; Paul Ekman. **Humor** 6:1 1993 pp.9 - 26.

704 On the validity of a weight-judging paradigm for the study of humor. Lambert Deckers. **Humor** 6:1 1993 pp.43 - 56.

705 Relationships between aggression and pubertal increases in testosterone — a panel analysis of adolescent males. Carolyn Tucker Halpern; J. Richard Udry; Benjamin Campbell; Chirayath Suchindran. **Soc. Biol.** 40:1-2 Spring-Summer:1993 pp.8 - 24.

706 A revised theory of aggression. Ana-Maria Rizzuto; Jerome I. Sashin; Dan H. Buie; W.W. Meissner. **Psychoanal. Rev.** 80:1 Spring:1993 pp.29 - 54.

707 Sex and salience in the appreciation of cartoon humor. Peter Derks; Sanjay Arora. **Humor** 6:1 1993 pp.57 - 69.

708 Special things: the management of an individual provision within a group care setting for emotionally disturbed children. Margarete Lucas. **Int. J. Therap. Comm. Support. Org.** 13:4 1992 pp.209 - 220.

709 Theories of love development, maintenance, and dissolution: octagonal cycle and differential perspectives. Oliver C. S. Tzeng [Ed.]. New York: Praeger, 1992. xv, 322p. *ISBN: 0275942341. Includes bibliographical references (p. [295]-307) and index.*

710 Unrequited love — on heartbreak, anger, guilt, scriptlessness, and humiliation. Roy F. Baumeister; Sara R. Wotman; Arlene M. Stillwell. **J. Pers. Soc. Psychol.** 64:3 3:1993 pp.377 - 394.

C.4: Groups
Groupes

711 [Advances in the Axelrod paradigm] *[Summary]*; *[Text in Japanese]*. Peter Kollock; Nahoko Hayashi; Ryuhei Tsuji; Toshio Yamagishi; Kenji Kosaka. **Rir. to ho.** 8:1 1993 pp.3 - 68. *Collection of 4 articles.*

712 Anticipated outgroup evaluations and intergroup bias. J.E. Vivian; N.H. Berkowitz. **Eur. J. Soc. Psychol.** 23:5 9-10:1993 pp.513 - 524.

713 Cohesion, equivalence, and similarity of behavior — a theoretical and empirical assessment. M.S. Mizruchi. **Soc. Networks** 15:3 9:1993 pp.275 - 307.

714 Collective action and group heterogeneity — voluntary provision versus selective incentives. Douglas D. Heckathorn. **Am. Sociol. R.** 58:3 6:1993 pp.329 - 350.

715 Collective action and network structure. Roger V. Gould. **Am. Sociol. R.** 58:2 4:1993 pp.182 - 196.

716 The common knowledge effect — information sharing and group judgment. Daniel Gigone; Reid Hastie. **J. Pers. Soc. Psychol.** 65:5 11:1993 pp.959 - 974.

717 The communal resource — transaction costs and the solution of collective action problems. Michael Taylor; Sara Singleton. **Polit. Soc.** 21:2 6:1993 pp.195 - 214.

C: Individuals. Groups. Organizations

718 The comparative utility of third party consultation and mediation within a complex simulation of intergroup conflict. Loraleigh Keashly; Ronald J. Fisher; Peter R. Grant. **Human Relat.** 46:3 3:1993 pp.371 - 393.

719 A comparison of social support and social networks of black parents and white parents with chronically ill children. Holly Ann Williams. **Soc. Sci. Med.** 37:12 12:1993 pp.1509 - 1520.

720 Computer brainstorms — more heads are better than one. Alan R. Dennis; Joseph S. Valacich. **J. Appl. Psychol.** 78:4 8:1993 pp.531 - 537.

721 The concept of intergroup mirroring — reality or illusion? Susan A. Wheelan; Marcia Abraham. **Human Relat.** 46:7 7:1993 pp.803 - 825.

722 Delineating personal support networks. Mart G.M. van der Poel. **Soc. Networks** 15:1 3:1993 pp.49 - 70.

723 Democracy in small groups: participation, decision making, and communication. John W. Gastil. Philadelphia: New Society, 1993. 213p. *ISBN: 0865712735, 0865712743. Includes bibliographical references and index.*

724 The determinants of differential group evaluations in distinctiveness-based illusory correlations in stereotyping. Craig Johnson; Brian Mullen. **Br. J. Soc. P.** 32:3 9:1993 pp.253 - 263.

725 Differential processing of in-group and out-group information. Thomas M. Ostrom; Sandra L. Carpenter; Constantine Sedikides; Fan Li. **J. Pers. Soc. Psychol.** 64:1 1:1993 pp.21 - 34.

726 The effects of intergroup discrimination and social values on level of self-esteem in the minimal group paradigm. M.G. Chin; C.G. McClintock. **Eur. J. Soc. Psychol.** 23:1 1-2:1993 pp.63 - 75.

727 Effects of intergroup similarity on intergroup relations. S. Roccas; S.H. Schwartz. **Eur. J. Soc. Psychol.** 23:6 11-12:1993 pp.581 - 595.

728 Ethnocentrism, group cohesion and constituent pressure on negotiators in intergroup conflict. Ruth Kinzel; Ronald J. Fisher. **Int. J. Confl. Manag.** 4:4 10:1993 pp.323 - 336.

729 Finding groups with a simple genetic algorithm. Linton C. Freeman. **J. Math. Sociol.** 17:4 1993 pp.227 - 241.

730 Formal models of collective action. Pamela E. Oliver. **Ann. R. Soc.** 19 1993 pp.271 - 300.

731 Gaining turns and achieving high influence ranking in small conversational groups. Sik Hung Ng; Dean Bell; Mark Brooke. **Br. J. Soc. P.** 32:3 9:1993 pp.265 - 275.

732 Group goals and group performance. Elizabeth Weldon; Laurie R. Weingart. **Br. J. Soc. P.** 32:4 12:1993 pp.307 - 334.

733 Group motivation: social psychological perspectives. Michael A. Hogg [Ed.]; Dominic Abrams [Ed.]. Hemel Hempstead: Harvester-Wheatsheaf, 1993. 240p. *ISBN: 0745012396.*

734 Group staffing levels and responses to prospective and new group members. Marie A. Cini; Richard L. Moreland; John M. Levine. **J. Pers. Soc. Psychol.** 65:4 10:1993 pp.723 - 734.

735 Group therapy with adults with learning difficulties who have committed sexual offences. Elisabeth Cormack. **Groupwork** 6:2 1993 pp.162 - 175.

736 A handbook of common groupwork problems. Tom Douglas. London, New York: Routledge, 1991. viii, 193p. *ISBN: 0415038979. Includes bibliographical references and index.*

C: Individus. Groupes. Organisations

737 The impact of consideration of issues and motivational orientation on group negotiation process and outcome. Laurie R. Weingart; Rebecca J. Bennett; Jeanne M. Brett. **J. Appl. Psychol.** 78:3 6:1993 pp.504 - 517.
738 Implicit and category-based allocations of decision-making power in majority-minority relations. Assaad E. Azzi. **J. Exp. S. Psychol.** 29:3 5:1993 pp.203 - 228.
739 Individual and group decision making: current issues. N. John Castellan [Ed.]. Hillsdale, N.J: L. Erlbaum, 1993. x, 315p. *Based on papers presented at the Science Weekend symposia of the 1990 convention of the American Psychological Association. Includes bibliographical references and index.*
740 The influence of power, distribution norms and task meeting structure on resource allocation in small group negotiation. Elizabeth A. Mannix. **Int. J. Confl. Manag.** 4:1 1:1993 pp.5 - 23.
741 Inside the juror: the psychology of juror decision making. Reid Hastie [Ed.]. Cambridge [England], New York: Cambridge University Press, 1992. 277p. *ISBN: 0521419883.* (*Series:* Cambridge series on judgment and decision making).
742 Interaction in cooperative groups: the theoretical anatomy of group learning. Norman Miller [Ed.]; Rachel Hertz-Lazarovits [Ed.]. Cambridge, New York: Cambridge University Press, 1992. viii, 294p. *ISBN: 0521403030. Includes bibliographical references and indexes.*
743 Linguistic intergroup bias and implicit attributions. Luciano Arcuri; Anne Maass; Giovanna Portelli. **Br. J. Soc. P.** 32:3 9:1993 pp.277 - 285.
744 Longitudinal approach to subgroup formation — re-analysis of Newcomb's fraternity data. Keiko Nakao; A. Kimball Romney. **Soc. Networks** 15:2 6:1993 pp.109 - 131.
745 Majority-minority status and perceived ingroup variability revisited. R.A. Bartsch; C.M. Judd. **Eur. J. Soc. Psychol.** 23:5 9-10:1993 pp.471 - 483.
746 Measuring the typicalness of behavior. B. Kuon. **Math. Soc. Sc.** 26:1 1993 pp.35 - 50.
747 Models of crossed categorization and intergroup relations. Miles Hewstone; Mir Rabiul Islam; Charles M. Judd. **J. Pers. Soc. Psychol.** 64:5 5:1993 pp.779 - 793.
748 Multivariate group comparisons of variable systems — MANOVA and structural equation modeling. David A. Cole; Scott E. Maxwell; Richard Arvey; Eduardo Salas. **Psychol . B.** 114:1 7:1993 pp.174 - 184.
749 Network structure and delinquent attitudes within a juvenile gang. S.W. Baron; D.B. Tindall. **Soc. Networks** 15:3 9:1993 pp.255 - 273.
750 On the asymmetry in the cognitive construal of ingroup and outgroup — a model of egocentric social categorization. B. Simon. **Eur. J. Soc. Psychol.** 23:2 3-4:1993 pp.131 - 147.
751 On the sociology of justice — theoretical notes from an actual jury deliberation. Douglas W. Maynard; John F. Manzo. **Sociol. Theory** 11:2 7:1993 pp.171 - 133.
752 Organizational and geopolitical approaches to international science and technology networks. Wesley Shrum; Carl Bankston. **Know. Pol.** 6:3+4 1993-1994 pp.119 - 133.
753 Patriotism as fundamental beliefs of group members. Daniel Bar-Tal; Michael Billig [Comments by]. **Polit. Indiv.** 3:2 1993 pp.45 - 66.
754 Perceptions of group variability. Constantine Sedikides [Ed.]; Thomas M. Ostrom [Ed.]; Emiko S. Kashima [Contrib.]; Yoshihisa Kashima [Contrib.]; Susan Kraus [Contrib.]; Carey S. Ryan [Contrib.]; Charles M. Judd [Contrib.]; Reid Hastie [Contrib.]; Bernadette Park [Contrib.]; Diane M. Mackie [Contrib.]; Jeffrey W.

C: Individuals. Groups. Organizations

Sherman [Contrib.]; Leila T. Worth [Contrib.]; Sandra Carpenter [Contrib.]; Patricia W. Linville [Contrib.]; Gregory W. Fischer [Contrib.]; Rupert Brown [Contrib.]; Lynne Wootton-Millward [Contrib.]; Marilynn B. Brewer [Contrib.]. **Soc. Cogn.** 11:1 Spring:1993 pp.1 - 174. *Collection of 8 articles.*

755 Personality and peer influence in juvenile corrections. Martin Gold; D. Wayne Osgood. Westport, Conn: Greenwood Press, 1992. xvii, 230p. *ISBN: 0313279705. Includes bibliographical references (p. [219]-224) and indexes. (Series:* Contributions in criminology and penology).

756 Psychological entrapment in group decision making — an assigned decision rule and a groupthink phenomenon. Tatsuya Kameda; Shinkichi Sugimori. **J. Pers. Soc. Psychol.** 65:2 8:1993 pp.282 - 292.

757 Les relations quotidiennes entre Romands et Suisses allemands: les cantons bilingues de Fribourg et du Valais. *[In French]*; [Every-day relations between French and German speaking Swiss: the bilingual districts of Fribourg and Valais]. Uli Windisch; Didier Froidevaux; Denise Maeder [Contrib.]; et al. Lausanne: Payot, 1992. *ISBN: 2601031115. Includes bibliographical references (v. 2, p. [525]-532).*

758 Relationship frames and cooperation. Harris Sondak; Marian Chapman Moore. **Group Decis. Negot.** 2:2 6:1993 pp.103 - 118.

759 Relationships in group decision and negotiation. Elizabeth A. Mannix [Ed.]; Harris Sondak [Contrib.]; Marian Chapman Moore [Contrib.]; Margaret A. Neale [Contrib.]; Jeffrey T. Polzer [Contrib.]; Patrick O. Glenn [Contrib.]; Pri Pradham Shah [Contrib.]; Karen A. Jehn [Contrib.]; Leonard Greenhalgh [Contrib.]; Roderick W. Gilkey [Contrib.]. **Group Decis. Negot.** 2:2 6:1993 pp.99 - 183. *Collection of 6 articles.*

760 The reliability of network density and composition measures. Peter V. Marsden. **Soc. Networks** 15:4 12:1993 pp.399 - 421.

761 Reward allocation preferences in groups and organizations. Ya-Ru Chen; Allan H. Church. **Int. J. Confl. Manag.** 4:1 1:1993 pp.25 - 59.

762 The role of communication in interindividual-intergroup discontinuity. Chester A. Insko; John Schopler; Stephen M. Drigotas; Kenneth A. Graetz; James Kennedy; Chante Cox; Garry Bornstein. **Confl. Resolut.** 37:1 3:1993 pp.108 - 138.

763 Service over secrecy: how lodge-style fraternalism yielded popularity to men's service clubs. Clifford Putney. **J. Pop. Cult.** 27:1 Summer:1993 pp.179 - 190.

764 Social networks as normal science. Norman P. Hummon; Kathleen Carley. **Soc. Networks** 15:1 3:1993 pp.71 - 106.

765 Social networks, marital status, and well-being. A.C. Acock; J.S. Hurlbert. **Soc. Networks** 15:3 9:1993 pp.309 - 344.

766 Social processes in small groups 1 — theoretical perspectives. Richard L. Moreland [Ed.]; Michael A. Hogg [Ed.]; James R. Larson [Contrib.]; Caryn Christensen [Contrib.]; Linda Argote [Contrib.]; Reuben M. Baron [Contrib.]; Stephen J. Misovich [Contrib.]; Sandra Robinson [Contrib.]; Elizabeth Weldon [Contrib.]; Richard A. Guzzo [Contrib.]; Paul R. Yost [Contrib.]; Richard J. Campbell [Contrib.]; Gregory P. Shea [Contrib.]. **Br. J. Soc. P.** 32:1 3:1993 pp.1 - 106. *Collection of 6 articles.*

767 Social processes in small groups 2 — studying social processes in small groups. Michael A. Hogg [Ed.]; Richard L. Moreland [Ed.]; Fabio Lorenzi-Cioldi [Contrib.]; Amy Marcus-Newhall [Contrib.]; Norman Miller [Contrib.]; Rolf Holtz [Contrib.]; Marilynn B. Brewer [Contrib.]; Deborah Rugs [Contrib.]; Martin F. Kaplan

C: Individus. Groupes. Organisations

[Contrib.]; Margaret Wilson [Contrib.]; David Canter [Contrib.]; David A. Kenny [Contrib.]; Byran W. Hallmark [Contrib.]; Patrick Sullivan [Contrib.]; Deborah A. Kashy [Contrib.]. **Br. J. Soc. P.** 32:2 6:1993 pp.107 - 190. *Collection of 6 articles.*

768 Support groups as open systems — a model for practice and research. Janice H. Schopler; Maeda J. Galinsky. **Health Soc. Work** 18:3 8:1993 pp.195 - 297.

769 Toward an empirical concept of group. Lloyd Sandelands; Lynda St. Clair. **J. Theory Soc. Behav.** 23:4 12:1993 pp.423 - 458.

770 Valori e identità sociale. Perché è ancora importante per la sociologia studiare i valori e i loro mutamenti. *[In Italian]*; (Values and social identity.) *[Summary]*. Loredana Sciolla. **Rass. It. Soc.** 34:3 9:1993 pp.341 - 359.

771 Variation of out-group presence and evaluation of the in-group. Ulrich Wagner; Phillip L. Ward. **Br. J. Soc. P.** 32:3 9:1993 pp.241 - 251.

772 Varieties of religious experience — continuity and change in religious involvement. Michael D. Mumford; Andrea F. Snell; Michael B. Hein. **J. Personal.** 61:2 6:1993 pp.265 - 297.

C.5: **Organizations**
Organisations

773 Accuracy and reliability of self-reported data in interorganizational networks. Michael Calloway; Joseph P. Morrissey; Robert I. Paulson. **Soc. Networks** 15:4 12:1993 pp.377 - 398.

774 Action research. Max Elden [Ed.]; Rupert F. Chisholm [Ed.]; Gerald E. Ledford [Contrib.]; Susan Albers Mohrman [Contrib.]; Davydd J. Greenwood [Contrib.]; William Foote Whyte; Ira Harkavy [Contrib.]; Morten Levin [Contrib.]; Per H. Engelstad [Contrib.]; Bjørn Gustavsen [Contrib.]; L. David Brown [Contrib.]. **Human Relat.** 46:2 2:1993 pp.121 - 298. *Collection of 7 articles.*

775 Akteurkompetenz im Organisationsdilemma. Grundprobleme strategisch ambitionierter Mitgliederverbände und zwei Techniken ihrer Überwindung. *[In German]*; (Competence of actors in an organizational dilemma. Fundamental problems encountered by ambitious members' associations and two ways of overcoming them.) *[Summary]*; *[Summary in French]*. Helmut Wiesenthal. **Berl. J. Soziol.** 3 1:1993 pp.3 - 18.

776 Alternative organizational formations — a typology of polycratic administrative systems. Malcolm Waters. **Sociol. Rev.** 41:1 2:1993 pp.54 - 81.

777 Approaches to organisational culture and ethics. Amanda Sinclair. **J. Busin. Ethics** 12:1 1:1993 pp.63 - 73.

778 Authority, organization, and societal context in multinational churches. Reed E. Nelson. **Adm. Sci. Qua.** 38:4 12:1993 pp.653 - 682.

779 Beyond bureaucracy: essays on the development and evolution of human organization. Warren G. Bennis. San Francisco: Jossey-Bass, 1993. xxvii, 254p. *ISBN: 1555425224.* (*Series:* Jossey-Bass management series).

780 Breaking the paradigm mentality. Hugh Willmott. **Organ. Stud.** 14:5 1993 pp.681 - 720.

781 Ciklićan razvitak znanosti i modela organizacije. *[In Serbo-Croatian (Roman)]*; (Cyclic development of science and model of organization.) *[Summary]*; *[Summary in Russian]*. Božidar Jušić. **Ekon. Preg.** 44:3-4 1993 pp.208 - 216.

C: Individuals. Groups. Organizations

782 Cognition in organizational analysis — who's minding the store? Susan C. Schneider; Reinhard Angelmar. **Organ. Stud.** 14:3 1993 pp.347 - 374.

783 The collapse of sensemaking in organizations: the Mann Gulch disaster. Karl E. Weick. **Adm. Sci. Qua.** 38:4 12:1993 pp.628 - 652.

784 Collective mind in organizations — heedful interrelating on flight decks. Karl E. Weick; Karlene H. Roberts. **Adm. Sci. Qua.** 38:3 9:1993 pp.357 - 381.

785 Comparing correlations based on individual-level and aggregated data. Cheri Ostroff. **J. Appl. Psychol.** 78:4 8:1993 pp.569 - 582.

786 Conflicting ideologies — structural and motivational consequences. Susan C. Schneider. **Human Relat.** 46:1 1:1993 pp.45 - 64.

787 Constraints on succession planning — the Nigerian public service experience; *[Summary in Arabic]; [Summary in French].* E.E. Aduaka. **Cah. Afr. Admin. Pub.** 38 1992 pp.47 - 60.

788 The context of interunit influence attempts. Christopher Gresov; Carroll Stephens. **Adm. Sci. Qua.** 38:2 6:1993 pp.252 - 276.

789 Corporate autonomy and institutional control: the crown corporation as a problem in organization design. Douglas Frederick Stevens. Montréal: McGill-Queen's University Press, 1993. 233p. *ISBN: 0773509003. Includes bibliographical references and index.* (*Series:* Canadian public administration series).

790 Creating readiness for organizational change. Achilles Armenakis; Stanley G. Harris; Kevin W. Mossholder. **Human Relat.** 46:6 6:1993 pp.681 - 703.

791 Cultural perspectives on organizations. Mats Alvesson. Cambridge: Cambridge University Press, 1993. ix, 137p. *ISBN: 0521401364. Includes bibliographical references.*

792 Cultures in organizations: three perspectives. Joanne Martin. New York: Oxford University Press, 1992. xi, 228p. *ISBN: 0195071638.*

793 A depletion of assets model of organizational learning. Martin Schulz. **J. Math. Sociol.** 17:2-3 1992 pp.145 - 174.

794 The design of organizations and the right to act. James S. Coleman. **Sociol. For.** 8:4 12:1993 pp.527 - 546.

795 Diversify with care — diversification strategies and organization development. Chung-Ming Lau. **Intern. J. Organiz. Anal.** 1:1 1:1993 pp.55 - 72.

796 The dynamics of organizational rules. Xueguang Zhou. **A.J.S.** 98:5 3:1993 pp.1134 - 1166.

797 The economics of organization — the principal-agent relationship. Trond Petersen. **Acta Sociol.** 36:3 1993 pp.277 - 293.

798 L'Economie sociale au Royaume-Uni. *[In French];* (The social economy in the United Kingdom.) Jeremy Kendall; Martin Knapp; Rob Paton; Alan Thomas. **R. Et. Coop. Mut. Ass.** 71:46(2) 1993 pp.51 - 75.

799 Emotion in organizations. Stephen Fineman [Ed.]. London: Sage Publications, 1993. 230p. *ISBN: 0803987331.*

800 Freedom and the organizational republic. Larry Michael Preston. New York; Berlin: Walter de Gruyter, 1992. x, 235p. *ISBN: 3110134187. Includes bibliographical references (p. [211]-230) and indexes.* (*Series:* De Gruyter studies on North America).

801 The gods and goddesses — personifying social life in the age of organization. Martin L. Bowles. **Organ. Stud.** 14:3 1993 pp.395 - 418.

C: Individus. Groupes. Organisations

802 Idee, Mentalität, Institution. Kultursoziologische Anmerkungen zu einer Theorie institutionellen Wandels. *[In German]*; [Ideas, mentality, institutions. Cultural sociological comments on the theory of institutional change]. Winfried Gebhardt. **Social. Int.** 31:1 1993 pp.41 - 62.

803 The implications of organizational learning for organizational communication — a review and reformulation. Craig C. Lundberg; Judi Brownell. **Intern. J. Organiz. Anal.** 1:1 1:1993 pp.29 - 53.

804 Incremental and revolutionary strategic change — an empirical test of common premises. Charles J. Fornaciari; Bruce T. Lamont; Ben Mason; James J. Hoffman. **Intern. J. Organiz. Anal.** 1:3 7:1993 pp.273 - 290.

805 Institutions and social conflict. Jack Knight. Cambridge [England], New York, N.Y: Cambridge University Press, 1992. xiii, 234p. *ISBN: 0521420520, 0521421896. Includes bibliographical references (p. 215-229) and index. (Series:* The political economy of institutions and decisions).

806 Interdisciplinary perspectives on organization studies. Siegwart Lindenberg [Ed.]; Hein Schreuder [Ed.]. Oxford, New York: Pergamon Press, 1993. 350p. *ISBN: 0080408141.*

807 [International organization of Hakoniwa therapy: reflexivity of institutional statuses and participation statuses]; *[Text in Japanese]*. Keiko Takayama. **Nen. Shak. Ron.** 6 1993 pp.83 - 202.

808 Interorganizational coordination — theory and practice. Ernest R. Alexander. **J. Plan. Lit.** 7:4 5:1993 pp.328 - 343.

809 Knowledge and value: a new perspective on corporate transformation. Solveig Wikstrom; Richard Normann. London: Routledge, 1993. 149p. *ISBN: 0415098173.*

810 The legalistic organization. Sim B. Sitkin [Ed.]; Robert J. Bies [Ed.]; Tom R. Tyler [Contrib.]; Nancy L. Roth [Contrib.]; Janet P. Near [Contrib.]; Terry Morehead Dworkin [Contrib.]; Marcia P. Miceli [Contrib.]; Marilyn R. Kaplan [Contrib.]; J. Richard Harrison [Contrib.]; Rikki Abzug [Contrib.]; Stephen J. Mezias [Contrib.]. **Organiz. Sci.** 4:3 8:1993 pp.345 - 453. *Collection of 6 articles.*

811 Market, bureaucracy and community: a student's guide to organisation. Hal K. Colebatch; Peter Larmour. Boulder, Colo; London: Pluto Press, 1993. 134p. *ISBN: 0745307620, 0745307639. Includes bibliographical references and index.*

812 Materialism and idealism in organizational research. Paul S. Adler; Bryan Borys. **Organ. Stud.** 14:5 1993 pp.657 - 680.

813 Modernization and the logic of interorganizational networks. Renate Mayntz. **Know. Pol.** 6:1 Spring:1993 pp.3 - 16.

814 News from behind my hand — gossip in organizations. Mike Noon; Rick Delbridge. **Organ. Stud.** 14:1 1993 pp.23 - 36.

815 Organisational commitment — from trust to altruism at work. Henry S.R. Kao; Sek-Hong Ng. **Psychol. Devel. Soc.** 5:1 1-6:1993 pp.43 - 60.

816 The organization of survival — women's and racial-ethnic voluntarist and activist organizations, 1955-1985. Debra C. Minkoff. **Soc. Forc.** 71:4 6:1993 pp.887 - 908.

817 Organization studies as a scientific and humanistic enterprise — toward a reconceptualization of the foundations of the field. Mayer N. Zald. **Organiz. Sci.** 4:4 11:1993 pp.513 - 528.

818 Organizational behavior: linking individuals and groups to organizational contexts. Richard T. Mowday; Robert I. Sutton. **Ann. R. Psych.** 44 1993 pp.195 - 230.

C: Individuals. Groups. Organizations

819 Organizational change and barriers to innovation: a case study in the Italian public sector. Jennifer Landau. **Human Relat.** 46:12 12:1993 pp.1411 - 1430.
820 Organizational cultures: types and transformations. Diana C. Pheysey. London, New York: Routledge, 1993. 340p. *ISBN: 0415082919, 0415082927.* Includes bibliographical references and index.
821 Organizational innovations in a long-term perspective: legitimacy and souls-of-fire as critical factors of change and viability. Torbjörn Stjernberg; Åke Philips. **Human Relat.** 46:10 10:1993 pp.1193 - 1220.
822 Organizational learning — a review of some literatures. Mark Dodgson. **Organ. Stud.** 14:3 1993 pp.375 - 394.
823 Organizational metapatterns — tacit relationships in organizational culture. Guy B. Adams. **Admin. Soc.** 25:2 8:1993 pp.139 - 159.
824 Organizational simulation and information systems design — an operations level example. Arundhati Kumar; Peng Si Ow; Michael J. Prietula. **Manag. Sci.** 39:2 2:1993 pp.218 - 237.
825 Organizational size and change — diversification in the savings and loan industry after deregulation. Heather A. Haveman. **Adm. Sci. Qua.** 38:1 3:1993 pp.20 - 50.
826 Organizations working together. Catherine Alter; Jerald Hage. Newbury Park, Calif: Sage Publications, 1992. 342p. *ISBN: 0803948263, 0803948271.* Includes bibliographical references and index. (*Series:* Sage library of social research).
827 Organizing and organizations: an introduction. David Sims; Stephen Fineman; Yiannis Gabriel. London: Sage, 1993. 324p. *ISBN: 080398703X.*
828 Organizing frameworks in emerging organizations — a cognitive approach to the analysis of change. Jan Löwstedt. **Human Relat.** 46:4 4:1993 pp.501 - 526.
829 Paradoxical thinking and change in the frames of reference. Ann Westenholz. **Organ. Stud.** 14:1 1993 pp.37 - 58.
830 Planning for disaster. Patrick A. O'Riordan. **Administration** 41:4 Winter:1993-1994 pp.411 - 432.
831 Planning responses to voluntary sector crises. Jennifer R. Wolch; Elizabeth M. Rocha. **Non. Manag. Leader.** 3:4 Summer:1993 pp.377 - 395.
832 Political and apolitical action — toward a reconciliation of contradictory models of organizational behavior. Blake E. Ashforth. **Intern. J. Organiz. Anal.** 1:4 10:1993 pp.363 - 384.
833 The postmodern organization: mastering the art of irreversible change. William H. Bergquist. San Francisco: Jossey-Bass Publishers, 1993. 277p. *ISBN: 155542533X.* (*Series:* The Jossey-Bass management series).
834 Power, social influence, and sense making — effects of network centrality and proximity on employee perceptions. Herminia Ibarra; Steven B. Andrews. **Adm. Sci. Qua.** 38:2 6:1993 pp.277 - 303.
835 The psychodynamics of organizations. Larry Hirschhorn [Ed.]; Carole K. Barnett [Ed.]. Philadelphia: Temple University Press, 1993. xviii, 266p. *ISBN: 1566390206. Includes bibliographical references and index.* (*Series:* Labor and social change).
836 Raising money or raising awareness: issues and tensions in the relationship between fund-raisers and service-providers. Joy MacKeith. London: LSE: Centre for Voluntary Organisation, 1992. 25p. *ISBN: 0853281521.* (*Series:* Working Paper 12).
837 Recruitment mode as a factor affecting informant response in organizational research. David A. Buchanan. **J. Manag. Stu.** 30:2 3:1993 pp.297 - 313.

C: Individus. Groupes. Organisations

838 The reforming organization? Nils Brunsson; Johan P. Olsen. New York; London: Routledge, 1993. 216p. *ISBN: 0415082870, 0415082889. Includes bibliographical references and index.*
839 The relationship between values and practice — organizational climates for wrongdoing. Janet P. Near; Melissa S. Baucus; Marcia P. Miceli. **Admin. Soc.** 25:2 8:1993 pp.204 - 226.
840 Resetting the clock — the dynamics of organizational change and failure. Terry L. Amburgey; Dawn Kelly; William P. Barnett. **Adm. Sci. Qua.** 38:1 3:1993 pp.51 - 73.
841 The role of nonprofit organizations among the Haredi (ultra-orthodox) Jewish community in Israel. Eliezer D. Jaffe. **J. Soc. Work Pol. Israel** 7-8 1993 pp.45 - 56.
842 Social networks and exchange of favours among middle-rank officials in formal organizations in Sri Lanka. S.T. Hettige. **Sri Lanka J. Soc. Sci.** 12:1/2 6/12:1989 pp.69 - 83.
843 Social organization and risk — some current controversies. Lee Clarke; James F. Short. **Ann. R. Soc.** 19 1993 pp.375 - 400.
844 Team organization: an enduring competitive advantage. Dean Tjosfold. Chichester: Wiley, 1991. 249p. *ISBN: 0471934836.*
845 Time and strategic action — a cross-cultural view. Michael Hay; Jean-Claude Usunier. **Time Soc.** 2:3 1993 pp.313 - 333.
846 Towards a measure of organisational effectiveness for non-governmental organisations. Swapan Garain. **Indian J. Soc. W.** LIV:2 4:1993 pp.251 - 270.
847 Transnationals, international organization and deindustrialization. Christos N. Pitelis. **Organ. Stud.** 14:4 1993 pp.527 - 548.
848 The tyranny of change — organizational development revised. Marie McKendall. **J. Busin. Ethics** 12:2 2:1993 pp.93 - 104.
849 Weidervereinigung als Organisationproblem: gesamtdeutsche Zusammenschlüsse von Parteien und Verbänden. *[In German]*; [Reunification as a problem of organization: the mergers of German parties and organizations]. Frank Löbler [Ed.]; Josef Schmid [Ed.]; Heinrich Tiemann [Ed.]; Rolf Berndt [Ed.]. Bochum: Dr. N. Brockmeyer, 1992. 211p. *ISBN: 3883399876.*

Management in organizations
Administration des organisations

850 Accounting practices and organizational decision making. Richard Colignon; Mark Covaleski. **Sociol. Q.** 34:2 5:1993 pp.299 - 317.
851 Evolutionary/systemic management of organizations — old ideas put to new use. Christine B. Wailand. **Wor. Futur.** 36:2-4 1993 pp.141 - 154.
852 Integrated system, autonomous departments — organizational invalidity and system change in a university. Faith Noble; Michael Newman. **J. Manag. Stu.** 30:2 3:1993 pp.195 - 219.
853 Knowledge workers and contemporary organizations. Michael Reed; Alan Whitaker; Frank Blackler; William H. Starbuck; Graham Winch; Eric Schneider; Harry Scarbrough; Nick Perry; David Knights; Fergus Murray; Hugh Willmott; Mats Alvesson. **J. Manag. Stu.** 30:6 11:1993 pp.851 - 1020. *Collection of 8 articles.*

C: Individuals. Groups. Organizations

854 Management by panacea — accounting for transience. John Gill; Sue Whittle. **J. Manag. Stu.** 30:2 3:1993 pp.281 - 295.

855 Management control and organizational behaviour. Phil Johnson; John Gill. London: Paul Chapman, 1993. 188p. *ISBN: 1853961639. Bibliography: p.160-181.*

856 Management research methodology — prospects and links to practice. George T. Duncan. **Intern. J. Organiz. Anal.** 1:3 7:1993 pp.255 - 272.

857 Managing the headquarters-foreign subsidiary relationship — the roles of strategy, conflict, and integration. Joy M. Pahl; Kendall Roth. **Int. J. Confl. Manag.** 4:2 4:1993 pp.139 - 165.

858 Managing through organisation: the management process, form of organisation, and the work of managers. Colin Hales. New York; London: Routledge, 1993. xxi, 279p. *ISBN: 0415010020. Includes bibliographical references (p. [243]-266) and index.* (*Series:* Organisational behaviour and management series).

859 The negotiated order of organizational reliability. Paul R. Schulman. **Admin. Soc.** 25:3 11:1993 pp.353 - 372.

860 Organizational change and the management of expertise. Janette Webb. London: Routledge, 1993. 175p. *ISBN: 0415091896.*

861 Organizational communication and management: a global perspective. Andrzej K. Koźmiński [Ed.]; Donald P. Cushman [Ed.]. Albany: SUNY Press, State University of New York Press, 1993. viii, 234p. *ISBN: 0791413055, 0791413063. Includes bibliographical references (p. 213-232) and index.* (*Series:* SUNY series in human communication processes).

862 Organizational perspectives and urban spatial structure — a review and appraisal. David Wilson. **J. Plan. Lit.** 7:3 2:1993 pp.227 - 237.

863 Organizations, uncertainties, and risk. James F. Short [Ed.]; Lee Ben Clarke [Ed.]. Boulder: Westview Press, 1992. xiv, 381p. *ISBN: 0813385628. Includes bibliographical references (p. [323]-355) and indexes.*

864 Performance appraisal and the emergence of management. Barbara Townley. **J. Manag. Stu.** 30:2 3:1993 pp.221 - 238.

865 Postmodernism and organizations. John Hassard [Ed.]; Martin Parker [Ed.]. London: Sage Publications, 1993. 240p. *ISBN: 0803988796.*

866 Procedural rationality in the strategic decision-making process. James W. Dean; Mark P. Sharfman. **J. Manag. Stu.** 30:4 7:1993 pp.587 - 610.

867 Racial dynamics in cross-race developmental relationships. David A. Thomas. **Adm. Sci. Qua.** 38:2 6:1993 pp.169 - 194.

868 The strategic management of corporate change. Dexter Dunphy; Doug Stace. **Human Relat.** 46:8 8:1993 pp.905 - 920.

869 Time in management and organizational studies. T.K. Das. **Time Soc.** 2:2 1993 pp.267 - 274.

870 Transferring management techniques to Eastern Europe — an institutional critique. J.-C. Spender. **Intern. J. Organiz. Anal.** 1:3 7:1993 pp.237 - 254.

871 Transforming the dinosaurs: how organisations learn. Douglas Chalmers Hague. London: Demos, 1993. 57p.

872 Uloga konflikata u poslovanju i organizaciji poduzeća. *[In Serbo-Croatian (Roman)]*; (The role of conflicts in operation and organization of enterprise.) *[Summary]*; *[Summary in Russian]*. Mijo Novak. **Ekon. Preg.** 44:5-6 1993 pp.337 - 357.

Organization theory
Théorie de l'organisation

873 Activity theory and the analysis of organizations. G. Richard Holt; Anthony W. Morris. **Human. Org.** 52:1 Spring:1993 pp.97 - 109.
874 Analogical reasoning and knowledge generation in organization theory. Haridimos Tsoukas. **Organ. Stud.** 14:3 1993 pp.323 - 346.
875 Assumptions concerning the social sciences — a comparative perspective. Ebtihaj Al-A'ali. **Am. J. Islam. Soc. Sci.** 10:4 Winter:1993 pp.485 - 490.
876 Basic issues in organizations — a comparative perspective. Avner Ben-Ner; John Michael Montias; Egon Neuberger. **J. Comp. Econ.** 17:2 6:1993 pp.207 - 242.
877 [The business civilization and organization theory]; *[Text in Japanese]*. Shuichi Suzuki. Tokyo: Gakubunsha, 1993. 322p.
878 Commitment to organizations and occupations — extension and test of a three-component conceptualization. John P. Meyer; Natalie J. Allen; Catherine A. Smith. **J. Appl. Psychol.** 78:4 8:1993 pp.538 - 551.
879 Decisions without hierarchy: feminist interventions in organization theory and practice. Kathleen P. Iannello. New York: Routledge, 1992. xii, 136p. *ISBN: 0415904285, 0415904293. Includes bibliographical references (p. 125-131) and index.*
880 Etica de la organizaciones o ética en las organizaciones — ¿contradicción o simple juedo de palabras? *[In Spanish]*; [Ethics of organizations or ethics in organizations — contradiction or a simple play on words?]. Josep Maria Lozano i Soler. **Rev. Fom. Soc.** 48:191 7-9:1993 pp.333 - 358.
881 Evolutionary guidance system in organizational design. Judy Irene Bach. **Wor. Futur.** 36:2-4 1993 pp.107 - 127.
882 The long and thorny way to an organizational taxonomy. Julio C. Sanchez. **Organ. Stud.** 14:1 1993 pp.73 - 92.
883 The new behaviorism — a critique of economics and organization. Roderick Martin. **Human Relat.** 46:9 9:1993 pp.1085 - 1101.
884 Organization theory and consumption in a post-modern era. David Knights; Glenn Morgan. **Organ. Stud.** 14:2 1993 pp.211 - 234.
885 The politics of organizational analysis. Richard Marsden. **Organ. Stud.** 14:1 1993 pp.93 - 123.
886 Power and involvement in organizations: an empirical examination of Etzioni's compliance theory. Helga Drummond. Aldershot: Avebury, 1993. 222p. *ISBN: 1856284743.*
887 The problem of experience in the study of organizations. Lloyd E. Sandelands; V. Srivatsan. **Organ. Stud.** 14:1 1993 pp.1 - 22.
888 The shortcomings of an organizational revolution that is out of step. Danièle Linhart. **Econ. Ind. Dem.** 14:1 2:1993 pp.49 - 64.
889 Sociology and organization theory: positivism, paradigms and postmodernity. John Hassard. Cambridge, New York: Cambridge University Press, 1993. 167p. *ISBN: 0521350344. Includes bibliographical references and index.*
890 Strength is ignorance — slavery is freedom — managing culture in modern organizations. Hugh Willmot. **J. Manag. Stu.** 30:4 7:1993 pp.515 - 552.
891 Technology, organization, freedom — the organizational theory of John Dewey. James A. Stever. **Admin. Soc.** 24:4 2:1993 pp.419 - 443.

C: Individuals. Groups. Organizations

892   Upward mobility in organizations — the effects of hierarchy and opportunity structure. Josef Brüderl; Peter Preisendörfer; Rolf Ziegler. **Eur. Sociol. R.** 9:2 9:1993 pp.173 - 188.

C.6: Power, leadership and social roles
Pouvoir, leadership et rôles sociaux

893   The bases of power — origins and recent developments. Bertram H. Raven. **J. Soc. Issues** 49:4 1993 pp.227 - 251.

894   Controlling other people — the impact of power on stereotyping. Susan T. Fiske. **Am. Psychol.** 48:6 6:1993 pp.621 - 628.

895   The decision seminar as an instrument of power and enlightenment. Andrew R. Willard; Charles H. Norchi. **Polit. Psych.** 14:4 12:1993 pp.575 - 606.

896   The development of a scientific speciality as diffusion through social relations — the case of role analysis. A.G. Michaelson. **Soc. Networks** 15:3 9:1993 pp.217 - 236.

897   Disaster, organizing, and role enactment — a structural approach. Gary A. Kreps; Susan Lovegren Bosworth. **A.J.S.** 99:2 9:1993 pp.428 - 463.

898   A generalization of the role expectation conflict theory with a methodological analysis. Martti Kuokkanen. **J. Math. Sociol.** 17:2-3 1992 pp.217 - 226.

899   The leader succession-performance relationship in a non-profit organization; *[Summary in French]*. Marc S. Mentzer. **Can. R. Soc. A.** 30:2 5:1993 pp.191 - 204.

900   Leadership instability in hospitals — the influence of board-CEO relations and organizational growth and decline. Jeffrey A. Alexander; Mary L. Fennell; Michael T. Halpern. **Adm. Sci. Qua.** 38:1 3:1993 pp.74 - 99.

901   Lying, deceit, and subterfuge — a model of dishonesty in the workplace. Steven L. Grover. **Organiz. Sci.** 4:3 8:1993 pp.478 - 495.

902   The motivational effects of charismatic leadership — a self-concept based theory. Boas Shamir; Robert J. House; Michael B. Arthur. **Organiz. Sci.** 4:4 11:1993 pp.577 - 594.

903   Organizational contexts and contingent leadership roles. a theoretical exploration. Kathreyn K. Eggleston; Rabi S. Bhagat. **Human Relat.** 46:10 10:1993 pp.1177 - 1192.

904   Politicheskoe liderstvo: optimal'nyi stil'. *[In Russian]*; (Political leadership: the optimum style.) G. Ashin. **Obshch. Nauki Sovrem.** 2 1993 pp.115 - 126.

905   [Possible existence of power relation between free actors]; *[Text in Japanese]*. Naoki Sudo. **Rir. to ho.** pp.199 - 214.

906   Power imbalance and the pattern of exchange in dyadic negotiation. Elizabeth A. Mannix; Margaret A. Neale. **Group Decis. Negot.** 2:2 6:1993 pp.119 - 133.

907   Role motivation theories. John B. Miner. New York; London: Routledge, 1993. 353p. *ISBN: 0415084865. Includes bibliographical references and index. (Series: People and organizations).*

908   Roles in the NBA — there's always room for a big man, but his role has changed. Avijit Ghosh; Joel H. Steckel. **Interfaces** 23:4 7-8:1993 pp.43 - 55.

909   The seeds of weak power — an extension of network exchange theory. Barry Markovsky; John Skvoretz; David Willer; Michael J. Lovaglia; Jeffrey Erger. **Am. Sociol. R.** 58:2 4:1993 pp.197 - 209.

C: Individus. Groupes. Organisations

910 Soziale Ungleichheit und gesellschaftliche Integration. Ein Vergleich von USA, Japan und Deutschland. *[In German]*; (Social inequality and social integration — a comparison between the USA, Japan and Germany.) *[Summary]*; *[Summary in French]*. Brigitte Hamm; Dieter Holtmann; Harold Kerbo; Hermann Strasser. **Berl. J. Soziol.** 3:2 1993 pp.215 - 226.
911 Stess and turnover intention — a comparative study among nurses. Yongqing Fang; Vishwanath V. Baba. **Int. J. Comp. Soc** XXXIV:1-2 1-4:1993 pp.24 - 38.
912 Upravlencheskaia triada: psikhologicheskaia sovmestimost' rukovoditelia i podchinennogo. *[In Russian]*; (Ruling triad — sociopsychological compatibility.) V.A. Tolochek. **Sot. Issle.** 5 1993 pp.69 - 73.
913 Upward power tendencies in a hierarchy — power distance theory versus bureaucratic rule. J.J. Bruins; H.A.M. Wilke. **Eur. J. Soc. Psychol.** 23:3 5-6:1993 pp.239 - 254.
914 Women's two roles: a contemporary dilemma. Phyllis Moen. New York: Auburn House, 1992. xii, 172p. *ISBN: 0865691983. Includes bibliographical references (p. [135]-165) and index.*

C.7: Opinions and attitudes
Opinions et attitudes

915 An analysis of public opinion toward undocumented immigration. Thomas J. Espenshade; Charles A. Calhoun. **Pop. Res. Pol. R.** 12:3 1993 pp.189 - 224.
916 As plain as 1, 2, 3... and 4 — ethics and organization structure. Linda DeLeon. **Admin. Soc.** 25:3 11:1993 pp.293 - 316.
917 Assessing the structure of prejudicial attitudes — the case of attitudes toward homosexuals. Geoffrey Haddock; Mark P. Zanna; Victoria M. Esses. **J. Pers. Soc. Psychol.** 65:6 12:1993 pp.1105 - 1118.
918 Atitudes dos estudantes universitários face às novas tecnologias de informação: construção de um modelo de análise. *[In Portuguese]*; (The attitudes of university students to new data-processing technology: building a model for analysis.) *[Summary]*; *[Summary in French]*. Jorge Vala; António Caetano. **Anál. Soc.** XXVIII:3(122) 1993 pp.523 - 554.
919 Attitude change following persuasive communication — integrating social judgment theory and the elaboration likelihood model. F.W. Siero; B.J. Doosje. **Eur. J. Soc. Psychol.** 23:5 9-10:1993 pp.541 - 554.
920 The attitude polarization phenomenon — role of reponse measure, attitude extremity, and behavioral consequences of reported attitude change. Arthur G. Miller; John W. McHoskey; Cynthia M. Bane; Timothy G. Dowd. **J. Pers. Soc. Psychol.** 64:4 4:1993 pp.561 - 574.
921 Attitudes and attitude change. James M. Olson; Mark P. Zanna. **Ann. R. Psych.** 44 1993 pp.117 - 154.
922 Beliefs about the native-migrant socio-economic gap in the Netherlands. Rob Eisinga; Albert Felling; Jan Lammers. **Polit. Indiv.** 3:2 1993 pp.67 - 92.
923 A brief report on hope in peace and war, and in good times and bad. Sara Staats; Christie Partlo. **Soc. Ind.** 29:2 6:1993 pp.229 - 243.
924 Bringing the good back in: values, objectivity and the future. Wendell Bell. **Int. Soc. Sci. J.** 137 8:1993 pp.333 - 348.

C: Individuals. Groups. Organizations

925   Conservatism and the political views of young men in Austria. Wolfgang Schulz; Hilde Weiss. **Eur. Sociol. R.** 9:1 5:1993 pp.79 - 93.

926   Cross-cultural comparison of attitudes toward welfare-state programs — path analysis with log-linear models. Ram A. Cnaan; Yeheskel Hasenfeld; Avital Cnaan; Jane Rafferty. **Soc. Ind.** 29:2 6:1993 pp.123 - 152.

927   The death fantasy scale — a measure based on metaphors of one's personal death. Jim McLennan; Glen W. Bates; Emelie Johnson; Ann R. Lavery; David De L. Horne. **J. Psychol.** 127:6 11:1993 pp.619 - 624.

928   Definition and assessment of accuracy in social stereotypes. Charles M. Judd; Bernadette Park. **Psychol. Rev.** 100:1 1:1993 pp.109 - 128.

929   Dimensions of inequality — a comparison of attitudes in Sweden and Britain. Stefan Svallfors. **Eur. Sociol. R.** 9:3 12:1993 pp.267 - 287.

930   Do laboratory experiences change college students' attitudes toward the elderly? Alta F. Shoemake; Virginia T. Rowland. **Educ. Geront.** 19:4 6:1993 pp.295 - 310.

931   Educating for change in attitudes toward nature and environment among oriental Jews in Israel. Abraham Stahl. **Envir. Behav.** 25:1 1:1993 pp.3 - 21.

932   The effect of hindsight bias on fear of future illness. Richard S. Brown; Christopher W. Williams; Paul R. Lees-Haley. **Envir. Behav.** 25:5 9:1993 pp.577 - 585.

933   Effects of HIV/AIDS information on attitudes toward AIDS — a cross-ethnic comparison of college students. David S. Goh. **J. Psychol.** 127:6 11:1993 pp.611 - 618.

934   Die ego-zentrierten Netzwerke von Meinungsbildnern („Opinion leaders"). *[In German]*; (The personal networks of opinion leaders.) *[Summary]*. Michael Schenk. **Kölner Z. Soz. Soz. psy.** 45:2 6:1993 pp.254 - 269.

935   Einstellungen zur staatlichen Regelung des Schwangerschaftsabbruchs in Ost- und Westdeutschland — Determinanten und politische Konsequenzen. *[In German]*; (Attitudes towards the abortion law in East and West Germany — determinants and political consequences.) *[Summary]*. Hans Rattinger. **Z. Soziol.** 22:2 4:1993 pp.111 - 124.

936   Employers' attitude towards people with disabilities. Sheila Honey; Nigel Meager; Matthew Williams. Brighton, Sussex: Institute of Manpower Studies, 1993. 196p. *ISBN: 1851841687*. (*Series:* IMS Report - 245).

937   Los españoles y la sexualidad. *[In Spanish]*; [The Spanish and sexuality]. Carlos A. Malo de Molina. Madrid: Temas de Hoy, 1992. 239p. *ISBN: 8478801634*.

938   Etnicheskie stereotipy i ikh vliianie na formirovanie obshchestvennogo mneniia. *[In Russian]*; [Ethnic stereotypes and their influence upon social opinion]. S. Chugov. **Mir. Ekon. Mezh. Otno.** 1 1993 pp.41 - 54.

939   Evangelicals in the new class — class versus subcultural predictors of ideology. John Schmalzbauer. **J. Sci. S. Relig.** 32:4 12:1993 pp.330 - 342.

940   Fear of crime — read all about it? The relationship between newspaper crime reporting and fear of crime. Paul Williams; Julie Dickinson. **Br. J. Crimin.** 33:1 Winter:1993 pp.33 - 56.

941   Genocide, a sociological perspective. Helen Fein. London, UK, Newbury Park, CA, US: Sage Publications, 1990. vi, 126p. *Includes bibliographical references: (p. [113]-126)*. (*Series:* Current sociology = La Sociologie contemporaine - 38, no. 1).

942   Eine Grid-Group-Analyse sozialer Gerechtigkeit. Die neuen und alten Bundesländer im Vergleich. *[In German]*; (A grid-group analysis of social justice — a

comparative study of former East and West Germany.) *[Summary]*. Bernd Wegener; Stefan Liebig. **Kölner Z. Soz. Soz. psy.** 45:4 12:1993 pp.668 - 690.
943 How children think and feel about war and peace — an Australian study. Robin Hall. **J. Peace Res.** 30:2 5:1993 pp.181 - 196.
944 How people think, reason, and feel about rights and liberties. Dennis Chong. **Am. J. Pol. Sc.** 37:3 8:1993 pp.867 - 899.
945 Ideology in action — a pragmatic approach to a contested concept. Gary Alan Fine; Kent Sandstrom. **Sociol. Theory** 11:1 3:1993 pp.21 - 38.
946 The impact of privacy and confidentiality concerns on survey participation: the case of the 1990 U.S. census. Eleanor Singer; Nancy A. Mathiowetz; Mick P. Couper. **Publ. Opin. Q.** 57:4 Winter:1993 pp.465 - 482.
947 In the path of Daedalus — middle-class Australians' attitudes to embryo research. Lucy Sullivan. **Br. J. Soc.** 44:2 6:1993 pp.271 - 302.
948 Inconsistency in beliefs about distributive justice — a cautionary note. Carol Burgoyne; Adam Swift; Gordon Marshall. **J. Theory Soc. Behav.** 23:4 12:1993 pp.327 - 342.
949 Indicators of modern health attitudes in an urban setting — an exploration of the attitude-behavior relationship. G.B. Fosu. **Soc. Ind.** 28:1 1:1993 pp.45 - 70.
950 Intensifiers in behavioral frequency questions. Colm A. O'Muircheartaigh; George D. Gaskell; Daniel B. Wright. **Publ. Opin. Q.** 57:4 Winter:1993 pp.552 - 565.
951 The interface between racism and sexism. Jim Sidanius. **J. Psychol.** 127:3 5:1993 pp.311 - 322.
952 Measuring satisfaction with organizations: predictions from information accessibility. Yaacov Schul; Miriam Schiff. **Publ. Opin. Q.** 57:4 Winter:1993 pp.536 - 551.
953 Numerical support, information processing and attitude change. C.K.W. de Dreu; N.K. de Vries. **Eur. J. Soc. Psychol.** 23:6 11-12:1993 pp.647 - 662.
954 Obshchestvennye nastroeniia v segodniashnei Rossii. *[In Russian]*; (State of minds in contemporary Russian society.) G. Vainstein. **Mir. Ek. Mez. Ot.** 8 1993 pp.18 - 28.
955 Panel analysis of the moderating effects of commitment on job satisfaction, intent to quit, and health following organizational change. Thomas M . Begley; Joseph M. Czajka. **J. Appl. Psychol.** 78:4 8:1993 pp.552 - 556.
956 Perceived political climate and job attitudes. Amos Drory. **Organ. Stud.** 14:1 1993 pp.59 - 71.
957 Perceptions of crime, fear of crime, and attitudes to police in Victoria: selected findings from the Australian Bureau of Statistics Crime and Crime Prevention Survey, Victoria, July 1987. Pat O'Malley. Bundoora, VIC: National Centre for Socio-Legal Studies, La Trobe University, 1991. 63p. *ISBN: 0858167972*. (*Series:* Research paper series - 1).
958 Polaków postawy pragmatyczne. *[In Polish]*; [The pragmatic attitudes of the Poles]. Jolanta Augustyniak-Kopka. **Prz. Soc.** XLI 1992 pp.129 - 144.
959 Presupposti psicosociali all'inchiesta demodossalogica. *[In Italian]*; [Psychosocial assumptions in surveys for research into the formation of public opinion]. Giulio D'Orazio. **Sociologia [Rome]** XXVII:1-3 1993 pp.479 - 498.
960 Punish and rehabilitate? Public attitudes towards six common crimes. Richard C. McCorkle. **Crime Delin.** 39:2 4:1993 pp.240 - 252.

C: Individuals. Groups. Organizations

961 Race, work, and welfare — attitudes toward the required employment of young mothers who use welfare. Cynthia Rexroat. **Pop. Res. Pol. R.** 12:2 1993 pp.123 - 138.

962 Reputation, image, and impression management. Dennis Basil Bromley. New York; Chichester: Wiley, 1993. 300p. *ISBN: 0471938696. Includes bibliographical references and indexes.*

963 Russia anni '90. La perestroika è fallita, la postperestroika è partita. *[In Italian]*; (Russia 1990's. Perestroika failed, postperestroika starts.) Vladimir Rukavishnikov. **Sociol. Urb. Rur.** XIII:36-37 1991-1992 pp.243 - 257.

964 Sinusondy obshchestvennogo mneniia. *[In Russian]*; [Social opinion]. I.V. Trubina; A.A. Neshchadin; V.K. Kashin. **Obshch. Ekon.** 3 1993 pp.63 - 75.

965 Social orientation of students in the Israeli state high school system. Yaacov J. Katz; Mirjam Schmida. **J. Psychol.** 127:3 5:1993 pp.303 - 310.

966 [A sociological study on the structure of "yoseba" discrimination]; *[Text in Japanese]*. Mitsutoshi Nakane. Hiroshima: Hiroshima Shudo University Press, 1993. 124p.

967 Sotsiologiia, vlast', obshchestvennoe mnenie. *[In Russian]*; (Sociology, power, public opinion.) M.N. Rutkevich. **Sot. Issle.** 7 1993 pp.3 - 13.

968 Southern intolerance — a fundamentalist effect? Christopher G. Ellison; Marc A. Musick. **Soc. Forc.** 72:2 12:1993 pp.379 - 398.

969 [A survey of student awareness regarding the human rights of Koreans living in Japan]; *[Text in Japanese]*. Katsuhide Yokoyama. **Ryuk. Kiyo** 14(2) 1993 pp.35 - 59.

970 Survey of the perceptions, values, expectations and stratification of the black youth of Port Elizabeth. C. N. Hoelsen. Port Elizabeth: Employment Research Unit/ Vista University, 1991. 98 leavesp. *ISBN: 1868280128.* (*Series:* Research report - 31).

971 What does the Lord require?: how American Christians think about economic justice. Stephen Hart. New York: Oxford University Press, 1992. xii, 253p. *ISBN: 0195067622. Includes bibliographical references (p. 225-246) and index.*

D: CULTURE
CULTURE

D.1: Culture
Culture

972 Alasdair MacIntyre: critic of modernity. Peter McMylor. London; New York: Routledge, 1993. 224p. *ISBN: 041504426X, 0415044278. Includes bibliographical references and index.*

973 Attachment and the transmission of culture — an evolutionary perspective. Daniel G. Freedman; Jane Gorman. **J. Soc. Evol. Sys.** 16:3 1993 pp.297 - 329.

974 Die Befreiung der Kulturen. Europas Kulturkreise nach dem „Ende der Systeme". *[In German]*; [The liberation of culture. Europe's cultural circles after the "collapse of the systems"]. Heinz-Jürgen Axt. **Südosteur. Mitteil.** 33:1 1993 pp.1 - 13.

975 Beyond boundaries: understanding, translation, and anthropological discourse. Pálsson Gísli [Ed.]. Providence, RI; Oxford, UK: Berg, 1993. xii, 260p. *ISBN: 085496813X. Includes bibliographical references (p. 231-248) and index. (Series:* Explorations in anthropology).

976 Budushchee Rossii vyrastaet iz proshlogo. *[In Russian]*; (Russia's future stems from the past. Post-communism as the logical phase of the development of Eurasian civilization.) *[Summary]*. V.B. Pastukhov. **Polis [Moscow]** 5-6 1992 pp.59 - 75.

977 »Chislo zveria«: k proiskhozhdeniiu sotsiologicheskogo proekta »Avtoritarnaia lichnost'«. *[In Russian]*; ("The number of beast" — on the origin of the sociological project "authoritarian person".) A.S. Dmitriev. **Sot. Issle.** 3 1993 pp.66 - 74.

978 Continuity and change: aspects of contemporary Norway. Anne Cohen-Kiel [Ed.]. Oslo: Scandinavian University Press, 1993. 266p. *ISBN: 8200211169.*

979 A critical and cultural theory reader. Antony Easthope [Ed.]; Kate McGowan [Ed.]. Buckingham: Open University Press, 1992. viii, 270p. *ISBN: 0335099459, 0335099440. Bibliography: p.263-267; includes index.*

980 Cultural identity and the formation of sub-national, national and transnational ideologies. Martin Peterson. **Scand. J. Devel. Altern.** XII:4 12:1993 pp.5 - 32.

981 Cultural imperialism in the late 20th century. James Petras. **J. Cont. Asia** 23:2 1993 pp.139 - 148.

982 [Cultural relativism and social policy]; *[Text in Japanese]*. Akihiro Sugino. **Over. Soc. Sec. News** 105 1993 pp.60 - 70.

983 Cultural rules and material relations. Douglas V. Porpora. **Sociol. Theory** 11:2 7:1993 pp.212 - 229.

984 Cultural studies. Fred Inglis. Oxford: Blackwell, 1993. 262p. *ISBN: 0631184538.*

985 The cultural studies reader. Simon During [Ed.]. London: Routledge, 1993. 478p. *ISBN: 0415077095, 0415077087.*

986 Cultural theory, ethics and politics. Oskar Gruenwald. **J. Interd. Stud.** IV:1/2 1992 pp.1 - 26.

987 Culture. Chris Jenks. New York; London: Routledge, 1993. 182p. *ISBN: 0415072786. Includes bibliographical references and index. (Series:* Key ideas).

988 Culture and anarchy and other writings. Matthew Arnold; Stefan Collini [Ed.]. New York; Cambridge: Cambridge University Press, 1993. 248p. *ISBN: 0521374405,*

D: Culture

052137796X. *Includes bibliographical references and index.* (*Series:* Cambridge texts in the history of political thought).

989 Culture and power: a media, culture & society reader. Paddy Scannell [Ed.]; Philip Schlesinger [Ed.]; Colin Sparks [Ed.]. London: SAGE, 1992. ix,357p. *ISBN: 0803986300, 0803986319. Includes bibliographies and index.* (*Series:* The Media, culture & society series).

990 Culture and society in new order Indonesia. Virginia Matheson Hooker [Ed.]. Kuala Lumpur, New York: Oxford University Press, 1993. xxiii, 302p. *ISBN: 0195886186. Includes bibliographical references and index.* (*Series:* South-East Asian social science monographs).

991 Culture, modernity, and nationalism — further reflections. Benjamin I. Schwartz. **Dædalus** 122:3 Summer:1993 pp.207 - 226.

992 The culture of complaint: the fraying of America. Robert Hughes. New York, Oxford: Oxford University Press, 1993. xiii,210p. *ISBN: 0195076761.*

993 The culture of love: Victorians to moderns. Stephen Kern. Cambridge, Mass.: Harvard University Press, 1992. x, 458p. *Includes bibliographical references and index.*

994 [Culture pluralism in an integrated world]; *[Text in Japanese].* Hideaki Hirano. **Shisō** 824 1993 pp.4 - 16.

995 Dead artists, live theories and other cultural problems. Stanley Aronowitz. London: Routledge, 1993. 323p. *ISBN: 0415907373.*

996 [The differences between "the general" and "the universal" in the cultural sciences]; *[Text in Japanese].* Keisuke Ikoshi. **Shak. Kenk. Nih. Shak. Gak.** 15 1993 pp.68 - 82.

997 Discourse analysis and racist talk. R. Wodak; R. Mitten; S. Jäger; F. Januschek; E. Petermann-Graubner; F. Stern; T. MacCreanor; Y. Tobin; M.I. Bresnahan; M. Sun Kim. **Folia Ling.** XXVII:3-4 1993 pp.185 - 363. *Collection of 7 articles.*

998 Eco-culture, development, and architecture. Chris Abel. **Know. Pol.** 6:3+4 1993-1994 pp.10 - 28.

999 Economía española, cultura y sociedad: homenaje a Juan Velarde Fuertes, ofrecido por la Universidad Complutense. *[In Spanish]*; [Spanish economy, culture and society: homage to Juan Velarde Fuertes, given by the Alcalá de Henares University]. José Luis García Delgado [Ed.]; José María Serrano Sanz [Ed.]. Madrid: EUDEMA, 1992. 3 vp. *ISBN: 8477541019. Includes bibliographical references.*

1000 Economies of signs and space. Scott Lash; John Urry. London: Sage Publications, 1993. 360p. *ISBN: 0803984715.* (*Series:* Theory, culture & society).

1001 Fictions of collective life: public drama in late modern culture. David Christopher Chaney. New York; London: Routledge, 1993. 228p. *ISBN: 0415032334, 0415093198. Includes bibliographical references and index.*

1002 Go with your feelings: Hong Kong and Taiwan popular culture in Greater China. Thomas B. Gold. **China Quart.** 136 12:1993 pp.907 - 925.

1003 Greeks: a portrait of self and others. Paul Cartledge. Oxford: Oxford University Press, 1993. 232p. *ISBN: 0192891472.* (*Series:* OPUS).

1004 Gunfighter nation: the myth of the frontier in twentieth-century America. Richard Slotkin. New York, Toronto, New York: Atheneum, Maxwell Macmillan Canada, Maxwell Macmillan International, 1992. xii, 850p. *ISBN: 0689121636. Includes bibliographical references (p. 767-828) and index.*

1005 Habermas, mass culture and the future of the public sphere. Nick Stevenson. **Berkeley J. Soc.** 38 1993-1994 pp.221 - 248.

1006 History, religion and identity in modern Britain. Keith Robbins. London: Hambledon, 1993. xi,301p. *ISBN: 1852851015.*

D: Culture

1007 [Human society of America]; *[Text in Japanese]*. Atsuhiro Terada. Tokyo: Sinsensha, 1993. 261p.
1008 La incómoda posición de la cultura en el desarrollo. *[In Spanish]*; [The inconvenient position of culture in development]. Paulina Gutiérrez. **Leviatán** II:53/54 Otoño/Invierno:1993 pp.155 - 166.
1009 Intercultural communication competence. Richard Lee Wiseman [Ed.]; Jolene Koester [Ed.]. Newbury Park, Calif: Sage, 1993. viii, 255p. *ISBN: 0803947194. Includes bibliographical references (p. 222-247) and index.* (*Series:* International and intercultural communication annual).
1010 Japan and the pursuit of a new American identity: work and education in a multicultural age. Walter Feinberg. London: Routledge, 1993. 216p. *ISBN: 0415906830.*
1011 Kryzys kultury. *[In Polish]*; (The crisis of culture.) *[Summary]*. Jan Szczepański. **Prz. Soc.** XL 1993 pp.95 - 100.
1012 Literary into cultural studies. Antony Easthope. New York; London: Routledge, 1991. xii, 202p. *ISBN: 0415066409, 0415066417. Bibliography: p.191-199; includes index.*
1013 The location of culture. Homi K. Bhabha. London: Routledge, 1993. 285p. *ISBN: 0415016355. Includes bibliographical references and index.*
1014 [Mass culture in the information society]; *[Text in Japanese]*. Takeshi Sato. **Gend. No Esup.** 312 1993 pp.5 - 24.
1015 Misconceptions of culture and perversions of multiculturalism. Louis Goldman. **Interchange** 24:4 1993 pp.397 - 408.
1016 Modernity, self-identity and the sequestration of death. Phillip A. Mellor; Chris Shilling. **Sociology** 27:3 8:1993 pp.411 - 431.
1017 Multiculturalism in Britain — fragmented reality or policy option?. John Fraser. **Aff. Soc. Int.** XXI:1 1993 pp.21 - 40.
1018 Multilevel structural analysis. Peter M. Blau. **Soc. Networks** 15:2 6:1993 pp.201 - 215.
1019 My space or yours? De Certeau, Frow and the meanings of popular culture. Tony Schirato. **Cult. St.** 7:2 5:1993 pp.282 - 291.
1020 National character, regional culture, and the values of Canadians and Americans; *[Summary in French]*. D. Baer; E. Grabb; W. Johnston. **Can. R. Soc. A.** 30:1 2:1993 pp.13 - 36.
1021 Nationalisms and national identities. Nahid Yeganeh [Contrib.]; Ann Curthoys [Contrib.]; Catherine Nash [Contrib.]; Máighréad Medbh [Contrib.]; Anne McClintock [Contrib.]; Suruchi Thapar [Contrib.]; Catherine Hall [Contrib.]; Clara Connolly [Contrib.]. **Feminist R.** 44 Summer:1993 pp.3 - 111.
1022 Nations, colonies and metropoles. Daniel A. Segal [Ed.]; Richard Handler [Ed.]; Pauline Turner Strong [Contrib.]; Barrik van Winkle [Contrib.]; Judith T. Irvine [Contrib.]; Pieter M. Judson [Contrib.]; Lora Wildenthal [Contrib.]; Karen Fog Olwig [Contrib.]; David Beriss [Contrib.]; Colleen Ballerino Cohen [Contrib.]; Frances E. Mascia-Lees. **Soc. Anal.** 33 9:1993 pp.9 - 151. *Collection of 7 articles.*
1023 O panorama civilizacional contemporâneo: uma ou mais civilizações modernas? *[In Portuguese]*; (The contemporary civilizational scene: one or many civilizations?) *[Summary]*; *[Summary in French]*. S.N. Eisenstadt. **Anál. Soc.** XXVIII:3(122) 1993 pp.475 - 488.

D: Culture

1024   O pesadelo da amnésia coletiva: um estudo sobre os conceitos de memória, tradição e traços do passado. *[In Portuguese]*; (The nightmare of collective amnesia: study of the concepts of memory, tradition and traces of the past.) *[Summary]*; *[Summary in French]*. Myrian Santos. **Rev. Bras. Ciên. Soc.** 8:23 10:1993 pp.70 - 84.

1025   L'Occident, miroir brisé. Une évaluation partielle de l'anthropologie sociale assorties de quelques perspectives. *[In French]*; (The West, the broken mirror.) *[Summary]*. Maurice Godelier. **Annales** 48:5 9-10:1993 pp.1183 - 1207.

1026   On edge: the crisis of contemporary Latin American culture. George Yúdice [Ed.]; Juan Flores [Ed.]; Jean Franco [Ed.]. Minneapolis: University of Minnesota Press, 1992. xiv, 234p. *ISBN: 0816619387, 0816619395.* Includes bibliographical references and index. (*Series:* Cultural politics).

1027   On the detachment of technique. Keith L. Raitz. **St. Philos. Educ.** 12:2-4 1993 pp.165 - 178.

1028   Pierre Bourdieu. Jill Forbes [Ed.]; Michael Kelly [Ed.]; Morag Shiach [Contrib.]; Margaret Archer [Contrib.]; Roy Boyne [Contrib.]; Mary McAllester-Jones [Contrib.]; Jacques Leenhardt [Contrib.]; Brian Rigby [Contrib.]; Ian MacLean [Contrib.]; Peter Collier [Contrib.]. **Fr. Cult. Stud.** 4(3):12 10:1993 pp.209 - 304. *Collection of 9 articles.*

1029   Pluralistic ignorance and alcohol use on campus — some consequences of misperceiving the social norm. Deborah A. Prentice; Dale T. Miller. **J. Pers. Soc. Psychol.** 64:2 2:1993 pp.243 - 256.

1030   Polarizing American culture. Paul Jerome Croce [Contrib.]; David E. Pearson [Contrib.]; Arthur Asa Berger [Contrib.]; Stanley Rothman [Contrib.]; Frederick R. Lynch [Contrib.]; Joshua Meyrowitz [Contrib.]; John Maguire [Contrib.]; Leo Bogart [Contrib.]. **Society** 30:5/Whole No. 205 7-8:1993 pp.11 - 56. *Collection of 7 articles.*

1031   Psychological impact of biculturalism — evidence and theory. Teresa LaFromboise; Hardin L.K. Coleman; Jennifer Gerton. **Psychol . B.** 114:3 11:1993 pp.395 - 412.

1032   Public space and the public sphere — political theory and the historical geography of modernity. P. Howell. **Envir. Plan. D.** 11:3 6:1993 pp.303 - 322.

1033   Rationality, romanticism and the individual — Max Weber's "modernism" and the confrontation with "modernity"; *[Summary in French]*. Andrew M. Koch. **Can. J. Poli.** XXVI:1 3:1993 pp.123 - 143.

1034   Repression, exile, and democracy: Uruguayan culture. Saúl Sosnowski; Louise B. Popkin. Durham: Duke University Press, 1993. viii, 259p. *ISBN: 0822312581, 0822312689.* Includes bibliographical references and index. (*Series:* Latin America in translation/en traducción/em tradução).

1035   Republic of signs: liberal theory and American popular culture. Anne Norton. Chicago: University of Chicago Press, 1993. viii, 195p. *ISBN: 0226595129, 0226595137.* Includes bibliographical references (p. 175-190) and index.

1036   Secular vocations: intellectuals, professionalism, culture. Bruce Robbins. New York; London: Verso, 1993. 263p. *ISBN: 0860914305.* Includes index. (*Series:* Haymarket series).

1037   Seducing the French: the dilemma of Americanization. Richard Francis Kuisel. Berkeley and Los Angeles, California: University of California Press, 1993. xiii, 296p. *ISBN: 0520079620.*

1038   Sex, art, and American culture: essays. Camille Paglia. New York: Vintage, 1992. xiii,337p. *ISBN: 0670846120, 067084800X.* Includes index.

D: Culture

1039 A sociology of modernity: liberty and discipline. Peter Wagner. New York; London: Routledge, 1993. 267p. *ISBN: 0415081858, 0415081866. Includes bibliographical references and index.*

1040 Socjologia kulturyw 40-leciu łódzkiego ośrodka socjologicznego. *[In Polish]*; (Sociology of culture on the 40th anniversary of the Lodz Centre of Sociology.) *[Summary]*. Zbigniew Bokszański. **Prz. Soc.** XL 1993 pp.41 - 48.

1041 [Some aspects of "French style of integration"]; *[Text in Japanese]*. Yuji Nakano. **Hos. Ken.** 60(2) 1993 pp.423 - 437.

1042 Standards-making organizations and the rationalization of American life. Marc A. Olshan. **Sociol. Q.** 34:2 5:1993 pp.319 - 336.

1043 Symposium — communication, culture, and identity. Philip Schlesinger [Contrib.]; Jesus-Martin Barbero [Contrib.]; Haluk Şahin [Contrib.]; Asu Aksoy [Contrib.]; Marjorie Ferguson [Contrib.]. **J. Comm.** 43:2 Spring:1993 pp.6 - 57. *Collection of 4 articles.*

1044 The tapestry vision of Canadian multiculturalism. Seymour V. Wilson. **Can. J. Poli.** XXVI:4 12:1993 pp.645 - 669.

1045 Theory of culture. Richard Münch [Ed.]; Neil Joseph Smelser [Ed.]. Berkeley: University of California Press, 1992. xiii, 410p. *ISBN: 0520075986. Based on papers from a conference held July 23-25, 1988 in Bremen, sponsored by the Theory Sections of the American Sociological Association and the German Sociological Association. Includes bibliographical references and index. (Series:* New directions in cultural analysis).

1046 Tradition and transition in Southern Africa: Festschrift for Philip and Iona Mayer. Andrew Spiegel [Ed.]; P. A. McAllister [Ed.]; Philip Mayer [Dedicatee]; Iona Mayer [Dedicatee]. Johannesburg, South Africa: Witwatersrand University Press, 1991. 274p. *ISBN: 1868142019. Includes bibliographical references. (Series:* African studies).

1047 Turkey and the West: changing political and cultural identities. Metin Heper [Ed.]; Heinz Kramer [Ed.]; Ayse Öncü [Ed.]. London: I.B. Tauris, 1993. 289p. *ISBN: 1850436118.*

1048 Voices of change: participatory research in the United States and Canada. Peter Park [Ed.]. Westport, Conn: Bergin & Garvey, 1993. xxii, 203p. *ISBN: 0897893344.*

1049 Wandel des Kulturbegriffs — ein Modell der Konkurrenz von Generationen? *[In German]*; (Changing conceptions of culture — a model of generational competition?) *[Summary]*; *[Summary in French]*. Albrecht Göschel. **Arc. Kommunal.** 32:1 1993 pp.71 - 86.

1050 Wasta: the hidden force in Middle Eastern society. Robert B. Cunningham; Yasin K. Sarayrah. Westport, Conn.; New York: Greenwood Press; Praeger, 1993. viii, 209p. *ISBN: 0275944026. Includes bibliographical references and index.*

1051 We have never been modern. Bruno Latour. Hemel Hempstead: Harvester Wheatsheaf, 1992. 153p. *ISBN: 0745006825.*

1052 What's so funny?: the comic conception of culture and society. Murray S. Davis. Chicago: University of Chicago Press, 1993. xiv, 386p. *ISBN: 0226138100. Includes bibliographical references and index.*

1053 When culture is everywhere — reflections on a favorite concept. Ulf Hannerz. **Ethnos** 58:1-2 1993 pp.95 - 111.

1054 Wrapping culture: politeness, presentation, and power in Japan and other societies. Joy Hendry. Oxford: Clarendon Press, 1993. 200p. *ISBN: 0198273894. Includes*

D: Culture

bibliographical references. (Series: Oxford studies in the anthropology of cultural forms).

Postmodernism
Postmodernisme

1055 Aesthetics, play and cultural memory — Giddens and Habermas on the postmodern challenge. Kenneth H. Tucker. **Sociol. Theory** 11:2 7:1993 pp.194 - 211.
1056 Against Finkielkraut's La Défense de la Pensée — culture, post-modernism and education. Michael Peters. **Fr. Cult. Stud.** 4:11 (Part 2) 6:1993 pp.91 - 106.
1057 The barbarian temperament: toward a postmodern critical theory. Stjepan Gabriel Mestrovic. London, New York: Routledge, 1993. 326p. *ISBN: 0415085721. Includes bibliographical references and index.*
1058 Beobachtungen der Moderne. *[In German]*; [Observations on the modern age]. Niklas Luhmann. Opladen: Westdeutscher Verlag, 1992. 220p. *ISBN: 3531122630. Includes bibliographical references.*
1059 Between modernism and postmodernism. Lawrence D. Berg. **Prog. H. Geog.** 17:4 12:1993 pp.490 - 507.
1060 En route to transnational postmodernism — Grace Jones, Josephine Baker and the African diaspora. Carolyn G. Anderson. **Soc. Sci. Info.** 32:3 1993 pp.491 - 512.
1061 From postmodern anthropology to deconstructive ethnography. Stephen Linstead. **Human Relat.** 46:1 1:1993 pp.97 - 120.
1062 The life and times of postmodernity. Keith Tester. New York, London: Routledge, 1993. 168p. *ISBN: 0415075459, 0415098327. Includes bibliographical references and index.*
1063 Postmodern revisionings of the political. Anna Yeatman. London: Routledge, 1993. 141p. *ISBN: 0415901979. (Series:* Thinking gender).
1064 Postmodern thought in symbolic interaction — reconstructing social inquiry in light of late-modern concerns. Michael A. Katovich; William A. Reese. **Sociol. Q.** 34:3 8:1993 pp.391 - 411.
1065 Postmodernism and philosophy of science — a critical engagement. Raphael Sassower. **Philos. S. Sc.** 23:4 12:1993 pp.426 - 445.
1066 Postmodernism and social theory: the debate over general theory. David George Wagner [Ed.]; Steven Seidman [Ed.]. Cambridge: Basil Blackwell, 1992. viii, 379p. *ISBN: 1557860483, 1557862842.*
1067 Postmodernism as pseudohistory. Craig Calhoun. **Theory Cult. Soc.** 10:1 2:1993 pp.75 - 96.
1068 Postmodernism, geography, and the social semiotics of space. A.P. Lagopoulos. **Envir. Plan. D.** 11:3 6:1993 pp.255 - 278.
1069 Postmodernity and the question of the other. H.Y. Jung [Ed.]; S.A. Tyler [Contrib.]; J. Flax [Contrib.]; L. Zhang [Contrib.]; K.W. Benston [Contrib.]; V.Y. Mudimbe [Contrib.]; R.A. Cohen [Contrib.]; M. Mahon [Contrib.]; S. Hekman [Contrib.]; J. Thomas [Contrib.]; W. Haver [Contrib.]; K.-M. Wu [Contrib.]; F. Dallmayr [Contrib.]. **Human St.** 16:1-2 1993 pp.1 - 235. *Collection of 14 articles.*
1070 Postmodern(ized) Simmel. Deena Weinstein; Michael A. Weinstein. New York; London: Routledge, 1993. 235p. *ISBN: 0415082692, 0415082706. Includes bibliographical references and index.*

D: Culture

1071 Principled positions: postmodernism and the rediscovery of value. Judith Squires [Ed.]. London: Lawrence & W, 1993. 211p. *ISBN: 0853157804.*
1072 Social systems theory, postmodernity and the region. Reza Banai. **Area** 24:4 12:1993 pp.386 - 399.
1073 A triptych: Freud's The Interpretation of Dreams, Rider Haggard's She, and Bulwer-Lytton's The Coming Race. Bruce Mazlish. **Comp. Stud. S.** 35:4 10:1993 pp.726 - 745.
1074 Twilight of the parasites — ultramodern capital and the new world order. Stephen Pfohl. **Soc. Prob.** 40:2 5:1993 pp.125 - 151.

Social norms, social control and value systems
Normes sociales, régulation sociale et systèmes de valeur

1075 A community-based theory of rebellion. Roger Petersen. **Eur. J. Soc.** XXXIV:1 1993 pp.41 - 78.
1076 Cultural reproduction. Chris Jenks [Ed.]. New York: Routledge, 1993. 257p. *ISBN: 0415071828, 0415071836. Includes bibliographical references and index.*
1077 Culture shift and popular protest in South Korea. Aie-Rie Lee. **Comp. Poli. S.** 26:1 4:1993 pp.63 - 80.
1078 The discourse of American civil society — a new proposal for cultural studies. Jeffrey C. Alexander; Philip Smith. **Theory Soc.** 22:2 4:1993 pp.151 - 207.
1079 [Folk society and public order in China]; *[Text in Japanese]*. Mamoru Sasaki. Tokyo: Toho Shoten, 1993. 263p.
1080 Les Français du coq à l'âne: histoire d'une révolution des mentalités. *[In French]*; [The French from one subject to another: history of a revolution of opinions]. Philippe Gavi. Paris: Plon, 1992. 309p. *ISBN: 2259024602.*
1081 Group solidarity and social order in Japan. Michael Hechter; Satoshi Kanazawa. **J. Theor. Pol.** 5:4 10:1993 pp.455 - 493.
1082 Herrschaft als soziale Praxis: historische und sozial-anthropologische Studien. *[In German]*; [Power as social practice: historical and socio-anthropological studies]. Alf Lüdtke [Ed.]. Göttingen: Vandenhoeck & Ruprecht, 1991. 594p. *ISBN: 3525356277. Includes bibliographical references.*
1083 Praise, pride and corporate compliance. T. Makkai; J. Braithwaite. **Int. J. S. Law** 21:1 3:1993 pp.73 - 91.
1084 The psychological reality of social construction. Philip C. Rodkin. **Ethn. Racial** 16:4 10:1993 pp.633 - 656.
1085 Reliable design under conflicting social values. Y. Veneris. **Envir. Plan. B.** 20:2 3:1993 pp.145 - 162.
1086 Repression and resistance — problems of regulation in contemporary urban culture (Part 1 — towards definition). C. Stanley. **Int. J. S. Law** 21:1 3:1993 pp.23 - 47.
1087 Social control and the censure(s) of sex. Paul Roberts. **Cr. Law Soc. Chan.** 19:2 3:1993 pp.171 - 186.
1088 Social control in health and law. Jeffrey J. Kamakahi [Ed.]; Deanna B K. Chang [Ed.]. Manoa: Department of Sociology, University of Hawaii, 1992. 229p. *(Series: Social process in Hawaii).*
1089 Social threat and social control. Allen E. Liska [Ed.]. Albany: State University of New York Press, 1992. xiii, 240p. *ISBN: 0791409031, 079140904X. Includes*

D: Culture

bibliographical references (p. 197-233) and index. (Series: SUNY series in deviance and social control).

1090 Soziale Normen und soziale Ordnung. Eine Kritik von Jon Elsters Theorie sozialer Normen. *[In German]*; (Social norms and the social system. A criticism of Jon Elster's theory of social norms.) *[Summary]*; *[Summary in French]*. Michael Schmid. **Berl. J. Soziol.** 3 1:1993 pp.19 - 41.

1091 Toward a dynamics for power and control in society. G.D. Allen. **J. Math. Sociol.** 17:1 1992 pp.1 - 38.

Socialization and alienation
Socialisation et aliénation

1092 Changements sociaux et exclusion sociale des handicapés. *[In French]*; [Social change and social exclusion of handicapped people]. Ammar Abderrazak. **R. Tun. Sci. Soc.** 29:109 1992 pp.373 - 399.

1093 Essai de conceptionalisation de la marginalisation sociale dans le processus de développement économique. *[In French]*; [Attempt at conceptualization of social marginalization in the process of economic development]. Choujaa Mustapha Lahzami. **R. Tun. Sci. Soc.** 29:109 1992 pp.13 - 42.

1094 Der Gast, der bleibt: Dimensionen von Georg Simmels Analyse des Fremdseins. *[In German]*; [The guest who ended up staying: dimensions of Georg Simmels' analysis of alienation]. Almut Loycke [Ed.]. Frankfurt am Main: Campus-Verlag, 1992. 224p. *ISBN: 359334727X*.

1095 Le handicap au quotidien. Empirisme médical et société traditionnelle. *[In French]*; [Handicap in daily life. Medical empiricism and traditional society]. Béchir Maaloul. **R. Tun. Sci. Soc.** 29:109 1992 pp.345 - 371.

1096 Marginalità ed emarginazione sociale: una ricerca empirica a Palermo. *[In Italian]*; [Marginality and social marginalization: empirical research in Palermo]. Caterina Lo Presti. Palermo: Dharba Editrice, 1991. 125p.

1097 The MOS alienation scale — an alternative to Srole's anomia scale. R. Travis. **Soc. Ind.** 28:1 1:1993 pp.71 - 92.

1098 Soziologie: Untersuchungen über die Formen der Vergesellschaftung. *[In German]*; [Sociology: a look at forms of socialization]. Georg Simmel; Otthein Rammstedt [Ed.]. Frankfurt am Main: Suhrkamp, 1992. 1051p. *ISBN: 3518284118*.

1099 Structures sociales contre la sous proletarisation — cas d'un douar du nord ouest et d'un lotissement pour jeunes techniciens et jeunes agriculteurs. *[In French]*; [Social structures protecting the underprivileged. The example of a "douar" from the northwest and a housing estate for young technicians and farmers]. Sabine Chennoufi. **R. Tun. Sci. Soc.** 29:109 1992 pp.183 - 210.

D.2: Everyday culture
Culture quotidienne

1100 Bilen och bilismen som kulturellt fenomen. *[In Swedish]*; (Automobiles and motorism as a cultural phenomenon.) Annette Rosengren. **Nord. Ny.** 52 1993 pp.4 - 14.

D: Culture

1101 [Contemporary life and human beings]; *[Text in Japanese]*. Kenichi Misawa [Ed.]. Kyoto: Koyo Shobo, 1993.

1102 Cultural politics of everyday life: social constructionism, rhetoric and knowing of the third kind. John Shotter. Buckingham: Open University Press, 1993. xv, 240p. *ISBN: 0335191207, 0335097626. Includes bibliographical references (p. 209-232) and index.*

1103 Dirty marks: the education of self, media, and popular culture. John F. Schostak. London: Pluto Press, 1993. 247p. *ISBN: 0745304303, 0745304311. Includes bibliographical references and index.*

1104 The effects of dieting on eating behavior — a three-factor model. Michael R. Lowe. **Psychol . B.** 114:1 7:1993 pp.100 - 121.

1105 The European diet — regional variations in food consumption in the 1980s. D. Grigg. **Geoforum** 24:3 1993 pp.277 - 290.

1106 The face of fashion: cultural studies in fashion. Jennifer Craik. New York; London: Routledge, 1993. 249p. *ISBN: 0415052610, 0415052629. Includes bibliographical references and index.*

1107 Fashion, culture, and identity. Fred Davis. Chicago: University of Chicago Press, 1992. xi, 226p. *ISBN: 0226138089. Includes bibliographical references (p. 207-216) and index.*

1108 Föremål och språk som symboler i en arbetarkultur. *[In Swedish]*; (Objects and language as symbols in a working class culture.) *[Summary]*. Gunilla Peterson. **Rig** 76:4 1993 pp.97 - 117.

1109 Der gemeine Machiavellismus. Zur dramatologischen Rekonstruktion erfolgsorientierten Alltagshandelns. *[In German]*; [The communal Machiavellianism. On the dramatological reconstruction of everyday behaviour orientated towards success]. Ronald Hitzler. **Social. Int.** 31:2 1993 pp.133 - 148.

1110 Géographie de la santé et mode de vie — l'obésité et l'hypertension artérielle chez les Cri et les Inuit du Nord du Québec. *[In French]*; [Medical geography and living habits — obesity and hypertension among the Cree and Inuit of Northern Quebec] *[Summary]*. J.P. Thouez; P. Foggin; J.M. Ekoe; M. Nadeau; A. Rannou. **Espace Géogr.** XXII:2 1993 pp.166 - 178.

1111 Inside culture: art and class in the American home. David Halle. Chicago: University of Chicago Press, 1993. xvi, 261p. *ISBN: 0226313670.*

1112 "Living" the house, "feeling" the house — Neapolitan issues in thought, organization and structure. Italo Pardo. **Eur. J. Soc.** XXXIII:2 1992 pp.251 - 279.

1113 The McDonaldization of society: the changing character of contemporary social life. George Ritzer. Newbury Park, Calif: Pine Forge Press, 1993. xv, 221p. *ISBN: 0803990006. Includes bibliographical references.*

1114 Nutritional patterns and transitions; *[Summary in French]*; *[Summary in Spanish]*. Barry M. Popkin. **Pop. Dev. Rev.** 19:1 3:1993 pp.138 - 157.

1115 Paradox of plenty: a social history of eating in modern America. Harvey A. Levenstein. New York: Oxford University Press, 1993. ix, 337p. *ISBN: 0195055438. Includes bibliographical references (p. [259]-322) and index.*

1116 Povesednevnost' v labirinte ratsional'nosti. *[In Russian]*; (Everyday life in the labyrinth of rationality.) A.V. Khudenko. **Sot. Issle.** 4 1993 pp.67 - 74.

1117 The refinement of America: persons, houses, cities. Richard L. Bushman. New York: Knopf, Distributed by Random House, 1992. xix, 504p. *ISBN: 0394550102. Includes bibliographical references (p. 449-484) and index.*

D: Culture

1118 The role of animals in human society. S. Plous [Ed.]; Stephen R. Kellert [Contrib.]; Susan Opotow [Contrib.]; Timothy J. Eddy [Contrib.]; Gordon G. Gallup [Contrib.]; Daniel J. Povinelli [Contrib.]; Harold A. Herzog [Contrib.]; Elizabeth Baldwin; Alan D. Bowd [Contrib.]; Kenneth J. Shapiro [Contrib.]; Jerrold Tannenbaum [Contrib.]; Judith M. Siegel [Contrib.]; Faye J. Crosby [Contrib.]. **J. Soc. Issues** 49:1 1993 pp.1 - 184. *Collection of 11 articles.*

1119 Sexy dressing, etc. Duncan Kennedy. Cambridge, Mass., London: Harvard University Press, 1993. 258p. *ISBN: 0674802942.*

1120 Small nations, big neighbour: Denmark and Quebec/Canada compare notes on American popular culture. William Gilsdorf; Ilja Wechselmann; Roger De La Garde [Ed.]. London: John Libbey, 1993. 239p. *ISBN: 0861963431.* (*Series:* Acamedia Research Monograph Series).

1121 Smoking: making the risky decision. W. Kip Viscusi. New York: Oxford University Press, 1992. x, 170p. *ISBN: 0195074866. Includes bibliographical references (p. 159-167) and index.*

1122 La sociologie des mœurs. *[In French]*; [The sociology of habits, customs and behaviour]. Henri Mendras [Ed.]; Bernard Valade; Hassane Ajérar; Irène Théry; Jean Kellerhals; Marianne Modak; Jean-François Perrin; Massimo Sardi; Lilyane Deroche-Gurcel; Michel Forsé; Olivier Galland; Yannick Lemel; Alain Degenne; Marie-Odile Lebeaux; Philippe Besnard; Cyril Grange; Nicolas Herpin. **Ann. Sociol.** 43 1993 pp.9 - 315. *Collection of 12 articles.*

1123 [Sociology of daily life]; *[Text in Japanese].* Sadamitsu Nakagiri. Tokyo: Kobundo, 1993. 209p.

1124 The sociology of death: theory, culture, practice. David Clark [Ed.]. Oxford, UK, Cambridge, MA: Blackwell Publishers/The Sociological Review, 1993. 302p. *ISBN: 0631190570. Includes bibliographical references and index.*

1125 "Sweet love" and women's place: Valentine's Day, Japan style. Millie R. Creighton. **J. Pop. Cult.** 27:3 Winter:1993 pp.1 - 20.

1126 Taste and fashion — the social function of fashion and style. Jukka Gronow. **Acta Sociol.** 36:2 1993 pp.89 - 100.

1127 Ten geleide. De stoffering van het dagelijks leven. *[In Dutch]*; [Introduction. The furnishing of everyday life]. Gerard Rooijakkers. **Volks. Bul.** 19:3 12:1993 pp.317 - 329.

1128 Unwrapping Christmas. Daniel Miller [Ed.]. Oxford: Clarendon Press, 1993. x, 239p. *ISBN: 0198279035. Includes bibliographical references and index.*

1129 What is "good taste". Jukka Gronow. **Soc. Sci. Info.** 32:2 1993 pp.279 - 301.

1130 [Yujinso: a new style Buddhist funeral by lay members]; *[Text in Japanese].* Tsuyoshi Nakano. Tokyo: Daisan Bunmeisha, 1993. 231p.

D.3: Ethics and morals
Éthique et morale

1131 »Als Mann und Frau..« — Grunddatum theologischer Anthropologie — Herausforderung christlicher Sozialethik. *[In German]*; ["When man and woman..." — The founding date of theological anthropology — the challenge of Christian social ethics]. Marianne Heimbach-Steins. **Jahr. Christ. Sozialwiss.** 34 1993 pp.165 - 189.

D: Culture

1132 Altruism. Ellen Frankel Paul [Ed.]; Jeffrey Paul [Ed.]; Fred Dycus Miller [Ed.]. Cambridge [England], New York, NY: Cambridge University Press, 1993. xii, 250p. *ISBN: 0521447593. Includes bibliographical references and index.*

1133 Certified public accountants — ethical perception skills and attitudes on ethics education. Suzanne Pinac Ward; Dan R. Ward; Alan B. Deck. **J. Busin. Ethics** 12:8 8:1993 pp.601 - 610.

1134 A cognitive style perspective on ethical questions. Roger P. McIntyre; Margaret M. Capen. **J. Busin. Ethics** 12:8 8:1993 pp.629 - 634.

1135 A companion to ethics. Peter Singer [Ed.]. Oxford: Basil Blackwell, 1991. 565p. *ISBN: 0631162119. Includes biblographies and index. (Series:* Blackwell companions to philosophy).

1136 A comparative examination of attitudes toward software piracy among business professors and executives. G. Stephen Taylor; J.P. Shim. **Human Relat.** 46:4 4:1993 pp.419 - 433.

1137 Comparative ideologies and alcoholism — the Protestant and proletarian ethics. Timothy P. Rouse; N. Prabha Unnithan. **Soc. Prob.** 40:2 5:1993 pp.213 - 227.

1138 Constructing community: moral pluralism and tragic conflicts. J. Donald Moon. Princeton, N.J: Princeton University Press, 1993. xi, 235p. *ISBN: 0691086427. Includes bibliographical references and index.*

1139 Contretemps: éloges des idéaux perdus. *[In French]*; [Contretemps: eulogies to lost ideals]. Régis Debray. Paris: Gallimard, 1992. 182p. *ISBN: 2070327132.*

1140 Creative morality. Don MacNiven. New York; London: Routledge, 1993. 238p. *ISBN: 0415000297, 0415000300.*

1141 Ekologiia i nravstvennost'. *[In Russian]*; (Ecology and morals.) V. Kosheleva. **Obshch. Nauki Sovrem.** 1 1993 pp.153 - 162.

1142 Empiricism in business ethics — suggested research directions. Diana C. Robertson. **J. Busin. Ethics** 12:8 8:1993 pp.585 - 599.

1143 An ethic of care: feminist and interdisciplinary perspectives. Mary Jeanne Larrabee [Ed.]. New York: Routledge, 1993. viii, 310p. *ISBN: 0415905672, 0415905680. Includes bibliographical references (p. 275-300) and index. (Series:* Thinking gender).

1144 Ethical attentiveness. Paul O'Leary. **St. Philos. Educ.** 12:2-4 1993 pp.139 - 152.

1145 The ethical crises of civilization: moral meltdown or advance. Leslie Lipson. Newbury Park, London: Sage Publications, 1993. xx,343p. *ISBN: 0803952430, 0803952422. Bibliography: p.320-326. Includes index..*

1146 Ethical or practical — an empirical study of students' choices in simulated business scenarios. Charles S. White; Robert S. Dooley. **J. Busin. Ethics** 12:8 8:1993 pp.643 - 651.

1147 Ethics and the environment. Christopher Charles Whiston Taylor [Ed.]. Oxford: Corpus Christi College, 1992. 97p. *ISBN: 095128441X. Proceedings of a conference held at Corpus Christi College, Oxford 20-21 September 1991.*

1148 Ethics as etiquette — the emblematic contribution of Erving Goffman. Laura Bovone. **Theory Cult. Soc.** 10:4 11:1993 pp.25 - 40.

1149 The European values study 1981-1990: summary report. David Gerard [Ed.]; Astrid Vloet [Ed.]. s.l.: Gordon Cook Foundation, 1992. 79p. *European Value Systems Study Group.*

1150 Exploring the relationship between personal values and moral reasoning. James Weber. **Human Relat.** 46:4 4:1993 pp.435 - 463.

D: Culture

1151 God and the marketplace: essays on the morality of wealth creation. Michael Novak; Jon Gower Davies [Ed.]. London: IEA Health and Welfare Unit, 1993. 145p. (*Series:* Choice in welfare series).

1152 The good life and the human good. Ellen Frankel Paul [Ed.]; Jeffrey Paul [Ed.]; Fred Dycus Miller [Ed.]. Cambridge, England, New York, NY: Cambridge University Press, 1992. xiv, 211p. *ISBN: 0521437598. Includes bibliographical references and index.*

1153 Human morality. Samuel Scheffler. New York: Oxford University Press, 1992. 150p. *ISBN: 0195074483.*

1154 An investigation into the acceptability of workplace behaviors of a dubious ethical nature. Peter E. Mudrack. **J. Busin. Ethics** 12:7 7:1993 pp.517 - 524.

1155 Jewish social ethics. David Novak. New York: Oxford University Press, 1992. xiii, 252p. *ISBN: 0195069242. Includes bibliographical references and index.*

1156 Justice, ethics, and New Zealand society. Graham Oddie [Ed.]; Roy W. Perrett [Ed.]. Auckland, Oxford: Oxford University Press, 1992. xvi, 233p. *ISBN: 0195582411. Includes index.*

1157 Justification and application: remarks on discourse ethics. Jurgen Habermas. Cambridge: Polity Press, 1993. 193p. *ISBN: 0745610439.*

1158 Kant and natural law ethics. J.B. Schneewind. **Ethics** 104:1 10:1993 pp.53 - 74.

1159 Killing in self-defense. Seumas Miller. **Publ. Aff. Q.** 7:4 10:1993 pp.325 - 339.

1160 Max Weber désenchanté. *[In French]*; [Max Weber disillusioned]. François-André Isambert. **Ann. Sociol.** 43 1993 pp.357 - 497.

1161 Moral boundaries: a political argument for an ethic of care. Joan C. Tronto. New York, London: Routledge, 1993. 226p. *ISBN: 0415906415.*

1162 Moral dilemmas, genuine and spurious: a comparative anatomy. Alan Donagan. **Ethics** 104:1 10:1993 pp.7 - 21.

1163 Moral systems as evolutionary systems — taking evolutionary ethics seriously. Franz M. Wuketits. **J. Soc. Evol. Sys.** 16:3 1993 pp.251 - 271.

1164 On human nature. Francis Hutcheson; Thomas Mautner. Cambridge, New York, NY: Cambridge University Press, 1993. 194p. *ISBN: 0521430895. Includes bibliographical references and index.*

1165 On measuring ethical judgements. Robert Skipper; Michael R. Hyman. **J. Busin. Ethics** 12:7 7:1993 pp.535 - 545.

1166 Operational modes for multinational corporations in post-apartheid South Africa — a proposal for a code of affirmative action in the marketplace. S. Prakash Sethi. **J. Busin. Ethics** 12:1 1:1993 pp.1 - 12.

1167 Personal and professional values underlying the ethical judgments of marketers. Anusorn Singhapakdi; Scott J. Vitell. **J. Busin. Ethics** 12:7 7:1993 pp.525 - 533.

1168 Persons and death — what's metaphysically wrong with our current statutory definition of death?. John P. Lizza. **J. Medic. Philos.** 18:4 8:1993 pp.351 - 374.

1169 Public relations ethics: Ivy Lee, Hill and Knowlton, and the Gulf War. R. Marlin. **Int. J. Moral Soc. S.** 8:3 Autumn:1993 pp.237 - 256.

1170 Quinn on the double effect — the problem of "closeness". John Martin Fischer; Mark Ravizza; David Copp. **Ethics** 103:4 7:1993 pp.707 - 725.

1171 Recent work on the American professional military ethic — an introduction and survey. James H. McGrath; Gustaf E. Anderson. **Am. Phil. Q.** 30:3 7:1993 pp.187 - 208.

D: Culture

1172 Remodelling the moral order in the Netherlands. Ruben Gowricharn. **Int. J. Soc. E.** 20:12 1993 pp.50 - 64.

1173 Risks and wrongs. Jules L. Coleman. Cambridge [England], New York: Cambridge University Press, 1992. xvii, 508p. *ISBN: 0521329507, 0521428610. Includes bibliographical references (p. 441-497) and index. (Series:* Cambridge studies in philosophy and law).

1174 The role of rights in a theory of social action; *[Summary in German].* James Coleman; Siegwart Lindenberg [Comments by]; Werner Raub [Comments by]. **J. Inst. Theo. Ec.** 149:1 3:1993 pp.213 - 251.

1175 [The significance of the Weber's concept of Gesinnungsethik]; *[Text in Japanese].* Michihiro Yokota. **Rin. Nenpo** 42 1993 pp.69 - 84.

1176 Social desirability bias in cross-cultural ethics research. Donna M. Randall; Y. Paul Huo; Patrice Pawelk. **Intern. J. Organiz. Anal.** 1:2 4:1993 pp.185 - 202.

1177 Sozialethik und Gemeinwohl: die Begründung einer realistischen Sozialethik bei Arthur F. Utz. *[In German]*; [Social ethics and public welfare: the foundations of a realistic social ethic in the work of Arthur F. Utz]. Bernd Kettern. Berlin: Duncker & Humblot, 1992. 194p. *ISBN: 3428074386. Originally presented as the author's thesis (doctoral) -- Universität Trier. Includes bibliographical references and index.*

1178 Value, welfare, and morality. Raymond G. Frey [Ed.]; Christopher W. Morris [Ed.]. Cambridge; New York: Cambridge University Press, 1993. x, 324p. *ISBN: 0521416965. Includes bibliographical references.*

D.4:   **Law**
             Loi

1179 Act and crime: the philosophy of action and its implications for criminal law. Michael S. Moore. Oxford: Clarendon, 1993. xiii,413p. *ISBN: 0198257910. Bibliography: p.391-403. - Includes index. (Series:* Clarendon law series).

1180 An analysis of right in Islamic law. H. Hasim Kamali. **Am. J. Islam. Soc. Sci.** 10:3 Fall:1993 pp.340 - 366.

1181 Anchored narratives: the psychology of criminal evidence. Willem Albert Wagenaar; P. J. van Koppen; Hans F. Crombag. Hemel Hempstead: Harvester Wheatsheaf, 1993. vii, 260p. *ISBN: 0745014585, 0745014593, 0312120303. Bibliography: p.247-252; includes index.*

1182 The brothel boy, and other parables of the law. Norval Morris. New York: Oxford University Press, 1992. 338p. *ISBN: 0195074432.*

1183 Coherence of the law. Luc J. Wintgens. **Arc. Recht. Soz.** 79:4 1993 pp.483 - 519.

1184 Cultural rights: technology, legality, and personality. Celia Lury. New York; London: Routledge, 1993. 239p. *ISBN: 0415031559, 0415095786. Includes bibliographical references and index. (Series:* The International library of sociology).

1185 Flexibility in long-term contractual relationships — the role of co-operation. David Campbell; Donald Harris. **J. Law Soc.** 20:2 Summer:1993 pp.166 - 191.

1186 The folly of the "social scientific" concept of legal pluralism. Brian Z. Tamanaha. **J. Law Soc.** 20:2 Summer:1993 pp.192 - 217.

1187 Geographies of judgment — the doctrine of changed conditions and the geopolitics of race. David Delaney. **Ann. As. Am. G.** 83:1 3:1993 pp.48 - 65.

D: Culture

1188 Gynaetopia — feminine genealogies of common law. Peter Goodrich. **J. Law Soc.** 20:3 Autumn:1993 pp.276 - 308.

1189 Hans Kelsen und die Rechtssoziologie. *[In German]*; [Hans Kelsen and the sociology of law]. Hans Kelsen; Hermann Kantorowicz; Eugen Ehrlich; Max Weber; Stanley L. Paulson [Ed.]. Aalen: Scientia Verlag, 1992. xiii,119p. *ISBN: 3511092078. Includes bibliographical references.*

1190 Islamic family law — ideals and realities. Ziba Mir-Hosseini [Ed.]; Richard Tapper [Contrib.]; Nancy Tapper [Contrib.]; Nadia Abu-Zahra [Contrib.]; Gabriele vom Bruck [Contrib.]; C.W. Watson [Contrib.]; Bernard Botiveau [Contrib.]; Dima Abdulrahim [Contrib.]. **Cam. Anthrop.** 16:2 1992/1993: pp.1 - 97. *Collection of 7 articles.*

1191 Iustititia distributiva. Zum Begriff und zu den Formen der Gerechtigkeit. *[In German]*; [Iustititia distributiva. The concept and the forms of justice]. Michael Köhler. **Arc. Recht. Soz.** 79:4 1993 pp.457 - 482.

1192 Law, language, and legal determinacy. Brian Bix. Oxford: Clarendon Press, 1993. x,221p. *ISBN: 0198257902. Includes bibliographical references and index.*

1193 Marx and law. Andrew Vincent. **J. Law Soc.** 20:4 Winter:1993 pp.371 - 397.

1194 Neue Risiken und neue Rechte. Subjektivierungstendenzen im Recht der Risikogesellschaft. *[In German]*; [New risks and new rights — subjectivization tendencies in the law of the risk society]. Reinhard Damm. **Arc. Recht. Soz.** 79:2 1993 pp.159 - 187.

1195 Nouvelles perspectives en matière de sanctions communautaires. *[In French]*; [New perspectives concerning EC sanctions]. Giovanni Grasso. **Rev. Sci. Crim. D. P.** 2 4-6:1993 pp.265 - 274.

1196 Panic and indifference: the politics of Canada's drug laws : a study in the sociology of law. P.J. Giffen; Shirley Jane Endicott; Sylvia Boorman. Ottawa: Canadian Centre on Substance Abuse, 1991. viii, 638p. *ISBN: 0969546807. Includes bibliographical references and index.*

1197 Philosophie, sociologie, droit. *[In French]*; [Philosophy, sociology, law]. André Berten [Contrib.]; Hervé Pourtois [Contrib.]; Niklas Luhmann [Contrib.]; Jean De Munck [Contrib.]; Olivier De Schutter [Contrib.]; Richard Perry [Contrib.]. **Recher. Sociolog.** XXIV:1-2 1993 pp.1 - 145. *Collection of 7 articles.*

1198 Putting sociology back into the sociology of law. Max Travers. **J. Law Soc.** 20:4 Winter:1993 pp.438 - 451.

1199 Rechts- und Sozialphilosophie in Deutschland heute: Beiträge zur Standortbestimmung. *[In German]*; [Current German legal and social philosophy: contributions to defining the position]. Robert Alexy [Ed.]; Ralf Dreier [Ed.]; Ulfrid Neumann [Ed.]. Stuttgart: F. Steiner, 1991. 440p. *ISBN: 3515058923. Includes bibliographical references and index.*

1200 Regulierung und Deregulierung. Zur Beschleunigung des Rechts. *[In German]*; (Regulation and deregulation. On the acceleration of law.) *[Summary]*. Barbara Rhode. **Soz. Welt.** 44:4 1993 pp.512 - 536.

1201 Réression de la tentative de complicité. Commentaire de l'article 28 du code pénal ivoirien. *[In French]*; [Repression of attempted complicity. Commentary on article 28 of the penal code of the Ivory Coast]. Isabelle Freij-Dalloz. **Rev. Sci. Crim. D. P.** 1 1-3:1993 pp.73 - 85.

1202 La responsabilité civile du fait pénal d'autrui. *[In French]*; [Civil liability for the criminal act of others]. Jean-Yves Lassalle. **Rev. Sci. Crim. D. P.** 1 1-3:1993 pp.19 - 32.

1203 The samurai, the mountie, and the cowboy: should America adopt the gun controls of other democracies?. David B. Kopel. Buffalo, N.Y: Prometheus Books, 1992. 470p. *ISBN: 0879757566. A Cato Institute book. Includes bibliographical references and index.*

1204 The social world of an English Crown Court: witness and professionals in the Crown Court Centre at Wood Green. Paul Rock. Oxford: Clarendon Press, 1993. 390p. *ISBN: 0198258437. Includes index. (Series:* Oxford socio-legal studies).

1205 Socialism and the law: Association for Legal and Social Philosophy, seveneenth annual conference, University of Bristol, 4-6 April 1991. William Watts Miller [Ed.]. Stuttgart: F. Steiner, 1992. 155p. *ISBN: 3515061908. Includes bibliographical references (p. [145]-155).*

1206 Testamentary behavior — issues and evidence about individuality, altruism and social influence. T.P. Schwartz. **Sociol. Q.** 34:2 5:1993 pp.337 - 355.

1207 Les transformations du droit pénal aux Etats-Unis. Pour un autre modèle de justice. *[In French]*; [Changes to the criminal law of the U.S.A. A different model of justice]. François Tulkens. **Rev. Sci. Crim. D. P.** 2 4-6:1993 pp.219 - 237.

1208 The "truth" about autopoiesis. Michael King. **J. Law Soc.** 20:2 Summer:1993 pp.218 - 236.

1209 Union européene et droit pénal européen — proposition pour l'avenir du droit pénal européen. *[In French]*; [European Union and European criminal law — a proposal for the future of European criminal law]. Ulrich Sieber. **Rev. Sci. Crim. D. P.** 2 4-6:1993 pp.249 - 264.

1210 The uses of discretion. Keith Hawkins [Ed.]. Oxford, New York: Clarendon Press, Oxford University Press, 1992. 431p. *ISBN: 0198257627. Includes index. (Series:* Oxford socio-legal studies).

1211 Zmiany społeczne i zmiany prawne w PRL. *[In Polish]*; (Social changes and legal changes in Poland. Typology of relations.) *[Summary]*. Małgorzata Fuszara. **Prz. Soc.** XL 1993 pp.135 - 151.

1212 Zuinig met recht. De Nederlandse rechtscultuur in vergelijking met de Westduitse. *[In Dutch]*; [Justice as last resort. Dutch legal culture compared to the German] *[Summary]*. Erhard Blankenburg. **Mens Maat.** 68:1 2:1993 pp.6 - 18.

D.5: Magic, mythology and religion
Magie, mythologie et religion

1213 The adaptation of Max Weber's theories of religion in Japan. Makoto. Hayashi; Yamanaka Hiroshi. **Jap. J. Relig. St.** 20:2-3 6-9:1993 pp.207 - 228.

1214 Addressing God as ruler. David Nicholls. **Br. J. Soc.** 44:1 3:1993 pp.125 - 141.

1215 African-American religion in the twentieth century: varieties of protest and accommodation. Hans A. Baer; Merrill Singer. Knoxville, Tennessee: University of Tennessee Press, 1992. xxiii, 265p. *ISBN: 0870497464, 0870497472.*

1216 Believing and belonging — religion in rural England. Michael Winter; Christopher Short. **Br. J. Soc.** 44:4 12:1993 pp.635 - 651.

D: Culture

1217 [Coping with society and culture in transition: comparison of Japanese and Sri Lankan village religious values]; *[Text in Japanese]*. Motoyoshi Omori. **Asia Bun. Ken.** 19 1993 pp.19 - 29.

1218 Les cultes orientaux et la nouvelle religiosité en Russie. *[In French]*; (Eastern religions and the new religious awareness in Russia.) Alexandre Agadjanian. **Rev. Ét. Comp.** 24:3-4 9-12:1993 pp.155 - 172.

1219 „Das Religiöse" in Max Webers Religionssoziologie. *[In German]*; [The religious in Max Weber's sociology of religion]. Hartmann Tyrell. **Saeculum** 43:2-3 1992 pp.172 - 230.

1220 De la religion diffuse à la religion des valeurs. *[In French]*; [From diffused religion to a religion of values] *[Summary]*. Roberto Cipriani. **Soc. Compass** 40:1 3:1993 pp.91 - 100.

1221 De ontwikkeling van de godsdienstsociologie in Nederland. *[In Dutch]*; (Sociology of religion in the Netherlands.) *[Summary]*. G. Dekker. **Mens Maat.** 67:3 8:1992 pp.296 - 310.

1222 Denominations as dual structures — an organizational analysis. Mark Chaves. **Soc. Relig.** 54:2 Summer:1993 pp.147 - 169.

1223 The effect of religion on work attitudes in the Netherlands; *[Summary in French]*. Marijke ter Voert. **Soc. Compass** 40:1 3:1993 pp.33 - 44.

1224 An empirical investigation of the discriminability of reported mystical experiences among religious contemplatives, psychotic inpatients, and normal adults. Kenneth Stifler; Joanne Greer; William Sneck; Robert Dovenmuehle. **J. Sci. S. Relig.** 32:4 12:1993 pp.366 - 372.

1225 Fetishism as cultural discourse. Emily S. Apter [Ed.]; William Pietz [Ed.]. Ithaca, N.Y: Cornell University Press, 1993. xi, 393p. *ISBN: 0801425220, 0801497574, 0801426537, 0801499526. Includes bibliographical references (p. 363-382) and index.*

1226 Fundamentalisms and society: reclaiming the sciences, the family, and education. R. Scott Appleby [Ed.]; Martin Emil Marty [Ed.]. Chicago: University of Chicago Press, 1993. ix, 592p. *ISBN: 0226508803. Includes bibliographical references and index.* American Academy of Arts and Sciences. (Series: The fundamentalism project).

1227 La géographie des religions, contexte et perspectives. *[In French]*; (The geography of religions — modern and historical perspectives.) Daniel Dory [Contrib.]; Jean-Luc Piveteau [Contrib.]; Steven Grosby [Contrib.]; Michel Bruneau [Contrib.]; David Ley [Contrib.]; R. Bruce Martin [Contrib.]; Guy Lubeigt [Contrib.]; Roland Breton [Contrib.]; Dean R. Louder [Contrib.]. **Soc. Compass** 40(2) 1993 pp.147 - 300. *Collection of 9 articles.*

1228 The growth of religious diversity: Britain from 1945. Volume 1. Traditions. Gerald Parsons [Ed.]. London: Routledge, [1993]. 352p. *ISBN: 0415083265.*

1229 The human predicament: its changing image : a study in comparative religion and history. Jaroslav Krejci; Anna Krejčová [Contrib.]. New York: St. Martin's Press, 1993. 194p. *ISBN: 031209101X. Includes bibliographical references and index.*

1230 I movimenti religiosi nelle società contemporanee. *[In Italian]*; [Religious movements in contemporary society]. Enzo Pace. **Quad. Sociol.** XXXVI:2 1992 pp.39 - 54.

1231 Ideological hegemony and the political symbolism of religious buildings in Singapore. L. Kong. **Envir. Plan. D.** 11:1 2:1993 pp.23 - 45.

D: Culture

1232 Innovations in religious traditions: essays in the interpretation of religious change. Michael A. Williams [Ed.]; Collett Cox [Ed.]; Martin S. Jaffee [Ed.]. Berlin, New York: Mouton de Gruyter, 1992. 373p. *ISBN: 3110127806. Revised papers from a seminar conducted by the Comparative Religion Program, Henry M. Jackson School of International Studies, University of Washington in 1988. Includes bibliographical references and index.* (*Series:* Religion and society).

1233 [Japanese religion in the occupation period]; *[Text in Japanese]*. Fujio Ikado. Tokyo: Miraisha, 1993. 650p.

1234 Jongeren over de dood en een hiernamaals. *[In Dutch]*; (Youth on death and a life after death.) *[Summary]*. Joep de Hart. **Sociol. Gids** 40:3 5-6:1993 pp.202 - 223.

1235 Masonería y pacifismo en la España contemporánea. *[In Spanish]*; [Freemasonry and pacificism in present day Spain]. José Antonio Ferrer Benimeli; Manuel A. de Paz Sánchez. Zaragoza: Universidad de Zaragoza, 1991. 209p. *ISBN: 847733241X.*

1236 Missions, social change, and resistance to authority — notes toward an understanding of the relative autonomy of religion. Jon Miller. **J. Sci. S. Relig.** 32:1 3:1993 pp.29 - 50.

1237 La mythologie programmée: l'économie des croyances dans la société moderne. *[In French]*; [Programmed mythology: the economy of beliefs in modern society]. Marie-Dominique Perrot; Gilbert Rist; Fabrizio Sabelli. Paris: Presses Universitaires de France, 1992. 217p. *ISBN: 2130445675. Bibliogr. p.213-217.*

1238 Oastea Domnului — the Army of the Lord in Romania. Tom Keppeler. **Relig. State Soc.** 21:2 1993 pp.221 - 227.

1239 Patterns of thought in Africa and the West: essays on magic, religion, and science. Robin Horton. Cambridge: Cambridge University Press, 1993. xi,471p. *ISBN: 0521360870.*

1240 Photographie d'un mouvement «mystique-ésotérique» de souche russe - le club cosmos. *[In French]*; (Picture of an "esoteric-mystic" movement of Russian origins — the Cosmos Club.) Kira Kovalkina. **Rev. Ét. Comp.** 24:3-4 9-12:1993 pp.173 - 182.

1241 Predicting tolerance of new religious movements — a multivariate analysis. John P. O'Donnell. **J. Sci. S. Relig.** 32:4 12:1993 pp.356 - 365.

1242 Règles d'échange, vœux monastiques et codes. *[In French]*; (Exchange rules and monastic vows.) *[Summary]*. Guy Jucquois. **Recher. Sociolog.** XXIII:3 1992 pp.27 - 42.

1243 Religion and attitudes toward the environment. Andrew Greeley. **J. Sci. S. Relig.** 32:1 3:1993 pp.19 - 28.

1244 Religion and philosophy. Martin Warner [Ed.]. Cambridge, New York: Cambridge University Press, 1992. 155p. *ISBN: 052142951X.* (*Series:* Royal Institute of Philosophy).

1245 Religion and rational choice — a critique of economic explanations of religious behavior. Steve Bruce. **Soc. Relig.** 54:2 Summer:1993 pp.193 - 206.

1246 Religion and the future: essays in honour of Prof. G. C. Oosthuizen. Gerald J. Pillay [Ed.]; Gerhardus Cornelis Oosthuizen [Ed.]. Pretoria, South Africa: HSRC Publishers, 1992. 209p. *ISBN: 0796912548.*

1247 Religion in the nineties. Wade Clark Roof [Ed.]; Martin E. Marty [Contrib.]; Roger Finke [Contrib.]; Laurence R. Iannaccone [Contrib.]; Edward A. Tiryakian [Contrib.]; Phillip E. Hammond [Contrib.]; Kee Warner [Contrib.]; Charles Y. Glock [Contrib.]; Barbara G. Wheeler [Contrib.]; J. Gordon Melton [Contrib.]; Jeffrey K.

D: Culture

Hadden [Contrib.]; Catherine L. Albanese [Contrib.]; Meredith B. McGuire [Contrib.]. **Ann. Am. Poli.** 527 5:1993 pp.8 - 170. *Collection of 11 articles.*

1248 Religious behaviour as a utility- and inclusive fitness-optimizing strategy. Marcel Roele; Roger D. Masters [Comments by]. **Soc. Sci. Info.** 32:3 1993 pp.387 - 423.

1249 Religious involvement and self-perception among black Americans. Christopher G. Ellison. **Soc. Forc.** 71:4 6:1993 pp.1027 - 1055.

1250 Religioznaia situatsiia v Rossii: realii, protivorechiia, prognozy. *[In Russian]*; (The religious situation in Russia.) M. Mchedlov. **Svobod. Mysl'** 5 3:1993 pp.52 - 62.

1251 Satanism in contemporary America — establishment or underground?. Diane E. Taub; Lawrence D. Nelson. **Sociol. Q.** 34:3 8:1993 pp.523 - 541.

1252 Secularization, rationalism, and sectarianism: essays in honour of Bryan R. Wilson. Bryan R. Wilson [Dedicatee]; Eileen Barker [Ed.]; James Arthur Beckford [Ed.]; Karel Dobbelaere [Ed.]. Oxford: Clarendon Press, 1993. 322p. *ISBN: 0198277210. Includes bibliographical references and index.*

1253 Sitting in oblivion as a Taoist practice of positive alienation — a response to negative alienation in the Tang dynasty. Tim Futing Liao. **Int. Sociol.** 8:4 12:1993 pp.479 - 492.

1254 The social adaptation of marginal religious movements in America. Charles L. Harper; Bryan F. le Beau. **Soc. Relig.** 54:2 Summer:1993 pp.171 - 192.

1255 The sociology of sacred texts. Jon Gower Davies [Ed.]; Isabel Wollaston [Ed.]. Sheffield: Sheffield Academic Press, 1993. 195p. *ISBN: 1850754047.*

1256 [Steps to an ecology of mind: Bateson's theory of religion and art]; *[Text in Japanese]*. Tsuyoshi Kato. **Jinbun-ronkyu** 43(3) 1993 pp.85 - 99.

1257 [Study in the sociology of Buddhism]; *[Text in Japanese]*. Seishun Hikita. Tokyo: Kokusho-kankokai, 1993. 302p.

1258 The study of religion in modern society. Ole Riis. **Acta Sociol.** 36:4 1993 pp.371 - 384.

1259 The truth of religious narratives. G.L. Comstock. **Int. J. Philos. Relig.** 34:3 12:1993 pp.131 - 150.

1260 Le «védisme», version païenne de l'idée russe. *[In French]*; ("Vedism", a pagan version of the Russian idea.) Evgenij Moroz. **Rev. Ét. Comp.** 24:3-4 9-12:1993 pp.183 - 198.

1261 Work in progress toward a new paradigm for the sociological study of religion in the United States. R. Stephen Warner. **A.J.S.** 98:5 3:1993 pp.1044 - 1093.

Christianity
Christianisme

1262 Ages, générations et christianisme en France et en Europe. *[In French]*; (Ages, generations and Christianity in France and in Europe.) *[Summary]*; *[Summary in German]*; *[Summary in Spanish]*. Yves Lambert. **Rev. Fr. Soc.** XXXIV:4 10-12:1993 pp.525 - 555.

1263 Les attitudes éthiques et politiques des protestants réformés en France. *[In French]*; [Ethical and political attitudes of reformed Protestants in France] *[Summary]*. Pierre Brechon. **Soc. Compass** 40:1 3:1993 pp.111 - 121.

D: Culture

1264 British Catholics in the Labour movement — a study of religious and political marginalization?; *[Summary in French]*. Michael P. Hornsby-Smith; Michael Foley. **Soc. Compass** 40:1 3:1993 pp.45 - 54.

1265 Caritas im geeinten Deutschland. *[In German]*; [Christian charity in a united Germany]. Peter Weiss [Ed.]. Freiburg im Breisgau: Lambertus, 1992. 150p. *ISBN: 3784105580. Deutscher Caritasverband.*

1266 Catholicism and abortion attitudes in the American states — a contextual analysis. Elizabeth Adell Cook; Ted G. Jelen; Clyde Wilcox. **J. Sci. S. Relig.** 32:3 9:1993 pp.223 - 230.

1267 Christliche Religiosität — Konzepte, Indikatoren, Meßinstrumente. *[In German]*; (Christian religiosity — concepts, indicators, instruments.) *[Summary]*. Robert Kecskes; Christof Wolf. **Kölner Z. Soz. Soz. psy.** 45:2 6:1993 pp.270 - 287.

1268 Communities in conflict: evangelicals and Jews. David A. Rausch. Philadelphia: Trinity Press International, 1991. x, 204p. *ISBN: 1563380293. Includes bibliographical references (p. 175-197) and index.*

1269 Conservative Protestantism and support for corporal punishment. Christopher G. Ellison; Darren E. Sherkat. **Am. Sociol. R.** 58:1 2:1993 pp.131 - 144.

1270 Cristianismo e ilustración; la construcción de la nueva Europa. *[In Spanish]*; [Christianity and illustration; the construction of the new Europe]. Juan Antonio Estrada Diaz. **Rev. Fom. Soc.** 48:192 10-12:1993 pp.471 - 498.

1271 Determinants of church involvement of young adults who grew up in Presbyterian churches. Dean R. Hoge; Benton Johnson; Donald A. Luidens. **J. Sci. S. Relig.** 32:3 9:1993 pp.242 - 255.

1272 Deviant spiritualism and ritual satanic abuse. Part one — possible Judeo-Christian influences. Stephen A. Kent. **Religion** 23:3 7:1993 pp.229 - 241.

1273 Dialog khristianskoi very i nauki. *[In Russian]*; (The dialogue of Christian faith with science.) L. Vasilenko. **Obshch. Nauki Sovrem.** 3 1993 pp.152 - 163.

1274 The economics of church decline in Scotland. Ian Smith. **Int. J. Soc. E.** 20:12 1993 pp.27 - 36.

1275 Ethique charismatique et esprit du capitalisme avancé — essai sur le mouvement charismatique catholique français. *[In French]*; [Charismatic ethics and the spirit of advanced capitalism — an essay on the French Catholic charismatism] *[Summary]*. Martine Cohen. **Soc. Compass** 40:1 3:1993 pp.55 - 63.

1276 Fazendo a "coisa certa": rastas, reggae e pentecostais em Salvador. *[In Portuguese]*; (Doing the "right thing": rastas, reggae and Pentecostals in Salvador.) *[Summary]*; *[Summary in French]*. Olívia Maria Gomes da Cunha. **Rev. Bras. Ciên. Soc.** 8:23 10:1993 pp.120 - 137.

1277 Firmness and accommodation — impression management in institutional Roman Catholicism. Mark R. Kowalewski. **Soc. Relig.** 54:2 Summer:1993 pp.207 - 217.

1278 Les Français sont-ils encore catholiques?: analyse d'un sondage d'opinion. *[In French]*; [Are the French still Catholic? An analysis from an opinion poll]. Guy Michelat; et al. Paris: Cerf, 1991. 332p. *ISBN: 220404346X. Includes bibliographical references.*

1279 Fundamentalism, Christian orthodoxy, and intrinsic religious orientation as predictors of discriminatory attitudes. Lee A. Kirkpatrick. **J. Sci. S. Relig.** 32:3 9:1993 pp.256 - 268.

D: Culture

1280 Godsdienst en kerk in België en Nederland. *[In Dutch]*; (Religion and church in Belgium and the Netherlands.) *[Summary]*. Loek Halman; Karel Dobbelaere; Ruud de Moor; Liliane Voyé. **Sociol. Gids** XXXIX:5-6 9-12:1992 pp.285 - 299.

1281 The Gospel and the Protestant churches of Europe — Christian responsibility for Europe from a Protestant perspective. Eberhard Jüngel. **Relig. State Soc.** 21:2 1993 pp.137 - 149.

1282 Die herausgeforderten Kirchen. Religiosität in Bewegung. *[In German]*; [Churches facing challenge. Religiosity on the move]. Roland Hitzler; Karl Gabriel; Michael N. Ebertz; Jürgen Eiben; Willy Viehöver; Volkhard Krech; Hedwig Meyer-Wilmes; Ulrich Willems; Harald Schroeter; Leo Jansen; Arno Klönne; Norbert Mette; Michael Schäfers; Volker Heins. **Fors.Jour. Soz. Beweg.** 3-4 1993 pp.28 - 138. *Collection of 9 articles.*

1283 Heresy: the battle of ideas in modern Ireland. Desmond Fennell. Belfast: Blackstaff, 1993. xiii, 289p. *ISBN: 0856405132, 0856405132, 0856405051.*

1284 Is American Catholicism anti-intellectual?. Daniel Rigney; Thomas J. Hoffman. **J. Sci. S. Relig.** 32:3 9:1993 pp.211 - 222.

1285 Market forces and Catholic commitment — exploring the new paradigm. Rodney Stark; James C. McCann. **J. Sci. S. Relig.** 32:2 6:1993 pp.111 - 124.

1286 The metamorphosis of Latin American Protestant groups — a sociohistorical perspective. Jean-Pierre Bastian. **Lat. Am. Res. R.** 28:2 1993 pp.33 - 62.

1287 La Misa Jíbara como campo de batalla sociopolítica en Puerto Rico. *[In Spanish]*; [The Misa Jíbara as socio-political battleground in Puerto Rico]; *[Summary in English]*. Ana María Díaz-Stevens. **Rev. Cien. Soc.** XXX:1-2 6:1993 pp.139 - 162.

1288 Le mouvement des fraternités orthodoxes en Russie. *[In French]*; (The Orthodox brotherhoods and their movement in Russia.) Kathy Rousselet. **Rev. Ét. Comp.** 24:3-4 9-12:1993 pp.121 - 138.

1289 Obedience and authority — religion and parental values reconsidered. Christopher G. Ellison; Darren E. Sherkat. **J. Sci. S. Relig.** 32:4 12:1993 pp.313 - 329.

1290 Optimal church size — the bigger the better?. Robert J. Stonebraker. **J. Sci. S. Relig.** 32:3 9:1993 pp.231 - 241.

1291 Patriarchal bargains and latent avenues of social mobility — nuns in the Roman Catholic Church. Helen Rose Ebaugh. **Gender Soc.** 7:3 9:1993 pp.400 - 414.

1292 Prevalence and correlates of New Age beliefs in six Protestant denominations. Michael J. Donahue. **J. Sci. S. Relig.** 32:2 6:1993 pp.177 - 184.

1293 Los protestantes en Guatemala. *[In Spanish]*; [The Protestants in Guatemala]. Jesus María Sarasa. S.l: s.n, 1991. 118p.

1294 Protestantism in contemporary China. Alan Hunter; Kim Kwong Chan. Cambridge, England: Cambridge University Press, 1993. 291p. *ISBN: 0521441617. Bibliography: p.281-287. (Series:* Cambridge studies in ideology & religion).

1295 Protestantism in El Salvador — conventional wisdom versus survey evidence. Edwin Eloy Aguilar; Jose Miguel Sandoval; Timothy J. Steigenga; Kenneth M. Coleman. **Lat. Am. Res. R.** 28:2 1993 pp.119 - 140.

1296 Les protestants en Russie. *[In French]*; (Protestants in Russia.) Igor V. Podberezskij. **Rev. Ét. Comp.** 24:3-4 9-12:1993 pp.139 - 154.

1297 La restructuration étatique du champ religieux. *[In French]*; (State reconstruction of the religious field.) Jacques Zylberberg [Contrib.]; Thomas Robbins [Contrib.]; Pauline Cote [Contrib.]; Roberto Blancarte [Contrib.]; Jean-Paul Willaime [Contrib.];

Antoine Messarra [Contrib.]; Françoise Champion [Contrib.]. **Soc. Compass** 40:4 1993 pp.499 - 609. *Collection of 7 articles.*

1298 The schism in the Bulgarian Orthodox Church. Janice Broun. **Relig. State Soc.** 21:2 1993 pp.207 - 220.

1299 The secret clergy in communist Czechoslovakia. Felix Corley. **Relig. State Soc.** 21:2 1993 pp.171 - 206.

1300 The sect-church dynamic and Christian expansion in the Roman Empire — persecution, penitential discipline, and schism in sociological perspective. Joseph M. Bryant. **Br. J. Soc.** 44:2 6:1993 pp.303 - 339.

1301 Sluzhiteli tserkvi o sebe. *[In Russian]*; (Churchmen on themselves.) T.V. Nikitina. **Sot. Issle.** 4 1993 pp.62 - 66.

1302 Strictly speaking... — Kelley's quandary and the Vineyard Christian fellowship. Robin D. Perrin; Armand L. Mauss. **J. Sci. S. Relig.** 32:2 6:1993 pp.125 - 135.

1303 Switching close to home — volatility or coherence in Protestant affiliation patterns. D. Paul Sullins. **Soc. Forc.** 72:2 12:1993 pp.399 - 419.

1304 Traditsionnaia dukhovnaia i material'naia kultura russkikh staroobriadcheskikh poselenii v stranakh Evropy, Azii i Ameriki: sbornik nauchnykh trudov. *[In Russian]*; [The traditional spirituality and material culture of the Russian Old Believers in Western Europe, Asia and America]. Nikolai Nikolaevich Pokrovskii; Richard A. Morris. Novosibirsk: Nauka, Sibirskoe otdelenie, 1992. 320p. *ISBN: 502029764X. Includes bibliographical references.*

1305 Weber's "Protestant ethic": origins, evidence, contexts. Hartmut F. Lehmann [Ed.]; Guenther Roth [Ed.]. Washington; Cambridge: German Historical Institute; Cambridge University Press, 1993. 397p. *ISBN: 0521440629.* (*Series:* Publications of the German Historical Institute).

1306 Zur Sozialgeschichte des protestantischen Milieus in der DDR. *[In German]*; [On the social history of the Protestant milieu in the GDR]. Christoph Kleßmann. **Gesch. Ges.** 19:1 1993 pp.29 - 53.

Islam
Islam

1307 Between general and particular "others" — some observations on fundamentalism. Dipankar Gupta. **Contr. I. Soc.** 27:1 1-6:1993 pp.119 - 137.

1308 Des musulmans dans la cité bouddhique: l'exemple de la Thaïlande. *[In French]*; [Muslims in a Buddhist city: the example of Thailand]. Jean Baffie. **R. Mon. Musul. Med.** 68-69 1993 pp.189 - 200.

1309 Fasting and feasting in Morocco: women's participation in Ramadan. Marjo Buitelaar. Oxford: Berg Publishers, 1993. 203p. *ISBN: 0854963219.* (*Series:* Mediterranea series).

1310 Islam and communication. Philip Schlesinger [Ed.]; Hamid Mowlana [Ed.]; Ziauddin Sardar [Contrib.]; Syed H. Pasha [Contrib.]; Waseem Sajjad [Contrib.]; Hujatol Islam Val Muslemin Muhammad Ali Taskhiri [Contrib.]; Arvind Rajagopal [Contrib.]; Lyman Chaffee [Contrib.]. **Media Cult. Soc.** 15:1 1:1993 pp.9 - 135. *Collection of 8 articles.*

1311 Islam in the Balkans: religion and society between Europe and the Arab world. Harry Thirlwall Norris. London: Hurst, 1993. 304p. *ISBN: 1850651671.*

D: Culture

1312 Islamic fundamentalism reconsidered: a critical outline of problems, ideas and approaches, part I. Sadik J. Al-Azm. **S.Asia B.** XIII:1+2 1993 pp.93 - 121.

1313 Muslim identity and social change in sub-Saharan Africa. Louis Brenner [Ed.]. London: C. Hurst, 1993. 250p. *ISBN: 1850651957.*

1314 Muslims: their religious beliefs and practices. Volume 2. The contemporary period. Andrew Rippin. London: Routledge, 1993. 171p. *ISBN: 0415045274.*

1315 New Jerusalems: reflections on Islam, fundamentalism and the Rushdie affair. Daniel Easterman. London: Grafton, 1992. 240p. *ISBN: 0586216723.*

1316 Recomposition du religieux et réaffirmation identitaire dans l'Europe de la fin du XXe siècle. *[In French]*; [The recomposition of religiosity and the reaffirmation of identity in the Europe of the late 20th Century]. Francois Laplantine.   pp.77 - 90.

1317 Religious revivalism in Southeast Asia. Hans-Dieter Evers [Contrib.]; Sharon Siddique [Contrib.]; Reuven Kahane [Contrib.]; Raymond L.M. Lee [Contrib.]; Jim Taylor [Contrib.]; Christian Kiem [Contrib.]; Susan E. Ackerman [Contrib.]; Apinya Fuengfusakul [Contrib.]. **Sojourn** 8:1 2:1993 pp.1 - 183. *Collection of 7 articles.*

1318 Some reflections on the question of Islam and social sciences in the contemporary Muslim world; *[Summary in French].* Mona Abaza. **Soc. Compass** 40(2) 1993 pp.301 - 321.

1319 Tamil Muslims and non-Brahmin atheists, 1925-1940. J.B.P. More. **Contr. I. Soc.** 27:1 1-6:1993 pp.83 - 104.

1320 Les "têtes nouvelles". Intrusion d'une forme rigoriste de l'islam chez les Jawi, Malais de Thaïlande. *[In French]*; [The "new heads". The intrusion of a form of Islamic rigorism with the Jawi, the Malays of Thailand]. Pierre Le Roux. **R. Mon. Musul. Med.** 68-69 1993 pp.201 - 214.

1321 Themes and symbols in the religious lesson — a Jordanian case study. Richard T. Antoun. **Int. J. M.E. Stud.** 25:4 11:1993 pp.607 - 624.

1322 Traditional qur'anic education in a southern Moroccan village. Jarmo Houtsonen. **Int. J. M.E. Stud.** 26:3 8:1993 pp.489 - 500.

1323 Das unbekannte Bosnien: Europas Brücke zur islamischen Welt. *[In German]*; [The unknown Bosnia: Europe's bridge to the Islamic world]. Smail Balić. Köln, Weimar, Wien: Böhlau, 1992. xx, 526p. *ISBN: 3412063916. Includes bibliographical references (p. [378]-459) and indexes.*

1324 Zerstörung der Moschee von Ayodhya — Indiens Schicksalsstunde? *[In German]*; [Destruction of the mosque in Ayodhya - was this India's fateful hour?]. Dietmar Rothermund. **Geogr. Rund.** 45:11 11:1993 pp.626 - 631.

Judaism
Judaïsme

1325 Avoidance and conflict — perceptions regarding contact between religious and non-religious Jewish youth in Israel. Ephraim Tabory. **J. Sci. S. Relig.** 32:2 6:1993 pp.148 - 162.

1326 Communities in conflict: evangelicals and Jews. David A. Rausch. Philadelphia: Trinity Press International, 1991. x, 204p. *ISBN: 1563380293. Includes bibliographical references (p. 175-197) and index.*

D: Culture

1327 The death of Herod: an essay in the sociology of religion. Richard K. Fenn. Cambridge: Cambridge University Press, 1992. x,200p. *ISBN: 0521414822, 0521425026. Includes bibliographical references (p. 192-195) and index.*

1328 Deviant spiritualism and ritual satanic abuse. Part one — possible Judeo-Christian influences. Stephen A. Kent. **Religion** 23:3 7:1993 pp.229 - 241.

1329 Father-adolescent religious consensus in the Jewish community — a preliminary report. Michael B. Herzbrun. **J. Sci. S. Relig.** 32:2 6:1993 pp.163 - 168.

1330 Jewish "apartheid" and a Jewish Gandhi. Nathan Katz; Ellen S. Goldberg. **Jew. Soc. Stud.** L:3-4 Summer-Fall:1988-1993 pp.147 - 176.

1331 One people?: tradition, modernity, and Jewish unity. Jonathan Sacks. London, UK, Washington, DC: Littman Library of Jewish Civilization, 1993. xviii, 254p. *ISBN: 1874774005, 1874774013, 0197100635. Includes bibliographical references (p. [229]-243) and index.*

1332 Recomposition du religieux et réaffirmation identitaire dans l'Europe de la fin du XXe siècle. *[In French]*; [The recomposition of religiosity and the reaffirmation of identity in the Europe of the late 20th Century]. Francois Laplantine.   pp.77 - 90.

1333 Soviet Jews, orthodox Judaism, and the Lubavitcher Hasidim. Jenny A. Freedman. **E.Eur. Jew. Aff.** 23:1 Summer:1993 pp.57 - 77.

D.6:   **Science and knowledge**
            Science et connaissance

1334 Agricultural biotechnology — whose efficiency?. Les Levidow. **Sci. Cult.** 3:3(16) 1993 pp.453 - 468.

1335 Bio-politics — the anthropology of the new genetics and immunology. Deborah Heath [Ed.]; Paul Rabinow [Ed.]; Sharon Traweek [Contrib.]; Michael J. Flower [Contrib.]; Usher Fleising [Contrib.]; Alan Smart [Contrib.]; Emily Martin [Contrib.]; Margot L. Lyon [Contrib.]. **Cult. Medic. Psych.** 17:1 3:1993 pp.1 - 98. *Collection of 6 articles.*

1336 [Ecology of science and technology]; *[Text in Japanese]*. Takeshi Hayashi [Ed.]. Tokyo: Agne-shufusha, 1993. 293p.

1337 The emergence of the Indian scientific community. V.V. Krishna. **Sociol. Bul.** 40:1-2 3-9:1991 pp.89 - 108.

1338 Experiment and the making of meaning: human agency in scientific observation and experiment. David Gooding. Dordrecht: Kluwer Academic, 1990. xviii, 310p. *ISBN: 0792307194. (Series:* Science and philosophy).

1339 Feminist epistemologies. Linda Alcoff [Ed.]; Elizabeth Potter [Ed.]. New York: Routledge, 1993. vii, 312p. *ISBN: 0415904501, 041590451X.   Includes bibliographical references (p. 295-301) and index. (Series:* Thinking gender).

1340 The Golem: what everyone should know about science. Harry M. Collins; Trevor J. Pinch. Cambridge: Cambridge University Press, 1993. 164p. *ISBN: 0521356016.*

1341 Knowledge and knowledge networks — in honor of Martin J. Beckmann. T.R. Lakshmanan [Ed.]; D.F. Batten [Ed.]; M. Beckmann [Contrib.]; Å.E. Andersson [Contrib.]; O. Persson [Contrib.]; W.-B. Zhang [Contrib.]; X. Han [Contrib.]; Y. Liang [Contrib.]; S. Mun [Contrib.]; K. Yoshikawa [Contrib.]; K. Kobayashi [Contrib.]. **Ann. Reg. Sci.** 27:1 1993 pp.1 - 94. *Collection of 6 articles.*

D: Culture

1342 A large community but few peers: a study of the scientific community in India. E. Haribabu. **Sociol. Bul.** 40:1-2 3-9:1991 pp.77 - 88.

1343 Modern science — institutionalization of knowledge and rationalization of power. Richard Harvey Brown. **Sociol. Q.** 34:1 Spring:1993 pp.153 - 168.

1344 Only a glancing blow — Roger Penrose and the critique of artificial intelligence. Bruce J. Berman. **Sci. Cult.** 3:3(16) 1993 pp.404 - 426.

1345 Patterns of thought in Africa and the West: essays on magic, religion, and science. Robin Horton. Cambridge: Cambridge University Press, 1993. xi,471p. *ISBN: 0521360870.*

1346 Popper's views on natural and social science. Colin George Frederick Simkin. Leiden, New York: E.J. Brill, 1993. viii, 207p. *ISBN: 9004096809. Includes bibliographical references (p. [200]-201) and index. (Series:* Brill's studies in epistemology, psychology, and psychiatry).

1347 [Reconstructing the sociology of science]; *[Text in Japanese].* Miwao Matsumoto. **Shak. Kenk. Nih. Shak. Gak.** 15 1993 pp.98 - 111.

1348 Science as salvation: a modern myth and its meaning. Mary Midgley. London, New York: Routledge, 1992. x, 239p. *ISBN: 0415062713. Based on Gifford lectures delivered at the University of Edinburgh in the Spring of 1990. Includes bibliographical references (p. 225-235) and index.*

1349 Science, technology and futures studies. Ian Miles. **Int. Soc. Sci. J.** 137 8:1993 pp.373 - 384.

1350 Scientific goods and their markets. Kamini Adhikari. **Sociol. Bul.** 40:1-2 3-9:1991 pp.133 - 150.

1351 Secrets of life, secrets of death: essays on language, gender, and science. Evelyn Fox Keller. New York: Routledge, 1992. x, 195p. *ISBN: 0415905249, 0415905257. Includes bibliographical references (p. 183-195).*

1352 Social constructivism — opening the black box and finding it empty. Langdon Winner. **Sci. Cult.** 3:3(16) 1993 pp.427 - 452.

1353 Social representations and the social basis of knowledge. Willem Doise [Ed.]; Gabriel Mugny [Ed.]; Mario von Cranach [Ed.]. Lewiston, NY: Hogrefe & Huber, 1992. xi, 220p. *ISBN: 0889370702, 3456821050. Includes bibliographical references and index. (Series:* Swiss monographs in psychology).

1354 The social theory of practices: tradition, tacit knowledge and presuppositions. Stephen P. Turner. Oxford: Polity Press, 1993. 145p. *ISBN: 0745605044.*

1355 A sociological theory of scientific change. Stephan Fuchs. **Soc. Forc.** 71:4 6:1993 pp.933 - 953.

1356 The sociology of scientific establishments today. John Wettersten. **Br. J. Soc.** 44:1 3:1993 pp.69 - 102.

1357 Teaching knowledge as conversation — a philosophical hermeneutical approach to education. Yedullah Kazmi. **St. Philos. Educ.** 11:4 1993 pp.339 - 357.

1358 [Towards the sociology of postmodern knowledge]; *[Text in Japanese].* Takeshi Mikami. Kyoto: Sekaishiso-sha, 1993. 213p.

1359 Wissenschaft im Kontext. Neuere Entwicklungstendenzen der Wissenschaftssoziologie. *[In German]*; (Science in context. A review of developments in the sociology of science.) *[Summary].* Bettina Heintz. **Kölner Z. Soz. Soz. psy.** 45:3 9:1993 pp.528 - 552.

D: Culture

D.7: **Language, communication and media**
Langage, communication et moyens de communication

1360 Acts in discourse — from monological speech acts to dialogical inter-acts. Per Linell; Ivana Marková. **J. Theory Soc. Behav.** 23:2 6:1993 pp.174 - 195.
1361 Adult comics: an introduction. Roger Sabin. New York; London: Routledge, 1993. 321p. *ISBN: 0415044189. Includes bibliographical references and index. (Series:* New accents).
1362 L'Afrique afro-francophone. *[In French]*; [Afro-Francophone Africa]. Ntole Kazadi. Aix-en-Provence, Paris: Institut d'Etudes Créoles et Francophones, UA 1041 du CNRS, Université de Provence, 1991. 183p. *ISBN: 2864601575. Published with the support of the Ministère français de la Coopération et du Développement. Includes bibliographical references (p. 175-179).*
1363 Albert Schäffle über Symbol, Verkehr und Wechselwirkung. *[In German]*; [Albert Schäffle on symbols, interaction and communication]. Jens Loenhoff. **Social. Int.** 31:2 1993 pp.197 - 220.
1364 The art of conversation. Peter Burke. Cambridge: Polity Press, 1993. viii, 178p. *ISBN: 0745611109, 0745612881. Includes bibliographical references (p. 143-173) and index.*
1365 Asymmetries in dialogue. Ivana Markovà [Ed.]; Klaus Foppa [Ed.]. Savage, MD: Barnes & Noble Books, 1991. vii, 284p. *ISBN: 0389209805. Includes bibliographical references.*
1366 Attitudinal identification, stimulus complexity and retrospective duration estimation. Dan Zakay; Jacob Lomranz. **Time Soc.** 2:3 1993 pp.381 - 397.
1367 Belief and behavior. John O'Leary-Hawthorne. **Mind Lang.** 8:4 Winter:1993 pp.461 - 486.
1368 The city in slang: New York life and popular speech. Irving Lewis Allen. New York: Oxford University Press, 1993. ix, 307p. *ISBN: 0195075919. Includes bibliographical references (p. 275-287) and indexes.*
1369 Coevolution of neocortical size, group size and language. R.I.M. Dunbar. **Behav. Brain Sci.** 16:4 12:1993 pp.681 - 735.
1370 Complimenting behaviour: a cross-cultural investigation. V. Ylänne-McEwen. **J. Multiling.** 14:6 1993 pp.499 - 510.
1371 A conceptual framework for the study of language standardization. Paul L. Garvin. **Int. J. S. Lang.** 100-101 1993 pp.37 - 54.
1372 Continuity as vagueness — the mathematical antecedents of Peirce's semiotics. Peter Ochs. **Semiotica** 96:3-4 1993 pp.231 - 255.
1373 Current concerns and electrodermal reactivity — responses to words and thoughts. Reiner Nikula; Eric Klinger; Mary Katherine Larson-Gutman. **J. Personal.** 61:1 3:1993 pp.63 - 84.
1374 Discourse marking and accounts of violence in Northern Ireland. John Wilson. **Text** 13:3 1993 pp.455 - 475.
1375 Discursive bias and ideology in the administration of minority group interests. David J. Corson. **Lang. Soc.** 22:2 6:1993 pp.165 - 191.
1376 Diversity and contestation in linguistic ideologies — German speakers in Hungary. Susan Gal. **Lang. Soc.** 22:3 9:1993 pp.337 - 359.

D: Culture

1377 Early sign language acquisition in children and gorillas — vocabulary content and sign iconicity. John D. Bonvillian; Francine G.P. Patterson. **Fst. Lang.** 13(3):39 1993 pp.315 - 338.
1378 Ecriture, recherche et pédagogie. *[In French]*; [Writing, research and education]; *[Summary in English]*. Wilfrid Bilodeau. **Interchange** 24:3 1993 pp.241 - 270.
1379 Effects of language intensity similarity on perceptions of credibility, relational attributions, and persuasion. R. Kelly Aune; Toshiyuki Kikuchi. **J. Lang. Soc. Psychol.** 12:3 9:1993 pp.224 - 238.
1380 En/gendering language: the poetics of Tamil identity. Sumathi Ramaswamy. **Comp. Stud. S.** 35:4 10:1993 pp.683 - 725.
1381 English in Malta. Gabriella Mazzon. **Eng. Wor.-wide** 14:2 1993 pp.171 - 208.
1382 English in South Africa: the Eastern Cape perspective. Vivian de Klerk; Barbara Bosch. **Eng. Wor.-wide** 14:2 1993 pp.209 - 230.
1383 Ethnolinguistic minorities in Perpignan. D. Marley. **J. Multiling.** 14:3 1993 pp.217 - 236.
1384 European economic integration and the fate of lesser-used languages; *[Summary in French]*. François Grin. **Lang. Prob. Lang. Plan.** 17:2 Summer:1993 pp.101 - 116.
1385 An examination of the relationship between social practices and the comprehension of narratives. Vaidehi Ramanathan-Abbott. **Text** 13:1 1993 pp.117 - 141.
1386 Forms for talk and talk for forms — oral and literate dimensions of language use in employment training interviews. Jo Longman; Neil Mercer. **Text** 13:1 1993 pp.91 - 116.
1387 Frauen in der Kommunikationswissenschaft: unterrepräsentiert — aber auf dem Vormarsch. *[In German]*; [Women in the communication sciences: under-represented but on the way up]. Romy Fröhlich; Christine Holtz-Bacha. **Publizistik** 38:4 10-12:1993 pp.527 - 541.
1388 The German language after unification — adapting assumptions and methodologies to the "new world order". Michael Clyne. **Int. J. S. Lang.** 100-101 1993 pp.11 - 28.
1389 Historia y sociedad — componentes básicos del lenguaje. *[In Spanish]*; [History and society — basic components of language]. Adolfo Elizaincin. **Int. J. S. Lang.** 100-101 1993 pp.29 - 35.
1390 Il est interdit d'interdire! Il n'est pas interdit d'imposer! Il est recommandé de promouvoir. *[In French]*; [It is forbidden to prohibt! It is not forbidden to impose! It is advisable to promote] *[Summary]*; *[Summary in Esperanto]*. Paul Pupier. **Lang. Prob. Lang. Plan.** 17:1 Spring:1993 pp.22 - 36.
1391 Images of money — cultural drift, capitalist fantasy and the prime-time female hero. Susan Kray. **Communication** 13:4 1993 pp.277 - 302.
1392 Information sequencing in modern standard Chinese in a genre of extended spoken discourse. Andy Kirkpatrick. **Text** 13:3 1993 pp.423 - 453.
1393 International visibility of periodicals from Ireland, India, and Latin America. Virginia Cano. **Know. Pol.** 6:3+4 1993-1994 pp.55 - 78.
1394 Jack in two boxes: a postmodern perspective on the transformation of persons into portraits. Maggie MacLure; Ian Stronach. **Interchange** 24:4 1993 pp.353 - 380.
1395 Japanese civilization in the modern world. 7. Language, literacy, and writing. Tadao Umesao [Ed.]; J. Marshall Unger [Ed.]; Osamu Sakiyama [Ed.]. Osaka: National Museum of Ethnology, 1992. i, 148p. *Papers presented at the Taniguchi International Symposium, Comparative Perspectives on Language, Literacy, and*

D: Culture

Writing, held at the National Museum of Ethnology, Suita, Osaka, Japan in March 1989. Includes bibliographical references. (*Series:* Senri ethnological studies).

1396 Kommunikationswissenschaft — ein Fach auf dem Weg zur Sozialwissenschaft. Eine wissenschaftsgeschichtliche Besinnungspause. *[In German]*; [Communication science - one subject on the way to becoming a social science. A scientific and historical pause for thought]. Hans Wagner. **Publizistik** 38:4 10-12:1993 pp.491 - 526.

1397 Language and social identity in the Caribbean. Richard K. Blot [Ed.]; Ellen M. Schnepel [Contrib.]; George Mentore [Contrib.]; John W. Pulis [Contrib.]. **Eth. Groups** 10:4 1993 pp.243 - 300. *Collection of 3 articles.*

1398 Language display — authenticating claims to social identity. C.M. Eastman; R.F. Stein. **J. Multiling.** 14:3 1993 pp.187 - 202.

1399 Language perceptions among the Inuit of Arctic Quebec — the future role of the heritage language. Donald M. Taylor; Stephen C. Wright; Karen M. Ruggiero; Mary C. Aitchison. **J. Lang. Soc. Psychol.** 12:3 9:1993 pp.195 - 206.

1400 Language revival: restoration or transformation?. A. Bentahila; E.E. Davies. **J. Multiling.** 14:5 1993 pp.355 - 374.

1401 Language rights, individual and communal; *[Summary in French]*. Pierre A. Coulombe. **Lang. Prob. Lang. Plan.** 17:2 Summer:1993 pp.140 - 152.

1402 Language, symbolism, and politics. Richard M. Merelman [Ed.]. Boulder: Westview Press, 1992. vii, 310p. *ISBN: 0813385814. Includes bibliographical references.*

1403 Language use in peer review texts. Agnes Weiyun He. **Lang. Soc.** 22:3 9:1993 pp.403 - 420.

1404 La lengua española en América cinco siglos después. *[In Spanish]*; (The Spanish language in America five centuries after.) *[Summary]*. Raúl Ávila. **Est. Sociol.** X:30 9-12:1992 pp.677 - 692.

1405 Literacy in contexts: Australian perspectives and issues. Pam Gilbert [Ed.]; Allan Luke [Ed.]. St Leonards, NSW: Allen & Unwin, 1993. 138p. *ISBN: 186373340X.*

1406 Migration and language in Friesland. A. van Langevelde. **J. Multiling.** 14:5 1993 pp.393 - 410.

1407 Minoritization of languages in their traditional historical territories: issues of autonomy and identity in the nation-state. Bud B. Khleif. **Social. Int.** 31:2 1993 pp.159 - 178.

1408 The negotiation and outcome of language and culture; *[Summary in Spanish]*; *[Summary in Esperanto]*. Robert F. Stein; Carol M. Eastman. **Lang. Prob. Lang. Plan.** 17:3 Fall:1993 pp.238 - 253.

1409 New directions in conversation analysis. Steven E. Clayman [Contrib.]; Elizabeth Holt [Contrib.]; Gene H. Lerner [Contrib.]; Jenny Mandelbaum [Contrib.]; John F. Manzo [Contrib.]; Anssi Peräkylä [Contrib.]. **Text** 13:2 1993 pp.159 - 316. *Collection of 6 articles.*

1410 Niesformalizowany obieg komunikowania jako instytucja społeczna. *[In Polish]*; (Non-formalized communication flow as social institution.) *[Summary]*. Piotr Łukasiewicz. **Prz. Soc.** XL 1993 pp.169 - 180.

1411 On determining the functions of language. Jan Nuyts. **Semiotica** 94:3-4 1993 pp.201 - 232.

1412 Perceptions of overaccommodation used by nurses in communication with the elderly. Helen Edwards; Patricia Noller. **J. Lang. Soc. Psychol.** 12:3 9:1993 pp.207 - 223.

D: Culture

1413 The performance of eight- to ten-year olds on measures of conversational skilfulness. Debra Schober-Peterson; Cynthia J. Johnson. **Fst. Lang.** 13(2):38 1993 pp.249 - 269.

1414 The power of silence: social and pragmatic perspectives. Adam Jaworski. Newbury Park, Calif: Sage, 1993. xiv, 191p. *ISBN: 0803949669, 0803949677. Includes bibliographical references and index.* (*Series:* Language and language behaviors).

1415 Real men don't speak Quiché — Quiché ethnicity, Ki-che ethnic movement, K'iche' nationalism; *[Summary in Spanish]*; *[Summary in Esperanto]*. M. Paul Lewis. **Lang. Prob. Lang. Plan.** 17:1 Spring:1993 pp.37 - 54.

1416 Red River Valley — geo-graphical studies in the landscape of language. O.M. Jensen. **Envir. Plan. D.** 11:3 6:1993 pp.295 - 301.

1417 Referential communication as teaching — adults tutoring their own and other children. Peter Lloyd. **Fst. Lang.** 13(3):39 1993 pp.339 - 357.

1418 The relevance of thresholds in language maintenance and shift: a theoretical examination. F. Grin. **J. Multiling.** 14:5 1993 pp.375 - 392.

1419 The rhetorical structure of US-American and Dutch fund-raising letters. Eric Abelen; Gisela Redeker; Sandra A. Thompson. **Text** 13:3 1993 pp.323 - 350.

1420 Rhetorik und Hermeneutik in der Selbstbeschreibung der Kommunikation. *[In German]*; [Rhetoric and hermeneutics in the self-description of communication]. Cornelia Bohn. **Social. Int.** 31:2 1993 pp.149 - 158.

1421 The roles of perceived and actual control in memory for spoken language. Elizabeth A.L. Stine; Margie E. Lachman; Arthur Wingfield. **Educ. Geront.** 19:4 6:1993 pp.331 - 349.

1422 The Romanian language press in America. G. James Patterson; Paul Petrescu. **E. Eur. Quart.** XXVII:2 Summer:1993 pp.261 - 270.

1423 The sad demise, mysterious disappearance, and glorious triumph of symbolic interactionism. Gary Alan Fine. **Ann. R. Soc.** 19 1993 pp.61 - 89.

1424 Semiotic modeling systems — the contribution of Thomas A. Sebeok. Bennetta Jules-Rosette. **Semiotica** 96:3-4 1993 pp.269 - 283.

1425 Semiotics in the United States and beyond: problems, people and perspectives. Thomas A. Sebeok; John Deely [Ed.]; Susan Petrilli [Ed.]; Lisa Block de Behar; José Luis Caivano; Patrizia Calefato; Svoboda Dimitrova; Jørgen Dines Johansen; Tzvetana Kristeva; Mariana Neţ; Ana Claudia Mei Alves de Oliveira; Augusto Ponzio; Maria N. Popova; Joëlle Réthoré; Lucia Santaella Braga [Comments by]; Elisabeth Saporiti; Erik van Vulpen; W.C. Watt. **Semiotica** 97:3-4 1993 pp.215 - 440. *Collection of 18 articles.*

1426 Semiotics of work and idleness. Nedda Strazhas. **Semiotica** 95:1-2 1993 pp.21 - 43.

1427 Social accountability in communication. Richard Buttny. London: Sage, 1993. x, 187p. *ISBN: 0803983077.*

1428 Social reactions towards education proposals. W.O. Lee. **J. Multiling.** 14:3 1993 pp.203 - 216.

1429 Sociology of language in Belgium (revisited). Albert F. Verdoodt [Contrib.]; Selma K. Sonntag [Contrib.]; Edmund A. Aunger [Contrib.]; Alexander B. Murphy [Contrib.]; Maureen Covell [Contrib.]; Casimiro Marques Balsa [Contrib.]. **Int. J. S. Lang.** 104 1993 pp.5 - 111. *Collection of 6 articles.*

1430 Species and individual differences in communication based on private states. D. Lubinski; T. Thompson. **Behav. Brain Sci.** 16:4 12:1993 pp.627 - 680.

1431 Structural coupling — simultaneity and difference between communication and thought. Claudio Baraldi. **Commun. Theory** 3:2 5:1993 pp.112 - 129.
1432 Survivor discourse — transgression or recuperation?. Linda Alcoff; Laura Gray. **Signs** 18:2 Winter:1993 pp.260 - 290.
1433 Taking humour seriously. Jerry Palmer. London, New York: Routledge, 1993. 203p. *ISBN: 0415102669, 0415102677. Includes bibliographical references (p.) and index.*
1434 Talk and social structure: studies in ethnomethodolgy and conversation analysis. Deirdre Boden [Ed.]; Don H. Zimmerman [Ed.]. Oxford: Polity Press, 1993. 305p. *ISBN: 0745612407.*
1435 A U.S. colony at a linguistic crossroads — the decision to make Spanish the official language of Puerto Rico; *[Summary in Spanish]*. Jorge A. Vélez; C. William Schweers. **Lang. Prob. Lang. Plan.** 17:2 Summer:1993 pp.117 - 139.
1436 Using and abusing language. John M. Wiemann [Ed.]; Howard Giles [Ed.]; C. Douglas McCann [Contrib.]; Richard N. Lalonde [Contrib.]; Daphne Blunt Bugental [Contrib.]; Cynthia Gallois [Contrib.]; Charles H. Tardy [Contrib.]; W. Peter Robinson [Contrib.]; Jonathan Potter [Contrib.]; Derek Edwards [Contrib.]; Margaret Wetherell [Contrib.]. **Am. Behav. Sc.** 36:3 1/2:1993 pp.262 - 401.
1437 Visual "literacy" — a theoretical synthesis. Paul Messaris. **Commun. Theory** 3:4 11:1993 pp.277 - 294.
1438 "You gotta know how to tell a story" — telling, tales, and tellers in American and Israeli narrative events at dinner. Shoshana Blum-Kulka. **Lang. Soc.** 22:3 9:1993 pp.361 - 402.

Advertising
Publicité

1439 Advertising and a democratic press. C. Edwin Baker. Princeton, N.J: Princeton University Press, 1993. 203p. *ISBN: 0691032580. Includes bibliographical references and index.*
1440 The American frontier and the contemporary real estate advertising magazine. Reuben J. Ellis. **J. Pop. Cult.** 27:3 Winter:1993 pp.119 - 134.
1441 Anzeigenanalysen als Weg zur historischen Leserschafts- und Medienwirkungsforschung. Ein Beitrag zu den Theorien von Johann Heinrich von Thünen und Walter Christaller. *[In German]*; (Analyses of advertising as a path to the historical research of readers and media effects — a contribution to the theories of Johann Heinrich von Thünen and Walter Christaller.) *[Summary]*; *[Summary in French]*; *[Summary in Spanish]*. Rudolf Stöber. **Publizistik** 38:2 4-6:1993 pp.187 - 205.
1442 Auflockerung oder Ablenkung? Die Wirkung von Zwischenblenden in der Fernsehwerbung? *[In German]*; (Relaxation or diversion? The effects of intercuts in TV commercials.) *[Summary]*; *[Summary in French]*. Hans-Bernd Brosius; Johanna Habermeier. **Publizistik** 38:1 1-3:1993 pp.76 - 89.
1443 A critique of commodity aesthetics of postmodern advertising on Korean television. Myung-Koo Kang. **Korean Soc. Sci. J.** XIX 1993 pp.7 - 22.
1444 Out of the garden: toys, TV, and children's culture in the age of marketing. Stephen Kline. London: Verso, 1993. x,406p. *ISBN: 086091397X.*

D: Culture

1445 PR-Anzeigen ausländischer Staaten in deutschen Zeitungen und Zeitschriften. Eine inhaltsanalytische Auswertung. *[In German]*; (PR-advertisement of foreign countries in German newspapers and magazines. A content analysis.) *[Summary]*; *[Summary in French]*. Michael Kunczik; Uwe Weber. **Publizistik** 38:1 1-3:1993 pp.46 - 66.

Information technology and telecommunications
Technologie de l'information et télécommunications

1446 Der Computer als Medium und Maschine. *[In German]*; (The computer as medium and as machine.) *[Summary]*. Elena Esposito. **Z. Soziol.** 22:5 10:1993 pp.338 - 354.

1447 Computerkulturen. Eine ethnographische Studie. *[In German]*; (Computer cultures — an ethnographic study.) *[Summary]*; *[Summary in French]*; *[Summary in Spanish]*. Roland Eckert; Waldemar Vogelgesang; Thomas A. Wetzstein. **Publizistik** 38:2 4-6:1993 pp.167 - 186.

1448 Electronic media and state control — the case of AZSCAM. David L. Altheide. **Sociol. Q.** 34:1 Spring:1993 pp.53 - 69.

1449 The future of the field — between fragmentation and cohesion. Karl Erik Rosengren [Contrib.]; James R. Beniger [Contrib.]; Robert T. Craig [Contrib.]; Klaus Krippendorff [Contrib.]; Brenda Dervin [Contrib.]; Joshua Meyrowitz [Contrib.]; Joli Jensen [Contrib.]; Barbara O'Keefe [Contrib.]; Gregory J. Shepherd [Contrib.]; Kurt Lang [Contrib.]; Gladys Engel Lang [Contrib.]; Paolo Mancini [Contrib.]; Austin S. Babrow [Contrib.]; Mary Anne Fitzpatrick [Contrib.]; Horace Newcomb [Contrib.]; Sandra Braman [Contrib.]; Dennis K. Davis [Contrib.]; James Jasinski [Contrib.]; Jennifer L. Monahan [Contrib.]; Lori Collins-Jarvis [Contrib.]; Eric W. Rothenbuhler [Contrib.]; James E. Grunig [Contrib.]; Robert K. Avery [Contrib.]; William F. Eadie [Contrib.]; W. Lance Bennett [Contrib.]; Douglas Gomery [Contrib.]; Eli Noam [Contrib.]; Willard D. Rowland [Contrib.]; H. Leslie Steeves [Contrib.]; David Docherty [Contrib.]; David Morrison [Contrib.]; Michael Tracey [Contrib.]. **J. Comm.** 43:3 Summer:1993 pp.6 - 238. *Collection of 26 articles.*

1450 The impact of information technology on the individual. Ruth A. Palmquist. **Ann. R. Info. Sci. Tech.** 27 1992 pp.3 - 42.

1451 The information society: a retrospective view. Herbert S. Dordick; Georgette Wang. London: Sage, 1993. 168p. *ISBN: 0803941870.*

1452 Information transfer policy: issues of control and access. Tamara Eisenschitz. London: Library Association, 1993. 175p. *ISBN: 0853658293.*

1453 Major issues in instructional/communication technology — an Islamic viewpoint. Dilnawaz Siddiqui. **Am. J. Islam. Soc. Sci.** 10:3 Fall:1993 pp.312 - 325.

1454 Professional communication: the social perspective. Nancy Roundy Blyler [Ed.]; Charlotte Thralls [Ed.]. Newbury Park, Calif.: Sage, 1993. xv, 292p. *ISBN: 0803939345, 0803939353. Includes bibliographical references (p. 257-279) and index.*

1455 Social equity and information technologies — moving toward information democracy. Ronald D. Doctor. **Ann. R. Info. Sci. Tech.** 27 1992 pp.43 - 96.

1456 Sozio-kulturelle Auswirkungen moderner Informations- und Kommunikationstechnologien: der Stand der Forschung in der Bundesrepublik Deutschland und in Frankreich. *[In German]*; [The socio-cultural effects of modern information- and communication technologies: the position of research in Germany

and France]. Jochen Hörisch; Gérard Baulet. Frankfurt am Main: Campus-Verlag, 1992. 119p. *ISBN: 3593347547.*
1457 Telematics for the community? An electronic village hall for east Manchester. K. Ducatel; P. Halfpenny. **Envir. Plan. C.** 11:4 11:1993 pp.367 - 379.
1458 Téléphone, communication et sociabilité des pratiques résidentielles différenciées. *[In French]*; (Telephone, communication and sociability: patterns diffenciation.) *[Summary]*. Gérard Claisse; Frantz Rowe. **Soc. Contemp.** 14/15 6-9:1993 pp.165 - 190.
1459 Telephone communication patterns in Austria — a comparison of the IPFP-based graph-theoretic and the intramax approaches. Manfred M. Fischer; Jürgen Esslezbichler; Helmut Gassler; Gerhard Trichtl. **Geogr. Anal.** 25:3 7:1993 pp.224 - 233.
1460 Time, information and communication technologies and the household. Roger Silverstone. **Time Soc.** 2:3 1993 pp.283 - 311.

Linguistics
Linguistique

1461 Agendas for second language literacy. Sandra Lee McKay. Cambridge [England], New York, NY: Cambridge University Press, 1993. xvii, 151p. *ISBN: 0521441188. Includes bibliographical references (p. 137-146) and index. (Series:* Cambridge language education).
1462 Arbitrariness, iconicity, and conceptuality. Flip G. Droste; John Fought. **Semiotica** 94:3-4 1993 pp.185 - 199.
1463 Children's linguistic choices — audience design and societal norms. Valerie Youssef. **Lang. Soc.** 22:2 6:1993 pp.257 - 274.
1464 Colonial knowledge and the fate of Hindustani. David Lelyveld. **Comp. Stud. S.** 35:4 10:1993 pp.665 - 682.
1465 Complaining and commiserating — exploring gender issues. Diana Boxer. **Text** 13:3 1993 pp.371 - 395.
1466 Conversational realities: constructing life through language. John Shotter. London: Sage, 1993. 201p. *ISBN: 0803989326, 0803989334. (Series:* Inquiries in social construction).
1467 Dialektvitalität links und rechts der belgischen Sprachgrenze. *[In German]*; (Dialect vitality left and right of the Belgian linguistic frontier.) *[Summary]; [Summary in Esperanto]*. Sonja Vandermeeren. **Lang. Prob. Lang. Plan.** 17:3 Fall:1993 pp.201 - 224.
1468 English in language shift: the history, structure, and sociolinguistics of South African Indian English. Rajend Mesthrie. Cambridge [England], New York: Cambridge University Press, 1992. xix, 252p. *ISBN: 0521415144. Includes bibliographical references (p. 237-247) and index.*
1469 English pronunciation in Cameroon: conflicts and consequences. A.S. Bobda. **J. Multiling.** 14:6 1993 pp.435 - 446.
1470 Esperanto as a first language — language acquisition with restricted input. Kees Versteegh. **Linguistics** 31 1993 pp.539 - 555.
1471 The existence of synonyms in a language — two forms but one, or rather two, meanings. Bob de Jonge. **Linguistics** 31 1993 pp.521 - 538.

D: Culture

1472 Formen sprachlicher Identitätskonstitution in inszenierter und dramatisierter mündlicher Kommunikation im spanischen Fernsehen. *[In German]*; (Forms of linguistic constitution of identity in stages and dramatized oral spoken communication on Spanish television.) Klaus Zimmermann. **Wissensch. Z. Humboldt-Univ.** 41:3 1992 pp.75 - 84.

1473 Language and causation — a discursive action model of description and attribution. Derek Edwards; Jonathan Potter. **Psychol. Rev.** 100:1 1:1993 pp.23 - 41.

1474 Language and discrimination: a study of communication in multi-ethnic workplaces. Celia Roberts; Evelyn Davies; Thomas Cyprian Jupp. London, New York: Longman, 1992. xvi, 422p. *ISBN: 0582552656. Includes bibliographical references (p. [394]-420) and indexes. (Series:* Applied linguistics and language study).

1475 Language development in special populations. David Messer [Ed.]; Geoffrey Turner [Ed.]; Leslie Rescorla [Contrib.]; Mary Hadicke-Wiley [Contrib.]; Elaine Escarce [Contrib.]; Elaine S. Andersen [Contrib.]; Anne Dunlea [Contrib.]; Linda Kekelis [Contrib.]; Hollis S. Scarborough [Contrib.]; Alana Fichtelberg [Contrib.]; Gisela E. Speidel [Contrib.]; Eva Magnusson [Contrib.]; Kerstin Nauclér [Contrib.]; Mabel L. Rice [Contrib.]; John V. Bode [Contrib.]; Ruth V. Watkins [Contrib.]; Candace C. Moltz [Contrib.]. **Fst. Lang.** 13(1):37 1993 pp.5 - 143. *Collection of 7 articles.*

1476 The language of vertical relationships and linguistic analysis. Patricia J. Wetzel. **Multilingua** 12:4 1993 pp.387 - 406.

1477 Lexical shift in working class New Zealand English: variation in the use of lexical pairs. Miriam Meyerhoff. **Eng. Wor.-wide** 14:2 1993 pp.231 - 248.

1478 Linguistic consequences of some sociopolitical changes in Iran. Yahya Modarresi. **Int. J. S. Lang.** 100-101 1993 pp.87 - 100.

1479 Linguistic politeness and universality. Sachiko Ide [Contrib.]; Richard W. Janney [Contrib.]; Horst Arndt [Contrib.]; B.J. Kwarciak [Contrib.]; Maria Sifianou [Contrib.]; Shinji Sanada [Contrib.]. **Multilingua** 12:1 1993 pp.7 - 94. *Collection of 5 articles.*

1480 Literature, strategies and metalanguage. Part 3 — poetical arts and metalanguage. Mariana Neţ. **Semiotica** 94:3-4 1993 pp.253 - 293.

1481 Literature, strategies and metalanguage. Part 4 — context, cotext, and metatext. Mariana Neţ. **Semiotica** 95:1-2 1993 pp.75 - 99.

1482 Loss of first language skills in the community — intermediate stage; *[Summary in German]*; *[Summary in Esperanto]*. Margit Waas. **Lang. Prob. Lang. Plan.** 17:3 Fall:1993 pp.225 - 237.

1483 Mesure de l'assimilation linguistique au moyen des recensements. *[In French]*; [Measurement of linguistic assimilation through censuses] *[Summary]*. Charles Castonguay. **Rech. Soc.graph** XXXIV:1 1-4:1993 pp.45 - 68.

1484 Mobilité géolinguistique de la population de langue maternelle française au Québec et en Ontario. *[In French]*; [Geolinguistic mobility of the French mother tongue population in Quebec and Ontario] *[Summary]*. André Langlois; Charles Castonguay. **Can. J. Soc.** 18:4 Fall:1993 pp.383 - 404.

1485 On puns, comebacks, verbal dueling, and play languages — speech play in Balinese verbal life. Joel Sherzer. **Lang. Soc.** 22:2 6:1993 pp.217 - 233.

1486 Out of the mouths of babes — an enquiry into the sources of language development. E. Urban. **J. Analyt. Psychol.** 38:3 7:1993 pp.237 - 256.

1487 Paralanguage: a linguistic and interdisciplinary approach to interactive speech and sound. Fernando Poyatos. Amsterdam, Philadelphia: J. Benjamins, 1993. 478p.

ISBN: 1556191499. Bibliography: p.453-465; includes indexes. (Series: Amsterdam studies in the theory and history of linguistic science. Current issues in linguistic theory. Series IV).

1488 Perceived ethnolinguistic vitality of Vietnamese and English in Australia. M. Willemyns; J. Pittam; C. Gallois. **J. Multiling.** 14:6 1993 pp.481 - 498.

1489 Reality and scientific construct — methodological pluralism in a sociolinguistic perspective. Lachman M. Khubchandani. **Int. J. S. Lang.** 100-101 1993 pp.55 - 72.

1490 Responsibility and evidence in oral discourse. Jane H. Hill [Ed.]; Judith T. Irvine [Ed.]. Cambridge: Cambridge University Press, 1993. viii, 316p. *ISBN: 0521415152, 0521425298. Includes bibliographical references (p. 289-305) and indexes. (Series:* Studies in the social and cultural foundations of language).

1491 Rol' gorodskoi rechi v protsesse formirovaniia natsional'nogo iazyka slovakov. *[In Russian];* (The role of urban speech in the formation of the national language of the Slovaks.) K.V. Lifanov. **Vest. Mosk. Univ. Ser. 9 Filol.** 3 5-6:1993 pp.3 - 10.

1492 The role of vowels in reading — a review of studies of English and Hebrew. Joseph Shimron. **Psychol . B.** 114:1 7:1993 pp.52 - 67.

1493 Semantic connectivity — an approach for analyzing symbols in semantic networks. Kathleen M. Carley; David S. Kaufer. **Commun. Theory** 3:3 8:1993 pp.183 - 213.

1494 The semantics of certainty in Quechua and its implications for a cultural epistemology. Janis B. Nuckolls. **Lang. Soc.** 22:2 6:1993 pp.235 - 255.

1495 A sociolinguistic analysis of the interpreter's role in simultaneous talk in interpreted interaction. Cynthia B. Roy. **Multilingua** 12:4 1993 pp.341 - 363.

1496 Some instantiations of the informational negativity effect — positive-negative asymmetry in category breadth and in estimated meaning similarity of trait adjectives. W. Claeys; L. Timmers. **Eur. J. Soc. Psychol.** 23:2 3-4:1993 pp.111 - 129.

1497 Towards a formalization of the semantics of some temporal prepositions. David S. Brée; Allel Feddag; Ian Pratt. **Time Soc.** 2:2 1993 pp.219 - 240.

Media
Moyens de communication

1498 Approche sociologique de la presse à Porto Rico et en Guadeloupe-Martinique. *[In French];* [A sociological approach to the press in Puerto Rico, Guadeloupe and Martinique]. Bernard Oreillard. **Carib. Stud.** 25:1-2 1-7:1992 pp.63 - 74.

1499 The baffling case of the smoking gun — the social ecology of political accounts in the Iran-Contra affair. Gray Cavender; Nancy C. Jurik; Albert K. Cohen. **Soc. Prob.** 40:2 5:1993 pp.152 - 166.

1500 Biased tidings — the media and the Cyril Burt controversy. Kevin Lamb. **Mankind Q.** XXXIII:2 Winter:1992 pp.203 - 225.

1501 Bibliographic guide to Caribbean mass communication. John A. Lent [Comp.]. Westport, Conn: Greenwood Press, 1992. xi, 301p. *ISBN: 0313282102. Includes indexes. (Series:* Bibliographies and indexes in mass media and communications).

1502 Bibliography of Cuban mass communications. John A. Lent [Comp.]. Westport, Conn: Greenwood Press, 1992. xi, 357p. *ISBN: 0313284555. Includes indexes. (Series:* Bibliographies and indexes in mass media and communications).

D: Culture

1503 Changing faces: a history of The Guardian 1956-88. Geoffrey Taylor. London: Fourth Estate, 1993. 354p. *ISBN: 1857021002*.

1504 Communication and citizenship: journalism and the public sphere. Peter Dahlgren [Ed.]; Colin Sparks [Ed.]. London: Routledge, 1993. 266p. *ISBN: 0415100674*.

1505 Communication, culture and hegemony: from the media to mediations. Jesus Martín-Barbero. London: Sage, 1993. 272p. *ISBN: 0803984898*. (*Series:* Communication and human values).

1506 Communication media and Mexican social issues — a focus on English-language and U.S.-origin communication media. Adalberto Aguirre. **Int. J. Comp. Soc** XXXIV:3-4 9-12:1993 pp.231 - 243.

1507 Communications and the Third World. Geoffrey W. Reeves. New York; London: Routledge, 1993. 277p. *ISBN: 0415047617*. *Includes bibliographical references.* (*Series:* Studies in culture and communication).

1508 Comunicazione e potere: mass media e politica in Italia. *[In Italian]*; [Communication and power: mass media and politics in Italy]. Gianpietro Mazzoleni. Naples: Liguori, 1992. 206p. *ISBN: 8820722054*.

1509 Critical studies of Canadian mass media. Marc Grenier [Ed.]. Markham, Ont: Butterworths, 1992. xvii, 384p. *ISBN: 0409906352*. *Includes bibliographical references (p. [341]-376) and index.*

1510 Culture and power: a media, culture & society reader. Paddy Scannell [Ed.]; Philip Schlesinger [Ed.]; Colin Sparks [Ed.]. London: SAGE, 1992. ix,357p. *ISBN: 0803986300, 0803986319*. *Includes bibliographies and index.* (*Series:* The Media, culture & society series).

1511 An der Schwelle zu einer neuen deutschen Rundfunkordnung: Grundlagen, Erfahrungen und Entwicklungsmöglichkeiten. *[In German]*; [On the threshold of a new order in German radio: basic principles, experiences and possibilities for development]. Winand Gellner [Ed.]; Manfred Anders [Ed.]. Berlin: VISTAS, 1991. 259p. *ISBN: 3891580665*. *Landeszentrale für politische Bildung Rheinland-Pfalz.*

1512 Disasters, relief and the media. Jonathan Benthall. London: I. B. Tauris, 1993. 267p. *ISBN: 1850436428*.

1513 Discourse of derision: the role of the mass media within the education policy process. Mike Wallace. **J. Educ. Pol.** 8:4 7-8:1993 pp.321 - 338.

1514 Distrust of representation — Habermas on the public sphere. John Durham Peters. **Media Cult. Soc.** 15:4 10:1993 pp.541 - 571.

1515 Dozentinnen und Dozenten in der Kommunikationswissenschaft, Publizistik, Journalistik. Ergebnisse einer Befragung in der Bundesrepublik Deutschland. *[In German]*; (Female and male professors in mass communication and journalism. Results of a survey in the Federal Republic of Germany.) *[Summary]*; *[Summary in French]*. Romy Fröhlich; Christina Holtz-Bacha. **Publizistik** 38:1 1-3:1993 pp.31 - 45.

1516 Essor et difficultés d'une presse indépendante en Mauritanie (juillet 1991-juillet 1992). *[In French]*; [The rise and difficulties of an independent press in Mauritania (July 1991-July 1992)]. Christian Roques. **R. Mon. Musul. Med.** 63-64 1992 pp.245 - 255.

1517 Fighting the war against crime — television, police, and audience. Philip Schlesinger; Howard Tumber. **Br. J. Crimin.** 33:1 Winter:1993 pp.19 - 32.

1518 The future of the field — between fragmentation and cohesion. Karl Erik Rosengren [Contrib.]; James R. Beniger [Contrib.]; Robert T. Craig [Contrib.]; Klaus

D: Culture

Krippendorff [Contrib.]; Brenda Dervin [Contrib.]; Joshua Meyrowitz [Contrib.]; Joli Jensen [Contrib.]; Barbara O'Keefe [Contrib.]; Gregory J. Shepherd [Contrib.]; Kurt Lang [Contrib.]; Gladys Engel Lang [Contrib.]; Paolo Mancini [Contrib.]; Austin S. Babrow [Contrib.]; Mary Anne Fitzpatrick [Contrib.]; Horace Newcomb [Contrib.]; Sandra Braman [Contrib.]; Dennis K. Davis [Contrib.]; James Jasinski [Contrib.]; Jennifer L. Monahan [Contrib.]; Lori Collins-Jarvis [Contrib.]; Eric W. Rothenbuhler [Contrib.]; James E. Grunig [Contrib.]; Robert K. Avery [Contrib.]; William F. Eadie [Contrib.]; W. Lance Bennett [Contrib.]; Douglas Gomery [Contrib.]; Eli Noam [Contrib.]; Willard D. Rowland [Contrib.]; H. Leslie Steeves [Contrib.]; David Docherty [Contrib.]; David Morrison [Contrib.]; Michael Tracey [Contrib.]. **J. Comm.** 43:3 Summer:1993 pp.6 - 238. *Collection of 26 articles.*

1519 The future of the field — between fragmentation and cohesion. Sonia M. Livingstone [Contrib.]; David Morley [Contrib.]; Klaus Bruhn Jensen [Contrib.]; Herbert J. Gans [Contrib.]; Gaye Tuchman [Contrib.]; Seth Geiger [Contrib.]; John Newhagen [Contrib.]; Robert M. Entman [Contrib.]; Frank Biocca [Contrib.]; Ito Youichi [Contrib.]; Barbie Zelizer [Contrib.]; Lawrence Grossberg [Contrib.]; Robert W. McChesney [Contrib.]; Eileen R. Meehan [Contrib.]; Vincent Mosco [Contrib.]; Janet Wasko [Contrib.]; Dan Schiller [Contrib.]; Everett M. Rogers [Contrib.]; Steven H. Chaffee [Contrib.]; John Durham Peters [Contrib.]; Susan Herbst [Contrib.]; Pamela J. Shoemaker [Contrib.]; Lana F. Rakow [Contrib.]; David L. Swanson [Contrib.]; Anandam P. Kavoori [Contrib.]; Michael Gurevitch [Contrib.]; José Marques de Melo [Contrib.]. **J. Comm.** 43:4 Autumn:1993 pp.5 - 191. *Collection of 22 articles.*

1520 Good news: social ethics and the press. Clifford G. Christians; John P. Ferré; Mark Fackler. New York: Oxford University Press, 1993. xvi, 265p. *ISBN: 0195074319. Includes bibliographical references and index.*

1521 A integração europeia e os meios de comunicação social. *[In Portuguese]*; [European integration and the means of social communication]. José Manuel Paquete de Oliveira. **Anál. Soc.** XXVII:4-5(118-119) 1992 pp.995 - 1024.

1522 Iukkorovskie izdaniia i perspektivy ikh razvitiia. *[In Russian]*; (Youth and children's newspapers and prospects for their development.) A.L. Miasnikova. **Vest. Mosk. Univ. Ser. 10 Zhur.** 3 5-6:1993 pp.41 - 47.

1523 Journalismus. *[In German]*; [Journalism]. Wolfgang R. Langenbucher [Contrib.]; Richard Münch [Contrib.]; Bernd Guggenberger [Contrib.]; Ulrich Saxer [Contrib.]; Anton Pelinka [Contrib.]; Jürgen Wilke [Contrib.]; Fritz Hausjell [Contrib.]; Beate Schneider [Contrib.]; Klaus Schönbach [Contrib.]; Dieter Stürzebecher [Contrib.]; Roman Hummel [Contrib.]; Petra E. Dorsch-Jungsberger [Contrib.]; Pierre A. Saffarnia [Contrib.]. **Publizistik** 38:3 7-9:1993 pp.261 - 425. *Collection of 11 articles.*

1524 Journalistinnen im Medienvergleich: mal mehr, mal weniger benachteiligt? Ergebnisse einer Telefonbefragung. *[In German]*; [A media comparison of women journalists: are they more disadvantaged than men? Results of a telephone survey]. Ute Schulz. **Publizistik** 38:4 10-12:1993 pp.542 - 556.

1525 Marktpublizistik. Oder — Wie alle - reihum - Presse und Rundfunk bezahlen. *[In German]*; (Market forms of public communication. Or — how everybody — one after the other — pays for newspapers and broadcasting.) *[Summary]*; *[Summary in French]*; *[Summary in Spanish]*. Manfred Rühl. **Publizistik** 38:2 4-6:1993 pp.125 - 152.

D: Culture

1526 The mass media and environmental issues. Anders Hansen [Ed.]. Leicester: Leicester University Press, 1993. 238p. *ISBN: 0718514440*. Includes bibliographical references and index. (*Series:* Studies in communication and society).

1527 The mass media, cultural identity, and the public sphere in the modern world. Nicholas Garnham. **Publ. Cult.** 5:2 Winter:1993 pp.251 - 266.

1528 Mass media, esoteric groups and folkloristics. Knut Djupedal. **J. Pop. Cult.** 26:4 Spring:1993 pp.69 - 78.

1529 Mass media in Greece: power, politics, and privatization. Thimios Zaharopoulos; Manny Paraschos. Westport, Conn: Praeger, 1993. xx, 214p. *ISBN: 027594106X*. Includes bibliographical references (p. [191]-206) and index.

1530 The media and disasters: Pan Am 103. Joan Deppa; Maria Russell; Dona Hayes; Elizabeth Lynne Flocke. London: David Fulton, 1993. 346p. *ISBN: 185346225X*.

1531 [Media audience studies in transition]; *[Text in Japanese]*. Kazuto Kojima. Tokyo: University of Tokyo Press, 1993. 223p.

1532 Media industry in Europe. Antonio Pilati [Ed.]. London: John Libbey for MIND Institute of Media Economics, 1993. 250p. *ISBN: 0861963989*.

1533 Médias et service public. *[In French]*; [Media and public service]. Robert Andersen; François Jongen. Brussels: Bruylant, 1992. 357p. *ISBN: 2802708015*. Includes bibliographical references. Université catholique de Louvain, Centre d'études constitutionnelles et administratives.

1534 Meinungsführer im Mediensystem — »Top-down«- und »Bottom-up«-Prozesse. *[In German]*; (Opinion leadership in the media system — »top-down« and »bottom-up«-processes.) *[Summary]*; *[Summary in French]*; *[Summary in Spanish]*. Rainer Mathes; Andreas Czaplicki. **Publizistik** 38:2 4-6:1993 pp.153 - 166.

1535 Nation, culture, text: Australian cultural and media studies. Graeme Turner. New York; London: Routledge, 1993. 260p. *ISBN: 0415088852, 0415088860*. Includes bibliographical references and index. (*Series:* Communication and society).

1536 Neue Lebenswelt - neue Medienwelt? Jugendliche aus der Ex- und Post-DDR im Transfer zu einer vereinten Medienkultur. *[In German]*; [A new world for us and for the media? Youth from the former and post-unification GDR in the transition to a united media culture]. Bernd Schorb [Ed.]; Hans-Jörg Stiehler [Ed.]. Opladen: Leske + Budrich, 1991. 162p. *ISBN: 3810009407*. Includes bibliographical references (p. 157-160).

1537 The New York Times' and Renmin Ribao's news coverage of the 1991 Soviet coup — a case study of international news discourse. Shujen Wang. **Text** 13:4 1993 pp.559 - 598.

1538 The phantom public sphere. Bruce Robbins [Ed.]. Minneapolis, MN: University of Minnesota Press, 1993. xxvi, 310p. *ISBN: 0816621241*. Includes bibliographical references and index. (*Series:* Cultural politics - 5).

1539 Pioneers and plain folks — cultural constructions of "place" in radio news. Barbie Zelizer. **Semiotica** 93:3-4 1993 pp.269 - 286.

1540 The politics of silence: the meaning of community and the uses of media in the new Europe. Kevin Robins. **New Form.** 21 Winter:1993 pp.80 - 101.

1541 Power, mass media and the Middle East. Joe Stork [Contrib.]; Laura Flanders [Contrib.]; Joel Beinin [Contrib.]; Susan Slyomovics [Contrib.]; Lila Abu-Lughod [Contrib.]; Hamid Naficy [Contrib.]; Fouad Moughrabi [Contrib.]; Hisham Milhem [Contrib.]; Muhammad Al-Saqr [Contrib.]; Serge Adda [Contrib.]; Sally Ethelston

[Ed.]; Martha Wenger [Contrib.]; Al Miskin [Contrib.]. **Middle E. Rep.** 23(1):180 1-2:1993 pp.2 - 40. *Collection of 9 articles.*

1542 The press and public access to the environment and development debate. Colin Lacey; David Longman. **Sociol. Rev.** 41:2 5:1993 pp.207 - 243.

1543 Prince Charles — our flexible friend — accounting for variations in constructions of identity. Nigel Edley. **Text** 13:3 1993 pp.397 - 422.

1544 Prosecuting the victim? A study of the reporting of barristers' comments in rape cases. Keith Soothill; Debbie Soothill. **Howard J. Crim. Just.** 32:1 2:1993 pp.12 - 24.

1545 Public relations and media strategies. John Corner [Ed.]; Philip Schlesinger [Ed.]; Howard Tumber [Contrib.]; John Tulloch [Contrib.]; David Miller [Contrib.]; Greg Philo [Contrib.]; Donn Tilson [Contrib.]; Susan Herbst [Contrib.]; Adigun Agbaje [Contrib.]; John L. Hochheimer [Contrib.]. **Media Cult. Soc.** 15:3 7:1993 pp.339 - 486. *Collection of 9 articles.*

1546 Revues and newspapers — on critics and rhetoric in local media. Erik Vangsnes. **J. Pop. Cult.** 26:4 Spring:1993 pp.101 - 114.

1547 The sacred meets the profane — baseball on strike. Maryellen Boyle. **Communication** 13:4 1993 pp.229 - 253.

1548 Sartre and the media. Michael Scriven. Basingstoke: Macmillan Press, 1993. 152p. *ISBN: 0333558138.*

1549 Shocking numbers and graphic accounts — quantified images of drug problems in the print media. James D. Orcutt; J. Blake Turner. **Soc. Prob.** 40:2 5:1993 pp.190 - 206.

1550 Social problems in Estonian mass media 1975-91. Mikko Lagerspetz. **Acta Sociol.** 36:4 1993 pp.357 - 370.

1551 Sociomedia: multimedia, hypermedia, and the social construction of knowledge. Edward Barrett [Ed.]. Cambridge, Mass: MIT Press, 1992. 580p. *ISBN: 0262023466. Most of the papers were originally presented at the first conference on "The Social Creation of Knowledge" at MIT in Spring, 1991. Includes bibliographical references and index. (Series: Technical communication and information systems).*

1552 Sowjetische Publizistik zwischen Öffnung und Umgestaltung: die Medien im Zeichen von Glasnost und Perestroika. *[In German]*; [Soviet journalism between openness and reorganization: the media, Glasnost and Perestroika] *[Summary]*; *[Summary in Russian]*. Winfried B. Lerg; Marianne Ravenstein; Sabine Schiller-Lerg. Münster: Lit, 1991. v, 301p. *ISBN: 3894730625. Includes bibliographical references.*

1553 Symposium — agenda setting revisited. Maxwell E. McCombs [Contrib.]; Donald L. Shaw [Contrib.]; Everett M. Rogers [Contrib.]; James W. Dearing [Contrib.]; Dorine Bregman [Contrib.]; Alex S. Edelstein [Contrib.]; Gerald M. Kosicki [Contrib.]. **J. Comm.** 43:2 Spring:1993 pp.58 - 127. *Collection of 4 articles.*

1554 The three paradigms of mass media research in mainstream communication journals. W. James Potter; Roger Cooper; Michel Dupagne. **Commun. Theory** 3:4 11:1993 pp.317 - 335.

1555 Timeshift: on video culture. Sean Cubitt. New York; London: Routledge, 1991. x, 206p. *ISBN: 0415055482, 0415016789. Includes bibliographical references (p. [188]-199) and index. (Series: Comedia series).*

D: Culture

1556 Über den Sender gehen. Lebensweltteffekte medialer Präsenz. *[In German]*; (To be on air — real-world effects of media presence.) *[Summary]*; *[Summary in French]*. Johannes Boettner. **Publizistik** 38:1 1-3:1993 pp.66 - 75.

1557 Virgin or vamp: how the press covers sex crimes. Helen Benedict. New York: Oxford University Press, 1992. vi, 309p. *ISBN: 0195066804. Includes bibliographical references (p. 295-299) and index.*

1558 We keep America on top of the world: journalism and the public sphere. Daniel C. Hallin. London, New York: Routledge, 1993. 187p. *ISBN: 041509142X, 0415091438. Includes bibliographical references and index. (Series: Communication and society).*

1559 Westdeutsche Journalisten im Vergleich — jung, professionell und mit Spaß an der Arbeit. *[In German]*; (West German journalists — young, professional and pleased with their profession — a comparative study.) *[Summary]*; *[Summary in French]*. Beate Schneider; Klaus Schönbach; Dieter Stürzebecher. **Publizistik** 38:1 1-3:1993 pp.5 - 30.

Multilingualism
Multilinguisme

1560 Balancing macro- and micro-sociolinguistic perspectives in language management — the case of Singapore; *[Summary in German]*; *[Summary in Esperanto]*. Eddie C.Y. Kuo; Björn H. Jernudd. **Lang. Prob. Lang. Plan.** 17:1 Spring:1993 pp.1 - 21.

1561 Bilingualism and national development. Andrew Gonzales [Contrib.]; John Edwards [Contrib.]; Gary Jones [Contrib.]; Peter W. Martin [Contrib.]; A.Conrad K. Ozóg [Contrib.]; Anne Pakir [Contrib.]; J.A. Oladejo [Contrib.]; Hugo Baetens Beardsmore [Contrib.]; Richard B. Baldauf [Contrib.]; Björn H. Jernudd [Contrib.]; Robert B. Kaplan [Contrib.]. **J. Multiling.** 14:1-2 1993 pp.5 - 172. *Collection of 10 articles.*

1562 Contextual influences on language politics in Canada and South Africa. Newell M. Stultz. **J. Comm. C. Pol.** XXXI:3 11:1993 pp.67 - 91.

1563 The emergent world language system. Abram de Swaan [Ed.]; David D. Laitin [Contrib.], Isabelle T. Kreindler [Contrib.]; Alamin M. Mazrui [Contrib.]; Ali A. Mazrui [Contrib.]; Hans R. Dua [Contrib.]. **Int. Pol. Sci Rev.** 14:3 7:1993 pp.219 - 308.

1564 Functional regional bilingualism. K.M. Pedersen. **J. Multiling.** 14:6 1993 pp.463 - 480.

1565 Language in power. J.A. Laponce [Contrib.]; Jonathan Pool [Contrib.]; David D. Laitin [Contrib.]; James W. Tollefson [Contrib.]; Stevan Harrell [Contrib.]; Harold F. Schiffman [Contrib.]; Carol Myers-Scotton [Contrib.]; Kevin Lang [Contrib.]. **Int. J. S. Lang.** 103 1993 pp.19 - 183. *Collection of 8 articles.*

1566 Tvasprakighet och lingvistisk medvetenhet: betydelsen av tvasprakighet och av undervisning för lingvistisk medvetenhet hos barn i aldern sex till atta ar. *[In Swedish]*; [Bilingualism and lingusitic development in children between the ages of six and eight] *[Summary]*. Anna-Lena Østern. Abo: Abo Akademis Förlag, 1991. 509p. *ISBN: 9519498931. Includes English summary.*

1567 The urban geolinguistics of Cape Town. I.J. van der Merwe. **Geojournal** 31:4 12:1993 pp.409 - 418.

D: Culture

1568 Welsh and English in the city of Bangor — a study in functional differentiation. Cora F. Lindsay. **Lang. Soc.** 22:1 3:1993 pp.1 - 17.
1569 'Why can't we speak Tagalog?' The problematic status of multilingualism in the international school. T. Ochs. **J. Multiling.** 14:6 1993 pp.447 - 462.

Television
Télévision

1570 Broadcast talk. Paddy Scannell [Ed.]. London, Newbury Park: Sage Publications, 1991. 231p. *ISBN: 0803983743, 0803983751. Includes bibliographical references and index.* (*Series:* Media, culture and society).
1571 Channels of resistance: global television and local enpowerment. Tony Dowmunt [Ed.]. London: BFI Publishing in association with Channel Four Television, 1993. 194p. *ISBN: 0851703925.*
1572 Citizen television: a local dimension to public service broadcasting. Dave Rushton [Ed.]. London: John Libbey, 1993. 232p. *ISBN: 0861964330.* (*Series:* Research monograph).
1573 Claiming identity — film and television in Hongkong. Rozanna Lilley. **Hist. Anthrop.** 6:2-3 1993 pp.261 - 292.
1574 En massa til masorna? Perspektiv på det moderna samhället. *[In Swedish]*; [A mass for the masses? Perspective on modern society]. Peter Dahlgren [Contrib.]; Johan Fornäs [Contrib.]; Kirsten Drotner [Contrib.]; Ole Breitenstein [Contrib.]; Seppo Luoma-Keturi [Contrib.]; Karin Becker [Contrib.]; Torunn Selberg [Contrib.]; Karin Lövgren [Contrib.]; Kirsten Rykind-Erikson [Contrib.]; Cilla Fredriksson [Contrib.]. **Nord. Ny.** 47 11:1992 pp.6 - 47. *Collection of 10 articles.*
1575 "Father knows best" and "The Cosby Show": nostalgia and the sitcom tradition. June M. Frazer; Timothy C. Frazer. **J. Pop. Cult.** 27:3 Winter:1993 pp.163 - 172.
1576 Formen sprachlicher Identitätskonstitution in inszenierter und dramatisierter mündlicher Kommunikation im spanischen Fernsehen. *[In German]*; (Forms of linguistic constitution of identity in stages and dramatized oral spoken communication on Spanish television.) Klaus Zimmermann. **Wissensch. Z. Humboldt-Univ.** 41:3 1992 pp.75 - 84.
1577 From TV talk to screen caption. Yung-O Biq. **Text** 13:3 1993 pp.351 - 369.
1578 Funding the BBC's future. Steven Barnett [Ed.]. London: BFI Publishing, 1993. 121p. *ISBN: 0851704255.* (*Series:* BBC Charter Review Series).
1579 "L'Heure de Vérité" — televised democracy?. Sheila Perry. **Fr. Cult. Stud.** 4:10 (Part 1) 2:1993 pp.1 - 14.
1580 A history of television in Belize. Dion Weaver. **Beliz. St.** 21:1 5:1993 pp.13 - 20.
1581 How you "act your age" when you watch TV. Mary Chayko. **Sociol. For.** 8:4 12:1993 pp.573 - 593.
1582 Interpreting soap operas and creating community: inside a computer-mediated fan club. Nancy K. Baym. **J. Folk. Res.** 30:2/3 5-12:1993 pp.143 - 176.
1583 It's time for my story: soap opera sources, structure, and response. Carol Traynor Williams. Westport, Conn: Praeger, 1992. x, 253p. *ISBN: 027594297X. Includes bibliographical references (p. [227]-237) and index.* (*Series:* Media and society series).

D: Culture

1584 Japanese daytime television, popular culture, and ideology. Andrew A. Painter. **J. Jpn. Stud.** 19:2 Summer:1993 pp.295 - 326.

1585 National identity and Europe: the television revolution. Phillip Drummond [Ed.]; Jane Willis [Ed.]; Richard Paterson [Ed.]. London: British Film Institute, 1993. x,140p. *ISBN: 0851703828. Includes index. (Series:* European media monographs).

1586 No primeiro aniversário da televisão privada em Portugal. *[In Portuguese]*; (Private television stations.) *[Summary]*; *[Summary in French]*. José Rebelo. **Anál. Soc.** XXVIII:3(122) 1993 pp.653 - 678.

1587 Our cultural perplexities — television and violent crime. Brandon S. Centerwall. **Publ. Inter.** 111 Spring:1993 pp.56 - 71.

1588 Les professionnels de la télévision. *[In French]*; [Television professionals]. Dominique Pasquier [Ed.]; Rémy Rieffel [Contrib.]; Dominique Mehl [Contrib.]; Sabine Chalvon-Demersay [Contrib.]; Jérôme Bourdon [Contrib.]; Norbert Alter [Contrib.]; Michel Feutrie [Contrib.]; Éric Verdier [Contrib.]. **Sociol. Trav.** XXXV 4:1993 pp.373 - 492. *Collection of 6 articles.*

1589 The regions, the nations and the BBC. Sylvia Harvey [Ed.]; Kevin Robins [Ed.]. London: BFI Publishing, 1993. 112p. *ISBN: 085170428X. (Series:* BBC Charter Review Series).

1590 Television and ritualization of everyday life. Torunn Selberg. **J. Pop. Cult.** 26:4 Spring:1993 pp.3 - 10.

1591 Television, ontological security and the transitional object. Roger Silverstone. **Media Cult. Soc.** 15:4 10:1993 pp.573 - 598.

1592 Watching television: hermeneutics, reception and popular culture. Tony Wilson. Cambridge, UK, Cambridge, MA: Polity Press, 1993. 230p. *ISBN: 0745607225. Includes bibliographical references and index.*

1593 You can't go home again... or can you? Reflections on the symbolism of TV families at Christmas time. Paul Nathanson. **J. Pop. Cult.** 27:2 Fall:1993 pp.149 - 162.

D.8: Art
Art

1594 The appeal of images. Jochen Becker [Ed.]; Àron Kibédi Varga [Ed.]; Annemiek Ouwerkerk [Contrib.]; Lex Bosman [Contrib.]; Jan Baptist Bedaux [Contrib.]; Paul van den Akker [Contrib.]; Bernard Vouilloux [Contrib.]; Jeroen Stumpel [Contrib.]. **Argumentation** 7:1 1993 pp.3 - 117. *Collection of 7 articles.*

1595 The arts in the 1970's: cultural closure. B. J. Moore-Gilbert [Ed.]. New York; London: Routledge, 1993. 312p. *ISBN: 0415099056, 0415099064. Includes bibliographical references and index.*

1596 The beast of the apocalypse: the post-colonial experience of the United States. Jon Stratton. **New Form.** 21 Winter:1993 pp.35 - 63.

1597 Books and reading in Australian society: a special publication of the Institute for Cultural Policy Studies, Faculty of Humanities, Griffith University. Jock Macleod [Ed.]; Pat Buckridge [Ed.]. Nathan/QLD: Griffith University, 1993. 154p. *ISBN: 0868574619.*

D: Culture

1598 Buildings and power: freedom and control in the origin of modern building types. Thomas A. Markus. New York; London: Routledge, 1993. 342p. *ISBN: 0415076641, 041507665X.*

1599 Cassette culture: popular music and technology in North India. Peter Lamarche Manuel. Chicago: University of Chicago Press, 1993. xix, 302p. *ISBN: 0226503992, 0226504018. Includes bibliographical references (p. 289-296) and index. (Series:* Chicago studies in ethnomusicology).

1600 Cinema and the urban poor in South India. Sara Dickey. Cambridge: Cambridge University Press, 1993. xii, 213p. *ISBN: 052144084X. Bibliography: p. 195-202. - Includes indexes. (Series:* Cambridge studies in social and cultural anthropology).

1601 Le cinéma déchaîné: mutation d'une industrie. *[In French]*; [Cinema unleashed: the change of an industry]. Joëlle Farchy. Paris: Presses du CNRS, 1992. 351p. *ISBN: 2876820633. Bibliogr.: p.329-351.*

1602 Cultural studies and social change — the war film as men's magic, and other fictions about fiction; *[Summary in French]*. Gaile McGregor. **Can. J. Soc.** 18:3 Summer:1993 pp.271 - 302.

1603 Cycles of repression and relaxation: politco-literary events in China, 1976-1989. Yuhuai He. Bochum: N. Brockmeyer, 1992. 584p. *ISBN: 3819600337.*

1604 Disrupted borders: an intervention in definitions of boundaries. Sunil Gupta [Ed.]. London: Rivers Oram Press, 1993. 222p. *ISBN: 1854890441.*

1605 Every picture tells a story — wall decorations as expressions of individuality, family unit and socio-cultural belonging. Eva Reme. **J. Pop. Cult.** 26:4 Spring:1993 pp.19 - 38.

1606 The evolution of narrative and the self. William L. Benzon. **J. Soc. Evol. Sys.** 16:2 1993 pp.129 - 155.

1607 The field of cultural production: essays on art and literature. Pierre Bourdieu; Randal Johnson [Ed.]. Cambridge: Polity Press, 1993. 322p. *ISBN: 0745609872.*

1608 Hunger for images, myths of femininity in the Sri Lankan cinema, 1947-1989. Laleen Jayamanne. **S.Asia B.** XII:1 1992 pp.57 - 75.

1609 Imagining women: cultural representations and gender. Frances Bonner [Ed.]. Cambridge: Polity Press in association with Blackwell Publishers and the Open University, 1992. viii, 361p. *ISBN: 0745609740, 0745609732. Includes bibliographical references (p. 330-347) and index.*

1610 Investeren in kennis voor een rendabel kunstbeleid. *[In Dutch]*; (Investing in knowledge to make arts policy pay.) *[Summary]*. M. Boorsma. **Mens Maat.** 68:2 5:1993 pp.107 - 132.

1611 Jazz — a people's music?. Charlie Hore. **Int. Soc.** 61 Winter:1993 pp.91 - 108.

1612 Der kultivierte Schrecken? Erlebnisweise von Horrorfilmen im Rahmen eines Zuschauerexperiments. *[In German]*; (Cultivated horror? How to experience horror movies — an audience experiment.) *[Summary]*; *[Summary in French]*; *[Summary in Spanish]*. Jürgen Grimm. **Publizistik** 38:2 4-6:1993 pp.206 - 217.

1613 Looking through a glass onion: rock and roll as modern manifestation of carnival. Paul R. Kohl. **J. Pop. Cult.** 27:1 Summer:1993 pp.143 - 162.

1614 The matter of images: essays on representations. Richard Dyer. London: Routledge, 1992. 172p. *ISBN: 0415057183.*

1615 Mimesis and alterity: a particular history of the senses. Michael T. Taussig. New York: Routledge, 1993. xix, 299p. *ISBN: 0415906865, 0415906873. Includes bibliographical references (p. 283-290) and index.*

D: Culture

1616 Musical self-image and cultural change — Lithuanian minority in Poland case study. M. Niewiadomska-Bugaj; S. Zeranska-Kiminek. **Behav. Sci.** 38:4 10:1993 pp.273 - 292.

1617 Now you see it: studies on lesbian and gay film. Richard Dyer. London: Routledge, 1990. 328p. *ISBN: 0415035554, 0415035562. Includes bibliography and index.*

1618 Panic sites: the Japanese imagination of disaster from Godzilla to Akira. Susan J. Napier. **J. Jpn. Stud.** 19:2 Summer:1993 pp.327 - 352.

1619 The pelvis as shock absorber: modern and African dance. Kees P. Epskamp; Feri de Geus. **J. Pop. Cult.** 27:1 Summer:1993 pp.55 - 66.

1620 Reframing the family photograph. Oddlaug Reiakvam. **J. Pop. Cult.** 26:4 Spring:1993 pp.39 - 68.

1621 Rock and popular music: politics, policies, institutions. Tony Bennett [Ed.]. New York; London: Routledge, 1993. 306p. *ISBN: 0415063698. Includes bibliographical references and index.* (*Series:* Culture).

1622 El "Sistema de Cristóbal Colón" y la "Biografía de Colón", una muestra de poesía popular Mexicana. *[In Spanish]*; ["The System of Christopher Columbus" and the "Biography of Columbus", an example of popular Mexican poetry]. Judith Orozco; Fernando Nava L.. **Cuad. Am.** 6:42 11-12:1993 pp.203 - 213.

1623 The socioeconomy of scholarly and cultural book publishing. Rowland Lorimer. **Media Cult. Soc.** 15:2 4:1993 pp.203 - 216.

1624 [The sociology of painting. 2]; *[Text in Japanese]*. Shigefumi Kurahashi. Kyoto: Koyo Shobo, 1993. 276p.

1625 Stages in the evolution of music. William L. Benzon. **J. Soc. Evol. Sys.** 16:3 1993 pp.273 - 296.

1626 Sur quelques progrès récents de la sociologie des œuvres. *[In French]*; [On recent progress in the sociology of works of art]. Jean-Louis Fabiani. **Genèses** 11 3:1993 pp.148 - 167.

1627 The texture of memory: Holocaust memorials and meaning in Europe, Israel, and America. James Edward Young. New Haven: Yale University Press, 1993. xvii, 398p. *ISBN: 0300053835. Includes bibliographical references and index.*

1628 Toward a unified theory of the arts. Victor A. Grauer. **Semiotica** 94:3-4 1993 pp.233 - 252.

1629 Tradition and novelty in concert programming — bringing the artist back into cultural analysis. Samuel Gilmore. **Sociol. For.** 8:2 6:1993 pp.221 - 242.

1630 Understanding rock 'n' roll: popular music in Britain 1955-1964. Dick Bradley. Buckingham, Philadelphia: Open University Press, 1992. vi, 191p. *ISBN: 0335097553, 0335097545. Includes bibliographical references and index.* (*Series:* Popular music in Britain).

1631 The United States of the Blues: on the crossing of African and European cultures in the 20th century. William L. Benzon. **J. Soc. Evol. Sys.** 16:4 1993 pp.401 - 438.

1632 Les vieillards dans l'art africain. *[In French]*; (The aged in African art.) *[Summary]*. Jacques Binet. **Afr. Cont.** 166 4-6:1993 pp.39 - 44.

1633 The view from the verandah — prospect, refuge and leisure. Brian Hudson. **Aust. Geogr. Stud.** 31:1 4:1993 pp.70 - 78.

1634 Views beyond the border country: Raymond Williams and cultural politics. Dennis L. Dworkin; Leslie G. Roman. New York: Routledge, 1993. xii, 364p. *ISBN: 0415902754, 0415902762. Includes bibliographical references (p. 295-353) and index.* (*Series:* Critical social thought).

1635 Where is the "Promised Land"? Class and gender in Bruce Springsteen's rock lyrics. Pamela Moss. **Geog.ann. B.** 74B:3 1992 pp.167 - 187.
1636 White on black: images of Africa and blacks in Western popular culture. Jan P. Nederveen Pieterse. New Haven: Yale University Press, 1992. 259p. *ISBN: 0300051433.*
1637 Yoshimoto Banana writes home: Shōjo culture and the nostalgic subject. John Whittier Treat. **J. Jpn. Stud.** 19:2 Summer:1993 pp.353 - 388.

D.9: **Education**
Éducation

1638 1 sur 500: la réussite scolaire en milieu populaire. *[In French]*; [1 out of 500: academic success in general education]. Jean-Paul Laurens. Toulouse: Presses Universitaires du Mirail, 1992. 259p. *ISBN: 2858161755.*
1639 Adolescents' cognitions and attributions for academic cheating — a cross-national study. Ellis D. Evans; Delores Craig; Gerd Mietzel. **J. Psychol.** 127:6 11:1993 pp.585 - 602.
1640 Africa's educational dilemma — roadblocks to universal literacy for social integration and change; *[Summary in German]*; *[Summary in French]*. Daphne W. Ntiri. **Int. R. Educat.** 39:5 9:1993 pp.357 - 372.
1641 Changing classroom cultures: anti-racism, politics and schools. Debbie Epstein. Stoke-on-Trent: Trentham, 1993. viii, 168p. *ISBN: 0948080655. Includes index. Bibliography: p. 149-162.*
1642 The choice alternative to school assignment. R.L. Church; O.B. Schoepfle. **Envir. Plan. B.** 20:4 7:1993 pp.447 - 457.
1643 Class, the labour process and work focus on education. Peter Edwin Watkins. Geelong, Vic: Deakin University : distributed by Deakin University Press, 1992. vi, 181p. *ISBN: 0730013812. Bibliography: p. 177-179.*
1644 Compulsory schooling disease: how children absorb fascist values. Chris Shute. Nottingham: Educational Heretics Press, 1993. 63p. *ISBN: 0951802224.*
1645 Cross-cultural approaches to literacy. Brian Vincent Street [Ed.]. Cambridge, New York: Cambridge University Press, 1993. 321p. *ISBN: 0521401674. Includes index.* (*Series:* Cambridge studies in oral and literate culture).
1646 Cultural diversity and the schools. James Lynch [Ed.]; Celia Modgil [Ed.]; Sohan Modgil [Ed.]. London, Washington, D.C: Falmer, 1992. *ISBN: 1850009899, 1850009910. Includes bibliographical references and indexes.*
1647 Cultural literacy: a positive view. Abraham Stahl. **Interchange** 24:3 1993 pp.287 - 298.
1648 Denominational schools and public schooling. Robin Barrow. **Interchange** 24:3 1993 pp.225 - 232.
1649 Disclaimer mannerisms of students — how to avoid being labelled as cheaters; *[Summary in French]*. Daniel Albas; Cheryl Albas. **Can. R. Soc. A.** 30:4 11:1993 pp.451 - 467.
1650 Education and political development among young adults. Kent Jennings. **Polit. Indiv.** 3:2 1993 pp.1 - 24.
1651 Education and society in Latin America. Orlando Albornoz. Basingstoke, Hampshire: Macmillan in association with St. Antony's College, Oxford, 1993. vii, 185p. *ISBN:*

D: Culture

      0333565630. Includes bibliographical references and index. (Series: St. Anthony's/Macmillan series).

1652 Education, inequality and social identity. Lawrence Angus [Ed.]. Washington, D.C, London: Falmer Press, 1993. 204p. *ISBN: 0750701722. Includes bibliographical references and index.*

1653 L'effet établissement. Construction d'une problématique. *[In French]*; (The establishment effect. Developing an issue.) *[Summary]*; *[Summary in German]*; *[Summary in Spanish]*. Olivier Cousin. **Rev. Fr. Soc.** XXXIV:3 7-9:1993 pp.395 - 419.

1654 Engineering persistence — past, present, and future factors and gender differences. Linda A. Jackson; Philip D. Gardner; Linda A. Sullivan. **High. Educ.** 26:2 9:1993 pp.227 - 246.

1655 Entitlement and achievement in education. Wally Morrow. **St. Philos. Educ.** 13:1 1993-1994 pp.33 - 48.

1656 Entry into school — the beginning school transition and educational stratification in the United States. Doris R. Entwisle; Karl L. Alexander. **Ann. R. Soc.** 19 1993 pp.401 - 424.

1657 Gender and practical tasks in science. Kok-Aun Toh. **Educat. Res.** 35:3 Winter:1993 pp.255 - 265.

1658 Identidad y educación en la Argentina. *[In Spanish]*; [Identity and education in Argentina]. Hugo E. Biagini. **R. Cen. Est. Consti.** 14 1-4:1993 pp.73 - 82.

1659 Integrating an East Asian focus into Australian business education. Murray Frazer. **Asian Prof.** 21:3 6:1993 pp.217 - 226.

1660 An interactive flow model for projecting school enrolments; *[Summary in French]*; *[Summary in German]*. Edward Gould. **Int. R. Educat.** 39:4 7:1993 pp.319 - 332.

1661 Intuition and the Socratic method: two opposed ways of knowing?. Anthony G. Rud, Jr. **St. Philos. Educ.** 13:1 1993-1994 pp.65 - 76.

1662 Karl Mannheim e la sociologia dell'educazione. *[In Italian]*; [Karl Mannheim and sociology of education]. C. Chiara Canta. **Sociologia [Rome]** XXVII:1-3 1993 pp.199 - 216.

1663 Knowledge, culture and power: international perspectives on literacy as policy and practice. Peter Freebody [Ed.]; Anthony R. Welch [Ed.]. London: Falmer Press, 1993. 244p. *ISBN: 1850008337, 1850008345. (Series:* Critical perspectives on literacy and education).

1664 Learning to go to school in Japan: the transition from home to preschool life. Lois Peak. Berkeley: University of California Press, 1991. xviii, 210p. *ISBN: 0520071514. Includes bibliographical references (p. 201-204) and index.*

1665 Life at school: an ethnographic study. Meenakshi Thapan. Delhi, Oxford: Oxford University Press, 1991. viii, 271p. *ISBN: 0195626273. Includes index. Bibliography: p. 257-263.*

1666 Literacy, myths, and legacies: lessons from the past/thoughts for the future. Harvey J. Graff. **Interchange** 24:3 1993 pp.271 - 286.

1667 Marketing education in the postmodern age. Jane Kenway; Chris Bigum; Lindsay Fitzclarence. **J. Educ. Pol.** 8:2 3-4:1993 pp.105 - 122.

1668 Medicaid — a potential source of revenue for special education. A. Jonathan Dugger; Russell S. Kirby; Charles R. Feild; Thomas J. Nosal; Linda Duncan Malone. **J. Child Fam. Stud.** 2:3 9:1993 pp.249 - 257.

D: Culture

1669 Modern to postmodern: social construction, dissonance, and education. Lynda Stone. **St. Philos. Educ.** 13:1 1993-1994 pp.49 - 64.

1670 No master high or low: libertarian education and schooling in Britain, 1890-1990. John Shotton. Bristol: Libertarian Education, 1993. 291p. *ISBN: 095139973X.* (*Series:* Libertarian education).

1671 Novas tendências da educação no leste Europeu. *[In Portuguese]*; [New trends in education in Eastern Europe] *[Summary].* Egídio F. Schmitz. **Est. Leop.** 29:134 9-10:1993 pp.29 - 46.

1672 Omitted-ability bias and increase in the return to schooling. McKinley L. Blackburn; David Neumark. **J. Labor Ec.** 11:3 7:1993 pp.521 - 544.

1673 Parents and schools: customers, managers or partners. Pamela Munn [Ed.]. London: New York, Routledge, 1993. 182p. *ISBN: 0415076927, 0415089263. Includes bibliographical references and index. (Series:* Educational management series).

1674 The place of religion in public education. Mark Holmes. **Interchange** 24:3 1993 pp.205 - 224.

1675 The politics of pedagogy/the pedagogy of culture(s). Henry A. Giroux [Contrib.]; Ava Collins [Contrib.]; Carol Becker [Contrib.]; Bell Hooks [Contrib.]; Michael Eric Dyson [Contrib.]; Roger I. Simon [Contrib.]; David Trend [Contrib.]; Abdul R. Jan Mohamed [Contrib.]; Peter McLaren [Contrib.]. **Cult. St.** 7:1 1:1993 pp.1 - 146. *Collection of 9 articles.*

1676 Principles of legitimation in educational discourses in Iceland and the production of progress. Michel Foucault [Subject of work]; Pierre Bourdieu [Subject of work]; Ingólfur Ásgeir Jóhannesson. **J. Educ. Pol.** 8:4 7-8:1993 pp.339 - 352.

1677 Pygmalion in the classroom: teacher expectation and pupils' intellectual development. Robert Rosenthal; Lenore F. Jacobson. New York: Irvington Publishers, 1992. 265p. *ISBN: 0030686857.*

1678 Reality and textuality: power, pedagogy and postmodernism. David D. Cooper. **J. Interd. Stud.** IV:1/2 1992 pp.27 - 45.

1679 Referent-centered and problem-centered knowledge — elements of an educational epistemology. Carl Bereiter. **Interchange** 23:4 1992 pp.337 - 352.

1680 Routes to adulthood in a changing society: the Portuguese experience. José Machado Pais. **J. Educ. Pol.** 8:1 1-2:1993 pp.9 - 16.

1681 School effectiveness: research, policy and practice. David Reynolds [Ed.]; Peter Cuttance [Ed.]. London: Cassell, 1992. xi, 196p. *ISBN: 0304322954, 0304322768. Includes index. (Series:* School development series).

1682 Les scolarités de la maternelle au lycée — etapes et processus dans la production des inégalités sociales. *[In French]*; (Schooling careers from kindergarten to upper secondary school — steps and mechanisms in the making of social inequalities.) *[Summary]*; *[Summary in Spanish]*; *[Summary in German].* Marie Duru-Bellat; Jean-Pierre Jarousse; Alain Mingat. **Rev. Fr. Soc.** XXXIV:1 1-3:1993 pp.43 - 60.

1683 The significance of schooling: life-journeys in an African society. Robert Serpell. Cambridge: Cambridge University Press, 1993. xv, 345p. *ISBN: 0521394783. Includes index.*

1684 Social status, types of family interaction and educational styles. Jean Kellerhals; Cléopâtre Montandon; Gilbert Ritschard. **Eur. J. Soc.** XXXIII:2 1992 pp.308 - 325.

1685 [Society and education]; *[Text in Japanese].* Shozan Shibano [Ed.]. Tokyo: Kyodo-shuppan, 1993. 279p.

D: Culture

1686 La sociología de la educatión en España: pasado inmediato y presente. *[In Spanish]*; [The sociology of education in Spain: the immediate past and present]. Manuel Rodriguez Carrajo; Paciano Fermoso Estebanez. Salamanca: Universidad Pontificia de Salamanca, 1991. 233p.

1687 Sociological theory and educational reality: education and society in Australia since 1949. Alan Barcan. Kensington, N.S.W: New South Wales University Press, [distributed in North America by] I.S.B.S., Portland, Oregon, 1993. xv, 411p. *ISBN: 0868401250. Includes index. Includes bibliographical references (p. [373]-405).*

1688 Special issue — history, philosophy, and science education. Michael R. Matthews [Ed.]; Ian Winchester [Ed.]; Maura C. Flannery [Contrib.]; Wim J. van der Steen [Contrib.]; Peter B. Sloep [Contrib.]; James W. Garrison; Kenneth S. Lawwill [Contrib.]; Derek Hodson [Contrib.]; David F. Jackson [Contrib.]; Pinchas Tamir [Contrib.]; Arthur Stinner [Contrib.]; Harvey Williams [Contrib.]; A.B. Arons [Contrib.]; Howard Woodhouse [Contrib.]; Theresa M. Ndongko [Contrib.]; Jacques Désautels [Contrib.]; Marie Larochelle [Contrib.]; Mansoor Niaz [Contrib.]. **Interchange** 24:1 & 2 1992 pp.1 - 199. *Collection of 14 articles.*

1689 Structural constraints in tribal education — a case study of tribal community in south Gujarat. S.P. Punalekar. **Ind. J. Soc. Sci.** 6:1 1-3:1993 pp.19 - 30.

1690 The struggle for pedagogies: critical and feminist discourses as regimes of truth. Jennifer Gore. New York: Routledge, 1993. xvi, 188p. *ISBN: 041590563X, 0415905648. Includes bibliographical references (p. 166-180) and index.*

1691 Succeeding generations: family resources and access to education in New Zealand: based on the Access and Opportunity Education Survey, 1989-91. Roy Nash; et al. Auckland: Oxford University Press, 1993. 222p. *ISBN: 0195582810.*

1692 "The teachers, they all had their pets" — concepts of gender, knowledge, and power. Wendy Luttrell. **Signs** 18:3 Spring:1993 pp.505 - 546.

1693 Teaching knowledge as conversation — a philosophical hermeneutical approach to education. Yedullah Kazmi. **St. Philos. Educ.** 11:4 1993 pp.339 - 357.

1694 Wissenschaftliches Interesse und politische Verantwortung: Dimensionen vergleichender Bildungsforschung : ausgewählte Schriften, 1967-1989. *[In German]*; [Academic interest and political responsibility: dimensions of comparative educational research: selective writings, 1967-1989]. Oskar Anweiler; Jürgen Henze [Ed.]; Wolfgang Hörner [Ed.]; Gerhard Schreier [Ed.]. Opladen: Leske + Budrich, 1990. 245p. *ISBN: 3810008885.*

1695 Young people and schooling in France at the close of the 20th century: reproduction and social change. Gérard Mauger. **J. Educ. Pol.** 8:1 1-2:1993 pp.73 - 85.

Education policy
Politique de l'éducation

1696 Adult education and the state. Peter Jarvis. London, New York: Routledge, 1993. 165p. *ISBN: 0415065321. Includes bibliographical references and index.*

1697 After the reforms: education and policy in Northern Ireland. Anthony M. Gallagher [Ed.]; Robert J. Cormack [Ed.]; Robert Osborne [Ed.]. Aldershot: Avebury, 1993. ix, 292p. *ISBN: 1856284018.*

1698 America's changing demographics — educational policy implications. Leonard A. Valverde [Contrib.]; Leobardo F. Estrada [Contrib.]; Josué M. González [Contrib.];

D: Culture

Eugene E. Garcia [Contrib.]; Geneva Gay [Contrib.]; Robert T. Stout [Contrib.]. **Educ. Urban. Soc.** 25:3 5:1993 pp.227 - 310. *Collection of 7 articles.*

1699 Bildungsplanung in den neuen Bundesländern: Entwicklungstrends, Perspektiven und Vergleiche. *[In German]*; [Educational planning in the new federal Länder: development trends, perspectives and comparisons]. Klaus Klemm; Wolfgang Böttcher; Michael Weegen. Weinheim: Juventa, 1992. 209p. *ISBN: 3779908387. Includes bibliographical references.*

1700 Calidad de la educación y redefinición del rol del estado en Chile, en el contexto de los proyectos de modernización. *[In Spanish]*; [Quality of education and redefinition of the role of the state in Chile, in the context of the modernization projects]. Marcelo Martínez Keim. **Rev. Parag. Sociol.** 30:86 1-4:1993 pp.139 - 160.

1701 Change forces: probing the depth of educational reform. Michael Fullan. London, New York: Falmer Press, 1993. x, 162p. *ISBN: 1850008256. Includes bibliographical references (p. 148-156) and index. (Series:* School development and management of change series).

1702 Chicago experience with an early childhood programme: the special case of the Child Parent Center Program. J.S. Fuerst; Dorothy Fuerst. **Educat. Res.** 35:3 Winter:1993 pp.237 - 254.

1703 Democracy, community and education. Graham Haydon [Ed.]; Amy Gutmann [Contrib.]; Kenneth A. Strike [Contrib.]; Susan Mendus [Contrib.]; Richard Smith [Contrib.]; Yael Tamir [Contrib.]; Wally Morrow [Contrib.]; Bin Li [Contrib.]; Natalya Lebedeva [Contrib.]. **St. Philos. Educ.** 12:1 1993 pp.1 - 101. *Collection of 9 articles.*

1704 Discourse of derision: the role of the mass media within the education policy process. Mike Wallace. **J. Educ. Pol.** 8:4 7-8:1993 pp.321 - 338.

1705 Educating all the children. Christopher Colclough; Keith M. Lewin. Oxford [England], New York: Clarendon Press, 1993. 332p. *ISBN: 019828747X, 0198287461. Includes bibliographical references and index.*

1706 Education and the making of modern Iran. David Menashri. Ithaca: Cornell University Press, 1992. xvii, 352p. *ISBN: 080142612X. Includes bibliographical references (p. 329-342) and index.*

1707 The education of an industrial middle class in Arab-Islamic countries; *[Summary in French]; [Summary in German].* Ibrahim Assad Odeh. **Int. R. Educat.** 39:4 7:1993 pp.307 - 317.

1708 Education policy, power relations and teachers' work. Stephen J. Ball. **Br. J. Educ. S.** XXXXI:2 6:1993 pp.106 - 121.

1709 Education rights or minority rights?. Holly Cullen. **Int. J. Law Fam.** 7:2 1993 pp.143 - 177.

1710 Education, the arts and urban regeneration: education strategies for the whole community : conference report, March 1990. Bob Catterall [Ed.]. London: London Research Centre, 1990. 166p. *ISBN: 1852611103.*

1711 The effect of post-4 June re-education campaigns on Chinese students. Stanley Rosen. **China Quart.** 134 6:1993 pp.310 - 334.

1712 Ethical policymaking in higher education — state regulation of religious colleges in Maryland. L. Leslie Bennett; David E. Sumler. **J. Chur. State** 35:3 Summer:1993 pp.547 - 557.

D: Culture

1713 Fe y Alegría. Una innovación educativa para proporcionar educación básica con calidad y equidad. *[In Spanish]*; ["Certificate and happiness". An innovation in education to provide basic education with quality and equity]. Fernando Relmers. **Rev. Parag. Sociol.** 29:85 9-12:1992 pp.41 - 58.

1714 Gender matters in educational administration and policy: a feminist introduction. Jill Blackmore [Ed.]; Jane Kenway [Ed.]. London: Falmer Press, 1993. 205p. *ISBN: 0750701471, 075070148X. Includes bibliographical references and index. (Series: Deakin studies in education).*

1715 The history of educational reform. Keiko Seki; N.K. Krupskaya [Subject of work]. **Hito. J. Soc. Stud.** 24:2 12:1992 pp.69 - 77.

1716 L'institution scolaire et la scolarisation — une perspective d'ensemble. *[In French]*; (School institution and its policy — a global view.) *[Summary]*; *[Summary in Spanish]*; *[Summary in German]*. Jean-Pierre Briand; Jean-Michel Chapoulie. **Rev. Fr. Soc.** XXXIV:1 1-3:1993 pp.3 - 42.

1717 LEA frameworks for the assessment of schools: an interrupted picture. Brian Wilcox; John Gray; Mark Tranmer. **Educat. Res.** 35:3 Winter:1993 pp.211 - 222.

1718 Markets or democracy for education. Stewart Ranson. **Br. J. Educ. S.** XXXXI:4 12:1993 pp.333 - 352.

1719 Modernization, youth and educational policy issues: a Finnish perspective. Lasse Siurala. **J. Educ. Pol.** 8:1 1-2:1993 pp.17 - 28.

1720 Mothers and education: inside out? Exploring family-education policy and experience. Miriam E. David [Ed.]; et al. Basingstoke: Macmillan Press, 1993. 241p. *ISBN: 0333565932.*

1721 New educational strategy and innovation in China. Seth Spaulding. **J. Asian Afr. Aff.** IV:2 Spring:1993 pp.12 - 32.

1722 New guiding principles in educational policy: the case of Germany. Manfred Weiss. **J. Educ. Pol.** 8:4 7-8:1993 pp.307 - 320.

1723 Paradigm shifts, feminist phase theory, and the missing variable in women's studies curriculum transformation projects. Joyce McCarl Neilsen; Jeana Abromeit. **Sociol. For.** 8:1 3:1993 pp.73 - 91.

1724 Parents as "consumers" of education in England and Wales and the Netherlands. Neville Harris; Sophie van Bijsterveld. **Int. J. Law Fam.** 7:2 1993 pp.178 - 204.

1725 Parents hearing their children read: a review. Rethinking the lessons of the Haringey project. Derek Toomey. **Educat. Res.** 35:3 Winter:1993 pp.223 - 236.

1726 Perspectives on deregulation of schooling in America. John Hardin Best. **Br. J. Educ. S.** XXXXI:2 6:1993 pp.122 - 133.

1727 Planning and implementing education policy in a developing country: a study of the shift system in Trinidad and Tobago. Norrel A. London. **J. Educ. Pol.** 8:4 7-8:1993 pp.353 - 364.

1728 Policy and experiment in mother tongue literacy in Nigeria; *[Summary in French]*; *[Summary in German]*. F. Niyi Akinnaso. **Int. R. Educat.** 39:4 7:1993 pp.255 - 285.

1729 Policy into practice — internal assessment at 16. Anne S. Buchan. **Educat. Res.** 35:2 Summer:1993 pp.171 - 179.

1730 The politics of linking schools and social services. Louise Adler; Unni Hagen; Felisa Tibbitts; Hanne B. Mawhinney; Julia E. Koppich; Patricia F. First; Joan L. Curcio; Dalton L. Young; Douglas E. Mitchell; Linda D. Scott; James R. Garvin; Alma H. Young; Jacqueline A. Stefkovich; Gloria J. Guba; Stephanie Kadel; Dorothy Routh; Michael S. Knapp; Kathryn Barnard; Richard N. Brandon; Nathalie J. Gehrke;

Albert J. Smith; Edward C. Teather; R. Michael Casto; Hal A. Lawson; Katharine Hooper-Briar; William Wilson; Patricia Karasoff; Barbara Nolan; Kip Tellez; Jo-Anne Schick; William A. White; Charles J. Russo; Jane Clark Lindle; Sid Gardner. **J. Educ. Pol.** 8:5-6 9-12:1993 pp.1 - 199. *Collection of 17 articles.*

1731 Post-apartheid education: towards non-racial, unitary and democratic socialization in the new South Africa. M. P. Mncwabe. Lanham, MD: University Press of America, 1993. 252p. *ISBN: 0819189693. Includes bibliographical references and index.*

1732 Primary headship, state policy and the challenge of the 1990s: an exceptional story that disproves total hegemonic rule. George Riseborough. **J. Educ. Pol.** 8:2 3-4:1993 pp.155 - 174.

1733 Problemas de aplicacion de la reforma educativa en Chile. *[In Spanish]*; [Problems of applying the education reforms in Chile]. Iván Nuñez. **Plan. Desarr.** XXIV:3 12:1993 pp.83 - 100.

1734 Problemas de aplicacion de la reforma educativa en Mexico. *[In Spanish]*; [Problems of applying the education reforms in Mexico]. José Angel Pescador Osuna. **Plan. Desarr.** XXIV:3 12:1993 pp.65 - 82.

1735 The recent process of decentralization and democratic management of education in Brazil; *[Summary in German]*; *[Summary in French]*. José Camilo dos Santos Filho. **Int. R. Educat.** 39:5 9:1993 pp.391 - 403.

1736 Reconsidering curriculum development: a framework for co-operation. Neil A. Johnson. **Interchange** 24:4 1993 pp.409 - 434.

1737 A review of community participation in school governance — an emerging culture in Australian education. D.T. Gamage. **Br. J. Educ. S.** XXXXI:2 6:1993 pp.134 - 149.

1738 Rückkehr der Bildungspolitik. *[In German]*; [The return of education policy]. Oskar Negt [Contrib.]; Dieter Wunder [Contrib.]; Ernst Rösner [Contrib.]; Gerhard Neuweiler [Contrib.]; Wilfried Kruse [Contrib.]; Angelika Paul-Kohlhoff [Contrib.]; Wolfgang Brezinka [Contrib.]; Hasso von Recum [Contrib.]. **Gewerk. Monat.** 44:11 11:1993 pp.657 - 721. *Collection of 7 articles.*

1739 School characteristics, school academic indicators and student outcomes: implications for policies to improve schools. Ronald H. Heck; Roberta A. Mayor. **J. Educ. Pol.** 8:2 3-4:1993 pp.143 - 154.

1740 Some problems in establishing equality of treatment in multi-ethnic schools. Peter Foster. **Br. J. Soc.** 44:3 9:1993 pp.519 - 535.

1741 Student perspective to the administration of educational equity in India. Sushila Singhal. **Psychol. Devel. Soc.** 5:1 1-6:1993 pp.61 - 80.

1742 Towards the "New South Africa" — equal opportunity policies at the University of Cape Town. Frank H. Herbstein. **High. Educ.** 26:2 9:1993 pp.183 - 198.

1743 Writing with word processors — a research overview. Ilana Snyder. **Educat. Res.** 35:1 Spring:1993 pp.49 - 68.

D: Culture

Education systems
Systèmes d'enseignement

1744 Academic freedom 2: a human rights report. et al; John Daniel. London: Zed Books, 1993. 168p. *ISBN: 1856492192.*

1745 L'administration de l'enseignement en Europe: actes du colloque tenu à Aix en octobre 1990. *[In French]*; [Education administration in Europe: proceedings from a conference held at Aix in October 1990] *[Summary].* Charles Debbasch [Ed.]. Paris: Editions du Centre National de la Recherche Scientifique, 1991. 248p. *ISBN: 2222046637.*

1746 Bildungsbeteiligung und Sozialstruktur in der Bundesrepublik: zu Stabilität und Wandel der Ungleichheit von Bildungschancen. *[In German]*; [Educational participation and social structure in the Federal Republic: on stability and change in inequality in educational opportunities]. Helmut Köhler. Berlin: Max-Planck-Institut für Bildungsforschung, 1992. 133p. *ISBN: 389404800X.*

1747 Charakterystyka systemu kształcenia w republice federalnej Niemiec. *[In Polish]*; (Characteristics of education system in the Federal Republic of Germany.) Ewa Sadowska-Kowalska. **Acta Univ. Łódz.** 130 1993 pp.63 - 72.

1748 [A comparative view of "public" and "private" in education between Japan and the U.S.]; *[Text in Japanese].* Mamoru Tsukada. **Kyo.-Shak. Ken.** 52 1993 pp.55 - 71.

1749 Desegregation in American schools: comparative intervention strategies. Brian L. Fife. New York: Praeger, 1992. xiv, 210p. *ISBN: 027594140X. Includes bibliographical references (p. [181]-203) and index.*

1750 Differentiating between distance/open education systems — parameters for comparison; *[Summary in French]*; *[Summary in German].* Sarah Guri-Rozenblit. **Int. R. Educat.** 39:4 7:1993 pp.287 - 306.

1751 Education, democracy and development. Raymond Ryba [Ed.]; Wolfgang Mitter [Contrib.]; Jiři Kotásek [Contrib.]; Gábor Halász [Contrib.]; Torsten Husén [Contrib.]; Stephen P. Heyneman [Contrib.]; Paul N'Da [Contrib.]; Candido A. Gomes [Contrib.]; Mark Bray [Contrib.]; W.O. Lee [Contrib.]; Kathleen Foreman [Contrib.]. **Int. R. Educat.** 39:6 11:1993 pp.463 - 575. *Collection of 9 articles.*

1752 Education for the community?. Carol Vincent. **Br. J. Educ. S.** XXXXI:4 12:1993 pp.366 - 380.

1753 Educational support agencies in some European countries; *[Summary in German]*; *[Summary in French].* J. Braaksma; A.L. Heinink. **Int. R. Educat.** 39:3 5:1993 pp.207 - 221.

1754 Importancia de las reformas educativas. *[In Spanish]*; [The importance of education reforms]. Noel McGinn. **Plan. Desarr.** XXIV:3 12:1993 pp.25 - 44.

1755 Law and education: regulation, consumerism and the education system. Neville Harris. London: Sweet & Maxwell, 1993. 268p. *ISBN: 0421474009. (Series:* Modern legal studies).

1756 Lessons from the National Alliance of Business Compact Project — business and public education reform. Sandra A. Waddock. **Human Relat.** 46:7 7:1993 pp.849 - 879.

1757 Multi-track and unified systems of post-compulsory education and "upper secondary education in Scotland" — an analysis of two debates. David Raffe. **Br. J. Educ. S.** XXXXI:3 9:1993 pp.223 - 252.

1758 New models of school management in South Africa — licence for change or loophole for separatism?. Clayton G. MacKenzie. **Br. J. Educ. S.** XXXXI:3 9:1993 pp.287 - 301.
1759 Official knowledge: democratic education in a conservative age. Michael W. Apple. New York, London: Routledge, 1993. ix,226p. *ISBN: 0415907489. Includes bibliographical references and index.*
1760 Personal autonomy and the flexible school; *[Summary in German]*; *[Summary in French]*. Aharon Aviram. **Int. R. Educat.** 39:5 9:1993 pp.419 - 433.
1761 Problems of reforming educational systems in post-communist countries; *[Summary in German]*; *[Summary in French]*. Nikola Pastuović. **Int. R. Educat.** 39:5 9:1993 pp.405 - 418.
1762 Researching autonomous schools — a survey of the first 100 GM schools. Marianne Coleman; Tony Bush; Derek Glover. **Educat. Res.** 35:2 Summer:1993 pp.107 - 126.
1763 School effectiveness studies using administrative data. Dougal Hutchison. **Educat. Res.** 35:1 Spring:1993 pp.27 - 47.
1764 Social selection in educational systems in Europe. Walter Müller; Wolfgang Karle. **Eur. Sociol. R.** 9:1 5:1993 pp.1 - 23.
1765 Why do different countries choose a different public-private mix of educational services?. Estelle James. **J. Hum. Res.** XXVIII:3 Summer:1993 pp.571 - 592.

Primary education
Enseignement primaire

1766 Educational provisions for our youngest children: European perspectives. Tricia David [Ed.]. London: Paul Chapman, 1993. 193p. *ISBN: 185396204X.*
1767 A orientação de codificação no contexto de socialização primária — implicações no (in)sucesso escolar. *[In Portuguese]*; (The orientation of social codes within the context of primary socialization: implications for school success/failure.) *[Summary]*; *[Summary in French]*. Isabel Neves; Ana Maria Morais. **Anál. Soc.** XXVIII:2 (121) 1993 pp.267 - 308.
1768 Primary education and economic development in China and India: overview and two case studies. Mrinalini Saran; Jean Drèze. London: London School of Economics and Political Science, 1993. 87p. *Suntory Toyota International Centre for Economics and Related Disciplines Development Economics Research Programme. (Series:* Development Economics Research Programme).
1769 Primary headship, state policy and the challenge of the 1990s: an exceptional story that disproves total hegemonic rule. George Riseborough. **J. Educ. Pol.** 8:2 3-4:1993 pp.155 - 174.
1770 The socialization through curricula control in Korea. Kwan Chun Lee. **Korea Obs.** XXIV:1 Spring:1993 pp.71 - 90.
1771 A survey of the nature and extent of bullying in junior/middle and secondary schools. Irene Whitney; Peter K. Smith. **Educat. Res.** 35:1 Spring:1993 pp.3 - 25.

D: Culture

Secondary education
Enseignement secondaire

1772 Education and training 14-19: continuity and diversity in the curriculum. Harry Tomlinson [Ed.]. Harlow: Longman, 1993. 239p. *ISBN: 0582091055.*
1773 Getting rid of troublemakers — high school disciplinary procedures and the production of dropouts. Christine Bowditch. **Soc. Prob.** 40:4 11:1993 pp.493 - 509.
1774 Multi-track and unified systems of post-compulsory education and "upper secondary education in Scotland" — an analysis of two debates. David Raffe. **Br. J. Educ. S.** XXXXI:3 9:1993 pp.223 - 252.
1775 The nonequivalence of high school equivalents. Stephen V. Cameron; James J. Hackman. **J. Labor Ec.** 11:1(1) 1:1993 pp.1 - 47.
1776 Non-government secondary schools in rural Bangladesh — school-level performance and determinants. Mahmudul Alam. **Bang. Dev. Stud.** XX:4 12:1992 pp.69 - 88.
1777 Policy into practice — internal assessment at 16. Anne S. Buchan. **Educat. Res.** 35:2 Summer:1993 pp.171 - 179.
1778 A survey of the nature and extent of bullying in junior/middle and secondary schools. Irene Whitney; Peter K. Smith. **Educat. Res.** 35:1 Spring:1993 pp.3 - 25.

Tertiary education
Enseignement post-scolaire

1779 Academic freedom. Conrad Sebastian Robert Russell. London, New York: Routledge, 1993. 119p. *ISBN: 041503714X, 0415037158.*
1780 Academic standards in South African universities and proposals for quality assurance. Andries H. Strydom; Noruwana. **High. Educ.** 25:4 6:1993 pp.379 - 393.
1781 El acceso a la educación superior. El ingreso irrestricto: ¿ una falacia? *[In Spanish]*; [Access to higher education. Non-restricted access: a fallacy?] *[Summary]*. Víctor Sigal. **Desar. Econ.** 33:130 7-9:1995 pp.265 - 280.
1782 Accessing higher education — the dilemma of schooling women, minorities, scheduled castes and scheduled tribes in contemporary India. Karuna Chanana. **High. Educ.** 26:1 7:1993 pp.69 - 92.
1783 Adult education and the state. Peter Jarvis. London, New York: Routledge, 1993. 165p. *ISBN: 0415065321. Includes bibliographical references and index.*
1784 Adult higher education from an international perspective. Carol E. Kasworm. **High. Educ.** 25:4 6:1993 pp.411 - 424.
1785 Adults in the colleges of further education. H. E. S. Marks; K. T. Elsdon. Nottingham: Department of Adult Education, University of Nottingham, 1991. iv, 162p. *ISBN: 1850410429. Bibliography: p.153-155. - Includes index. (Series:* Nottingham studies in the theory and practice of the education of adults).
1786 Affirmative action and the university: a philosophical inquiry. Steven M. Cahn [Ed.]. Philadelphia: Temple University Press, 1993. viii, 310p. *ISBN: 1566390303. Includes bibliographical references and index.*
1787 [Analysis of studies on higher education]; *[Text in Japanese]*. Kenshi Yamanouchi. **Dai. Ron.** 21 1992 pp.209 - 224.

D: Culture

1788 [A character of higher education research in Japan: with focus on the properties of researchers in higher education]; *[Text in Japanese]*. Soichiro Aihara. **Dai. Ron.** 22 1993 pp.225 - 249.
1789 Commitment, educative action and adults: learning programmes with a social purpose. Denis O'Sullivan. Aldershot: Avebury, 1992. 210p. *ISBN: 1856282929*.
1790 A comparative approach to assessing the quality of life of intercollegiate athletes. Mark A. Royal; Robert J. Rossi. **Soc. Ind.** 29:3 7:1993 pp.317 - 330.
1791 Developing drama at the University of Zimbabwe. R.M. McLaren. **Zambezia** 20:1 1993 pp.35 - 52.
1792 Ethical policymaking in higher education — state regulation of religious colleges in Maryland. L. Leslie Bennett; David E. Sumler. **J. Chur. State** 35:3 Summer:1993 pp.547 - 557.
1793 The European and American university since 1800: historical and sociological essays. Sheldon Rothblatt [Ed.]; Björn Wittrock [Ed.]. Cambridge, New York, NY: Cambridge University Press, 1993. 370p. *ISBN: 0521431654. Includes index.*
1794 Higher education in Latin America. Jorge Balán [Contrib.]; Simon Schwartzman [Contrib.]; Lúcia Klein [Contrib.]; José Joaquín Brunner [Contrib.]; Ricardo Lucio [Contrib.]; Mariana Serrano [Contrib.]; Rollin Kent [Contrib.]. **High. Educ.** 25:1 1:1993 pp.1 - 84. *Collection of 7 articles.*
1795 Higher education reform in India: experience and perspectives. Suma Chitnis [Ed.]; Philip Geoffrey Altbach [Ed.]. New Delhi, Newbury Park, Calif: Sage Publications, 1993. 438p. *ISBN: 0803991118, 8170363373. Papers prepared for a research project of the Comparative Education Center, State University of New York at Buffalo, and funded by the World Bank. Includes index.*
1796 How much education?. Peter Karmel. **J. Aust. Pop. Ass.** 10:1 5:1993 pp.17 - 30.
1797 The idea of the university in the 21st century — a British perspective. Peter Scott. **Br. J. Educ. S.** XXXXI:1 3:1993 pp.4 - 25.
1798 The idea of the university in the 21st century — an American perspective. Cameron Fincher. **Br. J. Educ. S.** XXXXI:1 3:1993 pp.26 - 45.
1799 The imperiled academy. Howard Dickman [Ed.]. London: Transaction Publishers, 1993. 281p. *ISBN: 156000097X. (Series:* Studies in social philosophy and policy).
1800 Improvements in equity in the participation of young people in higher education in Australia during the 1980s. Peter G. Carpenter; Martin Hayden. **High. Educ.** 26:2 9:1993 pp.199 - 216.
1801 The language question in higher education — trends and issues. N. Jayaram. **High. Educ.** 26:1 7:1993 pp.93 - 114.
1802 Learners of the future: preparing a policy for the third age. Tom Schuller; Anne Marie Bostyn. **J. Educ. Pol.** 8:4 7-8:1993 pp.365 - 379.
1803 The market oriented university and the changing role of knowledge. Howard Buchbinder. **High. Educ.** 26:3 10:1993 pp.331 - 347.
1804 NEA presidential address 1992 — policy issues in the post-secondary education of African Americans. Arthur T. King. **Rev. Bl. Pol. Ec.** 21:4 Spring:1993 pp.5 - 18.
1805 O sistema federal de ensino superior: problemas e alternativas. *[In Portuguese]*; (The federal system of higher education: problems and alternatives.) *[Summary]*; *[Summary in French]*. Eunice Ribeiro Durham. **Rev. Bras. Ciên. Soc.** 8:23 10:1993 pp.5 - 37.
1806 Participation in post-compulsory education in Scotland. C. Robertson. **J. Roy. Stat. Soc. A.** 156:3 1993 pp.423 - 442.

D: Culture

1807 Quality assurance for university teaching. Roger Ellis [Ed.]. Bristol, PA, USA: Open University Press, 1993. xi, 322p. *ISBN: 033519026X, 0335190251. Includes bibliographical references and indexes.*

1808 Research and relevant knowledge: American research universities since World War II. Roger L. Geiger. New York: Oxford University Press, 1993. xvi, 411p. *ISBN: 019505346X. Includes bibliographical references (p. 339-404) and index.*

1809 The roles of department chairs in Chinese higher education. Julie Q. Bao; John W. Creswell. **Asian Prof.** 21:5 10:1993 pp.369 - 380.

1810 [The strategy conversion in higher education management]; *[Text in Japanese]*. Katsumi Harada. Tokyo: Daiichihoki Shuppan, 1993.

1811 A struggle for choice: students with special needs in transition to adulthood. Jenny Corbett; Len Barton. London, New York: Routledge, 1992. ix, 131p. *ISBN: 0415080002, 0415080010. Includes bibliographical references (p. 114-124) and index.*

1812 Talcott Parsons, universalism and the educational revolution — democracy versus professionalism. Bryan S. Turner. **Br. J. Soc.** 44:1 3:1993 pp.1 - 24.

1813 Towards the "New South Africa" — equal opportunity policies at the University of Cape Town. Frank H. Herbstein. **High. Educ.** 26:2 9:1993 pp.183 - 198.

1814 U3A (the University of the Third Age) in Australia — a model for successful ageing. Richard Swindell. **Age. Soc.** 13:2 6:1993 pp.245 - 266.

1815 Universidad y sociedad en España: ¿el final de un ciclo? *[In Spanish]*; [University and society in Spain: the end of a cycle?]. José Ignacio Cubero Salmeron. **Rev. Fom. Soc.** 48:192 10-12:1993 pp.499 - 512.

1816 Universities and elites in Britain since 1800. Robert D. Anderson. Houndmills: Macmillan, 1992. 82p. *ISBN: 0333524349. (Series:* Studies in economic & social history).

1817 University libraries and scholarly communication: a study prepared for the Andrew W. Mellon Foundation. Anthony M. Cummings; et al. Washington, DC: Association of Research Libraries, 1993. 205p.

1818 University responses to research activity. Bruce Williams. London: Centre for Higher Education Studies, 1991. v,90p. *ISBN: 0854733493. (Series:* CHES policy series).

E: SOCIAL STRUCTURE
   STRUCTURE SOCIALE

E.1: Social system
   Système social

1819 L'anamorphose de l'Etat-nation — le cas italien. *[In French]*; [The anamorphosis of a nation-state — the Italian case] *[Summary]*. Salvatore Palidda. **Cah. Int. Soc.** XCIII 7-12:1992 pp.269 - 298.
1820 Czech and Slovak society. Jiří Musil. **Govt. Oppos.** 28:4 Autumn:1993 pp.479 - 495.
1821 Is society a self-organizing system?. Loet Leydesdorff. **J. Soc. Evol. Sys.** 16:3 1993 pp.331 - 349.
1822 The logics of social structure. Kyriakos M. Kontopoulos. Cambridge, New York: Cambridge University Press, 1993. x, 481p. *ISBN: 0521417791. Includes bibliographical references (p. 393-448) and index. (Series:* Structural analysis in the social sciences).
1823 May the Lord in His mercy be kind to Belfast. Tony Parker. London: Cape, 1993. 358p. *ISBN: 0224033123*.
1824 Obshchaia sotsiologiia. Tip obshchestva kak forma sotsial'nogo ritma. *[In Russian]*; [General sociology. Types of society as a form of social rhythm]. S.S. Andreev. **Sots.-Pol. Z.** 5-6 1993 pp.34 - 50.
1825 Paradigmi nazionali — percezioni del «particolarismo» in Italia e in Inghilterra. *[In Italian]*; (Paradigms of one's own society — perceptions of "particularism" in Britain and Italy.) *[Summary]*. Michael Eve. **Rass. It. Soc.** 34:3 9:1993 pp.361 - 390.
1826 Post-capitalist society. Peter Ferdinand Drucker. Oxford: Butterworth-Heinemann, 1993. 204p. *ISBN: 0750609214*.
1827 Power in modern societies. Marvin Elliot Olsen [Ed.]; Martin N. Marger [Ed.]. Boulder: Westview Press, 1993. xv, 327p. *ISBN: 0813312884. Includes bibliographical references*.
1828 La question du social. *[In French]*; [The social question] *[Summary]*. Danilo Martuccelli. **Cah. Int. Soc.** XCIII 7-12:1992 pp.367 - 387.
1829 Recurrent collapse of the fire service in New York City — the failure of paramilitary systems as a phase change. R. Wallace. **Envir. Plan. A.** 25:2 2:1993 pp.233 - 244.
1830 [Rediscover Italian society: sociological consideration for a 'composed' society]; *[Text in Japanese]*. Michinobu Niihara. **Jin. Ken.** 22 1993 pp.1 - 22.
1831 Social issues in Hong Kong. Benjamin K. P. Leung; Geoffrey H. Blowers. New York; Hong Kong: Oxford University Press, 1990. vii, 226p. *ISBN: 0195840089, 0195840097. Includes bibliographical references and index*.
1832 [Social system and crisis]; *[Text in Japanese]*. Satoshi Matsui. pp.117 - 145.
1833 Tradition in der post-traditionalen Gesellschaft. *[In German]*; (On tradition in the post-traditional society.) *[Summary]*. Anthony Giddens. **Soz. Welt.** 44:4 1993 pp.445 - 485.

E: Social structure

E.2: Social stratification
Stratification sociale

1834 Bildungsbeteiligung und Sozialstruktur in der Bundesrepublik: zu Stabilität und Wandel der Ungleichheit von Bildungschancen. *[In German]*; [Educational participation and social structure in the Federal Republic: on stability and change in inequality in educational opportunities]. Helmut Köhler. Berlin: Max-Planck-Institut für Bildungsforschung, 1992. 133p. *ISBN: 389404800X.*

1835 Class, powerlessness and political polarization. G. Evans. **Eur. J. Soc. Psychol.** 23:5 9-10:1993 pp.495 - 511.

1836 Cultivating differences: symbolic boundaries and the making of inequality. Michèle Lamont [Ed.]; Marcel Fournier [Ed.]. Chicago: University of Chicago Press, 1992. xvii, 346p. *ISBN: 0226468135, 0226468143. Includes bibliographical references and index.*

1837 Cultural representation and ideological domination. Richard Harvey Brown. **Soc. Forc.** 71:3 3:1993 pp.657 - 676.

1838 Dictionary of labour biography. Vol.9.. Joyce Margaret Bellamy [Ed.]; John Saville [Ed.]. Basingstoke: Macmillan, 1993. 328p. *ISBN: 033338783X.*

1839 Durkheims Beitrag zur Theorie der Integration sozialer Systeme. *[In German]*; (Durkheim's contribution to the theory of integration of social systems.) *[Summary]*; *[Summary in French]*. Talcott Parsons. **Berl. J. Soziol.** 3:4 1993 pp.447 - 468.

1840 Egalitarianism and natural lottery. Neven Sesardic. **Publ. Aff. Q.** 7:1 1:1993 pp.57 - 69.

1841 Das Ende der sozialen Schichtung?: Zürcher Arbeiten zur gesellschaftlichen Konstruktion von sozialer Lage und Bewusstsein in der westlichen Zentrumsgesellschaft. *[In German]*; [The end of social stratification? Zurich papers on the social construction of the social situation and consciousness in Western society]. Volker Bornschier [Ed.]. Zurich: Seismo-Verlag, 1991. 378p. *ISBN: 3908239028.*

1842 Hierarchy and democracy. Albert Somit [Ed.]; Rudolf Wildenmann [Ed.]. Carbondale: Southern Illinois University Press, 1991. 191p. *ISBN: 0809317915. Includes bibliographical references.*

1843 Hindu eschatology and the Indian caste system — an example of structural reversal. Murray Milner. **J. Asian St.** 52:2 5:1993 pp.298 - 319.

1844 Inequalities in access to community resources in a Chinese city. John R. Logan; Yanjie Bian. **Soc. Forc.** 72:2 12:1993 pp.555 - 576.

1845 The Japanese power elite. Albrecht Rothacher. New York: St. Martin's Press, 1993. xix, 311p. *ISBN: 0312102917. Includes bibliographical references (p. 288-292) and index.*

1846 Les jeunes diplômés: un groupe social en quête d'identité. *[In French]*; [Young qualified people: a social group in search of an identity]. Jean Lojkine. Paris: Presses Universitaires de France, 1992. 238p. *ISBN: 2130435491.*

1847 [Life course and social stratification 1]; *[Text in Japanese]*. Kazuo Katase. **Ron. (B. Toho. Gak. Univ.)** 106 1993 pp.87 - 116.

1848 Local history and societal history. C. Phythian-Adams. **Local. Pop. S.** 51 Autumn:1993 pp.30 - 45.

1849 Magyar polgárosodás. *[In Hungarian]*; [Hungarian embourgeoisement]. András Gerő. Budapest: Atlantisz, 1993. 434p. *ISBN: 963 7978 33 X.*

1850 Mediating claims to artistry — social stratification in a local visual arts community. Henry C. Finney. **Sociol. For.** 8:3 9:1993 pp.403 - 431.

E: Structure sociale

1851 Migration and status attainment among Norwegian men. Kristen Ringdal. **Acta Sociol.** 36:4 1993 pp.327 - 342.

1852 La mobilité sociale. *[In French]*; [Social mobility]. Dominique Merllié; Jean Prévot. Paris: La Découverte, 1991. 124p. *ISBN: 2707120367. Bibliogr. p.116-123.*

1853 Operários e mobilidade social na Bahia — análise de uma trajetória individual. *[In Portuguese]*; (Workers and social mobility in Bahia — analysis of an individual trajectory.) *[Summary]*; *[Summary in French]*. Antonio Sérgio Alfredo Guimarães. **Rev. Bras. Ciên. Soc.** 8:22 6:1993 pp.81 - 97.

1854 Perekhod ot pervobytnogo obshchestva k klassovomu: puti i varianty razvitiia (okonchanie). *[In Russian]*; (From primordial to class society: ways and variants fo development (conclusion).) Iu.I. Semenov. **Etnograf. Oboz.** 2 1993 pp.57 - 74.

1855 Regulirovanie sotsial'noi differentsiatsii: kriterii, tsikly, modeli. *[In Russian]*; [Regulating social differentiation: criteria, cycles and models]. N.F. Naumova. **Obshch. Ekon.** 3 1993 pp.3 - 21.

1856 Religion and economic change in Northern Ireland; *[Summary in French]*. Liam O'Dowd. **Soc. Compass** 40:1 3:1993 pp.15 - 24.

1857 Signs of status in bridal portraits. Allan Mazur. **Sociol. For.** 8:2 6:1993 pp.273 - 283.

1858 The silenced voice — female social mobility patterns with particular reference to the British Isles. Bernadette C. Hayes; Robert L. Miller. **Br. J. Soc.** 44:4 12:1993 pp.653 - 672.

1859 Social inequality in aboriginal North America — a test of Lenski's theory. Ain Haas. **Soc. Forc.** 72:2 12:1993 pp.295 - 313.

1860 Social mobility in the 1970s and 1980s — a study of men and women in England and Sweden. Jan O. Jonsson; Colin Mills. **Eur. Sociol. R.** 9:3 12:1993 pp.229 - 247.

1861 Social stratification among Muslim-Hindu community. A. F. Imam Ali. New Delhi, India: Commonwealth Publishers, 1992. 279p. *ISBN: 8171691935. Includes index. Includes bibliographical references (p. [250]-272).*

1862 (Social structure of experience: am attempt of work history analyses.); *[Text in Japanese]*. Fumiko Kohama. **Shak. Ronk.** 14 1993 pp.24 - 43.

1863 Soziale Differenzierung und Gesellschaftliche Reformen. Der politische Gehalt in Emile Durkheims Arbeitsteilung. *[In German]*; (Social differentiation and social reforms. The political substance of Emile Durkheim's De la division du travail social.) *[Summary]*; *[Summary in French]*. Hans-Peter Müller. **Berl. J. Soziol.** 3:4 1993 pp.507 - 519.

1864 The specter of capitalism and the promise of a classless society. Donald David Weiss. Atlantic Highlands, N.J: Humanities Press International, 1993. xii, 191p. *ISBN: 0391037528.*

1865 Stratifications et mobilités sociales. *[In French]*; [Social stratification and mobility]. André Delobelle [Ed.]; Wout Ultee [Contrib.]; Jean Remy [Contrib.]; Michel Loriaux [Contrib.]. **Recher. Sociolog.** XXIV:3 1993 pp.5 - 116. *Collection of 4 articles.*

1866 The structure and process of social stratification in Korea. Jong-Chun Cha. **Korean Soc. Sci. J.** XIX 1993 pp.95 - 115.

1867 Struggling for power and respectability in the Arab academic field. M'hammed Sabour. **Int. Soc. Sci. J.** 135 2:1993 pp.107 - 118.

E: Social structure

1868 Über sexuelle Arbeitsteilung. *[In German]*; (The division of labour by sex.) *[Summary]*; *[Summary in French]*. Gerhard Wagner. **Berl. J. Soziol.** 3:4 1993 pp.469 - 486.
1869 Untouchable concepts of person and society. Lynn Vincentnathan. **Contr. I. Soc.** 27:1 1-6:1993 pp.53 - 82.
1870 Upward dreams, downward mobility: the economic decline of the American middle class. Frederick R. Strobel. Savage, Md: Rowman & Littlefield Publishers, 1992. xv, 229p. *ISBN: 0847677567. Includes bibliographical references and index.*
1871 Wiederkehr der Klassen? Über Mechanismen der Integration und der Ausgrenzung in entwickelten Industriegesellschaften. *[In German]*; (Nationalism — the reaction of the excluded? On mechanisms of integration and of exclusion in developed industrial societies.) *[Summary]*. Ditmar Brock. **Soz. Welt.** 44:2 1993 pp.177 - 198.
1872 Wzory prestiżu a struktura społeczna. *[In Polish]*; [Occupational prestige and social structure]. Henryk Domański. Wrocław: Zakład Narod. im. Ossolińskich, 1991. 248p. *ISBN: 8304036452. Includes bibliographical references.*

Class
Classe

1873 L'acteur et le système des positions de classe. *[In French]*; [The actor and the system of class positions] *[Summary]*. Salvador Juan. **Cah. Int. Soc.** XCIII 7-12:1992 pp.339 - 366.
1874 Agrarian classes in Pakistan — an empirical test of Patnaik's labour-exploitation criterion. A. Haroon Akram-Lodhi. **J. Peasant Stud.** 20:4 7:1993 pp.557 - 589.
1875 [Anthony Giddens and the development of "structuration theory"]; *[Text in Japanese]*. Naoharu Shimoda. **Oyo-Shak. Ken.** 35 1993 pp.1 - 12.
1876 [Articulating of class structure and job autonomy]; *[Text in Japanese]*. Shonosuke Aoki. **S. Jap. Inst. Lab.** 5 1993 pp.75 - 93.
1877 Auf dem Weg in eine neue Klassengesellschaft? *[In German]*; [The path to a new class society?]. Ditmar Brock. **Gewerk. Monat.** 44:10 10:1993 pp.608 - 618.
1878 Changing classes: stratification and mobility in international sociology. Gosta Esping-Andersen [Ed.]. London: Sage Publications, 1993. 261p. *ISBN: 0803988974*.
1879 Class. Stephen Edgell. London, New York: Routledge, 1993. 149p. *ISBN: 0415060613. Includes bibliographical references and index. (Series:* Key ideas).
1880 Class — stories of concepts. From ordinary language to scientific language. Giampietro Gobo. **Soc. Sci. Info.** 32:3 1993 pp.467 - 489.
1881 Class and inequality: comparative perspectives. Malcolm B. Hamilton; Maria Hirszowicz. Hemel Hempstead: Harvester Wheatsheaf, 1993. 311p. *ISBN: 0745010008*.
1882 Class and stratification: an introduction to current debates. Rosemary Crompton. Cambridge; Cambridge, MA: Polity Press, 1993. 231p. *ISBN: 0745609465. Includes bibliographical references and index.*
1883 Class consciousness and national contexts — Canada, Sweden and the United States in historical perspective; *[Summary in French]*. William A. Johnston; Douglas Baer. **Can. R. Soc. A.** 30:2 5:1993 pp.271 - 295.
1884 Class consciousness and primordial values in the shaping of the Indian working class. Vinay Bahl. **S.Asia B.** XIII:1+2 1993 pp.152 - 172.

E: Structure sociale

1885 Class, gender, and expanded class consciousness in Steeltown. D.W. Livingstone; J. Marshall Mangan. **R. Soc. Move. Con. Cha.** 15 1993 pp.55 - 82.
1886 Class in Britain since 1979 — facts, theories and ideologies. John Westergaard. **Hito. J. Soc. Stud.** 25:1 7:1993 pp.25 - 62.
1887 Class interests, class politics and welfare state regime. Elim Papadakis. **Br. J. Soc.** 44:2 6:1993 pp.249 - 270.
1888 Class political organizing and welfare capitalism. Barbara G. Brents. **Crit. Sociol.** 19:1 pp.69 - 101.
1889 The classing gaze: sexuality, class and surveillance. Lynette Finch. St Leonards/NSW: Allen & Unwin, 1993. 197p. *ISBN: 1863734376.*
1890 Cognitive models of class structure and explanations of social outcomes. G. Evans. **Eur. J. Soc. Psychol.** 23:5 9-10:1993 pp.445 - 464.
1891 Colonialism, class formation, and underdevelopment in Sierra Leone. Eliphas G. Mukonoweshuro. Lanham, Md: University Press of America, 1993. x, 257p. *ISBN: 0819182826, 0819182834. Bibliography: p.243-250; includes index.*
1892 Cultura obrera en crisis — el caso de los cordeleros de Yucatán. *[In Spanish]*; [Working class culture in crisis — the case of ropemakers in Yucatán]. Luis A. Várguez Pasos. **Est. Sociol.** XI:31 1-4:1993 pp.93 - 110.
1893 Debate — are social classes dying?. Mike Hout [Contrib.]; Clem Brooks [Contrib.]; Jeff Manza [Contrib.]; Jan Pakulski [Ed.]; Terry Nichols Clark [Contrib.]; Seymour Martin Lipset [Contrib.]; Micheal Rempel [Contrib.]. **Int. Sociol.** 8:3 9:1993 pp.259 - 316. *Collection of 3 articles.*
1894 The decline of class divisions in Britain? Class and ideological preferences in the 1960s and the 1980s. Geoffrey Evans. **Br. J. Soc.** 44:3 9:1993 pp.449 - 471.
1895 Desarrollo de la clase dominante en la Argentina durante los años 70 y 80. *[In Spanish]*; [The development of the dominant class in Argentina in the 70's and 80's]. Jorge Mario Japaz. Buenos Aires: Centro Editor de America Latina, 1993. 2 v. (187 p.)p. *ISBN: 9502524152, 9502524152 (V. 1), 9502524160 (V. 2). Includes bibliographical references (p. 172-178).*
1896 The end of equality. Mickey Kaus. New York, NY: BasicBooks, 1992. 293p. *ISBN: 0465098142. Includes bibliographical references (p. [187]-282) and index.*
1897 Framing the underclass. Joan Vincent. **Crit. Anthr.** 13:3 1993 pp.215 - 230.
1898 Generating images of the shape of a class system. Thomas J. Fararo; Kenji Kosaka. **J. Math. Sociol.** 17:2-3 1992 pp.195 - 216.
1899 Gentrification und Lebensstile: eine empirische Untersuchung. *[In German]*; [Gentrification and life styles: an empirical investigation]. Jörg Blasius. Wiesbaden: Deutscher Universitäts Verlag, 1993. 290p. *ISBN: 382444125X. Also published as a dissertation (Universität Hamburg). Bibliography: p. [238]-250.*
1900 Intergenerational class mobility and political preferences between 1970 and 1986 in the Netherlands. Paul Nieuwbeerta; Nan Dirk de Graaf. **Neth. J. Soc. Sci.** 29:1 6:1993 pp.28 - 45.
1901 Journeyings: a biography of a middle-class generation, 1920-1990. Janet McCalman. Melbourne: Melbourne University Press, 1993. 348p. *ISBN: 052284569X.*
1902 Marx, class consciousness, and the transition to socialism. Dave Baxter. **Crit. Sociol.** 19:1 pp.19 - 43.
1903 Marx's analysis of the French class structure. Peter Hayes. **Theory Soc.** 22:1 2:1993 pp.99 - 123.

E: Social structure

1904 The new American black middle classes: their social structure and status ambivalence. Arthur S. Evans, Jr.. **Int. J. Pol. C. S.** 7:2 Winter:1993 pp.209 - 228.
1905 Over de homogeniteit van de arbeiderscultuur en de heterogeniteit van de cultuur van bedienden — een verkenning. *[In Dutch]*; (On the homogeneity of the blue-collar culture and the heterogeneity of the culture of white-collar workers — an exploratory study.) *[Summary]*. Hans de Witte. **Sociol. Gids** 40:4 7-8:1993 pp.295 - 319.
1906 The postindustrial paradox: growing class inequalities, declining class politics. Jerry Lee Lembcke [Comments by]; Raymond S. Frankliin [Comments by]; Raymond S. Franklin. **Crit. Sociol.** 20:1 1993-1994 pp.103 - 120.
1907 Proletarianization and the structure of Taiwan's working class. Yow-Suen Sen; Hagen Koo. **Crit. Sociol.** 19:1 pp.45 - 67.
1908 Protective discrimination for backward classes in India: sociological and legal dimensions. Rajendra Pandey. **R. Soc. Move. Con. Cha.** 16 1993 pp.139 - 190.
1909 The psychology of social class. Michael Argyle. London: Routledge, 1993. 305p. *ISBN: 0415079543, 0415079551. Includes bibliographical references and index.*
1910 Race and class. Alex Callinicos. London: Bookmarks, 1993. 86p. *ISBN: 0906224837.*
1911 Social class and educational attainment in historical perspective — a Swedish-English comparison part I. Jan O. Jonsson; Colin Mills. **Br. J. Soc.** 44:2 6:1993 pp.213 - 247.
1912 Social class and educational attainment in historical perspective — a Swedish-English comparison part II. Jan O. Jonsson; Colin Mills. **Br. J. Soc.** 44:3 9:1993 pp.403 - 428.
1913 Social class and social justice. Gordon Marshall; Adam Swift. **Br. J. Soc.** 44:2 6:1993 pp.187 - 211.
1914 Social stratification and socioeconomic inequality. Vol.1. A comparative biosocial analysis. Lee Ellis [Ed.]; Lionel Tiger [Foreword]. Westport, Conn: Praeger, 1993. 238p. *ISBN: 0275932621. Bibliography: p.175-216; includes indexes.*
1915 Structural inquiry, human agency and the contibution of Harré and Bhaskar — a case study of Wright's "classes". Barbara Adkins. **J. Theory Soc. Behav.** 23:2 6:1993 pp.157 - 172.
1916 The underclass, 'social isolation' and 'concentration effects'. The culture of poverty' revisited. Andrew H. Maxwell. **Crit. Anthr.** 13:3 1993 pp.231 - 246.
1917 Women and classes — gender and the class base of new social movements in the Netherlands. M. Nas. **Eur. J. Pol. R.** 23:3 4:1993 pp.343 - 355.
1918 The young ones: working-class culture, consumption and the category of youth. Jon Stratton. Perth, Australia: Black Swan Press, 1992. 210p. *ISBN: 0646096478. Includes bibliographical references (p. 199-204) and index.*

E.3: Social change
Changement social

1919 Abbruch und Aufbruch: Sozialwissenschaften im Transformationsprozess : Erfahrungen, Ansätze, Analysen. *[In German]*; [Breaking away and departure: social sciences in a transformation process: experiences, essays and analysis]. Michael

E: Structure sociale

Thomas [Ed.]. Berlin: Akademie Verlag, 1992. 335p. *ISBN: 3050021276. Includes bibliographical references.*

1920 Une Allemagne, deux sociétés distinctes: les causes et conséquences culturelles de la réunification. *[In French]*; [One Germany, two different societies: cultural causes and consequences of reunification] *[Summary]*. Laurence H. McFalls. **Can. J. Poli.** XXVI:4 12:1993 pp.721 - 743.

1921 L'ambivalence de la revitalisation religieuse dans les sociétés post-socialists. *[In French]*; [The ambivalent nature of religious renewal in post-socialist societies] *[Summary]*. Marko Kerševan. **Soc. Compass** 40:1 3:1993 pp.123 - 133.

1922 Badania statystyczne nad przemianami społecznymi w Polsce. *[In Polish]*; (Statistical research on social changes in Poland.) Antoni Rajkiewicz. **Pra. Zab. Społ.** XXXV:9 9:1993 pp.1 - 6.

1923 Bibliographie zur neueren deutschen Sozialgeschichte. *[In German]*; [Bibliography of recent German social history]. Hans-Ulrich Wehler. München: C.H. Beck, 1993. 439p. *ISBN: 3406373828.*

1924 Caribbean freedom: society and economy from emancipation to the present. Hilary Beckles [Ed.]; Verene Shepherd [Ed.]. Kingston, Jamaica; London: Randle; Currey, 1993. xiv, 581p. *ISBN: 9768100176, 0852557116. Includes bibliographical references.*

1925 Chinese intellectual discourse and society, 1978-1988 — the case of Li Zehou. Min Lin. **China Quart.** 132 12:1992 pp.969 - 998.

1926 Communications and the constitution of modernity. Graham Murdock. **Media Cult. Soc.** 15:4 10:1993 pp.521 - 539.

1927 Comparing world-systems — concepts and working hypotheses. Christopher Chase-Dunn; Thomas D. Hall. **Soc. Forc.** 71:4 6:1993 pp.851 - 886.

1928 Constructing culture and power in Latin America. Daniel H. Levine [Ed.]. Ann Arbor: Univeristy of Michigan Press, 1993. ix, 470p. *ISBN: 0472094564, 0472094564, 0472064568. Includes bibliographical references and index.* (*Series:* The Comparative studies in society and history book series).

1929 The critical mass in collective action: a micro-social theory. Gerald Marwell; Pamela Oliver. Cambridge; New York: Cambridge University Press, 1993. xii, 206p. *ISBN: 0521308399. Includes bibliographical references (p. [194]-200) and indexes.* (*Series:* Studies in rationality and social change).

1930 Domination, resistance, and social change in South Africa: the local effects of global power. Kathryn A. Manzo. Westport, Conn: Praeger, 1992. ix, 291p. *ISBN: 027594364X. Includes bibliographical references (p. [275]-283) and index.*

1931 Economia, sociologia e politica: il mutamento nella società italiana come differenziazione. *[In Italian]*; (Economics, sociology and politics: the change of Italian society as functional differentiation.) *[Summary]*. Davide La Valle. **Sociol. Lav.** 45 1992 pp.137 - 180.

1932 [Education and work in changing Denendeh: a survey report in the N.W.T., Canada]; *[Text in Japanese]*. Mitsuru Shimpo. Tokyo: Akashi Shoten, 1993. 251p.

1933 Farewell to democracy in Sarawak: theoretical explorations of socio-cultural transmissions, with reference to change, conflict and contradiction. Roy Bruton. Braunton: Merlin Bks, 1993. 278p. *ISBN: 0863036082.*

1934 Fragile resistance: social transformation in Iran from 1500 to the revolution. John Foran. Boulder: Westview Press, 1993. xiv, 452p. *ISBN: 0813384788. Includes bibliographical references and index.*

E: Social structure

1935 The future of social development in the developed world: learning from the Third World inside the First World. Elise Boulding. **Int. Soc. Sci. J.** 137 8:1993 pp.349 - 360.

1936 Futures studies and the trends towards unity and diversity. Eleonora Barbieri Masini. **Int. Soc. Sci. J.** 137 8:1993 pp.323 - 332.

1937 Futures studies in Latin America. Lourdes Yero. **Int. Soc. Sci. J.** 137 8:1993 pp.361 - 372.

1938 Gesellschaftlicher Umbruch, 1945-1990: Re-Demokratisierung und Lebensverhältnisse. *[In German]*; [A radical change in society, 1945-1990: re-democratization and living arrangements]. Uta Gerhard [Ed.]; Ekkehard Mochmann [Ed.]. Munich: Oldenbourg, 1992. 99p. *ISBN: 348655977X*. *Includes bibliographical references. Arbeitsgemeinschaft Sozialwissenschaftlicher Institute e.V..*

1939 The human face of political, economic, and social change in Eastern Europe. D. Kovacs; Sally Ward Maggard. **E. Eur. Quart.** XXVII:3 Fall:1993 pp.317 - 349.

1940 I mutamenti della società — un sistema da rimettere in movimento. *[In Italian]*; [Changes in society. A system to put back in motion]. Nadio Delai. **Riv. Pol. Ec.** LXXXIII(III):VIII-IX 8-9:1993 pp.43 - 76.

1941 Ideas, institutions and experience. Satish Saberwal. **Sociol. Bul.** 40:1-2 3-9:1991 pp.1 - 20.

1942 International relations of social change. Jan Aart Scholte. Buckingham: Open University Press, 1993. 186p. *ISBN: 0335093302*.

1943 Making the modern: industry, art, and design in America. Terry E. Smith. Chicago: University of Chicago Press, 1993. xv, 512p. *ISBN: 0226763463*. *Includes bibliographical references (p. 453-496) and index.*

1944 Mapping the futures: local cultures, global change. Jon Bird [Ed.]. London: Routledge, 1993. 288p. *ISBN: 0415070171*. (*Series:* Futures. new perspectives for cultural analysis).

1945 La mirada del otro. La imagen de España en el extranjero. *[In Spanish]*; [The look of the other. Spain's image abroad]. Emilio Lamo de Espinosa. **Infor. Com. Esp.** 722 10:1993 pp.11 - 26.

1946 Modernization in East Asia: political, economic, and social perspectives. Richard Harvey Brown [Ed.]; William T. Liu [Ed.]. Westport, Conn: Praeger, 1992. xiii, 186p. *ISBN: 0275932222*. *Includes bibliographical references (p. [167]-176) and index.*

1947 Monitoring social progress in the 1990s: data constraints, concerns and priorities. David G. Westendorff [Ed.]; Dharam Ghai [Ed.]. Aldershot, Hants: Avebury, 1993. 348p. *ISBN: 1856285650*.

1948 A new international research programme at UNESCO: 'management of social transformations' (MOST). Nadia Auriat; Paul de Guchteneire. **Int. Soc. Sci. J.** 137 8:1993 pp.395 - 402.

1949 Oigame! Oigame!: struggle and social change in a Nicaraguan urban community. Michael James Higgins; Tanya Leigh Coen. Boulder: Westview Press, 1992. xiv, 184p. *ISBN: 0813380839*. *Includes bibliographical references (p. 179-184)*. (*Series:* Conflict and social change).

1950 Population and social change in Israel. Calvin Goldscheider [Ed.]. Boulder, Colo: Westview Press, 1992. xvi, 192p. *ISBN: 0813385377*. *Includes bibliographical references*. (*Series:* Brown University studies in population and development).

E: Structure sociale

1951 Postmodernity USA: the crisis of social modernism in postwar America. Anthony Woodiwiss. London: SAGE, 1993. x, 181p. *ISBN: 0803987889, 0803987897. Includes bibliographical references (p. [162]-175) and index. (Series:* Theory, culture and society).

1952 Problems in China's social transformation. Peilin Li. **Soc. Sci. China** XIV:3 Autumn:1993 pp.23 - 34.

1953 Profil eines Standortes: die Bundesrepublik Deutschland in einem Europa des Umbruchs. *[In German]*; [Profile of a position: the Federal Republic of Germany in a Europe undergoing dramatic change]. Bernd Meier; Ingrid Rintelen. Cologne: Deutscher Instituts-Verlag, 1991. 512p. *ISBN: 3602143104. Institut der Deutschen Wirtschaft.*

1954 Prospects for civil society in China — a case study of Xiaoshan City. Gordon White. **Aust. J. Chin. Aff.** 29 1:1993 pp.63 - 87.

1955 Recent social trends in France, 1960-1990. Michel Forsé; et al; Liam Gavin [Tr.]. Frankfurt am Main; Montreal: Campus Verlag; McGill-Queen's University Press, 1993. xii, 368p. *ISBN: 3593348985, 0773508872. International Research Group on the Comparative Charting of Social Change in Advanced Industrial Nations. (Series:* Comparative charting of social change).

1956 Redefining Russian society and polity. Mary Buckley. Boulder, Colo: Westview Press, 1993. xviii, 346p. *ISBN: 0813315808, 0813315794. Includes bibliographical references and index.*

1957 A rendszerváltás és a gyermekjólét problémái. *[In Hungarian]*; (Changing social systems in Central and Eastern Europe and child welfare problems.) Sándor Sipos. **Acta Hum.** 9 1992 pp.25 - 50.

1958 Revolutionary outcomes in Iran and Nicaragua — coalition fragmentation, war, and the limits of social transformation. John Foran; Jeff Goodwin. **Theory Soc.** 22:2 4:1993 pp.209 - 247.

1959 Scandinavia in a new Europe. Thomas P. Boje [Ed.]; Sven E. Olsson [Ed.]. Oslo: Scandinavian University Press, 1993. 427p. *ISBN: 8200211835. Includes index and bibliographies. (Series:* Scandinavian library).

1960 Schüler erfahren die Wende: Schuljugendliche in Ostdeutschland im gesellschaftlichen Transformationprozess. *[In German]*; [Pupils experience political reform: school children in East Germany as part of the social transformation process]. Manfred Stock; Michael Tiedtke. Munich: Juventa, 1992. 112p. *ISBN: 3779908425.*

1961 Sikkim: democracy and social change. Madhumita Bhadra. Calcutta: Minerva, 1992. 168p.

1962 [The sixties: thoughts of the age of change]; *[Text in Japanese]*. Tetsuo Sakurai. Tokyo: Chikuma Shobo, 1993. 305p.

1963 Social and economic modernisation in East Germany from Honecker to Kohl. Mike Dennis. London: Pinter, 1993. viii, 252p. *ISBN: 0861871669. (Series:* New Germany series).

1964 Social change and social issues in the former USSR: selected papers from the fourth world congress for Soviet and East European Studies, Harrogate, 1990. Walter Joyce [Ed.]. New York: St. Martin's Press, 1992. 162p. *ISBN: 0333553284, 031207994X.*

1965 Social change in Hong Kong: Hong Kong man in search of majority. Hugh D.R. Baker. **China Quart.** 136 12:1993 pp.864 - 877.

E: Social structure

1966 Social development: its nature and companions. Leonard Trelawney Hobhouse. London: Thoemmes; Routledge, 1993. 348p.

1967 Socio-economic change and regional development. P. V. Rajeev. New Delhi: Deep and Deep, 1991. 135p. *ISBN: 8171003176.*

1968 [A sociological approach to social change and social deviance]; *[Text in Japanese].* Hiroto Fujita. Tokyo: Bunkashobo Hakubunsha, 1993. 257p.

1969 The sociology of social change. Piotr Sztompka. Oxford: Blackwell, 1993. xvi, 348p. *ISBN: 0631182055, 0631182055, 0631182063.*

1970 Soziologische Analysen zum politischen und sozialen Wandel in Ostdeutschland. *[In German]*; (Sociological analysis in respect of political and social change in East Germany.) Hasko Hüning [Contrib.]; Hildegard Maria Nickel [Contrib.]; Thomas Koch [Contrib.]; Michael Thomas [Contrib.]; Rudolf Woderich [Contrib.]; Rainer Münz [Contrib.]; Ralf Ulrich [Contrib.]; Irene Müller-Hartmann [Contrib.]; Elvir Ebert [Contrib.]; Gerhard Lippold [Contrib.]; Jürgen Dorbritz [Contrib.]; Sabine Schenk [Contrib.]; Uta Schlegel [Contrib.]; Wolfgang Kühnel [Contrib.]; Astrid Segert [Contrib.]; Irene Zierke [Contrib.]. **Berl. J. Soziol.** 3:3 1993 pp.257 - 430. *Collection of 10 articles.*

1971 Sugar and the origins of modern Philippine society. John A. Larkin. Berkeley: University of California Press, 1993. xvi, 337p. *ISBN: 0520079566. Includes bibliographical references and index.*

1972 Tahitian transformation: gender and capitalist development in a rural society. Victoria S. Lockwood. Boulder: Lynne Rienner Publishers, 1993. xii, 180p. *ISBN: 1555873170, 155587391X. Includes bibliographical references (p. 165-173) and index. (Series:* Women and change in the developing world).

1973 Themes of modernity in new religious movements and new social movements. Mario Diani. **Soc. Sci. Info.** 32:1 3:1993 pp.111 - 131.

1974 A theory of Third World social revolutions — Iran, Nicaragua, and El Salvador compared. John Foran. **Crit. Sociol.** 19:2 1992 pp.3 - 27.

1975 The transformation of European communist societies. David R. Segal [Contrib.]; Paul Hollander [Contrib.]; Randall Collins [Contrib.]; David Waller [Contrib.]; Gregory McLauchlan [Contrib.]; Johan Galtung [Contrib.]; David S. Meyer [Contrib.]; Sam Marullo [Contrib.]; Martin Patchen [Contrib.]; Christopher Chase-Dunn [Contrib.]; József Böröcz [Contrib.]; Christo Stojanov [Contrib.]; S.M. Miller [Contrib.]; Jerry W. Sanders [Contrib.]; Louis Kriesberg [Contrib.]. **R. Soc. Move. Con. Cha.** 14 1992 pp.1 - 297. *Collection of 13 articles.*

1976 Tu Galala: social change in the Pacific. David Robie [Ed.]. Wellington, N.Z, Annandale, NSW: Bridget Williams Books, Pluto Press Australia, 1992. 233p. *ISBN: 0908912145, 0949138851. Includes bibliographical references (p. 220-221) and index.*

1977 Una modernizzazione difficile: aspetti critici della società italiana. *[In Italian]*; [A difficult modernization: critical aspects of Italian society]. Riccardo Scartezzini [Ed.]; Carlo Tullio-Altan [Ed.]. Naples: Liguori, 1992. 184p. *ISBN: 8820720728.*

1978 Una perspectiva diferente del poder y el cambio social para la psicología social comunitaria. *[In Spanish]*; [A different perspective on power and social change for community social psychology] *[Summary].* Irma Serrano-García; Gerardo López Sánchez. **Rev. Cien. Soc.** XXIX:3-4 7-12:1990 pp.349 - 382.

E: Structure sociale

1979 Von der ständischen zur bürgerlichen Gesellschaft. *[In German]*; [From corporate to civil society]. Lothar Gall. München: Oldenbourg, 1993. viii,144p. *ISBN: 3486557548. Includes bibliographical references (p. [105]-136) and indexes.*

F: POPULATION. FAMILY. GENDER. ETHNIC GROUP
POPULATION. FAMILLE. SEXE. GROUPE ETHNIQUE

F.1: Demography
Démographie

1980 Aboriginal population prospects. Alan Gray; Habtemariam Tesfaghiorghis. **J. Aust. Pop. Ass.** 10:2 11:1993 pp.81 - 100.

1981 Application of the LIPRO model for protection of Poland's population by marital status and place of residence. Irena E. Kotowska. **Stud. Demogr.** 4(106) 1991 pp.3 - 26.

1982 Assessing post-census state poverty estimates. William P. O'Hare. **Pop. Res. Pol. R.** 12:3 1993 pp.261 - 276.

1983 Back projection and inverse projection — members of a wider class of constrained projection models. Jim Oeppen. **Pop. Stud.** 47:2 7:1993 pp.245 - 267.

1984 Census enumeration in remote Australia — issues for Aboriginal data analysis. John Taylor. **J. Aust. Pop. Ass.** 10:1 5:1993 pp.53 - 67.

1985 The changing population of Europe. Daniel Noin [Ed.]; Robert Woods [Ed.]. Oxford, UK, Cambridge, Mass: Blackwell, 1993. 260p. *ISBN: 0631176357, 0631189726. Includes bibliographical references (p. [230]-251) and index.*

1986 Clusteranalyse und Diskriminanzanalyse als Instrumente der Beschreibung der demographischen Transition. *[In German]*; (Cluster analysis and discriminance analysis as methods for the investigation of the demographic transition.). Bernd Rönz. **Wissensch. Z. Humboldt-Univ.** 41:2 1992 pp.69 - 95.

1987 Las consecuencias demográficas de la austeridad en América Latina — aspectos metodológicos. *[In Spanish]*; (The demographic consequences of austerity in Latin America — methodological aspects.) *[Summary]*. Ralph Hakkert. **Est. Demog. Urb.** 6:2 5-8:1991 pp.391 - 422.

1988 The contours of demography — estimates and projections. Samuel H. Preston. **Demography** 30:4 11:1993 pp.593 - 606.

1989 De toekomst van Europa's bevolking. Een scenariobenadering. *[In Dutch]*; (The future of Europe's population. A scenario approach.) *[Summary]*. Robert Cliquet; K. Kiernan; W. Lutz; F. Mesle; C. Prinz. **Bevolk. Gez.** 2 1993 pp.21 - 41.

1990 Demographic aspects of development — the Indian experience. Pravin Visaria. **Ind. J. Soc. Sci.** 6:3 7-9:1993 pp.219 - 242.

1991 Demographic infuences on the OECD labour market — is there a problem? Are there solutions? Fiorella Padoa Schioppa Kostoris. **Labour [Italy]** 7:1 Spring:1993 pp.181 - 208.

1992 The demographic transformation and the sociological enterprise. Maxine Baca Zinn; D. Stanley Eitzen. **Am. Sociol.** 24:2 Summer:1993 pp.5 - 12.

1993 Demography — the past 30 years, the present, and the future. Eileen M. Crimmins. **Demography** 30:4 11:1993 pp.579 - 591.

1994 The demography of Saudi Arabia. Abu Jafar Mohammad Sufian. **Popul. R.** 37:1-2 1-12:1993 pp.64 - 70.

1995 Dinamika zanaitosti naseleniia v nekotorykh strnakh Iugo-Votochnynoi Azii i Dal'nego Vostoka. *[In Russian]*; (The dynamics of population occupancy of certain

F: Population. Famille. Sexe. Groupe ethnique

countries of Southeast Asia and the Far East.). V.Iu. Bulantsev. **Vest. Mosk. Univ. Ser. 5 Geograf.** 3 1993 pp.67 - 75.

1996 Évolution démographique récente dans les T.O.M. du Pacifique, 1970-1990. *[In French]*; (Recent demographic trends in French Overseas Territories in the Pacific, 1970-1980.) *[Summary]*. Gérard Baudchon; Jean-Louis Rallu. **Population** 48:4 7-8:1993 pp.885 - 918.

1997 Families in context: a world history of population. Gladys Robina Quale. New York: Greenwood Press, 1992. xiv, 466p. *ISBN: 031327830X, 031327830X*. (*Series:* Contributions to the study of world history).

1998 House, home and the place of dwelling. P.T. Karjalainen. **Scand. Hous. Plan. R.** 10:2 1993 p.65.

1999 Household partition in rural Bangladesh. Andrew D. Foster. **Pop. Stud.** 47:1 3:1993 pp.97 - 114.

2000 Household registration, economic reform and migration. Xiushi Yang. **Int. Migr. Rev.** XXVII:4 Winter:1993 pp.796 - 818.

2001 The idea of demographic transition and the study of fertility change: a critical intellectual history. Simon Szreter. **Pop. Dev. Rev.** 19:4 12:1993 pp.659 - 702.

2002 Is demographic uniformity inevitable? Gavin W. Jones. **J. Aust. Pop. Ass.** 10:1 5:1993 pp.1 - 16.

2003 The link between population density and welfare participation. Mark R Rank; Thomas A. Hirschl. **Demography** 30:4 11:1993 pp.607 - 622.

2004 Living alone, marital status, gender and health. D. Cramer. **J. Comm. App. Soc. Psychol.** 3:1 4:1993 pp.1 - 15.

2005 Measurement errors in census counts and estimates of intercensal net migration. H.J. Kintner; D.A. Swanson. **J. Econ. Soc.** 19:2 1993 pp.97 - 120.

2006 Measuring demographic change — the split tract problem. Erick Howenstine. **Prof. Geogr.** 45:4 11:1993 pp.425 - 430.

2007 Methodology for population studies and development. Krishnan Mahadevan [Ed.]; Parameswara Krishnan [Ed.]. New Delhi ; Newbury Park: Sage Publications, 1992. 469p. *ISBN: 0803994311*. *Includes bibliographical references.*

2008 Możliwości zastosowania analizy ścieżkowej w demografii. *[In Polish]*; (Possibilities to apply path analysis in demography.). Elżbieta Gołata. **Stud. Demogr.** 4(110) 1992 pp.13 - 30.

2009 Na rubiecach demometrii. *[In Polish]*; (On the cross roads of demometries.) *[Summary]*. Irena Kotowska; Jan Paradysz. **Stud. Demogr.** 1(103) 1991 pp.3 - 12.

2010 Naselenie Moskvy: proshloe, nastoiashchee, budushchee. *[In Russian]*; [The population of Russia: the past, the present and the future]. Valentina Mikhailovna Moiseenko. Moskva: Izd-vo Moskovskogo universiteta, 1992. 116p. *ISBN: 5211021835*. *Includes bibliographical references.*

2011 Le nombre de ménages augmentera de moins en moins vite. *[In French]*; (The number of households will slow.). Claudie Louvot. **E & S** 267 7:1993 pp.31 - 48.

2012 O naturze prognozy demograficznej i o technologii jej ustalania. *[In Polish]*; (On the nature of demographic forecasting.). Maria Cieślak. **Stud. Demogr.** 4(110) 1992 pp.3 - 12.

2013 Old and new methods in historical demography. Roger S. Schofield [Ed.]; David-Sven Reher [Ed.]. Oxford: Clarendon Press, 1993. viii, 426p. *ISBN: 0198287933*. (*Series:* International studies in demography).

2014 (Overpopulation and depopulation problems: an approach by a model for population allocation between regions.) *[Summary]*; *[Text in Japanese]*. Kiyoko Hagihara. **Comp. Urban St.** 50 11:1993 pp.93 - 106.

F: Population. Family. Gender. Ethnic group

2015 Perspektiven der Künftigen Bevölkerungsentwicklung in Deutschland. Teil 2 — Regionale Bevölkerungsprognose 2000 der BFLR. *[In German]*; [Prospects for future demographic change in Germany. Part 2 — Regional prognosis model of the Federal Research Institute]. Hansjörg Bucher [Contrib.]; Hans-Peter Gatzweiler [Contrib.]; Mathias Siedhoff [Contrib.]; Gerhard Stiens [Contrib.]; Herwig Birg [Contrib.]. **Inf. Raum.** 11/12 1992 pp.809 - 876. *Collection of 3 articles.*

2016 [Population decrease shock]; *[Text in Japanese]*. Yoshihiko Furuta. Tokyo: PHP Institute, 1993. 238p.

2017 La population du Québec d'hier à demain. *[In French]*; [The population of Quebec from yesterday to tomorrow]. Jacques Henripin [Ed.]; Yves Martin [Ed.]. Montréal: Presses de l'Université de Montréal, 1991. 213p. *ISBN: 2760615499. Bibliography.*

2018 Population education; Education en matière de population. *[In French]*. Etienne Brunswic [Ed.]; Ferdinand J.C.M. Rath [Contrib.]; Mather Mahran [Contrib.]; M. Eugenia Dengo de Vargas [Contrib.]; Jorge Arias de Blois [Contrib.]; O.J. Sikes [Contrib.]; Jairo Palacio [Contrib.]; Beverley Kerr [Contrib.]; Jean Valérien [Contrib.]; John I. Clarke [Contrib.]; Mouna Liliane Samman [Contrib.]; Léon Gani [Contrib.]; Abdel Kader Fahem [Contrib.]; Fama Hane Ba [Contrib.]; Michel Louis Lévy [Contrib.]; George Muito [Contrib.]; Claude Georges [Contrib.]; Edouard El Wardini [Contrib.]; D.S. Muley [Contrib.]; Kaminieli Tagica [Contrib.]; César Birzéa [Contrib.]; Kimberley A. Crews [Contrib.]. **Int. R. Educat.** 39:1-2 3:1993 pp.5 - 149. *Collection of 23 articles.*

2019 Population et main-d'œuvre en corée du nord: évolution et conséquences. *[In French]*; (Population and labour in North Korea: trends and results.) *[Summary]*. Nicholas Eberstadt. **Population** 48:3 5-6:1993 pp.683 - 710.

2020 La population française dans son espace. *[In French]*; (The French population within its own space.). D. Pumain; J.-N. Biraben; A. Jacquot; J.-C. Fanouillet; G. Desplanques; T. Le Jeannic; B. Aubry; J.-P. Damais; J.-P. Charrié; R. Marconis; A.-M. Arnauné; M.-H. Cabanne; A. Etchelecou; J. Lavertu; A. Dittgen; G.-F. Dumont; F. Prioux; C. Blayo; J.-R. Bertrand; N. Sztokman; M. Castellan; M.-F. Goldberger; M. Marpsat; R. Séchet; C. Pihet; P. Violier; R. Hérin; J.-P. Augustin; P. George; M. Guillon; P. Simon; M. Poinard; C. Madinier; J.-P. Colliez; C. Chivallon; A. Calmont. **Espace Pop. Soc.** 2 1993 pp.165 - 434. *Collection of 31 articles.*

2021 Population growth and the demographic transition in Kenya; *[Summary in French]*. Robert A. Wortham. **Int. Sociol.** 8:2 6:1993 pp.197 - 214.

2022 Population movements and the Third World. Mike Parnwell. New York: Routledge, 1993. 158p. *ISBN: 041506953X. Inlcudes bibliographical references and index.* (*Series:* Routledge introductions to development).

2023 Population pressure, intensification of agriculture, and rural-urban migration. D. Salehi-Isfahani. **J. Dev. Econ.** 40:2 4:1993 pp.371 - 384.

2024 Population-environment dynamics: ideas and observations. Gayl DeForrest Ness [Ed.]; William D. Drake [Ed.]; Steven R. Brechin [Ed.]. Ann Arbor, MI: University of Michigan Press, 1993. xv, 456p. *ISBN: 0472103954. Includes bibliographical references (p. 407-437) and index.*

2025 Projections and forecasts. Martin Bell [Ed.]; Abbas Y. Adam [Contrib.]; Peter Davenport [Contrib.]; John O'Leary [Contrib.]; D.S. Ironmonger [Contrib.]; C.W. Lloyd-Smith [Contrib.]; Keith Spicer [Contrib.]; Ian Diamond [Contrib.]; Maire Ni Bhrolchain [Contrib.]; E.M. Webster [Contrib.]; Jim Skinner [Contrib.]. **J. Aust. Pop. Ass.** 9:2 11:1992 pp.103 - 235. *Collection of 7 articles.*

F: Population. Famille. Sexe. Groupe ethnique

2026 Przewidywane zmiany w stanie i strukturze lodności w wieku produkcyjnym w krajach europejskich i pozaeuropekskich w latach 1990-2010 i ich konsekwencje dla migracji zagaaaranicznych. *[In Polish]*; (Expected changes in size and structure of working — age population in European and non-European countries (in the period 1990-2010) and the consequences for international migration.) *[Summary]*. Kazimierz Dzienio; Krystyna Drzewieniecka. **Stud. Demogr.** 1(107) 1992 pp.39 - 55.

2027 Räumliche Auswirkungen und raumordnerische Konsequenzen der zukünftigen regionalen Bevölkerungsentwicklung. *[In German]*; [Spatial effects and environmental planning consequences of future regional population development]. Hansjörg Bucher; Hans-Peter Gatzweiler. **Inf. Raum.** 12 1993 pp.923 - 936.

2028 The right people, the right rates — making population estimates and forecasts with an interregional cohort-component model. Andrew M. Isserman. **J. Am. Plann.** 59:1 Winter:1993 pp.45 - 64.

2029 Rozwój demograficzny w trakcie przejścia demograficznego. *[In Polish]*; (Demographic development in the course of demographic transition.) *[Summary]*. Małgorzata Rószkiewicz. **Stud. Demogr.** 3(101) 1990 pp.3 - 19.

2030 Science that colonizes: a critique of fertility studies in Africa. Agnes Czerwinski Riedmann. Philadelphia: Temple University Press, 1993. xiv, 174p. *ISBN: 1566390427. Includes bibliographical references (p. 153-169) and index.*

2031 Sozialstaat und demographischer Wandel: Wechselwirkungen, Generationenverhältnisse, politisch-institutionelle Steuerung. *[In German]*; [Social state and demographic change: interactions, relations between generations, political-institutional control]. Lutz Leisering; Franz-Xaver Kaufmann [Intro.]. Frankfurt am Main, New York: Campus-Verlag, 1992. xvii, 327p. *ISBN: 3593343908. Includes bibliographical references (p. 301-327).*

2032 Synergetic conception of regional population and social-democratic processes taking place in the Czech Republic. P. Chalupa. **Geojournal** 31:4 12:1993 pp.435 - 438.

2033 Wielowymiarowa analiza porównawcza rozwoju demograficznego krajów europejskich. *[In Polish]*; (Multidimensional comparative analysis of demographic development of the European countries.) *[Summary]*. Józef Pociecha. **Stud. Demogr.** 4(102) 1990 pp.25 - 50.

2034 World Jewish population: trends and policies. Leah Cohen [Ed.]; Sergio Della Pergola [Ed.]. Jerusalem: Institute of Contemporary Jewry, Hebrew University of Jerusalem; Demographic Center, Ministry of Labour and Social Affairs; Association for Demographic Policy of the Jewish People, 1992. 334p. *ISBN: 9652222577. Selected proceedings of a Conference on World Jewish Population, 1987, Jerusalem. Includes bibliographical references. (Series:* Jewish population studies).

F.2: Age groups
Groupes d'âges

2035 Abkhaziia. Pozhiloi chelovek - gordost' obshchestva. *[In Russian]*; [Abkhazia. The middle aged person is the pride of society]. T. Sivertseva; M. Sivertsev. **Az. Afr. Seg.** 6 (432) 1993 pp.22 - 26.

2036 Analiza porównawcza zmian struktury ludności według wieku w wybranych krajach europejskich. *[In Polish]*; (Comparative analysis of changes of population age

F: Population. Family. Gender. Ethnic group

structure in selected European countries.) *[Summary]*. Jolanta Kurkiewicz. **Stud. Demogr.** 4(106) 1991 pp.45 - 63.

2037 Comparative patterns in retirement. Anne-Marie Guillemard; Martin Rein. **Ann. R. Soc.** 19 1993 pp.469 - 504.

2038 Contrasting age structures of Western Europe and of Eastern Europe and the former Soviet Union — demographic curiosity or labor resource? David A. Coleman. **Pop. Dev. Rev.** 19:3 9:1993 pp.523 - 555.

2039 Deutsche Lebensalter — Erkundungen in einer sächsischen Kleinstadt. *[In German]*; [Age in Germany as illustrated by a small town in Saxony]. Cordia Schlegelmilch. **Prokla** 23:2(91) 6:1993 pp.269 - 295.

2040 Livcyklus. *[In Norwegian]*; [Life cycles]. Birgitte Rørbye [Contrib.]; Lissie Åström [Contrib.]; Michèle Simonsen [Contrib.]; Bjørg Kjær [Contrib.]; Anne Isomursu [Contrib.]; Erling Bjurström [Contrib.]; Johan Wennhall [Contrib.]; Christine E. Swane [Contrib.]; Anne Leonora Blaakilde [Contrib.]; Finnur Magnusson [Contrib.]; Magnus Öhlander [Contrib.]; Lene Otto [Contrib.]. **Nord. Ny.** 49 2:1993 pp.5 - 116. *Collection of 13 articles.*

2041 The search for adolescent role exists and the transition to adulthood. John Hagan; Blair Wheaton. **Soc. Forc.** 71:4 6:1993 pp.955 - 980.

2042 The silent passage: menopause. Gail Sheehy. London: HarperCollins, 1993. viii,178p. *ISBN: 0002552140.*

2043 Sociodemographic correlates of the size and composition of informal caregiver networks among frail ethnic elderly; *[Summary in Spanish]*. Michael C. Thornton; Shelley I. White-Means; Kyong Choi Hye. **J. Comp. Fam. Stud.** XXIV:2 Summer:1993 pp.235 - 250.

Ageing
Vieillissement

2044 Ageing, independence and the life course. Sara Arber [Ed.]; Maria Evandrou [Ed.]. London: Jessica Kingsley Publishers, 1993. 256p. *ISBN: 1853021806.*

2045 Aging, money, and life satisfaction: aspects of financial gerontology. Neal E. Cutler [Ed.]; Davis Weinert Gregg [Ed.]; M. Powell Lawton [Ed.]. New York: Springer Pub. Co, 1992. xiii, 189p. *ISBN: 082617700X. Includes bibliographical references and index.*

2046 Are the old really obsolete? An explanatory study. Suparna Chandra; Deb Kumar Shome; Prafulla Chakraborti. **Man India** 73:3 9:1993 pp.215 - 228.

2047 Being old, old people and the burdens of burden. Anthony M. Warnes. **Age. Soc.** 13:3 9:1993 pp.297 - 338.

2048 The Berlin Aging Study. George L. Maddox [Ed.]; Paul B. Baltes [Contrib.]; Karl Ulrich Mayer [Contrib.]; Hanfried Helmchen [Contrib.]; Elisabeth Steinhagen-Thiessen [Contrib.]; Michael Wagner [Contrib.]; Jacqui Smith [Contrib.]; Michael Linden [Contrib.]; Markus Borchelt [Contrib.]; Margaret M. Baltes [Contrib.]; Ulrich Mayr [Contrib.]; Ineke Maas [Contrib.]; Hans-Ulrich Wilms [Contrib.]. **Age. Soc.** 13:4 12:1993 pp.483 - 680. *Collection of 6 articles.*

2049 Biological anthropology and human aging — some current directions in aging research. Douglas E. Crews. **Ann. R. Anthr.** 22 1993 pp.395 - 423.

F: Population. Famille. Sexe. Groupe ethnique

2050 Care of the elderly in Japan — changing norms and expectations. Naohiro Ogawa; Robert D. Retherford. **J. Marriage Fam.** 55:3 8:1993 pp.585 - 597.

2051 De gamla barnen. *[In Swedish]*; (The old children: the infantilization of the elderly.). Magnus Öhlander. **Nord. Ny.** 52 1993 pp.79 - 84.

2052 Demografisch profiel van de hoogbejaarden in België. *[In Dutch]*; (Demographic profile of the very elderly in Belgium.) *[Summary]*. Gilbert Dooghe. **Bevolk. Gez.** 2 1993 pp.65 - 93.

2053 The elderly population in developed and developing world: policies, problems and perspectives. Parameswara Krishnan [Ed.]; K. Mahadevan [Ed.]. Delhi: B. R. Publishing Corporation, 1992. 508p. *ISBN: 8170187249.*

2054 Envelliment i societat. *[In Catalan]*; [Old age and society]. Claudine Attias-Donfut [Contrib.]; Anne-Marie Guillemard [Contrib.]; Maria-Teresa Bazo [Contrib.]; Carmen Dominguez Alcón [Contrib.]; Mercé Pérez Salanova [Contrib.]; Pedro Sánchez Vera [Contrib.]; María Pía Barenys [Contrib.]; Elizabeth W. Markson [Contrib.]. **Papers** 40 1993 pp.13 - 160. *Collection of 8 articles.*

2055 Gender differences in economic well-being among the elderly of Java. Laura Rudkin. **Demography** 30:2 5:1993 pp.209 - 226.

2056 Geroethics: a new vision of growing old in America. Gerald A. Larue. Buffalo, NY: Prometheus Books, 1992. 267p. *ISBN: 0879757507. Includes bibliographical references. (Series:* Golden age books).

2057 Growing up and growing old: ageing and dependency in the life course. Jennifer Hockey; Allison James. London: Sage, 1993. 200p. *ISBN: 0803985592, 0803988338. Bibliography: p. 185-195. -Includes index. (Series:* Theory, culture & society).

2058 The health and well-being of Jewish people aged 65 to 85 years living at home in the East End of London. Ann Bowling; Morag Farquhar. **Age. Soc.** 13:2 6:1993 pp.213 - 244.

2059 Het mentaal functioneren van oudere weduwen — een multivariate analyse. *[In Dutch]*; [Mental functioning of elderly widows — a multivariate analysis] *[Summary]*. Lieve Vanderleyden. **Bevolk. Gez.** 2:1992 pp.49 - 65.

2060 Hilfebeziehungen und soziale Differenzierung im Alter. *[In German]*; (Social differentiation in old age and inequality of informal support.) *[Summary]*. Martin Diewald. **Kölner Z. Soz. Soz. psy.** 45:4 12:1993 pp.731 - 754.

2061 [Human science of aging]; *[Text in Japanese]*. Haruo Sagaza. Tokyo: Gakubunsha, 1993. 208p.

2062 Informele zorgverlening aan bejaarden. *[In Dutch]*; [Informal care of the aged]. Gilbert Dooghe. **Bevolk. Gez.** 3 1992 pp.29 - 49.

2063 [Introduction to gerontology: interdisciplinary approach]; *[Text in Japanese]*. Hiroshi Shibata [Ed.]. Tokyo: Kawashima Shoten, 1993. 242p.

2064 Joint role investments and synchronization of retirement — a sequential approach to couples' retirement timing. John C. Henretta; Angela M. O'Rand; Christopher G. Chan. **Soc. Forc.** 71:4 6:1993 pp.981 - 1000.

2065 "The land of old age" — society's changing attitudes toward urban built environments for elderly people. Glenda Laws. **Ann. As. Am. G.** 83:4 12:1993 pp.672 - 693.

2066 Life after 60: a profile of Britain's older population. Janet Askham; et al. London: Kings College, 1992. 89p. *Gerontology Data Service. Age Concern Institute of Gerentology.*

F: Population. Family. Gender. Ethnic group

2067 The meanings and motivations of learning during the retirement transition. Suzanne R. Adair; Richard Mowsesian. **Educ. Geront.** 19:4 6:1993 pp.317 - 330.

2068 Migration patterns and migration motives among the elderly — Swedish data in a comparative perspective. M. Ekström; B. Danermark. **Scand. Hous. Plan. R.** 10:2 1993 pp.75 - 89.

2069 Old age: a register of social research, 1985-1990. Gillian Crosby [Ed.]. London: Centre for Policy on Ageing, 1991. iv, 188p. *ISBN: 0904139786.*

2070 Opvattingen over de positie van ouderen en aspecten van de vergrijzing. *[In Dutch]*; [Views on the position of the aged and aspects of the ageing process]. Hans van den Brekel; Hein Moors. **Bevolk. Gez.** 3 1992 pp.51 - 76.

2071 La perspective future, facteur de santé mentale chez les personnes âgées. *[In French]*; (Mental health and elders' future perspectives.) *[Summary]*. Léandre Bouffard; Étienne Bastien. **San. Ment. Qué** XVII:2 Automne:1992 pp.227 - 249.

2072 Perspectives on later life. Peter Russell Day [Ed.]. London: Whiting & Birch Ltd./SCA, 1993. 178p. *ISBN: 1871177537.*

2073 The plight of the elderly in Poland. Frances Millard. **Comm. Dev. J.** 28:2 4:1993 pp.108 - 119.

2074 Policy and aging in contemporary China. Charlotte Ikels [Ed.]; Melvyn C. Goldstein [Ed.]; Deborah S. Davis [Contrib.]; Yachun Ku [Contrib.]; Jersey Liang [Contrib.]; Joan Bennett [Contrib.]; Shengzu Gu [Contrib.]; Cecilia Chan [Contrib.]; Christina Wu Harbaugh [Contrib.]; Loraine A. West [Contrib.]. **J. Cr-cult. Gerontol.** 8:3 7:1993 pp.173 - 280. *Collection of 6 articles.*

2075 Remembered lives: the work of ritual, storytelling, and growing older. Barbara G. Myerhoff; Marc Kaminsky [Ed.]; Barbara Kirshenblatt-Gimblett [Foreword]; Deena Metzger [Contrib.]; Jay Ruby [Contrib.]; Virginia Tufte [Contrib.]. Ann Arbor: University of Michigan Press, 1992. xxiv, 387p. *ISBN: 0472103172. Includes bibliographical references (p. 361-370) and index.*

2076 Reminiscence reviewed: evaluations, achievements, perspectives. Joanna Bornat [Ed.]. Milton Keynes [England], Bristol, Pa: Open University Press, 1993. 148p. *ISBN: 0335190421, 0335190413. Includes bibliographical references and index. (Series: Rethinking ageing).*

2077 La richesse de la vieillesse: la situation socio-économique des personnes âgées en Belgique : état actuel et prospective. *[In French]*; [Wealth and old age: the socio-economic position of old people in Belgium: current conditions and future prospects]. Herman Devos; Kurt Van Dender; Jozef Pacolet. Brussels: Fondation Roi Baudouin, 1991. 185p. *ISBN: 2872120637.*

2078 Roles, race and subjective well-being — a longitudinal analysis of elderly men. R.P.D. Burton; B. Rushing; C. Ritter; A. Rakocy. **Soc. Ind.** 28:2 2:1993 pp.137 - 156.

2079 Self-esteem and its sources — stability and change in later life. Peter G. Coleman; Christine Ivani-Chalian; Maureen Robinson. **Age. Soc.** 13:2 6:1993 pp.171 - 192.

2080 Sexuality in the later years. Richard A. Kaye. **Age. Soc.** 13:3 9:1993 pp.415 - 426.

2081 The social status of the elderly in the Philippines. C. Williams; L. Domingo. **J. Marriage Fam.** 55:2 5:1993 pp.415 - 426.

2082 Social status, physical, mental health, well being and self evaluation of elderly in China. Lucy C. Wu; Minqi Wang. **J. Cr-cult. Gerontol.** 8:2 4:1993 pp.147 - 159.

2083 Socio-economic status of the aged — a case study. K.C. Mahanta. **Man India** 73:3 9:1993 pp.201 - 214.

F: Population. Famille. Sexe. Groupe ethnique

2084 Understanding ageing: images, attitudes and professional practice. Simon Biggs. Buckingham: Open University Press, 1993. 195p. *ISBN: 0335157254, 0335157246. Includes bibliographical references and index.*
2085 Women come of age: perspectives on the lives of older women. Miriam Bernard [Ed.]; Kathy Mead [Ed.]. London: Edward Arnold, 1993. 230p. *ISBN: 0340552611.*

Children
Enfants

2086 America's childhood. Martha Minow [Contrib.]; Richard Weissbourd [Contrib.]; Mihaly Csikszentmihalyi [Contrib.]; Sandra K. Danziger [Contrib.]; Sheldon Danziger; David Finn [Contrib.]; Felton Earls [Contrib.]; Mary Carlson [Contrib.]; Thomas J. Cottle [Contrib.]; Maris A. Vinovskis [Contrib.]; David K. Cohen [Contrib.]; S.G. Grant [Contrib.]; Kim Marshall [Contrib.]; Jerome M. Ziegler [Contrib.]; John Condry [Contrib.]; Richard A. Shweder [Contrib.]. **Dædalus** 122:1 Winter:1993 pp.1 - 308. *Collection of 12 articles.*
2087 America's children: resources from family, government, and the economy. Donald J. Hernandez. New York: Russell Sage Foundation, 1993. 482p. *ISBN: 0871543818. National Committee for Research on the 1980 Census. Includes bibliographical references and index. (Series:* Census monograph series).
2088 Caring for children: the 1990 report: report for the European Commission's Childcare Network on childcare services and policies in the United Kingdom. Bronwen Cohen. London: Family Policy Studies Centre in association with the Scottish Child and Family Alliance, 1990. vi, 53p. *ISBN: 0907051545. (Series:* Occasional paper).
2089 Child care in JOBS employment and training programs — what difference does quality make? Marcia K. Meyers. **J. Marriage Fam.** 55:3 8:1993 pp.767 - 783.
2090 Child development: a first course. Kathy Sylva; Ingrid Lunt. Oxford: Blackwell, 1993. x, 261p. *ISBN: 0862160537, 0862160545.*
2091 Child protection adviser's resource pack. National Society for the Prevention of Cruelty to Children, Battered Child Research Team. London: NSPCC, 1992. *ISBN: 090249838X.*
2092 Child welfare: England, 1872-1989. Harry Hendrick. London: Routledge, 1993. 354p.
2093 Child welfare in Sarawak. Jomo K. Sundaram. **Born. R.** III:2 12:1992 pp.234 - 258.
2094 Childhood antecedents of young-adult judgability. C. Randall Colvin. **J. Personal.** 61:4 12:1993 pp.611 - 636.
2095 Childhood identities: self and social relationships in the experience of the child. Allison James. Edinburgh: Edinburgh University Press, 1993. 246p. *ISBN: 0748604561.*
2096 The Children Act 1989: conflict and compromise. Martin L. Parry [Ed.]. Hull: Hull University Law School, 1992. 62p. *ISBN: 0859587339. (Series:* Studies in law).
2097 Children and adolescents' conceptions of peace, war, and strategies to attain peace — a Dutch case study. Ilse Hakvoort; Louis Oppenheimer. **J. Peace Res.** 30:1 2:1993 pp.65 - 77.
2098 Children and household living standards. James Banks; Paul Johnson. London: Institute for Fiscal Studies, 1993. 84p. *ISBN: 1873357214.*

F: Population. Family. Gender. Ethnic group

2099 Children in time and place: developmental and historical insights. Glen H. Elder [Ed.]; John Modell [Ed.]; Ross D. Parke [Ed.]. Cambridge, New York, NY: Cambridge University Press, 1993. xiii, 289p. *ISBN: 0521417848. Includes bibliographical references (p. 251-276) and indexes. (Series:* Cambridge studies in social and emotional development).

2100 Children living away from home. Barbara Kahan. **Child. Soc.** 7:1 1993 pp.95 - 108.

2101 Children, rights, and childhood. David Archard. London, New York: Routledge, 1993. 188p. *ISBN: 041508251X, 0415082528. Includes bibliographical references. (Series:* Ideas).

2102 Children who care: inside the world of young carers. Jo Aldridge; Saul Becker. Loughborough, Leicestershire: Loughborough University of Technology, Department of Social Sciences, 1993. 91p. *ISBN: 0907274013.*

2103 Children's lifeworlds: gender, welfare and labour in the developing world. Olga Nieuwenhuys. London, New York: Routledge, 1993. 228p. *ISBN: 0415097509, 0415097517. Includes bibliographical references and index.*

2104 Children's peer relations — a meta-analytic review of popular, rejected, neglected, controversial, and average sociometric status. Andrew F. Newcomb; William M. Bukowski; Linda Pattee. **Psychol . B.** 113:1 1:1993 pp.99 - 128.

2105 Correlates of loneliness in nonreferred and psychiatrically hospitalized children. Robert T. Ammerman; Alan E. Kazdin; Vincent B. Van Hasselt. **J. Child Fam. Stud.** 2:3 9:1993 pp.187 - 202.

2106 The development of self-presentation — self-promotion in 6- to 10-year-old children. Patricia A. Aloise-Young. **Soc. Cogn.** 11:2 Summer:1993 pp.201 - 222.

2107 Do neighborhoods influence child and adolescent development? Jeanne Brooks-Gunn; Greg J. Duncan; Pamela Kato Klebanov; Naomi Sealand. **A.J.S.** 99:2 9:1993 pp.353 - 395.

2108 Estimating the quality of life for children around the world — NICQL '92. Thomas E. Jordan. **Soc. Ind.** 30:1 9:1993 pp.17 - 38.

2109 Goodness personified — the emergence of gifted children. Leslie Margolin. **Soc. Prob.** 40:4 11:1993 pp.510 - 532.

2110 The impact of the national child development study. Ron Davie. **Child. Soc.** 7:1 1993 pp.20 - 36.

2111 Making decisions about children: psychological questions and answers. H. Rudolph Schaffer. Oxford: Blackwell, 1990. xi, 260p. *ISBN: 0631171665, 0631171673. Bibliography: p.241-243; includes indexes. (Series:* Understanding children's worlds).

2112 No place to be a child: growing up in a war zone. James Garbarino; Kathleen Kostelny; Nancy Dubrow. Lexington: Lexington Books, 1991. 177p. *ISBN: 0669244414.*

2113 One scandal too many...: the case for comprehensive protection for children in all settings. Peter Newell [Ed.]. London: Calouste Gulbenkian Foundation, 1993. 225p. *ISBN: 0903319659.*

2114 Passivity in childminded children — problem or prejudice? Helen Barrett; David Jones. **Child. Soc.** 7:3 1993 pp.277 - 289.

2115 Protective factors and behavioral adjustment in preschool children of Iranian martyrs. Mehrdad Kalantari; William Yule; Frances Gardner. **J. Child Fam. Stud.** 2:2 6:1993 pp.97 - 108.

F: Population. Famille. Sexe. Groupe ethnique

2116 Significant harm: its management and outcome. Margaret Adcock [Ed.]; Anne Hollows [Ed.]; Richard White [Ed.]. Croydon: Significant Publications, 1991. 155p.
2117 The state of the child in Ontario. Richard Barnhorst [Ed.]; Laura Climenko Johnson [Ed.]. Toronto: Oxford University Press, 1991. xiii, 206p. *ISBN: 0195408268. Includes bibliographical references and index. Child, Youth and Family Policy Research Centre.*
2118 Temporal experiences and time knowledge in infancy and early childhood. Viviane Pouthas; Sylvie Droit; Anne-Yvonne Jacquet. **Time Soc.** 2:2 1993 pp.199 - 218.
2119 Trends in child health. Caroline Woodroffe; Myer Glickman. **Child. Soc.** 7:1 1993 pp.49 - 63.
2120 The trials of childhood — the development, reliability, and validity of the daily life stressors scale. Christopher A. Kearney; Ronald S. Drabman; Julie F. Beasley. **J. Child Fam. Stud.** 2:4 12:1993 pp.371 - 388.
2121 Under fives — thirty years of no progress. Sonia Jackson. **Child. Soc.** 7:1 1993 pp.64 - 81.
2122 Uwarunkowania występowania niskiej masy urodzeniowej noworodków rodzonych przez nastolatki w Polsce. *[In Polish]*; (Biodemographic determinants of low birthweight of babies born by teenagers in Poland.) *[Summary]*. Katarzyna Szamotulska. **Stud. Demogr.** 2 (108) 1992 pp.43 - 56.
2123 Videotaped versus in-court witness testimony — does protecting the child witness jeopardize due process? Janet K. Swim; Eugene Borgida; Kathy McCoy. **J. Appl. Soc. Psychol.** 23:8 4:1993 pp.603 - 631.
2124 Working with children and the Children Act: a practical guide for the helping professions. Martin Herbert. Leicester: BPS Books, 1993. 230p. *ISBN: 1854330934.*

Youth
Jeunesse

2125 Adolescence. Jacquelynne S. Eccles [Contrib.]; Carol Midgley [Contrib.]; Allan Wigfield [Contrib.]; Christy Miller Buchanan [Contrib.]; David Reuman [Contrib.]; Constance Flanagan [Contrib.]; Douglas MacIver [Contrib.]; Marilyn Jacobs Quadrel [Contrib.]; Baruch Fischhoff [Contrib.]; Wendy Davis [Contrib.]; Richard Jessor [Contrib.]; Alan E. Kazdin [Contrib.]; W. Rodney Hammond [Contrib.]; Betty Yung [Contrib.]; Anne C. Petersen [Contrib.]; Bruce E. Compas [Contrib.]; Jeanne Brooks-Gunn [Contrib.]; Mark Stemmler [Contrib.]; Sydney Ey [Contrib.]; Kathryn E. Grant [Contrib.]; Ann F. Garland [Contrib.]; Edward Zigler [Contrib.]; Gary L. Ackerman [Contrib.]; Martha J. Zaslow [Contrib.]; Ruby Takanishi [Contrib.]; Denise M. Dougherty [Contrib.]. **Am. Psychol.** 48:2 2:1993 pp.90 - 201. *Collection of 10 articles.*
2126 Adolescent female educational and occupational attainment. S. Wilson; G. Peterson; P. Wilson. **J. Marriage Fam.** 55:1 2:1993 pp.158 - 175.
2127 Arbeitslosigkeit und Lebensgeschichte: eine empirische Untersuchung unter jungen Langzeitarbeitslosen. *[In German]*; [Unemployment and life histories: an empirical investigation into young people that have been out of work for a long time]. Gerd Vonderach; Ruth Siebers; Ulrich Barr. Opladen: Leske + Budrich, 1992. 217p. *ISBN: 3810009881. Bibliography: p. 205-217.*

F: Population. Family. Gender. Ethnic group

2128 Biosocial models of adolescent problem behavior — extension to panel design. Stephen M. Drigotas; J. Richard Udry. **Soc. Biol.** 40:1-2 Spring-Summer:1993 pp.1 - 7.

2129 Black youth in crisis: facing the future. David Everatt [Ed.]; Community Agency for Social Enquiry South Africa; Elinor Sisulu [Ed.]. Braamfontein: Ravan Press, 1992. 89p. *ISBN: 0869754297. Includes bibliographical references.*

2130 Bushels of rubles: Soviet youth in transition. Kitty D. Weaver. Westport, Conn: Praeger, 1992. vi, 215p. *ISBN: 0275938441. Includes bibliographical references (p. 197-210) and indexes.*

2131 De jovenes y sus identidades: socioantropologia de la etnicidad en Euskadi. *[In Spanish]*; [Youth and their identity: the social anthropology of ethnicity in the Basque Country]. Eugenia Ramirez Goicoechea. Madrid: Siglo XXI de España Editores : Centro de Investigaciones Sociológicas, 1991. 440p. *ISBN: 8474761514.*

2132 De markt van vermaak en plezier. Over het ontstaan van een zelfstandige jeugdcultuur in België en Nederland. *[In Dutch]*; (The market of leisure and pleasure — the rise of an autonomous youth culture in Belgium and the Netherlands.) *[Summary]*. Henk Kleijer; Rudi Laermans; Ger Tillekens. **Sociol. Gids** XXXIX:5-6 9-12:1992 pp.384 - 399.

2133 Des jeunes en quête d'identité, Michael Jackson et ses fans à Bucarest. *[In French]*; [The young in search of an identity, Michael Jackson and his fans in Bucharest]. Costel Olaru. **Civilisations** LXII:2 12:1993 pp.249 - 254.

2134 Factores de riesgo de embarazo adolescente en el Paraguay. *[In Spanish]*; [The risk factors of adolescent pregnancies in Paraguay]. Edith Alejandra Pantelldes; Georgina Binstock. **Rev. Parag. Sociol.** 30:87 5-8:1993 pp.171 - 186.

2135 The family and peer relations of adolescents. P. Giordano; S. Cernkovich; A. DeMaris. **J. Marriage Fam.** 55:2 5:1993 pp.277 - 287.

2136 Growing up in the Federal Republic of Germany: chance and risk in a modern sozialstaat. René Bendit; Wolfgang Gaiser; Ursula Nissen. **J. Educ. Pol.** 8:1 1-2:1993 pp.43 - 60.

2137 Growing up with unemployment: a longitudinal study of its psychological impact. Anthony Harold Winefield. New York; London: Routledge, 1993. 200p. *ISBN: 0415074541, 041507455X. Includes bibliographical references and indexes. (Series:* Adolescence and society).

2138 Les jeunes des communautés culturelles. *[In French]*; (Youth from cultural communities.) *[Summary]*. Élena Alvarado. **San. Ment. Qué** XVII:1 Printemps:1993 pp.211 - 226.

2139 Jugend im deutsch-deutschen Vergleich: Die Lebenslage der jungen Generation im Jahr der Vereinigung. *[In German]*; [A comparison of youth in the two German nations: the living conditions of the young generation in the year of reunification]. Georg Neubauer [Ed.]; Wolfgang Melzer [Ed.]; Klaus Hurrelmann [Ed.]. Neuwied: Luchterhand, 1992. 214p. *ISBN: 3472010509. Includes bibliographical references (p. 207-214).*

2140 Jugend in der DDR: Daten und Ergebnisse der Jugendforschung vor der Wende. *[In German]*; [Youth in the GDR: data and results of youth research before political reform]. Werner Hennig [Ed.]; Walter Friedrich [Ed.]. Weinheim: Juventa, 1991. 243p. *ISBN: 3779904187. Includes bibliographical references (p. 236-243). Zentralinstitut für Jugendforschung.*

F: Population. Famille. Sexe. Groupe ethnique

2141 Jugendhilfe in Deutschland und Spanien. *[In German]*; [Youth in Germany in Spain]. Franz Hamburger; Rosario Alonso Alonso; Markus Höffer-Mehlmer. Rheinfelden: Schäuble, 1992. 155p. *ISBN: 387718586X*.

2142 Jugendliche Flüchtlinge in Heimen der Jugendhilfe: Situation und Zukunftsperspektiven. *[In German]*; [Young refugees in group homes for youth: current situation and future prospects]. Hans-Dieter Heun; Heide Kallert; Clemens Bacherl. Freiburg im Breisgau: Lambertus, 1992. 189p. *ISBN: 3784106366*. *Bibliography: p. 180-188.*

2143 Leaving care and after. Louise Garnett. London: National Children's Bureau, 1992. 132p. *ISBN: 090281799X*.

2144 Losing generations: adolescents in high-risk settings. National Research Council U.S Panel on High-Risk Youth. Washington, D.C: National Academy Press, 1993. ix, 276p. *ISBN: 0309048281*. *Includes bibliographical references and index.*

2145 The majority fallacy reconsidered. Willy Pedersen. **Acta Sociol.** 36:4 1993 pp.343 - 356.

2146 Neue Lebenswelt - neue Medienwelt? Jugendliche aus der Ex- und Post-DDR im Transfer zu einer vereinten Medienkultur. *[In German]*; [A new world for us and for the media? Youth from the former and post-unification GDR in the transition to a united media culture]. Bernd Schorb [Ed.]; Hans-Jörg Stiehler [Ed.]. Opladen: Leske + Budrich, 1991. 162p. *ISBN: 3810009407*. *Includes bibliographical references (p. 157-160).*

2147 Nonsuicidal physically self-damaging acts in adolescents. Carol Z. Garrison; Cheryl L. Addy; Robert E. McKeown; Steven P. Cuffe; Kirby L. Jackson; Jennifer L. Waller. **J. Child Fam. Stud.** 2:4 12:1993 pp.339 - 352.

2148 On the waves — a new kind of surf in Rio de Janeiro. José Arthur Rios. **Cr. Law Soc. Chan.** 20:2 9:1993 pp.161 - 175.

2149 Organized youth sports and the psychological development of nine-year-old males. Richard W. Seidel; N. Dickon Reppucci. **J. Child Fam. Stud.** 2:3 9:1993 pp.229 - 248.

2150 Osteuropäische Jugend im Wandel: Ergebnisse vergleichender Jugendforschung in der Sowjetunion, Polen, Ungarn und der ehemaligen DDR. *[In German]*; [Eastern European youth in transition: the results of comparative youth research in the USSR, Poland, Hungary and the former GDR]. Wolfgang Melzer [Ed.]. Weinheim: Juventa Verlag, 1991. 268p. *ISBN: 3779904195*. *Includes bibliographical references.*

2151 Parental behavior and tobacco use by young males. J. Melby; R. Conger; K. Conger; F. Lorenz. **J. Marriage Fam.** 55:2 5:1993 pp.439 - 454.

2152 Patterns and correlates of learning, behavior, and emotional problems of adolescents with and without serious emotional disturbance. Edward J. Sabornie; Douglas Cullinan; Michael H. Epstein. **J. Child Fam. Stud.** 2:2 6:1993 pp.159 - 175.

2153 Prévalence des attitudes et comportements inadaptés face à l'alimentation chez les adolescentes de la région de Montréal. *[In French]*; (Prevalence of unhealthy attitudes and behaviour of adolescent girls in regard to eating habits.) *[Summary]*. Daniel Bolduc; Howard Steiger; Freedom Leung. **San. Ment. Qué** XVIII:2 Autumn:1993 pp.183 - 196.

2154 Psychische Probleme von jungen Türken in Deutschland: psychiatrische Auffälligkeit von ausländischen Jungendlichen in der Adoleszenz, Schwerpunkt türkische Jungendliche ; eine epidemiologische Längsschnittunterssuchung. *[In German]*; [The psychological problems of young Turks in Germany: psychiatric conspicuousness of

F: Population. Family. Gender. Ethnic group

foreign adolescents, especially Turkish youths; an epidemiological longitudinal study]. Susanne Schlüter-Müller. Eschborn bei Frankfurt am Main: Dietmar Klotz, 1992. 89p. *ISBN: 3880742480.*

2155 Rave off: politics and deviance in contemporary youth culture. Steve Redhead [Ed.]. Aldershot: Avebury, 1993. 192p. *ISBN: 1856284654.* (*Series:* Popular cultural studies).

2156 Religiosity and adolescents' premarital sexual attitudes and behaviour — an empirical study of conceptual issues. P. Sheeran; D. Abrams; C. Abraham; R. Spears. **Eur. J. Soc. Psychol.** 23:1 1-2:1993 pp.39 - 52.

2157 Religiosity and delinquency among LDS adolescents. Bruce A. Chadwick; Brent L. Top. **J. Sci. S. Relig.** 32:1 3:1993 pp.51 - 67.

2158 Rites d'exhibition d'une adolescene marginale. Du rock au rap. *[In French]*; [The exhibition rites of a marginal adolescence. From rock to rap]. Claude Riviére. **Social. Int.** 31:1 1993 pp.63 - 82.

2159 Shut up and dance — youth culture and changing modes of femininity. Angela McRobbie. **Cult. St.** 7:3 10:1993 pp.406 - 426.

2160 [Social and political consciousness of the young in former D.D.R.: 1970s as a turning point]; *[Text in Japanese].* Takashi Kurihara. **J. Int. Rel.** 3(1) 1993 pp.41 - 75.

2161 Social bonds and teen pregnancy. LaWanda Ravoira; Andrew L. Cherry. Westport, Conn: Praeger, 1992. xvi, 175p. *ISBN: 0275941795. Includes bibliographical references (p. [161]-169) and index.*

2162 Social context and adolescent behavior — the impact of community on the transition to sexual activity. Karin L. Brewster; John O.G. Billy; William R. Grady. **Soc. Forc.** 71:3 3:1993 pp.713 - 740.

2163 Socialisatie, jeugd en levensloop. *[In Dutch]*; [Socialization, youth and the course of life]. Cees A.C. Klaassen [Ed.]; Henk Kleijer [Ed.]; Els Peters [Contrib.]; Erwin van Rooijen [Contrib.]; Harry Guit [Contrib.]; Aart C. Liefbroer [Contrib.]; Liesbeth Gerritsen [Contrib.]; Jenny de Jong Gierveld [Contrib.]; Karin Wittebrood [Contrib.]; Peter Cuyvers [Contrib.]; Frank von Meijenfeldt [Contrib.]; Haiee van Houten [Contrib.]; Frans Meijers [Contrib.]; Laurenz Veendrick [Contrib.]; Ger Tillekens [Contrib.]. **Sociol. Gids** 40.2 3-4:1993 pp.82 - 194. *Collection of 7 articles.*

2164 Socjologia młodzieży — nowy kierunek orientacji badawczej Zakładu Socjologii Ogólnej UŁ w latach osiemdziesiątych. *[In Polish]*; (Sociology of youth — new trend in research of chair of general sociology in the 1980.) *[Summary].* Wielisława Warzywoda-Kruszyńska. **Prz. Soc.** XL 1993 pp.73 - 84.

2165 Street youths, Bosozoku, and Vakuza — subculture formation and societal reactions in Japan. Joachim Kersten. **Crime Delin.** 39:3 7:1993 pp.277 - 295.

2166 Talented teenagers: the roots of success and failure. Mihaly Csikszentmihalyi; Kevin Raymond Rathunde; Maria Wong [Contrib.]; Samuel Whalen. Cambridge, New York: Cambridge University Press, 1993. x, 307p. *ISBN: 0521415780. Includes bibliographical references (p. 287-298) and index.*

2167 Those practical U.S.A. pants. Tom O'Dell. **Nord. Ny.** 53 1993 pp.41 - 55.

2168 Les troubles du comportement parmi les 13-16 ans selon la zone d'habitation. Approche épidémiologique. *[In French]*; (Behavioural problems among 13-16 year olds and housing zones. An epidemiological approach.). Marie Choquet; Hede Menke; Sylvie Ledoux; Robert Menfredi. **Population** 48:1 1-2:1993 pp.63 - 82.

F: Population. Famille. Sexe. Groupe ethnique

2169 Understanding youth: issues and methods in social education. David Marsland. St Albans: Claridge P, 1993. 252p. *ISBN: 1870626737*.

2170 Unter anderen: Rassismus und Jugendarbeit: zur Entwicklung angemessener Begriffe und Ansätze für eine verändernde Praxis (nicht nur) in der Arbeit mit Jugendlichen. *[In German]*; [Amongst others: racism and youth work: on the development of suitable concepts and approaches to a revised practice in working (not only) with young people]. Rudolf Leiprecht [Ed.]; Robert Miles [Contrib.]; et al. Duisburg: Deutsches Institut für Sprach-und Sozialforschung, 1992. 214p. *ISBN: 3-927388-33-5. Arbeitsgemeinschaft Jugendfreizeitstätten Ba Wü e.V.*.

2171 Young people in a changing society: The Netherlands. Manuela du Bois-Reymond; Ineke van der Zande. **J. Educ. Pol.** 8:1 1-2:1993 pp.61 - 72.

2172 Young people's leisure and lifestyles. Leo Brough Hendry [Ed.]. New York; London: Routledge, 1993. 209p. *ISBN: 0415043492. Includes bibliographical references and index. (Series:* Adolescence and society).

2173 Youth and inequality. Inge Bates [Ed.]; George Riseborough [Ed.]. Buckingham, England, Philadelphia, Pa: Open University Press, 1993. xi, 249p. *ISBN: 0335156959. Includes bibliographical references and index.*

2174 Youth and society in Chile. Alain Touraine. **Int. Soc. Sci. J.** 137 8:1993 pp.421 - 428.

2175 Youth drinking in Micronesia. Francis X.; S.J. Hezel. **J. Pacific Soc.** 15:4(57) 1:1993 pp.1 - 8.

2176 Youth transitions in Britain on the threshold of a 'new Europe'. Lynne Chisholm. **J. Educ. Pol.** 8:1 1-2:1993 pp.29 - 42.

2177 Zhiznennye puti odnogo pokoleniia. *[In Russian]*; [The life experiences of one generation]. M. Kh Titma. Moskva: Nauka, 1992. 184p. *ISBN: 5020134546. Includes bibliographical references.*

2178 Zwischen Aufstieg und Ausstieg: autoritäre Einstellungsmuster bei Judgendlichen / jungen Erwachsenen. *[In German]*; [Between climbing up or getting out: an authoritarian pattern of attitudes amongst youth / young adults]. Dieter Hoffmeister; Oliver Sill. Opladen: Leske + Budrich, 1992. 173p. *ISBN: 3810009202*.

F.3: **Demographic trends and population policy**
Tendances démographiques et politique démographique

2179 Les années 80 — les tendances démographiques inversées. *[In French]*; [The 80s — inverted demographic tendencies]. Thérèse Huissoud. **Schw. Z. Volk. Stat.** 128:3 9:1992 pp.383 - 397.

2180 Birth order effects on time allocation. Nancy Birdsall. **Res. Popul. Econ.** 7 1991 pp.191 - 213.

2181 Causes and implications of the recent increase in the reported sex ratio at birth in China. Zeng Yi; Tu Ping; Gu Baochang; Xu Yi; Li Bohua; Li Yongping. **Pop. Dev. Rev.** 19:2 6:1993 pp.283 - 302.

2182 Changing causes of death and the sex differential in the U.S.A. — recent trends and projections. Christin Knudsen; Robert McNown. **Pop. Res. Pol. R.** 12:1 1993 pp.27 - 41.

2183 Demograficzne korelaty rozwodów. *[In Polish]*; (Demographic correlates of divorce.) *[Summary]*. Paweł Rydzewski. **Stud. Demogr.** 1(107) 1992 pp.25 - 37.

F: Population. Family. Gender. Ethnic group

2184 Demographic change in nonmetropolitian America, 1980 to 1990. Kenneth M. Johnson. **Rural Sociol.** 58:3 Fall:1993 pp.347 - 365.

2185 Demographic profile of an Orissa village. Sujit Som. **Man India** 73:1 3:1993 pp.49 - 63.

2186 Demographic trends and patterns in the Soviet Union before 1991. Wolfgang Lutz; Sergei Scherbov [Ed.]; Andrei Volkov [Ed.]. London: Routledge, 1993. 496p. *ISBN: 0415101948.*

2187 Effects of oestrogen changes during menstrual cycle on spatial performance. Irwin Silverman; Krista Phillips. **Ethol. Socio.** 14:4 1993 pp.257 - 270.

2188 Food security, population, and environment; *[Summary in French]*; *[Summary in Spanish]*. Paul R. Ehrlich; Anne H. Ehrlich; Gretchen C. Daily. **Pop. Dev. Rev.** 19:1 3:1993 pp.1 - 32.

2189 L'héritage de l'indépendance professionnelle selon les lignées, le sexe et le rang dans la fratrie. *[In French]*; (The transmission of independant occupation between different generations by sex and birth order.) *[Summary]*. Bernard Zarca. **Population** 48:2 3-4:1993 pp.275 - 306.

2190 Human sex ratio as it relates to caloric availability. Robert J. Williams; Susan P. Gloster. **Soc. Biol.** 39:3-4 Fall-Winter:1992 pp.285 - 291.

2191 International evidence on the role of literacy in the demographic transition. Lawrence W. Kenny. **Res. Popul. Econ.** 7 1991 pp.113 - 128.

2192 Perspektiven der Künftigen Bevöikerungsentwicklung in Deutschland. Teil 1 — Fakten und Hypothesen. *[In German]*; [Prospects for future demograhic change in Germany. Part 1 — Facts and hypotheses]. Erika Schulz [Contrib.]; Josef Schmid [Contrib.]; Harmut Wendt [Contrib.]; Detlef Chruscz [Contrib.]; Franz-Josef Kemper [Contrib.]; Günter Thieme [Contrib.]; Clemens Geißler [Contrib.]; Dirk Heuwinkel [Contrib.]; Hans-Joachim Kujath [Contrib.]; Herbert Schubert [Contrib.]; Manfred Thebes [Contrib.]; Siegfried Grundmann [Contrib.]; Wolfram Ledenig [Contrib.]; Rainer Mackensen [Contrib.]; Ferdinand Böltken [Contrib.]; Hans-Joachim Hoffmann-Nowotny [Contrib.]; Bernd Knabe [Contrib.]; Martin Frey [Contrib.]. **Inf. Raum.** 9/10 1992 pp.669 - 778. *Collection of 13 articles.*

2193 Populační vývoj v ČSFR v roce 1992. *[In Czech]*; (Population development in the Czechoslovak Federal Republic in 1992.). Milan Alcš. **Demografie** XXXV:4 1993 pp.225 - 235.

2194 Population geography — disorder, death and future directions. Allan M. Findlay. **Prog. H. Geog.** 17:1 3:1993 pp.73 - 83.

2195 Population policies in the countries of the Gulf Co-operation Council — politics and society. Baquer Salman Al-Najjar. **Imm. Minor.** 12:2 7:1993 pp.200 - 218.

2196 Porządkowanie dendrytowe oraz hierarchizacja drzewkowa krajów europejskich ze względu na poziom rozwoju demograficznego. *[In Polish]*; (Dendrite ordering and tree classification of European countries with respect to demographic development.) *[Summary]*. Józef Pociecha. **Stud. Demogr.** 1(107) 1992 pp.3 - 24.

2197 La relocalización de poblaciones en el marco de las ciencias sociales. *[In Spanish]*; (The relocation of populations within the social sciences.) *[Summary]*. Alicia M. Barabas. **Am. Indígena** LII:1-2 1-6:1992 pp.303 - 320.

2198 The social implications of population displacement and resettlement — an overview with a focus on the Arab Middle East. Seteney Shami. **Int. Migr. Rev.** XXVII:1 Spring:1993 pp.4 - 33.

F: Population. Famille. Sexe. Groupe ethnique

2199 Structures démographiques et fécondité urbaine. *[In French]*; [Demographic structures and urban fertility]. Patrick Gubry; Valérie Guérin. **Afr. Cont.** 168 10-12:1993 pp.125 - 137.

2200 Struktura ludności według wieku w krajach Europy Wschodniej. Tendencje długookresowe. *[In Polish]*; (Population's age structure in the countries of Eastern Europe. The long-term tendencies.) *[Summary]*. Alicja Maksimowicz-Ajchel. **Stud. Demogr.** 4(102) 1990 pp.3 - 24.

2201 Towards renewed fears of population and family decline?; *[Summary in French]*. Anne Hélène Gauthier. **Eur. J. Pop.** 9:2 1993 pp.143 - 167.

2202 Urbanisation, population mobility and the evolution of cultural prejudice — some speculations on the geography of ignorance and the growth of national identity. D.J. Siddle. **Geog.ann. B.** 74B:3 1992 pp.155 - 166.

2203 When deaths exceed births — natural decrease in the United States. Kenneth M. Johnson. **Int. Reg. Sci. R.** 15:2 1993 pp.179 - 198.

2204 Zachowania demograficzne jako efekt procesu podejmowania decyzji — próba opisu. *[In Polish]*; (Demographic behaviour as an effect of decision-making process — an attempt to description.) *[Summary]*. Janina Jóźwiak; Tomasz Szapiro. **Stud. Demogr.** 2(100) 1990 pp.3 - 17.

Family planning
Planification de la famille

2205 Abortion on Guam — demographic trends and fertility data. Ann M. Workman; Randall L. Workman; Linda Cruz-Ortiz. **J. Micrones. Stud.** 1:2 Dry season:1992 pp.183 - 198.

2206 Abortion regimes. Kerry Anne Petersen. Aldershot, England, Brookfield, Vt: Dartmouth, 1993. 203p. *ISBN: 1855211599*. *(Series:* Medico-legal*)*.

2207 Adolescents and family planning — the case of Zambia. Vijayan K. Pillai; Paul P.W. Achola; Thomas Barton. **Popul. R.** 37:1-2 1-12:1993 pp.11 - 20.

2208 L'avortement en Pologne: la croix et la bannière. *[In French]*; [Abortion in Poland: the cross and the banner]. Jacqueline Heinen; Anna Matuchniak-Krasuska. France: L'Harmattan, 1992. 239p. *ISBN: 2738415857*.

2209 Babies for sale. Robin Fox. **Publ. Inter.** 111 Spring:1993 pp.14 - 40.

2210 Between two absolutes: public opinion and the politics of abortion. Elizabeth Adell Cook; Ted G. Jelen; William Clyde Wilcox. Boulder: Westview Press, 1992. xvii, 236p. *ISBN: 0813382866, 0813382874*. *Includes bibliographical references (p. [219]-228) and index.*

2211 The contraceptive pill and women's employment as factors in fertility change in Britain 1963-1980 — a challenge to the conventional view. Michael Murphy. **Pop. Stud.** 47:2 7:1993 pp.221 - 243.

2212 Contraceptive risk-taking in a medically underserved low-income population. Stephen E. Radecki; Linda J. Beckman. **Soc. Biol.** 40:3-4 Fall-winter:1993 pp.248 - 259.

2213 Corrrelates of family planning acceptance — a multivariate analysis. K. Sivaswamy Srikantan; Sanjeevanee Mulay; Anjali Radkar. **Art. Vij.** XXXIV:2 6:1992 pp.163 - 181.

F: Population. Family. Gender. Ethnic group

2214 A couple analysis of micro-level supply/demand factors in fertility regulation. F. Nii-Amoo Dodoo. **Pop. Res. Pol. R.** 12:2 1993 pp.93 - 101.

2215 Demograficzny wymiar aborcji. *[In Polish]*; (Demographic dimension of abortion.). Janina Jóźwiak; Jan Paradysz. **Stud. Demogr.** 1(111) 1993 pp.31 - 42.

2216 The diffusion of fertility control in Taiwan — evidence from pooled cross-section time-series models. Mark R. Montgomery; John B. Casterline. **Pop. Stud.** 47:3 11:1993 pp.457 - 480.

2217 Disembodying women: perspectives on pregnancy and the unborn. Barbara Duden; Lee Hoinacki [Ed.]. Cambridge, Mass., London: Harvard University Press, 1993. 126p. *ISBN: 0674212673. Translated from the German L. Hoinacki.*

2218 La donna italiana e la procreazione: situazione e scenari alternativi. *[In Italian]*; [The Italian woman and procreation: current situation and alternative scenarios]. Maria Grazia Piazza. Rome: Edizioni Dehoniane, 1993. 218p. *ISBN: 8839604804.*

2219 Essai de reconstitution de la pratique contraceptive en Algérie durant la période 1967-1987. *[In French]*; (A study of contraceptive practice in Algeria, 1967-1987.) *[Summary]*. Ali Kouaouci. **Population** 48:4 7-8:1993 pp.859 - 884.

2220 Estado e população: uma história do planejamento familiar no Brasil. *[In Portuguese]*; [State and population: a history of family planning in Brazil]. Délcio da Fonseca Sobrinho. Rio de Janeiro: Rosas dos Tempos, FNUAP, 1993. 203p. *ISBN: 858536369X. Includes bibliographical references (p. [193]-201).*

2221 The facts of life: science and the abortion controversy. Harold J. Morowitz; James S. Trefil. New York: Oxford University Press, 1992. xi, 179p. *ISBN: 0195079272. Includes bibliographical references (p. 169-174) and index.*

2222 Family planning and reproductive health. Malini Karkal. **Indian J. Soc. W.** LIV:2 4:1993 pp.297 - 306.

2223 Fertility and contraceptive use in poor urban areas of developing countries. Masuma Mamdani; Paul Garner; Trudy Harpman; Oona Campbell. **Health Pol. Plan.** 8:1 3:1993 pp.1 - 18.

2224 Genetic risk and reproduction. Evelyn Parsons; Paul Atkinson. **Sociol. Rev.** 41:4 11:1993 pp.679 - 706.

2225 The hidden agenda — abortion politics in Israel. Yael Yishai. **J. Soc. Pol.** 22:2 4:1993 pp.193 - 212.

2226 Life's dominion: an argument about abortion and euthanasia. Ronald Dworkin. London: HarperCollins, 1993. 272p. *ISBN: 0002159341.*

2227 Measurement of the quality of family planning services. James Veney; Robert Magnani; Pamina Gorbach. **Pop. Res. Pol. R.** 12:3 1993 pp.243 - 260.

2228 Medical technology assessment — a useful occupation or useless diversion? Janine Marie Morgall. **Wom. St. Inter. For.** 16:6 11-12:1993 pp.591 - 604.

2229 Medyczne następstwa przerywania ciąży. *[In Polish]*; (Medical consequences of induced abortion.). Bogdan Chazan. **Stud. Demogr.** 1(111) 1993 pp.103 - 112.

2230 A new look at the determinants of non-numeric response to desired family size — the case of Costa Rica. Ann P. Riley; Albert I. Hermalin; Luis Rosero-Bixby. **Demography** 30:2 5:1993 pp.159 - 174.

2231 The pattern of reproductive life in a Berber population of Morocco. Emile Crognier; Cristina Bernis; Silvia Elizondo; Carlos Varea. **Soc. Biol.** 40:3-4 Fall-winter:1993 pp.191 - 199.

2232 Preventing adolescent pregnancy: model programs and evaluations. Brent C. Miller; et al. Newbery Park, Calif: Sage Publications, 1992. viii, 296p. *ISBN: 0803943903,*

F: Population. Famille. Sexe. Groupe ethnique

0803943911. Includes bibliographical references and index. (*Series:* Sage focus editions).

2233 Problem aborcji na tle postaw i zachowań w zakresie regulacji urodzeń (wyniki ankietowego badania przemian rodziny i wzorców dzietności). *[In Polish]*; (Abortion problem against a background of contraceptive attitudes and behaviors (results of fertility and family survey).). Irena Kowalska. **Stud. Demogr.** 1(111) 1993 pp.43 - 86.

2234 Progress postponed: abortion in Europe in the 1990s. Karen Newman [Ed.]. London: International Planned Parenthood Federation, 1993. 173p. *ISBN: 0904983188*.

2235 Public attitudes toward fetal diagnosis and the termination of life. E. Singer. **Soc. Ind.** 28:2 2:1993 pp.117 - 136.

2236 Quality of care in family planning programmes — a rapid assessment in Burkina Faso. Ian Askew; Placide Tapsoba; Youssouf Ouédraogo; Claire Viadro; Didier Bakouan; Pascaline Sebago. **Health Pol. Plan.** 8:1 3:1993 pp.19 - 32.

2237 The regulation of reproduction — the relevance of public opinion for legislative policy formation. Charlene Miall. **Int. J. Law Fam.** 7:1 1993 pp.18 - 39.

2238 Reproductive technologies and the U.S. courts. Kim M. Blankenship; Beth Rushing; Suzanne Onorato; Renée White. **Gender Soc.** 7:1 3:1993 pp.8 - 31.

2239 Secrecy and openness in donor insemination. Ken R. Daniels; Karin Taylor; Rona Achilles [Comments by]; Eleonora Bielawska-Batorowicz [Comments by]; Annette Burfoot [Comments by]; Ian D. Cooke [Comments by]; Erica Haimes [Comments by]; Helen Bequaert Holmes [Comments by]; Bartha Maria Knoppers [Comments by]; Jacques Lansac [Comments by]; Judith N. Lasker [Comments by]; Alexina M. McWhinnie [Comments by]; Barbara Raboy [Comments by]; Robyn Rowland [Comments by]; Robert Snowden [Comments by]; John Triseliotis [Comments by]; Candace Turner [Comments by]. **Polit. Life** 12:2 8:1993 pp.155 - 203.

2240 Sexual behaviour and the acceptability of condoms to Ugandan males. Charles B. Rwabukwali. **E.Afr. Soc. Sci. Res. R.** VIII:1 1:1992 pp.33 - 45.

2241 Son preference and the one child policy in China: 1979-1988. Jiali Li; Rosemary Santana Cooney. **Pop. Res. Pol. R.** 12:3 1993 pp.277 - 296.

2242 "Surrogate mothering" and women's freedom — a critique of contracts for human reproduction. Mary Lyndon Shanley. **Signs** 18:3 Spring:1993 pp.618 - 639.

2243 Understanding the new politics of abortion. Malcolm L. Goggin [Ed.]. Newbury Park: Sage Publications, 1993. 323p. *ISBN: 0803952406*.

2244 Zmiany wzorcćow zachowań prokreacyjnych w ujęciu międzygeneracyjnym. *[In Polish]*; (Changing patterns of reproductive attitudes in intergenerational approach.) *[Summary]*. Hanna Augustyniak. **Stud. Demogr.** 2 (108) 1992 pp.21 - 42.

Fertility
Fécondité

2245 Appraisals of childbirth experience and newborn characteristics — the role of hardiness and affect. Beatrice Priel; Nilly Gonik; Betty Rabinowitz. **J. Personal.** 61:3 9:1993 pp.299 - 315.

2246 Betrachtungen zur Sexualproportion der Geborenen in der Bundesrepublik Deutschland. *[In German]*; (Studies of the sexual proportion of births in the Federal

F: Population. Family. Gender. Ethnic group

      Republic of Germany.). Erhard Förster. **Wissensch. Z. Humboldt-Univ.** 41:2 1992 pp.25 - 30.
2247 Biological and demographic determinants of reproduction. Ronald H. Gray [Ed.]; Henri Leridon [Ed.]; Alfred Spira. Oxford: Clarendon Press, 1992. xxi, 482p. *Includes bibliographical references and index. (Series:* International studies in demography).
2248 Birth intervals, gestational age, and low birth weight — are the relationships confounded? James Gribble. **Pop. Stud.** 47:1 3:1993 pp.133 - 146.
2249 Calculating cohort TFR from truncated distributions by completed parity. Nick Dworak; Karen Kirmeyer. **Stud. Demogr.** 4(106) 1991 pp.35 - 43.
2250 Causes and consequences of fertility decline in Western Europe. Seamus Grimes. **Administration** 41:1 Spring:1993 pp.57 - 71.
2251 Childless, no choice: the experience of involuntary childlessness. James H. Monach. London; New York: Routledge, 1993. 274p. *ISBN: 0415040906. Includes bibliographical references and index.*
2252 The compatibility of employment and childbearing in contemporary Sweden. Britta Hoem. **Acta Sociol.** 36:2 1993 pp.101 - 120.
2253 Cultural and economic approaches to fertility — proper marriage or mésalliance? Robert A. Pollak; Susan Cotts Watkins. **Pop. Dev. Rev.** 19:3 9:1993 pp.467 - 496.
2254 Cultural and reproductive success in industrial societies — testing the relationship at the proximate and ultimate levels. D. Pérusse. **Behav. Brain Sci.** 16:2 6:1993 pp.267 - 322.
2255 Cultural influences on the timing of first births in India — large differences that add up to little difference. Alaka Malwade Basu. **Pop. Stud.** 47:1 3:1993 pp.85 - 95.
2256 Determinants of fertility in urban and rural Kenya — estimates and a simulation of the impact of education policy. D.E. Hyatt; W.J. Milne. **Envir. Plan. A.** 25:3 3:1993 pp.371 - 382.
2257 Determinants of marital fertility in Pakistan: an application of the "synthesis framework". Mohammed Sabihuddin Butt; Haroon Jamal. **Pak. Dev. R.** 32:2 Summer:1993 pp.199 - 220.
2258 Development, urbanization and fertility in China. Li Li; John A. Ballweg. **Social Soc. Res.** 76:3 4.1992 pp.111 - 117.
2259 The dynamics of marital bargaining in male infertility. Judith Lorber; Lakshmi Bandlamudi. **Gender Soc.** 7:1 3:1993 pp.32 - 49.
2260 An economic analysis of teenage fertility in Oklahoma. W.L. Davis; K.W. Olson; L. Warner. **Am. J. Econ. S.** 52:1 1:1993 pp.85 - 99.
2261 The economic determinants of fertility — an analysis based on the 1980 U.S. census of population. Avery M. Horowitz. **Popul. R.** 37:1-2 1-12:1993 pp.52 - 63.
2262 Economic models of fertility dynamics — a study of Swedish fertility. James J. Heckman; James R. Walker. **Res. Popul. Econ.** 7 1991 pp.3 - 91.
2263 The effects of children's schooling on fertility limitation. William G. Axinn. **Pop. Stud.** 47:3 11:1993 pp.481 - 494.
2264 Effects of interpregnancy intervals on preterm birth, intrauterine growth retardation, and fetal loss. Jeffrey E. Kallan. **Soc. Biol.** 39:3-4 Fall-Winter:1992 pp.231 - 245.
2265 Effects of socio-demographic variables on birth intervals in Ghana; *[Summary in French]; [Summary in Spanish]*. Yaw Oheneba-Sakyi; Tim B. Heaton. **J. Comp. Fam. Stud.** XXIV:1 Spring:1993 pp.113 - 135.

F: Population. Famille. Sexe. Groupe ethnique

2266 Emergence of fertility differentials as evidence of fertility decline in India. K. Balasubramanian. **Art. Vij.** XXXIV:2 6:1992 pp.182 - 199.

2267 Enduring effects of women's early employment experiences on child-spacing — the Canadian evidence. Bali Ram; Abdur Rahim. **Pop. Stud.** 47:2 7:1993 pp.307 - 317.

2268 Equality and fertility in the kibbutz. L. Danziger; S. Neuman. **J. Pop. Ec.** 6:1 1993 pp.57 - 66.

2269 Fertility among Central American refugees and immigrants in Belize. Nancy Moss; Michael C. Stone; Jason B. Smith. **Human. Org.** 52:2 Summer:1993 pp.186 - 193.

2270 Fertility and contraceptive use in poor urban areas of developing countries. Masuma Mamdani; Paul Garner; Trudy Harpman; Oona Campbell. **Health Pol. Plan.** 8:1 3:1993 pp.1 - 18.

2271 Fertility and employment. Eva M. Bernhardt. **Eur. Sociol. R.** 9:1 5:1993 pp.25 - 42.

2272 Fertility and family planning among the elderly in Taiwan or integrating the demography of aging into population studies. Albert I. Hermalin. **Demography** 30:4 11:1993 pp.507 - 518.

2273 Fertility and social change in Oman — women's perspectives. Christine Eickelman. **Middle E. J.** 47:4 Autumn:1993 pp.652 - 666.

2274 Fertility in Botswana — the recent decline and future prospects. Naomi Rutenberg; Ian Diamond. **Demography** 30:2 5:1993 pp.143 - 157.

2275 The fertility of agricultural and non-agricultural traditional societies. Gillian R. Bentley; Tony Goldberg; Grażyna Jasieńska. **Pop. Stud.** 47:2 7:1993 pp.269 - 281.

2276 Fertility response to child survival in Nigeria — an analysis of microdata from Bendel state. Christiana E.E. Okojie. **Res. Popul. Econ.** 7 1991 pp.93 - 112.

2277 Fertility timing, wages, and human capital. M.L. Blackburn; D.E. Bloom; D. Neumark. **J. Pop. Ec.** 6:1 1993 pp.1 - 30.

2278 Gender preference and birthspacing in Matlab, Bangladesh. Mizanur Rahman; Julie da Vanzo. **Demography** 30:3 8:1993 pp.315 - 332.

2279 Hutterite fecundability by age and parity — strategies for frailty modeling of event histories. Ulla Larsen; James W. Vaupel. **Demography** 30:1 2:1993 pp.81 - 102.

2280 Indicador conjuntural ou descendência final? Da quebra à retoma da fecundidade nas sociedades europeias. *[In Portuguese]*; (Situational indicator or the ultimate descent? The fall and rise of birthrates in European societies.) *[Summary]*; *[Summary in French]*. João Peixoto. **Anál. Soc.** XVIII:1(120) 1993 pp.145 - 160.

2281 Maternal nativity status and pregnancy outcome among U.S.-born Filipinos. Greg R. Alexander; Gigliola Baruffi; Joanne Mor; Edith Kieffer. **Soc. Biol.** 39:3-4 Fall-Winter:1992 pp.278 - 284.

2282 Les mesures de la fécondité transversale. I. Construction des différents indices. *[In French]*; (Period fertility indices. I. The construction of different indices.). Jean-Louis Rallu; Laurent Toulemon. **Population** 48:1 1-2:1993 pp.7 - 26.

2283 Les mesures de la fécondité transversale. II. Application à la France de 1946 à 1989. *[In French]*; (Period fertility indices. II. France, 1946-1989.) *[Summary]*. Jean-Louis Rallu; Laurent Toulemon. **Population** 48:2 3-4:1993 pp.369 - 404.

2284 Modelling diffusion effects in fertility transition. Luis Rosero-Bixby; John B. Casterline. **Pop. Stud.** 47:1 3:1993 pp.147 - 167.

2285 The modern shift to below-replacement fertility — has Israel's population joined the process? Dov Friedlanger; Carole Feldmann. **Pop. Stud.** 47:2 7:1993 pp.295 - 306.

2286 Nuptialité et fécondité des hommes au Sud-Bénin: pour une approche stratégique de reproduction au Bénin. *[In French]*; [Nuptiality and male fertility in southern Benin:

F: Population. Family. Gender. Ethnic group

towards a strategic approach to reproduction in Benin]. Florentin Donadjè. Louvain-la-Neuve: Academia, 1992. 222p. *ISBN: 2872092056*. *Université Catholique de Louvain Département des Sciences de la Population et du Développement.*

2287 Parity progression and birth intervals in China — the influence of policy in hastening fertility decline; *[Summary in French]; [Summary in Spanish]*. Griffith Feeney; Wang Feng. **Pop. Dev. Rev.** 19:1 3:1993 pp.61 - 101.

2288 Patterns of intergenerational support and childbearing in the Third World. Daniel C. Clay; Jane E. Vander Haar. **Pop. Stud.** 47:1 3:1993 pp.67 - 83.

2289 Phosphoglucomutase genetic polymorphism and human fertility. Fulvia Gloria-Bottini; Nazzareno Lucarini; Antonio Scalamandré; Paola Borgiani; Ada Amante; Egidio Bottini. **Soc. Biol.** 39:3-4 Fall-Winter:1992 pp.246 - 256.

2290 Próba zintegrowanego badania płodności. *[In Polish]*; (Conceptional framework of the integral theory of fertility.) *[Summary]*. Malgorzata Rószkiewicz. **Stud. Demogr.** 1(103) 1991 pp.13 - 24.

2291 Przemiany płodności w Polsce i wybranych krajach Europy. *[In Polish]*; (Transformation of fertility in Poland and selected European countries in the light of history and the present day.) *[Summary]*. Krystyna Iglicka. **Stud. Demogr.** 3(113) 1993 pp.37 - 70.

2292 Re-evaluating the costs of teenage childbearing. Saul D. Hoffman; E. Michael Foster; Frank F. Furstenberg. **Demography** 30:1 2:1993 pp.1 - 13.

2293 Relative cohort size and fertility — the socio-political context of the Easterlin effect. Fred C. Pampel. **Am. Sociol. R.** 58:4 8:1993 pp.496 - 514.

2294 The resumption of fertility decline in Japan: 1973-92. Naohiro Ogawa; Robert D. Retherford. **Pop. Dev. Rev.** 19:4 12:1993 pp.703 - 742.

2295 The revolution in Asian fertility: dimensions, causes and implications. Richard Leete [Ed.]; Iqbal Alam [Ed.]. Oxford: Oxford University Press, 1993. 329p. *ISBN: 0198287917*. (*Series:* International studies in demography).

2296 Social dynamics of adolescent fertility in Sub-Saharan Africa. Caroline H. Bledsoe [Ed.]; Barney Cohen [Ed.]. Washington, D.C: National Academy Press, 1993. xv, 208p. *ISBN: 0309048974*. *Working Group on the Social Dynamics of Adolescent Fertility, Panel on the Population Dynamics of Sub-Saharan Africa, Committee on Population, Commission on Behavioral and Social Sciences and Education, National Research Council. Includes bibliographical references (p. 185-208).* (*Series:* Population dynamics of Sub-Saharan Africa).

2297 The South African fertility decline. John C. Caldwell; Pat Caldwell. **Pop. Dev. Rev.** 19:2 6:1993 pp.225 - 262.

2298 Studies in the fertility of Israel. E. Peritz [Ed.]; Mario Baras [Ed.]. Jerusalem: Institute of Contemporary Jewry, Hebrew University of Jerusalem, Demographic Center, Ministry of Labour and Social Affairs, Association for Demographic Policy of the Jewish People, 1992. 201p. *ISBN: 9652222585*. *Includes bibliographical references.* (*Series:* Jewish population studies).

2299 The supply-demand framework for the determinants of fertility — an alternative implementation. John Bongaarts. **Pop. Stud.** 47:3 11:1993 pp.437 - 456.

2300 Tendances récentes de la fécondité à l'île Maurice. *[In French]*; (Recent trends in birth rate in Mauritius.). Jean-Louis Rallu. **Population** 48:1 1-2:1993 pp.184 - 189.

2301 Terytorialne zróżnicowanie płodności w Polsce w świetle niektórych czynników. *[In Polish]*; (Selected factors of regional differences of fertility in Poland.). Krystyna Iglicka. **Stud. Demogr.** 4(110) 1992 pp.31 - 50.

F: Population. Famille. Sexe. Groupe ethnique

2302 The timing of first birth. Analysis and prediction of Swedish birth rates; *[Summary in French]*. Sten Martinelle. **Eur. J. Pop.** 9:3 1993 pp.265 - 286.

Morbidity
Morbidité

2303 AIDS impact assessment: modelling and scenario analysis. J. C. Jager [Ed.]; E. Joost Ruitenberg [Ed.]. Amsterdam, New York: Elsevier, 1992. xxiii, 319p. *ISBN: 0444895760. Includes proceedings of a workshop held at the National Institute of Public Health and Environmental Protection, Bilthoven, the Netherlands, 18-20 December 1989. Includes bibliographical references and index.*
2304 AIDS in Nicaragua — epidemiological, political, and sociocultural perspectives. Nicola Low; Matthias Egger; Anna Gorter; Peter Sandiford; Alcides González; Johanna Pauw; Jane Ferrie; George Davey Smith. **Int. J. Health. Ser.** 23:4 1993 pp.685 - 702.
2305 AIDS in South Africa: the myth and the reality. Mary Crewe. London: Penguin Books, 1992. 87p. *ISBN: 0140158499.* (*Series:* Penguin forum series).
2306 Chronic respiratory illness. Simon Johnson Williams. London, New York: Routledge, 1993. x, 145p. *ISBN: 0415096979, 0415076579. Includes bibliographical references (p. [135]-140) and index.* (*Series:* The experience of illness).
2307 Dimensions of mental health — life satisfaction, positive affect, anxiety and depression. Bruce Headey; Jonathan Kelley; Alex Wearing. **Soc. Ind.** 29:1 5:1993 pp.63 - 82.
2308 Directory of local disability information providers. Pamela Nadash. Poole, Dorset: Policy Studies Institute, 1993. 153p. *ISBN: 0853746117.*
2309 Disablism, planning, and the built environment. R.F. Imrie; P.E. Wells. **Envir. Plan. C.** 11:2 5:1993 pp.213 - 231.
2310 Distribution of culture-bound illnesses in the southern Peruvian Andes. James W. Carey. **Med. Anthr. Q.** 7:3 9:1993 pp.281 - 300.
2311 The effect of economic marital acquisitions on women's health. B. Hahn. **J. Marriage Fam.** 55:2 5:1993 pp.495 - 504.
2312 Facing up to AIDS: the socio-economic impact in Southern Africa. Sholto Cross [Ed.]; Alan Whiteside [Ed.]. New York: St. Martin's Press, 1993. xi, 331p. *ISBN: 0312091060. Includes bibliographical references and index.*
2313 Das freiwillig eingegangene HIV-Infektionsrisiko als konsumgesellschaftliches Sakrament: eine Fallgeschichte. *[In German]*; [Freely risking catching the HIV infection as a sacrament of the consumer society: a case history]; *[Summary in French]*. Hans Peter von Aarburg. **Ethnol. Helvet.** 17-18 1993-1994 pp.219 - 248.
2314 HIV seroprevalence and clinical characteristics of severe inpatient mentally ill homeless. Ilan Meyer; Francine Cournos; Maureen Empfield; Howell Schrage; Michael Silver; Myrna Rubin; Alan Weinstock. **J. Soc. Distr. Home.** 2:2 4:1993 pp.103 - 116.
2315 HIV/AIDS and the family — a review of research in the first decade. Robert Bor; Riva Miller; Eleanor Goldman. **J. Fam. Ther.** 15:2 5:1993 pp.187 - 204.

F: Population. Family. Gender. Ethnic group

2316 HIV-related risk practices among Glasgow male prostitutes — reframing concepts of risk behaviour. Michael J. Bloor; Marina A. Barnard; Andrew Finlay; Neil P. McKeganey. **Med. Anthr. Q.** 7:2 6:1993 pp.152 - 169.

2317 How coping mediates the effect of optimism on distress — a study of women with early stage breast cancer. Charles S. Carver; Christina Pozo; Suzanne D. Harris; Victoria Noriega; Michael F. Scheier; David S. Robinson; Alfred S. Ketcham; Frederick L. Moffat; Kimberley C. Clark. **J. Pers. Soc. Psychol.** 65:2 8:1993 pp.375 - 390.

2318 How people with disabilities fare when public policies change. Richard V. Burkhauser; Robert H. Haveman; Barbara L. Wolfe. **J. Policy An.** 12:2 1993 pp.251 - 269.

2319 Information enables: improving access to information services for disabled people. Policy Studies Institute. London: Policy Studies Institute, 1993. 67p. *ISBN: 0853746109.*

2320 Inner-city disease and the public health of the suburbs: the sociogeographic dispersion of point-source infection. R. Wallace; D. Wallace. **Envir. Plan. A.** 25:12 12:1993 pp.1707 - 1724.

2321 Migration und Gesundheit. Über den Umgang mit Krankheit türkischer Arbeitsmigranten in Deutschland und in der Türkei. *[In German]*; [Migration and health. On illness amongst Turkish migrant workers in Germany and Turkey]. Hanne Straube. **Hess. Blät. Volk.Kultur.** 29 1992 pp.125 - 144.

2322 Morbidity and multi-morbidity in Australia — evidence from the national health surveys. S.K. Jain. **J. Aust. Pop. Ass.** 10:1 5:1993 pp.31 - 52.

2323 The multiple jeopardy of race, class, and gender for AIDS risk among women. Marie Withers Osmond; K.G. Wambach; Dianne F. Harrison; Joseph Byers; Philippa Levine; Allen Imershein; David M. Quadagno. **Gender Soc.** 7:1 3:1993 pp.99 - 120.

2324 The nature and limits of the sub-Saharan African AIDS epidemic: evidence from geographic and other patterns. John C. Caldwell; Pat Caldwell. **Pop. Dev. Rev.** 19:4 12:1993 pp.817 - 848.

2325 Nombre passé de partenaires dans les modèles de transmission du SIDA par voie sexuelle. *[In French]*; (The number of previous partners in the transmission of AIDS through sexual intercourse.). Helmut Knolle. **Population** 48:1 1-2:1993 pp.111 - 124.

2326 Obraz zhizni, privychki, vliiaiushchie na zdorov'e moskvicheib i zakon o meditsinskom strakhovanii 1991-1993 g. *[In Russian]*; (Moscow's health habits and lifestyles prior to the start of 1991-1993 Health Insurance Act of Russia.). I. McKeehan; R. Campbell; S.V. Tumanov. **Sot. Issle.** 3 1993 pp.45 - 49.

2327 On the nature and dynamics of social construction — the case of AIDS. Philip H. [III] Pollock; Stuart A. Lilie; M. Elliot Vittes. **Soc. Sci. Q.** 74:1 3:1993 pp.123 - 135.

2328 Onchocerciasis in Chiapas, Mexico. Michael Vachon. **Geogr. Rev.** 83:2 4:1993 pp.141 - 149.

2329 Planning and evaluating disability information services. Rebecca Simpkins. London: Policy Studies Institute, 1993. 52p. *ISBN: 0853745730.*

2330 The production of infant health — input demand and health status differences related to gender of the infant. John S. Akin; David K. Guilkey; Barry M. Popkin. **Res. Popul. Econ.** 7 1991 pp.267 - 300.

F: Population. Famille. Sexe. Groupe ethnique

2331 Race, intervening variables, and two forms of low birth weight. Jeffrey E. Kallan. **Demography** 30:3 8:1993 pp.489 - 500.
2332 The relationship between socioeconomic status and health — a review of the literature. Jonathan S. Feinstein. **Milbank Q.** 71:2 1993 pp.279 - 322.
2333 Research needs for improving the health of Micronesian children. Usha K. Prasad. **J. Micrones. Stud.** 1:2 Dry season:1992 pp.251 - 260.
2334 Residential status and the physical health of a mentally ill population. Steven P. Segal; Debra J. vander Voort; Lawrence H. Liese. **Health Soc. Work** 18:3 8:1993 pp.208 - 214.
2335 Respiratory diseases of mothers and children and environmental factors among households in Jakarta. Charles Surjadi. **Environ. Urban.** 5:2 10:1993 pp.78 - 86.
2336 Risk and contraception — what women are not told about tubal ligation. Lyn Turney. **Wom. St. Inter. For.** 16:5 9-10:1993 pp.471 - 486.
2337 Risk as moral danger — the social and political functions of risk discourse in public health. Deborah Lupton. **Int. J. Health. Ser.** 23:3 1993 pp.425 - 435.
2338 La santé mentale sous l'occupation — le cas des enfants palestiniens. *[In French]*; [Mental health in the occupation — the case of Palestinian children]. Shafik Masalha. **R. Et. Palest.** 47 Spring:1993 pp.39 - 47.
2339 Schizophrenia and chronic mental illness in Micronesia — an epidemiological survey. Francis X. Hezel; A. Michael Wylie. **J. Micrones. Stud.** 1:2 Dry season:1992 pp.329 - 354.
2340 Selected correlates of morbidity in Pakistan. Zubeda Khan; M. Naseem Iqbal Farooqui [Comments by]. **Am. Anthrop.** 95:3 9:1993 pp.1037 - 1049.
2341 Socioeconomic aspects of HIV and AIDS in developing countries: a review and annotated bibliography. Susan Foster; Sue Lucas. London: London School of Hygiene and Tropical Medicine, 1991. viii, 116p. *Bibliography: p.114-115. - Includes index. (Series:* Public Health and Policy departmental publication - 3).
2342 Socioeconomic status — the prime indication of premature death in Australia. James F. Lawson; Deborah Black. **J. Biosoc. Sc.** 25:4 10:1993 pp.539 - 552.
2343 Source region effects in epidemic disease modeling — comparisons between influenza and HIV. Richard Thomas. **Pap. Reg. Sci.** 72:3 7:1993 pp.257 - 282.
2344 Spatial diffusion of the HIV /AIDS epidemic — modeling implications and case study of AIDS incidence in Ohio. Andrew Golub; Wilpen L. Gorr; Peter R. Gould. **Geogr. Anal.** 25:2 4:1993 pp.85 - 100.
2345 «Wer im Jahre 2001 kein AIDS hat, hat nicht gelebt». Zur Dialektik von Sicherheitsstreben und Intensitätssuche in den Industriegesellschaften. *[In German]*; ["Whoever has not got AIDS in 2001 will not have lived." On the dialectics of health safety attempts and the search for intensity in industrial societies]; *[Summary in French]*. Kathrin Oester. **Ethnol. Helvet.** 17-18 1993-1994 pp.249 - 268.
2346 Women, poverty and AIDS. Paul Farmer [Ed.]; Shirley Lindebaum [Ed.]; Mary-Jo DelVecchio Good [Ed.]; Geeta Rao Gupta [Contrib.]; Ellen Weiss [Contrib.]; Martha C. Ward [Contrib.]; Anitra Pivnick [Contrib.]; E.J. Sobo [Contrib.]; Nina Glick Schiller [Contrib.]. **Cult. Medic. Psych.** 17:4 12:1993 pp.387 - 512. *Collection of 6 articles.*
2347 Worlds of illness: biographical and cultural perspectives on health and disease. Alan Radley [Ed.]. New York; London: Routledge, 1993. 205p. *ISBN: 0415067693. Includes bibliographical references and indexes.*

F: Population. Family. Gender. Ethnic group

Mortality
Mortalité

2348 Alcool, tabac et mortalité en France depuis 1950. Essai d'évaluation du nombre des décès dus à la consommation d'alcool et de tabac en 1986. *[In French]*; (Alcohol, tobacco, and mortality in France since 1950. An estimate of the annual numbers of deaths in 1986.) *[Summary]*. Alfred Nizard; Francisco Munoz-Perez. **Population** 48:3 5-6:1993 pp.571 - 608.

2349 Alcool, tabac mortalité en France depuis 1950. Incidence de la consommation d'alcool et de tabac sur la mortalité. *[In French]*; (Alcohol, smoking and mortality in France since 1950. The effects on overall mortality and the excess mortality of males.) *[Summary]*. Alfred Nizard; Francisco Munoz-Perez. **Population** 48:4 7-8:1993 pp.975 - 1014.

2350 Assessing neonatal tetanus mortality levels and trends in developing countries with survey data. J. Ties Boerma; George Stroh. **Demography** 30:3 8:1993 pp.459 - 475.

2351 Assigning racial labels to the children of interracial marriages in Brazil — patterns in child mortality. Kathryn A. Sowards. **Soc. Sci. Q.** 74:3 9:1993 pp.631 - 644.

2352 Birth interval and family effects on postneonatal mortality in Brazil. Siân L. Curtis; Ian Diamond; John W. McDonald. **Demography** 30:1 2:1993 pp.33 - 43.

2353 Child mortality among twins in less developed countries. Guang Guo; Laurence M. Grummer-Strawn. **Pop. Stud.** 47:3 11:1993 pp.495 - 510.

2354 Economic status as a determinant of mortality among black and white older men — does poverty kill? Paul L. Menchik. **Pop. Stud.** 47:3 11:1993 pp.427 - 436.

2355 Effects on mortality of alcohol consumption, smoking, physical activity, and close personal relationships; *[Summary in French]*; *[Summary in Spanish]*. Jurgen Rehm; Manfred M. Fichter; Martin Elton. **Addiction** 88:1 1:1993 p.101-112.

2356 The geography of adult mortality: results from the fuzzy clumping method; *[Summary in Italian]*. G. Caselli; L. Cerbara; G. Leti. **Genus** IL:1-2 1-6:1993 pp.1 - 24.

2357 A global analysis of life expectancy and infant mortality. Clement F. Hobbs; Moses N. Kiggundu. Ottawa: Carleton University Press for the School of Business, Carleton University, 1992. 75p. *ISBN: 0886291844. Bibliography: p.31-32. (Series:* School of Business international development series).

2358 Il morente oggi, tra rimozione delle immagini di morte e desiderio di immortalità. *[In Italian]*; [Dying today, between repression of images of death and a desire for immortality]. Silvano Burgalassi. **Sociologia [Rome]** XXVII:1-3 1993 pp.217 - 238.

2359 The impact of advances in medicine on the biometric analysis of infant mortality. Andrew S. London. **Soc. Biol.** 40:3-4 Fall-winter:1993 pp.260 - 282.

2360 The influence of cohort effects on mortality trends in India — role of economic factors. K. Navaneetham. **Pop. Res. Pol. R.** 12:2 1993 pp.159 - 176.

2361 Low mortality and high morbidity in Kerala reconsidered; *[Summary in French]*; *[Summary in Spanish]*. B. Gopalakrishna Kumar. **Pop. Dev. Rev.** 19:1 3:1993 pp.103 - 121.

2362 Marriage selection and mortality patterns — inferences and fallacies. Noreen Goldman. **Demography** 30:2 5:1993 pp.189 - 208.

2363 "May God give sons to all" — gender and child mortality in India. Sunita Kishor. **Am. Sociol. R.** 58:2 4:1993 pp.247 - 265.

F: Population. Famille. Sexe. Groupe ethnique

2364 Modelo de estructura de covarianzas para el análisis de las diferencias espaciales de la mortalidad mexicana. *[In Spanish]*; (Covariance structure model for the analysis of spatial differences in Mexican mortality.) *[Summary]*. Olga López Ríos; Guillaume Wunsch. **Est. Demog. Urb.** 6:2 5-8:1991 pp.379 - 389.

2365 Morrendo à toa: causas da mortalidade no Brasil. *[In Portuguese]*; [Causes of mortality in Brazil]. Sergio Goes de Paula. São Paulo: Editora Atica, 1991. 160p. *ISBN: 8508039956. Includes bibliographical references (p. [157]-160).*

2366 Mortalidade infantil por causas na região metropolitana do Rio de Janeiro, 1976-1986: associação com variáveis socioeconômicas, climáticas e ligadas à poluição do ar. *[In Portuguese]*; (Infant mortality by cause of death, 1976-1986: association with socio-economic, climatic and air pollution variables in the Rio de Janeiro metropolitan area.) *[Summary]*. Milena P. Ducchiade; Kaizô I. Beltrão. **Rev. Brasil. Est. Popul.** 9:2 7-12:1992 pp.115 - 137.

2367 Mortalité et santé dans les villes africaines. *[In French]*; [Mortality and health in African villages]. Philippe Antoine; Amadou Ba. **Afr. Cont.** 168 10-12:1993 pp.138 - 146.

2368 Mortality on the move: methods of mortality projection. Bernard Benjamin; A. S. Soliman. Oxford: Actuarial Education Service, 1993. vi, 130p. *ISBN: 0952009803. Includes bibliographical references.*

2369 Mortality patterns and trends in the United States. Paul E. Zopf. Westport, Conn: Greenwood Press, 1992. xx, 281p. *ISBN: 0313267693. Includes bibliographical references (p. [257]-269) and index. (Series:* Studies in population and urban demography).

2370 Mortality trends and causes of death — a comparison between Eastern and Western Europe, 1960s-1980s; *[Summary in French]*. Guang Guo. **Eur. J. Pop.** 9:3 1993 pp.287 - 312.

2371 Niektóre społeczno-ekonomiczne uwarunkowanie umieralności (na przkładzie Wrocławia). *[In Polish]*; (Selected socio-economic determinants of mortality (case of Wrocław).) *[Summary]*. Czesław Brajczewski; Elżbieta Rogucka. **Stud. Demogr.** 1(107) 1992 pp.99 - 112.

2372 O úmrtnosti v České Republice. *[In Czech]*; (On mortality in the Czech Republic.). Ladislav Rabušic. **Demografie** XXXV:4 1993 pp.247 - 262.

2373 On the historical relationship between infant and adult mortality. Robert Woods. **Pop. Stud.** 47:2 7:1993 pp.195 - 219.

2374 Przemiany wzorca umieralności w Polsce. *[In Polish]*; (Changes of mortality pattern in Poland.) *[Summary]*. Alicja Maksimowicz-Ajchel. **Stud. Demogr.** 2(164) 1991 pp.3 - 45.

2375 Racial differentials in infant mortality in the U.S. — an examination of social and health determinants. Robert A. Hummer. **Soc. Forc.** 72:2 12:1993 pp.529 - 554.

2376 Reducing infant mortality — investment vs. food subsidy. J.W. Wickramasinghe. **Sri Lanka J. Soc. Sci.** 15:1/2 6-12:1992 pp.63 - 75.

2377 Regional mortality differences in Britain, 1931-1976 — a two dimensional analysis. Jon Anson. **J. Biosoc. Sc.** 25:3 7:1993 pp.383 - 396.

2378 Regres potencjału życiowego dorosłych mężczyzn w krajach Europy Wschodniej (1956-1985). *[In Polish]*; (Decline of the life potential of adult males in the countries of Eastern Europe (1956-1985).) *[Summary]*. Mieczysław Kędelski. **Stud. Demogr.** 2(164) 1991 pp.47 - 67.

F: Population. Family. Gender. Ethnic group

2379 Sex differences in mortality as a social indicator. Bali Ram. **Soc. Ind.** 29:1 5:1993 pp.83 - 108.
2380 Sex differentials in mortality early in the twentieth century — Sri Lanka and India compared. Christopher Langford; Pamela Storey. **Pop. Dev. Rev.** 19:2 6:1993 pp.263 - 282.
2381 Siblings' neonatal mortality risks and birth spacing in Bangladesh. Elizabeth Zenger. **Demography** 30:3 8:1993 pp.477 - 488.
2382 Skażenie środowiska i urbanizacja a umieralność na raka w Polsce w latach 1975-1987. *[In Polish]*; [Environmental pollution, urbanization and mortality from cancer in Poland 1875 -1987]. Zygmunt Gostkowski. **Prz. Soc.** XLI 1992 pp.145 - 153.
2383 Soziale Determinanten der Lebenserwartung. *[In German]*; (Social determinants of life-expectancy.) *[Summary]*. Thomas Klein. **Kölner Z. Soz. Soz. psy.** 45:4 12:1993 pp.712 - 730.
2384 Terytorialne zróżnicowanie umieralności w Polsce. *[In Polish]*; (Spatial differentiation of mortality in Poland.) *[Summary]*. Beata Pułaska-Turyna. **Stud. Demogr.** 3(101) 1990 pp.21 - 39.
2385 Umieralność mężczyzn w Polsce według wybranych przyczyn zgonów w latach 1960-1989. *[In Polish]*; (Male mortality in Poland by selected causes of death, 1960-1989.) *[Summary]*. Grzegorz Kaczorowski. **Stud. Demogr.** 1(107) 1992 pp.57 - 98.
2386 Use of sibling data to estimate family mortality effects in Guatemala. Guang Guo. **Demography** 30:1 2:1993 pp.15 - 32.
2387 Why people die — social representations of death and its causes. Lindsay Prior; Mick Bloor. **Sci. Cult.** 3:3(16) 1993 pp.346 - 374.
2388 Zróżnicowanie umieralności według stanu cywilnego. *[In Polish]*; (Mortality differentials by marital status.). Małgorzata Podogrodzka. **Stud. Demogr.** 3(109) 1992 pp.45 - 62.

Population ageing
Vieillissement de la population

2389 Bevolkingsveroudering en gezondheidszorg in Nederland: het demografisch effect voor de lange termijn. *[In Dutch]*; (Population ageing and public health care in the Netherlands: the long-term demographic effects.) *[Summary]*. P. Vossen. **Bevolk. Gez.** 2 1993 pp.1 - 19.
2390 Bevolkingsveroudering en stijgende collectieve lasten — bevolkingsbeleid als remedie? *[In Dutch]*; [Population ageing and rising collective problems — population policy as a remedy?]. Ad Vossen. **Bevolk. Gez.** 3 1992 pp.1 - 27.
2391 Demografické aspekty stárnutí obyvatelstva České republiky. *[In Czech]*; (Demographic aspects of population ageing in the Czech Republic.). Miroslava Mašková. **Demografie** XXXV:4 1993 pp.236 - 246.
2392 [Introduction to aging society]; *[Text in Japanese]*. Yoichi Okazaki. Tokyo: Chuohoki Shuppan, 1993. 122p.
2393 O desafio social do envelhecimento demográfico. *[In Portuguese]*; (The social challenge of demographic ageing.) *[Summary]*; *[Summary in French]*. Maria João Valente Rosa. **Anál. Soc.** XXVIII:3(122) 1993 pp.679 - 689.

F: Population. Famille. Sexe. Groupe ethnique

2394 Ontgroening en vergrijzing: een bevolkingsvraagstuk op mondiaal niveau. *[In Dutch]*; (Dejuvenation and aging of the population: a global issue.) *[Summary]*. J. de Jong Gierveld. **Bevolk. Gez.** 1993 pp.85 - 118.

2395 Opportunities and challenges in an ageing society. Wim J. A. van den Heuvel [Ed.]. North-Holland, Amsterdam: Royal Netherlands Academy of Arts and Sciences, 1992. vii, 189p. *ISBN: 0444857443. Includes bibliographical references. (Series:* Verhandelingen van der Koninklijke Nederlandse Akademie van Wetenschappen. Afd. Letterkunde.Nieuwe reeks).

2396 Starzenie się zasobów pracy w Polsce. *[In Polish]*; (Aging of labour force in Poland.) *[Summary]*. Irena Kotowska. **Stud. Demogr.** 3(101) 1990 pp.41 - 62.

F.4: Marriage and family
Mariage et famille

2397 About time: the revolution in work and family life. Patricia Hewitt. London: Rivers Oram P, 1993. 183p. *ISBN: 1854890395*.

2398 The adult legacy of childhood sexual abuse. Dick Agass; Mike Simes. **Practice** 6:1 1992-1993 pp.41 - 59.

2399 Adult siblings as sources of social support for the seriously mentally ill — a test of the serial model. Allan V. Horwitz. **J. Marriage Fam.** 55:3 8:1993 pp.623 - 632.

2400 American family decline, 1960-1990 — a review and appraisal. David Popenoe; Judith Stacey [Comments by]; Philip A. Cowan [Comments by]; David Popenoe [Comments by]. **J. Marriage Fam.** 55:3 8:1993 pp.527 - 555.

2401 Changing ideas about family care for the elderly in Japan. Kathryn Elliott; Ruth Campbell. **J. Cr-cult. Gerontol.** 8:2 4:1993 pp.119 - 135.

2402 Characteristics of families with no, one, or more than one gifted child. Kineret Weissler; Erika Landau. **J. Psychol.** 127:2 3:1993 pp.143 - 152.

2403 [Childbirth and child care in France; work and family]; *[Text in Japanese]*. Keiko Funabashi. **Jos. Kuk.** 10 1993 pp.107 - 120.

2404 Children and the family in a rural settlement in Gazankulu. J.C. Kotze. **Afr. Stud.** 51:2 1992 pp.143 - 166.

2405 A comparative study of the occupational attainment processes of white men and women in the United States — the effects of having ever married, spousal education, children and having ever divorced; *[Summary in Spanish]*. Linda A. Airsman; Bam Dev Sharda. **J. Comp. Fam. Stud.** XXIV:2 Summer:1993 pp.171 - 187.

2406 Darwin and the puzzle of primogeniture — an essay on biases in parental investment after death. Sarah Blaffer Hrdy; Debra S. Judge. **Hum. Nature** 4:1 1993 pp.1 - 45.

2407 Determinants of emotional well-being and parenting. R. Simons; J. Beaman; R. Conger; W. Chao. **J. Marriage Fam.** 55:2 5:1993 pp.385 - 398.

2408 Ėvoliutsiia sem'i i semeinaia politika v SSSR. *[In Russian]*; [The evolution of the family and family policy in the USSR]. Anatolii Grigor'evich Vishnevskii. Moskva: Nauka, 1992. 138p. *ISBN: 5020134473. Includes bibliographical references.*

2409 A dialogic perspective for family therapy — the contributions of Martin Buber and Gregory Bateson. Ivan B. Inger. **J. Fam. Ther.** 15:3 8:1993 pp.293 - 314.

2410 Division of family property in Taiwan. Rose Maris Li Yu Xie; Hui-Sheng Lin. **J. Cr-cult. Gerontol.** 8:1 1:1993 pp.49 - 69.

F: Population. Family. Gender. Ethnic group

2411 Does culture affect perceived family dynamics? A comparison of Arab and Jewish adolescents in Israel; *[Summary in Spanish]*. Victor Florian; Mario Mikulincer; Aron Weller. **J. Comp. Fam. Stud.** XXIV:2 Summer:1993 pp.189 - 201.

2412 The educational benefits of being spaced out — sibship density and educational progress. Brian Powell; Lala Carr Steelman. **Am. Sociol. R.** 58:3 6:1993 pp.367 - 397.

2413 The effects of family disruption on social mobility. Timothy J. Biblarz; Adrian E. Raftery. **Am. Sociol. R.** 58:1 2:1993 pp.97 - 109.

2414 Entre démographie et sociologie: la famille. *[In French]*; [Between demography and sociology: the family]. Louis Roussel. **Ann. Sociol.** 43 1993 pp.319 - 340.

2415 Ethnicity and informal support among filial caregivers — analysis of an Israeli sample. Howard Litwin; Leah Abramowitz. **J. Cr-cult. Gerontol.** 8:1 1:1993 pp.1 - 15.

2416 Familien im wiedervereinigten Deutschland. *[In German]*; [Families in the reunited Germany]. Bernhard Jans [Ed.]; Agathe Sering [Ed.]. Bonn: Vektor-Verlag, 1992. 172p. *ISBN: 3929304007. Papers presented at a conference organized by the Arbeitsgemeinschaft der Deutschen Familienorganisationen and held Nov. 18-19, 1991 in Gera, Germany. Includes bibliographical references.*

2417 Familien in der Schweiz. *[In German]*; Familles en Suisse. *[In French]*; [Families in Switzerland]. Pierre Gilliand [Ed.]; Kurt Lüscher [Ed.]; Thomas Fleiner-Gerster. Freiburg: Universitätsverlag, 1991. xxi, 623p. *ISBN: 3727807687. Text in German, French and Italian.*

2418 Les familles africaines face à la crise. *[In French]*; (African families facing the crises.) *[Summary]*. Thérèse Locoh. **Afr. Cont.** 166 4-6:1993 pp.3 - 14.

2419 Family and childhood adjustment in cystic fibrosis. Andres J. Pumariega; Deborah A. Pearson; Dan K. Seilheimer. **J. Child Fam. Stud.** 2:2 6:1993 pp.109 - 118.

2420 The family and the economy. Li Zong; Jock Collins; Vic Satzewich; G.S. Basran; Arthur Song; Peter S. Li. **J. Comp. Fam. Stud.** XXIV:3 Autumn:1993 pp.277 - 386. *Collection of 6 articles.*

2421 Family development. Murli Desai [Ed.]; Lina D. Kashyap [Contrib.]; Purnima Mane [Contrib.]; Jeroo Billimoria [Contrib.]; Rinki Bhattacharya [Contrib.]; Chhaya Datar [Contrib.]; Rosamma Vccdon [Contrib.]. **Indian J. Soc. W.** LIV:1 1:1993 pp.3 - 107. *Collection of 8 articles.*

2422 The family in the Western world from the Black Death to the industrial age. Beatrice Gottlieb. New York: Oxford University Press, 1993. x, 309p. *ISBN: 0195073444, 0195073444. Includes bibliographical references and index.*

2423 The family: is it just another lifestyle choice. Jon Gower Davies; Brigitte Berger; Allan C. Carlson. London: IEA Health and Welfare Unit, 1993. 109p. *ISBN: 0255362765. (Series:* Choice in welfare series).

2424 Family mediation in France. Benoit Bastard; Laura Cardia-Voneche. **Int. J. Law Fam.** 7:3 1993 pp.271 - 281.

2425 Family, motherhood and Zulu nationalism — the politics of the Inkatha women's brigade. Shireen Hassim. **Feminist R.** 43 Spring:1993 pp.1 - 25.

2426 Family, self, and society: toward a new agenda for family research. Philip A. Cowan [Ed.]; et al. Hillsdale, NJ: Lawrence Erlbaum Publishers, 1992. 502p. *ISBN: 0805809996. Includes bibliographical references and index.*

2427 Family support to single and married mothers. R. Jayakody; L. Chatters; R. Taylor. **J. Marriage Fam.** 55:2 5:1993 pp.261 - 276.

F: Population. Famille. Sexe. Groupe ethnique

2428 Family therapy and anthropology — a case for emotions. Inga-Britt Krause. **J. Fam. Ther.** 15:1 2:1993 pp.35 - 56.

2429 [Function of the kinship in Inobe]; *[Text in Japanese]*. Emiko Tamazato. **Chi. Sogoken.** 3 1993 pp.24 - 42.

2430 Future Polish family in the light of family attitudes of single young people. Walentyna Ignatczyk. **Stud. Demogr.** 3(105) 1991 pp.43 - 62.

2431 La genèse sociale des sentiments: aînés et cadets dans l'île grecque de Karpathos. *[In French]*; [The social genesis of feelings: older and younger children on the Greek island of Karpathos]. Bernard Vernier. Paris: Ecole des hautes études en sciences sociales, 1991. 312p. *ISBN: 2713209765.*

2432 Health care and family support systems of functionally impaired rural elderly men and women in Terengganu, Malaysia. Martin B. Tracy; Patsy D. Tracy. **J. Cr-cult. Gerontol.** 8:1 1:1993 pp.35 - 48.

2433 Hearth and home. Ronald Fletcher. **Society** 31:1 11-12:1993 pp.55 - 60.

2434 Houseworkers and paid workers — qualities of the work and effects on personal control. Chloe E. Bird; Catherine E. Ross. **J. Marriage Fam.** 55:4 11:1993 pp.913 - 925.

2435 Income growth among nonresident fathers — evidence from Wisconsin. Elizabeth Phillips; Irwin Garfinkel. **Demography** 30:2 5:1993 pp.227 - 241.

2436 Interdependence and the interpersonal sense of control — an analysis of family relationships. William L. Cook. **J. Pers. Soc. Psychol.** 64:4 4:1993 pp.587 - 601.

2437 Intra-family bargaining and time allocation. Paul S. Carlin. **Res. Popul. Econ.** 7 1991 pp.215 - 243.

2438 The Jamaican family: continuity and change. Elsa Leo-Rhynie. Kingston, Jamaica: Grace Kennedy Foundation, 1993. 57p. *ISBN: 9768041064.* (*Series:* Grace Kennedy Foundation lecture).

2439 Jetzt fühle ich mich sicherer in der Heimat. Beziehungen in türkischen Familien und ihre Beeinflussung durch Migration und Remigration. *[In German]*; ["Now I feel more secure in my homeland". Relations in Turkish families and their influences through migration and return migration]. Doris Stennert. **Hess. Blät. Volk.Kultur.** 29 1992 pp.175 - 187.

2440 Kindred matters: rethinking the philosophy of the family. Diana T. Meyers [Ed.]; Kenneth Kipnis [Ed.]; Cornelius F. Murphy [Ed.]. Ithaca, N.Y: Cornell University Press, 1993. x, 315p. *ISBN: 0801425948, 0801498864. Includes bibliographical references and index.*

2441 Kinkeeping and distress — gender, recipients of care, and work-family conflict. Naomi Gerstel; Sally K. Gallagher. **J. Marriage Fam.** 55:3 8:1993 pp.598 - 607.

2442 Kinscripts; *[Summary in Spanish]*. Carol B. Stack; Linda M. Burton. **J. Comp. Fam. Stud.** XXIV:2 Summer:1993 pp.157 - 170.

2443 The living arrangements of single mothers with dependent children. A.E. Winkler. **Am. J. Econ. S.** 52:1 1:1993 pp.1 - 18.

2444 Modernizzazione socio-economica, condizione femminile e nuovi comportamenti familiari e procreativi. *[In Italian]*; [Socio-economic modernization, conditions for women and new changes in family and fertility] *[Summary]*. Antonella Pinnelli. **Sta. Mer.** 36 12:1992 pp.401 - 428.

2445 Parenté et organisation sociale dans le Cambodge moderne et contemporain, vol 2. *[In French]*; [Kinship and social organization in modern and contemporary Cambodia, vol 2]. Jacques Népote. Geneva: Olizane / Centre de Documentation et

F: Population. Family. Gender. Ethnic group

de Recherche sur la Civilisation Khmère, 1992. 255, viip. *ISBN: 2880861020. Bibliography: p. 211-228; includes index.*

2446 A portrait of the nestleaving process in early adulthood. Frances Goldscheider; Arland Thornton; Linda Young-DeMarco. **Demography** 30:4 11:1993 pp.683 - 699.

2447 Proches et parents. *[In French]*; (Friends and relatives.). Catherine Bonvalet; Dominique Maison; Hervé le Bras; Lionel Charles. **Population** 48:1 1-2:1993 pp.83 - 110.

2448 Relative merits — family culture and kinship in small firms. Monder Ram; Ruth Holliday. **Sociology** 27:4 11:1993 pp.629 - 648.

2449 Religious belief, transmission, and the family — an Australian study. Bernadette C. Hayes; Yvonne Pittelkow. **J. Marriage Fam.** 55:3 8:1993 pp.755 - 766.

2450 Scottish prisoners and their families: The impact of imprisonment on family relationships. Stewart Asquith; Kate Peart; Save the Children Fund. Edinburgh: Scottish Divisional Office, Save the Children Fund, 1992. 24p. *ISBN: 1870322517.*

2451 She's leaving home — but why? An analysis of young people leaving the parental home. Nicholas Buck; Jacqueline Scott. **J. Marriage Fam.** 55:4 11:1993 pp.863 - 874.

2452 Siblings of children with mental retardation — family characteristics and adjustment. Denis J. Lynch; Lorraine Fay; Jeanne Funk; Rollin Nagel. **J. Child Fam. Stud.** 2:2 6:1993 pp.87 - 96.

2453 Some questions on the study of the Turkmen family. Shokhrat Kadyrov. **C.Asian Sur.** 12:3 1993 pp.393 - 400.

2454 SShA: izmeneniia v sfere semeiono-brachnykh otnoshenii. *[In Russian]*; [USA: changes in the sphere of family and marital relations]. O. Oskolkova. **Mir. Ek. Mez. Ot.** 6 1993 pp.110 - 121.

2455 Step by step: focus on stepfamilies. Margaret Robinson; Donna Smith. Hemel Hempstead: Harvester Wheatsheaf, 1993. xvii, 238p. *ISBN: 0745012817, 0745012825. Includes bibliographical references (p. 227-233) and index. National Stepfamily Association.*

2456 Substitute family placements of unaccompanied Mozambican refugee children — a field perspective. Stanley Phiri; Joan Duncan. **J. Soc. Devel. Afr.** 8:2 1993 pp.73 - 81.

2457 Task accomplishment versus household management in family work. H. Mederer. **J. Marriage Fam.** 55:1 2:1993 pp.133 - 145.

2458 Teen out-of-wedlock births and welfare receipt — the role of childhood events and economic circumstances. Chong-Bum An; Robert Haveman; Barbara Wolfe. **Rev. Econ. St.** LXXV:2 5:1993 pp.195 - 208.

2459 Three types of family environment scale profiles — functional, distressed, and abusive families. Brian A. Glaser; Thomas V. Sayger; Arthur M. Horne. **J. Fam. Viol.** 8:4 12:1993 pp.303 - 311.

2460 [The transformation of family life events]; *[Text in Japanese]*. Hideki Watanabe. **Kaz. Shak. Ken.** 5 1993 pp.67 - 74.

2461 Trauma-organized systems: physical and sexual abuse in families. Arnon Bentovim. London, New York: Karnac Books, 1992. xxi, 122p. *ISBN: 1855750120. Includes bibliographical references (p. 119-122). (Series:* Systemic thinking and practice series).

F: Population. Famille. Sexe. Groupe ethnique

2462 Trivers-Willard rules for sex allocation — when do they maximize expected grandchildren in humans? Judith L. Anderson; Charles B. Crawford. **Hum. Nature** 4:2 1993 pp.137 - 174.

2463 Umbrüche in der Privatsphäre: Familie und Haushalt zwischen Politik, Ökonomie und sozialen Netzen. *[In German]*; [Disruption in the private sphere: family and household between politics, economics and social networks]. Roland Reichwein; Alfons Cramer; Ferdinand Buer. Bielefeld: Kleine, 1993. 300p. *ISBN: 3893701702. Bibliography: p. 290-300.*

2464 Understanding family process: basics of family systems theory. Carlfred B. Broderick. Newbury Park, CA, London: Sage Pubns, 1993. 268p. *ISBN: 0803937784.*

2465 Wages for caring: compensating family care of the elderly. Nathan L. Linsk; et al. New York: Praeger, 1992. x, 281p. *ISBN: 027593635X. Includes bibliographical references (p. [261]-272) and index.*

2466 Women and the family in Northern Ireland — a review. Eithne McLaughlin. **Wom. St. Inter. For.** 16:6 11-12:1993 pp.553 - 568.

2467 Women, motherhood and childbearing. Diane Richardson. Basingstoke: Macmillan, 1993. 162p. *ISBN: 033353493X.* (*Series:* Women in society).

2468 Wpływ pracy zawodowej matek na postawy i zachowania prokreacyjne w cyklu życia rodziny. *[In Polish]*; (Effect of mother's work on reproductive attitudes and behaviour in family life cycle.). Alicja Szuman. **Stud. Demogr.** 4(110) 1992 pp.51 - 82.

Divorce
Divorce

2469 Altering support payments — does the bankruptcy court have the power? Scott E. Turner. **J. Fam. Law** 31:3 1992-1993 pp.629 - 647.

2470 Children's adjustment to divorce — theories, hypotheses, empirical support. P. Amato. **J. Marriage Fam.** 55:1 2:1993 pp.23 - 38.

2471 Co-operative parenting post-divorce — possibility or pipedream? Janet Walker. **J. Fam. Ther.** 15:3 8:1993 pp.273 - 292.

2472 Dividing the child: social and legal dilemmas of custody. Eleanor E. Maccoby; Charlene E. Depner [Contrib.]; H.. Elizabeth Peters [Contrib.]; Robert H. Mnookin. Cambridge, Mass: Harvard University Press, 1992. xi, 369p. *ISBN: 0674212940. Includes bibliographical references (p. [355]-363) and index.*

2473 Le divorce en Belgique: controverses & perspectives. *[In French]*; [Divorce in Belgium: controversies and perspectives]. Jacques de Gavre [Ed.]. Brussels: E. Story-Scientia, 1991. 310p. *ISBN: 906439668X. 2ème Association Famille & Droit, Colloque 1988, Bruxelles.*

2474 Divorce in Ireland: who should bear the cost. Peter Ward. Cork: Cork University Press, 1993. 65p. *ISBN: 0902561693.* (*Series:* Undercurrents).

2475 Divorce in the United States vs. in China. Linlin Pang. **J. Pop. Cult.** 27:2 Fall:1993 pp.91 - 100.

2476 The divorce of marriage and childbearing — changing attitudes and behavior in the United States. Deanna L. Pagnini; Ronald R. Rindfuss. **Pop. Dev. Rev.** 19:2 6:1993 pp.331 - 347.

F: Population. Family. Gender. Ethnic group

2477 Ecological determinants of divorce — a structural approach to the explanation of Japanese divorce. Hiroshi Fukurai; Jon P. Alston. **Soc. Biol.** 39:3-4 Fall-Winter:1992 pp.257 - 277.

2478 Enforcing divorce settlements — evidence from child support compliance and award modifications. H. Elizabeth Peters; Laura M. Argys; Eleanor E. Maccoby; Robert H. Mnookin. **Demography** 30:4 11:1993 pp.719 - 735.

2479 Female employment and first union dissolution in Puerto Rico. Karen Price Carver; Jay D. Teachmen. **J. Marriage Fam.** 55:3 8:1993 pp.686 - 698.

2480 Financial support on divorce — the right mixture of rules and discretion? Emily Jackson; Fran Washoff; Mavis Maclean; Rebecca Emerson Dobash. **Int. J. Law Fam.** 7:2 1993 pp.230 - 254.

2481 Impact of mortality decline on marital duration and length of post-dissolution life at different divorce levels; *[Summary in Italian]*; *[Summary in French]*. Purushottam M. Kulkarni. **Genus** XLVIII:3-4 7-12:1992 pp.45 - 62.

2482 Marital dissolutions in Iligan City. Luis Q. Lacar. **Phil. Stud.** 41 Second quarter:1993 pp.232 - 241.

2483 Marriage dissolution in Australia — models and explanations. Michael Bracher; Gigi Santow; S. Philip Morgan; James Trussell. **Pop. Stud.** 47:3 11:1993 pp.403 - 426.

2484 Measuring the effect of changing legislation on the frequency of divorce — the Netherlands, 1830-1990. Frans van Poppel; Joop de Beer. **Demography** 30:3 8:1993 pp.425 - 441.

2485 Parenting following divorce — a comparison of black and white single mothers; *[Summary in French]*; *[Summary in Spanish]*. Patrick C. McKenry; Mark A. Fine. **J. Comp. Fam. Stud.** XXIV:1 Spring:1993 pp.99 - 111.

2486 Promoting co-operative parenting after separation — a therapeutic/interventionist model of family mediation. Edward Kruk; Margaret Robinson [Comments by]. **J. Fam. Ther.** 15:3 8:1993 pp.235 - 271.

2487 The rhetoric of motives in divorce. Joseph Hopper. **J. Marriage Fam.** 55:4 11:1993 pp.801 - 813.

2488 Rottura di un rapporto di coppia e qualità della vita. *[In Italian]*; (Factors affecting quality of life of adult and children after marital separation.). Donata Francescato. **Rass. It. Soc.** XXXIV:4 12:1993 pp.539 - 560.

2489 Rozwód w cyklu życia rodziny. *[In Polish]*; (Divorce in family life cycle.). Paweł Rydzewski. **Stud. Demogr.** 3(109) 1992 pp.3 - 18.

2490 Social modernization and the increase in the divorce rate; *[Summary in German]*. Hartmut Esser; Karl-Dieter Opp [Comments by]; Ulrich Witt [Comments by]. **J. Inst. Theo. Ec.** 149:1 3:1993 pp.252 - 285.

2491 Social psychopathy, social distress, family breakdown, and custody disputes in the 1990s — implications for mental health professionals. Abe Fenster. **J. Soc. Distr. Home.** 2:1 1:1993 pp.35 - 59.

2492 Sociographie du divorce et divortialité. *[In French]*; (Divorce: beyond the sociographic approach.) *[Summary]*. Louis Roussel. **Population** 48:4 7-8:1993 pp.919 - 938.

2493 Visitation frequency, child support payment, and the father-child relationship postdivorce. Joyce A. Arditti; Timothy Z. Keith. **J. Marriage Fam.** 55:3 8:1993 pp.699 - 712.

F: Population. Famille. Sexe. Groupe ethnique

2494 Women and divorce in Canada: a sociological analysis. Aysan Sever. Toronto: Canadian Scholars' Press, 1992. xviii, 328p. *ISBN: 0921627653*. Includes bibliographical references: p. 295-328.
2495 Women, men, and the economic consequences of divorce — evidence from Canadian longitudinal data; *[Summary in French]*. Ross Finnie. **Can. R. Soc. A.** 30:2 5:1993 pp.205 - 241.

Family law
Droit de la famille

2496 Adoption Australia: a comparative study of Australian adoption legislation and policy. Peter Boss; Sue Edwards. Notting Hill, Vic: National Children's Bureau of Australia, 1992. vii, 460, 24p. *ISBN: 0646087290*. Bibliography: p. 445-447.
2497 An adult patient's right to refuse medical treatment for religious reasons — the limitations imposed by parenthood. Kristin M. Lomond. **J. Fam. Law** 31:3 1992-1993 pp.665 - 683.
2498 Children's rights and social placement — a cross-national comparison of legal and social policy towards children in one-parent families. W. Voegeli; B. Willenbacher. **Int. J. Law Fam.** 7:1 1993 pp.108 - 124.
2499 Family law in Czechoslovakia after the revolution. Milana Hrusakova. **Int. J. Law Fam.** 7:1 1993 pp.125 - 133.
2500 Illegitimate children's right to receive notice in probate proceedings involving putative father's estate. Cynthia S. Buttorff. **J. Fam. Law** 31:3 1992-1993 pp.649 - 664.
2501 Marriage on trial: a study of Islamic family law: Iran and Morocco compared. Ziba Mir-Hosseini. London: Tauris, 1993. 243p. *ISBN: 1850436851*. (*Series:* Society and culture in the modern Middle East).
2502 Mothers of a world: maternalist politics and the origins of Welfare States. Seth Koven [Ed.]; Sonya Michel [Ed.]. London: Routledge, 1993. 447p. *ISBN: 0415903130*.
2503 Natural parents' right to withdraw consent to adoption — how far should the right extend? Susan Yates Ely. **J. Fam. Law** 31:3 1992-1993 pp.685 - 705.
2504 Single-mother families in eight countries — economic status and social policy. Yin-Ling Irene Wong; Irwin Garfinkel; Sara McLanahan. **Soc. Ser. R.** 67:2 6:1993 pp.177 - 197.
2505 Sovremennaia sem'ia ideologiia i politika. *[In Russian]*; (Modern family — ideology and politics.). A. Vishnevsky. **Svobod. Mysl'** 11 7:1993 pp.110 - 120.

Family structure
Structure de la famille

2506 The American family transformed. David A. Hamburg. **Society** 30:2(202) 1/2:1993 pp.60 - 69.
2507 Aspects régionaux de la formation de la famille et de l'illégitimité en Autriche. *[In French]*; (Aspects of family formation and illegitimacy in the regions of Austria.) *[Summary]*. France Prioux. **Population** 48:3 5-6:1993 pp.711 - 734.

F: Population. Family. Gender. Ethnic group

2508 Change in extended family living among elderly people in South Korea, 1970-1980. Susan De Vos; Yean-Ju Lee. **Econ. Dev. Cult. Change** 41:2 1:1993 pp.377 - 393.

2509 Chicana/o family structure and gender personality — Chodorow, familism, and psychoanalytic sociology revisited. Denise A. Segura; Jennifer L. Pierce. **Signs** 19:1 Autumn:1993 pp.62 - 91.

2510 Children in single-parent households with same-sex parents. D. Downey; B. Powell. **J. Marriage Fam.** 55:1 2:1993 pp.55 - 71.

2511 Custodial fathers — myths, realities, and child support policy. D. Meyer; S. Garasky. **J. Marriage Fam.** 55:1 2:1993 pp.73 - 89.

2512 Domestic space, modes of control and problem behaviour. D. Sibley; G. Lowe. **Geog.ann. B.** 74B:3 1992 pp.189 - 198.

2513 Extended single-parent households and children's behavior. Andrea Stolba; Paul R. Amato. **Sociol. Q.** 34:3 8:1993 pp.543 - 549.

2514 Family and social change: the household as a process in an industrializing community. Angélique Janssens. Cambridge: Cambridge University Press, 1993. xxii, 317p. *ISBN: 0521416116. Includes bibliographical references and index.* (*Series:* Cambridge studies in population, economy and society in past time).

2515 Family customs in Portugal and Brazil — transatlantic parallels; *[Summary in French]*; *[Summary in German]*. Caroline B. Brettell; Alida C. Metcalf. **Contin. Change** 8:3 12:1993 pp.365 - 388.

2516 Family relationship history, contemporary parent-grandparent relationship quality, and the grandparent-grandchild relationship. Les B. Whitbeck; Danny R. Hoyt; Shirley M. Huck. **J. Marriage Fam.** 55:4 11:1993 pp.1025 - 1035.

2517 Family structure and the risk of a premarital birth. Lawrence L. Wu; Brian C. Martinson. **Am. Sociol. R.** 58:2 4:1993 pp.210 - 232.

2518 Family systems and social support. M. Farrell; G. Barnes. **J. Marriage Fam.** 55:1 2:1993 pp.119 - 132.

2519 Gender, family structure, and social support among parents. N. Marks; S. McLanahan. **J. Marriage Fam.** 55:2 5:1993 pp.481 - 493.

2520 Generalized extended family exchange — a case from the Philippines. Jean Treloggen Peterson. **J. Marriage Fam.** 55:3 8:1993 pp.570 - 584.

2521 Grandparents who parent their grandchildren — effects on lifestyle. Margaret Platt Jendrek. **J. Marriage Fam.** 55:3 8:1993 pp.609 - 621.

2522 Mate availability and family structure in metropolitan areas. M. Fossett; K. Kiecolt. **J. Marriage Fam.** 55:2 5:1993 pp.288 - 302.

2523 La matrifocalidad, el matrimonio y la familia en el Caribe. *[In Spanish]*; [Mother-centredness, marriage and the family in the Caribbean]; *[Summary in English]*. María Dolores Fernós. **Rev. Cien. Soc.** XXX:1-2 6:1993 pp.333 - 348.

2524 Der Monopolverlust der Familie. Vom Teilsystem Familie zum Teilsystem privater Lebensformen. *[In German]*; (The loss of the monopoly of the family. From the subsystem family towards a subsystem of private living-together.) *[Summary]*. Thomas Meyer. **Kölner Z. Soz. Soz. psy.** 45:1 1993 pp.23 - 40.

2525 Mothers, children, and cohabitation — the intergenerational effects of attitudes and behavior. William G. Axinn; Arland Thornton. **Am. Sociol. R.** 58:2 4:1993 pp.233 - 246.

2526 Neuer Totemismus? Überlegungen zur Genese und Semantik moderner Tierbestattung. *[In German]*; (New totemism? Reflections on formation and

F: Population. Famille. Sexe. Groupe ethnique

semantics of modern pet burial.) *[Summary]*. Rainer Wiedenmann. **Soz. Welt.** 44:2 1993 pp.199 - 222.

2527 New zodiacal influences on Chinese family formation — Taiwan, 1976. Daniel M. Goodkind. **Demography** 30:2 5:1993 pp.127 - 142.

2528 Research on the African-American family: a holistic perspective. Andrew Billingsley; Robert Bernard Hill; Wornie L. Reed [Ed.]. Westport, Connecticut: Auburn House, 1993. 195p. *ISBN: 0865690197. Prepared under the auspices of the William Monroe Trotter Insitute, University of Massachusetts at Boston. Bibliography: p.159-179.*

2529 Simplicity and complexity in the effects of parental structure on high school graduation. Roger A. Wojtkiewicz. **Demography** 30:4 11:1993 pp.701 - 717.

2530 Der soziale Wandel auf dem Lande — seine Bewältigung und Formen des Scheiterns. *[In German]*; (Social change in the country — coping and forms of failure. A comparison of three families.) *[Summary]*. Liselotte Bieback-Diel; Karl Friedrich Bohler; Bruno Hildenbrand; Helmut Oberle. **Soz. Welt.** 44:1 1993 pp.120 - 135.

2531 The structure of intergenerational exchanges in American families. Dennis P. Hogan; David J. Eggebeen; Clifford C. Clogg. **A.J.S.** 98:6 5:1993 pp.1428 - 1458.

2532 What do we mean by extended family? A closer look at Hispanic multigenerational families. Camilo Garcia. **J. Cr-cult. Gerontol.** 8:2 4:1993 pp.137 - 146.

Marriage and cohabitation
Mariage et cohabitation

2533 Age at return marriage and timing of first birth in Uttar Pradesh and Kerala, India. K.K. Singh; C.M. Suchindran; Vipin Singh; R. Ramakumar. **Soc. Biol.** 39:3-4 Fall-Winter:1992 pp.292 - 298.

2534 Alcohol use in male spouse abusers and their female partners. Ola W. Barnett; Ronald W. Fagan. **J. Fam. Viol.** 8:1 3:1993 pp.1 - 25.

2535 Attachment theory as applied to wartime and job-related marital separation. Julia K. Vormbrock. **Psychol . B.** 114:1 7:1993 pp.122 - 144.

2536 Availability of marriage partners in England and Wales — a comparison of three measures. Richard Lampard. **J. Biosoc. Sc.** 25:3 7:1993 pp.333 - 350.

2537 Becoming a married couple — the emergence of meaning in the first years of marriage. Terri L. Orbuch; Joseph Veroff; Diane Holmberg. **J. Marriage Fam.** 55:4 11:1993 pp.815 - 826.

2538 Being in control — a note on differences between caregiving and noncaregiving spouses. Audrey B. Sistler; Fredda Blanchard-Fields. **J. Psychol.** 127:5 9:1993 pp.537 - 542.

2539 Casamento em tempos de crise. *[In Portuguese]*; (Marriage and crisis: Brazil in the eighties.) *[Summary]*. Elza Berquó; Maria Coleta F.A. de Oliveira. **Rev. Brasil. Est. Popul.** 9:2 7-12:1992 pp.155 - 167.

2540 Catholicism and intermarriage in the United States. William Sander. **J. Marriage Fam.** 55:4 11:1993 pp.1037 - 1041.

2541 Catholicism and marriage in the United States. William Sander. **Demography** 30:3 8:1993 pp.373 - 384.

F: Population. Family. Gender. Ethnic group

2542 Changes in American marriage, 1972-1987 — availability and forces of attraction by age and education. Zhenchao Qian; Samuel Preston. **Am. Sociol. R.** 58:4 8:1993 pp.482 - 495.

2543 Changing nuptiality patterns in contemporary Spain; *[Summary in Italian]*. Teresa Castro Martin. **Genus** IL:1-2 1-6:1993 pp.79 - 96.

2544 Children and marital happiness of black Americans; *[Summary in Spanish]*. Richard E. Ball. **J. Comp. Fam. Stud.** XXIV:2 Summer:1993 pp.203 - 218.

2545 A comparative analysis of same-sex partnership protections — recommendations for American reform. Deborah M. Henson. **Int. J. Law Fam.** 7:3 1993 pp.282 - 313.

2546 A comparison of voluntarily childfree adults and parents. Marsha D. Somers. **J. Marriage Fam.** 55:3 8:1993 pp.643 - 650.

2547 A compressão do mercado matrimonial e o aumento de casamentos informais no Brasil. *[In Portuguese]*; (The marriage squeeze and the rise in informal marriage in Brazil.) *[Summary]*. Margaret E. Greene. **Rev. Brasil. Est. Popul.** 9:2 7-12:1992 pp.168 - 183.

2548 Conceptualizing gender in marriage — the case of marital care. Linda Thompson. **J. Marriage Fam.** 55:3 8:1993 pp.557 - 569.

2549 Concordance for depressive disorders and marital quality. Jane D. McLeod; Deborah A. Eckberg. **J. Marriage Fam.** 55:3 8:1993 pp.733 - 746.

2550 Coping in marital dyads — patterns and associations with psychological symptons. Carole T. Giunta; Bruce E. Compas. **J. Marriage Fam.** 55:4 11:1993 pp.1011 - 1017.

2551 Courtship as a waiting game. Theodore C. Bergstrom; Mark Bagnoli. **J. Polit. Ec.** 101:1 2:1993 pp.185 - 202.

2552 Disability, caring and marriage — the experience of younger couples when a partner is disabled after marriage. Gillian Parker. **Br. J. Soc. W.** 23:6 12:1993 pp.565 - 580.

2553 The division of household labor and wives' happiness — ideology, employment, and perceptions of support. Darlene L. Piña; Vern L. Bengtson. **J. Marriage Fam.** 55:4 11:1993 pp.901 - 912.

2554 Dual-earner couples in Singapore: an examination of work and nonwork sources of their experienced burnout. Samuel Aryee. **Human Relat.** 46:12 12:1993 pp.1441 - 1468.

2555 Economic conditions, spouse support, and psychological distress of rural husbands and wives. Frederick O. Lorenz; Rand D. Conger; Ruth B. Montague; K.A.S. Wickrama. **Rural Sociol.** 58:2 Summer:1993 pp.247 - 268.

2556 The economic costs of marital disruption for young women over the past two decades. Pamela J. Smock. **Demography** 30:3 8:1993 pp.353 - 371.

2557 Educational expansion and changes in entry into marriage and motherhood. The experience of Italian women; *[Summary in Italian]*; *[Summary in French]*. Hans-Peter Blossfeld; Alessandra de Rose. **Genus** XLVIII:3-4 7-12:1992 pp.73 - 92.

2558 Der Ehebegriff bei Kant und Hegel. *[In German]*; [The concept of marriage in the work of Hegel and Kant]. Karl Eckhart Heinz. **Arc. Recht. Soz.** 79:2 1993 pp.216 - 227.

2559 Employment status, gender role attitudes, and marital independence in later life. Maximiliane Szinovacz; Paula Harpster. **J. Marriage Fam.** 55:4 11:1993 pp.927 - 940.

F: Population. Famille. Sexe. Groupe ethnique

2560 The formation and stability of informal unions in Côte d'Ivoire; *[Summary in Spanish]*. Anastasia J. Gage-Brandon. **J. Comp. Fam. Stud.** XXIV:2 Summer:1993 pp.219 - 233.

2561 Integrating evolutionary and social exchange perspectives on relationships — effects of gender, self-appraisal, and involvement level on mate selection criteria. Douglas T. Kenrick; Gary E. Groth; Melanie R. Trost; Edward K. Sadalla. **J. Pers. Soc. Psychol.** 64:6 6:1993 pp.951 - 969.

2562 Interest in marriage among Canadian students at the end of the eighties; *[Summary in French]*; *[Summary in Spanish]*. Charles Hobart. **J. Comp. Fam. Stud.** XXIV:1 Spring:1993 pp.45 - 61.

2563 [Intermarriage and its consciousness on an island and in a mountain village]; *[Text in Japanese]*. Yasuo Natsukari. **J. Cult. R. Inst.** 24 1993 pp.1 - 15.

2564 Investigating spousal inconsistencies in temporal reports — a methodological framework. J. Hornik; J.Z. Shapiro. **J. Econ. Psyc.** 14:2 6:1993 pp.387 - 403.

2565 [Japan-Korean comparison of patterns of conjugal relations and marital satisfaction]; *[Text in Japanese]*. Hiroshi Motomura. **Kaz. Kank. Gaku** 12 1993 pp.13 - 24.

2566 A joint model of marital childbearing and marital disruption. Lee A. Lillard; Linda J. Waite. **Demography** 30:4 11:1993 pp.653 - 681.

2567 Lesbian and gay marriage: private commitments, public ceremonies. Suzanne Sherman [Ed.]. Philadelphia: Temple University Press, 1992. ix, 288p. *ISBN: 0877229740, 0877229759. Includes bibliographical references.*

2568 Logiques et pratiques de l'homogamie dans les familles du Bottin Mondain. *[In French]*; (The logic and practice of homogamy in the families from the Bottin Mondain.) *[Summary]*; *[Summary in German]*; *[Summary in Spanish]*. Luc Arrondel; Cyril Grange. **Rev. Fr. Soc.** XXXIV:4 10-12:1993 pp.597 - 626.

2569 Marital adjustment and subjective well-being in Indian-educated housewives and working women. S.S. Nathawat; Asha Mathur. **J. Psychol.** 127:3 5:1993 pp.353 - 358.

2570 Marital happiness and household equity. R. Ward. **J. Marriage Fam.** 55:2 5:1993 pp.427 - 438.

2571 Marital homophily on illicit drug use among young adults — assortative mating or marital influence? Kazuo Yamaguchi; Denise Kandel. **Soc. Forc.** 72:2 12:1993 pp.505 - 528.

2572 Marital name change — plans and attitudes of college students. Laurie Scheuble; David R. Johnson. **J. Marriage Fam.** 55:3 8:1993 pp.747 - 754.

2573 [Marital satisfaction in contemporary Japan]; *[Text in Japanese]*. Fumiko Kanbara. **Bung. Ron.** 41 1993 pp.37 - 66.

2574 Marital status and subjective well-being — a changing relationship? Arne Mastekaasa. **Soc. Ind.** 29:3 7:1993 pp.249 - 276.

2575 Marriage and cohabitation following premarital conception. Wendy D. Manning. **J. Marriage Fam.** 55:4 11:1993 pp.839 - 850.

2576 The meaning of marriage and status in exile: the experience of Iraqi women; *[Summary in French]*; *[Summary in Spanish]*. Madawi Al-Rasheed. **J. Refug. S.** 6:2 1993 pp.89 - 104.

2577 Mediators of male violence toward female intimates. Teresa W. Julian; Patrick C. McKenry. **J. Fam. Viol.** 8:1 3:1993 pp.39 - 56.

2578 Men and women's attribution of blame for domestic violence. Arthur L. Cantos; Peter H. Neidig; K.D. O'Leary. **J. Fam. Viol.** 8:4 12:1993 pp.289 - 302.

F: Population. Family. Gender. Ethnic group

2579 Mixed and matched: interreligious courtship and marriage in Northern Ireland. Raymond M. Lee. Lanham: University Press of America, 1992. 141p. *ISBN: 0819184802*. (*Series:* Class, ethnicity, gender and the democratic nation).

2580 Modeling remarriage — a simple modification of Hernes' model of first marriage. Thomas K. Burch. **Stud. Demogr.** 4(106) 1991 pp.27 - 33.

2581 Money in the bank — transaction costs and the economic organization of marriage. Judith Treas. **Am. Sociol. R.** 58:5 10:1993 pp.723 - 734.

2582 Mothers alone?: a study of women who gave birth outside marriage. Aileen O'Hare; et al. : Federation of Services for Unmarried Parents and their Children, 1993. 100p.

2583 Netzwerkorientierungen und Exklusivität der Paarbeziehung. Unterschiede zwischen Ehen, nichtehelichen Lebensgemeinschaften und Paarbeziehungen mit getrennten Haushalten. *[In German]*; (Network orientation and exclusivity of partnership in marital and nonmarital relationships, including bilocal nonmarital partnerships.) *[Summary]*. Martin Diewald. **Z. Soziol.** 22:4 8:1993 pp.279 - 297.

2584 On the economics of marriage: a theory of marriage, labor, and divorce. Shoshana Grossbard-Shechtman. Boulder: Westview Press, 1993. xviii, 149p. *ISBN: 081338527X. Includes bibliographical references and index.*

2585 Passionate love and marital satisfaction at key transition points in the family life cycle. Paula Tucker; Arthur Aron. **J. Soc. Clin. Psychol.** 12:2 Summer:1993 pp.135 - 147.

2586 Perceptions of marital interaction among black and white newlyweds. Jean Oggins; Joseph Veroff; Douglas Leber. **J. Pers. Soc. Psychol.** 65:3 9:1993 pp.494 - 511.

2587 Predicting marital dissolution — a 5-year prospective longitudinal study of newlywed couples. Lawrence A. Kurdek. **J. Pers. Soc. Psychol.** 64:2 2:1993 pp.221 - 242.

2588 Predicting marital quality with narrative assessments. J. Veroff; L. Sutherland; L. Chadiha; R. Ortega. **J. Marriage Fam.** 55:2 5:1993 pp.326 - 337.

2589 Race differences in marital well-being. Clifford L. Broman. **J. Marriage Fam.** 55:3 8:1993 pp.724 - 732.

2590 Race differences in the decision to marry. R. Bulcroft; K. Bulcroft. **J. Marriage Fam.** 55:2 5:1993 pp.338 - 356.

2591 Racial and ethnic differences in the desire to marry. S. South. **J. Marriage Fam.** 55:2 5:1993 pp.357 - 370.

2592 Racial distance and region in Brazil — intermarriage in Brazilian urban areas. Edward E. Telles. **Lat. Am. Res. R.** 28:2 1993 pp.141 - 162.

2593 Reconceptualizing family work — the effect of emotion work on perceptions of marital quality. Rebecca J. Erickson. **J. Marriage Fam.** 55:4 11:1993 pp.888 - 900.

2594 The religious composition of unions — its role as a determinant of marital stability. Evelyn L. Lehrer; Carmel U. Chiswick. **Demography** 30:3 8:1993 pp.385 - 404.

2595 Review essay — wife beating in Micronesia. Lee Ann Hoff. **J. Micrones. Stud.** 1:2 Dry season:1992 pp.199 - 221.

2596 The roles of identity development and psychosocial intimacy in marital success. Ken J. Rotenberg; George B. Schaut; Brian P. O'Connor. **J. Soc. Clin. Psychol.** 12:2 Summer:1993 pp.198 - 217.

2597 The sexuality of women in physically abusive marriages — a comparative study. Carol Apt; David Farley Hulbert. **J. Fam. Viol.** 8:1 3:1993 pp.57 - 69.

2598 The slowing metabolism of marriage — figures from 1988 U.S. marital status life tables. Robert Schoen; Robin M. Weinick. **Demography** 30:4 11:1993 pp.737 - 746.

F: Population. Famille. Sexe. Groupe ethnique

2599 Some women marry young — transitions to first marriage in metropolitan and nonmetropolitan areas. Diane K. McLaughlin; Daniel T. Lichter; Gail M. Johnston. **J. Marriage Fam.** 55:4 11:1993 pp.827 - 838.

2600 Spouse selection among the children of European immigrants — a study of marriage cohorts in the 1960 census. Matthijs Kalmijn. **Int. Migr. Rev.** XXVII:1 Spring:1993 pp.51 - 78.

2601 The spouse subsystem in the family context — couple interaction categories. Jane Akister; Emma Meekings; Joan Stevenson-Hinde. **J. Fam. Ther.** 15:1 2:1993 pp.1 - 21.

2602 Spouses' joint purchase decisions — determinants of influence tactics for muddling through the process. E. Kirchler. **J. Econ. Psyc.** 14:2 6:1993 pp.405 - 438.

2603 [The structures of marital decision making in Japan and the U.S.: changes from the 1950's to 1980's]; *[Text in Japanese]*. Noriko Iwai. **J. Ind. Manag.** 2 1993 pp.181 - 193.

2604 Testosterone and men's marriages. Alan Booth; James M. Dabbs. **Soc. Forc.** 72:2 12:1993 pp.463 - 477.

2605 Trends in black/white intermarriage. Matthijs Kalmijn. **Soc. Forc.** 72:1 9:1993 pp.119 - 146.

2606 Type A behavior and marital satisfaction — differential effects of achievement striving and impatience/irritability. Karyl MacEwen; Julian Barling. **J. Marriage Fam.** 55:4 11:1993 pp.1001 - 1010.

2607 Women behind the men — variations in wives' support of husbands' careers. Eliza K. Pavalko; Glen H. Elder. **Gender Soc.** 7:4 12:1993 pp.548 - 567.

2608 Writing the names — marriage style, living arrangements, and the first birth interval in a Nepali society. Tom Fricke; Jay D. Teachman. **Demography** 30:2 5:1993 pp.175 - 188.

Parent-child relations
Relations parents-enfants

2609 Childrearing orientations in Mexican American families — the influence of generation and sociocultural factors. Raymond Buriel. **J. Marriage Fam.** 55:4 11:1993 pp.987 - 1000.

2610 Cohabiting mothers: changing marriage and motherhood. Susan McRae. London: Policy Studies Institute, 1993. 184p. *ISBN: 0853745714*.

2611 Constitutional principle and the establishment of the legal relationship between the child and the non-marital father — a study of Germany, the Netherlands and England. Caroline Forder. **Int. J. Law Fam.** 7:1 1993 pp.40 - 107.

2612 Daughter-in-law's burden — an exploratory study of caregiving in Japan. Phyllis B. Harris; Susan O. Long. **J. Cr-cult. Gerontol.** 8:2 4:1993 pp.97 - 118.

2613 Determinants of parental behavior. R. Simons; J. Beaman; R. Conger; C. Wei. **J. Marriage Fam.** 55:1 2:1993 pp.91 - 106.

2614 The deviant mother and child — the development of adoption as an instrument of social control. Josephine Reeves. **J. Law Soc.** 20:4 Winter:1993 pp.412 - 426.

2615 La dynamique de la monoparentalité féminine au Canada. *[In French]*; [The dynamics of single motherhood in Canada] *[Summary]*. Hélène Desrosiers; Celine le Bourdais; Yves Péron. **Eur. J. Pop.** 9:2 1993 pp.197 - 224.

F: Population. Family. Gender. Ethnic group

2616 The effect of parental resources on patterns of leaving home among young adults in the Netherlands. Jenny de Jong Gierveld; Aart C. Liefbroer; Erik Beekink. **Stud. Demogr.** 3(105) 1991 pp.19 - 42.

2617 Effects of family, marital, and parent-child conflict on adolescent self-derogation and suicidal ideation. Shobha C. Shagle; Brian K. Barber. **J. Marriage Fam.** 55:4 11:1993 pp.964 - 974.

2618 Enhancing intuitive skills among adolescent mothers. Paul V. Trad. **J. Child Fam. Stud.** 1:4 12:1992 pp.351 - 370.

2619 Exploring the reliability of measures of family relations, parental attitudes, and parent-child relations in a disadvantaged minority population. Jacqueline McGuire; Felton Earls. **J. Marriage Fam.** 55:4 11:1993 pp.1042 - 1046.

2620 Family emergency procedures: a guide to child protection and domestic violence. Nicola Wyld; Nancy Carlton. London: Legal Action Group, 1993. 211p. *ISBN: 0905099389.*

2621 Family rituals in the early stages of parenthood. Barbara H. Fiese; Karen A. Hooker; Lisa Kotary; Janet Schwagler. **J. Marriage Fam.** 55:3 8:1993 pp.633 - 642.

2622 Family-peer relationships: modes of linkage. Ross D. Parke [Ed.]; Gary W. Ladd [Ed.]. Hillsdale, N.J: L. Erlbaum Associates, 1992. ix, 458p. *ISBN: 0805806008, 0805806016. Includes bibliographical references and index.*

2623 Fathering in the 20th century. Maxime P. Atkinson; Stephen P. Blackwelder. **J. Marriage Fam.** 55:4 11:1993 pp.975 - 986.

2624 Gender and close relationships. Barbara A. Winstead [Ed.]; Valerian J. Derlega [Ed.]; Joseph H. Pleck [Contrib.]; Freya L. Sonenstein [Contrib.]; Leighton C. Ku [Contrib.]; Letitia Anne Peplau [Contrib.]; Charles T. Hill [Contrib.]; Zick Rubin [Contrib.]; Karen K. Dion [Contrib.]; Kenneth L. Dion [Contrib.]; William Ickes [Contrib.]; Ted L. Huston [Contrib.]; Gilbert Geis [Contrib.]; Howard J. Markman [Contrib.]; Louise Silvern [Contrib.]; Mari Clements [Contrib.]; Shelley Kraft-Hanak [Contrib.]; Lawrence A. Kurdek [Contrib.]; Brenda Major [Contrib.]; Ann C. Crouter [Contrib.]; Susan M. McHale [Contrib.]; W. Todd Bartko [Contrib.]; Anita P. Barbee [Contrib.]; Michael R. Cunningham [Contrib.]; Mary R. Gulley [Contrib.]; Pamela A. Yankeelov [Contrib.]; Perri B. Druen [Contrib.]; Susan McWilliams [Contrib.]; Judith A. Howard [Contrib.]; Judith Worell [Contrib.]. **J. Soc. Issues** 49:3 1993 pp.1 - 218. *Collection of 13 articles.*

2625 Historical overview of child discipline in the United States — implication for mental health clinicians and researchers. Rex Forehand; Britton McKinney. **J. Child Fam. Stud.** 2:3 9:1993 pp.221 - 228.

2626 Individualisierung und Elternschaft — das Beispiel USA. *[In German]*; (Individualization and parenthood — the case of the USA.) *[Summary]*. Günter Burkart. **Z. Soziol.** 22:3 6:1993 pp.159 - 177.

2627 Infant affect and home environment. Tom Luster; Robert Boger; Kristi Hannan. **J. Marriage Fam.** 55:3 8:1993 pp.651 - 661.

2628 Investigating the antecedents of perceived social support — parents' views of and behavior toward their children. Barbara R. Sarason; Gregory R. Pierce; Ann Bannerman; Irwin G. Sarason. **J. Pers. Soc. Psychol.** 65:5 11:1993 pp.1071 - 1085.

2629 Laughter in mother-infant emotional communication. Evangeline Nwokah; Alan Fogel. **Humor** 6:2 1993 pp.137 - 161.

2630 Lives together/worlds apart: mothers and daughters in popular culture. Suzanna Danuta Walters. Berkeley: University of California Press, 1992. xiii, 281p. *ISBN:*

F: Population. Famille. Sexe. Groupe ethnique

0520078519. Filmography: p. 277-279. Includes bibliographical references (p. 253-276) and index.

2631 Maternal conversational control and the development of deaf children — a test of the stage hypothesis. Carol Musselman; Adele Churchill. **Fst. Lang.** 13(3):39 1993 pp.271 - 290.

2632 Maternal expectations and ex post rationalizations — the usefulness of survey information on the wantedness of children. Mark R. Rosenzweig; Kenneth I. Wolpin. **J. Hum. Res.** XXVIII:2 Spring:1993 pp.205 - 229.

2633 Mediators of negative contextual factors in parenting. L. Bank; M. Forgatch; G. Patterson; R. Fetrow. **J. Marriage Fam.** 55:2 5:1993 pp.371 - 384.

2634 Mothers' parenting and child mental health. M. Roosa; J. Tein; N. Groppenbacher; M. Michaels; L. Dumka. **J. Marriage Fam.** 55:1 2:1993 pp.107 - 118.

2635 Multigenerational households of caregiving families — negotiating shared space. Rachel A. Pruchno; Norah P. Dempsey; Paula Carder; Tanya Koropeckyj-Cox. **Envir. Behav.** 25:3 5:1993 pp.349 - 366.

2636 Parental assessment of the adjustment of children following abduction by the other parent. Rebecca L. Hegar; Geoffrey L. Greif. **J. Child Fam. Stud.** 2:2 6:1993 pp.143 - 158.

2637 Parental environment in families with gifted and nongifted children. Erika Landau; Kineret Weissler. **J. Psychol.** 127:2 3:1993 pp.129 - 142.

2638 Parenting: an ecological perspective. Tom Luster [Ed.]; Lynn Okagaki [Ed.]. Hillsdale, N.J: L. Erlbaum Associates, 1993. xiv, 272p. *ISBN: 0805807926, 0805808574. Includes bibliographical references and indexes.*

2639 Parenting style as context — an integrative model. Nancy Darling; Laurence Steinberg. **Psychol . B.** 113:3 5:1993 pp.487 - 496.

2640 Parenting under pressure: a study of forty families living in one street. Owen Gill. Cardiff: , 1992. 108p. *Bibliography: p. .106-108. Barnardo's South Wales and South West Division. Fulford Family Centre.*

2641 Patterns of influence and response in abusing and nonabusing families. Sharon Silber; Eric Bermann; Melinda Henderson; Adam Lehman. **J. Fam. Viol.** 8:1 3:1993 pp.27 - 38.

2642 Separation individuation of parents of adolescents — a "multiple identification" perspective of the parent-child interaction. Rachel B. Blass; H. Shmuel Erlich. **J. Child Adol. Gr. Ther.** 3:4 12:1993 pp.175 - 187.

2643 The spatial separation of parents and their adult children. Peter A. Rogerson; Richard H. Weng; Ge Lin. **Ann. As. Am. G.** 83:4 12:1993 pp.656 - 671.

2644 Le stress parental chez les mères d'enfants d'âge préscolaire — validation et normes québécoises pour l'Inventaire de Stress Parental. *[In French]*; (Parental stress of mothers with preschool children — Québec validation and standards in the Parental Stress Inventory.) *[Summary]*. Carl Lachrité; Louise Éthier; Christiane Piché. **San. Ment. Qué** XVII:2 Automne:1992 pp.183 - 203.

2645 Understanding your handicapped child. Valerie Sinason. London: Rosendale Press, 1993. 80p. *ISBN: 1872803652.* (Series: Understanding your child series).

2646 Voluntary parents to multiple children with special needs — a profile. Ann Goetting; Mark G. Goetting. **J. Child Fam. Stud.** 2:4 12:1993 pp.353 - 369.

2647 What's he doing at the family centre?: the dilemmas of men who care for children. Sandy Ruxton; Peter Moss. London: National Children's Home, 1992. 58p. *ISBN: 0900984252.*

F: Population. Family. Gender. Ethnic group

2648 Whom are Mexican infants said to resemble? Monitoring and fostering paternal confidence in the Yucatan. Jeanne M. Regalski; Steven J.C. Gaulin. **Ethol. Socio.** 14:2 1993 pp.97 - 113.

2649 Whose nest? A two-generational view of leaving home during the 1980s. Frances Goldscheider; Calvin Goldscheider. **J. Marriage Fam.** 55:4 11:1993 pp.851 - 862.

F.5: Gender
Sexe

2650 "Be true to your culture" — gender tensions among Somali Muslims in Britain. Camillia Fawzi El-Solh. **Imm. Minor.** 12:1 3:1993 pp.21 - 46.

2651 Bodies that matter: on the discursive limits of sex. Judith P. Butler. New York: Routledge, 1993. xii, 288p. *ISBN: 0415903661. Includes bibliographical references (p. [243]-284) and index.*

2652 Changes in the sex patterning of perceived threats of sanctions. Harold G. Grasmick; Brenda Sims Blackwell; Robert J. Bursik. **Law Soc. Rev.** 27:4 1993 pp.679 - 705.

2653 Chinese orphanages — saving China's abandoned girls. Kay Johnson. **Aust. J. Chin. Aff.** 30 7:1993 pp.61 - 87.

2654 Class, gender, and expanded class consciousness in Steeltown. D.W. Livingstone; J. Marshall Mangan. **R. Soc. Move. Con. Cha.** 15 1993 pp.55 - 82.

2655 Det kultiverade könet. *[In Norwegian]*; [The cultivated gender]. Michael Greifeneder [Ed.]; Petra Junus [Contrib.]; Birgitta Meurling [Contrib.]; Anna Lydia Svalastog [Contrib.]; Eva Lundgren [Contrib.]; Agneta Helmius [Contrib.]; Madeleine Sultán [Contrib.]; Anne-Loise Eriksson [Contrib.]. **Nord. Ny.** 50 4:1993 pp.7 - 109. *Collection of 8 articles.*

2656 Eastern Europe's silent revolution — gender. Peggy Watson. **Sociology** 27:3 8:1993 pp.471 - 487.

2657 An engaged state — sexuality, governance, and the potential for change. Davina Cooper. **J. Law Soc.** 20:3 Autumn:1993 pp.257 - 275.

2658 Engenderings: constructions of knowledge, authority, and privilege. Naomi Scheman. New York: Routledge, 1993. 254p. *ISBN: 041590739X, 0415907403. Includes bibliographical references and index. (Series:* Thinking gender).

2659 The evolution of women's asylums since 1500: from refuges for ex-prostitutes to shelters for battered women. Sherrill Cohen. New York: Oxford University Press, 1992. viii, 262p. *ISBN: 0195051645. Includes bibliographical references (p. 235-254) and index. (Series:* Studies in the history of sexuality).

2660 Ex-citoyennes dans l'ex-Yougoslavie. *[In French]*; [Ex-citizens in ex-Yugoslavia] *[Summary]*. Zarana Papic. **Peup. Médit.** 61 10-12:1992 pp.205 - 215.

2661 Familial hegemony — gender and production politics on Hong Kong's electronics shopfloor. Ching Kwan Lee. **Gender Soc.** 7:4 12:1993 pp.529 - 547.

2662 Fifth international congress on women's health issues. Angela Barron McBride; Ann Oakley; Karen Jensen; Inger Stauning; Kirsti Malterud; Elizabeth Ardayfio-Schandorf. **Health Care Wom. Int.** 14:4 7-8:1993 pp.315 - 386. *Collection of 6 articles.*

2663 Frauen zwischen Tradition und Moderne. *[In German]*; [Women between tradition and modernity]. Rosemarie Nave-Herz. Bielefeld: Kleine, 1992. 246p. *ISBN: 3893701567.*

F: Population. Famille. Sexe. Groupe ethnique

2664 FrauenEssen. Das Begehren der Geschichte/n. *[In German]*; (Women and eating. Craving as an individual and historical phenomenon.) *[Summary]*. Jutta Anna Kleber. **Z. Sexual.** 6:2 6:1993 pp.97 - 118.

2665 Fremde Frauen: von der Gastarbeiterin zur Bürgerin. *[In German]*; [Foreign women: from immigrant workers to citizens]. Marion Schulz [Ed.]. Frankfurt: Verlag für Interkulturelle Kommunikation, 1992. 227p. *ISBN: 388939048X. Includes bibliographical references (p. 147-225).*

2666 Gender and American history since 1890. Barbara Melosh [Ed.]. London, New York: Routledge, 1993. 308p. *ISBN: 0415076757, 0415076765. Includes bibliographical references and index. (Series:* Re-writing histories).

2667 Gender and illness — implications for family therapy. J. Altschuler. **J. Fam. Ther.** 15:4 11:1993 pp.381 - 401.

2668 Gender and political economy: explorations of South Asian systems. Alice Whitcomb Clark [Ed.]. Delhi, New York: Oxford University Press, 1993. viii, 375p. *ISBN: 0195631706. Includes bibliographical references and index.*

2669 Gender and restructuring. M.D. Garcia-Ramon [Contrib.]; M. Vilarino [Contrib.]; M. Baylina [Contrib.]; G. Canoves [Contrib.]; P. Breathnach; J. Momsen [Contrib.]; M. Ciechocińska [Contrib.]; J.G. Townsend [Contrib.]; J. Bain de Corcuera [Contrib.]; P. Raghuram [Contrib.]; A. Wickramasinghe [Contrib.]; F. Mackenzie [Contrib.]; L. Gray [Contrib.]. **Geoforum** 24:1 2:1993 pp.1 - 98. *Collection of 9 articles.*

2670 Gender and the effects of demographics, status, and work values on work centrality. Bilha Mannheim. **Work Occup.** 20:1 2:1993 pp.3 - 22.

2671 Gender choice and domestic space — preferences for kitchens in married households. Mary Joyce Hasell; Frieda Dell Peatross; Christine A. Bono. **J. Arch. Plan. Res.** 10:1 Spring:1993 pp.1 - 22.

2672 Gender class and citizenship in the comparative analysis of welfare states — theoretical and methodological issues. Julia S. O'Connor. **Br. J. Soc.** 44:3 9:1993 pp.501 - 518.

2673 Gender in Southern Africa: conceptual and theoretical issues. Ruth E. Meena [Ed.]. Harare: Sapes Books, 1992. 201p. *ISBN: 0797411623. Includes bibliographical references and indexes. (Series:* Southern Africa political economy series).

2674 Gender, work-family linkages, and economic success among small business owners. Karyn Loscocco; Kevin T. Leicht. **J. Marriage Fam.** 55:4 11:1993 pp.875 - 887.

2675 Grantley Dick Read and Sheila Kitzinger: towards a women-centred story of childbirth. Tess Cosslett. **J. Gender Studies** 1:1 5:1991 pp.29 - 43.

2676 Home truths — women and social change in Japan. Merry White. **Dædalus** 121:4 Fall:1992 pp.61 - 82.

2677 Ideology, female midlife, and the greying of Japan. Margaret Lock. **J. Jpn. Stud.** 19:1 Winter:1993 pp.43 - 78.

2678 If all we knew about women was what we read in Demography, what would we know? Susan C. Watykins. **Demography** 30:4 11:1993 pp.551 - 577.

2679 If pornography is the theory, is inequality the practice? Thelma McCormack. **Philos. S. Sc.** 23:3 9:1993 pp.298 - 326.

2680 The impact of family status on black, white, and Hispanic women's commuting. Valerie Preston; Sara McLafferty; Ellen Hamilton. **Urban Geogr.** 14:3 5-6:1993 pp.228 - 250.

2681 The interweave of public and private — women's challenge to society. H. Lopata. **J. Marriage Fam.** 55:1 2:1993 pp.176 - 190.

F: Population. Family. Gender. Ethnic group

2682 Magyar women: Hungarian women's lives, 1960s-1990s. Chris Corrin; Jo Campling [Ed.]. New York: St. Martin's Press, 1993. 312p. *ISBN: 0312106890, 1557786607. Includes bibliographical references and index.*

2683 The modern girl: girlhood and growing up. Lesley Johnson. Buckingham, Philadelphia: Open University Press, 1993. vi, 184p. *ISBN: 0335099998, 033509998X. Includes bibliographical references and index.*

2684 "Mother to mother" — a maternalist organization in late capitalist America. Linda M. Blum; Elizabeth A. Vandewater. **Soc. Prob.** 40:3 8:1993 pp.285 - 300.

2685 The Muslim woman in Soviet Central Asia. M.A. Tolmacheva. **C.Asian Sur.** 12:4 1993 pp.531 - 548.

2686 Nationalism and gender issues in South Africa. Patricia McFadden. **J. Gender Studies** 1:4 11:1992 pp.510 - 520.

2687 The new women workers — does money equal power? Helen I. Safa. **NACLA** XXVII:1 7-8:1993 pp.24 - 29.

2688 On gender. James Q. Wilson. **Publ. Inter.** 112 Summer:1993 pp.3 - 26.

2689 Palestinian women: identity and experience. Ebba Augustin [Ed.]. London: Zed Books, 1993. 209p. *ISBN: 1856492338.*

2690 Past and future in young women's experience of time. Carmen Leccardi; Marita Rampazi. **Time Soc.** 2:3 1993 pp.353 - 379.

2691 Pionierinnen, Feministinnen, Karrierefrauen?: zur Geschichte des Frauenstudiums in Deutschland. *[In German]*; [Women pioneers, feminists, career women?: On the history of women's studies in Germany]. Anne Schlüter [Ed.]. Pfaffenweiler: Centaurus, 1992. 352p. *ISBN: 3890854192. Includes bibliographical references.*

2692 The popular pleasures of female revenge (or rage bursting in a blaze of gunfire). Kirsten Marthe Lentz. **Cult. St.** 7:3 10:1993 pp.374 - 405.

2693 Reading the past — rewriting the present: Anna Banti and Artemisa Gentileschi. Derek Duncan. **J. Gender Studies** 1:2 11:1991 pp.152 - 167.

2694 Real and imagined women: gender, culture, and postcolonialism. Rajeswari Sunder Rajan. London, New York: Routledge, 1993. 153p. *ISBN: 0415085039, 0415085047.1*

2695 Relationships between the human sex ratio and the woman's microenvironment — four tests? Wade C. Mackey. **Hum. Nature** 4:2 1993 pp.175 - 198.

2696 Repricrocity in social science — gender issues. Patricia Uberoi. **Ind. J. Soc. Sci.** 6:3 7-9:1993 pp.243 - 258.

2697 Rupture épistemologie, mécanisme de protection des droits des femmes. *[In French]*; [Epistemological rupture, a mechanism for protecting women's rights]; *[Summary in Arabic]*. Lilia Labidi; Alia Belkhadi. **R. Tun. Sci. Soc.** 29:108 1992 pp.37 - 45.

2698 Sex and gender hierarchies. Barbara D. Miller [Ed.]. New York; Cambridge: Cambridge University Press, 1992. 401p. *ISBN: 0521412978. Includes index.*

2699 Sexing the self: gendered positions in cultural studies. Elspeth Probyn. London, New York: Routledge, 1993. 189p. *ISBN: 0415073553, 0415073561. Includes bibliographical references and index.*

2700 Sisters of the yam: black women and self-recovery. Bell Hooks. Toronto: Between The Lines, 1993. 194p. *ISBN: 0921284748, 0921284756.*

2701 Theologiegeschichtliche Frauenforschung als Veränderungspotential theologischer Ethik? *[In German]*; [Historical theological women's studies as the potential to change theological ethics?]. Elisabeth Gössmann. **Jahr. Christ. Sozialwiss.** 34 1993 pp.190 - 213.

F: Population. Famille. Sexe. Groupe ethnique

2702 Tracing the contours of women's citizenship; *[Summary in French]*. Ruth Lister. **Policy Pol.** 21:1 1:1993 pp.3 - 16.
2703 Transformations: recollective imagination and sexual difference. Drucilla Cornell. New York: Routledge, 1993. xi, 239p. *ISBN: 0415907462, 0415907470. Includes bibliographical references (p. 225-233) and index.*
2704 Uncovering reality — excavating women's rights in African family law. Alice Armstrong; Chaloka Beyani; Chuma Himonga; Janet Kabeberi-Macharia; Athaliah Molokomme; Welshman Ncube; Thandabantu Nhlapo; Bart Rwezaura; Julie Stewart. **Int. J. Law Fam.** 7:3 1993 pp.314 - 369.
2705 Viva: women and popular protest in Latin America. Sarah A. Radcliffe [Ed.]; Sallie Westwood [Ed.]. London: Routledge, 1993. 270p. *ISBN: 041507312X, 0415073138. Includes bibliographical references and index. (Series:* International studies of women and place).
2706 What do women want? rewriting the social contract. J. Thompson. **Int. J. Moral Soc. S.** 8:3 Autumn:1993 pp.257 - 272.
2707 Wide-verbal-repertoire speech — gender, language, and managerial influence. Susan Schick Case. **Wom. St. Inter. For.** 16:3 5-6:1993 pp.271 - 290.
2708 Women and development — the case of South Korea. Kyung Ae Park. **Comp. Polit.** 25:2 1:1993 pp.127 - 145.
2709 Women and property in early modern England. Amy Erickson. London: Routledge, 1993. 306p. *ISBN: 0415062675.*
2710 Women and social change in Bahrain. May Seikaly. **Int. J. M.E. Stud.** 26:3 8:1993 pp.415 - 426.
2711 Women in Polish society. Rudolf Jaworski [Ed.]; Bianka Pietrow-Ennker [Ed.]. New York; Boulder, Colo: Columbia University Press, 1992. x, 219p. *ISBN: 0880332417. Includes bibliographical references. (Series:* East European monographs).
2712 Women in the Middle East: perceptions, realities and struggles for liberation. Haleh Afshar [Ed.]. Basingstoke: Macmillan, 1993. 250p. *ISBN: 0333575652. (Series:* Women's studies at York/Macmillan).
2713 Women's decision-making: common themes - Irish voices. Nancy W. Veeder. Westport, Conn: Praeger, 1992. xii, 159p. *ISBN: 0275943542, 0275943542. Includes bibliographical references and index.*
2714 Women's equality, demography, and public policies: a comparative perspective. Alena Heitlinger. Basingstoke: Macmillan, 1993. xii, 383p. *ISBN: 0312096380. Includes index. Bibliography: p. 324-348.*
2715 The 'X' case: women and abortion in the Republic of Ireland, 1992. Ailbhe Smyth. **Fem. Leg. Stud.** I:2 8:1993 pp.163 - 178.
2716 Zwischen Anpassung und Widerspruch: Beiträge zur Frauenforschung am Osteuropa-Institut der Freien Universität Berlin. *[In German]*; [Between adaptation and contradiction: contributions to women's studies at the Eastern European Institute at the Freie Universität, Berlin]. Uta Grabmüller [Ed.]; Monika Katz [Ed.]. Wiesbaden: Harrassowitz, 1993. 387p. *ISBN: 3447033754. Includes bibliographical references and index. Freie Universität Berlin, Osteuropa-Institut.*

F: Population. Family. Gender. Ethnic group

Feminism
Féminisme

2717 Against fragmentation: the need for holism. Oshadi Mangena. **J. Gender Studies** 1:1 5:1991 pp.3 - 11.

2718 Anorexic bodies: a feminist and sociological perspective on anorexia nervosa. Morag MacSween. New york; London: Routledge, 1993. 273p. *ISBN: 0415028469. Includes bibliographical references and index.*

2719 Bad girls and dirty pictures: the challenge to reclaim feminism. Alison Assiter [Ed.]; Avedon Carol [Ed.]. London: Pluto Press, 1993. x, 185p. *ISBN: 0745305237.*

2720 The best of times, the worst of times — US feminism today. Johanna Brenner. **New Left R.** 200 7/8:1993 pp.101 - 159.

2721 Beyond economic man: feminist theory and economics. Marianne A. Ferber [Ed.]; Julie A. Nelson [Ed.]. Chicago: University of Chicago Press, 1993. 178p. *ISBN: 0226242005. Includes bibliographical references and index.*

2722 Birth control, contraception and women's rights — a Cape Town case study. Desirée Lewis; Elaine Salo. **Agenda** 17 1993 pp.59 - 68.

2723 Canadian feminism and women of color. Vijay Agnew. **Wom. St. Inter. For.** 16:3 5-6:1993 pp.217 - 228.

2724 Cinderella goes to market: citizenship, gender and women's movements in East Central Europe. Barbara Einhorn. London: Verso, 1993. 280p. *ISBN: 0860914100.*

2725 Contradictions and coherence in feminist responses to law. Emily Jackson. **J. Law Soc.** 20:4 Winter:1993 pp.398 - 411.

2726 Dans des genres différents:le féminisme au miroir transatlantique. *[In French]*; [In different perspectives: feminism in the transatlantic mirror]. Éric Fassin. **Esprit** 196 11:1993 pp.99 - 112.

2727 Depoliticising the personal — a feminist slogan in feminist therapy. Celia Kitzinger. **Wom. St. Inter. For.** 16:5 9-10:1993 pp.487 - 496.

2728 Differences and identities: feminism and the Albuquerque lesbian community. Trisha Franzen. **Signs** 18:4 Summer:1993 pp.891 - 906.

2729 Du musst dich halt behaupten: die gesellschaftliche Situation behinderter Frauen. *[In German]*; [You have to assert yourself: the social situation of disabled women]. Claudia Born; et al; Christine Burger [Ed.]. Würzburg: Bentheim, 1992. 323p. *ISBN: 3925265376.*

2730 Emma Goldman: sexuality and the impurity of the state. Bonnie Haaland. Montréal: Black Rose Books, 1993. 202p. *ISBN: 1895431654.*

2731 Erotic welfare: sexual theory and politics in the age of epidemic. Linda Singer; Judith P. Butler [Ed.]; Maureen MacGrogan [Ed.]. New York: Routledge, 1993. v, 210p. *ISBN: 0415902010. Includes bibliographical references (p. 199-203) and index. (Series:* Thinking gender).

2732 Érotisme et féminisme aux États-Unis: les exercices de la liberté. *[In French]*; [Eroticism and feminism in the USA: the exercise of freedom]. Michel Feher. **Esprit** 196 11:1993 pp.113 - 131.

2733 Feminism and geography: the limits of geographical knowledge. Gillian Rose. Cambridge: Polity Press, 1993. 205p. *ISBN: 0745608183. Includes bibliographical references.*

2734 Feminism and modern reproductive technology. Susan C. Ziehl. **S.Afr. Sociol. R.** 6:1 10:1993 pp.19 - 34.

F: Population. Famille. Sexe. Groupe ethnique

2735 Feminism and nationalism in Ireland: can we learn from history? Margaret Ward. **J. Gender Studies** 1:4 11:1992 pp.492 - 499.

2736 Feminismo y postmodernidad en Puerto Rico. *[In Spanish]*; [Feminism and postmodernity in Puerto Rico]; *[Summary in English]*. Madeline Román. **Rev. Cien. Soc.** XXX:1-2 6:1993 pp.57 - 68.

2737 Feminisms in South Africa. Desiree Lewis. **Wom. St. Inter. For.** 16:5 9-10:1993 pp.535 - 542.

2738 Feminist morality: transforming culture, society, and politics. Virginia Held. Chicago: University of Chicago Press, 1993. xi, 285p. *ISBN: 0226325911. Includes bibliographical references (p. 257-271) and index. (Series:* Women in culture and society).

2739 Feminist theory and Hannah Arendt's concept of public space. Seyla Benhabib. **Hist. Human Sci.** 6:2 5:1993 pp.97 - 114.

2740 Feminist theory and legal strategy. Anne Bottomley [Ed.]; Joanne Conaghan [Ed.]; Annie Bunting [Contrib.]; Deborah Cheney [Contrib.]; Denise Twomey [Contrib.]; Nicola Lacey [Contrib.]; Katherine de Gama [Contrib.]; Frances Olsen [Contrib.]. **J. Law Soc.** 20:1 Spring:1993 pp.1 - 144. *Collection of 9 articles.*

2741 Feminist voices: women's studies texts for Aotearoa/New Zealand. Rosemary Du Plessis [Ed.]; et al. Auckland, New York: Oxford University Press, 1992. xiv, 358p. *ISBN: 019558239X.*

2742 Gender, feminist consciousness, and war. Pamela Johnston Conover; Virginia Sapiro. **Am. J. Pol. Sc.** 37:4 11:1993 pp.1079 - 1099.

2743 The German feminist movement and the question of female aesthetics. Elisabeth Mermann-Jozwiak. **Wom. St. Inter. For.** 16:6 11-12:1993 pp.615 - 626.

2744 The hidden tradition: feminism, women and nationalism in Ireland. Carol Coulter. Cork: Cork University Press, 1993. vi, 69p. *ISBN: 0902561723. Includes bibliographical references. (Series:* Undercurrents).

2745 The history of doing: an illustrated account of movements for women's rights and feminism in India, 1800-1990. Radha Kumar. London, New York: Vision, 1993. 204p. *ISBN: 0860914550. Includes bibliographical references and index.*

2746 Home truths: recent feminist constructions. Robyn Dowling; Geraldine Pratt. **Urban Geogr.** 14:5 9-10:1993 pp.464 - 475.

2747 Indian women's movement: reform and revival. Maitrayee Chaudhuri. New Delhi: Radiant Publishers, 1993. x, 210p. *Includes index. Includes bibliographical references (p. [201]-205). (Series:* Women in the Third World).

2748 Introducing women's studies: feminist theory and practice. Diane Richardson [Ed.]; Victoria Robinson [Ed.]. Basingstoke: Macmillan, 1993. 421p. *ISBN: 0333541960.*

2749 The issues at stake: theory and practice in the contemporary women's movement in India. Nandita Gandhi; Nandita Shah. New Delhi: Kali for Women, 1992. 347p. *ISBN: 818510722X. Includes bibliographical references (p. [339]-347).*

2750 Issues for feminism. Shireen Hassim [Contrib.]; Lama Abu Odeh [Contrib.]; Jane Lewis [Contrib.]; Jenny Morris [Contrib.]; Anna Marie Smith [Contrib.]. **Feminist R.** 43 Spring:1993 pp.26 - 87. *Collection of 4 articles.*

2751 The last sex: feminism and outlaw bodies. Arthur Kroker [Ed.]; MariLouise Kroker [Ed.]. London: Macmillan, 1993. 249p. *ISBN: 0333605195. (Series:* Culture texts).

2752 Lebensfülle für alle — feministische Ethik zwischen den Lehrstühlen. *[In German]*; [The fullness of life for everybody — feminist ethics between the chairs of learning]. Beatrix Schiele. **Jahr. Christ. Sozialwiss.** 34 1993 pp.214 - 232.

F: Population. Family. Gender. Ethnic group

2753 The lonely mirror: Italian perspectives on feminist theory. Paola Bono [Ed.]; Sandra Kemp [Ed.]. London: Routledge, 1993. 251p. *ISBN: 0415037778.*

2754 Love and politics: radical feminist and lesbian theories. Carol Anne Douglas. San Francisco: ism Press, 1990. 11, 363p. *ISBN: 0910383170, 0910383189. Bibliography: p.337-351; includes index.*

2755 Making bodies, making history: feminism and German identity. Leslie A. Adelson. Lincoln: University of Nebraska Press, 1993. 196p. *ISBN: 0803210361. (Series:* Modern German culture & literature series).

2756 Materialist feminism and the politics of discourse. Rosemary Hennessy. New York: Routledge, 1993. xviii, 177p. *ISBN: 041590479X. Includes bibliographical references (p. 154-172) and index. (Series:* Thinking gender).

2757 A mind of one's own: feminist essays on reason and objectivity. Louise M. Antony [Ed.]; Charlotte Witt [Ed.]. Boulder: Westview Press, 1992. xvii, 302p. *ISBN: 0813379377, 0813379385. Includes index. (Series:* Feminist theory and politics).

2758 Nachdenken über Feminismus. *[In German];* (Some thoughts on feminism.) *[Summary].* Volkmar Sigusch. **Z. Sexual.** 6:1 3:1993 pp.36 - 51.

2759 New directions in feminist psychology: practice, theory, and research. Joan C. Chrisler [Ed.]; Doris Howard [Ed.]. New York: Springer Pub. Co, 1992. xiii, 257p. *ISBN: 0826175406. Includes bibliographical references and index. (Series:* Springer series, focus on women).

2760 Patriarchal feminism and the law of the father. Shelley Wright. **Fem. Leg. Stud.** I:2 8:1993 pp.115 - 140.

2761 Population policy & women's rights: transforming reproductive choice. Ruth Dixon-Mueller. Westport, Conn: Praeger, 1993. xiii, 287p. *ISBN: 0275945049, 0275946118. Includes bibliographical references (p. 254-276) and index.*

2762 Reflections on the women's movement in India: religion, ecology, development. Gabriele Dietrich. New Delhi: Horizon India Books, 1992. ix, 145p. *ISBN: 8185487014. Includes bibliographical references.*

2763 Reflexiones generales en torno a la construcción social del "género femenino". *[In Spanish];* [General reflections on the social construction of the "female gender"]. Otomie Vale. **Rev. Cien. Soc.** XXX:1-2 6:1993 pp.323 - 332.

2764 Sense-making in feminist social science research — a call to enlarge the methodological options of feminist studies. Vickie Rutledge Shields; Brenda Dervin. **Wom. St. Inter. For.** 16:1 1-2:1993 pp.65 - 81.

2765 The social bases of feminism in the European Community. Lee Ann Banaszak; Eric Plutzer. **Publ. Opin. Q.** 57:1 Spring:1993 pp.29 - 53.

2766 Space, place and gender relations — part 1. Feminist empiricism and the geography of social relations. Linda McDowell. **Prog. H. Geog.** 17:2 6:1993 pp.157 - 179.

2767 Starka kvinnor och kvinnlig framgångskultur. *[In Swedish];* (Strong women and the female culture of success.). Birgitta Conradson; Angela Rundquist. **Nord. Ny.** 52 1993 pp.50 - 54.

2768 Structuring feminist science. Muriel Lederman. **Wom. St. Inter. For.** 16:6 11-12:1993 pp.605 - 613.

2769 Theorizing black feminisms: the visionary pragmatism of black women. Stanlie Myrise James [Ed.]; Abena P. A. Busia [Ed.]. London, New York: Routledge, 1993. 300p. *ISBN: 0415073367, 0415073375. Includes bibliographical references and index.*

F: Population. Famille. Sexe. Groupe ethnique

2770 Theory on gender: feminism on theory. Paula England [Ed.]. New York: A. de Gruyter, 1993. xii, 377p. *ISBN: 020230437X. Includes bibliographical references and index. (Series:* Social institutions and social change).

2771 Two modes of power? Foucault, feminism and child sexual abuse. Vikki Bell. **J. Gender Studies** 1:2 11:1991 pp.168 - 184.

2772 Up against Foucault: explorations of some tensions between Foucault and feminism. Caroline Ramazanoglu [Ed.]. London, New York: Routledge, 1993. 271p. *ISBN: 0415050103, 0415050111. Includes bibliographical references and index.*

2773 Wenn Frauen wollen, kommt alles ins Rollen: der Frauenstreiktag vom 14. Juni 1991. *[In German]*; [When women act everything starts rolling: the example of the women's day of strike action, 14th June 1991]. Maja Wicki [Ed.]; Irena Breznà; et al. Zurich: Limmat-Verlag, 1991. 177p. *ISBN: 3857911921.*

2774 Whose breast is it anyway? A feminist consideration of advice and "treatment" for breast cancer. Sue Wilkinson; Celia Kitzinger. **Wom. St. Inter. For.** 16:3 5-6:1993 pp.229 - 238.

2775 Women and history. Vol 2. Creation of feminist consciousness: from the Middle Ages to eighteen-seventy. Gerda Lerner. New York: Oxford University Press, 1993. xii, 395p. *ISBN: 0195066049. Includes bibliographical references (p. 331-376) and index.*

2776 Women in Kuwait: the politics of gender. Haya Al-Mughni. London: Saqi, 1993. 174p. *ISBN: 0863561993. Bibliography: p. 161-167. - Includes index.*

2777 Women in South Africa — the historiography in English. Penelope Hetherington. **Int. J. Afr. H. S.** 26:2 1993 pp.241 - 270.

2778 "Women understand so little they call my good nature 'deceit'" — a feminist rethinking of seduction. Jane E. Larson. **Columb. Law.** 93:2 3:1993 pp.374 - 472.

2779 Women's culture and lesbian feminist activism — a reconsideration of cultural feminism. Verta Taylor; Leila J. Rupp. **Signs** 19:1 Autumn:1993 pp.32 - 61.

2780 The women's movement, feminism, and the national struggle in Palestine: unresolved contradictions. Kathy Glavanis. **J. Gender Studies** 1:4 11:1992 pp.463 - 474.

2781 Women's movements around the world — cross-cultural comparisons. Diane Rothbard Margolis. **Gender Soc.** 7:3 9:1993 pp.379 - 399.

2782 Women's studies and the women's movement in South Africa — defining a relationship. Shireen Hassim; Cherryl Walder. **Wom. St. Inter. For.** 16:5 9-10:1993 pp.523 - 534.

Gender differentiation
Différenciation sexuelle

2783 Age and gender differences in children's Halloween costumes. Shirley Matile Ogletree; Larry Denton; Sue Winkle Williams. **J. Psychol.** 127:6 11:1993 pp.633 - 637.

2784 Allein leben — Angleichung der Geschlechter oder Fortschreibung der Geschlechterdifferenz? Ergebnisse einer qualitativen Studie über die Berufs- und Beziehungsbiographien Alleinlebender. *[In German]*; (To be single — convergence of the sexes or continuation of their differences? Results of a qualitative study on

F: Population. Family. Gender. Ethnic group

career and educational biographies of singles.) *[Summary]*; *[Summary in French]*. Dorothea Krüger. **Berl. J. Soziol.** 3 1:1993 pp.75 - 88.

2785 Authority hierarchies at work — the impacts of race and sex. Gail M. McGuire; Barbara F. Reskin. **Gender Soc.** 7:4 12:1993 pp.487 - 506.

2786 Challenging gender inequalities in Africa. Nazneen Kanji [Contrib.]; Niki Jazdowska [Contrib.]; Hussaina Abdullah [Contrib.]; Dorthe von Bülow [Contrib.]; Anne Sørensen [Contrib.]; Emmanuel Nabuguzi [Contrib.]; Janet Bujra [Contrib.]; Beatrice Liatto-Katundo [Contrib.]; Kole Ahmed Shettima [Contrib.]; A. Zack-Williams [Contrib.]; Stephen Riley [Contrib.]; Rok Ajulu [Contrib.]; Akosua Adomako Ampofo [Contrib.]; Bience Gawanas [Contrib.]. **Rev. Afr. Pol. Ec.** 56 3:1993 pp.11 - 122. *Collection of 12 articles.*

2787 The consequences of gender stereotypes for women candidates at different levels and types of office. Leonie Huddy; Nayda Terkildsen. **Pol. Res. Q.** 46:3 9:1993 pp.503 - 525.

2788 Constructing difference — the making of gendered subcultures in a Japanese automobile assembly plant. Heidi Gottfried; Laurie Graham. **Sociology** 27:4 11:1993 pp.611 - 628.

2789 The construction of gender in sport — women, coaching, and the naturalization of difference. Nancy Theberge. **Soc. Prob.** 40:3 8:1993 pp.301 - 313.

2790 The cultural context of women's productive invisibility — a case study of a Pakistani village. Tassawar Saeed Ibraz. **Pak. Dev. R.** 32:1 Spring:1993 pp.101 - 125.

2791 Dance, gender, and culture. Helen Thomas [Ed.]. New York, N.Y: St. Martin's Press, 1993. 219p. *ISBN: 0312088817. Includes index.*

2792 Does enough work make women free? Part-time and full-time work strategies for women. Frances Olsen. **Indian J. Soc. W.** LIII:4 10:1992 pp.599 - 610.

2793 Economic and demographic effects on working women in Latin America. G. Psacharopoulos; Z. Tzannatos. **J. Pop. Ec.** 6:4 1993 pp.293 - 315.

2794 Equal value legislation and the unions: a case study in the UK. Sheila Cunnison. **J. Gender Studies** 1:1 5:1991 pp.12 - 28.

2795 Estimating the gender wage gap in Rawalpindi City. Javed Ashraf; Birjees Ashraf. **J. Dev. Stud.** 29:2 1:1993 pp.365 - 376.

2796 Evolved gender differences in mate preferences — evidence from personal advertisements. Michael W. Wiederman. **Ethol. Socio.** 14:5 1993 pp.331 - 352.

2797 Female entrepreneurs in the informal sector of Ouagadougou. Hanneke Dijkman; Meine Pieter Van Dijk. **Dev. Pol. R.** 11:3 9:1993 pp.273 - 288.

2798 Female representation in U.S. centralized private sector planning — the case of overlapping directorships. Kurt Stephenson; Steve Rakow. **J. Econ. Iss.** XXVII:2 6:1993 pp.459 - 470.

2799 Les femmes, le nationalisme et la guerre. *[In French]*; [Women, nationalism and war] *[Summary]*. Rada Ivekovic. **Peup. Médit.** 61 10-12:1992 pp.185 - 200.

2800 Gender and nation. Nira Yuval-Davis. **Ethn. Racial** 16:4 10:1993 pp.621 - 632.

2801 Gender and the labor market. Ōmori Maki. **J. Jpn. Stud.** 19:1 Winter:1993 pp.79 - 102.

2802 Gender and the relationship between job experiences and psychological distress — a study of dual-earner couples. Rosalind C. Barnett; Nancy L. Marshall; Stephen W. Raudenbush; Robert T. Brennan. **J. Pers. Soc. Psychol.** 64:5 5:1993 pp.794 - 806.

F: Population. Famille. Sexe. Groupe ethnique

2803 Gender and the social rights of citizenship — the comparative analysis of state policies and gender relations. Ann S. Orloff. **Am. Sociol. R.** 58:3 6:1993 pp.303 - 328.

2804 Gender differences in campaign messages — the political advertisements of men and women candidates for U.S. Senate. Kim Fridkin Kahn. **Pol. Res. Q.** 46:3 9:1993 pp.481 - 502.

2805 Gender differences in initiating requests for help. Mary I. Bresnahan. **Text** 13:1 1993 pp.7 - 27.

2806 Gender differences in job autonomy — the consequences of occupational segregation and authority position. Marina A. Adler. **Sociol. Q.** 34:3 8:1993 pp.449 - 465.

2807 Gender differences in mate preference among law students — divergence and convergence of criteria. John Marshall Townsend; Laurence W. Roberts. **J. Psychol.** 127:5 9:1993 pp.507 - 528.

2808 Gender differences in social persistence. Mary Beth Manolis; Richard Milich. **J. Soc. Clin. Psychol.** 12:4 Winter:1993 pp.385 - 405.

2809 Gender differences in training, capital, and wages. John M. Barron; Dan A. Black; Mark A. Loewenstein. **J. Hum. Res.** XXVIII:2 Spring:1993 pp.343 - 364.

2810 Gender divisions and social change. Nickie Charles. Hemel Hempstead, Hertfordshire, Lanham, MD: Harvester Wheatsheaf, Barnes & Noble Books, 1993. 306p. *ISBN: 0389210072. Includes bibliographical references and index.*

2811 Gender, education and employment in post-Mao China — issues in modernisation. Shirin M. Rai. **China R.** 29:1 1-3:1993 pp.1 - 14.

2812 The gender factor: women in New Zealand organisations. Suzann Olsson [Ed.]. Palmerston North, N.Z: Dunmore Press, 1992. 350p.

2813 Gender inequality and entrepreneurship — the Indian silk industry. Linda Mayoux. **Dev. Pol. R.** 11:4 12:1993 pp.413 - 426.

2814 The gender of time in professional occupations. Linda Hantrais. **Time Soc.** 2:2 1993 pp.139 - 157.

2815 Gender segregation in China. Karyn A. Loscocco; Xun Wang. **Social Soc. Res.** 76:3 4:1992 pp.118 - 126.

2816 Gender, work, and medicine: women and the medical division of labour. Elianne Riska [Ed.]; Katarina Wegar [Ed.]. London; Newbury Park, Calif: Sage Publications, 1993. viii, 196p. *ISBN: 0803989024, 0803989032. Includes bibliographical references and index. (Series:* Sage studies in international sociology).

2817 Gender-differentiated employment practices in the South Korean textile industry. Ok-Jie Lee. **Gender Soc.** 7:4 12:1993 pp.507 - 528.

2818 Gendered spaces and women's status. Daphne Spain. **Sociol. Theory** 11:2 7:1993 pp.137 - 151.

2819 Geschlechterverhältnis in der Wende. Individualisierung versus Solidarisierung? *[In German]*; [Gender relations during the transition. Individualization versus solidarity]. Hildegard Maria Nickel. **Deut. Arch.** 26:10 10:1993 pp.1127 - 1137.

2820 The growth in full-time work among Swedish women in the 1980s. Marianne Sundström. **Acta Sociol.** 36:2 1993 pp.139 - 150.

2821 He's no good: sexual division of labor and habitus among Nepal's Marpha Thakali. Barbara Parker; David W. Patterson. **S.Asia B.** XIII:1+2 1993 pp.81 - 89.

2822 Het aandeel van mannen in huishoudelijk werk. *[In Dutch]*; (The participation of men in household labour.) *[Summary]*. T. van der Lippe; A. van Doorne-Huiskes; J.J. Siegers. **Mens Maat.** 68:2 5:1993 pp.133 - 152.

F: Population. Family. Gender. Ethnic group

2823 How combat ideology structures military wives' domestic labour. Deborah Harrison; Lucie Laliberté. **Stud. Pol. Ec.** 42 Autumn:1993 pp.45 - 80.

2824 Industrial restructuring and gendered labour market processes. Lena Gonäs; Helén Westin. **Econ. Ind. Dem.** 14:3 8:1993 pp.423 - 458.

2825 Integration is not enough — gender inequality and empowerment in Nicaraguan agricultural co-operatives. Linda Mayoux. **Dev. Pol. R.** 11:1 3:1993 pp.67 - 89.

2826 Interactions en classe et réussite scolaire. Une analyse des différences filles-garçons. *[In French]*; (Class interactions and success at school. An analysis comparing boys and girls.) *[Summary]*; *[Summary in German]*; *[Summary in Spanish]*. Georges Felouzis. **Rev. Fr. Soc.** XXXIV:2 4-6:1993 pp.199 - 222.

2827 Iraqi rural women's participation in domestic decision-making; *[Summary in French]*; *[Summary in Spanish]*. Qais N. Al-Nouri. **J. Comp. Fam. Stud.** XXIV:1 Spring:1993 pp.81 - 97.

2828 Is more better? Mark II — with reference to women town planners in Britain. Clara H. Greed. **Wom. St. Inter. For.** 16:3 5-6:1993 pp.255 - 270.

2829 Letters of recommendation in academe — do women and men write in different languages? Susan E. Bell; C. Suzanne Cole; Liliane Floge. **Am. Sociol.** 23:3 Fall:1992 pp.7 - 22.

2830 "The madonna boom" — women in the Japanese diet. Iwai Tomoaki. **J. Jpn. Stud.** 19:1 Winter:1993 pp.103 - 120.

2831 Nationalism and women in Croatia. Ljiljana Gjurgjan. **J. Gender Studies** 1:4 11:1992 pp.521 - 529.

2832 A new measure of social status for men and women — the social distance scale. Bart F.M. Bakker. **Neth. J. Soc. Sci.** 29:2 12:1993 pp.113 - 129.

2833 "No freedom without the women" — mobilization and gender in South Africa, 1970-1992. Gay W. Seidman. **Signs** 18:2 Winter:1993 pp.291 - 320.

2834 The orthodox Jungian perspective on gender differences in consciousness — a re-examination. W.D. Hooke; S.L. Hooke. **J. Analyt. Psychol.** 38:3 7:1993 pp.273 - 302.

2835 Patriarchy and the politics of gender in modernizing societies: Iran, Pakistan and Afghanistan. Valentine M. Moghadam. **S.Asia B.** XIII:1+2 1993 pp.122 - 133.

2836 The practice of protective legislation for pregnant workers in Italy — limits, problems, and contradictions. Patrizia Romito. **Wom. St. Inter. For.** 16:6 11-12:1993 pp.581 - 590.

2837 Religion and the social positions of women and men; *[Summary in French]*. Moniek Steggerda. **Soc. Compass** 40:1 3:1993 pp.65 - 73.

2838 Renegotiating the domestic division of labour? A study of dual career households in north east and south east England. Nicky Gregson; Michelle Lowe. **Sociol. Rev.** 41:3 8:1993 pp.475 - 505.

2839 Returning to work after childbirth — opportunities and inequalities. Susan McRae. **Eur. Sociol. R.** 9:2 9:1993 pp.125 - 137.

2840 Rhetorical vision of men and women managers in Singapore. S.K. Jean Lee; Hwee Hoon Tan. **Human Relat.** 46:4 4:1993 pp.527 - 542.

2841 The silenced voice — female social mobility patterns with particular reference to the British Isles. Bernadette C. Hayes; Robert L. Miller. **Br. J. Soc.** 44:4 12:1993 pp.653 - 672.

F: Population. Famille. Sexe. Groupe ethnique

2842 Simultaneous determination of household and market-oriented activities of women in rural Pakistan. Harold Alderman; Salim Chishti. **Res. Popul. Econ.** 7 1991 pp.245 - 265.
2843 Social divisions in caring. Hilary Graham. **Wom. St. Inter. For.** 16:5 9-10:1993 pp.461 - 470.
2844 Social mobility of women from an intercountry perspective — theoretical context and methodological difficulties. Henryk Domański; Zbigniew Sawiński. **Soc. Sci. Info.** 32:1 3:1993 pp.87 - 109.
2845 Socio-legal status of Muslim women. Muniza Rafiq Khan. London: Sangam, 1993. xiv, 136p. *ISBN: 0861322916.*
2846 Stereotypical attitudes toward gender-based grade-level assignment of Japanese elementary school teachers. Hiromi Fukada; Seiko Fukada; Joe Hicks. **J. Psychol.** 127:3 5:1993 pp.345 - 351.
2847 Toward an integration of theory and research on the status of women. Karen Bradley; Diana Khor. **Gender Soc.** 7:3 9:1993 pp.347 - 378.
2848 The two facets of female violence — the public and the domestic domains. Sarah Ben-David. **J. Fam. Viol.** 8:4 12:1993 pp.345 - 359.
2849 Über sexuelle Arbeitsteilung. *[In German]*; (The division of labour by sex.) *[Summary]*; *[Summary in French]*. Gerhard Wagner. **Berl. J. Soziol.** 3:4 1993 pp.469 - 486.
2850 "Under the wife's feet"— renegotiating gender divisions in early retirement. Dallas Cliff. **Sociol. Rev.** 41:1 2:1993 pp.30 - 53.
2851 Waitering/waitressing — engendering the work of table servers. Elaine J. Hall. **Gender Soc.** 7:3 9:1993 pp.329 - 346.
2852 Whose interests? Problems in planning for women's practical needs. R. Alsop. **World Dev.** 21:3 3:1993 pp.367 - 377.
2853 Women and politics in New Zealand. Helena Catt [Contrib.]; Jennifer Curtin [Contrib.]; Heather Devere [Contrib.]; Bronwyn Hayward [Contrib.]; Elizabeth McLeay [Contrib.]; Raymond Miller [Contrib.]; Jean Drage [Contrib.]; Jacqueline Owens [Contrib.]; Peter Aimer [Contrib.]; Jack Vowles [Contrib.]; Stephen Levine [Contrib.]; Nigel S. Roberts [Contrib.]. **Poli. Sci.** 45:1 7:1993 pp.6 - 151. *Collection of 9 articles.*
2854 Women as farm landlords: does gender affect environmental decision-making on leased land? Denise M. Rogers; Ann M. Vandeman. **Rural Sociol.** 58:4 Winter:1993 pp.560 - 568.
2855 Women in Iran — the revolutionary ebb and flow. Nesta Ramazani. **Middle E. J.** 47:3 Summer:1993 pp.409 - 428.
2856 Women in the law — partners or tokens? Patricia MacCorquodale; Gary Jensen. **Gender Soc.** 7:4 12:1993 pp.582 - 593.
2857 Women, paid employment and ill-health in Britain and Finland. Sara Arber; Eero Lahelma. **Acta Sociol.** 36:2 1993 pp.121 - 138.
2858 Women's emancipation under communism — a re-evaluation. Lalith deSilva. **E. Eur. Quart.** XXVII:3 Fall:1993 pp.301 - 315.
2859 Women's power and the gendered division of domestic labor in the Third World. Laura Sanchez. **Gender Soc.** 7:3 9:1993 pp.434 - 459.
2860 Women's search for a place in public life in Singapore. Seet Ai Mee. **Sojourn** 8:2 8:1993 pp.275 - 292.

F: Population. Family. Gender. Ethnic group

2861 Women's work and social network use in Oaxaca City, Mexico. Katie Willis. **B. Lat. Am. Res.** 12:1 1:1993 pp.65 - 82.

Gender roles
Rôles de sexe

2862 20th century man - 21st century woman: how both sexes can bridge the century gap. Harriet Harman. London: Vermilion, 1993. 183p. *ISBN: 0091778190.*

2863 L'aide apportée par des tiers et les réactions des aidantes naturelles à la prise en charge de personnes âgées en perte d'autonomie. *[In French]*; (Support provided by third parties and the reactions from close female supporters with regard to caring for the elderly.) *[Summary].* Andrée Demers; Jean-Pierre Lavoie; Aline Drapeau. **San. Ment. Qué** XVII:2 Autumn:1992 pp.205 - 225.

2864 Belonging to others: cultural construction of womanhood among Muslims in a village in Bangladesh. Jitka Kotalová. Uppsala: Academiae Ubsaliensis, 1993. 252p. *ISBN: 9155431054. Based on the author's thesis (doctoral)--Uppsala University, 1993. Includes bibliographical references (p. [243]-252). (Series:* Acta Universitatis Upsaliensis. Uppsala studies in cultural anthropology).

2865 Body-images and the pornography of representation. Rosi Braidotti. **J. Gender Studies** 1:2 11:1991 pp.137 - 151.

2866 Changes in U.S. men's attitudes toward the family provider role, 1972-1989. Jane Riblett Wilkie. **Gender Soc.** 7:2 6:1993 pp.261 - 279.

2867 Changing work roles of black and white women. C. Herring; K. Wilson-Sadberry. **J. Marriage Fam.** 55:2 5:1993 pp.314 - 325.

2868 The Christmas imperative: leisure, family and women's work. Leslie Bella. Halifax, N.S: Fernwood Publishing, 1992. *ISBN: 1895686091. Includes bibliographical references.*

2869 Cultivating male allies — a focus on primate females, including homo sapiens. Bonnie Lori Hooks; Penny Anthon Green. **Hum. Nature** 4:1 1993 pp.81 - 107.

2870 Daughtering and mothering: female subjectivity reanalysed. Karlein Schreurs [Ed.]; Liesbeth Woertman [Ed.]; Janneke van Mens-Verhulst [Ed.]. London, New York: Routledge, 1993. 170p. *ISBN: 0415086493, 0415086507. Includes bibliographical references and index.*

2871 Déséquilibres psycho-sociaux et dynamique socio-économique dans les pays du triers-monde, notamment au Maghreb. *[In French]*; [Psycho-social disequilibria and socio-economic dynamics in developing countries, especially the Maghreb]. Ibrahima Sow. **R. Tun. Sci. Soc.** 29:109 1992 pp.329 - 344.

2872 Dilemmas of femininity — gender differences in the social construction of sexual imagery. Linda Kalof. **Sociol. Q.** 34:4 11:1993 pp.639 - 651.

2873 Dislocating masculinity: comparative ethnographies. Andrea Cornwall [Ed.]; Nancy Lindisfarne [Ed.]. London, New York: Routledge, 1993. 236p. *ISBN: 0415079411, 041507942X. Includes bibliographical references and index. (Series:* Male orders).

2874 Divided lives: American women in the twentieth century. Rosalind N. Rosenberg. London: Penguin, 1993. 291p. *ISBN: 0140174869.*

2875 [Early marriage, high fertility, women's position: an essay on the case of Muslims in rural Bangladesh]; *[Text in Japanese].* Mineo Takada. **J. Cen. Wom. Stud.** 2 1993 pp.1 - 25.

F: Population. Famille. Sexe. Groupe ethnique

2876 Ebenbild Gottes oder Hilfe des Mannes? Die Frau im Kontext der anthropologischen Aussagen von Genesis 1-3. *[In German]*; [An image of God or man's helper? Woman in the context of anthropological statements in Genesis 1-3]. Christoph Dohmen. **Jahr. Christ. Sozialwiss.** 34 1993 pp.152 - 164.

2877 Entretejiendo consensos — reflexiones sobre la dimensión social de la identidad de género de la mujer. *[In Spanish]*; [Interviewing consensus — reflections on the social dimension to women's gender identity]. Alejandro Cervantes Carson. **Est. Sociol.** XI:31 1-4:1993 pp.237 - 264.

2878 Erotics & politics: gay male sexuality, masculinity, and feminism. Timothy C. Edwards. London: Routledge, 1993. 192p. *ISBN: 041509903X. Includes bibliographical references and index. (Series:* Critical studies on men and masculinities).

2879 Etre femme et mère à Madagascar: Tañala d'Ifanadiana. *[In French]*; [To be a woman and mother in Madagascar: Tañala d'Ifanadiana]. Bodo Ravololomanga; Georges Condominas [Intro.]. Paris: L'Harmattan, 1992. 237p. *ISBN: 2738416985. Includes bibliographical references and index.*

2880 Femininity, post-Fordism, and the "new traditionalism". D.A. Leslie. **Envir. Plan. D.** 11:6 12:1993 pp.689 - 708.

2881 Une «féminisation des mœurs». *[In French]*; [Is there a "feminization " of manners?]. Claude Fischler. **Esprit** 196 11:1993 pp.9 - 28.

2882 Les femmes dans l'héroïsme sportif. *[In French]*; [Women and the heroism of sport]. Michèle Metoudi. **Esprit** 196 11:1993 pp.29 - 48.

2883 "Flexible" work, precarious future — some lessons from the Canadian clothing industry; *[Summary in French]*. Belinda Leach. **Can. R. Soc. A.** 30:1 2:1993 pp.64 - 82.

2884 Gender as a factor in the attribution of leadership traits. Deborah Alexander; Kristi Anderson. **Pol. Res. Q.** 46:3 9:1993 pp.527 - 545.

2885 Gender thinking. Steven G. Smith. Philadelphia: Temple University Press, 1992. xv,381p. *ISBN: 0877229635, 0877229643. Includes bibliographical references (p. 321-373) and index.*

2886 Geschlechterrollen und sozialpolitische Umorientierung. *[In German]*; [Gender roles and a reorientation of social policy]. Gerhard Bäcker; Brigitte Stolz-Willig. **Gewerk. Monat.** 44:7 7:1993 pp.414 - 432.

2887 Les habits neufs de la domination masculine. *[In French]*; [The new habits of masculine domination]. François de Singly. **Esprit** 196 11:1993 pp.54 - 64.

2888 Los hombres cambiantes, los machos impenitentes y las relaciones de género en México en los noventa. *[In Spanish]*; [Changing men, unrepentant chauvists and gender relations in Mexico in the 1990s]. Matthew C. Gutmann. **Est. Sociol.** XI:33 9-12:1993 pp.725 - 740.

2889 Homework and domestic work. Hilary Silver. **Sociol. For.** 8:2 6:1993 pp.181 - 204.

2890 "I can't come in today, the baby has chickenpox!" Gender and class processes in how parents in the labour force deal with the problem of sick children; *[Summary in French]*. Jenny Blain. **Can. J. Soc.** 18:4 Fall:1993 pp.405 - 429.

2891 Le immagini femminili nei programmi televisivi. Una panoramica sulle ricerche anglo-americane dagli anni 70 ad oggi. *[In Italian]*; (Women's images in television programs — a survey of American and English researches from 1970 to today.) *[Summary]*. Saveria Capecchi. **Rass. It. Soc.** 34:3 9:1993 pp.425 - 440.

F: Population. Family. Gender. Ethnic group

2892 The impact of family migration and family life cycle on the employment status of married, college-educated women. Lucy C. Yu; Min Qi Wang; Lynne Kaltreider; Ying-Ying Chien. **Work Occup.** 20:2 5:1993 pp.233 - 246.

2893 Kuwaiti women at a crossroads — privileged development and the constraints of ethnic stratification. Anh Nga Longva. **Int. J. M.E. Stud.** 25:3 8:1993 pp.443 - 456.

2894 Life is hard: machismo, danger, and the intimacy of power in Nicaragua. Roger N. Lancaster. Berkeley: University of California Press, 1993. xxiii, 340p. *ISBN: 0520079248. Includes bibliographical references and index.*

2895 Male premarital aggression and gender identity. J. Boye-Beaman; K. Leonard; M. Senchak. **J. Marriage Fam.** 55:2 5:1993 pp.303 - 313.

2896 Masculinities. R.W. Connell [Ed.]; Lynne Segal [Contrib.]; Mike Donaldson [Contrib.]; Rosa Linda Fregoso [Contrib.]; Anthony McMahon [Contrib.]; G.W. Dowsett [Contrib.]; Judith Stacey [Contrib.]; Michael A. Messner [Contrib.]; Irit Rogoff [Contrib.]; David van Leer [Contrib.]. **Theory Soc.** 22:5 10:1993 pp.595 - 762. *Collection of 10 articles.*

2897 Masculinity and male codes of honor in modern France. Robert A. Nye. New York: Oxford University Press, 1993. ix, 316p. *ISBN: 0195046498. Includes bibliographical references (p. 297-309) and index. (Series:* Studies in the history of sexuality).

2898 Masculinity and women. Teachers at Christian Brothers College. Lawrence B. Angus. **Organ. Stud.** 14:2 1993 pp.235 - 260.

2899 Menschenrechte — Männerrechte-Frauenrechte? *[In German]*; [Human rights — men's rights or women's rights?]. Konrad Hilpert. **Jahr. Christ. Sozialwiss.** 34 1993 pp.35 - 72.

2900 Migrant women: crossing boundaries and changing identities. Gina Buijs [Ed.]. Oxford: Berg, 1993. 204p. *ISBN: 085496729X, 0854968695. Includes bibliographical references and index. (Series:* Cross-cultural perspectives on women).

2901 Mothers' management of their combined workloads — clerical work and household needs; *[Summary in French]*. Melody Hessing. **Can. R. Soc. A.** 30:1 2:1993 pp.37 - 63.

2902 Mulheres e famílias operárias — a «esposa doméstica». *[In Portuguese]*; (Women and the working-class families — the housewife.) *[Summary]; [Summary in French]*. Ana Nunes de Almeida. **Anál. Soc.** XVIII:1(120) 1993 pp.105 - 134.

2903 Mutamenti del ruolo della donna in seno alla cultura pastorale abruzzese nel XX secolo. *[In Italian]*; [Changes in the role of women within the pastoral culture of the Abruzzi in the 20th century]. Anna Cavasinni. **Sociologia [Rome]** XXVII:1-3 1993 pp.357 - 388.

2904 Negotiating discourses of femininity. Sara Mills. **J. Gender Studies** 1:3 5:1992 pp.271 - 285.

2905 Obraz zhenshchiny v religioznom soznanii: proshloe, nastoiashchee, budushchee. *[In Russian]*; (The feminine image in religious consciousness: the past, the present and the future.). M. Stepaniants. **Obshch. Nauki Sovrem.** 4 1993 pp.177 - 183.

2906 Of Caldecotts and kings — gendered images in recent American children's books by black and non-black illustrators. Roger Clark; Rachel Lennon; Leanna Morris. **Gender Soc.** 7:2 6:1993 pp.227 - 245.

2907 On male femaling — some relations between sex, sexuality and gender. Richard Ekins. **Sociol. Rev.** 41:1 2:1993 pp.1 - 29.

F: Population. Famille. Sexe. Groupe ethnique

2908 The proper study of men. David Popenoe [Contrib.]; Andrew M. Greeley [Contrib.]; Richard B. Felson [Contrib.]; Stephen R. Felson [Contrib.]; Robin Fox [Contrib.]; Herbert I. London [Contrib.]; Michael S. Kimmel [Contrib.]; Ellen Frankel Paul [Contrib.]; Irving Louis Horowitz [Contrib.]. **Society** 30:6 9-10:1993 pp.5 - 45. *Collection of 8 articles.*

2909 "Proper women" and city pleasures — gender, class, and contested meanings in La Paz. L. Gill. **Am. Ethn.** 20:1 2:1993 pp.72 - 88.

2910 Resistance to "modernity" — southern Illinois farm women and the cult of domesticity. J. Adams. **Am. Ethn.** 20:1 2:1993 pp.89 - 113.

2911 The sexual metaphor. Helen Haste. London: Harvester Wheatsheaf, 1993. 302p. *ISBN: 071080282X.*

2912 Singaporean gifted adolescents under scrutiny — the gender factor; *[Summary in German]; [Summary in French].* Patrick C.F. Kwan. **Int. R. Educat.** 39:3 5:1993 pp.161 - 182.

2913 Smiling, deferring, and flirting — doing gender by giving "good service". Elaine J. Hall. **Work Occup.** 20:4 11:1993 pp.452 - 471.

2914 Social change and the position of women in Cyprus. Stavros Stavrou. **Cyprus Rev.** 4:2 Fall:1992 pp.67 - 92.

2915 [Sociological analysis about growing rate of unmarried women in Japan]; *[Text in Japanese].* Terue Ohashi. Tokyo: N.H.K. Books, 1993.

2916 Unreasonable men. Victor Jeleniewski Seidler. New York; London: Routledge, 1993. 254p. *ISBN: 0415082935, 0415082943. Includes bibliographical references and index. (Series:* Male orders).

2917 Urban women and violence — the life of a well-to-do-housewife. Kusum Gupta. **Soc. Act.** 43:2 4-6:1993 pp.183 - 192.

2918 Values under siege in Mexico — strategies for sheltering traditional values from change. Linda J. Hubbell. **J. Anthr. Res.** 49:1 Spring:1993 pp.1 - 16.

2919 Vécu dans les rôles féminins, soutien, conflit travail-famille et symptomatologie dépressive. *[In French];* (Women's life experiences, support, work-family conflicts and depressive symptomatology.) *[Summary].* Ursula Streit; Yolande Tanguay. **San. Ment. Qué** XVIII:2 Autumn:1993 pp.109 - 134.

2920 White women in darkest Africa: marginals as observers in no-woman's land; *[Summary in French].* Edward A. Tiryakian. **Civilisations** XLI:1-2 1993 pp.209 - 238.

2921 A woman's place....?: women and work. Elizabeth Templeton [Ed.]. Edinburgh: Saint Andrew's Press, 1993. 169p. *ISBN: 0861531620.*

2922 [Women, between family and work in present-day Japan]; *[Text in Japanese].* Hiroko Nishimura. **Soshiolojika** 17(1) 1993 pp.29 - 47.

2923 Women's "cocoon work" in new religious movements — sexual experimentation and feminine rites of passage. Susan J. Palmer. **J. Sci. S. Relig.** 32:4 12:1993 pp.343 - 355.

2924 Women's role in maintaining households — family welfare and sexual inequality in Ghana. Cynthia B. Lloyd; Anastasia J. Gage-Brandon. **Pop. Stud.** 47:1 3:1993 pp.115 - 131.

2925 Women's roles in the Afghanistan Jihad. Audrey C. Shalinsky. **Int. J. M.E. Stud.** 25:4 11:1993 pp.661 - 675.

2926 Zur Geschlechtersozialisation im Vorschulalter in der DDR — ein Nachtrag oder — als Mutti früh zur Arbeit ging. *[In German];* (On the socialization of the sexes in

F: Population. Family. Gender. Ethnic group

pre-school age in the GDR — a postscript. Or — when mummy went to work in the early morning.). Hartmut A.G. Bosinski. **Wissensch. Z. Humboldt-Univ.** 41:1 1992 pp.39 - 49.

2927 Zur Situation von Frauen in der Gesellschaft der Bundesrepublik Deutschland — Soziologische Perspektiven. *[In German]*; [The situation for women in German society — sociological perspectives]. Henny Engels. **Jahr. Christ. Sozialwiss.** 34 1993 pp.12 - 34.

Sex discrimination
Discrimination sexuelle

2928 Avoiding the exquisite trap: a critical look at the equal treatment/special treatment debate in law. Julia Adiba Sohrab. **Fem. Leg. Stud.** I:2 8:1993 pp.141 - 162.
2929 Barriers to women are barriers to local government. Su Maddock. **Loc. Govt. St.** 19:3 Autumn:1993 pp.341 - 350.
2930 "Close to home" in Johannesburg — gender oppression in township households. Caroline White. **Wom. St. Inter. For.** 16:2 3-4:1993 pp.149 - 163.
2931 Debunking the Social Democrats and the myth of equality. R. Amy Elman. **Wom. St. Inter. For.** 16:5 9-10:1993 pp.513 - 522.
2932 Dyskryminacja kobiet na rynku pracy w Polsce w latach 1990-1992. *[In Polish]*; (Women's discrimination in the labour market in Poland in 1990-1992.). Irena E. Kotowska. **Pra. Zab. Społ.** XXXV:4 4:1993 pp.14 - 27.
2933 Every woman is an occupied territory: the politics of militarism and sexism and the Israeli-Palestinian conflict. Simona Sharoni. **J. Gender Studies** 1:4 11:1992 pp.447 - 462.
2934 Gender and technology in the making. Cynthia Cockburn; Susan Ormrod. London: Sage, 1993. 185p. *ISBN: 0803988109*.
2935 Gender inequality in education and employment in the scheduled castes and tribes of India. Dana Dunn. **Pop. Res. Pol. R.** 12:1 1993 pp.53 - 70.
2936 The "glass ceiling" — the impasse of women in management in a county government workforce. Jerry Yaffe. **Loc. Govt. St.** 19:3 Autumn:1993 pp.431 - 446.
2937 Is there sex discrimination in the legal profession? Further evidence on tangible and intangible margins. David N. Laband; Bernard F. Lentz. **J. Hum. Res.** XXVIII:2 Spring:1993 pp.230 - 258.
2938 Jockeying for position — winnings and gender discrimination on the thoroughbred racetrack. Margaret A. Ray; Paul W. Grimes. **Soc. Sci. Q.** 74:1 3:1993 pp.46 - 61.
2939 A man's town: the subordination of women in rural Australia. Ken Dempsey. Melbourne: Oxford University Press, 1992. 325p. *ISBN: 019554997X, 019554997X. Includes index.*
2940 Now that we are here — discrimination, disparagement, and harassment at work and the experience of women lawyers. Janet Rosenberg; Harry Perlstadt; William R. Phillips. **Gender Soc.** 7:3 9:1993 pp.415 - 433.
2941 Sexism in research. Margrit Eichler [Contrib.]; Liz Stanley [Contrib.]; Sue Wise [Contrib.]; Maithreyi Krishnaraj [Contrib.]; Charles C. Langford [Contrib.]; Barbara J. Isely [Contrib.]; K. Ravindran [Contrib.]; Estela V. Welldon [Contrib.]; Malini Karkal [Contrib.]; Norbert Elliot [Contrib.]; Shirin Kudchedkar [Contrib.]; S.P. Sathe [Contrib.]. **Indian J. Soc. W.** LIII:3 7:1992 pp.329 - 483. *Collection of 11 articles.*

F: Population. Famille. Sexe. Groupe ethnique

2942 Survivors in a male preserve — a study of British women academics' experiences and perceptions of discrimination in a UK university. Barbara Bagilhole. **High. Educ.** 26:4 12:1993 pp.431 - 447.

2943 Umgekehrte Diskriminierung — ein ethisch geeigneter Weg zur Herstellung von Gleichheit? *[In German]*; [Discrimination in reverse — an ethically-appropriate road to equality?]. Dieter Witschen. **Jahr. Christ. Sozialwiss.** 34 1993 pp.73 - 100.

2944 Wayward puritans in the Ivory Tower — collective aspects of gender discrimination in academia. Mary J. Gallant; Jay E. Cross. **Sociol. Q.** 34:2 5:1993 pp.237 - 256.

F.6: Sexual behaviour
Comportement sexuelle

2945 5-a-androst-16en-3a-on — a male pheromone? A brief report. Karl Grammer. **Ethol. Socio.** 14:3 1993 pp.201 - 207.

2946 AIDS, identity and the space of desire. Jonathan Keane. **Tex. Prac.** 7:3 Winter:1993 pp.453 - 470.

2947 Aufstieg und Fall schwuler Identität. Ansätze zur Dekonstruktion der Kategorie Sexualität. *[In German]*; (Being gay — the rise and fall of an identity. Signs of deconstruction of the category sexuality.) *[Summary]*. Wolfgang Hegener. **Z. Sexual.** 6:2 6:1993 pp.132 - 150.

2948 Beruf: Hure. *[In German]*; [Occupation: whore]. Prostituiertenprojekt Hydra [Ed.]. Berlin: Ullstein, 1991. 251p. *ISBN: 354834786X*.

2949 Between women — lesbianism in pornography. Peter Benson. **Tex. Prac.** 7:3 Winter:1993 pp.412 - 427.

2950 Boots of leather, slippers of gold: the history of a lesbian community. Elizabeth Lapovsky Kennedy; Madeline D. Davis. New York: Routledge, 1993. xvii, 434p. *ISBN: 0415902932. Includes bibliographical references and index.*

2951 "Coming out" in the age of social constructionism — sexual identity formation among lesbian and bisexual women. Paula C. Rust. **Gender Soc.** 7:1 3:1993 pp.50 - 77.

2952 Cultural conflict and the Swedish sexual myth: the male immigrant's encounter with Swedish sexual and cohabitation culture. Sven-Axel Mansson. Westport, Conn: Greenwood Press, 1993. 246p. *ISBN: 0313289204. Includes bibliographical references (p. [225]-230) and index. (Series:* Contributions in sociology).

2953 The culture of sensibility: sex and society in eighteenth-century Britain. G. J. Barker-Benfield. Chicago: University of Chicago Press, 1992. xxxiv, 520p. *ISBN: 0226037134. Includes bibliographical references (p. [397]-503) and index.*

2954 Desperately seeking Susan — a geography of lesbian friendships. Gill Valentine. **Area** 25:2 6:1993 pp.109 - 116.

2955 Determinants and effects of waiting time to coitus. Koray Tanfer; Patricia Davis Hyle. **Soc. Biol.** 39:3-4 Fall-Winter:1992 pp.183 - 202.

2956 Dirty looks: women, pornography, power. Pamela Church Gibson [Ed.]; Roma Gibson [Ed.]; Carol J.. Clover [Ed.]. London: British Film Institute, 1993. 238p. *ISBN: 0851704034.*

2957 Discrepancies between men and women in reporting number of sexual partners — a summary from four countries. Tom W. Smith. **Soc. Biol.** 39:3-4 Fall-Winter:1992 pp.203 - 211.

F: Population. Family. Gender. Ethnic group

2958 Early proximity and intimacy between siblings and incestuous behavior — a test of the Westermarck theory. Irene Bevc; Irwin Silverman. **Ethol. Socio.** 14:3 1993 pp.171 - 181.

2959 Erotics & politics: gay male sexuality, masculinity, and feminism. Timothy C. Edwards. London: Routledge, 1993. 192p. *ISBN: 041509903X. Includes bibliographical references and index. (Series:* Critical studies on men and masculinities).

2960 Eu, mulher da vida. *[In Portuguese]*; [Myself, a prostitute]. Gabriela Silva Leite. Rio de Janeiro, RJ: Editora Rosa dos Tempos, 1992. 175p. *ISBN: 858536355X.*

2961 Factors affecting AIDS-related sexual behaviour change among Flemish gay men. John Vincke; Rodulf Mak; Ralph Bolton; Paul Jurica. **Human. Org.** 52:3 Fall:1993 pp.260 - 268.

2962 Footsteps and witnesses: lesbian and gay lifestories from Scotland. Bob Cant [Ed.]. Edinburgh: Polygon, 1993. 210p. *ISBN: 0748661700. (Series:* Living memory).

2963 Forms of desire: sexual orientation and the social constructionist controversy. Edward Stein [Ed.]. New York: Routledge, 1992. xi, 366p. *ISBN: 0415904854. Includes bibliographical references (p. [355]-366) and index.*

2964 Gay perspectives: essays in Australian gay culture. Robert Aldrich [Ed.]; Garry Wotherspoon [Ed.]. Sydney, NSW, Australia: Department of Economic History, University of Sydney, 1992. iv, 197p. *ISBN: 0867585633.*

2965 Gender, desire and child sexual abuse — accounting for the male majority. A. Mark Liddle. **Theory Cult. Soc.** 10:4 11:1993 pp.103 - 126.

2966 Gender differences in sexuality — a meta-analysis. Mary Beth Oliver; Janet Shibley Hyde. **Psychol . B.** 114:1 7:1993 pp.29 - 51.

2967 Le harcèlement sexuel, naissance d'un délit. *[In French]*; [Sexual harassment, the birth of a crime]. Alain Ehrenberg. **Esprit** 196 11:1993 pp.73 - 98.

2968 Heterosexuality: a feminism and psychology reader. Sue Wilkinson [Ed.]; Celia Kitzinger [Ed.]. London: Sage Publications, 1993. 282p. *ISBN: 0803988222, 0803988230.*

2969 Heterosexuality, bisexuality, and lesbianism — psychoanalytic views of women's sexual object choice. Beverley Burch. **Psychoanal. Rev.** 80:1 Spring:1993 pp.83 - 99.

2970 Homosexuality: a European Community issue: essays on lesbian and gay rights in European law and policy. Kees Waaldijk [Ed.]; Andrew Clapham [Ed.]. London: Martinus Nijhoff Publishers, 1993. xvi,426p. *ISBN: 0792320387. European Human Rights Foundation. (Series:* International studies in human rights).

2971 Homosexuality, the Bible, and us. Dennis Prager. **Publ. Inter.** 112 Summer:1993 pp.60 - 83.

2972 Household crowding and reproductive behavior. John N. Edwards; Theodore D. Fuller; Santhat Sermsri; Sairudee Vorakitphokatorn. **Soc. Biol.** 39:3-4 Fall-Winter:1992 pp.212 - 230.

2973 How to recognize a lesbian: the cultural politics of looking like what you are. Lisa M. Walker. **Signs** 18:4 Summer:1993 pp.866 - 890.

2974 Interpreting the evidence — competing paradigms and the emergence of lesbian and gay suicide as a "social fact". Kathleen Erwin. **Int. J. Health. Ser.** 23:3 1993 pp.437 - 453.

F: Population. Famille. Sexe. Groupe ethnique

2975 Interrogating incest: feminism, Foucault, and the law. Vikki Bell. London, New York: Routledge, 1993. 210p. *ISBN: 0415101042*. *Includes bibliographical references and index*. (*Series:* Sociology of law and crime).

2976 Intra-familial communication about contraception — a survey of black South African freshman. L. Nicholas. **Int. J. Advance. Counsel.** 16:4 12:1993 pp.291 - 300.

2977 Is beauty in the eye of the beholder? Victor Johnston; Melissa Franklin. **Ethol. Socio.** 14:3 1993 pp.183 - 199.

2978 Kondombenutzung von homosexuellen Männern in den Niederlanden. Ein Vergleich zwischen konsequenten Benutzern und Nichtbenutzerrn. *[In German]*; (Homosexual men using condoms in the Netherlands. A comparison between consistent users and non-users.) *[Summary]*. Theo G.M. Sandfort; Ernest M.M. de Vroome; Godfried J.P. van Griensven; Robert A.P. Tielman. **Z. Sexual.** 6:4 12:1993 pp.289 - 300.

2979 The lesbian heresy: a feminist perspective on the lesbian sexual revolution. Sheila Jeffreys. London: Women's Press, 1993. 262p. *ISBN: 0704343827*.

2980 Lesbian/gay studies in the house of anthropology. Kath Weston. **Ann. R. Anthr.** 22 1993 pp.339 - 367.

2981 Lonely hearts advertisements reflect sexually dimorphic mating strategies. Del Thiessen; Robert K. Young; Ramona Burroughs. **Ethol. Socio.** 14:3 1993 pp.209 - 229.

2982 Love styles, masculinity/femininity, physical attractiveness, and sexual behavior — a test of evolutionary theory. Anthony Walsh. **Ethol. Socio.** 14:1 1993 pp.25 - 38.

2983 Making trouble: essays on gay history, politics, and the university. John D'Emilio. New York: Routledge, 1992. xliv, 274p. *ISBN: 0415905095, 0415905109*. *Includes bibliographical references*.

2984 Modern homosexualities: fragments of lesbian and gay experiences. Kenneth Plummer [Ed.]. London, New York: Routledge, 1992. xix, 281p. *ISBN: 0415064201, 041506421X*. *Includes bibliographical references (p. 255-271) and indexes*.

2985 Nasilie na svidanii: prestuplenie ili momeng seksual'noi igry? *[In Russian]*; (The violence during meeting — crime or the moment of sexual game?). A.G. Levitskaia; E.N. Orlik; E.P. Porapova. **Sot. Issle.** 6 1993 pp.92 - 97.

2986 Neighborhood, family, and work — influences on the premarital behaviors of adolescent men. Leighton Ku; Freya L. Sonenstein; Joseph H. Pleck. **Soc. Forc.** 72:2 12:1993 pp.479 - 503.

2987 Perversity. Judith Squires [Ed.]; Anne McClintock [Contrib.]; Sue Golding [Contrib.]; Beverley Brown [Contrib.]; Grace Lau [Contrib.]; Stephen Johnstone [Contrib.]; John Gange [Contrib.]; David Curry [Contrib.]; Alasdair Pettinger [Contrib.]; Anna Douglas [Contrib.]; Leslie Moran [Contrib.]; Della Grace [Contrib.]; Parveen Adams [Contrib.]. **New Form.** 19 Spring:1993 pp.1 - 142. *Collection of 11 articles*.

2988 Pleasure principles: politics, sexuality and ethics. Victoria Harwood [Ed.]. London: Lawrence & Wishart, 1993. xvi, 192p. *ISBN: 085315791X*.

2989 The politics and poetics of camp. Moe Meyer [Ed.]. New York; London: Routledge, 1993. 203p. *ISBN: 0415082471, 041508248X*. *Includes bibliographical references and index*.

2990 Polygyny in American politics. Laura Betzig; Samantha Weber. **Polit. Life** 12:1 2:1993 pp.45 - 52.

2991 Prostitution de rue et législation — l'occultation de la dimension morale et technique de gestion pénale. *[In French]*; [Street prostitution and legislation-

F: Population. Family. Gender. Ethnic group

obscuring the moral dimension and penal control] *[Summary]*. Christiane Cardinal. **Can. R. Soc. A.** 30:2 5:1993 pp.153 - 171.

2992 Proust, Cole Porter, Michelangelo, Marc Almond and me: writings by gay men on their lives and lifestyles from the archives of the National Lesbian and Gay Survey. National Lesbian and Gay Survey Organization. London, New York: Routledge, 1993. 196p. *ISBN: 041508914X. Includes index.*

2993 Questions of conduct: sexual harassment, citizenship, government. Jeffrey Minson. Houndmills, Basingstoke: Macmillan, 1993. 279p. *ISBN: 0333465970. Includes bibliographical references (p.256-279) and index. (Series:* Language, discourse, society series).

2994 The representation of presence — outlining the anti-aesthetics of pornography. Pasi Falk. **Theory Cult. Soc.** 10:2 5:1993 pp.1 - 42.

2995 Rethinking sex: social theory and sexuality research. Gary W. Dowsett [Ed.]; Robert William Connell [Ed.]. Philadelphia: Temple University Press, 1993. x, 182p. *ISBN: 1566390729, 1566390737. Includes bibliographical (p. 144-167) references and index.*

2996 Sex and Russian society. Igor Semenovich Kon [Ed.]; James Riordan [Ed.]; Larissa I. Remennick; Lynne Attwood; Elizabeth Waters; Sergei Golod; Lev Shcheglov. Bloomington: Indiana University Press, 1993. viii, 168p. *ISBN: 0253332001, 025333201X. Includes bibliographical references and index.*

2997 Sexual activity among never-married men in northern Thailand. Mark J. van Landingham; Somboon Suprasert; Werasit Sittitrai; Chayan Vaddhanaphuti; Nancy Grandjean. **Demography** 30:3 8:1993 pp.297 - 313.

2998 Sexual attitudes of Greek Orthodox priests in Cyprus. George J. Georgiou. **Cyprus Rev.** 4:2 Fall:1992 pp.44 - 66.

2999 Sexual citizenship: the material construction of sexualities. David Trevor Evans. New York, N.Y: Routledge, 1993. 352p. *ISBN: 041505799X. Includes bibliographical references and index.*

3000 Sexualität und Bedeutung der Geschlechtszugehörigkeit bei lesbischen und heterosexuellen Paaren. Ergebnisse einer empirischen Studie in den Niederlanden. *[In German];* (Sex and the significance of gender in lesbian and heterosexual couples. Results of an empirical study in the Netherlands.) *[Summary]*. Karlein Schreurs. **Z. Sexual.** 6:4 12:1993 pp.321 - 334.

3001 Sexualité et sciences sociales. Les apports d'une enquête. *[In French];* (Sexuality and social sciences. What can be learnt from a survey.). Michel Bozon [Ed.]; Henri Leridon [Ed.]; Nathalie Bajos; Alfred Spira; Alain Giami; Benoît Riandey; Jean-Marie Firdion; Antoine Messiah; Emmanuelle Mouret-Fourme; Brenda Spencer; André Béjin; Alexis Ferrand; Lise Mounier; Béatrice Ducot; Jean-Paul Moatti; Nathalie Beltzer; William Dab; Françoise Le Pont. **Population** 48:5 9/10:1993 pp.1173 - 1550. *Collection of 15 articles.*

3002 Sexuality and ethnicity: variations in young women's sexual knowledge and practice. Janet Holland. London: Tufnell Press, 1993. 44p. *ISBN: 1872767850. (Series:* WRAP paper).

3003 Sexuality and partner selection — sex differences among college students. John Marshall Townsend. **Ethol. Socio.** 14:5 1993 pp.305 - 330.

3004 [Sexuality, subjectivation and pornography]; *[Text in Japanese]*. Manabu Akagawa. **Sociologos** 17 1993 pp.124 - 139.

F: Population. Famille. Sexe. Groupe ethnique

3005 Sexualverhalten in Zeiten von Aids in den USA. *[In German]*; (Sexual behavior in the USA in the face of AIDS.) *[Summary]*. Anke A. Ehrhardt; Sandra Yingling; Patricia A. Warne. **Z. Sexual.** 6:1 3:1993 pp.1 - 22.

3006 Sexuelle Kontakte zwischen Frauen und Kindern. Überlegungen zu einem nicht realisierbaren Forschungsprojekt. *[In German]*; (Sexual contacts between women and children. Some remarks on a research project which proved impracticable.) *[Summary]*. Marina Knopf. **Z. Sexual.** 6:1 3:1993 pp.23 - 35.

3007 Le SIDA en quête de sens. *[In French]*; [AIDS in search of sense]; *[Summary in German]*. Isabelle Girod. **Ethnol. Helvet.** 17-18 1993-1994 pp.269 - 294.

3008 Sida, sexe et société. *[In French]*; [Aids, sex and society]. Clémentine Coulaud; Claude Deslhiat; Christian Ruby; Kévin Nouvel; Julie Simonet; Philippe Mocellin; Jacques Martin; Virginie Parrault; Jean-Etienne Caire. **Regar. Actual.** 194-195 9-11:1993 pp.3 - 137. *Collection of 9 articles.*

3009 Sisters' and girlfriends' sexual and childbearing behavior — effects on early adolescent girls' sexual outcomes. Patricia L. East; Marianne E. Felice; Maria C. Morgan. **J. Marriage Fam.** 55:4 11:1993 pp.953 - 963.

3010 A six-month follow-up of adolescents' sexual risk-taking HIV/AIDS knowledge, and attitudes to condoms. D.A. Rosenthal; H. Shepherd. **J. Comm. App. Soc. Psychol.** 3:1 4:1993 pp.53 - 65.

3011 Soziale Isolation und safer Sex. Ergebnisse einer Studie von homosexuellen Männern in Österreich. *[In German]*; (Social isolation and safer sex. Results of a study of homosexual men in Austria.) *[Summary]*. Wolfgang Dür; Sabine Haas; Wolfgang Till. **Z. Sexual.** 6:4 12:1993 pp.301 - 320.

3012 Street harassment and the informal ghettoization of women. Cynthia Grant Bowman. **Harv. Law. Rev.** 106:3 1:1993 pp.517 - 580.

3013 Sustaining safe sex: gay communities respond to AIDS. Susan Kippax; et al. London: Falmer Press, 1993. 218p. *ISBN: 0750701331.* (*Series:* Social aspects of AIDS).

3014 A test of a model of male premarital sexual aggression. F. Christopher; L. Owens; H. Stecker. **J. Marriage Fam.** 55:2 5:1993 pp.469 - 479.

3015 The theory of reasoned action: its application to AIDS-preventive behaviour. Cynthia Gallois [Ed.]; Malcolm McCamish [Ed.]; Deborah J. Terry [Ed.]. Oxford: Pergamon Press, 1993. 326p. *ISBN: 0080419321.* (*Series:* International series in experimental social psychology).

3016 Über die fortschreitende Medikalisierung männlicher Sexualität. *[In German]*; (A progress report on the medicalization of male sexuality.) *[Summary]*. Leonore Tiefer. **Z. Sexual.** 6:2 6:1993 pp.119 - 131.

3017 Unwanted sexual activity among peers during early and middle adolescence — incidence and risk factors. Stephen A. Small; Donell Kerns. **J. Marriage Fam.** 55:4 11:1993 pp.941 - 952.

3018 Die Wahl der Qual. Ein Einblick in die kleine Lebens-Welt des Algophilen. *[In German]*; (A glimpse into the small realm of the algophile.) *[Summary]*. Ronald Hitzler. **Z. Sexual.** 6:3 9:1993 pp.228 - 242.

3019 Westermarck redivivus. Arthur P. Wolf. **Ann. R. Anthr.** 22 1993 pp.157 - 175.

3020 Wimp or gladiator: contradictions in acquiring masculine sexuality. Janet Holland; Caroline Ramazanoglu; Sue Sharpe. London: Tufnell Press, 1993. 40p. *ISBN: 1872767907. Women, Risk and AIDs Project. Men, Risk and AIDs Project.* (*Series:* WRAP/MRAP paper).

F: Population. Family. Gender. Ethnic group

3021 Women, AIDS, and power in heterosexual sex — a discourse analysis. Lesley Miles. **Wom. St. Inter. For.** 16:5 9-10:1993 pp.497 - 511.
3022 Women and bisexuality. Sue George. London: Scarlet Press, 1992. 245p.

    F.7:   Ethnic groups
                   Groupes ethniques

3023 Access to benefits: the information needs of minority ethnic groups. Alice Bloch. London: Policy Studies Institute, 1993. 97p. *ISBN: 0853745579*. *(Series:* PSI research report).
3024 The arguments for and against transracial placements. Clive Dean. Norwich: Social Work Monographs, 1993. 39p. *ISBN: 1857840135. Bibliography: p.37-39. (Series:* Social work monographs).
3025 Asian Indians in Australia — a statistical profile based on the 1986 census. James E. Coughlan. **Popul. R.** 37:1-2 1-12:1993 pp.21 - 45.
3026 Assimilation and stratification in the homeownership patterns of racial and ethnic groups. Richard D. Alba; John R. Logan. **Int. Migr. Rev.** XXVI:4 Winter:1992 pp.1314 - 1341.
3027 Black America — the street and the campus. Jan Carew [Contrib.]; Geronimo Ji-Jaga Pratt [Contrib.]; Mumia Abu-Jamal [Contrib.]; Ivor Miller [Contrib.]; Clarence Lusane [Contrib.]; Barbara Ransby [Contrib.]; Tracye Matthews [Contrib.]; Ruth Wilson Gilmore [Contrib.]; Cedric Robinson [Contrib.]; Sidney J. Lemelle [Contrib.]; Manning Marable [Contrib.]. **Race Class** 35:1 7-9:1993 pp.1 - 130. *Collection of 9 articles.*
3028 Black and white in America: the culture and politics of racial classification. Ernest Evans Kilker. **Int. J. Pol. C. S.** 7:2 Winter:1993 pp.229 - 258.
3029 The black Atlantic: modernity and double consciousness. Paul Gilroy. London, New York: Verso, 1993. xi, 261p. *ISBN: 0860914011, 0860916758. Includes bibliographical references (p. 225-252) and index.*
3030 Broadening the enclave debate — the labor market experiences of Dominican and Colombian men in New York City. Greta A. Gilbertson; Douglas T. Gurak. **Sociol. For.** 8:2 6:1993 pp.205 - 220.
3031 The career attainment of Caucasian and Asian engineers. Joyce Tang. **Sociol. Q.** 34:3 8:1993 pp.467 - 496.
3032 Changing identification among American Indians and Alaska natives. Karl Eschbach. **Demography** 30:4 11:1993 pp.635 - 652.
3033 Changing images of Asian Americans. Moon H. Jo; Daniel D. Mast. **Int. J. Pol. C. S.** 6:3 Spring:1993 pp.417 - 441.
3034 Convidados de piedra: los indios en el proceso urbano de Quito. *[In Spanish]*; (Silent guests: Indians in the urban process of Quito.) *[Summary]*. Marcelo F. Naranjo. **Am. Indígena** LI:2-3 4-9:1991 pp.251 - 272.
3035 Cultural hegemony and African American development. Clovis E. Semmes. Westport, Conn: Praeger, 1992. xiii, 272p. *ISBN: 0275939235. Includes bibliographical references (p. 255-264) and index.*
3036 Cultural parallelism: the golden mean between cultural nationalism and cultural assimilation — Asian Indians in Trinidad, West Indies. John Sahadat. **Asian Prof.** 21:2 4:1993 pp.165 - 182.

F: Population. Famille. Sexe. Groupe ethnique

3037 Cultural politics of Tamil nationalism. R. Cheran. **S.Asia B.** XII:1 1992 pp.42 - 56.

3038 Death and violence on the reservation: homicide, family violence, and suicide in American Indian populations. Ronet Bachman. New York: Auburn House, 1992. xiv, 167p. *ISBN: 0865690154. Includes bibliographical references (p. [149]-162) and index.*

3039 "Det mångkulturella sverige". *[In Swedish]*; (A multicultural Sweden does it exist?). Owe Ronström. **Nord. Ny.** 52 1993 pp.33 - 44.

3040 Diskurs, mentalitet och konstruktion av främlingskap. *[In Swedish]*; (Discourse, mentality and the construction of strangeness.). Björn Horgby. **Nord. Ny.** 53 1993 pp.70 - 79.

3041 The diverse Asians: a profile of six Asian communities in Australia. James E. Coughlan [Ed.]. Nathan/QLD: Ctr. Study Aust. Asian Relations, 1992. 196p. *ISBN: 0868574465.*

3042 Doubly elite: African Rhodes scholars, 1960-90. Anthony Kirk-Greene. **Imm. Minor.** 12:3 11:1993 pp.220 - 237.

3043 EM ethnic minorities directory: a commercial and social directory of African, Asian and Caribbean communities in Britain. . London: Hansib, 1993. 415p. *ISBN: 1870518853.*

3044 Die Entwicklung der jüdischen Minderheit in Deutschland (1780-1933): neuere Forschungen und offene Fragen. *[In German]*; [The development of the Jewish minority in Germany (1780-1933): recent research and open questions]. Trude Maurer. Tübingen: M. Niemeyer, 1992. 195p. *ISBN: 3484603836. Includes bibliographical references (p. [181]-190) and indexes.*

3045 Ethnic categorization and outgroup exclusion — cultural values and social stereotypes in the construction of ethnic hierarchies. Louk Hagendoorn. **Ethn. Racial** 16:1 1:1993 pp.26 - 51.

3046 Ethnic groups and language rights. Gudmund Sandvik [Ed.]; Lode Wils [Ed.]; Sergij Vilfan [Ed.]. New York, NY, Aldershot, Hants, England: Published for the European Science Foundation by New York University Press, Dartmouth Pub. Co, 1991. 321p. *ISBN: 0814787630. (Series:* Comparative studies on governments and non-dominant ethnic groups in Europe, 1850-1940).

3047 Ethnic leadership, ethnic communities' political powerlessness and the state in Belgium. Marco Martiniello. **Ethn. Racial** 16:2 4:1993 pp.236 - 255.

3048 Ethnies. *[In French]*; [Ethnic groups]. Angioni Giulio. **Civilisations** LXII:2 12:1993 pp.33 - 44.

3049 The face of survival: Jewish life in Eastern Europe past and present. Michael A. Riff; Hugo Gryn; Moses Rosen. London: Valentine Mitchell, 1992. 224p. *ISBN: 0853032203, 0853032297. Includes bibliography.*

3050 From school to work — public policy and underclass formation among young Turks in Germany during the 1980s. Thomas Faist. **Int. Migr. Rev.** XXVII:2 Summer:1993 pp.306 - 331.

3051 The global economy and the Latino populations in the United States — a world systems approach. William I. Robinson. **Crit. Sociol.** 19:2 1992 pp.29 - 59.

3052 El gran poder: fiesta del Aimara urbano. *[In Spanish]*; (The great power: the festival of the urban Aimara.) *[Summary]*. Xavier Albó; Matías Preiswerk. **Am. Indígena** LI:2-3 4-9:1991 pp.293 - 353.

F: Population. Family. Gender. Ethnic group

3053 Hasidic people: a place in the new world. Jerome R. Mintz. Cambridge, Mass: Harvard University Press, 1992. 434p. *ISBN: 0674381157*. *Includes bibliographical references and index.*

3054 Healing multicultural America: Mexican immigrants rise to power in rural California. Henry T. Trueba; et al. London, Washington, D.C: Falmer Press, 1993. 194p. *ISBN: 0750701501, 075070151X*. *Includes bibliographical references and index.*

3055 Immigration and ethnicity: American society - "melting pot" or "salad bowl". Michael D'Innocenzo [Ed.]; Josef P. Sirefman [Ed.]; Iska Alter; Christopher Sten; William E. Van Vugt; Ralph C. Wilcox; Steven Riess; Joyce Toney; Constance R. Sutton; Leonard Dinnerstein; Arthur C. Helton; Mark Gibney; George M. Szabad; Gary E. Rubin; Philip L. Martin; Leon F. Bouvier; Gregory DeFreitas. Westport, Conn: Greenwood Press, 1992. xi, 344p. *ISBN: 0313277591*. *Includes bibliographical references and index. Hofstra University.* (*Series:* Contributions in sociology).

3056 Indian South Africans — a contemporary portrait. J.R. Hiremath. **Afr. Q.** 32:1-4 1992-1993 pp.31 - 46.

3057 Indian South Africans in the transition to a post-apartheid South Africa. Yunus Carrim. **Afr. Q.** 32:1-4 1992-1993 pp.47 - 64.

3058 Indígenas en Quito. *[In Spanish]*; (Indigenous people in Quito.) *[Summary]*. Gladys Villavicencio de Mencías. **Am. Indígena** LI:2-3 4-9:1991 pp.223 - 250.

3059 Inside Babylon: Caribbean diaspora in Britain. Winston James; Clive Harris. London: Verso, 1993. 317p. *ISBN: 0860914712*.

3060 Interminority affairs in the U.S. — pluralism at the crossroads. Roy Simón Bryce-Laporte [Contrib.]; Milton D. Morris [Contrib.]; Gary E. Rubin [Contrib.]; Rita J. Simon [Contrib.]; Alejandro Portes [Contrib.]; Min Zhou [Contrib.]; Jeremy Hein [Contrib.]; Ronald Takaki [Contrib.]; Nathan Galzer [Contrib.]; Glen Grant [Contrib.]; Dennis M. Ogawa [Contrib.]; Robert L. Bach [Contrib.]; Lawrence H. Fuchs [Contrib.]; Peter I. Rose [Contrib.]. **Ann. Am. Poli.** 530 11:1993 pp.28 - 202. *Collection of 11 articles.*

3061 The invention of Ethiopian Jews : three models; *[Summary in French]*. Steven Kaplan. **Cah. Ét. Afr.** XXXIII(4):132 1993 pp.645 - 658.

3062 Islam vs. liberalism in Europe. Peter O'Brien. **Am. J. Islam. Soc. Sci.** 10:3 Fall:1993 pp.367 - 381.

3063 The Jewish heritage in British history: Englishness and Jewishness. Tony Kushner [Ed.]. London: Frank Cass, 1992. 234p. *ISBN: 0714634646*.

3064 The Jewish woman in contemporary society: transitions and traditions. Adrienne Baker; Susie Orbach. London: Macmillan, 1993. 234p. *ISBN: 0333537602*.

3065 The Jews of South Wales: historical studies. Ursula R. Q. Henriques [Ed.]. Cardiff: University of Wales Press, 1993. 238p. *ISBN: 0708311725*.

3066 Die Kaschuben — ihre Geschichte und Gegenwart. *[In German]*; [The Kashubes — their history and present situation]. József Borzyszkowski. **Eur. Ethn.** 50:1-2 1993 pp.39 - 50.

3067 Kisebbségnézőben. Beszélgetések és dokumentumok. *[In Hungarian]*; [Looking at the minorities. Conversations and documents]. István Schlett [Ed.]. Budapest: Kossuth, 1993. 269p. *ISBN: 963 09 3602 X*.

F: Population. Famille. Sexe. Groupe ethnique

3068 A land of dreams: study of Jewish and Caribbean migrant communities in England. Simon Taylor. New York: Routledge, 1993. 217p. *ISBN: 0415084474*. Includes bibliographical references and index.
3069 Leadership et pouvoir dans les communautés d'origine immigrée: l'exemple d'une communauté ethnique en Belgique. *[In French]*; [Leadership and power in communities of immigrant origin: the example of an ethnic community in Belgium]. Marco Martiniello. Paris: L'Harmattan, 1992. 317p. *ISBN: 2738415288*.
3070 Marginalization and survival strategies among young lower-class blacks of Surinamese descent in Amsterdam. Livio Sansone. **Neth. J. Soc. Sci.** 29:2 12:1993 pp.99 - 112.
3071 Modell einer autonomen öffentlichrechtlichen Vertretung der Slowenischen Volksgruppe in Kärnten. *[In German]*; [Model for an autonomous representation under public law of the Slovenian ethnic minority in Kärnten]. Peter Pernthaler. **Eur. Ethn.** 50:1-2 1993 pp.24 - 38.
3072 The multi-cultural planet: the report of a UNESCO international expert group. Ervin Laszlo [Ed.]. Oxford: Oneworld Pubns, 1993. 206p. *ISBN: 185168042X*.
3073 Myth or reality: adaptive strategies of Asian Americans in California. Henry T. Trueba; Lilly Cheng; Kenji Ima. London: Falmer, 1993. 193p. *ISBN: 0750700726*.
3074 Nationalismus, Nationalstaat und Minderheiten. Zu einer Soziologie der Minoritäten. *[In German]*; (Nationalism, nation-state and minorities. Toward a sociology of minorities.) *[Summary]*. Kurt Imhof. **Soz. Welt.** 44:3 1993 pp.327 - 357.
3075 [New ethnic issues in the European integration]; *[Text in Japanese]*. Takamichi Kajita. Tokyo: Chuo-koron Sha, 1993. 290p.
3076 New European countries and their minorities. Chauncy D. Harris. **Geogr. Rev.** 83:3 7:1993 pp.301 - 320.
3077 Paradoxes of ethnic politics — the case of Franco-Maghrebis in France. Miriam Feldblum. **Ethn. Racial** 16:1 1:1993 pp.52 - 74.
3078 Pastores quechuas en el oeste norteamericano. *[In Spanish]*; (Quechua shepherds in the North American west.) *[Summary]*. Teófilo Altamirano. **Am. Indígena** LI:2-3 4-9:1991 pp.203 - 222.
3079 La población indígena en la ciudad de México: algunos de sus problemas y éxitos. *[In Spanish]*; (The indigenous population in Mexico City: some of its problems and successes.) *[Summary]*. Anne Bar Din. **Am. Indígena** LII:1-2 1-6:1992 pp.153 - 168.
3080 Polacy w Kazachstanie — historia i współczesność. *[In Polish]*; (Poles in Kazakstan — their history and present day.) *[Summary]*. Elżbieta Budakowska. **Prz. Pol.** XVIII:4(66) 1992 pp.5 - 37.
3081 La presencia aimara en la ciudad de La Paz, Chuquiyawu Marka: entre la participación y la sobrevivencia. *[In Spanish]*; (The Aimara presence in the city of La Paz, Chuquiyawu Marka: between participation and survival.) *[Summary]*. Wigberto Rivero Pinto; Ives Encinas Cueto. **Am. Indígena** LI:2-3 4-9:1991 pp.273 - 292.
3082 Psychische Probleme von jungen Türken in Deutschland: psychiatrische Auffälligkeit von ausländischen Jungendlichen in der Adoleszenz, Schwerpunkt türkische Jungendliche ; eine epidemiologische Längsschnitttunterssuchung. *[In German]*; [The psychological problems of young Turks in Germany: psychiatric conspicuousness of foreign adolescents, especially Turkish youths; an epidemiological longitudinal

F: Population. Family. Gender. Ethnic group

study]. Susanne Schlüter-Müller. Eschborn bei Frankfurt am Main: Dietmar Klotz, 1992. 89p. *ISBN: 3880742480.*

3083 Reconstructing the multicultural community in Canada: discursive strategies of inclusion and exclusion. Karim H. Karim. **Int. J. Pol. C. S.** 7:2 Winter:1993 pp.189 - 208.

3084 Redefining California: Latino social engagement in a multicultural society. Aída Hurtado; et al. Los Angeles: Chicano Studies Research Center, University of California, Los Angeles, 1992. xv, 101p. *ISBN: 0895510936. Includes bibliographical references.*

3085 Rethinking race. Anthony M. Platt [Contrib.]; Elaine H. Kim [Contrib.]; Elizabeth Martínez [Contrib.]; John Brown Childs [Contrib.]; Roxanne Dunbar Ortiz [Contrib.]; Kathleen Daly [Contrib.]; Edward J. McCaughan [Contrib.]; Stuart Hall [Contrib.]; Dana Y. Takagi [Contrib.]; Justin M. Johnson [Contrib.]; Adalberto Aguirre [Contrib.]; David V. Baker [Contrib.]; Luis J. Rodriguez [Contrib.]; Francis A. Boyle [Contrib.]; Monique Fordham [Contrib.]. **Soc. Just.** 20:1-2 Spring-Summer:1993 pp.1 - 175. *Collection of 16 articles.*

3086 Self, group, and public interests motivating racial politics. Gregory Bovasso. **Polit. Psych.** 14:1 3:1993 pp.3 - 20.

3087 Small acts: thoughts on the politics of black cultures. Paul Gilroy. London: Serpent's Tail, 1993. 257p. *ISBN: 185242298X.*

3088 Soviet Jewish history, 1917-1991: an annotated bibliography. Yelena Luckert. New York: Garland, 1992. xxiii, 271p. *ISBN: 0824025830. Includes index. (Series: Garland reference library of social science).*

3089 Staat und Nation in multi-ethnischen Gesellschaften. *[In German]*; [State and nation in multi-ethnic societies]. Erich Fröschl [Ed.]; Maria Mesner [Ed.]; Uri Ra'anan [Ed.]. Vienna: Passagen-Verlag, 1991. 350p. *ISBN: 3900767831.*

3090 Stati, nazioni, etnie: il pluralismo etnico e nazionale nella teoria sociologica contemporanea. *[In Italian]*; [States, nations, ethnic groups: ethnic and national pluralism in contemporary sociological theory]. Daniele Petrosino. Milan: Angeli, 1991. 224p. *ISBN: 8820471582.*

3091 The structure and social functions of Korean immigrant churches in the United States. Pyong Gap Min. **Int. Migr. Rev.** XXVI:4 Winter:1992 pp.1370 - 1394.

3092 A szlovákiai magyarság sorsa. *[In Hungarian]*; [The life of Hungarians in Slovakia]. Károly Vigh. Budapest: Bereményi, 1992. 181p.

3093 Taquileños, quechuas del Lago Titicaca, en Lima. *[In Spanish]*; (Taquileños, Quechuas from Lake Titicaca, in Lima.) *[Summary]*. José Matos Mar. **Am. Indígena** LI:2-3 4-9:1991 pp.107 - 166.

3094 Towards a multicultural Europe? "Race" nation and identity in 1992 and beyond. Kum-Kum Bhavnani. **Feminist R.** 45 Autumn:1993 pp.30 - 45.

3095 [Trends in ethnic theories in the United States: theoretical overview about ethnic stratification]; *[Text in Japanese]*. Kaname Tsutsumi. **Shak. Hyor.** 44(2) 1993 pp.177 - 187.

3096 Underemployment and economic disparities among minority groups. Min Zhou. **Pop. Res. Pol. R.** 12:2 1993 pp.139 - 157.

3097 The Vietnamese concentration in Cabramatta — site of avoidance and deprivation, or island of adjustment and participation? Kevin M. Dunn. **Aust. Geogr. Stud.** 31:2 10:1993 pp.228 - 245.

F: Population. Famille. Sexe. Groupe ethnique

3098 Zagal'na kontseptsiia narodoznavchikh doslidzhen' ukrains'kogo zarubizhzhia. *[In Ukrainian]*; (General conception of people study investigations of Ukrainians abroad.). Grigorii Dem'ian. **Nav. Tvor. Etn.** 2 1993 pp.24 - 30.

3099 Zagovor protiv natsii: natsional"noe i natsionalisticheskoe v sud"bakh narodov. *[In Russian]*; [An agreement against the nation: the national and the nationalist in the fate of the people]. Ramazan Gadzhimuradovich Abdulatipov. Sankt-Peterburg: Lenizdat, 1992. 191p. *ISBN: 5289013539*.

Ethnicity
Ethnicité

3100 Acculturative stress among Hispanics — a bidimensional model of ethnic identification. Juan I. Sánchez; Diana M. Fernández. **J. Appl. Soc. Psychol.** 23:8 4:1993 pp.654 - 668.

3101 Age, race and ethnicity: comparative approach. Kenneth Blakemore; Margaret Boneham. Buckingham: Open University Press, 1993. 154p. *ISBN: 0335190863*. (*Series:* Rethinking Ageing).

3102 American Indian social, economic, political and cultural strategies for survival. Joane Nagel; C. Matthew Snipp. **Ethn. Racial** 16:2 4:1993 pp.203 - 235.

3103 Australia's Italians: culture and community in a changing society. Stephen Castles [Ed.]. North Sydney: Allen & Unwin, 1992. xxvii, 261p. *ISBN: 1863731709*. *Includes bibliographical references (p. 236-252) and index.*

3104 Beyond reason — the nature of the ethnonational bond. Walker Connor. **Ethn. Racial** 16:3 7:1993 pp.373 - 389.

3105 Une cohabitation ethno-réligieuse dans les balkans: le cas du Rhodope oriental. *[In French]*; [An ethno-religious cohabitation in the Balkans - the case of the eastern Rhodope]. Gueorguiva Tsvetana. **Civilisations** LXII:2 12:1993 pp.161 - 174.

3106 "Coloured" Afrikaans-speakers in Potchefstroom before and after 1950 — identity or political ideology. N.S. Jansen van Rensburg. **Afr. Stud.** 51:2 1992 pp.261 - 276.

3107 The construction of Jewish identity in Hungary in the 1980s. Eros Ferenc. **Civilisations** LXII:2 12:1993 pp.141 - 150.

3108 Constructions of race, place and nation. Peter Jackson [Ed.]; Jan Penrose [Ed.]. London: UCL Press, 1993. 216p. *ISBN: 1857280768*.

3109 Coping with two cultures: British Asian and Indo-Canadian adolescents. Paul A. Singh Ghuman. Clevedon: Multilingual Matters, 1993. 160p. *ISBN: 1853592021*.

3110 Demography and ethnic politics in independent Latvia — some basic facts. Elmars Vebers. **Nat. Pap.** XXI:2 Fall:1993 pp.179 - 194.

3111 Dve grani obshchestvennogo soznaniia: eticheskaia i natsional'naia. *[In Russian]*; [The two edges of social consciousness: the ethnic and the national]. V. Iurdanskii. **Mir. Ek. Mez. Ot.** 6 1993 pp.87 - 101.

3112 Dzieci, dzieciństwo i etniczność w stanach zjednoczonych do lat trzydziestych XX wieku. *[In Polish]*; (Children, their childhood and ethnic character in the U.S.A. till the 1930s.). Adam Walaszek. **Prz. Pol.** XIX:2 1993 pp.43 - 60.

3113 En/quète d'identité. *[In French]*; (In search of identity.). Vintila Mihailescu; Angioni Giulio; Christian Bromberger; Alain Morel; Francois Laplantine; Manfred Bornevasser; Cecile Zervudacki; Eros Ferenc; Rose Marie Lagrave; Gueorguiva Tsvetana; Irina Nicolau; Marianne Mesnil; Assia Popova; Ioana Popescu; Pierre

F: Population. Family. Gender. Ethnic group

Centlivres; Gerard Althabe; Zuzana Stefanikova; Zoltan Biro; Juliana Bodo; Andreas Bimmer; Costel Olaru; Claude Girard. **Civilisations** LXII:2 12:1993 p.. *Collection of 20 articles.*

3114 Ethnic cultural retention and transmission among first generation Hindu Asian Indians in a Canadian prairie city; *[Summary in French]*; *[Summary in Spanish].* Vanaja Dhruvarajan. **J. Comp. Fam. Stud.** XXIV:1 Spring:1993 pp.63 - 79.

3115 Ethnic living arrangements — cultural convergence or cultural manifestation. Jeffrey A. Burr; Jan E. Mutchler. **Soc. Forc.** 72:1 9:1993 pp.169 - 179.

3116 Ethnicismes, supranationalité ou démocratie nationale et internationale? *[In French]*; [Ethnic issues, supranational nature or national and international democracy?]. La Pensée. **Pensée** 296 11-12:1993 pp.5 - 14.

3117 Ethnicité et pouvoir au Moyen-Orient. *[In French]*; (Ethnicity and power in the Middle East.) *[Summary]*. Hosham Dawod. **Pensée** 296 11-12:1993 pp.59 - 68.

3118 Ethnicity and nationalism. Thomas Hylland Eriksen. London, Boulder, Colo: Pluto Press, 1993. 179p. *ISBN: 0745307019. Includes bibliographical references and index. (Series:* Perspectives in anthropology).

3119 Ethnicity and nationalism. Anthony David Smith [Ed.]. Leiden, New York: E.J. Brill, 1992. 130p. *ISBN: 9004096094. Includes bibliographical references. (Series:* International studies in sociology and social anthropology).

3120 L'étranger de l'étranger: les gens du voyage. *[In French]*; [The foreigner from foreign parts]. Rose Marie Lagrave. **Civilisations** LXII:2 12:1993 pp.151 - 160.

3121 Les familles Roms d'Europe de l'Est. *[In French]*; [Rom families of Eastern Europe]. Claire Auzias [Ed.]; Institut de l'Enfance et de Famille France. Paris: , 1993. 113p. *ISBN: 2110877065.*

3122 Identité et migration: l'exemple d'une communauté grecque en France. *[In French]*; [Identity and migration - the example of a Greek community in France]. Cecile Zervudacki. **Civilisations** LXII:2 12:1993 pp.119 - 140.

3123 L'identité ethnique en Roumanie. *[In French]*; [Ethnic identity in Romania] *[Summary]*. Michel Dion. **Cah. Int. Soc.** XCIII 7-12:1992 pp.251 - 268.

3124 Indigenous people today. Douglas Sanders [Contrib.]; Walter Fernandes [Contrib.]; Arundhuti Roy Choudhury [Contrib.]; Mari Thekkekara [Contrib.]; Nirmal Minz [Contrib.]; Sugna Pathy [Contrib.]; Mario Ibarra [Contrib.]; John McCarthy [Contrib.]; P. Ibrahim [Contrib.]. **Soc. Act.** 43:1 1-3:1993 pp.1 - 87. *Collection of 8 articles.*

3125 Internal ethnicity in the ethnic economy. Ivan Light; Georges Sabagh; Mehdi Bozorgmehr; Claudia Der-Martirosian. **Ethn. Racial** 16:4 10:1993 pp.581 - 597.

3126 Konflikt und Kohäsion — die Ethnogenese der Creoles (Afroamerikaner) in Nicaraguas Atlantikregion. *[In German]*; (Conflict and cohesion — the ethnogenesis of the Creoles (Afro-Americans) on Nicaragua's Atlantic coast.) *[Summary]*. Wolfgang Gabbert. **Sociologus** 43:2 1993 pp.136 - 145.

3127 Making ethnic choices: California's Punjabi Mexican Americans. Karen Isaksen Leonard. Philadelphia: Temple University Press, 1992. xii, 333p. *ISBN: 0877228906. Bibliography: p.293-319; includes index. (Series:* Asian American history and culture series).

3128 Making sense of Jewish ethnicity — identification patterns of New Zealanders of mixed parentage. H.B. Levine. **Ethn. Racial** 16:2 4:1993 pp.323 - 344.

3129 Nationalism and ethnicity. Craig Calhoun. **Ann. R. Soc.** 19 1993 pp.211 - 240.

F: Population. Famille. Sexe. Groupe ethnique

3130 Nomades en France: proximités et clivages. *[In French]*; [Nomads in France: proximity and divisions]. Daniel Bizeul. Paris, Bouguenais: Editions L'Harmattan, 1993. 286p. *ISBN: 2738420400. Includes bibliographical references (p. 275-283). URAGEV Association.*

3131 Paradigms of Jewish ethnicity — methodological and normative implications. Michael L. Gross. **Jew. J. Socio.** XXXV:1 6:1993 pp.5 - 34.

3132 La politización de la cultura regional: Zapotecos de la Sierra Juárez en la ciudad de México. *[In Spanish]*; (The politicization of regional culture: Zapotecs from the Sierra Juarez in Mexico City.) *[Summary]*. Lane Hirabayashi. **Am. Indígena** L1:4 10-12:1991 pp.185 - 213.

3133 The poverty of primordialism — the demystification of ethnic attachments. Jack David Eller; Reed M. Coughlan. **Ethn. Racial** 16:2 4:1993 pp.183 - 202.

3134 Priests, prophets, Jews and Germans — the political basis of Max Weber's conception of ethno-national solidarities. Y. Michal Bodemann. **Eur. J. Soc.** 34:2 1993 pp.224 - 247.

3135 The quest for Mennonite peoplehood — ethno-religious identity and the dilemma of definitions; *[Summary in French]*. Daphne Naomi Winland. **Can. R. Soc. A.** 30:1 2:1993 pp.110 - 138.

3136 Racial formation: towards a comparative study of collective identities in South Africa and the United States. Ran Greenstein. **Soc. Dyn.** 19:2 Summer:1993 pp.1 - 29.

3137 Region, race, ethnicity, and social inequality in Colombia. Peter Wade. **R. Soc. Move. Con. Cha.** 15 1993 pp.113 - 138.

3138 Religion and ethnicity in late twentieth-century America. Phillip E. Hammond; Kee Warner. **Ann. Am. Poli.** 527 5:1993 pp.55 - 66.

3139 Religious identity, citizenship, and welfare — the case of Muslims in Britain. Waqar I. Ahmad; Charles Husband. **Am. J. Islam. Soc. Sci.** 10:2 Summer:1993 pp.217 - 233.

3140 Territoire et ethnicité au Tatarstan. Une ancienne république soviétique en quête d'une identité. *[In French]*; [Territory and ethnicity in Tatarstan. A former Soviet republic searches for an identity]. Jean-Robert Raviot. **Eur. J. Soc.** 34:2 1993 pp.169 - 195.

3141 Les territoires de l'identité. Être juif à Arbreville. *[In French]*; [Territory and identity — to be Jewish in Arbreville]. Emmanuelle Saada. **Genèses** 11 3:1993 pp.111 - 136.

3142 Traditions of exclusiveness and ethnic identity in a changing African pastorialist society — the Fulbe of Adamawa, Nigeria. Catherine ver Eecke. **Eth. Groups** 10:4 1993 pp.301 - 321.

3143 Trinidad ethnicity. Kevin A. Yelvington [Ed.]. Knoxville, TN: University of Tennessee Press, 1993. 296p. *ISBN: 0870497790. Includes bibliographical references and index. (Series:* Warwick University Caribbean studies).

3144 Tschechen im Habsburgerreich und in Europa 1815-1914: sozialgeschichtliche Zusammenhänge der neuzeitlichen Nationsbildung und der Nationalitätenfrage in den böhmischen Ländern. *[In German]*; [Czechs in the Hapsburg Empire and Europe 1815-1914: the coherence of recent nation building and questions of nationality in Bohemian countries seen from the view of social history]. Jiří Kořalka. Vienna; Munich: Verlag für Geschichte und Politik; R. Oldenbourg, 1991. 324p. *ISBN:*

F: Population. Family. Gender. Ethnic group

3702803122, 3486559036. Jiří Kořalka: index of works 1955-1990: p. [298]-315. Includes bibliographical references and index.

Race relations
Relations raciales

3145 The Arab minority in Israel's economy: patterns of ethnic inequality. Noah Lewin-Epstein; Moshe Semyonov. Boulder: Westview Press, 1993. xvii, 169p. *ISBN: 0813315255. Includes bibliographical references and index.*

3146 A community in spite of itself: Soviet Jewish emigrés in New York. Fran Markowitz. Washington: Smithsonian Institution Press, 1993. 317p. *ISBN: 1560982004, 156098225X. Includes bibliographical references and index.*

3147 The contact hypothesis revisited — black-white interaction and positive racial attitudes. Lee Sigelman; Susan Welch. **Soc. Forc.** 71:3 3:1993 pp.781 - 795.

3148 Democracy and ethnic conflict — blacks in Costa Rica. Trevor W. Purcell; Kathleen Sawyers. **Ethn. Racial** 16:2 4:1993 pp.298 - 322.

3149 The ethnic responses of whites — what causes their instability, simplification, and inconsistency. Stanley Lieberson; Mary C. Waters. **Soc. Forc.** 72:2 12:1993 pp.421 - 450.

3150 Ethnische Minderheiten, Volk und Nation: Soziologie inter-ethnischer Beziehungen. *[In German]*; [Ethnic minorities, the people and nation: the sociology of interethnic relations]. Friedrich Heckmann. Stuttgart: F. Enke, 1992. x, 279p. *ISBN: 3432999712. Includes bibliographical references (p. [258]-272) and indexes.*

3151 Etnocentrisme in de Lage Landen — opinies over "eigen" en "ander" volk in Nederland en Vlaanderen. *[In Dutch]*; (Ethnocentrism in the Low Countries — opinions about "own" and "other" people in the Netherlands and Flanders.) *[Summary]*. J. Billiet; R. Eisinga; P. Scheepers. **Sociol. Gids** XXXIX:5-6 9-12:1992 pp.300 - 323.

3152 Etranger de tout poil ou comment on désigne l'autre. *[In French]*; [The wild foriegner or how we create the other]. Marianne Mesnil; Assia Popova. **Civilisations** LXII:2 12:1993 pp.179 - 198.

3153 Gedeelde waarden in racistisch en antiracistisch discours — Nederlandse buurtbewoners over etnische minderheden. *[In Dutch]*; (Shared values in racial and anti-racial discourse — Dutch inhabitants on the ethnic minorities in their neighbourhood.) *[Summary]*. M. Verkuyten; W. de Jong; C.N. Masson. **Sociol. Gids** 40:5 9-10:1993 pp.386 - 407.

3154 Indians in a changing South Africa. Ritha Ramphal. **East. Anthrop.** 46:1 1-3:1993 pp.77 - 84.

3155 Indígenas serranos en Quito y Guayaquil: relaciones interétnicas y urbanización de migrantes. *[In Spanish]*; (Highland indigenous people in Quito and Guayaquil: interethnic relations and urbanization of migrants.) *[Summary]*. Hernán Carrasco. **Am. Indígena** L1:4 10-12:1991 pp.159 - 184.

3156 Die indische Händlerminorität in Ostafrika. Ursachen und Verlauf eines ungelösten Konflikts. *[In German]*; (The Indian trading minority in East Africa. Causes and development of an unresolved conflict.) *[Summary]*. Christian G. Kiem. **Sociologus** 43:2 1993 pp.146 - 167.

F: Population. Famille. Sexe. Groupe ethnique

3157 L'invention d'une minorité: les Anglo-Québécois. *[In French]*; [The invention of a minority: the Anglo-Quebeckers]. Josée Legault. Montreal: Boréal, 1992. 282p. *ISBN: 2890524647. Includes bibliographical references (p. [263]-275) and index.*

3158 Knowledge and passion: essays in honour of John Rex. Herminio Martins [Ed.]. London: I. B. Tauris, 1993. 284p. *ISBN: 1850433232.*

3159 Living with conflict among Javanese and Tagalog Filipinos. Niels Mulder. **Phil. Stud.** 41:4 1993 pp.512 - 522.

3160 Lure and loathing: essays on race, identity, and the ambivalence of assimilation. Gerald Lyn Early [Ed.]. New York: Allen Lane, The Penguin Press, 1993. xxiv, 351p. *ISBN: 0713991011.*

3161 Minderheitenfragen in Südosteuropa: Beiträge der internationalen Konferenz : "The Minority Question in Historical Perspective 1900-1990" : Inter University Center, Dubrovnik, 8.-14. 1991. *[In German]*; [Minority questions in South East Europe: papers given at the international conference: "The Minority Question in Historical Perspective 1900-1990": Inter Univeristy Center, Dubrovnik, 1991]. Gerhard Seewann [Ed.]. München: Oldenbourg, 1992. 434p. *ISBN: 3486528815. Includes bibliographical references.*

3162 Minority proximity to whites in suburbs — an individual-level analysis of segregation. Richard D. Alba; John R. Logan. **A.J.S.** 98:6 5:1993 pp.1388 - 1427.

3163 Multi-ethnic work groups in the Dutch police — problems and potential. Sjiera de Vries. **Poli. Soc.** 3:3 1993 pp.177 - 188.

3164 Nomaden im Nationalstaat: zur Integration der Nomaden in Kenia. *[In German]*; [Nomads in the nation state: the integration of nomads in Kenya]. Gabriele Walz. Berlin: D. Reimer, 1992. xii,292p. *ISBN: 3496004088. Includes summary in English. Originally presented as the author's thesis (doctoral)--Freie Universität Berlin, 1989. Includes bibliographical references (p. 265-292).*

3165 Opposition to race-targeting — self-interest, stratification ideology, or racial attitudes? James R. Kluegel; Lawrence Bobo. **Am. Sociol. R.** 58:4 8:1993 pp.443 - 464.

3166 Opvattingen over etnische minderheden — etnocentrisme en discours-analyse. *[In Dutch]*; [Attitudes towards ethnic minorities — ethnocentrism and discourse analysis] *[Summary]*. M. Verkuyten; W. de Jong; C.N. Masson. **Mens Maat.** 68:1 2:1993 pp.19 - 38.

3167 Polska, Polacy, mniejszości narodowe. *[In Polish]*; [Poland, the Poles and ethnic minorities]. Ewa Grześkowiak-Łuczyk [Ed.]. Wrocław: Zakład Narodowy im. Ossolińskich, 1992. 421p. *ISBN: 8304038765. Includes bibliographical references and index.*

3168 Printsip »voronki«, ili Mekhanizm razvertyvaniia mezhEtnicheskogo konflikta. *[In Russian]*; ("Funnel" principle or the mechanism of interethnic conflict development.). V.A. Mikhailov. **Sot. Issle.** 5 1993 pp.57 - 63.

3169 Race and imprisonment decisions. John H. Kramer; Darrell Steffensmeier. **Sociol. Q.** 34:2 5:1993 pp.357 - 376.

3170 Race, class, and personal income — an empirical test of the declining significance of race thesis, 1968-1988. Melvin E. Thomas. **Soc. Prob.** 40:3 8:1993 pp.328 - 342.

3171 Race contacts and interracial relations: lectures on the theory and practice of race. Alain LeRoy Locke; Jeffrey C. Stewart [Ed.]. Washington, D.C: Howard University Press, 1992. lxv, 114p. *ISBN: 0882581376, 0882581589. Includes bibliographical references and index. (Series:* Moorland-Spingarn series).

F: Population. Family. Gender. Ethnic group

3172 Race equality strategy. Arun Misra. London: National Federation of Housing Associations, 1992. 16p. *ISBN: 0862972310.*
3173 Racialization of America. Yehudi O. Webster. New York: St. Martin's Press, U. S, 1992. 310p. *ISBN: 031207557X.*
3174 Radicalism, anti-racism, and representation. Alastair Bonnett. New York; London: Routledge, 1993. 221p. *ISBN: 0415072034. Includes bibliographical references and index. (Series:* Critical studies in racism and migration).
3175 Rasse, Blut und Gene: Geschichte der Eugenik und Rassenhygiene in Deutschland. *[In German]*; [Race, blood and genes: the history of eugenics in Germany]. Peter Weingart; Jürgen Kroll; Kurt Bayertz. Frankfurt am Main: Suhrkamp, 1992. 746p. *ISBN: 3518286226. Bibliogr. p. 685-727. Index p. 729-746.*
3176 Reading Rodney King/reading urban uprising. Robert Gooding-Williams. New York: Routledge, 1993. viii, 276p. *ISBN: 0415907349, 0415907357. Includes index.*
3177 Recensements et conflits «ethniques» dans les Balkans. *[In French]*; (Census and "ethnic" conflicts in the Balkans.) *[Summary]*. Jean-François Gossiaux. **Pensée** 296 11-12:1993 pp.23 - 31.
3178 Re-framing Europe — en-gendered racisms, ethnicities and nationalisms in contemporary Western Europe. Avtar Brah. **Feminist R.** 45 Autumn:1993 pp.9 - 28.
3179 Regional imbalances and the national question in Pakistan. S. Akbar Zaidi [Ed.]. Lahore: Vanguards, 1992. 361p.
3180 Relations ethniques et tensions identitaires en contexte pluriculturel. *[In French]*; (Ethnic relations and identity-based tensions in a multicultural context.) *[Summary]*. Anne Laperrière; Lejacques Compère; Mijid D' Khissy; René Dolce; Nicole Fleurant; Marianick Vendette. **San. Ment. Qué** XVII:2 Automne:1992 pp.133 - 155.
3181 Relations police-minorités ethniques. *[In French]*; (Police and ethnic minority relations.) *[Summary]*. Emerson Douyon. **San. Ment. Qué** XVII:1 Printemps:1993 pp.179 - 191.
3182 Sans distinction de ... race. *[In French]*; [Without distinction of ... race]. Simone Bonnafous [Ed.]; Bernard Herszberg [Ed.]; Jean-Jacques Israel [Ed.]. Paris: Presses de la Fondation Nationale des Sciences Politiques, 1992. 398p. *ISBN: 2724606221.*
3183 The scar of race. Paul M. Sniderman; Thomas Leonard Piazza. Cambridge, Mass: Belknap Press of Harvard University Press, 1993. xi, 212p. *ISBN: 0674790103. Includes bibliographical references (p. 203-207) and index.*
3184 Seeds of racial explosion. Timur Kuran. **Society** 30:6 9-10:1993 pp.55 - 67.
3185 Social psychological reactions to social change and social instability: fear of status loss, social discrimination and foreigner hostility; *[Summary in French]*. Manfred Bornevasser. **Civilisations** LXII:2 12:1993 pp.91 - 104.
3186 Some aspects of life of the Chinese communities in India. John Mao. **Man India** 73:1 3:1993 pp.29 - 40.
3187 Soziale Konflikte und offene Gewalt. Die Herausforderungen des Transformationsprozesses in den neuen Bundesländern. *[In German]*; [Social conflicts and open violence. The challenges of the transformation process in the new federal states]. Fred Klinger. **Deut. Arch.** 26:2 2:1993 pp.147 - 161.
3188 The state, ethnicity and violence. Anand Singh. **East. Anthrop.** 45:4 10-12:1992 pp.341 - 364.
3189 Südafrika: Apartheid und Menschenrechte in Geschichte und Gegenwart. *[In German]*; [South Africa: apartheid and human rights in the past and the present].

F: Population. Famille. Sexe. Groupe ethnique

Jörn Rüsen [Ed.]; Hildegard Vörös-Rademacher [Ed.]. Pfaffenweiler: Centaurus, 1992. 235p. *ISBN: 3890855504. Includes bibliographical references.*

3190 Who are the whites? Imposed census categories and the racial demography of Brazil. Marvin Harris; Josildeth Gomes Consorte; Joseph Lang; Bryan Byrne. **Soc. Forc.** 72:2 12:1993 pp.451 - 462.

3191 Wir und die anderen. Ethnozentrismus in den zwölf Ländern der europäischen Gemeinschaft. *[In German]*; ("We" and "the others" — ethnocentrism in the 12 countries of the European Community.) *[Summary]*. Dieter Fuchs; Jürgen Gerhards; Edeltraud Roller. **Kölner Z. Soz. Soz. psy.** 45:2 6:1993 pp.238 - 253.

Racial discrimination
Discrimination raciale

3192 American apartheid: segregation and the making of the underclass. Douglas S. Massey; Nancy A. Denton. Cambridge, Mass: Harvard University Press, 1993. x, 292p. *ISBN: 0674018206. Includes bibliographical references (p. [239]-284) and index.*

3193 Analyse sociologique et historique de l'antisémitisme en Pologne. *[In French]*; [Historical and sociological analysis of anti-semitism in Poland] *[Summary]*. Michel Wieviorka. **Cah. Int. Soc.** XCIII 7-12:1992 pp.237 - 249.

3194 The anatomy of racially motivated violence in New York City — a case study of youth in southern Brooklyn. Howard Pinderhughes. **Soc. Prob.** 40:4 11:1993 pp.478 - 492.

3195 Antisemitismus: das alte Gesicht des neuen Deutschland. *[In German]*; [Antisemitism: the old face of the new Germany]. Jürgen Elsässer. Berlin: Dietz, 1992. 158p. *ISBN: 3320017950.*

3196 Barbaric others: a manifesto on Western racism. Merryl Wyn Davies; Ashis Nandy; Ziauddin Sardar. London: Pluto Press, 1993. 99p. *ISBN: 0745307426, 0745307434.*

3197 Black, white, or mixed race?: race and racism in the lives of young people of mixed parentage. Barbara Tizard; Ann Phoenix. London, New York: Routledge, 1993. 192p. *ISBN: 0415088798, 0415097088. Includes bibliographical references and index.*

3198 Blacks on the bubble — the vulnerability of black executives in white corporations. Sharon M. Collins. **Sociol. Q.** 34:3 8:1993 pp.429 - 447.

3199 Construction de l'étranger dans les échanges quotidiens. *[In French]*; [Construction of the foreigner in daily exchanges]. Gerard Althabe. **Civilisations** LXII:2 12:1993 pp.217 - 228.

3200 Critical notes regarding the dislocation of Chicanos by the Spanish-language television industry in the United States. Adalberto Aguirre; Diana A. Bustamente. **Ethn. Racial** 16:1 1:1993 pp.121 - 132.

3201 Desigualdad racial en Brasil y en Estados Unidos: un estudio estadístico comparado. *[In Spanish]*; [Racial inequality in Brazil and the United States: a comparative statistical study] *[Summary]*. George Reid Andrews. **Desar. Econ.** 33:130 7-9:1995 pp.185 - 216.

3202 Discourse analysis and racist talk. R. Wodak; R. Mitten; S. Jäger; F. Januschek; E. Petermann-Graubner; F. Stern; T. MacCreanor; Y. Tobin; M.I. Bresnahan; M. Sun Kim. **Folia Ling.** XXVII:3-4 1993 pp.185 - 363. *Collection of 7 articles.*

F: Population. Family. Gender. Ethnic group

3203 Do black and white women hold different jobs in the same occupation? A critical analysis of the clerical and service sectors. Augustin K. Fosu. **Rev. Bl. Pol. Ec.** 21:4 Spring:1993 pp.68 - 82.

3204 Ethnic residential segregation in Suva — analysis of inter-censal rates of change. David King. **Reg. Sci. Urb. Econ.** 23:1 6:1992 pp.23 - 31.

3205 Etnicheskie stereotipy i ikh vliianie na formirovanie obshchestvennogo mneniia. *[In Russian]*; [Ethnic stereotypes and their influence upon social opinion]. S. Chugov. **Mir. Ekon. Mezh. Otno.** 1 1993 pp.41 - 54.

3206 An examination of racial attitudes of pre-school children in the English speaking Caribbean. Sharon-Ann Gopaul-McNicol. **Carib. Stud.** 25:3-4 1992 pp.389 - 400.

3207 Face au racisme. *[In French]*; [Facing racism. 2 vols.]. Pierre-André Taguieff [Ed.]. Paris: La Découverte, 1991. *ISBN: 2707119717, 2707120111. Includes bibliographical references.*

3208 Faces at the bottom of the well: the permanence of racism. Derrick A. Bell. New York, NY: BasicBooks, 1992. xiv, 222p. *ISBN: 0465068170. Includes bibliographical references (p. [201]-214) and index.*

3209 A first glance at the results of the survey "Poles, Jews and other ethnic groups". Helena Datner-Spiewak. **E.Eur. Jew. Aff.** 23:1 Summer:1993 pp.33 - 48.

3210 Die freundliche Zivilgesellschaft: Rassismus und Nationalismus in Deutschland. *[In German]*; [The friendly civil society: racism and nationalism in Germany]. . Berlin, Amsterdam: Edition ID-Archiv, 1992. 170p. *ISBN: 3894080191. Includes bibliographies.*

3211 The geography of economic development and racial discrimination in Brazil. Peggy A. Lovell. **Develop. Cha.** 24:1 1:1993 pp.83 - 101.

3212 Have the post-reform ethnic gains eroded? A seven-nation study. D. John Grove. **Ethn. Racial** 16:4 10:1993 pp.598 - 620.

3213 The invention of the white race. Vol.1. Racial oppression and social control. Theodore W. Allen. London: Verso, 1993. 310p. *ISBN: 0860914801.*

3214 Law, lawyers and racially segregated public transport in South Africa. G.H. Pirie. **Afr. Stud.** 51:2 1992 pp.243 - 260.

3215 Marginalidad de la población gitana española. *[In Spanish]*; [The marginalization of Spain's gypsy population]. Aurelio Cebrián Abellán. Murcia: Universidad de Murcia, 1992. 138p. *ISBN: 8476843208. Includes bibliographical references (p. 125-131).*

3216 Minority firms, racism and economic development. Monder Ram; John Sparrow. **Local. Ec.** 8:2 8:1993 pp.117 - 129.

3217 Montréal au pluriel: huit communautés ethno-culturelles de la région montréalaise. *[In French]*; [Montreal in the plural: eight ethno-cultural communities in the Montreal region]. Alberte Ledoyen. Quebec: Institut québécois de recherche sur la culture, 1992. 329p. *ISBN: 2892241782. Bibliographic references: p. 311-318. Commission des droits de la personne du Québec.*

3218 Ohne Gewalt läuft nichts!: Jugend und Gewalt in Deutschland. *[In German]*; [Nothing works without violence!: Youth and violence in Germany]. Klaus Farin; Eberhard Seidel-Pielen. Cologne: Bund-Verlag, 1993. *ISBN: 3766324306. Bibliography (p. 287-304).*

3219 The persistence of racism in America. Thomas F. Powell. Lanham: University Press of America, 1992. x, 355p. *ISBN: 0819185876. Includes bibliographical references (p. [311]-327) and indexes.*

F: Population. Famille. Sexe. Groupe ethnique

3220 The politics of antisemitic prejudice: the Waldheim phenomenon in Austria. Richard Mitten. Boulder: Westview Press, 1992. ix, 260p. *ISBN: 0813376300*. *Includes bibliographical references.*

3221 Psychological and cultural foundations of prejudice — the case of anti-Semitism in Quebec; *[Summary in French]*. Paul M. Sniderman; David A. Northrup; Joseph F. Fletcher; Peter H. Russell; Philip E. Tetlock. **Can. R. Soc. A.** 30:2 5:1993 pp.242 - 270.

3222 Race and class. Alex Callinicos. London: Bookmarks, 1993. 86p. *ISBN: 0906224837.*

3223 Racial harassment and the process of victimization — conceptual and methodological implications for the local crime survey. Benjamin Bowling. **Br. J. Crimin.** 33:2 Spring:1993 pp.231 - 250.

3224 Racial jurymandering: cancer or cure? A contemporary review of affirmative action in jury selection. Nancy J. King. **NY. U. Law. Re.** 68:4 10:1993 pp.707 - 776.

3225 Racism and planning. Charles Hoch. **J. Am. Plann.** 59:4 Autumn:1993 pp.451 - 460.

3226 Racism in the USA: history and political economy. Melvin M. Leiman. London, Concord, Mass: Pluto Press, 1992. 421p. *ISBN: 0745304885*. *Includes bibliographical references and index.*

3227 Racisme, continent obscure: clichés, stéréotypes et phantasmes à propos des noirs dans le Royaume de Belgique. *[In French]*; [Racism, dark continent: clichés, stereotypes and fantasy concerning blacks in the Kingdom of Belgium]. François Andrillon; et al. Brussels: , 1991. 215p. *ISBN: 9071665151*. *Coopération par l'Education et la Culture, Brussels. Centre National de Coopération au Développement.*

3228 Racist culture: philosophy and the politics of meaning. David Theo Goldberg. Cambridge, Mass: Blackwell, 1993. 313p. *ISBN: 063118077X, 0631180788, 0631175156*. *Includes bibliographical references and index.*

3229 Racist violence in Europe. Tore Björgo [Ed.]; Rob Witte [Ed.]. Basingstoke: Macmillan Press, 1993. ix, 261p. *ISBN: 0333601017, 0333601025, 0312102976*. *Includes index. Bibliography: p. 236-246.*

3230 Ras en nasionlisme ('n histories-sosiaalwetenskaplike studie). *[In Afrikaans]*; (Race and nationalism (a historical social scientific study).). Hannes Beyers. **S.Afr. J. Ethnol.** 16:4 12:1993 pp.101 - 109.

3231 A regional analysis of black male-white male wage differences. Jeremiah Cotton. **Rev. Bl. Pol. Ec.** 22:1 Summer:1993 pp.55 - 71.

3232 The state, racism, and domination in contemporary capitalist societies. Francis Adu-Febiri. **Berkeley J. Soc.** 38 1993-1994 pp.193 - 220.

3233 Territoriality and nonconscious racism at water fountains — intruders and drinkers (Blacks and Whites) are affected by race. R. Barry Ruback; Jason N. Snow. **Envir. Behav.** 25:2 3:1993 pp.250 - 267.

3234 Türken in der Bundesrepublik, Nordafrikaner in Frankreich: Ausländerproblematik im deutsch-französischen Vergleich. *[In German]*; [Turks in the BRD, North Africans in France: the problem of foreigners in a German-French comparison]. Klaus Manfrass. Bonn: Bouvier, 1991. xiii, 259p. *ISBN: 3416023579*. *Includes bibliographical references.*

F: Population. Family. Gender. Ethnic group

3235 Una comunità/cultura «diversa» in Italia — il caso degli zingari. *[In Italian]*; [A "different" community/culture in Italy — the case of the gypsies]. Roberto de Angelis. **Aff. Soc. Int.** XXI:1 1993 pp.79 - 92.

3236 Under the shadow of Weimar: democracy, law, and racial incitement in six countries. Louis I. Greenspan [Ed.]; Cyril Levitt [Ed.]. Westport, Conn: Praeger, 1993. viii, 235p. *ISBN: 0275940551. Includes bibliographical references (p. [213]-221) and index.*

3237 Undercurrents of racism in Italy. Angela Zanotti. **Int. J. Pol. C. S.** 7:2 Winter:1993 pp.173 - 188.

3238 Unemployment and racial competition in local labor markets. Leann M. Tigges; Deborah M. Tootle. **Sociol. Q.** 34:2 5:1993 pp.279 - 298.

3239 Unlucky Australians — labour market outcomes among Aboriginal Australians. F.L. Jones. **Ethn. Racial** 16:3 7:1993 pp.420 - 458.

3240 "A wary approach" — attitudes towards Jews and Jewish issues in Slovakia. Martin Butora; Zara Butorova. **E.Eur. Jew. Aff.** 23:1 Summer:1993 pp.5 - 20.

3241 "Was blind, but now I see" — white race consciousness and the requirement of discriminatory intent. Barbara J. Flagg. **MI. law. R.** 91:5 3:1993 pp.953 - 1017.

3242 Was macht Migranten in Deutschland krank?: zur Problematik von Rassismus und Ausländerfeindlichkeit und von Armutsdiskriminierung in psychosozialer und medizinischer Versorgung. *[In German]*; [What makes migrants in Germany ill?: the problems of racism amd hostility towards foreigners and discrimination against the poor seeking medical and psychosocial care]. Jürgen Collatz [Ed.]. Hamburg: Rissen, 1992. 193p. *ISBN: 3923002653. Papers from a conference held by the Ethnomedizinisches Zentrum in Hannover on 12th December 1991. Includes bibliographical references (p. 192-193).*

3243 What do we know about racial discrimination in mortgage markets? Cathy Cloud; George Galster. **Rev. Bl. Pol. Ec.** 22:1 Summer:1993 pp.101 - 120.

3244 What's wrong with the theory of racial inequality — toward a more effective theory of racial inequality in economic life. David H. Swinton. **Rev. Bl. Pol. Ec.** 21:3 Winter:1993 pp.25 - 40.

3245 When black first became worth less. Anton L. Allahar. **Int. J. Comp. Soc** XXXIV:1-2 1-4:1993 pp.39 - 65.

F.8: Migration
Migration

3246 [Asian foreigners in the Shinjuku district — a sociological portrait of their actual conditions]; *[Text in Japanese]*. Michihiro Okuda. Tokyo: Mekon, 1993. 313p.

3247 Beyond the killing fields: voices of nine Cambodian survivors in America. Usha Welaratna. Stanford, Calif: Stanford University Press, 1993. xxi, 285p. *ISBN: 0804721394. Includes bibliographical references ([281]-285). (Series:* Asian America).

3248 The challenge facing migration research — the case for a biographical approach. Keith H. Halfacree; Paul J. Boyle. **Prog. H. Geog.** 17:3 9:1993 pp.333 - 348.

3249 Changes in employment networks among undocumented Mexican migrants in Chicago. Maria de Lourdes Villar. **Urban Anthro.** 21:4 Winter:1992 pp.385 - 397.

F: Population. Famille. Sexe. Groupe ethnique

3250 Comportements migratoires individuels dans l'espace français. *[In French]*; [Migration on French territory — the behaviour of individuals] *[Summary]*. Brigitte Baccaïni. **Espace Géogr.** XXII:2 1993 pp.133 - 145.

3251 Consequences of return migrant status for employment in Puerto Rico. Clara G. Muschkin. **Int. Migr. Rev.** XXVII:1 Spring:1993 pp.79 - 102.

3252 Constructing a sense of home — place affiliation and migration across the life cycle. Lee Cuba; David M. Hummon. **Sociol. For.** 8:4 12:1993 pp.547 - 572.

3253 Dai due versanti delle Alpi: studi sull'emigrazione italiana in Francia. *[In Italian]*; [On two slopes of the Alps: studies on Italian emigration in France]. Gérard Claude; et al. Alexandria: Edizioni dell'Orso, 1991. 154p. *ISBN: 8876940790.*

3254 The demographics of immigration: a socio-demographic profile of the foreign-born population in New York State. Nadia H. Youssef. New York: Center for Migration Studies, 1992. xvi, 182p. *ISBN: 0934733600. Bibliography: p.169-177; includes index.*

3255 La dimension migratoire des Antilles. *[In French]*; [The migratory dimension of the Antilles]. Hervé Domenach; Michel Picouet. Paris: Economica, 1992. 254p. *ISBN: 2717823425. Biblio. p. 240-249.*

3256 "Einheimische Ausländer" und "Fremde Deutsche" im vereinigten Deutschland. *[In German]*; ["Indigenous foreigners" and "foreign Germans" in united Germany]. Klaus J. Bade. **Jahrb. Wirt. Gesch.** 2 1991 pp.9 - 27.

3257 Etnografické aspekty ozdravných a vzdělávacích pobytů dětí a mládeže českého původu z černobylské oblasti ukrajiny v ČSFR. *[In Czech]*; (On the ethnographic aspects regarding the curative and educational sojourn of children and young people of Czech descent from the Chernobyl areas of the Ukraine in the Czech and Slovak Federative Republic.). Helena Dluhošová. **Český Lid** 79:3 1992 pp.207 - 216.

3258 Evoluzione dei flussi migratori italiani dal dopoguerre ad oggi. *[In Italian]*; [Evolution of migratory flows from Italy from the immediate post-war years to today]. Alessandra Ruberti. **Aff. Soc. Int.** XXI:2 1993 pp.123 - 144.

3259 Der Fall Akar — eine Fallstudie zu den psychosozialen Konsequenzen der Arbeitsmigration für die zweite Generation. *[In German]*; [The case of Akar — a case study of the psycho-social consequences of labour migration for the second generation]. Werner Schiffauer. **Hess. Blät. Volk.Kultur.** 29 1992 pp.145 - 154.

3260 Fremde Frauen: von der Gastarbeiterin zur Bürgerin. *[In German]*; [Foreign women: from immigrant workers to citizens]. Marion Schulz [Ed.]. Frankfurt: Verlag für Interkulturelle Kommunikation, 1992. 227p. *ISBN: 388939048X. Includes bibliographical references (p. 147-225).*

3261 Geography and refugees: patterns and processes of change. Richard Black [Ed.]; Vaughan Robinson [Ed.]. London, New York; New York: Belhaven Press; Halsted Press, 1993. 220p. *ISBN: 1852932279, 0470219939. Includes bibliographical references and index.*

3262 Going home — the migration of Puerto Rican-born women from the United States to Puerto Rico. Adrian J. Bailey; Mark Ellis. **Prof. Geogr.** 45:2 5:1993 pp.148 - 158.

3263 Grounding a theory of African migration in recent data on Ghana; *[Summary in French]*. David Achanfuo-Yeboah. **Int. Sociol.** 8:2 6:1993 pp.215 - 226.

3264 Hindu children in Britain. Robert Jackson; Eleanor M. Nesbitt. Stoke on Trent: Trentham Books, 1993. 228p. *ISBN: 0948080736.*

F: Population. Family. Gender. Ethnic group

3265 Homeward bound — Yemeni return migration. Nora Ann Colton. **Int. Migr. Rev.** XXVII:4 Winter:1993 pp.870 - 882.

3266 Immigrant qualifications — recognition and relative wage outcomes. Bruce J. Chapman; Robyn Iredale. **Int. Migr. Rev.** XXVII:2 Summer:1993 pp.359 - 387.

3267 Immigrants and the American city. Thomas Muller. New York: New York University Press, 1993. ix, 372p. *ISBN: 0814754791.*

3268 Immigration and ethnic origin — the effect of demographic attributes on earnings of Israeli men and women. Yitchak Haberfeld. **Int. Migr. Rev.** XXVII:2 Summer:1993 pp.286 - 305.

3269 Immigration in Campania — social characteristics and evolutionary tendencies. Elena de Filippo; Enrica Morlicchio. **J. Reg. Pol.** 13:2 4-6:1993 pp.299 - 318.

3270 Immigration, language, and ethnicity: Canada and the United States. Barry R. Chiswick [Ed.]. Washington, D.C, Lanham, Md: AEI Press, Distributed by University Press of America, 1992. xix, 489p. *ISBN: 0844737615.*

3271 Immigration, nationality and citizenship. Satvinder Singh Juss. London: Mansell, 1993. 200p. *ISBN: 0720121493. Includes bibliographical references and index. (Series:* Citizenship and the law series).

3272 L'immigration, pour quoi faire? *[In French]*; [Why emigrate?]. Denise Helly. Quebec: Institut québécois de recherche sur la culture, 1992. 229p. *ISBN: 2892241731. Includes bibliographical references.*

3273 In the absence of their men: the impact of male migration on women. Leela Gulati. New Delhi, London: Sage Publications, 1993. 174p. *ISBN: 0803991282, 8170363543.*

3274 Inside the state: the Bracero program, immigration, and the I.N.S. Kitty Calavita. New York: Routledge, 1992. x, 243p. *ISBN: 0415905370. Includes bibliographical references (p. 219-234) and index. (Series:* After the law).

3275 Interdependencies in the timing of migration and mobility events. John Odland; J. Matthew Shumway. **Pap. Reg. Sci.** 72:3 7:1993 pp.221 - 237.

3276 The international legal protection of the child's right to a legal identity and the problem of statelessness. Douglas Hodgson. **Int. J. Law Fam.** 7:2 1993 pp.255 - 270.

3277 Irish illegals: transients between two societies. Mary P. Corcoran. Westport, Conn: Greenwood Press, 1993. xvii, 205p. *ISBN: 0313286248. Includes bibliographical references (p. [191]-199) and index. (Series:* Contributions in ethnic studies).

3278 Jugendliche Flüchtlinge in Heimen der Jugendhilfe: Situation und Zukunftsperspektiven. *[In German]*; [Young refugees in group homes for youth: current situation and future prospects]. Hans-Dieter Heun; Heide Kallert; Clemens Bacherl. Freiburg im Breisgau: Lambertus, 1992. 189p. *ISBN: 3784106366. Bibliography: p. 180-188.*

3279 [Live together with immigrant workers]; *[Text in Japanese].* Hiroshi Komai. Tokyo: Akashi Shoten, 1993. 381p.

3280 Long-distance commuting — a new approach to mining in Australia. D.S. Houghton. **Geogr. J.** 159:3 11:1993 pp.281 - 290.

3281 Mass migrations in Europe: the legacy and the future. Russell King [Ed.]. London, New York: Belhaven Press, 1993. 334p. *ISBN: 1852932244, 0470219270. Includes bibliographical references and index.*

3282 Migracja i społeczne konstruowanie tożsamości. *[In Polish]*; [Migration and the social construction of identity]. Zdzisław Mach. **Prz. Soc.** XLII 1993 pp.69 - 89.

F: Population. Famille. Sexe. Groupe ethnique

3283 Migracje powrotne na przykladzie województwa zamojskiego. *[In Polish]*; (Return migratory movements — the example of the Zamosc voivodeship.) *[Summary]*. Mieczyslaw Kowerski. **Stud. Demogr.** 1(103) 1991 pp.25 - 42.

3284 Migrancy, culture, identity. Iain Chambers. New York; London: Routledge, 1993. 154p. *ISBN: 0415088011, 041508802X*.

3285 Migrant status and labor market outcomes in urban and rural Hebei Province, China. William F. Stinner; Wu Xu; Jin Wei. **Rural Sociol.** 58:3 Fall:1993 pp.366 - 386.

3286 Migration — a review. Michael J. Greenwood [Ed.]; Timothy J. Bartik [Contrib.]; Alberta H. Charney [Contrib.]; Henry W. Herzog; Alan M. Schlottmann; Thomas P. Boehm [Contrib.]; Gary L. Hunt [Contrib.]; John M. McDowell [Contrib.]; Larry D. Singell [Contrib.]; William J. Milne [Contrib.]; David A. Plane [Contrib.]. **Reg. Stud.** 27:4 1993 pp.297 - 383.

3287 Migration and marriage in the life course — a method for studying synchronized events; *[Summary in French]*. Clara H. Mulder; Michael Wagner. **Eur. J. Pop.** 9:1 1993 pp.55 - 76.

3288 Migration and the new Europe. Robert Miles [Ed.]; F.W. Carter [Contrib.]; R.A. French [Contrib.]; J. Salt [Contrib.]; Roel Fernhout [Contrib.]; Giovanna Campani [Contrib.]; Martin Eaton [Contrib.]. **Ethn. Racial** 16:3 7:1993 pp.459 - 562. *Collection of 5 articles.*

3289 Les migrations dans le monde arabe. *[In French]*; [Migration in the Arab world]. Gilbert Beaugé [Ed.]; Friedmann Büttner [Ed.]; Institut de recherches et d'études sur le monde arabe et musulman. Paris: Editions du Centre national de la recherche scientifique, 1991. 327p. *ISBN: 2222045355. Includes bibliographical references (p. 325-327).*

3290 Migrations entre passé et avenir: flux et politiques migratoires en Europe et en Belgique. *[In French]*; [Migration between the past and the future: migratory flows and policies in Europe and in Belgium]. Felice Dassetto; Antonio Piaser. Louvain-la-Neuve: Academia, 1992. 137p. *ISBN: 2872091807. Includes bibliographical references.*

3291 A multilevel analysis of elderly migration. Jeffrey E. Kallan; Gary M. Fournier [Comments by]. **Soc. Sci. Q.** 74:2 6:1993 pp.403 - 419.

3292 The new geography of European migrations. Russell King [Ed.]. London, New York: Belhaven Press, 1993. 263p. *ISBN: 1852932910, 0470220368. Includes bibliographical references and index.*

3293 The new hosts — the case of Spain. Cristina Blanco Fdez. de Valderrama. **Int. Migr. Rev.** XXVII:1 Spring:1993 pp.169 - 181.

3294 Opvattingen over buitenlanders en over migratiebeleid. *[In Dutch]*; (Attitudes towards foreigners and migration policy.) *[Summary]*. Hans van den Brekel; Hein Moors. **Bevolk. Gez.** 1 1993 pp.1 - 24.

3295 [The overseas Chinese of Kobe in the era of globalisation]; *[Text in Japanese]*. Fang Guo [Ed.]. Kobe: Ministry of Education, 1993. 68p.

3296 Perú: ... y la vida continúa. *[In Spanish]*; (Peru: ... and life goes on.) *[Summary]*. Paul Doughty. **Am. Indígena** L1:4 10-12:1991 pp.49 - 80.

3297 Planned emigration — the Palestinian case. Hassan Elnajjar. **Int. Migr. Rev.** XXVII:1 Spring:1993 pp.34 - 50.

3298 Police et immigrés: images mutuelles, problèmes et solutions. *[In French]*; [Police and immigrants: images of each other, problems and solutions]. M.-T Casman; et al.

F: Population. Family. Gender. Ethnic group

Brugge: Vanden Broele, Politeia, 1991. 160p. *ISBN: 9062670598*. *Includes bibliographical references (p. 135-149)*.

3299 La pression migratoire — sentiment d'inquietude ou concept analytique? *[In French]*; [Migratory pressure — a feeling of anxiety or an analytical concept?]. G.P. Tapinos. **Aff. Soc. Int.** XXI:2 1993 pp.7 - 21.

3300 Propozycja zastosowania entropii do analizy migracji. *[In Polish]*; (A proposal to apply entropy to migration analysis.) *[Summary]*. Iwona Roeske-Słomka. **Stud. Demogr.** 2 (108) 1992 pp.3 - 20.

3301 The quetzal in flight: Guatemalan refugee families in the United States. Norita Vlach. Westport, Conn: Praeger, 1992. xvi, 175p. *ISBN: 0275939790*. *Includes bibliographical references (p. [163]-171) and index*.

3302 Refugees, immigrants, and the state. Jeremy Hein. **Ann. R. Soc.** 19 1993 pp.43 - 60.

3303 Rethinking measures of migration — on the decomposition of net migration. O.R. Galle; J.A. Burr; L.B. Potter. **Soc. Ind.** 28:2 2:1993 pp.157 - 171.

3304 Le retour au pays pour la retraite des personnes nées dans les DOM. *[In French]*; (When people born in French Overseas Departments return to retire - a survey of intentions.) *[Summary]*. Pascale Bessy; Corinne Riche. **E & S** 270 10:1993 pp.51 - 62.

3305 Ruimtelijke analyse van de migrates naar leeftijd. *[In Dutch]*; [Spatial analysis of migration by age groups]. Etienne van Hecke. **Bevolk. Gez.** 3 1992 pp.77 - 103.

3306 Settlers and refugees in Cyprus. Salâhi Ramsdan Sonyel. London: Cyprus Turkish Association, 1991. 135p. *ISBN: 0950488631*.

3307 [The social theories on global society and migrant workers]; *[Text in Japanese]*. Shin'ichi Asano. Okayama: Daigaku Kyoiku Shuppan, 1993. 291p.

3308 Soviet Jewish immigration and the 1992 Israeli Knesset elections. Bernard Reich; Noah Dropkin; Meyrav Wurmser. **Middle E. J.** 47:3 Summer:1993 pp.464 - 478.

3309 Stranieri e volontariato. *[In Italian]*; (Foreigners and voluntary service.) *[Summary]*. Guido Lazzarini; Maria Grazia Morchio. **Sociol. Urb. Rur.** XIII:36-37 1991-1992 pp.213 - 242.

3310 Tibetische Flüchtlinge in Südasien. *[In German]*; [Tibetan refugees in South Asia]. Thomas Methfessel. **Geogr. Rund.** 45:11 11:1993 pp.650 - 657.

3311 Toward a European migration policy. Thomas Straubhaar; Klaus F. Zimmermann. **Pop. Res. Pol. R.** 12:3 1993 pp.225 - 242.

3312 A typology of migration. David Joe Achanfuo-Yegoah. **Popul. R.** 37:1-2 1-12:1993 pp.71 - 77.

3313 Unaccompanied Mozambican children in Zimbabwe. Backson Muchini. **J. Soc. Devel. Afr.** 8:2 1993 pp.49 - 60.

3314 Vliianie migratsii na formirovanie rynka truda. *[In Russian]*; (The influence of Imigration on the labour-power market.). G.F. Morozova. **Sot. Issle.** 5 1993 pp.92 - 96.

3315 Westpendler, Ostpendler. Zum Arbeitspendeln im Umland vom Berlin. *[In German]*; [Commuters from the West and the East. On commuting in the area around Berlin]. Ines Schmidt. **Deut. Arch.** 26:10 10:1993 pp.1159 - 1170.

3316 Will a large-scale migration of Russians to the Russian Republic take place over the current decade? John B. Dunlop. **Int. Migr. Rev.** XXVII:3 Fall:1993 pp.605 - 629.

3317 Die zweite und dritte Ausländergeneration: ihre Situation und Zukunft in der Bundesrepublik Deutschland. *[In German]*; [The second and third generation of immigrants: their situation and future in the Federal Republic of Germany].

F: Population. Famille. Sexe. Groupe ethnique

Konstantin Lajios [Ed.]. Opladen: Leske + Budrich, 1991. 144p. *ISBN: 3810007714*. Papers presented at a meeting of the Landeszentrale für Politische Bildung des Landes Nordrhein-Westfalen. Includes bibliographical references.

Immigrant adaptation
Adaptation des immigrants

3318 Acculturation, stress et santé mentale chez des immigrants libanais à Montréal. *[In French]*; (Acculturative stress and mental health. Lebanese immigrants in Montreal.) *[Summary]*. Liliane Sayegh; Jean-Claude Lasry. **San. Ment. Qué** XVII:1 Printemps:1993 pp.21 - 51.

3319 Adaptation of migrants in the New Zealand labor market. Jacques Poot. **Int. Migr. Rev.** XXVII:1 Spring:1993 pp.121 - 139.

3320 Africans in the United Kingdom: an introduction. David Killingray. **Imm. Minor.** 12:3 11:1993 pp.2 - 27.

3321 L'approche interculturelle dans le processus d'aide. *[In French]*; (The intercultural approach in the support process.) *[Summary]*. Margalit Cohen-Emérique. **San. Ment. Qué** XVII:1 Printemps:1993 pp.71 - 91.

3322 Approche transculturelle des patients non francophones originaires du Sud-est asiatique dans le dispositif psychiatrique du XIIIème arrondissement de Paris. *[In French]*; (Transcultural approach of non Francophone patients originating from Southeast Asia in the psychiatric service network of Paris' XIIIth arrondissement.) *[Summary]*. Richard Rechtman; Geneviève Welsh. **San. Ment. Qué** XVII:1 Printemps:1993 pp.143 - 161.

3323 Beyond assimilation and pluralism — syncretic sociocultural adaptation of Korean immigrants in the United States. Kwang Chung Kim; Won Moo Hurh. **Ethn. Racial** 16:4 10:1993 pp.696 - 713.

3324 Ein- und Ausgliederung von Immigranten. Türken in Deutschland und mexikanische Amerikaner in den USA in den achziger Jahren. *[In German]*; (Inclusion and exclusion of immigrants. The transition from school to the world of work. Turks in Germany and Mexican Americans in the USA in the 80s.) *[Summary]*. Thomas Faist. **Soz. Welt.** 44:2 1993 pp.275 - 299.

3325 Electoral participation among immigrants in Sweden: integration, culture and participation. Maritta Soininen; Henry Bäck. **New Comm.** 20:1 10:1993 pp.111 - 130.

3326 The employment and wages of legalized immigrants. George J. Borjas; Marta Tienda. **Int. Migr. Rev.** XXVII:4 Winter:1993 pp.712 - 747.

3327 La famille, secret de l'intégration: enquête sur la France immigrée. *[In French]*; [The family, the secret of integration: survey of immigrant France]. Christian Jelen; Ilios Yannakakis [Ed.]. Paris: Laffont, 1993. *ISBN: 2221073878*.

3328 Family, work and women — the labor supply of Hispanic immigrant wives. Haya Stier; Marta Tienda. **Int. Migr. Rev.** XXVI:4 Winter:1992 pp.1291 - 1313.

3329 L'identité négative chez les jeunes immigrés. *[In French]*; (Negative identity and immigrant youth.) *[Summary]*. Hanna Malewska-Peyre. **San. Ment. Qué** XVII:1 Printemps:1993 pp.109 - 123.

3330 Immigranten im Wohlfahrtsstaat: am Beispiel der Rechtspositionen und Lebensverhältnisse von Aussiedlern. *[In German]*; [Immigrants in the welfare state:

F: Population. Family. Gender. Ethnic group

the legal position and living conditions of emigrants as an example]. Hubert Heinelt; Anne Lohmann; Eberhard Franz. Opladen: Leske + Budrich, 1992. 278p. *ISBN: 3810009822. Includes bibliographical references (p. 269-278).*

3331 Immigration and structural change — the Canadian experience 1971-86. Anthony H. Richmond. **Int. Migr. Rev.** XXVI:4 Winter:1992 pp.1200 - 1221.

3332 Immigration. Identités. Intégration. *[In French]*; [Immigration, identity and integration]. Jacques Barou [Contrib.]; Philippe Videlier [Contrib.]; Yvonne Knibiehler [Contrib.]; Jean-Pierre Hassoun [Contrib.]; Nicole Lapierre [Contrib.]; Maurizio Catani [Contrib.]. **Ethn. Fr.** 23:2 4-6:1993 pp.169 - 226. *Collection of 6 articles.*

3333 L'insertion de l'économie ethnique tertiaire libanaise en France. *[In French]*; [The integration of the Lebanese ethnic service economy in France] *[Summary]*. A. Abdulkarim. **Ann. Géogr.** 102:574 11-12:1993 pp.561 - 577.

3334 L'intégration des immigrants à Montréal dans les années 1970. *[In French]*; [The integration of immigrants in Montreal in the 1970s] *[Summary]*. Gary Caldwell. **Rech. Soc.graph** XXXIV:3 9-12:1993 pp.487 - 508.

3335 Integration of Vietnamese refugees into the Norwegian labor market — the impact of war trauma. Edvard Hauff; Per Vaglum. **Int. Migr. Rev.** XXVII:2 Summer:1993 pp.388 - 405.

3336 Integration südostasiatischer Flüchtlinge in der Bundesrepublik Deutschland und in Japan: eine international vergleichende Studie zur Lage einer neuen Minderheit. *[In German]*; [The integration of Southeast Asian refugees in the Federal Republic of Germany and Japan: an international comparative study of the social conditions of a new minority]. Fumiko Kosaka-Isleif. Saarbrücken: Breitenbach, 1991. 364p. *ISBN: 3881565175.*

3337 K adaptaci současné reemigrační vlny čechů z ukrajiny. *[In Czech]*; (To the adaptation of current reemigration waves of Czechs from the Ukraine.). Nad'a Valášková. **Český Lid** 79:3 1992 pp.193 - 206.

3338 Migration politique, migration économique — une lecture systémique du processus d'intégration des familles migrantes. *[In French]*; (Political and economical migration — a systematic look at the integration process of migrant families.) *[Summary]*. Jorge Barudy. **San. Ment. Qué** XVII.2 Automne.1992 pp.47 - 70.

3339 Le modèle français d'intégration. *[In French]*; [The French model of integration]. Chantal Saint-Blancat. **Aff. Soc. Int.** XXI:1 1993 pp.41 - 56.

3340 Nirgends zu Hause!?: türkische Schüler zwischen Integration in der BRD und Remigration in die Türkei : eine sozialpsychologisch-empirische Untersuchung. *[In German]*; [At home nowhere!?: Turkish school children between integration in the Federal Republic of Germany and return migration to Turkey: a sociopsychological-empirical investigation]. Ibrahim Firat. Frankfurt am Main: Verlag für Interkulturelle Kommunikation, 1991. 341p. *ISBN: 388939213X. Includes bibliographical references (p. 330-341).*

3341 Outsiders and outcasts: essays in honour of William J. Fishman. Geoffrey Alderman [Ed.]; Colin Holmes [Ed.]; William Jack Fishman. London: Duckworth, 1993. 214p. *ISBN: 0715624326.*

3342 Paths of community integration. Avery Guest; Keith Stamm. **Sociol. Q.** 34:4 11:1993 pp.581 - 595.

3343 Principes théoriques et méthodologiques de l'ethnopsychiatrie — un exemple du travail avec les enfants de migrants et leurs familles. *[In French]*; (Theoretical and methodological principles of ethnopsychiatry — the case of migrant children and their families.) *[Summary]*. Marie-Rose Moro. **San. Ment. Qué** XVII:2 Automne:1992 pp.71 - 98.

3344 [The problem of return migration in Czech: emigration, return migration and adaptation 1]; *[Text in Japanese]*. Toru Anami. **Jo. To Shak.** 3 1993 pp.77 - 90.

3345 Psychological traumas and depression in a sample of Vietnamese people in the United States. Thanh V. Tran. **Health Soc. Work** 18:3 8:1993 pp.184 - 194.

3346 [A reluctance to naturalize: social factors among Mexican immigrants in the U.S.]; *[Text in Japanese]*. Miyuki Enari. **Nen. Shak. Ron.** 6 1993 pp.215 - 226.

3347 Rethinking assimilation and ethnicity — the Chinese in Thailand. Chan Kwok Bun; Tong Chee Kiong. **Int. Migr. Rev.** XXVII:1 Spring:1993 pp.140 - 168.

3348 Seeking common ground: multidisciplinary studies of immigrant women in the United States. Donna Gabaccia [Ed.]. Westport, Conn: Praeger, 1992. xxvi, 237p. *ISBN: 0275943879. Includes bibliographical references (p. [221]-228) and index.* (*Series:* Contributions in women's studies).

3349 Soviet Jews in the United States — an analysis of their linguistic and economic adjustment. Barry R. Chiswick. **Int. Migr. Rev.** XXVII:2 Summer:1993 pp.260 - 285.

3350 La thérapie avec les familles immigrées. *[In French]*; (Therapy and the immigrant family.) *[Summary]*. Romano Scandariato. **San. Ment. Qué** XVII:1 Printemps:1993 pp.125 - 142.

3351 Vite sospese: il rischio dell'emigrante. *[In Italian]*; (Lives in suspence: the immigrants risk.). Adriana Luciano. **Rass. It. Soc.** XXXIV:4 12:1993 pp.515 - 538.

Internal migration
Migration interne

3352 The Bario exodus: a conception of Sarawak urbanisation. Lee Boon Thong; Tengku Shamsul Bahrin. **Born. R.** IV:2 12:1993 pp.113 - 127.

3353 Circular migration and families: a Yolmo Sherpa example. Naomi H. Bishop. **S.Asia B.** XIII:1+2 1993 pp.59 - 66.

3354 Circulatory mobility in post-Mao China — temporary migrants in Kaiping County, Pearl River delta region. Yuen-Fong Woon. **Int. Migr. Rev.** XXVII:3 Fall:1993 pp.578 - 604.

3355 Community, society, and migration: noneconomic migration in America. Patrick C. Jobes [Ed.]; William F. Stinner [Ed.]; John M. Wardwell [Ed.]. Lanham: University Press of America, 1992. xix, 389p. *ISBN: 0819187283. Includes bibliographical references.*

3356 The commuting of exurban home buyers. Judy S. Davis. **Urban Geogr.** 14:1 1-2:1993 pp.7 - 29.

3357 Counterurbanization and coastal development in New South Wales. M. Sant; P. Simons. **Geoforum** 24:3 1993 pp.291 - 306.

3358 De evolutie van de migratietendensen 1977-1990 in de Belgische ruimte. *[In Dutch]*; [The evolution of migration trends 1977-1990 in Belgium] *[Summary]*. Etienne van Hecke. **Bevolk. Gez.** 2:1992 pp.1 - 27.

F: Population. Family. Gender. Ethnic group

3359 Demographic and socioeconomic determinants of female rural to urban migration in sub-Saharan Africa. Martin Brockerhoff; Hongsook Eu. **Int. Migr. Rev.** XXVII:3 Fall:1993 pp.557 - 577.

3360 Determinants of 1980 to 1990 net migration in Texas counties — the role of sustenance specialization and dominance in international ecosystems. Steve H. Murdock; Md. Nazrul Hoque; Kenneth Backman. **Rural Sociol.** 58:2 Summer:1993 pp.190 - 209.

3361 An empirical analysis of inter-regional migration flows to and from South East England. . **Prog. Plan.** 39:2 1993 pp.79 - 137.

3362 An empirical analysis of motivations for mobility in Nigeria. Sarah O. Anyanwu. **Scand. J. Devel. Altern.** XII:4 12:1993 pp.125 - 138.

3363 Federal transfers, migration, and regional development in Canada — some policy lessons for India. M.R. Narayana. **Ind. J. Soc. Sci.** 6:1 1-3:1993 pp.1 - 18.

3364 (The financial aspect of uni-polarization.) *[Summary]*; *[Text in Japanese]*. Kiyoko Hagihara. **Comp. Urban Stud.** 48 3:1993 pp.57 - 68.

3365 The influence of rural-urban migration on migrant's fertility behavior in Cameroon. Bun Song Lee. **Int. Migr. Rev.** XXVI:4 Winter:1992 pp.1416 - 1447.

3366 The influence of rural-urban migration on migrants' fertility in Korea, Mexico and Cameroon. Bun Song Lee; Louis G. Pol. **Pop. Res. Pol. R.** 12:1 1993 pp.3 - 26.

3367 [Internal migration and social change in Egypt]; *[Text in Japanese]*. Hirofumi Tanada. **Nin. Kag. Ken.** 6(1) 1993 pp.73 - 96.

3368 Internal migration of scientific/technical and social sciences personnel in India — an analysis of DHTP survey 1981. D.P. Singh. **Indian J. Soc. W.** LIV:2 4:1993 pp.271 - 296.

3369 Inter-regional migration to and from South East England in the context of British regional development and planning. . **Prog. Plan.** 39:2 1993 pp.138 - 158.

3370 Migración y cambios socioeconómicos en la comunidad de Zoogocho, Oaxaca. *[In Spanish]*; (Migration and socioeconomic changes in the community of Zoogocho, Oaxaca.) *[Summary]*. Donato Ramos Pioquinto. **Est. Demog. Urb.** 6:2 5-8:1991 pp.313 - 345.

3371 Migration and remittances: inter-urban and rural-urban linkages. Jayasri Ray Chaudhuri. New Delhi, Newbury Park, Calif: Sage Publications, 1993. 261p. *ISBN: 0803994583. Includes bibliographical references.*

3372 Migration and the metropolis — recent research on the causes of migration to southeast England. A.J. Fielding. **Prog. H. Geog.** 17:2 6:1993 pp.195 - 212.

3373 Migration, inequality, and the informal economy: a critique of Eurocentric explanations of rural out-migration in the Third World. Abol Hassan Danesh. **R. Soc. Move. Con. Cha.** 16 1993 pp.51 - 68.

3374 Migration settlement and ethnic associations. K.P. Kumaran. New Delhi: Concept Pub. Co, 1992. 188p. *ISBN: 8170223903. Includes bibliographical references (p. [179]-185) and index.*

3375 Migration und Staat: inner- und intergesellschaftliche Prozesse am Beispiel Algerien, Türkei, Deutschland und Frankreich. *[In German]*; [Migration and the state: inner- and intersocial processes using the examples of Algeria, Turkey, Germany and France]. Rémy Leveau [Ed.]; Werner Ruf [Ed.]. Münster: Lit, 1991. 258p. *ISBN: 3886608018. Includes bibliographical references.*

3376 Les migrations de personnes âgées en Europe. *[In French]*; (Migration amongst the elderly in Europe.). F. Cribier [Ed.]; F. Dieleman [Ed.]; A.M. Warnes; P.

F: Population. Famille. Sexe. Groupe ethnique

Hooimeijer; M. Kuijperslinde; F.J. Kemper; A. Kych; S. Öberg; S. Scheele; G. Sundström; F. Bartiaux; A. Bonaguidi; R. Ford. **Espace Pop. Soc.** 3 1993 pp.445 - 532. *Collection of 8 articles.*

3377 Migratsionni protsesi v Bŭlgariia sled Vtorata svetovna vona. *[In Bulgarian]*; [Migration process in Bulgaria after the Second World War]. Boka Vasileva. Sofiia: Univ. izd-vo Sv. Kliment Okhridski, 1991. 249p. *Includes bibliographical references.*

3378 Le migrazioni interne in Bolivia. *[In Italian]*; [Internal migration in Bolivia]. Stefano Mondovì. **Sociologia [Rome]** XXVII:1-3 1993 pp.511 - 520.

3379 Mobilités spatiales et urbanisation. Asie, Afrique, Amérique. *[In French]*; (Spatial mobilities and urbanization. Asia, Africa, America.). Véronique Dupont; Christophe Z. Guilmoto; Galila El Kadi; Frédéric Landy; Marc le Pape; Alain Morice; Isabelle Bardem; Olivier Barbary; Françoise Dureau; Olivier Iyebi-Mandjek; Philippe Cadène; Éva Lelièvre; Jesus Arroyo Alejandre; Jean Papail; Gérard Heuzé; Emmanuel Grégoire; Pascal Labazée; Emmanuel Fauroux; Bernard Koto. **Cah. Sci. Hum.** 29:2-3 1993 pp.279 - 564. *Collection of 14 articles.*

3380 Modelling sparse interaction matrices: interward migration in Hereford and Worcester, and the underdispersion problem. P.J. Boyle; R. Flowerdew. **Envir. Plan. A.** 25:8 8:1993 pp.1201 - 1210.

3381 Naselenie SSSR: voprosy migratsii : ėkonomiko-statisticheskii obzor tendentsii 60-kh-80-kh godov. *[In Russian]*; [The population of the USSR - questions of migration: an economic and statistical overview of the sixties, seventies and eighties]. D. D. Moskvin. Moskva: Nauka, 1991. 157p. *ISBN: 502011992X.*

3382 Patrones de migración hacia Barranquilla, Cali, Medellín y Santa Fé de Bogotá. *[In Spanish]*; [Migration patterns in the direction of Barranquilla, Cali, Medellín and Santa Fé de Bogotá]. Wigberto Castañeda Hernández. **Coy. Soc.** 9 11:1993 pp.121 - 136.

3383 Plans to migrate in and out of Utah. William F. Stinner; Mollie van Loon; Yongchan Byun. **Social Soc. Res.** 76:3 4:1992 pp.131 - 137.

3384 Political economy of skill drain from rural India. B.N. Ghosh. **J. Cont. Asia** 23:3 1993 pp.327 - 353.

3385 El proceso de migración en el Perú: la revolución clandestina. *[In Spanish]*; (The process of migration in Peru: the underground revolution.) *[Summary]*. Harald Mossbrucker. **Am. Indígena** LI:2-3 4-9:1991 pp.167 - 202.

3386 The renewal of population loss in the nonmetropolitan Great Plains. Don E. Albrecht. **Rural Sociol.** 58:2 Summer:1993 pp.233 - 246.

3387 Requiem for the fixed-transition-probability migrant. David A. Plane. **Geogr. Anal.** 25:3 7:1993 pp.211 - 223.

3388 Rola krewnych i znajomych w kreowaniu strumieni mogracyjnych. *[In Polish]*; (Role of kith and kin in creating migration streams.) *[Summary]*. Mieczysław Kowerski. **Stud. Demogr.** 2(100) 1990 pp.45 - 60.

3389 Spatial redistribution of the Torres Strait Islander population: a preliminary analysis. J. Taylor; W.S. Arthur. **Aust. Geogr.** 24:2 11:1993 pp.26 - 38.

3390 Theoretical approaches to Mexican wage labor migration. Tamar Diana Wilson. **Lat. Am. Pers.** 20:3(78) Summer:1993 pp.98 - 129.

3391 Zachowania migracyjne ludności w nowych warunkach społeczno-ekonomicznych. *[In Polish]*; (Migrations in Poland under new socio-economic conditions.). Janusz Witkowski; et al. **Stud. Demogr.** 2(164) 1991 pp.91 - 133.

F: Population. Family. Gender. Ethnic group

International migration
Migration internationale

3392 Las áreas expulsoras de mano de obra del estado de Zacatecas. *[In Spanish]*; (The migration sending regions in the state of Zacatecas.) *[Summary]*. Jesús Tamayo; Fernando Lozano Ascencio. **Est. Demog. Urb.** 6:2 5-8:1991 pp.347 - 378.

3393 Asian and Pacific islander migration to the United States: a model of new global patterns. Elliott Robert Barkan. Westport, Conn: Greenwood Press, 1992. xiv, 259p. *ISBN: 0313275386*. Includes bibliographical references (p. [239]-252) and index. (*Series:* Contributions in ethnic studies).

3394 Aspetti socio-demografici dell'immigrazione extracomunitaria in Italia. *[In Italian]*; [Socio-demographic aspects of immigration from countries outside the EC into Italy]. Salvatore Geraci. **Aff. Soc. Int.** XXI:1 1993 pp.133 - 144.

3395 The choice of migration destination — Dominican and Cuban immigrants to the mainland United States and Puerto Rico. Edward Funkhouser; Fernando A. Ramos. **Int. Migr. Rev.** XXVII:3 Fall:1993 pp.537 - 556.

3396 Confrontation des statistiques de migrations intraEuropéennes: vers plus d'harmonisation? *[In French]*; (Confronting the statistics on inter-european migration: towards a greater harmonization?). Michel Poulain. **Eur. J. Pop.** 9:4 1993 pp.353 - 382.

3397 Current trends and patterns of female migration — evidence from Mexico. Katharine M. Donato. **Int. Migr. Rev.** XXVII:4 Winter:1993 pp.748 - 771.

3398 Le donne senegalesi nella loro esperienza migratoria in Italia. *[In Italian]*; [Senegalese women and their experience of migration to Italy]. R. de Luca; M.R. Panareo. **Critica Sociol.** 105 Spring:1993 pp.84 - 97.

3399 The elderly and international migration in Canada: 1971-1986; *[Summary in Italian]*. Margaret Michalowski. **Genus** IL:1-2 1-6:1993 pp.121 - 146.

3400 Emigrace ze Sovětského svazu v posledních letech II. *[In Czech]*; (Emigration from the Soviet Union during last years II.). Jana Pitlíková. **Demografie** XXXV:4 1993 pp.263 - 270.

3401 Emigratsiia iz Rossii: kul'turno- istoricheskii aspekt. *[In Russian]*; (Emigration from Russia — historico- cultural aspect.). A. Akhiyezer. **Svobod. Mysl'** 7 5:1993 pp.70 - 78.

3402 Ethiopian immigration to Israel: dream and reality. Ruben Schindler; David S. Ribner. **J. Soc. Work Pol. Israel** 7-8 1993 pp.31 - 44.

3403 The future of international labor migration. John Salt. **Int. Migr. Rev.** XXVI:4 Winter:1992 pp.1077 - 1111.

3404 Global restructuring in the world economy and migration — the globalization of migration dynamics. Hélène Pellerin. **Int. J.** XLVIII:2 Spring:1993 pp.240 - 254.

3405 History and the future of international migration. Göran Rystad. **Int. Migr. Rev.** XXVI:4 Winter:1992 pp.1168 - 1199.

3406 Imigranci z krajów Europy środkowo-wschodniej w USA i Kanadzie: aspekty socjo-demograficzne. *[In Polish]*; (Immigrants from Central and Eastern Europe in the USA and Canada: socio-demographic aspect.). Krystyna Slany. **Stud. Demogr.** 3(109) 1992 pp.19 - 44.

3407 Immigrazione in Europa: solidarietà e conflitto. *[In Italian]*; [Immigration in Europe: solidarity and conflict]. Marcella Delle Donne [Ed.]; Umberto Melotti [Ed.]; Stefano

F: Population. Famille. Sexe. Groupe ethnique

Petilli [Ed.]. Rome: Dipartimento di Sociologia, Università di Roma "La Sapienza", 1993. 663p. *Includes bibliographical references. CEDISS, Centro europeo di scienze sociali.*

3408 The Indonesian diaspora and Philippine-Indonesian relations. Evelyn Tan-Cullamar. **Phil. Stud.** 41 First quarter:1993 pp.38 - 50.

3409 International migration and control of communicable diseases. George A. Gellert. **Soc. Sci. Med.** 37:12 12:1993 pp.1489 - 1499.

3410 International migration in the nineties — causes and consequences. Gerald E. Dirks. **Int. J.** XLVIII:2 Spring:1993 pp.191 - 214.

3411 Latin American migration to Canada — new linkages in the hemispheric migration and refugee flow system. Alan B. Simmons. **Int. J.** XLVIII:2 Spring:1993 p.310.

3412 Matamoros-sur de Texas — el tránsito de los migrante de América Central por la frontera México-Estados Unidos. *[In Spanish]*; [Matamoros south of Texas — the movement of migrants from Central America to the Mexican-U.S. border]. Vicente Sánchez Munguía. **Est. Sociol.** XI:31 1-4:1993 pp.183 - 208.

3413 Mediterranean imbalances and the future of international migrations in Europe. Jean-Claude Chesnais. **SAIS R.** 13 Fall:1993 p.103.

3414 Mental health in Mariel Cubans and Haitian boat people. William W. Eaton; Roberta Garrison. **Int. Migr. Rev.** XXVI:4 Winter:1992 pp.1395 - 1415.

3415 Migrations et relations transnationales. *[In French]*; (Migrations and transnational relations.) Catherine Wihtol de Wenden [Ed.]; Bertrand Badie [Ed.]; Aristide R. Zolberg [Contrib.]; James F. Hollifield [Contrib.]; Marc Termote [Contrib.]; Alain Prujiner [Contrib.]; Nadji Safir [Contrib.]; Rémy Leveau [Contrib.]; Moustapha Diop [Contrib.]; Ottavia Schmidt di Friedberg [Contrib.]; Anne de Tinguy [Contrib.]. **Ét. Int.** XXIV:1 3:1993 pp.7 - 176. *Collection of 11 articles.*

3416 Nations of immigrants: Australia, the United States, and international migration. Gary P. Freeman; James Jupp. New York; Melbourne: Oxford University Press, 1992. xi, 250p. *ISBN: 0195534832. Includes bibliographical references and index.*

3417 New immigration policy and unskilled foreign workers in Japan. Keiko Yamanaka. **Pac. Aff.** 66:1 Spring:1993 pp.72 - 90.

3418 Les organisations syndicales et l'immigration en Europe. *[In French]*; [Trade union organizations and immigration in Europe]. Albert Bastenier; Patricia Targosz. Brussels: Système Bibliographique et Documentaire sur Immigration, 1991. 116p. *ISBN: 2872091599.*

3419 People of German descent in CIS states. H. Klüter. **Geojournal** 31:4 12:1993 pp.419 - 434.

3420 Restructuring of the labour market and the role of Third World migration in Europe. E. Pugliese. **Envir. Plan. D.** 11:5 10:1993 pp.513 - 522.

3421 The role of ethnic relations and education systems in migration from Southeast Asia to Australia. Gerard Sullivan; S. Gunasekaran. **Sojourn** 8:2 8:1993 pp.219 - 249.

3422 Stabilisation à la migration — un prologue à la mesure. *[In French]*; [Sensitization to migration — a prologue to the measure]. C.B. Keely. **Aff. Soc. Int.** XXI:2 1993 pp.23 - 44.

3423 The state, housing policy and Afro-Caribbean migration to France. Stephanie A. Condon; Philip E. Ogden. **Ethn. Racial** 16:2 4:1993 pp.256 - 297.

3424 Theories of international migration — a review and appraisal. Douglas S. Massey; Joaquín Arango; Graeme Hugo; Ali Kouaouci; Adela Pellegrino; J. Edward Taylor. **Pop. Dev. Rev.** 19:3 9:1993 pp.431 - 466.

F: Population. Family. Gender. Ethnic group

3425 Tutela previdenziale, assistenza socio-sanitaria e prospettive di elettorato amministrativo per i cittadini extracomunitari immigrati. *[In Italian]*; [Social security protection, health and social aid and the prospects of administrative electorate for immigrant citizens from outside the EC]. Antonio Zoina. **Aff. Soc. Int.** XXI:4 1993 pp.117 - 140.

3426 The uncertain connection — free trade and rural Mexican migration to the United States. Wayne A. Cornelius; Philip L. Martin. **Int. Migr. Rev.** XXVII:3 Fall:1993 pp.484 - 512.

3427 Weltweit auf der Flucht. *[In German]*; [Refugees all over the world]. Peter J. Opitz. **Geogr. Rund.** 45:11 11:1993 pp.680 - 685.

3428 Window on the Netherlands — international migration and population in the Netherlands. Hans van Amersfoort. **J. Econ. Soc. Geogr.** 84:1 1993 pp.65 - 74.

G: ENVIRONMENT. COMMUNITY. RURAL. URBAN
ENVIRONNEMENT. COMMUNAUTÉ. RURAL. URBAIN

G.1: Ecology. Geography. Human settlements
Écologie. Géographie. Établissements humains

3429 Alternative livelihood systems in the drylands: the need for a new paradigm. R. Méndez. **Geojournal** 31:1 9:1993 pp.67 - 76.

3430 Are people acting irrationally? Understanding public concerns about environmental threats. Abraham H. Wandersman; William K. Hallman. **Am. Psychol.** 48:6 6:1993 pp.681 - 686.

3431 Behavior and environment: psychological and geographical approaches. Tommy Gärling [Ed.]; Reginald G. Golledge [Ed.]. Amsterdam, New York: North-Holland, 1993. x, 483p. *ISBN: 0444896988. Includes bibliographical references and indexes. (Series:* Advances in psychology).

3432 Biotechnology: its place in geography. A. Mannion. **Geojournal** 31:4 12:1993 pp.347 - 354.

3433 The changing geography of China. Frank Leeming. Oxford, Cambridge, Mass: Blackwell, 1993. 197p. *ISBN: 0631176756, 0631181377. Includes bibliographical references and index. (Series:* IBG studies in geography).

3434 Children and the environment — ecological awareness among preschool children. Stewart Cohen; Diane Horm-Wingerd. **Envir. Behav.** 25:1 1:1993 pp.103 - 120.

3435 Constructing the dark continent — metaphor as geographic representation in Africa. L. Jarosz. **Geog.ann. B.** 74:2 1992 pp.105 - 116.

3436 Critical review of behavioral interventions to preserve the environment — research since 1980. William O. Dwyer; Frank C. Leeming; Melissa K. Cobern; Bryan E. Porter; John Mark Jackson. **Envir. Behav.** 25:3 5:1993 pp.275 - 321.

3437 Critical synthesis on the concept of 'region' in the sociospatial sciences: an instance of the social production of nature. C.O. Rambanapasi. **Soc. Epist.** 7:2 4-6:1993 pp.147 - 182.

3438 Desertification and society: a question of territory. P. Faggi. **Geojournal** 31:1 9:1993 pp.89 - 94.

3439 Desertification control and natural resource management in the aridity zones of the Third World. G. Winckler; A. Trux. **Geojournal** 31:1 9:1993 pp.101 - 120.

3440 Development and social problems — the impact of the offshore oil industry on suicide and homicide rates. Ruth Seydlitz; Shirley Laska; Daphne Spain; Elizabeth W. Triche; Karen L. Bishop. **Rural Sociol.** 58:1 Spring:1993 pp.93 - 110.

3441 Diverse world-views in an English village. Nigel Rapport. Edinburgh: Edinburgh University Press, 1993. 212p. *ISBN: 0748604170.*

3442 Ecological disturbance and nature tourism. Melissa Savage. **Geogr. Rev.** 83:3 7:1993 pp.290 - 300.

3443 Ecology, policy, and politics: human well-being and the natural world. John O'Neill. London, New York: Routledge, 1993. 227p. *ISBN: 0415072999, 0415073006. Includes bibliographical references and index. (Series:* Environmental philosophies).

3444 Ekologiia i nravstvennost'. *[In Russian]*; (Ecology and morals.). V. Kosheleva. **Obshch. Nauki Sovrem.** 1 1993 pp.153 - 162.

G: Environment. Community. Rural. Urban

3445 Energetyka jądrowa a społeczeństwo. *[In Polish]*; [Nuclear energy and society]. Zdzisław Celiński. Warszawa: Wydawnictwo naukowe PWN, 1992. 270p. *ISBN: 8301103655. Bibliography: p.254-[261].*

3446 Envaironmental'naia sotsiologiia vchera i segodnia. *[In Russian]*; (Environmental sociology yesterday and today.). O. Ianitskii. **Obshch. Nauki Sovrem.** 2 1993 pp.76 - 91.

3447 Environment and health: themes in medical geography. Rais Akhtar [Ed.]. New Delhi: Ashish Pub. House, 1991. xiii, 649p. *ISBN: 8170243327. Includes bibliographical references and index.*

3448 Environment and sustainable development — some sociological issues. S.T. Hettige. **Sri Lanka J. Soc. Sci.** 16:1-2 6-12:1993 pp.21 - 34.

3449 Environmental consciousness — an empirical study. Daniel Krause. **Envir. Behav.** 25:1 1:1993 pp.126 - 142.

3450 Environmental justice. Judith A. Perrolle [Ed.]; Stella M. Capek [Contrib.]; Edward Walsh [Contrib.]; Rex Warland [Contrib.]; D. Clayton Smith [Contrib.]; Suzanna Smith [Contrib.]; Michael Jepson [Contrib.]; Loren Lutzenhiser [Contrib.]; Bruce Hackett [Contrib.]; J. Timmons Roberts [Contrib.]; Elaine Draper [Contrib.]; Barbara Deutsch Lynch [Contrib.]. **Soc. Prob.** 40:1 2:1993 pp.1 - 124. *Collection of 8 articles.*

3451 [Environmental sociology]; *[Text in Japanese]*. Nobuko Ijima [Ed.]. Tokyo: Yuhikaku, 1993. 254p.

3452 Ethics and sustainability — a preliminary perspective. M.G. Reed; O. Slaymaker. **Envir. Plan. A.** 25:5 5:1993 pp.723 - 739.

3453 Feminism and the mastery of nature. Val Plumwood. London, New York: Routledge, 1993. 239p. *ISBN: 0415068096. Includes bibliographical references and index.* (*Series:* Opening out).

3454 A framework for the areal interpolation of socioeconomic data. M.F. Goodchild; L. Anselin; U. Deichmann. **Envir. Plan. A.** 25:3 3:1993 pp.383 - 397.

3455 Green politics and environmental ethics — a defence of human welfare ecology. David Wells. **Aust. J. Pol. Sci** 28:3 11:1993 pp.515 - 527.

3456 (Hetero)sexing space — lesbian perceptions and experiences of everyday spaces. G. Valentine. **Envir. Plan. D.** 11:4 8:1993 pp.395 - 413.

3457 Human behavior in spatial analysis. Gerard Rushton. **Urban Geogr.** 14:5 9-10:1993 pp.447 - 456.

3458 The human ecology of tornadoes. B.E. Aguirre; Rogelio Saenz; John Edmiston; Nan Yang; Elsa Agramonte; Dietra L. Stuart. **Demography** 30:4 11:1993 pp.623 - 633.

3459 Ideology, environment and legislation — South Australian attitudes to vegetation. Elaine Stratford. **Aust. Geogr. Stud.** 31:1 4:1993 pp.14 - 24.

3460 Implications of psychological research on stress and technological accidents. Andrew Baum; India Fleming. **Am. Psychol.** 48:6 6:1993 pp.665 - 672.

3461 Improving citizen participation in environmental decision making — the use of transformative mediator techniques. C.P. Ozawa. **Envir. Plan. C.** 11:1 2:1993 pp.103 - 117.

3462 Interpreting nature: cultural constructions of the environment. Ian Gordon Simmons. London: Routledge, 1993. 215p. *ISBN: 0415097053.*

3463 Inventing places: studies in cultural geography. Kay Anderson [Ed.]; Fay Gale [Ed.]. Melbourne: Longman Cheshire, 1992. xii, 285p. *ISBN: 0582868750. Includes bibliographical references and indexes.*

3464 John K. Wright and human nature in geography. Michael Handley. **Geogr. Rev.** 83:2 4:1993 pp.183 - 193.

G: Environnement. Communauté. Rural. Urbain

3465 Une justification écologique? Conflits dans l'aménagement de la nature. *[In French]*; (An ecological justification? Conflicts in the development of nature.) *[Summary]*; *[Summary in German]*; *[Summary in Spanish]*. Claudette LaFaye; Laurent Thévenot. **Rev. Fr. Soc.** XXXIV:4 10-12:1993 pp.495 - 524.

3466 Landscape, personhood, and culture — names of places and people in the Faeroe Islands. Dennis Gaffin. **Ethnos** 58:1-2 1993 pp.53 - 72.

3467 Landscape: politics and perspectives. Barbara Bender [Ed.]. Oxford: Berg Publishers, 1993. 351p. *ISBN: 0854963731*. (*Series:* Explorations in anthropology).

3468 Modern geography and contemporary reality. P. Claval. **Geojournal** 31:3 11:1993 pp.239 - 246.

3469 Motivation for reported involvement in local wetland preservation — the roles of knowledge, disposition, problem assessment, and arousal. Geoffrey J. Syme; Cynthia E. Beven; Neil R. Sumner. **Envir. Behav.** 25:5 9:1993 pp.586 - 606.

3470 Natural relations: ecology, animal rights and social justice. Ted Benton. London: Verso, 1993. 246p. *ISBN: 0860915905*.

3471 Neotraditional towns and urban villages — the cultural production of a geography of "otherness". K. Till. **Envir. Plan. D.** 11:6 12:1993 pp.709 - 732.

3472 Nomadism and desertification in Africa and the Middle East. D.L. Johnson. **Geojournal** 31:1 9:1993 pp.51 - 66.

3473 On economization and ecologization as civilizing processes. C. Schmidt. **Environ. Values** 2:1 Spring:1993 pp.33 - 46.

3474 Person-environment fit theory — some history, recent developments, and future directions. Robert D. Caplan; R. Van Harrison. **J. Soc. Issues** 49:4 1993 pp.253 - 275.

3475 Place and the politics of identity. Michael Keith [Ed.]; Steve Pile [Ed.]. London, New York: Routledge, 1993. 235p. *ISBN: 0415090083*. *Includes bibliographical references and index.*

3476 Place/culture/representation. James S. Duncan [Ed.]; David Ley [Ed.]. London: Routledge, 1993. 341p. *ISBN: 041509450X*.

3477 Planetary overload: global environmental change and the health of the human species. Anthony J. McMichael. Cambridge, New York, N.Y: Cambridge University Press, 1993. 352p. *ISBN: 0521441382*. *Includes bibliographical references and index.*

3478 Policy planning and the design and use of forums, arenas, and courts. J.M. Bryson; B.C. Crosby. **Envir. Plan. B.** 20:2 3:1993 pp.175 - 194.

3479 Politik in der Risikogesellschaft: Essays and Analysen. *[In German]*; [Politics in the risk society: essays and analyses]. Ulrich Beck; et al. Frankfurt am Main: Suhrkamp, 1991. 434p. *ISBN: 3518383310*. *Includes bibliographical references.*

3480 Population growth and land degradation. M. Mortimore. **Geojournal** 31:1 9:1993 pp.15 - 22.

3481 Post-modern geography or geography of the third modernity? J.-P. Ferrier. **Geojournal** 31:3 11:1993 pp.251 - 254.

3482 Public health spaces and the fabrication of identity. David Armstrong. **Sociology** 27:3 8:1993 pp.393 - 410.

3483 "Race" and sexuality — challenging the patriarchal structuring of urban social space. L. Peake. **Envir. Plan. D.** 11:4 8:1993 pp.415 - 432.

G: Environment. Community. Rural. Urban

3484 Raumauffassung und Kartographie bei schriftlosen Kulturen. *[In German]*; [Conceptions of space and cartography in cultures with no written language]. Andreas Dittmann. **Geogr. Rund.** 45:12 12:1993 pp.718 - 723.

3485 A reassessment of the human dimension of desertification. F.N. Ibrahim. **Geojournal** 31:1 9:1993 pp.5 - 10.

3486 The reinvention of cultural geography. Marie Price; Martin Lewis; Carl Saver [Subject of work]. **Ann. As. Am. G.** 83:1 3:1993 pp.1 - 17.

3487 (Re)mapping mother earth — a geographical perspective on environmental feminisms. C. Nesmith; S.A. Radcliffe. **Envir. Plan. D.** 11:4 8:1993 pp.379 - 334.

3488 Settlement frontiers revisited — the case of Israel and the West Bank. Aharon Kellerman. **J. Econ. Soc. Geogr.** 84:1 1993 pp.27 - 39.

3489 The social context of recycling. Linda Derksen; John Gartrell. **Am. Sociol. R.** 58:3 6:1993 pp.434 - 442.

3490 Social science perspectives on environment and sustainable development. N.E.H. Sanderatne. **Sri Lanka J. Soc. Sci.** 16:1-2 6-12:1993 pp.91 - 107.

3491 Sociology of natural resources in Pakistan and adjoining countries. Carol Carpenter [Ed.]; Michael R. Dove [Ed.]. Lahore: Vanguard, 1992. 458p. *ISBN: 9694020549.*

3492 Some socio-economic aspects of coral mining activities — a case study from the southwest coast of Sri Lanka. U. Weerakkody. **Sri Lanka J. Soc. Sci.** 15:1/2 6-12:1992 pp.89 - 104.

3493 Space, place and gender relations. Part II — identity, difference, feminist geometries and geographies. Linda McDowell. **Prog. H. Geog.** 17:3 9:1993 pp.305 - 318.

3494 Spatial-domain chaos in landscapes. Jonathan D. Phillips. **Geogr. Anal.** 25:2 4:1993 pp.101 - 117.

3495 Theory building in political ecology. Mark Somma. **Soc. Sci. Info.** 32:3 1993 pp.371 - 385.

3496 Therapeutic landscapes — theory and a case study of Epidauros, Greece. W.M. Gesler. **Envir. Plan. D.** 11:2 1993 pp.171 - 189.

3497 Towards a post-modern planning? O. Soubeyran. **Geojournal** 31:3 11:1993 pp.255 - 264.

3498 Viewing the world ecologically. Marvin Elliott Olsen; Dora G. Lodwick; Riley E. Dunlap. Boulder: Westview Press, 1992. xvi, 214p. *ISBN: 081338298X. Includes bibliographical references (p. 203-207) and index.*

3499 Women and desertification: the question of responsibility. E. Grawert. **Geojournal** 31:1 9:1993 pp.85 - 88.

3500 Women, ecology and health — rebuilding connections. Vandana Shiva [Contrib.]; Ann Danaiya Usher [Contrib.]; Penny Newman [Contrib.]; FASDSP Group [Contrib.]; Indira Jaising [Contrib.]; C. Sathyamala [Contrib.]; Gail Omvedt [Contrib.]; Loreta B. Ayupan [Contrib.]; Teresita G. Oliveros [Contrib.]; Rita Sebastian [Contrib.]. **Dev. Dialog.** 1-2 1992 pp.3 - 168. *Collection of 10 articles.*

G.2: Community
Communauté

3501 Ambivalent attachments to place in London — twelve Barbadian families. J. Western. **Envir. Plan. D.** 11:2 1993 pp.147 - 170.

G: Environnement. Communauté. Rural. Urbain

3502 Been-heres versus come-heres — negotiating conflicting community identities. Daphne Spain. **J. Am. Plann.** 59:2 Spring:1993 pp.156 - 171.
3503 Canada's social economy: co-operatives, non-profits and other community enterprises. Jack Quarter. Toronto: J. Lorimer, 1992. xii, 208p. *ISBN: 1550283871, 1550283863. Includes index. Includes bibliographical references: p. [199]-202.*
3504 Communities within cities: an urban social geography. Wayne Kenneth David Davies; David Herbert. London; New York: Belhaven Press; Halsted Press, 1993. 196p. *ISBN: 0470220228. Includes bibliographical references and index.*
3505 Community and public policy. Hugh Butcher [Ed.]; et al. London, Boulder: Pluto Press in association with Community Development Foundation, 1993. 281p. *ISBN: 0745308007, 0745308015. Includes bibliographical references and index.*
3506 Community development in Sierra Leone. Mathew L.S. Gboku. **Comm. Dev. J.** 28:2 4:1993 pp.167 - 175.
3507 Community economic development — some critical issues. John W. Handy. **Rev. Bl. Pol. Ec.** 21:3 Winter:1993 pp.41 - 64.
3508 Community economic development: policy formation in the US and UK. David Fasenfest [Ed.]. Basingstoke: Macmillan, 1993. 241p. *ISBN: 0333556577. (Series: Policy studies organization series).*
3509 Craft, class and control: the sociology of a shipbuilding community. Ian Roberts. Edinburgh: Edinburgh University Press (for the University of Durham), 1993. 228p. *ISBN: 0748603956.*
3510 The critical villager: beyond community participation. Eric Dudley. London: Routledge, 1993. 173p. *ISBN: 041507343X.*
3511 Diggers and dreamers, 1994-1995: the guide to communal living. Chris Coates [Ed.]; et al. Winslow: Communes Network, 1993. 220p. *ISBN: 095149452X.*
3512 Duurzaamheid en verloop in jongeren- en gezinswoongroepen. *[In Dutch]*; (Duration and development of communal households.) *[Summary]*. Harrie A.M. Jansen. **Bevolk. Gez.** 2 1993 pp.95 - 116.
3513 Essays on non-conventional community. Risto Eräsaari. Jyväskylä: Research Unit of Contemporary Culture, University of Jyväskylä, 1993. 216p. *ISBN: 9516809499. (Series:* Publication - 36).
3514 Estimating the first and (some of the) third faces of community power. Paul Schumaker. **Urban Aff. Q.** 28:3 3:1993 pp.441 - 461.
3515 Fighting back in Appalachia: traditions of resistance and change. Stephen L. Fisher [Ed.]. Philadelphia: Temple University Press, 1993. x, 365p. *ISBN: 0877229767. Includes bibliographical references (p. [339]-360).*
3516 (The formation of social integration system — the two systems of "life community".); *[Text in Japanese]*. Takashi Umezawa. **Shak. Ronso** 117 1993 pp.21 - 39.
3517 (Four types of community participation by the elderly of central Tokyo and their respective characteristics.) *[Summary]*; *[Text in Japanese]*. Yuetu Takahasi. **Comp. Urban Stud.** 48 3:1993 pp.5 - 22.
3518 Israeli Palestinian territorial perceptions. Izhak Schnell. **Envir. Behav.** 25:4 7:1993 pp.419 - 456.
3519 Kommunitäre Gruppen in Japan: alternative Mikrogesellschaften als kultureller Spiegel. *[In German]*; [Communitarian groups in Japan: alternative microsocieties as a cultural mirror]. Christoph Brumann. **Z. Ethn.** 117 1992 pp.119 - 138.

G: Environment. Community. Rural. Urban

3520 Locality and community coming to terms with places. Graham Day; Jonathan Murdoch. **Sociol. Rev.** 41:1 2:1993 pp.82 - 111.

3521 Moral communities: the Prideaux Lectures for 1992. Robin Gill. Exeter: University of Exeter, 1992. 87p. *ISBN: 085989391X.* (*Series:* Prideaux Lectures).

3522 Neighbourhood self-management in Jerusalem — planning issues and implementation dilemmas. Howard Litwin. **Admin. Soc.** 25:3 11:1993 pp.335 - 352.

3523 The partial unacceptability of money in repayment for neighborly help. Paul Webley; Stephen E.G. Lea. **Human Relat.** 46:1 1:1993 pp.65 - 76.

3524 A place to call home — identification with dwelling, community, and region. Lee Cuba; David M. Hummon. **Sociol. Q.** 34:1 Spring:1993 pp.111 - 131.

3525 Regenerating the coalfields: policy and politics in the 1980s and early 1990s. Royce Logan Turner. Aldershot: Avebury, 1993. 271p. *ISBN: 185628414X.*

3526 [Regional image and community development]; *[Text in Japanese]*. Toshikatsu Iwai. Tokyo: Gihodo Shuppan, 1993. 182p.

3527 Regionalbewußtsein und regionale Identität. Ein Konzept der Moderne als Forschungsfeld der Geschichtswissenschaft. *[In German]*; (Regional awareness and regional identity. A concept of modern features as a research field in the science of history.). Rüdiger Gans. **Inf. Raum.** 11 1993 pp.781 - 792.

3528 Regionalkultur? Muster und Werte regionaler Identität im Ruhrgebiet. *[In German]*; (Regional culture? Patterns and values of regional identity in the Ruhr.). Eckart Pankoke. **Inf. Raum.** 11 1993 pp.759 - 768.

3529 Ritual as action in a Javanese community — a network perspective on ritual and social structure. Thomas Schweizer; Elmar Klemm; Margarete Schweizer. **Soc. Networks** 15:1 3:1993 pp.19 - 48.

3530 Settlement planning and participation under principles of pluralism. T. Fenster. **Prog. Plan.** 39:3 1993 pp.167 - 242.

3531 Théorie et pratiques en organisation communautaire. *[In French]*; [Theory and praxis in community organization]. Laval Doucet [Ed.]; Louis Favreau [Ed.]; Yao Assogba [Contrib.]; et al. Sillery: Presses de l'Université du Québec, 1991. xvii, 468p. *ISBN: 2760506665. Bibliographic references: p. [453]-460.*

3532 Toward a political economy of inheritance — community and household among the Mennonites. Jeffrey Longhofer. **Theory Soc.** 22:3 6:1993 pp.337 - 362.

3533 (Towards a better understanding of the actual state of the local community.) *[Summary]*; *[Text in Japanese]*. Toru Amano; Yuetsu Takahashi. **Comp. Urban Stud.** 48 3:1993 pp.109 - 124.

3534 Die Verantwortung des Bürgers für seine Stadt. Reflexionen über eine verhaltensbeeinflussende Kommunalpolitik. *[In German]*; (Citizens' responsibility for their community.) *[Summary]*; *[Summary in French]*. Hasso Brühl; Paul von Kodolitsch. **Arc. Kommunal.** 32:1 1993 pp.47 - 70.

3535 "A world in a grain of sand" — towards a reconceptualisation of geographical scale. Richard Howitt. **Aust. Geogr.** 24:1 5:1993 pp.33 - 44.

G: Environnement. Communauté. Rural. Urbain

G.3: **Rural and urban sociology**
Sociologie rurale et urbaine

3536 Analysis of urban-rural population dynamics of China — a multiregional life table approach. J. Shen. **Envir. Plan. A.** 25:2 2:1993 pp.245 - 253.
3537 Causes of in-migration to Tel-Aviv inner city. Izhak Schnell; Iris Graicer. **Urban Stud.** 30:7 8:1993 pp.1187 - 1208.
3538 Comparative studies on the planned rural-urban migrants and spontaneous rural-urban migrants in China. Jinyu Xie. **China City Plan. R.** 8:4 12:1992 pp.25 - 41.
3539 (The concept of planning and theoretical and methodological studies on urban and rural planning.) *[Summary]*; *[Text in Japanese]*. Yorifusa Ishida. **Comp. Urban St.** 50 11:1993 pp.19 - 36.
3540 The effects of rural-to-urban migration of the poverty status of youth in the 1980s. DeeAnn Wenk; Constance Hardesty. **Rural Sociol.** 58:1 Spring:1993 pp.76 - 92.
3541 L'exode des jeunes du milieu rural — en quête d'un emploi ou d'un genre de vie. *[In French]*; [Exodus of the young from rural areas — in search of a job or a way of life] *[Summary]*. Jacques Roy. **Rech. Soc.graph** XXXIII:3 9-12:1992 pp.429 - 444.
3542 Landgemeinde und Stadtgemeinde in Mitteleuropa: ein struktureller Vergleich. *[In German]*; [Rural and urban communities in Central Europe: a structural comparison]. Peter Blickle [Ed.]; André Holenstein [Ed.]. München: Oldenbourg, 1991. vi,510p. *ISBN: 3486644130. Papers from a conference held Mar. 6-9, 1989, in Schloss Reisenburg and sponsored by the Volkswagen-Stiftung. Includes bibliographical references.*
3543 L'opposition villes-campagnes est-elle fatale? *[In French]*; [Is the town-country opposition fatal?]. François-Régis Mahleu. **Afr. Cont.** 168 10-12:1993 pp.108 - 124.
3544 Reconfiguración rural-urbana en la zona henequenera de Yucatán. *[In Spanish]*; [Rural-urban reconfiguration of Yucatan's Henequen zone] *[Summary]*. Othón Baños. **Est. Sociol.** XI:32 5-8:1993 pp.419 - 444.
3545 The rural-urban interface in Africa: expansion and adaptation. Jonathan David Baker; Poul Ove Pedersen. Uppsala: Nordiska Afrikainstitutet, 1992. 320p. *ISBN: 9171063293. Includes bibliographical references. Centre for Development Research, Copenhagen. (Series:* Seminar proceedings - 27).
3546 Upper and lower circuits in the context of urban-rural exchange relations. S.T. Hettige. **Sri Lanka J. Soc. Sci.** 13:1/2 6/12:1990 pp.19 - 31.

G.3.1: **Rural sociology**
Sociologie rurale

3547 Agrarian transition and social development in Orissa. Jayanta K. Mahapatra; Urmi Mala Das. **Ind. J. Pol. Sci.** LIV:2 4-6:1993 pp.292 - 312.
3548 Agricultural policy and the rural poor. M.V. Nadkarni [Contrib.]; Avadhoot Nadkarni [Contrib.]; Jagdish Pradhan [Contrib.]; K.T. Chandy [Contrib.]; Thomas Palakudy [Contrib.]; Sukhpal Singh [Contrib.]; B.C. Mehta [Contrib.]. **Soc. Act.** 43:3 7-9:1993 pp.271 - 357. *Collection of 6 articles.*
3549 Another country: real life beyond Rose Cottage. James Garo Derounian. London: National Council for Voluntary Organisations, 1993. 186p. *ISBN: 0719913950.*

G: Environment. Community. Rural. Urban

3550 Back to the land — the political dilemmas of agrarian reform in Nicaragua. Laura J. Enríquez; Marlen I. Llanes. **Soc. Prob.** 40:2 5:1993 pp.250 - 265.

3551 [Basic issues of the farm structure in Kyoto Pref]; *[Text in Japanese]*. Yoshio Kawamura. **J. Rural Prob.** 28(4) 1993 p.

3552 Behind the uneconomic size of the Malay's idle agricultural land. Buang Amriah. **Malay. J. Trop. Geogr.** 22:2 12:1991 pp.103 - 112.

3553 Canadian and Irish farm women — some similarities, differences and comments; *[Summary in French]*. Sally Shortall. **Can. R. Soc. A.** 30:2 5:1993 pp.172 - 190.

3554 Changing land tenure system in China: common problem, uncommon solution. Laurel Bossen. **Sociol. Bul.** 40:1-2 3-9:1991 pp.47 - 68.

3555 Collective resistance and sustainable development in rural Greece — the case of geothermal energy on the island of Milos. Maria Kousis. **Sociol. Rur.** XXXIII:1 1993 pp.3 - 24.

3556 Culture and agricultural land tenure. Sonya Salamon. **Rural Sociol.** 58:4 Winter:1993 pp.580 - 598.

3557 [Development and life histories in island and mountain village]; *[Text in Japanese]*. Motoo Yada [Ed.]. Tokyo: Inaho-shobo, 1993. 196p.

3558 Diffusion research in rural sociology: the record and prospects for the future. Frederick C. Fliegel; James J. Zuiches [Foreword]. Westport, Conn: Greenwood Press, 1993. xv, 132p. *ISBN: 0313264473. Under the auspices of the Rural Sociological Society. Includes bibliographical references (p. [117]-127) and index. (Series:* Contributions in sociology).

3559 Evolución de la economía campesina en Colombia, 1988-1992. *[In Spanish]*; [The development of the rural economy in Colombia, 1988-1992]. Miguel Gómez. **Coy. Soc.** 9 11:1993 pp.85 - 102.

3560 Factores socioculturales asociados a la erosión hídrica en un sistema hortícola: el caso de Cot y Tierra Blanca de Cartago. *[In Spanish]*; [Socio-cultural factors associated with the hydrographic erosion of an agricultural system: the case of Cot and Tierra Blanca in Cartago] *[Summary]*. Victor Manuel Cortes; Giovanni Oconitrillo. **An. Est. Cent.Am.** 19:1 1993 pp.79 - 90.

3561 Farm transfer and farm entry in the European Community; *[Summary in French]*; *[Summary in German]*. Michel Blanc; Philippe Perrier-Cornet. **Sociol. Rur.** XXXIII:3-4 1993 pp.319 - 335.

3562 Female farmers in Canada, 1971-1986. Gloria J. Leckie. **Prof. Geogr.** 45:2 5:1993 pp.180 - 193.

3563 Flexibilität Tradition. Zur Attraktivität der comunidad campesina in Peru. *[In German]*; (Flexibility contra tradition. On the attractivity of the Peruvian comunidad campesina.) *[Summary]*. Erdmute Alber. **Sociologus** 43:2 1993 pp.97 - 117.

3564 Green revolution technologies and dryland agriculture. G.S. Aurora. **Sociol. Bul.** 40:1-2 3-9:1991 pp.109 - 122.

3565 Growth promotion activities in rural areas — do they make a difference? Craig R. Humphrey; Kenneth P. Wilkinson. **Rural Sociol.** 58:2 Summer:1993 pp.175 - 189.

3566 Harvesting human capital — family structure and education among rural youth. Daniel T. Lichter; Gretchen T. Cornwell; David J. Eggbeen. **Rural Sociol.** 58:1 Spring:1993 pp.53 - 75.

3567 Housing assessment criteria of rural households. M.J. Weber; J. McCray; M. Ha. **Soc. Ind.** 28:1 1:1993 pp.21 - 44.

G: Environnement. Communauté. Rural. Urbain

3568 Identidad serrana, cultura silvícola y tradicíon forestal. La crisis de los aprovechamientos tradicionales en las tierras salmantinas y la opción forestal. *[In Spanish]*; [Mountain identity, forest culture and tradition. The crisis of traditional exploitation in the Salamanca area and options regarding the forests] *[Summary]*; *[Summary in French]*. Jose Manuel Llorente Pinto. **Agr. Soc.** 65 10-12:1992 pp.217 - 252.

3569 Imagens da integração — representações sociais sobre a integração da agricultura portuguesa na Comunidade Europeia. *[In Portuguese]*; [Images of integration — social representations on the integration of Portuguese agriculture into the European Communities]. Nelson Lourenço; José António Cabrita; Ana Maria Ventura. **Anál. Soc.** XXVII:4-5(118-119) 1992 pp.955 - 973.

3570 In the sticks: cultural identity in a rural police force. Malcolm Young. Oxford, New York: Clarendon Press, Oxford University Press, 1993. ix,309p. *ISBN: 0198762895. Includes bibliographical references and index.*

3571 Inside the Third World village. Petra Weyland. New York; London: Routledge, 1993. 257p. *ISBN: 0415088518. Includes bibliographical references and index.*

3572 Instytucjonalna koncepcja zmiany wiejskich społeczności lokalnych. *[In Polish]*; (Institutional conception of changes in rural local communities.) *[Summary]*. Paweł Starosta. **Prz. Soc.** XL 1993 pp.57 - 72.

3573 [Japanese rural community]; *[Text in Japanese]*. Hideki Takashima. Tokyo: Meisei University Press, 1993. 237p.

3574 The land question: are there answers? Gene Wunderlich. **Rural Sociol.** 58:4 Winter:1993 pp.547 - 559.

3575 Law as a resource in agrarian struggles. Menno Velde [Ed.]; Franz Benda-Beckmann [Ed.]; Jacqueling Vel; Mirjam de Bruijin; Han van Dijk; Franz von Benda-Beckmann; Tanja Taale; H.L.J. Spiertz; Abraham van Eldijk; Roland Brouwer; Viviane W.M.M. Ampt-Riksen; John W. van de Ven. Wageningen: Agricultural University Wageningen, 1992. viii, 319p. *ISBN: 9067542024. Includes bibliographical references. (Series:* Wageningse sociologische studies).

3576 The listing process in Scotland and the statutory protection of vernacular building types. Malcolm Horne. **Town Plan. R.** 64:4 10:1993 pp.375 - 393.

3577 A multidimensional index of financial stress in the farm sector. J.S. Shonkwiler; C.B. Moss. **Soc. Ind.** 29:3 7:1993 pp.307 - 316.

3578 The nature of symbolic beliefs and environmental behavior in a rural setting. John Cary. **Envir. Behav.** 25:5 9:1993 pp.555 - 576.

3579 Nonmetropolitan geography: migration, sense of place, and the American West. Gundars Rudzitis. **Urban Geogr.** 14:6 11-12:1993 pp.574 - 585.

3580 O estado-providência e a sociedade rural. Revalorização de recursos e reordenamento de estratégias num novo contexto: a agricultura de pluriactividade. *[In Portuguese]*; (The welfare state and rural society. The enhancement of resources and the redefinition of strategies in a new context: an agriculture involving multiple activities.) *[Summary]*; *[Summary in French]*. André Samouco. **Anál. Soc.** XXVIII:2 (121) 1993 pp.391 - 408.

3581 Organizational problems for the German Farmers' Association and alternative policy options. Rolf G. Heinze; Helmut Voelzkow. **Sociol. Rur.** XXXIII:1 1993 pp.25 - 41.

3582 Ownership: an overview. Charles Geisler. **Rural Sociol.** 58:4 Winter:1993 pp.532 - 546.

G: Environment. Community. Rural. Urban

3583 Pauperising agriculture: studies in agrarian change and demographic structure. N. Krishnaji. Bombay: Oxford University Press published for Sameeksha Trust, 1992. 259p. *ISBN: 0195631870. Includes index.*

3584 People's science: a perspective from the voluntary sector. Vithal Rajan. **Sociol. Bul.** 40:1-2 3-9:1991 pp.123 - 132.

3585 Persistent poverty in rural America. Emery N. Castle [Foreword]; Rural Sociological Society, Task Force on Persistent Rural Poverty. Boulder, Colo: Westview Press, 1993. 379p. *ISBN: 0813387124. Includes bibliographical references. (Series:* Rural studies series of the Rural Sociological Society).

3586 Perspectives on agrarian reform in East-Central Europe. Helga Répássy; David Symes. **Sociol. Rur.** XXXIII:1 1993 pp.81 - 91.

3587 Policy perspectives on social, agricultural, and rural sustainability. Ronald C. Wimberley. **Rural Sociol.** 58:1 Spring:1993 pp.1 - 29.

3588 La problemática social de la reforma de La P.A.C. — el caso de Castilla y León. *[In Spanish]*; [The social problem of reform of the C.A.P. — the case of Castilla y León]. Jesús Díezsánchez. **Rev. Fom. Soc.** 48:190 4-6:1993 pp.227 - 244.

3589 Property in land. Robert C. Ellickson. **Yale Law J.** 102:6 4:1993 pp.1315 - 1400.

3590 [A prospect on development of tourist industry and womens' work in depopulated mountain villages]; *[Text in Japanese]*. Sumie Goto. **B. Nihon Fuku. Univ.** 89 1993 pp.196 - 220.

3591 Regional development, remote communities and alternative transportation services. J. Jones; M.W. Rosenberg. **Geog.ann. B.** 74B:3 1992 pp.199 - 209.

3592 [Relationship of individual and group in Japanese farmers life]; *[Text in Japanese]*. Takashi Hosoya [Ed.]. Tokyo: Ochanomizu Shobo, 1993. 567p.

3593 The rise and demise of African agricultural production in Dinokana village, Bophuthatswana. James Drummond; Andy Manson. **Can. J. Afr. St.** 27:3 1993 pp.462 - 479.

3594 Rural action: a collection of community work case studies. Paul Henderson [Ed.]; David Francis [Ed.]. London: Pluto Press, 1993. 178p. *ISBN: 0745307337.*

3595 Rural community satisfaction and attachment in mass consumer society. Ralph B. Brown. **Rural Sociol.** 58:3 Fall:1993 pp.387 - 403.

3596 Rural crisis and rural research in the Netherlands; *[Summary in German]*; *[Summary in French]*. Henk de Haan [Contrib.]; Dirk Strijker [Contrib.]; Ad Nooij [Contrib.]; Hans Hillebrand [Contrib.]; Ursula Blom [Contrib.]; Wilma M. de Vries [Contrib.]; Jan G. Smit [Contrib.]; Jaap Frouws [Contrib.]; Jan van Tatenhove [Contrib.]; Jan Douwe van der Ploeg [Contrib.]; Niels Röling [Contrib.]; Cees Leeuwis [Contrib.]. **Sociol. Rur.** XXXIII:2 1993 pp.127 - 305. *Collection of 11 articles.*

3597 Rural household travel characteristics: the case of Kakamega district. Meleckidzedeck Khayesi. **J. E.Afr. Res. Devel.** 23 1993 pp.88 - 105.

3598 Rural income inequality in China since 1978. Chris Bramall; Marion E. Jones. **J. Peasant Stud.** 21:1 10:1993 pp.41 - 70.

3599 Rural poverty in India. B.C. Mehta. New Delhi: Concept Publishing Company, 1993. 200p. *ISBN: 8170224322.*

3600 Rural society: its integration and disintegration. Martine Dirven. **CEPAL R.** 51 12:1993 pp.69 - 88.

3601 Rural sociology in Canada. David A. Hay [Ed.]; G. S. Basran [Ed.]. Toronto: Oxford University Press, 1992. x, 333p. *ISBN: 0195408187. Includes index. Includes bibliographical references: p. 273-318.*

G: Environnement. Communauté. Rural. Urbain

3602 Socioeconomic heterogeneity of mining-dependent counties. Mark Nord; A.E. Luloff. **Rural Sociol.** 58:3 Fall:1993 pp.492 - 500.

3603 The solitude of collectivism: Romanian villagers to the revolution and beyond. David A. Kideckel. Ithaca: Cornell University Press, 1993. xix, 255p. *ISBN: 0801427460, 0801480256. Includes bibliographical references (p. 229-245) and index.* (*Series:* Anthropology of contemporary issues).

3604 Statement and process — designing "good" arguments about the rural energy problem in developing countries. W.W. Dougherty. **Envir. Plan. B.** 20:4 7:1993 pp.379 - 390.

3605 Tenures in transition, tenures in conflict: examples from the Zimbabwe social forest. John Bruce; Louise Fortmann; Calvin Nhira. **Rural Sociol.** 58:4 Winter:1993 pp.626 - 642.

3606 Titularidad y régimen de aprovechamiento de los montes catalogados en la comunidad Valenciana. *[In Spanish]*; [Entitled ownership and exploitation rules of registered woodlands in the Valencian community] *[Summary]*; *[Summary in French]*. Cristina Montiel Molina. **Agr. Soc.** 65 10-12:1992 pp.389 - 414.

3607 To farm or not to farm — rural dilemma in Russia and Ukraine. Alessandro Bananno; Andrei Kuznetsov; Simon Geletta; Mary Hendrickson. **Rural Sociol.** 58:3 Fall:1993 pp.404 - 423.

3608 Transformaciones de la vida rural y poder local. *[In Spanish]*; [Changes in rural life and local power]. Marielle Pepin-Lehalleur [Contrib.]; Odile Hoffmann [Contrib.]; Jean-Yves Marchal [Contrib.]; Marie-France Prévôt-Schapira [Contrib.]; Arturo Alvarado [Contrib.]; Nelson Minello [Contrib.]. **Est. Sociol.** X:30 9-12:1992 pp.517 - 650. *Collection of 5 articles.*

3609 Transitions in the South African countryside. Jonathan Crush; Alan Jeeves. **Can. J. Afr. St.** 27:3 1993 pp.351 - 360.

3610 Le village clanique en Corée du Sud: et son rôle dans la vie rurale. *[In French]*; [The clan village in South Korea: its role in rural life]. Chunson Yi. Paris: Collège de France, Centre d'études coréennes, 1992. 249p. *ISBN: 2905358149*.

3611 Villages astir: community development, tradition, and change in Korea. John Elliot Turner. Westport, Conn: Praeger, 1993. viii, 350p. *ISBN: 0275943720, 0275943720. Includes bibliographical references and index.*

Peasant studies
Études paysannes

3612 Amazonian caboclo society: an essay on invisibility and peasant economy. Stephen Lewis Nugent. Providence, RI: Berg, 1993. xxiii, 278p. *ISBN: 0854967567. Includes bibliographical references (p. 256-273) and index.* (*Series:* Explorations in anthropology).

3613 Die Bauern in der Geschichte der Schweiz. *[In German]*; Les paysans dans l'histoire de la Suisse. *[In French]*; [Peasantry in Swiss history]. Albert Tanner [Ed.]; Anne-Lise Head-König [Ed.]. Zurich: Chronos, 1992. 274p. *ISBN: 3905311054. In German and French. Includes bibliographical references.*

3614 El campesinado en Colombia hoy: diagnóstico y perspectivas. *[In Spanish]*; [Peasantry in Colombia today: diagnosis and points of view]. Edelmira Pérez Correa

G: Environment. Community. Rural. Urban

[Ed.]. Bogotá: Facultad de Ciencias Económicas y Administrativas, Pontificia Universidad Javeriana, 1991. 351p. *ISBN: 9586480267.*

3615 Camponeses, mediadores e Estado. *[In Portuguese]*; (Peasants, mediators and the state.) *[Summary]*; *[Summary in French].* Manuel Carlos Silva. **Anál. Soc.** XXVIII:3(122) 1993 pp.489 - 522.

3616 Disposições culturais, dinâmica afetiva e mudança de sentido — uma análise sociológica da pedagogia da pastoral da terra no Brasil. *[In Portuguese]*; [Cultural disposition, affective dynamics and change of direction — a sociological analysis of pastoral education in Brazil]. Luiz Inácio Gaiger. **Est. Leop.** 29:133 7-8:1993 pp.85 - 104.

3617 The distribution of land in rural China. Terry McKinley; Keith Griffin. **J. Peasant Stud.** 21:1 10:1993 pp.71 - 84.

3618 Embourgeoisement and the "cultural capital" variable — rural enterprise and concepts of prestige in northeastern Hungary; *[Summary in French].* Kathryn A. Szent-Gyötgyl. **Man** 28:3 9:1993 pp.515 - 532.

3619 In default: peasants, the debt crisis, and the agricultural challenge in Mexico. Marilyn Gates. Boulder, Colo: Westview Press, 1993. xii, 274p. *ISBN: 0813384559. Includes bibliographical references (p. 245-254) and index.* (*Series:* Latin American perspectives series).

3620 Producción campesina y cultura regional. *[In Spanish]*; (Peasant production and regional culture.) *[Summary].* William Mitchell. **Am. Indígena** L1:4 10-12:1991 pp.81 - 106.

3621 Soznanie krest'ianstva i agrarnye modernizatsii Rossii. *[In Russian]*; (Peasants' consciousness and agrarian modernisations of Russia.). S. Nikol'skii. **Svobod. Mysl'** 9 6:1993 pp.3 - 14.

3622 State and capital in the regeneration of a South African peasantry. Anne Vaughan; Alastair McIntosh. **Can. J. Afr. St.** 27:3 1993 pp.439 - 461.

Rural development
Développement rural

3623 El campesinado en Colombia hoy: diagnóstico y perspectivas. *[In Spanish]*; [Peasantry in Colombia today: diagnosis and points of view]. Edelmira Pérez Correa [Ed.]. Bogotá: Facultad de Ciencias Económicas y Administrativas, Pontificia Universidad Javeriana, 1991. 351p. *ISBN: 9586480267.*

3624 Development in a community under stress. John C. Allen. **Comm. Dev. J.** 28:2 4:1993 pp.154 - 166.

3625 Evolution of the rural dimension in Latin America and the Caribbean. Emiliano Ortega. **CEPAL R.** 47 8:1992 pp.115 - 136.

3626 From brigade to village community — the land tenure system and rural development in China. Zhu Ling; Jiang Zhongyi. **Camb. J. Econ.** 17:4 12:1993 pp.441 - 461.

3627 House construction in nonmetropolitan districts — economy, politics and rurality. Keith Hoggart. **Reg. Stud.** 27:7 1993 pp.651 - 664.

3628 Inscribing gender in rural development — industrial homework in two midwestern communities. Christina E. Gringeri. **Rural Sociol.** 58:1 Spring:1993 pp.30 - 52.

3629 Labour migration and rural development in Egypt — a study of return migration in six villages. Christoph Reichert. **Sociol. Rur.** XXXIII:1 1993 pp.42 - 60.

G: Environnement. Communauté. Rural. Urbain

3630 Ländliche Industrialisierung in der Volksrepublik China seit 1978. *[In German]*; [Rural industrialization in the People's Republic of China since 1978]. Hans-Peter Hüssen [Ed.]. Hamburg: Weltarchiv, 1991. 296p. *ISBN: 3878954212.*

3631 Le Québec rural dans tous ses états. *[In French]*; [Rural Quebec in all its states]. Bernard Vachon [Ed.]. Montreal: Boréal, 1991. 311p. *ISBN: 2890524450. D'Etats généraux du monde rural, 1991, Montreal, Quebec. Bibliographic references.*

3632 The rice-centric Korean village community on the road to industrialization. Mal-Soon Min. **Korea Obs.** XXIV:2 Summer:1993 pp.193 - 206.

3633 The road to Shangri La is paved: spatial development and rural transformation in Nepal. David N. Zurick. **S.Asia B.** XIII:1+2 1993 pp.35 - 44.

3634 Rural America blueprint for tomorrow. William E. Gahr [Ed.]; Emery N. Castle [Contrib.]; DeWitt John [Contrib.]; Ronald S. Cooper [Contrib.]; Cornelia Butler Flora [Contrib.]; Jan L. Flora [Contrib.]; C. Brice Ratchford [Contrib.]; Thomas G. Tate [Contrib.]; Leo V. Mayer [Contrib.]; G.W. Bird [Contrib.]; John Ikerd [Contrib.]; Dennis U. Fisher [Contrib.]; Brian Kelley [Contrib.]; Ruth McWilliams [Contrib.]; Ronald Saranich [Contrib.]; Jennifer Pratt [Contrib.]; H. Richard Anderson [Contrib.]; Anne Berblinger [Contrib.]; Ted K. Bradshaw [Contrib.]. **Ann. Am. Poli.** 529:9 9:1993 pp.12 - 175. *Collection of 14 articles.*

3635 Self help approach to rural transformation in Nigeria. Ephraim N. Madu; Emmanuel E. Umebali. **Comm. Dev. J.** 28:2 4:1993 pp.141 - 153.

3636 Una piedrita en los zapatos de los caciques. Ecos y repercusiones de las políticas de desarrollo rural en la Huasteca veracruzana. *[In Spanish]*; [A pebble in the shoes of the local bosses. Echoes and repercussions of rural development policies in the Huasteca region of Veracruz] *[Summary]*. Anath Ariel de Vidas. **Est. Sociol.** XI:33 9-12:1993 pp.741 - 768.

3637 Voluntarism and rural development in Bangladesh. Samiul Hasan. **Asian J. Pub. Admin.** 15:1 6:1993 pp.82 - 101.

G.3.2: **Urban sociology**
Sociologie urbaine

3638 Are Third World megacities sustainable? Jabotabek as an example. A. Atkinson. **J. Int. Dev.** 5:6 11-12:1993 pp.605 - 622.

3639 An argument for critical and comparative research on the urban economic geography of the Americas. V. Lawson; T. Klak. **Envir. Plan. A.** 25:8 8:1993 pp.1071 - 1084.

3640 At the end of the shift: mines and single-industry towns in Northern Ontario. Robert Matthew Bray [Ed.]; Ashley Thomson [Ed.]. Toronto: Dundurn Press, 1992. xiv, 208p. *ISBN: 1550021508. Papers presented at a conference held by Laurentian University's Institute of Northern Ontario Research and Development, 1990. Includes bibliographical references.*

3641 Auswirkungen demographischer Entwicklung auf das Städtewachstum. *[In German]*; [The effects of demographic development on city growth]; *[Summary in French]*. Peter Schaeffer. **Schw. Z. Volk. Stat.** 128:3 9:1992 pp.369 - 381.

3642 Les banlieues de Ouagadougou. *[In French]*; [The suburbs of Ouagadougou]. Sylvy Jaglin. **Afr. Cont.** 168 10-12:1993 pp.54 - 68.

G: Environment. Community. Rural. Urban

3643 Bolivia: La Paz/Chukiyawu: las dos caras de una ciudad. *[In Spanish]*; (Bolivia: La Paz/Chukiyawu: the two faces of a city.) *[Summary]*. Xavier Albó. **Am. Indígena** L1:4 10-12:1991 pp.107 - 158.

3644 Cellular automata and fractal urban form: a cellular modelling approach to the evolution of urban land-use patterns. R. White; G. Engelen. **Envir. Plan. A.** 25:8 8:1993 pp.1175 - 1200.

3645 Changing communications landscapes — threats and opportunities for UK cities. Stephen Graham. **Cities** 10:2 5:1993 pp.158 - 166.

3646 [The changing social life in Kyoto Nishijin]; *[Text in Japanese]*. Hiroshi Taniguchi [Ed.]. Kyoto: Horitsubunka Sha, 1993. 170p.

3647 Cities and children. Yuetsu Takahashi. **Loc. Govt. R. Jpn.** 21 1993 pp.57 - 70.

3648 Cities without suburbs. David Rusk. Washington: Woodrow Wilson Center Press, 1993. 147p. *ISBN: 0943875501*. (*Series:* Woodrow Wilson Center special studies).

3649 [Citizen's life and administrative problems, in the structure and change of local city: a case study of Shiogama city]; *[Text in Japanese]*. Masao Saito. **Kenkyunenpo (B. Ris. Univ.)** 9 1993 pp.60 - 77.

3650 La città fortezza. *[In Italian]*; (The fortified city.) *[Summary]*. Giandomenico Amendola. **Quad. Sociol.** XXXVII:4 1993 pp.63 - 78.

3651 City size and the rate and duration of unemployment — evidence from Israeli data. Gershon Alperovich. **J. Urban Ec.** 34:3 11:1993 pp.347 - 357.

3652 Comas: lo andino en la modernidad urbana. *[In Spanish]*; (Comas: the Andean element in urban modernity.) *[Summary]*. José Matos Mar; Alberto Cheng Hurtado. **Am. Indígena** LI:2-3 4-9:1991 pp.35 - 74.

3653 The conceptual basis of counterurbanisation — critique and development. Morgan Sant; Peter Simons. **Aust. Geogr. Stud.** 31:2 10:1993 pp.113 - 127.

3654 Conditions for healthy cities; diversity, game boards and social entrepreneurs. Leonard J. Duhl. **Environ. Urban.** 5:2 10:1993 pp.112 - 124.

3655 Contemporary urban sociology. William G. Flanagan. Cambridge, New York: Cambridge University Press, 1993. vi, 185p. *ISBN: 0521365198, 0521367433. Includes bibliographical references (p. 167-180) and indexes.*

3656 Coping with urban danger. Lodewijk Brunt. **Prague Occ. Pap. Ethn.** 2 1993 pp.19 - 39.

3657 Crime and the urban environment: the Scottish experience. Huw Roland Jones. Brookfield, Vt; Aldershot: Avebury, 1993. viii, 155p. *ISBN: 1856284689. Includes bibliographical references.*

3658 Crime prevention and the safer cities story. Nicholas Tilley. **Howard J. Crim. Just.** 32:1 2:1993 pp.40 - 57.

3659 Culturas regionales en ciudades de América Latina: un marco conceptual. *[In Spanish]*; (Regional cultures in Latin American cities: a conceptual framework.) *[Summary]*. Teófilo Altamirano; Lane Hirabayashi. **Am. Indígena** L1:4 10-12:1991 pp.17 - 48.

3660 Das Doppelgesicht der Metropolen — Tendenzen der amerikanischen Stadtentwicklung. Aspekte des Strukturwandels und der Stadtpolitik in den Ostküstenmetropolen New York, Philadelphia und Boston. *[In German]*; (The Janus face of big cities.) *[Summary]*; *[Summary in French]*. Jochen Schulz zur Wiesch. **Arc. Kommunal.** 32:1 1993 pp.24 - 46.

3661 East Germany's new towns in transition — a grassroots view of the impact of unification. Marilyn Rueschemeyer. **Urban Stud.** 30:3 4:1993 pp.495 - 506.

G: Environnement. Communauté. Rural. Urbain

3662 Economic activity and the quality of public space in inner cities — Amsterdam, for example. Ad Jansen. **J. Econ. Soc. Geogr.** 84:1 1993 pp.13 - 26.

3663 En jordnær drøm. *[In Danish]*; (A down-to-earth dream.). Johs. Nørregaard Frandsen. **Nord. Ny.** 53 1993 pp.56 - 69.

3664 Environmental problems in Third World cities. Jorge Enrique Hardoy; Diana Mitlin; David Satterthwaite. London: Earthscan Publications, 1992. 302p. *ISBN: 1853831468. Bibliography: p.253-273.*

3665 La escuela culturalista como crítica de la sociedad urbana. *[In Spanish]*; (The culturalist school as a critique of the urban society.) *[Summary]*. José Luis Lezama. **Est. Demog. Urb.** 6:2 5-8:1991 pp.225 - 259.

3666 European cities — changing urban structures in a changing world. Frans Dieleman [Ed.]; Hugo Priemus [Ed.]; Wim Baluw [Ed.]; Manuel Castells [Contrib.]; Jan Lambooy [Contrib.]; Lars-Erik Borgegård [Contrib.]; Robert Murdie [Contrib.]; Luděk Sýkora [Contrib.]; Duncan Maclennan [Contrib.]; Rein Jobse [Contrib.]; Sako Musterd [Contrib.]. **J. Econ. Soc. Geogr.** 84:4 1993 pp.247 - 311.

3667 La experiencia popular en Comas: 10 casos. *[In Spanish]*; (Popular experience in Comas: 10 cases.) *[Summary]*. José Matos Mar. **Am. Indígena** LI:2-3 4-9:1991 pp.75 - 106.

3668 The formation of a composite urban image. Eliahu Stern; Shaul Krakover. **Geogr. Anal.** 25:2 4:1993 pp.130 - 146.

3669 Fragmentation of the urban fabric — the experience of Middle Eastern and North African cities. Farhad Atash. **Cities** 10:4 11:1993 pp.313 - 325.

3670 Frustrated respectability — local culture and politics in London's Docklands. G. Morgan. **Envir. Plan. D.** 11:5 10:1993 pp.523 - 541.

3671 The future of the medium-sized city in Britain and Germany. Bernhard Blanke [Ed.]; Randall Smith [Ed.]. London: Anglo-German Foundation, 1993. 335p. *ISBN: 0905492811.*

3672 A growth machine for those who count. Melvin F. Hall; Leda McIntyre Hall. **Crit. Sociol.** 20:1 1993-1994 pp.79 - 102.

3673 Hacia una interpretación globalizante de la patología urbana. *[In Spanish]*; [Towards an inclusive interpretation of urban pathology]. Lopez Caballero. **Rev. Fom. Soc.** 48:190 4-6:1993 pp.245 - 260.

3674 Humanising the city?: social contexts of urban life at the turn of the millennium. Anthony Paul Cohen [Ed.]; Katsuyoshi Fukui [Ed.]. Edinburgh: Edinburgh U. P, 1993. 228p. *ISBN: 0748603883.*

3675 The impact on health of urban environments. David Satterthwaite. **Environ. Urban.** 5:2 10:1993 pp.87 - 111.

3676 Ein integriertes ökonomisch-ökologisches Informationssystem für städtische Agglomerationen. *[In German]*; [An integrated economic-ecological information system for city agglomerations]; *[Summary in French]*. Stephan Vaterlaus. **Schw. Z. Volk. Stat.** 128:3 9:1992 pp.511 - 523.

3677 International perspectives in urban studies. 1. Bill Lever [Ed.]; John Money [Ed.]; Ronan Paddison [Ed.]. London: J. Kingsley Publishers, 1993. 328p. *ISBN: 1853021636. (Series:* International perspectives in urban studies).

3678 [Komesodo in Tokyo city: the city and the complex of three urban lives]; *[Text in Japanese]*. Naoya Nakasuji. **Sociologos** 17 1993 pp.1 - 12.

3679 Kulturschock und Identitätsverlust. *[In German]*; [Culture shock and the loss of identity]. Ulrich Mai. **Geogr. Rund.** 45:4 4:1993 pp.232 - 237.

G: Environment. Community. Rural. Urban

3680 Language fundamentals for design-support architectures. J. Zucker; A. Demaid. **Envir. Plan. B.** 20:4 7:1993 pp.425 - 446.

3681 Linking business development and community development in inner cities. Marc Bendick; Mary Lou Egan. **J. Plan. Lit.** 8:1 8:1993 pp.3 - 19.

3682 [Linking mechanism between giant cities and communities - coordination at the local level]; *[Text in Japanese]*. Michihiro Okuda. Tokyo: Yushindo, 1993. 235p.

3683 The local and the global in the new urban politics — a critical view. K.R. Cox. **Envir. Plan. D.** 11:4 8:1993 pp.433 - 448.

3684 The location of services in the urban hierarchy and the regions of the United States. Breandán Ó hUallachán; Neal Reid. **Geogr. Anal.** 25:3 7:1993 pp.252 - 267.

3685 Locational returns to human capital — minority access to suburban community resources. John R. Logan; Richard D. Alba. **Demography** 30:2 5:1993 pp.243 - 268.

3686 Malyi gorod. Tekhnologiia vyzhivaniia i razvitiia. *[In Russian]*; (Small town. Technology for survival and development.). V. Glazychev. **Svobod. Mysl'** 7 5:1993 pp.9 - 18.

3687 Manufacturing location in a polycentric urban area — a study in the composition and attractiveness of employment subcenters. Paul Waddell; Vibhooti Shukla. **Urban Geogr.** 14:3 5-6:1993 pp.277 - 296.

3688 Meeting women's needs and priorities for water and sanitation in cities. Sara Jordan; Fritz Wagner. **Environ. Urban.** 5:2 10:1993 pp.135 - 145.

3689 La métropole lémanique dans tous ses état. *[In French]*; [The metropolis in the Léman in all its states]. Jean-Philippe Leresche; Dominique Joye; Michel Bassand. **R. Econ. Soc.** 51:1 3:1993 pp.23 - 39.

3690 Metropolitan structure and the suburban hierarchy. Holly L. Hughes. **Am. Sociol. R.** 58:3 6:1993 pp.417 - 433.

3691 Model of urban tourism for small Caribbean islands. David B. Weaver. **Geogr. Rev.** 83:2 4:1993 pp.134 - 140.

3692 New town, home town: the lessons of experience. Colin Ward. London: Calouste Gulbenkian Foundation, 1993. 159p. *ISBN: 0903319624.*

3693 El nuevo rostro de la cultura urbana del Perú. *[In Spanish]*; (The new face of urban culture in Peru.) *[Summary]*. José Matos Mar. **Am. Indígena** LI:2-3 4-9:1991 pp.11 - 34.

3694 [Phenomenology of 'city' and 'society']; *[Text in Japanese]*. Mikio Wakabayashi. **Jokyo** 4(3) 1993 pp.31 - 44.

3695 Public space. Stephen Carr; et al. Cambridge [England], New York: Cambridge University Press, 1992. xv, 400p. *ISBN: 0521351480, 0521359600. Includes bibliographical references (p. 371-383) and index. (Series:* Cambridge series in environment and behavior).

3696 Que peuvent faire les villes pour leur propre avenir? *[In French]*; [What can the cities do for their own future?]. Yvette Jaggi. **Schw. Z. Volk. Stat.** 128:3 9:1992 pp.271 - 278.

3697 Rape and fear in a New Zealand city. Eric Pawson; Glenn Banks. **Area** 25:1 3:1993 pp.55 - 63.

3698 Refining estimates of double taxation — lessons from law enforcement in a suburban county. Judy S. Davis; Sheldon M. Edner. **Urban Aff. Q.** 28:4 6:1993 pp.593 - 616.

3699 Représentations de Paris. *[In French]*; [Representations of Paris]. Yves Déloye [Ed.]; Florence Haegel [Ed.]; Alain Corbin [Contrib.]; Olivier Ihl [Contrib.]; Jean-Marc

G: Environnement. Communauté. Rural. Urbain

Berlière [Contrib.]; Jacques Lévy [Contrib.]; Dominique Reynié [Contrib.]; Pierre Christin [Contrib.]. **Politix** 21 1993 pp.7 - 141. *Collection of 7 articles.*

3700 Representing urban decline — postwar cities as narrative objects. Robert A. Beauregard. **Urban Aff. Q.** 29:2 12:1993 pp.187 - 202.

3701 Repression and resistance — problems of regulation in contemporary urban culture (part II — determining forces). C. Stanley. **Int. J. S. Law** 21:2 6:1993 pp.121 - 144.

3702 Salisbury, Harare: changer la vie, changer la ville. *[In French]*; [Salisbury, Harare: change life, change the town]. Philippe Gervais-Lambony. **Afr. Cont.** 168 10-12:1993 pp.41 - 53.

3703 [Social support system and disaster response in the suburban neighborhood]; *[Text in Japanese]*. Masaki Urano. **Shak.-Kag. Tok.** 113 1993 pp.201 - 233.

3704 [Sociological controversy in neighborhood institutions]; *[Text in Japanese]*. Hideki Takenaka. **Tos. Mon.** 84(11) 1993 pp.63 - 77.

3705 [Sociology of city and women]; *[Text in Japanese]*. Sumiko Yazawa [Ed.]. Tokyo: Saiensu-sha, 1993. 263p.

3706 Standortqualitäten und Entwicklungsmuster von Gross-, Mittel- und Kleinstädten in der Schweiz. *[In German]*; [The quality of location and development blueprint of large, middle-sized and small cities in Switzerland]; *[Summary in French]*. Elizabeth Bühler; Hans Elsasser; Christian Hanser; Hansruedi Meier; Christoph Muggli. **Schw. Z. Volk. Stat.** 128:3 9:1992 pp.355 - 367.

3707 Stressful environments and their effects on quality of life in Third World cities. Solvig Ekblad. **Environ. Urban.** 5:2 10:1993 pp.125 - 134.

3708 Strukturwandel der Städte: Städtesystem und Grundstücksmarkt in der "postfordistischen" Ära. *[In German]*; [Structural change in the towns: the urban system and real estate market in the "post-Fordism" era]. Stefan Krätke. Frankfurt am Main: Campus-Verlag, 1991. 210p. *ISBN: 3593345323.*

3709 Système de production territorial et rôle de l'espace urbain — le cas des villes de l'Arc jurassien. *[In French]*; [The territorial production system and the role of urban space — the case of the towns in the Arc Jurrassien region]; *[Summary in German]*. Denis Maillat; Gilles Léchot. **Schw. Z. Volk. Stat.** 128:3 9:1992 pp.339 - 354.

3710 A taxonomy of suburban office clusters — the case of Toronto. Gary Pivo. **Urban Stud.** 30:1 2:1993 pp.31 - 49.

3711 Towards a general theory of suburban office morphology in North America. Malcolm R. Matthew. **Prog. H. Geog.** 17:4 12:1993 pp.471 - 489.

3712 Trends in urban sociology in French-speaking countries from 1945 to 1980. J. Rémy. **Geojournal** 31:3 11:1993 pp.265 - 278.

3713 TV news, urban conflict, and the inner city. Simon Cottle. Leicester: Leicester University Press, 1993. 252p. *ISBN: 0718514475, 0718514629. Revision of the author's thesis (Ph. D. Centre for Mass Communications Research). Includes bibliographical references and index. (Series:* Studies in communication and society).

3714 Two Romes or more? The use and abuse of the center-periphery metaphor. John Agnew; Keith Bolling. **Urban Geogr.** 14:2 3-4:1993 pp.119 - 144.

3715 Urban agriculture in Kenya. Pyar Ali Memon; Diana Lee-Smith. **Can. J. Afr. St.** 27:1 1993 pp.25 - 42.

3716 Urban health in the Third world. Sarah J. Atkinson. **Environ. Urban.** 5:2 10:1993 pp.146 - 152.

G: Environment. Community. Rural. Urban

3717 Urban network and regional functions of towns. Lud'a Klusáková. **Prague Occ. Pap. Ethn.** 2 1993 pp.47 - 66.

3718 Urban sociology — the contribution and limits of political economy. John Walton. **Ann. R. Soc.** 19 1993 pp.301 - 320.

3719 Urban sociology, capitalism and modernity. Michael Savage; Alan Warde. Basingstoke: Macmillan, 1993. viii, 221p. *ISBN: 0333491637, 0333491645. Bibliography: p. 194-210. -Includes index.* (*Series:* Sociology for a changing world).

3720 [Urban space and time]; *[Text in Japanese].* Yoshikazu Nagai. **Soshioroji** 37(3) 1993 pp.36 - 46.

3721 Urban symbolism. Peter J. M. Nas [Ed.]. Leiden: E.J. Brill, 1993. 393p. *ISBN: 9004098550.* (*Series:* Studies in human society).

3722 Urban violence, citizenship and public policies; *[Summary in French].* Alba Zaluar. **Int. J. Urban** 17:1 3:1993 pp.56 - 66.

3723 Urbanität in Deutschland. *[In German];* [Urbanity in Germany]. Gerd Albers; Deutsches Institut für Urbanistik [Ed.]; et al. Stuttgart: W. Kohlhammer, 1991. 173p. *ISBN: 3170117483.*

3724 La ville intervalle: jeunes entre centre et banlieue. *[In French];* [The interval town: young people between the centre and the suburbs]. Laurence Roulleau-Berger. Paris: Méridiens Klincksieck, 1991. 211p. *ISBN: 2865632903.*

3725 Voices of decline: the postwar fate of US cities. Robert A. Beauregard. Oxford: Blackwell, 1993. 342p. *ISBN: 1557864411.*

3726 Wandel in der zentralörtlichen Gliederung Brandenburgs. *[In German];* [Change in the organiztion of the city centre of Brandenburg]. Karen Ziener. **Geogr. Rund.** 45:10 10:1993 pp.574 - 580.

3727 Will Dodoma ever be the new capital of Tanzania? J.M. Lusugga Kironde. **Geoforum** 24:4 1993 pp.435 - 453.

3728 (The young, the elderly, and the community.) *[Summary]; [Text in Japanese].* Yuetsu Takahashi. **Comp. Urban St.** 50 11:1993 pp.37 - 48.

Housing
Logement

3729 Affordable housing, exclusionary zoning, and American apartheid — using Title VIII to foster statewide racial integration. James J. Hartnett. **NY. U. Law. Re.** 68:1 4:1993 pp.89 - 135.

3730 Building for communities: a study of new housing association estates. David Page. York: Joseph Rowntree Foundation, 1993. 63p. *ISBN: 1872470785.*

3731 China's urban housing development in the shift from redistribution to decentralization. Xiangming Chen; Xiaoyuan Gao. **Soc. Prob.** 40:2 5:1993 pp.266 - 283.

3732 Controlling the housing land market: some examples from Europe. James Barlow. **Urban Stud.** 30:7 8:1993 pp.1129 - 1150.

3733 Conversions, condominiums and capital gains — the transformation of the Ontario rental housing market. Marion Steele. **Urban Stud.** 30:1 2:1993 pp.103 - 126.

3734 Co-operative housing. H. Schmalstieg [Contrib.]; C. Hachmann [Contrib.]; Hans H. Münkner [Contrib.]; T. Schaefers [Contrib.]; W. Wilkens [Contrib.]. **R. Int. Co-op.** 86:1 1993 pp.5 - 32. *Collection of 6 articles.*

G: Environnement. Communauté. Rural. Urbain

3735 The cultural meaning of urban space. Robert Louis Rotenberg [Ed.]; Gary W. McDonogh [Ed.]. Westport, Conn.: Greenwood Press; Bergin & Garvey, 1993. xix, 226p. *ISBN: 0897893190, 0897893204. Includes bibliographical references (p. [195]-214) and index. (Series:* Contemporary urban studies).

3736 Equo canone, primo decennio: come è cambiato il mercato delle abitazioni e per chi. *[In Italian]*; [Fair standards, first decade: how the housing market has changed and who has been affected]. Mariolina Toniolo Trivellato. **Arch. St. Urb. Region.** XXIII:43 1992 pp.131 - 156.

3737 Le financement du logement. *[In French]*; [Housing finance]. Alain Durance. Paris: Masson, 1992. vi, 138p. *ISBN: 2225827222. Bibliogr. and index.*

3738 La France au logis: étude sociologique des pratiques domestiques. *[In French]*; [French housing: sociological study of domestic practices]. Yvonne Bernard. Liège: Mardaga, 1992. 140p. *ISBN: 2870095244. Survey carried out by l'INSEE in 1988.*

3739 A geographical study of Kibera as an example of an uncontrolled settlement. Elizabeth Edna Wangui; Michael B.K. Darkoh. **J. E.Afr. Res. Devel.** 22 1992 pp.75 - 91.

3740 Großsiedlungen in Ostdeutschland. *[In German]*; [Housing estates in East Germany]. Uta Hohn; Andreas Hohn. **Geogr. Rund.** 45:3 3:1993 pp.146 - 152.

3741 Hacia una concepción de la vivienda y el desarrollo urbano. *[In Spanish]*; [Towards an understanding of the housing situation and urban development]. Fabio Giraldo Isaza. **Coy. Soc.** 9 11:1993 pp.55 - 84.

3742 An hierarchical approach to the segmentation of residential demand — theory and application. E. Feitelson. **Envir. Plan. A.** 25:4 4:1993 pp.553 - 569.

3743 Hong Kong's density policy towards public housing — a theoretical and empirical review. Lawrence Wai Chung Lai. **Third Wor. P.** 15:1 2:1993 pp.63 - 85.

3744 Household crowding and family relations in Bangkok. Theodore D. Fuller; John N. Edwards; Sairudee Vorakitphokatorn; Santhat Sermsri. **Soc. Prob.** 40:3 8:1993 pp.410 - 430.

3745 A household life cycle model for residential relocation behaviour. Peter Nijkamp; Leo van Wissen; Annemarie Rima. **Socio. Econ.** 27:1 1993 pp.35 - 53.

3746 Housing design standards for urban low-income people in Zimbabwe. Oscar Musandu-Nyamayaro. **Third Wor. P.** 15:4 11:1993 pp.329 - 354.

3747 (Housing problems in Tokyo: problems and policies.); *[Text in Japanese]*. Yorifusa Ishida; Kunio Takamizawa; Shunji Fukuoka; Tsutomu Isobe; Kiyoko Hagihara. **Comp. Urban Stud.** 48 3:1993 pp.125 - 155.

3748 Housing reform in Eastern Europe. Pal Baross [Ed.]; Raymond Struyk [Ed.]; Istvan Elter [Contrib.]; N.B. Kosareva [Contrib.]; Michael L. Hoffman [Contrib.]; Maya T. Koleva [Contrib.]; G. Thomas Kingsley [Contrib.]; Peter Tajćman [Contrib.]; Sarah W. Wines [Contrib.]; Srna Mandic [Contrib.]; Tone Rop [Contrib.]; Irena Herbst [Contrib.]; Alina Muziol-Weclawowicz [Contrib.]; József Hegedüs [Contrib.]; Katharine Mark [Contrib.]; Iván Tosics [Contrib.]. **Cities** 10:3 8:1993 pp.179 - 271. *Collection of 8 articles.*

3749 Housing stressors and mental health among marginalised urban populations. Robin A. Kearns; Christopher J. Smith. **Area** 25:3 9:1993 pp.267 - 278.

3750 Individual self-provision and the Scottish housing system. David Clapham; Keith Kintrea; Gordon McAdam. **Urban Stud.** 30:8 10:1993 pp.1355 - 1370.

G: Environment. Community. Rural. Urban

3751 Informal housing in a comparative perspective — on squatting, culture, and development in a Latin American and a Middle Eastern context. Nezar AlSayyad. **R. Urban. Region. Dev. S.** 5:1 1:1993 pp.3 - 18.

3752 Job-rich but housing-poor — the dilemma of a western amenity town. Patricia Gober; Kevin E. McHugh; Denis Leclerc. **Prof. Geogr.** 45:1 2:1993 pp.12 - 20.

3753 Kampung improvement in the small and medium sized cities of central Java. Pauline Milone. **R. Urban. Region. Dev. S.** 5:1 1:1993 pp.74 - 94.

3754 Land markets and the effect of regulation on formal-sector development in urban Indonesia. Bruce Ferguson; Michael Hoffman. **R. Urban. Region. Dev. S.** 5:1 1:1993 pp.51 - 73.

3755 Land rights for residential development in Jakarta, Indonesia — the colonial roots of contemporary urban dualism. Michael Leaf. **Int. J. Urban** 17:4 12:1993 pp.477 - 491.

3756 Land use controls and housing prices in Korea. Lawrence Hannah; Kyung-Hwan Kim; Edwin S. Mills. **Urban Stud.** 30:1 2:1993 pp.147 - 156.

3757 Marché suisse du logement et information. *[In French]*; [The Swiss rented market and information]; *[Summary in German]*. Christian Zimmermann. **Schw. Z. Volk. Stat.** 128:3 9:1992 pp.399 - 407.

3758 Models of housing adjustment and their implications for planning and politics. Roberto G. Quercia; William M. Rohe. **J. Plan. Lit.** 8:1 8:1993 pp.20 - 31.

3759 The mutinodal metropolis. Brian J.L. Berry [Contrib.]; Hak-Min Kim [Contrib.]; Paul Waddell [Contrib.]; Irving Och [Contrib.]; Vibhooti Shukla [Contrib.]; Wayne R. Archer [Contrib.]; Marc T. Smith [Contrib.]. **Geogr. Anal.** 25:1 1:1993 pp.1 - 82. *Collection of 6 articles.*

3760 Neighborhood aging and housing deterioration — predicting elderly owner housing distress in Cleveland and its suburbs. Harry L. Margulis. **Urban Geogr.** 14:1 1-2:1993 pp.30 - 47.

3761 La place du pauvre: histoire et géographie sociales de l'habitat HLM. *[In French]*; [The place of the poor: history and social geography of HLM housing]. Jacques Barou. Paris: Editions L'Harmattan, 1992. 135p. *ISBN: 2738411843. Bibliography and index.*

3762 Plakkery en informele vestiging in Port Elizabeth en Uitenhage. *[In Afrikaans]*; (Squatting and informal settlement in Port Elizabeth and Uitenhage.) *[Summary]*. P.P. Jacobs; H.J. Pauw. **S.Afr. J. Ethnol.** 16:2 6:1993 pp.53 - 63.

3763 Planning for social housing in London and the South East. Jane Brenan. **Plan. Pract. Res.** 8:4 12:1993 pp.15 - 26.

3764 Planning, housing and the community in a new socialist town — the case of Tychy, Poland. Marek S. Szczepański. **Town Plan. R.** 64:1 1:1993 pp.1 - 22.

3765 The polarization of a metropolis in a welfare state — the example of Stockholm. M. Johansson. **Scand. Hous. Plan. R.** 10:2 1993 pp.91 - 103.

3766 Private initiatives in lower income housing provisions in Korea. Woo-Suh Park. **Korea Obs.** XXIV:2 Summer:1993 pp.169 - 191.

3767 Privatization and restructuring public involvement in housing provision in Britain. A. Murie. **Scand. Hous. Plan. R.** 10:3 8:1993 pp.145 - 157.

3768 Public housing and overcrowding in Swedish municipalities. G. Lindberg. **Scand. Hous. Plan. R.** 10:3 8:1993 pp.129 - 143.

3769 Public housing and the concentration of poverty. Douglas S. Massey; Shawn M. Kanaiaupuni. **Soc. Sci. Q.** 74:1 3:1993 pp.109 - 122.

G: Environnement. Communauté. Rural. Urbain

3770 Race and residential mobility — individual determinants and structural constraints. Scott J. South; Glenn D. Deane. **Soc. Forc.** 72:1 9:1993 pp.147 - 167.

3771 Residential location, housing demand and labour supply decisions of one- and two-earner households — the case of Bogota, Colombia. Afsaneh Assadian; Jan Ondrich. **Urban Stud.** 30:1 2:1993 pp.73 - 86.

3772 Russia on the way to a housing market — a case study of St.Petersburg. N. Boyce. **Envir. Plan. A.** 25:7 7:1993 pp.975 - 986.

3773 Russian housing in the modern age: design and social history. William Craft Brumfield [Ed.]; Blair A. Ruble [Ed.]. Cambridge; Washington, D.C; New York: Woodrow Wilson Center Press; Cambridge University Press, 1993. xiv, 322p. *ISBN: 0521431972. Includes bibliographical references and index. (Series:* Woodrow Wilson Center series).

3774 Satisfaction with space around the home on large private sector estates — lessons from surveys in southern England and south Wales, 1985-1989. John Winter; Tessa Coombes; Stuart Farthing. **Town Plan. R.** 64:1 1:1993 pp.65 - 88.

3775 Self-provided housing: the first world's hidden housing arm. S.S. Duncan; A. Rowe. **Urban Stud.** 30:8 10:1993 pp.1331 - 1354.

3776 Services for shelter: infrastucture for urban low-income housing. Andrew Cotton; Richard Franceys; Rod Shaw [Illus.]. Liverpool: Liverpool University Press in association with Fairstead Press, 1991. vii, 147p. *ISBN: 0853232873. Loughborough University of Technology Water, Engineering and Development Centre. (Series:* Liverpool planning manual).

3777 Shelter poverty: new ideas on housing affordability. Michael Eric Stone. Philadelphia: Temple University Press, 1993. xi, 423p. *ISBN: 1566390508, 1566390923. Includes bibliographical references (p. [391]-415) and index.*

3778 Sozialatlas der Bundesrepublik Deutschland. Teil 2. Wohnungswesen. *[In German]*; [Social atlas of the Federal Republic of Germany. Part 2. Housing]. Hartmut Gottschild. Braunschweig: Maria Gottschild, 199o. 92p. *ISBN: 3928428209.*

3779 Spatiality and social change — domestic space use in Mexico and the United States. E. Pader. **Am. Ethn.** 20:1 2:1993 pp.114 - 137.

3780 Squatter access to land in Metro Manila. Ton van Naerssen. **Phil. Stud.** 41 First quarter:1993 pp.3 - 20.

3781 Squatter regularisation — problems and prospects — a case study from Trinidad. Jane Matthews Glenn; Ronald P. Labossiere; Jeanne M. Wolfe. **Third Wor. P.** 15:3 8:1993 pp.249 - 262.

3782 Squatting as rent-seeking and pressure-group competition — a South African case-study. Cedric D. Nathan; Zane A. Spindler. **Urban Stud.** 30:3 4:1993 pp.477 - 494.

3783 Squatting, culture, and development — a comparative analysis of informal settlements in Latin America and the Middle East. Nezar AlSayyad. **J. Dev. Soc.** IX:2 7-10:1993 pp.139 - 155.

3784 St. Petersburg. *[In German]*; [St. Petersburg]. Dorothee v. Ungern-Sternberg; N.S. Palćikov; R.B. Tov. **Geogr. Rund.** 45:3 3:1993 pp.153 - 159.

3785 Territorial justice and Thatcherism. G.A. Boyne; M. Powell. **Envir. Plan. C.** 11:1 2:1993 pp.35 - 53.

3786 Textured brick — speculations on the cultural production of domestic space. Louise C. Johnson. **Aust. Geogr. Stud.** 31:2 10:1993 pp.201 - 213.

3787 Types and forms of housing tenure — towards solving the comparison/translation problem. H. Ruonavaara. **Scand. Hous. Plan. R.** 10:1 2:1993 pp.3 - 20.

G: Environment. Community. Rural. Urban

3788 Urban housing for the better-off: gentrification in Europe. Sako Musterd [Ed.]; Jan van Weesep [Ed.]. Utrecht: Bureau Stedekijke Net-werken, 1991. 149p.

3789 Urban housing in developing economy. Om Parkash Miglani. New Delhi: Deep & Deep Publications, 1992. 199p. *ISBN: 8171003915*. Includes bibliographical references (p. [178]-196) and index.

3790 Urbanisme et logement: analyse d'une crise. *[In French]*; [Town planning and housing: an analysis of a crisis]. Georges Mesmin. Paris: Presses Universitaires de France, 1992. 173p. *ISBN: 2130448488*.

3791 The urbanization of capital: the contemporary French office real estate market. J. Maléziex. **Geojournal** 31:3 11:1993 pp.279 - 288.

3792 Why do shelter conditions differ in Ecuadoran cities and how do we know that they do?: a comparative locality study. T. Klak. **Envir. Plan. A.** 25:8 8:1993 pp.1115 - 1130.

3793 Wohnen und Stadtpolitik im Umbruch: Perspektiven der Stadterneuerung nach 40 Jahren DDR. *[In German]*; [Housing and urban policy facing radical change: perspectives on urban renewal after 40 years of the GDR]. Peter Marcuse [Ed.]; Fred Staufenbiel [Ed.]. Berlin: Akademie Verlag, 1991. 289p. *ISBN: 3050017473*.

3794 Wohnungspolitik und Wohnungswirtschaft in den neuen Ländern. *[In German]*; [Housing policy and housing economics in the new Länder]. Jörg Köhli. **Geogr. Rund.** 45:3 3:1993 pp.140 - 145.

Spatial and social differentiation
Différenciation spatio-sociale

3795 Black suburbanization in the 1980's. Mark Schneider; Thomas Phelan. **Demography** 30:2 5:1993 pp.269 - 279.

3796 Continued racial residential segregation in Detroit — "chocolate city, vanilla suburbs" revisited. Reynolds Farley; Charlotte Steeh; Tara Jackson; Maria Krysan; Keith Reeves. **J. Hous. Res.** 4:1 1993 pp.1 - 38.

3797 Dimensions of urban structure: an example of construct validation. Stephen L. Ross. **Urban Stud.** 30:7 8:1993 pp.1109 - 1128.

3798 Economic diversification and group stability in an urban system: the case of Canada, 1951-86. Wayne K.D. Davies; Daniel P. Donoghue. **Urban Stud.** 30:7 8:1993 pp.1165 - 1186.

3799 Environment, wealth and health; towards an analysis of intraurban differentials within greater Accra metropolitan area, Ghana. Jacob Songsore; Gordon McGranahan. **Environ. Urban.** 5:2 10:1993 pp.10 - 34.

3800 Exploring relationships between semi-variogram and spatial autoregressive models. Daniel A. Griffith; Ferenc Csillag. **Pap. Reg. Sci.** 72:3 7:1993 pp.283 - 295.

3801 Home, work, and locality — the case of Thorold, Ontario. Glen Norcliffe; Xiaofeng Liu. **Urban Geogr.** 14:3 5-6:1993 pp.251 - 276.

3802 Mobilidade intra-urbana no Rio de Janeiro: da estratificação social á segregação residencial no espaço. *[In Portuguese]*; (Intra-urban residential mobility in the city of Rio de Janeiro.) *[Summary]*. Martim Oscar Smolka. **Rev. Brasil. Est. Popul.** 9:2 7-12:1992 pp.97 - 114.

3803 Patterns of residential segregation and the gypsy minority in Budapest; *[Summary in French]*. János Ladányi. **Int. J. Urban** 17:1 3:1993 pp.30 - 41.

G: Environnement. Communauté. Rural. Urbain

3804 La política urbano-regional en México, 1978-1990. La ausencia de bases conceptuales más rigurosas. *[In Spanish]*; (Regional urban politics in Mexico, 1978-1990. The absence of more rigorous conceptual bases.) *[Summary]*. Adrián Guillermo Aguilar. **Est. Demog. Urb.** 6:2 5-8:1991 pp.283 - 311.

3805 Race and residential mobility — individual determinants and structural constraints. Scott J. South; Glenn D. Deane. **Soc. Forc.** 72:1 9:1993 pp.147 - 167.

3806 Residential segregation in Australian cities — a literature review. Seamus Grimes. **Int. Migr. Rev.** XXVII:1 Spring:1993 pp.103 - 120.

3807 Spatial indices of segregation. David W.S. Wong. **Urban Stud.** 30:3 4:1993 pp.559 - 572.

3808 Spazio e razzismo: strumenti urbanistici e segregazione etnica. *[In Italian]*; [Space and racism: urban instruments and ethnic segregation]. Paola Somma. Milan: Angeli, 1991. 172p. *ISBN: 8820471302.*

3809 La spécialisation spatiale à Los Angeles. *[In French]*; [Spatial specialization in Los Angeles] *[Summary]*. D. Mathieu. **Ann. Géogr.** 102:569 1-2:1993 pp.32 - 52.

3810 A suggested method of estimation for spatial interdependent models with autocorrelated errors, and an application to a county expenditure model. Harry H. Kelejian; Dennis P. Robinson. **Pap. Reg. Sci.** 72:3 7:1993 pp.297 - 312.

3811 [Urban thought: toward the reconstruction of spatial theory]; *[Text in Japanese]*. Naoki Yoshihara. Tokyo: Aoki Shoten, 1993. 318p.

3812 Using the transportation problem to measure the proximity between two sets of weighted points in a geographical space. Dominique Peeters; Joseph D. Ruhigira. **Pap. Reg. Sci.** 72:3 7:1993 pp.337 - 347.

Urban planning and development
Aménagement et développement urbain

3813 Alternative forums for citizen participation — formal mediation of urban land use disputes. David J. Allor. **Int. J. Confl. Manag.** 4:2 4:1993 pp.167 - 180.

3814 L'aménagement de territoire et le système national urbain: de l'armature urbaine aux réseaux de villes. Questions pour la recherche et l'action. *[In French]*; [Land use management and the national urban system: from urban structure to town networks. Questions for research and action] *[Summary]*. N. May. **R. Ec. Reg. Urb.** 5 1993 pp.823 - 832.

3815 L'aménagement urbain: promesses et défis. *[In French]*; [Urban management: promises and challenges]. Annick Germain [Ed.]. Quebec: Institut québécois de recherche sur la culture, 1991. 267p. *ISBN: 2892241588. Includes bibliographical references.*

3816 Appropriateness of traditional neighborhood concept for planning contemporary neighborhood units. H.M. Alshuwaikat. **Geojournal** 31:4 12:1993 pp.393 - 400.

3817 Arab cities. Constantine Municipality [Contrib.]; M.A. Al-Hammad [Contrib.]; Abdalmajeed Ismail Daghistani [Contrib.]; Municipality of Greater Amman [Contrib.]; Khaled Abdulgani [Contrib.]; Dammam Municipality [Contrib.]; M.S.S. Almaani [Contrib.]. **Cities** 10:1 2:1993 pp.13 - 80. *Collection of 8 articles.*

3818 Around the block — urban models with a street grid. John Yinger. **J. Urban Ec.** 33:3 5:1993 pp.305 - 330.

G: Environment. Community. Rural. Urban

3819 Australian metropolitan development — local government reform and urban growth into the 1990s. A.M.G. Jarman; A. Kouzmin. **Envir. Plan. C.** 11:2 5:1993 pp.143 - 160.

3820 Can politicians bargain with business? A theoretical and comparative perspective on urban development. Paul Kantor; H.V. Savitch. **Urban Aff. Q.** 29:2 12:1993 pp.230 - 255.

3821 Ceausescu's Bucharest. Darrick Danta. **Geogr. Rev.** 83:2 4:1993 pp.170 - 182.

3822 The central area of Alexandria Egypt — development implications and urban conservation. Osama M.A. Rahman. **Third Wor. P.** 15:1 2:1993 pp.37 - 54.

3823 (Cities and creativity: the future of metropolis.) *[Summary]*; *[Text in Japanese]*. Kiyoshi Kobayashi. **Comp. Urban Stud.** 49 9:1993 pp.5 - 22.

3824 The communicative work of development plans. P. Healey. **Envir. Plan. B.** 20:1 1993 pp.83 - 104.

3825 Community development and urban regeneration. Charlie McConnell [Ed.]; David Donnison [Contrib.]; Geoff Fordham [Contrib.]; Andrew A. McArthur [Contrib.]; Richard Penn [Contrib.]; Chris Wadhams [Contrib.]; Charles-Antoine Arnaud [Contrib.]; Angelika Krüger [Contrib.]; John Armstrong [Contrib.]. **Comm. Dev. J.** 28:4 10:1993 pp.293 - 361. *Collection of 8 articles.*

3826 Community in transition: mobility, integration, and conflict. Hanna Ayalon; Abraham Yogev; Eliezer Ben Rafael. Westport, Conn: Greenwood Press, 1993. xii, 195p. *ISBN: 031328699X. Includes bibliographical references and index. (Series:* Contributions in sociology).

3827 The convolution of urban planning with tradition in Lesotho, 1928-91. J.A. Kahimbaara. **Envir. Plan. A.** 25:7 7:1993 pp.1003 - 1020.

3828 The dependent city and intergovernmental aid — the impact of recent changes. David R. Morgan; Michael W. Hirlinger. **Urban Aff. Q.** 29:2 12:1993 pp.256 - 275.

3829 Designing renewal on Europe's multi-ethnic urban edge — the case of Bijlmermeer, Amsterdam. Thomas L. Blair; Edward D. Hulsbergen. **Cities** 10:4 11:1993 pp.283 - 298.

3830 Development interests and the attack on planning controls — "planning difficulties" in Bristol 1985-1990. J.V. Punter. **Envir. Plan. A.** 25:4 4:1993 pp.521 - 538.

3831 Développement urbain métropolitain et crise de la ville   un monde en transition. *[In French]*; [Urban development in metropolitan areas and the crisis of the cities — a world in transition]. J.B. Racine. **Schw. Z. Volk. Stat.** 128:3 9:1992 pp.241 - 260.

3832 Dodoma — an example of a growth centre shibboleth? M.B.K. Darkoh. **J. E.Afr. Res. Devel.** 23 1993 pp.106 - 120.

3833 Dublin: the shaping of a capital. Andrew MacLaran. New York; London: Belhaven Press, 1993. 242p. *ISBN: 0470220090, 0470220090, 1852931663. Includes bibliographical references and index. (Series:* World cities series).

3834 The economic restructuring of older industrial areas. Andrew M. Isserman [Contrib.]; William F. Lever [Contrib.]; Stephen F. Fournier [Contrib.]; Sten Axelsson [Contrib.]; Ronald L. Lewis [Contrib.]; Robin Boyle [Contrib.]; Brian J. Cushing [Contrib.]; Ronan Paddison [Contrib.]; Emily A. Spieler [Contrib.]; Ivan Turok [Contrib.]; Moira Munro [Contrib.]; Andrew McArthur [Contrib.]; Alan McGregor [Contrib.]; Robert Stewart [Contrib.]; Tom Hart [Contrib.]; Terance J. Rephann [Contrib.]. **Urban Stud.** 30:2 3:1993 pp.229 - 450. *Collection of 14 articles.*

G: Environnement. Communauté. Rural. Urbain

3835 Empleo y crecimiento urbano — aplicación del modelo de Czamanski al caso mexicano. *[In Spanish]*; (Employment and urban growth — an application of Czamanski's model to the Mexican case.) *[Summary]*. Basilio Verduzco Chávez. **Est. Demog. Urb.** 6:2 5-8:1991 pp.261 - 282.

3836 The entrepreneurial city — fabricating urban development in Syracuse, New York. Susan M. Roberts; Richard H. Schein. **Prof. Geogr.** 45:1 2:1993 pp.21 - 33.

3837 [An essay on urban politics and urban policy: the impact of expansion of the Tokyo metropolitan area]; *[Text in Japanese]*. Toshio Kumada. **Hogaku (J. Suru. Univ.)** 7(1) 1993 pp.223 - 242.

3838 Establishing urban land markets in the People's Republic of China. David E. Dowall. **J. Am. Plann.** 59:2 Spring:1993 pp.182 - 192.

3839 European cities: growth and change. Jan van Weesep [Ed.]; Frans M. Dieleman [Ed.]; Peter Hall; Jiří Musil; Jürgen Friedrichs; Frank Bruinsma; Piet Rietveld; W.F. Lever; Lila Leontidou; Jeroen Bosman; Marc de Smidt; Martine Meijer; Heinz-Jürgen Bremm; Peter Ache; Robert Hassink; Jens S. Dangschat; Roberto P. Camagni; Carlo Salone; Antony R. Walker. **Urban Stud.** 30:6 6:1993 pp.877 - 1080. *Collection of 14 articles.*

3840 Experiencing megalopolis in Princeton. Michael H. Ebner. **J. Urban Hist.** 19:2 2:1993 pp.11 - 55.

3841 Factors of evolution in the content of planning documents — downtown planning in a Canadian city, 1962-1992. P. Filion. **Envir. Plan. B.** 20:4 7:1993 pp.459 - 478.

3842 From megalopolis to megaroporisu. Jeffrey E. Hanes. **J. Urban Hist.** 19:2 2:1993 pp.56 - 94.

3843 Hacia una concepción de la vivienda y el desarrollo urbano. *[In Spanish]*; [Towards an understanding of the housing situation and urban development]. Fabio Giraldo Isaza. **Coy. Soc.** 9 11:1993 pp.55 - 84.

3844 Heritage, urban planning, and the postmodern city. Robert Freestone. **Aust. Geogr.** 24:1 5:1993 pp.17 - 24.

3845 Hong Kong's density policy towards public housing — a theoretical and empirical review. Lawrence Wai Chung Lai. **Third Wor. P.** 15:1 2:1993 pp.63 - 85.

3846 Kleinstädte und Dörfer in den neuen Bundesländern: Aufgabenfeld für die städtebauliche Erneuerung. *[In German]*; [Small towns and villages in the new federal Länder: areas of responsibility for urban renewal]. Rudolf Schäfer; Hans-Joachim Stricker; Daniela von Soest. Göttingen: O. Schwartz, 1992. 315p. *ISBN: 3509015983. Includes bibliographical references (p. 303-313).*

3847 The limits of property-led regeneration. R. Imrie; H. Thomas. **Envir. Plan. C.** 11:1 2:1993 pp.87 - 102.

3848 Managing community growth: policies, techniques, and impacts. Eric D. Kelly. Westport, Conn: Praeger, 1993. xiv, 248p. *ISBN: 0275944956. Includes bibliographical references (p. [225]-242) and index.*

3849 Managing fast growing cities: new approaches to urban planning and management in the developing world. Nick Devas [Ed.]; Carole Rakodi [Ed.]. Harlow; New York: Longman Scientific & Technical; Wiley, 1993. xii, 337p. *ISBN: 0470220465. Includes bibliographical references (p. 297-328) and index.*

3850 Managing metropolis: Metropolitan renaissance: new life for old city regions. Peter Roberts [Ed.]; Tony Struthers [Ed.]; Jeffrey Sacks [Ed.]. Aldershot, England, Brookfield, Vt: Avebury, 1993. 366p. *ISBN: 1856283836.*

G: Environment. Community. Rural. Urban

3851 Marketing the city: the role of flagship developments in urban regeneration. Hedley Smyth. London: E & F.N. Spon, 1993. 289p. *ISBN: 0419186107.*

3852 Metropolis 2000: planning, poverty and politics. Thomas Angotti. New York, NY: Routledge, 1993. 276p. *ISBN: 0415081351, 041508136X. Includes bibliographical references and index. (Series:* Development and underdevelopment).

3853 Models of housing adjustment and their implications for planning and politics. Roberto G. Quercia; William M. Rohe. **J. Plan. Lit.** 8:1 8:1993 pp.20 - 31.

3854 The mutinodal metropolis. Brian J.L. Berry [Contrib.]; Hak-Min Kim [Contrib.]; Paul Waddell [Contrib.]; Irving Och [Contrib.]; Vibhooti Shukla [Contrib.]; Wayne R. Archer [Contrib.]; Marc T. Smith [Contrib.]. **Geogr. Anal.** 25:1 1:1993 pp.1 - 82. *Collection of 6 articles.*

3855 Ökonomie und Politik in alten Industrieregionen Europas: Probleme der Stadt- und Regionalentwicklung in Deutschland, Frankreich, Grossbritannien und Italien. *[In German]*; [Economics and politics in the old industrial regions of Europe: problems of urban and regional development in Germany, France, Great Britain and Italy]. Hartmut Häussermann [Ed.]. Basel: Birkhäuser, 1992. 337p. *ISBN: 376432743X.*

3856 People in cities: a transatlantic policy exchange. Robin Hambleton [Ed.]; Marilyn Taylor [Ed.]. Bristol: University of Bristol, School for Advanced Urban Studies, 1993. 257p. (*Series:* SAUS Study).

3857 Philadelphia: neighborhoods, division, and conflict in a postindustrial city. Carolyn Teich Adams; et al. Philadelphia: Temple University Press, 1991. xiv, 210p. *ISBN: 0877228426. Includes bibliographical references (p. [189]-202) and index. (Series:* Comparative American cities).

3858 Plaidoyers pour les centres urbains secondaires en Afrique au sud du Sahara. *[In French]*; (Promotion of secondary urban centres in Africa south of the Sahara.). Monique Bertrand. **R. T-Monde** XXXIV:133 1-3:1993 pp.117 - 138.

3859 Planning and hazard. Christopher Miller; Claire Fricker. **Prog. Plan.** 40:3 1993 pp.175 - 260.

3860 Planning at the crossroads. J M. Simmie. London: UCL Press, 1993. 189p. *ISBN: 1857280245.*

3861 Planning for social housing in London and the South East. Jane Brenan. **Plan. Pract. Res.** 8:4 12:1993 pp.15 - 26.

3862 Policy making in Jerusalem — local discretion in a context that favours central control. Ira Sharkansky. **Cities** 10:2 5:1993 pp.115 - 124.

3863 Le politiche urbane di fronte ai cambiamenti sociali. *[In Italian]*; [Urban policies faced with social change]. Michele Sernini. **Arch. St. Urb. Region.** XXIII:43 1992 pp.71 - 112.

3864 The politics of cultural policy in urban regeneration strategies; *[Summary in French]*. Ron Griffiths. **Policy Pol.** 21:1 1:1993 pp.39 - 46.

3865 Power disparities in the planning of a mixed region — Arabs and Jews in the Galilee, Israel. Oren Yiftachel. **Urban Stud.** 30:1 2:1993 pp.157 - 182.

3866 PRIDE and prejudice — the economic impacts of growth controls in Pasadena. H.W. Richardson; P. Gordon; M.-J. Jun; M.H. Kim. **Envir. Plan. A.** 25:7 7:1993 pp.987 - 1002.

3867 Privatisation of public open space — the Los Angeles experience. Anastasia Loukaitou-Sideris. **Town Plan. R.** 64:2 4:1993 pp.139 - 168.

3868 Reconstructing the image of an industrial city. J.R. Short; L.M. Benton; W.B. Luce; J. Walton. **Ann. As. Am. G.** 83:2 6:1993 pp.207 - 224.

G: Environnement. Communauté. Rural. Urbain

3869 The reform of the urban land use system in Eastern Europe — a suggestion for Belgrade. Boris Begovic. **Pap. Reg. Sci.** 72:2 4:1993 pp.145 - 157.

3870 Reframing urban policy; *[Summary in French]*. William Solesbury. **Policy Pol.** 21:1 1:1993 pp.31 - 38.

3871 Renewing cities. Ross J. Gittell. Princeton, N.J: Princeton University Press, 1992. x, 232p. *ISBN: 0691042934. Includes bibliographical references (p. [217]-224) and index.*

3872 (The revised designation of land use regulation zones and the 1989 urban land use control policy for Tokyo.) *[Summary]*; *[Text in Japanese]*. Itsuki Nakabayashi; Kunio Takamizawa; Toru Fujiwara. **Comp. Urban Stud.** 48 3:1993 pp.69 - 108.

3873 The search for a centre — the recomposition of race, class and space in Los Angeles; *[Summary in French]*. Don Parson. **Int. J. Urban** 17:2 6:1993 pp.232 - 240.

3874 Small town development in socialist China — a functional analysis. G.C.S. Lin. **Geoforum** 24:3 1993 pp.327 - 338.

3875 S.O.S.Banlieues. *[In French]*; [SOS Suburbs]. Eric Raoult. Paris: L'Harmattan, 1993. 213p. *ISBN: 2738419488.*

3876 Stadtentwicklungspolitik über Großprojekte. Florenz, Wien und Zürich im Vergleich. *[In German]*; (Urban development through large-scale projects.) *[Summary]*; *[Summary in French]*. Sandro Cattacin. **J. Sozialfors.** 33:4 1993 pp.369 - 390.

3877 Sustainable communities: a new design synthesis for cities, suburbs, and towns. Peter Calthrope [Ed.]; Sim Van der Ryn [Ed.]. San Francisco: Sierra Club Books, 1991. 238p. *ISBN: 087156629X. Includes index.*

3878 Sustainable development and urban form. Michael J. Breheny [Ed.]. London: Pion, 1992. 292p. *ISBN: 0850861608. (Series:* European research in regional science).

3879 Understanding cities and regions: spatial political economy. Frank John Berkeley Stilwell. Leichhardt, NSW: Pluto Press Australia, 1992. 247p. *ISBN: 0949138886. Includes bibliographical references (p. 223-239) and index.*

3880 (Urban built form and the hidden urban designers in Japan.) *[Summary]*; *[Text in Japanese]*. Yorifusa Ishida; Halina Dunin-Woyseth. **Comp. Urban Stud.** 49 9:1993 pp.139 - 155.

3881 Urban development, collective consumption and the politics of metropolitan fragmentation. Kevin R. Cox; Andrew E.G. Jonas. **Pol. Geogr.** 12:1 1:1993 pp.8 - 37.

3882 Urban development in Nigeria: planning, housing and land policy. Robert W. Taylor [Ed.]. Aldershot: Avebury, 1993. 245p. *ISBN: 1856284565.*

3883 Urban landscape dynamics: a multi-level innovation process. Armando Montanari [Ed.]; Gerhard Curdes [Ed.]; Leslie Forsyth [Ed.]. Aldershot: Avebury, 1993. 395p. *ISBN: 1856282031. URBINNO Project. (Series:* Urban Europe Series).

3884 An urban pattern dynamics with capital and knowledge accumulation. W.-B. Zhlang. **Envir. Plan. A.** 25:3 3:1993 pp.357 - 370.

3885 Urban planning and development: issues and imperatives. Shamsher Singh. New Delhi: Ashish Pub. House, 1992. vii, 153p. *ISBN: 817024417X. Includes bibliographical references (p. [143]-148) and index.*

3886 Urban planning and the entrepreneurial state — the view from Victoria, Australia. I. Winter; T. Brooke. **Envir. Plan. C.** 11:3 8:1993 pp.263 - 278.

3887 Urban planning and the fragmented city of developing countries. Marcello Balbo. **Third Wor. P.** 15:1 2:1993 pp.23 - 35.

G: Environment. Community. Rural. Urban

3888 Urban planning in socialist China — theory and practice. Yichun Xie; Frank J. Costa. **Cities** 10:2 5:1993 pp.103 - 114.

3889 Urban social sustainability — the planning of an Australian city. Oren Yiftachel; David Hedgcock. **Cities** 10:2 5:1993 pp.139 - 157.

3890 Urbanisme et logement: analyse d'une crise. *[In French]*; [Town planning and housing: an analysis of a crisis]. Georges Mesmin. Paris: Presses Universitaires de France, 1992. 173p. *ISBN: 2130448488.*

3891 The value of conservation — a critical review of behavioural research. Philip Hubbard. **Town Plan. R.** 64:4 10:1993 pp.359 - 373.

3892 Vienna: bridge between cultures. Elisabeth Lichtenberger. London; New York: Belhaven Press; Halsted Press, 1993. xv, 212p. *ISBN: 1852930667, 0470220082. Includes bibliographical references (p. 196-201) and index. (Series:* World cities series).

3893 Vingt-cinq ans (1967-1992) de planification des transports urbains en France. *[In French]*; [25 years (1967-1992) of urban transport planning in France] *[Summary]*. J. Offner. **R. Ec. Reg. Urb.** 5 1993 pp.833 - 848.

3894 Zukunftsperspektiven der Raum- und Siedlungsentwicklung. *[In German]*; [Future perspectives on spatial and settlement development]. Hans-Peter Gatzweiler [Ed.]; Hansjörg Bucher; Martin Gornig; Markus Eltges; Steffen Maretzke; Aribert Peters; Stefan Schmitz; Gisela Beckmann; Siegfried Losch; Hanno Osenberg; Gerhard Stiens. **Inf. Raum.** 12 1993 pp.807 - 935. *Collection of 7 articles.*

Urban poverty
Pauvreté urbaine

3895 La criminalidad urbana en Colombia: una aproximación cuantitativa. *[In Spanish]*; [Urban crime in Colombia: a quantitive approximation]. Alvaro Camacho. **Coy. Soc.** 9 11:1993 pp.103 - 120.

3896 Environmental degradation in Mexico. David Barkin. **Mon. Rev.** 45:3 7-8:1993 pp.58 - 76.

3897 Estructura socio-ocupacional y pobreza en las ciudades Colombianas, 1986-1992. *[In Spanish]*; [Socio-occupational structure and poverty in Colombian cities, 1986-1992]. Oscar Fresneda. **Coy. Soc.** 9 11:1993 pp.137 - 164.

3898 In the name of the urban poor: access to basic amenities. Amitabh Kundu. New Delhi: Sage Publications, 1993. 299p. *ISBN: 0803991150.*

3899 Metropolis 2000: planning, poverty and politics. Thomas Angotti. New York, NY: Routledge, 1993. 276p. *ISBN: 0415081351, 041508136X. Includes bibliographical references and index. (Series:* Development and underdevelopment).

3900 El país de los excluídos: crecimiento y heterogeneidad de la pobreza en el conurbano Bonarense. *[In Spanish]*; [The country of the excluded: growth and heterogenity of poverty in the troubled Buenos Aires]. Inés Aguerrondo [Ed.]. Buenos Aires: CIPPA, 1991. 112p.

3901 La place du pauvre: histoire et géographie sociales de l'habitat HLM. *[In French]*; [The place of the poor: history and social geography of HLM housing]. Jacques Barou. Paris: Editions L'Harmattan, 1992. 135p. *ISBN: 2738411843. Bibliography and index.*

G: Environnement. Communauté. Rural. Urbain

3902 Selbsthilfe in den Armutsvierteln von Lima. Ein Rückgriff auf indianische Traditionen. *[In French]*; (Self-help in the shantytowns of Lima. A recourse to Indian traditions.) *[Summary]*. Cornelia Schweppe. **Sociologus** 43:2 1993 pp.118 - 135.

3903 Services for shelter: infrastucture for urban low-income housing. Andrew Cotton; Richard Franceys; Rod Shaw [Illus.]. Liverpool: Liverpool University Press in association with Fairstead Press, 1991. vii, 147p. *ISBN: 0853232873*. *Loughborough University of Technology Water, Engineering and Development Centre.* (Series: Liverpool planning manual).

3904 Shelter poverty: new ideas on housing affordability. Michael Eric Stone. Philadelphia: Temple University Press, 1993. xi, 423p. *ISBN: 1566390508, 1566390923. Includes bibliographical references (p. [391]-415) and index.*

3905 Squatter access to land in Metro Manila. Ton van Naerssen. **Phil. Stud.** 41 First quarter:1993 pp.3 - 20.

3906 Squatting, culture, and development — a comparative analysis of informal settlements in Latin America and the Middle East. Nezar AlSayyad. **J. Dev. Soc.** IX:2 7-10:1993 pp.139 - 155.

3907 Stedelijke armoede en etniciteit in de verzorgingsstaat — Amsterdam als voorbeeld. *[In Dutch]*; (Urban poverty and ethnicity in a welfare-state — the case of Amsterdam.) *[Summary]*. Sako Musterd; Wim Ostendorf. **Sociol. Gids** 40:6 11-12:1993 pp.466 - 481.

3908 The way to sustainability for poor cities. Richard L. Meier. **Environ. Urban.** 5:2 10:1993 pp.174 - 185.

Urban transport
Transport urbain

3909 Coûts externes du trafic routier — évaluation en milieu urbain. *[In French]*; [External costs of road traffic — evaluation in an urban environment]; *[Summary in German]*. Pascal Grosclaude; Nils Soguel. **Schw. Z. Volk. Stat.** 128:3 9:1992 pp.453 - 469.

3910 (Development of estimation method on obstructed homeward commuters after earthquake disaster.) *[Summary]*; *[Text in Japanese]*. Itsuki Nakabayashi. **Comp. Urban Stud.** 47 12:1992 pp.35 - 75.

3911 Externe Kosten des Agglomerationsverkehrs und Internalisierung. *[In German]*; [External costs of agglomeration transportation and internalization]; *[Summary in French]*. René Neuenschwander; Heini Sommer; Stefan Suter; Felix Walter. **Schw. Z. Volk. Stat.** 128:3 9:1992 pp.437 - 451.

3912 Global city characteristics and central London's employment. Martin Frost; Nigel Spence. **Urban Stud.** 30:3 4:1993 pp.547 - 558.

3913 "Go-slow" — the political economy of urban transport in Nigeria with an emphasis on Ado-Ekiti. J.T. Hathaway. **Geoforum** 24:2 1993 pp.165 - 182.

3914 Internalisieren der externen Kosten des Verkehrs. Fallbeispiel Agglomeration Zürich. *[In German]*; [Internalization of external costs of transportation. Using the Zürich agglomeration case as an example]; *[Summary in French]*. Markus Maibach; Rolf Iten; Samuel P. Mauch. **Schw. Z. Volk. Stat.** 128:3 9:1992 pp.471 - 493.

G: Environment. Community. Rural. Urban

3915 Mise en valeur des terrains de gare et renouveau du rail — vers une Suisse métropolitaine? *[In French]*; [Value of station areas and the redevelopment of railway land — towards a metropolitan Switzerland?]; *[Summary in German]*. Michel Rey. **Schw. Z. Volk. Stat.** 128:3 9:1992 pp.409 - 422.

3916 Road pricing für die Agglomeration Bern. Ein Vorschlag. *[In German]*; [Road pricing for the Bern agglomeration. A suggestion]; *[Summary in French]*. Georg Abay; Claude Zehnder. **Schw. Z. Volk. Stat.** 128:3 9:1992 pp.495 - 510.

3917 Simulating the evacuation of a small city — the effects of traffic factors. Zilla Sinuany-Stern; Eliahu Stern. **Socio. Econ.** 27:2 1993 pp.97 - 108.

3918 (A study of transportation and user-side subsidy for the elderly.) *[Summary]*; *[Text in Japanese]*. Masahiko Ohta; Tetsuo Akiyama; Hitoshi Yamakawa. **Comp. Urban Stud.** 48 3:1993 pp.45 - 56.

3919 Transport facilities and residential choice behavior — a model of multi-person choice processes. Aloys Borgers; Harry Timmermans. **Pap. Reg. Sci.** 72:1 1:1993 pp.45 - 61.

3920 Vingt-cinq ans (1967-1992) de planification des transports urbains en France. *[In French]*; [25 years (1967-1992) of urban transport planning in France] *[Summary]*. J. Offner. **R. Ec. Reg. Urb.** 5 1993 pp.833 - 848.

Urbanization
Urbanisation

3921 After modernism: global restructuring and the changing boundaries of city life. Michael Peter Smith [Ed.]. New Brunswick, NJ.: Transaction Publishers, 1992. 220p. *ISBN: 156000598X*. (*Series:* Comparative Urban and Community Research).

3922 Apartheid city in transition. Mark Swilling [Ed.]; Richard Humphries [Ed.]; Khehla Shubane [Ed.]. Cape Town, New York: Oxford University Press, 1991. xx, 377p. *ISBN: 0195705858. Includes bibliographical references and index.* (*Series:* Contemporary South African debates).

3923 Beaux quartiers et bidonvilles. *[In French]*; [Nice areas and shanty towns]. Xavier Crépin. **Afr. Cont.** 168 10-12:1993 pp.69 - 81.

3924 A catastrophe theory of urbanization — formalization and testing. Emilio Casetti. **Pap. Reg. Sci.** 72:3 7:1993 pp.203 - 220.

3925 Ciudad de Guatemala: dos estudios sobre su evolución urbana (1524-1950). *[In Spanish]*; [Guatemala City: two studies on its urban evolution (1524-1950)]. Gisela Gellert; Julio César Pinto Soria. Guatemala: Centro de Estudios Urbanos y Regionales, Universidad de San Carlos de Guatemala, 1990. 80p. *Includes bibliographical references.*

3926 Consideraciones teóricas sobre el proceso de urbanización en Mesoamérica. *[In Spanish]*; [Theoretical considerations on the urbanization process in Central America]. Noel Morelos García. **B. Antropol. Am.** 23 7:1991 pp.137 - 160.

3927 La crise des systèmes urbains et l'ajustement structurel. *[In French]*; [The crisis of urban systems and structural adjustment]. Philippe Hugon. **Afr. Cont.** 168 10-12:1993 pp.231 - 249.

3928 The cyclical urbanization model. A critical analysis. J. Nyström. **Geog.ann. B.** 74:2 1992 pp.133 - 144.

G: Environnement. Communauté. Rural. Urbain

3929 Envahir, conseiller et gouverner... la ville d'Amérique latine. *[In French]*; [Invade, advise and govern... the Latin American town]. Etienne Henry; Céline Sachs-Jeantet. **Soc. Sci. Info.** 32:2 1993 pp.303 - 361.

3930 Environmental degradation in Mexico. David Barkin. **Mon. Rev.** 45:3 7-8:1993 pp.58 - 76.

3931 Le financement de l'urbanisation. *[In French]*; [Financing urbanization]. Jean-Louis Venard. **Afr. Cont.** 168 10-12:1993 pp.207 - 217.

3932 From the history of the city to the history of the urbanized society. Samuel P. Hays. **J. Urban Hist.** 19:4 8:1993 pp.3 - 25.

3933 India's industrial cities: essays in economy and demography. Nigel Crook. Delhi: Oxford University Press, 1993. 181p. *ISBN: 0195631722. Includes bibliographical references (p. [167]-173) and index. (Series:* SOAS studies on South Asia).

3934 Japanese cities in the world economy. Kuniko Fujita [Ed.]; Richard Child Hill [Ed.]. Philadelphia: Temple University Press, 1993. xi, 311p. *ISBN: 1566390346. Includes bibliographical references and index. (Series:* Conflicts in urban and regional development).

3935 The Latin American inner city: differences of degree or of kind? P.M. Ward. **Envir. Plan. A.** 25:8 8:1993 pp.1131 - 1160.

3936 Montréal au XIX]e siècle: conformité et originalité par rapport au modèle occidental de croissance urbaine. *[In French]*; [Montreal in the 19th century: conformity and originality in relation to the model of urban growth in the Western countries] *[Summary]*. Marcel Bellavance. **Rech. Soc.graph** XXXIV:3 9-12:1993 pp.395 - 416.

3937 On the way to urbanization. Xiaochen Meng. **China City Plan. R.** 8:4 12:1992 pp.16 - 24.

3938 Los procesos de urbanización. *[In Spanish]*; [Urbanization processes]. Julio Vinuesa Angulo; María Jesús Vidal Domínguez. Madrid: Sintesis, 1991. 205p. *ISBN: 8477381100.*

3939 Procesos urbanos. *[In Spanish]*; [Urban processes]. Mario Lungo. San Salvador, El Salvador: ISTMO, 1992. 166p. *Includes bibliographical references (p. 161-166).*

3940 Skażenie środowiska i urbanizacja a umieralność na raka w Polsce w latach 1975-1987. *[In Polish]*; [Environmental pollution, urbanization and mortality from cancer in Poland 1875 -1987]. Zygmunt Gostkowski. **Prz. Soc.** XLI 1992 pp.145 - 153.

3941 Städte und Stadtentwicklung. *[In German]*; [Cities and urban development]. Heinz Heineberg [Contrib.]; Jorge Camberos Garibi [Contrib.]; Christoph Schäfers [Contrib.]; Jürgen Bähr [Contrib.]; Ulrich Jürgens [Contrib.]; Wolfgang Taubmann [Contrib.]; Burkhard Hofmeister [Contrib.]; Kenneth Hewitt [Contrib.]; Josef Nipper [Contrib.]; Manfred Nutz [Contrib.]. **Geogr. Rund.** 45:7-8 7-8:1993 pp.400 - 445. *Collection of 5 articles.*

3942 A theoretical foundation for the concept of differential urbanization. Hermanus S. Geyer; Thomas Kontuly. **Int. Reg. Sci. R.** 15:2 1993 pp.157 - 177.

3943 Third world cities: problems, policies and prospects. John D. Kasadra [Ed.]; Allan M. Parnell [Ed.]. Newbury Park, California: Sage, 1993. xvii, 310p. *ISBN: 0803944845, 0803944853. Includes bibliographical references and index.*

3944 Trends in the urbanization of Arab settlements in Galilee. Ghazi Falah. **Urban Geogr.** 14:2 3-4:1993 pp.145 - 164.

3945 "Urban management" in development assistance — an elusive concept. Richard Stren. **Cities** 10:2 5:1993 pp.125 - 138.

G: Environment. Community. Rural. Urban

3946 Urbanisation and the functions of the cities in the European Community. European Institute of Urban Affairs. Brussels, Luxembourg: Office for Official Publications of the European Communities, 1992. 230p. *ISBN: 9282648109. Includes bibliographical references (p. 215-230). (Series:* Regional development studies).

3947 Urbanisation et enjeux quotidiens: terrains ethnologiques dans la France actuelle. *[In French]*; [Urbanization and daily challenges: ethnological ground in present day France]. Gérard Althabe; Christian Marcadet; Michèle de la Pradelle; Monique Sélim. Paris: Editions L'Harmattan, 1993. 198p. *ISBN: 2738418422.*

3948 Urbanisation in post-independence Windhoek: with special emphasis on Katutura. Bruce Frayne. Windhoek: Namibian Institute for Social and Economic Research, 1992. 186p. *ISBN: 0947433252. Includes bibliographical references. (Series:* Research report - 6).

3949 Urbanisation in the Third World countries. Y.A. Parmar. **Indian J. Soc. W.** LIII:4 10:1992 pp.647 - 660.

3950 Urbanism and kinship bonds — a test of four generalizations. Thomas C. Wilson. **Soc. Forc.** 71:3 3:1993 pp.703 - 712.

3951 [Urbanization and the neighborhood association in Japanese modern ages]; *[Text in Japanese]*. Kazushi Tamano. Tokyo: Kojinsha, 1993. 297p.

3952 Urbanization in the Caribbean and trends of global convergence — divergence. Robert B. Potter. **Geogr. J.** 159:Part 1 3:1993 pp.1 - 21.

3953 Verstedeliking in Mhluzi. *[In Afrikaans]*; (Urbanization in Mhluzi.) *[Summary]*. J.S. Malan. **S.Afr. J. Ethnol.** 16:3 9:1993 pp.93 - 100.

3954 La ville coloniale: «lieu de colonisation» et métissage culturel. *[In French]*; [The colonial town: "place of colonization" and cultural crossing]. Catherine Coquery-Vidrovitch. **Afr. Cont.** 168 10-12:1993 pp.11 - 22.

3955 La ville, enveloppe et produit des sociétés mutantes. *[In French]*; (The city as a frame for, and a product of, changing societies.) *[Summary]*. René de Maximy. **Espace Géogr.** XXII:1 1993 pp.41 - 53.

3956 La ville: vers une nouvelle définition. *[In French]*; [The town: towards a new definition]. Jean Remy; Liliane Voyé. Paris: Editions L'Harmattan, 1992. 173p. *ISBN: 2738409563.*

H: ECONOMIC LIFE
VIE ÉCONOMIQUE

H.1: Economic sociology
Sociologie économique

3957 Applied economic psychology in the 1990s. Stephen E. G. Lea [Ed.]; Paul Webley [Ed.]; Brian Young [Ed.]. Exeter: Washington Singer Press, 1990. 1087p. *ISBN: 1873053002*. *15th International Colloquium on Economic Psychology, 1990, Exeter, England. International Association for Research in Economic Psychology.*

3958 The armchair economist: economics and everyday life. Steven E. Landsburg. Oxford: Maxwell Macmillan International, 1993. ix, 241p. *ISBN: 0029177758*.

3959 Belief — its role in economic thought and action. J.B. Rosser. **Am. J. Econ. S.** 52:3 7:1993 pp.355 - 368.

3960 Cultural determinants of economic performance. Mark Casson. **J. Comp. Econ.** 17:2 6:1993 pp.418 - 442.

3961 Economia e sociologia: una vecchia promessa. *[In Italian]*; (Economics and sociology: an old promise.) *[Summary]*. Arnaldo Bagnasco. **Sociol. Lav.** 45 1992 pp.15 - 36.

3962 Economics as an imperialist social science. Peter J. Buckley; Mark Casson. **Human Relat.** 46:9 9:1993 pp.1035 - 1052.

3963 Embeddedness and immigration — notes on the social determinants of economic action. Alejandro Portes; Julia Sensenbrenner. **A.J.S.** 98:6 5:1993 pp.1320 - 1350.

3964 Households: the moral architecture of the economy. William James Booth. Ithaca: Cornell University Press, 1993. xii, 305p. *ISBN: 0801427916, 080148068X. Includes bibliographical references and index.*

3965 Normative-affective choices. Amitai Etzioni. **Human Relat.** 46:9 9:1993 pp.1053 - 1069.

3966 Should economic psychology care about personality structure? H. Brandstätter. **J. Econ. Psyc.** 14:3 9:1993 pp.473 - 494.

H.2: Economic systems
Systèmes économiques

3967 Adam Smith and the ethics of contemporary capitalism. G.R. Bassiry; Marc Jones. **J. Busin. Ethics** 12:8 8:1993 pp.621 - 627.

3968 Against the economic orthodoxy — on the making of East Asian miracle. Jeffrey Henderson. **Econ. Soc.** 22:2 5:1993 pp.200 - 217.

3969 Asijský výrobní způsob v kontextu jihovýchodní Asie. *[In Czech]*; (Asiatic mode of production in the context of Southeast Asia.) *[Summary]*. Václav Hubinger. **Český Lid** 79 1992 pp.403 - 420.

3970 Bringing the economy home from the market. Ross V. G. Dobson. Montréal: Black Rose Books, 1992. *ISBN: 1895431514, 1895431506. Includes index.*

3971 Copyright made easier. Raymond Wall. London: Aslib, 1993. 393p. *ISBN: 0851423108*.

H: Economic life

3972 Differential interests, equity, and public good provision. Eric van Dijk; Henk Wilke. **J. Exp. S. Psychol.** 29:1 1:1993 pp.1 - 16.

3973 Economy and society at the close of the American century. James Ronald Stanfield [Contrib.]; Robert Heilbroner [Contrib.]; Doug Brown [Contrib.]; Elaine McCrate [Contrib.]; Jacqueline B. Stanfield [Contrib.]; Steven Shulman [Contrib.]; William M. Dugger [Contrib.]. **R. Soc. Econ.** L:4 Winter:1992 pp.366 - 471. *Collection of 7 articles.*

3974 An egalitarian democratic private ownership economy. Marc Fleurbaey. **Polit. Soc.** 21:2 6:1993 pp.215 - 233.

3975 The fair allocation of an indivisible good when monetary compensations are possible. K. Tadenuma; W. Thomson. **Math. Soc. Sc.** 25:2 2:1993 pp.117 - 132.

3976 For a crisiology. E. Morin. **Indust. Environ. Crisis** 7:1 1993 pp.5 - 21.

3977 From one economic ideology to another — Poland's transition from socialism to capitalism. Bronislaw Oyrzanowski; Magda Paleczny-Zapp. **Int. J. Pol. C. S.** 7:1 Fall:1993 pp.43 - 55.

3978 Has British capitalism changed since the First World War? W.G. Runciman. **Br. J. Soc.** 44:1 3:1993 pp.53 - 67.

3979 Host-country managerial behaviour and learning in Chinese and Hungarian joint ventures. John Child; Livia Markoczy. **J. Manag. Stu.** 30:4 7:1993 pp.611 - 631.

3980 The market and social forces — a comparative analysis of industrial change; *[Summary in French]*. Mauro Magatti. **Int. J. Urban** 17:2 6:1993 pp.213 - 231.

3981 Myths and realities of Kenyan capitalism. David Himbara. **J. Mod. Afr. S.** 31:1 3:1993 pp.93 - 107.

3982 National industrial structure and the global system. Kenneth A. Bollen; Stephen J. Appold. **Am. Sociol. R.** 58:2 4:1993 pp.283 - 301.

3983 The necessity of welfare: the systemic conflicts of the capitalist mixed economy. Geert Reuten; Michael Williams. **Sci. Soc.** 57:4 Winter:1993-1994 pp.420 - 440.

3984 Le pauvre, le hors-la-loi, le métis — la question de l'"économie informelle" en Afrique. *[In French]*; [The poor, those outside the law, those of mixed race — the question of the "informal economy" in Africa]. Gauthier de Villers. **Cah. CEDAF** 6 1992 pp.1 - 88.

3985 The peasant economy of refugee resettlement in Eastern Sudan. Johnathan Bascom. **Ann. As. Am. G.** 83:2 6:1993 pp.320 - 346.

3986 Popular attitudes to the transition to a market economy in the Soviet Union on the eve of reform. Simon Clarke. **Sociol. Rev.** 41:4 11:1993 pp.619 - 652.

3987 Prelude to the genesis of capitalism: the dynamics of the feudal mode of production. Dimitris Milonakis. **Sci. Soc.** 57:4 Winter:1993-1994 pp.390 - 419.

3988 Privatisation and economism — an investigation amongst "producers" in two privatised public utilities in Britian. Theo Nichols; Julia O'Connell. **Sociol. Rev.** 41:4 11:1993 pp.707 - 730.

3989 Problemy rekonstrukcji polskiej gospodarki. *[In Polish]*; (Problems of Polish economy reconstruction.). Józef Penc. **Pra. Zab. Społ.** XXXV:10-11 10-11:1993 pp.26 - 32.

3990 Quelles leçons d'une transition? *[In French]*; (What lessons can be learnt from a transition?) *[Summary]*. Jacques Sapir. **Pensée** 294-295 7-10:1993 pp.55 - 74.

3991 "Real'nyi sotsialism" i "aziatskii sposob proizvodstva". *[In Russian]*; ("Real socialism" and the "Asiatic mode of production".). A. Zakharov. **Obshch. Nauki Sovrem.** 3 1993 pp.164 - 172.

3992 Social effects produced by the system change. T. Kolosi; P. Róbert. **Acta Oecon.** 45:1-2 1993 pp.23 - 42.

H: Vie économique

3993 Die soziale Bedeutung der Privatisierung des Eigentums in der Sowjetunion und in Rußland. *[In German]*; [The social implications of privatization of property in the USSR and Russia]. Manfred Trapp. **Osteuropa** 43:4 4:1993 pp.341 - 357.
3994 Transition to Utopia — a reinterpretation of economics, ideas, and politics in Hungary, 1984-1990. Jason McDonald. **E.Eur. Pol. Soc.** 7:2 Spring:1993 pp.203 - 239.

H.3: Economic conditions and living standards
Conditions économiques et niveau de vie

3995 Aktywność zawodowa ludności wiejskiej w latach 1988-1992. *[In Polish]*; (Economic activity of rural population, 1988-1992.) *[Summary]*. Izasław Frenkel. **Stud. Demogr.** 3(113) 1993 pp.3 - 36.
3996 Armut im Alter? Ergebnisse der Berliner Altersstudie zur Einkommenslage alter und sehr alter Menschen. *[In German]*; (Poverty in old age? Results of the Berlin aging study on the income of the old and the very old.) *[Summary]*. Andreas Motel; Michael Wagner. **Z. Soziol.** 22:6 12:1993 pp.433 - 448.
3997 Assessing post-census state poverty estimates. William P. O'Hare. **Pop. Res. Pol. R.** 12:3 1993 pp.261 - 276.
3998 Breaking the cycle of poverty: the BRAC strategy. Catherine H. Lovell. West Hartford, Conn: Kumarian Press, 1992. x, 205p. *ISBN: 1565490053, 1565490045. Includes bibliographical references (p. 190-194) and index. (Series:* Kumarian Press library of management for development).
3999 Bringing it back home: remittances to Mexico from migrant workers in the United States. Aníbal Yáñez [Tr.]; Fernando Lozano Ascencio. La Jolla, CA: Center for U.S.-Mexican Studies University of California, San Diego, 1993. xii, 77p. *ISBN: 1878367110. Includes bibliographical references (p. [71]-77). (Series:* Monograph series - 37).
4000 The Canadian syndrome of regional polarities — an obituary; *[Summary in French]*. John Goyder. **Can. R. Soc. A.** 30:1 2:1993 pp.1 - 12.
4001 Changes in the male/female wage gap 1976/1985. Alison J. Wellington. **J. Hum. Res.** XXVIII:2 Spring:1993 pp.383 - 411.
4002 Cohort size effects on the wages of young men in Britain, 1961-1989. Stephen Nickell. **Br. J. Ind. R.** 31:3 9:1993 pp.459 - 469.
4003 Color or culture? Wage differences among non-Hispanic black males, Hispanic black males and hispanic white males. Jeremiah Cotton. **Rev. Bl. Pol. Ec.** 21:4 Spring:1993 pp.53 - 67.
4004 A compound index of national development. N.C. Lind. **Soc. Ind.** 28:3 3:1993 pp.267 - 284.
4005 Coping with a new reality — barriers and possibilities. Ursula Beer; Ursula Müller. **Camb. J. Econ.** 17:3 9:1993 pp.281 - 294.
4006 Counting the poor in Indonesia. Anne Booth. **B. Ind. Econ. St.** 29:1 4:1993 pp.53 - 83.
4007 Cross-cultural comparisons of quality of life of Thais and Americans. Orose Leelakulthanit; Ralph Day. **Soc. Ind.** 30:1 9:1993 pp.49 - 70.

H: Economic life

4008 Cross-cultural variations in predictors of life satisfaction — an historical view of differences among West European countries. Janet P. Near; Paula L. Rechner. **Soc. Ind.** 29:1 5:1993 pp.109 - 121.

4009 The culture of contentment. John Kenneth Galbraith. London: Penguin, 1993. 195p. *ISBN: 0140173668.*

4010 The decline of private-sector unionism and the gender wage gap. William E. Even; David A. Macpherson. **J. Hum. Res.** XXVIII:2 Spring:1993 pp.279 - 296.

4011 Des patrons "chinois" à Paris — ressources linguistiques, sociales et symboliques. *[In French]*; ("Chinese" employers in Paris — linguistic, social and symbolic resources.) *[Summary]*; *[Summary in Spanish]*; *[Summary in German]*. Jean-Pierre Hassoun. **Rev. Fr. Soc.** XXXIV:1 1-3:1993 pp.97 - 123.

4012 A different approach to the measurement of income inequality. Cecilia A. Conrad. **Rev. Bl. Pol. Ec.** 22:1 Summer:1993 pp.19 - 31.

4013 Dimensions of social inequality in the Third World: a cross-national analysis of income inequality and mortality decline. Edward Crenshaw; Ansari Ameen. **Pop. Res. Pol. R.** 12:3 1993 pp.297 - 314.

4014 The distributional impact of the 1980s — myth vs. reality. Lowell Gallaway; Richard Vedder. **Crit. Rev.** 7:1 Winter:1993 pp.61 - 79.

4015 Economic development — Rostow, Marx, and Durkheim. Sethard Fisher. **J. Dev. Soc.** 9:1 1-4:1993 pp.53 - 66.

4016 The economic effects of physical appearance. Eng Seng Loh. **Soc. Sci. Q.** 74:2 6:1993 pp.420 - 438.

4017 An economic model of subjective well-being — integrating economic and psychological theories. B. Heady. **Soc. Ind.** 28:2 2:1993 pp.97 - 116.

4018 The effects of comparable worth in the public sector on public private occupational relative wages. Greg Hundley. **J. Hum. Res.** XXVIII:2 Spring:1993 pp.318 - 342.

4019 Effects of family background on earnings and returns to schooling — evidence from Brazil. David Lam; Robert F. Schoeni. **J. Polit. Ec.** 101:4 8:1993 pp.710 - 740.

4020 L'evoluzione della qualita della vita nella provincia di Bologna: un'analisi su base comunale : 1961-1981. *[In Italian]*; [The development of quality of life in the province of Bologna: a community analysis: 1961-1981]. Guido Moretti. Rimini: Maggioli, 1992. 195p. *ISBN: 8838797684. Instituto di Architettura e Urbanistica. Universita Degli Studi di Bologna.*

4021 Female-headed households and family welfare in rural Ecuador. D.S. DeGraff; R.E. Bilsborrow. **J. Pop. Ec.** 6:4 1993 pp.317 - 336.

4022 Food and hunger nexus — availability and entitlement hypothesis reconsidered. Evidence from Bangladesh data. Khorshed Chowdhury. **J. Dev. Soc.** 9:1 1-4:1993 pp.88 - 104.

4023 Geographical differentials in the socioeconomic status of Puerto Ricans — human capital variations and labor market characteristics. Maria E. Enchautegui. **Int. Migr. Rev.** XXVI:4 Winter:1992 pp.1267 - 1290.

4024 Germany after unification — still a twofold society. Detlef Landua. **Int. J. Comp. Soc** XXXIV:1-2 1-4:1993 pp.75 - 86.

4025 The impact of adult ill-health on household income and nutrition in Khulna, Bangladesh. Jane Pryer. **Environ. Urban.** 5:2 10:1993 pp.35 - 49.

4026 The impact of democracy or repressiveness on the quality of life, income distribution and economic growth rates; *[Summary in French]*. Erich Weede. **Int. Sociol.** 8:2 6:1993 pp.177 - 195.

H: Vie économique

4027 The impact of population growth on the standard of living — demo-economic senarios for the Netherlands; *[Summary in French].* Jan H.M. Neilssen; Ad P. Vossen. **Eur. J. Pop.** 9:2 1993 pp.169 - 196.

4028 Income disparities and employment and occupational changes in New York; *[Summary in French]*; *[Summary in German].* Valerie Preston; Sara McLafferty. **Reg. Stud.** 27:3 1993 pp.223 - 236.

4029 Income inequality trends in the 1980s — a five-country comparison. Johan Fritzell. **Acta Sociol.** 36:1 1993 pp.47 - 62.

4030 Indicadores alternativos del desarrollo y mediciones de pobreza. *[In Spanish]*; [Alternative indicators of development and poverty measurement] *[Summary].* Julio Boltvinik. **Est. Sociol.** XI:33 9-12:1993 pp.605 - 640.

4031 Industrialization, modernization and the quality of life. Alex Inkeles. **Int. J. Comp. Soc** XXXIV:1-2 1-4:1993 pp.1 - 23.

4032 The inequality process and the distribution of income to blacks and whites. John Angle. **J. Math. Sociol.** 17:1 1992 pp.77 - 98.

4033 La informalidad urbana en años de expansión, crisis y restructuración económica. *[In Spanish]*; [The urban informal sector in the years of growth, crisis and economic restructuring]. Orlandina de Oliveira; Bryan Roberts. **Est. Sociol.** XI:31 1-4:1993 pp.33 - 58.

4034 An inquiry into well-being and destitution. Partha Dasgupta. Oxford: Clarendon Press, 1993. 661p. *ISBN: 0198287569. Bibliography: p.546-625; includes index.*

4035 Kak my zhivem? O dinamike denezhnykh dokhodov naseleniia v 1992godu. *[In Russian]*; (How do we live? On the dynamics of the population's money profits in 1992.). A. Surinov. **Svobod. Mysl'** 6 4:1993 pp.3 - 9.

4036 Lebensverhältnisse in Deutschland, Ungleichheit und Angleichung. *[In German]*; [Living conditions in Germany, inequality and alignment]. Wolfgang Glatzer [Ed.]; Heinz-Herbert Noll [Ed.]. Frankfurt am Main: Campus-Verlag, 1992. 328p. *ISBN: 3593347539. Includes bibliographies.*

4037 The legitimation of inequality — occupational earnings in nine nations. Jonathan Kelley; M.D.R. Evans. **A.J.S.** 99:1 7:1993 pp.75 - 125.

4038 Levensverwachting en kwaliteit van het leven. *[In Dutch]*; (Life expectancy and quality of life.) *[Summary].* Gilbert Dooghe. **Bevolk. Gez.** 1 1993 pp.25 - 44.

4039 Metoda i wyniki szacowania skal jednostek konsumpcyjnych. *[In Polish]*; (Method and results of the estimation of scales of consumer units.) *[Summary].* Alina Baran. **Stud. Demogr.** 2(164) 1991 pp.69 - 89.

4040 Modern poverty: the culture of distribution and structural unemployment in the foothills of Kerala. Peter Werff. New Delhi: Manohar, 1992. xii, 212p. *ISBN: 8185425612. Includes index and bibliographical references (p. [197]-210).*

4041 On formal educational certificates in earnings determination; *[Summary in French].* Alfred A. Hunter; Jean McKenzie Leiper. **Can. J. Soc.** 18:1 Winter:1993 pp.21 - 42.

4042 Pauvretés, inégalités, exclusions: renouveau des approches théoriques et des pratiques sociales. *[In French]*; Poverty, inequality, exclusion: new approaches to theory and practice. Gaudier. Geneva: International Institute for Labour Studies, 1993. xii, 208p. *ISBN: 9290145250.*

4043 Perekhodnyi period po otsenkam naseleniia. *[In Russian]*; (The transition to the market in the population's estimations.). V.S. Sycheva. **Sot. Issle.** 3 1993 pp.12 - 20.

H: Economic life

4044 Płaca jako narzędzie kierowania. *[In Polish]*; (Wages as instrument of management.). Alicja Sajkiewicz. **Pra. Zab. Społ.** XXXV:4 4:1993 pp.27 - 36.

4045 Politics, income perceptions and living standards. Peter Saunders; George Matheson. **Aust. J. Pol. Sci** 28:1 3:1993 pp.1 - 18.

4046 Population and economic development in Thailand: some critical household behavioral relations. Chalongphob Sussangkarn; et al. Bangkok: Human Resources and Social Development Program, Thailand Development Research Institute, 1991. xiv, 49p. *ISBN: 9748870073. Includes bibliographical references (p. 47-49). (Series:* Research monograph - 7).

4047 Positional power, class, and individual earnings inequality — advancing new structuralist explanations. Michael Wallace; Kevin T. Leicht; Don Sherman Grant. **Sociol. Q.** 34:1 Spring:1993 pp.85 - 109.

4048 Poverty and prosperity in the USA in the late twentieth century. Dimitri B. Papadimitriou [Ed.]; Edward N. Wolff [Ed.]. New York, N.Y: St. Martin's Press, 1993. 390p. *ISBN: 0312094736. Includes index.*

4049 Poverty in Karachi: incidence, location, characteristics, and upward mobility. Mir Anjum Altaf; Aly Ercelawn; Kaiser Bengali; Abdul Rahim. **Pak. Dev. R.** 32:2 Summer:1993 pp.159 - 178.

4050 The quality of life. Martha Craven Nussbaum [Ed.]; Amartya Sen [Ed.]. New York; Oxford: Oxford University Press, 1992. 453p. *ISBN: 0198283954. Papers presented at a conference sponsored by the World Institute for Development Economics Research. Includes index. (Series:* Studies in development economics).

4051 Region and class specific determinants of rural poverty in India. B.C. Mehta. **Ind. J. Reg. Sci.** XXV:1 1993 pp.59 - 70.

4052 The relationship between income and subjective well-being — relative or absolute? Ed Diener; Ed Sandvik; Larry Seidlitz; Marrisa Diener. **Soc. Ind.** 28:3 3:1993 pp.195 - 223.

4053 Rich kids, poor kids — changing income inequality among American children. Daniel T. Lichter; David J. Eggebeen. **Soc. Forc.** 71:3 3:1993 pp.761 - 780.

4054 La richesse de la vieillesse: la situation socio-économique des personnes âgées en Belgique : état actuel et prospective. *[In French]*; [Wealth and old age: the socioeconomic position of old people in Belgium: current conditions and future prospects]. Herman Devos; Kurt Van Dender; Jozef Pacolet. Brussels: Fondation Roi Baudouin, 1991. 185p. *ISBN: 2872120637.*

4055 Social aspects of economic readjustment in Hungary — a consideration of the role of social-economic indicators. Charles L. Choguill; Erwin S. Solomon; Robert Machin. **Soc. Ind.** 29:2 6:1993 pp.205 - 227.

4056 Social change and economic reform in Africa. Peter Gibbon [Ed.]. Uppsala: Nordiska Afrikainstitutet, 1993. 381p. *ISBN: 9171063315. Papers of a workshop held in Harare, Zimbabwe in March 1992. Includes bibliographical references (p. [360]-378).*

4057 Social polarization — a comparison of evidence from Britain and the United States. S. Pinch. **Envir. Plan. A.** 25:6 6:1993 pp.779 - 795.

4058 Social responses to Mexico's economic crisis of the 1980s. Mercedes González de la Rocha [Ed.]; Agustín Escobar Latapí [Ed.]. San Diego: University of California, San Diego: Center for U.S.-Mexican Studies, 1991. 245p. *ISBN: 187836703X. Includes bibliographical references. (Series:* U.S.-Mexico contemporary perspectives series).

4059 The spatial concentration of affluence and poverty during the 1970s. Douglas S. Massey; Mitchell L. Eggers. **Urban Aff. Q.** 29:2 12:1993 pp.299 - 315.
4060 Spatial patterns of "socio-economic well-being" in Sri Lanka. M.B. Wijedasa. **Reg. Sci. Urb. Econ.** 23:1 6:1992 pp.51 - 60.
4061 Statek morski a deprywacja potrzeb. *[In Polish]*; (Sea-going vessel and deprivations of needs.) *[Summary]*. Ludwik Janiszewski. **Prz. Soc.** XL 1993 pp.181 - 195.
4062 Struggle and survival in the modern Middle East. Edmund Burke III [Ed.]. London: I.B. Tauris, 1993. 400p. *ISBN: 1850436053*. (*Series:* Society and culture in the modern Middle East).
4063 Subjective well-being among Russian students. Galina Balatsky; Ed Diener. **Soc. Ind.** 28:3 3:1993 pp.225 - 243.
4064 Théories du rapport salarial et question de la transition dans les économies de type soviétique (E.T.S.) — bilan et perspectives. *[In French]*; (Theories on the wage relationship, and the problem of transition in Soviet type-economies (STE) — appraisal and future prospects.) *[Summary]*. Patrick Dieuaide; Ramine Motamed-Nejad. **Rev. Ét. Comp.** XXIV:2 6:1993 pp.5 - 45.
4065 Umverteilen: Schritte zur sozialen und wirtschaftlichen Einheit Deutschlands. *[In German]*; [Redistribution: steps towards social and economic unity in Germany]. Rudolf Hickel [Ed.]; Ernst-Ulrich Huster [Ed.]; Heribert Kohl [Ed.]. Cologne: Bund-Verlag, 1993. 416p. *ISBN: 3766323733*.
4066 Union presence, class, and individual earnings inequality. Kevin T. Leicht; Michael Wallace; Don Sherman Grant. **Work Occup.** 20:4 11:1993 pp.429 - 451.
4067 Union-non-union wage differentials — individual level and organizational level effects. Arne Mastekaasa. **Eur. Sociol. R.** 9:2 9:1993 pp.109 - 124.
4068 Urban poverty profiles of regions in India. B.C. Mehta; Sunanda Devpura. **Ind. J. Reg. Sci.** XXV:2 1993 pp.29 - 40.
4069 The varied economic returns to post-secondary education — new evidence from the class of 1972. W. Norton Grubb. **J. Hum. Res.** XXVIII:2 Spring:1993 pp.365 - 382.

H.4: Enterprises and production systems
Entreprises et systèmes de production

4070 Back to the sweatshop or ahead to the informal sector?; *[Summary in French]*. Roger Waldinger; Michael Lapp. **Int. J. Urban** 17:1 3:1993 pp.6 - 29.
4071 Black Americans' business ownership factors: a theoretical perspective. Sol Ahiarah. **Rev. Bl. Pol. Ec.** 22:2 Fall:1993 pp.15 - 40.
4072 Brewery and Brauerei — the organizational ecology of brewing. Glenn R. Carroll; Peter Preisendoerfer; Anand Swaminathan; Gabriele Wiedenmayer. **Organ. Stud.** 14:2 1993 pp.155 - 188.
4073 Business and bureaucracy in a Chinese city: an ethnography of private business households in contemporary China. Ole Bruun. Berkeley, CA: Institute of East Asian Studies; University of California; Berkeley, 1993. 273p. *ISBN: 1557290423*. (*Series:* China research monograph).
4074 Canadian recruitment of East Asian automobile transplants — cultural, economic, and political perspectives; *[Summary in French]*. Ernest J. Yanarella; William C. Green. **Can. J. Soc.** 18:4 Fall:1993 pp.359 - 381.

H: Economic life

4075 Central business districts of the two Laredos. James R. Curtis. **Geogr. Rev.** 83:11:1993 pp.54 - 65.
4076 City and countryside in the onset of Brazilian industrialization. Mauricio A. Font. **Stud. Comp. ID.** 27:3 Fall:1992 pp.26 - 56.
4077 Coffee co-operatives and culture: an anthropological study of a coffee co-operative in Kenya. Hans Hedlund. Oxford: Oxford University Press (E. Africa), 1992. 205p. *ISBN: 0195727584.*
4078 A constructivist framework for understanding entrepreneurship performance. Hamid Bouchikhi. **Organ. Stud.** 14:4 1993 pp.549 - 570.
4079 Corporate networks, international telecommunications and interdependence: perspectives from geography and information systems. Henry Bakis [Ed.]; Ronald Abler [Ed.]; Edward M. Roche [Ed.]. London: Belhaven Press, 1992. 232p. *ISBN: 1852931426.*
4080 Culture and capitalism in contemporary Ireland. Paul Keating; Dermot Desmond. Aldershot: Avebury, 1992. 238p. *ISBN: 1856283623.*
4081 De la mano de obra excedente a la empresa dinámica: perspectivas de competencia del sector informal latinoamericano. *[In Spanish]*; [From oversupply of labour to the dynamic enterprise: competing perspectives on the Latin America informal sector] *[Summary]*. Alejandro Portes; Richard Schauffler. **Est. Sociol.** XI:33 9-12:1993 pp.817 - 850.
4082 Defense-less territory — workers, communities, and the decline of military production in Los Angeles. R.M. Law; J.R. Wolch; L.M. Takahashi. **Envir. Plan. C.** 11:3 8:1993 pp.291 - 315.
4083 Deux communautés paysannes du café au Costa Rica: Tucurrique et Pejibaye, 1850-1992. *[In French]*; [Two communities of peasant coffee growers in Costa Rica: Tucurrique et Pejibaye, 1850-1992]; *[Summary in Spanish]*. Carine Craipeau. **Caravelle** 61 1993 pp.75 - 92.
4084 The enterprise culture and the inner city. Nicholas D. Deakin; John Edwards. London: Tavistock, Routledge, 1993. 273p. *ISBN: 0415035481, 041503549X. Includes bibliographical references and index.*
4085 Equalizing opportunity through small business development: a South African perspective. Bruce Phillips. **Rev. Bl. Pol. Ec.** 22:2 Fall:1993 pp.141 - 150.
4086 Firmy i ikh rukovoditeli. *[In Russian]*; [Enterprises and their leaders]. D.D. Bachugov; V.R. Vesnin. **Sots.-Pol. Z.** 5-6 1993 pp.93 - 102.
4087 Fordism, flexible specialization and agri-industrial restructuring — the case of the U.S. broiler industry. Chul-Kyoo Kim; James Curry. **Sociol. Rur.** XXXIII:1 1993 pp.61 - 80.
4088 From peasant to entrepreneur: the survival of the family economy in Italy. Anna Cento Bull; Paul Corner. Oxford: Berg, 1993. 174p. *ISBN: 085496309X.*
4089 From production systems to learning systems — lessons from Japan. J. Patchell. **Envir. Plan. A.** 25:6 6:1993 pp.797 - 815.
4090 Die Funktion von Managementstrategien und -entscheidungen bei der Modernisierung des betrieblichen Produktionsapparats. *[In German]*; (The function of management strategies and decisions in the modernization of the industrial production plant.) *[Summary]*. Rainer Freriks; Peter Hauptmanns; Josef Schmid. **Z. Soziol.** 22:6 12:1993 pp.399 - 415.
4091 Gender, entrepreneurship and socioeconomic reparation in South Africa. Fred Ahwireng-Obeng. **Rev. Bl. Pol. Ec.** 22:2 Fall:1993 p.151.

4092 Good and evil in the chairmen's "boiler plate" — an analysis of corporate visions of the 1970s. Julie E. Kendall. **Organ. Stud.** 14:4 1993 pp.571 - 592.
4093 The Greek and Greek-Cypriot economic ethos — a sociocultural analysis. Ceasar V. Mavratsas. **Cyprus Rev.** 4:2 Fall:1992 pp.7 - 43.
4094 Inside a Japanese transplant — a critical perspective. Laurie Graham. **Work Occup.** 20:2 5:1993 pp.147 - 173.
4095 Interorganizational imitation: the impact of interlocks on corporate acquisition activity. Pamela R. Haunschild. **Adm. Sci. Qua.** 38:4 12:1993 pp.564 - 592.
4096 The invention of corporate culture — a history of the histories of Cadbury. Michael Rowlinson; John Hassard. **Human Relat.** 46:3 3:1993 pp.299 - 326.
4097 'It's gotta be da shoes': domestic manufacturing, international subcontracting, and the production of athletic footwear. R. Barff; J. Austen. **Envir. Plan. A.** 25:8 8:1993 pp.1103 - 1114.
4098 Japanese inward investment in the northeast of England — reassessing "Japanisation". F. Peck; I. Stone. **Envir. Plan. C.** 11:1 2:1993 pp.55 - 67.
4099 The Japanese world of work and North American factories. Carl H.A. Dassbach. **Crit. Sociol.** 20:1 1993-1994 pp.3 - 30.
4100 Die Kleinen ganz groß? Der Wandel der Betriebsgrößenstruktur im Branchenvergleich. *[In German]*; (Big future for small scale production?) *[Summary]*. René Leicht; Reinhard Stockmann. **Soz. Welt.** 44:2 1993 pp.243 - 274.
4101 Legislating organizational probation — state capacity, business power, and corporate crime control. William S. Lofquist. **Law Soc. Rev.** 27:4 1993 pp.741 - 783.
4102 Lideranças empresariais e problemas da estratégia liberal no Brasil. *[In Portuguese]*; (Entrepreneur's leadership and problems of the liberal strategy in Brazil.) *[Summary]*; *[Summary in French]*. Eli Diniz; Renato Boschi. **Rev. Bras. Ciên. Soc.** 8:23 10:1993 pp.101 - 119.
4103 The limits of local initiatives — a reassessment of urban entrepreneurialism for urban development. Helga Leitner; Mark Garner. **Urban Geogr.** 14:1 1-2:1993 pp.57 - 77.
4104 Making capitalism: the social and cultural construction of a South Korean conglomerate. Roger L. Janelli; Dawnhee Yim Janelli [Contrib.]. Stanford, Calif: Stanford University Press, 1993. x, 276p. *ISBN: 0804716099. Includes bibliographical references (p. [245]-262) and index.*
4105 Management, masculinity and manipulation — from paternalism to corporate strategy in financial services in Britain. Deborah Kerfoot; David Knights. **J. Manag. Stu.** 30:4 7:1993 pp.659 - 677.
4106 Markets, design, and local agglomeration — the role of the small independent retailer in the workings of the fashion system. L. Crewe; Z. Forster. **Envir. Plan. D.** 11:2 1993 pp.213 - 229.
4107 Minority contractors' views of government purchasing and procurement practices. Susan A. MacManus. **Econ. Devel. Q.** 7:1 2:1993 pp.30 - 49.
4108 Modernisation and employment: the coir industry in Kerala. T. M. Thomas Isaac; Paul van Stuijvenberg; K. N. Nair. New Delhi, Newbury Park, Calif: Sage, 1992. 249p. *ISBN: 080399446X, 8170363047. Includes bibliographical references and index. (Series:* Indo-Dutch studies on development alternatives).
4109 Multinational culture: social impacts of a global economy. Cheryl R. Lehman [Ed.]; Russell M. Moore [Ed.]. Westport, Conn: Greenwood Press, 1992. xviii, 340p. *ISBN: 0313278229. Prepared under the auspices of Hofstra University. Includes*

H: Economic life

bibliographical references and index. (*Series:* Contributions in economics and economic history).

4110 Novye predprinimateli i staraia kul'tura. *[In Russian]*; (New businessmen and old culture.). S.G. Klimova; L.V. Dunaevskii. **Sot. Issle.** 5 1993 pp.64 - 69.

4111 Occupational and industrial diversification in the United States — implications of the new spatial division of labor. Sharmistba Bagchi-Sen; Bruce Wm. Pigozzi. **Prof. Geogr.** 45:1 2:1993 pp.44 - 54.

4112 On the semiosis of corporate culture. Lise Boily. **Semiotica** 93:1/2 1993 pp.5 - 31.

4113 Opinie pracowników o procesie restrukturyzacji przedsiębiorstw przemysłowych. *[In Polish]*; (Workers' opinions about the process of restructuring industrial enterprises.). Emilia Pankowska. **Pra. Zab. Społ.** XXXV:7 7:1993 pp.30 - 37.

4114 Organization theory and the multinational corporation. Sumantra Ghoshal [Ed.]; D. Eleanor Westney [Ed.]. New York, N.Y: St. Martin's Press, 1993. xiv, 358p. *ISBN: 0312079354, 0333546229. Includes bibliographical references (p. 313-341) and index.*

4115 Organizational obstacles — links with financial performance, customer satisfaction, and job satisfaction in a service environment. Karen A. Brown; Terence R. Mitchell. **Human Relat.** 46:6 6:1993 pp.725 - 757.

4116 Ownership patterns and centralization — a China and U.S. comparison. Richard H. Hall; Shanhe Jiang; Karyn A. Loscocco; John K. Allen. **Sociol. For.** 8:4 12:1993 pp.595 - 608.

4117 Personal contacts, subcontracting linkages, and development in the Hong Kong-Zhujiang Delta region. Chi Kin Leung. **Ann. As. Am. G.** 83:2 6:1993 pp.272 - 302.

4118 Perspektivy predprinimatel'stva i privatizatsii v Rossii: politika i obshchestvennoe mnenie. *[In Russian]*; (Perspectives on entrepreneurship and privatization in Russia — policy and public opinion.). L.D. Nel'son; L.V. Babaeva; R.O. Babaev. **Sot. Issle.** 1 1993 pp.7 - 18.

4119 A political and economic case for the democratic enterprise. Samuel Bowles; Herbert Gintis. **Econ. Philos.** 9:1 4:1993 pp.75 - 100.

4120 Private Selbständigkeit in Ostdeutschland. Erste Schritte in einem neuen Forschungsfeld. *[In German]*; (Private entrepreneurship in East Germany — first steps in a new field of research.) *[Summary]*. Michael Thomas. **Soz. Welt.** 44:2 1993 pp.223 - 242.

4121 Privatisation and entrepreneurial development in Hungary — an overview. Lester Lloyd-Reason. **Slovo** 6:1 9:1993 pp.54 - 67.

4122 The producer service complex of Edmonton — the role and organization of producer services firms in a peripheral city. W.Z. Michalak; K.J. Fairburn. **Envir. Plan. A.** 25:6 6:1993 pp.761 - 777.

4123 Progress and success in the development of black-owned franchise units. Matthew C. Sonfield. **Rev. Bl. Pol. Ec.** 22:2 Fall:1993 pp.73 - 88.

4124 Public policy and employee ownership: designing economic institutions for a good society. Kieron Swaine. **Policy Sci.** 26:4 1993 pp.289 - 316.

4125 Rapid industrialization in Thailand 1986-1991. Antonia Hussey. **Geogr. Rev.** 83:1 1:1993 pp.14 - 28.

4126 Representations of restructuring in the meat-packing industry of Victoria. R. Francis. **Envir. Plan. A.** 25:12 12:1993 pp.1725 - 1742.

4127 Risky business?: youth and the enterprise culture. Robert MacDonald; Frank Coffield. London: Falmer Press, 1991. 295p. *ISBN: 1850008973, 1850008981.*

4128 Rural minority business development. Frank A. Fratoe. **Rev. Bl. Pol. Ec.** 22:2 Fall:1993 pp.41 - 72.
4129 Small business enterprise: an economic analysis. Gavin C. Reid. London, New York, N.Y: Routledge, 1993. 327p. *ISBN: 0415056810. Includes bibliographical references and index.*
4130 Small-scale manufacturing enterprises and the informal sector in a medium-sized urban center in the Philippines. H. Schneider. **Reg. Sci. Urb. Econ.** 23:1 6:1992 pp.33 - 43.
4131 The social limits of the family-operated firm in a German town — the demise of a traditional institution in the context of rapid development. Norbert Dannhaeuser. **J. Dev. Soc.** 9:1 1-4:1993 pp.11 - 32.
4132 Sociological and religious origins of the non-profit sector in Israel; *[Summary in French]*. Eliezer David Jaffe. **Int. Sociol.** 8:2 6:1993 pp.159 - 176.
4133 Sportartikelindustrie in Pakistan. *[In German]*; [Manufacture of sports equipment in Pakistan]. Jörg Zimmermann. **Geogr. Rund.** 45:11 11:1993 pp.658 - 665.
4134 Studied trust — building new forms of cooperation in a volatile economy. Charles F. Sabel. **Human Relat.** 46:9 9:1993 pp.1133 - 1170.
4135 Success patterns of Cuban-American enterprises — implications for entrepreneurial communities. Mark F. Peterson; Jaime Roquebert. **Human Relat.** 46:8 8:1993 pp.921 - 937.
4136 Systèmes productifs — les modèles en question. *[In French]*; [Productive systems — different models in the spotlight]. Pierre Veltz [Contrib.]; Philippe Zarifian [Contrib.]; Jean-Louis Laville [Contrib.]; Denis Segrestin [Contrib.]; Danièle Linhart [Contrib.]; Norbert Alter [Contrib.]; Marc Maurice [Contrib.]. **Sociol. Trav.** XXXV:1 1993 pp.3 - 98. *Collection of 6 articles.*
4137 The ties that bind. Informal and formal sector linkages in streetvending: the case of Peru's ambulantes. M. Hays-Mitchell. **Envir. Plan. A.** 25:8 8:1993 pp.1085 - 1102.
4138 Transaction cost economics and organization theory. O.E. Williamson. **Indust. Corpor. Change** 2:2 1993 pp.107 - 156.
4139 Two roads left — stategies of resistances to steel plant closings in the Monongahela valley. Sidney Plotkin; William E. Scheuerman. **R. Soc. Move. Con. Cha.** 15 1993 pp.157 - 179.
4140 Vom volkseigenen Betrieb zum Unternehmen. Transformationsprobleme betrieblicher Produkt-, Organisations- und Personalkonzepte in Ostdeutschland. *[In German]*; (From socialist company to private enterprise — some problems of transforming East European product, organizational and staffing policies.) *[Summary]*. Martin Heidenreich. **Kölner Z. Soz. Soz. psy.** 45:1 1993 pp.76 - 96.
4141 Women in business: perspectives on women entrepreneurs. Sheila Allen [Ed.]; Carole Truman [Ed.]. London, New York: Routledge, 1993. 180p. *ISBN: 0415063116. Includes bibliographical references and indexes. (Series:* Social analysis).
4142 Working for the Japanese: the economic and social consequences of Japanese investment in Wales. Jonathan Morris; Max Munday; Barry Wilkinson. London: Athlone Press, 1993. 156p. *ISBN: 0485114380. Bibliography: p.148-152.*

H: Economic life

Technology
Technologie

4143 Composing robot production systems — Japan as a flexible manufacturing system. J. Patchell. **Envir. Plan. A.** 25:7 7:1993 pp.923 - 944.

4144 The diffusion of flexible manufacturing systems in Japan, Europe and the United States. Edwin Mansfield. **Manag. Sci.** 39:2 2:1993 pp.149 - 159.

4145 Große technische Systeme und ihre gesellschaftstheoretische Bedeutung. *[In German]*; (The societal relevance of large technical systems.) *[Summary]*. Renate Mayntz. **Kölner Z. Soz. Soz. psy.** 45:1 1993 pp.97 - 108.

4146 Implementing advanced manufacturing technologies in mature industrial regions — towards a social model of technology production. Meric S. Gertler. **Reg. Stud.** 27:7 1993 pp.665 - 680.

4147 Innovation diffusion: some new technological substitution models. Vinod Kumar; Uma Kumar. **J. Math. Sociol.** 17:2-3 1992 pp.175 - 194.

4148 Innovation et organisation — deux légitimités concurrence. *[In French]*; (Innovation and organization — two competing legitimacies.) *[Summary]*; *[Summary in German]*; *[Summary in Spanish]*. Norbert Alter. **Rev. Fr. Soc.** XXXIV:2 4-6:1993 pp.175 - 197.

4149 Innovative networks and the technopolis phenomenon — the case of Sophia-Antipolis. C. Longhi; M. Quéré. **Envir. Plan. C.** 11:3 8:1993 pp.317 - 330.

4150 Knowledge in production. Jim Davis; Michael Stack. **Race Class** 34:3 1-3:1993 pp.1 - 14.

4151 Learning, trust, and technological collaboration. Mark Dodgson. **Human Relat.** 46:1 1:1993 pp.77 - 95.

4152 Models of technological change — a critical review of current knowledge. Govindan Parayil. **Hist. Technol.** 10:3 1993 pp.105 - 126.

4153 Skill, autonomy, and technological change in Canada. J. Paul Grayson. **Work Occup.** 20:1 2:1993 pp.23 - 45.

4154 A systems approach to the transfer of mutually dependent technologies. Christian N. Madu; Assumpta A. Madu. **Socio. Econ.** 27:4 1993 pp.269 - 287.

4155 Teams, markets, and systems: business innovation and information technology. Claudio Ciborra. Cambridge; New York: Cambridge University Press, 1993. 250p. *ISBN: 0521404630. Includes bibliographical references and index.*

H.5: Markets and consumption
Marchés et consommation

4156 Advertising and publicity — an information processing perspective. K.R. Lord; S. Putrevu. **J. Econ. Psyc.** 14:1 3:1993 pp.57 - 84.

4157 Aging of the population and spending patterns in Canada: 1984 and 1986; *[Summary in Italian]*. William L. Marr; Douglas Mccready. **Genus** IL:1-2 1-6:1993 pp.97 - 120.

4158 Appropriate meal occasions — understanding conventions and exploring situational influences on food choice. David Marshall. **Int. R. Ret. Dist. Res.** 3:3 7:1993 pp.279 - 301.

H: Vie économique

4159 The authority of the consumer. Russell Keat [Ed.]; Nicholas Abercrombie [Ed.]; Nigel Whiteley [Ed.]. London, New York, NY: Routledge, 1993. 281p. *ISBN: 0415089182, 0415089190. The papers presented in this volume derive from conferences and workshops organized by the Center for the Study of Cultural Values at the University of Lancaster. Includes bibliographical references and index.*

4160 Causal linkages between psychographic and demographic determinates of outshopping behaviour. Denise G. Jarratt; Michael J. Polonsky. **Int. R. Ret. Dist. Res.** 3:3 7:1993 pp.303 - 319.

4161 Chain image and store-choice modeling — the effects of income and race. A.S. Fotheringham; R. Trew. **Envir. Plan. A.** 25:2 2:1993 pp.179 - 196.

4162 Cognitive styles and personal involvement of market initiators for "healthy" food brands — implications for adoption theory. G.R. Foxall; S. Bhate. **J. Econ. Psyc.** 14:1 3:1993 pp.33 - 56.

4163 A conceptual model of retail image influences on loyalty patronage behaviour. M.Z. Osman. **Int. R. Ret. Dist. Res.** 3:2 4:1993 pp.133 - 148.

4164 Consumer behaviour in China: customer satisfaction and cultural values. Oliver H. M. Yau. New York: Routledge, 1993. 285p. *ISBN: 0415004365. Includes bibliographical references and index. (Series:* Consumer research and policy series).

4165 Consumer culture reborn: the cultural politics of consumption. Martyn J. Lee. London, New York: Routledge, 1993. 190p. *ISBN: 041508413X, 0415084148. Includes bibliographical references and index.*

4166 Consumption. Robert Bocock. New York; London: Routledge, 1993. 131p. *ISBN: 0415069629. Includes bibliographical references and index. (Series:* Key ideas).

4167 Consumption theories and consumers' assessments of subjective well-being. Maurice MacDonald; Robin A. Douthitt. **J. Consum. Aff.** 26:2 Winter:1992 pp.243 - 261.

4168 Corporate culture and shared knowledge. J. Crémer. **Indust. Corpor. Change** 2:3 1993 pp.351 - 386.

4169 Deceptive nature of dial-a-porn commercials and public policy alternative? Shaheen Borna; Joseph Chapman; Dennis Menezes. **J. Busin. Ethics** 12:7 7:1993 pp.503 - 509.

4170 Demografia, marketing e innovazione. *[In Italian]*; [Demography, marketing and innovation]. Giuseppe de Bartolo. **Aff. Soc. Int.** XXI:2 1993 pp.101 - 122.

4171 Does the career/non-career dichotomy distinguish shopping segments of working women? Marilyn Lavin. **Int. R. Ret. Dist. Res.** 3:3 7:1993 pp.321 - 340.

4172 The economic psychology of consumer debt. S.E.G. Lea; P. Webley; R.M. Levine. **J. Econ. Psyc.** 14:1 3:1993 pp.85 - 119.

4173 Effects of female adolescent locus of control on shopping behaviour, fashion orientation and information search. William K. Darley; Denise M. Johnson. **Int. R. Ret. Dist. Res.** 3:2 4:1993 pp.149 - 166.

4174 Factors affecting borrower choice between fixed and adjustable rate mortgages. Mark Lino. **J. Consum. Aff.** 26:2 Winter:1992 pp.262 - 273.

4175 Firma ishchet rynok (marketingovye issledovaniia potrebitel'skogo sprosa sotsial'nykh sloev obshchestva: teoriia i metodologiia). *[In Russian]*; [The enterprises seek the market]. Iu.V. Merkulova. **Obshch. Ekon.** 1 1993 pp.97 - 111.

4176 Follow the leader: mimetic isomorphism and entry into new markets. Heather A. Haveman. **Adm. Sci. Qua.** 38:4 12:1993 pp.593 - 627.

H: Economic life

4177 Graphical energy labels and consumers' decisions about home appliances — a process tracing approach. B. Verplanken; M.W.H. Weenig. **J. Econ. Psyc.** 14:4 12:1993 pp.739 - 752.
4178 Household finance management and the labour market — a case study in Hartlepool. Lydia Morris. **Sociol. Rev.** 41:3 8:1993 pp.506 - 536.
4179 Individual perceptions of organizational cultures — a methodological treatise on levels of analysis. Geert Hofstede; Michael Harris Bond; Chung-leung Luk. **Organ. Stud.** 14:4 1993 pp.483 - 503.
4180 The "magic of the mall" — an analysis of form, function, and meaning in the contemporary retail built economy. Jon Goss. **Ann. As. Am. G.** 83:1 3:1993 pp.18 - 47.
4181 Market niche. Ronald S. Burt; Ilan Talmud. **Soc. Networks** 15:2 6:1993 pp.133 - 149.
4182 A model of multi-purpose shopping trip behavior. Theo Arentze; Aloys Borgers; Harry Timmermans. **Pap. Reg. Sci.** 72:3 7:1993 pp.239 - 256.
4183 Modeling strategies of the spatial search problem. Harvey J. Miller. **Pap. Reg. Sci.** 72:1 1:1993 pp.63 - 85.
4184 "Numbers and souls" — retailing and the de-differentiation of economy and culture. Paul du Gay. **Br. J. Soc.** 44:4 12:1993 pp.563 - 587.
4185 Ondernemers, markt en milieu. Het lot van de T-Ford. *[In Dutch]*; (Entrepreneurs, markets and environment. The fate of the model T.) *[Summary]*. R. Stokvis. **Sociol. Gids** XL:1 1-2:1993 pp.34 - 48.
4186 Placing the market and marketing place — tourist advertising of the Hawaiian islands, 1972-92. J.D. Goss. **Envir. Plan. D.** 11:6 12:1993 pp.663 - 688.
4187 Price knowledge and search behavior for habitual, low involvement food purchases. J.T. Kujala; M.D. Johnson. **J. Econ. Psyc.** 14:2 6:1993 pp.249 - 265.
4188 The relationship between expenditure-based plans and development plans — with specific reference to housing. N. Carter [Ed.]; T. Brown [Ed.]; T. Abbott [Ed.]. **Prog. Plan.** 39:1 1993 pp.11 - 66. *Collection of 7 articles.*
4189 Shopping with Freud. Rachel Bowlby. London: Routledge, 1993. 134p. *ISBN: 0415060060.*
4190 A status-based model of market competition. Joel M. Podolny. **A.J.S.** 98:4 1:1993 pp.829 - 872.
4191 The structure and determinants of consumer complaint intentions and behavior. M.F. Maute; W.R. Forrester. **J. Econ. Psyc.** 14:2 6:1993 pp.219 - 247.
4192 Temptations: sex, selling and the department store. Gail Reekie. Sydney: Allen & Unwin, 1993. 257p. *ISBN: 1863733426. Includes bibliographical references and index. (Series:* Australian cultural studies).
4193 Time and money: the making of consumer culture. Gary S. Cross. New York, N.Y: Routledge, 1993. 294p. *ISBN: 0415070023, 0415088550. Includes bibliographical references and index.*
4194 A tournament of value — strategies of presentation in Japanese advertising. Brian Moeran. **Ethnos** 58:1-2 1993 pp.73 - 93.
4195 Transformation: die blockierten Konsumenten. *[In German]*; (Transformation: the blocked consumers.). Wolfgang Hahn. **Wissensch. Z. Humboldt-Univ.** 41:10 1992 pp.99 - 104.
4196 The use and abuse of consumer credit — application of psychological theory and research. H. Tokunaga. **J. Econ. Psyc.** 14:2 6:1993 pp.285 - 316.

4197 The world of consumption. Ben Fine; Ellen Leopold. London, New York: Routledge, 1993. 361p. *ISBN: 0415095883, 0415095891. Includes bibliographical references and index.*

H.6: Finance
Finance

4198 An analysis of small, high performing minority and nonminority banks' strategies, 1980-1988. Don P. Holdren; Jafar Alavi; Wilton E. Heyliger. **Rev. Bl. Pol. Ec.** 22:2 Fall:1993 pp.109 - 140.
4199 Children's saving: a study in the development of economic behaviour. Edmund J. S. Sonuga-Barke; Paul Webley. Hove: Lawrence Erlbaum, 1993. xii, 153p. *ISBN: 0863772331. (Series:* Essays in developmental psychology).
4200 Le contrôle de la bourse et l'incrimination du délit d'initié aux Pays-Bas. *[In French]*; [Stock market control and the accusation of initiation in the Netherlands]. John Vervaele. **Rev. Sci. Crim. D. P.** 1 1-3:1993 pp.1 - 18.
4201 From redlining to reinvestment: community responses to urban disinvestment. Gregory D. Squires [Ed.]. Philadelphia: Temple University Press, 1992. viii, 288p. *ISBN: 0877229848. Includes bibliographical references. (Series:* Conflicts in urban and regional development).
4202 A geography of institutional stock ownership in the United States. Milford B. Green. **Ann. As. Am. G.** 83:1 3:1993 pp.66 - 89.
4203 How well is debt managed by nonprofits? Howard P. Tuckman; Cyril F. Chang. **Non. Manag. Leader.** 3:4 Summer:1993 pp.347 - 361.
4204 Information in the marketplace — media explanations of the '87 crash. Kee Warner; Harvey Molotch. **Soc. Prob.** 40:2 5:1993 pp.167 - 188.
4205 Institutional investment patterns in troubled corporations — a sociological analysis. R. Eckstein; K. Delaney. **Am. J. Econ. S.** 52:3 7:1993 pp.291 - 306.
4206 Modernisation, conflit et inflation. Notes sur le cas brésilien. *[In French]*; [Modernization, conflict and inflation. Notes on the case of Brazil]; *[Summary in Spanish]*. Fabio S.A. Earp. **Cah. Amer. Lat.** 15 1993 pp.5 - 22.
4207 The performance of minority banks in a deregulated banking environment. Don P. Holdren; Wilton E. Heyliger. **Rev. Bl. Pol. Ec.** 22:2 Fall:1993 pp.89 - 108.
4208 Savers and borrowers — strategies of personal financial management. S. Livingstone; P. Lunt. **Human Relat.** 46:8 8:1993 pp.963 - 985.
4209 The state and fiscal sociology. John L. Campbell. **Ann. R. Soc.** 19 1993 pp.163 - 186.

H.7: Economic policy and planning
Politique économique et planification

4210 Ajustements et démocratisation en Afrique francophone. *[In French]*; (Adjustments and democratization in Francophone Africa.). Myriam Gervais [Ed.]; Raymond R. Gervais [Ed.]; Kengne Fodouop; Tiékoura Koné; Bonnie Campbell; Suzanne Dansereau. **Labour Cap. Soc.** 26:1 4:1993 pp.7 - 127. *Collection of 8 articles.*

H: Economic life

4211 Aufbau ohne fremde Hilfe. Die iranische Aufbauorganisation Gehād e Sāzandegi. *[In German]*; (Reconstruction without foreign assistance. The Iranian Reconstruction Organization Gehād e Sāzandegi.) *[Summary]*. Shahnaz Nadjmabadi. **Sociologus** 43:2 1993 pp.168 - 182.

4212 Community controversy and the adoption of economic development policies. Todd Donovan. **Soc. Sci. Q.** 74:2 6:1993 pp.386 - 402.

4213 Contradictions and limits of a developmental state — with illustrations from the South Korean case. Eun Mee Kim. **Soc. Prob.** 40:2 5:1993 pp.228 - 249.

4214 Cuestiones de estados. *[In Spanish]*; [Questions of state]. María Eugenia Caumel [Ed.]; Francisco Comín [Contrib.]; José A. García Durán [Contrib.]; Joan Subirats [Contrib.]; Carlos Rodríguez Braun [Contrib.]; Matilde Mas [Contrib.]; Francisco Pérez [Contrib.]; Joan Esteban [Contrib.]. **Infor. Com. Esp.** 712 12:1992 pp.3 - 58. *Collection of 7 articles.*

4215 Decentralised planning: the Karnataka experiment. Abdul Aziz. New Delhi, London: Sage, 1993. 148p. *ISBN: 0803991134, 817036339X.*

4216 Economic reforms in Poland — the dilemma of privatization or partition. Edward K. Zajicek; James B. Heisler. **Int. J. Pol. C. S.** 7:1 Fall:1993 pp.19 - 42.

4217 High-technology industries as a vehicle for growth in Israel's peripheral regions. D. Shefer; E.(Lambert) Bar-El. **Envir. Plan. C.** 11:3 8:1993 pp.245 - 261.

4218 Historia y planificación regional — un encuentro posible. *[In Spanish]*; [History and regional planning — a possible meeting]. Susana Bandieri. **Rev. Int.Am. Plan.** XXVI:101-102 1-6:1993 pp.78 - 94.

4219 Die Kulturalisierung der Regionalpolitik. *[In German]*; [The culturalization of regional policy]. Hartmut Häußermann; Walter Siebel. **Geogr. Rund.** 45:4 4:1993 pp.218 - 223.

4220 The main approaches to measuring regional development and welfare. Gabriel Lipshitz. **Soc. Ind.** 29:2 6:1993 pp.163 - 181.

4221 Marxisms, modernities, and moralities — development praxis and the claims of distant strangers. S. Corbridge. **Envir. Plan. D.** 11:4 8:1993 pp.449 - 472.

4222 Migrační atraktivita v regionálním pohledu (okresy ČR v letech 1961-1991). *[In Czech]*; (Migration attractiveness in regional aspects (districts of the Czech Republic in 1961-1991).) *[Summary]*; *[Summary in Russian]*. Dagmar Bartoňová; Dušan Drbohlav. **Demografie** XXXV:2 1993 pp.95 - 107.

4223 Parametros sociales para la planificación en Colombia. *[In Spanish]*; [Social parameters for planning in Colombia]. Curtis R. Glick. **Rev. Int.Am. Plan.** XXVI:101-102 1-6:1993 pp.95 - 111.

4224 Regional aspects of economic restructuring in the former Soviet Union. Mikhail I. Popov [Ed.]; William N. Trumbull [Ed.]; Leonard A. Kozlov [Contrib.]; Boris M. Shtoulberg [Contrib.]; Nikolai G. Chumachenko [Contrib.]; Sergey I. Doroguntsov [Contrib.]; Vladimir F. Onishchenko; Ruvin I. Shnieper [Contrib.]; Oleg S. Pchelintsev [Contrib.]; William Alonso [Contrib.]; Boris Pleskovic [Contrib.]. **Int. Reg. Sci. R.** 15:3 1993 pp.229 - 315. *Collection of 9 articles.*

4225 Rethinking regional planning. Frank J. Popper. **Society** 30:6 9-10:1993 pp.46 - 54.

4226 Science parks — a critical assessment. Hooshang Amirahmadi; Grant Saff. **J. Plan. Lit.** 8:2 11:1993 pp.107 - 123.

4227 SotsioEkonomicheskie zakony i reforma v Rossii. *[In Russian]*; (Social and economic laws and the reform in Russia.). D. Tenivik. **Svobod. Mysl'** 6 4:1993 pp.10 - 24.

4228 Spatial inequalities in Sandinista Nicaragua. David L. Wall. **Geogr. Rev.** 83:1 1:1993 pp.1 - 13.
4229 State autonomy and structural constraints — software wars in Brazil. Sara Schoonmaker. **Crit. Sociol.** 19:1 pp.3 - 18.
4230 Thirty years of Spanish regional change — interregional dynamics and sectoral transformation. Luis Suarez-Villa; Juan R. Cuadrado Roura. **Int. Reg. Sci. R.** 15:2 1993 pp.121 - 156.
4231 Tragfähigkeitsveränderung durch Bevölkerungsverlust. *[In German]*; [The capacity for change through a reduction of population numbers]. Peter M. Müller. **Geogr. Rund.** 45:3 3:1993 pp.173 - 179.
4232 The utility of impulse response functions in regional analysis — some critical issues. Jeff B. Cromwell; Michael J. Hannan. **Int. Reg. Sci. R.** 15:2 1993 pp.199 - 222.
4233 Wealth or poverty?: critical choices for South Africa. Robert A. Schrire [Ed.]. Oxford: Oxford Universtiy Press, 1992. 680p. *ISBN: 0195706439*. (*Series:* Contemporary South African debates).

I: LABOUR
TRAVAIL

I.1: Sociology of industry and work
Sociologie de l'industrie et du travail

4234 Beyond industrial sociology: the work of men and women. Claire Williams; Billy Thorpe. North Sydney, NSW, Australia: Allen & Unwin, 1992. 286p. *ISBN: 1863730842*. *Includes bibliographical references (p. 248-271) and index*. (Series: Studies in society).

4235 Deadlock, lock-out or reconciliation? Industrial psychology and industrial relations. C.M. Tustin. **Ind. Rel. J. S.Afr.** 12:1/2 1992 pp.37 - 46.

4236 Different trajectories in the social divisions of labour: the cutlery industry in Sheffield, England, and Tsubame, Japan. Roger Hayter; Jerry Patchell. **Urban Stud.** 30:8 10:1993 pp.1427 - 1446.

4237 L'emploi, l'entreprise et la société: débats économie-sociologie. *[In French]*; [Employment, the enterprise and society: socio-economic debates]. François Michon [Ed.]; Denis Segrestin [Ed.]. Paris: Economica, 1990. 301p. *ISBN: 2717820000*. *MIRE. Ministère du Travail, de la formation professionnnelle et de l'emploi, France*.

4238 Gender inequality and industrial development — the household connection; *[Summary in French]*; *[Summary in Spanish]*. Gay Young. **J. Comp. Fam. Stud.** XXIV:1 Spring:1993 pp.1 - 20.

4239 Die Rationalität von Rationalisierung: betrieblicher Wandel und die Industriesoziologie. *[In German]*; [The rationality of rationalization: change within enterprises and industrial sociology]. Heiner Minssen. Stuttgart: Ferdinand Enke Verlag, 1992. 137p. *ISBN: 3432251211*. *Includes index and bibliography*.

4240 The sociology of work and occupations. Andrew Abbott. **Ann. R. Soc.** 19 1993 pp.187 - 210.

4241 Socjologia pracy — kilka refleksji. *[In Polish]*; (Some reflections on sociology of work.) *[Summary]*. Piotr Tobera. **Prz. Soc.** XL 1993 pp.85 - 94.

I.2: Employment and labour market
Emploi et marché du travail

4242 Affirmative action during the transition: some practical suggestions. Linda Human. **Ind. Soc. Rel.** 13:3-4 1993 pp.125 - 138.

4243 Bargaining success of Chinese factories. Kevin O'Brien. **China Quart.** 132 12:1992 pp.1086 - 1100.

4244 Bauarbeiter aus der DDR: eine empirische Untersuchung über gruppenspezifische Merkmale bei Flüchtlingen und Übersiedlern der Jahre 1989 und 1990. *[In German]*; [Construction workers from the GDR: an empirical investigation on group characteristics of refugees and immigrants in 1989 and 1990]. Peter Brenske. Berlin: Duncker & Humblot, 1992. 273p. *ISBN: 3428073215*. *Includes bibliographical references and index*.

4245 Beschäftigungspolitische Konzeptionen verschiedener gesellschaftlicher Gruppen in Frankreich: eine Analyse der theoretischen Grundlagen und der Auswirkungen auf den Arbeitsmarkt. *[In German]*; [Employment policy's concepts of different social groups in France: an analysis of theoretical principles and effects on the labour market]. Mirjam Nauschütz. Pfaffenweiler: Centaurus, 1992. 307p. *ISBN: 3890856659*.

4246 Black-white wage differential — the relative importance of human capital and labor market structure. Kwabena Gyimah-Brempong; Rudy Fichtenbaum. **Rev. Bl. Pol. Ec.** 21:4 Spring:1993 pp.19 - 52.

4247 Citizenship and employment: investigating post-industrial options. Jocelyn Pixley. Cambridge, New York: Cambridge University Press, 1993. vii, 229p. *ISBN: 0521417937, 0521446155. Includes bibliographical references and index.*

4248 Culture or society? A research report on work-related values in the two Germanies. Bernhard Wilpert; Hans Maimer. **Soc. Sci. Info.** 32:2 1993 pp.259 - 278.

4249 Differentiation of life courses? Changing patterns of labour market sequences in West Germany. Peter A. Berger; Peter Steinmüller; Peter Sopp. **Eur. Sociol. R.** 9:1 5:1993 pp.43 - 61.

4250 Dilemmas in tackling child labour — the case of scavenger children in the Philippines. Susan E. Gunn; Zenaida Ostos. **Int. Lab. Rev.** 131:6 1992 pp.629 - 646.

4251 Does the targeted jobs tax credit create jobs at subsidized firms? John H. Bishop; Mark Montgomery. **Ind. Relat.** 32:3 Fall:1993 pp.289 - 306.

4252 East Asia labour market symposium. Alan Williams [Ed.]; Yoko Sano [Contrib.]; Yoshio Sasajima [Contrib.]; Malcolm Warner [Contrib.]; Lynn McFarlane Shore [Contrib.]; Bruce W. Eagle [Contrib.]; Michael Jay Jedel [Contrib.]; Chimezie A.B. Osigweh [Contrib.]; Yg Huo [Contrib.]; Y. Paul Huo [Contrib.]; Zhong-Ming Wang [Contrib.]; Frank A. Heller [Contrib.]; Maragtas S.V. Amante [Contrib.]; Stephen Chiu [Contrib.]; David A. Levin [Contrib.]; Samuel Aryee [Contrib.]; Yaw A. Debrah [Contrib.]; Yue Wah Chay [Contrib.]; Irene K.H. Chew [Contrib.]; Albert C.Y. Teo [Contrib.]. **Int. J. Hum. Res. Man.** 4:1 2:1993 pp.11 - 240. *Collection of 11 articles.*

4253 The economic problems of disabled people. Richard Berthoud; Jane Lakey; Stephen McKay. London: Policy Studies Institute, 1993. 139p. *ISBN: 085374551X. (Series:* PSI research report).

4254 Economics of seasonal migration. D. V. Kasar. New Delhi: Classical Pub. Co, 1992. 220p. *ISBN: 8170541727*.

4255 Edad, empleo y jubilación — nuevos datos internacionales. *[In Spanish]*; [Age, employment and retirement — new international data] *[Summary]*; *[Summary in Catalan]*. Anne-Marie Guillemard. **Papers** 40 1993 pp.35 - 56.

4256 Employment equity goal setting and external availability data. Edward B. Harvey; John H. Blakely. **Soc. Ind.** 28:3 3:1993 pp.245 - 266.

4257 Employment legislation — Thatcher and after. Kenneth Miller; Mairi Steele. **Ind. Relat. J.** 24:3 9:1993 pp.224 - 235.

4258 Equal opportunity law and the construction of internal labor markets. Frank Dobbin; John R. Sutton; John W. Meyer; W. Richard Scott. **A.J.S.** 99:2 9:1993 pp.396 - 427.

4259 L'exemple de jeunes en emploi précaire face aux politiques sociales. *[In French]*; (The social construction of transition periods: young people in precarious employment and social policies.) *[Summary]*. Laurence Roulleau-Berger. **Soc. Contemp.** 14/15 6-9:1993 pp.191 - 209.

4260 The "flexible firm" — strategy and segmentation. Laurie Hunter; Alan McGregor; John MacInnes; Alan Sproull. **Br. J. Ind. R.** 31:3 9:1993 pp.383 - 407.

I: Labour

4261 Formirovanie rynka truda i politika zaniatosti v Vostochnoi Evrope. *[In Russian]*; (Creation of a labour market and employment policy in Eastern Europe.). S. Glinkina; N. Kulikova; I. Sintsina. **Mir. Ekon. Mezh. Otno.** 11 1993 pp.26 - 38.

4262 From bureaucrat to professional: skill and work in the Commonwealth employment service. Glenda Maconachie. **J. Ind. Relat.** 35:2 6:1993 pp.221 - 241.

4263 The gender and race composition of jobs and the male/female, white/black pay gaps. Donald Tomaskovic-Devey. **Soc. Forc.** 72:1 9:1993 pp.45 - 76.

4264 A human capital policy for the cities. Nathan Glazer. **Publ. Inter.** 112 Summer:1993 pp.27 - 49.

4265 Human resources development in Sri Lanka — a sociological perspective. S.T. Hettige. **Sri Lanka J. Soc. Sci.** 14:1-2 6-12:1991 pp.49 - 64.

4266 The implications of work force diversification in the U.S. forest service. Greg Brown; Charles C. Harris. **Admin. Soc.** 25:1 5:1993 pp.85 - 113.

4267 L'informazione statistica per il monitoraggio e la valutazione degli interventi di politica del lavoro. *[In Italian]*; (Statistical information for the monitoring and evaluation of labour policy measures.) *[Summary]*. Alberto Martini; Pietro Garibaldi. **Ec. Lav.** XXVII:1 1-3:1993 pp.3 - 22.

4268 International employment contracts — the applicable law. Raymond Smith; Valerie Cromack. **Ind. Law J.** 22:1 3:1993 pp.1 - 13.

4269 Job mobility in post-Mao cities — increases on the margins. Deborah Davis. **China Quart.** 132 12:1992 pp.1062 - 1085.

4270 Kapitalizm i rabochii klass na poroge XXI veka: opyt kompleksnogo issledovaniia. *[In Russian]*; [Capitalism and the working class on the eve of the 21 century: the evidence of complex research]. Oleg Ivanovich Grigor'ev. Leningrad: Izd-vo Leningradskogo universiteta, 1991. 209p. *ISBN: 5288005656.*

4271 Die Krise der Datenverarbeitungs-Industrie. *[In German]*; [The crisis of the data processing industry]. Klaus-Dieter Bornemann. **Marx. Blät** 31:4 7-8:1993 pp.38 - 44.

4272 Labor market tightness and business confidence — an international comparison. Christopher Heye. **Polit. Soc.** 21:2 6:1993 pp.169 - 193.

4273 Labour institutions and economic growth — a survey and a "regulationist" approach. Robert Boyer. **Labour [Italy]** 7:1 Spring:1993 pp.25 - 72.

4274 Die Lebens- und Arbeitsbedingungen deutscher Firmenvertreter in Rußland. *[In German]*; (Living and working conditions of German business representatives in Russia.) *[Summary]*. Frank Gieth; Bernd Knabe. **Ost. Wirt.** 38:2 6:1993 pp.160 - 170.

4275 Literacy, socialisation and employment. Catherine Stercq. Bristol, Pennsylvania: J. Kingsley Publishers, 1993. 103p. *ISBN: 1853022098. UNESCO Institute for Education.*

4276 "The long-averted clash": farm labour competition in the South African countryside. Jonathan Crush. **Can. J. Afr. St.** 27:3 1993 pp.404 - 423.

4277 Manufacturing consent and resistance in peripheral production: the labor process among Egyptian migrant workers and Egyptian national development. James Toth. **Dialect. Anthrop.** 18:3-4 12:1993 pp.291 - 336.

4278 Married couples and their labour market status. Kène Henkens; Gerbert Kraaykamp; Jacques Siegers. **Eur. Sociol. R.** 9:1 5:1993 pp.67 - 78.

I: Travail

4279 Mercado de trabajo juvenil y políticas de empleo. *[In Spanish]*; [The youth labour market and employment policy] *[Summary]*; *[Summary in Catalan]*. Enric Sanchis. **Papers** 39 1992 pp.59 - 76.

4280 Mismatch in the Spanish labor market — overeducation? Alfonso Alba-Ramírez. **J. Hum. Res.** XXVIII:2 Spring:1993 pp.259 - 278.

4281 Mobilität und Diskriminierung: deutsche und ausländische Arbeiter auf einem betrieblichen Arbeitsmarkt. *[In German]*; [Mobility and discrimination: German and foreign workers in a company's labour market]. Hans Grüner. Frankfurt am Main: Campus-Verlag, 1992. 288p. *ISBN: 3593345617*.

4282 Movilidad en el empleo — una comparación de trabajo asalariado y por cuenta propia en Puebla. *[In Spanish]*; [Mobility in employment — a comparison of wage earning work and self-employment in Puebla] *[Summary]*. Ludger Pries. **Est. Sociol.** XI:32 5-8:1993 pp.475 - 496.

4283 Organizacja rynku pracy w Polsce. *[In Polish]*; (Organization of labour market in Poland.). Halina Mortimer-Szymczak. **Pra. Zab. Społ.** XXXV:5-6 5-6:1993 pp.1 - 11.

4284 Part-time employment and the utilisation of labour resources. Lei Delsen. **Labour [Italy]** 7:3 Autumn:1993 pp.73 - 91.

4285 Perceptions des difficultés d'insertion en emploi et raisons de fin d'emploi — les cas du Québec et du Canada. *[In French]*; [Perceptions of the difficulties of entering work and reasons for leaving work — the cases of Quebec and Canada] *[Summary]*. Guy Fréchet. **Can. R. Soc. A.** 30:4 11:1993 pp.468 - 487.

4286 Politics, pragmatism and ideology — the "wellsprings" of conservative union legislation (1979-1992). Patricia Fosh; Huw Morris; Roderick Martin; Paul Smith; Roger Undy. **Ind. Law J.** 22:1 3:1993 pp.14 - 31.

4287 Procesy zmian dynamiki i struktury zatrudnienia i płac w 1992 roku (I). *[In Polish]*; (Changes of dynamic and structure of employment and wages in 1992 (I).). Wiesław Krencik. **Pra. Zab. Społ.** XXXV:8 8:1993 pp.20 - 32.

4288 Procesy zmian dynamiki i struktury zatrudnienia i płac w 1992 roku (II). *[In Polish]*; (Changes of dynamic and structure of employment and wages in 1992 (II).). Wiesław Krencik. **Pra. Zab. Społ.** XXXV:9 9:1993 pp.7 - 20.

4289 Projection of the Mexican national labor force, 1980-2005. James B. Pick; Edgar W. Butler; Raul Gonzalez Ramirez. **Soc. Biol.** 40:3-4 Fall-winter:1993 pp.161 - 190.

4290 The psychological impact of merger and acquisition on the individual — a study of building society managers. Sue Cartwright; Cary L. Cooper. **Human Relat.** 46:3 3:1993 pp.327 - 347.

4291 Rynok truda v Rossii: regulirovanie, prognozy. *[In Russian]*; [The labour market in Russia — regulation and forecasts]. A. Kashenov. **Ekonomist** 3 3:1993 pp.59 - 68.

4292 Segregated and integrated occupations — a new approach to analysing social change. Catherine Hakim; Martin Watts [Comments by]; Catherine Hakim [Comments by]. **Eur. Sociol. R.** 9:3 12:1993 pp.289 - 324.

4293 Self employment: a selected annotated bibliography. Madhuri Bose; International Labour Office; Aurelio Parisotto. Geneva: International Labour Office, 1991. 39p. *ISBN: 922107899X*.

4294 Self-employment — a study of seventeen OECD countries. Udo Staber; Dieter Bögenhold. **Ind. Relat. J.** 24:2 6:1993 pp.126 - 137.

4295 Shafted — the social impact of down-scaling on the free state goldfields. Gay W. Seidman. **S.Afr. Sociol. R.** 5:(2) 4:1993 pp.14 - 34.

I: Labour

4296 The social dimension after Maastricht: setting a new agenda for the labour market. Martin Rhodes. **Int. J. Comp. L. L. I. R.** 9:4 Winter:1993 pp.297 - 325.
4297 Socio-economic determinants of labour mobility in Pakistan. Ather Maqsood Ahmed; Ismail Sirageldin. **Pak. Dev. R.** 32:2 Summer:1993 pp.139 - 158.
4298 Socio-economic profile of child workers of hosiery industries in Tirupur Town, Tamil Nadu. T.V. Yamuna; N. Jaya. **Man India** 73:2 6:1993 pp.151 - 162.
4299 The sources of suburban employment growth. Sammis B. White; Lisa S. Binkley; Jeffrey D. Osterman. **J. Am. Plann.** 59:2 Spring:1993 pp.193 - 204.
4300 Sovremennye trebovaniia trudiashchikhsia k sotsial'no-ekonomicheskoi politike. *[In Russian]*; (Present-day demands of working people to social and economic policy.). G. Rakitskaya. **Vop. Ekon.** 4 1993 pp.64 - 76.
4301 Szara sfera rynku pracy w Polsce (I). *[In Polish]*; (A shadowy labour market in Poland (I).). Henryk Zarychta. **Pra. Zab. Społ.** XXXV:12 12:1993 pp.10 - 22.
4302 Tehnološke promjene i njihov utjecaj na razvitak ljudskih potencijala. *[In Serbo-Croatian (Roman)]*; (Technological changes and their influence upon human potentials.) *[Summary]*; *[Summary in Russian]*. Mira Lenardić. **Ekon. Preg.** 44:5-6 1993 pp.358 - 371.
4303 Trayectorias laborales y constitución de identidades — los trabajadores indígenas en la ciudad de Guatemala. *[In Spanish]*; [Labour trajectories and constitution of identities — indigenous workers in Guatemala City] *[Summary]*. Juan Pablo Pérez Sáinz; Manuela Camus; Santiago Bastos. **Est. Sociol.** XI:32 5-8:1993 pp.515 - 546.
4304 Trud: gde glavnaia tochka otscheta? *[In Russian]*; (Labour — where is the crucial point?). V.D. Ozmitin. **Sot. Issle.** 3 1993 pp.21 - 29.
4305 The use of Chinese rural labour resources and its impact on the rural environment; *[Summary in French]*. Lu Xueyi. **Int. Sociol.** 8:2 6:1993 pp.227 - 237.
4306 Vieillir en emploi. *[In French]*; [Getting old in employment]. Rodrigue Blouin [Ed.]; et al. Sainte-Foy: Département des relations industrielles de l'Université Laval, 1991. xii, 199p. *ISBN: 2763772714. 46th Conference of industrial relations at Lavel University, 1991].*
4307 Vstuplenie novykh pokolenii v trudovuiu zhizn' v usloviiakh politicheskikh i sotsial'no-ekonomicheskikh reform. *[In Russian]*; [A new generation of workers enters the world of employment in the conditions of political and socio-economic reform]. V. N. Shubkin [Ed.]. Moscow: Institut sravnitel'noi politologii i problem rabochego dvizheniia RAN, 1992. 199p.
4308 What about the workers?: workers and the transition to capitalism in Russia. Simon Clarke. London: Verso, 1993. 248p. *ISBN: 086091402X.*
4309 Who is fed-up working, and why: employment in Ashkelon. Gideon M. Kressel. **East. Anthrop.** 46:4 10-12:1993 pp.341 - 370.

Gender issues
Questions de sexe

4310 Agricultural restructuring and the spatial dynamics of U.S. women's employment in the 1970s. Irene Padavic. **Rural Sociol.** 58:2 Summer:1993 pp.210 - 232.
4311 The Australian government's affirmative action legislation: achieving social change through human resource management. Valerie Braithwaite. **Law Policy** 15:4 10:1993 pp.327 - 354.

I: Travail

4312 Bezrobotne kobiety w Polsce: fakty i opinie. *[In Polish]*; (Unemployed women in Poland: facts and opinions.). Krystyna Kluzowa; Krystyna Slany. **Pra. Zab. Społ.** XXXV:12 12:1993 pp.31 - 36.

4313 Bijstandsvrouwen en de arbeidsmarkt. *[In Dutch]*; (Women on welfare and the labour market.) *[Summary]*. Rudi Wielers; Jolanda Tuinstra; Rie Borman. **Sociol. Gids** 40:4 7-8:1993 pp.320 - 332.

4314 Day care in Europe and mothers' forgone earnings. Heather Joshi; Hugh Davies. **Int. Lab. Rev.** 131:6 1992 pp.561 - 579.

4315 De arbeidsparticipatie van de gehuwde vrouw en de gezinsopbouw — gedragen Nederlandse vrouwen zich anders dan Vlaamse vrouwen? *[In Dutch]*; [Work participation of the married woman and family structure — do Dutch women behave differently to Flemish women]. Noortje Mertens; Peter van der Meer; Joop Schippers; Jacques Siegers. **Bevolk. Gez.** 3 1992 pp.105 - 129.

4316 De culturele en economische dimensie van beroepen — een nieuw meetinstrument voor de beroepsstatus van mannen en vrouwen. *[In Dutch]*; (The cultural and economic dimensions of occupations — a new measure for male and female occupational status.) *[Summary]*. A. Blees-Booij. **Mens Maat.** 68:2 5:1993 pp.153 - 174.

4317 De invloed van de geboorte van kinderen op veranderingen in de arbeids- en wooncarrière. *[In Dutch]*; (The influence of childbirth on changes in the labour market and careers.) *[Summary]*. Ronald Camstra. **Bevolk. Gez.** 2 1993 pp.43 - 63.

4318 The decision to work by married immigrant women. Harriet Orcutt Duleep; Seth Sanders. **Ind. Lab. Rel.** 46:4 7:1993 pp.677 - 690.

4319 The economics of equal value. Jill Rubery. **Labour [Italy]** 7:3 Autumn:1993 pp.117 - 131.

4320 Employment after childbearing in post-war Britain — cohort-study evidence on contrasts within and across generations. Heather Joshi; P.R. Andrew Hinde. **Eur. Sociol. R.** 9:3 12:1993 pp.203 - 227.

4321 Equal pay and the value of work in industrialized countries. François Eyraud. **Int. Lab. Rev.** 132:1 1993 pp.33 - 48.

4322 Family and labour in the Low Countries. Roel Jansweijer [Contrib.]; Walter van Dongen [Contrib.]; Dorien Manting [Contrib.]; Anton Kuijsten [Contrib.]; Janneke Helleman [Contrib.]; Kène Henkens [Contrib.]; Jacques Siegers; Karel van den Bosch [Contrib.]; Janneke Plantenga [Contrib.]; Bea Cantillon [Contrib.]; Yolanda Grift [Contrib.]. **Bevolk. Gez.** 1 1992 pp.1 - 125. *Collection of 9 articles.*

4323 Female labour supply in farm households — farm and off-farm participation. Tim Callan; Arthur van Soest. **Econ. Soc. R.** 24:4 7:1993 pp.313 - 334.

4324 Femmes au travail: l'introuvable égalité? *[In French]*; (Women at work in search of equality.). Michèle Ferrand [Ed.]; Pierre Merle; Raymond Magro; Nicky le Feuvre; Patricia Walters; Anne-Marie Rieu; Bernard Zarca; Jacqueline Martin; Anne-Marie Daune-Richard; Cécile Brossollet. **Soc. Contemp.** 16 12:1993 pp.5 - 164. *Collection of 9 articles.*

4325 French and British mothers at work. Shirley Dex; Patricia Walters; David M. Alden. Basingstoke: Macmillan, 1993. 213p. *ISBN: 0333582330.*

4326 Gender and economic outcomes — the role of wage structure. Francine D. Blau. **Labour [Italy]** 7:1 Spring:1993 pp.73 - 92.

4327 Gender and the effects of demographics, status, and work values on work centrality. Bilha Mannheim. **Work Occup.** 20:1 2:1993 pp.3 - 22.

I: Labour

4328 Gender and the labour market in Europe — Britain, Germany and France compared. Christel Lane. **Sociol. Rev.** 41:2 5:1993 pp.274 - 301.

4329 Gender, contracts and wage work — agricultural restructuring in Brazil's São Francisco valley. Jane L. Collins. **Develop. Cha.** 24:1 1:1993 pp.53 - 82.

4330 Gender differences in occupational mobility and structure of employment in the British Civil Service. Ron Roberts; Eric Brunner; Ian White; Michael Marmot. **Soc. Sci. Med.** 37:12 12:1993 pp.1415 - 1425.

4331 Gender differences in organizational commitment — influences of work positions and family roles. Peter V. Marsden; Arne L. Kalleberg; Cynthia R. Cook. **Work Occup.** 20:3 8:1993 pp.368 - 390.

4332 Le harcèlement sexuel au travail: le régime juridique de protection. *[In French]*; [Sexual harassment at work: the legal system of protection]. Maurice Drapeau. Cowansville, Quebec: D'Editions Y. Blais, 1991. 213p. *ISBN: 2890737616. Includes several passages in English. Commission des droits de la personne du Québec.*

4333 The illusions of comparable worth. Gabriël Moens; Suri Ratnapala. St. Leonards, N.S.W: Centre for Independent Studies, 1992. xvi, 106p. *ISBN: 0949769762. Bibliography: p.99-103; includes index. (Series:* CIS policy monographs).

4334 Japanese women working. Janet Hunter [Ed.]. London, New York: Routledge, 1993. 245p. *ISBN: 0415061881. Includes bibliographical references and index.*

4335 Labour force participation and the growth of women's employment, Ireland 1971-1991. Brendan M. Walsh. **Econ. Soc. R.** 24:4 7:1993 pp.369 - 400.

4336 The labour market for women and employment perspectives in the aftermath of German unification. Friederike Maier. **Camb. J. Econ.** 17:3 9:1993 pp.267 - 280.

4337 The labour supply of married and cohabiting women in the Netherlands, 1981-1989. Kène Henkens; Liana Meijer; Jacques Siegers. **Eur. J. Pop.** 9:4 1993 pp.331 - 352.

4338 Maternity issues in the Natal textile industry. Carmel R. Matthias. **Ind. Soc. Rel.** 13:3-4 1993 pp.157 - 172.

4339 Men's participation in child care and women's work attachment. David J. Maume; Karen R. Mullin. **Soc. Prob.** 40:4 11:1993 pp.533 - 546.

4340 Multiple gender contexts and employee rewards. Patricia Yancey Martin; Steve Harkreader. **Work Occup.** 20.3 8.1993 pp.296 - 336.

4341 On the question of the feminization of production on part-time farms — evidence from Norway. Arild Blekesaune; Wava G. Haney; Marit S. Haugen. **Rural Sociol.** 58:1 Spring:1993 pp.111 - 129.

4342 Opleiding en verschillen in arbeidsmarktparticipatie en vruchtbaarheidsgedrag van vrouwen. *[In Dutch]*; (Education and differences in female labour force participation and fertility behaviour.) *[Summary]*. Rina F. de Vries. **Bevolk. Gez.** 1 1993 pp.45 - 63.

4343 Part-time work and child care choices for mothers of preschoolers. K. Folk; A. Beller. **J. Marriage Fam.** 55:1 2:1993 pp.146 - 157.

4344 Le passage à la retraite d'une génération féminine: une projection par simulation individuelle. *[In French]*; (The transition to retirement of a female cohort. A projection by individual simulation.) *[Summary]*. Sophie Pennec. **Population** 48:3 5-6:1993 pp.655 - 682.

4345 Pay differences among the highly paid — the male-female earnings gap in lawyers' salaries. Robert G. Wood; Mary E. Corcoran; Paul N. Courant. **J. Labor Ec.** 11:3 7:1993 pp.417 - 441.

4346 Les programmes d'accès à l'égalité en emploi. *[In French]*; [Programmes for equality in employment]. Lucie Lamarche. Montreal: L. Courteau, 1990. 264p. *ISBN: 2892391180. Some works in English. Bibliographic references.*

4347 Sex discrimination and occupational segregation in the Australian labour market. Michael P. Kidd. **Econ. Rec.** 69:204 3:1993 pp.44 - 55.

4348 Sexual harassment: legal redress for the victim and the need for company policies. Lisa Dancaster. **Ind. Soc. Rel.** 13:3-4 1993 pp.145 - 156.

4349 A simple model for interpreting cross-tabulations of family size and women's labour force participation; *[Summary in French]*. Didier Blanchet; Sophie Pennec. **Eur. J. Pop.** 9:2 1993 pp.121 - 142.

4350 Slouching towards equality — gender discrimination, market efficiency, and social change. Edward J. McCaffery. **Yale Law J.** 103:3 12:1993 pp.595 - 675.

4351 Sozialarbeit, ein deutscher Frauenberuf: Kontinuitäten und Brüche in 20. Jahrhundert. *[In German]*; [Social work, a career for German women: continuity and disruption in the 20th century]. Verena Fesel [Ed.]; Barbara Rose [Ed.]; Monika Simmel [Ed.]. Pfaffenweiler: Centaurus, 1992. 122p. *ISBN: 3890856357. Papers from a conference held in 1991. Includes bibliographical references.*

4352 Suburban pink collar ghettos — the spatial entrapment of women? Kim V.L. England. **Ann. As. Am. G.** 83:2 6:1993 pp.225 - 242.

4353 Sugar and spice and everything nice — health effects of the sexual division of labor among train cleaners. Karen Messing; Ghislaine Doniol-Shaw; Chantal Haëntjens. **Int. J. Health. Ser.** 23:1 1993 pp.133 - 146.

4354 Sytuacja kobiet na brytyjskim rynku pracy. *[In Polish]*; (Situation of women on British labour market.). Jadwiga Florczak-Bywalec. **Acta Univ. Łódz.** 130 1993 pp.47 - 62.

4355 Theoretical and measurement issues in the study of sex segregation in the workplace — research note. Jerry A. Jacobs. **Eur. Sociol. R.** 9:3 12:1993 pp.325 - 330.

4356 Le travail au féminin: analyse démographique de la discontinuité professionnelle des femmes au Canada. *[In French]*; [Women workers: demographic analysis of the professional discontinuity of women in Canada]. Marianne Kempeneers. Montreal: Presses de l'Université de Montréal, 1992. 216p. *ISBN: 2760615456.*

4357 Union views of women as management negotiators. D.S. Maloon; J.T. Cook. **S. Afr. J. Labour Relat.** 17:3 9:1993 pp.12 - 30.

4358 We're worth it: women and collective action in the insurance workplace. Cynthia Butler Costello. Urbana: Illinois University Press, 1991. 154p. *ISBN: 0252018036.*

4359 Where women are leaders: the SEWA movement in India. Kalima Rose. London: Zed Books, 1992. 286p. *ISBN: 1856490831.*

4360 Women and work in South Asia: regional patterns and perspectives. Saraswati Raju [Ed.]; Deipica Bagchi [Ed.]. London, New York: Routledge, 1993. 282p. *ISBN: 0415042496. Includes bibliographical references and index.*

4361 Women in the European community. . **Ind. Soc. Rel.** 13:3-4 1993 pp.201 - 224.

4362 Women's labour force participation and socioeconomic development — influences of local context and individual characteristics in Brazil. M.D.R. Evans; Helcio U. Saraiva. **Br. J. Soc.** 44:1 3:1993 pp.25 - 51.

4363 Work participation behaviour of married women with living husbands — a case of rural and urban Pondicherry. V. Nirmala; K. Sham Bhat; Md. Mohsin; B. Kamaiah. **Art. Vij.** XXXIV:3 9:1992 pp.315 - 336.

I: Labour

Unemployment
Chômage

4364 Arbeitslosigkeit und Alkoholismus: epidemiologische, ätiologische und diagnostische Zusammenhänge. *[In German]*; [Unemployment and alcoholism: epidemiological, etiological and diagnostical connections]. Dieter Henkel. Weinheim: Deutscher Studien Verlag, 1992. 200p. *ISBN: 3892712689.*

4365 Arbeitslosigkeit und Lebensgeschichte: eine empirische Untersuchung unter jungen Langzeitarbeitslosen. *[In German]*; [Unemployment and life histories: an empirical investigation into young people that have been out of work for a long time]. Gerd Vonderach; Ruth Siebers; Ulrich Barr. Opladen: Leske + Budrich, 1992. 217p. *ISBN: 3810009881. Bibliography: p. 205-217.*

4366 Armut, Arbeitslosigkeit, Selbsthilfe: Armuts- und Arbeitslosenprojekte zwischen Freizeit und Markt. *[In German]*; [Poverty, unemployment, self-help: projects for the poor and unemployed between free-time and market]. Lutz Finkeldey. Bochum: SWI-Verlag, 1992. 255p. *ISBN: 3925895388. Bibliography: p. 246-255.*

4367 Le chômage de longue durée — la théorie et l'action. *[In French]*; (Long-term unemployment — theory and action.) *[Summary]; [Summary in German]; [Summary in Spanish]*. Emmanuèle Reynaud. **Rev. Fr. Soc.** XXXIV:2 4-6:1993 pp.271 - 291.

4368 Desocupados precoces: ¿otra cara de la maquila? *[In Spanish]*; [Young unemployed men: the other face of the factory?] *[Summary]*. Fernando Cortés; Rosa María Rubalcava. **Est. Sociol.** XI:33 9-12:1993 pp.695 - 724.

4369 La disoccupazione strutturale — un'analisi della letteratura. *[In Italian]*; (Structural unemployment — an analysis of the literature.) *[Summary]*. Floro E. Caroleo. **Ec. Lav.** XXVII:1 1-3:1993 pp.43 - 56.

4370 Education-employment linkages — the macro profile. Patricia J. Alailima. **Sri Lanka J. Soc. Sci.** 15:1/2 6-12:1992 pp.1 - 45.

4371 The effect of immigration on aggregate native unemployment — an across-city estimation. Julian L. Simon; Stephen Moore; Richard Sullivan. **J. Labor Res.** XIV:3 Summer:1993 pp.299 - 316.

4372 The effect of social networks and concentrated poverty on black and Hispanic youth unemployment. K.M. O'Regan. **Ann. Reg. Sci.** 27:4 1993 pp.327 - 342.

4373 Facing the unemployment crisis in Ireland. Kieran Anthony Kennedy. Cork: Cork University Press, 1993. 63p. *ISBN: 0902561677. Bibliography.* (*Series: Undercurrents*).

4374 Factors influencing unemployment duration with a special emphasis on migration — an investigation using SIPP data and event history methods. J. Matthew Shumway. **Pap. Reg. Sci.** 72:2 4:1993 pp.159 - 176.

4375 Human resources deployment and urban unemployment in Dar es Salaam, Tanzania — a symptom of perverse socio-economic structure. C.M.F. Lwoga. **J. E.Afr. Res. Devel.** 22 1992 pp.60 - 74.

4376 Job insecurity: CAB evidence on employment problems in the recession. National Association of Citizens Advice Bureaux. London: National Association of Citizens Advice Bureau, 1993. 55p.

4377 Metodología cuantitativa para una caracterización diacrónica de recursos humanos desocupados. *[In Spanish]*; [Quantitative analysis for a diachronic description of unemployed human resources]. Marta Ceballos. **Rev. Parag. Sociol.** 29:85 9-12:1992 pp.157 - 170.

I: Travail

4378 Profils et trajectoires des chômeurs de longue durée: le cas Lausannois. *[In French]*; [Profiles and trajectories of the long-term unemployed: the case of Lausanne]. Laurence Marti; Geneviève Corajoud. Lausanne: Editions du Bourg, 1992. 217p.

4379 Proximity to job opportunities and African American male unemployment — a test of the spatial mismatch hypothesis in Indianapolis. Thomas J. Cooke. **Prof. Geogr.** 45:4 11:1993 pp.407 - 415.

4380 Psychological and behavioral consequences of job loss — a covariance structure analysis using Weiner's (1985) attribution model. Gregory E. Prussia; Angelo J. Kinicki; Jeffrey S. Bracker. **J. Appl. Psychol.** 78:3 6:1993 pp.382 - 394.

4381 Racial differences in men's unemployment. Leslie S. Stratton. **Ind. Lab. Rel.** 46:3 4:1993 pp.451 - 463.

4382 Rechtvaardigheid van sancties in de sociale zekerheid. *[In Dutch]*; (The justice of sanctions in social security.) *[Summary]*. D. Houtman. **Mens Maat.** 68:3 8:1993 pp.234 - 256.

4383 Réflexions sur le chômage de longue durée. *[In French]*; (Reflections on long-term unemployment.) *[Summary]*; *[Summary in German]*; *[Summary in Spanish]*. Jean Vincens. **Rev. Fr. Soc.** XXXIV:3 7-9:1993 pp.327 - 344.

4384 Social security or economic insecurity? The concentration of unemployment (and research) within households. Sarah Irwin; Lydia Morris. **J. Soc. Pol.** 22:3 7:1993 pp.349 - 372.

4385 Stadt und Arbeitslosigkeit: örtliche Arbeitsmarktpolitik im Vergleich. *[In German]*; [The town and unemployment: comparing local labour market policy]. Susanne Benzler; Hubert Heinelt; Bernhard Blanke [Intro.]. Opladen: Leske + Budrich, 1991. 426p. *ISBN: 381000877X. Includes bibliographical references (p. 404-419).*

4386 Stress e condizioni di non lavoro. Teorie interpretative, metodologia della ricerca, strumenti di valutazione ed evidenze empiriche dell'impatto psicosociale della perdita di lavoro. *[In Italian]*; [Stress and conditions caused by not working. Interpretative theories, research methods, valuation instruments and scientific evidence on the psychosocial impact of the loss of employment]. Paolo Crepet. **Sociol. Lav.** 44 1991 pp.124 - 154.

4387 Structural/frictional and demand-deficient unemployment in local labor markets. Harry J. Holzer. **Ind. Relat.** 32:3 Fall:1993 pp.307 - 328.

4388 Systemumbruch, Arbeitslosigkeit und individuelle Bewältigung in der Ex-DDR. *[In German]*; [System change, unemployment and individual responses to coping in the former GDR]. Thomas Kieselbach [Ed.]; Peter Voigt [Ed.]; Regine Hildebrandt [Intro.]. Weinheim: Deutscher Studien Verlag, 1992. 544p. *ISBN: 3892713111. Includes bibliographical references (p. 513-534).*

4389 Unemployment and marital status in Great Britain. William Sander. **Soc. Biol.** 39:3-4 Fall-Winter:1992 pp.299 - 305.

4390 Unemployment and search for work — exploratory analyses of labour market attachment and its dynamics. Enrico Rettore; Nicola Torelli; Ugo Trivellato. **Labour [Italy]** 7:3 Autumn:1993 pp.133 - 159.

4391 Unemployment benefit levels and search activity. John Schmitt; Jonathan Wadsworth. **Ox. B. Econ. S.** 55:1 2:1993 pp.1 - 24.

4392 Unemployment in South Africa. A. de Vries. **Ind. Rel. J. S.Afr.** 12:3 1992 pp.29 - 45.

I: Labour

4393 Unemployment in urban China — an analysis of survey data from Shanghai. Gangzhan Fu; Athar Hussain; Stephen Pudney; Limin Wang. **Labour [Italy]** 7:1 Spring:1993 pp.93 - 123.

4394 Von der Finanzierung der Arbeitslosigkeit zur Subventionierung niedriger Erwerbseinkommen. *[In German]*; [From financing unemployment to subsidizing low incomes]. Fritz W. Scharpf. **Gewerk. Monat.** 44:7 7:1993 pp.433 - 443.

4395 Zeitstrukturkrisen: biographische Interviews mit Arbeitslosen. *[In German]*; [Crisis in the structure of time: biographical interviews with the unemployed]. Siegfried Heinemeier. Opladen: Leske + Budrich, 1991. 313p. *ISBN: 3810009121.*

I.3: Personnel management and working conditions
Administration du personnel et conditions de travail

4396 All our labours: oral histories of working life in twentieth century Sydney. John Shields [Ed.]. Kensington, NSW, Australia: New South Wales University Press, 1992. xi, 252p. *ISBN: 086840117X. Includes bibliographical references and index.*

4397 Arbeitsmotivation in der Planwirtschaft: Führungskräfte der DDR im Vergleich. *[In German]*; [Work motivation in a planned economy: a comparison of GDR executives]. Bodo Neumann. Wermelskirchen: WFT, Verlag für Wissenschaft, Forschung und Technik, 1992. 249p. *ISBN: 3929095025.*

4398 The articulation of work through interaction. Juliet Corbin; Anselm Strauss. **Sociol. Q.** 34:1 Spring:1993 pp.71 - 83.

4399 Assessing newcomers' changing commitments to the organization during the first 6 months of work. Robert J. Vandenberg; Robin M. Self. **J. Appl. Psychol.** 78:4 8:1993 pp.557 - 568.

4400 Att värdera tankar. *[In Swedish]*; (Evaluating thoughts - the suggestion committee in an industrial workshop.). Eva Fägerborg. **Nord. Ny.** 52 1993 pp.20 - 32.

4401 Britain's secret slaves: an investigation into the plight of overseas domestic workers in the United Kingdom. Bridget Anderson. London: Anti-Slavery International, 1993. 128p. *ISBN: 0900918292.* (*Series:* Human rights series).

4402 Changes in work hours of male employees, 1940-1988. Mary T. Coleman; John Pencavel. **Ind. Lab. Rel.** 46:2 1:1993 pp.262 - 283.

4403 Computing and social change — new technology and the workplace transformation, 1980-1990. D. Hakken. **Ann. R. Anthr.** 22 1993 pp.107 - 132.

4404 The contract labour system and its effects on family and social life in Namibia: a historical perspective. Ndeutala Selma Hishongwa. Windhoek, Namibia: Gamsberg Macmillan, 1992. 116p. *ISBN: 1868487571. Includes bibliographical references (p. 113-115).*

4405 Control, technology and the management offensive in newspapers. Mike Noon. **New Tech. Work. Empl.** 8:2 9:1993 pp.102 - 110.

4406 The corporate construction of occupational health and safety — a labour process; *[Summary in French]*. Alan Hall. **Can. J. Soc.** 18:1 Winter:1993 pp.1 - 20.

4407 Correlates of employee attitudes toward functional flexibility. John Cordery; Peter Sevastos; Wally Mueller; Sharon Parker. **Human Relat.** 46:6 6:1993 pp.705 - 723.

4408 Culture, self-identity, and work. Miriam Erez; P. Christopher Earley. New York, NY: Oxford University Press, 1993. xiv, 260p. *ISBN: 0195075803. Includes bibliographical references (p. [235]-253) and index.*

4409 Donut shops and speed traps — evaluating models of supervision on police behaviour. John Brehm; Scott Gates. **Am. J. Pol. Sc.** 37:2 5:1993 pp.555 - 581.

4410 The effects of leader-member exchange on employee citizenship and impression management behavior. Sandy J. Wayne; Shawn A. Green. **Human Relat.** 46:12 12:1993 pp.1431 - 1440.

4411 Emploi, protection sociale et cycle de vie — résultats d'une comparaison internationale des dispositifs de sortie anticipée d'activité. *[In French]*; (Employment, welfare and the life-course — the results of an international comparison of early withdrawal from the labor force.) *[Summary]*. Anne-Marie Guillemard. **Sociol. Trav.** XXXVI:3 1993 pp.257 - 284.

4412 Employment and working conditions of low-skilled information-processing workers in less developed countries. Ruth Pearson; Swasti Mitter. **Int. Lab. Rev.** 132:1 1993 pp.49 - 64.

4413 Empowered teams: creating self-directed work teams that improve quality, productivity and participation. Richard S. Wellins; Jeanne M. Wilson [Ed.]; William C. Byham [Ed.]. San Francisco, Oxford: Jossey-Bass, 1991. 258p. *ISBN: 1555423531. Bibliography: p.247-250. (Series:* Jossey-Bass management series).

4414 Expectancy, valence, and motivational force functions in goal-setting research — an empirical test. Mark E. Tubbs; Donna M. Boehne; James G. Dahl. **J. Appl. Psychol.** 78:3 6:1993 pp.361 - 373.

4415 Factors influencing the cost of workers' compensation claims: the effects of settlement method, injury characteristics, and demographics. Gavin A. Wood; David L. Morrison; Sally Macdonald. **J. Occupat. Rehabil.** 3:4 12:1993 pp.201 - 212.

4416 Firm level decisions and human resource development in an Islamic economy. Abdul Aziz. **Am. J. Islam. Soc. Sci.** 10:2 Summer:1993 pp.201 - 216.

4417 Gender and turnover — a re-examination of the impact of sex on intent and actual job changes. Jacob Weisberg; Alan Kirschenbaum. **Human Relat.** 46:8 8:1993 pp.987 - 1006.

4418 How companies respond to new safety regulations — a Canadian investigation. J. Saari; S. Bedard; V. Dufort; J. Hryniewiecki; G. Theriault. **Int. Lab. Rev.** 132:1 1993 pp.65 - 74.

4419 The impact of new office information technology on job quality of female and male employees. Richard J. Long. **Human Relat.** 46:8 8:1993 pp.939 - 961.

4420 Incentives and penalties as a means of influencing attendance — a study in the UK public sector. Joan Harvey; Nigel Nicholson. **Int. J. Hum. Res. Man.** 4:4 12:1993 pp.841 - 858.

4421 Individual and cultural differences in adaptation to environmental risks. Elaine Vaughan. **Am. Psychol.** 48:6 6:1993 pp.673 - 680.

4422 The influence of rater and ratee age on judgments of work-related attributes. Kevin J. Gibson; Wilfred J. Zerbe; R.E. Franken. **J. Psychol.** 127:3 5:1993 pp.271 - 280.

4423 Interactional, formal, and distributive justice in the workplace — an exploratory study. Julian Barling; Michelle Phillips. **J. Psychol.** 127:6 11:1993 pp.649 - 656.

4424 Jeder irgendwie für sich allein? Probleme und Chancen sozialer Interaktion am Arbeitsplatz. *[In German]*; ("Everyone somehow on their own"? Problems and opportunities for social interaction at the place of work.) *[Summary]*. Lothar Peter. **Z. Soziol.** 22:6 12:1993 pp.416 - 432.

4425 Job evaluation as institutional myth. Maeve Quaid. **J. Manag. Stu.** 30:2 3:1993 pp.239 - 260.

I: Labour

4426 Leadership style and incentives. Julio J. Rotemberg; Garth Saloner. **Manag. Sci.** 39:11 11:1993 pp.1299 - 1318.

4427 Lo stress nel lavoro manageriale e le organizzazioni patogene. *[In Italian]*; [Stress in managerial work and pathogenic organizations]. Francesco Novara. **Sociol. Lav.** 44 1991 pp.111 - 123.

4428 Making the difference: women and men in the workplace. Pat Dixon. London: Heineman, Lime Tree, 1993. 215p. *ISBN: 0413456218*.

4429 Massenarbeiter und Personalpolitik in Deutschland und Frankreich. *[In German]*; [Mass workers and personnel policy in Germany and France]. Klaus Düll; Günter Bechtle; Manfred Moldaschl. Frankfurt am Main: Campus-Verlag, 1991. 344p. *ISBN: 3593345498. Groupe de Sociologie du Travail, Université Paris VII.*

4430 New technology and Hong Kong telephone workers. John Ure. **New Tech. Work. Empl.** 8:2 9:1993 pp.91 - 101.

4431 Office relocation and environmental change — a case study. Kent F. Spreckelmeyer. **Envir. Behav.** 25:2 3:1993 pp.181 - 204.

4432 Organizing engineering work — a comparative analysis. Peter Meiksins; Chris Smith. **Work Occup.** 20:2 5:1993 pp.123 - 146.

4433 Organizzazione del lavoro, decisione, fatica mentale e stress. *[In Italian]*; [Work organization, decisions, mental tiredness and stress]. Sebastiano Bagnara; Antonio Rizzo; Michela Vian. **Sociol. Lav.** 44 1991 pp.21 - 49.

4434 Pay-allocations by managers — a policy-capturing approach. Satish P. Deshpande; Peter P. Schoderbek. **Human Relat.** 46:4 4:1993 pp.465 - 479.

4435 Performance as a function of increased minority hiring. Jay M. Silva; Rick R. Jacobs. **J. Appl. Psychol.** 78:4 8:1993 pp.591 - 601.

4436 Personality and occupational behavior — Myers-Briggs type indicator correlates of managerial practices in two cultures. Adrian Furnham; Paul Stringfield. **Human Relat.** 46:7 7:1993 pp.827 - 848.

4437 Productivity and extra-role behavior — the effects of goals and incentives on spontaneous helping. Patrick M. Wright; Jennifer M. George; S. Regena Farnsworth; Gary C. McMahan. **J. Appl. Psychol.** 78:3 6:1993 pp.374 - 381.

4438 Le recrutement et l'observation des ouvriers par le patron. Etude d'un fichier d'entreprise. *[In French]*; (Recruitment and observation of employees by employers. Studying a company's records.) *[Summary]*; *[Summary in German]*; *[Summary in Spanish]*. Jean Peneff. **Rev. Fr. Soc.** XXXIV:4 10-12:1993 pp.557 - 596.

4439 Réduire le temps de travail. *[In French]*; [Reducing working time]. Ewald Ackerman; Martino Rossi; Serge Gaillard; Hans Baumann; Samuel König. **R. Synd. Suisse** 85:4 1993 pp.85 - 107. *Collection of 5 articles.*

4440 Regulating employers and employees — health and safety in the workplace. Bridget M. Hutter. **J. Law Soc.** 20:4 Winter:1993 pp.452 - 470.

4441 The role of the supervisor in successful adjustment to work with a disabling condition: issues for disability policy and practice. Lauren B. Gates. **J. Occupat. Rehabil.** 3:4 12:1993 pp.179 - 190.

4442 Santé et identité dans les organisations — une revue de la littérature. *[In French]*; (Health and identity in organization — a review of the literature.) *[Summary]*. Thomas Périlleux. **Recher. Sociolog.** XXIII:3 1992 pp.91 - 120.

4443 Sex segregation in the workplace. Barbara Reskin. **Ann. R. Soc.** 19 1993 pp.241 - 270.

I: Travail

4444 The show must go on — the response to fatalities in multiple employer workplaces. Fiona Haines. **Soc. Prob.** 40:4 11:1993 pp.547 - 563.

4445 Sicherheitswissenschaft in Theorie und Praxis im wiedervereinigten Deutschland: Konzepte - Realitäten - Defizite. *[In German]*; [Safety in theory and in practice in a unified Germany: concepts - realities - deficiencies. Peter C. Compes [Ed.]. Wuppertal: Gesellschaft für Sicherheitswissenschaft, 1992. 184p. *ISBN: 389429129X*. *Papers given at the 12th international summer symposium of Gesellschaft für Sicherheitswissenschaft.*

4446 Skills, control and "careers at work" — possibilities for worker control in the South African motor industry. Glenn Adler. **S.Afr. Sociol. R.** 5:(2) 4:1993 pp.35 - 64.

4447 Status politics, labor-management status, and gender — leaders' views on employers and workers' family obligations. Patricia Yancey Martin; Myrna M. Courage; Karolyn L. Godbey; Sandra Fields Seymour; Richard Tate. **R. Soc. Move. Con. Cha.** 15 1993 pp.83 - 112.

4448 Storytelling: an instrument for understanding the dynamics of corporate relationships. Carol D. Hansen; William M. Kahnweiler. **Human Relat.** 46:12 12:1993 pp.1391 - 1410.

4449 The strategic interaction between managers and workers in Soviet industrial enterprises — work-place motivation and economic performance. Adil E.A. Abdalla; Michael L. Wyzan. **Econ. Plan.** 26:3 1993 pp.209 - 228.

4450 Stress e piloti. *[In Italian]*; [Stress and pilots]. Michele Visciola. **Sociol. Lav.** 44 1991 pp.155 - 174.

4451 Technological evolution, working time and remuneration. William Grossin. **Time Soc.** 2:2 1993 pp.159 - 177.

4452 Telecommuting innovation and organization — a contingency theory of labor process change. Donald Tomaskovic-Devey; Barbara J. Risman. **Soc. Sci. Q.** 74:2 6:1993 pp.367 - 385.

4453 Telework, the local community and ways of life. K. Storgaard. **Scand. Hous. Plan. R.** 10:1 2:1993 pp.21 - 35.

4454 Times are changing: working time in 14 industrialised countries. Gerhard Bosch [Ed.]; Peter Dawkins [Ed.]; François Michon [Ed.]. Geneva: International Institute for Labour Studies, 1994. 323p. *ISBN: 9290145269*.

4455 Transnational perspectives on job burnout — replication of phase model results among Japanese respondents. Robert T. Golembiewski; Robert Boudreau; Keiichi Goto; Tadamasa Murai. **Intern. J. Organiz. Anal.** 1:1 1:1993 pp.7 - 27.

4456 Understanding the leader-strategy interface — application of the strategic relationship interview method. Manfred F.R. Kets de Vries; Danny Miller; Alain Noël. **Human Relat.** 46:1 1:1993 pp.5 - 22.

4457 Windowlessness in the workplace — a reexamination of the compensation hypothesis. Paul M. Biner; Darrell L. Butler; Theresa E. Lovegrove; Rachel L. Burns. **Envir. Behav.** 25:2 3:1993 pp.205 - 227.

4458 Within and beyond the time economy of employment relations — conceptual issues pertinent to research on time and work. Barbara Adam. **Soc. Sci. Info.** 32:2 1993 pp.163 - 184.

4459 Work stressors in health care and social service settings. Jeanne A. Schaefer [Ed.]; R. H. Moos [Ed.]; K.R. Parkes [Contrib.]; C. von Rabenau [Contrib.]; N.L. Marshall [Contrib.]; R.C. Barnett [Contrib.]; D.A. Revicki [Contrib.]; T.W. Whitley [Contrib.]; M.E. Gallery [Contrib.]; E.J. Allison [Contrib.]; P. Dewe [Contrib.]; M.

I: Labour

Shinn [Contrib.]; H. Mørch [Contrib.]; P.E. Robinson [Contrib.]; R.A. Neuner [Contrib.]; S. Reynolds [Contrib.]; E. Taylor [Contrib.]; D. Shapiro [Contrib.]. **J. Comm. App. Soc. Psychol.** 3:4 11:1993 pp.235 - 337. *Collection of 8 articles.*
4460 Work without wages — the motivation for volunteer firefighters. A.M. Thompson; B.A. Bono. **Am. J. Econ. S.** 52:3 7:1993 pp.323 - 343.

Job satisfaction
Satisfaction au travail

4461 Affect and managerial performance — a test of the sadder-but-wiser vs. happier-and-smarter hypothesis. Barry M. Staw; Sigal G. Barsade. **Adm. Sci. Qua.** 38:2 6:1993 pp.304 - 331.
4462 The affective consequences of service work — managing emotions on the job. Amy S. Wharton. **Work Occup.** 20:2 5:1993 pp.205 - 232.
4463 Boredom at work — a neglected concept. Cynthia D. Fisher. **Human Relat.** 46:3 3:1993 pp.395 - 417.
4464 Career strategies in capitalism and socialism — work values and job rewards in the United States and Hungary. Arne L. Kalleberg; David Stark. **Soc. Forc.** 72:1 9:1993 pp.181 - 198.
4465 Consequences of adolescent drug use on young adult job behavior and job satisfaction. Judith A. Stein; Gene M. Smith; Sybille M. Guy; P.M. Bentler. **J. Appl. Psychol.** 78:3 6:1993 pp.463 - 474.
4466 Determinants of employee job satisfaction — an empirical test of a causal model. Augustine O. Agho; Charles W. Mueller; James L. Price. **Human Relat.** 46:8 8:1993 pp.1007 - 1027.
4467 Does affective disposition moderate the relationship between job satisfaction and voluntary turnover? Timothy A. Judge. **J. Appl. Psychol.** 78:3 6:1993 pp.395 - 401.
4468 Effect of dysfunctional thought processes on subjective well-being and job satisfaction. Timothy A. Judge; Edwin A. Locke. **J. Appl. Psychol.** 78:3 6:1993 pp.475 - 490.
4469 Everyday forms of employed resistance. James Tucker. **Sociol. For.** 8:1 3:1993 pp.25 - 45.
4470 Follow-up and extension of the interdisciplinary costs and benefits of enlarged jobs. Michael A. Campion; Carol L. McClelland. **J. Appl. Psychol.** 78:3 6:1993 pp.339 - 351.
4471 The influence of cognitive and effective based job satisfaction measures on the relationship between satisfaction and organizational citizenship behavior. Robert H. Moorman. **Human Relat.** 46:6 6:1993 pp.759 - 776.
4472 Job demands and worker health — three-dimensional reexamination of the relationship between person-environment fit and strain. Jeffrey R. Edwards; R. van Harrison. **J. Appl. Psychol.** 78:4 8:1993 pp.628 - 648.
4473 The role of protegés' needs in seeking mentoring functions. Hann-Ol Kim; Jin-Kyu Lee. **Korean Soc. Sci. J.** XIX 1993 pp.65 - 76.

Personnel management
Gestion du personnel

4474 Arbeiten im Kleinbetrieb: Interessenvertretung im deutschen Alltag. *[In German]*; [Working in a small business: representation of interests in everyday life in Germany]. Wolfram Wassermann; Wolfgang Rudolph. Cologne: Bund-Verlag, 1992. 139p. *ISBN: 3766323091. Includes bibliographical references (p. 135-139).*
4475 [Corporate social responsibility?]; *[Text in Japanese]*. Mariko Inoue. **J. Hum. Sci.** 10 1993 pp.15 - 38.
4476 Developing a "European" model of human resource management. Chris Brewster. **Int. J. Hum. Res. Man.** 4:4 12:1993 pp.765 - 784.
4477 Dialogue and development: theory of communication, action research and the restructuring of working life. Björn Gustavsen. Assen, Stockholm: Van Gorcum, Swedish Center for Working Life, 1992. viii, 127p. *ISBN: 9023226917. Includes bibliographical references (p. 121-126). (Series:* Social science for social action).
4478 Effects of performance appraisal format on perceived goal characteristics, appraisal process satisfaction, and changes in rated job performance — a field experiment. Aharon Tziner; Richard E. Kopelman; Neomi Livneh. **J. Psychol.** 127:3 5:1993 pp.281 - 291.
4479 Human resource management in the Canadian manufacturing sector. Ignace Ng; Dennis Maki. **Int. J. Hum. Res. Man.** 4:4 12:1993 pp.897 - 916.
4480 Human resource management in the Japanese financial institution abroad — the case of the London office. Carolyn L. Evans. **Br. J. Ind. R.** 31:3 9:1993 pp.347 - 364.
4481 An integrative framework of strategic international human resource management. Randall S. Schuler; Peter J. Dowling; Helen de Cieri. **Int. J. Hum. Res. Man.** 4:4 12:1993 pp.717 - 764.
4482 The new economics of personnel. Edward P. Lazear. **Labour [Italy]** 7:1 Spring:1993 pp.3 - 23.
4483 Organizational and environmental factors related to human resource management practices in Hong Kong — a cross-cultural expanded replication. James B. Shaw; Sara F.Y. Tang; Cynthia D. Fisher; Paul S. Kirkbride. **Int. J. Hum. Res. Man.** 4:4 12:1993 pp.785 - 815.
4484 The politics of personnel transfer in Indian state bureaucracies. Frank de Zwart. **Neth. J. Soc. Sci.** 29:2 12:1993 pp.147 - 163.
4485 Strategies for coping with employee retention problems in small and medium enterprises (SMEs) in Singapore. Yaw A. Debrah. **Entrepren. Innov. Change** 2:2 6:1993 pp.143 - 172.
4486 Workplace policies as social policy. Susan J. Lambert. **Soc. Ser. R.** 67:2 6:1993 pp.237 - 260.

I.4: Vocational training, occupations and careers
Formation professionnelle, professions et carrières

4487 Age and sex in the occupational structure — a United States-Japan comparison. Mary C. Brinton; Hang-Yue Ngo. **Sociol. For.** 8:1 3:1993 pp.93 - 111.
4488 Algunas determinantes de la inserción laboral en la industria maquiladora de exportación de Matamoros. *[In Spanish]*; [Some determinants of labour insertion in

I: Labour

the Matamoros maquiladora export industry]. Fernando Cortés; Rosa María Rubalcava. **Est. Sociol.** XI:31 1-4:1993 pp.59 - 92.

4489 Are skill requirements rising? Evidence from production and clerical jobs. Peter Cappelli. **Ind. Lab. Rel.** 46:3 4:1993 pp.515 - 530.

4490 Basic skills and jobs: a report on the basic skills needed at work. John Atkinson; Mark Spilsbury. London: Adult Literacy and Basic Skills Unit, 1993. 59p.

4491 Black female clerical workers — movement toward equality with white women? Marilyn Power; Sam Rosenberg. **Ind. Relat.** 32:2 Spring:1993 pp.223 - 237.

4492 Britain's low skill equilibrium — a problem of demand? Sean Glynn; Howard Gospel. **Ind. Relat. J.** 24:2 6:1993 pp.112 - 125.

4493 Career commitments of American women — the issue of side bets. Helena Znaniecka Lopata. **Sociol. Q.** 34:2 5:1993 pp.257 - 277.

4494 Child and adult day care professions converging in the 1990s?: Implications for training and research. Shirley S. Travis; Andrew J. Stremmel; Paula A. Duprey. **Educ. Geront.** 19:4 6:1993 pp.283 - 294.

4495 Coming out of the blue: British police officers talk about their lives in "the job" as lesbians, gays and bisexuals. Marc E. Burke. London: Cassell, 1993. 259p. *ISBN: 0304327166, 030432714X.*

4496 Concepts of misconduct and malafides — practical deployment in vigilance cases. A.K. Garde. **Indian J. Publ. Admin.** XXXIX:2 4-6:1993 pp.128 - 138.

4497 De vervangingsvraag op de Nederlandse arbeidsmarkt. *[In Dutch]*; [Replacement demand on the Dutch labour market] *[Summary]*. Peter Ekamper. **Bevolk. Gez.** 2:1992 pp.29 - 47.

4498 Diverging pathways: social structure and career deflections. Alan C. Kerckhoff. Cambridge, New York: Cambridge University Press, 1993. xxii, 254p. *ISBN: 0521433975. Includes index. Bibliography: p. 241-247.*

4499 A Dutch prison officer's work — balancing between prison policy, organizational structure and professional autonomy. Max M. Kommer. **Neth. J. Soc. Sci.** 29:2 12:1993 pp.130 - 146.

4500 Education and human resources development. Swarna Jayaweera. **Sri Lanka J. Soc. Sci.** 14:1-2 6-12:1991 pp.11 - 28.

4501 Enwicklungslinien im Berufsbild des kaufmannisch-ökonomischen Facharbeiters in der Deutschen Demokratischen Republik: (1949 bis 1990). *[In German]*; [Occupational development of the commercial-economic skilled worker in the German Democratic Republic (1949-1990)]. Franz-Josef Hücker. Frankfurt am Main: Peter Lang, 1992. 316p. *ISBN: 3631445121.*

4502 Executive reward systems — a cross-national comparison. Johannes M. Pennings. **J. Manag. Stu.** 30:2 3:1993 pp.261 - 280.

4503 Farewell to the self-employed: deconstructing a socioeconomic and legal solipsism. Marc Linder. New York: Greenwood Press, 1992. viii, 189p. *ISBN: 0313284660. Bibliography: p.163-185; and index. (Series:* Contributions in labor studies).

4504 A force for change: how leadership differs from management. John P. Kotter. New York; London: Free Press; Collier Macmillan, 1990. 180p. *ISBN: 0029184657.*

4505 Het verband tussen de beroepsposities van huwelijkspartners in acht landen van de Europese Gemeenschap, 1975-1989. *[In Dutch]*; [The association between husbands' and wives' occupational positions in eight EC-countries, 1975-1989] *[Summary]*. Jeroen Smits; Wout Ultee; Jan Lammers. **Mens Maat.** 68:1 2:1993 pp.39 - 58.

4506 Implications of technological advances for human resource development. W.E. Ratnayake. **Sri Lanka J. Soc. Sci.** 14:1-2 6-12:1991 pp.29 - 35.
4507 Management reform in Eastern and Central Europe: use of pre-communist cultures. Magoroh Maruyama [Ed.]. Aldershot: Dartmouth, 1993. 180p. *ISBN: 1855213435.*
4508 Managerial quality, team success, and individual player performance in major league baseball. Lawrence M. Kahn. **Ind. Lab. Rel.** 46:3 4:1993 pp.531 - 547.
4509 Masculinity and the British organization man since 1945. Michael Roper. Oxford: Oxford University Press, 1993. 259p. *ISBN: 0198256930.*
4510 New measures of job control, cognitive demand, and production responsibility. Paul R. Jackson; Toby D. Wall; Robin Martin; Keith Davids. **J. Appl. Psychol.** 78:5 10:1993 pp.753 - 762.
4511 [Occupation structure and society]; *[Text in Japanese].* Shigeru Susato. Tokyo: Gakubunsha, 1993. 226p.
4512 On the proletarianization of Asian-American women in Hawaii. James A. Geschwender; Rita Argiros. **R. Soc. Move. Con. Cha.** 15 1993 pp.29 - 54.
4513 Organizational vacancy chains and the attainment process. Peter Hedström. **J. Math. Sociol.** 17:1 1992 pp.63 - 76.
4514 Os negros que dão certo: mercado de trabalho, mobilidade e desiguladades ocupacionais. *[In Portuguese]*; (Blacks that scored right: labour market, mobility and occupational inequalities.) *[Summary].* Nadya A. Castro; Vanda S. de Sá Barreto. **Rev. Brasil. Est. Popul.** 9:2 7-12:1992 pp.138 - 154.
4515 Les ouvriers et leurs carrières: enracinements et mobilité. *[In French]*; (Blue-collar workers' occupational stability and change throughout the life-course.) *[Summary].* Alain Chenu. **Soc. Contemp.** 14/15 6-9:1993 pp.79 - 92.
4516 Pojęcie „kariery". Perspektywa strukturalno-funkcjonalna i interakcjonistyczna. *[In Polish]*; [The notion of "career". A structural, functional and interactional perspective]. Ewa Rokicka. **Prz. Soc.** XLI 1992 pp.115 - 128.
4517 A profile of Canadian correctional workers. Gareth V. Hughes; Edward Zamble. **Int. J. Offen.** 37:2 Summer:1993 pp.99 - 113.
4518 Recasting steel labour: the Stelco story. June Shirley Corman; et al. Halifax, N.S: Fernwood, 1993. *ISBN: 1895686199. Includes bibliographical references and index.*
4519 Shattering the glass ceiling: the woman manager. Marilyn J. Davidson; Cary Lynn Cooper. London: Paul Chapman, 1992. iv, 185p. *ISBN: 1853961329. Includes bibliographical references (p. [174]-183) and index.*
4520 The skills and economic status of American Jewry — trends over the last half-century. Barry R. Chiswick. **J. Labor Ec.** 11:1(1) 1:1993 pp.229 - 242.
4521 Socioeconomic status and depression — the role of occupations involving direction, control, and planning. Bruce G. Link; Mary Clare Lennon; Bruce P. Dohrenwend. **A.J.S.** 98:6 5:1993 pp.1351 - 1387.
4522 Still serving the tea — domestic workers in Zimbabwe 1980-90. John Pape. **J. S.Afr. Stud.** 19:3 9:1993 pp.387 - 404.
4523 The wealth of a nation: practical partnerships between industry and education. David Warwick [Ed.]. London: Nicholas Brealey Publishing, 1993. 261p. *ISBN: 1857880129.*
4524 Women's work in the EC — five career profiles. Marianne Kempeneers; Eva Lelièvre. **Eur. J. Pop.** 9:1 1993 pp.77 - 92.
4525 Working for Nissan. Philip Garrahan; Paul Stewart. **Sci. Cult.** 3:3(16) 1993 pp.319 - 345.

I: Labour

Managers
Cadres

4526 [Alternatives to firing: the art of placing executives]; *[Text in Japanese]*. Yasuaki Muto. Tokyo: Chukei Shuppan, 1993. 221p.

4527 Differences in leadership behaviour and influence between public and private organizations in Greece. Dimitris Bourantas; Nancy Papalexandris. **Int. J. Hum. Res. Man.** 4:4 12:1993 pp.859 - 871.

4528 An ethical argument for host country workforce training and development in the expatriate management assignment. Charles M. Vance; Eduardo S. Paderon. **J. Busin. Ethics** 12:8 8:1993 pp.635 - 641.

4529 The information environment of managers. Jeffrey Katzer; Patricia T. Fletcher. **Ann. R. Info. Sci. Tech.** 27 1992 pp.227 - 263.

4530 Management and human resource development. G. Nanayakkara. **Sri Lanka J. Soc. Sci.** 14:1-2 6-12:1991 pp.37 - 43.

4531 Method and progress in management science. D.B. Learner; Fred Young Phillips. **Socio. Econ.** 27:1 1993 pp.9 - 24.

4532 The Persean ethic — consistency of belief and action in managerial practice. Joseph A. Raelin. **Human Relat.** 46:5 5:1993 pp.575 - 621.

4533 Purgatory or place of safety? The managerial plateau and organizational agegrading. Nigel Nicholson. **Human Relat.** 46:12 12:1993 pp.1369 - 1390.

4534 The relationship of career mentoring to early career outcomes. William T. Whitely; Pol Coetsier. **Organ. Stud.** 14:3 1993 pp.419 - 441.

Professional workers
Travailleurs professionnels

4535 Accounting for change — facilitating power and accountability. J. Cousins; P. Sikka. **Crit. Persp. Acc.** 4:1 3:1993 pp.53 - 72.

4536 Accounting for change — the institutions of accountancy. A. Mitchell; P. Sikka. **Crit. Persp. Acc.** 4:1 3:1993 pp.29 - 52.

4537 Australian academics — career patterns, work roles, and family life-cycle commitments of men and women. Susanne Romanin; Ray Over. **High. Educ.** 26:4 12:1993 pp.411 - 429.

4538 Berufliche Bildung in den neuen Bundesländern: Betrieb, Schule, Mitbestimmung, Arbeitsmarkt, Europa. *[In German]*; [Professional education in the new federal Länder: business, school, participation, labour market, Europe]. Irmgard Kroymann; S. Oliver Lübke. Cologne: Bund-Verlag, 1992. 155p. *ISBN: 3766324187*.

4539 Berufliche Umschulung: Konzepte und Erfahrungen beruflicher Qualifizierung mit Aussiedlern aus osteuropäischen Staaten. *[In German]*; [Professional retraining: concepts and the experiences of qualifying as a professional of immigrants from Eastern European states]. Rolf Dobischat [Ed.]; Antonius Lipsmeier [Ed.]. Stuttgart: F. Steiner, 1992. 189p. *ISBN: 3515062297*.

4540 Between markets and the state — scientists in comparative perspective. Etel Solingen. **Comp. Polit.** 26:1 10:1993 pp.31 - 51.

4541 Careers and partnerships — the strategies of secondary headteachers. Julia Evetts. **Sociol. Rev.** 41:2 5:1993 pp.302 - 327.

4542 «Carrera» professional i cicle vital — continuïtat i canvi en la socialització ocupacional dels docents. *[In Catalan]*; [Professional career and the life cycle — continuity and change in the occupational sozialization of teachers] *[Summary]*; *[Summary in Spanish]*. Lluís Samper. **Papers** 39 1992 pp.11 - 22.

4543 Comparing national patterns of medical specialization — a contribution to the theory of professions. Marian Döhler. **Soc. Sci. Info.** 32:2 1993 pp.185 - 231.

4544 The crisis years: the history of the Association of University Teachers from 1969 to 1983. Charles Geoffrey Stuttard. London: AUT, 1992. 105p. *ISBN: 090010712X*.

4545 Critical realist ethnography — the case of racism and professionalism in a medical setting. Sam Porter. **Sociology** 27:4 11:1993 pp.591 - 609.

4546 Eliot Freidson's contribution to the sociology of professions. Steven Brint. **Work Occup.** 20:3 8:1993 pp.259 - 278.

4547 The European medical profession and 1992 — the problem of numbers. Leon Hurwitz. **J. Dev. Soc.** 9:1 1-4:1993 pp.1 - 10.

4548 Factores para la eficcacia en la organización profesional — una aproximación teórica y empírica en el sector sanitario. *[In Spanish]*; [Factor for efficiency in professional organizations — a theoretical and empirical approximation in the health sector]. Alfonso Carlos Morales Gutierrez. **Rev. Fom. Soc.** 48:191 7-9:1993 pp.383 - 404.

4549 Falling from a tightrope? Doctors and lawyers between the market and the state. Margaret Brazier; Jill Lovecy; Michael Moran; Margaret Potton. **Politic. Stud.** XLI:2 6:1993 pp.197 - 213.

4550 Female labour force participation and the choice of occupation — the supply of teachers. P.J. Dolton; G.H Makepeace. **Eur. Econ. R.** 37:7 10:1993 pp.1393 - 1411.

4551 Informatiker zwischen Professionalisierung und Proletarisierung. Zur Standardisierung beruflichen Wissens im EDV-Bereich. *[In German]*; (Computerscientists between professionalization and proletarianization. On the standardization of occupational knowledge in the computer-sector.) *[Summary]*. Michael Hartmann. **Soz. Welt.** 44:3 1993 pp.392 - 419.

4552 International Conference on Teacher Thinking. Ron Hoz [Ed.]; Jude Butcher [Contrib.]; Grace E. Grant [Contrib.]; A.H. Corporaal [Contrib.]; F. Boei [Contrib.]; F.K. Kieviet [Contrib.]. **J. Struct. Learn.** 11:4 1993 pp.299 - 348. *Collection of 3 articles.*

4553 Legal data banks, the glut of lawyers, and the German legal profession. Michael Hartmann. **Law Soc. Rev.** 27:2 1993 pp.421 - 442.

4554 Perspectives de carrière et évolution du corps des magistrats, 1990-2030. *[In French]*; (Career perspectives and trends in the magistracy, 1990-2030.). Francisco Munoz-Perez; Michèle Tribalat. **Population** 48:1 1-2:1993 pp.27 - 62.

4555 Rank advancement in academic careers — sex differences and the effects of productivity. J. Scott Long; Paul D. Allison; Robert McGinnis. **Am. Sociol. R.** 58:5 10:1993 pp.703 - 722.

4556 Shifting gender boundaries — women's inroads into academic sociology. Patricia A. Roos; Katharine W. Jones. **Work Occup.** 20:4 11:1993 pp.395 - 428.

4557 Sotsial'nyi status meditsinskogo rabotnika. *[In Russian]*; (Social status of medics.). M.D. Rozenbaum. **Sot. Issle.** 3 1993 pp.36 - 40.

I: Labour

4558 Stress and burnout among teachers in Italy and France. Luigi Pedrabissi; J.P. Rolland; M. Santinello. **J. Psychol.** 127:5 9:1993 pp.529 - 535.
4559 Structural reform of the vetinary profession in Africa and the new institutional economics. David K. Leonard. **Develop. Cha.** 24:2 4:1993 pp.227 - 267.
4560 The temporal dimension of gender inequality in academia. Nina Toren. **High. Educ.** 25:4 6:1993 pp.439 - 456.
4561 What do lawyers do? Reflections on the market for lawyers. I.M. Ramsay. **Int. J. S. Law** 21:4 12:1993 pp.355 - 389.
4562 The work environments of male and female professionals — objective and subjective characteristics. Jo Phelan; Evelyn J. Bromet; Joseph E. Schwartz; Mary Amanda Dew; E. Carroll Curtis. **Work Occup.** 20:1 2:1993 pp.68 - 89.

Training
Formation

4563 Achieving the national education and training targets: a report to the Employment Department. Mark Spilsbury; Mike Everett. Brighton, Sussex: Institute of Manpower Studies, 1993. 68p. *ISBN: 1851841792*. (*Series:* IMS Report - 256).
4564 Building microcomputing skills in public adminstration graduate education — an assessment of MPA programs. Jeffrey L. Brudney; Ronald John Hy; William L. Waugh. **Admin. Soc.** 25:2 8:1993 pp.183 - 203.
4565 Employment and skills in Brazil — the implications of new technologies. Howard Rush; João Carlos Ferraz. **Int. Lab. Rev.** 132:1 1993 pp.75 - 93.
4566 Entry-level employment and employees — problems, policies, and prospects. James T. Bennett [Contrib.]; Dwight R. Lee [Contrib.]; Walter John Wessels [Contrib.]; Arnold Packer [Contrib.]; Lisa M. Lynch [Contrib.]; June O'Neill [Contrib.]; Robert Rector [Contrib.]. **J. Labor Res.** XIV:3 Summer:1993 pp.197 - 297. *Collection of 7 articles.*
4567 Formation et jeunes entreprises — quelles actions conduire pour les pépinières d'entreprises? *[In French]*; (Training programmes and young business — which actions would be brought out of incubation?) *[Summary]*. Emmanuelle Dontenwill; Stéphane Marion. **Gestion** 9:6 12:1993 pp.119 - 140.
4568 Human resource development in Sri Lanka — challenges and priorities. G.L. Peiris. **Sri Lanka J. Soc. Sci.** 14:1-2 6-12:1991 pp.1 - 10.
4569 The impact of government-assisted management training and development on small and medium-sized enterprises in Britain. J.N. Marshall; N. Alderman; C. Wong; A. Thwaites. **Envir. Plan. C.** 11:3 8:1993 pp.331 - 348.
4570 Impact of task experience and individual factors on training-emphasis ratings. J. Kevin Ford; Eleanor M. Smith; Douglas J. Sego; Miguel A. Quiñones. **J. Appl. Psychol.** 78:4 8:1993 pp.583 - 590.
4571 Making Japan work: the origins, education and training of the Japanese salaryman. James Edward Thomas. Folkstone: Japan Library, 1993. 143p. *ISBN: 1873410182*.
4572 Mirrors, butterflies, and training policy. Judith Marquand. **Human Relat.** 46:9 9:1993 pp.1071 - 1084.
4573 Occupation and skill change in the European retail sector. Mark Spilsbury; Janet Toye; Claire Davies. Brighton: Institute of Manpower Studies, University of Brighton, 1993. 187p. *ISBN: 1851841709*. Commission of the European

I: Travail

Communities Task Force Human Resources. Institute of Manpower Studies. CECD. EURO-FIET. (Series: IMS Report).

4574 Roads to work — school-to-work transition patterns in Germany and the United States. Christoph F. Buechtemann; Juergen Schupp; Dana Soloff. **Ind. Relat. J.** 24:2 6:1993 pp.97 - 111.

4575 Training for urban local government in Sri Lanka: a study of the training component of the performance improvement programme for urban local authorities, 1985-89. David Pasteur. Birmingham: Development Administration Group, University of Birmingham, 1992. 150p. *ISBN: 0704411814. (Series:* Papers in the administration of development).

4576 Umdenken bei der Programmgestaltung — Managerkurse bereiten Frustration. *[In German]*; (New considerations for drafting programs — management courses provide frustrations.) *[Summary]*. Hans-Peter Müller. **Ost. Wirt.** 38:2 6:1993 pp.109 - 114.

I.5: Labour relations
Relations du travail

4577 Accounting for delay in grievance arbitration. Kenneth W. Thornicroft. **Lab. Law J.** 44:9 9:1993 pp.543 - 553.

4578 Arbeit, Organisation und Arbeitsbeziehungen in Ostdeutschland. *[In German]*; (Work, organization and industrial relations in Eastern Germany.) *[Summary]*; *[Summary in French]*. Arndt Sorge. **Berl. J. Soziol.** 3:4 1993 pp.549 - 567.

4579 The Australian workplace industrial relations survey and comparative industrial relations — Canadian reflections. C.H.J. Gilson. **J. Labor Res.** XIV:3 Summer:1993 pp.335 - 353.

4580 The big dark cloud of workers' compensation — does it have a silver lining? Cecily Raiborn; Dinah Payne. **Lab. Law J.** 44:9 9:1993 pp.554 - 563.

4581 Collective bargaining in the domestic labour sector. Lirieka Meintjes-Van der Walt. **Ind. Soc. Rel.** 13:3-4 1993 pp.189 - 200.

4582 A comparison of the United States and Chinese managerial cultures in a transitional period — implications for labor relations and joint ventures. Paul G. Wilhelm; Ang Xia. **Intern. J. Organiz. Anal.** 1:4 10:1993 pp.405 - 426.

4583 Contracts and commitment — economic and sociological perspectives on employment relations. Arne L. Kalleberg; Torger Reve. **Human Relat.** 46:9 9:1993 pp.1103 - 1132.

4584 Decline and fall — national bargaining in British water. Stuart Ogden. **Ind. Relat. J.** 24:1 3:1993 pp.44 - 58.

4585 Determinants of management's organizational structure in the public sector. Rafael Gely; Timothy D. Chandler. **J. Labor Res.** XIV:4 Fall:1993 pp.381 - 397.

4586 The effects of employee ownership on employee attitudes — an integrated causal model and path analysis. Aaron A. Buchko. **J. Manag. Stu.** 30:4 7:1993 pp.633 - 657.

4587 Efficiency and equity at work: the need for labour market regulation in Australia. John Buchanan; Ron Callus. **J. Ind. Relat.** 35:4 12:1993 pp.515 - 537.

4588 Employee stock ownership plans and productivity in Japanese manufacturing firms. Derek C. Jones; Takao Kato. **Br. J. Ind. R.** 31:3 9:1993 pp.331 - 346.

I: Labour

4589 The erosion of paternalism on South African gold mines. Wilmot G. James. **Ind. Rel. J. S.Afr.** 12:1/2 1992 pp.1 - 16.

4590 European collective bargaining: a triumph of the will? Antonio Ojeda-Avilés. **Int. J. Comp. L. L. I. R.** 9:4 Winter:1993 pp.279 - 296.

4591 Formal and informal institutions in the labor market, with applications to the construction sector in Egypt. R. Assaad. **World Dev.** 21:6 6:1993 pp.925 - 939.

4592 Gender differences in the acquisition of salary negotiation skills — the role of goals, self-efficacy, and perceived control. Stevens Cynthia Kay; Anna G. Bavetta; Marilyn E. Gist. **J. Appl. Psychol.** 78:5 10:1993 pp.723 - 735.

4593 Industrial relations and the construction of the Channel Tunnel. John Fisher. **Ind. Relat. J.** 24:3 9:1993 pp.211 - 223.

4594 Industrial relations in ASEAN and other capitalist countries. Melanie Beresford; Di Kelly. **Econ. Ind. Dem.** 14:1 2:1993 pp.89 - 107.

4595 Industrial relations in local government — the impact of privatisation. Deborah Foster. **Pol. Quart.** 64:1 1-3:1993 pp.49 - 59.

4596 Industrial relations theory: its nature, scope, and pedagogy. Noah M. Meltz [Ed.]; Roy James Adams [Ed.]. Metuchen, N.J: IMLR Press/Rutgers University, Scarecrow Press, 1993. vi, 403p. *ISBN: 081082678X. Includes bibliographical references and index. (Series:* Institute of Management and Labor Relations series).

4597 Internalization v. decentralization — an analysis of recent developments in pay bargaining. Janet Walsh. **Br. J. Ind. R.** 31:3 9:1993 pp.409 - 432.

4598 Japanese production management and labour relations in Brazil. John Humphrey. **J. Dev. Stud.** 30:1 10:1993 pp.92 - 114.

4599 Job creation through collective bargaining: the preferred alternative to government regulations. Wayne Jett. **Lab. Law J.** 44:12 12:1993 pp.742 - 754.

4600 Justice for all? Union versus management responses to unjust acts and social accounts. Raymond A. Friedman; Robert J. Robinson. **Int. J. Confl. Manag.** 4:2 4:1993 pp.99 - 117.

4601 Kollektivvertragspolitik in Österreich 1985-1990. *[In German]*; [Collective agreement policy in Austria 1985-1990]. Theodor Tomandl; Carl-George Vogt; Jürgen Winkler; et al. Vienna: Wirtschaftsverlag Dr. Anton Orac, 1992. 136p. *ISBN: 3700703279. Includes bibliographical references.*

4602 Labor relations in education: an international perspective. Bruce S. Cooper [Ed.]; Charles T. Kerchner [Foreword]. Westport, Conn: Greenwood Press, 1992. xviii, 355p. *ISBN: 0313267073. Includes bibliographical references and index. (Series:* Contributions to the study of education).

4603 Labour resistance in Cameroon: managerial strategies & labour resistance in the agro-industrial plantations of the Cameroon Development Corporation. Piet Konings. London, Portsmouth, N.H: J. Currey, Heinemann, 1993. x, 203p. *ISBN: 0435080865, 0435080873. Includes bibliographical references (p. [185]-197) and index.*

4604 Lokaut jako jedna z podstawowych instytucji w prawie sporów zbiorowych Republiki Federalnej Niemiec. *[In Polish]*; (Lock-out as one of a basic institutions in collective bargaining in Germany.). Bogusław Cudowski. **Pra. Zab. Społ.** XXXV:5-6 5-6:1993 pp.49 - 57.

4605 Mandatory voluntarism — negotiating technology in Denmark. Philip Kraft; Jørgen Bansler. **Ind. Relat.** 32:3 Fall:1993 pp.329 - 342.

4606 The metamorphosis of Australian industrial relations. Keith Hancock; Don Rawson. **Br. J. Ind. R.** 31:4 12:1993 pp.489 - 513.

4607 The micro-politics of paternalism — the discourses of management and resistance on South African fruit and wine farms. Andries du Toit. **J. S.Afr. Stud.** 19:2 6:1993 pp.314 - 336.
4608 Nepalese indigenous labour relations. Jana Fortier. **Contrib. Nepal. Stud.** 20:1 1:1993 pp.105 - 118.
4609 On trust in employment relationships — the case of child-minders. Rudi Wielers. **Neth. J. Soc. Sci.** 29:1 6:1993 pp.46 - 63.
4610 Patterns of continuity and change in managerial attitudes and behaviour in industrial relations 1980-1990. Michael Poole; Roger Mansfield. **Br. J. Ind. R.** 31:1 3:1993 pp.11 - 35.
4611 The political economy of control — an organizational theory of structural inequality. John H. Godard. **Work Occup.** 20:3 8:1993 pp.337 - 367.
4612 Rabochee dvizhenie v postsotsialisticheskoi Rossii. *[In Russian]*; (The working class movement in post-socialist Russia.). L. Gordon; A. Temkina. **Obshch. Nauki Sovrem.** 3 1993 pp.31 - 44.
4613 Regulierung der Arbeitsbeziehungen und Unternehmerinteressen. Das Beispiel der Leiharbeit. *[In German]*; (Regulation of labor relations and business interests. The case of agency work.) *[Summary]*. Stephan Voswinkel; Ingo Bode. **Z. Soziol.** 22:4 8:1993 pp.298 - 316.
4614 Researching industrial relations: methods and methodology. Diana Kelly [Ed.]. Sydney: Australian Centre for Industrial Relations, Research and Teaching, 1991. 155p. *ISBN: 0867585579*. (*Series:* ACIRRT monograph).
4615 Rugby league and the union game. Braham Dabscheck. **J. Ind. Relat.** 35:2 6:1993 pp.242 - 273.
4616 South African management perceptions of research in human resource management and industrial relations. R.S. Moore. **Ind. Rel. J. S.Afr.** 12:1/2 1992 pp.17 - 36.
4617 Towards a regionalization of industrial relations; *[Summary in French]*. Paolo Perulli. **Int. J. Urban** 17:1 3:1993 pp.98 - 113.
4618 Whither solidarity? Transitions in Swedish public-sector pay policy. Lois Recascino Wise. **Br. J. Ind. R.** 31:1 3:1993 pp.75 - 95.
4619 Women's productivity: productivity bargaining and service workers. Kathy McDermott. **J. Ind. Relat.** 35:4 12:1993 pp.538 - 553.
4620 Workplace industrial relations: Australian case studies. Russell Duncan Lansbury; Duncan MacDonald. Melbourne: Oxford University Press, 1992. 252p. *ISBN: 0195532759. Includes bibliographical references and index.* (*Series:* Australian studies in labour relations).

Labour disputes
Conflits du travail

4621 An analysis of labour disputes in Korea and Japan — the search for an alternative model. Dong-One Kim. **Eur. Sociol. R.** 9:2 9:1993 pp.139 - 154.
4622 The anatomy of a rural strike: power and space in the Transvaal lowveld. Charles Mather. **Can. J. Afr. St.** 27:3 1993 pp.424 - 438.
4623 Delay in conciliation proceedings — a systemic malaise. Debi S. Saini. **Indian J. Soc. W.** LIV:2 4:1993 pp.231 - 240.

I: Labour

4624 Hard-pressed in the heartland: the Hormel strike and the future of the labor movement. Peter J. Rachleff. Boston: South End Press, 1992. *ISBN: 0896084515, 0896084507. Includes bibliographical references and index.*

4625 Internal dispute resolution — the transformation of civil rights in the workplace. Lauren B. Edelman; Howard S. Erlanger; John Lande. **Law Soc. Rev.** 27:3 1993 pp.497 - 534.

4626 New perspectives on industrial disputes. David Metcalf [Ed.]; Simon Milner [Ed.]. New York; London: Routledge, 1993. 275p. *ISBN: 0415091519. Includes bibliographies.*

4627 Sotsial'no-trudovye konflikti pri perekhode k rynochnoi ekonomike. *[In Russian]*; [Social and labour disputes in the transition to a market economy]. L.A. Gordon; V.I. Kabalina; A.K. Nazimova. **Obshch. Ekon.** 2 1993 pp.3 - 20.

4628 Strike duration and the degree of disagreement. Jan I. Ondrich; John F. Schnell. **Ind. Relat.** 32:3 Fall:1993 pp.412 - 431.

4629 Tribunal policy and dispute settlement: the nurses' case 1986-87. Carol Fox. **J. Ind. Relat.** 35:2 6:1993 pp.292 - 315.

Labour law
Droit du travail

4630 Allgemeiner Kündigungsschutz in ausgewählten europäischen Ländern. Ein internationaler Vergleich aus theoretischer und empirischer Sicht. *[In German]*; [Comprehensive protection against dismissal in selected European countries. An international comparison from a theoretical and empirical perspective] *[Summary]*. Heinz-Dieter Hardes. **Jahr. Soz.schaft.** 44:1 1993 pp.78 - 103.

4631 Arbeitsgesetze der Bundesrepublik Deutschland 1993: mit den Besonderheiten in den neuen Bundesländern und Ost-Berlin. *[In German]*; [Labour laws in the Federal Republic of Germany 1993: the peculiarities of the new Länder and East Berlin]. Günter Halbach [Ed.]. Bonn: Stollfuss, 1993. 754p. *ISBN: 3083691939.*

4632 Borrowing and bending: the development of South Africa's unfair labour practice jurisprudence. Clive Thompson. **Int. J. Comp. L. L. I. R.** 9:3 Autumn:1993 pp.183 - 205.

4633 Le droit social à l'épreuve du SIDA. *[In French]*; [Social law tested by AIDS]. Philippe Auvergnon [Ed.]. Talence, France: Editions de la Maison des sciences de l'homme d'Aquitaine, 1992. 154p. *ISBN: 2858921806. Université de Bordeaux I Centre de droit comparé du travail travail et de la sécurité sociale.*

4634 "Government by injunction" — the U.S. judiciary and strike action in the late 19th and 20th centuries. Holly J. McCammon. **Work Occup.** 20:2 5:1993 pp.174 - 204.

4635 Labour law and German unification: transition from central planning to a market economy. Otfried Wlotzke. **Int. J. Comp. L. L. I. R.** 9:4 Winter:1993 pp.326 - 350.

4636 Labour law's little sister: the Employment Standards Act and the feminization of labour. Judy Fudge. Ottawa, Ont: Canadian Centre for Policy Alternatives, 1991. iv, 112p. *ISBN: 0886271045. Includes bibliographical references.*

4637 Labour legislation and institutional aspects of the Brazilian labour market. Edward J. Amadeo; José Márcio Camargo. **Labour [Italy]** 7:1 Spring:1993 pp.157 - 180.

4638 Mrs Thatcher's labour laws — slouching toward utopia? Simon Auerbach. **Pol. Quart.** 64:1 1-3:1993 pp.37 - 48.

I: Travail

4639 Ökonomische und rechtliche Konsequenzen der deutschen Vereinigung: wirtschaftspolitische sowie arbeits- und unternehmensrechtliche Gestaltungsaspekte der Systemtransformation. *[In German]*; [Economic and legal consequences of German unification: aspects of system transformation from the view of economic policy as well as labour and company law]. Dirk Ipsen [Ed.]; Egbert Nickel [Ed.]. Marburg: Metropolis, 1992. 267p. *ISBN: 392657058X. Papers from a conference held in Darmstadt. Includes bibliographical references.*

4640 Protecting employee rights in successorship. Stephen B. Goldstein. **Lab. Law J.** 44:1 1:1993 pp.18 - 29.

4641 Protective legislation and women's labour market participation. Charles Harvie; Chris Nyland; Stuart Svensen. **J. Ind. Relat.** 35:4 12:1993 pp.554 - 570.

4642 Przesrrzeganie prawa pracy w świetle sprawozdania z działalności Państwowej Inspekcji Pracy w 1992 roku (I). *[In Polish]*; (Obeying the labour law in the light of the report of state labour supervision activity (I).). Jacek Olesiński. **Pra. Zab. Społ.** XXXV:8 8:1993 pp.33 - 45.

4643 Psychology and law — the labour law interface. M.W. van Wyk. **S. Afr. J. Labour Relat.** 17:3 9:1993 pp.47 - 62.

4644 Reflections on matters of independence and industrial tribunals in Australia. S.A. Kennedy. **J. Ind. Relat.** 35:2 6:1993 pp.274 - 291.

4645 Sexual orientation and the workplace — a rapidly developing field. Arthur S. Leonard. **Lab. Law J.** 44:9 9:1993 pp.574 - 583.

4646 The state and industrial relations — background to the adoption of compulsory arbitration law in Australia and Nigeria. Paul Omojo Omaji. **Br. J. Ind. R.** 31:1 3:1993 pp.37 - 55.

4647 Using arbitration to avoid litigation. Todd H. Thomas. **Lab. Law J.** 44:1 1:1993 pp.3 - 17.

4648 Wege zur Gleichberechtigung: Vergleich des Arbeitsrechts der Bundesrepublik Deutschland und der Vereinigten Staaten. *[In German]*; [Paths to justice: comparison of labour law in the Federal Republic of Germany and the USA]. Monika Schlachter. München: C.H. Beck, 1993. xlii, 455p. *ISBN: 340637364X. The author's Habilitationsschrift (Georg-August-Universität Göttingen, 1992). Includes bibliographical references (p. [xix]-xlii) and index.*

Trade unions
Syndicats

4649 "All those in favour" — computerised trade union membership lists as sampling frames for postal surveys. David J. Owens; Teresa Rees; Nina Parry-Langdon. **Sociol. Rev.** 41:1 2:1993 pp.141 - 152.

4650 Ballots and union government in the 1980s. Paul Smith; Patricia Fosh; Roderick Martin; Huw Morris; Roger Undy. **Br. J. Ind. R.** 31:3 9:1993 pp.365 - 382.

4651 Battling against the odds — the emergence of senior women trade unionists. Theresa Dorgan; Margaret Grieco. **Ind. Relat. J.** 24:2 6:1993 pp.151 - 164.

4652 Black South African unions — relative wage effects in international perspective. Peter G. Moll. **Ind. Lab. Rel.** 46:2 1:1993 pp.245 - 261.

I: Labour

4653 Business associations and labor unions in comparison — theoretical perspectives and empirical findings on social class, collective action and associational organizability. Franz Traxler. **Br. J. Soc.** 44:4 12:1993 pp.673 - 691.

4654 The collective organization of Australian academic staff 1949-1983. John M. O'Brien. **J. Ind. Relat.** 35:2 6:1993 pp.185 - 220.

4655 Correlates of union membership and joining intentions in a unit of federal employees. Hugh D. Hindman; Charles G. Smith. **J. Labor Res.** XIV:4 Fall:1993 pp.439 - 454.

4656 Decline of the farm labor movement in California — organizational crisis and political change. Theo J. Majka; Linda C. Majka. **Crit. Sociol.** 19:3 1992 pp.3 - 36.

4657 The development of members' attitudes toward their unions — Sweden and Canada. Sarosh Kuruvilla; Daniel G. Gallagher; Kurt Wetzel. **Ind. Lab. Rel.** 46:3 4:1993 pp.499 - 514.

4658 Dimensions of local union effectiveness. Tove H. Hammer; David L. Wazeter. **Ind. Lab. Rel.** 46:2 1:1993 pp.302 - 319.

4659 Dylematy ochrony działaczy związkowych przed zwolnieniem z pracy. *[In Polish]*; (Dilemmas of union workers' protection against dismissal.). Walerian Sanetra. **Pra. Zab. Społ.** XXXV:3 3:1993 pp.21 - 34.

4660 Dylematy ochrony działaczy związkowych przed zwolnieniem z pracy (jeszcze raz). *[In Polish]*; (Dilemmas of active union members' protection against dismissals.). Józef Iwulski. **Pra. Zab. Społ.** XXXV:12 12:1993 pp.23 - 30.

4661 Dylematy tożsamości związkowej. *[In Polish]*; [Dilemmas of the identity of unions]. Anna Matuchniak-Krasuska. **Prz. Soc.** XLII 1993 pp.137 - 152.

4662 La economía informal y las modificaciones del movimiento sindical en Bolivia. *[In Spanish]*; [The informal economy and changes in the trade union movement in Bolivia]. H.C.F. Mansilla. **Rev. Parag. Sociol.** 30:86 1-4:1993 pp.113 - 126.

4663 The effect of unionization on faculty salaries and compensation — estimates from the 1980s. Daniel I. Rees. **J. Labor Res.** XIV:4 Fall:1993 pp.399 - 422.

4664 An empirical analysis of union election outcomes in the electric utility industry. Clyde Scott; Jim Simpson; Sharon Oswald. **J. Labor Res.** XIV:3 Summer:1993 pp.355 - 365.

4665 An enduring flame: the history of the Toronto gas workers. Jamie Swift. Toronto: Energy and Chemical Workers' Union, Local 001, 1991. 122p. *ISBN: 0969559801. Includes bibliographical references.*

4666 Engineering and its discontents: Taylorism, unions, and employers. Stephane Castonguay. **Soc. Epist.** 7:3 7-9:1993 pp.293 - 312.

4667 From compliance to confrontation: 140 years of teachers' unions in South Australia, 1851-1991. Bernard Keith Hyams. Adelaide: Auslib Press, 1992. 148p. *ISBN: 1875145168.*

4668 Gewerkschaften und Angestelltenverbände in der schweizerischen Privatwirtschaft: Entstehung, Mitgliedschaft, Organisation und Politik seit 1940. *[In German]*; [Trade unions and white-collar associations in the Swiss private economy: foundation, membership, organization and politics since 1940]. Robert Fluder; et al. Zurich: Seismo-Verlag, 1991. 782p. *ISBN: 3908239060.*

4669 Gewerkschaften und die „Neue Politik". Eine quantitative Inhaltsanalyse von Protokollen deutscher und schwedischer Gewerkschaftskongresse. *[In German]*; (Trade unions and new politics — a quantitative content analysis of the minutes of

German and Swedish trade union congresses.) *[Summary]*. Detlef Jahn. **Z. Soziol.** 22:3 6:1993 pp.192 - 208.

4670 Gewerkschaftsreform. *[In German]*; [Trade union reform]. Oskar Negt [Contrib.]; Jürgen Hoffmann [Contrib.]; Reiner Hoffman [Contrib.]; Dietrich Lange [Contrib.]; Ulrich Mückenberger [Contrib.]; Seppel Kraus [Contrib.]; Ulrich von Alemann [Contrib.]; Josef Schmid [Contrib.]; Wolfgang Uellenberg-van Dawen [Contrib.]; Günther Häckl [Contrib.]. **Gewerk. Monat.** 44:5 5:1993 pp.265 - 327. *Collection of 6 articles.*

4671 L'image du pouvoir syndical au Québec (1950-1991). *[In French]*; [The image of trade union power in Quebec (1950-1991)] *[Summary]*. Jacques Rouillard. **Rech. Soc.graph** XXXIV:2 5-8:1993 pp.279 - 304.

4672 Inventar zu den Nachlässen der deutschen Arbeiterbewegung für die zehn westdeutschen Länder und West-Berlin. *[In German]*; [Inventory of the inheritance of the German workers' movement for the ten West German Länder and West Berlin]. Hans-Holger Paul [Ed.]; Karl Kollmann. Munich, New York: K.G. Saur, 1993. x, 996p. *ISBN: 3598111045. Includes bibliographical references and indexes. Archiv der Sozialen Demokratie der Friedrich-Ebert-Stiftung.*

4673 Japanese employment practices and industrial relations — the road to union "compliance". Hasegawa Harukiyo. **Jpn. Forum** 5:1 4:1993 pp.21 - 36.

4674 Jetzt erst recht! Dokumente zur Geschichte der Arbeiterbewegung in Mannheim 1945-1990. *[In German]*; [Legal for the first time! Documents on the history of the workers' movement in Mannheim 1945-1990]. Josef Kaiser [Intro.]. Mannheim: Edition Quadrat, 1993. 584p. *ISBN: 3923003471. Includes bibliographical references and indexes. Industriegewerkschaft Metall, Verwaltungsstelle Mannheim.*

4675 Membership participation in workplace unionism — the possibility of union renewal. Patricia Fosh. **Br. J. Ind. R.** 31:4 12:1993 pp.577 - 592.

4676 Multi-unionism, size of bargaining group and strikes. David Metcalf; Jonathan Wadsworth; Peter Ingram. **Ind. Relat. J.** 24:1 3:1993 pp.3 - 13.

4677 New immigrants, old unions: organizing undocumented workers in Los Angeles. Héctor L. Delgado. Philadelphia: Temple University Press, 1993. x, 186p. *ISBN: 1566390443. Includes bibliographical references (p. [163]-177) and index.*

4678 Nonwage benefits as a limited-dependent variable — implications for the impact of unions. Augustin Kwasi Fosu. **J. Labor Res.** XIV:1 Winter:1993 pp.29 - 43.

4679 'On the doorstep of management': upward mobility of African workers in the metal industry and its implications for trade union organisation. Owen Crankshaw. **S.Afr. Sociol. R.** 6:1 10:1993 pp.1 - 18.

4680 Polycentric society and the fate of unionism. Franco Ferrarotti. **Int. Soc. Sci. J.** 137 8:1993 pp.385 - 394.

4681 Rabochee dvizhenie v postsotsialisticheskoi Rossii. *[In Russian]*; (The labour movement in post-socialist Russia.). L. Gordon; E. Klopov. **Mir. Ek. Mez. Ot.** 5 1993 pp.5 - 16.

4682 Recent developments in the US — trade union strategies. Steven Deutsch [Contrib.]; Margaret Hallock [Contrib.]; Susan Schurman [Contrib.]; Steven Hecker [Contrib.]. **Econ. Ind. Dem.** 14:3 8:1993 pp.327 - 367. *Collection of 4 articles.*

4683 Die Rentnergewerkschaft. Ein neuer Akteur der Alterspolitik? *[In German]*; (The pensioners' trade unions — a new actor in old age politics?) *[Summary]*. Harald Künemund; Sighard Neckel; Jürgen Wolf. **Soz. Welt.** 44:4 1993 pp.537 - 554.

I: Labour

4684 Reprezentatywność jako cecha zwi,azku zawodowego. (Na przykładzie Niezależnego, Samorządnego Związku Zawodowego „Solidarność 80"). *[In Polish]*; ("Representativeness" as attribute of trade union.). Walery Masewicz. **Pra. Zab. Społ.** XXXV:5-6 5-6:1993 pp.17 - 24.

4685 Sindicalismo, democracia y desarrollo. *[In Spanish]*; [Trade unions, democracy and development]. Jean Bunel. **Est. Sociol.** XI:31 1-4:1993 pp.133 - 153.

4686 The Tories and employment law in Northern Ireland — seeing unions in a different light? Terry Cradden. **Ind. Relat. J.** 24:1 3:1993 p.59-70.

4687 Trabajo y organización gremial en Matamoros. *[In Spanish]*; [Labour and union organization in Matamoros] *[Summary]*. Arturo Alvarado Mendoza. **Est. Sociol.** XI:33 9-12:1993 pp.661 - 694.

4688 Trade union membership concentration, 1892-1987 — development and causation. Jeremy Waddington. **Br. J. Ind. R.** 31:3 9:1993 pp.433 - 457.

4689 Trade union membership in Europe 1960-90 — rediscovering local unions. Bob Hancké. **Br. J. Ind. R.** 31:4 12:1993 pp.593 - 613.

4690 Trade unions and research. Keith Forrester [Ed.]; Colin Thorne [Ed.]. Aldershot: Avebury, 1993. 215p. *ISBN: 1856283542. Collected papers originate from a Conference entitled: Research as Engagement: An International Conference on Developing Relationships Between Trade Unions and Research Organizations; held at Ruskin College, Oxford, 15-18 July 1991. (Series:* Avebury Business School Library).

4691 Understanding the new labor movements in the "Third World" — the emergence of social movement unionism. Kim Scipes. **Crit. Sociol.** 19:2 1992 pp.81 - 101.

4692 Union effects on municipal employment and wages — a longitudinal approach. Robert G. Valletta. **J. Labor Ec.** 11:3 7:1993 pp.545 - 574.

4693 Union exclusion and the decollectivization of industrial relations in contemporary Britain. Paul Smith; Gary Morton. **Br. J. Ind. R.** 31:1 3:1993 pp.97 - 114.

4694 Union membership and perceived powerlessness in Southern US textiles. Rhonda Zingraff; Jeffrey Leiter. **Sociol. Rev.** 41:1 2:1993 pp.112 - 140.

4695 Union organisation: why countries differ. Jelle Visser. **Int. J. Comp. L. L. I. R.** 9:3 Autumn:1993 pp.206 - 226.

4696 Union participation in occupational health and safety in Western Australia. P. Warren-Langford; D.R. Biggins; M. Phillips. **J. Ind. Relat.** 35:4 12:1993 pp.585 - 606.

4697 Union recognition and non-unionism — shifting fortunes in the electronics industry in Scotland. Patricia Findlay. **Ind. Relat. J.** 24:1 3:1993 pp.28 - 43.

4698 Union rent appropriation and ex post analysis. Ted W. Chiles; James B. Stewart. **J. Labor Res.** XIV:3 Summer:1993 pp.317 - 333.

4699 Union structural change. Bengt Abrahamsson. **Econ. Ind. Dem.** 14:3 8:1993 pp.399 - 421.

4700 Unionization among racial and ethnic minorities. Gregory DeFreitas. **Ind. Lab. Rel.** 46:2 1:1993 pp.284 - 301.

4701 Unions and work attitudes in the United States and Japan. James R. Lincoln; Joan N. Boothe. **Ind. Relat.** 32:2 Spring:1993 pp.159 - 187.

4702 Variations in union presence and density in Australia: evidence from AWIRS. Richard Harris. **J. Ind. Relat.** 35:4 12:1993 pp.571 - 584.

4703 Von der stalinistischen zur marktvermittelten Konvergenz? Zur Transformation der Struktur und Politik der Gewerkschaften in Osteuropa. *[In German]*; (From a

Stalinist to a market-led convergence? A cross-national study in the conversion of union structures and politics in Eastern Europe.) *[Summary]*. Gerd Schienstock; Franz Traxler. **Kölner Z. Soz. Soz. psy.** 45:3 9:1993 pp.484 - 506.

4704 Why American engineers aren't unionized — a comparative perspective. Peter Meiksins; Chris Smith. **Theory Soc.** 22:1 2:1993 pp.57 - 97.

4705 Worker perceptions of procedural justice in workers' compensation claims — do unions make a difference? Sandra E. Gleason; Karen Roberts. **J. Labor Res.** XIV:1 Winter:1993 pp.45 - 58.

4706 Workplace unions and workplace industrial relations — the Italian experience. Michael Terry. **Ind. Relat. J.** 24:2 6:1993 pp.138 - 150.

4707 Works councils and unions in the Netherlands — rivals or allies? Jelle Visser. **Neth. J. Soc. Sci.** 29:1 6:1993 pp.64 - 92.

4708 Zwischen Krise und Solidarität: Perspektiven gewerkschaftlicher Sozialpolitk. *[In German]*; [Between crisis and solidarity: perspectives on the social policy of trade unions]. Horst Schmitthenner [Ed.]. Hamburg: VSA-Verlag, 1992. 247p. *ISBN: 3879756015.*

Workers participation
Participation des travailleurs

4709 Democratic firms, financial participation and economic democratization. Niels Mygind [Ed.]; Charles P. Rock [Ed.]; Milica Uvalic [Contrib.]; Daniel Vaughan-Whitehead [Contrib.]; Ove Langeland [Contrib.]; Yvan Comeau [Contrib.]; Benoît Lévesque [Contrib.]; A. Melissa Moye [Contrib.]; Lars Engberg [Contrib.]. **Econ. Ind. Dem.** 14:2 5:1993 pp.163 - 300. *Collection of 7 articles.*

4710 La experiencia del grupo cooperativo Mondragón. *[In Spanish]*; [The experience of the cooperative group Mondragón]. Alfonso Gorroñogoitia González. **Rev. Fom. Soc.** 48:192 10-12:1993 pp.547 - 560.

4711 The influence of managerial relations on waves of employee involvement. Mick Marchington; Adrian Wilkinson; Peter Ackers; John Goodman. **Br. J. Ind. R.** 31:4 12:1993 pp.553 - 576.

4712 The involvement of trade unions in quality — evidence from EC enterprises. Colin Gill. **New Tech. Work. Empl.** 8:2 9:1993 pp.122 - 133.

4713 Is worker solidarity undermined by autonomy and participation? Patterns from the ethnographic literature. Randy Hodson; Sandy Welsh; Sabine Rieble; Cheryl Sorenson Jamison; Sean Creighton. **Am. Sociol. R.** 58:3 6:1993 pp.398 - 416.

4714 Japanisation? Some early lessons from the British Post Office. Keith Grint. **Ind. Relat. J.** 24:1 3:1993 pp.14 - 27.

4715 Management und Partizipation in der Automobilindustrie: zum Wandel der Arbeitsbeziehungen in Deutschland und Frankreich. *[In German]*; [Management and participation in the automobile industry: on the change in labour relations in Germany and France]. Leo Kissler [Ed.]. Frankfurt am Main: Campus-Verlag, 1992. 296p. *ISBN: 3593346400.*

4716 Udział pracowników w zarządzaniu przedsiębiorstwami w krajach Wspólnoty Europejskiej. *[In Polish]*; (Workers' participation in enterprise management in EC countries.). Jerzy Wratny. **Pra. Zab. Społ.** XXXV:7 7:1993 pp.1 - 13.

I: Labour

4717 Worker cooperatives in the plantation system — a study of tribal tea plantation workers in Eastern India. Sharit K. Bhowmik. **Labour Cap. Soc.** 25:2 11:1992 pp.180 - 197.
4718 Workplace participation in Chinese local industries. Wen Fang Tang. **Am. J. Pol. Sc.** 37:3 8:1993 pp.920 - 940.

I.6: Leisure
Loisir

4719 Bali revisited — death, rejuvenation, and the tourist cycle. J. Connell. **Envir. Plan. D.** 11:6 12:1993 pp.641 - 661.
4720 Black women, recreation and organised sport. Cheryl Roberts. **Agenda** 17 1993 pp.8 - 17.
4721 Correlates of self-reported leisure among adults with mental retardation. Barbara A. Hawkins; Patti A. Freeman. **Leis. Sci.** 15:2 5-6:1993 pp.131 - 148.
4722 Dosug kak faktor sotsial'noi reabilitatsii invalidov. *[In Russian]*; (Leisure as a factor of the invalid's social rehabilitation.). S.S. Kuchinskii; S.P. Shevshuk; I.A. Shames. **Sot. Issle.** 5 1993 pp.87 - 91.
4723 Ecotourism in the small island Caribbean. D.B. Weaver. **Geojournal** 31:4 12:1993 pp.457 - 465.
4724 "Enkelt luggad blev den kille, som ej dribbling lära ville". Hammerby idrätsförening. *[In Swedish]*; (Football tradition in Stockholm.). Mats Franzén. **Nord. Ny.** 53 1993 pp.80 - 89.
4725 Ethnic factors and the use of public outdoor recreation areas: the case of Mexican Americans. Myron F. Floyd; James H. Gramann; Rogelio Saenz. **Leis. Sci.** 15:2 5-6:1993 pp.83 - 98.
4726 Feminist perspectives on leisure constraints. Karla Henderson. **Agenda** 17 1993 pp.29 - 40.
4727 Foul play: a class analysis of sport. Dave Hammond. London: Ubique, 1993. 92p.
4728 History from below: women's underwear and the rise of women's sport. Janet Phillips; Peter Phillips. **J. Pop. Cult.** 27:2 Fall:1993 pp.129 - 148.
4729 The influence of outcome messages on reference prices. Ronald E. McCarville; John L. Crompton; Jane A. Sell. **Leis. Sci.** 15:2 5-6:1993 pp.115 - 130.
4730 Just gaming — allegory and economy in computer games. Julian Stallabrass. **New Left R.** 198 3/4:1993 pp.83 - 106.
4731 Leisure, tourism and "Australianness". David Rowe. **Media Cult. Soc.** 15:2 4:1993 pp.253 - 269.
4732 Mediated messages: gender, class, and cosmos in home video games. Christine Ward Gailey. **J. Pop. Cult.** 27:1 Summer:1993 pp.81 - 98.
4733 A motivational model of leisure participation in the elderly. Gaëtan F. Losier; Paul Bourque; Robert Vallerand. **J. Psychol.** 127:2 3:1993 pp.153 - 170.
4734 Naherholung im Verflechtungsraum Berlin — Brandenburg. *[In German]*; [Recreation in the area around Berlin-Brandenburg]. Gabriele Saupe. **Geogr. Rund.** 45:10 10:1993 pp.608 - 614.
4735 Nature and process of leisure constraints: an empirical test. Leslie Raymore; Geoffrey Godbey; Duane Crawford; Alexander von Eye. **Leis. Sci.** 15:2 5-6:1993 pp.99 - 114.

I: Travail

4736 The passion and the fashion: football fandom in the new Europe. Steve Redhead. Aldershot: Avebury, 1993. 205p. *ISBN: 185628462X, 1856284646. (Series:* Popular cultural studies).

4737 Planning and rural recreation in Britain. David Groome. Aldershot: Avebury, 1993. 346p. *ISBN: 1856284549. Includes bibliographical references and index.*

4738 The positive and negative effects of tourism development in Cyprus. Michael Kammas. **Cyprus Rev.** 5:1 Spring:1993 pp.70 - 89.

4739 The pull of the fruit machine — a sociological typology of young players. Sue Fisher. **Sociol. Rev.** 41:3 8:1993 pp.446 - 474.

4740 The relationship between work stress and leisure style — British and German managers. Bruce D. Kirkcaldy; Cary L. Cooper. **Human Relat.** 46:5 5:1993 pp.669 - 680.

4741 The role of sport in the process of modernisation — the Kenyan case. Peter Mahlmann. **J. E.Afr. Res. Devel.** 22 1992 pp.120 - 131.

4742 [Sociology for sports and rural development]; *[Text in Japanese]*. Kazunori Matsumura. Tokyo: Dowa Shoin, 1993. 279p.

4743 Sport and national identity in the European media. Neil Blain; Raymond Boyle; Hugh O'Donnell. Leicester: Leicester University Press, 1993. vii, 209p. *ISBN: 0718514513. Includes bibliographical references (p. [200]-203) and index. (Series:* Sport, politics, and culture).

4744 Sport, culture and politics. Clyde Binfield [Ed.]; John Stevenson [Ed.]. Sheffield: Sheffield Academic Press, 1993. 192p. *ISBN: 1850753652.*

4745 Time use research. M. Bittman [Contrib.]; P. Eglite [Contrib.]; I. Zarins; W. Michelson [Contrib.]; M.L. Cantwell [Contrib.]; M.M. Sanik [Contrib.]; I. Glorieux [Contrib.]; K. Victor Ujimoto [Contrib.]; A.S. Harvey [Ed.]; I. Niemi [Contrib.]; J. Geurts [Contrib.]; J. de Ree [Contrib.]. **Soc. Ind.** 30:2-3 11:1993 pp.91 - 284. *Collection of 10 articles.*

4746 Le Tour de France et ses mythes. *[In French]*; [The Tour de France and its myths]. . **Regar. Actual.** 192 6:1993 pp.45 - 53.

4747 Tourism and heritage attractions. Richard Prentice. London, New York: Routledge, 1993. 253p. *ISBN: 041508525X. Includes bibliographical references and index. (Series:* Issues in tourism series).

4748 Tourism and society in four Austrian alpine communities. H.G. Kariel. **Geojournal** 31:4 12:1993 pp.449 - 456.

4749 Tourism in Ireland: a critical analysis. Michael Cronin; Barbara O'Connor. Cork: Cork University Press, 1993. 278p. *ISBN: 0902561618.*

4750 Le tourisme des nationaux au Maroc (une nouvelle approche du tourisme dans les pays en développement). *[In French]*; [Domestic tourism in Morocco (a new approach to tourism in developing countries] *[Summary]*. M. Berriane. **Ann. Géogr.** 102:570 3-4:1993 pp.131 - 161.

4751 Ways of escape: modern transformations in leisure and travel. Chris Rojek. Basingstoke: Macmillan, 1993. 251p. *ISBN: 0333475771.*

4752 Women and 'adventure travel' tourism. Anne Beezer. **New Form.** 21 Winter:1993 pp.119 - 130.

J: POLITICS. STATE. INTERNATIONAL RELATIONS
POLITIQUE. ÉTAT. RELATIONS INTERNATIONALES

J.1: Political sociology
Sociologie politique

4753 Explorations in political psychology. William James McGuire [Ed.]; Shanto Iyengar [Ed.]. Durham: Duke University Press, 1993. 481p. *ISBN: 0822313014, 0822313243. Includes bibliographical references (p. [407]-466) and index. (Series:* Duke studies in political psychology).

4754 Political psychology. Jon Elster. Cambridge [England], New York: Cambridge University Press, 1993. viii, 204p. *ISBN: 0521411106, 0521422868. Includes bibliographical references (p. 192-198) and index.*

4755 Les relations de service comme régulations. *[In French]*; (Service relations acting as regulators.) *[Summary]*; *[Summary in Spanish]*; *[Summary in German]*. Philippe Warin. **Rev. Fr. Soc.** XXXIV:1 1-3:1993 pp.69 - 95.

4756 Simmel e la sociologia della politica. *[In Italian]*; (Simmel's interest in political sociology.) *[Summary]*. Carlo Mongardini. **Rass. It. Soc.** XXXIII:4 12:1992 pp.489 - 506.

4757 Sociologie des crises politiques: la dynamique des mobilisations multisectorielles. *[In French]*; [The sociology of political crises: the dynamics of multisector mobilization]. Michel Dobry. Paris: Presses de la Fondation nationale des sciences politiques, 1992. 319p. *ISBN: 2724606108. Bibliogr.: [293]-306 and index.*

4758 Soziologie als Politik: Schriften von 1949 bis 1991. *[In German]*; [Sociology as politics: writings from 1949 to 1991]. Theo Pirker; Rainer Weinert [Ed.]. Berlin: Schelzky und Jeep, 1991. 275p. *ISBN: 392302441X.*

J.2: Political thought
Pensée politique

4759 Analytical Marxism — the race for respectability. Tim Nickel. **Crit. Sociol.** 19:3 1992 pp.81 - 106.

4760 Aufklärung und Ideologie: die Rolle von Philosophie und Soziologie im gesellschaftlichen Umbruch der "realsozialistischen" Staaten. *[In German]*; [Enlightenment and ideology: the role of philosophy and sociology in the radical social change of "real socialist" states]. Johannes Weiss [Ed.]; Wolfdietrich Schmied-Kowarzik [Ed.]. Kassel: Jenior & Pressler, 1992. xii, 137p. *ISBN: 3928172220. Papers given at the East-West Congress in Kassel in 1990.*

4761 Beyond individualism: reconstituting the liberal self. Jack Crittenden. New York: Oxford University Press, 1992. x, 230p. *ISBN: 0195073304. Includes bibliographical references (p. 209-223) and index.*

4762 Citizenship and social theory. Bryan Stanley Turner [Ed.]. London: Sage Publications, 1993. 194p. *ISBN: 0803986114. (Series:* Politics and culture).

4763 Český národní zájem a geopolitika. *[In Czech]*; [The Czech people are interested in geopolitics]. Oskar Krejčí. Praha: Universe, 1993. 179p. *ISBN: 8090150624. Bibliography: p.173-177.*

J: Politique. État. Relations internationales

4764 Explanation and emancipation in Marxism and feminism. Erik Olin Wright. **Sociol. Theory** 11:1 3:1993 pp.39 - 54.

4765 Foundations of class compromise — a theoretical basis for understanding diverse patterns of regime outcomes. Kevin Neuhouser. **Sociol. Theory** 11:1 3:1993 pp.96 - 116.

4766 Gumanizm i obshchestvo budushchego. *[In Russian]*; (Humanism and society of the future.). Iu.G. Volkov; V.S. Malitskii. **Sot. Issle.** 5 1993 pp.51 - 56.

4767 The inner ocean: individualism and democratic culture. George Kateb. Ithaca, N.Y: Cornell University Press, 1992. xi, 274p. *ISBN: 0801427355, 0801480140. Includes bibliographical references and index. (Series:* Contestations).

4768 Konservativnaia mysl'. *[In Russian]*; (Conservative thought.). K. Mannheim. **Sot. Issle.** 4 1993 pp.135 - 146.

4769 The legacy of communism — poisoned minds and souls. Elisabeth Tamedly Lenches. **Int. J. Soc. E.** 20:5/6/7 1993 pp.14 - 34.

4770 Liberal conduct. Duncan Ivison; John Locke [Subject of work]. **Hist. Human Sci.** 6:3 8:1993 pp.25 - 59.

4771 Liberalism and the economic order. Norman Barry [Contrib.]; John Gray [Contrib.]; James M. Buchanan [Contrib.]; Svetozar Pejovich [Contrib.]; William H. Riker [Contrib.]; David L. Weimer [Contrib.]; Don Lavoie [Contrib.]; Russell Hardin [Contrib.]; Richard J. Arneson [Contrib.]; Daniel M. Hausman [Contrib.]; Peter C. Ordeshook [Contrib.]; Allen Buchanan [Contrib.]; Robert H. Frank [Contrib.]; Joshua Cohen [Contrib.]; Joel Rogers [Contrib.]. **Soc. Philos. Pol.** 10:2 Summer:1993 pp.1 - 312. *Collection of 13 articles.*

4772 Liberalism, multiculturalism, and toleration. John P. Horton [Ed.]. Basingstoke: Macmillan, 1993. 209p. *ISBN: 0333571029.*

4773 Marx's theory of rebellion — a cross-national analysis of class exploitation, economic development, and violent revolt. Terry Boswell; William J. Dixon. **Am. Sociol. R.** 58:5 10:1993 pp.681 - 702.

4774 Name, hero, icon: semiotics of nationalism through heroic biography. Anna Makolkin. Berlin, New York: Mouton de Gruyter, 1992. 264p. *ISBN: 3110130122. Includes bibliographical references and index. (Series:* Approaches to semiotics).

4775 Nationalism and civil society — democracy, diversity and self-determination. Craig Calhoun. **Int. Sociol.** 8:4 12:1993 pp.387 - 411.

4776 Nationalstaat und Gesellschaftstheorie. Anthony Giddens, John A. Halls und Michael Manns Beiträge zu einer notwendigen Diskussion. *[In German]*; (Nation-state and social theory — Anthony Giddens', John A. Hall's and Michael Mann's contributions to a necessary debate.) *[Summary].* Wolfgang Knöbl. **Z. Soziol.** 22:3 6:1993 pp.221 - 235.

4777 Nietzsche, feminism, and political theory. Paul Patton [Ed.]. London, New York: Routledge, 1993. 247p. *ISBN: 0415082552, 0415082560. Includes bibliographical references and index.*

4778 Pitirim A. Sorokin's sociological anarchism. Gary Dean Jaworski. **Hist. Human Sci.** 6:3 8:1993 pp.61 - 77.

4779 Poststructuralism and the epistemological basis of anarchism. Andrew M. Koch. **Philos. S. Sc.** 23:3 9:1993 pp.327 - 351.

4780 Power, process, and popular sovereignty. Julie Mostov. Philadelphia: Temple University Press, 1992. xi, 218p. *ISBN: 0877229708, 0877229708. Includes bibliographical references (p. 173-212) and index.*

4781 Proć jsem konzervativcem? *[In Czech]*; [Why are we conservative?]. Václav Klaus. Praha: TOP Agency, 1992. 118p. *ISBN: 8090062679.*

J: Politics. State. International relations

4782 Regionalismus im (west)europäischen Kontext. *[In German]*; (Regionalism in the (Western) European context.). Gerhard Brunn. **Inf. Raum.** 11 1993 pp.739 - 748.
4783 Social movements, political parties, and democratic theory. Herbert Kitschelt. **Ann. Am. Poli.** 528 7:1993 pp.13 - 29.
4784 The social origins of democratic socialism in Jamaica. Nelson W. Keith; Novella Zett Keith. Philadelphia: Temple University Press, 1992. xxiv, 320p. *ISBN: 0877229066. Includes bibliographical references (p. [293]-309) and index.*
4785 Toward a humanist political economy. Harold Chorney; Phillip Birger Hansen. Montréal: Black Rose Books, 1992. 214p. *ISBN: 1895431220, 1895431220.*

J.3: Political systems
Systèmes politiques

4786 Accountable policing: effectiveness, empowerment and equity. Robert Reiner [Ed.]; Sarah Spencer [Ed.]. London: Institute for Public Policy Research, 1993. 191p.
4787 Appropriate skill-task matching or gender bias in deployment of male and female police officers? Jennifer Brown; Anita Maidment; Ray Bull. **Poli. Soc.** 3:2 1993 pp.121 - 136.
4788 L'arrêt de la Cour européenne des droits de l'homme, du 27 août 1992, Tomasi c/France — mauvais traitements et délai déraisonnable. *[In French]*; [The decision of the European Court of Human Rights of 27th August 1992, Tomasi v. France — poor treatment and unreasonable delay]. Frédéric Sudre. **Rev. Sci. Crim. D. P.** 1 1-3:1993 pp.33 - 43.
4789 Attitudes to the police of ethnic minorities in a provincial city. Tony Jefferson; Monica A. Walker. **Br. J. Crimin.** 33:2 Spring:1993 pp.251 - 266.
4790 La Belgique entre les piliers et les "mondes linguistiques". Quelques réflexions sur la question des formes sociales. *[In French]*; (Belgium between vertical structures and linguistic worlds.) *[Summary]*. Bernard Poche. **Recher. Sociolog.** XXIII:3 1992 pp.43 - 68.
4791 Bringing society back into democratic transition theory after 1989 — pact making and regime collapse. Daniel V. Friedheim. **E.Eur. Pol. Soc.** 7:3 Fall:1993 pp.482 - 512.
4792 Bürger machen mobil. Über die neue soziale Sicherheits-bewegung. *[In German]*; [Citizens mobilize. The new social law enforcement movements]. Roland Hitzler. **Fors.Jour. Soz. Beweg.** 3-4 1993 pp.16 - 27.
4793 Civil society — an inquiry into the usefulness of an historical term. Krishan Kumar. **Br. J. Soc.** 44:3 9:1993 pp.375 - 395.
4794 Civil society and the public sphere. Craig Calhoun. **Publ. Cult.** 5:2 Winter:1993 pp.267 - 280.
4795 Community policing in Canada. James Chacko [Ed.]; Stephen E. Nancoo [Ed.]. Toronto: Canadian Scholars' Press, 1993. *ISBN: 1-55130-016-8.*
4796 A comparative analysis of the social requisites of democracy. Seymour Martin Lipset; Kyuong-Ryung Seong; John Charles Torres. **Int. Soc. Sci. J.** 136 5:1993 pp.155 - 175.
4797 Crime and justice: a review of research. Vol.15. Modern policing. Michael H. Tonry [Ed.]; Norval Morris [Ed.]. Chicago: University of Chicago Press, 1992. viii, 606p. *ISBN: 0226808130, 0226808149. Includes bibliographical references and index.*

J: Politique. État. Relations internationales

4798 Defining good policing — the instrumental and moral in approaches to good practice and competence. Clive Norris; Nigel Norris. **Poli. Soc.** 3:3 1993 pp.205 - 221.

4799 The developments of civil society in communist systems. Robert F. Miller [Ed.]. North Sydney, Australia: Allen & Unwin, 1992. 187p. *ISBN: 1863731717. Includes bibliographical references (p. 148-178) and index.*

4800 Dimensions of perceived stress in a British police force. Graham Crowe; Stephen G. Stradling. **Poli. Soc.** 3:2 1993 pp.137 - 150.

4801 Dividing public and private: law, politics, and social theory. Gerald Turkel. Westport, Conn: Praeger, 1992. xii, 255p. *ISBN: 027594154X. Includes bibliographical references (p. [239]-250) and index.*

4802 Dying in a ditch: the use of police powers in public order. P.A.J. Waddington. **Int. J. S. Law** 21:4 12:1993 pp.335 - 354.

4803 Equal opportunities in policing — a comparative examination of anti-discrimination policy and practice in British policing. I.K. McKenzie. **Int. J. S. Law** 21:2 6:1993 pp.159 - 174.

4804 Integrating calls for service with community- and problem-oriented policing — a case study. David A. Kessler. **Crime Delin.** 39:4 10:1993 pp.485 - 508.

4805 Internal police records and the control of juveniles — politics and policing in a suburban town. Albert J. Meehan. **Br. J. Crimin.** 33:4 Autumn:1993 pp.504 - 524.

4806 Modern governance: new government-society interactions. Jan Kooiman [Ed.]. London: Sage, 1993. 280p. *ISBN: 0803988907, 0803988915. Bibliography: p. 267-280.*

4807 Modernist and postmodernist metaphors of the policy process — control and stability vs. chaos and reflexive understanding. Laurent Dobuzinskis. **Policy Sci.** 25:4 11:1992 pp.355 - 380.

4808 La notion d'autorité politique et l'idéologie étatique. *[In French]*; [The notion of political authority and state ideology] *[Summary]*. Lahouri Addi. **Cah. Int. Soc.** XCIV 1-6:1993 pp.145 - 160.

4809 Outline of a theory of human rights. Bryan S. Turner. **Sociology** 27:3 8:1993 pp.489 - 512.

4810 Police and policing in India: a select bibliography. Nehal Ashraf [Ed.]. New Delhi, India: Commonwealth Publishers, 1992. viii, 256p.

4811 Police and the use of force: the Savannah study. Richard R.E. Kania [Foreword]; Vance McLaughlin. Westport, Conn: Praeger, 1992. xvi, 154p. *ISBN: 0275943445. Includes bibliographical references (p. [141]-147) and index.*

4812 La police: approche socio-politique. *[In French]*; [The police: a socio-political approach]. Jean-Louis Loubet del Bayle. Paris: Montchrestien, 1992. 158p. *ISBN: 2707605352. Index and bibliogr..*

4813 Police et immigrés: images mutuelles, problèmes et solutions. *[In French]*; [Police and immigrants: images of each other, problems and solutions]. M.-T Casman; et al. Brugge: Vanden Broele, Politeia, 1991. 160p. *ISBN: 9062670598. Includes bibliographical references (p. 135-149).*

4814 La police et le secret des données d'ordre personnel en droit français. *[In French]*; [Police and confidential personal information under French law]. Etienne Picard. **Rev. Sci. Crim. D. P.** 2 4-6:1993 pp.275 - 310.

4815 Police interview techniques — establishing truth or proof? John Baldwin. **Br. J. Crimin.** 33:3 Summer:1993 pp.325 - 352.

J: Politics. State. International relations

4816 Policing and social change. G.M. Stephenson [Contrib.]; T.M. Williamson [Contrib.]; S. Moston [Contrib.]; G.H. Gudjonsson [Contrib.]; S.G. Stradling [Contrib.]; G. Crowe [Contrib.]; A.P. Tuohy [Contrib.]. **J. Comm. App. Soc. Psychol.** 3:2 6:1993 pp.87 - 147. *Collection of 5 articles.*

4817 Policing for a new South Africa. Michael Brogden; Clifford D. Shearing. London: Routledge, 1993. 234p. *ISBN: 0415083214.*

4818 Policing South Africa: the South African Police and the transition from apartheid. Gavin Cawthra. London: Zed Books, 1993. 226p. *ISBN: 1856490653. Includes bibliographical references (p. 209-218) and index.*

4819 The politics of interest in post-communist East Europe. David Ost. **Theory Soc.** 22:4 8:1993 pp.453 - 485.

4820 Politics, society, and democracy: the case of Spain. Richard Gunther [Ed.]; Juan José Linz. Boulder: Westview Press, 1993. xvi, 272p. *ISBN: 0813385458. Includes bibliographical references. (Series: Essays in honor of Juan J. Linz).*

4821 A power index for multi-stage and multi-agent decision systems. Tatsuaki Kuroda. **Behav. Sci.** 38:4 10:1993 pp.255 - 272.

4822 Prospects of a free and democratic society in Hungary. Gyorgy Andrássy; Miklós Fülöp. **J. Interd. Stud.** IV:1/2 1992 pp.121 - 138.

4823 Protection des droits de l'homme — situation actuelle et développement. *[In French]*; [Protecting human rights — actual situation and development]; *[Summary in Arabic]*. Khaïreddine Abdessamad. **R. Tun. Sci. Soc.** 29:108 1992 pp.21 - 35.

4824 Public images of the police in Northern Ireland. John D. Brewer. **Poli. Soc.** 3:3 1993 pp.163 - 176.

4825 Requiem for communism — the case of Hungary. Lewis E. Hill; István Magas. **Int. J. Soc. E.** 20:5/6/7 1993 pp.35 - 43.

4826 The rise and fall of the new class. Ivan Kuvacic. **Int. J. Pol. C. S.** 7:1 Fall:1993 pp.5 - 18.

4827 Sind soziale Rechte universalisierbar? *[In German]*; (Are social rights universalizable?) *[Summary]*. Heiner Ganßmann. **Z. Soziol.** 22:5 10:1993 pp.385 - 394.

4828 La situación y los derechos de los pueblos indígenas de América. *[In Spanish]*; (Situation and human rights of American indigenous peoples.) *[Summary]*. Rodolfo Stavenhagen. **Am. Indígena** LII:1-2 1-6:1992 pp.63 - 118.

4829 The socialist system and its collapse in Hungary — an interpretation in terms of modernisation theory. Rudolf Andorka. **Int. Sociol.** 8:3 9:1993 pp.317 - 337.

4830 Socialist visions, Naples and the Neapolitans — value, control and representation in the agency/structure relationship. Italo Pardo. **J. Mediter. St.** 3:1 1993 pp.77 - 98.

4831 Society, state & politics in Australia. Michael Muetzelfeldt [Ed.]. Leichhardt: Pluto Press, 1992. 393p. *ISBN: 0949138592. Includes bibliographical references (p. [360]-382) and index. (Series: Sociology/politics).*

4832 Socjalistyczne "welfare state": studium z psychologii społecznej Polski ludowej. *[In Polish]*; [The socialist welfare state: studies on the social psychology of the Polish working class]. Winicjusz Narojek. Warszawa: Wydawn. Nauk. PWN, 1991. 119p. *ISBN: 8301106158. Includes bibliographical references.*

4833 Sotsiokul'turnyi bazis perestroiki. *[In Russian]*; [The socio-cultural basis of perestroika]. I. E. Diskin. Moskva: Nauka, 1992. 103p. *ISBN: 5020134910.*

4834 Społeczeństwo i polityka w okresie transformacji systemu. *[In Polish]*; [Politics and society in the era of transformation]. Anita Miszalska. **Prz. Soc.** XLI 1992 pp.11 - 30.
4835 Tainaia poliitsiia kak tainoe obshchestvo: strakh i vera b SSSR. *[In Russian]*; (The secret police as a secret society: fear and belief in the USSR.). L.A. Abrahamian. **Etnograf. Oboz.** 5 1993 pp.35 - 42.
4836 Targeting community beat officers — organisational constraints and resistance. M.R. Chatterton. **Poli. Soc.** 3:3 1993 pp.189 - 203.
4837 Term-limitation express. Mark P. Petracca; Darci Jump. **Society** 31:1 11-12:1993 pp.61 - 69.
4838 Totalitarian interaction: a systems approach. Vessela Misheva. **Social. Int.** 31:2 1993 pp.179 - 196.
4839 Understanding political change in Eastern Europe — a sociological perspective. Barbara A. Misztal. **Sociology** 27:3 8:1993 pp.451 - 470.

J.4: Public administration
Administration publique

4840 Another century for local democracy? Decentralization, deregulation and participation in Scandinavia in times of European integration; *[Summary in French]*. Søren Villadsen. **Int. J. Urban** 17:1 3:1993 pp.42 - 55.
4841 Après la décentralisation. L'action publique flexible. *[In French]*; (After decentralization — flexible public actions.) *[Summary]*. Dominique Lorrain. **Sociol. Trav.** XXXVI:3 1993 pp.285 - 307.
4842 Assessment of intergovernmental revenue transfers. Agha Iqbal Ali; Catherine S. Lerme; Robert A. Nakosteen. **Socio. Econ.** 27:2 1993 pp.109 - 118.
4843 Autopoiesis and the science of (public) administration — essence, sense and nonsense. Walter J.M. Kickert. **Organ. Stud.** 14:2 1993 pp.261 - 278.
4844 Back to the classics — relevance of Western organisation theory in developing nations. Jonathan N. Moyo. **Indian J. Publ. Admin.** XXXVIII:4 10-12:1992 pp.539 - 555.
4845 Black and Hispanic council representation — does council size matter? Nicholas O. Alozie; Lynne L. Manganaro. **Urban Aff. Q.** 29:2 12:1993 pp.276 - 298.
4846 Care, justice, and public administration. Philip H. Jos; Samuel M. Hines. **Admin. Soc.** 25:3 11:1993 pp.373 - 392.
4847 Eléments pour une compréhension subversive de la technocratie. *[In French]*; [The elements necessary for a subversive understanding of technocracy] *[Summary]*. Gilbert Larochelle. **Cah. Int. Soc.** XCIV 1-6:1993 pp.121 - 143.
4848 From centralised state to local government. The case of Poland in the light of Western European experience. H.T. Jensen; V. Plum. **Envir. Plan. D.** 11:5 10:1993 pp.565 - 581.
4849 Im Bannkreis der Machtfrage — Entwicklung und Stand der lokalen Selbstverwaltung in Rußland. *[In German]*; (Local self-administration in Russia.) *[Summary]*; *[Summary in French]*. Hellmut Wollman. **Arc. Kommunal.** 32:1 1993 pp.1 - 23.
4850 Länderneugliederung in Deutschland. *[In German]*; [The restructuring of the Länder]. Eugen Ernst. **Geogr. Rund.** 45:7-8 7-8:1993 pp.446 - 458.

J: Politics. State. International relations

4851 La modernisation de l'administration et les projets de service: l'expérience burkinabé. *[In French]*; [The modernization of administration and service projects: the experience of Burkina Faso]. Loïtéohin Félix Ye. **Cah. Afr. Admin. Pub.** 40 1993 pp.45 - 54.

4852 La modernisation de l'administration et les projets de service: l'expérience gabonaise. *[In French]*; [The modernization of public administration and service projects: the Gabon experience]. Lindzondzo Mambanya. **Cah. Afr. Admin. Pub.** 40 1993 pp.55 - 58.

4853 La modernisation de l'administration et les projets de service: l'expérience malienne. *[In French]*; [The modernization of public administration and service projects: the experience of Mali]. Bouaré Lassine. **Cah. Afr. Admin. Pub.** 40 1993 pp.59 - 64.

4854 The new Leviathan — the dynamics and limits of technocracy. Miguel Angel Centeno. **Theory Soc.** 22:3 6:1993 pp.307 - 335.

4855 Racial politics — does it pay? Timothy Bates; Darrell L. Williams. **Soc. Sci. Q.** 74:3 9:1993 pp.507 - 522.

4856 Regulation theory, the local state, and the transition of urban politics. M. Goodwin; S. Duncan; S. Halford. **Envir. Plan. D.** 11:1 2:1993 pp.67 - 88.

4857 The rhetorical way of knowing and public administration. Richard T. Green; Robert C. Zinke. **Admin. Soc.** 25:3 11:1993 pp.317 - 334.

4858 The role of the administration in central-local relations — the legislative and executive control. Shirani A. Bandaranayake. **Sri Lanka J. Soc. Sci.** 14:1-2 6-12:1991 pp.65 - 77.

4859 'What big teeth you have!': identifying the motivations for exclusionary zoning. William T. Bogart. **Urban Stud.** 30:10 12:1993 pp.1669 - 1682.

J.5: Political parties, pressure groups and political movements
Partis politiques, groupes de pression et mouvements politiques

4860 1968 in Frankreich — die große Parallelaktion. *[In German]*; (1968 in France — the great parallel action.) *[Summary]*; *[Summary in French]*. Ingrid Gilcher-Holtey. **Berl. J. Soziol.** 3:4 1993 pp.539 - 548.

4861 Acting locally — environmental injustice and the emergence of grass-roots environmental organizations. Sherry Cable; Michael Benson. **Soc. Prob.** 40:4 11:1993 pp.464 - 477.

4862 Action collective et démocratie locale: les mouvements urbains montréalais. *[In French]*; [Collective action and local democracy: Montreal urban movements]. Pierre Hamel. Montréal: Presses de l'Université de Montréal, 1991. 239p. *ISBN: 2760615464. Includes bibliographical references: p. [223]-236.*

4863 Activating theory: lesbian, gay, bisexual politics. Joseph Bristow [Ed.]; Angie Wilson [Ed.]. London: Lawrence & Wishart, 1993. 266p. *ISBN: 0853157901.*

4864 Auf dem Weg in die „Bewegungsgesellschaft"? Über die Stabilisierbarkeit sozialer Bewegungen. *[In German]*; (Towards a society of social movements. On the stabilization of social movements.) *[Summary]*. Friedhelm Neidhardt; Dieter Rucht. **Soz. Welt.** 44:3 1993 pp.305 - 326.

4865 Auf der Suche nach der postkommunistischen Gesellschaft — das Beispiel Polen. *[In German]*; (In search of a post-communist society — the example of Poland.) *[Summary]*. Zygmunt Bauman. **Soz. Welt.** 44:2 1993 pp.157 - 176.

J: Politique. État. Relations internationales

4866 Bewegungen und Protest in Italien. Mögliche Szenarien für die 90er Jahre. *[In German]*; [Movements and protest in Italy. Possible scenarios for the 1990s]. Donatella della Porta. **Fors.Jour. Soz. Beweg.** 1 1993 pp.59 - 68.

4867 Beyond resource mobilization? Emerging trends in social movement theory. Steven M. Buechler. **Sociol. Q.** 34:2 5:1993 pp.217 - 235.

4868 Birmingham confrontation reconsidered — an analysis of the dynamics and tactics of mobilization. Aldon D. Morris. **Am. Sociol. R.** 58:5 10:1993 pp.621 - 636.

4869 Bürgerinitiativen und Parteien im Umweltschutz in Portugal. *[In German]*; [Citizens' initiative and political parties for environmental protection in Portugal]. Alexander Carius; Helge Jörgens. **Fors.Jour. Soz. Beweg.** 1 1993 pp.76 - 86.

4870 Bürgerinitiativen und Parteien im Umweltschutz in Spanien. *[In German]*; [Citizens' initiative and political parties for environmental protection in Spain]. Alexander Carius. **Fors.Jour. Soz. Beweg.** 1 1993 pp.69 - 75.

4871 Commitment across the miles — ideological and microstructural sources of membership support in a national anti-hunger organization. Steven E. Barkan; Steven F. Cohn; William H. Whitaker. **Soc. Prob.** 40:3 8:1993 pp.362 - 373.

4872 Les conflits scolaires 1991-1992. *[In French]*; [The education conflicts of 1991-1992]. J.E. Charlier; Y. Collard. **Ann. Soc.** 1992 pp.75 - 109.

4873 Contesting power: resistance and everyday social relations in South Asia. Douglas E. Haynes [Ed.]; Gyan Prakash [Ed.]. Berkeley: University of California Press, 1992. 310p. *ISBN: 0520075854.*

4874 Coordinating demands for social change. Dennis Chong. **Ann. Am. Poli.** 528 7:1993 pp.126 - 141.

4875 The <u>damnificados</u> of Guadalajara — the politics of domination and social movement protest. Jon Shefner; John Walton. **Int. J. Urban** 17:4 12:1993 pp.611 - 622.

4876 De l'utopie au pragmatisme?: le mouvement occitan, 1976-1990. *[In French]*; [From utopia to pragmatism?: the Occitan movement, 1976-1990]. Henri Jeanjean. Perpinyà: Llibres del Trabucaire, 1992. 211p. *ISBN: 290582834X. Includes bibliographical references (p. 206-209).*

4877 Dissident groups, personal networks, and spontaneous cooperation — the East German revolution of 1989. Karl-Dieter Opp; Christiane Gern. **Am. Sociol. R.** 58:5 10:1993 pp.659 - 680.

4878 The dynamics of protest waves — West Germany, 1965 to 1989. Ruud Koopmans. **Am. Sociol. R.** 58:5 10:1993 pp.637 - 658.

4879 The ecological movements in the light of social movements' development — the cases of four contemporary industrialized societies. Guy Fréchet; Barbara Wörndl. **Int. J. Comp. Soc** XXXIV:1-2 1-4:1993 pp.56 - 74.

4880 Einstellungen bei Mitgliedern von Umweltorganisationen — Veränderungen und Stabilität im "neuen Europa" am Beispiel Schwedens. *[In German]*; [Views of members of environmental organizations. Changes and stability in "new Europe" — the example of Sweden]. Martin Barnulf. **Fors.Jour. Soz. Beweg.** 1 1993 pp.33 - 41.

4881 Environmentalism in Ireland — two versions of development and modernity. Hilary Tovey. **Int. Sociol.** 8:4 12:1993 pp.413 - 430.

4882 Envolvimento político-social de adolescentes no episódio Collor. *[In Portuguese]*; [The socio-political involvement of adolescents in the demonstrations against President Collor] *[Summary]*. Marli Möller. **Est. Leop.** 29:134 9-10:1993 pp.47 - 60.

J: Politics. State. International relations

4883 État et idéologie du bénévolat au Québec — les enjeux dans un contexte néo-libéral. *[In French]*; (State and the volunteer ideology in Quebec — issues in a neo-liberal setting.) *[Summary]*. Gilbert Larochelle. **Recher. Sociolog.** XXIII:3 1992 pp.65 - 90.

4884 Fighting back — vulnerabilities, blunders, and countermobilization by the targets in three animal rights campaigns. James M. Jasper; Jane Poulsen. **Sociol. For.** 8:4 12:1993 pp.639 - 657.

4885 Frame disputes within the nuclear disarmament movement. Robert D. Benford. **Soc. Forc.** 71:3 3:1993 pp.677 - 701.

4886 "From confusion to Lusaka" — the youth revolt in Sekhukhuneland. Ineke van Kessel. **J. S.Afr. Stud.** 19:4 12:1993 pp.593 - 614.

4887 From unidimensionality to multidimensionality — some observations on the dynamics of social movements. Tamar Hermann. **R. Soc. Move. Con. Cha.** 15 1993 pp.181 - 202.

4888 A growing crisis — changing patterns of South African violence. Christopher Hewitt. **R. Soc. Move. Con. Cha.** 15 1993 pp.139 - 156.

4889 Hotbild, hopp och etik i miljörörelser. *[In Swedish]*; (The environmental movement and threatening images.). Knut Weibust. **Nord. Ny.** 52 1993 pp.98 - 104.

4890 Impact of social movements on European party systems. Robert Rohrschneider. **Ann. Am. Poli.** 528 7:1993 pp.157 - 170.

4891 Individual environmental responsibility and its role in public environmentalism. S.E. Eden. **Envir. Plan. A.** 25:12 12:1993 pp.1743 - 1758.

4892 Khristianskaia demokratiia v Rossii. *[In Russian]*; (Christian democracy in Russia.). R. Sakva. **Sot. Issle.** 7 1993 pp.122 - 131.

4893 Khristianskaia demokratiia v Rossii. Ch.i. *[In Russian]*; (Christian democracy in Russia P.I.). R.-Kh. Sakva. **Sot. Issle.** 4 1993 pp.126 - 134.

4894 The making of social movements in Latin America: identity, strategy, and democracy. Arturo Escobar [Ed.]; Sonia E. Alvarez [Ed.]. Boulder, Colo: Westview Press, 1992. xvi, 383p. *ISBN: 081331206X, 0813312078. Includes bibliographical references (p. 334-364) and index. (Series:* Series in political economy and economic development in Latin America).

4895 Mass social movements and social class; *[Summary in French]*. Jan Pakulski. **Int. Sociol.** 8:2 6:1993 pp.131 - 158.

4896 Mobilization potential for environmental protest. Hanspeter Kriesi; Willem E. Saris; Anchrit Wille. **Eur. Sociol. R.** 9:2 9:1993 pp.155 - 171.

4897 Mobilizing against nuclear energy: a comparison of Germany and the United States. Christian Joppke. Berkeley: University of California Press, 1993. xv, 307p. *ISBN: 0520078136.*

4898 Modern social movements as active risk observers — a systems-theoretical approach to collective action. Jost Halfmann; Klaus P. Japp. **Soc. Sci. Info.** 32:3 1993 pp.427 - 446.

4899 Moderne soziale Bewegungen in der Bundesrepublik Deutschland — Reichweite und Wirkungen. *[In German]*; (Modern social movements in the Federal Republic of Germany — scope and impacts.) *[Summary]*; *[Summary in French]*. Jost Halfmann. **Berl. J. Soziol.** 3:2 1993 pp.205 - 214.

4900 Movements and media as interacting systems. William A. Gamson; Gadi Wolfsfeld. **Ann. Am. Poli.** 528 7:1993 pp.114 - 125.

4901 Movimenti sociali e sistema politico. Un confronto fra Italia e Germania. *[In Italian]*; (Social movements and the political system: Italy and Germany compared.)

J: Politique. État. Relations internationales

[Summary]. Donatella della Porta; Dieter Rucht. **Riv. It. Sci. Pol.** XXII:3 12:1992 pp.501 - 538.

4902 El movimiento de mujeres y el sistema político mexicano — análisis de la lucha por la liberalización del aborto, 1976-1990. *[In Spanish]*; [The women's movement and the Mexican political system — analysis of the struggle for the liberalisation of abortion, 1976-1990] *[Summary]*. María Luisa Tarrés. **Est. Sociol.** XI:32 5-8:1993 pp.365 - 398.

4903 The neoliberal assault and Latin American countermobilization. David Sheinin. **Crit. Sociol.** 20:1 1993-1994 pp.121 - 128.

4904 Neue soziale Bewegungen in einer alten Stadt: Versuch einer vorläufigen Bilanz am Beispiel Bremens. *[In German]*; [New social movements in an old town: an attempt at current analysis using Bremen as an example]. Christoph Butterwegge [Ed.]; Hans G. Jansen [Ed.]; Ralf Fücks [Intro.]. Bremen: Steintor, 1992. 286p. *ISBN: 3926028777. Includes bibliographical references (p. 259-285).*

4905 New directions in the study of social movements. William K. Carroll [Contrib.]; Barry D. Adam [Contrib.]; Jane Jenson [Contrib.]; Leslie Kenny [Contrib.]; Warren Magnusson [Contrib.]; Sharon D. Stone [Contrib.]; Lorna Erwin [Contrib.]. **Can. R. Soc. A.** 30:3 8:1993 pp.316 - 420.

4906 The new politics of class: social movements and cultural dynamics in advanced societies. Klaus Eder. London: Sage Publications, 1993. 223p. *ISBN: 0803988680.* (*Series:* Theory, culture and society).

4907 New social movements in the South: empowering the people. Ponna Wignaraja [Ed.]. London: Zed Books, 1993. 275p. *ISBN: 1856491072.*

4908 Der Niedergang von Bewegungsorganisationen. Zur Analyse von organisatorischen Laufbahnen. *[In German]*; (The decline of social movement organizations. A contribution to the analysis of organizational trajectories.) *[Summary]*. Sandro Cattacin; Florence Passy. **Kölner Z. Soz. Soz. psy.** 45:3 9:1993 pp.419 - 438.

4909 Nuclear summer: the clash of communities at the Seneca women's peace encampment. Louise Krasniewicz. Ithaca, N.Y: Cornell University Press, 1992. xiii, 259p. *ISBN: 0801426359, 0801499380. Includes bibliographical references (p. [240]-249) and index.* (*Series:* Anthropology of contemporary issues).

4910 O perspektivakh konservativnoi partiinoi politiki v Rossii. *[In Russian]*, (On the perspective of conservative party politics in Russia.). V.F. Shapovalov. **Sot. Issle.** 4 1993 pp.106 - 115.

4911 La ocupación de tierras como lucha social — los rescates de terreno en Puerto Rico — 1968-1976. *[In Spanish]*; [The occupation of land as social struggle — land invasion in Puerto Rico — 1968-1976] *[Summary]*. Liliana Cotto. **Rev. Cien. Soc.** XXIX:3-4 7-12:1990 pp.409 - 428.

4912 La organización popular y el rol de las ONGDs — una aproximación. *[In Spanish]*; (Popular organizations and the role of NGOs — an approximation.) *[Summary]*. Héctor Béjar. **Soc. Part.** 63 11:1993 pp.39 - 58.

4913 Outsiders: class, gender, and nation. Dorothy Thompson. New York; London: Verso, 1993. 186p. *ISBN: 0860914909. Includes bibliographical references.*

4914 Parties, interest groups, and administered mass organizations. Gregory J. Kasza. **Comp. Poli. S.** 26:1 4:1993 pp.81 - 110.

4915 The people and the mob: the ideology of civil conflict in modern Europe. Peter Hayes. Westport, Conn: Praeger, 1992. xx, 162p. *ISBN: 0275943364. Includes bibliographical references (p. [147]-157) and index.*

J: Politics. State. International relations

4916 Political generations and protest — the old left and the new left. Roger Neustadter. **Crit. Sociol.** 19:3 1992 pp.37 - 55.
4917 Political mobilization and social change: the Dutch case in comparative perspective. Hanspeter Kriesi. Aldershot: Avebury, 1993. 292p. *ISBN: 1856285189*. (*Series: Public policy and social welfare*).
4918 Power and protest: movements for change in Australian society. Verity Burgmann. Sydney: Allen & Unwin, 1992. xiv, 302p. *ISBN: 186373211X. Includes index. Bibliography.*
4919 Protesters, counterprotesters, and the authorities. Diarmuid Maguire. **Ann. Am. Poli.** 528 7:1993 pp.101 - 113.
4920 Qué puede hacer uno ante los grandes problemas mundiales? Una perspectiva pedagógica. *[In Spanish]*; [What can be done about the great global problems? A pedagogical perspective]. Josep Miralles. **Rev. Fom. Soc.** 48:192 10-12:1993 pp.535 - 546.
4921 Quebec-as-distinct-society as conventional wisdom — the constitutional silence of Anglo-Canadian sociologists; *[Summary in French]*. Claude Denis. **Can. J. Soc.** 18:3 Summer:1993 pp.251 - 263.
4922 Representing solidarity — class, gender and the crisis in social-democratic Sweden. Jane Jenson; Rianne Mahon. **New Left R.** 201 9-10:1993 pp.76 - 100.
4923 Repression and popular collective action — evidence from the West Bank. Marwan Khawaja. **Sociol. For.** 8:1 3:1993 pp.47 - 71.
4924 Resource mobilization in Africa — the role of local organizations in the Tanganyika Independence Movement. Nancy L. Spalding. **J. Dev. Areas** 28:1 10:1993 pp.89 - 109.
4925 Rethinking critical theory: emancipation in the age of global social movements. Larry J. Ray. London: Sage Publications, 1993. 202p. *ISBN: 0803983646*.
4926 Die Rolle sozialer Bewegungen bei der Gestaltung einer neuen politischen Symbolik in Rußland. *[In German]*; [The role of social movements in the formation of a new political symbolism in Russia]. Elena Zdravomyslova. **Fors.Jour. Soz. Beweg.** 2:3 1993 pp.59 - 69.
4927 Shall we overcome? The sense of movement power among Gulf War protesters. Eric Swank. **Crit. Sociol.** 20:1 1993-1994 pp.31 - 52.
4928 Social movements. Charles Tilly; Suzanne Staggenborg; Donna Eder; Lori Sudderth; John L. Boies; Nelson A. Pichardo; Sean D. Stryker; Timothy Ingalsbee; David S. Meyer; Will Hathaway; Alberto Melucci. **Berkeley J. Soc.** 38 1993-1994 pp.1 - 192. *Collection of 7 articles.*
4929 Social movements and the policy process. Thomas R. Rochon; Daniel A. Mazmanian. **Ann. Am. Poli.** 528 7:1993 pp.75 - 87.
4930 Social movements in Chile today. James Petras; Rosa Canadell. **Labour Cap. Soc.** 25:2 11:1992 pp.198 - 217.
4931 [Sociometrical analysis of social movements]; *[Text in Japanese]*. Nobuyoshi Kurita. Tokyo: Nihon Hyoronsha, 1993. 167p.
4932 Sotsial"naia baza dvizheniia kraine pravykh v Zapadnoi Evrope. *[In Russian]*; [The social basis for extreme right movements in Western Europe]. I. N. Barygin. Leningrad: Izd-vo Leningradskogo universiteta, 1990. 159p. *ISBN: 5288005419. Bibliography.*
4933 Soziale Bewegungen im Übergang zu politischen Parteien in Ost-Mitteleuropa — Polen, die Tschechische Republik, Slowakei und Ungarn. *[In German]*; [Social

movements in transition to political parties in East-Central Europe. Poland, the Czech Republic, Slovakia and Hungary]. Helmut Fehr. **Fors.Jour. Soz. Beweg.** 2:3 1993 pp.25 - 40.
4934 The specifics of Dutch political parties. Ruud A. Koole. **Neth. J. Soc. Sci.** 29:2 12:1993 pp.164 - 182.
4935 Specifying the relationship between social ties and activism. Doug McAdam; Ronnelle Paulsen. **A.J.S.** 99:3 11:1993 pp.640 - 667.
4936 The structure of social protest, 1961-1983. Peter S. Bearman; Kevin D. Everett. **Soc. Networks** 15:2 6:1993 pp.171 - 200.
4937 Terrorizm postperestroechnoi Epokhi. *[In Russian]*; (Terrorism of the post-perestroika epoch.). V.V. Vitiuk. **Sot. Issle.** 7 1993 pp.42 - 50.
4938 A theoretical framework for comparisons of social movement participation. Bert Klandermans. **Sociol. For.** 8:3 9:1993 pp.383 - 402.
4939 Tradition and the new social movements — the politics of Isthmus Zapotec culture. Howard Campbell. **Lat. Am. Pers.** 20:3(78) Summer:1993 pp.83 - 97.
4940 Umweltgruppen in den Niederlanden und der EG — Produktorientierung und europäische Implikationen. *[In German]*; [Environment groups in the Netherlands and the European Communities. Product orientation and European implications]. Frank Boons. **Fors.Jour. Soz. Beweg.** 1 1993 pp.42 - 49.
4941 Urban social movements and local democracy in Brazil; *[Summary in Spanish]*. Willem Assies. **R. Eur. Lat.am. Caribe** 55 12:1993 pp.39 - 58.
4942 Vnutri konflikta. *[In Russian]*; (Inside the conflict.). Iu.G. Zaprudskii. **Sot. Issle.** 7 1993 pp.51 - 58.
4943 Whale politics and green legitimacy — a critique of the anti-whaling campaign. Arne Kalland. **Anthr. Today** 9:6 12:1993 pp.3 - 7.
4944 Whose common future?: reclaiming the commons. Ecologist. London: Earthscan Publications, 1993. 216p. *ISBN: 1853831492.*
4945 "You could be the hundreth monkey" — collective action frames and vocabularies of motive within the nuclear disarmament movement. Robert D. Benford. **Sociol. Q.** 34:2 5:1993 pp.195 - 216.

**J.6: Political behaviour and elections
Comportement politique et élections**

4946 Backlash effects in attack politics. Neal J. Roese; Gerald N. Sande. **J. Appl. Soc. Psychol.** 23:8 4:1993 pp.632 - 653.
4947 Campaign '92 — new frontiers in political communication. James L. Golden [Contrib.]; Dee Dee Myers [Contrib.]; Robert Dole [Contrib.]; Patrick Downey [Contrib.]; J. Gregory Payne [Ed.]; Alan L. Golden [Contrib.]; Scott C. Ratzan [Contrib.]; David A. Brenders [Contrib.]; Valeria Fabj [Contrib.]; Judith S. Trent [Contrib.]; Paul A. Mongeau [Contrib.]; Jimmie D. Trent [Contrib.]; Kathleen E. Kendall [Contrib.]; Ronald B. Cushing [Contrib.]; Wayne Jacques [Contrib.]; Frank Meilinger [Contrib.]; Michael Balmoris [Contrib.]; Cynthia Gerns [Contrib.]; Steven Denby [Contrib.]; Edwin Diamond [Contrib.]; Martha McKay [Contrib.]; Robert Silverman [Contrib.]; Robert H. Wicks [Contrib.]; Montague Kern [Contrib.]; L. Patrick Devlin [Contrib.]; Kevin Mercuri [Contrib.]; Kenneth E. Andersen [Contrib.];

J: Politics. State. International relations

Matthew J. Sobnosky [Contrib.]; Arthur Miller [Contrib.]; Doris A. Graber [Contrib.]. **Am. Behav. Sc.** 37:2 11-12:1993 pp.173 - 336. *Collection of 18 articles.*

4948 Les chemins de l'abstention: une comparaison franco-américaine. *[In French]*; [The paths of abstention: a Franco-American comparison]. Françoise Subileau; Marie-France Toinet. Paris: La Découverte, 1993. 221p. *ISBN: 2707121886. Includes bibliographical references (p. 215-[216]) and index.*

4949 Citizenship and the place of the public sphere — law, community, and political culture in the transition to democracy. Margaret R. Somers. **Am. Sociol. R.** 58:5 10:1993 pp.587 - 620.

4950 Comparing the decline of nationalisms in Western Europe: the generational dynamic. Mattei Dogan. **Int. Soc. Sci. J.** 136 5:1993 pp.177 - 198.

4951 Composició sociològica dels delegats del VIII Congrés del PSUC a l'Assemblea Constituent d'IC. *[In Catalan]*; [The sociological composition of the delegates to the 8th PSUC Congress at the Constituent Assembly of the IC] *[Summary]*; *[Summary in Spanish]*. Gabriel Colomé. **Papers** 39 1992 pp.43 - 58.

4952 Cultura política e cidadania no Brasil — uma análise longitudinal. *[In Portuguese]*; [Political culture and citizenship in Brazil — a longitudinal analysis] *[Summary]*. Marcello Baquero; Jussara Reis Prá. **Est. Leop.** 28:129/130 9-12:1992 pp.87 - 110.

4953 Culture and democracy in the South Pacific. Ronald Gordon Crocombe [Ed.]; Fanaafi Le Tagaloa Aiono; et al. Suva, Fiji: Institute of Pacific Studies, University of the South Pacific, 1992. x, 280p. *ISBN: 9820200792. Includes bibliographical references and index.*

4954 Demography and federal elections in Germany, 1953-1990 — and beyond. Hans Rattinger. **Elec. Stud.** 11:3 9:1992 pp.223 - 247.

4955 The dilemma of cultural identity on the margin of Europe. Çağlar Keyder. **Rev. F. Braudel. Ctr.** XVI:1 Winter:1993 pp.19 - 33.

4956 L'elettore tra razionalità e identificazione. *[In Italian]*; [Voters between rationality and identification]. Francesco Francioso; Paolo Natale. **Quad. Sociol.** XXXVI:2 1992 pp.95 - 118.

4957 Fra vecchie e nuove fratture culturali in Italia. *[In Italian]*; [Between new and old cultural fractures in Italy]. Roberto Cartocci. **Aff. Soc. Int.** XXI:1 1993 pp.57 - 77.

4958 Fragmented vision: culture and politics in contemporary Malaysia. Joel S. Kahn [Ed.]; Francis Kok-Wah Loh [Ed.]. North Sydney: Asian Studies Association of Australia, in association with Allen & Unwin, 1992. vi, 327p. *ISBN: 1863731679, 1863732179. Includes bibliographical references and index. (Series:* Southeast Asia publications series).

4959 "Geschäftspolitiker" in Italien — Überlegungen im Anschluß an eine Studie über politische Korruption. *[In German]*; ("Business politicians" in Italy — some reflections on a study on political corruption in Italy.) *[Summary]*. Allessandro Pizzorno; Donatella della Porta. **Kölner Z. Soz. Soz. psy.** 45:3 9:1993 pp.439 - 464.

4960 Incumbency and the news media in U.S. Senate elections: an experimental investigation. Kim Fridkin Kahn. **Pol. Res. Q.** 46:4 12:1993 pp.715 - 740.

4961 Institutions, society or protest? Explaining invalid votes in Australian elections. Ian McAllister; Toni Makkai. **Elec. Stud.** 12:1 3:1993 pp.23 - 40.

4962 Intergenerationele klassenmobiliteit en politieke voorkeur in Nederland tussen 1970 en 1986. *[In Dutch]*; (Intergenerational class mobility and political preferences in the Netherlands between 1970 and 1986.) *[Summary]*. Paul Nieuwbeerta; Nan Dirk de Graaf. **Mens Maat.** 67:3 8:1992 pp.255 - 272.

J: Politique. État. Relations internationales

4963 Is talk really cheap? Prompting conversation between critical theory and rational choice. James Johnson. **Am. Poli. Sci.** 87:1 3:1993 pp.74 - 86.
4964 Kuwaiti national assembly 1992. J. Karam. **Geojournal** 31:4 12:1993 pp.383 - 392.
4965 The landslide victory that wasn't — the bias toward consistency in recall of election support. James K. Beggan; Scott T. Allison. **J. Appl. Soc. Psychol.** 23:8 4:1993 pp.669 - 677.
4966 Left-right self-identification and (post)materialism in the ideological space. Cees P. Middendorp. **Elec. Stud.** 11:3 9:1992 pp.249 - 260.
4967 Notes on the servicing of triumphant sub-groupism; *[Summary in French]*. James N. Rosenau. **Int. Sociol.** 8:1 3:1993 pp.77 - 90.
4968 Old brigades, money bags, new breeds and the ironies of reform in Nigeria. William Reno. **Can. J. Afr. St.** 27:1 1993 pp.66 - 87.
4969 On the controversy over Huntington's equations. When are such equations meaningful? R. Wille; U. Wille. **Math. Soc. Sc.** 25:2 2:1993 pp.173 - 180.
4970 Open institutions: the hope for democracy. John W. Murphy [Ed.]; Dennis L. Peck [Ed.]; Susan E. Cozzens; John E. Jalbert; Jeffrey W. Riemer; Kimberly A. Folse; Judith A. Burry; Eric M. Kramer; Herbert J. Rubin; William Vega; Amalia Gonzalez del Valle; Richard A. Wright; John W. Murphy; Jung Min Choi; Algis Mickunas. Westport, Conn: Praeger, 1993. viii, 201p. *ISBN: 0275940284. Includes bibliographical references (p. [193]-194) and index.*
4971 Opkomst bij verkiezingen van vrouwen en mannen — uit balans? *[In Dutch]*; (Voting of women and men — out of balance?) *[Summary]*. J.J.G. Schmeets; F.W.J. Otten. **Mens Maat.** 68:2 5:1993 pp.175 - 185.
4972 Partis politiques municipaux: une étude de sociologie électorale. *[In French]*; [Municipal political parties: a study in electoral sociology]. Louise Quesnel-Ouellet; Serge Belley; Jacques Léveillée [Contrib.]. Montréal: Agence d'ARC, 1991. 285p. *ISBN: 2890222489. Includes bibliographical references: p. 277-285.*
4973 Personnes âgées et le vote. Les significations plurielles de la participation électorale dans la vieillesse. *[In French]*; (The elderly and the vote. Plural meanings of electoral participation during old age.) *[Summary]*. Hélène Thomas. **Politix** 22 1993 pp.104 - 118.
4974 The phantom public sphere. Bruce Robbins [Ed.]. Minneapolis, MN: University of Minnesota Press, 1993. xxvi, 310p. *ISBN: 0816621241. Includes bibliographical references and index. (Series:* Cultural politics - 5).
4975 The political consequences of social mobility. P. Clifford; A.F. Heath. **J. Roy. Stat. Soc. A.** 156:1 1993 pp.51 - 61.
4976 Political time — the problem of time and chance. Donald F. Miller. **Time Soc.** 2:2 1993 pp.179 - 197.
4977 La politique à l'épreuve des images. *[In French]*; [Politics tested by images] *[Summary]*. Georges Balandier. **Cah. Int. Soc.** XCIV 1-6:1993 pp.9 - 20.
4978 Praviashchaia Elita i obshchestvo. *[In Russian]*; (The ruling elite and society.). G. Ashin. **Svobod. Mysl'** 7 5:1993 pp.58 - 69.
4979 The presence of the past: chronicles, politics, and culture in Sinhala life. Steven Kemper. Ithaca: Cornell University Press, 1991. xiv, 244p. *ISBN: 0801423953. Includes bibliographical references (p. [227]-239) and index. (Series:* The Wilder House series in politics, history, and culture).
4980 Proces powstawania niezależnych struktur obywatelskich na przykładzie kampanii wyborczej WKO „solidarność" w łodzi. *[In Polish]*; [The emergence of an

J: Politics. State. International relations

independent structure of citizenship, the example of Solidarity's electoral campaign in Łodz]. Paweł Kowalski. **Prz. Soc.** XLI 1992 pp.49 - 76.

4981 Rational choice theory, public policy and the liberal state. Jenny Stewart. **Policy Sci.** 26:4 1993 pp.317 - 330.

4982 Rechtsextremismus und Beziehungserfahrungen. *[In German]*; (Right-wing extremism and social relations in the family.) *[Summary]*. Christel Hopf. **Z. Soziol.** 22:6 12:1993 pp.449 - 463.

4983 Rodinné hodnoty v měnícím se Československu. *[In Czech]*; (Family values in the transforming Czechoslovakia.) *[Summary]*. Josef Kandert. **Český Lid** 80:1 1993 pp.1 - 6.

4984 Le rôle des individualités au cours des mutations historiques. *[In French]*; [The role of personalities in affecting the course of history] *[Summary]*. Michèle Ansart-Dourlen. **Cah. Int. Soc.** XCIV 1-6:1993 pp.71 - 96.

4985 Shaping a candidate's image in the press: Ronald Reagan and the 1980 presidential election. Cary R. Covington; Kent Kroeger; Glenn Richardson; J. David Woodard. **Pol. Res. Q.** 46:4 12:1993 pp.783 - 798.

4986 The social group dynamics of partisan evaluations. Arthur H. Miller; Christopher Wlezien. **Elec. Stud.** 12:1 3:1993 pp.5 - 22.

4987 Society transformed? Rethinking the social roots of perestroika. Donna Bahry. **Slavic R.** 52:3 Fall:1993 pp.512 - 554.

4988 State political cultures and public opinion about abortion. Elizabeth Adell Cook; Ted G. Jelen; Clyde Wilcox. **Pol. Res. Q.** 46:4 12:1993 pp.771 - 782.

4989 Theologies of black South Africans and the rhetoric of peace versus violence. Karla Poewe. **Can. J. Afr. St.** 27:1 1993 pp.43 - 65.

4990 Vers une évaluation des services publics par les usagers. *[In French]*; (Will users be asked to evaluate public services?) *[Summary]*. Philippe Warin. **Sociol. Trav.** XXXVI:3 1993 pp.309 - 331.

4991 Voter preference and behavior in the presidential election of 1988. Bernice Lott; Albert Lott; Renee Saris. **J. Psychol.** 127:1 1:1993 pp.87 - 97.

4992 Zertsalo iunosti. *[In Russian]*; (The mirror of youth.). B. Dubin. **Svobod. Mysl'** 9 6:1993 pp.54 - 65.

J.7: Armed forces
Forces armées

4993 Armées et défis démocratiques en Afrique. *[In French]*; [Armies and democratic challenges in Africa]. Dominique Bangoura. **Afr. 2000** 12 1-3:1993 pp.111 - 122.

4994 Chinese women in the People's Liberation Army — professionals or quasi-professionals? Xiaolin Li. **Arm. Forces Soc.** 20:1 Fall:1993 pp.69 - 83.

4995 Conduct unbecoming: lesbians and gays in the U.S. military, Vietnam to the Persian Gulf. Randy Shilts. p.. *Bibliography: p.767-770. -Includes index.*

4996 Homosexuality and the military culture. John Sibley Butler [Contrib.]; John Money [Contrib.]; Charles L. Davis [Contrib.]; James Burk [Contrib.]; David R. Segal [Contrib.]; Paul A. Gade [Contrib.]; Edgar M. Johnson [Contrib.]; A.J. Bacevich [Contrib.]. **Society** 31:1 11-12:1993 pp.13 - 47. *Collection of 6 articles.*

J: Politique. État. Relations internationales

4997 Improving learning persistence of military personnel by enhancing motivation in a technical training program. Betty V. Whitehill; Barbara A. McDonald. **Simulat. Gam.** 24:3 9:1993 pp.294 - 313.
4998 The military and society in Haiti. Michel S. Laguerre. Basingstoke: Macmillan, 1993. 223p. *ISBN: 033358239X*.
4999 Patterns of militarism in Israel. Baruch Kimmerling. **Eur. J. Soc.** 34:2 1993 pp.196 - 223.
5000 Performance assessment for the workplace. Alexandra K. Wigdor [Ed.]; Bert F. Green [Ed.]. Washington, D.C: National Academy Press, 1991. *ISBN: 030904538X, 0309045398. Includes bibliographical references and index. National Research Council U.S Committee on the Performance of Military Personnel.*
5001 Personal attributes as predictors of superiors' and subordinates' perceptions of military academy leadership. Leanne E. Atwater; Francis J. Yammarino. **Human Relat.** 46:5 5:1993 pp.645 - 668.
5002 Sexual orientation and military service — a social science perspective. Gregory M. Herek. **Am. Psychol.** 48:5 5:1993 pp.538 - 549.
5003 Soldiers, sovereignty and silences: Gurkhas as diplomatic currency. Mary Des Chene. **S.Asia B.** XIII:1+2 1993 pp.67 - 80.
5004 Van adelborst tot admiraal. De carrière van marine-officieren en de dynamiek van een interne arbeidsmarkt. *[In Dutch]*; (Dynamics of the internal labour market. An empirical analysis of naval officer careers.) *[Summary]*. G. Oosterhuis. **Mens Maat.** 67:3 8:1992 pp.231 - 254.

J.8: International relations
Relations internationales

5005 [The aspect of late 20th century: capital, state, nation and 'internationalization']; *[Text in Japanese]*. Machi Okuyama. Tokyo: Yachiyo Shuppan, 1993. 285p.
5006 Borrowing against the future — children and Third World indebtedness. York W. Bradshaw; Rita Noonan; Laura Gash; Claudia Buchmann Sershen. **Soc. Forc.** 71:3 3:1993 pp.629 - 656.
5007 Conflict resolution theory and practice: integration and application. Dennis J. D. Sandole [Ed.]; Hugo van der Merwe [Ed.]. New York: St. Martin's Press, 1993. 298p. *ISBN: 0719037476, 0719037484. Includes index.*
5008 Contending dramas: a cognitive approach to international organizations. Martha L. Cottam [Ed.]; Chih-yu Shih [Ed.]. New York: Praeger, 1992. xi, 264p. *ISBN: 0275935264. Includes bibliographical references and index.*
5009 Dividing the world — the dichotomous rhetoric of Ronald Reagan. Helena Halmari. **Multilingua** 12:2 1993 pp.143 - 176.
5010 Ethnic discourse and the new world "dysorder". Majid Tehranian. **Iran. J. Int. Aff.** V:2 Summer:1993 pp.287 - 310.
5011 El fin de una historia. La comunicación intercultural y el nuevo orden internacional en formación. *[In Spanish]*; [The end of an age. Intercultural communication and the formation of a new international order]. Andrés Ordóñez. **Cuad. Am.** 6:42 11-12:1993 pp.101 - 111.
5012 Foreign debt in the new East-Central Europe — a threat to European integration? R.A. Gibb; W.Z. Michalak. **Envir. Plan. C.** 11:1 2:1993 pp.69 - 85.

J: Politics. State. International relations

5013 Israel and its enemies. Louis René Beres. **Society** 30:5 (205) 7-8:1993 pp.68 - 77.
5014 Kuril'skaia tema v mestnom masshtabe. *[In Russian]*; (Kuril's theme in the local scale.). V.V. Mindogulov; S.A. Chernyshov. **Sot. Issle.** 5 1993 pp.100 - 106.
5015 The Litani River of Lebanon. Hussein A. Amery. **Geogr. Rev.** 83:3 7:1993 pp.229 - 237.
5016 Mezhnatsional'naia napriazhennost' v regional'nom aspekte. *[In Russian]*; (International tension in regional aspect.). V.N. Ivanov. **Sot. Issle.** 7 1993 pp.58 - 66.
5017 The new East-West conflict? Japan and the Bush administration's "new world order". Geraóid Ó. Tuatahil. **Area** 25:2 6:1993 pp.127 - 135.
5018 O kontse evrotsentristskogo mira i novoi konfiguratsii geopoliticheskikh sil. Ch.i. *[In Russian]*; (On the end of Eurocentrical world and new configuration of the geopolitical forces P.I.). K.S. Gadzhiev. **Sot. Issle.** 4 1993 pp.29 - 37.
5019 A peace dividend — towards a kinder and gentler Third World development. Proshanta K. Nandi; Ashim K. Basu. **J. Dev. Soc.** 9:1 1-4:1993 pp.33 - 52.
5020 Political geography, the new world order, and the city. Fred M. Shelley. **Urban Geogr.** 14:6 11-12:1993 pp.557 - 567.
5021 Psychological research on the Persian Gulf War. Darrin R. Lehman [Ed.]; Jessica Wolfe [Contrib.]; Pamela J. Brown [Contrib.]; John M. Kelley [Contrib.]; Patricia B. Sutker [Contrib.]; Madeline Uddo [Contrib.]; Kevin Brailey [Contrib.]; Albert N. Allain [Contrib.]; Charles R. Figley [Contrib.]; Julian D. Ford [Contrib.]; David Shaw [Contrib.]; Shirley Sennhauser [Contrib.]; David Greaves [Contrib.]; Barbara Thacker [Contrib.]; Patricia Chandler [Contrib.]; Lawrence Schwartz [Contrib.]; Valerie McClain [Contrib.]; Norman (Noach) Milgram [Contrib.]; James W. Pennebaker [Contrib.]; Kent Harber [Contrib.]; Barbara A. Spellman [Contrib.]; Jodie B. Ullman [Contrib.]; Keith J. Holyoak [Contrib.]; Jon A. Krosnick [Contrib.]; Laura A. Brannon [Contrib.]; Peter Suedfeld [Contrib.]; Michael D. Wallace [Contrib.]; Kimberly L. Thachuk [Contrib.]; David R. Mandel [Contrib.]; Lawrence J. Axelrod [Contrib.]. **J. Soc. Issues** 49:4 1993 pp.1 - 215. *Collection of 11 articles.*
5022 Regime theory and international relations. Volker Rittberger [Ed.]; Peter Mayer. New York; Oxford: Oxford University Press, 1993. 470p. *ISBN: 0198277830. Includes bibliographical references and index.*
5023 Revolution and world order: the revolutionary state in international society. James David Armstrong. New York; Oxford: Oxford University Press; Clarendon Press, 1993. 328p. *ISBN: 0198275285. Includes bibliographical references.*
5024 Rossiia: somosoznanie obshchestva i vneshniaia politika. *[In Russian]*; (Russia: self-awareness of society and foreign policy.). N. Kosolapov. **Mir. Ek. Mez. Ot.** 5 1993 pp.36 - 50.
5025 Ruptures et innovations dans l'approche sociologique des relations internationales. *[In French]*; [Splits and innovations in the sociological approach to international relations]. Bertrand Badie. **R. Mon. Musul. Med.** 68-69 1993 pp.65 - 74.
5026 Seeking justice: ethics and international affairs. Rachel M. McCleary [Ed.]. Boulder, Colo: Westview Press, 1992. xiii, 165p. *ISBN: 0813380588. Includes bibliographical references. (Series:* Case studies in international affairs).
5027 [The structure of mutual images between the Japanese and Chinese]; *[Text in Japanese]*. Kazufumi Manabe. **Asia Jiho** 275 1993 pp.66 - 74.

J: Politique. État. Relations internationales

5028 Thucydides, Hobbes, and the interpretation of realism. Laurie M. Johnson. DeKalb, IL: Northern Illinois University Press, 1993. xiv, 259p. *ISBN: 0875801757. Includes bibliographical references and index.*
5029 Time-space compression and the continental divide in German subjectivity. John Borneman. **New Form.** 21 Winter:1993 pp.102 - 118.
5030 Transnationalism. Mohammed A. Bamyeh. **Curr. Sociol.** 41:3 Winter:1993 pp.1 - 78.
5031 Tschechoslowakei oder Tschechische Republik und Slowakische Republik? *[In German]*; [Czechoslavakia or the Czech Republic and the Slovak Republic]. Peter Daněk; Radan Květ. **Geogr. Rund.** 45:3 3:1993 pp.160 - 165.
5032 Turkey and the West: changing political and cultural identities. Metin Heper [Ed.]; Heinz Kramer [Ed.]; Ayse Öncü [Ed.]. London: I.B. Tauris, 1993. 289p. *ISBN: 1850436118.*
5033 War and militarism in the thought of Herbert Spencer. Fabrizio Battistelli. **Int. J. Comp. Soc** XXXIV:3-4 9-12:1993 pp.192 - 209.
5034 War stories — British elite narratives of the 1982 Falklands/Malvinas War. K.-J. Dodds. **Envir. Plan. D.** 11:6 12:1993 pp.619 - 640.
5035 World peace and the human family. Roy Weatherford. New York; London: Routledge, 1993. 172p. *ISBN: 0415063027. Includes bibliographical references and index.* (*Series:* Points of conflict).

K: SOCIAL PROBLEMS. SOCIAL SERVICES. SOCIAL WORK
PROBLÈMES SOCIAUX. SERVICES SOCIAUX. TRAVAIL SOCIAL

K.1: Social problems
Problèmes sociaux

5036 Capitalism, culture, and decline in Britain, 1750-1990. W. D. Rubinstein. London, New York: Routledge, 1993. 182p. *ISBN: 0415037182. Includes bibliographical references and index.*

5037 Death on the streets: cars and the mythology of road safety. Robert Davis. Hawes: Leading Edge Press, 1992. 302p. *ISBN: 0948135468.*

5038 Disaster education, household preparedness, and stress responses following Hurricane Hugo. Charles E. Faupel; Susan P. Styles. **Envir. Behav.** 25:2 3:1993 pp.228 - 249.

5039 [Epistemology of social problems]; *[Text in Japanese].* Hisao Shikata. **Gend. No Shak. Byo.** 8 1993 pp.3 - 25.

5040 The failure to construct an MMPI-based incest perpetrator scale. John M. Goeke; Michele C. Boyer. **Int. J. Offen.** 37:3 Fall:1993 pp.271 - 277.

5041 From the community mental health movement to the war on drugs — a study in the definition of social problems. Keith Humphreys; Julian Rappaport. **Am. Psychol.** 48:8 8:1993 pp.892 - 901.

5042 Goliath: Britain's dangerous places. Beatrix Campbell. London: Methuen, 1993. 324p. *ISBN: 0413454118.*

5043 Institutional isomorphism and informal social control — evidence from a community mediation center. Calvin Morrill; Cindy McKee. **Soc. Prob.** 40:4 11:1993 pp.445 - 463.

5044 Made to fail — the mythical option of legal abortion for the survivors of rape and incest. Desirée Hansson; Diana Russell. **S. Afr. J. Human Rights** 9:4 1993 pp.500 - 524.

5045 La misère du monde. *[In French];* [The misery of the world]. Pierre Bourdieu; et al. Paris: Ed. Du Seuil, 1993. 949p. *ISBN: 2020196743. Index.*

5046 The mistreatment of elderly people. Peter Decalmer [Ed.]; Frank Glendenning [Ed.]. London: Sage, 1993. 192p. *ISBN: 0803987129.*

5047 La nuit. *[In French];* [Night]. Bertrand Sachs [Contrib.]; Pierre Sansot [Contrib.]; Michel de Fornel [Contrib.]; Anne Boisset [Contrib.]; M.-J. Guedj [Contrib.]; C. Hoang [Contrib.]; Pablo Pastor [Contrib.]; Brigitte Roussillon [Contrib.]; Paule Paillet [Contrib.]; Françoise Gailliard [Contrib.]; Monique Gally [Contrib.]; Véronique Nizou [Contrib.]; Pascale Pichon [Contrib.]; Frédérique Paolini [Contrib.]; Dominique Lallemand [Contrib.]; Odile Peiger [Contrib.]; Bernard Fily [Contrib.]; Lise Mingasson [Contrib.]. **Inf. Soc.** 29 1993 pp.4 - 103. *Collection of 15 articles.*

5048 Observer le social. *[In French];* [Observing social issues]. Michel Legros [Contrib.]; Patrick Viveret [Contrib.]; Alain Lebaube [Contrib.]; Bernard Simonin [Contrib.]; Annie Fouquet [Contrib.]; Pierre Nardin [Contrib.]; Béatrix Andrade [Contrib.]; Bernard Langevin [Contrib.]; Jean-Louis Sanchez [Contrib.]; Pierre Anglaret [Contrib.]; René Squarzoni [Contrib.]; Alberto Lopez [Contrib.]; Michel Villac

K: Problèmes sociaux. Services sociaux. Travail social

[Contrib.]; Patrice Sauvage [Contrib.]; Francis Calcoen [Contrib.]. **Inf. Soc.** 27 1993 pp.4 - 118. *Collection of 15 articles.*

5049 [Phenomenological explication of social pathology]; *[Text in Japanese].* Toshiro Sakai. **Gend. No Shak. Byo.** 8 1993 pp.102 - 139.

5050 Policy analysis and problem-solving for social systems: toward understanding, monitoring, and managing complex real world problems. P. N. Rastogi. New Delhi, Newbury Park, Calif: Sage Publications, 1992. 150p. *ISBN: 8170362784, 8170362784 (INDIA), 0803994257 (U.S.). Includes bibliographical references (p. [147]-150).*

5051 Politicheskie i sotsial'nye problemy sovremennykh ekonomicheskikh reform v Rossii. *[In Russian];* [The political and social problems of the current economic reform in Russia]. A.S. Bim. **Obshch. Ekon.** 1 1993 pp.3 - 19.

5052 Politique de la ville et lutte contre l'exclusion. *[In French];* [Urban policy and the fight against exclusion]. Jean-Marie Delarue; Jean-Bernard Campion; Marie-Françoise Goldberger; Maryse Marpsat; Philippe Estèbe; Jacques Donzelot; Jacques Ion. **Regar. Actual.** 196 12:1993 pp.3 - 49. *Collection of 4 articles.*

5053 The quest for social justice II: the Morris Fromkin memorial lectures, 1981-1990. Alan D. Corré; Morris Fromkin. Milwaukee, Wisconsin: Golda Meir Library, University of Wisconsin--Milwaukee, 1992. xi, 217p. *ISBN: 1879281058. Includes bibliographical references (p. 210-214) and index.*

5054 Social problems: an Australian perspective. George H. Morgan; Inta Allegritti. Wentworth, NSW: Social Science Press, 1992. 183p. *ISBN: 094921826X. (Series:* Social health and welfare series).

5055 Social problems and the family. Rudi Dallos [Ed.]; Eugene McLaughlin [Ed.]. London: Sage Publications in association with the Open University, 1993. 274p. *ISBN: 0803988370. (Series:* Family life and social policy).

5056 Social problems in Russia. David E. Powell. **Curr. Hist.** 92:576 10:1993 pp.325 - 330.

5057 [Social problems language game and researcher's language game: a clarification of methodological problems in constructionist sociology of social problems]; *[Text in Japanese].* Nobutoshi Nakagawa. **JIn. Kiyo** 25(2) 1993 pp.57 - 81.

5058 Sotsial'no-ekonomicheskii krizis v postranstvennom izmerenii. *[In Russian];* (Socio-economic crisis: regional aspects.). O. Pchelintsev. **Obshch. Nauki Sovrem.** 2 1993 pp.30 - 38.

5059 Sotsial'nye konflikty v usloviiakh perekhodnogo perioda (»kruglyi stol«). *[In Russian];* (Social conflicts in the transition period conditions ("round table").). V.V. Panferova [Ed.]. **Sot. Issle.** 4 1993 pp.15 - 25.

5060 Toward better problems: new perspectives on abortion, animal rights, the environment, and justice. Anthony Weston. Philadelphia: Temple University Press, 1992. xiii, 214p. *ISBN: 0877229473, 0877229481. Includes bibliographical references (p. 183-207) and index. (Series:* Ethics and action).

Child abuse
Enfants martyrs

5061 Les abus sexuels et mécanismes de protection chez la petite fille. *[In French];* [Sex abuse and mechanisms for protecting young girls]; *[Summary in Arabic].* Hela Chelli; Lilia Labidi; I. Lebbi; Y. Drissi. **R. Tun. Sci. Soc.** 29:108 1992 pp.47 - 55.

K: Social problems. Social services. Social work

5062 Bébés en pièces détachées — une nouvelle «légende» latino-américaine. *[In French]*; [Babies in detached pieces — a new Latin American "legend"] *[Summary]*. Véronique Campion-Vincent. **Cah. Int. Soc.** XCIII 7-12:1992 pp.299 - 319.

5063 Beyond blame: child abuse tragedies revisited. Peter Reder; Sylvia Duncan; Moira Gray. London: Routledge, 1993. 191p. *ISBN: 0415066786, 0415 066794. Includes bibliographical references and indexes.*

5064 Child abuse and child abusers: protection and prevention. Olive Stevenson; Lorraine Waterhouse [Ed.]. London: J. Kingsley Publrs, 1993. 236p. *ISBN: 1853021334.* (*Series:* Research highlights in social work).

5065 Child abuse and the social environment. George E. Fryer. Boulder: Westview Press, 1993. xv, 139p. *ISBN: 0813318033. Includes bibliographical references (p. [114]- 134) and index.*

5066 Child abuse inquiries and the report of the Kilkenny incest investigation: a critical analysis. Harry Ferguson. **Administration** 41:4 Winter:1993-1994 pp.385 - 410.

5067 Child abuse: towards a knowledge base. Brian Corby. Buckingham, Philadelphia: Open University Press, 1993. 195p. *ISBN: 0335157475, 0335157467. Includes bibliographical references and index.*

5068 Child sexual abuse and the symbolic geographies of Cleveland. J. Cream. **Envir. Plan. D.** 11:2 1993 pp.231 - 246.

5069 Childhood sexual victimization and lack of empathy in child molesters: explanation or excuse? N. Zoe Hilton. **Int. J. Offen.** 37:4 Winter:1993 pp.287 - 296.

5070 Children's freedom from sexual exploitation: international protection and implementation. Diane Goodman. Oslo: Norwegian Institute of Human Rights, 1992. 94p. (*Series:* Publication - 9).

5071 Decisions to register children as at risk of abuse. Liza Bingley Miller; Terry Fisher; Ian Sinclair. **Soc. Work Soc. Sci. R.** 4:2 1993 pp.101 - 118.

5072 Defining child neglect — evolution, influences, and issues. Susan J. Rose; William Meezan. **Soc. Ser. R.** 67:2 6:1993 pp.279 - 293.

5073 Deprivation and child abuse — implications for strategic planning in children's services. Norma Baldwin; Nick Spencer. **Child. Soc.** 7:4 1993 pp.357 - 375.

5074 Emotional and psychological abuse of children. Kieran O'Hagan. Buckingham, Philadelphia: Open University Press, 1992. vii, 167p. *ISBN: 0335098894, 0335098843. Includes bibliographical references and index.*

5075 Etiology of child maltreatment — a developmental-ecological analysis. Jay Belsky. **Psychol . B.** 114:3 11:1993 pp.413 - 434.

5076 Impact of sexual abuse on children — a review and synthesis of recent empirical studies. Kathleen A. Kendall-Tackett; Linda Meyer Williams; David Finkelhor. **Psychol . B.** 113:1 1:1993 pp.164 - 180.

5077 Important links between child abuse, neglect, and delinquency. Robert G. Scudder; William R. Blount; Kathleen M. Heide; Ira J. Silverman. **Int. J. Offen.** 37:4 Winter:1993 pp.315 - 324.

5078 Initial emotional response to childhood sexual abuse — emotion profiles of victims and relationship to later adjustment. Patricia J. Long; Joan L. Jackson. **J. Fam. Viol.** 8:2 6:1993 pp.167 - 181.

5079 Innocence destroyed: a study of child sexual abuse. Jean Renvoize. London, New York: Routledge, 1992. 181p. *ISBN: 0415062837. Includes bibliographical references and index.*

K: Problèmes sociaux. Services sociaux. Travail social

5080 Long-term consequences of childhood physical abuse. Robin Malinosky-Rummell; David J. Hansen. **Psychol . B.** 114:1 7:1993 pp.68 - 79.
5081 Making monsters. Richard Ofshe; Ethan Watters. **Society** 30:3 3-4:1993 pp.4 - 16.
5082 Neglect, physical abuse, and sexual molestation in Palau. Richard Shewman. **J. Pacific Soc.** 16:1(58) 6:1993 pp.1 - 9.
5083 Perpetrator gender and type of child maltreatment: overcoming limited conceptualizations and obtaining representative samples. Craig M. Allen; Douglas L. Epperson. **Child Wel.** LXXII:6 11-12:1993 pp.543 - 554.
5084 Postpartum depression syndrome as a defense to criminal behavior. G. LaVerne Williamson. **J. Fam. Viol.** 8:2 6:1993 pp.151 - 165.
5085 Psychosexual, attitudinal, and developmental characteristics of juvenile female sexual perpetrators in a residential treatment setting. John A. Hunter; Lenard J. Lexier; Dennis W. Goodwin; Patsy A. Browne; Christine Dennis. **J. Child Fam. Stud.** 2:4 12:1993 pp.317 - 326.
5086 School-based child sexual abuse prevention programs. Jeanne Kohl. **J. Fam. Viol.** 8:2 6:1993 pp.137 - 150.
5087 Sex, money, and paternity: the evolutionary psychology of domestic violence. Aurelio José Figueredo; Laura Ann McCloskey. **Ethol. Socio.** 14:6 1993 pp.353 - 380.
5088 The sexual abuse of children: theory and research. William T. O'Donohue [Ed.]; James Geer [Ed.]. Hillsdale, N.J: L. Erlbaum, 1991. viii, 419p. *ISBN: 0805803394. Includes bibliographical references and index.*
5089 Victimized daughters — sexual violence and the empathic female self. Janet Liebman Jacobs. **Signs** 19:1 Autumn:1993 pp.126 - 145.

Crime
Délits

5090 American skinheads: the criminology and control of hate crime. Mark S. Hamm. Westport, Conn: Praeger, 1993. xvii, 243p. *ISBN: 0275943550. Bibliography: p.223-235; includes index. (Series:* Praeger series in criminology and crime control policy).
5091 Anxiety over crime; *[Summary in Spanish]; [Summary in French].* K. Gönczöl. **Ann. Inter. Crimin.** 31:1-2 1993 pp.19 - 34.
5092 Assault on men — masculinity and male victimization. Elizabeth A. Stanko; Kathy Hobdell. **Br. J. Crimin.** 33:3 Summer:1993 pp.400 - 415.
5093 Atmospheric and temporal correlates of sex crimes — endogenous factors do not explain seasonal differences in rape. James Rotton. **Envir. Behav.** 25:5 9:1993 pp.625 - 642.
5094 Attitudes toward women and rape among male adolescents convicted of sexual versus nonsexual crimes. Kevin J. Epps; Rebecca Haworth; Tracey Swaffer. **J. Psychol.** 127:5 9:1993 pp.501 - 506.
5095 Bad guys and good guys: moral polarization and crime. Daniel S. Claster. Westport, Conn: Greenwood Press, 1992. xi, 302p. *ISBN: 031328489X. Includes bibliographical references (p. [257]-289) and index. (Series:* Contributions in criminology and penology).

K: Social problems. Social services. Social work

5096 Changements économiques et répression pénale: plus de chômage, plus d'emprisonnement. *[In French]*; [Economic change and penal repression: more unemployment, more imprisonment]. Thierry Godefroy; Bernard Laffargue. Paris: CESDIP, 1991. 284p. *ISBN: 2907370227.*

5097 Community structural change and fear of crime. Ralph B. Taylor; Jeanette Covington. **Soc. Prob.** 40:3 8:1993 pp.374 - 397.

5098 Context and linkage — reflections on comparative research and internationalism in criminology. Jon Vagg. **Br. J. Crimin.** 33:4 Autumn:1993 pp.541 - 554.

5099 Contextual effects in models of criminal victimization. Terance D. Miethe; David McDowall. **Soc. Forc.** 71:3 3:1993 pp.741 - 759.

5100 Crime. Chris Platts [Ed.]; Tony Gibson [Contrib.]; John Pilgrim [Contrib.]; Colin Ward [Contrib.]; Jeremy Cameron [Contrib.]; Stephen Cullen [Contrib.]; Hans Ramaer [Contrib.]; Thom Holterman [Contrib.]; John Myhill [Contrib.]; Donald Rooum [Contrib.]; Clarence Darrow [Contrib.]; David Hartley [Contrib.]. **Raven** 6:2(22) 4-6:1993 pp.97 - 190. *Collection of 10 articles.*

5101 Crime and justice in a changing world; *[Summary in French]*; *[Summary in Spanish]*. A.J. Reiss, Jr. **Ann. Inter. Crimin.** 31:1-2 1993 pp.35 - 44.

5102 Crime and masculinities in Australia, Germany and Japan. Joachim Kersten. **Int. Sociol.** 8:4 12:1993 pp.461 - 678.

5103 Crime and the urban environment: the Scottish experience. Huw Roland Jones. Brookfield, Vt; Aldershot: Avebury, 1993. viii, 155p. *ISBN: 1856284689. Includes bibliographical references.*

5104 Crime as strategy — testing an evolutionary ecological theory of expropriative crime. Bryan J. Vila; Lawrence E. Cohen. **A.J.S.** 98:4 1:1993 pp.873 - 912.

5105 Crime, class, and community — an emerging paradigm. John Hagan [Contrib.]; Robert J. Bursik [Contrib.]; Harold G. Grasmick [Contrib.]; Robert J. Sampson [Contrib.]; John H. Laub [Contrib.]; Martha A. Myers [Contrib.]; Allen E. Liska [Contrib.]; Austin T. Turk [Contrib.]. **Law Soc. Rev.** 27:2 1993 pp.255 - 360. *Collection of 6 articles.*

5106 Crime prevention discourses and the multi-agency approach. D. Gilling. **Int. J. S. Law** 21:2 6:1993 pp.145 - 157.

5107 Crime prevention in America: a British perspective. Jon Bright. Chicago: Office of International Criminal Justice, University of Illinois at Chicago, 1992. xi, 113p. *ISBN: 0942511522. Includes index.*

5108 Criminal choice: the economic theory of crime and its implications for crime control. Cathy Buchanan; Peter R. Hartley. St. Leonards, N.S.W., Australia: The Centre for Independent Studies, 1992. xvi, 80p. *ISBN: 0949769819. Includes bibliographical references and index. (Series:* CIS policy monographs).

5109 Criminal involvement of cocaine users enrolled in a methadone treatment program. Sung-Yeon Kang; George de Leon. **Addiction** 88:3 3:1993 pp.395 - 404.

5110 Criminalità organizzata e finanza d'avventura. *[In Italian]*; (Organized crime and financial crime.) *[Summary]*. Letizia Paoli. **Rass. It. Soc.** 34:3 9:1993 pp.391 - 423.

K: Problèmes sociaux. Services sociaux. Travail social

5111 Criminology and criminalization: defiance and the science of the criminal sanction; *[Summary in French]*; *[Summary in Spanish]*. L.W. Sherman. **Ann. Inter. Crimin.** 31:1-2 1993 pp.79 - 94.

5112 De l'anthropologie à la criminologie comparée. "Quatre leçons au collège de France". *[In French]*; [From anthropology to comparative criminology. "Four lessons at the College of France"]. Denis Zabo. **R. Tun. Sci. Soc.** 29:109 1992 pp.55 - 141.

5113 Deviancia. *[In Hungarian]*; [Deviant behaviour]. Béla Kolozsi. Budapest: Gondolat, 1992. 113p. *ISBN: 963 282 674 4.*

5114 Dewiacja i kontrola społeczna w krajach Europy Zachodniej i w Polsce Wybrane zagadnienia. *[In Polish]*; (Deviance and social control in West Europe and Poland.) *[Summary]*. Halina Wantuła. **Prz. Soc.** XL 1993 pp.153 - 167.

5115 Did shoplifting really decrease? David P. Farrington; John N. Burrows. **Br. J. Crimin.** 33:1 Winter:1993 pp.57 - 69.

5116 The dragon breathes fire — Chinese organized crime in New York City. Robert J. Kelly; Ko-Lin Chin; Jeffrey A. Fagan. **Cr. Law Soc. Chan.** 19:3 4:1993 pp.245 - 269.

5117 Drinking and driving, self-control, and gender — testing a general theory of crime. Carl Keane; Paul S. Maxim; James J. Teevan. **J. Res. Crim. Delin.** 30:1 2:1993 pp.30 - 46.

5118 L'economia ribelle — le operazioni di mercato nero nelle organizzazioni guerrigliere. *[In Italian]*; (The insurgent economy — black market operations by guerrilla organizations.) *[Summary]*. R.T. Naylor. **Rass. It. Soc.** 34:2 6:1993 pp.243 - 293.

5119 Enduring individual differences and rational choice theories of crime. Daniel S. Nagin; Raymond Paternoster. **Law Soc. Rev.** 27:3 1993 pp.467 - 496.

5120 Fear of victimization in Mexico. L. Ramos Lira; P. Andrade-Palos. **J. Comm. App. Soc. Psychol.** 3:1 4:1993 pp.41 - 51.

5121 Femmes et criminelles. *[In French]*; [Women and women offenders]. Robert Cario. Toulouse: Erès, 1992. 330p. *ISBN: 2865861937. Includes bibliographical references (p. [291]-312) and indexes.*

5122 Giving crime prevention top priority. Herman Schwendinger; Julia Schwendinger. **Crime Delin.** 39:4 10:1993 pp.425 - 446.

5123 Global crime connections: dynamics and control. Frank Pearce [Ed.]; Michael Woodiwiss [Ed.]. London: Macmillan, 1991. 269p. *ISBN: 0333522540. (Series: Insights).*

5124 Hit and run: mugging in Amsterdam. Gert Vogel. **Prague Occ. Pap. Ethn.** 2 1993 pp.165 - 184.

5125 Homicide between inpatients in a mental institution ward. Stefano Ferracuti; George B. Palermo; Mario Manfredi. **Int. J. Offen.** 37:4 Winter:1993 pp.331 - 338.

5126 How to stop the rapists? A question of strategy in two rape crisis centers. Ellen Kaye Scott. **Soc. Prob.** 40:3 8:1993 pp.343 - 361.

5127 I molti aspetti della criminalità organizzata negli Stati Uniti. *[In Italian]*; (The many faces of organized crime in the United States.) *[Summary]*. Robert J. Kelly. **Rass. It. Soc.** 34:2 6:1993 pp.201 - 242.

K: Social problems. Social services. Social work

5128 Immigration and rising criminality in the U.S.A.. John Tanton; Wayne Lutton. **J. Soc. Pol. E.** 18:2 Summer:1993 pp.217 - 234.

5129 Implications of cross-border crime risks in an open Europe. Petrus van Duyne. **Cr. Law Soc. Chan.** 20:2 9:1993 pp.99 - 111.

5130 The incidence and prevalence of woman abuse in Canadian university and college dating relationships; *[Summary in French]*. Walter DeKeseredy; Katharine Kelly. **Can. J. Soc.** 18:2 Spring:1993 pp.137 - 159.

5131 Informe. Víctimas de robos y agresiones violentas en la ciudad de Vitoria-Gasteiz. *[In Spanish]*; [Report. Victims of burglaries and violent aggression in the town of Vitoria-Gasteiz] *[Summary]*; *[Summary in French]*. J.L. de la Cuesta Arzamendi. **Ann. Inter. Crimin.** 31:1-2 1993 pp.107 - 126.

5132 Korruptionsneigung bei unterschiedlichen Erwartungskonstellationen in der Handlungssituation. Ein Quasi-Experiment mit Studenten. *[In German]*; (Tendency towards corruption under different expectation patterns of the situation.) *[Summary]*. Hartmut Lüdtke; Hartmut Schweitzer. **Kölner Z. Soz. Soz. psy.** 45:3 9:1993 pp.465 - 483.

5133 Learning by criming and learning by policing — who learns more? Andrew J. Buck; Joseph Deutsch; Simon Hakim; Uriel Spiegel. **Publ. Finan.** 47 2:1992 pp.173 - 184.

5134 Left realism, local crime surveys and policing of racial minorities. A further analysis of data from the first sweep of the Islington Crime Survey. Brian D. MacLean. **Cr. Law Soc. Chan.** 19:1 1:1993 pp.51 - 86.

5135 Modes of defensive behavior in a violent society. George B. Palermo; Richard Knudten; Douglas Simpson; Vitaliano Turci; Hugh Davis. **Int. J. Offen.** 37:3 Fall:1993 pp.251 - 261.

5136 The Montreal massacre. Louise Malette [Ed.]; Marie Chalouh [Ed.]. Charlottetown, P.E.I: Gynergy, 1991. 177p. *ISBN: 0921881142*.

5137 The moral minorities — a self-report study of low-consensus deviance. Robert W. Winslow; Phillip T. Gay. **Int. J. Offen.** 37:1 Spring:1993 pp.17 - 27.

5138 Neighbourhood incivilities and the study of crime in place. David T. Herbert. **Area** 25:1 3:1993 pp.45 - 54.

5139 Nigerian crime networks in the United States. Mark Jones. **Int. J. Offen.** 37:1 Spring:1993 pp.59 - 73.

5140 Offenders and victims : theory and policy. David P. Farrington [Ed.]; Sandra Walklate [Ed.]. London: The British Society of Criminology, 1992. 260p. *ISBN: 0901541273. Includes bibliographical references. Selected papers (of the Conference), Vol.1. Institute for the Study and Treatment of Delinquency, King's College.*

5141 Organized crime and business crime - enterprises in the Netherlands. Petrus C. van Duyne. **Cr. Law Soc. Chan.** 19:2 3:1993 pp.103 - 142.

5142 Organized crime in the West and in the former USSR — an attempted comparison. Alexander S. Nikiforov. **Int. J. Offen.** 37:1 Spring:1993 pp.5 - 15.

5143 Parents, peers, and delinquency. Mark Warr. **Soc. Forc.** 72:1 9:1993 pp.247 - 264.

5144 La prévention de la criminalité urbaine. *[In French]*; [The prevention of urban crime]. Gilbert Bonnemaison [Ed.]; Université de Droit, d'Économie et des Sciences d'Aix-Marseille, Institut de sciences pénales et de criminologie. Aix-en-Provence: Presses Universitaires d'Aix-Marseille, 1992. 267p.

5145 Profits, pressure and corporate lawbreaking. Anne Jenkins; John Braithwaite. **Cr. Law Soc. Chan.** 20:3 10:1993 pp.221 - 232.

K: Problèmes sociaux. Services sociaux. Travail social

5146 The psychology of crime: a social science textbook. Maurice Philip Feldman. Cambridge, New York: Cambridge University Press, 1993. xiv, 526p. *ISBN: 052133120X, 0521337321. Includes bibliographical references (p. 450-508) and indexes.*

5147 Race, riots and policing: lore and disorder in a multi-racist society. Michael Keith. London: UCL Press, 1993. 280p. *ISBN: 1857281098.*

5148 Racial segregation and black urban homicide. Ruth D. Peterson; Lauren J. Krivo. **Soc. Forc.** 71:4 6:1993 pp.1001 - 1026.

5149 Racism and criminology. Dee Cook [Ed.]; Barbara Hudson [Ed.]. London: Sage Publications, 1993. 175p. *ISBN: 0803987633.*

5150 Regolazione e devianza: sociologia e questione criminale in Italia. *[In Italian]*; [Regulation and deviance: sociology and criminal questions in Italy]. Franca Faccioli; Università di Roma Dipartimento di Sociologia. Milan: FrancoAngeli, 1991. 125p. *ISBN: 8820469065.*

5151 La regolazione sociale violenta. Il ruolo della criminalità organizzata nell'Italia meridionale. *[In Italian]*; (Violent social regulation in southern Italy.) *[Summary].* Raimondo Catanzaro. **Quad. Sociol.** XXXVII:4 1993 pp.79 - 89.

5152 Religiosity, religious climate, and delinquency among ethnic groups in the Netherlands. Marianne Junger; Wim Polder. **Br. J. Crimin.** 33:3 Summer:1993 pp.416 - 435.

5153 Responses to crime. Volume 2. Penal policy in the making. David James George Hennessy Windlesham. Oxford: Clarendon Press, 1993. 484p. *ISBN: 0198254164.*

5154 Routine activities and a subculture of violence — a study of violence on the street. Leslie W. Kennedy; Stephen W. Baron. **J. Res. Crim. Delin.** 30:1 2:1993 pp.88 - 112.

5155 The seasonality of violent crime — the case of robbery and homicide in Israel. Simha F. Landau; Daniel Fridman. **J. Res. Crim. Delin.** 30:2 5:1993 pp.163 - 191.

5156 The severity of preaddiction criminal behavior among urban, male narcotic addicts and two nonaddicted control groups. David N. Nurco; Timothy Kinlock; Mitchell B. Balter. **J. Res. Crim. Delin.** 30:3 8:1993 pp.293 - 316.

5157 Sex crimes on trial: the use of sexual evidence in Scottish courts. Beverley Brown; Michele Burman; Lynn Jamieson. Edinburgh: Edinburgh University Press, 1993. 234p. *ISBN: 0748604081. (Series:* Edinburgh law & society series).

5158 The Sicilian Mafia: the business of private protection. Diego Gambetta. Cambridge, Mass: Harvard University Press, 1993. 335p. *ISBN: 0674807413. Includes bibliographical references and index.*

5159 The situational analysis of crime and deviance. Christopher Birkbeck; Gary LaFree. **Ann. R. Soc.** 19 1993 pp.113 - 138.

5160 The situational context of violent female offending. Ira Sommers; Deborah R. Baskin. **J. Res. Crim. Delin.** 30:2 5:1993 pp.136 - 162.

5161 Social changes, crime and police. József Vigh [Ed.]; Géza Katona [Ed.]. Budapest: Eötvös Loránd Univ. Press, 1993. 395p.

5162 [Social psychological criminology]; *[Text in Japanese].* Yoshiyuki Takahashi. Tokyo: Reibunsya, 1993. 201p.

5163 The structuring effects of social control; *[Summary in French]; [Summary in Spanish].* M. Cusson. **Ann. Inter. Crimin.** 31:1-2 1993 pp.45 - 60.

5164 A study of patterns in criminal homicides in Greece. Peter D. Chimbos. **Int. J. Comp. Soc** XXXIV:3-4 9-12:1993 pp.260 - 271.

K: Social problems. Social services. Social work

5165 Tendentsii prestupnosti: mirovye, regional'nye, rossiiskie. *[In Russian]*; [The trends of criminality — global, regional and Russian]. V.V. Luneev. **Gos. Pravo** 5 1993 pp.3 - 19.

5166 Testing for core empirical implications of Gottfredson and Hirschi's general theory of crime. Harold G. Grasmick; Charles R. Tittle; Robert J. Bursik; Bruce J. Arneklev. **J. Res. Crim. Delin.** 30:1 2:1993 pp.5 - 29.

5167 Trends in violent crime against women, 1973-89. M. Dwayne Smith; Ellen S. Kuchta. **Soc. Sci. Q.** 74:1 3:1993 pp.28 - 45.

5168 Type of place, urbanism, and delinquency — further testing the determinist theory. A. Leigh Ingram. **J. Res. Crim. Delin.** 30:2 5:1993 pp.192 - 212.

5169 Understanding and preventing violence. Albert J. Reiss [Ed.]; Jeffrey A. Roth [Ed.]. Washington, D.C: National Academy Press, 1993. xiv, 464p. *ISBN: 0309045940. Includes bibliographical references and index.*

5170 Understanding criminal victimization: an introduction to theoretical victimology. Ezzat A. Fattah. Scarborough, Ontario: Prentice-Hall Canada, 1991. 412p. *ISBN: 0139295976. Bibliography: p.359-400.*

5171 Urban crimes in mainland China — a social ecological approach. Yuefeng Wang. **Iss. Stud.** 29:8 8:1993 pp.101 - 117.

5172 Urban-rural residence and criminal victimization; *[Summary in French]*. Vincent F. Sacco; Holly Johnson; Robert Arnold. **Can. J. Soc.** 18:4 Fall:1993 pp.431 - 451.

5173 Violence against women. Pauline Bart [Ed.]; Eileen Geil Moran [Ed.]. Newbury Park, Calif: Sage, 1993. xvii, 294p. *ISBN: 0803950446, 0803950454. Includes bibliographical references. (Series:* Gender & society readers).

5174 Violent crime in small shops. Malcolm Hibberd; Joanna Shapland. London: Police Foundation, 1993. 81p. *ISBN: 0947692290.*

5175 White-collar crime. Gilbert Geis [Ed.]; P. Paul Jesilow [Ed.]. Newbury Park: Sage Pubns, 1993. 210p. *ISBN: 0803946880. (Series:* Annals of the American Academy of Political and Social Science).

5176 Winkeldiefstal, een te riskante zaak? *[In Dutch]*; (Shoplifting, a too risky business?). Hans Moerland. Arnhem: Gouda Quint BV, 1991. 342p. *Proefschrift thesis Erasmus Universiteit 1991.*

5177 Women, violence and crime prevention: a West Yorkshire study. Jalna Hanmer; Sheila Saunders. Aldershot: Avebury, 1993. 407p. *ISBN: 1856282376.*

5178 Work situation and behavioural patterns: an analysis of female criminality. M. Bilmoria Rani. **East. Anthrop.** 46:2 4-6:1993 pp.199 - 204.

Criminal justice
Justice criminelle

5179 Anatomie de la prison. *[In French]*; [Anatomy of prison]. Guy Lemire. Montréal: Presses de l'Université de Montréal, 1990. 195p. *ISBN: 2760615332, 2717819843. Bibliographic references.*

5180 Bad guys and good guys: moral polarization and crime. Daniel S. Claster. Westport, Conn: Greenwood Press, 1992. xi, 302p. *ISBN: 031328489X. Includes bibliographical references (p. [257]-289) and index. (Series:* Contributions in criminology and penology).

K: Problèmes sociaux. Services sociaux. Travail social

5181 Beschuldigtennationalität und polizeiliche Ermittlungspraxis. Plädoyer für eine qualitative Polizeiforschung. *[In German]*; (The nationality of suspected persons and investigations by the police. A plea for the use of qualitative research methods.) *[Summary]*. Jo Reichertz; Norbert Schröer. **Kölner Z. Soz. Soz. psy.** 45:4 12:1993 pp.755 - 771.

5182 A case report — alcohol-induced blackouts during sexual intercourse: legal responsibility. Dan E. Neal; Edward M. Scott; Raymond A. Grimsbo. **Int. J. Offen.** 37:4 Winter:1993 pp.325 - 330.

5183 Changes in prison culture — prison gangs and the case of the "Pepsi generation". Geoffrey Hunt; Stephanie Riegel; Tomas Morales; Dan Waldorf. **Soc. Prob.** 40:3 8:1993 pp.398 - 409.

5184 Children visiting Holloway prison: inside and outside perspectives on the all day visits scheme at HMP Holloway. Eva Lloyd [Ed.]. London: Save the Children Fund, 1992. 64p. *ISBN: 1870322460*.

5185 A comparison of recidivism of Florida's community control and prison — a five year survival analysis. Linda G. Smith; Ronald L. Akers. **J. Res. Crim. Delin.** 30:3 8:1993 pp.267 - 292.

5186 Corruption and reform. M. Johnston [Ed.]; S. Riley [Ed.]; A. Doig [Ed.]; Keith Maguire [Contrib.]; Nikos Passas [Contrib.]; Nick Fielding [Contrib.]; Hugh D. Barlow [Contrib.]; Rowan Bosworth-Davies [Contrib.]; Hazel Croall [Contrib.]. **Cr. Law Soc. Chan.** 20:4 11:1993 pp.273 - 372. *Collection of 6 articles*.

5187 Crime and justice in a changing world; *[Summary in French]*; *[Summary in Spanish]*. A.J. Reiss, Jr. **Ann. Inter. Crimin.** 31:1-2 1993 pp.35 - 44.

5188 Crime control as industry: towards gulags, Western style. Nils Christie. Oslo; London, New York: Scandinavian University Press; Routledge, 1993. 192p. *ISBN: 041509478X*. *Includes bibliographical references and index*.

5189 Crime, juvenile delinquency and deterrence policy in China. Børge Bakken. **Aust. J. Chin. Aff.** 30 7:1993 pp.29 - 60.

5190 Criminal justice : theory and practice. Allan Keith Bottomley [Ed.]. London: British Society of Criminology in association with the Institute for the Study & Treatment of Delinquency, 1992. 325p. *ISBN: 0901541281*. *Selected papers from the British Criminology Conference, 1991, volume 2*.

5191 The criminal justice system and mental retardation: defendants and victims. Ronald W. Conley; Ruth Luckasson; George N. Bouthilet. Baltimore: Paul H. Brookes, 1992. 299p. *ISBN: 1557660700*.

5192 The criminal justice system and the politics of scrutiny. Jon Spencer. **Soc. Pol. Admin.** 27:1 3:1993 pp.18 - 32.

5193 Criminology and criminalization: defiance and the science of the criminal sanction; *[Summary in French]*; *[Summary in Spanish]*. L.W. Sherman. **Ann. Inter. Crimin.** 31:1-2 1993 pp.79 - 94.

5194 Different substance abusing offenders require a unique program. Wagdy Loza. **Int. J. Offen.** 37:4 Winter:1993 pp.351 - 364.

5195 Disciplina social y organización interna de la cárcel. Síntesis del estudio de una prisión catalana. *[In Spanish]*; [Social discipline and internal organization of the prison. Synthesis of a case study of a Catalonian prison] *[Summary]*; *[Summary in Catalan]*. José Adelantado Gimeno. **Papers** 39 1992 pp.77 - 100.

5196 Discrimination in punishment and deterrence effects. Uri Ben-Zion; Seiichi Kawasaki; Uriel Spiegel. **Publ. Finan.** 48:1 1993 pp.10 - 18.

K: Social problems. Social services. Social work

5197 Drugs and justice — the impact of drugs on criminal justice in a metropolitan community. John M. Klofas. **Crime Delin.** 39:2 4:1993 pp.204 - 224.
5198 Evaluating and responding to private prisons in the United Kingdom. M. Ryan. **Int. J. S. Law** 21:4 12:1993 pp.319 - 334.
5199 L'évaluation des expériences de médiation entre délinquants et victimes — l'exemple britannique. *[In French]*; [Evaluating mediation between offenders and victims — the British example]. Marie-Clet Desdevises. **Rev. Sci. Crim. D. P.** 1 1-3:1993 pp.45 - 61.
5200 An evaluation of juvenile sexual offender treatment. Steven P. Lab; Glenn Shields; Connie Schondel. **Crime Delin.** 39:4 10:1993 pp.543 - 553.
5201 Giving victims a voice — a New Zealand experiment. Allison Morris; Gabrielle M. Maxwell; Jeremy P. Robertson. **Howard J. Crim. Just.** 32:4 11:1993 pp.304 - 321.
5202 Growing fears, rising crime — juveniles and China's justice system. Daniel J. Curran; Sandra Cook. **Crime Delin.** 39:3 7:1993 pp.296 - 315.
5203 Innovations in policing domestic violence: evidence from metropolitan London. James William Edward Sheptycki. Aldershot: Avebury, 1993. 167p. *ISBN: 1856283887.*
5204 Intensive probation for young adult offenders — evaluating the impact of a non-custodial sentence. Ian D. Brownlee; Derrick Joanes. **Br. J. Crimin.** 33:2 Spring:1993 pp.216 - 230.
5205 Intermediate punishment — redistributing or extending social control? Thomas G. Blomberg; William Bales; Karen Reed. **Cr. Law Soc. Chan.** 19:2 3:1993 pp.187 - 201.
5206 Judgments regarding rape — a comparison of rape counselors, police, hospital staff, and citizens. Patricia J. Blake; Martin Heesacker; Lawrence I. Marks. **J. Soc. Clin. Psychol.** 12:3 Fall:1993 pp.248 - 261.
5207 Judicial rape. Sue Lees. **Wom. St. Inter. For.** 16:1 1-2:1993 pp.11 - 36.
5208 Jugend(kriminal)recht in Deutschland und Frankreich: auf der Suche nach neuen Wegen. *[In German]*; [Juvenile (criminal) law in Germany and France: the search for new ways forward]. Caroline Steindorff [Ed.]; Jaques Borricand [Ed.]; Gisela Losseff-Tillmanns [Ed.]. Bonn: Forum-Verlag Godesberg, 1992. 164p. *ISBN: 3927066516. Deutsch-Französische Jugendwerke.*
5209 Juvenile (in)justice and the criminal court alternative. Barry C. Feld. **Crime Delin.** 39:4 10:1993 pp.403 - 424.
5210 Law's knowledge — the judge, the expert, the battered woman, and her syndrome. Katherine O'Donovan. **J. Law Soc.** 20:4 Winter:1993 pp.427 - 437.
5211 Long economic cycles and the criminal justice system in U.S.. David E. Barlow; Melissa Hickman Barlow; Theodore G. Chiricos. **Cr. Law Soc. Chan.** 19:2 3:1993 pp.143 - 169.
5212 A "missed opportunity" re-assessed — the influence of the day training centre experiment on the criminal justice system and probation policy and practice. Maurice Vanstone. **Br. J. Soc. W.** 23:3 6:1993 pp.213 - 229.
5213 Modèle tutélaire ou modèle légaliste dans la justice pénale des mineurs? Réflexions inspirées par l'arrêt de la cour d'appel de Reims du 30 juillet 1992 et les «dispositions applicables aux mineurs» de la loi du 4 janvier 1993. *[In French]*; [Criminal justice for minors based on the tutelary or the legalistic model? Thoughts inspired by the decision of the Reims appeal court on 30th July 1992 and the

K: Problèmes sociaux. Services sociaux. Travail social

"clauses applicable to minors" of the law of 4th January 1993]. Denis Salas. **Rev. Sci. Crim. D. P.** 2 4-6:1993 pp.238 - 248.

5214 A new methodology for assessing the level of risk in incarcerated offenders. D.A. Clark; M.J. Fisher; C. McDougall. **Br. J. Crimin.** 33:3 Summer:1993 pp.436 - 448.

5215 Penal policy and social justice. Barbara Hudson. Basingstoke: Macmillan, 1993. x, 222p. *ISBN: 0333495756, 0333495764. Includes bibliographical references and index.*

5216 The persistent prison?: rethinking decarceration and penal reform. Maeve Winifred McMahon. Toronto: University of Toronto Press, 1992. xxvi, 274p. *ISBN: 0802028179, 0802076890. Includes index. Includes bibliographical references: p. [237]-264.*

5217 Policing the deinstitutionalized mentally ill — toward an understanding of its function. Sandra Wachholz; Robert Mullaly. **Cr. Law Soc. Chan.** 19:3 4:1993 pp.281 - 300.

5218 Prison reform in England — an overview. Michael Kaye Carlie. **Int. J. Offen.** 37:3 Fall:1993 pp.197 - 219.

5219 Prisons after Woolf: reform through riot. Elaine Player [Ed.]; Michael Jenkins [Ed.]. London, New York: Routledge, 1993. 278p. *ISBN: 041507956X. Includes bibliographical references and index.*

5220 Prisons and women. Blanche Hampton. Kensington NSW, Australia: New South Wales University Press, 1993. xviii, 220p. *ISBN: 0868402214. Includes bibliographical references (p. [207]-215) and index.*

5221 Probation work with sex offenders: a survey of current practice. Leah Warwick. Norwich: Social Work Monographs, 1991. 49p. *ISBN: 0946751900. Bibliography: p.43-49. (Series: Probation monographs).*

5222 The prosecutor fine and social control — the introduction of the fiscal fine to Scotland. Peter Duff. **Br. J. Crimin.** 33:4 Autumn:1993 pp.481 - 503.

5223 Psychology in prisons. David J. Cooke; Pamela J. Baldwin; Jacqueline Howison. London: Routledge, 1990. viii,147p. *ISBN: 0415005337. Includes index.*

5224 Punishing drugs — criminal justice and drug use. Mike Collison. **Br. J. Crimin.** 33:3 Summer:1993 pp.382 - 399.

5225 Race, riots and policing: lore and disorder in a multi-racist society. Michael Keith. London: UCL Press, 1993. 280p. *ISBN: 1857281098.*

5226 Reinventing juvenile justice — research directions. Barry Krisberg [Ed.]; Ira M. Schwartz [Contrib.]; Shenyang Guo [Contrib.]; John J. Kerbs [Contrib.]; Edmund F. McGarrell [Contrib.]; Michael J. Dale [Contrib.]; Carl Sanniti [Contrib.]; Richard G. Wiebush [Contrib.]; James R. Maupin [Contrib.]; Michael B. Greene [Contrib.]. **Crime Delin.** 39:1 1:1993 pp.3 - 124. *Collection of 7 articles.*

5227 Responses to crime. Volume 2. Penal policy in the making. David James George Hennessy Windlesham. Oxford: Clarendon Press, 1993. 484p. *ISBN: 0198254164.*

5228 The rise and fall of tagging as a criminal justice measure in Britain. S.J. Fay. **Int. J. S. Law** 21:4 12:1993 pp.301 - 318.

5229 The Scottish prison service — changing the culture. E.W. Frizzell. **Howard J. Crim. Just.** 32:3 8:1993 pp.203 - 214.

5230 Sex crimes on trial: the use of sexual evidence in Scottish courts. Beverley Brown; Michele Burman; Lynn Jamieson. Edinburgh: Edinburgh University Press, 1993. 234p. *ISBN: 0748604081. (Series:* Edinburgh law & society series).

5231 Solitary confinement. Robert Rogers. **Int. J. Offen.** 37:4 Winter:1993 pp.339 - 350.

K: *Social problems. Social services. Social work*

5232 Les surveillants de prison — le prix de la sécurité. *[In French]*; (Prison warders — the price to be paid for security.) *[Summary]*; *[Summary in German]*; *[Summary in Spanish]*. Antoinette Chauvenet; Georges Benguigui; Françoise Orlic. **Rev. Fr. Soc.** XXXIV:3 7-9:1993 pp.345 - 366.

5233 Trends and conditions of imprisonment in Nigeria. Etannibi E.O. Alemika. **Int. J. Offen.** 37:2 Summer:1993 pp.147 - 162.

5234 Well kept — comparing quality of confinement in private and public prisons. Charles H. Logan. **J. Crim. Law Criminol.** 83:3 Fall:1992 pp.577 - 613.

5235 Zero-tolerance policies — do they inhibit or stimulate illicit drug consumption? Jonathan P. Caulkins. **Manag. Sci.** 39:4 4:1993 pp.458 - 476.

Domestic violence
Violence domestique

5236 The abuse of elderly people — considerations for practice. Bridget Penhale. **Br. J. Soc. W.** 23:2 4:1993 pp.95 - 112.

5237 Battered spouse as a special concern in work with families in two semi-rural communities of Nigeria. W.J. Kalu. **J. Fam. Viol.** 8:4 12:1993 pp.361 - 373.

5238 The battered woman scale and gender identities. Martin D. Schwartz; Christine L. Mattley. **J. Fam. Viol.** 8:3 9:1993 pp.277 - 287.

5239 Differential patterns of partner-to-woman violence — a comparison of samples of community, alcohol-abusing, and battered women. William R. Downs; Brenda A. Miller; Denise D. Panek. **J. Fam. Viol.** 8:2 6:1993 pp.113 - 135.

5240 Domestic violence: action for change. Gill Hague; Ellen Malos. Cheltenham: New Clarion Press, 1993. 234p. *ISBN: 1873797079.*

5241 Domestic violence as a human rights issue. Dorothy Q. Thomas; Michele E. Beasley. **Hum. Rights Q.** 15:1 1993 pp.36 - 62.

5242 Explaining women's double jeopardy — factors that mediate the association between harsh treatment as a child and violence by a husband. Ronald L. Simons; Christine Johnson; Jay Beaman; Rand D. Conger. **J. Marriage Fam.** 55:3 8:1993 pp.713 - 723.

5243 Gender, intimacy, and lethal violence — trends from 1976 through 1987. Angela Browne; Kirk R. Williams. **Gender Soc.** 7:1 3:1993 pp.78 - 98.

5244 Homosexuals as a new class of domestic violence subjects under the New Jersey Prevention of Domestic Violence Act of 1991. Mac D. Hunter. **J. Fam. Law** 31:3 1992-1993 pp.557 - 627.

5245 The impact of arrest on domestic assault. Eve S. Buzawa [Ed.]; Carl G. Buzawa [Ed.]; Richard J. Gelles [Contrib.]; Murray A. Straus [Contrib.]; Janell D. Schmidt [Contrib.]; Lawrence W. Sherman [Contrib.]; Thomas Austin [Contrib.]; Barbara Hart [Contrib.]; Peter K. Manning [Contrib.]; Evan Stark [Contrib.]. **Am. Behav. Sc.** 36:5 5/6:1993 pp.558 - 680. *Collection of 8 articles.*

5246 Innovations in policing domestic violence: evidence from metropolitan London. James William Edward Sheptycki. Aldershot: Avebury, 1993. 167p. *ISBN: 1856283887.*

5247 Intervening with male batterers — a study of social workers perceptions of domestic violence. Margaret S. Malloch; Stephen A. Webb. **Soc. Work Soc. Sci. R.** 4:2 1993 pp.119 - 147.

5248 Law's knowledge — the judge, the expert, the battered woman, and her syndrome. Katherine O'Donovan. **J. Law Soc.** 20:4 Winter:1993 pp.427 - 437.
5249 Perceived helpfulness and use of professional services by abused women. Bonita Hamilton; John Coates. **J. Fam. Viol.** 8:4 12:1993 pp.313 - 324.
5250 «Perché se n'è andata»? L'esplicitazione pubblica del maltrattamento come esempio di discontinuità biografica. *[In Italian]*; («Why did she go away?» The act of making ill-treatment public as an example of «biographical discontinuity».). Anna Rosa Favretto. **Rass. It. Soc.** XXXIV:4 12:1993 pp.561 - 582.
5251 A predictive model of male spousal violence. Sandra M. Stith; Sarah C. Farley. **J. Fam. Viol.** 8:2 6:1993 pp.183 - 201.
5252 Researching elder abuse. Jim Ogg; Carol Munn-Giddings. **Age. Soc.** 13:3 9:1993 pp.389 - 413.
5253 The return of the "battered husband syndrome" through the typification of women as violent. Martin D. Schwartz; Walter S. Dekeseredy. **Cr. Law Soc. Chan.** 20:3 10:1993 pp.249 - 265.
5254 Sex, money, and paternity: the evolutionary psychology of domestic violence. Aurelio José Figueredo; Laura Ann McCloskey. **Ethol. Socio.** 14:6 1993 pp.353 - 380.
5255 Violence against women. Pauline Bart [Ed.]; Eileen Geil Moran [Ed.]. Newbury Park, Calif: Sage, 1993. xvii, 294p. *ISBN: 0803950446, 0803950454. Includes bibliographical references. (Series:* Gender & society readers).
5256 Violence against women by male partners — prevalence, outcomes, and policy implications. Angela Browne. **Am. Psychol.** 48:10 10:1993 pp.1077 - 1087.
5257 Wife-battering — an Australian perspective. Renata Alexander. **J. Fam. Viol.** 8:3 9:1993 pp.229 - 251.

Homelessnes
Sans-abri

5258 Blaming the victim, blaming society, or blaming the discipline — fixing responsibility for homelessness. Susan Wright. **Sociol. Q.** 34:1 Spring:1993 pp.1 - 16.
5259 Broken promises: a survey of resettlement unit replacement packages. Joseph Oldman. London: CHAR, 1993. 52p. *ISBN: 0906951380.*
5260 Caught in the mix: an oral portrait of homelessness. Philip Michael Bulman. Westport, Conn: Auburn House, 1993. x, 211p. *ISBN: 0865692297. Includes index.*
5261 Creating family forms. The exclusion of men and teenage boys from families in the New York City shelter system, 1987-91. Ida Susser. **Crit. Anthr.** 13:3 1993 pp.267 - 284.
5262 Developing interagency collaboration on behalf of homeless children. Maria Grace Yon; Roslyn Arlin Mickelson; Iris Carlton-Laney. **Educ. Urban. Soc.** 25:4 8:1993 pp.410 - 423.
5263 The duration of homeless careers — an exploratory study. Irving Piliavin; Michael Sosin; Alex H. Westerfelt; Ross L. Matsueda. **Soc. Ser. R.** 67:4 12:1993 pp.576 - 598.

K: Social problems. Social services. Social work

5264 Education of younger homeless children in urban settings. E. Anne Eddowes. **Educ. Urban. Soc.** 25:4 8:1993 pp.381 - 393.

5265 Fear of crime among vulnerable populations — homeless women. Charisse T.M. Coston; James O. Finckenauer. **J. Soc. Distr. Home.** 2:1 1:1993 pp.1 - 21.

5266 A follow-up study of homeless women. Céline Mercier; Guylaine Racine. **J. Soc. Distr. Home.** 2:3 7:1993 pp.207 - 222.

5267 HIV/AIDS and homelessness. James R. McDonell; Linda Persse; Louise Valentine; Richard Priebe. **J. Soc. Distr. Home.** 2:3 7:1993 pp.159 - 175.

5268 Homeless children — coping with material losses. Ronald Paul Hill. **J. Consum. Aff.** 26:2 Winter:1992 pp.274 - 287.

5269 Homeless families since 1980 — implications for education. Kay Young McChesney. **Educ. Urban. Soc.** 25:4 8:1993 pp.361 - 380.

5270 Homelessness: a good practice guide : how local authorities can apply homelessness law and the Code of Guidance. Lesley Moroney; John Goodwin. London: Shelter, 1992. 196p.

5271 Homelessness, health care, and welfare provision. Kevin John Fisher [Ed.]; John William Collins [Ed.]. London, New York: Routledge, 1993. 214p. *ISBN: 0415049997, 0415050006. Includes bibliographical references and index.*

5272 Housing needs, family values and single homeless people. Patricia Garside. **Policy Pol.** 21:4 10:1993 pp.319 - 328.

5273 L'intervention en santé mentale — le mandat inattendu des maisons d'hébergement pour femmes sans abri. *[In French]*; (Intervention in mental health. An unexpected function of shelters for homeless women.) *[Summary]*. Guylaine Racine. **San. Ment. Qué** XVII:1 Printemps:1993 pp.251 - 268.

5274 Malign neglect: homelessness in an American city. Jennifer R. Wolch; Michael J. Dear. San Francisco: Jossey-Bass Publishers, 1993. xxviii, 378p. *ISBN: 155542564X. Includes bibliographical references and index. (Series:* Public administration series).

5275 The medicalization of homelessness and the theater of repression. Arline Mathieu. **Med. Anthr. Q.** 7:2 6:1993 pp.170 - 184.

5276 My address is not my home: hidden homelessness and single women in Scotland. Sarah Webb. Edinburgh: Scottish Council for Single Homeless, 1992. 204p. *ISBN: 090705045X.*

5277 A nation in denial: the truth about homelessness. Alice S. Baum; Donald W. Burnes. Boulder: Westview Press, 1993. xiv, 247p. *ISBN: 0813382440, 0813382459. Includes bibliographical references and index.*

5278 Neither homed nor homeless — contested definitions and the personal worlds of the poor. April R. Veness. **Pol. Geogr.** 12:4 7:1993 pp.319 - 340.

5279 Reaching the hard to reach — educating homeless adolescents in urban settings. Jane L. Powers; Barbara Jaklitsch. **Educ. Urban. Soc.** 25:4 8:1993 pp.394 - 409.

5280 Resident adaptations in an Alcoholics Anonymous-based residential program for the urban homeless. Gordon Bazemore; Peter L. Cruise. **Soc. Ser. R.** 67:4 12:1993 pp.599 - 616.

5281 Sociodemographic and health-related risk factors among African-American, Caucasian, and Hispanic homeless men — a comparative study. Laurie A. Davis; Marilyn A. Winkleby. **J. Soc. Distr. Home.** 2:2 4:1993 pp.83 - 101.

K: *Problèmes sociaux. Services sociaux. Travail social*

5282 Street addicts in the political economy. Alisse Waterston. Philadelphia: Temple University Press, 1993. xix, 280p. *ISBN: 0877229929. Includes bibliographical references (p. [257]-273) and index.*

5283 Street children in North and Latin America: preliminary data from Proyecto Alternativos in Tegucigalpa and some comparisons with the U.S. case. James D. Wright; Martha Wittig; Donald C. Kaminsky. **Stud. Comp. ID.** 28:2 Summer:1993 pp.81 - 92.

5284 Value, attitude, and belief determinants of willingness to accept a facility for the homeless. Frances B. Somerman. **J. Soc. Distr. Home.** 2:3 7:1993 pp.177 - 192.

Juvenile delinquency
Délinquance juvénile

5285 Anti-Sozial-Front: vom Fussballfan zum Hooligan. *[In German]*; [The anti-social front: from football fan to hooligan]. Beate Matthesius. Opladen: Leske + Budrich, 1992. 245p. *ISBN: 3810010235.*

5286 Beschuldigtennationalität und polizeiliche Ermittlungspraxis. Plädoyer für eine qualitative Polizeiforschung. *[In German]*; (The nationality of suspected persons and investigations by the police. A plea for the use of qualitative research methods.) *[Summary]*. Jo Reichertz; Norbert Schröer. **Kölner Z. Soz. Soz. psy.** 45:4 12:1993 pp.755 - 771.

5287 Children and trouble: a study of juvenile justice issues for local government. Association of Metropolitan Authorities. London: Association of Metropolitan Authorities, 1993. 81p. (*Series:* Child care series).

5288 Crime in the making: pathways and turning points through life. Robert J. Sampson; John H. Laub. Cambridge, Mass: Harvard University Press, 1993. ix, 309p. *ISBN: 0674176049. Includes bibliographical references (p. [287]-304) and index.*

5289 Crime, juvenile delinquency and deterrence policy in China. Børge Bakken. **Aust. J. Chin. Aff.** 30 7:1993 pp.29 - 60.

5290 Délinquance systématisée des jeunes et vulnérabilité sociétale. *[In French]*; [Systemized juvenile delinquence and society's vulnerability]. Lode Walgrave. Geneva: Editions Médecine et Hygiène, Méridiens Klincksieck, 1992. 154p. *ISBN: 2880490642, 2865633128. Bibliogr. : p 139-154.*

5291 Effects of parenting practices and peer relations on early adolescent delinquency. Jung-Hye Kwon; Bong-Keon Lee; Soo-Hyun Kim. **Korean Soc. Sci. J.** XIX 1993 pp.23 - 39.

5292 An evaluation of juvenile sexual offender treatment. Steven P. Lab; Glenn Shields; Connie Schondel. **Crime Delin.** 39:4 10:1993 pp.543 - 553.

5293 Fifth grade school adjustment and later arrest rate — a longitudinal study of middle school antisocial boys. Hill M. Walker; Steve Stieber; Elizabeth Ramsey; Robert O'Neill. **J. Child Fam. Stud.** 2:4 12:1993 pp.295 - 315.

5294 Growing fears, rising crime — juveniles and China's justice system. Daniel J. Curran; Sandra Cook. **Crime Delin.** 39:3 7:1993 pp.296 - 315.

5295 Heavy metal music preference, delinquent friends, social control, and delinquency. Simon I. Singer; Murray Levine; Susyan Jou. **J. Res. Crim. Delin.** 30:3 8:1993 pp.317 - 329.

K: Social problems. Social services. Social work

5296 Important links between child abuse, neglect, and delinquency. Robert G. Scudder; William R. Blount; Kathleen M. Heide; Ira J. Silverman. **Int. J. Offen.** 37:4 Winter:1993 pp.315 - 324.

5297 Jugend(kriminal)recht in Deutschland und Frankreich: auf der Suche nach neuen Wegen. *[In German]*; [Juvenile (criminal) law in Germany and France: the search for new ways forward]. Caroline Steindorff [Ed.]; Jaques Borricand [Ed.]; Gisela Losseff-Tillmanns [Ed.]. Bonn: Forum-Verlag Godesberg, 1992. 164p. *ISBN: 3927066516. Deutsch-Französische Jugendwerke.*

5298 Modèle tutélaire ou modèle légaliste dans la justice pénale des mineurs? Réflexions inspirées par l'arrêt de la cour d'appel de Reims du 30 juillet 1992 et les «dispositions applicables aux mineurs» de la loi du 4 janvier 1993. *[In French]*; [Criminal justice for minors based on the tutelary or the legalistic model? Thoughts inspired by the decision of the Reims appeal court on 30th July 1992 and the "clauses applicable to minors" of the law of 4th January 1993]. Denis Salas. **Rev. Sci. Crim. D. P.** 2 4-6:1993 pp.238 - 248.

5299 Offenders and victims : theory and policy. David P. Farrington [Ed.]; Sandra Walklate [Ed.]. London: The British Society of Criminology, 1992. 260p. *ISBN: 0901541273. Includes bibliographical references. Selected papers (of the Conference), Vol.1. Institute for the Study and Treatment of Delinquency, King's College.*

5300 Perspectivas de las investigaciones sobre la delincuencia y la conducta delictiva. *[In Spanish]*; [Perspectives on the investigations into delinquency and criminal behaviour] *[Summary]*; *[Summary in French]*. E.R. Zaffaroni. **Ann. Inter. Crimin.** 31:1-2 1993 pp.61 - 78.

5301 Psychosexual, attitudinal, and developmental characteristics of juvenile female sexual perpetrators in a residential treatment setting. John A. Hunter; Lenard J. Lexier; Dennis W. Goodwin; Patsy A. Browne; Christine Dennis. **J. Child Fam. Stud.** 2:4 12:1993 pp.317 - 326.

5302 Putting the brakes on car crime: a local study of auto-related crime among young people. Maureen McGillivray; Anne Crowley; Howell Edwards. London: Children's Society, 1993. 84p. *ISBN: 0907324835.*

5303 Reflections on urban juvenile crime in the Mao era. Yuefeng Wang. **Iss. Stud.** 29:2 2:1993 pp.76 - 104.

5304 Reinventing juvenile justice — research directions. Barry Krisberg [Ed.]; Ira M. Schwartz [Contrib.]; Shenyang Guo [Contrib.]; John J. Kerbs [Contrib.]; Edmund F. McGarrell [Contrib.]; Michael J. Dale [Contrib.]; Carl Sanniti [Contrib.]; Richard G. Wiebush [Contrib.]; James R. Maupin [Contrib.]; Michael B. Greene [Contrib.]. **Crime Delin.** 39:1 1:1993 pp.3 - 124. *Collection of 7 articles.*

5305 The role of juvenile gangs in facilitating delinquent behavior. Terence P. Thornberry; Marvin D. Krohn; Alan J. Lizotte; Deborah Chard-Wierschem. **J. Res. Crim. Delin.** 30:1 2:1993 pp.55 - 87.

5306 Self-concept comparisons of British and American delinquents. Robert C. Evans; Gary D. Copus; Thomas E. Sullenberger; F. Peter Hodgkinson. **Int. J. Offen.** 37:4 Winter:1993 pp.297 - 314.

5307 Self-control and juvenile delinquency: theoretical issues and an empirical assessment of selected elements of a general theory of crime. David Brownfield; Ann Marie Sorenson. **Dev. Beh.** 14:3 1993 pp.243 - 264.

K: Problèmes sociaux. Services sociaux. Travail social

5308 Symposium on the future of research in crime and delinquency. Jeffrey Fagan [Ed.]; John Braithwaite [Contrib.]; Marcus Felson [Contrib.]; Joan McCord [Contrib.]; Robert J. Sampson [Contrib.]; Lawrence W. Sherman [Contrib.]; Alfred Blumstein [Contrib.]; Elliott Currie [Contrib.]; John Hagan [Contrib.]; C. Ray Jeffery [Contrib.]; Joan Petersilia [Contrib.]; Albert J. Reiss [Contrib.]; Ann Dryden Witte [Contrib.]; Franklin E. Zimring [Contrib.]; Gordon Hawkins [Contrib.]. **J. Res. Crim. Delin.** 30:4 11:1993 pp.383 - 530. *Collection of 13 articles.*

5309 Uchastie roditelei nesovershennoletnikh podozrevaemykh i obviniaemykh v ugolovnom protsesse. *[In Russian]*; [The participation of parents of minors, suspected or accused of crimes, in the criminal procedure]. V.I. Nikandrov. **Gos. Pravo** 8 1993 pp.99 - 106.

5310 Why do they do it? An examination of the intervening mechanisms between "social control" variables and delinquency. Robert Agnew. **J. Res. Crim. Delin.** 30:3 8:1993 pp.245 - 266.

Poverty
Pauvreté

5311 Analyse des différentes méthodes de calcul des seuils de pauvreté en Tunisie. Quels enseignements? *[In French]*; [Analysis of the different methods of calculating poverty thresholds in Tunisia. What can we learn from it?]. Abdeljelil Bedoui. **R. Tun. Sci. Soc.** 29:109 1992 pp.161 - 180.

5312 Argentine — nouvelle et ancienne pauvreté. *[In French]*; (Argentina — new and old poverty.) *[Summary]*; *[Summary in Spanish]*. Laura Golbert; Emilio Tenti Fanfani. **Prob. Am.Lat.** 8 1-3:1993 pp.51 - 64.

5313 Armut im Rheinland: Dokumente zur Geschichte von Armut und Fürsorge im Rheinland vom Mittelalter bis heute. *[In German]*; [Poverty in the Rhineland: documents on the history of poverty and welfare form the Middle Ages to the present day]. Friedhelm Weinforth [Ed.]. Kleve: Boss, 1992. 304p. *ISBN: 3894131705.*

5314 Armut in der "DDR"-Bevölkerung: Lebensstandard und Konsumtionsniveau vor und nach der Wende. *[In German]*; [Poverty amongst the population of the GDR: living standards and levels of consumption before and after German unification]. Günter Manz; Wolfgang Voges [Intro.]. Augsburg: Maro Verlag, 1992. xi, 151p. *ISBN: 3875121775. Includes bibliographical references (p. 144-147) and index.*

5315 Armut in Hamburg: soziale und gesundheitliche Risiken; Arbeitslosigkeit, Sozialhilfe, Wohnungsnot, Verschuldung, Stadtteil-Ungleichheit, Krankheit und Sterblichkeit. *[In German]*; [Poverty in Hamburg: social and health risks: unemployment, welfare, housing shortage, debt, urban inequality, illness and mortality]. Waldemar Süss [Ed.]; Alf Trojan [Ed.]. Hamburg: VSA-Verlag, 1992. 184p. *ISBN: 3879755841.*

5316 Bébés en pièces détachées — une nouvelle «légende» latino-américaine. *[In French]*; [Babies in detached pieces — a new Latin American "legend"] *[Summary]*. Véronique Campion-Vincent. **Cah. Int. Soc.** XCIII 7-12:1992 pp.299 - 319.

5317 Child abuse and the social environment. George E. Fryer. Boulder: Westview Press, 1993. xv, 139p. *ISBN: 0813318033. Includes bibliographical references (p. [114]- 134) and index.*

K: Social problems. Social services. Social work

5318 Child poverty and the ameliorative effects of public assistance. Leif Jensen; David J. Eggebeen; Daniel T. Lichter. **Soc. Sci. Q.** 74:3 9:1993 pp.542 - 559.

5319 Comparing measures of poverty and relative deprivation. An example for Belgium. B. Delhausse; A. Luttgens; S. Perelman. **J. Pop. Ec.** 6:1 1993 pp.83 - 102.

5320 The culture of achievement among the poor. The case of mothers and children in a Head Start program. Delmos J. Jones. **Crit. Anthr.** 13:3 1993 pp.247 - 266.

5321 Dangerous classes: the underclass and social citizenship. Lydia Morris. London, New York: Routledge, 1993. 177p. *ISBN: 0415050138. Includes bibliographical references and index.*

5322 Developing interagency collaboration on behalf of homeless children. Maria Grace Yon; Roslyn Arlin Mickelson; Iris Carlton-Laney. **Educ. Urban. Soc.** 25:4 8:1993 pp.410 - 423.

5323 Education of younger homeless children in urban settings. E. Anne Eddowes. **Educ. Urban. Soc.** 25:4 8:1993 pp.381 - 393.

5324 Exclusion sociale et pauvreté. L'urban underclass chez les sociologues américains. *[In French]*; (The urban underclass according to American sociologists — social exclusion and poverty.) *[Summary]*; *[Summary in German]*; *[Summary in Spanish]*. Nicolas Herpin. **Rev. Fr. Soc.** XXXIV:3 7-9:1993 pp.421 - 439.

5325 Gaining ground — poverty in the postwar United States. Daniel T. Slesnick. **J. Polit. Ec.** 101:1 2:1993 pp.1 - 38.

5326 Geografía de la pobreza y la desigualdad. *[In Spanish]*; [The geography of poverty and inequality]. Juan Cordoba Ordoñez; José M. García Alvarado. Madrid: Sintesis, 1991. 255p. *ISBN: 8477380805.*

5327 Gli studi sulla poverta in Italia. *[In Italian]*; [Studies on poverty in Italy]. Paolo Guidicini [Ed.]. Milan: Angeli, 1991. 337p. *ISBN: 8820471914.*

5328 Homeless families since 1980 — implications for education. Kay Young McChesney. **Educ. Urban. Soc.** 25:4 8:1993 pp.361 - 380.

5329 In the name of the urban poor: access to basic amenities. Amitabh Kundu. New Delhi: Sage Publications, 1993. 299p. *ISBN: 0803991150.*

5330 Informal shelter providers — low income households sheltering the homeless. Edward F. Vacha; Marguerite V. Marin. **J. Soc. Distr. Home.** 2:2 4:1993 pp.117 - 133.

5331 Inner-city concentrated poverty and neighborhood distress — 1970 to 1990. John D. Kasarda. **Hous. Pol. Deb.** 4:3 1993 pp.253 - 302.

5332 Lives on the edge: single mothers and their children in the other America. Valerie Polakow. Chicago: University of Chicago Press, 1993. ix, 222p. *ISBN: 0226671836.*

5333 Neither homed nor homeless — contested definitions and the personal worlds of the poor. April R. Veness. **Pol. Geogr.** 12:4 7:1993 pp.319 - 340.

5334 The new urban poverty and the underclass. Enzo Mingione [Ed.]; Herbert J. Gans [Contrib.]; Hilary Silver [Contrib.]; Peter Marcuse [Contrib.]; Loïc J.D. Wacquant [Contrib.]; Norman Fainstein [Contrib.]; L.D. Morris [Contrib.]; Enrica Morlicchio [Contrib.]. **Int. J. Urban** 17:3 9:1993 pp.324 - 428. *Collection of 8 articles.*

5335 Nutrition and poverty. Siddiqur Rahman Osmani [Ed.]. Oxford, New York, NY: Clarendon Press, 1991. 366p. *ISBN: 0198283962. Includes bibliographical references and index. (Series:* Studies in development economics).

5336 On opulence driven poverty traps. C. van Marrewijk; J. Verbeek. **J. Pop. Ec.** 6:1 1993 pp.67 - 81.

K: Problèmes sociaux. Services sociaux. Travail social

5337 El país de los excluídos: crecimiento y heterogeneidad de la pobreza en el conurbano Bonarense. *[In Spanish]*; [The country of the excluded: growth and heterogenity of poverty in the troubled Buenos Aires]. Inés Aguerrondo [Ed.]. Buenos Aires: CIPPA, 1991. 112p.

5338 La pobreza en la España de la transición. *[In Spanish]*; [Poverty in a changing Spain]. María Encarnación Guillén Sadaba. Madrid: Instituto de Sociología Aplicada, 1991. 80p. *ISBN: 8486111102. Includes bibliographical references (p. 73-80).*

5339 La pobreza más de cerca: las estrategias de supervivencia de las fammilias más pobres de Mendoza. *[In Spanish]*; [Poverty close-up: the survival techniques of the poorest families in Mendoza]. Azucena Beatriz Reyes Suarez. Mendoza: Editorial de la Universidad Nacional de Cuyo, 1992. 320p. *ISBN: 9503900158.*

5340 Population, poverty and social transformation — an alternative paradigm. Vasant P. Pethe. **Art. Vij.** XXXIV:2 6:1992 pp.200 - 208.

5341 Poverty in Karachi: incidence, location, characteristics, and upward mobility. Mir Anjum Altaf; Aly Ercelawn; Kaiser Bengali; Abdul Rahim. **Pak. Dev. R.** 32:2 Summer:1993 pp.159 - 178.

5342 Poverty monitoring: an international concern. Richard Anker [Ed.]; Rolph Van Der Hoeven [Ed.]. Basingstoke, Hants: Macmillan Press, 1993. 224p. *ISBN: 0333593537.*

5343 Poverty, parenting, and children's mental health. Jane D. McLeod; Michael J. Shanahan. **Am. Sociol. R.** 58:3 6:1993 pp.351 - 366.

5344 Power, poverty, and poison: disaster and response in an Indian city. James Manor. New Delhi, Newbury Park, CA: Sage Publications, 1993. 197p. *ISBN: 0803994664. Includes bibliographical references and index.*

5345 Revisiting the relationship between growth and poverty. Golam Azam; Alonzo Redmon. **Rev. Bl. Pol. Ec.** 22:1 Summer:1993 pp.5 - 18.

5346 Rural poverty in India. B.C. Mehta. New Delhi: Concept Publishing Company, 1993. 200p. *ISBN: 8170224322.*

5347 The satisfied poor. G.I. Olson; B.I. Schober. **Soc. Ind.** 28:2 2:1993 pp.173 - 193.

5348 Sociologists, social policy and the estranged poor: the selective inattention to the limits of success. Richard H.P. Mendes. **Am. Sociol.** 24:2 Summer:1993 pp.16 - 36.

5349 The space of vulnerability — the causal structure of hunger. Michael J. Watts; Hans G. Bohle. **Prog. H. Geog.** 17:1 3:1993 pp.43 - 67.

5350 Structural adjustment programmes and poverty creation — evidence from Sudan. Ali Abdel Gadir Ali. **E.Afr. Soc. Sci. Res. R.** VIII:1 1:1992 pp.1 - 21.

5351 Le tunisien pauvre face à sa pauvreté. *[In French]*; [The poor Tunisian faced with his poverty]. Mustapha Nasraoui. **R. Tun. Sci. Soc.** 29:109 1992 pp.243 - 292.

5352 Understanding poverty. Pete Alcock. Basingstoke: Macmillan, 1993. 286p. *ISBN: 0333567587.*

5353 Understanding the changing fortunes of metropolitan neighborhoods — 1980 to 1990. George C. Galster; Ronald B. Mincy. **Hous. Pol. Deb.** 4:3 1993 pp.303 - 352.

5354 Welfare, poverty and development in Latin America. Christopher Abel [Ed.]; Colin M. Lewis [Ed.]. Basingstoke: Macmillan Press, 1993. 485p. *ISBN: 0333517377. (Series:* St. Antony's Macmillan series).

5355 Women, poverty and AIDS. Paul Farmer [Ed.]; Shirley Lindebaum [Ed.]; Mary-Jo DelVecchio Good [Ed.]; Geeta Rao Gupta [Contrib.]; Ellen Weiss [Contrib.]; Martha C. Ward [Contrib.]; Anitra Pivnick [Contrib.]; E.J. Sobo [Contrib.]; Nina Glick Schiller [Contrib.]. **Cult. Medic. Psych.** 17:4 12:1993 pp.387 - 512. *Collection of 6 articles.*

K: Social problems. Social services. Social work

5356 Work and welfare among single mothers in poverty. Kathleen Mullan Harris. **A.J.S.** 99:2 9:1993 pp.317 - 352.
5357 Zwischen Verdrängung und Dramatisierung. Zur Wissenssoziologie der Armut in der bundesrepublikanischen Gesellschaft. *[In German]*; (Between ignorance and dramatization. Poverty in the Federal Republic of Germany — a study in the sociology of knowledge.) *[Summary]*. Lutz Leisering. **Soz. Welt.** 44:4 1993 pp.486 - 511.

Substance abuse
Usage des stupéfiants

5358 Addiction as a social construction — a postempirical view. Franklin Truan. **J. Psychol.** 127:5 9:1993 pp.489 - 499.
5359 Alcohol problems: a resource directory and bibliography. Larry Harrison. London: Central Council for Education and Training in Social Work, 1993. 135p. *ISBN: 1857190440.*
5360 Alcohol-control policies and motor-vehicle fatalities. Frank J. Chaloupka; Henry Saffer; Michael Grossman. **J. Leg. Stud.** XXII:1 1:1993 pp.161 - 186.
5361 Alcoholism in North America, Europe, and Asia. J.ohn E. Helzer [Ed.]; Glorisa J. Canino [Ed.]. New York: Oxford University Press, 1992. xix, 325p. *ISBN: 0195050908. Includes bibliographical references and index.*
5362 Alcoholism, work, and income. John Mullahy; Jody L. Sindelar. **J. Labor Ec.** 11:3 7:1993 pp.494 - 520.
5363 Alcohol-related knowledge and attitudes in people with a mild learning disability — the effects of a "sensible drinking" group. C.G. McCusker; I.C.H. Clare; C. Cullen; J. Reep. **J. Comm. App. Soc. Psychol.** 3:1 4:1993 pp.29 - 40.
5364 Arbeitslosigkeit und Alkoholismus: epidemiologische, ätiologische und diagnostische Zusammenhänge. *[In German]*; [Unemployment and alcoholism: epidemiological, etiological and diagnostical connections]. Dieter Henkel. Weinheim: Deutscher Studien Verlag, 1992. 200p. *ISBN: 3892712689.*
5365 Being female and less deviant — the direct and indirect effects of gender on alcohol abuse and tobacco smoking. James DeFronzo; Rebecca Pawlak. **J. Psychol.** 127:6 11:1993 pp.639 - 647.
5366 Brief interventions for alcohol problems — a review. Thomas H. Bien; William R. Miller; J. Scott Tonigan. **Addiction** 88:3 3:1993 pp.315 - 336.
5367 A case report — alcohol-induced blackouts during sexual intercourse: legal responsibility. Dan E. Neal; Edward M. Scott; Raymond A. Grimsbo. **Int. J. Offen.** 37:4 Winter:1993 pp.325 - 330.
5368 Characteristics of homeless alcohol and drug abusers identified through an assertive outreach program. David C. Cohen; Mary Ann Krating. **J. Soc. Distr. Home.** 2:3 7:1993 pp.193 - 206.
5369 Characteristics of substance-abusing offenders — implications for treatment programming. Lynn Lightfoot; David C. Hodgins. **Int. J. Offen.** 37:3 Fall:1993 pp.239 - 250.
5370 Cocaine and crack: supply and use. Philip Bean [Ed.]. New York, N.Y: St. Martin's Press, 1993. viii, 176p. *ISBN: 0312089392. Includes bibiographical references and index.*

K: Problèmes sociaux. Services sociaux. Travail social

5371 The co-morbidity of depression, anxiety and substance abuse among American Indians and Alaska natives. Jack D. Maser [Ed.]; Norman Dinges [Ed.]; Byron J. Good [Contrib.]; Theresa D. O'Nell [Contrib.]; William H. Sack [Contrib.]; Morton Beiser [Contrib.]; Norman Phillips [Contrib.]; Gloria Baker-Brown [Contrib.]; Quang Duong-Tran [Contrib.]; Philip D. Somervell [Contrib.]; Janette Beals [Contrib.]; J. David Kinzie [Contrib.]; James Boehnlein [Contrib.]; Paul Leung [Contrib.]; Spero M. Manson [Contrib.]; Joseph Westermeyer [Contrib.]; John Neider [Contrib.]; Michelle Westermeyer [Contrib.]; G.L. Brown [Contrib.]; B.J. Albaugh [Contrib.]; R.W. Robin [Contrib.]; S.G. Goodson [Contrib.]; M. Trunzo [Contrib.]; D.K. Wynne [Contrib.]; D. Goldman [Contrib.]; Don Matsunaga [Contrib.]; Robert Johnson [Contrib.]; James H. Shore [Contrib.]; R. Dale Walker [Contrib.]; M. Dow Lambert [Contrib.]; Patricia Silk Walker [Contrib.]; Daniel R. Kivlahan [Contrib.]. **Cult. Medic. Psych.** 16:4 1992-1993 pp.409 - 572. *Collection of 10 articles.*

5372 Confronting drug policy: illicit drugs in a free society. Ronald Bayer [Ed.]; Gerald M. Oppenheimer [Ed.]. Cambridge [England], New York, NY, USA: Cambridge University Press, 1993. vii, 369p. *ISBN: 0521441153. Includes bibliographical references and index.*

5373 La construction de l'alcoolique entre nature et culture. *[In French]*; [Construction of the alcoholic between nature and culture]; *[Summary in German].* Sylvie Fainzang. **Ethnol. Helvet.** 17-18 1993-1994 pp.169 - 190.

5374 Criminal involvement of cocaine users enrolled in a methadone treatment program. Sung-Yeon Kang; George de Leon. **Addiction** 88:3 3:1993 pp.395 - 404.

5375 Demanda de drogas psicoactivas y drogadiccion. *[In Spanish]*; [The demand for psychoactive and addictive drugs]. Francisco Thoumi. **Plan. Desarr.** XXIV:3 12:1993 pp.455 - 496.

5376 Different substance abusing offenders require a unique program. Wagdy Loza. **Int. J. Offen.** 37:4 Winter:1993 pp.351 - 364.

5377 Differential patterns of partner-to-woman violence — a comparison of samples of community, alcohol-abusing, and battered women. William R. Downs; Brenda A. Miller; Denise D. Panek. **J. Fam. Viol.** 8:2 6:1993 pp.113 - 135.

5378 Don't be your own best customer — drug use of San Francisco gang drug sellers. Dan Waldorf. **Cr. Law Soc. Chan.** 19:1 1:1993 pp.1 - 15.

5379 Drinking and driving, self-control, and gender — testing a general theory of crime. Carl Keane; Paul S. Maxim; James J. Teevan. **J. Res. Crim. Delin.** 30:1 2:1993 pp.30 - 46.

5380 Drinking and schooling. P.J. Cook; M.J. Moore. **J. Health Econ.** 12:4 1993 pp.411 - 429.

5381 Drogenboom im Osten? *[In German]*; [Is there a drugs boom in the East?]. Gundula Barsch; Rolf Bergmann. Berlin: Morgenbuch, 1992. 127p. *ISBN: 3371003353.*

5382 Drogenkonsum und Drogenpolitik: Deutschland und die Niederlande im Vergleich. *[In German]*; [Consuming drugs and drugs policy: Germany and the Netherlands in comparison]. Karl-Heinz Reuband. Opladen: Leske + Budrich, 1993. 174p. *ISBN: 3810010022.*

5383 Drug policy in the Americas. Peter H. Smith [Ed.]. Boulder: Westview Press, 1992. x, 366p. *ISBN: 0813382394, 0813382408. Result of a series of workshops held at the University of California, San Diego in 1990-1991 under the auspices of the Project on Hemispheric Cooperation for the Prevention of Drug Abuse and Traffic. Includes bibliographical references and index.*

K: Social problems. Social services. Social work

5384 Drug policy in the time of AIDS — the development of outreach in San Francisco. Robert S. Broadhead; Eric Margolis. **Sociol. Q.** 34:3 8:1993 pp.497 - 522.

5385 Drugs and justice — the impact of drugs on criminal justice in a metropolitan community. John M. Klofas. **Crime Delin.** 39:2 4:1993 pp.204 - 224.

5386 Drugs, law, and the state. Harold Traver [Ed.]; Mark S. Gaylord [Ed.]. New Brunswick, U.S.A: Transaction Publishers, 1992. xxix, 176p. *ISBN: 1560000821. Includes bibliographical references and index.*

5387 Drugs, people and services: final report of the Drug Information Project to the Lewisham Safer Cities Project. Heidi Safia Mirza; Geoffrey Pearson; Stewart Phillips. London: Drug Information Project, Goldsmiths' College, University of London, 1991. 65p.

5388 The effect of parents' alcohol problems on children's behaviour as reported by parents and teachers; *[Summary in French]*; *[Summary in Spanish]*. Gary M. Connolly; Sally Casswell; Joanna Stewart; Phil A. Silva; Mary K. O'Brien. **Addiction** 88:10 10:1993 pp.1383 - 1390.

5389 Effects of maternal employment patterns on adolescents' substance use and other risk-taking behaviors. Stephen B. Hillman; Shlomo S. Sawilowsky; Marilyn J. Becker. **J. Child Fam. Stud.** 2:3 9:1993 pp.203 - 219.

5390 Estimating actual rates of drug abuse. John M. Gleason; Darold T. Barnum. **Socio. Econ.** 27:3 9:1993 pp.199 - 208.

5391 A follow-up study of homeless women. Céline Mercier; Guylaine Racine. **J. Soc. Distr. Home.** 2:3 7:1993 pp.207 - 222.

5392 Generality and specificity in health behavior — application to warning-label and social influence expectancies. Alan W. Stacy; David P. MacKinnon; Mary Ann Pentz. **J. Appl. Psychol.** 78:4 8:1993 pp.611 - 627.

5393 Geography's impact on the success of focused local drug enforcement operations. Jonathan P. Caulkins; Richard C. Larson; Thomas F. Rich. **Socio. Econ.** 27:2 1993 pp.119 - 130.

5394 La légalisation des drogues: pour mieux en prévenir les abus. *[In French]*; [Would the legalization of drugs be a better way to prevent abuse?]. Line Beauchesne. Montreal: Méridien, 1991. 381p. *ISBN: 2894150482. Bibliographic references: p. [341]-375.*

5395 Life satisfaction and adjustment of children of alcoholics — the effects of parental drinking, family disorganization and survival roles. Valerie Braithwaite; Cindy Devine. **Br. J. Clin. Psycho.** 32:4 11:1993 pp.417 - 429.

5396 The limitations of drug screening in the workplace. Scott MacDonald; Samantha Wells; Richard Fry. **Int. Lab. Rev.** 132:1 1993 pp.95 - 113.

5397 The medicine society. Paul Scriven. East Lansing, Michigan: Michigan State University Press, 1992. xiii, 217p. *ISBN: 0870133152.*

5398 Mi guerra en Medellín. *[In Spanish]*; [My war in Medellín]. Augusto Bahamón Dussán. Santafé de Bogotá: Intermedio, 1991. 152p. *ISBN: 9586371719.*

5399 National audit of drug misuse in Britain, 1992. Mike Ashton [Ed.]. London: Institute for the Study of Drug Dependence, 1993. 83p. *ISBN: 094883076X.*

5400 Outreach among drug users — combining the role of ethnographic field assistant and health educator. Claire Sterk-Elifson. **Human. Org.** 52:2 Summer:1993 pp.162 - 168.

5401 Political pharmacology — thinking about drugs. Mathea Falco [Contrib.]; Peter Reuter [Contrib.]; Mark A.R. Kleiman [Contrib.]; Ethan A. Nadelmann [Contrib.];

K: Problèmes sociaux. Services sociaux. Travail social

Jerome H. Skolnick [Contrib.]; Thomas Szasz [Contrib.]; David C. Lewis [Contrib.]; Mark Schlesinger [Contrib.]; Robert A. Dorwart [Contrib.]; Patricia G. Erickson [Contrib.]; Dwight B. Heath [Contrib.]; Jerri A. Husch [Contrib.]. **Dædalus** 121:3 Summer:1992 pp.1 - 304. *Collection of 11 articles.*

5402 Prediction of controlled drinking by alcoholics and problem drinkers. Harold Rosenberg. **Psychol . B.** 113:1 1:1993 pp.129 - 139.

5403 A preliminary survey of Italian intravenous heroin users in London. Maurice Lipsedge; Gianni Dianin; Eblish Duckworth. **Addiction** 88:11 11:1993 pp.1565 - 1572.

5404 Prevalence of volatile solvent inhalation among junior high school students in Japan and background life style of users; *[Summary in French]*; *[Summary in Spanish]*. Kiyoshi Wada; Susumu Fukui. **Addiction** 88:1 1:1993 pp.89 - 100.

5405 Punishing drugs — criminal justice and drug use. Mike Collison. **Br. J. Crimin.** 33:3 Summer:1993 pp.382 - 399.

5406 Race, class, and gender differences in substance abuse — evidence of middle-class/underclass polarization among black males. Kellie E.M. Barr; Michael P. Farrell; Grace M. Barnes; John W. Welte. **Soc. Prob.** 40:3 8:1993 pp.314 - 327.

5407 Recruiting and retaining out-of-treatment injecting drug users in Puerto Rico AIDS prevention project. H. Ann Finlinson; Rafaela R. Robles; Héctor M. Colón; J. Bryan Page. **Human. Org.** 52:2 Summer:1993 pp.169 - 175.

5408 Resident adaptations in an Alcoholics Anonymous-based residential program for the urban homeless. Gordon Bazemore; Peter L. Cruise. **Soc. Ser. R.** 67:4 12:1993 pp.599 - 616.

5409 Risk factors for suicide and undetermined death among in-patient alcoholics in Scotland; *[Summary in French]*; *[Summary in Spanish]*. John Duffy; Norman Kreitman. **Addiction** 88:6 6:1993 pp.757 - 766.

5410 The severity of preaddiction criminal behavior among urban, male narcotic addicts and two nonaddicted control groups. David N. Nurco; Timothy Kinlock; Mitchell B. Balter. **J. Res. Crim. Delin.** 30:3 8:1993 pp.293 - 316.

5411 Le SIDA et les consommateurs de drogue: la prévention à l'épreuve de la ville. *[In French]*; [AIDS and drug users: how the town affects prevention]. Dominique Malatesta. **Ethnol. Helvet.** 17-18 1993-1994 pp.201 - 218.

5412 Street addicts in the political economy. Alisse Waterston. Philadelphia: Temple University Press, 1993. xix, 280p. *ISBN: 0877229929. Includes bibliographical references (p. [257]-273) and index.*

5413 Studying drugs in rural areas — notes from the field. Ralph A. Weisheit. **J. Res. Crim. Delin.** 30:2 5:1993 pp.213 - 232.

5414 Suicide and adolescence. Tracey E. Harris; Chris J. Lennings. **Int. J. Offen.** 37:3 Fall:1993 pp.263 - 270.

5415 War on drugs: studies in the failure of U.S. narcotics policy. Alfred W. McCoy [Ed.]; Alan A. Block [Ed.]. Boulder: Westview Press, 1992. xi, 359p. *ISBN: 0813385512. Includes bibliographical references.*

5416 What is the size and nature of the "drug problem" in the UK? Matthew Sutton; Alan Maynard. York: The Centre for Health Economics/University of York, 1993. 105p. (*Series:* Yartic occacisonal paper).

5417 The will to win — determinants of public support for the drug war in Belize. Bruce Wiegand; Richard Bennett. **Cr. Law Soc. Chan.** 19:2 3:1993 pp.203 - 220.

K: *Social problems. Social services. Social work*

5418 Women drug users: an ethnography of a female injecting community. Avril Taylor. Oxford: Clarendon, 1993. 182p. *ISBN: 0198257961.*
5419 Women with alcohol problems — do they relapse for reasons different to their male counterparts?; *[Summary in French]*; *[Summary in Spanish].* Bill Saunders; Sally Baily; Mike Phillips; Steve Allsop. **Addiction** 88:10 10:1993 pp.1413 - 1422.
5420 Zero-tolerance policies — do they inhibit or stimulate illicit drug consumption? Jonathan P. Caulkins. **Manag. Sci.** 39:4 4:1993 pp.458 - 476.
5421 Zwischen Legalisierung und Normalisierung: Ausstiegsszenarien aus der repressiven Drogenpolitik. *[In German]*; [Between legalization and normalization: getting away from a repressive drugs policy]. Jürgen Neumeyer [Ed.]; Gudrun Schaich-Walch [Ed.]. Marburg: Schüren, 1992. 202p. *ISBN: 3894722495. Includes bibliographies.*

Suicide
Suicide

5422 Age, gender, and suicide — a cross-national analysis. Chris Girard. **Am. Sociol. R.** 58:4 8:1993 pp.553 - 574.
5423 Alcohol and the 1950-90 Hungarian suicide trend — is there a causal connection? Ole-Jørgen Skog; Zsuzsanna Elekes. **Acta Sociol.** 36:1 1993 pp.33 - 46.
5424 The co-morbidity of depression, anxiety and substance abuse among American Indians and Alaska natives. Jack D. Maser [Ed.]; Norman Dinges [Ed.]; Byron J. Good [Contrib.]; Theresa D. O'Nell [Contrib.]; William H. Sack [Contrib.]; Morton Beiser [Contrib.]; Norman Phillips [Contrib.]; Gloria Baker-Brown [Contrib.]; Quang Duong-Tran [Contrib.]; Philip D. Somervell [Contrib.]; Janette Beals [Contrib.]; J. David Kinzie [Contrib.]; James Boehnlein [Contrib.]; Paul Leung [Contrib.]; Spero M. Manson [Contrib.]; Joseph Westermeyer [Contrib.]; John Neider [Contrib.]; Michelle Westermeyer [Contrib.]; G.L. Brown [Contrib.]; B.J. Albaugh [Contrib.]; R.W. Robin [Contrib.]; S.G. Goodson [Contrib.]; M. Trunzo [Contrib.]; D.K. Wynne [Contrib.]; D. Goldman [Contrib.]; Don Matsunaga [Contrib.]; Robert Johnson [Contrib.]; James H. Shore [Contrib.]; R. Dale Walker [Contrib.]; M. Dow Lambert [Contrib.]; Patricia Silk Walker [Contrib.]; Daniel R. Kivlahan [Contrib.]. **Cult. Medic. Psych.** 16:4 1992-1993 pp.409 - 572. *Collection of 10 articles.*
5425 Marital status, alcohol consumption, and suicide — an analysis of national data. Steven Stack; Ira Wasserman. **J. Marriage Fam.** 55:4 11:1993 pp.1018 - 1024.
5426 Risk factors for suicide and undetermined death among in-patient alcoholics in Scotland; *[Summary in French]*; *[Summary in Spanish].* John Duffy; Norman Kreitman. **Addiction** 88:6 6:1993 pp.757 - 766.
5427 Suicide: a European perspective. Nils Retterstøl. New York, NY: Cambridge University Press, 1993. 261p. *ISBN: 0521420997. Includes bibliographical references and index.*
5428 Suicide and adolescence. Tracey E. Harris; Chris J. Lennings. **Int. J. Offen.** 37:3 Fall:1993 pp.263 - 270.
5429 Suicide in Japan and in the West — evidence for Durkheim's theory. Charles R. Chandler; Yung-Mei Tsai. **Int. J. Comp. Soc** XXXIV:3-4 9-12:1993 pp.244 - 259.
5430 Suicide mortality in Australia, 1970-1991. L.T. Ruzicka; C.Y. Choi. **J. Aust. Pop. Ass.** 10:2 11:1993 pp.101 - 118.

K: Problèmes sociaux. Services sociaux. Travail social

5431 "Therefore choose life": reflections on a suicide epidemic. Avshalom C. Elitzur. **J. Soc. Work Pol. Israel** 7-8 1993 p.145.

5432 An update on American Indian suicide in New Mexico, 1980-1987. Nancy Westlake van Winkle; Philip A. May. **Human. Org.** 52:3 Fall:1993 pp.304 - 315.

Violence
Violence

5433 Les formes de la violence. *[In French]*; [Forms of violence]. J. Molino [Contrib.]; E. Ascher [Contrib.]; G. Berthoud [Contrib.]; J. Freund [Contrib.]; J. Bergeret [Contrib.]; R. Verdier [Contrib.]; M. Cosandey [Contrib.]; L. Sfez [Contrib.]; G. Moser [Contrib.]; J. Beauchard [Contrib.]; A. Aliman [Contrib.]; M. Killias [Contrib.]; D. Welzer-Lang [Contrib.]; M. Wieviorka [Contrib.]; J.-P. Siméon [Contrib.]; A. Delessert [Contrib.]. **Rev. Eur. Sci. Soc.** XXX:94 1992 pp.7 - 176. *Collection of 15 articles.*

5434 Gesellschaft und Gewalt — ein Aufriß. *[In German]*; (Society and violence — an outline.) *[Summary]*. Roland Eckert. **Soz. Welt.** 44:3 1993 pp.358 - 374.

5435 Gewalt. *[In German]*; [Force]. Tilmann Moser [Contrib.]; Hans-Joachim Maaz [Contrib.]; Eike Hennig [Contrib.]; Eberhard Seidel-Pielen [Contrib.]; Eugen E. Jungjohann [Contrib.]; Helga Theunert [Contrib.]; Franz Josef Krafeld [Contrib.]. **Gewerk. Monat.** 44:4 4:1993 pp.203 - 264. *Collection of 7 articles.*

5436 Informe. Víctimas de robos y agresiones violentas en la ciudad de Vitoria-Gasteiz. *[In Spanish]*; [Report. Victims of burglaries and violent aggression in the town of Vitoria-Gasteiz] *[Summary]*; *[Summary in French]*. J.L. de la Cuesta Arzamendi. **Ann. Inter. Crimin.** 31:1-2 1993 pp.107 - 126.

5437 Modes of defensive behavior in a violent society. George B. Palermo; Richard Knudten; Douglas Simpson; Vitaliano Turci; Hugh Davis. **Int. J. Offen.** 37:3 Fall:1993 pp.251 - 261.

5438 Ohne Gewalt läuft nichts!: Jugend und Gewalt in Deutschland. *[In German]*; [Nothing works without violence!: Youth and violence in Germany]. Klaus Farin; Eberhard Seidel-Pielen. Cologne: Bund-Verlag, 1993. *ISBN: 3766324306. Bibliography (p. 287-304).*

5439 Patterns of violence: case studies of conflict in Natal. Anthony Minaar [Ed.]. Pretoria: Human Science Research Council, 1992. 264p. *ISBN: 0796913471. Includes bibliographical references.*

5440 The political subject of violence. David Campbell [Ed.]; Michael Dillon [Ed.]. Manchester, UK, New York, NY: Manchester University Press, distributed by St. Martin's Press, 1993. 185p. *ISBN: 0719038499.*

5441 A public health approach to the violence epidemic in the United States. Larry Cohen; Susan Swift. **Environ. Urban.** 5:2 10:1993 pp.50 - 66.

5442 The seasonality of violent crime — the case of robbery and homicide in Israel. Simha F. Landau; Daniel Fridman. **J. Res. Crim. Delin.** 30:2 5:1993 pp.163 - 191.

5443 Trends in violent crime against women, 1973-89. M. Dwayne Smith; Ellen S. Kuchta. **Soc. Sci. Q.** 74:1 3:1993 pp.28 - 45.

5444 Understanding and preventing violence. Albert J. Reiss [Ed.]; Jeffrey A. Roth [Ed.]. Washington, D.C: National Academy Press, 1993. xiv, 464p. *ISBN: 0309045940. Includes bibliographical references and index.*

K: Social problems. Social services. Social work

5445 Violence and law. Costas Douzinas [Ed.]; Peter Goodrich [Ed.]; Sara Cobb; Richard Devlin; Deborah Cheney; Christopher Stanley; Denis J. Brion. **Law Crit.** IV:2 1993 pp.131 - 252. *Collection of 5 articles.*

5446 Violence in the urban slums — a case study of Delhi. Somen Chakraborty; Geeta Rana. **Soc. Act.** 43:2 4-6:1993 pp.153 - 164.

5447 Violent crime in small shops. Malcolm Hibberd; Joanna Shapland. London: Police Foundation, 1993. 81p. *ISBN: 0947692290.*

5448 Violent incidents in a secure unit. David Torpy; Marianne Hall. **J. For. Psy.** 4:3 12:1993 pp.517 - 544.

5449 Women, violence and crime prevention: a West Yorkshire study. Jalna Hanmer; Sheila Saunders. Aldershot: Avebury, 1993. 407p. *ISBN: 1856282376.*

K.2: Social security
Sécurité sociale

5450 "Age speaks for itself in Europe". Robert Leaper [Contrib.]; B. de Clercq [Contrib.]; R. Maus [Contrib.]; W. Vanderleen [Contrib.]; D. Verté [Contrib.]; Serge Mayence [Contrib.]; Joe Larragy [Contrib.]; Marie-Odile Frattini [Contrib.]; Irène Sipos [Contrib.]. **Soc. Pol. Admin.** 27:3 9:1993 pp.191 - 265. *Collection of 6 articles.*

5451 Beyond privatization and service integration — organizational models for service delivery. John O'Looney. **Soc. Ser. R.** 67:4 12:1993 pp.501 - 534.

5452 Beyond the problem projects paradigm — defining and revitalizing "severely distressed" public housing. Lawrence J. Vale; Richard C. Gentry [Comments by]; Jeffrey K. Lines [Comments by]. **Hous. Pol. Deb.** 4:2 1993 pp.147 - 198.

5453 Child and family benefits in Eastern and Central Europe and in the West — learning from the transition. S.B. Kamerman; A.J. Kahn. **Envir. Plan. C.** 11:2 5:1993 pp.199 - 211.

5454 Choisir ses voisins? *[In French]*; (Choosing one's neighbors?) *[Summary]*; *[Summary in German]*; *[Summary in Spanish]*. Hubert Cukrowicz. **Rev. Fr. Soc.** XXXIV:3 7-9:1993 pp.367 - 393.

5455 Citizen involvement: a practical guide for change. Peter Beresford; Suzy Croft. Basingstoke: Macmillan Press Ltd, 1993. 240p. *ISBN: 0333483006.* (*Series:* Practical social work).

5456 Citizenship, dependency, and the welfare mix — problems of inclusion and exclusion. Peter Taylor-Gooby. **Int. J. Health. Ser.** 23:3 1993 pp.455 - 474.

5457 Community care and control: a guide to the legislation. Colin Fishwick. Birmingham: Pepar Publications, 1992. 224p. *ISBN: 0948680253.*

5458 Community law centres — problems and proposals. Mike Stephens. **J. Soc. Pol.** 22:1 1:1993 pp.49 - 68.

5459 Community or ghetto?: an analysis of day centres for single homeless people in England and Wales. Jacqueline Waters. London: CHAR, 1992. viii,119p. *ISBN: 090695133X.*

5460 Community social work, older people and informal care: a romantic illusion. David S. Gordon; Sheena C. Donald. Aldershot: Avebury, 1993. 186p. *ISBN: 1856285561.*

5461 De ontwikkeling van corporatieve verzorgingsstaten in België en Nederland. *[In Dutch]*; (The development of corporative welfare states in Belgium and the

K: Problèmes sociaux. Services sociaux. Travail social

Netherlands.) *[Summary]*. S. Hellemans; R. Schepers. **Sociol. Gids** XXXIX:5-6 9-12:1992 pp.346 - 364.

5462 Do community-based, longterm care services reduce nursing home use? A transition probability analysis. Vernon L. Greene; Mary E. Lovely; Jan I. Ondrich. **J. Hum. Res.** XXVIII:2 Spring:1993 pp.297 - 317.

5463 Der Dritte Sektor zwischen Markt und Staat - ökonomische und politologische Theorieansätze. *[In German]*; [The third sector between the market and the state]. Annette Zimmer; Martina Scholz. **Fors.Jour. Soz. Beweg.** 4 1992 pp.21 - 39.

5464 Droit et pauvreté: droits de l'homme, sécurité sociale, aide sociale. *[In French]*; [Law and poverty: human rights, social security and social aid]. Jacques Fierens. Bruxelles: E. Bruylant, 1992. xv, 456p. *ISBN: 280270804X. Includes bibliographical references (p. [427]-443) and index.*

5465 Dual welfare and sex segregation of access to social benefits — income maintenance policies in the UK, the US, the Netherlands and Sweden. Diane Sainsbury. **J. Soc. Pol.** 22:1 1:1993 pp.69 - 98.

5466 Efficient targeting of community care — the case of the home help service. Andrew Bebbington; Bleddyn Davies. **J. Soc. Pol.** 22:3 7:1993 pp.373 - 391.

5467 Equality of treatment for housewives in tax and benefit systems — a proposal. Rolande Cuvillier. **J. Soc. Pol.** 22:4 10:1993 pp.439 - 460.

5468 [Establishing need — judgement criteria and estimating site of need for social services for the elderly]; *[Text in Japanese]*. Shogo Takegawa. **Kiyo Shak.** 151 1993 pp.51 - 76.

5469 Family self-sufficiency and housing. Anne B. Shlay. **Hous. Pol. Deb.** 4:3 1993 pp.457 - 498.

5470 Federalism and suitable housing for the frail elderly — a comparison of policies in Canada and the United States. Phoebe S. Liebig. **Hous. Pol. Deb.** 4:2 1993 pp.199 - 237.

5471 Führungs- und Kontrollprobleme bei Nonprofitorganisationen in staatlich dominierter Umgebung. Eine historische Fallstudie. *[In German]*; [Leadership and control problems in non-profit organizations in a state dominated environment. An historical case study]. Melissa Middleton-Stone. **Fors.Jour. Soz. Beweg.** 4 1992 pp.59 - 76.

5472 [Fundamantal theory of welfare — a social philosophical approach]; *[Text in Japanese]*. Tomio Saikawa. **Ken. Kiyo (J. Aomori Univ.)** 15(2) 1993 pp.47 - 69.

5473 The growth of government. Warren J. Samuels. **Crit. Rev.** 7:4 Fall:1993 pp.445 - 460.

5474 Huishoudenssituatie van ouderen in Nederland — implicatie voor de vraag naar zorgvoorzieningen. *[In Dutch]*; [Household situation of elderly in the Netherlands — implication for the demand for care facilities] *[Summary]*. Hanne van Solinge; Ingrid Esveldt. **Bevolk. Gez.** 2:1992 pp.67 - 91.

5475 Im Wettstreit der Ideen: Reform des Sozialstaats. *[In German]*; [A competition of ideas: reform of the social state]. Monika Wulf-Mathies [Ed.]. Cologne: Bund-Verlag, 1991. 282p. *ISBN: 3766321781.*

5476 Improving information for social policy decisions: the uses of microsimulation modeling. Volume 1. Review and recommendations. Constance Forbes Citro [Ed.]; Eric Alan Hanushek [Ed.]. Washington, DC: National Academy Press, 1991. *ISBN: 030904541X. National Research Council, U.S, Panel to Evaluate Microsimulation Models for Social Welfare Programs. Includes bibliographical references and index.*

K: Social problems. Social services. Social work

5477 Informing people about social services. Jane Steele. London: Policy Studies Institute, 1993. *ISBN: 085374565X*. (*Series:* PSI Report).
5478 Integrating carers into the service system — six strategic responses. Julia Twigg. **Age. Soc.** 13:2 6:1993 pp.141 - 170.
5479 Is family care on the decline? A longitudinal investigation of the substitution of formal long-term care services for informal care. Sharon L. Tennstedt; Sybil L. Crawford; John B. McKinlay. **Milbank Q.** 71:4 1993 pp.601 - 625.
5480 Last in line — housing assistance for households with children. Sandra J. Newman; Ann B. Schnare. **Hous. Pol. Deb.** 4:3 1993 pp.417 - 455.
5481 Leadership counts: lessons for public managers from the Massachusetts welfare, training, and employment program. Robert D. Behn. Cambridge, Mass: Harvard University Press, 1991. xiii, 248p. *ISBN: 0674518527. Includes bibliographical references (p. [221]-244) and index.*
5482 Lo stato sociale da Brodolini ad oggi. *[In Italian]*; [Welfare state from Brodolini to today]. Ugo Ascoli; et al. Venice: Marsilio, 1991. 167p. *ISBN: 8831756001*.
5483 The long term impact of staying put. Philip Leather; Sheila Mackintosh. **Age. Soc.** 13:2 6:1993 pp.193 - 211.
5484 Long-term care, Medicaid, and impoverishment of the elderly. Frank A. Sloan; May W. Shayne. **Milbank Q.** 71:4 1993 pp.575 - 599.
5485 Managing appeals — the control of housing benefit internal reviews by local authority officers. Tony Eardley; Roy Sainsbury. **J. Soc. Pol.** 22:4 10:1993 pp.461 - 485.
5486 Managing poverty: the limits of social assistance. Carol Walker. London: New York, Routledge, 1993. 204p. *ISBN: 0415084547, 0415084555. Includes bibliographical references and index.* (*Series:* The state of welfare).
5487 Needs as claims. Paul Spicker. **Soc. Pol. Admin.** 27:1 3:1993 pp.7 - 17.
5488 Nonprofit housing development — status, trends, and prospects. Christopher Walker. **Hous. Pol. Deb.** 4:3 1993 pp.369 - 414.
5489 Nonprofits for hire: the welfare state in the age of contracting. Steven Rathgeb Smith; Michael Lipsky. Cambridge, MA.: Harvard University Press, 1993. 292p. *ISBN: 0674626389*.
5490 La place du pauvre: histoire et géographie sociales de l'habitat HLM. *[In French]*; [The place of the poor: history and social geography of HLM housing]. Jacques Barou. Paris: Editions L'Harmattan, 1992. 135p. *ISBN: 2738411843. Bibliography and index.*
5491 Planning for social housing in London and the South East. Jane Brenan. **Plan. Pract. Res.** 8:4 12:1993 pp.15 - 26.
5492 Political parties and public pensions: a quantitative analysis. Evelyne Huber; John D. Stephens. **Acta Sociol.** 36:4 1993 pp.309 - 326.
5493 The politics of linking schools and social services. Louise Adler; Unni Hagen; Felisa Tibbitts; Hanne B. Mawhinney; Julia E. Koppich; Patricia F. First; Joan L. Curcio; Dalton L. Young; Douglas E. Mitchell; Linda D. Scott; James R. Garvin; Alma H. Young; Jacqueline A. Stefkovich; Gloria J. Guba; Stephanie Kadel; Dorothy Routh; Michael S. Knapp; Kathryn Barnard; Richard N. Brandon; Nathalie J. Gehrke; Albert J. Smith; Edward C. Teather; R. Michael Casto; Hal A. Lawson; Katharine Hooper-Briar; William Wilson; Patricia Karasoff; Barbara Nolan; Kip Tellez; Jo-Anne Schick; William A. White; Charles J. Russo; Jane Clark Lindle; Sid Gardner. **J. Educ. Pol.** 8:5-6 9-12:1993 pp.1 - 199. *Collection of 17 articles.*

K: Problèmes sociaux. Services sociaux. Travail social

5494 Poor children and welfare reform. Olivia Ann Golden. Westport, Conn: Auburn House, 1992. xiv, 193p. *ISBN: 0865690456. Bibliography: p.179-187; and index.*
5495 Public housing and the concentration of poverty. Douglas S. Massey; Shawn M. Kanaiaupuni. **Soc. Sci. Q.** 74:1 3:1993 pp.109 - 122.
5496 Replacing the social fund: a strategy for change. Gary Craig. York: University of York Social Policy Research Unit, 1992. 105p. *ISBN: 1871713056.*
5497 Rethinking the social role of public housing. Lewis H. Spence. **Hous. Pol. Deb.** 4:3 1993 pp.355 - 368.
5498 Satisfaction with public housing in Papua New Guinea — the case of West Taraka housing scheme. Sababu Kaitilla. **Envir. Behav.** 25:4 7:1993 pp.514 - 545.
5499 A service for people: origins and development of the personal social services of Northern Ireland. Brian Caul; Stanley C. Herron. Belfast: December Publications, 1992. 184p. *ISBN: 0951706810.*
5500 El sistema público de servicios sociales en España. *[In Spanish]*; [The public system of the social services in Spain]. María del Carmen Alemán Bracho. Granada: Impredisur, Taller de Edición, 1991. 349p. *ISBN: 8479330155. Includes bibliographical references (p. [325]-349).*
5501 Social exchange and welfare development. Luis Moreno [Ed.]. Madrid: C.S.I.C./Instituto de Estudios Sociales Avanzados, 1993. 284p. *ISBN: 8400073789.*
5502 [Social lives and welfare: an essay on clinical sociology]; *[Text in Japanese].* Toru Yamaguchi. Tokyo: Kobundo Shuppansha, 1993. 220p.
5503 Social networks and social care in Tanzania. Felician Tungaraza. **Soc. Pol. Admin.** 27:2 6:1993 pp.141 - 150.
5504 Social policy in poor countries. Joseph L. Scarpaci. **Urban Geogr.** 14:5 9-10:1993 pp.476 - 488.
5505 Social security reform in Central Europe — issues and stategies; *[Summary in French].* Vladimir Rys. **J. Europe. Soc. Pol.** 3:3 1993 pp.163 - 175.
5506 Sotsial'noe obespechenia v zapadnykh strankh: problemy. *[In Russian]*; (Social security in western countries: problems of the nineties.). L. Solov'eva. **Mir. Ek. Mez. Ot.** 12 1993 pp.114 - 125.
5507 Sozialatlas der Bundesrepublik Deutschland. Teil 1. Sozialhilfe. *[In German]*; [Social atlas of the Federal Republic of Germany. Part 1. Welfare]. Harmut Gottschild. Braunschweig: Maria Gottschild, 1991. 95p. *ISBN: 392842811X.*
5508 Soziale Bewegung und soziale Ordnung im Konzept des Wohlfahrtsmix. *[In German]*; [Social movements and social order in the concept of the welfare mix]. Adalbert Evers. **Fors.Jour. Soz. Beweg.** 4 1992 pp.49 - 58.
5509 Sozialpolitik in deutscher und europäischer Sicht: Rolle und Zukunft der freien Wohlfahrtspflege zwischen EG-Binnenmarkt und Beitrittsländern. *[In German]*; [Social policy from a German and a European viewpoint: the role and future of free services on the welfare state between the single European market and member states]. Rudolph Bauer [Ed.]. Weinheim: Deutscher Studien Verlag, 1992. 230p. *ISBN: 3892713499. Includes bibliograpic references.*
5510 Staat — Wohlfahrtsstaat — Sozialwissenschaftliche Diskurse. *[In German]*; (State — welfare state — the discourse in social sciences.) *[Summary].* Gerda Bohmann [Contrib.]; Eva Kreisky [Contrib.]; Emmerich Tálos [Contrib.]; Nikolaus Dimmel [Contrib.]; Lorenz Lassnigg [Contrib.]; Georg Vobruba [Contrib.]. **Öster. Z. Polit.** 22:1 1993 pp.5 - 92. *Collection of 6 articles.*

K: Social problems. Social services. Social work

5511 State, politics and the idea of social justice in Chile. Patricio Silva. **Develop. Cha.** 24:3 7:1993 pp.465 - 486.

5512 Le statut des travailleurs immigrés dans la sécurité sociale suisse. *[In French]*; [The status of migrant workers under Swiss social security]. Jean Meyer. Basle; Frankfurt am Main: Helbing & Lichtenhahn, 1990. xii, 144p. *ISBN: 3719011127.*

5513 Tolley's social security and state benefits. 1992-93.. Jim Matthewman [Ed.]. Croydon: Tolley, 1992. 612p. *ISBN: 0854596445.*

5514 Training in partnership: translating intentions into practice in social services. Clive Newton; Peter Marsh. York: Joseph Rowntree Foundation, 1993. 98p. *ISBN: 1872470858.*

5515 Understanding the welfare state: crisis, critics, and countercritics. Theodore R. Marmor. **Crit. Rev.** 7:4 Fall:1993 pp.461 - 478.

5516 Waarom frauderen alle mensen niet met uitkeringen? *[In Dutch]*; (Why is fraud with social benefits not more prevalent?) *[Summary]*. J.J. Godschalk. **Mens Maat.** 68:3 8:1993 pp.257 - 270.

5517 Welfarism, socialism and religion — on T.G. Green and others. Mark Bevir. **Rev. Polit.** 55:4 Fall:1993 pp.639 - 661.

5518 What's happening in housing? Changing roles for the public and private sectors. Royal Institute of the Architects of Ireland. Dublin: Environmental Research Unit, 1990. 355p. *ISBN: 185053134X. Proceedings of the National Housing Conference, 1987, Wexford, Ireland.*

5519 Zorg voor ouderen in Vlaanderen — nu en straks. *[In Dutch]*; [Care for the elderly in Flanders — today and tomorrow] *[Summary]*. Lut vanden Boer. **Bevolk. Gez.** 2:1992 pp.93 - 122.

5520 Die Zukunft der sozialen Sicherung in Deutschland. *[In German]*; [The future of social security in Germany]. Klaus-Dirk Henke [Ed.]; Joachim Jens Hesse [Ed.]; Gunnar Folke Schuppert [Ed.]. Baden-Baden: Nomos-Verlagsgesellschaft, 1991. 272p. *ISBN: 3789024708.*

Child care
Aide à l'enfance

5521 Assuring child support: an extension of social security. Irwin Garfinkel. New York: Russell Sage Foundation, 1992. xii, 161p. *ISBN: 0871543001. Includes bibliographical references and index.*

5522 Child support — the British solution. Mavis Maclean; John Eekelaar. **Int. J. Law Fam.** 7:2 1993 pp.205 - 229.

5523 Child support and welfare dynamics — evidence from Wisconsin. Daniel R. Meyer. **Demography** 30:1 2:1993 pp.45 - 62.

5524 Child support in lone-parent families — policies in Australia and the UK. Jane Millar; Peter Whiteford. **Policy Pol.** 21:1 1:1993 pp.59 - 72.

5525 Children first: working with children and disability. Laura Middleton. Birmingham: Venture P, 1992. vii, 127p. *ISBN: 0900102926.*

5526 The contract culture — mix or muddle? Christine Walby. **Child. Soc.** 7:4 1993 pp.343 - 356.

5527 Contracting — opportunity or threat? Michael Jarman. **Child. Soc.** 7:4 1993 pp.331 - 342.

K: Problèmes sociaux. Services sociaux. Travail social

5528 Day-care supply by Dutch municipalities. Liset Van Dijk; Alice H.E.B. Koot-Du Buy; Jacques J. Siegers. **Eur. J. Pop.** 9:4 1993 pp.315 - 330.
5529 From prevention to partnership — child welfare services across three decades. Jean Packman. **Child. Soc.** 7:2 1993 pp.183 - 195.
5530 [An introduction to child welfare]; *[Text in Japanese].* Kazuko Enomoto. Tokyo: Genbunsha, 1993. 199p.
5531 The Job Opportunities and Basic Skills Training Program and child care — initial state developments. Jan L. Hagen; Irene Lurie. **Soc. Ser. R.** 67:2 6:1993 pp.198 - 216.
5532 Mothers, markets and the state — a Scandinavian "model"? Arnlaug Leira. **J. Soc. Pol.** 22:3 7:1993 pp.329 - 347.
5533 National styles of regulation — child care in three countries. William T. Gormley; B. Guy Peters. **Policy Sci.** 25:4 11:1992 pp.381 - 399.
5534 Organizational factors in the integration of services for children. Marcia K. Meyers. **Soc. Ser. R.** 67:4 12:1993 pp.547 - 575.
5535 Private agencies as public agents? Developments in child welfare in New South Wales. Martin Mowbray. **Soc. Ser. R.** 67:4 12:1993 pp.535 - 546.
5536 Secure accommodation in child care: between hospital and prison or thereabouts. Robert Harris; Noel Timms. London, New York: Tavistock/Routledge, 1993. 196p. *ISBN: 0415062810, 0415062829. Includes bibliographical references and index.*
5537 The supply of child care labor. David M. Blau. **J. Labor Ec.** 11:2 4:1993 pp.324 - 347.

K.3: Social work
Travail social

5538 Adapting treatment techniques to children's needs. Tammie Ronen. **Br. J. Soc. W.** 23:6 12:1993 pp.581 - 596.
5539 Adolescents' perceptions of the efficacy of short-term, inpatient group therapy. Jeffrey L. Chase; Mary Margaret Kelly. **J. Child Adol. Gr. Ther.** 3:3 9:1993 pp.155 - 161.
5540 AIDS-related knowledge and attitudes of social workers in South Carolina. Leiyu Shi; Michael E. Samuels; Donna L. Richter; Carleen H. Stoskopf; Samuel L. Baker; Francisco S. Sy. **Health Soc. Work** 18:4 11:1993 pp.268 - 280.
5541 Alcohol, social work, and helping. Stewart Collins [Ed.]. London: Routledge, 1990. vii,176p. *ISBN: 0415025788. Includes bibliographies and index.*
5542 All equal under the Act?: a practical guide to the Children Act 1989 for social workers. Sheila Macdonald. London: Race Equality Unit, Personal Social Services, 1991. xiii,137p. *ISBN: 1873912013.*
5543 Assessment of competence in social work law. Michael Preston-Shoot [Ed.]; John Murrell [Contrib.]; Robert Adams [Contrib.]; Suzy Braye [Contrib.]; Chris Gwenlan [Contrib.]; Veronica Matthew [Contrib.]; Dave Ward [Contrib.]; Bryan Hogg [Contrib.]. **Soc. Work. Ed.** 1993 pp.5 - 78. *Collection of 7 articles.*
5544 Away with experts? — self-help groupwork in Germany. Jurgen Matzat. **Groupwork** 6:1 1993 pp.30 - 42.
5545 Bereavement and loss. Lynne Muir [Ed.]; Sheila Finlayson [Contrib.]; Estelle Hopmeyer [Contrib.]; Annette Werk [Contrib.]; Hardev Notta [Contrib.]; Joyce

K: Social problems. Social services. Social work

Rimmer [Contrib.]; Frank Parkinson [Contrib.]. **Groupwork** 6:2 1993 pp.93 - 151. *Collection of 5 articles.*
5546 Black perspectives in social work. Bandana Ahmad. Birmingham: Venture Press, 1990. [8], 100p. *ISBN: 0900102780. Includes bibliographies and index.*
5547 A case for social work evaluation of social work education. Imogen Taylor. **Br. J. Soc. W.** 23:2 4:1993 pp.123 - 138.
5548 The challenge of social work in Africa — starting the indigenisation process. Kwaku Osei-Hwedie. **J. Soc. Devel. Afr.** 8:1 1993 pp.19 - 30.
5549 Child abuse revisited: children, society, and social work. David Michael Cooper. Buckingham, [England], Philadelphia: Open University Press, 1993. 118p. *ISBN: 0335157270, 0335157262. Includes bibliographical references and index.*
5550 Children in secure accommodation. Robert Harris; Noel Timms. **Br. J. Soc. W.** 23:6 12:1993 pp.597 - 612.
5551 Children's views of child protection social work. Roger Barford. Norwich: University of East Anglia, 1993. 44 leavesp. *ISBN: 1857840097. (Series:* Social work monographs).
5552 Children's welfare, surrogacy and social work. Eric Blyth. **Br. J. Soc. W.** 23:3 6:1993 pp.259 - 276.
5553 Choosing social work as a profession — behavioural indicators of a developmental process. Yael Enoch. **Soc. Work. Ed.** 12:2 1993 pp.54 - 66.
5554 Common knowledge: a coordinated approach to information-giving. Susan Tester. London: Centre for Policy on Ageing, 1992. 100p. *ISBN: 0904139824. (Series:* CPA reports).
5555 Community social work with children and families — a positive step forward. Steve Rogowski; Leza Harrison. **App. Commun. Stud.** 1:3 1992 pp.4 - 20.
5556 Comparison of the initial phase of group therapy in adult and latency age groups. Max Sugar. **J. Child Adol. Gr. Ther.** 3:3 9:1993 pp.131 - 141.
5557 Controversial issues in social work. Eileen D. Gambrill [Ed.]; Robert Pruger [Ed.]. Boston: Allyn and Bacon, 1992. xiii, 394p. *ISBN: 0205129021. Includes bibliographies.*
5558 The cost of a child: living standards for the 1990s. Nina Oldfield; Autumn C. S. Yu. London: Child Poverty Action Group, 1993. 73p. *ISBN: 0946744564.*
5559 Counseling values and objectives — a comparison of western and Islamic perspectives. Mumtaz F. Jafari. **Am. J. Islam. Soc. Sci.** 10:3 Fall:1993 pp.326 - 339.
5560 Counselling problem drinkers. Robin Davidson [Ed.]; Stephen Rollnick [Ed.]; Ian MacEwan [Ed.]. London: Routledge, 1991. xiv, 164p. *ISBN: 0415031605. Includes bibliographies and index. New Directions in the Study of Alcohol Group.*
5561 Counselling survivors of childhood sexual abuse. Claire Burke Draucker. London: Sage Publications, 1992. 168p. *ISBN: 0803985703, 0803985711. Includes bibliographical references (p. [158]-163) and index. (Series:* Counselling in practice).
5562 A crisis in care?: challenges to social work. John Clarke [Ed.]. London: Sage Publications in association with the Open University, 1993. 176p. *ISBN: 0803988435.*
5563 Cross-cultural counseling — a systematic approach to understanding the issues. W.H. James; J.F. Hastings. **Int. J. Advance. Counsel.** 16:4 12:1993 pp.319 - 332.
5564 Des réactions des intervenants dans un centre de jour en santé mentale et de l'évitement de l'institutionnalisation des défenses individuelles. *[In French]*;

K: Problèmes sociaux. Services sociaux. Travail social

(Reactions from social workers in a day centre for mental health patients and the avoidance of institutionalization of individual defense mechanisms.) *[Summary]*. Alain Barbeau. **San. Ment. Qué** XVII:2 Automne:1992 pp.251 - 263.

5565 Differential validity in social work measurement. William R. Nugent. **Soc. Ser. R.** 67:4 12:1993 pp.631 - 650.

5566 Disabled people find a voice — will it be heard in the move towards community care? Audrey Mullender. **Practice** 6:1 1992-1993 pp.5 - 16.

5567 The evaluation of a unified theory for HIV/AIDS counselling. D.H. Balmer. **Int. J. Advance. Counsel.** 16:4 12:1993 pp.269 - 280.

5568 An evaluation of freestanding alcoholism treatment for Medicare recipients; *[Summary in French]*; *[Summary in Spanish]*. Annie Lo; Albert Woodward. **Addiction** 88:1 1:1993 pp.53 - 68.

5569 The family reunification role-play. Gail B. Werrbach. **Child Wel.** LXXII:6 11-12:1993 pp.555 - 568.

5570 Groupwork versus casework in a group. Roselle Kurland; Robert Salmon. **Groupwork** 6:1 1993 p.5-16.

5571 Groupwork with siblings of children with special needs — a pilot study. Georgina Ferraro; Julie Tucker. **Groupwork** 6:1 1993 pp.43 - 50.

5572 Guidance and counselling in various societies. Lothar Martin [Ed.]; J.G. Paterson [Contrib.]; H.L. Janzen [Contrib.]; M. Israelashvili [Contrib.]; Q. Al-Sarraf [Contrib.]; L.C. Rodriguez [Contrib.]; R. Blanco-Beledo [Contrib.]; G.L. Hermansson [Contrib.]; S.B. Webb [Contrib.]; S.A. Stickel [Contrib.]; J. Yang [Contrib.]. **Int. J. Advance. Counsel.** 16:3 9:1993 pp.151 - 264. *Collection of 8 articles.*

5573 How shelter counselors' views of responsibility for wife abuse relate to services they provide to battered women. A. Jay McKell; Michael J. Sporokowski. **J. Fam. Viol.** 8:2 6:1993 pp.101 - 112.

5574 Identité professionnelle et formation permanente des assistantes sociales. *[In French]*; [Professional identity and permanent training of social workers]. Gisèle Morand. Paris: Bayard Éditions, 1992. 269p. *ISBN: 2227120320*.

5575 The importance of levels of knowledge in developing a unified theory for HIV/AIDS counselling — a comparison of two culturally different samples. C. Wilson; L.L. Stewin. **Int. J. Advance. Counsel.** 16:4 12:1993 pp.281 - 289.

5576 Independent women's projects in Germany — between the women's movement and social work. Margrit Brückner. **App. Commun. Stud.** 1:3 1992 pp.41 - 56.

5577 Infertility counselling — the need for psychosocial perspective. Ken Daniels. **Br. J. Soc. W.** 23:5 10:1993 pp.501 - 515.

5578 Innovative integration of human resources development programme with community development — social work intevention in the global programme of development. Meher C. Nanavatty. **Indian J. Soc. W.** LIV:2 4:1993 pp.241 - 250.

5579 International parental abduction and its implications for social work practice — Great Britain to the United States. Geoffrey L. Greif; Rebecca L. Hegar. **Child. Soc.** 7:3 1993 pp.269 - 276.

5580 The large group — the heart of the system in group care. Adrian Ward. **Groupwork** 6:1 1993 pp.64 - 77.

5581 Learning the hard way — practice issues in supporting parents with learning difficulties. Wendy Booth; Tim Booth. **Soc. Work Soc. Sci. R.** 4:2 1993 pp.148 - 162.

K: Social problems. Social services. Social work

5582 The Leicestershire inquiry 1992: the report of an inquiry into aspects of the management of childen's homes in Leicestershire between 1973 and 1986. Andrew Kirkwood. Leicester: Leicestershire County Council, 1993. 355p.

5583 Life story work: a therapeutic tool for social work. Jess Usher. Norwich: University of East Anglia, 1993. 41p. *ISBN: 1857840046. Bibliography: p.40-41. (Series:* Social work monographs).

5584 Making a case in child protection. Corrine Wattam. Harlow, Essex: Longman, 1992. x, 207p. *ISBN: 0582092817. Published in association with the NSPCC.*

5585 Making a difference?: social work after Hillsborough. Tim Newburn. London: National Institute for Social Work, 1993. 78p. *ISBN: 0902789813.*

5586 Mental health. Julian Lousada; Dick Agass [Ed.]; Suzy Braye; Michael Preston-Shoot; Angela Foster; Malcolm T. Firth; Gill Martin; Angela Rosenfeld; Ann C. Dawson; Susan Taylor; Peter Stratton; Helga Hanks; Howard Campbell; Simon Hatcher. **J. Soc. Work. Practice** 7:2 Autumn:1993 pp.103 - 194. *Collection of 8 articles.*

5587 Les métiers du social à l'épreuve de l'exclusion. *[In French]*; [Careers in social work put to the test by exclusion]. Jacques Ion. **Regar. Actual.** 196 12:1993 pp.39 - 49.

5588 The NCH factfile: children in Britain 1992. National Children's Home. London: NCH, 1992. 96p. *ISBN: 090098421X.*

5589 Neutralisation of group control in youth gangs. T. Wing Lo. **Groupwork** 6:1 1993 pp.51 - 63.

5590 Out of bounds: sexual exploitation in counselling and therapy. Janice Russell. London: Sage, 1993. 159p. *ISBN: 0803985339.*

5591 Over-chastisement, child non-compliance and parenting skills — a behavioural intervention by a family centre social worker. D.F. Bourn. **Br. J. Soc. W.** 23:5 10:1993 pp.481 - 499.

5592 Parenting with learning difficulties — lessons for practitioners. Tim Booth; Wendy Booth. **Br. J. Soc. W.** 23:5 10:1993 pp.459 - 480.

5593 Partnership practice — responding to the challenge, realizing the potential. Suzy Braye; Michael Preston-Shoot. **Soc. Work. Ed.** 12:2 1993 pp.35 - 53.

5594 Pathways to adoption: research project. Mervyn Murch. London: HMSO, 1993. 276p. *ISBN: 0113215886.*

5595 Perceptions of the triad model's efficacy in training family counsellors for diverse South African groups. M. Strous; M. Skuy; J. Hickson. **Int. J. Advance. Counsel.** 16:4 12:1993 pp.307 - 318.

5596 Race in child protection: a code of practice. Norma Baldwin; Paul Johansen; Alexandra Seale. London: NISW Race Equality Unit, 1990. 35p. *ISBN: 1873912005.*

5597 Reflections upon the functions of food in a children's psychotherapy group. Sharon R. Kahn. **J. Child Adol. Gr. Ther.** 3:3 9:1993 pp.143 - 153.

5598 Regulation in child protection — policy failure? Mai Walton. **Br. J. Soc. W.** 23:2 4:1993 pp.139 - 156.

5599 Rehabilitation of juvenile delinquents in India. M.S. Pawar. **Ind. J. Soc. Sci.** 6:1 1-3:1993 pp.41 - 64.

5600 Residential child care: an international reader. Meir Gottesmann [Ed.]. London: Whiting and Birch, 1991. 300p. *ISBN: 1871177170.*

K: Problèmes sociaux. Services sociaux. Travail social

5601 Secure accommodation in child care: between hospital and prison or thereabouts. Robert Harris; Noel Timms. London, New York: Tavistock/Routledge, 1993. 196p. *ISBN: 0415062810, 0415062829*. *Includes bibliographical references and index.*

5602 Services for children and families: report on a survey of children and parents who have had contact with Kent Social Services. Kent Social Services Department. London: British Market Research Bureau, 1992. 198p.

5603 Serving the urban poor. David Fanshel; Stephen J. Finch; John F. Grundy. Westport, Conn: Praeger, 1992. viii, 348p. *ISBN: 0275940756*. *Includes bibliographical references (p. [341]-343) and index.*

5604 Silent conspiracies: scandals and successes in the care and education of vulnerable young people. Andrew Miller [Ed.]; David A. Lane [Ed.]. Stoke on Trent: Trentham Books, 1993. 254p. *ISBN: 0948080698*.

5605 Situations d'incompréhensions interculturelles dans les services sociaux — problématique. *[In French]*; (Issues involved in cases of intercultural misunderstanding relating to social services.) *[Summary]*. Gisèle Legault; Myriam Lafrenière. **San. Ment. Qué** XVII:2 Automne:1992 pp.113 - 131.

5606 Social policy, community service development, and religious organizations. Robert J. Wineburg. **Non. Manag. Leader.** 3:3 Spring:1993 pp.283 - 297.

5607 Social work: disabled people and disabling environments. Michael Oliver. London: Jessica Kingsley, 1991. 203p. *ISBN: 1853020427*. (*Series:* Research highlights in social work).

5608 Social work discourse and the social work interview. Kevin Stenson. **Econ. Soc.** 22:1 2:1993 pp.42 - 76.

5609 Social work in Europe — an ERASMUS initiative. Greta Bradley; Robert Harris. **Soc. Work. Ed.** 12:3 1993 pp.51 - 66.

5610 Social work in prisons. David Smith. **Practice** 6:2 1992-1993 pp.135 - 146.

5611 Social work practice in Botswana — principles and relevance. Gloria Jacques. **J. Soc. Devel. Afr.** 8:1 1993 pp.31 - 49.

5612 Social work profession in Asia. Murli Desai [Ed.]; David Drucker [Contrib.]; Rama S. Pandey [Contrib.]; Meher C. Nanavatty [Contrib.]; P.D. Kulkarni [Contrib.]; M. Abu Taher [Contrib.]; A.S.M. Atiqur Rahman [Contrib.]; Chack-Kie Wong [Contrib.]; David Cox [Contrib.]; Brij Mohan [Contrib.]; Mukunda Rao [Contrib.]. **Indian J. Soc. W.** LIV:4 10:1993 pp.513 - 612. *Collection of 9 articles.*

5613 Social work today. Chris Jones; Tony Novak. **Br. J. Soc. W.** 23:3 6:1993 pp.195 - 212.

5614 Social workers as entrepreneurs. Uri Yanay. **Soc. Pol. Admin.** 27:2 6:1993 pp.151 - 161.

5615 Sozialarbeit, ein deutscher Frauenberuf: Kontinuitäten und Brüche in 20. Jahrhundert. *[In German]*; [Social work, a career for German women: continuity and disruption in the 20th century]. Verena Fesel [Ed.]; Barbara Rose [Ed.]; Monika Simmel [Ed.]. Pfaffenweiler: Centaurus, 1992. 122p. *ISBN: 3890856357*. *Papers from a conference held in 1991. Includes bibliographical references.*

5616 Soziale Arbeit und Erziehung in der Risikogesellschaft. *[In German]*; [Social work and education in the risk society]. Thomas Rauschenbach [Ed.]; Hans Gängler [Ed.]. Neuwied; Berlin: Luchterhand; Kriftel, 1992. 204p. *ISBN: 3472004983*.

5617 Stress management consultation to Israeli social workers during the Gulf War. Julie G. Cwikel; Lea Kacen; Vered Slonim-Nevo. **Health Soc. Work** 18:3 8:1993 pp.172 - 183.

K: Social problems. Social services. Social work

5618 Support groups for battered women — research on their efficacy. Leslie M. Tutty; Bruce A. Bidgood; Michael A. Rotherty. **J. Fam. Viol.** 8:4 12:1993 pp.325 - 343.
5619 Techniques of intervention with groups. Moshe Sonnheim. **J. Soc. Work Pol. Israel** 7-8 1993 pp.125 - 144.
5620 Teenagers in foster care: a survey by the National Foster Care Association. Kevin Lowe. London: NFCA, 1992. 68p.
5621 Theory for approved social work — the use of the compulsory admissions assessment schedule. Michael Sheppard. **Br. J. Soc. W.** 23:3 6:1993 pp.231 - 257.
5622 Trends in assaults on social work staff — the experience of one Scottish department. David Leadbetter. **Br. J. Soc. W.** 23:6 12:1993 pp.613 - 623.
5623 Türkische Kolonie im Wandel: Ausländersozialarbeit und Ausländerpädagogik in Schleswig-Holstein. *[In German]*; [Change in the Turkish colony: social work with migrants and minority education in Schleswig-Holstein]. Rüdiger Wurr; et al. Frankfurt am Main: Peter Lang, 1992. 202p. *ISBN: 3631453671*.
5624 Understanding and modifying identifications in an adolescent boys therapy group. Steven Kuchuck. **J. Child Adol. Gr. Ther.** 3:4 12:1993 pp.189 - 201.
5625 Understanding social work research. Betty G. Dawson. Needham Heights, MA: Allyn and Bacon, 1991. 446p. *ISBN: 0205128149*.
5626 Unter anderen: Rassismus und Jugendarbeit: zur Entwicklung angemessener Begriffe und Ansätze für eine verändernde Praxis (nicht nur) in der Arbeit mit Jugendlichen. *[In German]*; [Amongst others: racism and youth work: on the development of suitable concepts and approaches to a revised practice in working (not only) with young people]. Rudolf Leiprecht [Ed.]; Robert Miles [Contrib.]; et al. Duisburg: Deutsches Institut für Sprach-und Sozialforschung, 1992. 214p. *ISBN: 3-927388-33-5. Arbeitsgemeinschaft Jugendfreizeitstätten Ba Wü e.V..*
5627 What does equity in health mean? João Pereira. **J. Soc. Pol.** 22:1 1:1993 pp.19 - 48.
5628 Who we are: the social work labor force as reflected in the NASW membership. Margaret Gibelman; Philip H. Schervish. Washinton, D.C: NASW Press, 1993. xv, 152p. *ISBN: 0871012251. Includes bibliographical references and index.*
5629 Why groupwork is not put into practice — reflections on the social work scene in Denmark. Ulla Habermann. **Groupwork** 6:1 1993 pp.17 - 29.
5630 Women, management and care. Cordelia Grimwood; Ruth Popplestone; Julia Phillipson. Basingstoke: Macmillan, 1993. 171p. *ISBN: 0333551478. (Series: Practical social work).*

K.4: Health care
Soins médicaux

5631 Access to health care for people from black and ethnic minorities. Anthony Hopkins [Ed.]; Veena Bahl [Ed.]. London: Royal College of Physicians, 1993. 226p. *ISBN: 1873240600*.
5632 Access to health care in America. Michael L. Millman [Ed.]; Institute of Medicine, U.S, Committee on Monitoring Access to Personal Health Care Services. Washington, D.C: National Academy Press, 1993. vii, 229p. *ISBN: 0309047420. Includes bibliographical references and index.*
5633 Advances in medical sociology: a research annual. Vol. 1.. Gary L. Albrecht [Ed.]. Greenwich, Conn: JAI, 1990. 329p. *ISBN: 1559380926*.

K: Problèmes sociaux. Services sociaux. Travail social

5634 AIDS: intervening with hidden grievers. Barbara O. Dane; Samuel O. Miller. New York: Auburn House, 1992. viii, 225p. *ISBN: 0865690286.*

5635 Analiza regresji i korelacji w badaniu rozbieżności warunków życia w miastach i na wsi. Ilustracja metody na przykładzie wskaźników opieki zdrowotnej, 1975-1985. *[In Polish]*; (Regression and correlation analysis in a study of divergences in life conditions of the cities and the countryside. Illustration of the method with the use of health care indicators, 1975-1985.). Zygmunt Gostkowski. **Prz. Soc.** XL:2 1993 pp.149 - 162.

5636 Applications of O.R. in health in developing countries — a review. S. Datta. **Soc. Sci. Med.** 37:12 12:1993 pp.1441 - 1450.

5637 Birth management, part 1. Michael E. Lamb [Ed.]; Maris A. Vinovskis; Wenda R. Trevathan; Peter Curtis; Vern L. Katz; Sheryl Burt Ruzek. **Hum. Nature** 4:4 1993 pp.232 - 408. *Collection of 6 articles.*

5638 Black people and health care in contemporary Britain. Femi Nzegwu. Reading: International Institute for Black Research, 1993. 280p. *ISBN: 1874387028.*

5639 Caste & utilization of health resources. S.N.M. Kopparty. **East. Anthrop.** 45:4 10-12:1992 pp.365 - 383.

5640 The coming crisis of public health in the suburbs. Rodrick Wallace; Deborah Wallace. **Milbank Q.** 71:4 1993 pp.543 - 564.

5641 La construction médicale de la relation thérapeutique: pour une définition des enjeux. *[In French]*; (The medical construction of the therapeutic relationship: towards a definition of the issues.). Monique Membrado. **Ethn. Fr.** 23:4 12:1993 pp.526 - 533.

5642 The construction of patienthood in medical advertising. Deborah Lupton. **Int. J. Health. Ser.** 23:4 1993 pp.805 - 825.

5643 Control of health care. Jane Jones [Contrib.]; John MacDonald [Contrib.]; Cathy McCormack [Contrib.]; Nina Wallerstein [Contrib.]; Victor Amaya [Contrib.]; Maria Black [Contrib.]; Julie Cliff [Contrib.]; Marie McCusker [Contrib.]; Ruby Johnston [Contrib.]; Janet Pelly [Contrib.]; Hester van der Walt [Contrib.]; Lies Hoogendoorn [Contrib.]; R.M. Mazibuko [Contrib.]. **Comm. Dev. J.** 28:3 7:1993 pp.199 - 279. *Collection of 10 articles.*

5644 Dental care utilization over time. Tryfon Beazoglou; L. Jackson Brown; Dennis Heffley. **Soc. Sci. Med.** 37:12 12:1993 pp.1461 - 1472.

5645 Disabling barriers: enabling environments. John Swain [Ed.]; et al. London: Sage Publications, 1993. 307p. *ISBN: 0803988249.*

5646 Doctors as managers: experiences in the front-line of the NHS. Roger Hadley [Ed.]; Don Forster [Ed.]. Harlow: Longman, 1993. xii,183p. *ISBN: 0582228611.*

5647 The double-edged sword of social service contracting — public accountability versus nonprofit autonomy. James M. Ferris. **Non. Manag. Leader.** 3:4 Summer:1993 pp.363 - 376.

5648 The effect of physician and corporate interests on the formation of health maintenance organizations. Douglas R. Wholey; Jon B. Christianson; Susan M. Sanchez. **A.J.S.** 99:1 7:1993 pp.164 - 200.

5649 The effects of population aging on the physician services market — a computable equilibrium analysis. Martcia Wade. **Manag. Sci.** 39:2 2:1993 pp.135 - 148.

5650 Equity and equality in health and health care. A.J. Culyer; A. Wagstaff. **J. Health Econ.** 12:4 1993 pp.431 - 457.

K: Social problems. Social services. Social work

5651 The future of health care in Canada. Neena L. Chappell. **J. Soc. Pol.** 22:4 10:1993 pp.487 - 505.

5652 Geographic influences on the uptake of infant immunisations — 1. Concepts, models, and aggregate analyses. M.L. Senior; S.J. New; A.C. Gatrell; B.J. Francis. **Envir. Plan. A.** 25:3 3:1993 pp.425 - 436.

5653 Geographic influences on the uptake of infant immunisations — 2. disaggregate analyses. M.L. Senior; S.J. New; A.C. Gatrell; B.J. Francis. **Envir. Plan. A.** 25:4 4:1993 pp.467 - 479.

5654 Hardship and health in women's lives. Hilary Graham. Hemel Hempstead: Harvester Wheatsheaf, 1993. 221p. *ISBN: 0745012655.*

5655 The health and lifestyle survey: seven years on: a longitudinal study of a nationwide sample, measuring changes in physical and mental health, attitudes and lifestyle. Brian D. Cox [Ed.]; Felicia A. Huppert [Ed.]; Margaret J. Whichelow [Ed.]. Aldershot: Dartmouth Publishing, 1993. 400p. *ISBN: 1855214105.*

5656 Health and wellbeing: a reader. Alan Beattie [Ed.]. Basingstoke: Macmillan Press Ltd, 1993. 322p. *ISBN: 0333587162.*

5657 The health of woman: a global perspective. Marjorie A. Koblinsky [Ed.]; Judith Timyan [Ed.]; Jill Gay [Ed.]. Boulder: Westview Press, 1993. viii,291p. *ISBN: 0813385008, 0813316081. Includes bibliographical references and index.*

5658 Histories of immune systems. Emily Martin. **Cult. Medic. Psych.** 17:1 3:1993 pp.67 - 76.

5659 Ideology in the reemergence of North American midwifery. Beth Rushing. **Work Occup.** 20:1 2:1993 pp.46 - 67.

5660 The importance of assessing the effectiveness of care — the case of hospices. Maria K. Goddard. **J. Soc. Pol.** 22:1 1:1993 pp.1 - 17.

5661 [Introduction of primary health care for all]; *[Text in Japanese].* Masami Matsuda. Tokyo: Kakiuchi Shuppan, 1993. 205p.

5662 Lay participation in health care decision making: a conceptual framework. Cathy Charles; Suzanne DeMaio. **J. Health Polit. Pol. Law** 18:4 Winter:1993 pp.881 - 904.

5663 Lichnye sviazi v sisteme zdravookhraneniia i »kar'era bolezni«. *[In Russian]*; (Personal connections in public health care system.). Dzh.V. Braun; N.L. Rusinova. **Sot. Issle.** 3 1993 pp.30 - 36.

5664 Locating health: sociological and historical explorations. Stephen David Platt [Ed.]. Aldershot: Avebury, 1993. 253p. *ISBN: 1856283674. (Series:* Explorations in sociology).

5665 Managing quality of care in population programs. Anrudh K. Jain [Ed.]. West Hartford, Conn: Kumarian Press, 1992. xx, 162p. *ISBN: 1565490134. Includes bibliographical references and index. (Series:* Kumarian Press library of management for development).

5666 Maternal and infant care — comparisons between Western Europe and the United States. C. Arden Miller. **Int. J. Health. Ser.** 23:4 1993 pp.655 - 664.

5667 Measures of the quality of life: and the uses to which such measures may be put. Anthony Hopkins [Ed.]. London: Royal College of Physicians, 1992. xii, 153p. *ISBN: 1873240457. The chapters in this book were presented for mutual discussion at a Workshop held at the Royal College of Physicians on 10th October 1991.*

5668 Medical authority and its discontents — the case of organized non-compliance. Ivan Emke. **Crit. Sociol.** 19:3 1992 pp.57 - 80.

K: Problèmes sociaux. Services sociaux. Travail social

5669 Medical confidentiality and legal privilege. Jean Vanessa McHale. London, New York: Routledge, 1993. 160p. *ISBN: 0415046955*. Includes bibliographical references and index. (*Series:* Social ethics and policy).

5670 A medical practice as a vehicle for evolutionary learning. Donald L. McGee. **Wor. Futur.** 36:2-4 1993 pp.129 - 139.

5671 Medical technology and inequity in health care — the case of Korea. Bong-Min Yang. **Health Pol. Plan.** 8:4 12:1993 pp.385 - 393.

5672 The midwife's tale: an oral history from handywoman to professional midwife. Nicky Leap; Billie Hunter. London: Scarlet Press, 1993. 215p. *ISBN: 1857270363*.

5673 La misurazione della produttività nei servizi sanitari. *[In Italian]*; (The productivity measurement in the health care.) *[Summary]*. Felice Paolo Arcuri. **Sociol. Lav.** 46 1992 pp.88 - 105.

5674 Paediatric care and immunisation among Jordanian children. Carla Makhlouf Obermeyer; Eva Deykin; Joseph Potter. **J. Biosoc. Sc.** 25:3 7:1993 pp.371 - 382.

5675 Patients' compliance with medical treatments in the Third World. What do we know? Nuria Homedes; Antonio Ugalde. **Health Pol. Plan.** 8:4 12:1993 pp.291 - 314.

5676 Patients' rights. Amar Jesani [Ed.]; Vimla Nadkarni [Ed.]; Arun Bal [Contrib.]; Anil Pilgaonkar [Contrib.]; Ravi Duggal [Contrib.]; Padma Prakash [Contrib.]; Annie George [Contrib.]; Rupande Panalal [Contrib.]; Sunil K. Pandya [Contrib.]. **Indian J. Soc. W.** LIV:2 4:1993 pp.173 - 222. *Collection of 6 articles.*

5677 Perspectives on organizational change in the US medical care sector. Mary L. Fennell; Jeffrey A. Alexander. **Ann. R. Soc.** 19 1993 pp.89 - 111.

5678 [Physically disabled as a way of life]; *[Text in Japanese]*. Takehiko Hirakawa. **Bung. Ron.** 41 1993 pp.85 - 104.

5679 Physician uncertainty and the art of persuasion. John A. Rizzo. **Soc. Sci. Med.** 37:12 12:1993 pp.1451 - 1459.

5680 Política internacional y atención primaria de salud en Costa Rica. *[In Spanish]*; [International politics and primary health care in Costa Rica] *[Summary]*. Lynn Morgan. **An. Est. Cent.Am.** 19:1 1993 pp.91 - 108.

5681 Predicting birth weight — relative importance of sociodemographic, medical, and prenatal care variables. Terri Combs-Orme; Christina Risley-Curtiss; Ronald Taylor. **Soc. Ser. R.** 67:4 12:1993 pp.617 - 630.

5682 Predprinimatel'stvo v zdravookhranenii. *[In Russian]*; (Business and public health care.). N.G. Shamshurina. **Sot. Issle.** 3 1993 pp.40 - 45.

5683 Preparing and updating systematic reviews of randomized controlled trials of health care. Iain Chalmers; Murray Enkin; Marc J.N.C. Keirse. **Milbank Q.** 71:3 1993 pp.411 - 437.

5684 Preparing for the welfare state? A reexamination of the decision to establish the social service department of the Va'ad le'Ummi. Frank M. Loewenberg. **J. Soc. Work Pol. Israel** 7-8 1993 pp.21 - 30.

5685 The private/public mix in health care in India. Ramesh Bhat. **Health Pol. Plan.** 8:1 3:1993 pp.43 - 56.

5686 Professionalism, educated labour and the state — hospital medicine and the new managerialism. Mike Dent. **Sociol. Rev.** 41:2 5:1993 pp.244 - 273.

5687 The public/private mix and human resources for health. Julio Frenk. **Health Pol. Plan.** 8:4 12:1993 pp.315 - 326.

K: Social problems. Social services. Social work

5688 "Race" and health in contemporary Britain. Waqar Ihsan-Ullah Ahmad [Ed.]. Milton Keynes: Open University Press, 1993. 247p. *ISBN: 0335156983*.

5689 The racial integration of health facilities. David Barton Smith. **J. Health Polit. Pol. Law** 18:4 Winter:1993 pp.851 - 870.

5690 Racism, gender, class, and health. Evelyn L. Barbee [Ed.]; William W. Dressler [Contrib.]; Eileen M. Jackson [Contrib.]; Lauren Clark [Contrib.]. **Med. Anthr. Q.** 7:4 12:1993 pp.323 - 402. *Collection of 4 articles*.

5691 Retailing research — increasing the role of evidence in clinical services for childbirth. Jonathan Lomas. **Milbank Q.** 71:3 1993 pp.439 - 475.

5692 The rise and decline of the cooperative medical system in rural China. Xiao-ming Chen; Teh-wei Hu; Zihau Lin. **Int. J. Health. Ser.** 23:4 1993 pp.731 - 742.

5693 Round and round it goes — the epidemiology of childhood lead poisoning, 1950-1990. Barbara Berney. **Milbank Q.** 71:1 1993 pp.3 - 39.

5694 The science of prevention — a conceptual framework and some directions for a national research program. John D. Coie; Norman F. Watt; Stephen G. West; J. David Hawkins; Joan R. Asarnow; Howard J. Markman; Sharon L. Ramey; Myrna B. Shure; Beverly Long. **Am. Psychol.** 48:10 10:1993 pp.1013 - 1022.

5695 A social comparison perspective of treatment seeking by the homeless. Randall E. Osborne; John E. Karlin; Donald Baumann; Mary Osborne; Doyle Nelms. **J. Soc. Distr. Home.** 2:2 4:1993 pp.135 - 154.

5696 Social dimensions of health: the Israeli experience. Judith T. Shuval. Westport, Conn: Praeger, 1992. x, 213p. *ISBN: 0275934950. Includes bibliographical references (p. [195]-206) and index*.

5697 (Social service though bureaucracy system.); *[Text in Japanese]*. Hiroyuki Watanabe. **Shak.-Sen. Kiyo** 16 1993 pp.117 - 148.

5698 Sociology of health and health care: an introduction for nurses. Steve D. Taylor [Ed.]; David Field [Ed.]. Oxford: Blackwell, 1993. 228p. *ISBN: 0632034025*.

5699 The stork and the syringe: a political history of reproductive medicine. Naomi Pfeffer. Cambridge: Polity Press, 1993. 235p. *ISBN: 0745608213*. (*Series:* Feminist perspectives series).

5700 The study of medical institutions — Eliot Freidson's legacy. Sydney Halpern; Renee R. Anspach. **Work Occup.** 20:3 8:1993 pp.279 - 295.

5701 Typification in a neuro-rehabilitation centre — Scheff revisited? Lesley Griffiths; David Hughes. **Sociol. Rev.** 41:3 8:1993 pp.415 - 445.

5702 Übertragungskonflikte in der gynäkologischen Praxis. *[In German]*; (Transference conflicts in gynaecology.) *[Summary]*. Ulrike Körbitz. **Z. Sexual.** 6:3 9:1993 pp.199 - 217.

5703 Use of research knowledge in policy formulation: differences between decision makers and social service deliverers. Yehudit Elraz. **J. Soc. Work Pol. Israel** 7-8 1993 pp.89 - 108.

5704 Utilization of maternal health-care services in Peru — the role of women's education. Irma T. Elo. **Health Trans. R.** 2:1 4:1992 pp.49 - 70.

5705 Was macht Migranten in Deutschland krank?: zur Problematik von Rassismus und Ausländerfeindlichkeit und von Armutsdiskriminierung in psychosozialer und medizinischer Versorgung. *[In German]*; [What makes migrants in Germany ill?: the problems of racism amd hostility towards foreigners and discrimination against the poor seeking medical and psychosocial care]. Jürgen Collatz [Ed.]. Hamburg: Rissen, 1992. 193p. *ISBN: 3923002653*. *Papers from a conference held by the*

K: Problèmes sociaux. Services sociaux. Travail social

Ethnomedizinisches Zentrum in Hannover on 12th December 1991. Includes bibliographical references (p. 192-193).

5706 Work roles and responsibilities in genitourinary medicine clinics. Isobel Allen; Debra Hogg. London: Policy Studies Institute, 1993. 238p. *ISBN: 0853745706.* (*Series:* PSI research report).

Community care
Garde communitaire

5707 Afvigelse fra hvad? De psykisk udviklingshæmmede og samfundet. *[In Norwegian]*; [Homes for the mentally handicapped and community care]. Edith Mandrup Rønn [Ed.]; Janie Olsen [Ed.]; Else Marie Kofod [Contrib.]; Birgit Kirkebœk [Contrib.]; Vibeke Hedemand [Contrib.]; Annedorte Hybel [Contrib.]; Lisbeth Haastrup [Contrib.]; Christina Ax [Contrib.]; Mikkel V. Pedersen [Contrib.]; Siri Ytrehus [Contrib.]; Dieter Sebelin [Contrib.]; David A. Goode [Contrib.]. **Nord. Ny.** 51 1993 pp.3 - 106. *Collection of 11 articles.*
5708 Care for frail elders: developing community solutions. N. Leutz; et al. Westport, Conn: Auburn House, 1992. xiii, 300p. *ISBN: 0865690294. Includes bibliographical references (p. [273]-290) and index.*
5709 Care management: tasks and workloads. Joan Orme; Bryan Glastonbury. Basingstoke: Macmillan Press, 1993. 209p. *ISBN: 0333544102.* (*Series:* Practical social work).
5710 Case management and care management in community care. Peter Huxley. **Br. J. Soc. W.** 23:4 8:1993 pp.365 - 381.
5711 Changing practice — participation, rights and community care. Nina Biehal. **Br. J. Soc. W.** 23:5 10:1993 pp.443 - 458.
5712 Community care in China and Hong Kong. Linda Wong. **Asian J. Pub. Admin.** 15:2 12:1993 pp.159 - 176.
5713 Community psychiatric nursing. Vol.2. A research perspective. Charlie Brooker [Ed.]; Edward White [Ed.]. London: Chapman and Hall, 1993. 245p. *ISBN: 0412436000.*
5714 Community-based AIDS services — formalization and depoliticization. Roy Cain. **Int. J. Health. Ser.** 23:4 1993 pp.665 - 684.
5715 Conflicts in case management — the use of staff time in community care. Gail Wilson. **Soc. Pol. Admin.** 27:2 6:1993 pp.109 - 123.
5716 Costing community care: theory and practice. Ann Netten [Ed.]; Jennifer Beechem [Ed.]. Aldershot: Ashgate, 1993. 214p. *ISBN: 1857420985.*
5717 Group homes and community integration of developmentally disabled people: micro-institutionalisation. Janice C. Sinson. London: J. Kingsley Publishers, 1993. 202p. *ISBN: 1853021253.*
5718 Home health care and elders — international perspectives. Charlotte Ikels [Ed.]; Nana Araba Apt [Contrib.]; Luiz R. Ramos [Contrib.]; Monica Perracini [Contrib.]; Tereza E. Rosa [Contrib.]; Alex Kalache [Contrib.]; Majda Slajmer-Japelj; Laihua Wang [Contrib.]; Joseph W. Schneider [Contrib.]; Vladislav V. Bezrukov [Contrib.]; Joseph F. Larragy [Contrib.]; Jenny Brodsky [Contrib.]; Denise Naon [Contrib.]; Lennarth Johansson [Contrib.]; Carol L. Schaffer [Contrib.]; Jacqueline J. Birmingham [Contrib.]; A.J.P. Schrijvers [Contrib.]; P.J.M. Dingemans [Contrib.];

K: Social problems. Social services. Social work

Nobuo Meada [Contrib.]; Seiichi Takahashi [Contrib.]; Pamela Doty [Contrib.]. **J. Cr-cult. Gerontol.** 8:4 10:1993 pp.301 - 461. *Collection of 13 articles.*

5719 Independent lives?: community care and disabled people. Jenny Morris. Basingstoke: Macmillan Press, 1993. 189p. *ISBN: 0333593723.*

5720 Integrated mental health care. Ian R. H. Falloon; Grainne Fadden. Cambridge, New York: Cambridge University Press, 1992. 335p. *ISBN: 0521394279.*

5721 Long-term care in an aging society: choices and challenges for the '90s. Gerald A. Larue [Ed.]; Rich Bayly [Ed.]. Buffalo, N.Y: Prometheus Books, 1992. 170p. *ISBN: 0879756950, 0879757124. Includes bibliographical references. (Series:* Golden age books).

5722 The myth of community care: an alternative neighbourhood model of care. Steve Baldwin. London: Chapman & Hall, 1993. 176p. *ISBN: 0412478307.*

5723 Older people, poverty and community care under the Tories: out of sight, out of mind, out of pocket. David Barrett. Aldershot: Avebury, 1993. 205p. *ISBN: 1856284034. Includes bibliographical references and index.*

5724 Punishing children for caring — the hidden cost of young carers. Jo Aldridge; Saul Becker. **Child. Soc.** 7:4 1993 pp.376 - 387.

5725 Quasi-markets and community care. Julian Le Grand. Bristol: University of Bristol/School for Advanced Urban Studies, 1993. 31p. *(Series:* Studies in decentralisation and quasi-markets).

5726 [Urban aging society and community care]; *[Text in Japanese].* Isami Kaneko. Kyoto: Minerva Shobo, 1993.

5727 User involvement in community care — origins, purposes and applications. Gerald Wistow; Marian Barnes. **Publ. Admin.** 71:3 Autumn:1993 pp.279 - 299.

5728 Users and providers — different perspectives on community care services. Gail Wilson. **J. Soc. Pol.** 22:4 10:1993 pp.507 - 526.

5729 Working together for better community care. Randall Smith [Ed.]; et al. Bristol: University of Bristol, School for Advanced Urban Studies, 1993. vii,242p. *ISBN: 1873575416. Bibliography: p.229-233. - Includes index. (Series:* SAUS study).

Geriatrics
Gériatrie

5730 Care for frail elders: developing community solutions. N. Leutz; et al. Westport, Conn: Auburn House, 1992. xiii, 300p. *ISBN: 0865690294. Includes bibliographical references (p. [273]-290) and index.*

5731 Changing behaviour in a residential group setting for elderly people with learning difficulties. Katy Cigno. **Br. J. Soc. W.** 23:6 12:1993 pp.629 - 642.

5732 Cold comfort: a national survey of elderly people in cold weather. Ann V. Salvage. London: Age Concern England, 1993. 256p. *ISBN: 0862421225. (Series:* Research report - 7).

5733 Development and consequences of group living in Sweden. A new mode of care for the demented elderly. Lena Annerstedt. **Soc. Sci. Med.** 37:12 12:1993 pp.1529 - 1538.

5734 Do elderly Medicaid patients experience reduced access to nursing home care? S.L. Ettner. **J. Health Econ.** 12:3 1993 pp.259 - 280.

K: Problèmes sociaux. Services sociaux. Travail social

5735 Effects of literacy on health care of the aged: implications for health professionals. Peggy W. Murphy; Terry C. Davis; Robert H. Jackson; Barbara C. Decker; Sandra W. Long. **Educ. Geront.** 19:4 6:1993 pp.311 - 316.

5736 Ethical aspects of health care for the elderly: an annotated bibliography. Marshall B. Kapp [Comp.]. Westport, Conn: Greenwood Press, 1992. xviii, 175p. *ISBN: 0313274908. (Series:* Bibliographies and indexes in gerontology).

5737 Evaluation of a carer support scheme for elderly people — the importance of "coping". Derek Milne; Irene Pitt; Neil Sabin. **Br. J. Soc. W.** 23:2 4:1993 pp.157 - 168.

5738 Home health care and elders — international perspectives. Charlotte Ikels [Ed.]; Nana Araba Apt [Contrib.]; Luiz R. Ramos [Contrib.]; Monica Perracini [Contrib.]; Tereza E. Rosa [Contrib.]; Alex Kalache [Contrib.]; Majda Slajmer-Japelj; Laihua Wang [Contrib.]; Joseph W. Schneider [Contrib.]; Vladislav V. Bezrukov [Contrib.]; Joseph F. Larragy [Contrib.]; Jenny Brodsky [Contrib.]; Denise Naon [Contrib.]; Lennarth Johansson [Contrib.]; Carol L. Schaffer [Contrib.]; Jacqueline J. Birmingham [Contrib.]; A.J.P. Schrijvers [Contrib.]; P.J.M. Dingemans [Contrib.]; Nobuo Meada [Contrib.]; Seiichi Takahashi [Contrib.]; Pamela Doty [Contrib.]. **J. Cr-cult. Gerontol.** 8:4 10:1993 pp.301 - 461. *Collection of 13 articles.*

5739 Involvement of informal elderly-care networks in contacts with public social services. Howard Litwin; Gail K. Auslander. **J. Soc. Work Pol. Israel** 7-8 1993 pp.7 - 20.

5740 Long-term care in an aging society: choices and challenges for the '90s. Gerald A. Larue [Ed.]; Rich Bayly [Ed.]. Buffalo, N.Y: Prometheus Books, 1992. 170p. *ISBN: 0879756950, 0879757124. Includes bibliographical references. (Series:* Golden age books).

5741 A model for the comprehensive assessment of older people and their carers. Beverley Hughes. **Br. J. Soc. W.** 23:4 8:1993 pp.345 - 364.

5742 Older people, poverty and community care under the Tories: out of sight, out of mind, out of pocket. David Barrett. Aldershot: Avebury, 1993. 205p. *ISBN: 1856284034. Includes bibliographical references and index.*

5743 Partners in care?: hospices and health authorities. David Clark. Aldershot: Avebury, 1993. 155p. *ISBN: 1856282279.*

5744 Residents' rights: a strategy in action in homes for older people. Norma Baldwin; et al. Aldershot: Avebury, 1992. 215p. *ISBN: 1856283666.*

Health economics
Économie de la santé

5745 Consumer access to health care — basic right 21st century challenge. Mary Gardiner Jones. **J. Consum. Aff.** 26:2 Winter:1992 pp.221 - 242.

5746 Costing community care: theory and practice. Ann Netten [Ed.]; Jennifer Beechem [Ed.]. Aldershot: Ashgate, 1993. 214p. *ISBN: 1857420985.*

5747 Does the geographic distribution of physicians reflect market failure? — An examination of the New Zealand experience, 1981-87. J.R. Barnett. **Envir. Plan. A.** 25:6 6:1993 pp.827 - 846.

5748 Financing long term care: the crucial debate. William Laing. London: Age Concern England, 1993. 176p. *ISBN: 0862421233.*

K: *Social problems. Social services. Social work*

5749 How expenditure caps and expenditure targets really work. William A. Glaser. **Milbank Q.** 71:1 1993 pp.97 - 127.
5750 Informed consent to rationing decisions. Mark A. Hall. **Milbank Q.** 71:4 1993 pp.645 - 668.
5751 Paying for the Kasongo hospital in Zaire — a conceptual framework. Bart Criel; Harrie van Balen. **Health Pol. Plan.** 8:1 3:1993 pp.61 - 71.
5752 Reasonable efforts revisited — reforming federal financing of children's mental health services. Gary B. Sutnick. **NY. U. Law. Re.** 68:1 4:1993 pp.136 - 184.
5753 The social impact of AIDS in the United States. National Research Council, U.S, Panel on Monitoring the Social Impact of the AIDS Epidemic. Washington, D.C: National Academy Press, 1993. xi, 322p. *ISBN: 0309046289. Includes bibliographical references and index.*

Health policy
Politique sanitaire

5754 Area, class and health — should we be focusing on places or people? Sally Macintyre; Sheila Maciver; Anne Sooman. **J. Soc. Pol.** 22:2 4:1993 pp.213 - 234.
5755 Can an employer-based health insurance system be just? Nancy S. Jecker. **J. Health Polit. Pol. Law** 18:3 Fall:1993 pp.657 - 674.
5756 Childhood immunization programs — an analysis of policy issues. Gary L. Freed; W. Clayton Bordley; Gordon H. DeFriese. **Milbank Q.** 71:1 1993 pp.65 - 96.
5757 Community health policy and practice in Australia. Frances Baum [Ed.]; Denise Fry [Ed.]; Ian Lennie [Ed.]. Sydney: Pluto Press; Australian Community Health Association, 1992. 314p. *ISBN: 0949138827. Includes index.*
5758 Devolution and centralism in the National Health Service. Calum Paton. **Soc. Pol. Admin.** 27:2 6:1993 pp.83 - 108.
5759 The future for palliative care: issues of policy and practice. David Clark [Ed.]. Buckingham, Philadelphia: Open University Press, 1993. xi, 180p. *ISBN: 0335157653, 0335157645. Includes bibliographical references and index.*
5760 Has socialism failed? An analysis of health indicators under capitalism and socialism. Vicente Navarro. **Sci. Soc.** 57:1 Spring:1993 pp.6 - 30.
5761 Health care reform in the United States. Pauline Vaillancourt Rosenau [Ed.]; Milton I. Roemer [Contrib.]; Michael D. Intriligator [Contrib.]; Lu Ann Aday [Contrib.]; Colleen M. Grogan [Contrib.]; Russell L. Hanson [Contrib.]; Mark A. Peterson [Contrib.]; Linda A. Bergthold [Contrib.]; J. Peter Nixon [Contrib.]; Karen M. Ignagni [Contrib.]; Robert H. Binstock [Contrib.]; Chris Hafner-Eaton [Contrib.]; Michael R. Cousineau [Contrib.]; John N. Lozier [Contrib.]. **Am. Behav. Sc.** 36:6 7-8:1993 pp.689 - 886. *Collection of 13 articles.*
5762 High risk and high stakes: health professionals, politics, and policy. Robert Perrucci [Foreword]; Earl Wysong. Westport, Conn: Greenwood Press, 1992. xiv, 172p. *ISBN: 031328475X. Includes bibliographical references (p. [147]-163) and index.* (*Series:* Contributions in sociology).
5763 An historical perspective on home care policy. A.E. Benjamin. **Milbank Q.** 71:1 1993 pp.129 - 166.
5764 The home birth movement in the United States. Bonnie B. O'Connor. **J. Medic. Philos.** 18:2 4:1993 pp.147 - 174.

K: Problèmes sociaux. Services sociaux. Travail social

5765 How state policy affects rural hospital consortia — the rural health care delivery system. Joan M. Kiel. **Milbank Q.** 71:4 1993 pp.625 - 643.

5766 Improving the use of research-based evidence in policy making — effective care in pregnancy and childbirth in the United States. Jane E. Sisk. **Milbank Q.** 71:3 1993 pp.477 - 496.

5767 Informed consent to rationing decisions. Mark A. Hall. **Milbank Q.** 71:4 1993 pp.645 - 668.

5768 Is health care different? Popular support of federal health and social policies. Mark Schlesinger; Tae-Ku Lee. **J. Health Polit. Pol. Law** 18:3 Fall:1993 pp.551 - 628.

5769 Is reasonable access what we want? Implications of, and challenges to, current Canadian policy on equity in health care. Stephen Birch; Julia Abelson. **Int. J. Health. Ser.** 23:4 1993 pp.629 - 653.

5770 Management of HIV/AIDS in the Australian federal system. Barbara Misztal. **Soc. Pol. Admin.** 27:2 6:1993 pp.124 - 140.

5771 National health systems of the world. 2. The issues. Milton Irwin Roemer. New York: Oxford University Press, 1993. viii, 356p. *ISBN: 0195078454. Bibliographical references and index.*

5772 The new face of the NHS. Peter Spurgeon [Ed.]. Harlow: Longman, 1993. 267p. *ISBN: 0582219981.*

5773 New medical technologies — economic, ethical, and political considerations for policy. Sandra S. Tangri [Ed.]; Teresa E. Levitin [Ed.]; Irene H. Butter [Contrib.]; Deborah J. Bowen [Contrib.]; Nicole Urban [Contrib.]; David Carrell [Contrib.]; Susan Kinne [Contrib.]; Mary S. Henifin [Contrib.]; Ruth R. Faden [Contrib.]; Nancy E. Kass [Contrib.]; Daryl Evans [Contrib.]; Katherine D. Seelman [Contrib.]; Jeffrey M. Prottas [Contrib.]; Marshall B. Kapp [Contrib.]; Bruce Jennings [Contrib.]; Thomas H. Murray [Contrib.]; Eric T. Juengst [Contrib.]. **J. Soc. Issues** 49:2 1993 pp.1 - 210. *Collection of 12 articles.*

5774 Policies for curbing the HIV epidemic in the United States — implications of a simulation model. Allan M. Salzberg; Duncan MacRae. **Socio. Econ.** 27:3 9:1993 pp.153 - 170.

5775 The politics of participation: primary health care in Costa Rica. Lynn Marie Morgan. New York, NY: Cambridge University Press, 1993. 181p. *ISBN: 0521418984. Includes bibliographical references. (Series:* Cambridge studies in medical anthropology).

5776 Politique de santé — les trois options stratégiques. *[In French]*; (Health policy — three strategic options.) *[Summary]*. Eric de la Moussaya; Pierre Jacquemot. **Afr. Cont.** 166 4-6:1993 pp.15 - 26.

5777 A review of recent structural changes to district health authorities as purchasing organisations. M. Exworthy. **Envir. Plan. C.** 11:3 8:1993 pp.279 - 289.

5778 Santé et démocratie. *[In French]*; [Health and democracy]. Maria Maïlat [Contrib.]; Patricia Croutte [Contrib.]; Andrée Mizrahi [Contrib.]; Arié Mizrahi [Contrib.]; Dominique Beaux [Contrib.]; Michel Joubert [Contrib.]; Ketty Guilloux [Contrib.]; Marguerite Arene [Contrib.]; Marie Rey [Contrib.]; Françoise Dagallier [Contrib.]; Renée David [Contrib.]; André Lazarus [Contrib.]; Robert Castel [Contrib.]; Michel Bass [Contrib.]; Bernard Hours [Contrib.]; Denis Couet [Contrib.]. **Inf. Soc.** 26 1993 pp.4 - 120. *Collection of 15 articles.*

5779 Segregation, poverty, and empowerment — health consequences for African Americans. Thomas A. LaVeist. **Milbank Q.** 71:1 1993 pp.41 - 64.

K: Social problems. Social services. Social work

5780 Structural adjustment and health policy in Africa. Rene Loewenson. **Int. J. Health. Ser.** 23:4 1993 pp.717 - 730.
5781 Theory for approved social work — the use of the compulsory admissions assessment schedule. Michael Sheppard. **Br. J. Soc. W.** 23:3 6:1993 pp.231 - 257.
5782 Thinking and rethinking AIDS — implications for health policy. Elizabeth Fee; Nancy Krieger. **Int. J. Health. Ser.** 23:2 1993 pp.323 - 346.
5783 Universal health insurance that really works: foreign lessons for the United States. William A. Glaser. **J. Health Polit. Pol. Law** 18:3 Fall:1993 pp.695 - 722.

Medical ethics
Code déontologique médical

5784 The abortion debate — the search for common ground, Part 1. Nancy (Ann) Davis. **Ethics** 103:3 4:1993 pp.516 - 539.
5785 Abortion logic and paternal responsibility — one more look at Judith Thomson's A Defense of Abortion. Keith J. Pavlischek. **Publ. Aff. Q.** 7:4 10:1993 pp.341 - 361.
5786 Abortion, moral responsibility, and self-defense. Tom L. Huffman. **Publ. Aff. Q.** 7:4 10:1993 pp.287 - 302.
5787 Aktive und passive Euthanasie. *[In German]*; [Active and passive euthanasia]. Jean-Claude Wolf. **Arc. Recht. Soz.** 79:3 1993 pp.393 - 415.
5788 Animal models in biomedical research — some epistemological worries. Hugh LaFollette; Niall Shanks. **Publ. Aff. Q.** 7:2 4:1993 pp.113 - 130.
5789 Bioethics in a liberal society. Maxwell John Charlesworth. New York: Cambridge University Press, 1993. 172p. *ISBN: 0521445035, 0521449529. Includes bibliographical references and index.*
5790 Bioethics in artificial reproduction in the Muslim world. Gamal I. Serour. **Bioethics** 7:2-3 4:1993 pp.207 - 217.
5791 Brain dead, brain absent, brain donors: human subjects or human objects. Peter John McCullagh. Chichester, New York: Wiley, 1993. vi, 261p. *ISBN: 0471937363. Includes bibliographical references and index.*
5792 Dances with data. Johannes J.M. van Delden; Loes Pijnenborg; Paul J. van der Maas. **Bioethics** 7:4 7:1993 pp.323 - 329.
5793 Death rites: law and ethics at the end of life. Robert Gregory Lee [Ed.]; Derek Morgan [Ed.]. London, New York: Routledge, 1993. 308p. *ISBN: 0415062608. Includes bibliographical references and index.*
5794 Deficiencies in the National Institute of Health's guidelines for the care and protection of laboratory animals. Wendell Stephenson. **J. Medic. Philos.** 18:4 8:1993 pp.375 - 388.
5795 Doing what the patient orders — maintaining integrity in the doctor-patient relationship. Jeffrey Blustein. **Bioethics** 7:4 7:1993 pp.289 - 314.
5796 Economic perspectives on bioethics. John A. Baden. **J. Medic. Philos.** 18:4 8:1993 pp.389 - 397.
5797 Elimination of morality: reflections on utilitarianism and bioethics. Anne Maclean. London: Routledge, 1993. 219p. *ISBN: 0415010810.*
5798 Essays on bioethics. Richard Mervyn Hare. Oxford, New York: Clarendon Press, Oxford University Press, 1993. 248p. *ISBN: 0198239831. Includes bibliographical references and index.*

K: Problèmes sociaux. Services sociaux. Travail social

5799 Ethical aspects of germline gene therapy. Maurice de Wachter. **Bioethics** 7:2-3 4:1993 pp.166 - 177.

5800 Ethical aspects of health care for the elderly: an annotated bibliography. Marshall B. Kapp [Comp.]. Westport, Conn: Greenwood Press, 1992. xviii, 175p. *ISBN: 0313274908. (Series:* Bibliographies and indexes in gerontology).

5801 Ethics and biotechnology. Anthony Dyson [Ed.]; John Harris [Ed.]. New York; London: Routledge, 1993. 274p. *ISBN: 0415091403. Includes bibliographical references. (Series:* Social ethics and policy).

5802 The ethics and politics of human experimentation. Paul Murray McNeill. Cambridge, [Eng.], New York: Cambridge University Press, 1993. 315p. *ISBN: 0521416272. Includes bibliographical references and index.*

5803 The ethics of reproductive technology. Kenneth D. Alpern [Ed.]. New York: Oxford University Press, 1992. xvi, 354p. *ISBN: 0195074351. Includes bibliographical references (p. 353-354).*

5804 Euthanasia and other medical decisions concerning the ending of life. P.J. van der Maas; L. Pijnenborg; J.J.M. van Delden. Amsterdam: Elsevier, 1992. 262p. *ISBN: 0444892788. Netherlands Commission of Inquiry into the Medical Practice concerning Euthanasia. (Series:* Health policy monographs - 2).

5805 Euthanasia: the good of the patient, the good of society. Robert I. Misbin [Ed.]. Frederick, Maryland: University Publishing Group, 1992. x, 223p. *ISBN: 155572017X.*

5806 Evaluating ethics committees — a view from the outside. Diane E. Hoffmann. **Milbank Q.** 71:4 1993 pp.677 - 701.

5807 Formulating selection policies for assisted reproduction. Ken Daniels; Karyn Taylor. **Soc. Sci. Med.** 37:12 12:1993 pp.1473 - 1480.

5808 Fruchtbarkeit als Todeskult im Patriarchat — Historisch-philosophische Hintergründe des modernen Menschenopfers. *[In German]*; [Fertility as a death-cult in patriarchy. The historical and philosophical background to modern human sacrifice]. Anna Bergmann. **Prokla** 22:4(89) 12:1992 pp.647 - 660.

5809 Human gene therapy — down the slippery slope? Nils Holtug. **Bioethics** 7:5 10:1993 pp.402 - 419.

5810 Identity and the ethics of gene therapy. Robert Elliot. **Bioethics** 7:1 1993 pp.27 - 40.

5811 The intellectual basis of bioethics in Southern European countries. Diego Gracia. **Bioethics** 7:2-3 4:1993 pp.97 - 107.

5812 Is gene therapy a form of eugenics? John Harris. **Bioethics** 7:2-3 4:1993 pp.178 - 187.

5813 Issues in clinical ethics. Laurence B. McCullough [Ed.]; Richard M. Zaner [Contrib.]; Kevin Wm. Wildes [Contrib.]; Howard J. Curzer [Contrib.]; Raymond J. Devettere [Contrib.]; Franklin G. Miller [Contrib.]. **J. Medic. Philos.** 18:1 2:1993 pp.1 - 98. *Collection of 6 articles.*

5814 Legal euthanasia — ethical issues in an era of legalized aid in dying. Margaret P. Battin [Ed.]; Thomas J. [III] Bole [Ed.]; Albert R. Jonsen [Contrib.]; Grant R. Gillet [Contrib.]; Michael M. Burgess [Contrib.]; Martin Gunderson [Contrib.]; David J. Mayo [Contrib.]; Leslie Pickering Francis [Contrib.]; Kevin Wm. Wildes [Contrib.]. **J. Medic. Philos.** 18:3 6:1993 pp.237 - 341. *Collection of 8 articles.*

5815 Life and death: philosophical essays in biomedical ethics. Dan W. Brock. Cambridge, New York: Cambridge University Press, 1993. xi, 435p. *ISBN:*

K: Social problems. Social services. Social work

0521417856, 0521428335. *Includes bibliographical references and index. (Series:* Cambridge studies in philosophy and public policy).
5816 Medical ethics today: its practice and philosophy. Ann Sommerville [Ed.]. London: British Medical Journal Publishing Group, 1993. 374p. *From the BMA's Ethics, Science and Information Division.*
5817 Medicine, money, and morals: physicians' conflicts of interest. Marc A. Rodwin. New York: Oxford University Press, 1993. xvii, 411p. *ISBN: 0195080963. Includes bibliographical references (p. 271-389) and index.*
5818 Moral philosophy and public policy — the case of the new reproductive technologies. Will Kymlicka. **Bioethics** 7:1 1993 pp.1 - 26.
5819 Moral reasoning and political conflict — the abortion controversy. Jonathan Kelley; M.D.R. Evans; Bruce Headey. **Br. J. Soc.** 44:4 12:1993 pp.589 - 611.
5820 Moral sensibilities and moral standing — Caplan on xenograft "donors". James Lindemann Nelson. **Bioethics** 7:4 7:1993 pp.315 - 322.
5821 Morality, mortality. Volume 1. Death and whom to save from it. Frances Myrna Kamm. New York: Oxford University Press, 1993. 344p. *ISBN: 019507789X. (Series:* Oxford ethics series).
5822 The patient's ordeal. William F. May. Bloomington: Indiana University Press, 1991. 218p. *ISBN: 0253337178. (Series:* Medical ethics series).
5823 The personhood of the human embryo. John F. Crosby. **J. Medic. Philos.** 18:4 8:1993 pp.399 - 417.
5824 Rationing fairly — programmatic considerations. Norman Daniels. **Bioethics** 7:2-3 4:1993 pp.224 - 233.
5825 Should a brain-dead pregnant-woman carry her child to full term? The case of the "Erlanger baby". Christoph Anstötz. **Bioethics** 7:4 7:1993 pp.340 - 350.
5826 Teaching bioethics as a new paradigm for health professionals. Juan Carlos Tealdi. **Bioethics** 7:2-3 4:1993 pp.188 - 199.
5827 Unrequested termination of life — is it permissable? Gerrit van der Wal. **Bioethics** 7:4 7:1993 pp.330 - 339.
5828 The use of parental diagnosis for sex selection — the Indian scene. Kusum. **Bioethics** 7:2-3 4:1993 pp.149 - 165.
5829 The view from somewhere — particularism in bioethics. Kevin Wm. Wildes [Ed.]; Gerald P. McKenny [Contrib.]; Stanley S. Harakas [Contrib.]; Louis E. Newman [Contrib.]; B. Andrew Lustig [Contrib.]. **J. Medic. Philos.** 18:6 12:1993 pp.505 - 587. *Collection of 5 articles.*
5830 What bioethics has to offer the developing countries. Ren-Zong Qiu. **Bioethics** 7:2-3 4:1993 pp.108 - 125.

Mental health
Santé mentale

5831 Afvigelse fra hvad? De psykisk udviklingshæmmede og samfundet. *[In Norwegian]*; [Homes for the mentally handicapped and community care]. Edith Mandrup Rønn [Ed.]; Janie Olsen [Ed.]; Else Marie Kofod [Contrib.]; Birgit Kirkebœk [Contrib.]; Vibeke Hedemand [Contrib.]; Annedorte Hybel [Contrib.]; Lisbeth Haastrup [Contrib.]; Christina Ax [Contrib.]; Mikkel V. Pedersen [Contrib.]; Siri Ytrehus

K: Problèmes sociaux. Services sociaux. Travail social

[Contrib.]; Dieter Sebelin [Contrib.]; David A. Goode [Contrib.]. **Nord. Ny.** 51 1993 pp.3 - 106. *Collection of 11 articles.*

5832   Care programming in mental health — assimilation and adaptation. Justine Schneider. **Br. J. Soc. W.** 23:4 8:1993 pp.383 - 403.

5833   Case management in mental health. Steve Onyett. London: Chapman & Hall, 1992. xiv, 265p. *ISBN: 0412393301. Bibliography: p.242-254. - Includes index.*

5834   Community psychiatric nursing. Vol.2. A research perspective. Charlie Brooker [Ed.]; Edward White [Ed.]. London: Chapman and Hall, 1993. 245p. *ISBN: 0412436000.*

5835   Crisis support in the aftermath of disaster — a longitudinal perspective. Stephen Joseph; William Yule; Ruth Williams; Bernice Andrews. **Br. J. Clin. Psycho.** 32:2 5:1993 pp.177 - 185.

5836   Experiencing psychiatry: user's views of services. Anne Rogers; David Pilgrim; Ron Lacey. Basingstoke: Macmillan in association with Mind, 1993. xiii,205p. *ISBN: 0333452585, 0333452593. Includes bibliographies and index. (Series:* Issues in mental health).

5837   Experiments with Nigerian village communities in the dual roles of western psychiatric treatment centres and homes for indigenous Nigerian inhabitants. Okeke Azu-Okeke. **Int. J. Therap. Comm. Support. Org.** 13:4 1992 pp.221 - 228.

5838   Families in China — an undervalued resource for mental health? Veronica Pearson. **J. Fam. Ther.** 15:2 5:1993 pp.163 - 185.

5839   Geistige Behinderung: Normalisierung und soziale Abhängigkeit. *[In German]*; [The mentally disabled: normalization and social dependency]. Jürgen Wendeler. Heidelberg: HVA, Edition Schindele, 1992. 156p. *ISBN: 3891491840.*

5840   Integrated mental health care. Ian R. H. Falloon; Grainne Fadden. Cambridge, New York: Cambridge University Press, 1992. 335p. *ISBN: 0521394279.*

5841   Integrating systems of care in California for youth with severe emotional disturbance III — answers that lead to questions about out-of-home placements and the AB377 evaluation project. Abram Rosenblatt; Clifford Attkisson. **J. Child Fam. Stud.** 2:2 6:1993 pp.119 - 141.

5842   Making monsters. Richard Ofshe; Ethan Watters. **Society** 30:3 3-4:1993 pp.4 - 16.

5843   Measuring mental health needs. John Kenneth Wing [Ed.]; Chris Brewin [Ed.]; Graham Thornicroft [Ed.]. London: Gaskell, 1992. 328p. *ISBN: 0902241516.*

5844   Mental health services in the context of health insurance reform. David Mechanic. **Milbank Q.** 71:3 1993 pp.349 - 364.

5845   Organizational determinants of performance of outpatient mental health programs. A.P. Schinnar; E. Kamis-Gould; L. Enama-Markson; A.B. Rothbard; N. Ramachandran. **Socio. Econ.** 27:3 9:1993 pp.209 - 218.

5846   Reasonable efforts revisited — reforming federal financing of children's mental health services. Gary B. Sutnick. **NY. U. Law. Re.** 68:1 4:1993 pp.136 - 184.

5847   Siblings as caregivers for the seriously mentally ill. Allan V. Horwitz. **Milbank Q.** 71:2 1993 pp.323 - 339.

5848   Small staffed houses for people with a severe learning disability and challenging behaviour. Jim Mansell; Fran Beasley. **Br. J. Soc. W.** 23:4 8:1993 pp.329 - 344.

5849   The social organization of mental illness. Lindsay Prior. London: Sage, 1993. 225p. *ISBN: 0803985002. Bibliography: p.200-215.*

K: Social problems. Social services. Social work

5850 A sociology of mental health and illness. David Pilgrim; Anne Rogers. Buckingham, Philadelphia: Open University Press, 1993. ix, 198p. *ISBN: 0335190146, 0335190138. Includes bibliographical references (p. [177]-190) and index.*

5851 Südostasiatische Flüchtlinge in der Westschweiz. Bedarfsnachweis für einen psychosozialen Dienst und ein Begegnungszentrum (PSIND-Romandie). *[In German]*; [Southeast Asian refugees in west Switzerland. Proof of a need for psycho-social help and a centre of meeting other sufferers (PSIND-Romandie)]. Martine Verwey. **Ethnol. Helvet.** 17-18 1993-1994 pp.127 - 150.

5852 The support networks of people with severe, long-term mental health problems. Barbara Hatfield; Peter Huxley; Hadi Mohamad. **Practice** 6:1 1992-1993 pp.25 - 40.

5853 Theory for approved social work — the use of the compulsory admissions assessment schedule. Michael Sheppard. **Br. J. Soc. W.** 23:3 6:1993 pp.231 - 257.

5854 Torture and its consequences: current treatment approaches. Metin Başoğlu [Ed.]. Cambridge, New York: Cambridge University Press, 1992. xxiii, 527p. *ISBN: 0521392993. Includes bibliographical references and index.*

5855 You in mind — a preventive mental health television series. Chris Barker; Nancy Pistrang; David A. Shapiro; Suzanne Davies; Irene Shaw. **Br. J. Clin. Psycho.** 32:3 9:1993 pp.281 - 293.

AUTHOR INDEX
INDEX DES AUTEURS

Aarburg, H. von 2313
Abay, G. 3916
Abaza, M. 1318
Abbott, A. 242, 4240
Abbott, T. 4188
Abdalla, A. 4449
Abderrazak, A. 1092
Abdessamad, K. 4823
Abdulatipov, R. 3099
Abdulgani, K. 3817
Abdulkarim, A. 3333
Abdullah, H. 2786
Abdulrahim, D. 1190
Abel, C. 998, 5354
Abel, T. 133, 134
Abele, A. 511
Abelen, E. 1419
Abell, P. 242
Abelson, J. 5769
Abercrombie, N. 4159
Abler, R. 4079
Abraham, C. 2156
Abraham, G. 159
Abraham, M. 721
Abrahamian, L. 4835
Abrahamsen, A. 504
Abrahamsson, B. 4699
Abramowitz, L. 2415
Abrams, D. 733, 2156
Abromeit, J. 1723
Abu-Jamal, M. 3027
Abu-Lughod, L. 1541
Abu-Saud, M. 239
Abu-Zahra, N. 1190
Abzug, R. 810
Achanfuo-Yeboah, D. 3263, 3312
Ache, P. 3839
Achilles, R. 2239
Achola, P. 2207
Ackerman, E. 4439

Ackerman, G. 2125
Ackerman, S. 1317
Ackers, P. 4711
Acock, A. 765
Adair, S. 2067
Adam, A. 2025
Adam, B. 4458, 4905
Adams, B. 217
Adams, C. 3857
Adams, G. 823
Adams, J. 2910
Adams, P. 2987
Adams, R. 4596, 5543
Aday, L. 5761
Adcock, M. 2116
Adda, S. 1541
Addi, L. 4808
Addy, C. 2147
Adelantado Gimeno, J. 5195
Adelson, L. 2755
Adhikari, K. 1350
Adkins, B. 1915
Adler, G. 4446
Adler, L. 1730, 5493
Adler, M. 2806
Adler, P. 812
Adomako Ampofo, A. 2786
Aduaka, E. 787
Adu-Febiri, F. 3232
Afshar, H. 2712
Agadjanian, A. 1218
Agass, D. 2398, 5586
Agassi, J. 145
Agbaje, A. 1545
Agee, M. 681
Agger, B. 120
Agho, A. 4466
Agnew, J. 3714
Agnew, R. 5310
Agnew, V. 2723

Author index

Agramonte, E. 3458
Aguerrondo, I. 3900, 5337
Aguilar, A. 3804
Aguilar, E. 1295
Aguirre, A. 1506, 3085, 3200
Aguirre, B. 3458
Ahiarah, S. 4071
Ahmad, B. 5546
Ahmad, W. 3139, 5688
Ahmed, A. 4297
Ahwireng-Obeng, F. 4091
Aihara, S. 1788
Aimer, P. 2853
Aiono, F. 4953
Airsman, L. 2405
Aitchison, M. 1399
Ajérar, H. 1122
Ajulu, R. 2786
Akagawa, M. 3004
Akers, R. 5185
Akhiyezer, A. 3401
Akhtar, R. 3447
Akimoto, R. 130
Akimoto, S. 109
Akin, J. 2330
Akinnaso, F. 1728
Akister, J. 2601
Akiyama, T. 3918
Akker, P. van den 1594
Akram-Lodhi, A. 1874
Aksoy, A. 1043
Akyürek, A. 424
Al-A'ali, E. 875
Alailima, P. 4370
Alam, I. 2295
Alam, M. 1776
Alavi, J. 4198
Al-Azm, S. 1312
Alba, R. 3026, 3162, 3685
Albanese, C. 1247
Alba-Ramírez, A. 4280
Albas, C. 1649
Albas, D. 1649
Albaugh, B. 5371, 5424
Alber, E. 3563
Albers, G. 3723
Albert, H. 145
Albin, C. 657

Albó, X. 3052, 3643
Albornoz, O. 1651
Albrecht, D. 3386
Albrecht, G. 5633
Alcock, P. 5352
Alcoff, L. 1339, 1432
Alden, D. 4325
Alderman, G. 438, 3341
Alderman, H. 2842
Alderman, N. 4569
Alderson, A. 237
Aldor, R. 590
Aldrich, R. 2964
Aldridge, J. 228, 2102, 5724
Alemán Bracho, M. 5500
Alemann, U. von 4670
Alemika, E. 5233
Aleš, M. 2193
Alexander, D. 2884
Alexander, E. 808
Alexander, G. 2281
Alexander, J. 900, 1078, 5677
Alexander, K. 1656
Alexander, R. 5257
Alexy, R. 1199
Alfano, M. 577
Al-Hammad, M. 3817
Ali, A. 1861, 4842, 5350
Aliman, A. 5433
Allahar, A. 3245
Allain, A. 403, 5021
Allegritti, I. 5054
Allen, C. 5083
Allen, G. 267, 326, 1091
Allen, I. 1368, 5706
Allen, J. 3624, 4116
Allen, N. 878
Allen, S. 4141
Allen, T. 3213
Allgeier, E. 697
Allison, E. 4459
Allison, P. 4555
Allison, S. 4965
Allor, D. 3813
Allsop, S. 5419
Almaani, M. 3817
Almeida, A. de 2902
Almeida, G. 244

Index des auteurs

Al-Mughni, H. 2776
Al-Najjar, B. 2195
Al-Nouri, Q. 2827
Aloise-Young, P. 2106
Alonso, R. 2141
Alonso, W. 4224
Alozie, N. 4845
Alpern, K. 5803
Alperovich, G. 3651
Al-Rasheed, M. 2576
Al-Saqr, M. 1541
Al-Sarraf, Q. 5572
AlSayyad, N. 3751, 3783, 3906
Alshuwaikat, H. 3816
Alsop, R. 2852
Alston, J. 2477
Altaf, M. 4049, 5341
Altamirano, T. 3078, 3659
Altbach, P. 1795
Alter, C. 826
Alter, I. 3055
Alter, N. 1588, 4136, 4148
Althabe, G. 3113, 3199, 3947
Altheide, D. 1448
Altschuler, J. 2667
Altukhov, V. 249
Alvarado, A. 3608
Alvarado, É. 2138
Alvarado Mendoza, A. 4687
Alvarez, S. 4894
Alves de Oliveira, A. 1425
Alvesson, M. 791, 853
Alwin, D. 341, 345
Amadeo, E. 4637
Amano, T. 3533
Amante, A. 2289
Amante, M. 4252
Amato, P. 2470, 2513
Amaya, V. 5643
Amburgey, T. 840
Ameen, A. 4013
Amendola, G. 3650
Amersfoort, H. van 3428
Amery, H. 5015
Amirahmadi, H. 4226
Ammentorp, W. 439
Ammerman, R. 2105
Ampt-Riksen, V. 3575

Amriah, B. 3552
An, C. 2458
Anami, T. 3344
Anders, M. 1511
Andersen, E. 1475
Andersen, K. 4947
Andersen, R. 1533
Anderson, B. 4401
Anderson, C. 1060
Anderson, G. 1171
Anderson, H. 3634
Anderson, J. 2462
Anderson, K. 136, 2884, 3463
Anderson, R. 1816
Andersson, Å. 1341
Andorka, R. 46, 4829
Andrade, B. 5048
Andrade-Palos, P. 5120
Andrássy, G. 4822
Andreev, S. 1824
Andrews, B. 5835
Andrews, G. 3201
Andrews, S. 834
Andrillon, F. 3227
Angelis, R. de 3235
Angelmar, R. 782
Anglaret, P. 5048
Angle, J. 4032
Anglin, M. 56
Angotti, T. 3852, 3899
Angus, L. 1652, 2898
Anker, R. 5342
Annerstedt, L. 5733
Anooshian, L. 534
Ansart, P. 30
Ansart-Dourlen, M. 4984
Anselin, L. 3454
Anson, J. 2377
Anspach, R. 5700
Anstötz, C. 5825
Antoine, P. 2367
Antone, C. 384
Antony, L. 2757
Antoun, R. 1321
Anurin, V. 303
Anweiler, O. 1694
Anyanwu, S. 3362
Aoki, S. 1876

Author index

Apfelbaum, E. 404
Apothéloz, D. 150
Apple, M. 1759
Appleby, R. 1226
Appold, S. 3982
Apt, C. 2597
Apt, N. 5718, 5738
Apter, E. 1225
Aqueci, F. 150
Aquilino, W. 333
Arango, J. 3424
Arber, S. 2044, 2857
Archard, D. 2101
Archer, J. 449
Archer, M. 1028
Archer, W. 3759, 3854
Arcuri, F. 5673
Arcuri, L. 743
Ardayfio-Schandorf, E. 2662
Arditti, J. 2493
Arene, M. 5778
Arentze, T. 4182
Argiros, R. 4512
Argote, L. 766
Argyle, M. 1909
Argys, L. 2478
Arimoto, A. 59
Arluke, A. 636
Armacost, R. 340
Armenakis, A. 790
Armstrong, A. 2704
Armstrong, D. 3482
Armstrong, J. 3825, 5023
Arnaud, C. 3825
Arnauné, A. 2020
Arndt, H. 1479
Arneklev, B. 5166
Arneson, R. 4771
Arnold, M. 988
Arnold, R. 5172
Aron, A. 2585
Aronowitz, S. 995
Arons, A. 1688
Arora, S. 707
Arrondel, L. 2568
Arroyo Alejandre, J. 3379
Arthur, M. 902
Arthur, W. 3389

Arvey, R. 748
Aryee, S. 2554, 4252
Asano, S. 3307
Asarnow, J. 5694
Ascher, E. 210, 5433
Ascoli, U. 5482
Ashforth, B. 832
Ashin, G. 904, 4978
Ashraf, B. 2795
Ashraf, J. 2795
Ashraf, N. 4810
Ashton, M. 5399
Askew, I. 2236
Askham, J. 2066
Aspinwall, L. 582
Asquith, S. 2450
Assaad, R. 4591
Assadian, A. 3771
Assies, W. 4941
Assiter, A. 2719
Association of Metropolitan Authorities 5287
Assogba, Y. 3531
Assor, A. 590
Åström, L. 2040
Atash, F. 3669
Atkinson, A. 3638
Atkinson, D. 248
Atkinson, J. 4490
Atkinson, M. 2623
Atkinson, P. 2224
Atkinson, S. 3716
Attardo, S. 496
Atteslander, P. 356
Attias-Donfut, C. 2054
Attkisson, C. 5841
Attwood, L. 2996
Atwater, L. 5001
Aubry, B. 2020
Auerbach, S. 4638
Augustin, E. 2689
Augustin, J. 2020
Augustyniak, H. 2244
Augustyniak-Kopka, J. 958
Aune, R. 1379
Aunger, E. 1429
Auriat, N. 536, 1948
Aurora, G. 3564

Index des auteurs

Auslander, G.   5739
Austen, J.   4097
Austin, T.   5245
Auvergnon, P.   4633
Auzias, C.   3121
Avery, R.   1449, 1518
Ávila, R.   1404
Aviram, A.   483, 1760
Ax, C.   5707, 5831
Axelrod, L.   403, 5021
Axelsson, S.   3834
Axinn, W.   2263, 2525
Axt, H.   974
Ayalon, H.   3826
Ayupan, L.   3500
Azam, G.   5345
Aziz, A.   4215, 4416
Azu-Okeke, O.   5837
Azzi, A.   738
Ba, A.   2367
Ba, F.   2018
Baaren, K. van   524
Baba, V.   911
Babaev, R.   4118
Babaeva, L.   4118
Babrow, A.   1449, 1518
Baccaïni, B.   3250
Bacevich, A.   4996
Bach, J.   881
Bach, R.   3060
Bacherl, C.   2142, 3278
Bachman, R.   3038
Bachugov, D.   4086
Bäck, H.   3325
Bäcker, G.   2886
Backman, K.   3360
Bade, K.   3256
Baden, J.   5796
Badhwar, N.   603
Badie, B.   209, 3415, 5025
Baechler, J.   150, 210
Baenninger, M.   606
Baenninger, R.   606
Baer, D.   1020, 1883
Baer, H.   1215
Baetens Beardsmore, H.   1561
Baffie, J.   1308
Bagchi, D.   4360

Bagchi-Sen, S.   4111
Bagilhole, B.   2942
Bagnara, S.   4433
Bagnasco, A.   3961
Bagnoli, M.   2551
Bagozzi, R.   550
Bahamón Dussán, A.   5398
Bahl, V.   1884, 5631
Bähr, J.   3941
Bahrin, T.   3352
Bahry, D.   4987
Baier, A.   135
Bailey, A.   3262
Bailey, D.   244
Bailey, F.   458
Bailey, K.   197
Bailin, S.   439
Baily, S.   5419
Bain de Corcuera, J.   2669
Bajos, N.   3001
Baker, A.   3064
Baker, C.   1439
Baker, D.   3085
Baker, H.   1965
Baker, J.   3545
Baker, L.   374
Baker, S.   5540
Baker-Brown, G.   5371, 5424
Bakirov, V.   253
Bakis, H.   4079
Bakken, B.   5189, 5289
Bakker, B.   2832
Bakouan, D.   2236
Bal, A.   5676
Balán, J.   1794
Balandier, G.   4977
Balasubramanian, K.   2266
Balatsky, G.   4063
Balbo, M.   3887
Baldauf, R.   1561
Baldwin, E.   1118
Baldwin, J.   4815
Baldwin, M.   656
Baldwin, N.   5073, 5596, 5744
Baldwin, P.   5223
Baldwin, S.   5722
Balen, H. van   5751
Bales, W.   5205

Author index

Balić, S. 1323
Ball, R. 2544
Ball, S. 1708
Ballweg, J. 2258
Balmer, D. 5567
Balmoris, M. 4947
Baloche, L. 439
Balsa, C. 1429
Balter, M. 5156, 5410
Baltes, M. 2048
Baltes, P. 2048
Baluw, W. 3666
Bamyeh, M. 5030
Banai, R. 1072
Bananno, A. 3607
Banaszak, L. 2765
Bandaranayake, S. 4858
Bandieri, S. 4218
Bandlamudi, L. 2259
Bane, C. 920
Bangoura, D. 4993
Bank, L. 573, 2633
Banks, G. 3697
Banks, J. 2098
Bankston, C. 752
Bannerman, A. 2628
Baños, O. 3544
Bansler, J. 4605
Bao, J. 1809
Baochang, G. 2181
Baquero, M. 4952
Barabas, A. 2197
Baraldi, C. 1431
Baran, A. 4039
Baras, M. 2298
Barbalet, J. 436
Barbary, O. 3379
Barbeau, A. 5564
Barbee, A. 2624
Barbee, E. 5690
Barber, B. 2617
Barbero, J. 1043
Barbieri Masini, E. 1936
Barbour, R. 358
Barcan, A. 1687
Barclay, C. 528
Bardem, I. 3379
Bar-El, E. 4217

Barenys, M. 2054
Barff, R. 4097
Barford, R. 5551
Barkan, E. 3393
Barkan, S. 4871
Barker, C. 5855
Barker, E. 1252
Barker-Benfield, G. 2953
Barkin, D. 3896, 3930
Barling, J. 2606, 4423
Barlow, D. 5211
Barlow, H. 5186
Barlow, J. 3732
Barlow, M. 5211
Barnard, K. 1730, 5493
Barnard, M. 358, 2316
Barnes, G. 2518, 5406
Barnes, M. 5727
Barnett, C. 835
Barnett, J. 5747
Barnett, N. 583
Barnett, O. 2534
Barnett, R. 2802, 4459
Barnett, S. 1578
Barnett, W. 840
Barnhorst, R. 2117
Barnulf, M. 4880
Barnum, D. 5390
Baron, J. 401
Baron, L. 560
Baron, R. 620, 766
Baron, S. 749, 5154
Baross, P. 3748
Barou, J. 3332, 3761, 3901, 5490
Barr, K. 5406
Barr, U. 2127, 4365
Barresi, J. 494
Barreto, V. 4514
Barrett, D. 5723, 5742
Barrett, E. 1551
Barrett, H. 2114
Barrett, J. 611
Barron, D. 263
Barron, J. 2809
Barrow, R. 1648
Barry, N. 4771
Barsade, S. 4461
Barsch, G. 5381

Index des auteurs

Bart, P.   5173, 5255
Bar-Tal, D.   753
Bartholomew, D.   304
Bartiaux, F.   3376
Bartik, T.   3286
Bartko, W.   2624
Bartolo, G. de   4170
Barton, L.   1811
Barton, T.   2207
Bartoňová, D.   4222
Bartsch, R.   745
Barudy, J.   3338
Baruffi, G.   2281
Barygin, I.   4932
Barzvi, A.   594
Basadur, M.   439
Bascom, J.   3985
Baskin, D.   5160
Başoğlu, M.   5854
Basran, G.   2420, 3601
Bass, M.   5778
Bassand, M.   3689
Bassin, E.   304
Bassiry, G.   3967
Bastard, B.   2424
Bastenier, A.   3418
Bastian, J.   1286
Bastien, É.   2071
Bastos, S.   4303
Basu, A.   2255, 5019
Bates, G.   927
Bates, I.   2173
Bates, R.   1
Bates, T.   4855
Batten, D.   1341
Battin, M.   5814
Battistelli, F.   5033
Baucus, M.   839
Baudchon, G.   1996
Bauer, R.   5509
Baulet, G.   1456
Baum, A.   3460, 5277
Baum, F.   5757
Bauman, Z.   4865
Baumann, D.   5695
Baumann, H.   4439
Baumann, P.   184
Baumeister, R.   595, 600, 710

Bavetta, A.   4592
Baxter, D.   1902
Bayer, R.   5372
Bayertz, K.   3175
Baylina, M.   2669
Bayly, R.   5721, 5740
Baym, N.   1582
Bazemore, G.   5280, 5408
Bazo, M.   2054
Beals, J.   5371, 5424
Beaman, J.   2407, 2613, 5242
Bean, P.   5370
Bearman, P.   4936
Beasley, F.   5848
Beasley, J.   2120
Beasley, M.   5241
Beattie, A.   5656
Beau, B. le   1254
Beauchard, J.   5433
Beauchesne, L.   5394
Beaugé, G.   3289
Beauregard, R.   3700, 3725
Beaux, D.   5778
Beazoglou, T.   5644
Bebbington, A.   5466
Bechtel, W.   512
Bechtle, G.   4429
Beck, U.   466, 3479
Becker, C.   1675
Becker, E.   3
Becker, G.   441
Becker, J.   1594
Becker, K.   1574
Becker, M.   5389
Becker, S.   2102, 5724
Beckford, J.   1252
Beck-Gernsheim, E.   466
Beckles, H.   1924
Beckman, L.   2212
Beckmann, G.   3894
Beckmann, M.   1341
Bedard, S.   4418
Bedaux, J.   1594
Bedoui, A.   5311
Beechem, J.   5716, 5746
Beekink, E.   2616
Beer, J. de   2484
Beer, U.   4005

Author index

Beezer, A. 4752
Beggan, J. 4965
Begley, T. 955
Begovic, B. 3869
Behar, L. de 1425
Behn, R. 5481
Beinin, J. 1541
Beiser, M. 5371, 5424
Béjar, H. 4912
Béjin, A. 3001
Belkhadi, A. 2697
Bell, D. 731, 3208
Bell, M. 2025
Bell, S. 2829
Bell, V. 2771, 2975
Bell, W. 924
Bella, L. 2868
Bellamy, J. 1838
Bellavance, M. 3936
Beller, A. 4343
Belley, S. 4972
Belsky, J. 5075
Beltrão, K. 2366
Beltzer, N. 3001
Ben-Ari, E. 175
Benda-Beckmann, F. von 3575
Ben-David, S. 2848
Bendel, K. 169
Bender, B. 3467
Bendick, M. 3681
Bendit, R. 2136
Benedict, H. 1557
Benford, R. 4885, 4945
Bengali, K. 4049, 5341
Bengtson, V. 2553
Benguigui, G. 5232
Benhabib, S. 2739
Beniger, J. 1449, 1518
Benjamin, A. 5763
Benjamin, B. 2368
Ben-Ner, A. 876
Bennett, J. 2074, 4566
Bennett, L. 1712, 1792
Bennett, R. 737, 5417
Bennett, T. 1621
Bennett, W. 1449, 1518
Bennis, W. 779
Ben-Rafael, E. 145, 3826

Benson, M. 629, 4861
Benson, P. 2949
Benston, K. 1069
Bentahila, A. 1400
Benthall, J. 1512
Bentler, P. 271, 4465
Bentley, G. 2275
Benton, L. 3868
Benton, T. 3470
Bentovim, A. 2461
Ben-Zion, U. 5196
Benzler, S. 4385
Benzon, W. 1606, 1625, 1631
Berblinger, A. 3634
Bereiter, C. 1679
Beres, L. 5013
Beresford, M. 4594
Beresford, P. 5455
Berg, L. 1059
Bergeman, C. 553
Berger, A. 1030
Berger, B. 2423
Berger, P. 4249
Bergeret, J. 5433
Bergmann, A. 5808
Bergmann, R. 5381
Bergquist, W. 833
Bergstrom, T. 2551
Bergthold, L. 5761
Beriss, D. 1022
Berkowitz, N. 712
Berlière, J. 3699
Berman, B. 1344
Bermann, E. 2641
Bernard, M. 2085
Bernard, Y. 3738
Berndt, R. 849
Berney, B. 5693
Bernhardt, E. 2271
Bernis, C. 2231
Berquó, E. 2539
Berriane, M. 4750
Berry, B. 3759, 3854
Berry, D. 573
Berry, W. 319
Bershady, H. 467
Berten, A. 1197
Berthoud, G. 5433

Index des auteurs

Berthoud, R. 4253
Bertrand, J. 2020
Bertrand, M. 3858
Besnard, P. 1122
Bessy, P. 3304
Best, J. 1726
Betancourt, H. 423
Bettman, J. 518
Betzig, L. 2990
Bevc, I. 2958
Beven, C. 3469
Bevir, M. 5517
Beyani, C. 2704
Beyers, H. 3230
Bezrukov, V. 5718, 5738
Bhabha, H. 1013
Bhadra, M. 1961
Bhagat, R. 903
Bhargava, S. 37
Bhat, K. 4363
Bhat, R. 5685
Bhate, S. 4162
Bhattacharya, R. 2421
Bhavnani, K. 3094
Bhowmik, S. 4717
Biagini, H. 1658
Bian, Y. 1844
Biblarz, T. 2413
Bidgood, B. 5618
Bieback-Diel, L. 2530
Biedebach, M. 439
Biehal, N. 5711
Biek, M. 393
Bielawska-Batorowicz, E. 2239
Bien, T. 5366
Bienenstock, E. 265
Biervert, B. 42
Bies, R. 688, 810
Biggart, D. 151
Biggins, D. 4696
Biggs, E. 109
Biggs, S. 2084
Bigum, C. 1667
Bijsterveld, S. van 1724
Billiet, J. 3151
Billig, M. 753
Billimoria, J. 2421
Billingsley, A. 2528

Billy, J. 2162
Bilodeau, W. 1378
Bilsborrow, R. 4021
Bilu, Y. 431
Bim, A. 5051
Bimmer, A. 3113
Bindra, R. 578
Biner, P. 4457
Binet, J. 1632
Binfield, C. 4744
Binkley, L. 4299
Binstock, G. 2134
Binstock, R. 5761
Biocca, F. 1519
Biq, Y. 1577
Biraben, J. 2020
Birch, S. 5769
Bird, C. 2434
Bird, G. 3634
Bird, J. 1944
Birdsall, N. 2180
Birg, H. 2015
Birkbeck, C. 5159
Birkelbach, K. 482
Birmingham, J. 5718, 5738
Birnbaum, N. 204
Biro, Z. 3113
Birt, R. 562
Birzéa, C. 2018
Bishop, J. 4251
Bishop, K. 3440
Bishop, N. 3353
Bittman, M. 4745
Bix, B. 1192
Bizeul, D. 3130
Björgo, T. 3229
Bjurström, E. 2040
Blaakilde, A. 2040
Black, D. 2342, 2809
Black, M. 5643
Black, R. 3261
Black, T. 232
Blackburn, M. 1672, 2277
Blackler, F. 853
Blackmore, J. 1714
Blackwelder, S. 2623
Blackwell, B. 2652
Blaikie, N. 227

Author index

Blain, J.   2890
Blain, N.   4743
Blair, T.   3829
Blake, P.   5206
Blakely, J.   4256
Blakemore, K.   3101
Blanc, M.   3561
Blancarte, R.   1297
Blanchard-Fields, F.   2538
Blanchet, D.   4349
Blanck, P.   639
Blanckaert, C.   2
Blanco-Beledo, R.   5572
Blanke, B.   3671, 4385
Blankenburg, E.   1212
Blankenship, K.   2238
Blasius, J.   1899
Blasius, M.   96
Blass, R.   2642
Blatt, S.   569, 579
Blau, D.   5537
Blau, F.   4326
Blau, P.   1018
Blayo, C.   2020
Bledsoe, C.   2296
Bleedorn, B.   439
Blees-Booij, A.   4316
Blekesaune, A.   4341
Bless, H.   386
Blickle, P.   3542
Blien, U.   71
Bloch, A.   3023
Block, A.   5415
Block, J.   549
Blois, J. de   2018
Blom, U.   3596
Blomberg, T.   5205
Bloom, D.   2277
Bloor, M.   2316, 2387
Blossfeld, H.   2557
Blot, R.   1397
Blouin, R.   4306
Blount, W.   5077, 5296
Blowers, G.   1831
Blum, L.   2684
Blum-Kulka, S.   1438
Blumstein, A.   5308
Blundell, V.   57

Blustein, J.   5795
Blyler, N.   1454
Blyth, E.   5552
Bobda, A.   1469
Bobo, L.   3165
Bochkareva, V.   33
Bocock, R.   4166
Bode, I.   4613
Bode, J.   1475
Bodemann, Y.   3134
Boden, D.   1434
Bodo, J.   3113
Boehm, T.   3286
Boehne, D.   4414
Boehnlein, J.   5371, 5424
Boei, F.   4552
Boer, L. vanden   5519
Boerma, J.   2350
Boettner, J.   1556
Bogart, L.   1030
Bogart, W.   4859
Bogdan, R.   374
Bogen, D.   137
Bögenhold, D.   4294
Boger, R.   2627
Bohan, J.   410
Bohle, H.   5349
Bohler, K.   2530
Bohmann, G.   5510
Bohn, C.   1420
Bohner, G.   594
Bohua, L.   2181
Boies, J.   4928
Boily, L.   4112
Bois-Reymond, M.   2171
Boisset, A.   5047
Boje, T.   1959
Bokszański, Z.   1040
Bolduc, D.   2153
Bole, T.   5814
Bollen, K.   237, 3982
Bolling, K.   3714
Böltken, F.   2192
Bolton, R.   2961
Boltvinik, J.   4030
Bonacich, E.   244, 245
Bonacich, P.   265
Bonaguidi, A.   3376

Index des auteurs

Bonanno, G.   569
Bond, M.   416
Boneham, M.   3101
Bongaarts, J.   2299
Bonnafous, S.   3182
Bonnemaison, G.   5144
Bonner, F.   1609
Bonnett, A.   3174
Bono, B.   4460
Bono, C.   2671
Bono, P.   2753
Bonvalet, C.   2447
Bonvillian, J.   1377
Boons, F.   4940
Boorman, S.   1196
Boorsma, M.   1610
Booth, A.   2604, 4006
Booth, T.   5581, 5592
Booth, W.   3964, 5581, 5592
Boothe, J.   4701
Booth-Kewley, S.   340
Bor, R.   2315
Borchelt, M.   2048
Bordley, W.   5756
Borgatti, S.   298, 318
Borgegård, L.   3666
Borgers, A.   3919, 4182
Borgiani, P.   2289
Borgida, E.   2123
Boriani, F.   201
Borjas, G.   3326
Borkenau, P.   547, 573
Borlandi, M.   150
Borman, R.   4313
Born, C.   2729
Borna, S.   4169
Bornat, J.   2076
Borneman, J.   5029
Bornemann, K.   4271
Bornevasser, M.   3113, 3185
Bornschier, V.   1841
Bornstein, G.   762
Bornstein, R.   457
Böröcz, J.   1975
Borricand, J.   5208, 5297
Bortz, J.   695
Borys, B.   812
Borzyszkowski, J.   3066

Bosch, B.   1382
Bosch, G.   4454
Bosch, K. van den   4322
Boschi, R.   4102
Bose, M.   4293
Bosinski, H.   2926
Bosman, J.   3839
Bosman, L.   1594
Boss, P.   2496
Bossen, L.   3554
Bostyn, A.   1802
Boswell, T.   4773
Bosworth, S.   897
Bosworth-Davies, R.   5186
Bot, Y. le   209
Botiveau, B.   1190
Böttcher, W.   1699
Bottini, E.   2289
Bottomley, A.   2740, 5190
Bouchard, T.   554
Bouchikhi, H.   4078
Boudon, R.   145, 209
Boudreau, R.   4455
Bouffard, L.   2071
Bouhuijs, F.   591
Boulding, E.   1935
Bourantas, D.   4527
Bourdais, C. le   2615
Bourdieu, P.   1607, 5045
Bourdon, J.   1588
Bourn, D.   5591
Bourque, P.   4733
Bouthilet, G.   5191
Bouton, M.   529
Bouvier, L.   3055
Bovasso, G.   3086
Bovone, L.   1148
Bowd, A.   1118
Bowditch, C.   1773
Bowen, D.   5773
Bowlby, R.   4189
Bowles, M.   801
Bowles, S.   4119
Bowling, A.   2058
Bowling, B.   3223
Bowman, C.   3012
Boxer, D.   1465
Boyce, N.   3772

Author index

Boye-Beaman, J.   2895
Boyer, M.   5040
Boyer, R.   4273
Boyle, F.   3085
Boyle, M.   1547
Boyle, P.   3248, 3380
Boyle, R.   3834, 4743
Boyne, G.   3785
Boyne, R.   1028
Bozon, M.   3001
Bozorgmehr, M.   3125
Braaksma, J.   1753
Bracher, M.   2483
Bracker, J.   4380
Bradley, D.   1630
Bradley, G.   5609
Bradley, K.   2847
Bradshaw, S.   240
Bradshaw, T.   3634
Bradshaw, Y.   5006
Brah, A.   3178
Braidotti, R.   2865
Brailey, K.   403, 5021
Braithwaite, J.   1083, 5145, 5308
Braithwaite, V.   4311, 5395
Brajczewski, C.   2371
Bramall, C.   3598
Braman, S.   1449, 1518
Brandon, R.   1730, 5493
Brandstätter, H.   3966
Brannon, L.   403, 5021
Bras, H.   2447
Bratman, M.   486
Braun, D.   5663
Bravo, M.   420
Bray, M.   1751
Bray, R.   3640
Braye, S.   5543, 5586, 5593
Brazier, M.   4549
Breakwell, G.   624
Breathnach, P.   2669
Brechin, S.   2024
Brechon, P.   1263
Brée, D.   1497
Bregman, D.   1553
Breheny, M.   3878
Brehm, J.   4409
Breitenstein, O.   1574

Brekel, H. van den   2070, 3294
Bremm, H.   3839
Brenan, J.   3763, 3861, 5491
Brenders, D.   4947
Brennan, R.   2802
Brenner, J.   2720
Brenner, L.   1313
Brenske, P.   4244
Brents, B.   1888
Bresnahan, M.   997, 2805, 3202
Breton, R.   1227
Brett, J.   737
Brettell, C.   2515
Breuer, S.   183
Brewer, B.   484
Brewer, D.   538
Brewer, J.   4824
Brewer, M.   754, 767
Brewin, C.   5843
Brewster, C.   4476
Brewster, K.   2162
Brezinka, W.   1738
Breznà, I.   2773
Briand, J.   1716
Briesen, D.   34
Bright, J.   5107
Brint, S.   4546
Brinton, M.   4487
Brion, D.   5445
Bristow, J.   4863
Britton, S.   448
Broadhead, R.   5384
Brock, D.   1871, 1877, 5815
Brockerhoff, M.   3359
Broderick, C.   2464
Brodsky, J.   5718, 5738
Brogden, M.   4817
Broman, C.   2589
Bromberger, C.   3113
Bromet, E.   4562
Bromley, D.   962
Brooke, M.   731
Brooke, T.   3886
Brooker, C.   5713, 5834
Brooks, C.   1893
Brooks-Gunn, J.   2107, 2125
Brosius, H.   1442
Brossollet, C.   4324

Index des auteurs

Broun, J. 1298
Brouwer, R. 3575
Brower, R. 139
Brown, B. 2987, 5157, 5230
Brown, D. 3973
Brown, F. 530
Brown, G. 4266, 5371, 5424
Brown, J. 4787
Brown, K. 4115
Brown, L. 774, 5644
Brown, P. 403, 5021
Brown, R. 754, 932, 1343, 1837, 1946, 3595
Brown, T. 4188
Browne, A. 5243, 5256
Browne, P. 5085, 5301
Brownell, J. 803
Brownfield, D. 5307
Brownlee, I. 5204
Bruce, J. 3605
Bruce, S. 1245
Bruck, G. vom 1190
Bruckner, E. 678
Brückner, M. 5576
Brüderl, J. 892
Brudney, J. 4564
Brühl, H. 3534
Bruijin, M. de 3575
Bruins, J. 913
Bruinsma, F. 3839
Brumann, C. 3519
Brumfield, W. 3773
Bruneau, M. 1227
Brunn, G. 4782
Brunner, E. 4330
Brunner, J. 1794
Brunsson, N. 838
Brunswic, E. 2018
Brunt, L. 3656
Brüseke, F. 155
Bruton, R. 1933
Bruun, O. 4073
Bryant, J. 1300
Bryce-Laporte, R. 3060
Brycz, H. 559
Bryson, J. 3478
Buchan, A. 1729, 1777
Buchanan, A. 4771

Buchanan, C. 5108
Buchanan, D. 837
Buchanan, J. 4587, 4771
Buchbinder, H. 1803
Bucher, H. 2015, 2027, 3894
Buchko, A. 4586
Buck, A. 5133
Buck, N. 2451
Buckley, M. 1956
Buckley, P. 3962
Buckridge, P. 1597
Budakowska, E. 3080
Buechler, S. 4867
Buechtemann, C. 4574
Buer, F. 2463
Bugental, D. 1436
Bühler, E. 3706
Buie, D. 706
Buijs, G. 2900
Buitelaar, M. 1309
Bujra, J. 2786
Bukowski, W. 2104
Bulantsev, V. 1995
Bulcroft, K. 2590
Bulcroft, R. 2590
Bull, K. 439
Bull, R. 4787
Bulman, P. 5260
Bulmer, M. 75
Bülow, D. von 2786
Bun, C. 3347
Bunel, J. 4685
Bunting, A. 2740
Burch, B. 2969
Burch, T. 2580
Burfoot, A. 2239
Burgalassi, S. 2358
Burger, C. 2729
Burger, T. 146
Burgess, M. 5814
Burgmann, V. 4918
Burgoon, J. 601, 696
Burgoyne, C. 948
Buri, J. 473
Buriel, R. 2609
Burk, J. 4996
Burkart, G. 466, 2626
Burke III, E. 4062

Author index

Burke, M. 4495
Burke, P. 1364
Burkhauser, R. 2318
Burman, E. 276
Burman, M. 5157, 5230
Burnes, D. 5277
Burns, R. 4457
Burr, J. 3115, 3303
Burroughs, R. 2981
Burrows, J. 5115
Burry, J. 4970
Bursik, R. 2652, 5105, 5166
Burt, R. 4181
Burton, L. 2442
Burton, R. 2078
Bush, T. 1762
Bushaw, V. 245
Bushman, R. 1117
Busia, A. 2769
Busino, G. 150, 210
Bustamente, D. 3200
Butcher, H. 3505
Butcher, J. 4552
Butler, D. 4457
Butler, E. 4289
Butler, J. 2651, 2731, 4996
Butora, M. 3240
Butorova, Z. 3240
Butt, M. 2257
Butter, I. 5773
Butterwegge, C. 4904
Büttner, F. 3289
Buttny, R. 1427
Button, G. 99
Buttorff, C. 2500
Buunk, B. 543, 650
Buy, A. 5528
Buzawa, C. 5245
Buzawa, E. 5245
Bybee, D. 354
Byers, J. 2323
Byham, W. 4413
Byrd, K. 599
Byrne, B. 3190
Byrne, R. 382
Bytheway, B. 228
Byun, Y. 3383
Caballero, L. 3673

Cabanne, M. 2020
Cable, S. 4861
Cabrita, J. 3569
Cadène, P. 3379
Caetano, A. 918
Cahn, S. 1786
Cain, R. 5714
Caire, J. 3008
Caivano, J. 1425
Calavita, K. 3274
Calcoen, F. 5048
Caldwell, G. 3334
Caldwell, J. 2297, 2324
Caldwell, P. 2297, 2324
Calefato, P. 1425
Calhoun, C. 915, 1067, 3129, 4775, 4794
Callan, T. 4323
Callinicos, A. 1910, 3222
Calloway, M. 773
Callus, R. 4587
Calmont, A. 2020
Calsyn, R. 267, 326
Calthrope, P. 3877
Camacho, A. 3895
Camagni, R. 3839
Camargo, J. 4637
Cameron, J. 5100
Cameron, S. 1775
Camic, C. 217
Campani, G. 3288
Campbell, B. 705, 4210, 5042
Campbell, C. 440
Campbell, D. 1185, 5440
Campbell, H. 4939, 5586
Campbell, J. 4209
Campbell, K. 374
Campbell, O. 2223, 2270
Campbell, R. 766, 2326, 2401
Campion, J. 5052
Campion, M. 4470
Campion-Vincent, V. 5062, 5316
Campling, J. 2682
Camstra, R. 4317
Camus, M. 4303
Canadell, R. 4930
Cancian, F. 245
Canino, G. 420, 5361

Index des auteurs

Cano, V. 1393
Canoves, G. 2669
Cant, B. 2962
Canta, C. 1662
Canter, D. 624, 767
Cantillon, B. 4322
Cantos, A. 2578
Cantwell, M. 4745
Capecchi, S. 2891
Capek, S. 3450
Capen, M. 1134
Caplan, R. 3474
Cappella, J. 696
Cappelli, P. 4489
Carder, P. 2635
Cardia-Voneche, L. 2424
Cardinal, C. 2991
Carew, J. 3027
Carey, J. 2310
Cario, R. 5121
Carius, A. 4869, 4870
Carjuzáa, J. 452
Carley, K. 764, 1493
Carlie, M. 5218
Carlin, P. 2437
Carling, A. 153
Carlson, A. 2423
Carlson, M. 2086
Carlston, D. 533
Carlton, N. 2620
Carlton-Laney, I. 5262, 5322
Carnevale, P. 686
Carol, A. 2719
Caroleo, F. 4369
Carpenter, C. 3491
Carpenter, P. 1800
Carpenter, S. 725, 754
Carr, S. 3695
Carrasco, H. 3155
Carrell, D. 5773
Carreras, M. 150
Carrim, Y. 3057
Carroll, D. 407
Carroll, G. 4072
Carroll, W. 4905
Carroy, J. 404
Carter, F. 3288
Carter, N. 4188

Cartledge, P. 1003
Cartocci, R. 4957
Cartwright, S. 4290
Carver, C. 2317
Carver, K. 2479
Cary, J. 3578
Case, S. 2707
Caselli, G. 2356
Casetti, E. 3924
Casman, M. 3298, 4813
Casson, M. 3960, 3962
Casswell, S. 5388
Castañeda Hernández, W. 3382
Castel, R. 5778
Castellan, M. 2020
Castellan, N. 523, 739
Castells, M. 3666
Casterline, J. 2216, 2284
Castle, E. 3585, 3634
Castles, A. 498
Castles, S. 3103
Casto, R. 1730, 5493
Castonguay, C. 1483, 1484
Castonguay, S. 4666
Castro Martin, T. 2543
Castro, N. 4514
Catani, M. 3332
Catanzaro, R. 5151
Catt, H. 2853
Cattacin, S. 3876, 4908
Catterall, B. 1710
Caul, B. 5499
Caulkins, J. 5235, 5393, 5420
Caumel, M. 4214
Cavasinni, A. 2903
Cavender, G. 1499
Cawthra, G. 4818
Ceballos, M. 4377
Cebrián Abellán, A. 3215
Celiński, Z. 3445
Centeno, M. 4854
Centerwall, B. 1587
Centlivres, P. 3113
Cento Bull, A. 4088
Cerbara, L. 2356
Ceri, P. 143
Cernea, M. 251
Cernkovich, S. 2135

Author index

Cervantes Carson, A. 2877
Cha, J. 1866
Chacko, J. 4795
Chadiha, L. 2588
Chadwick, B. 2157
Chafetz, J. 217
Chaffee, L. 1310
Chaffee, S. 1519
Chakib, A. 192
Chakraborti, P. 2046
Chakraborty, S. 5446
Chalcraft, D. 147
Chalmers, I. 5683
Chalongphob Sussangkarn 4046
Chalouh, M. 5136
Chaloupka, F. 5360
Chalupa, P. 2032
Chalvon-Demersay, S. 1588
Chambers, I. 3284
Champion, F. 1297
Chan, C. 2064, 2074
Chan, K. 696, 1294
Chan, W. 271
Chanana, K. 1782
Chandler, C. 5429
Chandler, P. 403, 5021
Chandler, T. 4585
Chandra, S. 2046
Chandy, K. 3548
Chaney, D. 1001
Chang, C. 4203
Chang, D. 1088
Chao, W. 2407
Chaplin, W. 573
Chapman, B. 3266
Chapman, J. 4169
Chapoulie, J. 1716
Chappell, N. 5651
Chard-Wierschem, D. 5305
Charles, C. 5662
Charles, L. 2447
Charles, N. 2810
Charlesworth, M. 5789
Charlier, J. 4872
Charney, A. 3286
Charrié, J. 2020
Chase, J. 5539
Chase-Dunn, C. 1927, 1975

Chatters, L. 2427
Chatterton, M. 4836
Chaudhuri, M. 2747
Chauvenet, A. 5232
Chaves, M. 1222
Chay, Y. 4252
Chayko, M. 1581
Chazan, B. 2229
Chazel, F. 7
Chelli, H. 5061
Chen, G. 660
Chen, X. 3731, 5692
Chen, Y. 761
Chene, M. 5003
Cheney, D. 2740, 5445
Cheng Hurtado, A. 3652
Cheng, L. 3073
Chennoufi, S. 1099
Chenu, A. 4515
Cheran, R. 3037
Chernyshov, S. 5014
Cherry, A. 2161
Chesham, D. 415
Chesnais, J. 3413
Chew, I. 4252
Chien, Y. 2892
Child, J. 3979
Childs, J. 3085
Chiles, T. 4698
Chimbos, P. 5164
Chin, K. 5116
Chin, M. 726
Chipuer, H. 553
Chiricos, T. 5211
Chisholm, L. 2176
Chisholm, R. 774
Chishti, S. 2842
Chiswick, B. 3270, 3349, 4520
Chiswick, C. 2594
Chitnis, S. 1795
Chiu, S. 4252
Chivallon, C. 2020
Cho, S. 65
Choguill, C. 4055
Choi, C. 5430
Choi, J. 4970
Chong, D. 944, 4874
Choquet, M. 2168

Index des auteurs

Chorney, H. 4785
Chou, C. 56
Choudhury, A. 3124
Chowdhury, K. 4022
Chrisler, J. 2759
Christensen, C. 766
Christians, C. 1520
Christianson, J. 5648
Christie, J. 16
Christie, N. 5188
Christin, P. 3699
Christopher, F. 3014
Chruscz, D. 2192
Chugov, S. 938, 3205
Chumachenko, N. 4224
Church, A. 334, 761
Church, R. 1642
Churchill, A. 2631
Churchland, P. 374
Ciborra, C. 4155
Ciechocińska, M. 2669
Cieri, H. de 4481
Cieślak, M. 2012
Cigno, K. 5731
Cini, M. 734
Cipolla, C. 100
Cipriani, R. 1220
Citro, C. 5476
Claeys, W. 1496
Claisse, G. 1458
Clancy, S. 586
Clapham, A. 2970
Clapham, D. 3750
Clare, I. 5363
Clark, A. 367, 374, 517, 2668
Clark, D. 1124, 5214, 5743, 5759
Clark, K. 2317
Clark, L. 669, 5690
Clark, R. 2906
Clark, T. 1893
Clarke, J. 2018, 5562
Clarke, L. 843, 863
Clarke, S. 3986, 4308
Claster, D. 5095, 5180
Claude, G. 3253
Claval, P. 3468
Clay, D. 2288
Clayman, S. 609, 1409

Clémence, A. 408
Clements, M. 2624
Clercq, B. de 5450
Cliff, D. 2850
Cliff, J. 5643
Clifford, P. 4975
Cliquet, R. 1989
Clogg, C. 2531
Cloud, C. 3243
Clover, C. 2956
Clyde, R. 439
Clyne, M. 1388
Cnaan, A. 926
Cnaan, R. 926
Coates, C. 3511
Coates, J. 5249
Cobb, S. 5445
Cobern, M. 3436
Cochrane, R. 407
Cockburn, C. 2934
Cockerham, W. 133, 134
Coen, T. 1949
Coetsier, P. 4534
Coffield, F. 4127
Cohen, A. 1499, 3674
Cohen, B. 2088, 2296
Cohen, C. 1022
Cohen, D. 2086, 5368
Cohen, E. 175, 354
Cohen, J. 4771
Cohen, L. 2034, 5104, 5441
Cohen, M. 1275
Cohen, R. 1069
Cohen, S. 2659, 3434
Cohen-Emérique, M. 3321
Cohen-Kiel, A. 978
Cohn, S. 4871
Coie, J. 5694
Colclough, C. 1705
Cole, C. 2829
Cole, D. 748
Colebatch, H. 811
Coleman, D. 2038
Coleman, H. 1031
Coleman, J. 200, 440, 794, 1173, 1174
Coleman, K. 1295
Coleman, M. 1762, 4402

Author index

Coleman, P. 2079
Colignon, R. 850
Collard, Y. 4872
Collatz, J. 3242, 5705
Collier, G. 404
Collier, P. 1028
Colliez, J. 2020
Collini, S. 988
Collins, A. 1675
Collins, H. 1340
Collins, J. 2420, 4329, 5271
Collins, L. 395
Collins, R. 146, 1975
Collins, S. 3198, 5541
Collins-Jarvis, L. 1449, 1518
Collison, M. 5224, 5405
Colomé, G. 4951
Colón, H. 5407
Colton, N. 3265
Colvin, C. 558, 573, 2094
Combs-Orme, T. 5681
Comeau, Y. 4709
Comín, F. 4214
Community Agency for Social Enquiry South Africa 2129
Compas, B. 2125, 2550
Compère, L. 3180
Compes, P. 4445
Comstock, G. 1259
Conaghan, J. 2740
Condominas, G. 2879
Condon, S. 3423
Condry, J. 2086
Conger, K. 2151
Conger, R. 2151, 2407, 2555, 2613, 5242
Conley, R. 5191
Connell, J. 4719
Connell, R. 2896, 2995
Connolly, C. 1021
Connolly, G. 5388
Connor, W. 3104
Conover, P. 2742
Conrad, C. 4012
Conradson, B. 2767
Consorte, J. 3190
Constantine Municipality 3817
Cook, C. 4331

Cook, D. 5149
Cook, E. 1266, 2210, 4988
Cook, J. 4357
Cook, P. 5380
Cook, S. 5202, 5294
Cook, W. 2436
Cooke, D. 5223
Cooke, I. 2239
Cooke, T. 4379
Coombes, T. 3774
Cooney, R. 2241
Cooper, B. 4602
Cooper, C. 4290, 4519, 4740
Cooper, D. 1678, 2657, 5549
Cooper, R. 1554, 3634
Copp, D. 1170
Copus, G. 5306
Coquery-Vidrovitch, C. 3954
Corajoud, G. 4378
Corbett, J. 1811
Corbin, A. 3699
Corbin, J. 4398
Corbridge, S. 4221
Corby, B. 5067
Corcoran, M. 3277, 4345
Corcoran, R. 531
Corder, L. 320
Cordery, J. 4407
Cordier, A. 404
Cordoba Ordoñez, J. 5326
Cordonnier, R. 209
Corley, F. 1299
Cormack, E. 735
Cormack, R. 1697
Corman, J. 4518
Cornelius, W. 3426
Cornell, D. 2703
Corner, J. 1545
Corner, P. 4088
Cornwall, A. 2873
Cornwell, B. 490
Cornwell, G. 3566
Corporaal, A. 4552
Corré, A. 5053
Corrin, C. 2682
Corson, D. 1375
Cortés, F. 4368, 4488
Cortes, V. 3560

Index des auteurs

Cosandey, M. 5433
Cosslett, T. 2675
Costa, F. 3888
Costa, P. 445, 553
Costello, C. 4358
Coston, C. 5265
Cote, P. 1297
Cottam, M. 5008
Cotterill, P. 228
Cottle, S. 3713
Cottle, T. 2086
Cotto, L. 4911
Cotton, A. 3776, 3903
Cotton, J. 3231, 4003
Couet, D. 5778
Coughlan, J. 3025, 3041
Coughlan, R. 3133
Coulaud, C. 3008
Coulombe, P. 1401
Coulter, C. 2744
Couper, M. 946
Courage, M. 537, 4447
Courant, P. 4345
Cournos, F. 2314
Cousin, O. 1653
Cousineau, M. 5761
Cousins, J. 4535
Covaleski, M. 850
Covell, M. 1429
Covington, C. 4985
Covington, J. 5097
Cowan, N. 385
Cowan, P. 2400, 2426
Cowen, T. 603
Cox, B. 5655
Cox, C. 762, 1232
Cox, D. 5612
Cox, K. 3683, 3881
Coxon, A. 353
Cozzarelli, C. 563
Cozzens, S. 4970
Cradden, T. 4686
Craig, D. 1639
Craig, G. 5496
Craig, R. 1449, 1518
Craik, J. 1106
Craipeau, C. 4083
Cramer, A. 2463

Cramer, D. 2004
Cranach, M. von 1353
Crankshaw, O. 351, 4679
Crawford, C. 2462
Crawford, D. 4735
Crawford, S. 5479
Cream, J. 5068
Creese, G. 61
Creighton, M. 1125
Creighton, S. 4713
Crémer, J. 4168
Crenshaw, E. 4013
Crepet, P. 4386
Crépin, X. 3923
Crespi, F. 145
Creswell, J. 1809
Crewe, L. 4106
Crewe, M. 2305
Crews, D. 2049
Crews, K. 2018
Cribier, F. 3376
Criel, B. 5751
Crimmins, E. 1993
Crittenden, J. 4761
Croall, H. 5186
Croce, P. 1030
Crocker, J. 490
Crocombe, R. 4953
Croft, S. 5455
Crognier, E. 2231
Cromack, V. 4268
Crombag, H. 1181
Crompton, J. 4729
Crompton, R. 1882
Cromwell, J. 4232
Cronin, M. 4749
Crook, N. 3933
Crosby, B. 3478
Crosby, F. 1118
Crosby, G. 2069
Crosby, J. 5823
Cross, G. 4193
Cross, J. 2944
Cross, M. 32
Cross, S. 2312
Crouter, A. 2624
Croutte, P. 5778
Crowe, G. 4800, 4816

Author index

Crowley, A. 5302
Cruise, P. 5280, 5408
Crundall, I. 375
Crush, J. 3609, 4276
Cruz-Ortiz, L. 2205
Csikszentmihalyi, M. 2086, 2166
Csillag, F. 3800
Cuba, L. 3252, 3524
Cubero Salmeron, J. 1815
Cubitt, S. 1555
Cudowski, B. 4604
Cuesta Arzamendi, J. de la 5131, 5436
Cuffe, S. 2147
Cukrowicz, H. 5454
Cullen, C. 5363
Cullen, H. 1709
Cullen, S. 5100
Cullinan, D. 2152
Culyer, A. 5650
Cummings, A. 1817
Cunha, O. da 1276
Cunningham, M. 2624
Cunningham, R. 1050
Cunnison, S. 2794
Curcio, J. 1730, 5493
Curdes, G. 3883
Curran, D. 5202, 5294
Currie, E. 5308
Curry, D. 2987
Curry, J. 4087
Curthoys, A. 1021
Curtin, J. 2853
Curtis, E. 4562
Curtis, J. 4075
Curtis, P. 5637
Curtis, S. 2352
Curzer, H. 5813
Cushing, B. 3834
Cushing, R. 4947
Cushman, D. 861
Cussins, A. 374
Cusson, M. 5163
Cutler, N. 2045
Cuttance, P. 1681
Cuvillier, R. 5467
Cuyvers, P. 2163
Cwikel, J. 5617

Czaja, S. 519
Czajka, J. 955
Czaplicki, A. 1534
Dab, W. 3001
Dabbs, J. 2604
Dabscheck, B. 4615
Dagallier, F. 5778
Daghistani, A. 3817
Dahl, J. 4414
Dahlgren, P. 1504, 1574
Daily, G. 2188
Dale, A. 60
Dale, M. 5226, 5304
Dallmayr, F. 1069
Dallos, R. 5055
Daly, K. 3085
Damais, J. 2020
Damm, R. 1194
Dammam Municipality 3817
Dancaster, L. 4348
Dance, K. 585
Dane, B. 5634
Daněk, P. 5031
Danermark, B. 2068
Danesh, A. 3373
Dangschat, J. 3839
Daniel, J. 1744
Daniels, K. 2239, 5577, 5807
Daniels, N. 5824
Dannhaeuser, N. 4131
Dansereau, S. 4210
Danta, D. 3821
Danziger, L. 2268
Danziger, S. 2086, 2086
Darkoh, M. 3739, 3832
Darley, W. 4173
Darling, N. 2639
Darrow, C. 5100
Das, T. 869
Das, U. 3547
Dasgupta, P. 604, 4034
Dassbach, C. 4099
Dassetto, F. 3290
Datar, C. 2421
Datner-Spiewak, H. 3209
Datta, S. 5636
Daune-Richard, A. 4324
Davenport, P. 2025

Index des auteurs

David, M. 1720
David, R. 5778
David, T. 1766
Davids, K. 4510
Davidson, K. 573
Davidson, M. 4519
Davidson, R. 5560
Davie, R. 2110
Davies, B. 5466
Davies, C. 4573
Davies, E. 1400, 1474
Davies, H. 4314
Davies, J. 1151, 1255, 2423
Davies, M. 228, 3196
Davies, P. 353
Davies, S. 5855
Davies, W. 3504, 3798
Davis, C. 4996
Davis, D. 1449, 1518, 2074, 4269
Davis, F. 1107
Davis, H. 5135, 5437
Davis, J. 3356, 3698, 4150
Davis, L. 5281
Davis, M. 1052, 2950
Davis, N. 5784
Davis, P. 569
Davis, R. 5037
Davis, T. 5735
Davis, W. 283, 2125, 2260
Davydov, I. 19
Dawkins, P. 4454
Dawod, H. 3117
Dawson, A. 5586
Dawson, B. 5625
Day, G. 3520
Day, P. 2072
Day, R. 4007
De Munck, J. 1197
De Schutter, O. 1197
Deakin, N. 4084
Dean, C. 3024
Dean, J. 866
Deane, G. 299, 3770, 3805
Dear, M. 5274
Dearing, J. 1553
Debbasch, C. 1745
Debrah, Y. 4252, 4485
Debray, R. 1139

Decalmer, P. 5046
Dechamps, I. 9
Deck, A. 1133
Decker, B. 5735
Deckers, L. 704
Deely, J. 1425
DeFreitas, G. 3055, 4700
DeFriese, G. 5756
DeFronzo, J. 5365
Degenne, A. 1122
DeGraff, D. 4021
Dehue, F. 516
Deichmann, U. 3454
Dejours, C. 400
Dekeseredy, W. 5130, 5253
Dekker, G. 1221
Delai, N. 1940
Delaney, D. 1187
Delaney, K. 4205
Delarue, J. 5052
Delbridge, R. 814
Delden, J. van 5792, 5804
DeLeon, L. 916
Delessert, A. 5433
Delgado, H. 4677
Delhausse, B. 5319
Della Pergola, S. 2034
Delle Donne, M. 3407
Delobelle, A. 1865
Déloye, Y. 3699
Delsen, L. 4284
DelVecchio Good, M. 2346, 5355
Demaid, A. 3680
DeMaio, S. 5662
DeMaris, A. 2135
Demers, A. 2863
Dem'ian, G. 3098
Demo, D. 629
Dempsey, K. 2939
Dempsey, N. 2635
Denby, S. 4947
Denis, C. 4921
Dennett, D. 508
Dennis, A. 720
Dennis, C. 5085, 5301
Dennis, M. 1963
Dent, M. 5686
Denton, F. 290

Author index

Denton, L.   2783
Denton, M.   527
Denton, N.   3192
DePaulo, B.   619
Depner, C.   2472
Deppa, J.   1530
Derks, P.   707
Derksen, L.   3489
Derlega, V.   2624
Der-Martirosian, C.   3125
Deroche-Gurcel, L.   1122
Derounian, J.   3549
Dervin, B.   1449, 1518, 2764
Desai, M.   2421, 5612
Désautels, J.   1688
Desdevises, M.   5199
Deshpande, S.   4434
DeSilva, L.   2858
Deslhiat, C.   3008
Desmond, D.   4080
Desplanques, G.   2020
Desrosiers, H.   2615
Deutsch, J.   5133
Deutsch, S.   4682
Deutsches Institut für Urbanistik   3723
Devas, N.   3849
Devere, H.   2853
Devettere, R.   5813
Devine, C.   5395
Devine, P.   659
Devlin, L.   4947
Devlin, R.   5445
Devos, H.   2077, 4054
Devpura, S.   4068
Dew, M.   4562
Dewe, P.   4459
Dex, S.   4325
Dey, I.   306
Deykin, E.   5674
Dhaouadi, M.   55
Dhruvarajan, V.   3114
Diamond, E.   4947
Diamond, I.   2025, 2274, 2352
Diani, M.   1973
Dianin, G.   5403
Díaz-Stevens, A.   1287
Dickey, S.   1600
Dickinson, H.   228

Dickinson, J.   940
Dickman, H.   1799
Dieleman, F.   3376, 3666, 3839
Diener, E.   493, 4052, 4063
Diener, M.   4052
Dierkes, M.   42
Dietrich, G.   2762
Dieuaide, P.   4064
Diewald, M.   2060, 2583
Díezsánchez, J.   3588
Dijk, E. van   3972
Dijk, H. van   3575
Dijk, L.   5528
Dijkink, G.   111, 194
Dijkman, H.   2797
Dillard, J.   696
Dillman, L.   601
Dillon, M.   5440
Dimitrova, S.   1425
Dimmel, N.   5510
Din, A.   3079
Dingemans, P.   5718, 5738
Dinges, N.   5371, 5424
Diniz, E.   4102
Dinnerstein, L.   3055
Dion, K.   2624, 2624
Dion, M.   3123
Diop, M.   3415
Dirks, G.   3410
Dirven, M.   3600
Diskin, I.   4833
Dittgen, A.   2020
Dittmann, A.   3484
Dixon, P.   4428
Dixon, W.   4773
Dixon-Mueller, R.   2761
Djupedal, K.   1528
Dluhošová, H.   3257
Dmitriev, A.   977
Doba, G.   701
Dobash, R.   2480
Dobbelaere, K.   1252, 1280
Dobbin, F.   4258
Dobischat, R.   4539
Döbner, R.   500
Dobry, M.   4757
Dobson, R.   3970
Dobuzinskis, L.   4807

Index des auteurs

Docherty, D. 1449, 1518
Dockrell, J. 502
Doctor, R. 1455
Dodds, K. 5034
Dodge, K. 667
Dodgson, M. 822, 4151
Dogan, M. 4950
Döhler, M. 4543
Dohmen, C. 2876
Dohrenwend, B. 4521
Doig, A. 5186
Doise, W. 408, 1353
Dolce, R. 3180
Dole, R. 4947
Dollinger, S. 586
Dolton, P. 4550
Domański, H. 1872, 2844
Domenach, H. 3255
Domingo, L. 2081
Dominguez Alcón, C. 2054
Donadjè, F. 2286
Donagan, A. 1162
Donahue, E. 580
Donahue, M. 1292
Donald, S. 5460
Donaldson, M. 2896
Donati, P. 188
Donato, K. 3397
Dongen, W. van 4322
Doniol-Shaw, G. 4353
Donnison, D. 3825
Donoghue, D. 3798
Donovan, T. 4212
Dontenwill, E. 4567
Donzelli, M. 404
Donzelot, J. 5052
Dooghe, G. 2052, 2062, 4038
Dooley, R. 1146
Doorne-Huiskes, A. van 2822
Doosje, B. 650, 919
Doran, C. 168
Dorbritz, J. 1970
Dordick, H. 1451
Dorgan, T. 4651
Döring, N. 695
Dorn, R. 491
Doroguntsov, S. 4224
Dorsch-Jungsberger, P. 1523

Dorwart, R. 5401
Dory, D. 1227
Doty, P. 5718, 5738
Doubt, K. 217
Doucet, L. 3531
Dougherty, D. 2125
Dougherty, W. 3604
Doughty, P. 3296
Douglas, A. 2987
Douglas, C. 2754
Douglas, M. 167
Douglas, T. 736
Douthitt, R. 4167
Douyon, E. 3181
Douzinas, C. 5445
Dove, M. 3491
Dovenmuehle, R. 1224
Dowall, D. 3838
Dowd, T. 920
Dowling, P. 4481
Dowling, R. 2746
Dowmunt, T. 1571
Downey, D. 2510
Downey, P. 4947
Downs, W. 5239, 5377
Dowsett, G. 2896, 2995
Drabman, R. 2120
Drage, J. 2853
Draguns, J. 476
Drake, W. 2024
Drapeau, A. 2863
Drapeau, M. 4332
Draper, D. 282
Draper, E. 3450
Draucker, C. 5561
Drbohlav, D. 4222
Dreier, R. 1199
Dressler, W. 5690
Dreu, C. de 953
Drew, P. 671
Drèze, J. 1768
Drigotas, S. 762, 2128
Drissi, Y. 5061
Droit, S. 2118
Dropkin, N. 3308
Drory, A. 956
Droste, F. 1462
Drotner, K. 1574

Author index

Drucker, D. 5612
Drucker, P. 1826
Druen, P. 2624
Drummond, H. 886
Drummond, J. 3593
Drummond, P. 1585
Drzewieniecka, K. 2026
Du Plessis, R. 2741
Dua, H. 1563
Dubin, B. 4992
Dubrow, N. 2112
Ducatel, K. 1457
Ducchiade, M. 2366
Duckitt, J. 417
Duckworth, E. 5403
Ducot, B. 3001
Duden, B. 2217
Dudley, E. 3510
Duff, P. 5222
Duffy, J. 5409, 5426
Dufort, V. 4418
Duggal, R. 5676
Dugger, A. 1668
Dugger, W. 3973
Duhamel, A. 394
Duhl, L. 3654
Duke, J. 280
Duleep, H. 4318
Düll, K. 4429
Dumka, L. 2634
Dumont, G. 2020
Dunaevskii, L. 4110
Dunbar, R. 1369
Duncan, D. 2693
Duncan, G. 856, 2107
Duncan, J. 2456, 3476
Duncan, N. 119
Duncan, S. 3775, 4856, 5063
Duncan, T. 573
Dunegan, K. 521
Dunin-Woyseth, H. 3880
Dunlap, R. 3498
Dunlea, A. 1475
Dunlop, J. 3316
Dunn, D. 2935
Dunn, G. 421
Dunn, K. 3097
Dunnington, R. 340

Dunphy, D. 868
Duong-Tran, Q. 5371, 5424
Dupagne, M. 1554
Dupont, V. 3379
Duprey, P. 4494
Dür, W. 3011
Durance, A. 3737
Durand, G. 114
Durand, J. 284
Durand, R. 284
Dureau, F. 3379
Durham, E. 1805
During, S. 985
Duru-Bellat, M. 1682
Dutka, S. 340
Dutton, J. 525
Duyne, P. van 5129, 5141
Dworak, N. 2249
Dworkin, D. 1634
Dworkin, R. 2226
Dwyer, W. 3436
Dyer, R. 1614, 1617
Dyson, A. 5801
Dyson, M. 1675
Dzienio, K. 2026
Eadie, W. 1449, 1518
Eagle, B. 4252
Eardley, T. 5485
Earley, P. 4408
Earls, F. 2086, 2619
Early, G. 3160
Earp, F. 4206
East, P. 3009
Easterman, D. 1315
Easthope, A. 979, 1012
Eastman, C. 1398, 1408
Eaton, M. 3288
Eaton, W. 3414
Ebaugh, H. 1291
Eberstadt, N. 2019
Ebert, E. 1970
Ebertz, M. 1282
Ebner, M. 3840
Eccles, J. 2125
Eckberg, D. 2549
Eckert, R. 1447, 5434
Eckstein, R. 4205
Ecologist 4944

Index des auteurs

Eddowes, E.   5264, 5323
Eddy, T.   1118
Edelman, L.   4625
Edelstein, A.   1553
Eden, D.   483
Eden, S.   4891
Eder, D.   4928
Eder, K.   4906
Edgell, S.   1879
Edles, L.   122
Edley, N.   1543
Edmiston, J.   3458
Edner, S.   3698
Edwards, D.   1436, 1473
Edwards, H.   1412, 5302
Edwards, J.   340, 1561, 2972, 3744, 4084, 4472
Edwards, K.   691
Edwards, S.   2496
Edwards, T.   2878, 2959
Eecke, C. ver   3142
Eekelaar, J.   5522
Egan, M.   3681
Eggebeen, D.   2531, 3566, 4053, 5318
Egger, M.   2304
Eggers, M.   4059
Eggertsson, T.   200
Eggleston, K.   903
Eglite, P.   4745
Ehrenberg, A.   2967
Ehrhardt, A.   3005
Ehrlich, A.   2188
Ehrlich, E.   1189
Ehrlich, P.   2188
Ehrlich, S.   668
Eiben, J.   1282
Eichler, M.   2941
Eickelman, C.   2273
Einhorn, B.   2724
Eisenschitz, T.   1452
Eisenstadt, S.   1023
Eisinga, R.   922, 3151
Eitzen, D.   1992
Ekamper, P.   4497
Ekblad, S.   3707
Ekins, R.   2907
Ekman, P.   703

Ekoe, J.   1110
Ekström, M.   2068
Elaad, E.   617
Elden, M.   774
Elder, G.   2099, 2607
Eldijk, A. van   3575
Elekes, Z.   5423
Elitzur, A.   5431
Elizaincin, A.   1389
Elizondo, S.   2231
Ellemers, N.   443
Eller, J.   3133
Ellickson, R.   3589
Elliot, N.   2941
Elliot, R.   5810
Elliott, K.   2401
Ellis, C.   257
Ellis, L.   1914
Ellis, M.   3262
Ellis, R.   1440, 1807
Ellison, C.   968, 1249, 1269, 1289
Ellsworth, P.   691
Elman, J.   507
Elman, R.   2931
Elnajjar, H.   3297
Elo, I.   5704
Elraz, Y.   5703
Elsasser, H.   3706
Elsässer, J.   3195
Elsdon, K.   1785
Elster, J.   200, 4754
Elter, I.   3748
Elteren, M. van   404
Eltges, M.   3894
Elton, M.   2355
Ely, S.   2503
D'Emilio, J.   2983
Emke, I.   5668
Empfield, M.   2314
Enama-Markson, L.   5845
Enari, M.   3346
Enchautegui, M.   4023
Encinas Cueto, I.   3081
Endicott, S.   1196
Engberg, L.   4709
Engelen, G.   3644
Engels, H.   2927
Engelstad, P.   774

Author index

Engelsted, N. 418
England, K. 4352
England, P. 2770
English, C. 584
Enkin, M. 5683
Enoch, Y. 5553
Enomoto, K. 5530
Enríquez, L. 3550
Enriquez, V. 378
Entman, R. 1519
Entwisle, B. 237
Entwisle, D. 1656
Epperson, D. 5083
Epps, K. 5094
Epskamp, K. 1619
Epstein, D. 1641
Epstein, M. 2152
Epstein, R. 604
Eräsaari, R. 3513
Erben, M. 228
Ercelawn, A. 4049, 5341
Erez, M. 4408
Erger, J. 909
Erickson, A. 2709
Erickson, P. 5401
Erickson, R. 2593
Eriksen, T. 3118
Eriksson, A. 2655
Erlanger, H. 4625
Erlich, H. 2642
Erneling, C. 148
Ernst, E. 4850
Erwin, K. 2974
Erwin, L. 4905
Erwin, P. 630
Escarce, E. 1475
Eschbach, K. 3032
Escobar, A. 4894
Escobar Latapí, A. 4058
Espenshade, T. 915
Esping-Andersen, G. 1878
Esposito, E. 1446
Esser, H. 2490
Esses, V. 917
Esslezbichler, J. 1459
Esteban, J. 4214
Estèbe, P. 5052
Estrada Diaz, J. 1270

Estrada, L. 1698
Esveldt, I. 5474
Etchelecou, A. 2020
Ethelston, S. 1541
Éthier, L. 2644
Ettner, S. 5734
Etzioni, A. 3965
Eu, H. 3359
European Institute of Urban Affairs 3946
Evandrou, M. 2044
Evans, C. 4480
Evans, D. 2999, 5773
Evans, E. 1639
Evans, G. 200, 1835, 1890, 1894
Evans, J. 382, 510
Evans, Jr., A. 1904
Evans, M. 228, 4037, 4362, 5819
Evans, R. 5306
Eve, M. 1825
Even, W. 4010
Everatt, D. 2129
Everett, J. 583
Everett, K. 4936
Everett, M. 298, 318, 4563
Evers, A. 5508
Evers, H. 1317
Evetts, J. 4541
Exworthy, M. 5777
Ey, S. 2125
Eye, A. von 4735
Eyraud, F. 4321
Fabiani, J. 1626
Fabj, V. 4947
Fabrega, H. 427
Fabrigar, L. 472
Faccioli, F. 5150
Fackler, M. 1520
Fadden, G. 5720, 5840
Faden, R. 5773
Fagan, J. 5116, 5308
Fagan, R. 2534
Fägerborg, E. 4400
Faggi, P. 3438
Fahem, A. 2018
Fainstein, N. 5334
Fainzang, S. 5373
Fairburn, K. 4122

Index des auteurs

Fairchild, H. 361
Fairclough, B. 578
Faist, T. 3050, 3324
Falah, G. 3944
Falco, M. 5401
Falk, P. 2994
Falloon, I. 5720, 5840
Fanfani, E. 5312
Fang, Y. 911
Fanouillet, J. 2020
Fanshel, D. 5603
Fararo, T. 234, 242, 1898
Farchy, J. 1601
Farin, K. 3218, 5438
Farley, R. 3796
Farley, S. 5251
Farmer, P. 2346, 5355
Farnsworth, S. 4437
Farooqui, M. 2340
Farquhar, M. 2058
Farrell, M. 2518, 5406
Farrington, D. 5115, 5140, 5299
Farthing, S. 3774
FASDSP Group 3500
Fasenfest, D. 3508
Fassin, É. 2726
Fattah, E. 5170
Faupel, C. 5038
Fauroux, E. 3379
Favell, A. 127
Favreau, L. 3531
Favretto, A. 5250
Fawzi El-Solh, C. 2650
Fay, L. 2452
Fay, S. 5228
Feddag, A. 1497
Fee, E. 5782
Feeney, G. 2287
Feher, M. 2732
Fehr, H. 4933
Feige, M. 446
Feild, C. 1668
Fein, H. 941
Feinberg, W. 1010
Feingold, A. 471
Feinstein, J. 2332
Feitelson, E. 3742
Feld, B. 5209

Feldblum, M. 3077
Feldman, M. 5146
Feldmann, C. 2285
Felice, M. 3009
Felling, A. 922
Felouzis, G. 2826
Felson, M. 5308
Felson, R. 2908
Felson, S. 2908
Feng, W. 2287
Fenn, R. 1327
Fennell, D. 1283
Fennell, M. 900, 5677
Fenster, A. 2491
Fenster, T. 3530
Ferber, M. 2721
Ferenc, E. 3107, 3113
Ferguson, B. 3754
Ferguson, H. 5066
Ferguson, M. 1043
Fermoso Estebanez, P. 1686
Fernandes, W. 3124
Fernández, D. 3100
Fernhout, R. 3288
Fernós, M. 2523
Ferracuti, S. 5125
Ferrand, A. 3001
Ferrand, M. 51, 4324
Ferraro, G. 5571
Ferrarotti, F. 122, 230, 4680
Ferraz, J. 4565
Ferré, J. 1520
Ferrer Benimeli, J. 1235
Ferrie, J. 2304
Ferrier, J. 3481
Ferris, J. 5647
Fesel, V. 4351, 5615
Fetrow, R. 2633
Feutrie, M. 1588
Feuvre, N. le 4324
Fey, J. 696
Fichtelberg, A. 1475
Fichtenbaum, R. 4246
Fichter, M. 2355
Field, D. 5698
Field, J. 240
Fielding, A. 3372
Fielding, N. 5186

Author index

Fierens, J. 5464
Fiese, B. 2621
Fife, B. 1749
Figley, C. 403, 5021
Figueredo, A. 5087, 5254
Filion, P. 3841
Filippo, E. de 3269
Filippov, A. 44
Fily, B. 5047
Finch, L. 1889
Finch, S. 5603
Fincher, C. 1798
Finckenauer, J. 5265
Findlay, A. 2194
Findlay, P. 4697
Fine, B. 4197
Fine, G. 945, 1423
Fine, M. 2485
Fineman, S. 799, 827
Finke, R. 1247
Finkeldey, L. 4366
Finkelhor, D. 5076
Finlay, A. 2316
Finlayson, S. 5545
Finlinson, H. 5407
Finn, D. 2086
Finney, H. 1850
Finnie, R. 2495
Firat, I. 3340
Firdion, J. 3001
First, P. 1730, 5493
Firth, M. 5586
Fischer, G. 754
Fischer, J. 1170
Fischer, M. 1459
Fischhoff, B. 2125
Fischler, C. 2881
Fisher, C. 4463, 4483
Fisher, D. 3634
Fisher, J. 4593
Fisher, K. 5271
Fisher, M. 5214
Fisher, R. 718, 728
Fisher, S. 3515, 4015, 4739
Fisher, T. 5071
Fishman, W. 3341
Fishwick, C. 5457
Fiske, S. 662, 894

Fitness, J. 702
Fitzclarence, L. 1667
Fitzpatrick, M. 696, 1449, 1518
Fivush, R. 535
Flagg, B. 3241
Flanagan, C. 2125
Flanagan, W. 3655
Flanders, L. 1541
Flannery, M. 1688
Flax, J. 1069
Fleiner-Gerster, T. 2417
Fleising, U. 1335
Fleming, I. 3460
Fleming, J. 575
Fletcher, B. 625
Fletcher, G. 645, 702
Fletcher, J. 3221
Fletcher, P. 4529
Fletcher, R. 2433
Flett, G. 363
Fleurant, N. 3180
Fleurbaey, M. 3974
Fliegel, F. 3558
Flocke, E. 1530
Floge, L. 2829
Flora, C. 3634
Flora, J. 3634
Florczak-Bywalec, J. 4354
Flores, J. 1026
Florian, V. 433, 2411
Flower, M. 1335
Flowerdew, R. 3380
Floyd, M. 4725
Fluder, R. 4668
Foddy, M. 375
Foddy, W. 328
Fodouop, K. 4210
Fogel, A. 2629
Foggin, P. 1110
Foley, M. 1264
Folk, K. 4343
Folse, K. 4970
Fong, G. 520
Fonseca Sobrinho, D. da 2220
Font, M. 4076
Foppa, K. 1365
Foran, J. 219, 1934, 1958, 1974
Forbes, J. 1028

Index des auteurs

Ford, J. 403, 4570, 5021
Ford, R. 3376
Forder, C. 2611
Fordham, G.382Fordham, M. 3085
Forehand, R. 2625
Foreman, K. 1751
Forester, J. 245
Forgatch, M. 2633
Fornaciari, C. 804
Fornäs, J. 1574
Fornel, M. de 5047
Forrester, K. 4690
Forrester, W. 4191
Forsé, M. 1122, 1955
Forster, D. 5646
Förster, E. 2246
Forster, Z. 4106
Forsyth, L. 3883
Fortier, J. 4608
Fortmann, L. 3605
Fosh, P. 4286, 4650, 4675
Fossett, M. 2522
Foster, A. 1999, 5586
Foster, D. 4595
Foster, E. 2292
Foster, P. 1740
Foster, S. 2341
Fosu, A. 3203, 4678
Fosu, G. 949
Fotheringham, A. 4161
Foucault, M. 96
Fought, J. 1462
Fouquet, A. 5048
Fourastié, B. 114
Fournier, G. 3291
Fournier, M. 1836
Fournier, S. 3834
Fox, C. 4629
Fox, E. 648
Fox, R. 2209, 2908
Foxall, G. 4162
Frable, D. 435
Francescato, D. 2488
Franceys, R. 3776, 3903
Francioso, F. 4956
Francis, B. 5652, 5653
Francis, D. 3594
Francis, L. 5814

Francis, R. 4126
Francis X. 2175
Franco, J. 1026
Frandsen, J. 3663
Frank, A. 481
Frank, M. 703
Frank, R. 4771
Frankel, L. 340
Franken, R. 4422
Franklin, M. 2977
Franklin, R. 1906
Franz, E. 3330
Franzén, M. 4724
Franzen, T. 2728
Fraser, J. 1017
Fratoe, F. 4128
Frattini, M. 5450
Frayne, B. 3948
Frazer, J. 1575
Frazer, M. 1659
Frazer, T. 1575
Fréchet, G. 4285, 4879
Freddolino, P. 354
Fredriksson, C. 1574
Freebody, P. 1663
Freed, G. 5756
Freedman, D. 973
Freedman, J. 1333
Freeman, G. 3416
Freeman, L. 729
Freeman, M. 540
Freeman, P. 4721
Freestone, R. 3844
Fregoso, R. 2896
Freij-Dalloz, I. 1201
French, R. 3288
French, S. 248
Frenk, J. 5687
Frenkel, I. 3995
Freriks, R. 4090
Fresneda, O. 3897
Freudenburg, W. 203
Freund, J. 150, 210, 5433
Frevert, U. 12
Frey, B. 200
Frey, J. 576
Frey, M. 2192
Frey, R. 1178

Author index

Fricke, T. 2608
Fricker, C. 3859
Fricker, E. 374
Fridman, D. 5155, 5442
Friedberg, O. di 3415
Friedheim, D. 4791
Friedkin, N. 260
Friedlanger, D. 2285
Friedman, R. 4600
Friedrich, W. 2140
Friedrichs, J. 3839
Friese, H. 92
Frisby, D. 171
Fritzell, J. 4029
Frizzell, E. 5229
Fröhlich, R. 1387, 1515
Froidevaux, D. 757
Fromkin, M. 5053
Fröschl, E. 3089
Frost, M. 3912
Frouws, J. 3596
Frudà, L. 241
Fry, D. 684, 5757
Fry, R. 5396
Fryer, G. 5065, 5317
Fu, G. 4393
Fuchs, D. 3191
Fuchs, L. 3060
Fuchs, S. 145, 1355
Fücks, R. 4904
Fudge, J. 4636
Fuengfusakul, A. 1317
Fuerst, D. 1702
Fuerst, J. 1702
Fujita, H. 1968
Fujita, K. 3934
Fujiwara, T. 3872
Fukada, H. 2846
Fukada, S. 2846
Fukui, K. 3674
Fukui, S. 5404
Fukuoka, S. 3747
Fukurai, H. 2477
Fullan, M. 1701
Fuller, T. 2972, 3744
Fülop, M. 4822
Funabashi, K. 2403
Funder, D. 573

Funk, J. 2452
Funkhouser, E. 3395
Furnham, A. 391, 4436
Fürstenau, U. von 356
Furstenberg, F. 2292
Furuta, Y. 2016
Fuszara, M. 1211
Gabaccia, D. 3348
Gabbert, W. 3126
Gabriel, K. 1282
Gabriel, Y. 827
Gade, P. 4996
Gadzhiev, K. 5018
Gaffin, D. 3466
Gage-Brandon, A. 2560, 2924
Gahr, W. 3634
Gaiger, L. 3616
Gailey, C. 4732
Gaillard, S. 4439
Gailliard, F. 5047
Gaiser, W. 2136
Gal, S. 1376
Galaskiewicz, J. 260
Galbraith, J. 4009
Gale, F. 3463
Galenkamp, M. 455
Galin, K. 675
Galinsky, M. 768
Gall, L. 1979
Gallagher, A. 1697
Gallagher, D. 4657
Gallagher, S. 2441
Galland, O. 1122
Gallant, M. 2944
Gallaway, L. 4014
Galle, O. 3303
Gallery, M. 4459
Gallois, C. 673, 696, 1436, 1488, 3015
Gallup, G. 1118
Gally, M. 5047
Galster, G. 3243, 5353
Galston, W. 603
Galtung, J. 1975
Galzer, N. 3060
Gama, K. de 2740
Gamage, D. 1737
Gambetta, D. 5158

Index des auteurs

Gambrill, E. 5557
Gamson, W. 4900
Gandhi, N. 2749
Gane, M. 633
Gange, J. 2987
Gangestad, S. 393, 548
Gängler, H. 5616
Gani, L. 2018
Gans, H. 1519, 5334
Gans, R. 3527
Ganßmann, H. 4827
Gao, X. 3731
Garain, S. 846
Garasky, S. 2511
Garbarino, J. 2112
García Alvarado, J. 5326
Garcia, C. 2532
García Delgado, J. 999
García Durán, J. 4214
Garcia, E. 1698
Garcia-Ramon, M. 2669
Garde, A. 4496
Garde, R. De La 1120
Gardiner, M. 165
Gardner, F. 2115
Gardner, H. 439
Gardner, P. 1654
Gardner, S. 1730, 5493
Gareau, F. 13
Garfinkel, I. 2435, 2504, 5521
Garibaldi, P. 4267
Garibi, J. 3941
Garland, A. 2125
Gärling, T. 3431
Garner, M. 4103
Garner, P. 2223, 2270
Garnett, L. 2143
Garnham, N. 1527
Garrahan, P. 4525
Garrison, C. 2147
Garrison, J. 1688
Garrison, R. 3414
Garside, P. 5272
Gartrell, J. 3489
Garvin, J. 1730, 5493
Garvin, P. 1371
Gash, L. 5006
Gaskell, G. 950

Gassler, H. 1459
Gastil, J. 723
Gateaux-Mennecier, J. 404
Gates, L. 4441
Gates, M. 3619
Gates, S. 4409
Gatrell, A. 5652, 5653
Gatzweiler, H. 2015, 2027, 3894
Gaudier, M. 4042
Gaulin, S. 2648
Gauthier, A. 2201
Gavanski, I. 392
Gavi, P. 1080
Gavre, J. 2473
Gawanas, B. 2786
Gay, G. 1698
Gay, J. 5657
Gay, P. 5137
Gay, P. du 4184
Gaylord, M. 5386
Gboku, M. 3506
Gebhardt, W. 802
Gecas, V. 576
Geddes, D. 432
Geer, J. 5088
Geer, J. Van De 294
Gehrke, N. 1730, 5493
Geiger, R. 1808
Geiger, S. 1519
Geis, G. 2624, 5175
Geisler, C. 3582
Geißler, C. 2192
Geletta, S. 3607
Gellert, G. 3409, 3925
Gelles, R. 5245
Gellner, W. 1511
Gely, R. 4585
Gentry, R. 5452
George, A. 5676
George, J. 4437
George, L. 489
George, P. 2020
George, S. 3022
Georges, C. 2018
Georgiou, G. 2998
Gephart, W. 142
Geraci, S. 3394
Gerard, D. 1149

Author index

Gerhard, U. 1938
Gerhards, J. 3191
Gerholm, L. 336
Germain, A. 3815
Gern, C. 4877
Gerns, C. 4947
Gerő, A. 1849
Gerritsen, L. 2163
Gerstel, N. 2441
Gertler, M. 4146
Gerton, J. 1031
Gervais, M. 4210
Gervais, R. 4210
Gervais-Lambony, P. 3702
Geschwender, J. 4512
Gesler, W. 3496
Geurts, J. 4745
Geus, F. 1619
Geyer, H. 3942
Ghai, D. 1947
Ghosh, A. 908
Ghosh, B. 3384
Ghoshal, S. 4114
Ghuman, P. 3109
Giacalone, R. 437
Giami, A. 404, 3001
Gibb, R. 5012
Gibbon, P. 4056
Gibelman, M. 5628
Gibney, M. 3055
Gibson, K. 4422
Gibson, P. 2956
Gibson, R. 2956
Gibson, T. 5100
Giddens, A. 1833
Gieth, F. 4274
Giffen, P. 1196
Gigone, D. 716
Gilbert, M. 602
Gilbert, N. 264
Gilbert, P. 373, 1405
Gilbertson, G. 3030
Gilcher-Holtey, I. 4860
Giles, H. 1436
Gilkey, R. 680, 759
Gill, B. 3
Gill, C. 4712
Gill, J. 854, 855

Gill, L. 2909
Gill, O. 2640
Gill, R. 3521
Gillet, G. 5814
Gillett, G. 514
Gilliand, P. 2417
Gilling, D. 5106
Gilmore, R. 3027
Gilmore, S. 1629
Gilroy, P. 3029, 3087
Gilsdorf, W. 1120
Gilson, C. 4579
Giner, S. 210
Ginsburg, G. 607
Gintis, H. 4119
Giordano, P. 2135
Girard, C. 3113, 5422
Giri, A. 272
Girod, I. 3007
Giroux, H. 1675
Gísli, P. 975
Gist, M. 4592
Gittell, R. 3871
Giulio, A. 3048, 3113
Giunta, C. 2550
Gjurgjan, L. 2831
Glance, N. 301
Glaser, B. 2459
Glaser, W. 5749, 5783
Glastonbury, B. 5709
Glatzer, W. 4036
Glavanis, K. 2780
Glazer, N. 4264
Glazychev, V. 3686
Gleason, J. 5390
Gleason, S. 4705
Glendenning, F. 5046
Glenn, J. 3781
Glenn, P. 623, 759
Glenwick, D. 560
Glick, C. 4223
Glickman, M. 2119
Glinkina, S. 4261
Glock, C. 1247
Gloria-Bottini, F. 2289
Glorieux, I. 4745
Gloster, S. 2190
Glover, D. 1762

Index des auteurs

Glynn, S.   4492
Gober, P.   3752
Gobo, G.   1880
Godard, J.   4611
Godbey, G.   4735
Godbey, K.   4447
Goddard, M.   5660
Godefroy, T.   5096
Godelier, M.   1025
Godschalk, J.   5516
Goeke, J.   5040
Goertzel, B.   405
Goetting, A.   2646
Goetting, M.   2646
Goggin, M.   2243
Goh, D.   933
Gołata, E.   2008
Golbert, L.   5312
Gold, M.   755
Gold, T.   1002
Goldberg, D.   3228
Goldberg, E.   1330
Goldberg, T.   2275
Goldberger, M.   2020, 5052
Golden, A.   4947
Golden, J.   4947
Golden, O.   5494
Goldenberg, S.   152
Golding, D.   206
Golding, S.   2987
Goldman, D.   5371, 5424
Goldman, E.   2315
Goldman, H.   146
Goldman, L.   1015
Goldman, N.   2362
Goldscheider, C.   1950, 2649
Goldscheider, F.   2446, 2649
Goldstein, M.   2074
Goldstein, S.   4640
Golembiewski, R.   4455
Golledge, R.   3431
Golod, S.   2996
Golub, A.   2344
Gomery, D.   1449, 1518
Gomes, C.   1751
Gómez, M.   3559
Gomperts, W.   571
Gonäs, L.   2824

Gönczöl, K.   5091
Gonik, N.   2245
Gonzales, A.   1561
González, A.   2304
González de la Rocha, M.   4058
Gonzalez del Valle, A.   4970
González, J.   1698
Good, B.   5371, 5424
Goodchild, M.   3454
Goode, D.   5707, 5831
Gooding, D.   1338
Gooding-Williams, R.   3176
Goodkind, D.   2527
Goodman, D.   5070
Goodman, J.   4711
Goodrich, P.   1188, 5445
Goodson, S.   5371, 5424
Goodwin, D.   5085, 5301
Goodwin, J.   1958, 5270
Goodwin, M.   4856
Goor, H. van   285
Gopaul-McNicol, S.   3206
Gorbach, P.   2227
Gordon, D.   5460
Gordon, L.   4612, 4627, 4681
Gordon, P.   3866
Gore, J.   1690
Gorman, J.   973
Gormley, W.   5533
Gornig, M.   3894
Gorr, W.   2344
Gorroñogoitia González, A.   4710
Gorsuch, R.   487
Gorter, A.   2304
Göschel, A.   1049
Gospel, H.   4492
Goss, J.   4180, 4186
Gosselin, G.   312
Gossiaux, J.   3177
Gössmann, E.   2701
Gostkowski, Z.   2382, 3940, 5635
Gotchev, A.   41
Goto, K.   4455
Goto, S.   3590
Gottdiener, M.   178
Gottesmann, M.   5600
Gottfried, H.   2788
Gottlieb, B.   2422

Author index

Gottschild, H. 3778, 5507
Gould, E. 1660
Gould, P. 2344
Gould, R. 715
Govier, T. 626, 674
Gowricharn, R. 1172
Goyder, J. 4000
Graaf, N. de 1900, 4962
Graaff, J. 222
Grabb, E. 1020
Graber, D. 4947
Grabmüller, U. 2716
Grace, D. 2987
Gracia, D. 5811
Grady, W. 2162
Graetz, K. 762
Graff, H. 1666
Graham, H. 2843, 5654
Graham, L. 2788, 4094
Graham, S. 3645
Graicer, I. 3537
Gramann, J. 4725
Grammer, K. 2945
Grandjean, N. 2997
Grange, C. 1122, 2568
Grant, D. 4047
Grant, G. 3060, 4552
Grant, K. 2125
Grant, P. 718
Grant, S. 2086
Grasmick, H. 2652, 5105, 5166
Grasso, G. 1195
Grauer, V. 1628
Grawert, E. 3499
Gray, A. 1980
Gray, J. 1717, 4771
Gray, L. 1432, 2669
Gray, M. 5063
Gray, R. 2247
Grayson, J. 4153
Graziano, W. 664
Greaves, D. 403, 5021
Greed, C. 2828
Greek, C. 28
Greeley, A. 1243, 2908
Green, B. 593, 5000
Green, D. 279
Green, G. 358

Green, M. 4202
Green, P. 2869
Green, R. 4857
Green, S. 4410
Green, W. 4074
Greenberg, H. 287
Greenberg, J. 581
Greene, J. 432
Greene, M. 2547, 5226, 5304
Greene, V. 5462
Greenfeld, A. 459
Greenhalgh, L. 680, 759
Greenspan, L. 3236
Greenstein, R. 3136
Greenwood, D. 774
Greenwood, M. 3286
Greer, J. 1224
Gregersen, H. 38
Gregg, D. 2045
Grégoire, E. 3379
Gregson, N. 2838
Greif, G. 2636, 5579
Greifeneder, M. 2655
Grémy, J. 76, 349
Grenier, M. 1509
Gresov, C. 788
Gribble, J. 2248
Grieco, M. 4651
Griensven, G. van 2978
Griffin, K. 3617
Griffith, D. 3800
Griffiths, L. 5701
Griffiths, R. 3864
Grift, Y. 4322
Grigg, D. 1105
Grigor'ev, O. 4270
Grimes, P. 2938
Grimes, S. 2250, 3806
Grimm, J. 1612
Grimsbo, R. 5182, 5367
Grimwood, C. 5630
Grin, F. 1384, 1418
Gringeri, C. 3628
Grint, K. 4714
Grize, J. 150, 210
Grogan, C. 5761
Gronow, J. 1126, 1129
Groome, D. 4737

Index des auteurs

Groot, J. de   68
Groppenbacher, N.   2634
Grosby, S.   1227
Grosclaude, P.   3909
Gross, M.   3131
Grossbard-Shechtman, S.   2584
Grossberg, L.   1519
Grossin, W.   4451
Grossman, M.   570, 5360
Groth, A.   448
Groth, G.   2561
Groth-Marnat, G.   462
Grove, D.   3212
Grover, S.   901
Grubb, W.   4069
Gruenwald, O.   986
Grummer-Strawn, L.   2353
Grundmann, S.   2192
Grundy, J.   5603
Grüner, H.   4281
Grunig, J.   1449, 1518
Grützmann, K.   296
Gryn, H.   3049
Grześkowiak-Łuczyk, E.   3167
Gu, S.   2074
Guba, G.   1730, 5493
Gubry, P.   2199
Guchteneire, P. de   1948
Gudjonsson, G.   388, 4816
Guedj, M.   5047
Guérin, B.   414
Guérin, V.   2199
Guest, A.   3342
Guggenberger, B.   1523
Guichaoua, A.   209
Guidicini, P.   5327
Guilkey, D.   2330
Guillemard, A.   2037, 2054, 4255, 4411
Guillén Sadaba, M.   5338
Guillon, M.   2020
Guilloux, K.   5778
Guilmoto, C.   3379
Guimarães, A.   1853
Guit, H.   2163
Gulati, L.   3273
Gulley, M.   2624
Gunasekaran, S.   3421

Gunderson, M.   5814
Gunn, S.   4250
Gunther, R.   4820
Guo, F.   3295
Guo, G.   2353, 2370, 2386
Guo, S.   5226, 5304
Gupta, D.   1307
Gupta, G.   2346, 5355
Gupta, K.   2917
Gupta, S.   1604
Gurak, D.   3030
Gurevitch, M.   1519
Guri-Rozenblit, S.   1750
Gurtman, M.   546
Gustavsen, B.   774, 4477
Gutiérrez, P.   1008
Gutmann, A.   1703
Gutmann, M.   2888
Guy, S.   4465
Guzzo, R.   766
Gwenlan, C.   5543
Gyimah-Brempong, K.   4246
Ha, M.   3567
Haag, G.   296
Haaken, J.   632
Haaland, B.   2730
Haan, H. de   3596
Haan, J. de   70
Haar, J. Vander   2288
Haas, A.   1859
Haas, E.   404
Haas, S.   3011
Haastrup, L.   5707, 5831
Haberfeld, Y.   3268
Habermann, U.   5629
Habermas, J.   500, 1157
Habermeier, J.   1442
Hachmann, C.   3734
Hackett, B.   3450
Häckl, G.   4670
Hackman, J.   1775
Hadden, J.   1247
Haddock, G.   917
Hadicke-Wiley, M.   1475
Hadley, R.   5646
Haegel, F.   3699
Haëntjens, C.   4353
Hafner-Eaton, C.   5761

Author index

Hagan, J. 2041, 5105, 5308
Hage, J. 826
Hagen, J. 5531
Hagen, U. 1730, 5493
Hagendoorn, L. 3045
Hagihara, K. 2014, 3364, 3747
Hague, D. 871
Hague, G. 5240
Hahn, B. 2311
Hahn, W. 4195
Haimes, E. 2239
Haines, F. 4444
Hakim, C. 4292, 4292
Hakim, S. 5133
Hakken, D. 4403
Hakkert, R. 1987
Hakvoort, I. 2097
Halaby, C. 54
Halász, G. 1751
Halbach, G. 4631
Hales, C. 858
Halfacree, K. 3248
Halfmann, J. 4898, 4899
Halford, S. 4856
Halfpenny, P. 1457
Hall, A. 4406
Hall, B. 244
Hall, C. 1021
Hall, E. 2851, 2913
Hall, L. 3672
Hall, M. 3672, 5448, 5750, 5767
Hall, P. 3839
Hall, R. 244, 943, 4116
Hall, S. 3085
Hall, T. 1927
Halle, D. 1111
Haller, M. 23
Hallin, D. 1558
Hallman, W. 3430
Hallmark, B. 767
Hallock, M. 4682
Halman, L. 1280
Halmari, H. 5009
Halpern, C. 705
Halpern, M. 900
Halpern, S. 5700
Hambleton, R. 3856
Hamburg, D. 2506

Hamburger, F. 2141
Hamel, J. 229
Hamel, P. 4862
Hamilton, B. 5249
Hamilton, E. 2680
Hamilton, M. 1881
Hamm, B. 910
Hamm, M. 5090
Hammer, T. 4658
Hammersley, M. 58, 250
Hammond, D. 4727
Hammond, P. 1247, 3138
Hammond, W. 2125
Hampton, B. 5220
Hampton, J. 603
Han, X. 1341
Hancké, B. 4689
Hancock, K. 4606
Hand, D. 421
Handler, R. 1022
Handley, M. 3464
Handy, J. 3507
Hanes, J. 3842
Haney, W. 4341
Hanks, H. 5586
Hanmer, J. 5177, 5449
Hannah, L. 3756
Hannah, M. 89
Hannan, B. 374
Hannan, K. 2627
Hannan, M. 4232
Hannerz, U. 1053
Hansen, A. 1526
Hansen, C. 4448
Hansen, D. 5080
Hansen, P. 4785
Hanser, C. 3706
Hanson, R. 5761
Hansson, D. 5044
Hantrais, L. 2814
Hanushek, E. 5476
Harada, K. 1810
Harakas, S. 5829
Harbaugh, C. 2074
Harber, K. 403, 5021
Hardes, H. 4630
Hardesty, C. 3540
Hardin, R. 115, 604, 4771

Index des auteurs

Hardoy, J. 3664
Hardy, M. 308
Hare, R. 5798
Haribabu, E. 1342
Harkavy, I. 774
Harkess, S. 352
Harkreader, S. 4340
Harman, H. 2862
Haroche, C. 610
Harper, C. 1254
Harpman, T. 2223, 2270
Harpster, P. 2559
Harrell, S. 1565
Harris Bond, M. 4179
Harris, C. 3059, 3076, 4266
Harris, D. 1185
Harris, J. 5801, 5812
Harris, K. 5356
Harris, M. 3190
Harris, N. 1724, 1755
Harris, P. 2612
Harris, R. 4702, 5536, 5550, 5601, 5609
Harris, S. 790, 2317
Harris, T. 5414, 5428
Harrison, B. 228
Harrison, D. 2323, 2823
Harrison, J. 810
Harrison, L. 5359, 5555
Harrison, R. van 4472
Hart, B. 5245
Hart, J. de 285, 1234
Hart, S. 971
Hart, T. 3834
Hartley, D. 5100
Hartley, P. 637, 5108
Hartmann, M. 4551, 4553
Hartnett, J. 3729
Harukiyo, H. 4673
Harvey, A. 4745
Harvey, E. 4256
Harvey, J. 4420
Harvey, S. 1589
Harvie, C. 4641
Harwood, V. 2988
Hasan, S. 3637
Hasell, M. 2671
Hasenfeld, Y. 926

Hashimoto, A. 321
Hashizume, D. 72
Hashtroudi, S. 541
Hassard, J. 865, 889, 4096
Hassim, S. 2425, 2750, 2782
Hassink, R. 3839
Hassoun, J. 3332, 4011
Haste, H. 2911
Hastie, R. 716, 741, 754
Hastings, J. 5563
Hatch, M. 668
Hatcher, S. 5586
Hatfield, B. 5852
Hathaway, J. 3913
Hathaway, W. 4928
Hauff, E. 3335
Haugen, M. 4341
Haunschild, P. 4095
Hauptmanns, P. 4090
Hausjell, F. 1523
Hausman, D. 4771
Häußermann, H. 3855, 4219
Haveman, H. 825, 4176
Haveman, R. 2318, 2458
Haver, W. 1069
Hawkins, B. 4721
Hawkins, G. 5308
Hawkins, J. 5694
Hawkins, K. 1210
Haworth, R. 5094
Hay, D. 3601
Hay, M. 845
Hayashi, C. 273
Hayashi, N. 711
Hayashi, T. 1336
Hayden, M. 1800
Haydon, G. 1703
Hayes, B. 1858, 2449, 2841
Hayes, D. 1530
Hayes, P. 1903, 4915
Haynes, D. 4873
Haynes, K. 506
Hays, S. 3932
Hays-Mitchell, M. 4137
Hayter, R. 4236
Hayward, B. 2853
Hayward, M. 288
He, A. 1403

Author index

He, Y. 1603
Headey, B. 2307, 5819
Head-König, A. 3613
Heady, B. 4017
Healey, P. 3824
Heath, A. 4975
Heath, D. 1335, 5401
Heatherton, T. 595, 600
Heaton, T. 2265
Hechter, M. 1081
Heck, R. 1739
Heckathorn, D. 714
Hecke, E. van 3305, 3358
Hecker, S. 4682
Heckman, J. 2262
Heckmann, F. 3150
Hedemand, V. 5707, 5831
Hedgcock, D. 3889
Hedlund, H. 4077
Hedström, P. 4513
Heesacker, M. 5206
Heffley, D. 5644
Hegar, R. 2636, 5579
Hegedüs, J. 3748
Hegener, W. 2947
Heide, K. 5077, 5296
Heidenreich, M. 4140
Heijden, P. van der 270
Heikes, E. 339
Heilbroner, R. 3973
Heimbach-Steins, M. 1131
Hein, J. 3060, 3302
Hein, M. 772
Heineberg, H. 3941
Heinelt, H. 3330, 4385
Heinemeier, S. 4395
Heinen, J. 2208
Heinink, A. 1753
Heins, V. 1282
Heintz, B. 1359
Heinz, K. 2558
Heinze, R. 3581
Heise, D. 242
Heisler, J. 4216
Heitlinger, A. 2714
Hekman, S. 1069
Held, V. 2738
Helleman, J. 4322

Hellemans, S. 5461
Heller, F. 4252
Helly, D. 3272
Helmchen, H. 2048
Helmius, A. 2655
Helton, A. 3055
Helzer, J. 5361
Henderson, J. 3968
Henderson, K. 4726
Henderson, M. 2641
Henderson, P. 3594
Hendrick, H. 2092
Hendrickson, M. 3607
Hendry, J. 1054
Hendry, L. 2172
Henifin, M. 5773
Henke, K. 5520
Henkel, D. 4364, 5364
Henkens, K. 4278, 4322, 4337
Hennessy, R. 2756
Hennig, E. 5435
Hennig, W. 2140
Hennis, W. 159
Henretta, J. 2064
Henripin, J. 2017
Henriques, U. 3065
Henry, E. 3929
Henson, D. 2545
Henze, J. 1694
Heper, M. 1047, 5032
Herbert, D. 3504, 5138
Herbert, M. 2124
Herbst, I. 3748
Herbst, S. 1519, 1545
Herbstein, F. 1742, 1813
Herden, G. 313
Herek, G. 5002
Hérin, R. 2020
Heritage, J. 671
Hermalin, A. 2230, 2272
Herman, C. 595
Hermann, T. 4887
Hermans, H. 588
Hermansson, G. 5572
Hermer, P. 511
Hernandez, D. 2087
Herpin, N. 1122, 5324
Herring, C. 2867

Index des auteurs

Herron, S. 5499
Herszberg, B. 3182
Hertz-Lazarovits, R. 742
Herzbrun, M. 1329
Herzog, H. 1118, 3286
Hesse, J. 5520
Hessing, M. 2901
Hetherington, P. 2777
Hettige, S. 842, 3448, 3546, 4265
Heun, H. 2142, 3278
Heuvel, W. van den 2395
Heuwinkel, D. 2192
Heuzé, G. 3379
Hewitt, C. 4888
Hewitt, K. 3941
Hewitt, P. 2397
Hewstone, M. 747
Heye, C. 4272
Heyink, J. 233
Heyliger, W. 4198, 4207
Heyneman, S. 1751
Hezel, F. 2339
Hezel, S. 2175
Hibberd, M. 5174, 5447
Hickel, R. 4065
Hicks, J. 2846
Hickson, J. 5595
Higgins, E. 515
Higgins, M. 1949
Hikita, S. 1257
Hildebrandt, R. 4388
Hildenbrand, B. 2530
Hill, C. 2624
Hill, J. 1490
Hill, L. 4825
Hill, R. 2528, 3934, 5268
Hill, T. 121, 603
Hillebrand, H. 3596
Hillman, S. 5389
Hilpert, K. 2899
Hilton, N. 5069
Himbara, D. 3981
Himonga, C. 2704
Hinde, P. 4320
Hinde, R. 611
Hindman, H. 4655
Hines, S. 4846
Hirabayashi, L. 3132, 3659

Hirakawa, T. 5678
Hirano, H. 994
Hiremath, J. 3056
Hirlinger, M. 3828
Hiroshi, Y. 1213
Hirschhorn, L. 835
Hirschl, T. 2003
Hirszowicz, M. 1881
Hishongwa, N. 4404
Hitzler, R. 1109, 1282, 3018, 4792
Hoang, C. 5047
Hobart, C. 2562
Hobbs, C. 2357
Hobdell, K. 5092
Hobhouse, L. 1966
Hoch, C. 3225
Hochheimer, J. 1545
Hockey, J. 2057
Hodges, J. 282
Hodgins, D. 5369
Hodgins, H. 364
Hodgkinson, F. 5306
Hodgkinson, P. 400
Hodgson, D. 3276
Hodson, D. 1688
Hodson, R. 4713
Hoelsen, C. 970
Hoem, B. 2252
Hoeven, R. Van Der 5342
Hofer, M. 689
Hoff, L. 2595
Höffer-Mehlmer, M. 2141
Hoffman, J. 804
Hoffman, M. 3748, 3754
Hoffman, R. 4670
Hoffman, S. 277, 2292
Hoffman, T. 1284
Hoffmann, D. 5806
Hoffmann, J. 4670
Hoffmann, O. 3608
Hoffmann-Nowotny, H. 2192
Hoffmeister, D. 2178
Hofmeister, B. 3941
Hofstede, G. 4179
Hogan, D. 2531
Hoge, D. 1271
Hogg, B. 5543
Hogg, D. 5706

Author index

Hogg, M.   733, 766, 767
Hoggart, K.   3627
Hohn, A.   3740
Hohn, U.   3740
Hoinacki, L.   2217
Hokanson, J.   574
Holdren, D.   4198, 4207
Holenstein, A.   3542
Holland, C.   567
Holland, J.   3002, 3020
Hollander, P.   1975
Holliday, R.   2448
Hollifield, J.   3415
Hollows, A.   2116
Holmberg, D.   2537
Holmes, C.   3341
Holmes, H.   2239
Holmes, J.   658
Holmes, M.   1674
Holt, E.   1409
Holt, G.   873
Holterman, T.   5100
Holtmann, D.   910
Holtug, N.   5809
Holtz, R.   767
Holtz-Bacha, C.   1387, 1515
Holyoak, K.   403, 5021
Holzer, H.   4387
Homedes, N.   5675
Hondagneu-Sotelo, P.   245
Honderich, T.   125
Honey, S.   936
Hoogendoorn, L.   5643
Hooimeijer, P.   3376
Hooke, S.   2834
Hooke, W.   2834
Hooker, K.   2621
Hooker, V.   990
Hooks, B. 1675, 2700, 2869
Hookway, C.   513
Hooper-Briar, K.   1730, 5493
Hoorens, V.   470
Hopf, C.   4982
Hopkins, A.   5631, 5667
Hopmeyer, E.   5545
Hopper, J.   2487
Hopstaken, L.   650
Hoque, M.   3360

Hore, C.   1611
Horgan, T.   374
Horgby, B.   3040
Hörisch, J.   1456
Horm-Wingerd, D.   3434
Horn, R.   315
Horne, A.   2459
Horne, D.   927
Horne, M.   3576
Hörner, W.   1694
Hornik, J.   2564
Hornsby-Smith, M.   1264
Horowitz, A.   2261
Horowitz, I.   2908
Horton, J.   4772
Horton, R.   1239, 1345
Horwitz, A.   2399, 5847
Hosoya, T.   3592
Hosseini, J.   340
Hotta, M.   404
Houghton, D.   3280
Houle, D.   606
Houle, L.   566
Hours, B.   5778
House, R.   902
Hout, M.   1893
Houten, H. van   2163
Houtman, D.   4382
Houtsonen, J.   1322
Howard, D.   2759
Howard, J.   2624
Howe, M.   537
Howell, P.   1032
Howenstine, E.   2006
Howes, M.   530
Howison, J.   5223
Howitt, R.   3535
Hoyle, R.   485
Hoyt, D.   2516
Hoz, R.   4552
Hrdy, S.   2406
Hrusakova, M.   2499
Hryniewiecki, J.   4418
Hser, Y.   56
Hu, T.   5692
Hubbard, P.   3891
Hubbell, L.   2918
Huber, E.   5492

Index des auteurs

Huber, K. 82
Huberman, B. 301
Hubinger, V. 3969
Huck, S. 2516
Hücker, F. 4501
Huddy, L. 2787
Hudson, B. 1633, 5149, 5215
Hudson, J. 535
Huebner, E. 438
Huffman, T. 5786
Hughes, B. 5741
Hughes, D. 5701
Hughes, G. 4517
Hughes, H. 3690
Hughes, R. 992
Hugo, G. 3424
Hugon, P. 3927
Huissoud, T. 2179
Hulbert, D. 2597
Hulsbergen, E. 3829
Human, L. 4242
Hummel, R. 1523
Hummer, R. 2375
Hummon, D. 3252, 3524
Hummon, N. 764
Humphrey, C. 3565
Humphrey, J. 4598
Humphrey, N. 381
Humphrey, R. 228
Humphreys, K. 5041
Humphries, R. 3922
Hundley, G. 4018
Hüning, H. 1970
Hunt, A. 162, 353
Hunt, G. 3286, 5183
Hunter, A. 1294, 4041
Hunter, B. 5672
Hunter, J. 4334, 5085, 5301
Hunter, L. 4260
Hunter, M. 5244
Huo, Y. 1176, 4252, 4252
Huppert, F. 5655
Hurh, W. 3323
Hurlbert, J. 765
Hurrelmann, K. 2139
Hurtado, A. 3084
Hurwitz, L. 4547
Husband, C. 3139

Husch, J. 5401
Husén, T. 1751
Huspek, M. 163
Hussain, A. 4393
Hussain, S. 103
Hüssen, H. 3630
Hussey, A. 4125
Huster, E. 4065
Huston, T. 2624
Hutcheson, F. 1164
Hutchison, D. 1763
Hutter, B. 4440
Huxley, P. 5710, 5852
Hy, R. 4564
Hyams, B. 4667
Hyatt, D. 2256
Hybel, A. 5707, 5831
Hyde, J. 2966
Hye, K. 2043
Hyle, P. 2955
Hyman, M. 1165
Iakovets, I. 255
Ianitskii, O. 3446
Iannaccone, L. 1247
Iannello, K. 879
Ibarra, H. 834
Ibarra, M. 3124
Ibrahim, F. 3485
Ibrahim, P. 3124
Ibraz, T. 2790
Ickes, W. 573, 2624
Ide, S. 1479
Iglicka, K. 2291, 2301
Ignagni, K. 5761
Ignatczyk, W. 2430
Ihl, O. 3699
Ijima, N. 3451
Ikado, F. 1233
Ikels, C. 2074, 5718, 5738
Ikerd, J. 3634
Ikoshi, K. 996
Illingworth, K. 597
Ima, M. 3073
Imbert, F. 51
Imershein, A. 2323
Imhof, K. 3074
Imrie, R. 2309, 3847
Ingalsbee, T. 4928

407

Author index

Inger, I. 2409
Inglis, F. 984
Ingram, A. 5168
Ingram, P. 4676
Inkeles, A. 4031
Inman, M. 620
D'Innocenzo, M. 3055
Inoue, M. 4475
Insko, C. 762
Institut de l'Enfance et de Famille France 3121
Institut de recherches et d'études sur le monde arabe et musulman 3289
Institute of Medicine, U.S, Committee on Monitoring Access to Personal 5632
International Labour Office 4293
Intriligator, M. 5761
Ion, J. 5052, 5587
Ipsen, D. 4639
Iredale, R. 3266
Ironmonger, D. 2025
Irvine, J. 1022, 1490
Irwin, S. 4384
Isaac, T. 4108
Isambert, F. 1160
Isaza, F. 3741, 3843
Isely, B. 2941
Isham, J. 533
Ishida, Y. 3539, 3747, 3880
Ishikawa, H. 321
Islam, M. 747
Isobe, T. 3747
Isomursu, A. 2040
Israel, J. 3182
Israelashvili, M. 5572
Isserman, A. 2028, 3834
Iten, R. 3914
Iurdanskii, V. 3111
Ivani-Chalian, C. 2079
Ivanov, V. 5016
Ivekovic, R. 2799
Ivison, D. 4770
Iwai, N. 2603
Iwai, T. 3526
Iwulski, J. 4660
Iyebi-Mandjek, O. 3379
Iyengar, S. 4753

Izard, C. 572
Jackson, D. 1688
Jackson, E. 2480, 2725, 5690
Jackson, F. 374
Jackson, J. 424, 3436, 5078
Jackson, K. 2147
Jackson, L. 1654
Jackson, P. 3108, 4510
Jackson, R. 3264, 5735
Jackson, S. 2121
Jackson, T. 3796
Jacob, A. 377
Jacobs, J. 4355, 5089
Jacobs, P. 3762
Jacobs Quadrel, M. 2125
Jacobs, R. 4435
Jacobson, K. 469
Jacobson, L. 1677
Jacquemot, P. 5776
Jacques, G. 5611
Jacques, W. 4947
Jacquet, A. 2118
Jacquot, A. 2020
Jafari, M. 5559
Jaffe, E. 841, 4132
Jaffee, M. 1232
Jager, J. 2303
Jäger, S. 997, 3202
Jaggi, Y. 3696
Jaglin, S. 3642
Jahn, D. 4669
Jahn, T. 3
Jain, A. 5665
Jain, S. 2322
Jaising, I. 3500
Jaklitsch, B. 5279
Jalbert, J. 4970
Jamal, H. 2257
James, A. 2057, 2095
James, E. 1765
James, S. 2769
James, W. 3059, 4589, 5563
Jamieson, L. 5157, 5230
Jamison, C. 4713
Jamuna, D. 399
Janelli, D. 4104
Janelli, R. 4104
Janiszewski, L. 4061

Index des auteurs

Janney, R.   1479
Jans, B.   2416
Jans, L.   650
Jansen, A.   3662
Jansen, H.   3512, 4904
Jansen, L.   1282
Janssens, A.   2514
Jansweijer, R.   4322
Januschek, F.   997, 3202
Janzen, H.   5572
Japaz, J.   1895
Japp, K.   4898
Jarman, A.   3819
Jarman, M.   5527
Jarosz, L.   3435
Jarousse, J.   1682
Jarratt, D.   4160
Jarvis, P.   1696, 1783
Jary, D.   73
Jary, J.   73
Jasieńska, G.   2275
Jasinski, J.   1449, 1518
Jasper, J.   4884
Jasso, G.   242
Jaworski, A.   1414
Jaworski, G.   4778
Jaworski, R.   2711
Jaya, N.   4298
Jayakody, R.   2427
Jayamanne, L.   1608
Jayaram, N.   1801
Jayaweera, S.   4500
Jazdowska, N.   2786
Jeanjean, H.   4876
Jeannic, T.   2020
Jecker, N.   5755
Jedel, M.   4252
Jeeves, A.   3609
Jefferson, T.   4789
Jeffery, C.   5308
Jeffreys, S.   2979
Jehn, K.   618, 759
Jelen, C.   3327
Jelen, T.   1266, 2210, 4988
Jendrek, M.   2521
Jenkins, A.   5145
Jenkins, M.   5219
Jenks, C.   987, 1076

Jennings, B.   5773
Jennings, K.   1650
Jensen, A.   475
Jensen, G.   2856
Jensen, H.   4848
Jensen, J.   1449, 1518
Jensen, K.   1519, 2662
Jensen, L.   5318
Jensen, O.   1416
Jensen-Campbell, L.   664
Jenson, J.   4905, 4922
Jeongkoo, Y.   651
Jepson, M.   3450
Jernudd, B.   1560, 1561
Jesani, A.   5676
Jesilow, P.   5175
Jessor, R.   2125
Jett, W.   4599
Jevning, R.   439
Jiang, S.   4116
Jo, M.   3033
Joanes, D.   5204
Joas, H.   196
Jobes, P.   3355
Jobse, R.   3666
Jóhannesson, I.   1676
Johansen, J.   1425
Johansen, P.   5596
Johansson, L.   5718, 5738
Johansson, M.   3765
John, D.   3634
John, O.   573
Johnson, A.   240
Johnson, B.   1271
Johnson, C.   724, 1413, 5242
Johnson, D.   439, 2572, 3472, 4173
Johnson, E.   518, 927, 4996
Johnson, H.   5172
Johnson, J.   3085, 4963
Johnson, K.   2184, 2203, 2653
Johnson, L.   2117, 2683, 3786, 5028
Johnson, M.   541, 4187
Johnson, N.   1736
Johnson, P.   855, 2098
Johnson, R.   439, 1607, 5371, 5424
Johnson, T.   331
Johnsson, B.   439
Johnston, C.   616

Author index

Johnston, G. 2599
Johnston, M. 5186
Johnston, R. 5643
Johnston, V. 2977
Johnston, W. 1020, 1883
Johnstone, S. 2987
Joiner, T. 577
Jonas, A. 3881
Jones, C. 5613
Jones, D. 2114, 4588, 5320
Jones, F. 625, 3239
Jones, G. 1561, 2002
Jones, H. 3657, 5103
Jones, J. 3591, 5643
Jones, K. 4556
Jones, M. 3598, 3967, 5139, 5745
Jones, R. 164
Jones, T. 687
Jong Gierveld, J. de 2163, 2394, 2616
Jong, W. de 3153, 3166
Jonge, B. de 1471
Jongen, F. 1533
Jonsen, A. 5814
Jonsson, J. 1860, 1911, 1912
Joppke, C. 4897
Jordan, K. 581
Jordan, S. 3688
Jordan, T. 2108
Jörgens, H. 4869
Joron, P. 114
Jos, P. 4846
Joseph, S. 5835
Joshi, H. 4314, 4320
Jou, S. 5295
Joubert, M. 5778
Joyce, W. 1964
Joye, D. 3689
Jóźwiak, J. 2204, 2215
Juan, S. 1873
Juckes, T. 494
Jucquois, G. 1242
Judd, C. 745, 747, 754, 928
Judge, D. 2406
Judge, T. 4467, 4468
Judson, P. 1022
Juengst, E. 5773
Jules-Rosette, B. 1424

Julian, T. 2577
Jump, D. 4837
Jun, M. 3866
Jung, H. 1069
Jüngel, E. 1281
Junger, M. 5152
Jungjohann, E. 5435
Junus, P. 2655
Jupp, J. 3416
Jupp, T. 1474
Jürgens, U. 3941
Jurica, P. 2961
Jurik, N. 1499
Jušić, B. 781
Juss, S. 3271
Jussim, L. 573
Kabalina, V. 4627
Kabasakal, H. 681
Kabeberi-Macharia, J. 2704
Kabyshcha, A. 295
Kacen, L. 5617
Kaczorowski, G. 2385
Kadel, S. 1730, 5493
Kadi, G. 3379
Kadyrov, S. 2453
Kağitçibaşi, Ç. 402
Kahan, B. 2100
Kahane, R. 1317
Kahimbaara, J. 3827
Kahlbaugh, P. 389
Kahn, A. 5453
Kahn, J. 4958
Kahn, K. 2804, 4960
Kahn, L. 4508
Kahn, S. 5597
Kahnweiler, W. 4448
Kaiser, J. 4674
Kaitilla, S. 5498
Kajita, T. 3075
Kalache, A. 5718, 5738
Kalantari, M. 2115
Kalberg, S. 25
Kalbfleisch, P. 638
Kallan, J. 2264, 2331, 3291
Kalland, A. 4943
Kalleberg, A. 4331, 4464, 4583
Kallert, H. 2142, 3278
Kalmijn, M. 2600, 2605

Index des auteurs

Kalof, L. 2872
Kaltreider, L. 2892
Kalu, W. 5237
Kaluzny, A. 331
Kamaiah, B. 4363
Kamakahi, J. 1088
Kamali, H. 1180
Kameda, T. 756
Kamerman, S. 5453
Kaminsky, D. 5283
Kaminsky, M. 2075
Kamis-Gould, E. 5845
Kamm, F. 5821
Kammas, M. 4738
Kanaiaupuni, S. 3769, 5495
Kanazawa, S. 1081
Kanbara, F. 2573
Kandel, D. 2571
Kandert, J. 4983
Kane, E. 342
Kaneko, I. 5726
Kanfer, A. 573
Kang, M. 1443
Kang, S. 5109, 5374
Kania, R. 4811
Kaniasty, K. 672
Kanji, N. 2786
Kanno, H. 198, 477
Kanno, M. 180
Kantor, P. 3820
Kantorowicz, H. 1189
Kao, H. 815
Kaplan, M. 767, 810
Kaplan, R. 1561
Kaplan, S. 3061
Kapp, M. 5736, 5773, 5800
Karam, J. 4964
Karasoff, P. 1730, 5493
Karau, S. 488
Kariel, H. 4748
Karim, K. 3083
Karjalainen, P. 1998
Karkal, M. 2222, 2941
Karle, W. 1764
Karlin, J. 5695
Karmel, P. 1796
Karmiloff-Smith, A. 367, 517
Karoly, P. 463

Kasadra, J. 3943
Kasar, D. 4254
Kasarda, J. 5331
Kashenov, A. 4291
Kashima, E. 754
Kashima, Y. 673, 754
Kashin, V. 964
Kashy, D. 767
Kashyap, L. 2421
Kasof, J. 102
Kass, N. 5773
Kasworm, C. 1784
Kasza, G. 4914
Katase, K. 1847
Kateb, G. 4767
Kato, T. 1256, 4588
Katona, G. 5161
Katovich, M. 214, 1064
Katz, M. 2716
Katz, N. 1330
Katz, V. 5637
Katz, Y. 965
Katzer, J. 4529
Kaufer, D. 1493
Kaufman, R. 275
Kaufmann, F. 2031
Kaus, M. 1896
Kavoori, A. 1519
Kawakami, S. 202
Kawamura, Y. 3551
Kawasaki, S. 5196
Kaye, R. 2080
Kazadi, N. 1362
Kazdin, A. 2105, 2125
Kazmi, Y. 1357, 1693
Kazuto, M. 522
Keane, C. 5117, 5379
Keane, J. 2946
Kearney, C. 2120
Kearns, R. 3749
Keashly, L. 718
Keat, R. 4159
Keating, P. 4080
Kecskes, R. 1267
Kędelski, M. 2378
Keely, C. 3422
Keinan, G. 699
Keirse, M. 5683

Author index

Keith, M. 3475, 5147, 5225
Keith, N. 4784, 4784
Keith, T. 2493
Kekelis, L. 1475
Kelejian, H. 3810
Keller, E. 1351
Kellerhals, J. 1122, 1684
Kellerman, A. 3488
Kellert, S. 1118
Kelley, B. 3634
Kelley, J. 403, 2307, 4037, 5021, 5819
Kelly, D. 245, 840, 4594, 4614
Kelly, E. 3848
Kelly, K. 5130
Kelly, M. 1028, 5539
Kelly, R. 5116, 5127
Kelsen, H. 1189
Keltner, D. 682, 691
Kemp, S. 2753
Kempen, H. 588
Kempeneers, M. 4356, 4524
Kemper, F. 2192, 3376
Kemper, S. 4979
Kendall, J. 798, 4092
Kendall, K. 4947
Kendall-Tackett, K. 5076
Kennedy, D. 1119
Kennedy, E. 2950
Kennedy, J. 762
Kennedy, K. 4373
Kennedy, L. 5154
Kennedy, S. 4644
Kenney, K. 598
Kenny, D. 573, 619, 767
Kenny, L. 2191, 4905
Kenrick, D. 698, 2561
Kent, R. 1794
Kent, S. 1272, 1328
Kent Social Services Department 5602
Kenway, J. 1667, 1714
Keough, K. 384
Keppeler, T. 1238
Kerbo, H. 910
Kerbs, J. 5226, 5304
Kerchner, C. 4602
Kerckhoff, A. 4498

Kerfoot, D. 4105
Kern, M. 4947
Kern, S. 993
Kerns, D. 3017
Kerr, B. 2018
Kerševan, M. 1921
Kersten, J. 2165, 5102
Kessel, I. van 4886
Kessler, D. 4804
Ketcham, A. 2317
Ketner, K. 26
Kettern, B. 1177
Kettler, D. 144
Keyder, Ç. 4955
Khan, M. 2845
Khan, Z. 2340
Khawaja, M. 4923
Khayesi, M. 3597
Khissy, M. D' 3180
Khleif, B. 1407
Khor, D. 2847
Khubchandani, L. 1489
Khudenko, A. 1116
Kibbee, D. 164
Kickert, W. 4843
Kidd, M. 4347
Kideckel, D. 3603
Kiecolt, K. 2522
Kieffer, E. 2281
Kiel, J. 5765
Kiem, C. 1317, 3156
Kiernan, K. 1989
Kieselbach, T. 4388
Kieviet, F. 4552
Kiggundu, M. 2357
Kikuchi, T. 1379
Kilker, E. 3028
Killias, M. 5433
Killingray, D. 3320
Kim, C. 4087
Kim, D. 4621
Kim, E. 3085, 4213
Kim, H. 3759, 3854, 4473
Kim, J. 429
Kim, K. 3323, 3756
Kim, M. 997, 3202, 3866
Kim, S. 5291
Kimmel, M. 2908

Index des auteurs

Kimmerling, B. 4999
King, A. 1804
King, D. 3204
King, M. 1208
King, N. 3224
King, R. 3281, 3292
Kingsley, G. 3748
Kinicki, A. 4380
Kinkade, P. 214
Kinlock, T. 5156, 5410
Kinne, S. 5773
Kintner, H. 2005
Kintrea, K. 3750
Kinzel, R. 728
Kinzie, J. 5371, 5424
Kiong, T. 3347
Kipnis, K. 2440
Kippax, S. 3013
Kirby, R. 1668
Kirchler, E. 2602
Kirino, K. 419
Kirkbride, P. 4483
Kirkcaldy, B. 4740
Kirkebœk, B. 5707, 5831
Kirk-Greene, A. 3042
Kirkpatrick, A. 1392
Kirkpatrick, L. 1279
Kirkwood, A. 5582
Kirmeyer, K. 2249
Kironde, J. 3727
Kirschenbaum, A. 4417
Kirshenblatt-Gimblett, B. 2075
Kishor, S. 2363
Kissler, L. 4715
Kitcher, P. 627
Kitschelt, H. 4783
Kitzinger, C. 2727, 2774, 2968
Kitzinger, J. 358
Kivlahan, D. 5371, 5424
Kjœr, B. 2040
Klaassen, C. 2163
Klak, T. 3639, 3792
Klandermans, B. 4938
Klaus, V. 4781
Klebanov, P. 2107
Kleber, J. 2664
Kleijer, H. 2132, 2163
Kleiman, M. 5401

Klein, L. 1794
Klein, T. 2383
Klein-Allermann, E. 670
Kleinke, C. 656
Kleinman, S. 257
Klemm, E. 3529
Klemm, K. 1699
Klerk, V. de 1382
Kleßmann, C. 1306
Kliemt, H. 145
Klimova, S. 4110
Kline, S. 1444
Klinger, E. 1373
Klinger, F. 3187
Klofas, J. 5197, 5385
Klönne, A. 1282
Klopov, E. 4681
Kluegel, J. 3165
Klusáková, L. 3717
Klüter, H. 3419
Klüver, J. 181
Kluzowa, K. 4312
Knabe, B. 2192, 4274
Knapp, M. 798, 1730, 5493
Knapp, S. 74
Knaup, K. 678
Kniazeva, E. 311
Knibiehler, Y. 3332
Knight, G. 593
Knight, J. 805
Knights, D. 853, 884, 4105
Knippenberg, A. van 443
Knippenberg, D. 591
Knöbl, W. 4776
Knoke, D. 260
Knolle, H. 2325
Knopf, M. 3006
Knoppers, B. 2239
Knowlton, B. 542
Knudsen, C. 2182
Knudten, R. 5135, 5437
Kobayashi, K. 1341, 3823
Koblinsky, M. 5657
Koch, A. 1033, 4779
Koch, T. 1970
Kodama, M. 161
Kodolitsch, P. von 3534
Koester, J. 1009

Author index

Kofod, E.   5707, 5831
Kohama, F.   1862
Kohl, H.   4065
Kohl, J.   5086
Kohl, P.   1613
Köhler, H.   1746, 1834
Köhler, M.   1191
Köhli, J.   3794
Kojima, K.   1531
Koleva, M.   3748
Kollmann, K.   4672
Kollock, P.   711
Kolosi, T.   3992
Kolozsi, B.   5113
Komai, H.   3279
Kommer, M.   4499
Kon, I.   2996
Koné, T.   4210
Konecki, K.   256
Kong, L.   1231
König, S.   4439
Konings, P.   4603
Kontopoulos, K.   1822
Kontuly, T.   3942
Koo, H.   1907
Kooiman, J.   4806
Koole, R.   4934
Koopmans, R.   4878
Kopel, D.   1203
Kopelman, R.   4478
Koper, G.   591
Kopparty, S.   5639
Koppen, P. van   1181
Koppich, J.   1730, 5493
Kořalka, J.   3144
Körbitz, U.   5702
Koropeckyj-Cox, T.   2635
Korsgaard, C.   603
Kosaka, K.   242, 711, 1898
Kosaka-Isleif, F.   3336
Kosareva, N.   3748
Kosheleva, V.   1141, 3444
Kosicki, G.   1553
Kosolapov, N.   5024
Kostelny, K.   2112
Kostoris, F.   1991
Kotalová, J.   2864
Kotary, L.   2621

Kotásek, J.   1751
Koto, B.   3379
Koto, Y.   185
Kotowska, I.   1981, 2009, 2396, 2932
Kotter, J.   4504
Kotthoff, H.   679
Kotze, J.   2404
Kouaouci, A.   2219, 3424
Kousis, M.   3555
Kouzmin, A.   3819
Kovacs, D.   1939
Kovalkina, K.   1240
Koven, S.   2502
Kowalewicz, K.   348
Kowalewski, M.   1277
Kowalska, I.   2233
Kowalski, P.   4980
Kowalski, R.   641
Kowerski, M.   3283, 3388
Kowner, R.   613
Kozlov, L.   4224
Koźmiński, A.   861
Kraaykamp, G.   4278
Krafeld, F.   5435
Kraft, P.   4605
Kraft-Hanak, S.   2624
Krakover, S.   3668
Kramer, E.   4970
Kramer, H.   1047, 5032
Kramer, J.   3169
Krames, L.   363
Krasniewicz, L.   4909
Krating, M.   5368
Krätke, S.   3708
Kraus, S.   754, 4670
Krause, D.   3449
Krause, I.   2428
Krausz, E.   156
Kray, S.   1391
Krech, V.   1282
Kreindler, I.   1563
Kreisky, E.   5510
Kreiswirth, B.   245
Kreitman, N.   5409, 5426
Krejci, J.   1229
Krejčí, O.   4763
Krejćová, A.   1229
Krencik, W.   4287, 4288

Index des auteurs

Kreps, G. 897
Kressel, G. 4309
Krieger, N. 5782
Kriesberg, L. 1975
Kriesi, H. 4896, 4917
Krimsky, S. 206
Krippendorff, K. 1449, 1518
Krisberg, B. 5226, 5304
Krishna, V. 1337
Krishnaji, N. 3583
Krishnan, P. 2007, 2053
Krishnaraj, M. 2941
Kristeva, T. 1425
Krivo, L. 5148
Kroeger, K. 4985
Krohn, M. 5305
Kroker, A. 2751
Kroker, M. 2751
Kroll, J. 3175
Krosnick, J. 403, 5021
Kroymann, I. 4538
Krüger, A. 3825
Krüger, D. 2784
Kruk, E. 2486
Krukonis, A. 457
Kruse, L. 696
Kruse, W. 1738
Krysan, M. 3796
Ku, L. 2624, 2986
Ku, Y. 2074
Kubiak, A. 344
Kuchinskii, S. 4722
Kuchta, E. 5167, 5443
Kuchuck, S. 5624
Kudchedkar, S. 2941
Kugler, P. 492
Kühnel, W. 1970
Kuijperslinde, M. 3376
Kuijsten, A. 4322
Kuiper, N. 450, 585
Kuisel, R. 1037
Kujala, J. 4187
Kujath, H. 2192
Kulikova, N. 4261
Kulkarni, P. 2481, 5612
Kumada, T. 3837
Kumar, A. 824
Kumar, B. 2361

Kumar, K. 4793
Kumar, R. 2745
Kumar, U. 4147
Kumar, V. 4147
Kumaran, K. 3374
Kumpf, M. 670
Kunczik, M. 1445
Kunda, Z. 520
Kundu, A. 3898, 5329
Künemund, H. 4683
Kuo, E. 1560
Kuokkanen, M. 898
Kuon, B. 746
Kurahashi, S. 1624
Kuran, T. 3184
Kurdek, L. 2587, 2624
Kurdiumov, S. 311
Kurihara, T. 2160
Kurita, N. 4931
Kurkiewicz, J. 2036
Kurland, R. 5570
Kuroda, T. 4821
Kuruvilla, S. 4657
Kushner, T. 3063
Kusum 5828
Kuvacic, I. 4826
Kuznetsov, A. 3607
Květ, R. 5031
Kwan, P. 2912
Kwarciak, B. 1479
Kwon, J. 5291
Kwun, S. 649
Kych, A. 67, 3376
Kymlicka, W. 5818
Lab, S. 5200, 5292
Laband, D. 2937
Labazée, P. 3379
Labidi, L. 2697, 5061
Labossiere, R. 3781
Lacar, L. 2482
Lacey, C. 1542
Lacey, N. 2740
Lacey, R. 5836
Lachman, M. 1421
Lachrité, C. 2644
Ladányi, J. 3803
Ladd, G. 2622
Lado, C. 252

Author index

Laermans, R.   2132
LaFaye, C.   3465
Laffargue, B.   5096
LaFollette, H.   5788
LaFree, G.   5159
Lafrenière, M.   5605
LaFromboise, T.   1031
Lagerspetz, M.   1550
Lagopoulos, A.   1068
Lagrave, R.   3113, 3120
Laguerre, M.   4998
Lahelma, E.   2857
Lahzami, C.   1093
Lai, L.   3743, 3845
Laing, W.   5748
Laitin, D.   1563, 1565
Lajios, K.   3317
Lakey, J.   4253
Lakshmanan, T.   1341
Laliberté, L.   2823
Lallemand, D.   5047
Lalljee, M.   607
Lalonde, R.   1436
Lam, D.   440, 4019
Lamarche, L.   4346
Lamb, K.   1500
Lamb, M.   5637
Lamb, R.   607
Lambert, M.   5371, 5424
Lambert, S.   4486
Lambert, Y.   1262
Lambooy, J.   3666
Lammers, J.   922, 4505
Lamo de Espinosa, E.   1945
Lamont, B.   804
Lamont, M.   1836
Lampard, R.   2536
Lancaster, R.   2894
Lance, C.   478
Land, K.   299, 335
Landau, E.   2402, 2637
Landau, J.   819
Landau, S.   5155, 5442
Lande, J.   4625
Landingham, M. van   2997
Landis, S.   244
Landsburg, S.   3958
Landua, D.   355, 4024

Landy, F.   3379
Lane, C.   4328
Lane, D.   5604
Lang, F.   631
Lang, G.   1449, 1518
Lang, J.   3190
Lang, K.   1449, 1518, 1565
Lange, D.   4670
Langeland, O.   4709
Langenbucher, W.   1523
Langevelde, A. van   1406
Langevin, B.   5048
Langford, C.   2380, 2941
Langlois, A.   1484
Lansac, J.   2239
Lansbury, R.   4620
Laperrière, A.   3180
Lapierre, N.   3332
Laplantine, F.   1316, 1332, 3113
Lapointe, R.   150
Laponce, J.   1565
Lapp, M.   4070
Larkin, J.   1971
Larmour, P.   811
Larochelle, G.   4847, 4883
Larochelle, M.   1688
Larrabee, M.   1143
Larragy, J.   5450, 5718, 5738
Larsen, U.   2279
Larson, J.   292, 629, 766, 2778
Larson, R.   5393
Larson-Gutman, M.   1373
Larue, G.   2056, 5721, 5740
Lash, S.   1000
Laska, S.   6, 3440
Lasker, J.   2239
Lasry, J.   3318
Lassalle, J.   1202
Lassine, B.   4853
Lassnigg, L.   5510
Laszlo, E.   3072
Lather, P.   88
Latoszek, M.   259
Latour, B.   1051
Lau, C.   795
Lau, G.   2987
Laub, J.   5105, 5288
Laurens, J.   1638

Index des auteurs

LaVeist, T.   5779
Lavertu, J.   2020
Lavery, A.   927
Laville, J.   4136
Lavin, M.   4171
Lavoie, D.   4771
Lavoie, G.   404
Lavoie, J.   2863
Lavoie, L.   404
Law, R.   4082
Lawler, E.   422, 651
Laws, G.   2065
Lawson, H.   1730, 5493
Lawson, J.   2342
Lawson, V.   3639
Lawton, M.   2045
Lawwill, K.   1688
Lazarus, A.   5778
Lazarus, R.   447, 506
Lazear, E.   4482
Lazinier, E.   404
Lazzarini, G.   3309
Le Grand, J.   5725
Le Pont, F.   3001
Le Roux, P.   1320
Lea, S.   3523, 3957, 4172
Leach, B.   2883
Leadbetter, D.   5622
Leaf, M.   3755
Leap, N.   5672
Leaper, R.   5450
Learner, D.   4531
Leather, P.   5483
Lebaube, A.   5048
Lebbi, I.   5061
Lebeaux, M.   1122
Lebedeva, N.   1703
Leber, D.   2586
Leccardi, C.   2690
Léchot, G.   3709
Leckie, G.   3562
Leclerc, D.   3752
Lecocq, G.   404
Ledenig, W.   2192
Lederman, M.   2768
Ledford, G.   774
Ledoux, S.   2168
Ledoyen, A.   3217

Lee, A.   302, 1077
Lee, B.   3365, 3366, 5291
Lee, C.   2661
Lee, D.   65, 4566
Lee, J.   102, 4473
Lee, K.   1770
Lee, M.   4165
Lee, O.   2817
Lee, R.   231, 1317, 2579, 5793
Lee, S.   411, 2840
Lee, T.   5768
Lee, W.   1428, 1751
Lee, Y.   2508
Leelakulthanit, O.   4007
Leeming, F.   3433, 3436
Leenhardt, J.   1028
Leer, D. van   2896
Lees, S.   5207
Lees-Haley, P.   932
Lee-Smith, D.   3715
Leete, R.   2295
Leeuw, F.   70
Leeuw, J. de   270
Leeuwis, C.   3596
Legault, G.   5605
Legault, J.   3157
Legoux, L.   76
Legrenzi, P.   145
Legros, M.   5048
Lehman, A.   2641
Lehman, C.   4109
Lehman, D.   403, 5021
Lehmann, H.   1305
Lehmann, J.   160
Lehrer, E.   2594
Leicht, K.   2674, 4047, 4066
Leicht, R.   4100
Leiman, M.   3226
Leiprecht, R.   2170, 5626
Leira, A.   5532
Leisering, L.   2031, 5357
Leite, G.   2960
Leiter, J.   4694
Leitner, H.   4103
Lelièvre, E.   3379, 4524
Lelyveld, D.   1464
Lembcke, J.   1906
Lemel, Y.   1122

Author index

Lemelle, S. 3027
Lemire, G. 5179
Lenardić, M. 4302
Lenches, E. 4769
Lennie, I. 5757
Lennings, C. 5414, 5428
Lennon, M. 4521
Lennon, R. 2906
Lent, J. 1501, 1502
Lentz, B. 2937
Lentz, K. 2692
Leon, G. de 5109, 5374
Leonard, A. 4645
Leonard, D. 4559
Leonard, K. 2895, 3127
Leontidou, L. 3839
Leopold, E. 4197
Leo-Rhynie, E. 2438
Lepsius, M. 69
Leresche, J. 3689
Lerg, W. 1552
Leridon, H. 2247, 3001
Lerme, C. 4842
Lerner, G. 1409, 2775
Leroke, W. 141
Leslie, D. 2880
Letherby, G. 228, 646
Leti, G. 2356
Leung, B. 1831
Leung, C. 4117
Leung, F. 566, 2153
Leung, P. 5371, 5424
Leutz, N. 5708, 5730
Leveau, R. 3375, 3415
Léveillée, J. 4972
Levenstein, H. 1115
Lever, B. 3677
Lever, W. 3834, 3839
Lévesque, B. 4709
Levidow, L. 1334
Levin, D. 4252
Levin, M. 774
Levine, A. 141
Levine, D. 1928
Levine, H. 3128
Levine, J. 515, 734
Levine, M. 5295
Levine, P. 2323

Levine, R. 4172
Levine, S. 2853
Levitin, T. 5773
Levitskaia, A. 2985
Levitt, C. 3236
Lévy, J. 3699
Lévy, M. 2018
Lewin, K. 1705
Lewin-Epstein, N. 3145
Lewis, C. 468, 5354
Lewis, D. 223, 2722, 2737, 5401
Lewis, J. 2750
Lewis, M. 1415, 3486
Lewis, R. 3834
Lexier, L. 5085, 5301
Ley, D. 111, 194, 1227, 3476
Leydesdorff, L. 316, 1821
Lezama, J. 3665
Li, B. 1703
Li, F. 725
Li, J. 439, 2241
Li, L. 2258
Li, P. 1952, 2420
Li, X. 4994
Liang, J. 2074
Liang, Y. 1341
Liao, T. 1253
Liatto-Katundo, B. 2786
Liberman, V. 526
Libero, D. 572
Lichtblau, K. 205
Lichtenberger, E. 3892
Lichter, D. 2599, 3566, 4053, 5318
Liddle, A. 2965
Liden, R. 644
Lieberson, S. 3149
Liebig, P. 5470
Liebig, S. 942
Liebler, A. 547, 573
Liebrand, W. 516
Liefbroer, A. 2163, 2616
Liese, L. 2334
Lieske, J. 307
Lifanov, K. 1491
Light, I. 3125
Lightfoot, L. 5369
Lilie, S. 2327
Lillard, L. 2566

Index des auteurs

Lilley, R.   1573
Lin, G.   2643, 3874
Lin, H.   2410
Lin, M.   1925
Lin, Z.   5692
Lincoln, J.   4701
Lind, N.   4004
Lindberg, G.   3768
Lindebaum, S.   2346, 5355
Linden, M.   2048
Lindenberg, S.   145, 200, 806, 1174
Linder, M.   4503
Lindisfarne, N.   2873
Lindle, J.   1730, 5493
Lindner, R.   50
Lindsay, C.   1568
Lindsay, D.   541
Linell, P.   1360
Lines, J.   5452
Ling, Z.   3626
Linger, D.   380
Linhart, D.   888, 4136
Link, B.   4521
Lino, M.   4174
Linsk, N.   2465
Linstead, S.   1061
Linville, P.   754
Linz, J.   4820
Lipkus, I.   653, 677
Lippe, T. van der   2822
Lippold, G.   1970
Lipsedge, M.   5403
Lipset, S.   1893, 4796
Lipshitz, G.   4220
Lipsky, M.   5489
Lipsmeier, A.   4539
Lipson, L.   1145
Lira L. Ramos   5120
Liska, A.   1089, 5105
Lister, R.   2702
Litwin, H.   2415, 3522, 5739
Liu, W.   1946
Liu, X.   3801
Livingstone, D.   1885, 2654
Livingstone, S.   1519, 4208
Livneh, N.   4478
Lizotte, A.   5305
Lizza, J.   1168

Llanes, M.   3550
Llorente Pinto, J.   3568
Lloyd, C.   2924
Lloyd, E.   5184
Lloyd, M.   124
Lloyd, P.   1417
Lloyd-Reason, L.   4121
Lloyd-Smith, C.   2025
Lo, A.   5568
Lo Presti, C.   1096
Lo, T.   5589
Löbler, F.   849
Lock, M.   2677
Locke, A.   3171
Locke, E.   4468
Lockwood, V.   1972
Locoh, T.   2418
Lodwick, D.   3498
Loenhoff, J.   1363
Loewenberg, F.   5684
Loewenson, R.   5780
Loewenstein, M.   2809
Lofland, J.   220
Lofquist, W.   4101
Loftus, E.   539
Logan, C.   5234
Logan, J.   1844, 3026, 3162, 3685
Loh, E.   4016
Loh, F.   4958
Lohmann, A.   3330
Lojkine, J.   1846
Lomas, J.   5691
Lombard, J.   209
Lomond, K.   2497
Lomranz, J.   1366
London, A.   2359
London, H.   2908
London, N.   1727
Long, B.   5694
Long, J.   4555
Long, P.   5078
Long, R.   603, 4419
Long, S.   2612, 5735
Long, V.   589
Longhi, C.   4149
Longhofer, J.   3532
Longman, D.   1542
Longman, J.   1386

Author index

Longva, A. 2893
Loon, M. van 3383
Lopata, H. 2681, 4493
Lopez, A. 5048
López Ríos, O. 2364
López, S. 423
López Sánchez, G. 1978
Lorber, J. 2259
Lord, K. 4156
Lore, R. 693
Lorenz, E. 376
Lorenz, F. 2151, 2555
Lorenzi-Cioldi, F. 408, 767
Loriaux, M. 1865
Lorimer, R. 1623
Lorrain, D. 4841
Losch, S. 3894
Loscocco, K. 2674, 2815, 4116
Losier, G. 4733
Losseff-Tillmanns, G. 5208, 5297
Lott, A. 4991
Lott, B. 4991
Loubet del Bayle, J. 4812
Louder, D. 1227
Loukaitou-Sideris, A. 3867
Lourdes Villar, M. de 3249
Lourenço, N. 3569
Lousada, J. 5586
Louvot, C. 2011
Lovaglia, M. 909
Lovecy, J. 4549
Lovegrove, T. 4457
Lovell, C. 3998
Lovell, P. 3211
Lovely, M. 5462
LoVerde, M. 340
Lövgren, K. 1574
Low, N. 2304
Lowe, G. 2512
Lowe, K. 5620
Lowe, M. 1104, 2838
Lowis, M. 451
Löwstedt, J. 828
Loycke, A. 1094
Loza, W. 5194, 5376
Lozano Ascencio, F. 3392, 3999
Lozano i Soler, J. 880
Lozier, J. 5761

Lubeigt, G. 1227
Lubek, I. 404
Lubinski, D. 1430
Lübke, S. 4538
Luca, R. de 3398
Lucarini, N. 2289
Lucas, M. 708
Lucas, S. 2341
Lucchini, R. 150
Luce, W. 3868
Luciano, A. 3351
Lucio, R. 1794
Luckasson, R. 5191
Luckert, Y. 3088
Lüdtke, A. 1082
Lüdtke, H. 5132
Luhmann, N. 213, 224, 1058, 1197
Luidens, D. 1271
Luk, C. 4179
Łukasiewicz, P. 1410
Luke, A. 1405
Lukes, S. 145
Luloff, A. 3602
Lundberg, C. 803
Lundgren, E. 2655
Lundgren, S. 664
Luneev, V. 5165
Lungo, M. 3939
Lunt, I. 2090
Lunt, P. 4208
Luoma-Keturi, S. 1574
Lupton, D. 2337, 5642
Lurie, I. 5531
Lury, C. 1184
Lusane, C. 3027
Lüschen, G. 134
Lüscher, K. 2417
Luster, T. 2627, 2638
Lustig, B. 5829
Luthar, S. 579
Luttgens, A. 5319
Lutton, W. 5128
Luttrell, W. 1692
Lutyńska, K. 347
Lutyński, J. 53, 62
Lutz, W. 1989, 2186
Lutzenhiser, L. 3450
Lwoga, C. 4375

Index des auteurs

Lykken, D. 554
Lynch, B. 3450
Lynch, D. 2452
Lynch, F. 1030
Lynch, J. 1646
Lynch, L. 4566
Lynch, M. 596
Lynd, M. 244
Lyon, D. 166
Lyon, E. 228
Lyon, M. 1335
Maaloul, B. 1095
Maas, I. 2048
Maas, P. van der 5792, 5804
Maass, A. 743
Maaz, H. 5435
McAdam, D. 4935
McAdam, G. 3750
McAllester-Jones, M. 1028
McAllister, I. 4961
McAllister, P. 1046
McArthur, A. 3825, 3834
Macauley, L. 342
McBride, A. 2662
McCabe, D. 525
McCaffery, E. 4350
McCall, P. 335
MacCallum, R. 472
McCalman, J. 1901
McCamish, M. 673, 3015
McCammon, H. 4634
McCann, C. 1436
McCann, J. 1285
McCarthy, J. 3124
McCarville, R. 4729
McCaughan, E. 3085
McChesney, K. 5269, 5328
McChesney, R. 1519
McClain, V. 403, 5021
McClearn, G. 553
McCleary, R. 5026
McClelland, C. 4470
McClendon, M. 345
McClintock, A. 1021, 2987
McClintock, C. 516, 726
McCloskey, L. 5087, 5254
Maccoby, E. 2472, 2478
McCombs, M. 1553

McConnell, C. 3825
McCord, J. 5308
McCorkle, R. 960
McCormack, C. 5643
McCormack, T. 2679
MacCorquodale, P. 2856
McCoy, A. 5415
McCoy, K. 2123
McCrae, R. 445, 553
McCrate, E. 3973
McCray, J. 3567
Mccready, D. 4157
MacCreanor, T. 997, 3202
McCullagh, P. 5791
McCullough, L. 5813
McCusker, C. 5363
McCusker, M. 5643
McDermott, K. 4619
McDonald, B. 4997
MacDonald, D. 567, 4620
McDonald, J. 2352, 3994
MacDonald, J. 5643
MacDonald, M. 4167
MacDonald, R. 4127
Macdonald, S. 4415, 5396, 5542
McDonell, J. 5267
McDonogh, G. 3735
McDougall, C. 5214
McDowall, D. 5099
McDowell, J. 3286
McDowell, L. 2766, 3493
MacEwan, I. 5560
MacEwen, K. 2606
McFadden, P. 2686
McFalls, L. 1920
McGarrell, E. 5226, 5304
McGee, D. 5670
McGillivray, M. 5302
McGinn, N. 1754
McGinnis, R. 4555
McGowan, K. 979
McGranahan, G. 3799
McGrath, J. 1171
McGregor, A. 3834, 4260
McGregor, G. 1602
MacGrogan, M. 2731
McGuckin, R. 343
McGue, M. 554

Author index

McGuire, G. 404, 2785
McGuire, J. 2619
McGuire, M. 1247
McGuire, W. 4753
Mach, Z. 3282
McHale, J. 5669
McHale, S. 2624
Mchedlov, M. 1250
Machin, R. 4055
McHoskey, J. 920
McHugh, K. 3752
MacInnes, J. 4260
McIntosh, A. 3622
McIntyre, R. 1134
Macintyre, S. 5754
MacIver, D. 2125
Maciver, S. 5754
McKay, M. 4947
McKay, S. 1461, 4253
McKee, C. 5043
McKeehan, I. 2326
McKeganey, N. 2316
MacKeith, J. 836
McKell, A. 5573
McKendall, M. 848
McKendy, J. 700
McKenny, G. 5829
McKenry, P. 2485, 2577
Mackensen, R. 2192
MacKenzie, C. 1758
Mackenzie, F. 2669
McKenzie, I. 4803
McKenzie Leiper, J. 4041
McKeown, R. 2147
Mackey, W. 2695
Mackie, D. 754
McKinlay, J. 5479
McKinley, T. 3617
McKinney, B. 2625
MacKinnon, D. 5392
Mackintosh, S. 5483
McLafferty, S. 2680, 4028
McLain, R. 223
McLanahan, S. 2504, 2519
MacLaran, A. 3833
McLaren, P. 1675
McLaren, R. 1791
McLauchlan, G. 1975

McLaughlin, D. 2599
McLaughlin, E. 2466, 5055
McLaughlin, V. 4811
Maclean, A. 5797
MacLean, B. 5134
MacLean, I. 1028
Maclean, M. 2480, 5522
McLeay, E. 2853
Maclennan, D. 3666
McLennan, J. 927
Macleod, J. 1597
McLeod, J. 2549, 5343
MacLure, M. 1394
McMahan, G. 4437
McMahon, A. 2896
McMahon, M. 5216
MacManus, S. 4107
McManus, T. 353
McMichael, A. 3477
McMullen, M. 392
McMylor, P. 972
Macnamara, J. 366
McNeill, P. 5802
MacNiven, D. 1140
McNown, R. 2182
Maconachie, G. 4262
Macpherson, D. 4010
MacRae, D. 5774
McRae, S. 2610, 2839
McRobbie, A. 2159
McShane, J. 502, 503
MacSween, M. 2718
McWhinnie, A. 2239
McWilliams, R. 3634
McWilliams, S. 2624
Maddock, S. 2929
Maddox, G. 2048
Madinier, C. 2020
Madu, A. 4154
Madu, C. 4154
Madu, E. 3635
Maeder, D. 757
Maffesoli, M. 114
Magas, I. 4825
Magatti, M. 3980
Maggard, S. 1939
Magnani, R. 2227
Magnusson, D. 555

Index des auteurs

Magnusson, E. 1475
Magnusson, F. 2040
Magnusson, W. 4905
Magro, R. 4324
Maguire, D. 4919
Maguire, J. 1030
Maguire, K. 5186
Mahadevan, K. 2007, 2053
Mahajan, G. 8
Mahanta, K. 2083
Mahapatra, J. 3547
Mahleu, F. 3543
Mahlmann, P. 4741
Mahon, M. 1069
Mahon, R. 4922
Mahran, M. 2018
Mai, U. 3679
Maibach, M. 3914
Maidment, A. 4787
Maier, F. 4336
Maïlat, M. 5778
Maillat, D. 3709
Maimer, H. 4248
Maines, D. 243
Maison, D. 2447
Majewski, M. 108
Majka, L. 4656
Majka, T. 4656
Major, B. 490, 2624
Mak, R. 2961
Makepeace, G. 4550
Maki, . 2801
Maki, D. 4479
Makkai, T. 1083, 4961
Makolkin, A. 4774
Makoto. Hayashi 1213
Maksimowicz-Ajchel, A. 2200, 2374
Malan, J. 3953
Malatesta, D. 5411
Malette, L. 5136
Malewska-Peyre, H. 3329
Maléziex, J. 3791
Malinosky-Rummell, R. 5080
Malitskii, V. 4766
Malloch, M. 5247
Mallows, C. 282
Malmberg, B. 297
Malo de Molina, C. 937

Malone, L. 1668
Maloon, D. 4357
Malos, E. 5240
Malterud, K. 2662
Mambanya, L. 4852
Mamdani, M. 2223, 2270
Manabe, K. 274, 5027
Mancini, P. 1449, 1518
Mandel, D. 403, 5021
Mandelbaum, J. 1409
Mandic, S. 3748
Mane, P. 2421
Manfrass, K. 3234
Manfredi, M. 5125
Mangan, J. 1885, 2654
Manganaro, L. 4845
Mangena, O. 2717
Mann, T. 552
Manne, S. 635
Mannheim, B. 2670, 4327
Mannheim, K. 4768
Manning, K. 457
Manning, P. 5245
Manning, W. 2575
Mannion, A. 3432
Mannix, E. 740, 759, 906
Manolis, M. 2808
Manor, J. 5344
Mansell, J. 5848
Mansfield, E. 4144
Mansfield, R. 4610
Mansilla, H. 4662
Manson, A. 3593
Manson, S. 5371, 5424
Mansson, S. 2952
Manting, D. 4322
Manton, K. 320
Manuel, P. 1599
Manz, G. 5314
Manza, J. 1893
Manzo, J. 751, 1409
Manzo, K. 1930
Mao, J. 3186
Marable, M. 3027
Marcadet, C. 3947
Marchal, J. 3608
Marchington, M. 4711
Marchman, V. 505

Author index

Marconis, R. 2020
Marcuse, P. 3793, 5334
Marcus-Newhall, A. 767
Maretzke, S. 3894
Marger, M. 1827
Margolin, L. 2109
Margolis, D. 2781
Margolis, E. 5384
Margulis, H. 3760
Marin, M. 5330
Marion, S. 4567
Mark, K. 3748
Markman, H. 2624, 5694
Markman, K. 392
Markoczy, L. 3979
Markovà, I. 1360, 1365
Markovsky, B. 422, 909
Markowitz, F. 3146
Marks, H. 1785
Marks, L. 5206
Marks, N. 2519
Markson, E. 2054
Markus, T. 1598
Marley, D. 1383
Marlin, R. 1169
Marmor, T. 5515
Marmot, M. 4330
Maroszek, A. 559
Marpsat, M. 2020, 5052
Marquand, J. 4572
Marques de Melo, J. 1519
Marr, W. 4157
Marrewijk, C. van 5336
Marsden, P. 260, 760, 4331
Marsden, R. 885
Marsh, H. 592
Marsh, P. 5514
Marshall, D. 4158
Marshall, G. 948, 1913
Marshall, J. 4569
Marshall, K. 2086
Marshall, N. 2802, 4459
Marsland, D. 2169
Martelli, S. 122
Marti, L. 4378
Martin, C. 384
Martin, E. 1335, 5658
Martin, G. 5586

Martin, J. 792, 3008, 4324
Martin, L. 612, 5572
Martin, P. 1561, 3055, 3426, 4340, 4447
Martin, R. 450, 585, 883, 1227, 4286, 4510, 4650
Martin, Y. 2017
Martín-Barbero, J. 1505
Martinelle, S. 2302
Martínez, E. 3085
Martinez, J. 404
Martínez Keim, M. 1700
Martini, A. 4267
Martiniello, M. 3047, 3069
Martins, H. 3158
Martinson, B. 2517
Martuccelli, D. 1828
Marty, M. 1226, 1247
Marullo, S. 1975
Maruyama, M. 4507
Marwell, G. 1929
Mas, M. 4214
Masalha, S. 2338
Mascia-Lees, F. 1022
Maser, J. 5371, 5424
Masewicz, W. 4684
Mašková, M. 2391
Mason, B. 804
Massaro, D. 385
Massey, D. 3192, 3424, 3769, 4059, 5495
Masson, C. 3153, 3166
Mast, D. 3033
Mastekaasa, A. 2574, 4067
Masters, R. 1248
Mastrosimone, C. 457
Mather, C. 4622
Mathes, R. 286, 1534
Matheson, G. 4045
Mathieu, A. 5275
Mathieu, D. 3809
Mathiowetz, N. 946
Mathur, A. 2569
Matos Mar, J. 3093, 3652, 3667, 3693
Matsuda, M. 5661
Matsueda, R. 5263
Matsui, S. 1832
Matsumoto, M. 1347

Index des auteurs

Matsumura, K. 4742
Matsunaga, D. 5371, 5424
Matsuzaki, N. 158
Matthesius, B. 5285
Matthew, M. 3711
Matthew, V. 5543
Matthewman, J. 5513
Matthews, M. 1688
Matthews, T. 3027
Matthias, C. 4338
Mattley, C. 5238
Matuchniak-Krasuska, A. 2208, 4661
Matzat, J. 5544
Mauch, S. 3914
Mauger, G. 1695
Maume, D. 4339
Maupin, J. 5226, 5304
Maurer, A. 356
Maurer, T. 3044
Maurice, M. 4136
Maus, R. 5450
Mauss, A. 1302
Maute, M. 4191
Mautner, T. 1164
Mavratsas, C. 4093
Mawhinney, H. 1730, 5493
Maxim, P. 5117, 5379
Maximy, R. de 3955
Maxwell, A. 1916
Maxwell, G. 5201
Maxwell, S. 748
May, N. 3814
May, P. 5432
May, W. 5822
Mayence, S. 5450
Mayer, K. 2048
Mayer, L. 3634
Mayer, P. 5022
Maynard, A. 5416
Maynard, D. 751
Maynard, M. 68
Mayntz, R. 813, 4145
Mayo, D. 5814
Mayor, R. 1739
Mayoux, L. 2813, 2825
Mayr, U. 2048
Mazibuko, R. 5643
Mazlish, B. 1073

Mazmanian, D. 4929
Mazrui, A. 1563, 1563
Mazur, A. 1857
Mazzella, R. 471
Mazzoleni, G. 1508
Mazzon, G. 1381
Mead, K. 2085
Meada, N. 5718, 5738
Meager, N. 936
Mechanic, D. 5844
Médard, J. 209
Medbh, M. 1021
Mederer, H. 2457
Mee, S. 2860
Meehan, A. 4805
Meehan, E. 1519
Meekings, E. 2601
Meena, R. 2673
Meer, P. van der 4315
Meezan, W. 5072
Mehl, D. 1588
Mehta, B. 3548, 3599, 4051, 4068, 5346
Meier, B. 1953
Meier, H. 3706
Meier, R. 3908
Meijenfeldt, F. von 2163
Meijer, L. 4337
Meijer, M. 3839
Meijers, F. 2163
Meiksins, P. 4432, 4704
Meilinger, F. 4947
Meissner, W. 706
Meja, V. 144
Melby, J. 2151
Mellers, B. 401
Mellor, P. 1016
Melosh, B. 2666
Melotti, U. 3407
Melton, J. 1247
Meltsner, M. 642
Meltz, N. 4596
Melucci, A. 4928
Melzer, W. 2139, 2150
Membrado, M. 5641
Memon, P. 3715
Menashri, D. 1706
Menchik, P. 2354

Author index

Mendes, R.   5348
Méndez, R.   3429
Mendras, H.   1122
Mendus, S.   1703
Menezes, D.   4169
Menfredi, R.   2168
Meng, X.   3937
Menke, H.   2168
Menssen, S.   439
Mens-Verhulst, J. van   2870
Mentore, G.   1397
Mentzer, M.   899
Mercer, N.   1386
Mercier, C.   5266, 5391
Mercuri, K.   4947
Merelman, R.   1402
Merkulova, I.   4175
Merle, P.   4324
Merllié, D.   64, 1852
Mermann-Jozwiak, E.   2743
Mertens, N.   4315
Merwe, H. van der   5007
Merwe, I. van der   1567
Mesle, F.   1989
Mesmin, G.   3790, 3890
Mesner, M.   3089
Mesnil, M.   3113, 3152
Messaris, P.   1437
Messarra, A.   1297
Messer, D.   1475
Messiah, A.   3001
Messing, K.   4353
Messner, M.   2896
Mesthrie, R.   1468
Mestrovic, S.   1057
Metalsky, G.   577
Metcalf, A.   2515
Metcalf, D.   4626, 4676
Methfessel, T.   3310
Metoudi, M.   2882
Mette, N.   1282
Metzger, A.   429
Metzger, D.   2075
Metzger, T.   29
Meulemann, H.   325, 482
Meurling, B.   2655
Meyer, D.   1975, 2511, 4928, 5523
Meyer, I.   2314

Meyer, J.   179, 878, 4258, 5512
Meyer, M.   2989
Meyer, T.   2524
Meyerhoff, M.   1477
Meyers, D.   2440
Meyers, M.   2089, 5534
Meyer-Wilmes, H.   1282
Meyrowitz, J.   1030, 1449, 1518
Mezias, S.   810
Miall, C.   2237
Miasnikova, A.   1522
Miceli, M.   810, 839
Michaels, M.   2634
Michaelson, A.   896
Michaelson-Kanfer, A.   242
Michalak, W.   4122, 5012
Michalowski, M.   3399
Michel, S.   2502
Michelat, G.   1278
Micheloni, M.   150
Michelson, W.   4745
Michon, F.   4237, 4454
Michon, J.   424
Mickelson, R.   5262, 5322
Mickunas, A.   4970
Middendorp, C.   4966
Middleton, L.   5525
Middleton-Stone, M.   5471
Midgley, C.   2125
Midgley, M.   1348
Miethe, T.   5099
Mietzel, G.   1639
Miglani, O.   3789
Mihailescu, V.   3113
Mikami, T.   1358
Mikhailov, V.   3168
Mikulincer, M.   433, 2411
Miles, I.   1349
Miles, L.   3021
Miles, R.   2170, 3288, 5626
Miley, J.   217
Milgram, N.   403, 5021
Milhem, H.   1541
Milich, R.   2808
Millar, J.   5524
Millard, F.   2073
Miller, A.   920, 4947, 4986, 5604
Miller, B.   2232, 2698, 5239, 5377

Index des auteurs

Miller Buchanan, C.   2125
Miller, C.   3859, 5666
Miller, D.   1029, 1128, 1545, 4456, 4976
Miller, F.   1132, 1152, 5813
Miller, H.   4183
Miller, I.   3027
Miller, J.   190, 1236
Miller, K.   4257
Miller, L.   5071
Miller, M.   327
Miller, N.   228, 742, 767
Miller, R.   1858, 2315, 2841, 2853, 4799
Miller, S.   1159, 1975, 5634
Miller, T.   327
Miller, W.   5366
Millman, M.   5632
Mills, C.   1860, 1911, 1912
Mills, E.   3756
Mills, S.   2904
Milne, D.   5737
Milne, W.   2256, 3286
Milner, M.   1843
Milner, S.   4626
Milonakis, D.   3987
Milone, P.   3753
Min, M.   3632
Min, P.   3091
Minaar, A.   5439
Mincy, R.   5353
Mindogulov, V.   5014
Minello, N.   3608
Miner, J.   907
Mingasson, L.   5047
Mingat, A.   1682
Mingione, E.   5334
Minkoff, D.   816
Minow, M.   2086
Minson, J.   2993
Minssen, H.   4239
Minton, H.   404
Mintz, J.   3053
Minz, N.   3124
Miralles, J.   4920
Mir-Hosseini, Z.   1190, 2501
Mirowski, P.   3
Mirza, H.   5387

Misawa, K.   1101
Misbin, R.   5805
Misheva, V.   4838
Miskin, A.   1541
Misovich, S.   766
Misra, A.   3172
Miszalska, A.   4834
Misztal, B.   4839, 5770
Mitchell, A.   4536
Mitchell, D.   1730, 5493
Mitchell, T.   4115
Mitchell, W.   3620
Mitlin, D.   3664
Mitten, R.   997, 3202, 3220
Mitter, S.   4412
Mitter, W.   1751
Miyake, K.   608
Mizrahi, A.   5778, 5778
Mizruchi, M.   260, 713
Mncwabe, M.   1731
Mnookin, R.   2472, 2478
Moatti, J.   3001
Moberg, D.   357
Mocellin, P.   3008
Mochmann, E.   1938
Modak, M.   1122
Modarresi, Y.   1478
Modell, J.   2099
Modgil, C.   1646
Modgil, S.   1646
Moen, P.   914
Moens, G.   4333
Moeran, B.   4194
Moerland, H.   5176
Moffat, F.   2317
Moffesoli, M.   122
Moghadam, V.   2835
Mohamad, H.   5852
Mohamed, A.   1675
Mohan, B.   5612
Mohrman, S.   774
Mohsin, M.   4363
Moiseenko, V.   2010
Moldaschl, M.   4429
Molino, J.   5433
Moll, P.   4652
Möller, M.   4882
Molm, L.   654

Author index

Molokomme, A.   2704
Molotch, H.   4204
Moltz, C.   1475
Momsen, J.   2669
Monach, J.   2251
Monahan, J.   1449, 1518
Mondadori, M.   145
Mondovì, S.   3378
Money, J.   3677, 4996
Monfries, M.   462
Mongardini, C.   4756
Mongeau, P.   4947
Monmonier, M.   238
Montague, R.   2555
Montanari, A.   3883
Montandon, C.   1684
Monteith, M.   659
Montello, D.   387
Montesano, A.   145
Montgomery, D.   439
Montgomery, M.   2216, 4251
Montias, J.   876
Montiel Molina, C.   3606
Moodey, R.   217
Moody, J.   696
Mooijaart, A.   270
Moon, J.   1138
Moor, R. de   1280
Moore, M.   758, 759, 1179, 5380
Moore, R.   4109, 4616
Moore, S.   4371
Moore-Gilbert, B.   1595
Moorman, R.   4471
Moors, H.   2070, 3294
Moos, R.   4459
Mor, J.   2281
Morais, A.   1767
Morales Gutierrez, A.   4548
Morales, T.   5183
Moran, E.   5173, 5255
Moran, L.   2987
Moran, M.   4549
Morand, G.   5574
Mørch, H.   4459
Morchio, M.   3309
More, J.   1319
Morehead Dworkin, T.   810
Morel, A.   3113

Moreland, R.   734, 766, 767
Morelos García, N.   3926
Moreno, L.   5501
Moretti, G.   4020
Morgall, J.   2228
Morgan, D.   228, 3828, 5793
Morgan, G.   884, 3670, 5054
Morgan, L.   5680, 5775
Morgan, M.   3009
Morgan, S.   2483
Morgan, T.   439
Morice, A.   3379
Morin, E.   400, 3976
Morley, D.   1519
Morlicchio, E.   3269, 5334
Moro, M.   3343
Moroney, L.   5270
Morowitz, H.   2221
Moroz, E.   1260
Morozova, G.   3314
Morrill, C.   5043
Morrill, R.   11
Morris, A.   873, 4868, 5201
Morris, B.   495
Morris, C.   1178
Morris, G.   340
Morris, H.   4286, 4650
Morris, J.   2750, 4142, 5719
Morris, L.   2906, 4178, 4384, 5321, 5334
Morris, M.   260, 3060
Morris, N.   1182, 4797
Morris, R.   1304
Morrison, D.   1449, 1518, 4415
Morrissey, J.   773
Morrow, W.   1655, 1703
Morse, G.   267, 326
Mortimer-Szymczak, H.   4283
Mortimore, M.   3480
Morton, G.   4693
Mosco, V.   1519
Moscovici, S.   404, 426
Moser, G.   5433
Moser, T.   5435
Moskowitz, D.   621
Moskvin, D.   3381
Moss, C.   3577
Moss, N.   2269

Index des auteurs

Moss, P. 1635, 2647
Mossbrucker, H. 3385
Mossholder, K. 790
Moston, S. 4816
Mostov, J. 4780
Motamed-Nejad, R. 4064
Motel, A. 3996
Motomura, H. 2565
Moughrabi, F. 1541
Mounier, L. 3001
Mouret-Fourme, E. 3001
Moussaya, E. de la 5776
Mouzelis, N. 195
Mowbray, C. 354
Mowbray, M. 5535
Mowday, R. 818
Mowlana, H. 1310
Mowsesian, R. 2067
Moye, A. 4709
Moyo, J. 4844
Muchini, B. 3313
Mückenberger, U. 4670
Mudimbe, V. 1, 1069
Mudrack, P. 1154
Mueller, C. 4466
Mueller, R. 473
Mueller, W. 4407
Muetzelfeldt, M. 4831
Muggli, C. 3706
Mugny, G. 1353
Muir, L. 5545
Muito, G. 2018
Mukonoweshuro, E. 1891
Mulay, S. 2213
Mulder, C. 3287
Mulder, N. 3159
Muley, D. 2018
Mullahy, J. 5362
Mullaly, R. 5217
Mullen, B. 724
Mullender, A. 5566
Müller, H. 212, 1863, 4576
Müller, K. 3
Müller, P. 4231
Muller, T. 3267
Müller, U. 4005
Müller, W. 71, 1764
Müller-Hartmann, I. 1970

Müller-Schneider, T. 322
Mullin, K. 4339
Mumford, M. 772
Mumma, G. 476
Mun, S. 1341
Münch, R. 1045, 1523
Munday, M. 4142
Municipality of Greater Amman 3817
Münkner, H. 3734
Munn, P. 1673
Munn-Giddings, C. 5252
Munoz-Perez, F. 2348, 2349, 4554
Munro, M. 3834
Munz, D. 561
Münz, R. 1970
Murai, T. 4455
Murch, M. 5594
Murdie, R. 3666
Murdoch, J. 3520
Murdock, G. 1926
Murdock, S. 3360
Murie, A. 3767
Murnighan, J. 429
Murphy, A. 1429
Murphy, C. 2440
Murphy, J. 4970, 4970
Murphy, M. 2211
Murphy, P. 5735
Murray, F. 853
Murray, H. 413
Murray, J. 568
Murray, S. 658
Murray, T. 5773
Murrell, J. 5543
Musandu-Nyamayaro, O. 3746
Muschkin, C. 3251
Musen, G. 542
Musick, M. 968
Musil, J. 40, 1820, 3839
Musselman, C. 2631
Musterd, S. 3666, 3788, 3907
Mutchler, J. 3115
Muthien, Y. 141
Muto, Y. 4526
Mutti, A. 453
Muziol-Weclawowicz, A. 3748
Myerhoff, B. 2075
Myers, D. 4947

Author index

Myers, M. 5105
Myers-Scotton, C. 1565
Mygind, N. 4709
Myhill, J. 5100
Nabuguzi, E. 2786
Nadash, P. 2308
Nadeau, M. 1110
Nadeau, R. 145
Nadelmann, E. 5401
Nadjmabadi, S. 4211
Nadkarni, A. 3548
Nadkarni, M. 3548
Nadkarni, V. 5676
Naerssen, T. van 3780, 3905
Naficy, H. 1541
Nagai, Y. 3720
Nagel, J. 3102
Nagel, R. 2452
Nagin, D. 5119
Nair, K. 4108
Naito, K. 211
Naka, Y. 208
Nakabayashi, I. 3872, 3910
Nakagawa, N. 5057
Nakagiri, S. 1123
Nakane, M. 966
Nakano, T. 1130
Nakano, Y. 1041
Nakao, K. 744
Nakasuji, N. 3678
Nakosteen, R. 4842
Nanavatty, M. 5578, 5612
Nanayakkara, G. 4530
Nancoo, S. 4795
Nandi, P. 5019
Nandy, A. 3196
Naon, D. 5718, 5738
Napier, S. 1618
Naranjo, M. 3034
Narayana, M. 3363
Nardin, P. 5048
Narojek, W. 4832
Nas, M. 1917
Nas, P. 3721
Nash, C. 1021
Nash, F. 245
Nash, R. 1691
Nasraoui, M. 5351

Nassehi, A. 173
Natale, P. 4956
Nathan, C. 3782
Nathanson, P. 1593
Nathawat, S. 2569
National Association of Citizens Advice Bureaux 4376
National Children's Home 5588
National Lesbian and Gay Survey Organization 2992
National Research Council U.S Panel on High-Risk Youth 2144
National Research Council, U.S, Panel on Monitoring the Social Impact of 5753
National Society for the Prevention of Cruelty to Children 2091
Natsukari, Y. 2563
Nattrass, N. 141
Nauclér, K. 1475
Naumova, N. 1855
Nauschütz, M. 4245
Nava L., F. 1622
Navaneetham, K. 2360
Navarro, V. 5760
Nave-Herz, R. 2663
Naylor, R. 5118
Nazimova, A. 4627
Ncube, W. 2704
N'Da, P. 1751
Ndongko, T. 1688
Neal, D. 5182, 5367
Neale, M. 623, 759, 906
Near, J. 810, 839, 4008
Neckel, S. 4683
Negt, O. 1738, 4670
Neider, J. 5371, 5424
Neidhardt, F. 4864
Neidig, P. 2578
Neilsen, J. 1723
Neilssen, J. 4027
Nel, P. 141
Nelms, D. 5695
Nelson, J. 2721, 5820
Nelson, L. 1251, 4118
Nelson, R. 778
Népote, J. 2445
Nesbitt, E. 3264

Index des auteurs

Neshchadin, A. 964
Nesmith, C. 3487
Ness, G. 2024
Nesselroade, J. 553
Neţ, M. 1425, 1480, 1481
Netten, A. 5716, 5746
Neubauer, G. 2139
Neuberger, E. 876
Neuenschwander, R. 3911
Neuhouser, K. 4765
Neuman, S. 2268
Neumann, B. 4397
Neumann, U. 1199
Neumark, D. 1672, 2277
Neumeyer, J. 5421
Neuner, R. 4459
Neustadter, R. 4916
Neuweiler, G. 1738
Neves, I. 1767
Nevo, O. 699
New, S. 5652, 5653
Newburn, T. 5585
Newcomb, A. 2104
Newcomb, H. 1449, 1518
Newell, P. 2113
Newhagen, J. 1519
Newman, K. 2234
Newman, L. 634, 5829
Newman, M. 852
Newman, P. 3500
Newman, S. 5480
Newstead, S. 382
Newton, C. 5514
Ng, I. 4479
Ng, S. 696, 731, 815
Ngo, H. 4487
Nhira, C. 3605
Nhlapo, T. 2704
Ni Bhrolchain, M. 2025
Niaz, M. 1688
Nicholas, L. 2976
Nicholls, D. 1214
Nichols, T. 3988
Nicholson, N. 4420, 4533
Nicholson, P. 379
Nickel, E. 4639
Nickel, H. 1970, 2819
Nickel, T. 4759

Nickell, S. 4002
Nicolau, I. 3113
Niemi, I. 4745
Nieuwbeerta, P. 1900, 4962
Nieuwenhuys, O. 2103
Nieuwoudt, J. 451
Niewiadomska-Bugaj, M. 1616
Nii-Amoo Dodoo, F. 2214
Niihara, M. 1830
Nijkamp, P. 3745
Nikandrov, V. 5309
Nikiforov, A. 5142
Nikitina, T. 1301
Nikol'skii, S. 3621
Nikula, R. 1373
Nipper, J. 3941
Nippert, R. 22
Nirmala, V. 4363
Nishimura, H. 2922
Nissen, U. 2136
Nixon, J. 5761
Nizard, A. 2348, 2349
Nizou, V. 5047
Noam, E. 1449, 1518
Noble, F. 852
Noble, W. 107
Noël, A. 4456
Noin, D. 1985
Nolan, B. 1730, 5493
Noll, H. 4036
Noller, P. 696, 1412
Nollert, M. 683
Nooij, A. 3596
Noon, M. 814, 4405
Noonan, R. 5006
Norchi, C. 895
Norcliffe, G. 3801
Nord, M. 3602
Nordenfelt, L. 474
Norem, J. 597
Noriega, V. 2317
Normann, R. 809
Norrick, N. 479
Norris, C. 4798
Norris, F. 672
Norris, H. 1311
Norris, N. 4798
Northrup, D. 3221

Author index

Norton, A. 1035
Noruwana 1780
Nosal, T. 1668
Notta, H. 5545
Nouvel, K. 3008
Novak, D. 1155
Novak, M. 872, 1151
Novak, T. 5613
Novara, F. 4427
Novelli, L. 439
Novikov, N. 18
Nowotny, H. 35
Nsamenang, A. 402
Ntiri, D. 1640
Nuciari, M. 176
Nuckolls, J. 1494
Nugent, S. 3612
Nugent, W. 5565
Nunes, T. 402
Nuñez, I. 1733
Nunner-Winkler, G. 500
Nurco, D. 5156, 5410
Nurius, P. 532
Nussbaum, M. 4050
Nuttin, J. 470
Nutz, M. 3941
Nuyts, J. 1411
Nwokah, E. 2629
Nyden, P. 244
Nye, R. 2897
Nyland, C. 4641
Nyström, J. 3928
Nzegwu, F. 5638
Oakeshott, M. 647
Oakley, A. 2662
O'Barr, J. 1
Öberg, S. 3376
Oberle, H. 2530
Obermeyer, C. 5674
O'Brien, J. 4654
O'Brien, K. 4243
O'Brien, M. 5388
O'Brien, P. 3062
Och, I. 3759, 3854
Ochs, P. 1372
Ochs, T. 1569
Oconitrillo, G. 3560
O'Connell, J. 3988

O'Connor, B. 2596, 4749, 5764
O'Connor, J. 2672
O'Connor, K. 599
Oddie, G. 3684
Odeh, I. 1707
Odeh, L. 2750
O'Dell, T. 2167
Odland, J. 3275
O'Donnell, H. 4743
O'Donnell, J. 1241
O'Donohue, W. 5088
O'Donovan, K. 5210, 5248
O'Dowd, L. 1856
Oeppen, J. 1983
Oester, K. 2345
Offner, J. 3893, 3920
Ofshe, R. 5081, 5842
Ogasawara, S. 17
Ogawa, D. 3060
Ogawa, N. 2050, 2294
Ogawa, T. 613
Ogden, P. 3423
Ogden, S. 4584
Ogg, J. 5252
Oggins, J. 2586
Ogino, M. 663
Ogletree, S. 2783
Ogryzko-Wiewiórowski, H. 112
O'Hagan, K. 5074
O'Hara, K. 501
O'Hare, A. 2582
O'Hare, W. 1982, 3997
Ohashi, T. 2915
Ohayon, A. 404
Oheneba-Sakyi, Y. 2265
Öhlander, M. 2040, 2051
Ohlsson, R. 225
Ohta, M. 3918
O'hUallachán, B. 3684
Ojeda-Avilés, A. 4590
Okagaki, L. 2638
Okazaki, Y. 2392
O'Keefe, B. 1449, 1518
Okojie, C. 2276
Okuda, M. 3246, 3682
Okuyama, M. 5005
Oladejo, J. 1561
Olaru, C. 2133, 3113

Index des auteurs

Oldfield, N. 5558
Oldman, J. 5259
O'Leary, J. 2025
O'Leary, K. 2578
O'Leary, P. 1144
O'Leary-Hawthorne, J. 1367
Olesiński, J. 4642
Olinger, L. 585
Oliveira, J. de 1521
Oliveira, M. de 2539
Oliveira, O. de 4033
Oliver, M. 2966, 5607
Oliver, P. 730, 1929
Oliveros, T. 3500
O'Looney, J. 5451
Olsen, F. 2740, 2792
Olsen, J. 838, 5707, 5831
Olsen, M. 1827, 3498
Olsen, N. 655
Olshan, M. 1042
Olson, G. 5347
Olson, J. 921
Olson, K. 2260
Olsson, S. 1959, 2812
Olwig, K. 1022
Omaji, P. 4646
O'Malley, P. 957
Omori, M. 1217
O'Muircheartaigh, C. 950
Omvedt, G. 3500
Öncü, A. 1047, 5032
Ondrich, J. 3771, 4628, 5462
O'Neill, J. 3443, 4566
O'Neill, R. 5293
O'Nell, T. 5371, 5424
Onishchenko, V. 4224
Onizuka, R. 677
Onorato, S. 2238
Onyett, S. 5833
Oosterhuis, G. 5004
Oosthuizen, G. 1246
Opitz, P. 3427
Opotow, S. 1118
Opp, K. 2490, 4877
Oppenheimer, G. 5372
Oppenheimer, L. 2097
O'Rand, A. 2064
D'Orazio, G. 959

Orbach, S. 3064
Orbuch, T. 2537
Orcutt, J. 1549
Ordeshook, P. 4771
Ordóñez, A. 5011
O'Regan, K. 4372
Oreillard, B. 1498
Orford, J. 369
O'Riordan, P. 830
Orlic, F. 5232
Orlik, E. 2985
Orloff, A. 2803
Orme, J. 5709
Ormrod, S. 2934
Orozco, J. 1622
Ortega, E. 3625
Ortega, G. 402
Ortega, R. 2588
Ortiz, R. 3085
Osborne, M. 5695
Osborne, R. 1697, 5695
Osei-Hwedie, K. 5548
Osenberg, H. 3894
Osgood, D. 755
Osigweh, C. 4252
Oskolkova, O. 2454
Osman, M. 4163
Osmani, S. 5335
Osmond, M. 2323
Osorio, J. 4
Ost, D. 4819
Ostendorf, W. 3907
Osterman, J. 4299
Østern, A. 1566
Ostos, Z. 4250
Ostroff, C. 785
Ostrom, T. 725, 754
O'Sullivan, D. 1789
Oswald, S. 4664
Otten, F. 4971
Otto, L. 2040
Ouédraogo, Y. 2236
Ouwerkerk, A. 1594
Over, R. 4537
Ow, P. 824
Owens, D. 4649
Owens, J. 2853
Owens, L. 3014

Author index

Oyrzanowski, B. 3977
Oyserman, D. 643
Ozawa, C. 3461
Ozer, D. 573
Özkan, S. 685
Ozmitin, V. 4304
Ozóg, A. 1561
Pace, E. 1230
Pacholczykowa, A. 81
Packer, A. 4566
Packman, J. 5529
Pacolet, J. 2077, 4054
Padavic, I. 4310
Paddison, R. 3677, 3834
Pader, E. 3779
Paderon, E. 4528
Padova, L. di 139
Page, D. 3730
Page, J. 5407
Pagès, R. 404
Paglia, C. 1038
Pagnini, D. 2476
Pahl, J. 857
Paicheler, H. 404
Paillet, P. 5047
Painter, A. 1584
Pais, J. 1680
Pakir, A. 1561
Pakulski, J. 1893, 4895
Palacio, J. 2018
Palakudy, T. 3548
Palćikov, N. 3784
Paleczny-Zapp, M. 3977
Palermo, G. 5125, 5135, 5437
Palidda, S. 1819
Palmer, J. 1433
Palmer, R. 437
Palmer, S. 2923
Palmquist, B. 279
Palmquist, R. 1450
Pampel, F. 2293
Panalal, R. 5676
Panareo, M. 3398
Pandey, R. 1908, 5612
Pandya, S. 5676
Panek, D. 5239, 5377
Panferova, V. 5059
Pang, L. 2475

Pankoke, E. 3528
Pankowska, E. 4113
Pantelldes, E. 2134
Panter, A. 573
Paoli, L. 5110
Paolini, F. 5047
Papadakis, E. 1887
Papadimitriou, D. 4048
Papail, J. 3379
Papalexandris, N. 4527
Pape, J. 4522
Pape, M. le 3379
Papic, Z. 2660
Paradysz, J. 2009, 2215
Paraschos, M. 1529
Parayil, G. 4152
Pardo, I. 1112, 4830
Parisotto, A. 4293
Park, B. 754, 928
Park, K. 2708
Park, P. 244, 1048
Park, W. 3766
Parke, R. 2099, 2622
Parker, B. 2821
Parker, G. 2552
Parker, I. 276
Parker, M. 865
Parker, S. 4407
Parker, T. 1823
Parkes, K. 4459
Parkinson, F. 5545
Parmar, Y. 3949
Parnell, A. 3943
Parnwell, M. 2022
Parrault, V. 3008
Parrott, W. 694
Parry, M. 2096
Parry-Langdon, N. 4649
Parson, D. 3873
Parsons, E. 2224
Parsons, G. 1228
Parsons, J. 331
Parsons, T. 1839
Partlo, C. 923
Pasha, S. 1310
Pasquier, D. 1588
Passas, N. 5186
Passeron, J. 199, 210

Passy, F. 4908
Pasteur, D. 4575
Pastor, P. 5047
Pastorino, R. 676
Pastukhov, V. 976
Pastuović, N. 1761
Patchell, J. 4089, 4143, 4236
Patchen, M. 1975
Pater, B. de 111, 194
Paternoster, R. 5119
Paterson, J. 5572
Paterson, R. 1585
Pathy, S. 3124
Paton, C. 5758
Paton, R. 798
Pattee, L. 2104
Patterson, D. 2821
Patterson, F. 1377
Patterson, G. 573, 1422, 2633
Pattison, P. 261
Patton, P. 4777
Pauchant, T. 400
Paul, E. 1132, 1152, 2908
Paul, H. 4672
Paul, J. 1132, 1152
Paul, R. 439
Paula, S. 2365
Paul-Kohlhoff, A. 1738
Paulsen, R. 4935
Paulson, R. 773
Paulson, S. 1189
Pauw, H. 3762
Pauw, J. 2304
Pavalko, E. 2607
Pavlischek, K. 5785
Pawar, M. 5599
Pawelk, P. 1176
Pawlak, R. 5365
Pawson, E. 3697
Payne, D. 4580
Payne, G. 32
Payne, J. 518, 4947
Paz Sánchez, M. de 1235
Pchelintsev, O. 4224, 5058
Peacock, M. 91
Peak, L. 1664
Peake, L. 3483
Pearce, F. 5123

Pearson, D. 1030, 2419
Pearson, G. 5387
Pearson, R. 4412
Pearson, V. 5838
Peart, K. 2450
Peatross, F. 2671
Pecchinenda, G. 101
Peck, D. 4970
Peck, F. 4098
Peck, S. 343
Pedersen, K. 1564
Pedersen, M. 5707, 5831
Pedersen, N. 553
Pedersen, P. 3545
Pedersen, W. 2145
Pedrabissi, L. 4558
Peeters, D. 3812
Peiger, O. 5047
Peirce, R. 519
Peiris, G. 4568
Peixoto, J. 2280
Pejovich, S. 4771
Pelham, B. 587
Pelinka, A. 1523
Pellegrin, M. 404
Pellegrino, A. 3424
Pellerin, H. 3404
Pelly, J. 5643
Penc, J. 3989
Pencavel, J. 4402
Peneff, J. 4438
Penhale, B. 5236
Penn, R. 3825
Pennant, G. 78
Pennebaker, J. 403, 5021
Pennec, S. 4344, 4349
Pennings, J. 4502
Penrose, J. 3108
La Pensée 3116
Pentz, M. 5392
Pepin-Lehalleur, M. 3608
Peplau, L. 2624
Peräkylä, A. 1409
Pereira, J. 5627
Perelman, S. 5319
Pérez Correa, E. 3614, 3623
Pérez, F. 4214
Pérez Sáinz, J. 4303

Author index

Pérez Salanova, M. 2054
Périlleux, T. 4442
Peritz, E. 2298
Perlstadt, H. 2940
Pernthaler, P. 3071
Péron, Y. 2615
Perracini, M. 5718, 5738
Perrett, R. 1156
Perrier-Cornet, P. 3561
Perrin, J. 1122
Perrin, R. 1302
Perrolle, J. 3450
Perrot, M. 1237
Perrucci, R. 5762
Perry, N. 853
Perry, R. 1197
Perry, S. 1579
Persse, L. 5267
Persson, O. 1341
Perulli, P. 4617
Pérusse, D. 2254
Pescador Osuna, J. 1734
Peschl, M. 105
Peter, L. 4424
Petermann-Graubner, E. 997, 3202
Peters, A. 3894
Peters, B. 5533
Peters, E. 2163
Peters, H. 2472, 2478
Peters, J. 1514, 1519
Peters, M. 1056
Petersen, A. 2125
Petersen, K. 2206
Petersen, R. 1075
Petersen, T. 247, 797
Petersilia, J. 5308
Peterson, D. 513
Peterson, G. 1108, 2126
Peterson, J. 2520
Peterson, M. 980, 4135, 5761
Peterson, R. 5148
Pethe, V. 5340
Petilli, S. 3407
Petitat, A. 150
Petracca, M. 4837
Petras, E. 245
Petras, J. 981, 4930
Petrescu, P. 1422

Petrilli, S. 1425
Petroni, A. 98
Petrosino, D. 3090
Pettinger, A. 2987
Pettit, P. 368, 374
Peukert, H. 189
Pfeffer, N. 5699
Pfohl, S. 1074
Pheby, J. 20
Phelan, J. 4562
Phelan, T. 3795
Pheysey, D. 820
Philips, Å. 821
Phillips, B. 4085
Phillips, E. 2435
Phillips, F. 4531
Phillips, J. 3494, 4728
Phillips, K. 2187
Phillips, M. 4423, 4696, 5419
Phillips, N. 5371, 5424
Phillips, P. 4728
Phillips, S. 5387
Phillips, W. 2940
Phillipson, J. 5630
Philo, G. 1545
Phiri, S. 2456
Phoenix, A. 3197
Phythian-Adams, C. 1848
Piaser, A. 3290
Piazza, M. 2218
Piazza, T. 3183
Picard, E. 4814
Pichardo, N. 4928
Piché, C. 2644
Pichon, P. 5047
Pick, H. 387
Pick, J. 4289
Pickering, A. 24
Picouet, M. 3255
Piedmont, R. 445
Pienkowski, R. 559
Pierce, G. 2628
Pierce, J. 2509
Pieterse, J. 1636
Pietrow-Ennker, B. 2711
Pietz, W. 1225
Pigozzi, B. 4111
Pihet, C. 2020

Index des auteurs

Pijnenborg, L.   5792, 5804
Pikowsky, B.   689
Pilati, A.   1532
Pile, S.   3475
Pilgaonkar, A.   5676
Pilgrim, D.   5836, 5850
Pilgrim, J.   5100
Piliavin, I.   5263
Pillai, V.   2207
Pillay, G.   1246
Pimm, D.   390
Piña, D.   2553
Pinch, S.   4057
Pinch, T.   1340
Pinderhughes, H.   3194
Pinel, E.   581
Ping, T.   2181
Pinnelli, A.   2444
Pinto Soria, J.   3925
Pioquinto, D.   3370
Piparo, F.   150
Piper, D.   357
Pirie, G.   3214
Pirker, T.   4758
Pistrang, N.   5855
Pitelis, C.   847
Pitlíková, J.   3400
Pitt, I.   5737
Pittam, J.   1488
Pittelkow, Y.   2449
Piveteau, J.   1227
Pivnick, A.   2346, 5355
Pivo, G.   3710
Pixley, J.   4247
Pizzorno, A.   145, 4959
Plane, D.   3286, 3387
Plantenga, J.   4322
Platt, A.   3085
Platt, J.   36
Platt, S.   5664
Platts, C.   5100
Plaut, T.   244
Player, E.   5219
Pleck, J.   2624, 2986
Pleskovic, B.   4224
Pligt, J. van der   524
Ploeg, J. van der   3596
Plomin, R.   553

Plotkin, S.   4139
Plous, S.   1118
Plum, V.   4848
Plummer, K.   2984
Plumwood, V.   3453
Plunkett, K.   505, 509
Plutzer, E.   2765
Poche, B.   4790
Pociecha, J.   2033, 2196
Podberezskij, I.   1296
Podogrodzka, M.   2388
Podolny, J.   4190
Poel, M. van der   722
Poewe, K.   4989
Pöhler, W.   22
Poinard, M.   2020
Pokrovskii, N.   1304
Pol, L.   3366
Polakow, V.   5332
Polder, W.   5152
Policy Studies Institute   2319
Polivy, J.   595
Pollak, R.   2253
Pollock, P.   2327
Polonsky, M.   4160
Polzer, J.   623, 759
Ponzio, A.   1425
Pool, J.   1565
Poole, M.   4610
Poot, J.   3319
Pope, L.   506
Popenoe, D.   2400, 2908
Popescu, I.   3113
Popkin, B.   1114, 2330
Popkin, L.   1034
Popov, M.   4224
Popova, A.   3113, 3152
Popova, M.   1425
Poppel, F. van   2484
Popper, F.   4225
Popplestone, R.   5630
Porapova, E.   2985
Porpora, D.   245, 983
Porta, D. della   4866, 4901, 4959
Portelli, G.   743
Porter, B.   3436
Porter, J.   464
Porter, S.   4545

437

Author index

Portes, A.   3060, 3963, 4081
Post, S.   398
Potter, E.   1339
Potter, J.   1436, 1473, 5674
Potter, L.   3303
Potter, R.   3952
Potter, W.   1554
Potton, M.   4549
Poulain, M.   3396
Poulsen, J.   4884
Pourtois, H.   1197
Pouthas, V.   2118
Povinelli, D.   1118
Powell, B.   2412, 2510
Powell, D.   5056
Powell, M.   3785
Powell, T.   3219
Power, M.   4491
Powers, D.   278
Powers, J.   5279
Poyatos, F.   1487
Pozo, C.   2317
Prá, J.   4952
Praag, B. van   281
Pradelle, M. de la   3947
Prades, J.   122
Pradhan, J.   3548
Prager, D.   2971
Prakash, G.   4873
Prakash, P.   5676
Prasad, U.   2333
Pratt, G.   2746, 3027
Pratt, I.   1497
Pratt, J.   3634
Pregibon, D.   282
Preisendörfer, P.   892, 4072
Preiswerk, M.   3052
Prentice, D.   1029
Prentice, R.   4747
Preston, L.   800
Preston, S.   440, 1988, 2542
Preston, V.   2680, 4028
Preston-Shoot, M.   5543, 5586, 5593
Prévot, J.   1852
Prévôt-Schapira, M.   3608
Price, J.   4466
Price, M.   3486
Priebe, R.   5267

Priel, B.   2245
Priemus, H.   3666
Pries, L.   4282
Prietula, M.   824
Prinz, C.   1989
Prior, L.   2387, 5849
Prioux, F.   2020, 2507
Pripp, O.   236
Probyn, E.   2699
Prostituiertenprojekt Hydra   2948
Prottas, J.   5773
Pruchno, R.   2635
Pruger, R.   5557
Pruitt, D.   519, 686
Prujiner, A.   3415
Prussia, G.   4380
Pryer, J.   4025
Psacharopoulos, G.   2793
Pudney, S.   4393
Pugh, D.   442
Pugliese, E.   3420
Pułaska-Turyna, B.   2384
Pulis, J.   1397
Pullen, J.   210
Pumain, D.   2020
Pumariega, A.   2419
Punalekar, S.   1689
Punter, J.   3830
Pupier, P.   1390
Purcell, T.   3148
Purkhardt, S.   428
Purvis, T.   162
Pusey, M.   21
Pusić, V.   52
Putnam, P.   572
Putney, C.   763
Putrevu, S.   4156
Pyszczynski, T.   581
Qian, Z.   2542
Qiu, R.   5830
Quadagno, D.   2323
Quah, S.   65
Quaid, M.   4425
Quale, G.   1997
Quarter, J.   3503
Quercia, R.   3758, 3853
Quéré, M.   4149
Quesnel-Ouellet, L.   4972

Index des auteurs

Quine, L. 415
Quiñones, M. 4570
Quinsey, V. 544
Quintana, F. 27
Quist, T. 654
Ra'anan, U. 3089
Rabenau, C. von 4459
Rabinow, P. 1335
Rabinowitz, B. 2245
Raboy, B. 2239
Rabušic, L. 2372
Rachleff, P. 4624
Racine, G. 5266, 5273, 5391
Racine, J. 3831
Radcliffe, S. 2705, 3487
Radecki, S. 2212
Radkar, A. 2213
Radley, A. 2347
Radnitzky, G. 132
Raelin, J. 4532
Raffe, D. 1757, 1774
Rafferty, J. 926
Raftery, A. 2413
Raghuram, P. 2669
Rahim, A. 2267, 4049, 5341
Rahman, A. 5612
Rahman, M. 2278
Rahman, O. 3822
Rai, S. 2811
Raiborn, C. 4580
Raitz, K. 1027
Rajagopal, A. 1310
Rajan, V. 3584
Rajanti, T. 131
Rajeev, P. 1967
Rajkiewicz, A. 1922
Raju, S. 4360
Rakitskaya, G. 4300
Rakocy, A. 2078
Rakodi, C. 3849
Rakow, L. 1519
Rakow, S. 2798
Rallu, J. 1996, 2282, 2283, 2300
Ram, B. 2267, 2379
Ram, M. 2448, 3216
Ramachandran, N. 5845
Ramaer, H. 5100
Ramakumar, R. 2533

Ramamurti, P. 399
Ramanathan-Abbott, V. 1385
Ramaswamy, S. 1380
Ramazani, N. 2855
Ramazanoglu, C. 2772, 3020
Rambanapasi, C. 3437
Ramey, S. 5694
Ramirez Goicoechea, E. 2131
Ramirez, R. 4289
Rammstedt, O. 1098
Ramos, F. 3395
Ramos, L. 5718, 5738
Rampazi, M. 2690
Ramphal, R. 3154
Ramsay, I. 4561
Ramsey, E. 5293
Rana, G. 5446
Randall, D. 1176
Rani, M. 5178
Rank, M. 2003
Rannou, A. 1110
Ransby, B. 3027
Ranson, S. 1718
Rao, M. 5612
Raoult, E. 3875
Rappaport, J. 5041
Rapport, N. 3441
Raskin, V. 496
Rastogi, P. 5050
Ratajczak, M. 559
Ratchford, C. 3634
Rath, F. 2018
Rath, S. 465
Rathunde, K. 2166
Ratnapala, S. 4333
Ratnayake, W. 4506
Rattinger, H. 935, 4954
Ratzan, S. 4947
Raub, W. 1174
Raudenbush, S. 2802
Rausch, D. 1268, 1326
Rauschenbach, T. 5616
Raven, B. 893
Ravenstein, M. 1552
Ravindran, K. 2941
Raviot, J. 3140
Raviv, A. 409
Ravizza, M. 1170

Author index

Ravoira, L. 2161
Ravololomanga, B. 2879
Rawson, D. 4606
Ray Chaudhuri, J. 3371
Ray, L. 4925
Ray, M. 2938
Raymond, P. 594
Raymore, L. 4735
Reardon, K. 245
Rebelo, J. 1586
Reber, E. 520
Rechner, P. 4008
Rechtman, R. 3322
Rector, R. 4566
Recum, H. von 1738
Redeker, G. 1419
Reder, P. 5063
Redhead, S. 2155, 4736
Redmon, A. 5345
Ree, J. de 4745
Reed, K. 5205
Reed, M. 853, 3452
Reed, W. 2528
Reekie, G. 4192
Reep, J. 5363
Rees, C. 353
Rees, D. 4663
Rees, T. 4649
Reese, W. 1064
Reeves, G. 1507
Reeves, J. 2614
Reeves, K. 3796
Regalski, J. 2648
Regan, P. 77
Reher, D. 2013
Rehm, J. 2355
Reiakvam, O. 1620
Reich, B. 3308
Reich, J. 635
Reichert, C. 3629
Reichertz, J. 5181, 5286
Reichle, A. 620
Reichwein, R. 2463
Reid, G. 4129
Reid, J. 573
Reid, N. 3684
Reilly, A. 400
Rein, M. 2037

Reiner, R. 4786
Reis, H. 655
Reiss, A. 5169, 5308, 5444
Reiss, Jr, A. 5101, 5187
Relmers, F. 1713
Reme, E. 1605
Remennick, L. 2996
Remery, C. 70
Remland, M. 687
Rempel, M. 1893
Remy, J. 1865, 3712, 3956
Reno, W. 4968
Rensburg, N. van 3106
Renvoize, J. 5079
Répássy, H. 3586
Rephann, T. 3834
Reppucci, N. 2149
Rescorla, L. 1475
Reskin, B. 2785, 4443
Resnick, L. 515
Retherford, R. 2050, 2294
Réthoré, J. 1425
Retterstøl, N. 5427
Rettore, E. 4390
Reuband, K. 5382
Reuman, D. 2125
Reuten, G. 3983
Reuter, P. 5401
Reve, T. 4583
Revicki, D. 4459
Rexroat, C. 961
Rey, M. 3915, 5778
Reyes Suarez, A. 5339
Reynaud, E. 4367
Reynié, D. 404, 3699
Reynolds, D. 1681
Reynolds, S. 4459
Reznikoff, M. 560
Rhode, B. 1200
Rhodes, M. 4296
Rhodes, V. 449
Riandey, B. 3001
Ribbens, J. 228
Ribisl, K. 354
Ribner, D. 3402
Rice, M. 1475
Rich, T. 5393
Richardson, D. 2467, 2748

Index des auteurs

Richardson, G. 4985
Richardson, H. 3866
Richardson, K. 497
Richardson, L. 193
Riche, C. 3304
Richmond, A. 3331
Richter, D. 5540
Richter, R. 23
Ridgeway, C. 422
Rieble, S. 4713
Riedmann, A. 2030
Rieffel, R. 1588
Riegel, S. 5183
Riemer, J. 4970
Riess, S. 3055
Rietveld, P. 3839
Rieu, A. 4324
Riff, M. 3049
Rigby, B. 1028
Rigney, D. 1284
Riis, O. 1258
Rijks, T. 588
Riker, W. 4771
Riley, A. 2230
Riley, S. 2786, 5186
Rima, A. 3745
Rimmer, J. 5545
Rindfuss, R. 2476
Ringdal, K. 1851
Rintelen, I. 1953
Riordan, J. 2996
Rios, J. 2148
Rippin, A. 1314
Riseborough, G. 1732, 1769, 2173
Riska, E. 2816
Risley-Curtiss, C. 5681
Risman, B. 4452
Rist, G. 1237
Ritschard, G. 1684
Rittberger, V. 5022
Ritter, C. 2078
Ritzer, G. 1113
Rivero Pinto, W. 3081
Riviére, C. 209, 2158
Rizzo, A. 4433
Rizzo, J. 5679
Rizzuto, A. 706
Robbins, B. 1036, 1538, 4974

Robbins, K. 1006
Robbins, T. 1297
Róbert, P. 3992
Roberts, B. 580, 4033
Roberts, C. 1474, 4720
Roberts, F. 94
Roberts, I. 3509
Roberts, J. 3450
Roberts, K. 784, 4705
Roberts, L. 2807
Roberts, N. 2853
Roberts, P. 1087, 3850
Roberts, R. 4330
Roberts, S. 3836
Robertson, C. 1806
Robertson, D. 1142
Robertson, J. 5201
Robie, D. 1976
Robin, R. 5371, 5424
Robins, K. 1540, 1589
Robins, R. 491, 573, 580
Robinson, C. 3027
Robinson, D. 2317, 3810
Robinson, G. 480
Robinson, M. 2079, 2455, 2486
Robinson, P. 4459
Robinson, R. 557, 682, 4600
Robinson, S. 439, 766
Robinson, V. 2748, 3261
Robinson, W. 1436, 3051
Robles, R. 5407
Robson, C. 246
Roccas, S. 727
Rocha, E. 831
Roche, E. 4079
Rochon, T. 4929
Rock, C. 4709
Rock, P. 1204
Rodkin, P. 1084
Rodríguez Braun, C. 4214
Rodriguez Carrajo, M. 1686
Rodriguez, L. 3085, 5572
Rodwin, M. 5817
Roele, M. 1248
Roemer, J. 140
Roemer, M. 5761, 5771
Roese, N. 4946
Roeske-Słomka, I. 3300

Author index

Rogers, A. 5836, 5850
Rogers, D. 2854
Rogers, E. 1519, 1553
Rogers, J. 4771
Rogers, R. 5231
Rogerson, P. 2643
Rogoff, I. 2896
Rogowski, S. 5555
Rogucka, E. 2371
Rohe, W. 3758, 3853
Rohrschneider, R. 4890
Rojas, R. 3
Rojek, C. 10, 4751
Rokicka, E. 4516
Rokkan, S. 338
Röling, N. 3596
Rolland, J. 4558
Roller, E. 286, 3191
Rollnick, S. 5560
Roman, L. 1634
Román, M. 2736
Romanin, S. 4537
Romano, R. 150
Romito, P. 2836
Romney, A. 744
Roncek, D. 323
Ronen, T. 5538
Roniger, L. 446
Rønn, E. 5707, 5831
Ronström, O. 3039
Rönz, B. 1986
Roof, W. 1247
Rooijakkers, G. 1127
Rooijen, E. van 2163
Roos, P. 4556
Roosa, M. 2634
Root, M. 138
Rooum, D. 5100
Rop, T. 3748
Roper, M. 4509
Roquebert, J. 4135
Roques, C. 1516
Rørbye, B. 2040
Rosa, M. 2393
Rosa, T. 5718, 5738
Rose, A. de 2557
Rose, B. 4351, 5615
Rose, D. 289

Rose, G. 2733
Rose, K. 4359
Rose, P. 3060
Rose, S. 5072
Rosen, M. 3049
Rosen, S. 1711
Rosenau, J. 4967
Rosenberg, H. 5402
Rosenberg, J. 2940
Rosenberg, M. 3591
Rosenberg, R. 2874
Rosenberg, S. 4491
Rosenblatt, A. 5841
Rosenfeld, A. 5586
Rosenfeld, P. 340
Rosengren, A. 1100
Rosengren, K. 1449, 1518
Rosenthal, D. 3010
Rosenthal, R. 317, 1677
Rosenzweig, M. 402, 2632
Rosero-Bixby, L. 2230, 2284
Rosie, A. 228
Rösner, E. 1738
Ross, C. 2434
Ross, D. 14
Ross, S. 3797
Rosser, J. 3959
Rossi, M. 4439
Rossi, R. 1790
Rossner, S. 457
Rostocki, W. 344
Rószkiewicz, M. 2029, 2290
Rotemberg, J. 4426
Rotenberg, K. 2596
Rotenberg, R. 3735
Roth, G. 1305
Roth, J. 5169, 5444
Roth, K. 857
Roth, N. 810
Rothacher, A. 1845
Rothbard, A. 5845
Rothblatt, S. 1793
Rothenbuhler, E. 1449, 1518
Rothermund, D. 1324
Rotherty, M. 5618
Rothman, A. 384
Rothman, S. 1030
Rotton, J. 5093

Index des auteurs

Rouillard, J. 4671
Roulleau-Berger, L. 3724, 4259
Roura, J. 4230
Rouse, T. 1137
Roussel, L. 2414, 2492
Rousselet, K. 1288
Roussillon, B. 5047
Routh, D. 1730, 5493
Rowe, A. 3775
Rowe, D. 4731
Rowe, F. 1458
Rowe, R. 544
Rowland, R. 2239
Rowland, V. 930
Rowland, W. 1449, 1518
Rowlinson, M. 4096
Roy, C. 1495
Roy, J. 3541
Royal Institute of the Architects of Ireland 5518
Royal, M. 1790
Rozell, E. 557
Rozenbaum, M. 4557
Ruan, D. 640
Ruback, R. 3233
Rubalcava, R. 4368, 4488
Ruberti, A. 3258
Rubery, J. 4319
Rubin, G. 3055, 3060
Rubin, H. 4970
Rubin, M. 2314
Rubin, Z. 2624
Rubinstein, D. 187
Rubinstein, W. 5036
Rubio-Stipec, M. 420
Ruble, B. 3773
Ruby, C. 3008
Ruby, J. 2075
Ruch, W. 465, 496
Rucht, D. 4864, 4901
Rud, Jr, A. 1661
Rudder, C. 43
Rudkin, L. 2055
Rudman, L. 575
Rudolph, W. 4474
Rudzitis, G. 3579
Rueschemeyer, M. 3661
Ruf, W. 3375

Ruggiero, K. 1399
Rugs, D. 767
Ruhigira, J. 3812
Rühl, M. 1525
Ruitenberg, E. 2303
Rukavishnikov, V. 963
Rumiati, R. 145
Runciman, W. 3978
Runco, M. 439
Rundell, J. 480
Rundquist, A. 2767
Ruonavaara, H. 3787
Rupp, L. 2779
Rural Sociological Society, Task Force on Persistent Rural Poverty 3585
Rusbult, C. 653, 677
Rüsen, J. 3189
Rush, H. 4565
Rushing, B. 2078, 2238, 5659
Rushton, D. 1572
Rushton, G. 3457
Rusinova, N. 5663
Rusk, D. 3648
Russell, C. 1779
Russell, D. 5044
Russell, J. 5590
Russell, M. 402, 1530
Russell, P. 3221
Russo, C. 1730, 5493
Russo, N. 593
Rust, P. 2951
Rutenberg, N. 2274
Rutkevich, M. 967
Rutter, D. 415
Ruxton, S. 2647
Ruzek, S. 5637
Ruzicka, L. 5430
Rwabukwali, C. 2240
Rwezaura, B. 2704
Ryan, C. 754
Ryan, M. 5198
Ryba, R. 1751
Rydzewski, P. 2183, 2489
Rykind-Erikson, K. 1574
Rys, V. 5505
Rystad, G. 3405
Saada, E. 3141
Saari, J. 4418

Author index

Saavedra, L. 191
Saavedra, R. 649
Sabagh, G. 3125
Sabel, C. 4134
Sabelli, F. 1237
Saberwal, S. 1941
Sabin, N. 5737
Sabin, R. 1361
Sabornie, E. 2152
Sabour, M. 1867
Sacco, V. 5172
Sachs, B. 5047
Sachs-Jeantet, C. 3929
Sack, W. 5371, 5424
Sacks, J. 599, 1331, 3850
Sadalla, E. 2561
Sadowska-Kowalska, E. 1747
Saenz, R. 3458, 4725
Safa, H. 2687
Saff, G. 4226
Saffarnia, P. 1523
Saffer, H. 5360
Safi, L. 221
Safir, N. 3415
Sagaza, H. 2061
Sahadat, J. 3036
Şahin, H. 1043
Sahoo, F. 383
Saikawa, T. 5472
Sailer, L. 38
Saini, D. 4623
Sainsbury, D. 5465
Sainsbury, R. 5485
St. Clair, L. 769
Saint-Blancat, C. 3339
Saito, M. 3649
Sajjad, W. 1310
Sajkiewicz, A. 4044
Sakai, T. 5049
Sakiyama, O. 1395
Sakurai, T. 1962
Sakuta, K. 95
Sakva, R. 4892, 4893
Salamon, S. 3556
Salas, D. 5213, 5298
Salas, E. 748
Salazar, P. 114
Salehi-Isfahani, D. 2023

Salmon, R. 5570
Salo, E. 2722
Salone, C. 3839
Saloner, G. 4426
Salovey, P. 384
Salt, J. 3288, 3403
Salvage, A. 5732
Salvaggio, S. 145
Salzberg, A. 5774
Samman, M. 2018
Samouco, A. 3580
Samper, L. 4542
Sampson, R. 5105, 5288, 5308
Samuels, M. 5540
Samuels, W. 5473
Sanada, S. 1479
Sanbonmatsu, D. 109
Sanchez, J. 882, 3100, 5048
Sanchez, L. 2859
Sánchez, M. 244
Sánchez Munguía, V. 3412
Sanchez, S. 5648
Sánchez Vera, P. 2054
Sanchis, E. 4279
Sande, G. 4946
Sandelands, L. 769, 887
Sander, W. 2540, 2541, 4389
Sanderatne, N. 3490
Sanders, C. 636
Sanders, D. 3124
Sanders, J. 1975
Sanders, S. 4318
Sandfort, T. 2978
Sandiford, P. 2304
Sandole, D. 5007
Sandoval, J. 1295
Sandstrom, K. 945
Sandvik, E. 493, 4052
Sandvik, G. 3046
Sanetra, W. 4659
Sanik, M. 4745
Sanitioso, R. 520
Sanniti, C. 5226, 5304
Sano, Y. 4252
Sansone, L. 3070
Sansot, P. 5047
Sant, M. 3357, 3653
Santaella Braga, L. 1425

Index des auteurs

Santinello, M. 4558
Santos Filho, J. dos 1735
Santos, M. 1024
Santow, G. 2483
Sapir, J. 3990
Sapiro, V. 2742
Saporiti, E. 1425
Sar, N. van der 281
Saraiva, H. 4362
Saran, M. 1768
Saranich, R. 3634
Sarasa, J. 1293
Sarason, B. 2628
Sarason, I. 2628
Sarayrah, Y. 1050
Sardar, Z. 1310, 3196
Sardi, M. 1122
Saris, R. 4991
Saris, W. 4896
Sasajima, Y. 4252
Sasaki, M. 273, 1079
Sashin, J. 706
Sassower, R. 1065
Sathe, S. 2941
Sathyamala, C. 3500
Sato, T. 1014
Sato, Y. 207
Satorra, A. 266
Satterthwaite, D. 3664, 3675
Satzewich, V. 2420
Saunders, B. 5419
Saunders, P. 4045
Saunders, S. 5177, 5449
Saupe, G. 4734
Sauvage, P. 5048
Savage, M. 3442, 3719
Save the Children Fund 2450
Saville, J. 1838
Savitch, H. 3820
Sawilowsky, S. 5389
Sawiński, Z. 350, 2844
Sawyers, K. 3148
Saxer, U. 1523
Sayegh, L. 3318
Sayger, T. 2459
Scaff, L. 146
Scalamandré, A. 2289
Scandariato, R. 3350

Scannell, P. 989, 1510, 1570
Scarborough, H. 1475
Scarbrough, H. 853
Scarpaci, J. 5504
Scartezzini, R. 1977
Schaefer, C. 487
Schaefer, J. 4459
Schaefers, T. 3734
Schaeffer, N. 330
Schaeffer, P. 3641
Schäfer, R. 3846
Schäfers, C. 3941
Schäfers, M. 1282
Schaffer, C. 5718, 5738
Schaffer, H. 2111
Schaich-Walch, G. 5421
Scharpf, F. 4394
Schatzki, T. 149
Schauffler, R. 4081
Schaut, G. 2596
Scheele, S. 3376
Scheepers, P. 3151
Scheffler, S. 1153
Scheier, M. 2317
Schein, R. 3836
Scheler, M. 467
Scheman, N. 2658
Schenk, M. 934
Schenk, S. 1970
Schepers, R. 5461
Scherbov, S. 2186
Schervish, P. 5628
Scheuble, L. 2572
Scheuch, E. 338
Scheuerman, W. 4139
Schick, J. 1730, 5493
Schie, E. van 524
Schiele, B. 2752
Schienstock, G. 4703
Schiff, J. 696
Schiff, M. 952
Schiffauer, W. 3259
Schiffman, H. 1565
Schiller, D. 1519
Schiller, N. 2346, 5355
Schiller-Lerg, S. 1552
Schindler, R. 3402
Schinnar, A. 5845

Author index

Schippers, J. 4315
Schirato, T. 1019
Schlachter, M. 4648
Schlegel, U. 1970
Schlegelmilch, C. 2039
Schlemmer, B. 209
Schlesinger, M. 5401, 5768
Schlesinger, P. 989, 1043, 1310, 1510, 1517, 1545
Schlett, I. 3067
Schlottmann, A. 3286
Schlüter, A. 2691
Schlüter-Müller, S. 2154, 3082
Schmalstieg, H. 3734
Schmalzbauer, J. 939
Schmeets, J. 4971
Schmid, J. 849, 2192, 4090, 4670
Schmid, M. 1090
Schmida, M. 965
Schmidt, C. 3473
Schmidt, I. 3315
Schmidt, J. 5245
Schmidtz, D. 603
Schmied-Kowarzik, W. 4760
Schmitt, J. 4391
Schmitthenner, H. 4708
Schmitz, E. 1671
Schmitz, S. 3894
Schnare, A. 5480
Schneewind, J. 1158
Schneider, B. 1523, 1559
Schneider, E. 853
Schneider, H. 4130
Schneider, J. 5718, 5738, 5832
Schneider, M. 3795
Schneider, S. 782, 786
Schnell, I. 3518, 3537
Schnell, J. 4628
Schnepel, E. 1397
Schober, B. 5347
Schober-Peterson, D. 1413
Schoderbek, P. 4434
Schoen, R. 2598
Schoeni, R. 4019
Schoepfle, O. 1642
Schofield, R. 2013
Scholte, J. 1942
Scholz, M. 5463

Schönbach, K. 1523, 1559
Schondel, C. 5200, 5292
Schoonmaker, S. 4229
Schopler, J. 762, 768
Schorb, B. 1536, 2146
Schostak, J. 1103
Schrage, H. 2314
Schreier, G. 1694
Schreuder, H. 806
Schreurs, K. 2870, 3000
Schrijvers, A. 5718, 5738
Schrire, R. 4233
Schröer, N. 5181, 5286
Schroeter, H. 1282
Schubert, H. 2192
Schuessler, K. 304
Schul, Y. 430, 952
Schuler, R. 4481
Schuller, T. 1802
Schulman, P. 859
Schultz, L. 693
Schulz, E. 2192
Schulz, M. 793, 2665, 3260
Schulz, U. 1524
Schulz, W. 925
Schulz zur Wiesch, J. 3660
Schumaker, J. 462
Schumaker, P. 3514
Schupp, J. 4574
Schuppert, G. 5520
Schurman, S. 4682
Schütze, Y. 631
Schwagler, J. 2621
Schwartz, B. 604, 991
Schwartz, G. 569
Schwartz, I. 5226, 5304
Schwartz, J. 4562
Schwartz, L. 403, 5021
Schwartz, M. 5238, 5253
Schwartz, S. 727
Schwartz, T. 1206
Schwartzman, S. 1794
Schwarz, N. 386, 594
Schweers, C. 1435
Schweitzer, H. 5132
Schweizer, M. 3529
Schweizer, T. 3529
Schwendinger, H. 5122

Index des auteurs

Schwendinger, J. 5122
Schweppe, C. 3902
Schwerzel, M. 75
Schwinn, T. 182
Sciolla, L. 770
Scipes, K. 4691
Sciulli, D. 217
Sclavi, M. 454
Scott, C. 4664
Scott, E. 396, 5126, 5182, 5367
Scott, J. 2451
Scott, L. 1730, 5493
Scott, P. 1797
Scott, W. 4258
Scriven, M. 1548
Scriven, P. 5397
Scudder, R. 5077, 5296
Scutt, T. 501
Sealand, N. 2107
Seale, A. 5596
Sebago, P. 2236
Sebastian, R. 3500
Sebelin, D. 5707, 5831
Sebeok, T. 1425
Seca, J. 404
Séchet, R. 2020
Sedikides, C. 655, 725, 754
Seelman, K. 5773
Seewann, G. 3161
Seff, M. 576
Segal, D. 1022, 1975, 4996
Segal, L. 2896
Segal, S. 2334
Segert, A. 1970
Sego, D. 4570
Segrestin, D. 4136, 4237
Segrin, C. 665, 696
Segura, D. 2509
Seibel, R. 476
Seibert, P. 534
Seidel, R. 2149
Seidel-Pielen, E. 3218, 5435, 5438
Seidler, V. 2916
Seidlitz, L. 493, 4052
Seidman, G. 2833, 4295
Seidman, S. 1066
Seikaly, M. 2710
Seilheimer, D. 2419

Seki, K. 1715
Selberg, T. 1574, 1590
Self, R. 4399
Sélim, M. 3947
Sell, J. 4729
Sellier, F. 404
Semenov, I. 1854
Semmes, C. 3035
Semyonov, M. 3145
Sen, A. 4050
Sen, Y. 1907
Senchak, M. 2895
Senior, M. 5652, 5653
Sennhauser, S. 403, 5021
Sensenbrenner, J. 3963
Seong, K. 4796
Sering, A. 2416
Serlin, R. 357
Sermsri, S. 2972, 3744
Sernini, M. 3863
Serour, G. 5790
Serpell, R. 1683
Serrano, M. 1794
Serrano Sanz, J. 999
Serrano-García, I. 1978
Sershen, C. 5006
Sesardic, N. 1840
Sethi, S. 1166
Sevastos, P. 4407
Sever, A. 2494
Seydlitz, R. 3440
Seymour, S. 4447
Sfez, L. 5433
Sgroi, E. 444
Shagle, S. 2617
Shah, N. 2749
Shah, P. 618, 759
Shakespeare, P. 248
Shalinsky, A. 2925
Sham, P. 421
Shames, I. 4722
Shami, S. 2198
Shamir, B. 902
Shamshurin, V. 177
Shamshurina, N. 5682
Shanahan, M. 5343
Shanks, N. 5788
Shanley, M. 2242

Author index

Shapiro, D. 4459, 5855
Shapiro, J. 2564
Shapiro, K. 1118
Shapland, J. 5174, 5447
Shapovalov, V. 4910
Sharda, B. 2405
Sharfman, M. 866
Sharkansky, I. 3862
Sharma, A. 170
Sharoni, S. 2933
Sharp, J. 119
Sharpe, S. 3020
Sharrock, R. 388
Sharrock, W. 99
Shaw, D. 403, 1553, 5021
Shaw, I. 5855
Shaw, J. 4483
Shayne, M. 5484
Shcheglov, L. 2996
Shea, G. 766
Shea, J. 462
Shearing, C. 4817
Shebilske, L. 664
Sheehy, G. 2042
Sheeran, P. 2156
Sheets, V. 698
Shefer, D. 4217
Shefner, J. 4875
Sheinin, D. 4903
Shelley, F. 5020
Shen, J. 3536
Shepherd, G. 1449, 1518
Shepherd, H. 3010
Shepherd, J. 57
Shepherd, V. 1924
Sheppard, M. 5621, 5781, 5853
Sheptycki, J. 5203, 5246
Sheridan, D. 228
Sherkat, D. 1269, 1289
Sherman Grant, D. 4066
Sherman, J. 754
Sherman, L. 5111, 5193, 5245, 5308
Sherman, S. 392, 2567
Sherzer, J. 1485
Shettima, K. 2786
Shevshuk, S. 4722
Shewman, R. 5082
Shi, L. 5540

Shiach, M. 1028
Shibano, S. 1685
Shibata, H. 2063
Shields, G. 5200, 5292
Shields, J. 4396
Shields, V. 2764
Shih, C. 5008
Shikata, H. 5039
Shilling, C. 154, 1016
Shilts, R. 4995
Shim, J. 1136
Shimoda, N. 1875
Shimpo, M. 1932
Shimron, J. 1492
Shinn, M. 4459
Shiva, V. 3500
Shlay, A. 5469
Shnieper, R. 4224
Shoemake, A. 930
Shoemaker, P. 1519
Shome, D. 2046
Shonkwiler, J. 3577
Shore, J. 5371, 5424
Shore, L. 4252
Short, C. 1216
Short, J. 111, 194, 843, 863, 3868
Short, K. 616
Shortall, S. 3553
Shotter, J. 90, 1102, 1466
Shotton, J. 1670
Shrout, P. 573
Shrum, W. 752
Shtoulberg, B. 4224
Shubane, K. 3922
Shubkin, V. 4307
Shukla, V. 3687, 3759, 3854
Shulman, S. 3973
Shumway, J. 3275, 4374
Shure, M. 5694
Shute, C. 1644
Shuval, J. 5696
Shweder, R. 372, 2086
Sibley, D. 2512
Sica, A. 146
Sidanius, J. 951
Siddique, S. 1317
Siddiqui, D. 1453
Siddle, D. 2202

448

Index des auteurs

Siebel, W. 4219
Sieber, U. 1209
Siebers, R. 2127, 4365
Siedhoff, M. 2015
Siegel, J. 1118
Siegel, M. 530
Siegers, J. 2822, 4278, 4315, 4322, 4337, 5528
Siero, F. 919
Sifianou, M. 1479
Sigal, V. 1781
Sigelman, L. 3147
Sigmund, S. 172
Sigusch, V. 2758
Sikes, O. 2018
Sikka, P. 4535, 4536
Silber, S. 2641
Sill, O. 2178
Silva, J. 4435
Silva, M. 3615
Silva, P. 5388, 5511
Silver, H. 2889, 5334
Silver, M. 2314
Silverman, I. 2187, 2958, 5077, 5296
Silverman, R. 4947
Silvern, L. 2624
Silverstone, R. 1460, 1591
Siméon, J. 5433
Simes, M. 2398
Simkin, C. 1346
Simmel, G. 1098
Simmel, M. 4351, 5615
Simmie, J. 3860
Simmons, A. 3411
Simmons, I. 3462
Simon, B. 750
Simon, J. 4371
Simon, L. 581
Simon, P. 2020
Simon, R. 1675, 3060
Simonds, W. 499
Simonet, J. 3008
Simonin, B. 5048
Simons, P. 3357, 3653
Simons, R. 2407, 2613, 5242
Simonsen, M. 2040
Simonson, L. 245
Simpkins, R. 2329

Simpson, D. 5135, 5437
Simpson, J. 393, 548, 4664
Sims, D. 827
Sinason, V. 2645
Sinclair, A. 777
Sinclair, I. 5071
Sindelar, J. 5362
Singell, L. 3286
Singer, E. 946, 2235
Singer, H. 262
Singer, J. 569
Singer, L. 2731
Singer, M. 1215
Singer, P. 1135
Singer, S. 5295
Singh, A. 3188
Singh, B. 47
Singh, D. 3368
Singh, K. 2533
Singh, S. 3548, 3885
Singh, V. 2533
Singhal, S. 1741
Singhapakdi, A. 1167
Singleton, S. 717
Singly, F. 2887
Sinha, J. 402
Sinha, Y. 110
Sinson, J. 5717
Sintsina, I. 4261
Sinuany-Stern, Z. 3917
Sipos, I. 5450
Sipos, S. 1957
Sirageldin, I. 4297
Sirefman, J. 3055
Sisk, J. 5766
Sistler, A. 2538
Sisulu, E. 2129
Sitkin, S. 688, 810
Sittitrai, W. 2997
Siurala, L. 1719
Sivertsev, M. 2035
Sivertseva, T. 2035
Sjögren, A. 236
Skagestad, P. 116
Skinner, J. 2025
Skipper, R. 1165
Skog, O. 200, 5423
Skolnick, J. 5401

Author index

Skowronski, J. 533
Skuy, M. 5595
Skvoretz, J. 242, 909
Slajmer-Japelj, M. 5718, 5738
Slany, K. 3406, 4312
Slaymaker, O. 3452
Slesina, W. 22
Slesnick, D. 5325
Sloan, C. 478
Sloan, F. 5484
Sloep, P. 1688
Slonim-Nevo, V. 5617
Slotkin, R. 1004
Slugoski, B. 607
Slyomovics, S. 1541
Small, S. 3017
Smart, A. 1335
Smelser, N. 1045
Smidt, M. de 3839
Śmiłowski, E. 350
Smirnova, N. 254
Smit, J. 3596
Smith, A. 1730, 2750, 3119, 5493
Smith, C. 217, 506, 878, 3749, 4432, 4655, 4704
Smith, D. 2455, 3450, 5610, 5689
Smith, E. 4570
Smith, G. 2304, 4465
Smith, I. 1274
Smith, J. 117, 2048, 2269
Smith, L. 5185
Smith, M. 84, 3759, 3854, 3921, 5167, 5443
Smith, P. 416, 1078, 1771, 1778, 4286, 4650, 4693, 5383
Smith, R. 267, 326, 583, 694, 1703, 3671, 4268, 5729
Smith, S. 2885, 3450, 5489
Smith, T. 309, 528, 1943, 2957
Smither, R. 545
Smits, J. 4505
Smock, P. 2556
Smolka, M. 3802
Smoll, F. 583
Smyth, A. 2715
Smyth, H. 3851
Sneck, W. 1224
Snell, A. 772

Sniderman, P. 3183, 3221
Snipp, C. 3102
Snow, J. 3233
Snowden, R. 2239
Snyder, I. 1743
Sober, E. 141
Sobnosky, M. 4947
Sobo, E. 2346, 5355
Soest, A. van 4323
Soest, D. von 3846
Soguel, N. 3909
Sohrab, J. 2928
Soininen, M. 3325
Solesbury, W. 3870
Soliman, A. 2368
Solinge, H. van 5474
Solingen, E. 4540
Soloff, D. 4574
Solomon, E. 4055
Solomon, S. 581
Solov'eva, L. 5506
Som, S. 2185
Somerman, F. 5284
Somers, M. 2546, 4949
Somervell, P. 5371, 5424
Somit, A. 1842
Somma, M. 3495
Somma, P. 3808
Sommer, H. 3911
Sommers, I. 5160
Sommerville, A. 5816
Sondak, H. 758, 759
Sonenstein, F. 2624, 2986
Sonfield, M. 4123
Song, A. 2420
Songsore, J. 3799
Sonnheim, M. 5619
Sonntag, S. 1429
Sonuga-Barke, E. 4199
Sonyel, S. 3306
Sooman, A. 5754
Soothill, D. 1544
Soothill, K. 1544
Sopp, P. 4249
Sørensen, A. 2786
Sorenson, A. 5307
Sorge, A. 4578
Sosin, M. 5263

Index des auteurs

Sosnowski, S.   1034
Soubeyran, O.   3497
South, S.   2591, 3770, 3805
Sow, I.   2871
Sowards, B.   485
Sowards, K.   2351
Sozański, T.   268
Spain, D.   2818, 3440, 3502
Spalding, N.   4924
Sparks, C.   989, 1504, 1510
Sparling, K.   82
Sparrow, J.   3216
Spaulding, S.   1721
Spears, R.   2156
Speicher, B.   661
Speidel, G.   1475
Spellman, B.   403, 5021
Spence, L.   5497
Spence, N.   3912
Spencer, B.   290, 3001
Spencer, J.   337, 5192
Spencer, N.   5073
Spencer, S.   596, 4786
Spender, J.   870
Spero, M.   425
Spicer, K.   2025
Spicker, P.   5487
Spiegel, A.   1046
Spiegel, U.   5133, 5196
Spieler, E.   3834
Spiertz, H.   3575
Spilsbury, M.   4490, 4563, 4573
Spindler, Z.   3782
Spira, A.   2247, 3001
Sporokowski, M.   5573
Spreckelmeyer, K.   4431
Sprondel, W.   15
Sproull, A.   4260
Spurgeon, P.   5772
Squarzoni, R.   5048
Squire, L.   542
Squires, G.   4201
Squires, J.   1071, 2987
Srikantan, K.   2213
Srivatsan, V.   887
Staats, S.   923
Staber, U.   4294
Stace, D.   868

Stacey, J.   2400, 2896
Stack, C.   2442
Stack, M.   4150
Stack, S.   5425
Stacy, A.   5392
Staggenborg, S.   4928
Stahl, A.   931, 1647
Stallabrass, J.   4730
Stallard, E.   320
Stamm, K.   3342
Stanfield, J.   3973, 3973
Stangl, W.   564
Stanko, E.   5092
Stanley, C.   1086, 3701, 5445
Stanley, L.   104, 228, 2941
Starbuck, W.   853
Stark, D.   4464
Stark, E.   5245
Stark, R.   1285
Starosta, P.   3572
Staszyńska, K.   324
Statsevich, T.   346
Staufenbiel, F.   3793
Stauning, I.   2662
Stauth, G.   186
Stavenhagen, R.   4828
Stavrou, S.   2914
Staw, B.   4461
Steckel, J.   908
Stecker, H.   3014
Steeh, C.   3796
Steele, C.   596
Steele, H.   391
Steele, J.   5477
Steele, M.   3733, 4257
Steelman, L.   2412
Steen, W. van der   1688
Steeves, H.   1449, 1518
Stefanikova, Z.   3113
Steffensmeier, D.   3169
Stefkovich, J.   1730, 5493
Steggerda, M.   2837
Steigenga, T.   1295
Steiger, H.   566, 2153
Stein, E.   2963
Stein, J.   4465
Stein, R.   1398, 1408
Steinberg, L.   2639

Author index

Steindorff, C. 5208, 5297
Steinhagen-Thiessen, E. 2048
Steinmüller, P. 4249
Stemmler, M. 2125
Sten, C. 3055
Stennert, D. 2439
Stenson, K. 5608
Stepaniants, M. 2905
Stephens, C. 788
Stephens, J. 5492
Stephens, M. 5458
Stephenson, G. 4816
Stephenson, K. 2798
Stephenson, W. 5794
Stercq, C. 4275
Sterelny, K. 374
Sterk-Elifson, C. 5400
Stern, E. 3668, 3917
Stern, F. 997, 3202
Stern, L. 601
Stets, J. 614
Steury, E. 371
Stevens C. 4592
Stevens, D. 789
Stevenson, J. 4744
Stevenson, N. 1005
Stevenson, O. 5064
Stevenson-Hinde, J. 2601
Stever, J. 891
Stewart, J. 2704, 3171, 4698, 4981, 5388
Stewart, M. 400
Stewart, P. 4525
Stewart, R. 3834
Stewin, L. 5575
Stickel, S. 5572
Stieber, S. 5293
Stiehler, H. 1536, 2146
Stiens, G. 2015, 3894
Stier, H. 3328
Stifler, K. 1224
Still, J. 128
Stillwell, A. 710
Stilwell, D. 644
Stilwell, F. 3879
Stine, E. 1421
Stinner, A. 1688
Stinner, W. 3285, 3355, 3383

Stith, S. 5251
Stjernberg, T. 821
Stöber, R. 1441
Stock, M. 1960
Stockmann, R. 4100
Stoecker, R. 244, 245
Stojanov, C. 1975
Stokvis, R. 4185
Stolba, A. 2513
Stolz-Willig, B. 2886
Stone, I. 4098
Stone, L. 1669
Stone, M. 2269, 3777, 3904
Stone, S. 4905
Stonebraker, R. 1290
Storey, P. 2380
Storgaard, K. 4453
Stork, J. 1541
Stoskopf, C. 5540
Stout, R. 1698
Strack, F. 386
Stradling, S. 4800, 4816
Straker, G. 628
Strang, D. 179, 314
Strasser, H. 910
Stratford, E. 3459
Stratton, J. 1596, 1918
Stratton, L. 4381
Stratton, P. 5586
Straube, H. 2321
Straubhaar, T. 3311
Straus, M. 5245
Strauss, A. 4398
Strazhas, N. 1426
Street, B. 1645
Streit, U. 2919
Stremmel, A. 4494
Stren, R. 3945
Stricker, H. 3846
Strijker, D. 3596
Strike, K. 1703
Stringfield, P. 4436
Strobel, F. 1870
Stroh, G. 2350
Strohmayer, U. 83
Stronach, I. 1394
Strong, P. 1022
Strous, M. 5595

Index des auteurs

Struthers, T. 3850
Struyk, R. 3748
Strydom, A. 1780
Stryker, S. 4928
Stuart, D. 3458
Stuijvenberg, P. van 4108
Stultz, N. 1562
Stumpel, J. 1594
Stumpf, H. 551
Stürzebecher, D. 1523, 1559
Stuttard, C. 4544
Styles, S. 5038
Suarez-Villa, L. 4230
Subileau, F. 4948
Subirats, J. 4214
Suchindran, C. 705, 2533
Sudderth, L. 4928
Sudo, N. 905
Sudre, F. 4788
Suedfeld, P. 403, 5021
Sufian, A. 1994
Sugar, M. 5556
Sugden, R. 603
Sugimori, S. 756
Sugino, A. 982
Sullenberger, T. 5306
Sullins, D. 1303
Sullivan, G. 3421
Sullivan, L. 947, 1654
Sullivan, M. 372
Sullivan, O. 289
Sullivan, P. 767
Sullivan, R. 4371
Sultán, M. 2655
Sumler, D. 1712, 1792
Sumner, N. 3469
Sundaram, J. 2093
Sunder Rajan, R. 2694
Sundström, G. 3376
Sundström, M. 2820
Suprasert, S. 2997
Surinov, A. 4035
Surjadi, C. 2335
Susato, S. 4511
Süss, W. 5315
Susser, I. 5261
Suter, S. 3911
Sutherland, L. 2588

Sutker, P. 403, 5021
Sutnick, G. 5752, 5846
Sutton, C. 3055
Sutton, J. 4258
Sutton, M. 5416
Sutton, R. 818
Suzuki, H. 31
Suzuki, S. 877
Suzuki, T. 273
Svalastog, A. 2655
Svallfors, S. 929
Svensen, S. 4641
Svintsov, V. 461
Swaan, A. de 1563
Swaffer, T. 5094
Swain, J. 5645
Swaine, K. 4124
Swaminathan, A. 4072
Swane, C. 2040
Swank, E. 4927
Swanson, D. 1519, 2005
Sweetman, M. 561
Swift, A. 948, 1913
Swift, J. 4665
Swift, S. 5441
Swilling, M. 3922
Swim, J. 2123
Swindell, R. 1814
Swinton, D. 3244
Sy, F. 5540
Sycheva, V. 4043
Sykes, W. 75
Sýkora, L. 3666
Sylva, K. 2090
Syme, G. 3469
Symes, D. 3586
Szabad, G. 3055
Szalai, A. 338
Szamotulska, K. 2122
Szapiro, T. 2204
Szasz, T. 5401
Szczepański, J. 1011
Szczepański, M. 3764
Szent-Gyötgyl, K. 3618
Szinovacz, M. 2559
Szreter, S. 2001
Sztabiński, F. 329
Sztabiński, P. 258

Author index

Sztokman, N. 2020
Sztompka, P. 1969
Szuman, A. 2468
Taale, T. 3575
Tabory, E. 1325
Tacussel, P. 114
Tadenuma, K. 3975
Tagica, K. 2018
Taguieff, P. 3207
Taher, M. 5612
Tajćman, P. 3748
Takada, M. 2875
Takagi, D. 3085
Takahashi, L. 4082
Takahashi, N. 652
Takahashi, S. 5718, 5738
Takahashi, Y. 3517, 3533, 3647, 3728, 5162
Takaki, R. 3060
Takamizawa, K. 3747, 3872
Takanhashi, Y. 692
Takanishi, R. 2125
Takashima, H. 3573
Takayama, K. 807
Takegawa, S. 5468
Takenaka, H. 3704
Talmud, I. 4181
Tálos, E. 5510
Tamanaha, B. 1186
Tamano, K. 3951
Tamás, P. 49
Tamayo, J. 3392
Tamazato, E. 2429
Tamir, P. 1688
Tamir, Y. 1703
Tamplin, A. 611
Tan, H. 2840
Tanada, H. 3367
Tanaka, J. 573
Tan-Cullamar, E. 3408
Tanfer, K. 2955
Tang, J. 3031
Tang, S. 4483
Tang, W. 4718
Tangri, S. 5773
Tanguay, Y. 2919
Taniguchi, H. 3646
Tannenbaum, J. 1118

Tanner, A. 3613
Tanton, J. 5128
Tapinos, G. 3299
Tapper, N. 1190
Tapper, R. 1190
Tapsoba, P. 2236
Tardy, C. 1436
Targosz, P. 3418
Tarifa, F. 48
Tarrés, M. 4902
Tarumoto, H. 216
Taskhiri, H. 1310
Tate, R. 574, 4447
Tate, T. 3634
Tatenhove, J. van 3596
Taub, D. 1251
Taubmann, W. 3941
Taussig, M. 1615
Taylor, A. 5418
Taylor, B. 66
Taylor, C. 1147
Taylor, D. 1399
Taylor, E. 4459
Taylor, G. 1136, 1503
Taylor, I. 57, 5547
Taylor, J. 1317, 1984, 3389, 3424
Taylor, K. 2239, 5807
Taylor, M. 717, 3856
Taylor, R. 2427, 3882, 5097, 5681
Taylor, S. 439, 582, 3068, 5586, 5698
Taylor, V. 2779
Taylor-Gooby, P. 5456
Teachman, J. 288, 2608
Teachmen, J. 2479
Tealdi, J. 5826
Teather, E. 1730, 5493
Teevan, J. 5117, 5379
Tehranian, M. 5010
Tein, J. 2634
Tellegen, A. 554
Telles, E. 2592
Tellez, K. 1730, 5493
Temkina, A. 4612
Tempelhoff, B. 267, 326
Templeton, E. 2921
Tenivik, D. 4227
Tennstedt, S. 5479
Teo, A. 4252

Index des auteurs

Terada, A. 1007
Terkildsen, N. 2787
Termote, M. 3415
Terpstra, D. 557
Terry, D. 3015
Terry, M. 4706
Tesfaghiorghis, H. 1980
Teshimovsky-Arditi, M. 699
Tesser, A. 612
Tessier, R. 122
Tester, K. 1062
Tester, S. 5554
Tetlock, P. 3221
Thachuk, K. 403, 5021
Thacker, B. 403, 5021
Thackrey, M. 599
Thapan, M. 1665
Thapar, S. 1021
Theberge, N. 2789
Thebes, M. 2192
Thekkekara, M. 3124
Theriault, G. 4418
Théry, I. 1122
Theunert, H. 5435
Thévenot, L. 3465
Thibaudeau, J. 566
Thieme, G. 2192
Thiessen, D. 2981
Thimm, C. 696
Thomas, A. 798
Thomas, C. 615
Thomas, D. 867, 5241
Thomas, H. 2791, 3847, 4973
Thomas, J. 1069, 4571
Thomas, M. 340, 1919, 1970, 3170, 4120
Thomas, R. 2343
Thomas, T. 4647
Thompson, A. 4460
Thompson, C. 4632
Thompson, D. 4913
Thompson, J. 2706
Thompson, K. 122
Thompson, L. 2548
Thompson, P. 531
Thompson, S. 1419
Thompson, T. 1430
Thomson, A. 3640

Thomson, E. 330
Thomson, W. 3975
Thong, L. 3352
Thorn, B. 675
Thornberry, T. 5305
Thorne, C. 4690
Thornicroft, G. 5843
Thornicroft, K. 4577
Thornton, A. 2446, 2525
Thornton, M. 2043
Thorpe, B. 4234
Thouez, J. 1110
Thoumi, F. 5375
Thralls, C. 1454
Thwaites, A. 4569
Tibbitts, F. 1730, 5493
Tice, D. 600
Tiedtke, M. 1960
Tiefer, L. 3016
Tielman, R. 2978
Tiemann, H. 849
Tienda, M. 3326, 3328
Tiger, L. 1914
Tigges, L. 3238
Till, K. 3471
Till, W. 3011
Tillekens, G. 2132, 2163
Tilley, N. 3658
Tilly, C. 4928
Tilson, D. 1545
Timmermans, H. 3919, 4182
Timmers, L. 1496
Timms, N. 5536, 5550, 5601
Timyan, J. 5657
Tindall, D. 749
Tinguy, A. de 3415
Tiryakian, E. 1247, 2920
Titma, M. 2177
Tittle, C. 5166
Tizard, B. 3197
Tjosfold, D. 844
Tobayiwa, C. 332
Tobera, J. 360
Tobera, P. 4241
Tobin, Y. 997, 3202
Toh, K. 1657
Toho Gakkai 80
Toinet, M. 4948

Author index

Toit, A. du 4607
Tokunaga, H. 4196
Tollefson, J. 1565
Tolmacheva, M. 2685
Tolochek, V. 912
Tomandl, T. 4601
Tomasi, L. 122
Tomaskovic-Devey, D. 4263, 4452
Tomaszewicz, Ł. 291
Tomlinson, H. 1772
Tomoaki, I. 2830
Toney, J. 3055
Tonigan, J. 5366
Tonry, M. 4797
Toomey, D. 1725
Tootle, D. 3238
Top, B. 2157
Torelli, N. 4390
Toren, K. 439
Toren, N. 4560
Törestad, B. 555
Torpy, D. 5448
Torres, J. 4796
Tosics, I. 3748
Toth, J. 4277
Toulemon, L. 2282, 2283
Touraine, A. 209, 2174
Tov, R. 3784
Tovey, H. 4881
Townley, B. 864
Townsend, J. 2669, 2807, 3003
Toye, J. 4573
Tracey, M. 1449, 1518
Tracy, K. 452
Tracy, M. 2432
Tracy, P. 2432
Trad, P. 2618
Tran, T. 3345
Tranmer, M. 1717
Trapp, M. 3993
Traver, H. 5386
Travers, M. 1198
Travis, R. 1097
Travis, S. 4494
Traweek, S. 1335
Traxler, F. 4653, 4703
Treas, J. 2581
Treat, J. 1637

Trefil, J. 2221
Trend, D. 1675
Trent, J. 4947, 4947
Trevathan, W. 5637
Trevor, J. 244
Trew, R. 4161
Tribalat, M. 4554
Triche, E. 3440
Trichtl, G. 1459
Trifiletti, R. 45
Trifonas, P. 97
Trimboli, A. 696
Triseliotis, J. 2239
Trist, E. 413
Trivellato, M. 3736
Trivellato, U. 4390
Trojan, A. 5315
Tronto, J. 1161
Trost, M. 2561
Truan, F. 5358
Trubina, I. 964
Trueba, H. 3054, 3073
Truman, C. 4141
Trumbull, W. 4224
Trunzo, M. 5371, 5424
Trussell, J. 2483
Trux, A. 3439
Tsai, Y. 5429
Tsoukas, H. 874
Tsuji, R. 711
Tsukada, M. 1748
Tsutsumi, K. 3095
Tsvetana, G. 3105, 3113
Tuatahil, G. 5017
Tubbs, M. 4414
Tuchman, G. 1519
Tucker, J. 4469, 5571
Tucker, K. 1055
Tucker, P. 2585
Tuckman, H. 4203
Tufte, V. 2075
Tuinstra, J. 4313
Tul'chinskii, M. 295
Tulea, G. 156
Tulkens, F. 1207
Tullio-Altan, C. 1977
Tulloch, J. 1545
Tuma, N. 314

Index des auteurs

Tumanov, S. 2326
Tumber, H. 1517, 1545
Tungaraza, F. 5503
Tuohy, A. 4816
Turci, V. 5135, 5437
Turk, A. 5105
Turkel, G. 4801
Turner, B. 10, 1812, 4762, 4809
Turner, C. 2239
Turner, G. 1475, 1535
Turner, J. 1549, 3611
Turner, R. 3525
Turner, S. 87, 1354, 2469
Turney, L. 2336
Turok, I. 3834
Tustin, C. 4235
Tutty, L. 5618
Tversky, A. 526
Twigg, J. 5478
Twomey, D. 2740
Tyler, S. 1069
Tyler, T. 810
Tymstra, T. 233
Tyrell, H. 1219
Tzannatos, Z. 2793
Tzeng, O. 709
Tziner, A. 4478
Uberoi, P. 2696
Uchino, B. 472
Uddo, M. 403, 5021
Udéhn, L. 200
Udry, J. 705, 2128
Uellenberg-van Dawen, W. 4670
Ugalde, A. 5675
Ujimoto, K. 4745
Ullman, J. 403, 5021
Ulrich, R. 1970
Ultee, W. 1865, 4505
Umebali, E. 3635
Umesao, T. 1395
Umezawa, T. 3516
Undy, R. 4286, 4650
Unger, J. 1395
Ungern-Sternberg, D. v. 3784
Università di Roma, Dipartimento di Sociologia 5150
Université de Droit, d'Économie et des Sciences d'Aix-Marseille 5144

Unnithan, N. 1137
Urano, M. 3703
Urban, E. 1486
Urban, N. 5773
Ure, J. 4430
Urry, J. 1000
Usher, A. 3500
Usher, J. 5583
Ussher, J. 379
Usunier, J. 845
Uvalic, M. 4709
Uyl, D. 603
Vacha, E. 5330
Vacher, O. 404
Vachon, B. 3631
Vachon, M. 2328
Vaddhanaphuti, C. 2997
Vagg, J. 5098
Vaglum, P. 3335
Vaillancourt Rosenau, P. 5761
Vainstein, G. 954
Vala, J. 918
Valacich, J. 720
Valade, B. 1122
Valášková, N. 3337
Valderrama, C. de 3293
Vale, L. 5452
Vale, O. 2763
Valentine, G. 2954, 3456
Valentine, L. 5267
Valérien, J. 2018
Valle, D. La 1931
Vallerand, R. 4733
Valletta, R. 4692
Valverde, L. 1698
Van Dender, K. 2077, 4054
Van der Ryn, S. 3877
Van Dijk, M. 2797
Van Harrison, R. 3474
Van Hasselt, V. 2105
Vance, C. 4528
Vandeman, A. 2854
Vandenberg, R. 4399
Vanderleen, W. 5450
Vanderleyden, L. 2059
Vandermeeren, S. 1467
Vandevelde, T. 145
Vandewater, E. 2684

Author index

Vangsnes, E. 1546
Vanstone, M. 5212
Vanzo, J. da 2278
Vardomatskii, A. 310
Varea, C. 2231
Varga, À. 1594
Vargas, M. de 2018
Várguez Pasos, L. 1892
Vasilenko, L. 1273
Vasileva, B. 3377
Vaterlaus, S. 3676
Vaughan, A. 3622
Vaughan, E. 4421
Vaughan-Whitehead, D. 4709
Vaupel, J. 2279
Vaux, A. 666
Vebers, E. 3110
Vedder, R. 4014
Veeder, N. 2713
Veedon, R. 2421
Veendrick, L. 2163
Vega, W. 4970
Vel, J. 3575
Velde, M. 3575
Vélez, J. 1435
Veltz, P. 4136
Ven, J. van de 3575
Venard, J. 3931
Vendette, M. 3180
Veneris, Y. 1085
Veness, A. 5278, 5333
Veney, J. 2227
Ventura, A. 3569
Verba, S. 338
Verbeek, A. 305
Verbeek, J. 5336
Verdier, É. 1588
Verdier, R. 5433
Verdoodt, A. 1429
Verduzco Chávez, B. 3835
Verkuyten, M. 3153, 3166
Vermés, G. 404
Vermunt, R. 591
Vernier, B. 2431
Veroff, J. 2537, 2586, 2588
Verplanken, B. 4177
Versteegh, K. 1470
Verté, D. 5450

Vervaele, J. 4200
Verwey, M. 5851
Vesnin, V. 4086
Viadro, C. 2236
Vian, M. 4433
Vidal Domínguez, M. 3938
Vidas, A. de 3636
Videlier, P. 3332
Viehöver, W. 1282
Vigh, J. 5161
Vigh, K. 3092
Vila, B. 5104
Vilakazi, H. 141
Vilarino, M. 2669
Vilfan, S. 3046
Villac, M. 5048
Villadsen, S. 4840
Villavicencio de Mencías, G. 3058
Villers, G. de 3984
Vincens, J. 4383
Vincent, A. 1193
Vincent, C. 1752
Vincent, J. 1897
Vincentnathan, L. 1869
Vincke, J. 2961
Vinovskis, M. 2086, 5637
Vinuesa Angulo, J. 3938
Violier, P. 2020
Visaria, P. 1990
Visciola, M. 4450
Viscusi, W. 1121
Vishnevsky, A. 2408, 2505
Visser, J. 4695, 4707
Vitell, S. 1167
Vitiuk, V. 4937
Vittes, M. 2327
Viveret, P. 5048
Vivian, J. 712
Vlach, N. 3301
Vlaenderen, H. van 406
Vloet, A. 1149
Vobruba, G. 5510
Voegeli, W. 2498
Voelzkow, H. 3581
Voert, M. ter 1223
Vogel, G. 5124
Vogelgesang, W. 1447
Voges, W. 5314

Index des auteurs

Vogt, C. 4601
Voigt, P. 4388
Volkov, A. 2186
Volkov, I. 4766
Vollmer, F. 456
Vonderach, G. 2127, 4365
Vonk, R. 556
Voort, D. vander 2334
Vorakitphokatorn, S. 2972, 3744
Vormbrock, J. 2535
Vörös-Rademacher, H. 3189
Vos, S. De 2508
Vossen, A. 2390, 4027
Vossen, P. 2389
Voswinkel, S. 4613
Vouilloux, B. 1594
Vowles, J. 2853
Voyé, L. 1280, 3956
Vredenburg, K. 363
Vries, A. de 4392
Vries, M. de 4456
Vries, N. de 953
Vries, R. de 4342
Vries, S. de 3163
Vries, W. de 3596
Vroome, E. de 2978
Vugt, W. Van 3055
Vulpen, E. van 1425
Waaldijk, K. 2970
Waas, M. 1482
Waast, R. 209
Wachholz, S. 5217
Wachter, M. de 5799
Wacquant, L. 5334
Wada, K. 5404
Waddell, P. 3687, 3759, 3854
Waddington, J. 4688
Waddington, P. 4802
Waddock, S. 1756
Wade, M. 5649
Wade, P. 3137
Wadhams, C. 3825
Wadsworth, J. 240, 4391, 4676
Wagenaar, W. 1181
Wagner, D. 1066
Wagner, F. 3688
Wagner, G. 174, 1868, 2849
Wagner, H. 1396

Wagner, M. 2048, 3287, 3996
Wagner, P. 63, 1039
Wagner, U. 771
Wagstaff, A. 5650
Wailand, C. 851
Waite, L. 2566
Wakabayashi, M. 3694
Wakasa, K. 215
Wakefield, J. 604
Wal, G. van der 5827
Walaszek, A. 3112
Walby, C. 5526
Walder, C. 2782
Waldinger, R. 4070
Waldorf, D. 5183, 5378
Walgrave, L. 5290
Walker, A. 3839
Walker, C. 129, 5486, 5488
Walker, H. 5293
Walker, J. 2262, 2471
Walker, L. 2973
Walker, M. 260, 696, 4789
Walker, P. 5371, 5424
Walker, R. 5371, 5424
Walker, W. 544
Walklate, S. 5140, 5299
Wall, D. 4228
Wall, R. 3971
Wall, T. 4510
Wallace, D. 2320, 5640
Wallace, J. 666
Wallace, M. 403, 1513, 1704, 4047, 4066, 5021
Wallace, R. 1829, 2320, 5640
Waller, D. 1975
Waller, J. 2147
Wallerstein, N. 5643
Walsh, A. 2982
Walsh, B. 4335
Walsh, E. 3450
Walsh, J. 4597
Walt, H. van der 5643
Walt, L. der 4581
Walter, F. 3911
Walters, P. 4324, 4325
Walters, S. 2630
Walton, J. 3718, 3868, 4875
Walton, M. 5598

Author index

Walz, G. 3164
Wambach, K. 2323
Wandersman, A. 3430
Wang, G. 1451
Wang, L. 4393, 5718, 5738
Wang, M. 2082, 2892
Wang, S. 1537
Wang, X. 2815
Wang, Y. 5171, 5303
Wang, Z. 402, 4252
Wangui, E. 3739
Wantuła, H. 5114
Ward, A. 5580
Ward, C. 3692, 5100
Ward, D. 1133, 5543
Ward, M. 2346, 2735, 5355
Ward, P. 771, 2474, 3935
Ward, R. 2570
Ward, S. 1133
Warde, A. 3719
Wardini, E. El 2018
Wardle, J. 578
Wardwell, J. 3355
Warf, B. 111, 194
Warin, P. 4755, 4990
Warland, R. 3450
Warne, P. 3005
Warnecke, R. 331
Warner, K. 1247, 3138, 4204
Warner, L. 2260
Warner, M. 1244, 4252
Warner, R. 1261
Warnes, A. 2047, 3376
Warr, M. 5143
Warren, B. 397
Warren, C. 352
Warren-Langford, P. 4696
Warwick, D. 4523
Warwick, L. 5221
Warzywoda-Kruszyńska, W. 2164
Washington, R. 464
Washoff, F. 2480
Wasko, J. 1519
Wasserman, E. 370
Wasserman, I. 5425
Wassermanm, S. 260
Wassermann, W. 4474
Watanabe, H. 2460, 5697

Waterhouse, L. 5064
Waters, E. 2996
Waters, J. 5459
Waters, M. 776, 3149
Waterston, A. 5282, 5412
Watier, P. 114
Watkins, P. 1643
Watkins, R. 1475
Watkins, S. 2253
Watson, C. 1190
Watson, P. 2656
Watt, N. 5694
Watt, W. 1425
Wattam, C. 5584
Watters, E. 5081, 5842
Watts, M. 4292, 5349
Watts Miller, W. 86, 1205
Watykins, S. 2678
Waugh, W. 4564
Wayne, S. 644, 4410
Wazeter, D. 4658
Weakliem, D. 54, 269
Wearing, A. 2307
Weatherall, A. 696
Weatherburn, P. 353
Weatherford, R. 5035
Weaver, D. 1580, 3691, 4723
Weaver, K. 2130
Webb, J. 860
Webb, S. 5247, 5276, 5572
Weber, J. 1150
Weber, M. 1189, 3567
Weber, S. 2990
Weber, U. 1445
Webley, P. 3523, 3957, 4172, 4199
Webster, E. 2025
Webster, Y. 3173
Wechselmann, I. 1120
Weede, E. 4026
Weegen, M. 1699
Weenig, M. 4177
Weerakkody, U. 3492
Weesep, J. van 3788, 3839
Weesie, J. 305
Wegar, K. 2816
Wegener, B. 942
Wegener, D. 472
Wehler, H. 1923

Index des auteurs

Wehling, P. 3
Wei, C. 2613
Wei, J. 3285
Weibust, K. 4889
Weick, K. 783, 784
Weigert, A. 223
Weimer, D. 4771
Weinberger, D. 569
Weiner, J. 605
Weinert, R. 4758
Weinforth, F. 5313
Weingart, L. 732, 737
Weingart, P. 3175
Weinick, R. 2598
Weinstein, D. 1070
Weinstein, M. 1070
Weinstock, A. 2314
Weisberg, J. 4417
Weisbrod, C. 594
Weisfeld, G. 690
Weisheit, R. 5413
Weiss, D. 1864
Weiss, E. 2346, 5355
Weiss, H. 925
Weiss, J. 4760
Weiss, M. 1722
Weiss, P. 1265
Weissbourd, R. 2086
Weissler, K. 2402, 2637
Weitz, B. 123
Weizman, F. 361
Wejland, A. 235, 359
Welaratna, U. 3247
Welch, A. 1663
Welch, S. 3147
Weldon, E. 732, 766
Welker, R. 437
Welland, D. 290
Welldon, E. 2941
Weller, A. 433, 2411
Wellings, K. 240
Wellington, A. 4001
Wellins, R. 4413
Wellman, B. 260
Wells, D. 3455
Wells, P. 2309
Wells, S. 5396
Welsh, G. 3322

Welsh, J. 245
Welsh, S. 4713
Welte, J. 5406
Welzer-Lang, D. 5433
Wendeler, J. 5839
Wenden, C. de 3415
Wendt, H. 2192
Weng, R. 2643
Wenger, M. 126, 1541
Wenk, D. 3540
Wennhall, J. 2040
Werff, P. 4040
Werk, A. 5545
Wero, J. 573
Werrbach, G. 5569
Wessels, W. 4566
West, L. 2074
West, S. 573, 5694
Westcombe, A. 578
Westenberg, P. 549
Westendorff, D. 1947
Westenholz, A. 829
Westerfelt, A. 5263
Westergaard, J. 1886
Westermeyer, J. 5371, 5424
Westermeyer, M. 5371, 5424
Western, J. 3501
Westin, H. 2824
Westney, D. 4114
Weston, A. 5060
Weston, K. 2980
Westwood, S. 2705
Wetherell, M. 1436
Wettersten, J. 1356
Wetzel, K. 4657
Wetzel, P. 1476
Wetzstein, T. 1447
Weyer, J. 218
Weyland, P. 3571
Whalen, S. 2166
Whang, P. 475
Wharton, A. 4462
Wheaton, B. 2041
Wheelan, S. 721
Wheeler, B. 1247
Wheeler, J. 39
Wheeler, R. 561
Whichelow, M. 5655

Author index

Whitaker, A. 853
Whitaker, W. 4871
Whitbeck, L. 2516
White, C. 1146, 2930
White, E. 5713, 5834
White, G. 1954
White, I. 4330
White, M. 2676
White, R. 2116, 2238, 3644
White, S. 4299
White, W. 1730, 5493
Whiteford, P. 5524
Whitehill, B. 4997
Whiteley, N. 4159
Whitely, W. 4534
White-Means, S. 2043
Whiteside, A. 2312
Whitley, T. 4459
Whitney, I. 1771, 1778
Whittle, S. 854
Wholey, D. 5648
Whyte, W. 774
Wicki, M. 2773
Wickrama, K. 2555
Wickramasinghe, A. 2669
Wickramasinghe, J. 2376
Wicks, R. 4947
Widmer, C. 5, 150, 210
Wiebush, R. 5226, 5304
Wiedenmann, R. 2526
Wiedenmayer, G. 4072
Wiederman, M. 697, 2796
Wiegand, B. 5417
Wielers, R. 4313, 4609
Wiemann, J. 1436
Wiesenthal, H. 775
Wieviorka, M. 3193, 5433
Wiewel, W. 244
Wigdor, A. 5000
Wigfield, A. 2125
Wignaraja, P. 4907
Wijedasa, M. 4060
Wikstrom, S. 809
Wilcox, B. 1717
Wilcox, C. 1266, 4988
Wilcox, R. 3055
Wilcox, W. 2210
Wildenmann, R. 1842

Wildenthal, L. 1022
Wildes, K. 5813, 5814, 5829
Wilhelm, P. 4582
Wilke, H. 443, 591, 913, 3972
Wilke, J. 1523
Wilkens, W. 3734
Wilkie, J. 2866
Wilkins, R. 228
Wilkinson, A. 4711
Wilkinson, B. 4142
Wilkinson, K. 3565
Wilkinson, S. 2774, 2968
Willaime, J. 1297
Willard, A. 895
Wille, A. 4896
Wille, R. 4969
Wille, U. 4969
Willems, U. 1282
Willemyns, M. 1488
Willenbacher, B. 2498
Willer, D. 242, 909
Williams, A. 85, 4252
Williams, B. 1818
Williams, C. 339, 622, 932, 1583, 2081, 4234
Williams, D. 4855
Williams, H. 719, 1688
Williams, K. 488, 5243
Williams, L. 5076
Williams, M. 936, 1232, 3983
Williams, P. 940
Williams, R. 2190, 5835
Williams, S. 2306, 2783
Williamson, G. 5084
Williamson, O. 4138
Williamson, T. 4816
Willis, J. 1585
Willis, K. 2861
Willke, H. 106
Willmot, H. 890
Willmott, H. 780, 853
Wilms, H. 2048
Wilpert, B. 4248
Wils, L. 3046
Wilson, A. 4863
Wilson, C. 5575
Wilson, D. 862
Wilson, G. 5715, 5728

Index des auteurs

Wilson, J.   1374, 2688, 4413
Wilson, M.   767
Wilson, P.   2126
Wilson, S.   629, 1044, 2126
Wilson, T.   1592, 3390, 3950
Wilson, W.   1730, 5493
Wilson-Sadberry, K.   2867
Wimberley, R.   3587
Winch, G.   853
Winchester, I.   1688
Winckler, G.   3439
Windisch, U.   757
Windlesham, D.   5153, 5227
Wineburg, R.   5606
Winefield, A.   2137
Wines, S.   3748
Wing, J.   5843
Wingfield, A.   1421
Winkel, M.   434
Winkle, B. van   1022
Winkle, N. van   5432
Winkleby, M.   5281
Winkler, A.   2443
Winkler, J.   4601
Winland, D.   3135
Winner, L.   1352
Winslow, R.   5137
Winstead, B.   2624
Winter, D.   412, 565
Winter, I.   3886
Winter, J.   3774
Winter, M.   1216
Wintgens, L.   1183
Wirth, H.   71
Wise, L.   4618
Wise, S.   2941
Wiseley, P.   654
Wiseman, R.   1009
Wissen, L. van   3745
Wistow, G.   5727
Witkowski, J.   3391
Witschen, D.   2943
Witt, C.   2757
Witt, U.   2490
Witte, A.   5308
Witte, H. de   1905
Witte, R.   3229
Wittebrood, K.   285, 2163

Wittig, M.   5283
Wittrock, B.   1793
Witztum, E.   431
Wlezien, C.   4986
Wlotzke, O.   4635
Wodak, R.   997, 3202
Woderich, R.   1970
Woertman, L.   2870
Wojciszke, B.   559
Wojtkiewicz, R.   2529
Wolch, J.   831, 4082, 5274
Wolf, A.   3019
Wolf, C.   1267
Wolf, J.   4683, 5787
Wolfe, B.   2318, 2458
Wolfe, J.   403, 3781, 5021
Wolff, E.   4048
Wolfsfeld, G.   4900
Wollaston, I.   1255
Wollman, H.   4849
Wolpin, K.   2632
Wong, C.   4569, 5612
Wong, D.   3807
Wong, L.   5712
Wong, M.   2166
Wong, Y.   2504
Wood, G.   4415
Wood, R.   4345
Wood, W.   570
Woodard, J.   4985
Woodbury, M.   320
Woodbury-Farina, M.   420
Woodhouse, H.   1688
Woodiwiss, A.   1951
Woodiwiss, M.   5123
Woodroffe, C.   2119
Woods, R.   1985, 2373
Woodward, A.   5568
Woon, Y.   3354
Wootton-Millward, L.   754
Worell, J.   2624
Workman, A.   2205
Workman, R.   2205
Wörndl, B.   4879
Worth, L.   754
Wortham, R.   2021
Wortman, P.   300
Wotherspoon, G.   2964

Author index

Wotman, S. 710
Wouters, A. 93
Wratny, J. 4716
Wright, C. 374
Wright, D. 950
Wright, E. 141, 4764
Wright, J. 5283
Wright, P. 4437
Wright, R. 4970
Wright, S. 1399, 2760, 5258
Wu, J. 357
Wu, K. 1069
Wu, L. 2082, 2517
Wuketits, F. 1163
Wulf-Mathies, M. 5475
Wunder, D. 1738
Wunderlich, G. 3574
Wunsch, G. 2364
Wurmser, M. 3308
Wurr, R. 5623
Wuthnow, R. 604
Wyatt, G. 361
Wyk, M. van 4643
Wyld, N. 2620
Wylie, A. 2339
Wynne, D. 5371, 5424
Wysong, E. 5762
Wyzan, M. 4449
Xia, A. 4582
Xiberras, M. 114
Xie, J. 3538
Xie, Y. 3888
Xu, W. 3285
Xueyi, L. 4305
Yada, M. 79, 3557
Yaffe, J. 2936
Yamagishi, T. 711
Yamaguchi, K. 2571
Yamaguchi, T. 5502
Yamakawa, H. 3918
Yamanaka, K. 3417
Yamanouchi, K. 1787
Yammarino, F. 5001
Yamuna, T. 4298
Yanarella, E. 4074
Yanay, U. 5614
Yang, B. 5671
Yang, J. 5572

Yang, N. 3458
Yang, X. 2000
Yankeelov, P. 2624
Yannakakis, I. 3327
Yau, O. 4164
Yazawa, S. 3705
Ybema, J. 543
Ye, L. 4851
Yeatman, A. 1063
Yeaton, W. 300
Yee, A. 361
Yeganeh, N. 1021
Yeich, S. 354
Yelvington, K. 3143
Yero, L. 1937
Yetoim, Ü. 460
Yi, C. 65, 3610
Yi, X. 2181
Yi, Z. 2181
Yiftachel, O. 3865, 3889
Yin, R. 226
Yinger, J. 3818
Yingling, S. 3005
Yishai, Y. 2225
Ylänne-McEwen, V. 1370
Yogev, A. 3826
Yokota, M. 1175
Yokoyama, K. 969
Yon, M. 5262, 5322
Yongping, L. 2181
Yoshihara, N. 3811
Yoshikawa, K. 1341
Yost, P. 766
Youichi, I. 1519
Young, A. 1730, 5493
Young, B. 3957
Young, D. 1730, 5493
Young, G. 4238
Young, J. 1627
Young, M. 3570
Young, R. 2981
Young, R. De 365
Young-DeMarco, L. 2446
Youssef, N. 3254
Youssef, V. 1463
Ytrehus, S. 5707, 5831
Yu, A. 5558
Yu, L. 2892

Index des auteurs

Yu Xie, R.   2410
Yúdice, G.   1026
Yule, W.   2115, 5835
Yung, B.   2125
Yuval-Davis, N.   2800
Zabo, D.   5112
Zack-Williams, A.   2786
Zaffaroni, E.   5300
Zaharopoulos, T.   1529
Zaidi, S.   3179
Zajicek, E.   4216
Zakay, D.   1366
Zakharov, A.   3991
Zald, M.   817
Zaluar, A.   3722
Zamble, E.   4517
Zande, I.   2171
Zaner, R.   5813
Zanna, M.   362, 917, 921
Zanotti, A.   3237
Zappalà, G.   293
Zaprudskii, I.   4942
Zarca, B.   2189, 4324
Zarifian, P.   4136
Zarins, I.   4745
Zarychta, H.   4301
Zaslow, M.   2125
Zautra, A.   635
Zdravomyslova, E.   4926
Zehnder, C.   3916
Zelizer, B.   1519, 1539
Zemelman, H.   113
Zenger, E.   2381
Zeranska-Kiminek, S.   1616
Zerbe, W.   4422
Zervudacki, C.   3113, 3122
Zeytinoğlu, I.   527
Zhang, J.   277
Zhang, L.   1069
Zhang, W.   1341
Zhlang, W.   3884
Zhongyi, J.   3626
Zhou, M.   3060, 3096
Zhou, X.   796
Ziegler, J.   2086
Ziegler, R.   892
Ziehl, S.   2734
Ziener, K.   3726

Zierke, I.   1970
Zigler, E.   2125
Zimmer, A.   5463
Zimmerman, D.   1434
Zimmermann, C.   3757
Zimmermann, J.   4133
Zimmermann, K.   1472, 1576, 3311
Zimring, F.   5308
Zingraff, R.   4694
Zinke, R.   4857
Zinn, M.   1992
Zoina, A.   3425
Zolberg, A.   3415
Zong, L.   2420
Zopf, P.   2369
Zucker, J.   3680
Zuckerman, M.   364, 608
Zuiches, J.   3558
Zuidema, J.   157
Zurbrugg, N.   118
Zurick, D.   3633
Zuwerink, J.   659
Zwart, F. de   4484
Zylberberg, J.   1297

PLACENAME INDEX
INDEX DES ENDROITS

Afghanistan 2835, 2925
Africa 1, 1060, 1239, 1345, 1565, 1619, 1632, 1636, 1640, 2018, 2199, 2214, 2367, 2418, 2662, 2704, 2920, 3142, 3227, 3263, 3435, 3472, 3543, 3545, 3642, 3702, 3923, 3927, 3931, 3954, 3984, 4559, 4993, 5548, 5780
see also: East Africa, Francophone Africa, North Africa, Southern Africa, Sub-Saharan Africa, West Africa
Alabama 4868
Alaska 2005, 3032, 5371, 5424
Albania 48
Alberta 4122
Algeria 2219, 3375
Alps 4748
Amazon 3612
Americas 1404, 3639, 3792, 3935, 4097, 4137, 4828
see also: Central America, Latin America, North America
Arctic Region 1399
Argentina 1310, 1658, 1781, 1794, 1895, 3900, 4218, 4377, 5034, 5337, 5339
Arizona 3752
Asia 774, 2295, 3393, 4011, 4074, 4252, 5361, 5612
see also: Central Asia, East Asia, South Asia, Southeast Asia
Assam 2083
Australia 462, 943, 947, 957, 1405, 1488, 1535, 1597, 1633, 1643, 1652, 1667, 1687, 1736, 1737, 1796, 1800, 1814, 1918, 1980, 1984, 2025, 2137, 2322, 2342, 2449, 2483, 2496, 2683, 2939, 2964, 3025, 3041, 3103, 3239, 3280, 3389, 3416, 3421, 3806, 3819, 3889, 4017, 4045, 4234, 4311, 4333, 4347, 4454, 4579, 4587, 4606, 4615, 4620, 4629, 4644, 4646, 4702, 4731, 4831, 4918, 4961, 5054, 5102, 5108, 5220, 5257, 5430, 5524, 5757, 5770
see also: New South Wales, South Australia, Victoria, Western Australia
Austria 23, 925, 1459, 1523, 2507, 3071, 3220, 3876, 3892, 4454, 4601, 4748
Bahia 1276, 1853, 4514
Bahrain 2710
Bali 1485, 3575, 4719
Bangladesh 747, 1861, 1999, 2278, 2381, 2864, 2875, 3637, 3998, 4022, 4025
Belgium 536, 1280, 1429, 1467, 2052, 2077, 2132, 2473, 2961, 3047, 3069, 3151, 3227, 3290, 3298, 3358, 4054, 4315, 4322, 4454, 4790, 4813, 4872, 5319, 5450, 5461, 5464, 5519
Belize 1580, 2269, 5417
Benin 2286
Bolivia 2909, 3052, 3081, 3378, 3643, 4231, 4662
Borneo
see: Brunei, Sarawak
Botswana 2274, 5611
Brazil 380, 1735, 1794, 1805, 2220, 2351, 2352, 2365, 2515, 2539, 2547, 2592, 2960, 3190, 3201, 3211, 3379, 3612, 3616, 3722, 4019, 4076, 4102, 4206, 4229, 4329, 4362, 4412, 4565, 4598, 4637, 4882, 4903, 4941, 5718, 5738
see also: Bahia, Rio de Janeiro, Rio Grande do Sul
British Columbia 61, 3109
Brunei 1561
Bulgaria 41, 1298, 3105, 3377, 3748
Burkina Faso 2236, 2797, 3642, 4851

Placename index

Burma 1182
C.I.S. 870, 3419
California 445, 915, 2075, 2472, 2532, 3054, 3073, 3078, 3084, 3125, 3127, 3176, 3809, 3860, 3866, 3867, 3873, 4082, 4656, 4677, 5274, 5378, 5384, 5841
Cambodia 2445, 3247
Cameroon 1469, 3365, 3366, 3955, 4603
Canada 290, 527, 789, 1020, 1043, 1044, 1048, 1196, 1509, 1562, 1736, 1883, 2237, 2267, 2420, 2494, 2495, 2562, 2615, 2723, 2883, 2991, 3083, 3114, 3135, 3270, 3331, 3399, 3406, 3411, 3503, 3553, 3562, 3601, 3798, 3841, 4000, 4029, 4074, 4153, 4157, 4256, 4332, 4346, 4356, 4418, 4425, 4454, 4479, 4517, 4577, 4657, 4795, 4905, 4921, 4946, 5130, 5136, 5394, 5401, 5470, 5572, 5651, 5662, 5769, 5783
see also: Alberta, British Columbia, Manitoba, Northwest Territories, Ontario, Quebec
Caribbean 1397, 1501, 1924, 3206, 3255, 3625, 3691, 3952, 4723
Central America 3412, 3926, 3939
Central Asia 2685
Central Europe 1957, 2724, 3067, 3542, 3586, 3717, 4507, 4576, 5012, 5453, 5505
Chile 1700, 1733, 1794, 2174, 4930, 5511
China 29, 495, 598, 640, 1002, 1079, 1294, 1565, 1603, 1711, 1721, 1768, 1809, 1844, 1925, 1952, 1965, 2000, 2074, 2082, 2241, 2258, 2420, 2475, 2527, 2653, 2811, 2815, 3186, 3285, 3354, 3433, 3536, 3538, 3554, 3598, 3617, 3626, 3630, 3731, 3838, 3874, 3888, 3979, 4073, 4116, 4117, 4164, 4243, 4252, 4269, 4305, 4393, 4436, 4582, 4718, 4994, 5027, 5189, 5202, 5289, 5294, 5303, 5692, 5712, 5718, 5738, 5838

Colombia 1754, 1794, 3137, 3382, 3559, 3614, 3623, 3741, 3771, 3843, 3895, 3897, 4223, 5375, 5398
Colorado 3078
Costa Rica 1639, 2230, 3148, 3560, 4083, 5680, 5775
Croatia 2831
Cuba 1502, 2523
Cyprus 2914, 2998, 3306, 4093, 4738
Czech Republic 40, 1820, 2032, 2291, 2372, 2391, 3257, 3344, 4222, 4763, 4933, 5031
see also: Czechoslovakia
Czechoslovakia 1299, 2193, 2499, 3748, 4781, 5031
see also: Czech Republic, Slovakia
Denmark 1120, 1564, 3466, 3663, 4453, 4605, 5629, 5707, 5831
Dominican Republic 2687
East Africa 1563, 3156
East Asia 1659, 1946, 1995, 3968, 4213
Eastern Europe 52, 870, 1671, 1919, 1939, 1957, 1970, 2038, 2192, 2200, 2370, 2378, 2656, 2716, 2724, 3049, 3076, 3121, 3311, 3717, 3748, 3869, 4140, 4261, 4507, 4703, 4771, 4791, 4819, 4826, 4839, 4933, 5453
Ecuador 1494, 3034, 3058, 3155, 3379, 3792, 3955, 4021
Egypt 3367, 3379, 3571, 3629, 3822, 4277, 4591
El Salvador 1295, 1974, 5643
England 1188, 1204, 1216, 1457, 1710, 1724, 1860, 1911, 1912, 2092, 2251, 2480, 2640, 2709, 2838, 3068, 3109, 3341, 3361, 3369, 3372, 3376, 3380, 3441, 3501, 3570, 3627, 3670, 3671, 3763, 3851, 3861, 3928, 4098, 4127, 4236, 4480, 4525, 4563, 5068, 5177, 5203, 5218, 5246, 5387, 5403, 5449, 5450, 5459, 5491, 5582, 5602, 5720, 5840
Eritrea 3985
Estonia 1550
Ethiopia 3061
Europe 35, 42, 77, 647, 974, 1043, 1105, 1149, 1195, 1209, 1262, 1270,

Index des endroits

1281, 1532, 1540, 1563, 1585, 1627, 1631, 1745, 1753, 1764, 1766, 1793, 1953, 1959, 1975, 1985, 1989, 2026, 2033, 2196, 2234, 2280, 2740, 3046, 3062, 3075, 3076, 3094, 3144, 3229, 3281, 3290, 3292, 3396, 3407, 3413, 3415, 3418, 3650, 3666, 3788, 3829, 3839, 3883, 4144, 4284, 4314, 4436, 4476, 4505, 4573, 4593, 4630, 4689, 4736, 4743, 4788, 4840, 4890, 4940, 4955, 5129, 5361, 5427, 5609, 5718, 5738, 5811
see also: Central Europe, Eastern Europe, Scandinavia, Southeast Europe, Western Europe
Falkland Islands   5034
Fiji   3204
Finland   284, 1566, 1719, 2857, 3787
Florida   5185
France   10, 63, 394, 404, 888, 1037, 1041, 1080, 1122, 1262, 1263, 1275, 1278, 1383, 1456, 1548, 1579, 1653, 1695, 1846, 1852, 1873, 1903, 1955, 1996, 2020, 2283, 2348, 2349, 2403, 2424, 2897, 2967, 3001, 3008, 3113, 3120, 3122, 3130, 3141, 3182, 3234, 3250, 3253, 3304, 3321, 3322, 3327, 3332, 3333, 3339, 3375, 3376, 3413, 3423, 3699, 3712, 3724, 3732, 3737, 3738, 3761, 3790, 3791, 3855, 3875, 3890, 3893, 3901, 3920, 3947, 4011, 4245, 4255, 4314, 4324, 4325, 4328, 4353, 4429, 4454, 4502, 4558, 4633, 4715, 4746, 4814, 4860, 4876, 4879, 4948, 5047, 5048, 5096, 5208, 5297, 5334, 5450, 5490, 5574, 5778
Francophone Africa   1362, 4210
French Polynesia   1972
Gabon   4852
Georgia   2035
Georgia (U.S.A.)   4811
Germany   69, 172, 775, 849, 910, 935, 997, 1045, 1049, 1070, 1118, 1199, 1212, 1265, 1388, 1445, 1456, 1511, 1523, 1536, 1639, 1694, 1699, 1722, 1738, 1746, 1747, 1834, 1871, 1899, 1919, 1920, 1923, 1938, 1953, 1979, 2015, 2031, 2127, 2136, 2139, 2141, 2142, 2146, 2154, 2170, 2178, 2192, 2246, 2291, 2321, 2416, 2463, 2665, 2691, 2743, 2755, 2819, 2927, 3044, 3050, 3082, 3150, 3175, 3195, 3202, 3210, 3218, 3234, 3242, 3260, 3278, 3315, 3317, 3324, 3330, 3336, 3340, 3375, 3419, 3528, 3581, 3661, 3671, 3723, 3726, 3740, 3778, 3794, 3846, 3855, 3894, 3996, 4024, 4029, 4036, 4065, 4131, 4195, 4248, 4249, 4281, 4314, 4328, 4336, 4351, 4365, 4366, 4385, 4388, 4395, 4429, 4445, 4474, 4538, 4539, 4553, 4574, 4604, 4631, 4635, 4639, 4648, 4669, 4670, 4672, 4674, 4708, 4715, 4734, 4740, 4850, 4879, 4897, 4901, 4904, 4954, 5029, 5102, 5208, 5285, 5297, 5313, 5314, 5315, 5357, 5381, 5382, 5421, 5438, 5507, 5509, 5520, 5533, 5544, 5572, 5576, 5615, 5623, 5626, 5705
Germany (East)   942, 1523, 1960, 1963, 1970, 2039, 2140, 2150, 2160, 2926, 3187, 3679, 3734, 3793, 4120, 4244, 4397, 4501, 4578, 4877
Germany (West)   942, 1515, 1559, 3376, 4454, 4878, 4899
Ghana   949, 2265, 2786, 2924, 3263, 3799
Greece   1003, 1529, 2431, 3496, 3555, 4093, 4527, 5164
Guadeloupe   1498
Guatemala   1293, 1415, 2386, 3301, 3925, 4303
Gujarat   1689
Haiti   4998
Hawaii   1088, 4186, 4512
Holland
   see: Netherlands
Hong Kong   411, 1002, 1428, 1573, 1831, 1965, 2661, 3743, 3845, 4117, 4252, 4430, 4483, 5712
Hungary   46, 49, 1849, 1975, 2150, 2682, 3107, 3618, 3748, 3803, 3979, 3992, 3994, 4055, 4121, 4454, 4464, 4822, 4825, 4829, 4933, 5091, 5423
Iceland   1676
Idaho   3078
Illinois   50, 1702, 2910, 3249

Placename index

India 37, 170, 399, 495, 1021, 1310, 1319, 1324, 1330, 1337, 1342, 1350, 1393, 1464, 1563, 1565, 1599, 1665, 1741, 1768, 1795, 1843, 1869, 1884, 1908, 1941, 1967, 1990, 2266, 2360, 2363, 2380, 2669, 2694, 2745, 2747, 2749, 2762, 2813, 2845, 2935, 2941, 3124, 3186, 3353, 3368, 3371, 3374, 3379, 3384, 3447, 3564, 3583, 3584, 3599, 3885, 3898, 3933, 4051, 4068, 4254, 4359, 4484, 4810, 4873, 5329, 5340, 5346, 5599, 5639, 5685, 5828
see also: Assam, Gujarat, Karnataka, Kerala, Maharashtra, Orissa, Pondicherry, Punjab, Sikkim, Tamil Nadu, Tripura, Uttar Pradesh, West Bengal
Indiana 4379
Indonesia 65, 990, 2335, 3408, 3575, 3638, 3754, 3755, 4006
see also: Bali, Java
Iran 1021, 1478, 1706, 1934, 1958, 1974, 2115, 2501, 2835, 2855, 4211
Iraq 403, 2827, 5021
Ireland 1021, 1283, 1393, 2474, 2582, 2669, 2713, 2715, 2735, 2744, 3213, 3553, 3833, 4080, 4323, 4335, 4373, 4749, 4881, 5066, 5450, 5518, 5643
Israel 409, 425, 433, 446, 643, 841, 926, 965, 1325, 1438, 1627, 1950, 2225, 2268, 2285, 2298, 2411, 2415, 2689, 3145, 3268, 3308, 3402, 3488, 3518, 3522, 3530, 3537, 3651, 3826, 3862, 3865, 3944, 4132, 4217, 4309, 4999, 5013, 5015, 5155, 5431, 5442, 5614, 5617, 5619, 5684, 5696, 5703, 5718, 5738, 5739
see also: Israeli Occupied Territories
Israeli Occupied Territories 2780, 2933, 3488, 4923
Italy 404, 819, 1096, 1112, 1230, 1508, 1819, 1825, 1830, 1931, 1977, 2075, 2218, 2291, 2356, 2557, 2659, 2693, 2753, 2903, 3235, 3237, 3253, 3258, 3269, 3288, 3309, 3351, 3376, 3394, 3398, 3415, 3425, 3650, 3714, 3855, 3863, 3876, 3961, 4020, 4088, 4369, 4390, 4454, 4558, 4706, 4830, 4866, 4901, 4919, 4956, 4957, 4959, 5110, 5150, 5151, 5158, 5327, 5334
Ivory Coast 1201, 2560, 3379
Jamaica 2438, 4412, 4784
Japan 80, 82, 321, 404, 462, 613, 910, 966, 969, 1010, 1054, 1081, 1118, 1125, 1130, 1213, 1217, 1233, 1395, 1479, 1584, 1618, 1637, 1664, 1748, 1787, 1788, 1832, 1845, 1898, 2050, 2165, 2294, 2401, 2429, 2477, 2563, 2565, 2573, 2603, 2612, 2676, 2677, 2788, 2830, 2846, 2915, 2922, 3246, 3295, 3336, 3364, 3417, 3517, 3519, 3533, 3539, 3551, 3557, 3573, 3592, 3646, 3647, 3649, 3678, 3728, 3747, 3837, 3842, 3872, 3880, 3910, 3918, 3934, 3951, 4089, 4094, 4098, 4099, 4142, 4143, 4144, 4194, 4236, 4252, 4264, 4334, 4454, 4455, 4475, 4487, 4571, 4588, 4621, 4701, 4714, 5014, 5027, 5039, 5102, 5404, 5429, 5718, 5738
Java 2055, 3529, 3753
Jordan 1321, 3817, 5674
Karnataka 4215, 5344
Kazakhstan 3080
Kenya 252, 2021, 2256, 2786, 3164, 3597, 3715, 3739, 3981, 4077, 4741
Kerala 1967, 2361, 2533, 3273, 4040, 4108
Korea 1443, 1770, 2565, 3365, 3366, 3611, 3756, 4621, 5671
see also: North Korea, South Korea
Kuwait 2776, 2893, 4964, 5572
Latin America 4, 1026, 1043, 1286, 1393, 1651, 1713, 1794, 1928, 1937, 1987, 2705, 2793, 3411, 3600, 3625, 3639, 3734, 3751, 3783, 3906, 3929, 3935, 4033, 4081, 4894, 4903, 5062, 5283, 5316, 5354, 5383
Latvia 3110
Lebanon 5015
Lesotho 3827
Madagascar 2879, 3379
Maharashtra 2213, 4254
Malaysia 65, 1317, 1561, 1933, 2432, 3552, 4412, 4958
see also: Sarawak

Index des endroits

Mali 4853
Malta 1381
Manitoba 3591
Maryland 1712, 1792
Massachusetts 2713, 5481
Mauritania 1516
Mauritius 2300
Mediterranean Region 3413, 3415
Mexico 1506, 1622, 1734, 1892, 2328, 2364, 2648, 2861, 2888, 2918, 3079, 3132, 3365, 3366, 3370, 3379, 3390, 3392, 3397, 3412, 3544, 3608, 3619, 3636, 3779, 3804, 3835, 3896, 3930, 3999, 4033, 4058, 4075, 4282, 4289, 4368, 4488, 4687, 4875, 4902, 4903, 4939, 5120, 5572
Michigan 755, 3796
Micronesia 2175, 2595
Middle East 403, 1050, 1541, 2195, 2198, 2712, 2855, 3117, 3289, 3472, 3669, 3751, 3783, 3906, 4062, 5015, 5021
Morocco 1309, 1322, 2231, 2501, 3332, 4750
Mozambique 5643
Namibia 3948, 4404
Nepal 2263, 2608, 2821, 3353, 3633, 4608
Netherlands 70, 404, 922, 1127, 1172, 1212, 1221, 1223, 1280, 1406, 1419, 1610, 1681, 1724, 1900, 1917, 2097, 2132, 2163, 2171, 2389, 2484, 2514, 2616, 3000, 3070, 3151, 3153, 3163, 3166, 3376, 3428, 3512, 3575, 3656, 3662, 3829, 3907, 4027, 4200, 4313, 4315, 4316, 4317, 4322, 4337, 4382, 4454, 4497, 4499, 4502, 4707, 4917, 4934, 4940, 4966, 4971, 5004, 5124, 5141, 5152, 5176, 5382, 5461, 5465, 5474, 5516, 5528, 5804, 5805
New Jersey 2950, 3840, 4859, 5244
New Mexico 5432
New South Wales 3097, 3357, 3844, 4396
New York 1368, 1829, 2950, 3030, 3053, 3146, 3194, 3254, 3277, 3836, 3868, 4028, 4070, 4909, 5116, 5197, 5261, 5385, 5603

New Zealand 997, 1156, 1477, 1691, 2741, 2812, 2853, 3128, 3202, 3319, 3697, 3749, 5201, 5572, 5747
Nicaragua 1949, 1958, 1974, 2304, 2825, 2894, 3126, 3550, 4228
Niger 3379
Nigeria 787, 1561, 1728, 2030, 2276, 2786, 3142, 3362, 3635, 3882, 3913, 4646, 4968, 5233, 5237, 5837
North Africa 2871, 3077, 3669
North America 1859, 3639, 3711, 4099, 5283, 5361, 5659
North Korea 2019
Northern Ireland 1374, 1697, 1823, 1856, 2466, 2579, 2713, 2735, 4686, 4824, 4919, 5186, 5499
Northwest Territories 1932
Norway 774, 978, 1528, 1546, 1590, 1605, 1620, 1730, 3335, 4943, 5493, 5707, 5831
Ohio 2344, 3760
Oklahoma 2260
Oman 2273
Ontario 1484, 1885, 2117, 2654, 3640, 3710, 3733, 3801, 4518, 4636, 4665, 5216
Orissa 2185, 3547
Pacific Region 1976, 3393, 4953
see also: Micronesia
Pakistan 1874, 2257, 2790, 2795, 2835, 2842, 3179, 3491, 4049, 4133, 4297, 5341
Palau 5082
Papua New Guinea 5498
Paraguay 2134
Pennsylvania 3857, 4139
Peru 2310, 3093, 3296, 3385, 3563, 3620, 3652, 3693, 3902, 4137, 4912, 5704
Philippines 65, 378, 1565, 1971, 2081, 2482, 2520, 3159, 3408, 3500, 3780, 3905, 4130, 4250, 4252, 5643
Poland 53, 62, 81, 344, 347, 958, 1040, 1616, 1872, 1922, 1981, 2029, 2073, 2122, 2150, 2208, 2244, 2291, 2301, 2371, 2374, 2382, 2384, 2385, 2396, 2430, 2669, 2711, 2932, 3066, 3167, 3193, 3209, 3283, 3300, 3388,

Placename index

3391, 3445, 3748, 3764, 3940, 3977, 3989, 3995, 4216, 4283, 4287, 4288, 4301, 4312, 4684, 4819, 4832, 4848, 4865, 4933, 4980, 5114, 5635
Pondicherry   4363
Portugal   918, 1586, 1680, 1767, 2393, 2515, 2902, 3288, 3575, 3580, 3615
Puerto Rico   420, 1287, 1435, 1498, 2479, 2523, 2687, 2736, 3251, 3262, 3395, 4911, 5407
Punjab   3789
Quebec   229, 1110, 1120, 1390, 1484, 2017, 3157, 3217, 3221, 3272, 3318, 3334, 3631, 3815, 3936, 4285, 4332, 4353, 4671, 4862, 4879, 4883, 4921, 4972
Rio de Janeiro   2148, 2366, 3802
Rio Grande do Sul   4952
Romania   1422, 2133, 3113, 3123, 3603, 3821
Russia   18, 33, 249, 904, 954, 963, 964, 976, 1141, 1218, 1240, 1250, 1260, 1288, 1296, 1522, 1855, 1956, 2010, 2291, 2326, 2505, 2996, 3099, 3111, 3140, 3316, 3401, 3444, 3446, 3607, 3621, 3748, 3772, 3773, 3784, 3993, 4035, 4043, 4063, 4086, 4110, 4118, 4227, 4274, 4291, 4300, 4307, 4612, 4627, 4681, 4849, 4892, 4893, 4910, 4926, 4937, 4978, 5024, 5051, 5056, 5059, 5165, 5663
Sarawak   1933, 2093, 3352
Saudi Arabia   1994, 3817
Scandinavia   1959, 4477, 4840, 5532
Scotland   1274, 1806, 2316, 2450, 2480, 2962, 3576, 3657, 3750, 4129, 4697, 5103, 5157, 5222, 5229, 5230, 5276, 5409, 5418, 5426, 5622
Senegal   3415
Serbia   3869
Sierra Leone   1891, 3506
Sikkim   1961
Singapore   65, 1231, 1560, 1561, 2554, 2840, 2860, 2912, 4252, 4485
Slovakia   1491, 1820, 2291, 3092, 3113, 3240, 4933, 5031
  see also: Czechoslovakia
Slovenia   3748

South Africa   141, 351, 970, 1046, 1166, 1382, 1468, 1562, 1567, 1731, 1742, 1758, 1780, 1813, 1930, 2129, 2297, 2305, 2404, 2420, 2686, 2722, 2737, 2777, 2782, 2833, 2930, 2976, 3021, 3056, 3057, 3106, 3136, 3154, 3188, 3189, 3214, 3230, 3593, 3609, 3622, 3762, 3782, 3922, 3953, 4085, 4091, 4233, 4235, 4242, 4276, 4338, 4392, 4446, 4581, 4589, 4607, 4616, 4622, 4632, 4652, 4679, 4817, 4818, 4886, 4888, 4989, 5439, 5595, 5643
South America
  see: Amazon
South Asia   1380, 2668, 3310, 3491, 4360
South Australia   3459, 4667
South Carolina   5540
South Korea   65, 1077, 2508, 2708, 2817, 3610, 4104, 4213
Southeast Asia   1317, 1995, 3322, 3336, 3421, 3969, 4594
Southeast Europe   1311, 3113, 3161, 3177, 4576
Southern Africa   2312, 2673
Spain   122, 191, 937, 999, 1235, 1472, 1576, 1686, 1815, 1945, 2054, 2131, 2141, 2543, 2669, 3215, 3293, 3568, 3588, 4214, 4230, 4280, 4710, 4820, 4870, 4951, 5131, 5195, 5326, 5338, 5436, 5500
Sri Lanka   842, 1217, 1608, 2376, 2380, 2669, 3492, 3500, 3546, 3575, 4060, 4265, 4370, 4568, 4575, 4979
Sub-Saharan Africa   1313, 2023, 2296, 2324, 3359, 3858, 4056, 5776
Sudan   2669, 3985, 5350
Sweden   236, 774, 929, 1860, 1883, 1911, 1912, 2068, 2167, 2252, 2262, 2302, 2820, 2824, 2931, 2952, 3039, 3040, 3325, 3376, 3732, 3765, 3768, 3787, 3928, 4029, 4255, 4314, 4324, 4454, 4513, 4618, 4657, 4669, 4699, 4724, 4880, 4922, 5465, 5533, 5733
Switzerland   757, 2417, 2773, 3113, 3613, 3706, 3876, 3914, 3915, 3916, 4378, 4439, 4668, 5512, 5851

Index des endroits

Taiwan 65, 1002, 1907, 1965, 2216, 2272, 2410, 5572
Tamil Nadu 1600
Tanzania 2786, 3727, 3832, 4375, 4924, 5503
Texas 3360
Thailand 1308, 1317, 1320, 2997, 3347, 3500, 3744, 4007, 4046, 4125
Trinidad and Tobago 1727, 3036, 3143, 3781
Tripura 4717
Tunisia 1099, 5311, 5351
Turkey 460, 681, 1043, 1047, 3340, 3375, 4955, 5032
Turkmenistan 2453
U.S.A. 14, 17, 28, 204, 302, 307, 371, 423, 475, 499, 598, 660, 661, 681, 708, 741, 879, 910, 914, 926, 946, 971, 981, 992, 997, 1004, 1007, 1010, 1020, 1030, 1035, 1037, 1038, 1042, 1043, 1048, 1078, 1111, 1113, 1115, 1117, 1118, 1119, 1120, 1121, 1137, 1169, 1171, 1203, 1207, 1215, 1247, 1249, 1251, 1254, 1261, 1266, 1268, 1277, 1284, 1326, 1333, 1419, 1422, 1435, 1438, 1439, 1440, 1499, 1506, 1520, 1541, 1557, 1558, 1565, 1575, 1596, 1627, 1631, 1639, 1650, 1656, 1681, 1698, 1726, 1730, 1739, 1748, 1749, 1756, 1759, 1773, 1786, 1793, 1798, 1799, 1804, 1808, 1817, 1870, 1883, 1896, 1897, 1904, 1916, 1943, 1951, 2045, 2065, 2075, 2086, 2087, 2099, 2144, 2161, 2167, 2182, 2184, 2203, 2210, 2226, 2232, 2238, 2243, 2261, 2281, 2292, 2320, 2346, 2354, 2369, 2375, 2400, 2405, 2413, 2440, 2454, 2465, 2475, 2476, 2504, 2506, 2528, 2531, 2540, 2541, 2542, 2544, 2545, 2556, 2567, 2584, 2594, 2598, 2600, 2603, 2605, 2609, 2625, 2626, 2643, 2666, 2684, 2700, 2720, 2726, 2769, 2798, 2804, 2866, 2874, 2891, 2906, 2910, 2963, 2974, 2983, 2990, 3005, 3027, 3028, 3031, 3032, 3033, 3035, 3038, 3051, 3055, 3060, 3064, 3085, 3091, 3095, 3112, 3115, 3131, 3136, 3165, 3171, 3173, 3192, 3200, 3201, 3202, 3208, 3213, 3219, 3225, 3226, 3247, 3262, 3267, 3270, 3274, 3286, 3291, 3301, 3323, 3324, 3326, 3345, 3346, 3348, 3349, 3355, 3386, 3392, 3393, 3395, 3406, 3412, 3416, 3426, 3498, 3500, 3508, 3515, 3532, 3556, 3579, 3585, 3602, 3634, 3648, 3660, 3672, 3683, 3684, 3698, 3700, 3725, 3729, 3769, 3777, 3779, 3828, 3848, 3856, 3871, 3877, 3904, 3973, 3999, 4007, 4009, 4023, 4029, 4032, 4048, 4053, 4057, 4071, 4075, 4087, 4111, 4116, 4124, 4135, 4144, 4201, 4202, 4263, 4264, 4266, 4310, 4318, 4332, 4346, 4358, 4408, 4454, 4464, 4487, 4493, 4502, 4520, 4574, 4582, 4624, 4634, 4648, 4682, 4694, 4700, 4701, 4704, 4725, 4879, 4897, 4927, 4928, 4947, 4948, 4960, 4985, 4986, 4988, 4991, 4995, 5000, 5017, 5043, 5053, 5060, 5065, 5090, 5095, 5099, 5105, 5107, 5122, 5127, 5128, 5139, 5148, 5169, 5173, 5175, 5180, 5191, 5211, 5255, 5260, 5271, 5277, 5278, 5282, 5283, 5306, 5317, 5321, 5324, 5325, 5332, 5333, 5334, 5348, 5355, 5371, 5372, 5397, 5401, 5412, 5415, 5424, 5441, 5444, 5465, 5470, 5476, 5489, 5493, 5494, 5495, 5521, 5531, 5533, 5557, 5563, 5568, 5572, 5579, 5606, 5628, 5632, 5648, 5666, 5677, 5689, 5690, 5693, 5708, 5718, 5721, 5730, 5738, 5740, 5745, 5749, 5753, 5755, 5756, 5761, 5762, 5763, 5764, 5766, 5768, 5774, 5779, 5782, 5783, 5784, 5805, 5817
see also: Alabama, Alaska, Arizona, California, Colorado, Florida, Hawaii, Idaho, Illinois, Indiana, Maryland, Massachusetts, Michigan, New Jersey, New Mexico, New York, Ohio, Oklahoma, Pennsylvania, South Carolina, Texas, Utah, Wisconsin, Wyoming
U.S.S.R. 44, 448, 1105, 1137, 1333, 1537, 1552, 1956, 1964, 1975, 2038, 2130, 2150, 2177, 2186, 2408, 2685, 2996, 3088, 3168, 3349, 3381, 3400,

Placename index

3986, 3993, 4064, 4224, 4307, 4308, 4449, 4454, 4771, 4833, 4835, 4987, 5142
see also: Estonia, Georgia, Kazakhstan, Latvia, Russia, Turkmenistan, Ukraine
Uganda   2240, 2786
Ukraine   3337, 3607
United Kingdom   20, 32, 75, 78, 578, 798, 836, 871, 929, 936, 988, 1006, 1017, 1124, 1204, 1228, 1264, 1452, 1513, 1545, 1572, 1589, 1630, 1641, 1670, 1673, 1681, 1696, 1704, 1708, 1717, 1720, 1725, 1729, 1755, 1757, 1772, 1774, 1777, 1779, 1783, 1785, 1797, 1807, 1811, 1816, 1818, 1825, 1838, 1858, 1886, 1894, 2056, 2066, 2069, 2085, 2088, 2091, 2096, 2098, 2102, 2113, 2116, 2124, 2143, 2155, 2169, 2173, 2176, 2211, 2308, 2319, 2329, 2368, 2377, 2397, 2536, 2576, 2610, 2620, 2647, 2650, 2794, 2828, 2841, 2857, 2891, 2942, 2953, 2992, 3002, 3023, 3024, 3042, 3043, 3059, 3063, 3064, 3087, 3101, 3139, 3172, 3216, 3264, 3271, 3320, 3376, 3505, 3508, 3509, 3511, 3525, 3549, 3645, 3692, 3713, 3730, 3732, 3750, 3767, 3774, 3785, 3825, 3830, 3855, 3856, 3860, 3870, 3971, 3978, 3988, 4002, 4029, 4057, 4084, 4105, 4253, 4255, 4257, 4286, 4314, 4320, 4324, 4325, 4328, 4330, 4354, 4376, 4389, 4401, 4420, 4428, 4454, 4490, 4492, 4495, 4509, 4544, 4569, 4584, 4593, 4610, 4676, 4693, 4714, 4727, 4737, 4740, 4747, 4800, 4803, 4928, 4944, 5034, 5036, 5037, 5042, 5046, 5063, 5064, 5074, 5134, 5147, 5153, 5174, 5177, 5184, 5190, 5192, 5199, 5219, 5221, 5225, 5227, 5228, 5236, 5240, 5259, 5270, 5271, 5281, 5287, 5302, 5306, 5321, 5334, 5370, 5399, 5416, 5447, 5449, 5455, 5456, 5457, 5460, 5465, 5477, 5486, 5496, 5513, 5514, 5522, 5524, 5525, 5529, 5536, 5541, 5542, 5546, 5549, 5551, 5554, 5558, 5562, 5579, 5583, 5584, 5588, 5594, 5596, 5601, 5604, 5607, 5620, 5630, 5631, 5638, 5645, 5646, 5654, 5655, 5664, 5669, 5672, 5688, 5698, 5706, 5709, 5713, 5717, 5719, 5722, 5723, 5725, 5729, 5732, 5742, 5743, 5744, 5748, 5758, 5772, 5793, 5834, 5836, 5843, 5849
see also: England, Northern Ireland, Scotland, Wales
Uruguay   1034
Utah   3078, 3383
Uttar Pradesh   2533
Victoria   957, 1901, 3886, 4126
Wales   1568, 1724, 3065, 3520, 3627, 4142, 5459
West Africa   3415, 3575
West Bengal   4717
Western Australia   4696
Western Europe   2038, 2250, 2370, 2444, 3178, 3311, 3376, 4008, 4716, 4782, 4932, 4950, 5114, 5666
Wisconsin   2435
Wyoming   3078
Yugoslavia   1565
see also: Croatia, Serbia, Slovenia
Zaire   5751
Zambia   1683, 2207, 2786
Zimbabwe   1791, 2786, 3313, 3605, 3702, 3746, 4522

SUBJECT INDEX

Ability 375, 543
Aborigines 1859, 1980, 1984, 3239
Abortion 563, 603, 935, 1266, 2181, 2205, 2206, 2208, 2210, 2215, 2221, 2225, 2226, 2229, 2233, 2234, 2235, 2243, 2715, 2853, 4902, 4988, 5044, 5060, 5784, 5785, 5786, 5819, 5823
Absenteeism 4420
Abuse of the aged 5046, 5236
Academic achievement 997, 1010, 1638, 1653, 1655, 1657, 1677, 1681, 1741, 1775, 1780, 1911, 2412, 3202, 4498, 4520
Academic freedom 159, 1744, 1779, 1799
Academic profession 452, 1515, 1786, 1867, 2829, 2942, 2944, 4537, 4544, 4555, 4556, 4560, 4654, 4663
Academic success 1655, 1767, 2826
Access to education 1691, 1781
Access to employment 4253, 4376
Access to information 430, 1452, 2308, 3023
Accidents
  see: Nuclear accidents, Traffic accidents, Work accidents
Accountability 4535, 4786, 5647, 5662
Accountants 1133, 4535, 4536
Accounting 850
  see also: Social accounting
Acculturation 1046, 3055, 3100
Achievement motivation 565, 907
  see also: Academic achievement
Action research 774, 1048
Action theory 218
Activists 1853
Adaptation to change 518, 3073
Addiction 1121, 5358
  see also: Drug addiction
Addicts
  see: Drug addicts
Administration 891, 1375, 1741, 4849, 4858, 5720, 5840
  see also: Development administration, Education administration, Financial administration, Health administration, Public administration, School administration
Administrative efficiency 859
Administrative organization 776
Administrative science 429, 783, 4095, 4176, 4844
Adolescence 755, 2094, 2125, 2158, 2232, 5414, 5428
Adolescents 280, 579, 629, 705, 1612, 1639, 2041, 2097, 2107, 2126, 2128, 2134, 2135, 2145, 2147, 2152, 2153, 2156, 2157, 2161, 2162, 2163, 2166, 2168, 2207, 2296, 2411, 2421, 2518, 2616, 2617, 2618, 2912, 2986, 3009, 3010, 3109, 3724, 4173, 4465, 4882, 5080, 5094, 5279, 5291, 5310, 5389, 5539, 5620
Adorno, Theodor 977
Adult education 1696, 1783, 1784, 1785, 1789, 1802, 1811, 1814, 4490, 4571
Adults 469, 666, 735, 1417, 2041, 2356, 2378, 2399, 2488, 2497, 2546, 2643, 4025, 4721, 5556
Advertising 1439, 1440, 1441, 1442, 1443, 1444, 1445, 2796, 2880, 4156, 4169, 4186, 4189, 4192, 4194, 5642
Aesthetics 7, 1055, 1443, 1628
Affiliation 565, 1303, 3252
  see also: Religious affiliation
Affirmative action 1166, 3165, 3184, 3224, 4242, 4311, 4435
Africans 3042, 3320
Age
  see: Old age

Subject index

Age at marriage 2542, 2543, 2551, 2557, 2599, 2875
Age distribution 4487
Age groups 1581, 2035, 2038, 2040, 2200, 2536, 2622, 3305, 4255, 4533, 5422
Aged 930, 1412, 1632, 1802, 1814, 2044, 2045, 2046, 2050, 2051, 2053, 2054, 2055, 2056, 2058, 2059, 2063, 2066, 2067, 2068, 2069, 2070, 2071, 2072, 2073, 2077, 2078, 2079, 2081, 2082, 2083, 2085, 2354, 2394, 2395, 2401, 2410, 2432, 2465, 2508, 2570, 2612, 2635, 3291, 3376, 3399, 3517, 3728, 3918, 4054, 4306, 4733, 4745, 4973, 5468, 5470, 5474, 5478, 5483, 5519, 5554, 5708, 5721, 5723, 5726, 5730, 5731, 5732, 5736, 5740, 5742, 5743, 5744, 5748, 5800
see also: Abuse of the aged, Care of the aged
Ageing 228, 399, 2018, 2040, 2044, 2048, 2049, 2056, 2057, 2060, 2061, 2064, 2065, 2071, 2074, 2075, 2084, 2272, 2390, 2396, 2643, 2677, 3760, 3996, 4157
Aggregate analysis 785
Agrarian reform 3547, 3550, 3586, 3621
Agrarian society 1874, 2275, 3614, 3623, 4323
Agrarian structure 3985
Agricultural cooperatives 2825, 4077
Agricultural development 3584, 3634
see also: Green Revolution
Agricultural enterprises 2910, 3551, 3561, 3607, 4323
see also: Family farms
Agricultural extension 3596
Agricultural history 1971, 4083
Agricultural industry 4087, 4603
Agricultural innovations 3558
Agricultural labour 3562, 4276, 4622, 4656
Agricultural policy 3548, 3564, 3575, 3583, 3587, 3588, 3619, 4210
Agricultural production 2188, 3560, 3575, 3593, 4083
Agricultural productivity 3564, 3584
Agricultural sector 3577, 4324
Agricultural technology 3564
Agricultural trade 3575
Agricultural workers 3274, 4254, 4421, 4603
Agriculture 1334, 3491, 3558, 3568, 3569, 3580, 3606, 3715, 4310
Agrofood industry 4329
Aid 2805, 3828, 3945
see also: Development aid, Foreign aid, State aid
AIDS 810, 933, 1409, 2303, 2304, 2305, 2312, 2315, 2320, 2323, 2324, 2325, 2327, 2341, 2344, 2345, 2346, 2731, 2946, 2961, 2978, 2997, 3001, 3002, 3005, 3007, 3008, 3010, 3013, 3015, 3021, 3500, 4633, 5267, 5355, 5384, 5400, 5407, 5411, 5540, 5567, 5575, 5634, 5668, 5669, 5714, 5753, 5770, 5782
Air pollution 2366
Air transport 1530, 4450
Airlines 395
Alcohol 1029, 2348, 2349, 2355, 2534, 2634, 5117, 5182, 5360, 5365, 5367, 5379, 5380, 5396, 5423, 5425
Alcoholic beverages 2175, 5344
see also: Beer
Alcoholism 632, 1137, 4364, 5239, 5266, 5280, 5359, 5361, 5362, 5364, 5366, 5368, 5371, 5373, 5377, 5388, 5391, 5392, 5395, 5402, 5408, 5409, 5419, 5424, 5426, 5541, 5560, 5568
Algebra 261
Algorithms 318, 729
Alienation 1094, 1096, 1097, 1253
Alliances 826, 1091
Almond, Marc 2992
Altruism 603, 604, 627, 815, 1132, 1206, 5773
Amerindians 1859, 3102, 3115, 4303, 5371, 5424, 5432, 5563
see also: North Amerindians, South Amerindians
Anarchism 4778, 5100
Anarchy 988

Subject index

Animal experimentation 1118, 5788, 5794
Animal protection 3443
Animals 370, 636, 1118, 4559, 4884, 5060, 5796, 5820
see also: Domestic animals, Sheep
Anonymity 71
Anorexia nervosa 2153, 2664, 2718
Anthropological methodology 336
see also: Participant observation
Anthropology 5, 210, 1061, 2428, 5112
see also: Cultural anthropology, Economic anthropology, Linguistic anthropology, Medical anthropology, Philosophical anthropology, Social anthropology, Urban anthropology
Anti-nuclear movements 4897, 4909
Anti-semitism 309, 941, 997, 3044, 3193, 3195, 3202, 3220, 3221, 3240
Anti-social behaviour 2168, 5285
Antiquity
see: Roman Antiquity
Anxiety 581, 641, 2307, 3299
Apartheid 1330, 1930, 3057, 3189, 3214, 4818
Appeals 5213, 5298
Applied sociology 32, 5502
Apprenticeship 4148
Arab countries 1050, 1707, 1867, 2198, 3289, 3669, 3817
Arabs 643, 2411, 3865, 3944
Arbitration 688, 718, 4577, 4629, 4646, 4647
see also: Compulsory arbitration
Architecture 998, 1594, 1598, 1633, 2671, 3576, 3680, 3891, 3955
see also: Domestic architecture, Urban architecture
Arendt, Hannah 2739
Arid zones 3439
Armaments industry 4082
Armed forces 403, 763, 4993, 4995, 4996, 4997, 5000, 5021
Armies 4994
Arms limitation 4885

Art 439, 993, 1038, 1111, 1256, 1604, 1607, 1609, 1615, 1627, 1629, 1632, 1636, 1943
see also: Contemporary art, Dramatic art, History of art, Sociology of art, Visual arts, Works of art
Artificial insemination 5807
Artificial intelligence 1344
Artificial reproduction 5790
Artists 1629, 1850
Arts 1034, 1480, 1595, 1603
Arts policy 1610
ASEAN 4594
Asian studies 1659
Asians 578, 660, 3025, 3031, 3033, 3036, 3041, 3043, 3073, 3085, 3101, 3109, 3114, 3216, 3246, 3322, 3336, 3393, 4318, 4512, 4789
Asiatic mode of production 3969, 3991
Assets 793
Assistance 3945, 5480
Associations 775, 798, 3374, 3581, 3951, 4653
Astrology 2527
Asylum 3055, 3427
Atlases 3778, 5507
Attitude change 766, 920, 921, 2476, 4399
Attitude formation 3147, 4657
Attitudes 47, 102, 109, 240, 281, 304, 310, 341, 345, 374, 486, 506, 653, 659, 749, 917, 918, 919, 920, 921, 922, 923, 927, 929, 930, 931, 932, 933, 935, 936, 937, 942, 943, 944, 949, 951, 953, 954, 957, 958, 960, 961, 965, 968, 970, 971, 1133, 1136, 1223, 1243, 1366, 1382, 1383, 1846, 2065, 2127, 2156, 2160, 2178, 2235, 2430, 2476, 2559, 2562, 2572, 2619, 2765, 2846, 2866, 2998, 3001, 3002, 3149, 3218, 3240, 3294, 3434, 3449, 3459, 3489, 3986, 4113, 4171, 4365, 4461, 4610, 4789, 4950, 5094, 5284, 5363, 5438, 5450, 5540, 5551
see also: Management attitudes, Political attitudes, Racial attitudes, Religious attitudes

Subject index

Attitudes to work 956, 1523, 4407, 4409, 4414, 4455, 4478, 4586, 4701
Audience 1517, 1531, 1592, 1612
Augustine [Saint] 148
Authoritarianism 544, 545, 977, 1034, 5445
Authority 54, 184, 778, 1236, 2658, 2785, 2806, 4159, 5777
 see also: Political authority, Religious authorities
Autobiography 228, 257, 259, 528, 540, 2960
Automobile industry 2788, 4074, 4446, 4525, 4715
Automobiles 1100, 4074, 4185, 5037, 5302, 5360
Avoidance 3097, 5564
Bahamón Dussán, Augusto 5398
Bakhtin, M.M. 90, 165
Ball games 4615
Bank loans 4201
Banking 4115
Bankruptcy 2469
Banks 4198, 4207
 see also: Savings banks, World Bank
Banti, Anna 2693
Bargaining 651, 657, 2259, 2437, 4243, 4619
 see also: Collective bargaining, Wage bargaining
Bargaining power 623
Basic education 1713, 4490
Basic needs 3898, 4061, 5329
 see also: Housing needs
Basic rights 5745
Basques 2131
Bateson, Gregory 454, 1256, 2409
Baudrillard, Jean 10, 118
Beck, Frank 5582
Becker, Gary 200
Bedouin 3530
Beer 4072
Behaviour in groups 746
Behavioural sciences 239, 472, 883, 2104, 3431, 3436, 3457
Beliefs 374, 942, 948, 1020, 1237, 1318, 3578, 3959, 4835
 see also: Ethnomedical beliefs, Folk beliefs, Religious beliefs
Benjamin, Walter 131
Bereavement 5545, 5634
Beverages
 see: Alcoholic beverages
Bible 2876
Bibliographies 74, 82, 1501, 1502, 1923, 2341, 3088, 4042, 4293, 4810, 5359, 5736, 5800
Biculturalism 1031
Bilingual education 1561
Bilingualism 1561, 1562, 1564, 1565, 1566, 1568
Binet, Alfred 404
Biographies 81, 228, 259, 1394, 1838, 2076, 4774
Biological anthropology 2049
Biology
 see: Human biology
Biotechnology 1334, 3432, 5801
Birth 2181, 2218, 2245, 2246, 2248, 2264, 2288, 2331, 2403, 2533, 2675, 5637, 5683, 5691, 5764, 5766, 5825
Birth control 2220, 2231, 2232, 2273, 2722, 2761, 2996, 5665
Birth intervals 2255, 2265, 2287, 2352, 2608
Birth order 2180, 2189
Birth rate 1986, 2192, 2250, 2280, 2300, 2302
Birth spacing 2244, 2264, 2267, 2278, 2381, 2412
Black market 5186
Blacks 78, 719, 970, 1215, 1249, 1276, 1631, 1636, 1731, 1904, 2129, 2135, 2331, 2354, 2427, 2485, 2522, 2528, 2544, 2586, 2588, 2590, 2591, 2605, 2680, 2700, 2723, 2769, 2867, 2895, 2906, 2976, 3027, 3028, 3029, 3035, 3043, 3055, 3060, 3068, 3070, 3085, 3087, 3147, 3148, 3160, 3165, 3169, 3173, 3184, 3192, 3198, 3208, 3226, 3227, 3231, 3233, 3238, 3245, 3423, 3501, 3507, 3770, 3795, 3796, 3805, 4032, 4071, 4123, 4372, 4379, 4402, 4491, 4514, 4652, 4679, 4720, 4789, 4845, 4855, 4989, 5118, 5134,

478

Subject index

5147, 5148, 5225, 5281, 5406, 5563, 5631, 5638, 5688, 5779
Blindness   2328
Blood   3008
Bodin, Jean   150
Body mutilations   2987
Body symbolism   2664
Body techniques
  see: Tattooing
Bogdanov, Alexander   151
Books   1597, 1623
Border politics   5031
Borders   3488
Boredom   4463
Borrowing   4208, 5006
Bourdieu, Pierre   1028, 1676
Bourgeois culture   1022
Bourgeoisie   1849
Boys   5261, 5293
Brain   517, 1369, 5791
Brain drain   5612
Braudel, Fernand   150
Breweries   4072
Brides   1857
Britons   3055
Broadcasting   409, 1184, 1511, 1525, 1558, 1570, 1586, 1589
Brodolini, Giacomo   5482
Brotherhoods   1288
Browne, Robert S.   3244, 3507
Buber, Martin   2409
Buddhism   495, 1130, 1218, 1257, 1317
Buddhists   1308
Budgetary policy   4210
Budgets   270
  see also: Time budgets
Buffon, G.L.L.   2
Buildings   505, 1231, 1598, 2309, 3576, 3844, 3880
Bureaucracy   779, 796, 800, 811, 842, 913, 4073, 4243, 5697
Burial   1327
Burt, Cyril   1500
Buses   3918
Bush, George   403, 5021
Business cycles   3286, 3759, 3854, 5211

Business history   4096
Business investment   4205
Business management   861, 872, 4086, 4116, 4260, 4716
Business organization   525, 819, 845, 872, 4448, 4532
Camus, Albert   459
Cancer   932, 2317, 2382, 2774, 3430, 3940, 5773
Candidates   2787, 2804
Capital   2809, 3727, 3791, 3884, 5005
  see also: Foreign capital
Capital accumulation   3884
Capital cities   3727, 3833
Capital gains   3733
Capitalism   1074, 1151, 1275, 1305, 1864, 1881, 1888, 1891, 1975, 2999, 3226, 3719, 3967, 3977, 3978, 3981, 3983, 3987, 3990, 4080, 4104, 4270, 4308, 4464, 4765, 4784, 5036, 5760
Capitalist countries   4594
Capitalist development   1972, 4126, 5211
Capitalist enterprises   1888
Capitalist society   3232, 4856
Care of the aged   2040, 2043, 2047, 2050, 2062, 2065, 2074, 2084, 2401, 2415, 2432, 2612, 2863, 4494, 5145, 5236, 5450, 5460, 5462, 5470, 5474, 5478, 5479, 5484, 5519, 5718, 5728, 5733, 5734, 5735, 5737, 5738, 5739, 5741, 5761
Career development   3031, 4317, 4473, 4493, 4501, 4516, 4534, 4537, 4541, 4554, 4566, 5004
Caring   615, 628, 1161, 2102, 2441, 2465, 2538, 2548, 2552, 2612, 2635, 2667, 2843, 2863, 4494, 5630, 5724, 5847
Carnivals   1613
Cartoons   707
Caste   1782, 1843, 1861, 1869, 1884, 2935, 5639
Catalan language   1383
Catastrophe theory   3924
Cather, Willa   3055
Catholic Church   1265, 1282, 1283, 1291, 1297, 1299, 5511

Subject index

Catholicism 1266, 1284, 1287, 2540, 2541, 5829
Catholics 1264, 1275, 1278, 1285, 1289, 2579
Causal analysis 2008
Causality 8, 102, 109
Causes of death 2365, 2366, 2385, 2387
Censorship 1034, 1439, 2719, 2750
Censuses 1483, 3173, 3389
  see also: Population censuses
Central business districts 4075
Central government 2657, 3767
Central-local government relations 4858
Centralization 4848
Centrally-planned economies 4635
Centre-periphery relations 1022, 3714, 3830
Chaos theory 3, 38, 155, 157, 3494
Character 95
  see also: National character
Charisma 902, 1275, 4984
Charitable organizations 798, 1265
Chicago School 36, 50
Child abuse 568, 2116, 2123, 2398, 2461, 2636, 2641, 2771, 2965, 3019, 5061, 5062, 5063, 5064, 5065, 5066, 5067, 5068, 5069, 5070, 5071, 5073, 5074, 5075, 5076, 5077, 5078, 5079, 5080, 5081, 5082, 5083, 5084, 5085, 5086, 5087, 5088, 5254, 5296, 5301, 5316, 5317, 5445, 5549, 5555, 5561, 5582, 5584, 5596, 5842
Child adoption 2496, 2503, 2614, 2646, 3024, 5594
Child care 1957, 2089, 2091, 2113, 2114, 2124, 2143, 2403, 2478, 2491, 2521, 2609, 2645, 2647, 2862, 2890, 4339, 4343, 4459, 4486, 4494, 4609, 5072, 5521, 5522, 5523, 5524, 5525, 5526, 5527, 5528, 5529, 5531, 5532, 5533, 5534, 5535, 5536, 5537, 5552, 5558, 5569, 5582, 5588, 5600, 5601, 5604, 5620, 5666
Child costs 2292
Child development 404, 498, 503, 1377, 1486, 1587, 2090, 2095, 2099, 2106, 2107, 2110, 2111, 2114, 2631, 2639, 2645, 2688
Child fostering 676, 2646, 2648, 5569, 5841
Child health 420, 719, 2093, 2108, 2115, 2119, 2122, 2330, 2331, 2333, 2350, 2381, 2634, 5343, 5534, 5653, 5674, 5681, 5693, 5752, 5756, 5846
Child labour 2103, 4250, 4298
Child mortality 2108, 2276, 2351, 2352, 2353, 2363, 2386
Child neglect 5072, 5077, 5082, 5296
Child protection 2091, 2092, 2096, 2113, 2116, 2124, 2620, 5064, 5070, 5551, 5583, 5596, 5603
Child psychology 2095, 2111, 4199
Child rearing 1664, 2431, 2467, 2638, 2645, 5524
Child rearing practices 5291
Childhood 537, 568, 2040, 2094, 2104, 2120, 2419, 2458, 3112, 5078, 5080
  see also: Early childhood
Children 148, 390, 391, 438, 498, 502, 505, 535, 560, 583, 611, 616, 708, 943, 1377, 1444, 1463, 1475, 1522, 1564, 1702, 1725, 1730, 1771, 1778, 2086, 2087, 2088, 2097, 2098, 2099, 2101, 2103, 2105, 2108, 2112, 2117, 2121, 2149, 2263, 2335, 2338, 2404, 2405, 2443, 2452, 2456, 2462, 2470, 2472, 2488, 2498, 2510, 2511, 2513, 2525, 2544, 2638, 2644, 2646, 2783, 2906, 3112, 3206, 3259, 3264, 3313, 3343, 3434, 3647, 4053, 4199, 4739, 5006, 5071, 5076, 5184, 5262, 5264, 5268, 5283, 5318, 5320, 5322, 5323, 5343, 5388, 5395, 5435, 5493, 5494, 5521, 5530, 5538, 5542, 5552, 5555, 5558, 5571, 5582, 5597, 5598, 5600, 5602, 5604, 5613, 5674, 5724
  see also: Disabled children, Gifted children, Migrants' children
Children in care 2088, 2100, 2143, 5536, 5550, 5601, 5613
Children's rights 2096, 2100, 2101, 2496, 2500, 3276, 5061, 5070, 5542
Chin, Yao-chi 29

480

Subject index

Chinese 411, 475, 2527, 3295, 3347, 4011, 4305, 5116
Chodorow, Nancy 2509
Christaller, Walter 1441
Christian Churches 245, 899, 1280, 1282, 1290, 1300
 see also: Catholic Church, Greek Orthodox Church, Hutterites, Mennonites, Mormonism, Orthodox Church, Presbyterianism, Protestant churches, Russian Orthodox Church
Christian democracy 4892, 4893
Christian theology 1131, 2655, 2701, 2752, 2876
Christianity 28, 1214, 1262, 1267, 1268, 1270, 1272, 1273, 1279, 1281, 1294, 1303, 1316, 1326, 1328, 1332, 1674, 5819
 see also: Catholicism, Pentecostalism
Christians 971, 1302
Christmas 1128, 1593, 2868
Church and state 1296, 1297
Church history 1006, 1293
Church membership 1274
Churches 778, 1231, 3091
Cinema 1608, 2956, 2996
Circumcision 2324
Cities 1844, 2482, 2909, 3058, 3093, 3097, 3132, 3267, 3296, 3385, 3504, 3542, 3545, 3638, 3640, 3641, 3645, 3647, 3648, 3649, 3650, 3651, 3652, 3654, 3656, 3658, 3659, 3660, 3664, 3665, 3666, 3669, 3671, 3676, 3677, 3678, 3681, 3682, 3688, 3694, 3696, 3700, 3706, 3713, 3721, 3723, 3725, 3726, 3744, 3753, 3758, 3769, 3790, 3796, 3797, 3817, 3823, 3828, 3831, 3839, 3847, 3848, 3852, 3853, 3856, 3868, 3879, 3882, 3890, 3891, 3892, 3897, 3899, 3900, 3908, 3912, 3917, 3925, 3932, 3933, 3934, 3935, 3938, 3941, 3943, 3946, 3955, 3956, 4076, 4084, 4269, 5020, 5107, 5124, 5144, 5274, 5337, 5387, 5495
 see also: Capital cities
Citizen participation 3534, 3813, 5455, 5514, 5662

Citizens 327, 444, 3461, 3649, 4869, 4870, 4933
Citizenship 1021, 1812, 2665, 2672, 2803, 2993, 3139, 3260, 3271, 3722, 4471, 4762, 4809, 4949, 4952, 4980, 5456
Civil code 1122
Civil proceedings 810, 1173
Civil religion 1297
Civil rights 944, 1034, 4625
 see also: Right to education, Right to vote
Civil servants 4484
Civil service 4330
Civil society 1078, 1954, 1979, 4771, 4775, 4790, 4793, 4794, 4799
Civil-military relations 4993, 4998
Civilization 302, 1003, 1023, 1037, 1054, 1120, 1145, 1229, 1323, 1535, 1966, 2741, 4080, 4958
 see also: Islamic civilization, Modern civilization, Western civilization
Clans 3610
Class 54, 133, 144, 440, 939, 1022, 1111, 1635, 1643, 1746, 1764, 1834, 1835, 1841, 1861, 1864, 1877, 1878, 1879, 1880, 1881, 1882, 1889, 1890, 1894, 1896, 1898, 1902, 1906, 1909, 1910, 1911, 1913, 1914, 1915, 1917, 1918, 1940, 2119, 2173, 2323, 2342, 2672, 2763, 2826, 2839, 2890, 2909, 2918, 3085, 3170, 3198, 3222, 3226, 3509, 3529, 3873, 4037, 4047, 4051, 4057, 4066, 4653, 4727, 4732, 4773, 4784, 4826, 4895, 4906, 4913, 4922, 5105, 5406, 5690, 5754
 see also: Bourgeoisie, Lower class, Middle class, Ruling class, Underclass, Working class
Class behaviour 1900
Class conflict 3987, 4765
Class consciousness 1883, 1884, 1885, 1902, 2654
Class formation 1874, 1891
Class identification 4962
Class interest 1887
Class society 1854, 1871, 3969

Subject index

Class structure 1684, 1843, 1873, 1875, 1876, 1886, 1888, 1893, 1895, 1897, 1907, 1916
Classification 312, 882, 2196, 3028, 3797, 3798
Clergy 1299
Clergymen 2655
Clientelism 842, 3615, 4473
Climate 2366, 5093
Clinical psychology 379
Clothes 1108, 2167
Clothing industry 2883, 4070, 4298
Clubs 763
Cluster analysis 313
Co-operatives 798, 1902, 3503, 3730, 4717
    see also: Agricultural co-operatives, Housing co-operatives, Industrial co-operatives, Production co-operatives
Coal mines 3525
Coalitions 1958
Coasts 3357, 3492
Cocaine 5109, 5370, 5374, 5415
Coffee 4076, 4077, 4083
Cognition 105, 366, 370, 424, 502, 510, 511, 513, 515, 516, 535, 680, 750, 782, 828, 873, 1134, 1639, 4162, 5008
    see also: Social cognition
Cognitive development 367, 389, 501, 503, 504, 508, 509, 512, 514, 517
Cohabitation 2525, 2547, 2567, 2575, 2610, 4337
Cohorts 2249, 2293
Coleman, James 127
Collective action 200, 301, 715, 730, 3555, 4324, 4862, 4898, 4923, 4945, 5126
Collective agreements 4601
Collective bargaining 4357, 4581, 4584, 4585, 4590, 4599, 4604, 4638, 4676
Collective behaviour 609, 784, 1929, 4915
Collective farming 3607
Collectivism 455, 3603
Colonial history 1464, 2920, 3755
Colonialism 378, 1837, 1891

Colonies 1022
Colonization 3954
Columbus, Christopher 1622
Comedy 1433
Comics 1361
Commerce 1659
Commercial workers 4501
Commodities 1443
Common law 1188
Communal violence 3187
Communalism 3542
Communes 3512
Communication 386, 676, 689, 696, 701, 723, 762, 803, 861, 1043, 1310, 1363, 1369, 1375, 1378, 1393, 1402, 1403, 1410, 1412, 1413, 1414, 1417, 1420, 1424, 1427, 1430, 1436, 1438, 1446, 1449, 1458, 1459, 1460, 1472, 1504, 1505, 1506, 1508, 1514, 1518, 1521, 1525, 1576, 1926, 2421, 2829, 2976, 3823, 3824, 4079, 4453, 4477, 4963, 4977
    see also: Intercultural communication, Interpersonal communication, Mass communication, Non-verbal communication, Oral communication, Political communication, Verbal communication, Visual communication
Communication economics 1449, 1518
Communication networks 1582
Communication research 1456, 1515, 1519
Communication sciences 1387, 1396, 1454
Communication systems 1519
Communism 1881, 2858, 4760, 4769, 4822, 4832
Communist parties 4830, 4951
Community 244, 335, 369, 406, 717, 811, 1075, 1138, 1540, 1582, 1689, 1703, 1713, 1752, 1844, 1850, 1978, 2162, 3186, 3342, 3370, 3506, 3513, 3516, 3519, 3520, 3521, 3522, 3524, 3529, 3532, 3534, 3589, 3626, 3632, 3681, 3682, 3764, 4082, 4212, 4761, 4836, 4859, 4949, 4970, 5041, 5043,

482

Subject index

5097, 5185, 5237, 5239, 5377, 5458, 5555, 5578, 5707, 5712, 5831
see also: Ethnic communities, Local communities, Religious communities, Rural communities, Scientific communities, Urban communities
Community care   2074, 3703, 5270, 5274, 5457, 5466, 5468, 5554, 5586, 5603, 5708, 5709, 5710, 5711, 5712, 5713, 5714, 5715, 5716, 5717, 5718, 5719, 5720, 5721, 5722, 5723, 5724, 5725, 5726, 5727, 5728, 5729, 5730, 5731, 5738, 5740, 5742, 5746, 5834, 5840
Community development   245, 3505, 3507, 3508, 3510, 3521, 3525, 3526, 3531, 3611, 3681, 3825, 3877, 3970, 4201
Community law   2970
Community life   3056, 3511, 3513, 4247
Community organization   3503, 3508, 3509, 3511, 3515, 3531, 3730, 5757
Community participation   717, 3505, 3510, 3517, 4792, 5680
Community power   3514, 4944
Community services   3594, 4795, 5259, 5459, 5460, 5462, 5606, 5708, 5730
Commuting   2320, 3280, 3315, 3356, 3910, 4352
Company law   4268, 4639
Company management
see: Business management
Comparative analysis   25, 237, 272, 911, 1753, 1927, 1973, 2377, 2536, 2672, 2803, 3234, 3538, 4018, 4432, 4740, 4901, 4948, 5001, 5142
Comparative politics   338
Compensation   3975, 4415, 4580, 4705, 5201
Competition   305, 844, 1049, 4032
see also: Interpersonal competition, Perfect competition
Competitiveness   1751
Compulsory arbitration   4646
Computer industry   4412
Computer programmes   181

Computerization   4229, 4324, 4649
Computers   116, 166, 340, 720, 1136, 1446, 1447, 1743, 3596, 4271, 4403, 4551, 4564, 4730
see also: Microcomputers
Comte, Auguste   404
Concentration camps   5188
Conciliation   4623
Conditions of employment   4262, 4268
Confidentiality   4814
Conflict   676, 687, 689, 1856, 2554, 3126, 4872, 5702
see also: Class conflict, Cultural conflicts, Interethnic conflict, International conflicts, Interpersonal conflicts, Marital conflict, Political conflicts, Racial conflict, Religious conflicts, Role conflicts
Conflict resolution   676, 679, 681, 682, 683, 684, 685, 686, 688, 718, 872, 895, 1050, 1935, 4448, 4469, 4621, 4625, 4647, 5007
Confucianism   495
Congregations   1290
Conservation   365, 3576, 3891
see also: Nature conservation, Resource conservation
Conservatism   925, 939, 3615, 4286, 4768, 4781
Conservative parties   4686, 5723, 5742
Conservatives   4910
Constitution   1920, 4771
Constitutional reforms   1297
Construction activity   4593
Construction industry   4244, 4591
Consumer behaviour   2602, 4158, 4159, 4160, 4162, 4163, 4164, 4171, 4173, 4174, 4177, 4182, 4183, 4187, 4189, 4191, 4196
Consumer credit   4172
Consumer education   4159
Consumer society   1129
Consumerism   1637, 1724, 4184, 4193, 4195, 5727
Consumers   1444, 4115, 4156, 4192, 4195, 5745

Subject index

Consumption 884, 3881, 4159, 4165, 4166, 4175, 4180, 4192, 4193, 4197, 5314
  see also: Food consumption, Household consumption, Mass consumption
Consumption patterns 4249
Consumption theory 4167
Contemporary art 2040
Contraception 673, 2211, 2212, 2216, 2219, 2233, 2240, 2263, 2722, 2955, 2976, 3008
Contraceptive methods 2162
Contracts 1122, 1173, 1185, 2242, 4329, 5489
  see also: Labour contract, Social contract
Copyright 1184, 3971
Corporate crime 4101
Corporate culture 791, 792, 820, 877, 890, 4096, 4104, 4112, 4114, 4168, 4179, 4448, 4483
Corporate planning 4105, 4406
Correlation 785
Corruption 5132, 5186
  see also: Political corruption
Cosmology 103
Cost of living 2098, 5314
Costs 3911, 3914, 4138, 5558
  see also: Child costs
Costumes 1106, 1107, 3113
Counselling 409, 642, 700, 2421, 5206, 5559, 5560, 5561, 5567, 5572, 5577, 5590
Counsellors 5573, 5595
Counterculture 3519
Counties 2936
Countries
  see: Arab countries
Countryside 4076
Coup d'état 1537
Courtesy 1370
Courts 2469, 5157, 5230
  see also: Criminal courts, Juvenile courts, Labour courts
Courtship 614, 629, 641, 2551, 2579, 2624
Covariance 266, 271, 472, 2364

Craft workers 4324
Creativity 439, 480, 3823
Credit 4196, 4251
  see also: Consumer credit
Cree 1110
Creole languages 1470
Creoles 3126
Crime 656, 957, 960, 1081, 1517, 1557, 2652, 2985, 3038, 3223, 3229, 3236, 3650, 3656, 3657, 3895, 4888, 5090, 5091, 5093, 5094, 5095, 5096, 5097, 5100, 5101, 5102, 5103, 5104, 5105, 5108, 5109, 5110, 5114, 5120, 5122, 5123, 5124, 5127, 5128, 5129, 5131, 5133, 5134, 5136, 5138, 5141, 5143, 5144, 5145, 5146, 5147, 5148, 5150, 5151, 5153, 5155, 5156, 5159, 5161, 5163, 5166, 5168, 5169, 5171, 5172, 5173, 5175, 5176, 5180, 5187, 5189, 5208, 5225, 5227, 5255, 5265, 5285, 5287, 5289, 5297, 5300, 5302, 5303, 5307, 5308, 5309, 5374, 5386, 5410, 5436, 5442, 5444
  see also: Corporate crime, International crime, Organized crime, Victims of crime
Crime prevention 3658, 5101, 5106, 5107, 5144, 5163, 5169, 5174, 5177, 5187, 5415, 5444, 5447, 5449, 5555
Criminal courts 1204
Criminal jurisdiction 5095, 5153, 5180, 5227
Criminal justice 539, 1181, 1207, 2991, 4797, 4970, 5105, 5157, 5186, 5188, 5190, 5191, 5192, 5197, 5200, 5201, 5202, 5208, 5210, 5211, 5213, 5216, 5222, 5228, 5230, 5245, 5248, 5287, 5292, 5294, 5297, 5298, 5385
Criminal law 371, 1179, 1182, 5153, 5182, 5188, 5227, 5367
Criminal sentencing 3169, 5182, 5196, 5207, 5367
Criminal sociology 5119, 5160
Criminality 2157, 3895, 5128, 5143, 5152, 5165, 5178
  see also: Economic criminality
Criminology 5069, 5077, 5091, 5098, 5101, 5108, 5111, 5112, 5123, 5125,

Subject index

5131, 5140, 5144, 5146, 5149, 5150, 5162, 5163, 5182, 5187, 5193, 5194, 5220, 5231, 5296, 5299, 5300, 5306, 5308, 5367, 5376, 5436
Crisis management   400
Critical theory   120, 131, 977, 979, 1057, 1063, 1514, 4925, 4963, 5445
Criticism   159, 439, 979, 988, 995, 1036
  see also: Literary criticism
Crop
  see: Fruit crops
Cross-cultural analysis   302, 338, 416, 1009, 1120, 1176, 1203, 1615, 2698, 2873, 2900, 4436, 5386
Cross-national analysis   338, 3201
Crowds   404, 4915
Cubans   3115, 3395, 3414, 4135
Cults   2910
Cultural adaptation   420
Cultural anthropology   986
Cultural assimilation   1483, 1871, 3036, 3160
Cultural behaviour   380
Cultural change   1077, 1217, 1391, 1616, 3132, 5229
Cultural conflicts   1010, 1013, 1310, 2138, 2952, 3052, 3081, 3150, 3329, 3343, 5605
Cultural crises   1026
Cultural development   212, 998
Cultural differentiation   1385
Cultural diffusion   1026, 1047, 3072, 5032
Cultural diversity   254, 693, 1020, 1646, 1920, 2002, 2740, 3693
Cultural dynamics   4906
Cultural environment   1127
Cultural factors   3486, 4316
Cultural heritage
  see: Preservation of cultural heritage
Cultural history   3066, 3401
Cultural identity   980, 998, 1008, 1015, 1047, 1407, 1527, 1573, 1658, 2155, 2964, 3058, 3087, 3093, 3113, 3124, 3267, 3296, 3570, 3659, 4408, 4955, 5027, 5032
Cultural industry   1623

Cultural influence   1037, 1113, 2255, 4083
Cultural integration   994, 3256, 3324
Cultural nationalism   3036
Cultural patterns   4249
Cultural policy   1026, 1034, 1045, 1049, 1535, 1597, 3864
Cultural practices   1597
Cultural relations   1120, 3284
Cultural reproduction   1028
Cultural studies   57, 984, 985, 986, 995, 1012, 1078, 1519, 1602, 1675, 2699, 3665
Cultural tradition   495, 1933, 3034, 3103
Cultural values   3045
Culture   29, 167, 186, 204, 225, 230, 372, 404, 423, 461, 514, 578, 676, 690, 696, 772, 791, 823, 890, 973, 974, 975, 976, 979, 982, 987, 988, 989, 990, 991, 993, 999, 1000, 1001, 1006, 1011, 1013, 1015, 1020, 1022, 1030, 1033, 1036, 1040, 1043, 1049, 1052, 1053, 1055, 1056, 1060, 1073, 1076, 1077, 1086, 1102, 1111, 1184, 1212, 1408, 1449, 1510, 1518, 1538, 1596, 1604, 1607, 1634, 1647, 1663, 1836, 2411, 2448, 2515, 2650, 2779, 2791, 2903, 3035, 3072, 3091, 3115, 3139, 3228, 3471, 3556, 3568, 3620, 3679, 3701, 3786, 4003, 4009, 4080, 4165, 4219, 4248, 4953, 4958, 4974, 4979, 5183, 5371, 5373, 5401, 5424
  see also: Bourgeois culture, Corporate culture, Cultural diversity, Mass culture, Material culture, Musical culture, National culture, Political culture, Right to culture, Subculture, Theory of culture, Universality of culture, Working class culture, Youth culture
Culture and development   1008
Culture of poverty   5320
Curriculum   1666, 1723, 1757, 1770, 1772, 1774
Curriculum development   1647, 1736
Customs   1080, 1083, 1122, 2515, 2964

see also: Family customs, Sex customs
Cyclical analysis   781
Czechs   3144
Damage   2147
Dance   1619, 2791
Darwin, Charles   2406
Data analysis   56, 263, 264, 266, 267, 268, 271, 273, 274, 275, 279, 282, 283, 287, 289, 293, 294, 295, 300, 301, 304, 305, 306, 310, 312, 314, 318, 320, 322, 323, 326, 744, 2276, 3248, 5462
Data bases   74, 76, 4553
Data collection   267, 326, 331, 332, 334, 337, 339, 340, 346, 353, 354, 355, 357, 773
Data processing   306, 918, 4271
Data protection   71, 77
Dating   536, 614, 638, 5130
Daughters   689, 1329, 2630, 2760, 2870, 5089
Day care centres   4314, 4494, 5528
Deafness   2631
Dealer
 see: Drug dealers
Death   147, 257, 927, 1016, 1124, 1234, 1327, 1409, 2182, 2194, 2358, 2370, 2377, 2387, 2421, 2526, 5409, 5426, 5759, 5791, 5793, 5821
see also: Causes of death
Debt   4172, 4203, 5315
see also: External debt
Debt management   4203
Decentralization   1735, 1737, 3731, 4215, 4597, 4618, 4680, 4840, 4841, 4967
Decision   759, 4318, 4416, 4433
see also: Siting decisions
Decision making   260, 268, 392, 400, 401, 518, 519, 520, 521, 522, 523, 524, 525, 526, 527, 714, 738, 739, 741, 756, 784, 831, 850, 863, 866, 879, 895, 1121, 1150, 2204, 2437, 2602, 2603, 2713, 2827, 2854, 3461, 3965, 4090, 4116, 4416, 4434, 4821, 4857, 5071, 5476, 5662, 5679, 5703, 5817, 5822
see also: Group decision making

Decision models   296, 317, 767
Decision theory   4981
Deconstruction   160, 1061
Decorative art   1605
Deforestation   4210
Delinquency   5536, 5601
 see also: Juvenile delinquency
Delinquent rehabilitation   960
Demand   3771, 4472, 4497, 4874, 5474
Democracy   4, 29, 210, 723, 988, 1455, 1579, 1703, 1812, 1842, 1933, 1961, 3057, 3116, 3148, 4026, 4685, 4767, 4771, 4775, 4780, 4783, 4820, 4822, 4840, 4894, 4953, 4970, 5778
 see also: Christian democracy, Liberal democracy, Social democracy
Democratic regimes   4796
Democratization   122, 1731, 1938, 1945, 2656, 4210, 4791, 4796, 4839, 4941, 4949, 4993, 5511
Demographic change   1698, 1986, 1990, 1991, 1992, 1996, 2001, 2006, 2015, 2018, 2021, 2026, 2029, 2031, 2033, 2179, 2184, 2186, 2191, 2192, 2193, 2196, 2198, 2203, 2205, 2276, 2291, 2389, 2453, 3286, 3357, 3413, 3565, 3641, 3666
Demographic indicators   557
Demographic research   2030
Demography   1988, 1993, 1994, 2001, 2002, 2007, 2008, 2011, 2017, 2019, 2020, 2028, 2032, 2036, 2122, 2185, 2189, 2199, 2215, 2219, 2244, 2247, 2282, 2283, 2300, 2325, 2348, 2349, 2414, 2492, 2507, 3110, 3190, 3268, 3300, 3583, 3933, 4170, 4344, 4554, 4954, 5340
 see also: Ethnic demography, Historical demography
Dentistry   5644
Dependence relationships   579, 2057
Dependence theory   4229
Dependency rehabilitation   632, 5194, 5376
Deprivation   4061, 5073
Depth interviews   339, 352, 358
Deregulation   1200, 1726, 3767, 4840

Subject index

Desegregation 1749
Desertification 3429, 3438, 3439, 3472, 3480, 3485, 3499
Determinism 125
Deterrence 5189, 5196, 5289
Developing countries 209, 402, 1013, 1166, 1282, 1507, 1705, 1727, 1907, 1935, 1987, 2007, 2022, 2103, 2223, 2270, 2288, 2341, 2350, 2357, 2859, 2871, 3373, 3375, 3399, 3407, 3420, 3439, 3510, 3571, 3604, 3638, 3664, 3707, 3716, 3721, 3776, 3816, 3849, 3887, 3903, 3937, 3943, 3949, 3982, 4013, 4034, 4229, 4691, 4750, 4844, 4907, 5006, 5019, 5504, 5636, 5643, 5665, 5675, 5830
see also: Less developed countries
Development
see: Economic development, Rural development, Socio-economic development, Sustainable development, Urban development
Development administration 2669
Development aid 3945
Development planning 1937, 2852
Development policy 3634, 3636
Development programmes 5348
Development projects 3555
Development strategies 4074
Development studies 209, 4221
Deviance 1968, 2974, 5113, 5114, 5137, 5150
Devolution 5758
Dewey, John 123, 891
Dialectics 93
Dialects 1467, 4876
Diaspora 3059, 3098, 3408
Dictionaries 73, 1838
Diet 584, 595, 1110, 1115
Dietary change 1104, 1114
Dietary disorders 2153
Diffusion theory 179, 314
Directories 75, 78, 2308, 3043, 3511
Disability 670, 2318
Disabled children 502, 2631, 2645, 5525
Disabled persons 670, 936, 1092, 1095, 1811, 2308, 2309, 2319, 2329, 2552, 2729, 2750, 4253, 5566, 5607, 5645, 5717, 5719, 5773
Disabled workers 4441
Disaster relief 1512
Disasters 830, 897, 1512, 1530, 3460, 3703, 3910, 5038, 5344, 5585, 5835
see also: Natural disasters
Discourse analysis 162, 276, 975, 997, 1365, 1374, 1385, 1403, 1434, 1466, 1472, 1490, 1537, 1576, 2756, 2904, 3202, 5009
Discrimination 726, 966, 1279, 1565, 1641, 1646, 1786, 2932, 2942, 3079, 3185, 3242, 3475, 4645, 5645, 5705
see also: Employment discrimination, Racial discrimination, Sex discrimination, Wage discrimination
Diseases 481, 932, 2304, 2305, 2306, 2310, 2313, 2317, 2320, 2321, 2328, 2335, 2341, 2343, 2345, 2347, 2350, 2356, 2419, 2667, 2774, 3007, 3409, 5373, 5411, 5634, 5695, 5701, 5753
see also: AIDS, Anorexia nervosa, Epilepsy, Occupational diseases, Sexually transmitted diseases, Tuberculosis
Dismissals 4295, 4630, 4659, 4660
Dissidents 4877
Distribution 440, 740, 2249, 2310, 4026, 4040
Distributive justice 761, 948, 4423, 5755
Districts 5777
Diversification 795, 825, 4111, 4266
Division of labour 1863, 1868, 2457, 2553, 2570, 2593, 2816, 2821, 2822, 2838, 2849, 2859, 2889, 2930, 4089, 4236, 4292, 4324
Divorce 2183, 2405, 2424, 2469, 2470, 2471, 2472, 2473, 2474, 2475, 2477, 2478, 2479, 2481, 2482, 2483, 2484, 2485, 2486, 2487, 2489, 2490, 2492, 2493, 2494, 2495, 2501, 2584, 2704, 5579
Divorced persons 2481
Domestic animals 2526
Domestic architecture 1117, 3773

Subject index

Domestic violence   684, 700, 2461, 2534, 2577, 2578, 2595, 2597, 2620, 2636, 2641, 2659, 2763, 5087, 5173, 5203, 5210, 5236, 5238, 5239, 5240, 5241, 5242, 5243, 5244, 5245, 5246, 5247, 5248, 5250, 5251, 5252, 5253, 5254, 5255, 5257, 5377, 5573
Domestic workers   2859, 4401, 4522
Domination   545, 3232, 4875
Dominicans   3030, 3395
Donagan, Alan   121, 486
Double taxation   3698
Drama   1582, 1583, 1593, 1791
Dramatic art   1594
Drawing   1594
Dress   1119, 1126, 4728
Drinkers   3233, 5380
Dropouts   1773
Drug abuse   1196, 1549, 1964, 2145, 4465, 5041, 5224, 5235, 5266, 5282, 5368, 5370, 5372, 5375, 5381, 5382, 5384, 5386, 5387, 5390, 5391, 5393, 5394, 5396, 5397, 5399, 5400, 5401, 5403, 5405, 5407, 5412, 5413, 5416, 5418, 5420, 5421
Drug addiction   56, 5370, 5375, 5387, 5399, 5416
Drug addicts   5156, 5282, 5410, 5411, 5412
Drug dealers   5378
Drug trafficking   5129, 5375, 5383, 5386, 5397, 5398, 5415, 5417
Drugs   1196, 2571, 5197, 5224, 5372, 5385, 5393, 5400, 5405, 5407
  see also: Cocaine, Drug trafficking, Heroin
Dummer, Ethel Sturges   36
Durable goods   4185
Durkheim, Emile   86, 87, 114, 122, 143, 160, 164, 201, 211, 1839, 1863, 1868, 2849, 4015, 5429
Dynamic models   284
Dynamics   796, 867, 1091, 2411, 3536, 3884, 4230, 5004
Dyslexia   498
Early childhood   530, 2118
Early motherhood   2122, 2260, 2292, 2296, 2458, 2517, 2618, 3009

Early retirement   4439
Earnings   54, 3268, 4019, 4037, 4041, 4047, 4066, 4282, 4513
Earthquakes   3910
East-West relations   5009, 5017
Ecological movements   4861, 4879, 4880, 4881, 4889, 4940, 4943
Ecologism   165, 2762, 4891
Ecology   107, 1141, 1336, 3434, 3442, 3443, 3444, 3453, 3455, 3465, 3470, 3473, 3495, 4072, 4670
  see also: Human ecology
Economic activity   3429, 3995
Economic analysis   291, 2260, 4324
Economic anthropology   4073
Economic behaviour   3959, 4046, 4093, 4199
Economic change   1008, 1856, 1916, 1939, 1967, 3977, 4043, 4055, 4064, 4102, 4120, 4140, 4308, 4627, 4771, 5096
Economic conditions   978, 999, 1046, 1870, 1895, 1924, 1938, 1961, 1963, 2045, 2066, 2077, 2127, 2186, 2555, 2709, 2871, 3059, 3164, 3179, 3226, 3508, 3612, 3662, 3671, 3857, 3894, 3923, 3934, 3985, 3994, 4020, 4035, 4037, 4054, 4059, 4062, 4080, 4142, 4206, 4233, 4365, 4373, 4388, 4397, 5036, 5282, 5354, 5412
Economic cooperation   4134
Economic criminality   4200, 5186
Economic crisis   1987, 2539, 3976, 3994, 4058, 4064, 5058
Economic decline   5036
Economic development   1093, 1451, 1768, 1864, 1990, 2708, 3211, 3216, 3440, 3507, 3820, 3839, 3931, 3968, 4015, 4046, 4074, 4211, 4212, 4213, 4224, 4230, 4231, 4232, 4416, 4773, 5354
Economic differentiation   3798
Economic equality   4065
Economic geography   3639
Economic growth   1945, 3565, 3934, 4026, 4220, 4273, 4796, 5345
Economic independence   4224
Economic indicators   315, 3577, 4055

Subject index

Economic inequality   929, 1840, 1914, 2048, 4042, 4045, 4206, 5258
Economic integration   3333
Economic justice   971
Economic life   3244
Economic methodology   3962
Economic models   2262, 2437, 4017
Economic organization   4124, 4138
Economic performance   3960, 4115, 4124, 4449
Economic planning   4215
Economic policy   1870, 1991, 3508, 3855, 4214, 4215, 4217, 4228, 4233, 4300, 4639, 4781
   see also: Industrial policy
Economic prospects   1936, 4272
Economic psychology   3957, 3966, 4172
Economic reform   1953, 1963, 2000, 3986, 3989, 4056, 4216, 4227, 5051
Economic relations
   see: International economic relations
Economic rights   4615
Economic sociology   1931, 3958, 3961, 3963
Economic status   2083, 2332, 2354, 2366, 2504, 4011, 4316
Economic structure   3125, 3666, 3964
Economic systems   798, 3974
Economic theory   886, 2721, 3244, 5108
Economic thought   157, 3958, 3959, 3994, 4009
Economics and politics   3338, 4229, 4855
Economics of education   1667, 1794, 1803, 4275
Ecosystems   998
Education   40, 41, 123, 390, 439, 1027, 1056, 1378, 1638, 1640, 1641, 1643, 1644, 1647, 1650, 1651, 1652, 1655, 1658, 1659, 1665, 1666, 1667, 1671, 1672, 1673, 1675, 1678, 1680, 1682, 1683, 1685, 1688, 1689, 1690, 1700, 1706, 1710, 1721, 1724, 1731, 1735, 1738, 1740, 1741, 1745, 1762, 1782, 1791, 1814, 1815, 1840, 1864, 1932, 1933, 2086, 2136, 2169, 2171, 2176, 2232, 2405, 2412, 2645, 2784, 2983, 3054, 3421, 3566, 4019, 4041, 4280, 4370, 4500, 4544, 4563, 5038, 5264, 5279, 5323, 5510, 5547, 5576
   see also: Access to education, Adult education, Basic education, Bilingual education, Consumer education, Economics of education, Family education, Health education, Higher education, History of education, Industrial education, Intercultural education, Minority education, Parent's education, Parent-teacher relations, Population education, Post-secondary education, Preschool education, Primary education, Private education, Public education, Religious education, Secondary education, Special education, Tertiary education, Theory of education, Vocational education, Women's education
Education administration   1714, 1717, 1736
Education policy   1513, 1644, 1663, 1696, 1697, 1698, 1700, 1703, 1704, 1705, 1706, 1708, 1710, 1711, 1712, 1713, 1714, 1716, 1717, 1718, 1719, 1720, 1721, 1722, 1723, 1727, 1728, 1729, 1731, 1732, 1733, 1734, 1736, 1738, 1755, 1759, 1769, 1773, 1777, 1781, 1783, 1792, 1794, 1804, 1805, 2256, 3324, 4264, 4654
Education reform   1676, 1697, 1701, 1715, 1730, 1733, 1734, 1738, 1752, 1754, 1756, 1761, 1762, 1795, 4970, 5493
Education systems   1686, 1697, 1747, 1750, 1751, 1752, 1753, 1754, 1755, 1757, 1759, 1760, 1761, 1764, 1765, 1774, 1789, 4324
Educational development   1751
Educational expenditure   1648
Educational institutions   1716
Educational needs   1709
Educational opportunities   1746, 1834
Educational output   1815
Educational philosophy   1357, 1693

Educational planning   1660, 1699, 1701
Educational psychology   390
Educational research   43, 1394, 1643, 1681, 1686, 1694, 1787, 1788
Educational sociology   1103, 1662, 1684, 1686, 1687, 1691, 1692, 4498
Effects   641, 680, 955, 1442, 1556, 2955, 3540, 4016, 5389
see also: Environmental effects, Psychological effects
Egalitarianism   140, 1840
Ego   549, 600
Elections   3325, 4954, 4971, 4977
see also: Gubernatorial elections, Local elections, Parliamentary elections, Presidential elections
Elections to the upper chamber   4960
Electoral campaigning   2804, 4946, 4947, 4960, 4964, 4980, 4985
Electoral college   5112
Electoral results   4664, 4965
Electoral sociology   4956, 4972
Electrical industries   4429
Electricity   4664
Electronics   166, 1448, 1457
Electronics industry   2661, 4697
Elites   331, 1122, 1565, 1816, 1845, 1895, 3042, 4102, 4104, 4928, 4978, 5034, 5036
see also: Political elites
Emancipation   2858, 4764, 4925
see also: Women's emancipation
Emigrants   3256, 3310
Emigration   1950, 3253, 3289, 3297, 3327, 3344, 3400, 3401
Emotions   167, 228, 436, 447, 453, 454, 467, 506, 530, 534, 550, 569, 570, 572, 581, 590, 646, 691, 692, 694, 696, 697, 699, 701, 702, 703, 704, 708, 709, 799, 1436, 1998, 2152, 2407, 2428, 2585, 2593, 2629, 2953, 3133, 4380, 4462, 5078
Empirical research   303, 1220
Empirical tests   804, 3170
Empiricism   117, 769, 1095, 1142, 2766

Employees   644, 829, 834, 956, 4124, 4340, 4358, 4407, 4410, 4438, 4440, 4466, 4474, 4475, 4571, 4573, 4586, 4588, 4640, 4655, 4677
Employers   4011, 4438, 4440, 4475, 4609, 4666
Employment   936, 1811, 1876, 1907, 2020, 2089, 2137, 2252, 2396, 2479, 2553, 2584, 2817, 2921, 3145, 3239, 3249, 3326, 3912, 4028, 4057, 4224, 4237, 4242, 4255, 4256, 4263, 4282, 4287, 4288, 4291, 4299, 4303, 4306, 4307, 4309, 4316, 4320, 4346, 4352, 4355, 4356, 4411, 4412, 4435, 4439, 4444, 4490, 4510, 4514, 4565, 4566, 4578, 4673, 4686, 4692
see also: Access to employment, Conditions of employment, Full employment, Full time employment, Part-time employment, Rural employment, Temporary employment, Urban employment, Women's employment, Youth employment
Employment creation   4251, 4599
Employment discrimination   936, 1474, 3324, 4253, 4281, 4311
Employment opportunities   3379, 4336, 4376, 4379, 5531
Employment policy   4245, 4247, 4251, 4257, 4261, 4267, 4279, 4286, 4375, 4388, 4486, 4693
Employment services   4262, 5481
Employment situation   4615
Employment subsidies   4251
Energy
see: Geothermal energy, Nuclear energy
Energy efficiency   4177
Energy planning   3604
Engineering   4432, 4666
Engineers   1654, 3031, 4704
English language   679, 1368, 1370, 1381, 1382, 1405, 1468, 1469, 1488, 1492, 1561, 1563, 1568
Enterprises   713, 877, 1756, 3216, 4073, 4078, 4084, 4086, 4092, 4119, 4124, 4138, 4205, 4237, 4251, 4260, 4416, 4475, 4569, 5141

Subject index

see also: Agricultural enterprises, Capitalist enterprises, Family firms, Foreign enterprises, Industrial enterprises, Location of enterprises, Multinational enterprises, Private enterprises, Public enterprises
Entrepreneurs   2797, 4102, 4103, 4110, 4120, 4135, 4141, 4185, 4567
Entrepreneurship   2813, 3545, 3836, 4078, 4080, 4088, 4091, 4093, 4118, 4121, 4123
Environment   203, 1147, 1526, 1542, 1998, 2024, 2065, 2188, 2854, 3447, 3448, 3452, 3459, 3461, 3462, 3474, 3477, 3490, 3495, 3799, 3911, 4185, 4562, 5060
see also: Cultural environment, Family environment, Occupational environment, Social environment, Urban environment, Work environment
Environmental degradation   998, 2382, 3450, 3480, 3492, 3896, 3909, 3930, 3940, 4861
Environmental effects   3449
Environmental impact studies   4210
Environmental management   1243, 3578, 3638
Environmental planning   2027, 3764, 3894
Environmental policy   3430, 3443, 3473, 3498, 3877
Environmental protection   365, 3436, 3469, 3489, 4869, 4870, 4891, 4943
Environmental psychology   387, 3431
Environmental sociology   6, 3446, 3451, 4421
Epidemiology   260, 2303, 2320, 2324, 2339, 2344, 5361, 5693
Epilepsy   531
Epistemology   27, 100, 101, 103, 104, 110, 112, 113, 114, 115, 116, 626, 1339, 1679, 4779, 5039
Equal opportunities   1742, 1800, 1813, 4242, 4258, 4346, 4803
Equal pay   2794, 4319, 4321, 4326, 4333

Equality   123, 128, 140, 988, 1896, 2268, 2928, 4350, 5467, 5650
see also: Economic equality, Sex equality, Social equality
Equilibrium
see: Social equilibrium
Equity   1455, 1741, 1800, 3972, 4210, 4256, 5650, 5769
Eroticism   2732, 2878, 2959
Ethics   121, 122, 137, 142, 150, 210, 228, 398, 486, 880, 916, 986, 1122, 1131, 1133, 1135, 1136, 1137, 1138, 1140, 1143, 1144, 1145, 1147, 1148, 1151, 1152, 1153, 1154, 1155, 1156, 1157, 1158, 1160, 1162, 1163, 1164, 1165, 1167, 1169, 1170, 1175, 1176, 1177, 1263, 1275, 1520, 1639, 1712, 1792, 2337, 2701, 2752, 2885, 2943, 2988, 3452, 3455, 3462, 3521, 3967, 4528, 5026, 5028, 5755, 5761, 5788, 5801, 5805, 5823
see also: Medical ethics, Professional ethics, Protestant ethics, Work ethic
Ethnic assimilation   3160
Ethnic communities   3047, 3057, 3125, 3191, 4512
Ethnic demography   3190
Ethnic groups   307, 933, 1048, 1270, 2605, 3023, 3025, 3026, 3033, 3036, 3041, 3045, 3046, 3048, 3061, 3075, 3095, 3097, 3105, 3110, 3113, 3115, 3118, 3122, 3154, 3187, 3201, 3204, 3209, 3215, 3219, 3240, 3242, 3333, 3518, 3770, 3805, 3806, 4263, 4967, 5031, 5152, 5705
Ethnic minorities   78, 816, 922, 1031, 1616, 1740, 1992, 2154, 2420, 2619, 3043, 3044, 3047, 3051, 3056, 3066, 3067, 3071, 3074, 3076, 3079, 3082, 3092, 3096, 3097, 3150, 3153, 3156, 3161, 3162, 3163, 3166, 3167, 3181, 3199, 3224, 3254, 3264, 3320, 3336, 3374, 3419, 3530, 3808, 4071, 4085, 4091, 4107, 4123, 4128, 4198, 4207, 4700, 4789, 4828, 5623, 5631
Ethnic policy   3201
Ethnicity   423, 938, 1084, 1313, 1380, 1407, 1415, 1488, 1541, 1647, 1782,

Subject index

1856, 1992, 2043, 2131, 2415, 2592, 2650, 3002, 3027, 3034, 3040, 3048, 3052, 3055, 3061, 3070, 3079, 3085, 3089, 3090, 3091, 3093, 3094, 3100, 3101, 3102, 3103, 3104, 3105, 3106, 3107, 3109, 3110, 3111, 3112, 3113, 3114, 3116, 3117, 3118, 3119, 3120, 3121, 3123, 3124, 3125, 3127, 3128, 3129, 3131, 3132, 3133, 3134, 3135, 3137, 3138, 3140, 3141, 3142, 3143, 3149, 3151, 3152, 3153, 3177, 3178, 3185, 3188, 3205, 3268, 3270, 3308, 3570, 3796, 3907, 4303, 4725, 5010
Ethnocentrism   119, 728, 3151, 3166, 3191, 3196, 3221
Ethnography   85, 1061, 1394, 1447, 3066, 3135, 4545, 4713
Ethnolinguistics   1488
Ethnology   3947
Ethnomedical beliefs   2313, 2345, 3007, 5373, 5411
Ethnomethodology   1434, 1466, 3095
Ethnomusicology   1616
Ethnopsychiatry   3343
Ethnopsychology   3144
Ethology   5087, 5254
Etiology   2718, 5075
Etiquette   1148, 1370
Etzioni, Amitai   886
Eugenics   3175, 5812
European Communities   1195, 1209, 2765, 3191, 3407, 3418, 3561, 3588, 4524, 4547, 4712, 4716, 4940, 5510
see also: Single European market
European Court of Justice   4788
European integration   1384, 1521, 3075
European Union   3311, 3839, 3946, 4296, 4361, 4590
Euthanasia   2226, 5787, 5792, 5793, 5804, 5805, 5808, 5814, 5827
Evaluation   281, 375, 437, 526, 656, 771, 1780, 1807, 2858, 4267, 5335, 5476, 5567, 5568, 5632, 5720, 5840
see also: Job evaluation, Programme evaluation
Evangelism   1268, 1282, 1326

Everyday life   1095, 1101, 1102, 1109, 1116, 1123, 1127, 1590, 2120, 3199, 3456, 3958, 4745, 4928
Evidence   1181, 1204, 1490, 2123, 2266, 2322
Evolution   3258
see also: Human evolution
Evolutionary psychology   5087, 5254
Exchange   265, 650, 906, 1363, 2520, 2531, 3546
see also: Social exchange
Exchange theory   883
Executives   3198, 4092, 4397, 4502, 4509, 4519, 4526, 4858
Exhibitions   1604
Exile
see: Political exile
Expectation   639, 1677, 4414, 5132
see also: Role expectations
Expenditure
see: Health expenditure, Public expenditure
Experimental psychology   362, 392
Experimentation   2923, 5802
see also: Animal experimentation
Experiments   94, 1338
Experts   860, 4816
Explanation   8, 83, 688, 1890, 4764
Export-oriented industry   4488, 4687
External debt   3619, 5006, 5012
External migration   3353
Extreme right   4932, 4982, 5435
Extremism   4982
Facial expressions   675
Factor analysis   283
Factories   4099
Failure   997, 2808, 3202
see also: School failure
Fairy tales   5586
Faith   1273
Falkland War   5034
Family   616, 914, 1021, 1575, 1605, 1620, 1684, 1691, 1767, 1997, 2087, 2125, 2180, 2201, 2213, 2222, 2237, 2269, 2315, 2352, 2386, 2400, 2401, 2404, 2408, 2409, 2410, 2411, 2414, 2415, 2416, 2419, 2422, 2423, 2425, 2426, 2430, 2431, 2432, 2437, 2438,

Subject index

2440, 2442, 2444, 2447, 2448, 2452, 2453, 2456, 2459, 2464, 2466, 2468, 2476, 2489, 2496, 2499, 2504, 2505, 2506, 2508, 2514, 2523, 2524, 2528, 2530, 2532, 2543, 2568, 2585, 2593, 2611, 2612, 2617, 2622, 2635, 2647, 2648, 2674, 2680, 2866, 2868, 2892, 2919, 2924, 2986, 3038, 3327, 3328, 3350, 3566, 3744, 4315, 4322, 4331, 4349, 4404, 4905, 4983, 5055, 5143, 5184, 5237, 5261, 5269, 5272, 5328, 5339, 5343, 5395, 5469, 5479, 5581, 5594, 5595, 5603
  see also: One-parent families, Sociology of the family
Family customs 2406
Family disintegration 2413, 2491, 5395
Family education 1226
Family environment 2433, 4019
Family farms 2910, 3556, 3561, 3580, 3596
Family firms 4073, 4088, 4131
Family income 2480, 4053
Family law 1190, 2424, 2472, 2473, 2501, 2611, 2704
Family life 1460, 1970, 2397, 2403, 2417, 2421, 2447, 2460, 2461, 2463, 2526, 4537
Family planning 2207, 2214, 2216, 2220, 2223, 2227, 2230, 2236, 2239, 2241, 2263, 2269, 2270, 2272, 2278, 2527, 3499
Family policy 2087, 2101, 2124, 2408, 2418, 2440, 2465, 2496
Family relations 403, 1720, 2086, 2402, 2421, 2426, 2436, 2439, 2450, 2451, 2454, 2460, 2464, 2465, 2512, 2516, 2531, 2619, 2620, 2637, 2641, 2645, 2649, 2746, 2922, 4982, 5021, 5569
Family size 2244
Family structure 278, 2180, 2412, 2420, 2507, 2509, 2515, 2517, 2529, 2892, 3950, 3973
Family therapy 2421, 5545, 5586
Farm management 2854

Farmers 1099, 3385, 3561, 3562, 3581, 3592
Farming 3078, 3560, 3607, 4323
  see also: Collective farming, Part-time farming, Small-scale farming
Farrell, James T. 50
Fascism 1644, 4915, 4932
Fashion 1106, 1107, 1126, 1129, 4106, 4173
Fasting 1309
Fatherhood 2648
Fathers 685, 1329, 2238, 2435, 2500, 2611, 2623, 2625, 2760, 5785
Fear 394, 932, 940, 957, 1612, 3697, 4835, 5120, 5265, 5445
Federal states 3187, 4954
Federalism 4790, 5470, 5761
Feelings 435, 3299
Female labour 2840, 4328, 4342, 4349, 4550
Female offenders 5121, 5220
Femininity 589, 1087, 1608, 2159, 2651, 2870, 2872, 2880, 2881, 2882, 2887, 2904, 2905, 2908, 2967, 2982
Feminism 85, 104, 124, 228, 379, 410, 632, 700, 1021, 1161, 1449, 1518, 1690, 2228, 2502, 2655, 2656, 2663, 2669, 2682, 2683, 2691, 2694, 2696, 2700, 2705, 2706, 2717, 2718, 2719, 2720, 2723, 2724, 2725, 2726, 2727, 2728, 2729, 2730, 2732, 2733, 2734, 2735, 2736, 2737, 2738, 2739, 2741, 2742, 2743, 2744, 2745, 2747, 2749, 2750, 2751, 2752, 2755, 2758, 2760, 2761, 2763, 2764, 2765, 2768, 2769, 2770, 2771, 2773, 2776, 2778, 2779, 2780, 2791, 2853, 2865, 2878, 2908, 2928, 2931, 2959, 2979, 3453, 3487, 4777, 4905, 5510, 5659
Feminist theory 633, 879, 1063, 1143, 1339, 1714, 1723, 2651, 2658, 2675, 2699, 2703, 2717, 2721, 2731, 2738, 2739, 2740, 2746, 2748, 2753, 2754, 2756, 2757, 2759, 2766, 2769, 2770, 2772, 2775, 2777, 2843, 2853, 2878, 2896, 2928, 2941, 2959, 2968, 2975, 3493, 4726, 5445

Subject index

Fertility   330, 440, 1989, 2001, 2008, 2019, 2030, 2038, 2191, 2192, 2199, 2205, 2211, 2214, 2216, 2223, 2231, 2233, 2244, 2249, 2250, 2252, 2253, 2254, 2256, 2257, 2258, 2260, 2261, 2262, 2265, 2266, 2268, 2269, 2270, 2271, 2272, 2273, 2274, 2275, 2276, 2277, 2279, 2282, 2283, 2284, 2285, 2286, 2288, 2289, 2290, 2291, 2295, 2296, 2297, 2298, 2301, 2418, 2444, 2453, 2875, 3366, 4317, 4342, 4349, 4356, 5808
   see also: Soil fertility
Fertility decline   2280, 2287, 2294, 2299
Fertility rate   2002
Festivals   1125, 1309, 3052, 4928
Fetishism   1225, 2987
Feudalism   3987
Field work   336, 337, 358
Filipinos   2281
Film industry   1601
Films   1573, 1574, 1578, 1596, 1600, 1602, 1612, 1614, 1617, 1618, 5445
Finance   836, 1578, 3737, 5716, 5746
   see also: Local finance
Financial administration   4203
Financial crisis   4204, 4210
Financial information   4204
Financial institutions   4290, 4480
Financial management   4178, 5118
Financial services   4105
Finkielkraut, Alain   1056
Fire   2433
Fire services   1829, 4460
Firearms   1203, 4811
Fiscal policy   4771, 4842
Fishing   3124
Flexible hours of work   2397
Flexible specialization   4087
Floods   2197
Folk beliefs   374
Folk culture   445, 1079
Folk songs   1616
Folklore   1438
Folkloristics   1528
Food   2376, 4162, 4187, 5597
Food consumption   1105

Food habits   1113, 1115, 4158
Food marketing   3575
Food price policy   2376
Food production   3584, 4087
Food security   2188, 5349
Food supply   4022
Forced migration   2197
Forecasts   2026, 2302, 5402
   see also: Population forecasts
Foreign aid   4211
Foreign capital   4229
Foreign enterprises   4098
Foreign investment   4074, 4098, 4142
Foreign policy   562, 5024
Foreign relations   1047, 1362, 5013, 5017, 5032
Foreign workers   3242, 3256, 3289, 3375, 3417, 3418, 3425, 3921, 4274, 4281, 4401, 5512, 5705
Foreigners   997, 1429, 2952, 3040, 3152, 3185, 3199, 3202, 3246, 3271, 3294, 3309, 3317
Forest development   3568
Forest resources   3605
Forests   4266
Formalization   1497
Foster, Peter   58
Foucault, Michel   89, 124, 162, 166, 190, 885, 1676, 2771, 2772, 2865, 2975
Fraternities   744, 763
Fraud   5110, 5129, 5139, 5141, 5186, 5516
Free trade   3426
Freedom   125, 800, 891, 944, 1039, 1598, 2242, 2715, 2833, 4822
   see also: Academic freedom
Freedom of conscience   1296
Freedom of religion   1250
Freedom of speech   2732, 4894
Freedom of the press   1439
Freemasonry   1235
Freidson, Eliot   4546, 5700
French language   229, 1362, 1483, 1484
Freud, Sigmund   377
Frictional unemployment   4387

Subject index

Friendship 621, 631, 678, 2135, 2145, 2447, 2624
Fruit crops 4607
Fulani 3575
Fulbe 3142
Full employment 4247
Full time employment 2792
Functional analysis 3874
Functionalism 197, 1411
Funerals 1130
Funerary rites
  see: Burial, Funerals
Furniture industry 4677
Gambling 4739
Game
  see: Ritual games
Game theory 268, 429, 1563, 4963
Games 265, 305, 317, 4732, 5057
Gangs 749, 5090, 5154, 5378
Gas 4665
Gender 12, 339, 342, 379, 527, 593, 594, 621, 631, 697, 1021, 1084, 1107, 1351, 1465, 1609, 1635, 1657, 1692, 1714, 1741, 1858, 1885, 1972, 2004, 2103, 2189, 2246, 2278, 2311, 2323, 2330, 2363, 2504, 2509, 2519, 2536, 2561, 2570, 2654, 2655, 2658, 2661, 2664, 2666, 2667, 2668, 2672, 2673, 2686, 2690, 2694, 2696, 2699, 2707, 2724, 2732, 2763, 2770, 2784, 2787, 2788, 2799, 2801, 2802, 2803, 2807, 2809, 2813, 2816, 2824, 2833, 2835, 2841, 2854, 2867, 2881, 2882, 2884, 2907, 2909, 2911, 2934, 2935, 2965, 2966, 3000, 3085, 3245, 3262, 3450, 3562, 3628, 4091, 4238, 4328, 4329, 4345, 4350, 4352, 4550, 4556, 4732, 4913, 4922, 4971, 5083, 5117, 5130, 5238, 5243, 5365, 5379, 5532, 5690, 5828
Gender differentiation 593, 678, 680, 696, 1188, 1654, 1858, 1868, 2055, 2181, 2182, 2187, 2380, 2410, 2548, 2624, 2652, 2669, 2670, 2702, 2703, 2742, 2758, 2783, 2785, 2793, 2795, 2796, 2804, 2805, 2806, 2807, 2808, 2809, 2810, 2814, 2815, 2817, 2818, 2821, 2826, 2829, 2834, 2837, 2838, 2841, 2846, 2848, 2849, 2851, 2852, 2853, 2859, 2872, 2939, 2944, 2957, 2966, 4001, 4010, 4263, 4319, 4326, 4327, 4330, 4331, 4340, 4355, 4417, 4428, 4537, 4555, 4560, 4562, 4592, 4787, 5406, 5419, 5422, 5465
Gender relations 641, 700, 2238, 2482, 2548, 2650, 2655, 2656, 2671, 2726, 2746, 2766, 2786, 2800, 2827, 2850, 2887, 2888, 2916, 2930, 2933, 2967, 2985, 3016, 3021, 3493, 4178, 4324, 4389
Gender roles 589, 638, 754, 2059, 2548, 2554, 2559, 2624, 2674, 2688, 2783, 2789, 2790, 2810, 2822, 2840, 2863, 2866, 2869, 2877, 2883, 2886, 2889, 2890, 2895, 2896, 2900, 2906, 2908, 2912, 2913, 2917, 2918, 2926, 4316, 4353, 4428
General theories 3711, 5117, 5166, 5379
Generalization 996
Generation differences 1262, 1900, 2039, 2531, 4320
Generations 440, 2040, 2609, 3114
Genes 5799, 5810, 5812
Genetic engineering 5810
Genetic psychology 548, 553
Genetics 548, 553, 729, 2289
  see also: Human genetics
Genocide 941
Gentileschi, Artemisia 2693
Geographic distribution 5747
Geographic location 5653
Geographical information systems 3454, 4079
Geography 111, 194, 1068, 1110, 2733, 2766, 3211, 3261, 3333, 3389, 3431, 3432, 3433, 3435, 3441, 3447, 3464, 3468, 3471, 3481, 3484, 3487, 3493, 5068, 5393
  see also: Economic geography, Historical geography, Human geography, Political geography, Population geography, Urban geography
Geometry 3493

Subject index

Geopolitics   752, 1187, 3476, 3985, 4763, 5018, 5020
Geothermal energy   3555
Geriatrics   5733, 5734
German language   679, 1376, 1564
German unification   849, 1388, 1920, 1963, 1970, 2139, 2192, 2416, 2819, 3661, 3679, 4024, 4065, 4336, 4336, 4635, 4639, 5029, 5314
Gerontology   2040, 2044, 2045, 2046, 2056, 2061, 2063, 2076, 2083, 2612
Giddens, Anthony   174, 222, 1055, 1875, 4776
Gift   1128
Gifted children   2109, 2166, 2402, 2637, 2912
Girls   2153, 2653, 2683, 5085, 5301
Global warming   3450
Glueck, Sheldon   5288
Goddesses   2655
Goffman, Erving   45, 1148
Gold mines   4295, 4589
Goldman, Emma   2730
Gorbachev, Mikhail   448
Government   1756, 4806
   see also: Central government, Local government, State government
Government policy   2096, 2502, 3210, 3234, 3272, 3375, 4253, 4569, 5259, 5372, 5421
Graduates   1846, 4564
Gramsci, Antonio   13
Grandparents   2521
Greek Orthodox Church   2998, 3122
Greeks   1003
Green Revolution   3564
Green, Thomas Hill   5517
Gross domestic product   4004
Group behaviour   545, 664, 702, 716, 733, 756, 1029, 2586, 2587, 3104
Group cohesiveness   728
Group composition   714, 744
Group decision making   523, 723, 737, 739, 759, 767
Group dynamics   618, 623, 721
Group identity   745, 753, 770, 1107, 1119, 1675, 1935, 3135
Group interaction   720, 731, 742, 762

Group membership   714, 725, 734, 753
Group participation   807, 3529
Group performance   488, 618, 732
Group protest   4920
Group psychotherapy   735, 736
Group theory   769, 818
Gubernatorial elections   4965
Guerrillas   5118
Gulf War   403, 425, 433, 1169, 1541, 3415, 4927, 5021, 5617
Gurvitch, Georges   208
Gustafson, James   5829
Gypsies   3113, 3120, 3121, 3130, 3215, 3235, 3803
Habermas, Jürgen   21, 137, 189, 1005, 1055, 1157, 1197, 1514
Habits   1122
   see also: Food habits, Reading habits
Haitians   3414
Hall, John A.   4776
Happiness   474, 2544
Harré, R.   90
Harvesting   3566
Hasidism   3053
Hauerwas, Stanley   5829
Hayek, Friedrich A. von   91, 132
Hazardous waste   3460
Healing   2313, 2345, 3007, 5373, 5411, 5851
Health   134, 248, 357, 384, 391, 415, 457, 474, 511, 955, 1088, 1110, 1121, 2074, 2078, 2304, 2305, 2311, 2313, 2321, 2322, 2342, 2347, 2355, 2367, 2375, 2432, 2857, 3007, 3447, 3477, 3647, 3654, 3675, 3716, 3799, 4330, 4353, 4406, 4440, 4548, 4722, 4740, 5315, 5373, 5392, 5400, 5411, 5636, 5655, 5656, 5664, 5696, 5732, 5754, 5763, 5769, 5777, 5851
   see also: Child health, Mental health, Public health, Women's health
Health administration   5709
Health care   786, 949, 2125, 2236, 2389, 2394, 2662, 2853, 3425, 3496, 4459, 5366, 5478, 5568, 5627, 5631, 5632, 5635, 5638, 5643, 5648, 5649, 5650, 5651, 5660, 5662, 5665, 5667,

Subject index

5669, 5671, 5673, 5674, 5675, 5676, 5682, 5683, 5687, 5688, 5689, 5690, 5691, 5692, 5694, 5698, 5701, 5704, 5706, 5707, 5713, 5717, 5718, 5720, 5727, 5732, 5734, 5735, 5738, 5743, 5744, 5745, 5747, 5748, 5753, 5755, 5756, 5760, 5765, 5766, 5768, 5769, 5773, 5783, 5805, 5809, 5813, 5829, 5831, 5834, 5837, 5840, 5845, 5849, 5855
see also: Medical care, Primary health care, Private health care
Health economics   5747, 5751
Health education   2357, 2976
Health expenditure   2389, 5748, 5749, 5750, 5753, 5767
Health insurance   2326, 5755, 5761, 5771, 5773, 5783, 5844
Health planning   5824, 5826
Health policy   2205, 4970, 5755, 5757, 5762, 5763, 5768, 5769, 5770, 5771, 5773, 5774, 5775, 5776, 5778, 5780, 5782, 5783
Health services   457, 2227, 5387, 5632, 5635, 5639, 5644, 5646, 5663, 5680, 5706, 5722, 5743, 5751, 5752, 5757, 5758, 5761, 5771, 5772, 5777, 5833, 5836, 5839, 5843, 5844, 5846
Hegel, Georg Friedrich W.   136, 2558
Hegemony   380, 1231, 1505, 2661, 2909, 3973
Heidegger, Martin   605
Heresies   1283
Hermeneutics   8, 96, 286, 1357, 1420, 1592, 1693
Herod   1327
Heroes   4774
Heroin   5403, 5415
Heterosexuality   2968, 3000
Hierarchy   807, 892, 913, 1842, 2658, 2785, 4735
High technology   4226
Higher education   204, 1651, 1712, 1781, 1785, 1786, 1787, 1788, 1790, 1792, 1793, 1794, 1795, 1796, 1799, 1800, 1805, 1806, 1809, 1810, 1818, 4654
Hinduism   1259, 1307, 1319, 1843

Hindus   1324, 1843, 1861, 1869, 3114, 3264
Hirsch, Jr., E.D.   1647
Hispanics   2509, 2532, 2591, 2680, 3051, 3084, 3085, 3100, 3115, 3200, 4003, 4372, 4845, 5281, 5563
Historians   14
Historic sites   4747
Historical analysis   25
Historical demography   1997, 2013
Historical geography   1032
Historical museums   4747
Historiography   404, 1006, 2666, 2777
History   12, 15, 34, 164, 1067, 1503, 1666, 2693, 3063, 3213, 3226, 3527, 3542, 4096, 4218
see also: Agricultural history, Business history, Church history, Colonial history, Cultural history, Industrial history, Labour history, Language history, Local history, Oral history, Political history, Religious history, Social history, Urban history
History of art   1594
History of education   1670, 1688, 1715, 1793, 1816
History of law   1197
History of medicine   5664, 5699
History of political ideas   4777
History of science   1335, 1340
History of sociology   7, 17, 19, 21, 29, 50, 61, 210
History of the social sciences   1, 20
HIV   810, 933, 2313, 2314, 2315, 2316, 2320, 2341, 2343, 2344, 2346, 2978, 3001, 3008, 3010, 3011, 5267, 5355, 5400, 5567, 5575, 5770, 5774
Hmong   3332
Hobbes, Thomas   5028
Hobson, John Atkinson   20
Holism   2717
Holocaust   560, 941, 1627, 3107
Home ownership   3026
Homeless people   267, 326, 5259, 5260, 5262, 5263, 5264, 5265, 5266, 5269, 5271, 5272, 5277, 5278, 5279, 5280, 5282, 5284, 5322, 5323, 5328,

497

Subject index

5333, 5391, 5408, 5412, 5459, 5695, 5761
Homelessness 267, 326, 354, 1097, 5047, 5259, 5260, 5261, 5267, 5268, 5270, 5273, 5274, 5275, 5276, 5277, 5283
Homicide 698, 3440, 5125, 5148, 5155, 5164, 5243, 5442
see also: Murder
Homogamy 2568
Homosexuality 353, 659, 917, 1614, 1617, 2327, 2545, 2567, 2624, 2728, 2878, 2896, 2946, 2947, 2950, 2959, 2961, 2962, 2963, 2964, 2969, 2970, 2971, 2973, 2974, 2978, 2980, 2983, 2984, 2989, 2992, 3001, 3011, 3013, 3456, 4495, 4645, 4863, 4995, 4996, 5244, 5445
Hormones 705, 2187, 2604
Horse-racing 2938
Hospital treatment 5621, 5695, 5781, 5853
Hospitals 5206, 5671, 5673, 5686, 5689, 5743, 5751, 5759, 5765, 5806, 5845
see also: Mental hospitals
Host countries 4528
Hours of work 4193, 4454
see also: Flexible hours of work
Household consumption 4039
Household equipment 4177
Household expenditure 4157, 4178
Household income 3598, 4025, 4157
Households 1111, 1460, 1999, 2000, 2011, 2025, 2098, 2180, 2437, 2463, 2508, 2513, 2520, 2532, 2570, 2635, 2746, 2822, 2838, 2842, 2861, 2901, 2921, 2924, 2972, 3273, 3512, 3532, 3597, 3742, 3744, 3745, 3771, 3964, 4021, 4034, 4046, 4057, 4238, 4384, 5038, 5240, 5261, 5330, 5474, 5480
Housewives 2902, 2917, 2921, 2922, 4317, 5467
Housework 1122, 2434, 2457, 2553, 2570, 2671, 2822, 2823, 2838, 2889, 4057, 4324
Housing 1099, 1112, 1998, 2168, 2334, 3372, 3567, 3729, 3730, 3731, 3732, 3734, 3736, 3737, 3738, 3739, 3740, 3749, 3750, 3751, 3752, 3753, 3756, 3759, 3760, 3761, 3762, 3763, 3764, 3765, 3766, 3767, 3768, 3770, 3771, 3773, 3774, 3775, 3778, 3779, 3781, 3784, 3785, 3786, 3787, 3789, 3790, 3791, 3792, 3801, 3805, 3825, 3854, 3861, 3890, 3901, 4188, 4589, 5315, 5452, 5469, 5470, 5480, 5483, 5488, 5490, 5491, 5497, 5518, 5744
see also: Social housing, Urban housing
Housing co-operatives 3734
Housing construction 3627, 3741, 3843
Housing market 3733, 3736, 3742, 3745, 3754, 3757, 3772, 3791
Housing needs 354, 4911, 5272, 5470
Housing policy 3172, 3423, 3729, 3743, 3747, 3748, 3758, 3777, 3793, 3794, 3845, 3853, 3904, 5498
Housing prices 3759, 3777, 3854, 3904
Housing reform 3666, 3748
Housing shortage 3741, 3843
Human biology 2247
Human body 72, 149, 154, 1106, 2095, 2217, 2865, 5641
Human ecology 3443, 3458, 3462, 3467, 3479, 3491, 3498, 3612
Human evolution 2254, 5637
Human genetics 255, 554, 1335, 2224, 2289, 5799, 5809, 5812
Human geography 2733, 3292, 3463, 3475, 3476, 3504
Human nature 370, 1164, 3464
Human race 1369
Human relations 605, 4448
Human resources 437, 439, 2014, 2277, 3286, 3566, 3685, 4023, 4246, 4252, 4264, 4265, 4305, 4375, 4377, 4416, 4456, 4480, 4500, 4506, 4530, 4568, 4616, 5578, 5687
Human rights 5, 150, 455, 969, 1744, 2197, 2740, 2899, 3189, 3415, 3470, 4788, 4799, 4809, 4823, 4828, 5241, 5464, 5612
Human settlements 351, 3894

Subject index

Humanism   4766, 4785
Humanities   1, 238
Humanity   2655
Humour   451, 454, 471, 668, 690, 704, 1052, 1433, 2629
   see also: Jokes
Hunger   1104
Husbands   536, 2554, 2607, 5253
Hutcheson, Francis   1164
Hutterites   2279
Hygiene   3482
Hypothesis   364, 3147
Idealism   126, 297, 812
Identification   262, 283, 1366, 3032, 3128, 5624
   see also: Class identification
Identity   154, 258, 443, 450, 452, 464, 500, 584, 586, 643, 754, 770, 1010, 1016, 1043, 1316, 1332, 1397, 1398, 1573, 1658, 2095, 2133, 2185, 2596, 2651, 2728, 2870, 2946, 2951, 3048, 3094, 3105, 3106, 3107, 3113, 3120, 3122, 3136, 3139, 3152, 3180, 3185, 3252, 3276, 3282, 3284, 3329, 3332, 3475, 3482, 3493, 3502, 3524, 5810
   see also: Cultural identity, Group identity, National identity, Professional identity, Regional identity, Social identity
Ideology   120, 122, 162, 168, 178, 682, 700, 939, 945, 980, 1137, 1139, 1231, 1269, 1287, 1375, 1547, 1584, 1837, 1886, 1894, 1941, 2505, 2677, 2823, 2908, 3165, 3459, 3977, 4286, 4595, 4783, 4808, 4915, 4966, 4988, 5009, 5659
   see also: Political ideology
Illegal immigrants   3274, 3277, 3288, 4677
Illegal immigration   915
Illegitimacy   2507
Images   114, 521, 1074, 1391, 1437, 1543, 1614, 1898, 1945, 2358, 2865, 2872, 2876, 2891, 2905, 2906, 3033, 3152, 3569, 3668, 3868, 4824, 4889, 5027
Imagination   94, 114, 480, 1466
IMF   4210

Imitations   1615
Immigrant adaptation   2138, 3180, 3317, 3318, 3319, 3321, 3329, 3332, 3336, 3337, 3338, 3340, 3341, 3343, 3344, 3349, 3350, 3620
Immigrant assimilation   3055, 3060, 3270, 3323, 3325, 3330, 3332, 3334, 3335, 3338, 3346, 3347, 3348, 5851
Immigrants   236, 245, 560, 1017, 2020, 2269, 2900, 3030, 3039, 3050, 3054, 3055, 3056, 3068, 3069, 3077, 3101, 3103, 3112, 3114, 3125, 3146, 3180, 3234, 3254, 3257, 3266, 3267, 3270, 3272, 3298, 3302, 3306, 3309, 3318, 3320, 3325, 3326, 3329, 3345, 3346, 3348, 3350, 3395, 3406, 3425, 4135, 4244, 4309, 4318, 4539, 4813, 4961, 5127
   see also: Illegal immigrants
Immigration   1950, 2740, 3041, 3055, 3253, 3267, 3268, 3269, 3271, 3277, 3289, 3293, 3308, 3309, 3327, 3333, 3339, 3394, 3402, 3407, 3416, 3963, 4371, 5128
   see also: Illegal immigration
Immigration policy   3274, 3290, 3294, 3311, 3417
Imperialism   981, 1013
Imports   4074
Impoverishment   5484
In-group   725, 743, 745, 750, 754, 767, 771, 3086
In-service training   4575, 5514
Incest   2958, 2975, 5040, 5044, 5066, 5082, 5087, 5089, 5254
Incest taboo   3019
Income   1970, 2074, 2435, 3799, 3996, 4026, 4035, 4045, 4052, 4161, 4167, 5524
   see also: Family income, Household income, Low income
Income determination   4611
Income distribution   3170, 4014, 4032, 4034, 4048, 4206
Income inequality   3598, 4012, 4013, 4028, 4029, 4032, 4037, 4053, 4059, 4066, 4263, 4340
Income maintenance   4247

Subject index

Income measurement   4030, 4068
Income redistribution   3580, 3804, 3972, 4065, 4214
Incomes policy   5465
Independence   2559, 4644, 4924
  see also: Economic independence
Independence movements   1516
Indians   1468, 3056, 3057, 3114, 3156
Indicators   668, 4030, 4436
  see also: Demographic indicators, Economic indicators, Social indicators
Indigenous populations   2197, 3034, 3058, 3079, 3093, 3124, 3155, 3643, 3667, 4303, 4371, 4828, 5127, 5837
Individual and society   316, 446, 458, 461, 466, 477, 494, 715, 3592, 4779
Individual behaviour   432, 441, 511, 906, 1496, 2125, 3250, 4094
Individualism   455, 800, 1206, 3513, 4761, 4767, 4780, 4950
Individuality   173, 212, 466, 577, 819, 1033, 1605, 2626
Individuals   96, 114, 388, 435, 443, 444, 457, 458, 461, 486, 487, 488, 516, 523, 544, 547, 549, 550, 556, 563, 565, 570, 574, 575, 592, 597, 643, 650, 653, 739, 785, 818, 1430, 1431, 1853, 2317, 2628, 3474, 3770, 3805, 4047, 4067, 4179, 4421, 4508, 5119, 5564, 5823
Indonesians   3408
Induction   152
Industrial adjustment   4126
Industrial areas   3640, 3868, 3933
Industrial co-operatives   4710
Industrial development   3525, 3832, 3980, 4102, 4217, 4229
Industrial education   1707
Industrial enterprises   4113, 4449
Industrial history   3936
Industrial management   4090, 4104, 4155, 4239, 4504
Industrial organization   3834, 4236, 4620
Industrial policy   4127, 4673
Industrial production   4090, 4277
Industrial productivity   1010

Industrial psychology   835, 4235
Industrial society   1230, 1828, 2254, 3973
Industrial sociology   835, 1643, 4234, 4237, 4239
Industrial statistics   343
Industrial workers   1853, 4108, 4449, 4488, 4489, 4510, 4518
Industrialization   1907, 2514, 3630, 3632, 3982, 4031, 4076, 4125, 4238
Industrialized countries   4321
Industry   825, 888, 1943, 2514, 3355, 3440, 4151, 4217, 4298, 4523
  see also: Agricultural industry, Agrofood industry, Armaments industry, Automobile industry, Clothing industry, Computer industry, Construction industry, Cultural industry, Electrical industries, Electronics industry, Export-oriented industry, Film industry, Furniture industry, Location of industry, Manufacturing, Meat industry, Metal industry, Petrochemical industry, Pharmaceutical industry, Record industry, Service industry, Shipbuilding, Shoe industry, Small-scale industry, Textile industry
Infancy   2118, 2209, 5062, 5316, 5681
Infant mortality   2350, 2357, 2359, 2366, 2373, 2375, 2376, 2381, 5666
Infanticide   2181
Infertility   2251, 2259, 5577, 5699, 5807
Inflation   4206
Informal sector   2797, 3984, 4033, 4070, 4081, 4130, 4137, 4210, 4662
Information   77, 341, 353, 824, 953, 1392, 1449, 1460, 1517, 1518, 3676, 4168, 4187, 4267, 4529, 4814, 5048
  see also: Access to information, Political information
Information exchange   364, 1452
Information networks   1341
Information processing   385, 516, 725, 4156
Information services   78, 1452, 2308, 2319, 2329, 3023, 5477, 5554

Subject index

Information society   1014, 1451
Information systems   852, 1014, 1393, 1457, 4079
Information technology   918, 1184, 1450, 1451, 1453, 1454, 1455, 1456, 4144, 4155, 4403, 4419, 4453, 4836
Inheritance   2406, 2500, 3532, 3561
Initiation   4200
Injuries   395
Inkatha   2425
Innovation   819, 821, 1629, 1721, 3883, 4148, 4170, 4452, 5578
  see also: Agricultural innovations
Innovation diffusion   3558, 4147
Innovation policies   1350
Insemination
  see: Artificial insemination
Insider dealing   557, 5186
Institutionalism   883
Institutionalization   1343, 5564
Institutions   63, 200, 802, 805, 870, 1375, 1941, 2088, 2143, 3615, 4536, 4604, 4801, 5582, 5588, 5600, 5717, 5744
  see also: Educational institutions, Financial institutions
Insurance
  see: Health insurance
Insurance companies   4358
Insurgency   5118
Intellectual property   1184
Intellectuals   46, 452, 1028, 1034, 1036, 1284, 1925, 3027, 3029
Intelligence   116, 370, 388, 440, 475, 497, 547
  see also: Artificial intelligence
Intercultural communication   416, 1009, 1026, 1054, 1474, 5011, 5030
Intercultural dialogue   5030
Intercultural education   1474, 1645, 1646, 3054, 3174
Interdependence   2436, 3973
Interdisciplinary research   3, 9
Interest   2562
Interest groups   3782, 4914, 4928
Interethnic conflict   3117, 3148, 3159, 3168, 3177, 3500

Interethnic relations   1046, 2592, 3046, 3055, 3060, 3068, 3088, 3099, 3144, 3145, 3146, 3150, 3155, 3157, 3161, 3163, 3167, 3171, 3176, 3179, 3242, 3317, 3327, 3421, 5705
Intergenerational relations   2031, 2040, 2288, 2525, 2635, 5435
Intergroup relations   712, 721, 726, 727, 728, 745, 747, 767, 768
Intermarriage   2540, 2563, 2579, 2592, 2605
Internal migration   351, 2000, 2022, 2192, 3032, 3286, 3352, 3353, 3354, 3355, 3358, 3360, 3361, 3362, 3363, 3367, 3368, 3369, 3370, 3372, 3374, 3375, 3376, 3377, 3378, 3380, 3381, 3383, 3386, 3387, 3388, 3389, 3391, 3502, 3537, 3653, 3659, 3762, 4254
International conflicts   5003, 5016
International crime   5123
International economic relations   861, 999, 4109, 5030
International integration   3421
International law   3124, 5023
International migration   2018, 2026, 2038, 2192, 3286, 3305, 3311, 3392, 3395, 3396, 3397, 3399, 3402, 3403, 3404, 3405, 3408, 3409, 3410, 3411, 3412, 3413, 3415, 3416, 3419, 3422, 3424, 3426, 3427, 3428, 4289
International organizations   807, 847, 5008, 5035
International politics   5680
International relations   403, 1942, 1945, 1959, 3415, 5003, 5008, 5009, 5013, 5014, 5021, 5022, 5023, 5025, 5026, 5028, 5030
International trade   4074
  see also: Imports
Internationalism   5098
Internationalization   1270, 1563, 3295, 5005, 5030
Interpersonal attraction   653, 2542
Interpersonal behaviour   3233
Interpersonal communication   601, 607, 637, 638, 661, 674, 1398, 1417, 1465, 1476, 1495
Interpersonal competition   758

Interpersonal conflicts 679, 680, 689
Interpersonal influence 280, 546
Interpersonal perception 573, 616, 680, 2094
Interpersonal relations 337, 457, 488, 560, 577, 590, 602, 610, 611, 617, 619, 620, 626, 628, 635, 639, 640, 642, 644, 645, 648, 650, 651, 652, 657, 658, 660, 664, 665, 671, 673, 675, 677, 678, 690, 694, 695, 696, 701, 702, 708, 709, 710, 716, 734, 756, 759, 905, 906, 1029, 1122, 1412, 1436, 1479, 2169, 2355, 2586, 2587, 3001, 4935, 5852
Interracial marriages 2351, 3127
Interviewers 342, 346
Interviews 51, 286, 325, 328, 329, 331, 333, 336, 348, 359, 360, 420, 837, 1386, 4396, 4456, 4815, 4816, 5260
Intimacy 2596, 2958, 5243
Intraregional migration 3286
Inuit 1110, 1399
Invasions 4911
Inventions 4096
Inventories 567
Investment 2376, 4205
  see also: Business investment, Foreign investment
Investment returns
  see: Rent
Iranians 3125
Iron and steel industry 4139, 4236, 4518
Irrigation 2197, 3575
Islam 103, 239, 1021, 1180, 1307, 1308, 1309, 1311, 1312, 1314, 1315, 1316, 1318, 1319, 1320, 1321, 1332, 1453, 2845, 2925, 3062, 5559, 5790
  see also: Koran
Islam and politics 1310, 1317, 1934
Islamic civilization 55, 1310
Islamic countries 1318, 1323, 1707, 2750
Islamic economics 4416
Islamic law 221, 1190, 2501
Islands 2563, 3097, 3555, 3557, 4723
Italian language 1471

Italians 3047, 3069, 3103, 3253, 3258, 5403
Itinerants 3130
Japanese 2477, 4194, 4480
Jaspers, Karl 129
Jazz 1611, 1631
Jealousy 694, 697, 702
Jews 431, 643, 841, 931, 941, 1325, 1327, 1333, 1627, 2034, 2058, 2075, 2415, 3044, 3049, 3053, 3055, 3060, 3061, 3063, 3064, 3065, 3068, 3088, 3107, 3113, 3125, 3128, 3134, 3141, 3146, 3209, 3220, 3240, 3349, 3865, 4520
  see also: Lubavitch
Job change 4417
Job evaluation 4425, 4478
Job loss 449, 4380, 4386
Job requirements 4262, 4489
Job satisfaction 955, 4008, 4115, 4331, 4461, 4463, 4464, 4465, 4466, 4467, 4468, 4470, 4471, 4472, 4473, 4477, 4510, 4533, 4701
Job search 483, 4382, 4390, 4391
Job security 4268
Job vacancies 4513
Joint ventures 3979, 4582
Jokes 479, 2040
Jones, Grace 1060
Journalism 1504, 1519, 1520, 1523, 1552, 1558
Journalists 1524, 1559, 4405
Judaism 1155, 1268, 1272, 1316, 1326, 1328, 1330, 1331, 1332, 1333, 2971, 5829
  see also: Hasidism
Judgement 526, 612, 620, 716, 754, 1167, 1187, 4422, 4788, 4965, 5206
  see also: Social judgement, Value judgement
Judges 4554
Judicial behaviour 1210
Jung, Carl 377, 492, 2834
Juries 741, 751, 1409, 2123, 3224
Jurisdiction
  see: Criminal jurisdiction
Jurisprudence 4632

Subject index

Justice 123, 444, 539, 654, 657, 738, 751, 810, 1156, 1173, 1191, 1212, 3450, 3785, 4382, 4600, 4846, 5028, 5101, 5187, 5212, 5213, 5224, 5226, 5298, 5304, 5405
see also: Criminal justice, Distributive justice, Economic justice, Social justice
Juvenile courts 5209
Juvenile delinquency 599, 749, 755, 4805, 5077, 5085, 5140, 5181, 5189, 5200, 5202, 5208, 5213, 5226, 5285, 5286, 5287, 5288, 5289, 5290, 5291, 5292, 5293, 5294, 5295, 5296, 5297, 5298, 5299, 5300, 5301, 5302, 5303, 5304, 5305, 5306, 5307, 5308, 5309, 5310, 5589, 5599
Kant, Immanuel 121, 129, 1158, 2558
Kelabit 3352
Kibbutzim 2268
King, Rodney 3176
Kinship 2429, 2441, 2442, 2445, 2448, 3104, 3388, 3950, 4117, 5503
Kinship systems 2456
Kitzinger, Sheila 2675
Knowledge 24, 55, 99, 103, 105, 106, 113, 132, 253, 439, 607, 674, 716, 809, 853, 874, 1073, 1102, 1341, 1343, 1346, 1350, 1354, 1357, 1464, 1663, 1679, 1692, 1693, 1803, 2658, 2662, 3884, 4150, 4400, 4551, 4857, 4928, 5357, 5363, 5540, 5575, 5668
see also: Sociology of knowledge
Kohlberg, L. 880
Koran 1322
Koreans 3085, 3091
Krupskaya, N.K. 1715
Labelling 508
Labour 293, 1426, 1838, 1868, 1907, 2019, 2038, 2584, 2822, 2849, 2890, 3239, 3384, 4099, 4285, 4300, 4304, 4305, 4352, 4384, 4406, 4452, 4486, 4497, 4613, 4687, 5686
see also: Agricultural labour, Child labour, Division of labour, Female labour
Labour contract 4583
Labour courts 4644

Labour demand 3894, 4497
Labour disputes 4126, 4623, 4625, 4626, 4627, 4628, 4629
Labour economics 4482
Labour force 2026, 2396, 2420, 2842, 3937, 4271, 4289, 4302, 4318, 4333, 4362, 4490
Labour force utilization 4260
Labour history 1862, 4396, 4544, 4665, 4667, 4672, 4674
Labour law 2794, 3575, 4605, 4631, 4632, 4633, 4634, 4635, 4636, 4637, 4638, 4639, 4641, 4642, 4643, 4644, 4645, 4646, 4648, 4659, 4686
Labour market 203, 1991, 2025, 2670, 2801, 2824, 2901, 2932, 3030, 3238, 3285, 3286, 3314, 3319, 3324, 3335, 3372, 3389, 3420, 3541, 3894, 4023, 4178, 4249, 4252, 4258, 4261, 4263, 4272, 4273, 4278, 4279, 4281, 4283, 4284, 4285, 4291, 4296, 4301, 4313, 4316, 4317, 4320, 4322, 4327, 4328, 4336, 4347, 4354, 4369, 4379, 4382, 4385, 4387, 4390, 4487, 4488, 4514, 4533, 4538, 4587, 4591, 4637, 4639, 4641
Labour market structure 4246, 4280, 5004
Labour migration 3382, 3390, 3403, 3544, 3629, 4303
Labour mobility 3286, 3355, 4269, 4281, 4282, 4297, 4438, 4539
Labour movements 1264, 4308, 4624, 4662, 4672, 4681, 4691, 4938
Labour policy 4251, 4257, 4267, 4355, 4629
Labour redundancy 4295
Labour relations 4235, 4262, 4329, 4429, 4430, 4449, 4458, 4474, 4577, 4578, 4579, 4582, 4583, 4585, 4587, 4588, 4592, 4594, 4595, 4596, 4598, 4600, 4601, 4602, 4603, 4605, 4606, 4607, 4608, 4611, 4613, 4614, 4615, 4616, 4617, 4619, 4620, 4621, 4623, 4626, 4628, 4629, 4630, 4638, 4640, 4641, 4644, 4646, 4647, 4653, 4654, 4663, 4671, 4673, 4682, 4692, 4693, 4695, 4696, 4702, 4706, 4707

Subject index

Labour supply 3328, 3377, 3771, 3894, 4081, 4245, 4275, 4281, 4284, 4323, 4337, 4498, 5537
Labour turnover 4467
Land market 3732, 3754, 3838
Land policy 3554, 3882
Land property 3582, 3589
Land reform 3554, 3583
Land settlement 3530, 3751
Land tenure 2854, 3554, 3556, 3574, 3582, 3589, 3605, 3606, 3626, 3754, 4828
Land use 2023, 3552, 3560, 3564, 3584, 3606, 3644, 3708, 3756, 3780, 3813, 3814, 3848, 3865, 3867, 3869, 3872, 3883, 3905, 4737, 4859
Landowners 3574, 3582, 3606, 3617
Landscape 1416, 3463, 3466, 3467, 3494
Language 137, 164, 445, 1108, 1192, 1214, 1351, 1362, 1367, 1373, 1377, 1379, 1386, 1390, 1395, 1397, 1398, 1399, 1406, 1408, 1411, 1416, 1417, 1421, 1426, 1429, 1430, 1436, 1463, 1473, 1475, 1476, 1479, 1481, 1485, 1541, 1570, 1628, 1880, 2707, 2805, 2829, 3349, 3680, 4790, 4876, 5057
see also: Official languages
Language acquisition 148, 505, 507, 1461, 1463, 1470, 1475, 1486, 1561, 1566
Language change 1384
Language disorder
see: Dyslexia
Language history 1468
Language planning 1371
Language policy 1390, 1400, 1401, 1418, 1428, 1435, 1464, 1561, 1562, 1565, 1567, 1801, 3046, 3270, 4946
Laughter 459
Law 150, 935, 1122, 1180, 1183, 1190, 1194, 1200, 1206, 1207, 2096, 2499, 2704, 2760, 2845, 2928, 3214, 3575, 3698, 4227, 4258, 4633, 4643, 4801, 4949, 5157, 5230, 5458, 5543, 5793
see also: Common law, Community law, Company law, Criminal law, Family law, History of law, International law, Islamic law, Labour law, Natural law, Philosophy of law, Public law, Sociology of law
Law and order 957, 1079, 1196, 5107, 5108, 5144
Law enforcement 412, 4792, 5137, 5393, 5417
Law of the air 395
Lawyers 561, 1204, 1544, 2807, 2856, 2940, 3214, 4345, 4553, 4561
Leaders 899, 912
see also: Political leaders
Leadership 404, 439, 894, 900, 902, 903, 906, 1534, 2884, 3047, 3069, 4410, 4426, 4504, 4527, 4740, 5471
see also: Political leadership
Learning 148, 507, 508, 529, 697, 735, 742, 766, 793, 822, 1377, 1475, 1666, 1789, 2067, 2752, 3979, 4089, 4151, 4997, 5133, 5581
Learning difficulties 404, 502, 1475, 2452, 5191, 5363, 5592, 5731, 5848
Least-squares estimations 299, 746
Lee, Ivy 1169
Left 997, 3202, 4901, 4916
Legal aspects 371, 444, 810, 1168, 1190, 1193, 1201, 1212, 4639, 4647, 4814, 4902, 5213, 5298, 5394, 5458, 5787, 5794
Legal profession 2937, 4324, 4553
Legal protection 2697, 3276, 4332, 4823
Legal reform 1207, 1211
Legal science 9
Legal status 2709, 5542
Legal systems 1183, 1208
Legal theory 1187
Legislation 2836, 3459, 4210, 4257, 4311, 4641
Legislative process 2237, 2237
Legislature 4837
Legitimacy 184, 443, 821
Legitimation 1676, 4037
Leisure 1633, 2132, 2172, 2868, 4193, 4720, 4721, 4722, 4725, 4726, 4729, 4731, 4733, 4735, 4739, 4740, 4745, 4751

504

Subject index

Leite, Gabriela Silva   2960
Lenin, V.I.   448
Lesbians   1617, 2545, 2728, 2754, 2779, 2949, 2950, 2951, 2954, 2962, 2969, 2970, 2973, 2974, 2979, 2980, 2984, 3000, 3456, 4495, 4863, 4995, 5445
Less developed countries   2299, 2353, 4154
Level of education   1912, 2542, 4324, 4342, 5380
Lewin, Kurt   404
Li, Zehou   1925
Liability   1173, 1202
Liberal democracy   4819
Liberalism   939, 1035, 1056, 1138, 1896, 3062, 4102, 4761, 4770, 4771, 4772, 4783, 4785, 4981
see also: Neoliberalism
Liberalization   974, 4902
Liberation   4994
Libertarianism   1670
Libraries   1817
Life cycles   489, 2057, 2468, 2481, 2489, 2643, 2892, 3351, 3745
Life expectancy   2052, 2357, 2378, 4038
Life satisfaction   355, 438, 460, 474, 478, 493, 2045, 2071, 2108, 3595, 4024, 4031
Life stories   540, 2992, 3557
Life styles   1122, 1127, 1899, 1970, 2172, 2423, 2521, 2992, 3512, 3541, 3647, 4163, 5655, 5667
Linear models   574
Linear programming   287
Linguistic anthropology   1490
Linguistic contact   757, 1468
Linguistic groups   757
Linguistic minorities   1376, 1383, 1400, 1406, 1407, 1418, 1474, 1564, 3046, 3270
Linguistics   743, 1022, 1462, 1463, 1472, 1473, 1475, 1476, 1479, 1481, 1483, 1484, 1487, 1491, 1493, 1576, 3349
see also: Sociolinguistics
Listeners   409

Literacy   1385, 1395, 1405, 1461, 1640, 1645, 1647, 1663, 1666, 1728, 2191, 4275, 5735
Literary criticism   97, 1012
Literature   26, 50, 97, 993, 1013, 1028, 1480, 1481, 1596, 1603, 1607, 1634, 1637, 2693, 3055
see also: Novels, Poetry, Popular literature
Livestock industry   4087
Living arrangements   1938, 2004, 2100, 2443, 2446, 2513, 2583, 2616, 3512, 3744, 4021
Living conditions   2108, 2139, 3115, 3330, 3647, 4007, 4008, 4036, 4274, 5339
Loans   825, 4174
see also: Bank loans
Local communities   3533, 3535, 3572, 3670, 3825, 4453
Local elections   3636, 4972
Local finance   3364, 4859
Local government   327, 1930, 3648, 3764, 3819, 3820, 3830, 3876, 3893, 3920, 4575, 4595, 4845, 4848, 4849, 4855, 4856, 4862, 5270, 5287, 5485, 5528
Local history   1848
Local politics   3534, 3881, 4941
Local power   1571, 3608
Location of enterprises   3759, 3854
Location of industry   3355, 3687
Locke, John   4770
Lockouts   4235, 4604
Logic   43, 382, 405, 439
Loneliness   462, 695, 1122, 2105, 5047
Low income   2212, 2861, 3746, 3766, 3776, 3825, 3903, 4394, 5330
Lower class   1122
Loyalty   645, 4163
Lubavitch   1333
Luhmann, Niklas   169, 216, 477, 1197
Lukes, Stephen   216
Maastricht Treaty   4296, 4590
Machiavellianism   1109
MacIntyre, Alasdair   972
Macroeconomics   291

Subject index

Mafia 5158
Magic 1239, 1345
Mail surveys 4649
Majority groups 738
Male-female relationships 393, 606, 614, 629, 633, 638, 641, 655, 2535, 2547, 2593, 2606, 2624, 2778, 2869, 2871, 2981, 2985, 3017, 5251
see also: Partners
Malnutrition 4034, 5335
Management 439, 851, 852, 853, 854, 855, 858, 860, 865, 867, 868, 869, 870, 871, 886, 1113, 1708, 1735, 2707, 2901, 4044, 4105, 4114, 4357, 4427, 4436, 4461, 4507, 4528, 4530, 4582, 4585, 4600, 4607, 4715, 4718, 4787, 5617, 5770
see also: Crisis management, Environmental management, Farm management, Financial management, Industrial management, Personnel management, Production management, Public management, Resource management, Risk management, Top management, University management, Urban management
Management attitudes 758, 866, 3979, 4410
Management development 856, 4569
Management research 4531, 4616
Management techniques 851, 4094, 4508, 4532, 4714
Managers 787, 858, 2840, 2929, 2936, 4252, 4290, 4434, 4436, 4449, 4527, 4529, 4532, 4533, 4534, 4610, 5630, 5646
Mankind 2
Mann, Michael 4776
Mannheim, Karl 130, 144, 1662
Manual workers 4515
Manufacturing 343, 3687, 4130, 4136, 4143, 4144, 4146, 4277, 4479, 4488, 4489, 4513, 4588, 4676, 4687
Maori 997, 3202
Mapping 238, 3484
Maps 534
Marcuse, Herbert 120, 136

Marginality 2158
Marginalized people 3749
Marine resources 3450
Marital conflict 2578, 2617
Marital interaction 696, 2259, 2538, 2550, 2555, 2559, 2571, 2586, 2602
Marital life 2481, 2543, 2565, 2568, 2573, 2603
Marital roles 1122, 2563, 2565, 2603
Marital satisfaction 2539, 2544, 2546, 2549, 2565, 2573, 2585, 2588, 2589, 2596, 2606, 2624
Marital separation 2482, 2483, 2486, 2488, 2535, 2556, 2566, 2587
Marital stability 2008, 2594
Marital status 765, 2004, 2557, 2574, 2598, 4389, 5425
Market 811, 1285, 1803, 2842, 3285, 4162, 4175, 4181, 4185, 4350, 4540, 5118, 5463, 5532, 5747
see also: Black market, Housing market, Labour market, Land market
Market economy 3986, 3990, 4043, 4227, 4635, 4771
Market entry 4176
Market forces 1718, 3980
Market research 4175
Market socialism 4825
Marketing 1134, 1167, 1667, 3868, 4170, 4186
see also: Advertising, Food marketing
Marriage 333, 702, 2286, 2296, 2362, 2405, 2420, 2421, 2453, 2454, 2476, 2501, 2523, 2533, 2535, 2536, 2539, 2541, 2542, 2544, 2547, 2548, 2552, 2558, 2560, 2561, 2562, 2564, 2567, 2575, 2576, 2579, 2580, 2581, 2583, 2584, 2590, 2591, 2592, 2598, 2599, 2600, 2601, 2604, 2605, 2608, 2704, 2850, 2862, 3287
see also: Age at marriage, Intermarriage, Interracial marriages, Remarriage
Married persons 333, 625, 2257, 2362, 2388, 2537, 2552, 2569, 2597, 4278, 4337, 4505
Married women 2311, 2553, 2572, 4318, 4363

506

Subject index

Marx, Karl 93, 162, 1193, 1225, 1902, 1903, 4015, 4773
Marxian analysis 126, 153, 204, 1893, 2756
Marxism 141, 1864, 1902, 3983, 3987, 4221, 4759, 4764, 5445
Masculinity 589, 1087, 2624, 2660, 2873, 2878, 2881, 2882, 2887, 2888, 2894, 2896, 2897, 2898, 2908, 2916, 2959, 2967, 2982, 3020, 4105, 4509, 5092, 5102, 5433
Mass communication 896, 1501, 1502, 1508, 1509, 1558
Mass consumption 1122
Mass culture 1005, 1014
Mass organizations 4914
Mass society 1505
Mate selection 608, 2421, 2522, 2561, 2600, 2796, 2807, 2869, 2945, 2977, 2981, 3003
Material culture 983, 1117, 1127, 1871, 4074
Materialism 374, 812, 1128, 4966
Maternity benefits 5666
Maternity leave 4338
Mathematical analysis 2009, 5104
Mathematical models 261, 268, 793, 1091
Mathematics 4324
Maya 3926
Mead, George 223
Measurement 279, 281, 292, 309, 383, 1165, 1483, 2005, 2227, 5319, 5565, 5673
Meat industry 4126
Media 403, 896, 989, 1030, 1043, 1074, 1103, 1169, 1310, 1441, 1445, 1448, 1449, 1498, 1499, 1500, 1501, 1502, 1505, 1506, 1507, 1508, 1509, 1510, 1512, 1513, 1514, 1515, 1517, 1518, 1519, 1520, 1521, 1523, 1524, 1525, 1526, 1527, 1528, 1529, 1530, 1531, 1532, 1533, 1534, 1535, 1536, 1537, 1538, 1540, 1541, 1544, 1545, 1546, 1548, 1549, 1550, 1551, 1552, 1553, 1554, 1555, 1556, 1557, 1558, 1559, 1570, 1574, 1579, 1609, 1675, 1704, 2146, 2891, 4194, 4204, 4743, 4900, 4947, 4960, 4970, 4974, 4985, 5021, 5048, 5435
see also: Press
Media policy 1533, 1586
Mediation 642, 676, 676, 686, 718, 728, 2424, 2486, 3813, 5007, 5043, 5199
Medical anthropology 1110, 1335, 2313, 2345, 3007, 5373, 5411
Medical care 2497, 2816, 5271, 5631, 5637, 5638, 5642, 5670, 5670, 5677, 5686, 5692, 5736, 5759, 5763, 5771, 5775, 5799, 5800, 5812, 5817, 5843
Medical ethics 1118, 2239, 5736, 5789, 5791, 5793, 5795, 5798, 5800, 5802, 5803, 5804, 5806, 5808, 5809, 5810, 5813, 5815, 5816, 5820, 5821, 5822, 5825, 5829
Medical occupations 4543
Medical personnel 2816, 4459, 4545, 4557, 5081, 5668, 5672, 5706, 5715, 5735, 5762, 5813, 5826, 5842
Medical research 947, 5753, 5788
Medical sociology 3242, 5700, 5705, 5850
Medicine 2359, 3016, 3447, 5275, 5641, 5675
see also: History of medicine, Social medicine, Surgery, Traditional medicine
Memoirs 259
Memory 528, 529, 530, 531, 532, 533, 534, 535, 536, 537, 538, 539, 540, 541, 542, 569, 674, 725, 1024, 1421, 5081, 5842
Men 339, 656, 678, 700, 763, 1415, 1602, 1860, 2078, 2151, 2259, 2349, 2378, 2385, 2405, 2413, 2432, 2495, 2534, 2577, 2578, 2604, 2647, 2804, 2822, 2829, 2832, 2840, 2866, 2873, 2888, 2895, 2896, 2897, 2899, 2907, 2916, 2953, 2957, 2961, 2965, 2978, 2992, 2997, 3011, 3014, 3016, 3020, 3268, 4002, 4316, 4339, 4381, 4419, 4537, 4971, 5092, 5156, 5247, 5251, 5256, 5261, 5410
Mennonites 3135, 3532
Menopause 2042, 2750

Menstruation 2187
Mental deficiencies 4721
Mental health 363, 431, 449, 484, 569, 577, 579, 593, 616, 635, 786, 2048, 2082, 2153, 2307, 2334, 2338, 2398, 2491, 2625, 2634, 2919, 3242, 3414, 3749, 5041, 5081, 5343, 5586, 5621, 5655, 5705, 5720, 5752, 5781, 5832, 5833, 5836, 5837, 5840, 5841, 5842, 5843, 5844, 5845, 5846, 5850, 5851, 5852, 5853, 5854, 5855
Mental hospitals 5125, 5849
Mental illness 267, 326, 396, 468, 568, 656, 667, 1224, 1436, 2105, 2314, 2339, 2549, 3345, 4442, 5084, 5217, 5281, 5414, 5428, 5586, 5838, 5847, 5849, 5850
Mental stress 395, 403, 412, 421, 433, 447, 487, 491, 568, 574, 585, 625, 628, 650, 669, 672, 911, 2115, 2120, 2317, 2419, 2550, 2554, 2635, 2644, 2802, 2919, 2974, 3100, 3318, 3460, 3707, 4386, 4427, 4433, 4450, 4459, 4472, 4517, 4521, 4558, 4740, 4800, 5021, 5038, 5371, 5395, 5424, 5545, 5586, 5617, 5835
Mentality 381, 802, 3040
Mentally disabled 5191, 5707, 5831, 5839
Mergers 4290
Messages 384
Mestizos 3132
Metal industry 4679
Metaphor 927, 1378, 3435
Methodology 8, 58, 138, 152, 189, 221, 226, 227, 229, 239, 240, 247, 287, 338, 856, 1066, 1388, 1394, 2007, 2013, 2028, 2518, 2672, 2844, 3539, 4425, 4572, 5057, 5214
see also: Anthropological methodology, Economic methodology, Sociological methodology
Metropolitan areas 2599, 3648, 3653, 3684, 3690, 3725, 3759, 3799, 3819, 3831, 3835, 3850, 3854, 3881, 3915
Mexicans 2609, 3054, 3115, 3127, 3324, 3346, 3390, 3426, 4902

Michelangelo 2992
Microcomputers 4564
Microsociology 1929
Middle age 2035
Middle Ages 5313
Middle class 947, 1117, 1707, 1870, 1889, 1891, 1899, 1901, 1904, 2167, 2918, 3788, 4104, 5175, 5406
Midwives 5637, 5659, 5672, 5764
Migrant workers 2665, 3249, 3260, 3274, 3279, 3307, 3353, 3354, 3417, 3999, 4254, 4277, 4404, 5512
Migrants 1541, 2163, 3058, 3078, 3081, 3093, 3098, 3155, 3242, 3251, 3259, 3284, 3285, 3295, 3296, 3319, 3321, 3322, 3338, 3342, 3343, 3351, 3354, 3366, 3398, 3412, 3417, 3538, 3642, 3659, 3667, 3693, 3734, 5623, 5705
Migrants' children 3317, 3340, 3343
Migration 1270, 1851, 1970, 1989, 2000, 2005, 2014, 2022, 2023, 2026, 2321, 2439, 2892, 3061, 3113, 3122, 3186, 3248, 3250, 3252, 3255, 3256, 3258, 3262, 3263, 3273, 3275, 3281, 3282, 3286, 3287, 3288, 3290, 3291, 3292, 3294, 3299, 3303, 3305, 3312, 3314, 3316, 3358, 3359, 3378, 3384, 3385, 3393, 3395, 3420, 3421, 3423, 3426, 3428, 3540, 3579, 3620, 3693, 4222, 4374, 5403
see also: External migration, Forced migration, Internal migration, International migration, Intraregional migration, Labour migration, Return migration, Rural-urban migration, Urban-rural migration
Militants 176
Militarism 2933, 4776, 4999, 5033
Military 1171, 2823, 4996
Military and politics 4997
Military industrial complex 4082
Military personnel 2933, 5000, 5001, 5002, 5003, 5004
Military regimes 5445
Mines
 see: Coal mines, Gold mines
Minimum wages 4566

Subject index

Mining   3280, 3492, 3602, 3640, 4210
Minorities   464, 738, 1375, 1616, 1709, 1782, 1786, 3023, 3060, 3070, 3074, 3076, 3096, 3144, 3172, 3179, 3216, 3217, 3229, 3239, 3327, 3685, 4435, 4845, 5215, 5456, 5546
see also: Ethnic minorities, Linguistic minorities, Religious minorities
Minority education   5623
Minority groups   968, 1375, 3803, 4372
Miscegenation   3197
Mixed economy   3983
Mode of production   3987
Modelling   748, 4183
Models   262, 269, 270, 278, 279, 280, 283, 297, 299, 446, 472, 485, 510, 522, 677, 730, 747, 768, 781, 832, 1049, 1104, 1207, 1660, 1814, 1890, 1981, 2128, 2364, 2483, 2486, 2580, 2639, 3014, 3071, 3919, 3928, 4146, 4147, 4466, 4513, 4586, 4733, 5251, 5532, 5595, 5774
see also: Decision models, Dynamic models, Economic models, Linear models, Mathematical models, Non-linear models, Statistical models
Modern civilization   1051, 1057, 1145, 1826
Modernism   118, 480, 1033, 1059, 1943, 1951, 4807
Modernity   172, 972, 991, 1016, 1023, 1032, 1039, 1270, 1331, 1926, 1973, 2910, 3029, 3193, 3481, 3652, 3719, 4221
Modernization   29, 35, 180, 209, 813, 1618, 1680, 1700, 1719, 1921, 1935, 1945, 1946, 1963, 1975, 1977, 2490, 2708, 2835, 3600, 3621, 3717, 4031, 4076, 4108, 4206, 4741, 4851, 4852, 4853
Modes of production
  see: Asiatic mode of production
Monarchy   1543
Money   836, 1391, 4035
Monks   1242
Montesquieu, Charles de Secondat   86
Moral crisis   3976, 5808

Moral development   1143, 1648
Moral philosophy   127, 132, 3964, 5818
Morality   135, 137, 645, 1138, 1140, 1144, 1145, 1153, 1159, 1162, 1178, 1282, 4830, 5026, 5137, 5785, 5786, 5797
see also: Political morality
Morals   122, 225, 404, 1127, 1135, 1141, 1144, 1150, 1163, 1172, 2337, 2991, 3444, 5095, 5180, 5786, 5817, 5819, 5820
Morbidity   2203, 2322, 2333, 2340, 2361
Mormonism   2157, 3383
Mortality   1168, 1964, 1986, 1989, 2192, 2348, 2349, 2354, 2355, 2356, 2358, 2360, 2361, 2362, 2365, 2367, 2368, 2369, 2370, 2371, 2372, 2373, 2374, 2375, 2377, 2379, 2380, 2381, 2382, 2383, 2384, 2385, 2388, 2418, 3940, 4013, 5315, 5821
see also: Child mortality, Infant mortality
Mortality decline   2481
Mortgages   3243, 4174, 4201
Mortuary customsMosques   1231
Mother tongue   1380, 1399, 1482
Motherhood   616, 2252, 2255, 2425, 2467, 2502, 2525, 2557, 2610, 2615, 2618, 2632, 2684, 2734
see also: Surrogate motherhood
Mothers   689, 914, 961, 1720, 2238, 2335, 2443, 2485, 2504, 2523, 2582, 2614, 2630, 2631, 2633, 2634, 2644, 2675, 2870, 2879, 2901, 4317, 4343, 5084, 5320, 5356, 5532, 5586, 5654, 5704
see also: Early motherhood, Unmarried mothers, Working mothers
Motivation   330, 437, 565, 590, 733, 737, 3469, 4380, 4414, 4437, 4997, 5773
see also: Achievement motivation
Mountains   3557, 3568
Multiculturalism   236, 994, 1010, 1015, 1017, 1030, 1044, 1648, 1675, 1992, 3027, 3039, 3083, 3085, 3089,

Subject index

3094, 3180, 3643, 3652, 3659, 3693, 4772
Multidimensional analysis   2033
Multiethnic countries   3039, 3212, 3829
Multilingualism   1560, 1563, 1567, 1569
Multinational enterprises   847, 857, 861, 1166, 4109, 4114, 4480, 4481
Multivariate analysis   294, 748, 2059, 2213
Municipal council   4845
Murder   3038, 5136
Museums   236
see also: Historical museums
Music   1596, 1611, 1616, 1625, 5295
see also: Ethnomusicology, Pop music, Rock music
Musical culture   1631
Muslims   1308, 1310, 1311, 1313, 1318, 1319, 1320, 1323, 1324, 1861, 2650, 2685, 2845, 2864, 2875, 3062, 3125, 3139
Myth   2, 1237, 1666, 2305, 2655, 4014
Mythology   1237
Names   538, 1122, 2572, 3332, 3466, 4774
Narcissism   560
Narcotics   5156, 5410
Narratives   104, 242, 243, 257, 481, 540, 588, 658, 1385, 1606, 2588, 5034
Nation   1022, 1380, 3090, 3094, 3099, 3150, 4913, 4921, 5005
Nation building   3144
Nation state   1407, 1819, 2657, 3074, 3164, 4776
National character   378, 1020, 1080, 5024
National culture   1125, 2165, 3960
National development   1561, 4004, 4277
National identity   1003, 1006, 1020, 1021, 1022, 1287, 1585, 1675, 2131, 2202, 2755, 3134, 3140, 3271, 3518, 4731, 4743, 4950
National stereotypes   1945

Nationalism   991, 1006, 1015, 1021, 1022, 1260, 1308, 1415, 1585, 1871, 2425, 2686, 2735, 2744, 2800, 2831, 3037, 3074, 3089, 3099, 3104, 3108, 3111, 3118, 3119, 3129, 3161, 3178, 3210, 3230, 4763, 4774, 4775, 4776, 4905, 4950, 4979, 5010, 5025
see also: Cultural nationalism
Nationalist movements   2780, 2833
Nationality   3144, 5181, 5286
Natural disasters   672, 3458, 5038
Natural history   2
Natural law   1155, 1158, 3470
Natural resources   3439, 3491, 4266
Natural sciences   3, 1346
Naturalization   3113
Nature   931, 3437, 3443, 3453, 3462, 3465, 3578, 5373
Nature conservation   3442, 3575
Navy   5004
Nazism   1523, 3175
Neighbourhood associations   3704, 4941
Neighbourhoods   2074, 2986, 3522, 3816, 3857, 3951, 5138, 5331
Neighbouring relationships   3523, 3703, 5099
Neoconservatism   4905
Neoliberalism   4883, 4903
Network analysis   260, 298, 316, 713, 760, 773, 813, 909, 1493, 4079, 4117, 4372
New international economic order   5011
New technology   918, 2235, 4403, 4430, 4565, 4605, 5830
New towns   3692, 3826
News   814, 1410, 1449, 1518, 1537, 1539, 1558
Nietzsche, Friedrich   186, 4777
Night work   5047
Nomadism   3472
Nomads   3130, 3164
Non-governmental organizations   774, 846, 1935, 4912
Non-linear models   284, 311
Non-profit organizations   841, 899, 3503, 4132, 5471, 5489

Subject index

Non-verbal communication 393, 687, 1377, 1487
North Amerindians 1097, 1110, 3032, 3038, 3085
Nostalgia 1575
Novels 26, 997, 1606, 3202
Novghorodtsev, P.I. 177
Nuclear accidents 3257, 3460
Nuclear energy 3445, 4897
Nuclear weapons 4945
Nuptiality 2286, 2539
Nursery schools 1664
Nurses 911, 1412, 4629, 5698, 5713, 5834
Nutrition 1105, 1114, 1115, 2093, 4025, 5335
Obesity 490, 584, 1104, 1110
Objectivity 113, 1520
Obligation 458
Observation 106, 4438, 5048
Occitan language 4876
Occupational achievement 2405, 2607, 4498
Occupational choice 4550, 5553
Occupational diseases 4442, 5762
Occupational environment 4459, 4472
Occupational groups 4018
Occupational mobility 2643, 4028, 4269, 4330, 4417, 4491, 4497, 4515, 4547, 4679
Occupational prestige 1872
Occupational qualification 3266, 4324, 4539
Occupational roles 911
Occupational safety 4406, 4418, 4421, 4440, 4445, 4696, 5396
Occupational segregation 2806, 4028, 4292, 4347, 4353, 4355
Occupational sociology 4542, 4546
Occupational status 1851, 2559, 2784, 2851, 4278, 4505, 4520, 4521
Occupational stratification 4316
Occupational structure 4487, 4511, 4514
Occupations 2189, 2913, 3897, 4037, 4111, 4240, 4446, 4493, 4516, 4534, 4541, 4542, 4559, 4562, 5263, 5628, 5659

see also: Academic profession, Legal profession, Medical occupations
OECD 1991
Offenders 371, 388, 599, 960, 1202, 1207, 1209, 2965, 5069, 5077, 5091, 5094, 5107, 5108, 5111, 5119, 5125, 5133, 5140, 5144, 5156, 5160, 5163, 5164, 5172, 5182, 5191, 5192, 5193, 5194, 5196, 5197, 5199, 5201, 5212, 5213, 5214, 5215, 5221, 5224, 5226, 5228, 5231, 5232, 5233, 5245, 5288, 5295, 5296, 5298, 5299, 5300, 5304, 5306, 5309, 5367, 5376, 5385, 5405, 5410, 5599
see also: Female offenders
Office workers 3203, 3711, 4352, 4431, 4470, 4489, 4491
Official languages 1429, 1435, 1562, 1565
Oil 3440
Old age 631, 2040, 2045, 2048, 2052, 2060, 2065, 2069, 2080, 2393, 3996, 4683
Older workers 4422
One-parent families 2407, 2427, 2443, 2458, 2459, 2480, 2485, 2498, 2504, 2510, 2511, 2513, 2582, 2615, 2633, 2927, 5065, 5317, 5332, 5356, 5522, 5524
Ontology 104, 1591
Operations research 5636
Opinion 934, 954, 1534
see also: Political opinions, Public opinion
Optimism 561, 597, 2317
Oral communication 671, 1364, 1365, 1466, 1490
Oral history 4396, 5672
Oral tradition 3484
Organization 773, 777, 781, 784, 789, 797, 800, 811, 816, 823, 827, 839, 842, 843, 846, 847, 850, 859, 862, 865, 881, 897, 2684, 4067, 4148, 4203, 4283, 4433, 4578, 4670, 4871, 4912, 4924, 5118, 5673
see also: Administrative organization, Business organization, Community organization, Economic organization,

Industrial organization, Sociology of organizations, Work organization
Organization of space   3786
Organization theory   429, 866, 873, 874, 875, 876, 877, 878, 879, 880, 881, 882, 883, 884, 885, 886, 887, 888, 889, 890, 891, 892, 4096, 4114, 4136, 4138, 4611, 4653, 4844
Organizational analysis   260, 775, 780, 782, 795, 885, 1222, 1277, 4548
Organizational behaviour   37, 758, 788, 791, 799, 803, 815, 818, 820, 832, 834, 835, 838, 855, 857, 858, 861, 867, 2812, 3296, 4095, 4176, 4471, 4828
Organizational change   774, 779, 790, 804, 809, 819, 820, 821, 825, 828, 829, 833, 838, 840, 848, 860, 868, 871, 900, 955, 2898, 4155, 4452, 5648, 5677
Organizational effectiveness   784, 844, 851, 851, 858, 871, 907, 5845
Organizational research   340, 782, 812, 817, 837
Organizational size   825, 4100
Organizational structure   776, 786, 807, 816, 824, 903, 916, 4090, 4499, 4513, 4585
Organizations   340, 469, 668, 717, 721, 778, 783, 785, 787, 792, 793, 794, 796, 808, 810, 813, 814, 826, 828, 830, 849, 851, 853, 854, 863, 876, 880, 952, 1042, 4101, 4151, 4168, 4181, 4331, 4398, 4456, 4908
see also: International organizations, Mass organizations, Non-governmental organizations, Non-profit organizations, Peasant organizations, Professional organizations, Voluntary organizations, Women's organizations
Organized crime   5116, 5118, 5127, 5139, 5142, 5151, 5158
Orphanages   2653
Ortega y Gasset, José   223
Orthodox Church   1298, 1301, 5829
Out-groups   712, 725, 743, 750, 754, 767, 771, 1375, 3045, 3086

Overpopulation   2014, 3768
Overseas territories   1996, 2020, 3304
Owners   3760, 4124
Paganism   1260
Painting   1594, 1605, 1624, 5445
Palestinians   2689, 2780, 2933, 3145, 3297, 3518
Panafricanism   3027
Panel surveys   275, 355
Paradigms   18, 249, 529, 780, 889, 2974
Parent's education   1725
Parent-child relations   685, 1289, 1329, 2102, 2115, 2163, 2471, 2486, 2493, 2611, 2611, 2612, 2617, 2619, 2621, 2622, 2623, 2624, 2625, 2626, 2627, 2628, 2629, 2630, 2631, 2632, 2636, 2640, 2642, 2644, 2645, 2649, 2941, 5065, 5317, 5343, 5579, 5637
Parent-teacher relations   1673
Parenthood   2440, 2471, 2476, 2486, 2497, 2546, 2566, 2621, 2626, 2638, 2639, 2640, 2908
Parents   473, 684, 719, 1673, 1702, 1725, 2503, 2518, 2519, 2546, 2613, 2616, 2637, 2643, 2644, 2646, 2890, 5143, 5309, 5388, 5581, 5591, 5592, 5602, 5620
see also: Step-parents
Pareto, Vilfredo   150, 189, 210, 453
Park, Robert   14
Parliamentary elections   284, 3308, 4964
Parsons, Talcott   189, 192, 1812
Part-time employment   2397, 2792, 4284, 4343
Part-time farming   4341
Participant observation   1048
Partisanship   4966
Partners   608, 677, 2064, 2163, 2214, 2524, 2536, 2545, 2560, 2564, 2578, 2583, 2602, 2838, 2856, 3000, 4178, 4278, 4541, 5256, 5593
Party members   4951
Past   40, 1024, 2690
Pastoralism   2903, 3472
Paternalism   648, 4105, 4589, 4607
Pathology   3673

Subject index

Patients 411, 2497, 3322, 5409, 5426, 5564, 5634, 5642, 5658, 5662, 5675, 5676, 5795, 5805, 5822
Patriarchy 2406, 2835, 3483, 5808
Patriotism 753
Pay 4263, 4434, 4451, 4618
 see also: Equal pay
Payment agreements 2469
Payments 2493
Peace 923, 943, 4989, 5019, 5035
Peace movements 4885, 4909, 4927, 4938, 4945
Peace negotiations 728
Peasant movements 3500
Peasant organizations 3636, 4912
Peasantry 3613, 3614, 3623, 3985, 4088
Peasants 3081, 3385, 3612, 3615, 3616, 3617, 3618, 3619, 3620, 3621, 3622, 4083
Peer groups 649, 755, 2104, 2163, 5143
Peirce, Charles Sanders 1372, 1425
Penal codes 1201, 3656
Penal policy 1207, 2991, 5153, 5189, 5192, 5215, 5222, 5227, 5235, 5289, 5420
Penal sanctions 5111, 5193
Penitential rites 1300
Penrose, Roger 1344
Pensions 2045, 3580, 4411, 5492
Pentecostalism 1276
Perception 12, 107, 465, 476, 525, 674, 754, 834, 1029, 1249, 1379, 1399, 1412, 1825, 2942, 3456, 3668, 4045, 4179, 4285, 4977, 5001, 5247, 5450, 5539, 5595
 see also: Interpersonal perception, Social perception
Perception of others 533, 606, 620, 622, 634, 643, 649, 724, 743, 1069, 1325, 4422
Perestroika 963, 1552, 1956, 4833, 4987
Perfect competition 4273
Periodicals 1393, 1440

Personal aggression 544, 684, 693, 705, 706, 1771, 1778, 2895, 3014, 4982, 5433
Personality 393, 544, 545, 547, 549, 550, 552, 554, 555, 557, 558, 559, 560, 561, 562, 563, 564, 565, 566, 567, 568, 569, 570, 572, 573, 576, 586, 587, 592, 597, 643, 650, 755, 977, 1184, 2317, 2628, 3966, 4436, 4456, 4984, 5516
Personality disorders 571
Personality measurement 2094
Personality traits 556, 634, 641
Personnel management 4311, 4474, 4475, 4476, 4477, 4478, 4479, 4480, 4481, 4482, 4483, 4484, 4485, 4486, 4508, 4616, 5000
Persuasion 919, 1366, 2436, 5679
Pessimism 597, 691
Pesticides 4421
Petrochemical industry 4514
Pharmaceutical industry 1282
Pharmacology 5401
Phenomenology 201, 605, 3694
Philosophers 127
Philosophical anthropology 2885, 5028
Philosophical thought 148, 1027, 1135, 1144, 1661, 1678
Philosophy 8, 16, 43, 117, 124, 125, 129, 131, 132, 135, 136, 138, 143, 250, 367, 513, 987, 1039, 1058, 1145, 1182, 1197, 1244, 1246, 1348, 1351, 1615, 1644, 1688, 2733, 2757, 4760
 see also: Educational philosophy, Moral philosophy, Political philosophy, Social philosophy
Philosophy of law 1173, 1179, 1191, 1192, 1199, 1205
Philosophy of science 1065, 1338, 1346
Phonology 1492
Photography 230, 598, 1620
Physical appearance 606, 608, 613, 630, 1857, 2648, 2973, 2977, 4016
Physically disabled 5678
Physician-patient relationship 5702

Subject index

Physicians 4547, 4549, 5641, 5646, 5648, 5649, 5658, 5668, 5669, 5679, 5686, 5701, 5747, 5795, 5817
Piaget, Jean 880
Pilot surveys 2612
Planning methods 830
Planning systems 3478, 4188
Planning theory 3497
Plant fibres 4108
Plant shutdowns 4139
Plantations 4603, 4717
Play 1055, 2040
Pluralism 1138, 1282, 1646, 3054, 3060, 3090, 3174, 3407, 4772
    see also: Religious pluralism, Social pluralism
Poetry 1480, 1622, 5446
Police 412, 957, 1517, 3163, 3181, 3298, 3570, 4409, 4495, 4786, 4789, 4792, 4795, 4797, 4800, 4802, 4810, 4811, 4812, 4813, 4814, 4817, 4818, 4824, 4836, 5147, 5161, 5181, 5190, 5206, 5225, 5286
    see also: Secret police
Policing 4787, 4798, 4803, 4804, 4805, 4816, 4836, 5047, 5133, 5134, 5203, 5217, 5246
Policy analysis 5050
Policy implementation 1727
Policy making 1712, 1730, 1792, 3862, 4807, 5048, 5476, 5493, 5703
Political action 124, 832, 2705, 4883
Political activity 2853, 4863, 4913, 4935
Political attitudes 200, 925, 939, 1263, 1650, 1835, 1900, 2039, 4986
Political authority 4808
Political behaviour 4976, 4986
Political change 976, 1478, 1933, 1936, 1939, 1970, 1975, 2150, 2656, 2657, 3057, 3992, 4005, 4102, 4388, 4595, 4638, 4656, 4818, 4826, 4829, 4834, 4839, 5059
Political communication 1409, 1519, 4946, 4947
Political conditions 978, 1603, 1920, 1923, 3994, 4822, 4825
Political conflicts 1933, 5819

Political consciousness 2160
Political corruption 1499, 4959
Political crises 3976, 4757
Political culture 338, 986, 1035, 1282, 1928, 1944, 3596, 4767, 4926, 4949, 4952, 4957, 4970, 4988
Political development 1650
Political economy 1897, 2668, 3384, 3532, 3718, 3913, 4785
Political elites 4978
Political exile 2576
Political forces
    see: Pressure groups
Political generations 4916
Political geography 5020
Political history 1034, 4822, 4979
Political ideas 602
    see also: History of political ideas
Political ideology 3106, 4760
Political influences 1644, 4695
Political information 1499
Political leaders 4985
Political leadership 491, 904, 2884, 4984, 5481
Political mobilization 4886, 4896, 4917, 4938
Political morality 1499
Political movements 4861, 4902, 4903
    see also: Anti-nuclear movements, Revolutionary movements
Political opinions 29, 4962
Political opposition 3636, 4873
Political participation 1949, 3325, 4869, 4870, 4882, 4907, 4917, 4933, 4952, 4969, 4981
Political parties 849, 4783, 4869, 4870, 4890, 4910, 4914, 4933, 4934, 4964, 4972, 4980, 5492
    see also: Communist parties, Conservative parties, Right wing parties, Social democratic parties, Socialist parties
Political philosophy 127, 132, 157, 1191, 1842, 3228
Political power 1343, 1508, 1529, 3047, 3423
Political protest 1077, 1282, 2705, 4878, 4882, 4903, 4916

514

Subject index

Political psychology 1402, 4753, 4754, 5008
Political reform 1960, 3922, 4791, 4987, 5338
Political refugees 2576, 3247
Political regimes 4765, 4769, 5022
see also: Military regimes
Political representation 4830
Political science 30, 368, 404, 5463
Political socialization 4806, 4983
Political sociology 610, 1538, 4756, 4757, 4758, 4831, 4972, 4974
Political speech 5009
Political structure 1888, 4828
Political systems 380, 1819, 4829, 4838, 4901, 4902
Political theory 1032, 2706, 4777, 4783, 4807
Political thought 1033, 4770, 4778
Political violence 4888, 5440
Politicians 491, 1579, 2990, 3820, 4837, 4959
Politicization 3132, 4992
Politics 885, 1558, 1931, 2225, 2830, 3077, 4045, 4801, 4820
Polls
see: Public opinion polls
Pollution 2382, 3500, 3664, 3859, 3940, 5693
see also: Air pollution
Polygamy 2418
Polygyny 2990
Poor 2223, 2270, 3761, 3777, 3901, 3904, 3984, 4006, 4053, 4366, 5137, 5278, 5321, 5333, 5335, 5348, 5351, 5464, 5490, 5494, 5723, 5742
Pop music 1613, 2163
Popper, Karl Raimund 100, 101, 1346
Popular culture 979, 992, 1001, 1002, 1004, 1012, 1019, 1035, 1038, 1103, 1120, 1368, 1505, 1535, 1536, 1555, 1575, 1584, 1592, 1600, 1609, 1618, 1636, 1637, 1675, 2146, 2630, 3027, 4724
Popular literature 1622
Popular music 1276, 1599, 1621, 1630, 5295
Popularity 4960

Population 1950, 1981, 1995, 1997, 2007, 2010, 2013, 2017, 2019, 2020, 2021, 2023, 2024, 2034, 2036, 2186, 2198, 2225, 2272, 3289, 3386, 3428, 3536, 4035, 4046, 4356, 5340
see also: Indigenous populations, Rural population, School population, Urban population, World population
Population ageing 1802, 2036, 2294, 2389, 2391, 2392, 2393, 2394, 2395, 2396, 4284, 5649, 5721, 5726, 5740
Population censuses 67, 536, 1980, 1982, 2005, 2261, 3025, 3997
Population composition 2200
Population decline 2014, 2016, 4231
Population density 2003, 2972, 3743, 3744, 3845
Population distribution 4230
Population dynamics 1484, 2020, 2026, 2184, 2250, 2297, 2302, 2396, 3338
Population education 2018
Population forecasts 1980, 1985, 1988, 1989, 2012, 2025, 2027, 2028, 2368, 3894
Population geography 2194
Population growth 2002, 2188, 3480, 3499, 3666, 4027, 4081
Population movements 251, 2014, 2197, 2202, 3080, 3357, 3379, 3415
Population policy 2031, 2195, 2201, 2220, 2241, 2287, 2334, 2390, 2394, 2761, 2941
Population projections 1981, 1983
Population statistics 3396
Population transfers 3248
Populism 997, 3202
Pornography 2679, 2719, 2750, 2865, 2949, 2956, 2994, 3004, 4169, 5445
Porter, Cole 2992
Ports 3762
Positivism 114, 201, 217, 889, 924
Post-communist societies 976, 1751, 1761, 1864, 1975, 2073, 2150, 3140, 3586, 3603, 3992, 4064, 4224, 4248, 4507, 4612, 4681, 4769, 4771, 4781, 4793, 4819, 4825, 4826, 4829, 4834, 4865, 4937

515

Subject index

Post-Fordism   2880, 3708, 4126
Post-industrial society   253, 1893, 1906, 1975, 4745, 4928
Post-secondary education   1804, 4069
Post-structuralism   88, 97, 4779
Postal services   334, 4714
Postmodernism   10, 110, 111, 118, 119, 120, 122, 126, 156, 178, 194, 195, 492, 833, 865, 889, 1055, 1056, 1057, 1058, 1059, 1060, 1061, 1062, 1063, 1064, 1065, 1066, 1067, 1068, 1069, 1070, 1071, 1072, 1073, 1074, 1122, 1197, 1310, 1358, 1394, 1443, 1667, 1669, 1678, 1944, 1951, 2736, 3481, 3497, 3521, 3844, 4807
Poverty   1916, 1982, 2073, 2119, 2346, 2354, 3242, 3540, 3543, 3769, 3896, 3897, 3907, 3930, 3996, 3997, 3998, 4006, 4030, 4034, 4040, 4042, 4048, 4049, 4059, 4210, 4233, 4372, 5062, 5065, 5226, 5273, 5281, 5283, 5304, 5311, 5313, 5314, 5315, 5316, 5317, 5318, 5319, 5324, 5325, 5326, 5327, 5330, 5331, 5332, 5335, 5336, 5338, 5339, 5340, 5341, 5342, 5343, 5345, 5347, 5349, 5350, 5351, 5352, 5353, 5354, 5355, 5356, 5357, 5401, 5486, 5495, 5705, 5723, 5742, 5779
see also: Culture of poverty, Rural poverty, Urban poverty
Power   565, 651, 654, 696, 740, 810, 834, 886, 893, 894, 895, 905, 906, 909, 913, 967, 989, 1082, 1510, 1565, 1598, 1663, 1692, 1751, 1827, 1928, 1978, 2662, 2687, 2771, 2772, 2894, 2916, 3021, 3069, 3117, 3865, 4047, 4535, 4694, 4780, 4821, 4873, 4928, 4944, 5659
Power generation   4664
Power supply   4670
Pragmatics   140, 945, 1414
Pragmatism   196, 958, 4286
Prairies   3114
Prayer   1214
Pregnancy   2134, 2161, 2217, 2232, 2264, 2281, 2533, 2575, 2675, 2836, 5637, 5683, 5691, 5764, 5766, 5825, 5828

Prejudice   417, 917, 997, 1646, 3201, 3202, 3219, 3220
see also: Racial prejudice
Presbyterianism   1271
Preschool education   1664, 1702, 2121
Preservation of cultural heritage   3844, 3864, 4747
Presidential elections   4947, 4985, 4991
Press   940, 1441, 1445, 1498, 1503, 1512, 1516, 1520, 1522, 1523, 1525, 1542, 1543, 1546, 1547, 1549, 1557, 4405, 4905, 4985
Pressure groups   1439, 4861
Prestige   3618
see also: Occupational prestige
Price policy
see: Food price policy
Prices   3756, 4187, 4729
see also: Housing prices, Relative prices
Pricing   3916, 4190
Priests   1299, 1301, 2998
Primary education   1732, 1766, 1768, 1769, 1770
Primary health care   5639, 5652, 5653, 5661, 5670, 5670, 5680, 5775
Primary schools   1767, 2846
Primates   1377, 2698, 2869
Primitive religion   1239, 1345
Printing   1184
Prisoner's dilemma   711, 762
Prisoners   442, 2450, 3169, 5179, 5184, 5231
Prisons   166, 396, 2450, 4499, 4517, 5122, 5179, 5183, 5184, 5185, 5188, 5195, 5198, 5214, 5216, 5218, 5219, 5220, 5223, 5229, 5231, 5232, 5233, 5234, 5610
Privacy   77, 946, 1197, 3735
Private education   1748, 1765
Private enterprises   800, 4140, 4527
Private health care   5685, 5687
Private property   3589
Private schools   1901
Private sector   2798, 3774, 5198

Subject index

Privatization 1026, 1529, 3607, 3767, 3772, 3867, 3977, 3988, 3993, 4118, 4121, 4216, 4584, 4595, 5451, 5535
Probability 290, 323, 371, 5462
Probation system 4101, 5204, 5212, 5221
Problem solving 382, 442, 476, 766, 895, 1679, 5050
Procreation 2218
Producers 4122
Product quality 4190
Production 2661, 4089, 4146, 4150, 4341, 4510
see also: Agricultural production, Industrial production
Production co-operatives 4247
Production management 4598
Production systems 376, 4090, 4136, 4143, 4149
Productivity 4413, 4437, 4555, 4587, 4588, 4619, 5673
see also: Agricultural productivity, Industrial productivity
Professional ethics 1171, 4798, 5817
Professional identity 5574
Professional organizations 4538, 4548
Professional workers 1588, 1730, 2814, 4534, 4538, 4539, 4546, 4549, 4551, 4559, 5493
Professionalism 1036, 4545, 4994, 5686
Professionalization 4551
Professors 1136, 1515, 1815
Profit 4035
Programme evaluation 4267
Programming
see: Linear programming
Proletarianization 1907
Proletariat 1137
Propaganda 1169
Property 2410, 2709, 3672, 3847, 3993
see also: Intellectual property, Land property, Private property
Property rights 2410, 3974, 4771
Prosperity 4048
Prostitution 2316, 2948, 2960, 2991

Protest movements 4866, 4874, 4875, 4877, 4919, 4927
Protestant churches 1271, 1286, 1293, 1295, 1297
Protestant ethics 147, 1305
Protestantism 1137, 1269, 1281, 1295
Protestants 1263, 1289, 1292, 1293, 1294, 1296, 1303, 1306, 2579
Proust, Marcel 2992
Psychiatry 371, 396, 398, 411, 420, 421, 427, 2048, 2154, 3082, 3322, 4459, 5047, 5586, 5713, 5834, 5836
see also: Social psychiatry
Psychoanalysis 404, 473, 5445
Psychological effects 395, 665, 4290
Psychological factors 438, 448, 562, 616, 2048
Psychologists 2491, 4235
Psychology 246, 366, 367, 372, 374, 377, 378, 382, 385, 389, 399, 400, 401, 402, 405, 406, 409, 410, 412, 418, 499, 515, 545, 667, 755, 873, 1052, 1143, 1473, 1500, 1683, 1909, 2154, 2699, 2713, 2727, 2759, 2873, 2953, 2968, 3082, 4196, 4455, 4643, 5146, 5223
see also: Child psychology, Clinical psychology, Economic psychology, Educational psychology, Environmental psychology, Evolutionary psychology, Experimental psychology, Genetic psychology, Industrial psychology, Political psychology, Social psychology
Psychometrics 550, 567
Psychopathology 129, 373, 574
Psychosociology 959, 3259, 4386
Psychotherapy 390, 425, 431, 539, 2759, 3350, 5586
see also: Group psychotherapy
Public administration 4214, 4564, 4806, 4842, 4843, 4845, 4846, 4850, 4851, 4852, 4853, 4854, 4857
Public choice 640, 1173, 4780
Public education 1648, 1674, 1748, 1756, 1765
Public enterprises 789, 4527

Public expenditure 3810, 4188, 4210, 5473
Public goods 3972, 3975, 4859, 4944
Public health 2229, 2320, 2337, 2345, 3008, 3482, 5441, 5640, 5663, 5682, 5753, 5771
Public interest 3086
Public law 3071
Public management 4484, 5481
Public opinion 344, 345, 915, 926, 938, 946, 960, 962, 963, 964, 967, 1037, 1278, 1519, 1534, 1557, 1938, 2210, 2217, 2235, 2237, 2243, 2327, 3205, 3209, 3227, 4118, 4671, 4824, 4988, 4990, 5014, 5347, 5417, 5768
Public opinion polls 274, 327, 950, 952
Public opinion research 959
Public ownership 3582
Public policy 1449, 1518, 1730, 2318, 2714, 3050, 3505, 3722, 3767, 4124, 4169, 4821, 4842, 4929, 4981, 5226, 5304, 5493, 5598, 5777, 5818
Public relations 1169, 1445, 1523, 1545, 4786
Public sector 819, 3286, 4018, 4420, 4439, 4585, 4618, 4655, 4692, 4729, 5526, 5647, 5687, 5727
Public servants 4496, 4575
Public services 787, 1533, 3684, 3785, 3988, 4755, 4990
Public transport 3214
Publishing 1422
Puerto Ricans 3115, 4023
Punishment 654, 960, 1182, 1269, 5095, 5101, 5111, 5180, 5187, 5190, 5193, 5196, 5205, 5215, 5220, 5235, 5300, 5420
Punjabi 3127
Pupils 245, 332, 1677, 1720, 1960, 2327, 3340, 5404
Qualitative analysis 256, 306, 313, 1780
Quality of life 474, 1790, 2108, 2394, 2488, 3567, 3707, 4007, 4020, 4026, 4034, 4036, 4038, 4050, 4063, 4068, 5045, 5183, 5635, 5667, 5811
Quality standards 2227, 4712

Quantitative analysis 256, 294, 408, 4377
Quechua 3078, 3093
Questionnaires 51, 324, 328, 329, 344, 347, 349, 350, 351, 359
Quiché 1415
Quinn, Warren 1170
Race 361, 423, 961, 1084, 1910, 2323, 2589, 2785, 2885, 3024, 3026, 3028, 3055, 3085, 3094, 3101, 3108, 3136, 3137, 3160, 3169, 3170, 3172, 3182, 3197, 3213, 3222, 3230, 3241, 3483, 3770, 3805, 3873, 4032, 4161, 4491, 5226, 5304, 5334, 5406, 5596, 5638
Race relations 867, 1675, 1930, 2592, 2605, 3068, 3115, 3143, 3147, 3153, 3158, 3171, 3173, 3174, 3175, 3176, 3182, 3183, 3184, 3185, 3189, 3190, 3192, 3208, 3218, 3219, 3226, 3327, 3407, 3770, 3805, 3857, 3922, 5438
Racial attitudes 3040, 3147, 3153, 3165, 3166, 3191, 3194, 3198, 3199, 3206
Racial conflict 3086
Racial differentiation 2331, 2375, 2589, 2590, 2591, 3170, 3770, 3805, 4003, 4246, 4263, 5779
Racial discrimination 3139, 3156, 3181, 3192, 3210, 3211, 3212, 3215, 3217, 3223, 3224, 3230, 3233, 3235, 3238, 3241, 3243, 3385, 4381, 5688
Racial inequality 3145, 3201, 3231, 3244, 4012, 4242, 4514
Racial prejudice 3206, 3221
Racial segregation 3162, 3214, 3729, 3796, 5148, 5689
Racism 58, 417, 941, 951, 997, 1187, 1646, 1910, 2170, 2700, 2782, 3085, 3171, 3175, 3178, 3183, 3187, 3194, 3196, 3197, 3202, 3207, 3208, 3210, 3213, 3216, 3219, 3222, 3225, 3226, 3227, 3228, 3229, 3230, 3232, 3233, 3236, 3237, 3242, 3245, 3288, 3808, 4545, 5090, 5147, 5149, 5225, 5433, 5546, 5626, 5690, 5705
Radicalism 1970, 2754, 3174
Radio 409, 1511, 1539, 1570, 1589

Subject index

Railways 3915
Rape 544, 594, 2715, 2956, 3017, 3697, 5087, 5093, 5094, 5126, 5157, 5173, 5182, 5206, 5230, 5254, 5255, 5367, 5445
Rastifarianism 1276
Rational behaviour 4963
Rational choice 200, 234, 441, 1081, 1245, 4963, 5119
Rationalism 142, 1252
Rationality 134, 169, 203, 210, 866, 1033, 1116, 1629, 3965, 4847, 4956
Rationalization 1113, 4239, 4429
Rationing 5750, 5767, 5824
Rawls, John 123, 150
Read, Grantley Dick 2675
Readers 97, 1441, 1725
Reading habits 1492, 1597, 1725
Reagan, Ronald 4985, 5009
Real estate 1440, 3708, 3759, 3854
Realism 91, 201, 1466, 5028, 5134
Reasoning 199, 382, 510, 874, 1150, 3015
Rebellions 380, 1075, 4773
Recession 1172, 4376
Recidivism 599, 5185
Reciprocity 601, 650, 690, 3523
Record industry 1599
Recording 1599
Recreation 4720, 4725, 4729, 4734, 4737
Recruitment 837, 1825, 4438, 4935
Recycling 3489
Red Cross 5851
Reforestation 3568
Reform 1263, 3212, 3819, 3838, 3869, 4670, 4968, 5218, 5229, 5755, 5761, 5768, 5783
  see also: Agrarian reform, Constitutional reforms, Economic reform, Education reform, Housing reform, Land reform, Legal reform, Political reform, Social reform
Refugees 2142, 2269, 3055, 3261, 3276, 3278, 3288, 3297, 3301, 3302, 3306, 3310, 3320, 3322, 3335, 3336, 3410, 3411, 3427, 3985, 4244, 5851
  see also: Political refugees

Reggae 1276
Regime transition 3977, 3990, 3992, 4791, 4796, 4834
Regional analysis 2027, 2324, 3894, 4068, 4068, 4617
Regional development 1967, 3369, 3591, 3855, 3894, 4117, 4220, 4222, 4224, 4226
Regional disparities 2020, 2301, 2507, 3179, 4000, 4036, 4051, 4060, 4224, 4230, 4232
Regional economics 4226, 5058
Regional identity 34, 980, 998, 3113, 3526, 3527, 3528
Regional integration 4840
Regional planning 3857, 3879, 3894, 4215, 4218, 4223, 4225
Regional policy 4219
Regional variation 307, 1105
Regionalism 111, 194, 1429, 4782
Regionalization 3404, 4617
Regions 1072, 2015, 2343, 3137, 3437
Regression analysis 278, 299, 308, 319, 320, 1982, 3997, 5568, 5635
Regulation 485, 1086, 1200, 2214, 2237, 3701, 3732, 3754, 4273, 4291, 4440, 4549, 4587, 4613, 4856, 5151, 5533, 5598
Relative deprivation 5319
Relative prices 200
Relative wages 3266
Relativism 982
Reliability 341, 760, 773, 859, 2619
Religion 122, 142, 397, 1215, 1220, 1223, 1228, 1229, 1230, 1233, 1239, 1243, 1244, 1246, 1247, 1256, 1261, 1264, 1268, 1269, 1280, 1283, 1289, 1326, 1345, 1348, 1856, 1921, 2594, 2762, 2837, 2905, 3529, 4132, 5517
  see also: Civil religion, Primitive religion, Sociology of religion, World religions
Religion and politics 1281, 1282, 1287, 1297, 1299, 5819
Religiosity 1267, 1279, 1282, 1316, 1332, 2156, 2157, 2415, 5152
Religious affiliation 1303

Subject index

Religious attitudes   482, 1262, 2971
Religious authorities   1222
Religious behaviour   1245, 1248, 1325
Religious beliefs   1216, 1217, 1248, 1249, 1250, 1314, 2449, 2497, 3052
Religious change   1220, 1232, 1263, 1270, 1277, 1286
Religious communities   1235, 1302, 1304, 3146
Religious conflicts   1324
Religious conversion   1276
Religious education   1321, 1322, 1648, 1674, 1712, 1792, 3616
Religious experiences   772, 1224
Religious fundamentalism   1226, 1279, 1282, 1307, 1310, 1312, 1315, 1317
Religious groups   1218, 1302, 1892, 2579, 5606
Religious history   28, 1006, 1300
Religious influences   1127
Religious life   1278, 1309
Religious minorities   3105
Religious missions   1236
Religious movements   398, 1238, 1240, 1241, 1254, 1260, 1282, 1288, 1973, 2923
Religious orders   1242
Religious participation   1274, 1285
Religious persecution   1300
Religious pluralism   1285
Religious practice   1271, 1302, 1314
Religious revival   1317
Religious songs   1287
Remarriage   2455, 2580
Remittances   3371, 3999
Rent   3757
Rent-seeking   3782
Repression   569, 1086, 1201, 3701, 4026, 4923
Reproductive technology   2209, 2224, 2228, 2237, 2237, 2238, 2259, 2734, 5699, 5773, 5790, 5803, 5818
Research   37, 40, 41, 58, 232, 237, 244, 337, 339, 403, 856, 1441, 1808, 2315, 3460, 3539, 3677, 3961, 4425, 4690, 5021, 5181, 5286, 5691, 5703
see also: Action research, Communication research, Demographic research, Educational research, Empirical research, Interdisciplinary research, Management research, Medical research, Operations research, Organizational research, Public opinion research, Scientific research, Social research, Social science research, Sociological research
Research and development   1805, 1808, 1818
Research centres   70, 252
Research methods   59, 226, 231, 233, 240, 246, 256, 259, 273, 282, 293, 318, 328, 353, 360, 363, 551, 1378, 2426, 4614
see also: Field work
Research programmes   1948
Residence   5172
Residential areas   3663, 3666, 3735, 3742, 3755, 3774
Residential differentiation   3809
Residential mobility   351, 1484, 1851, 3275, 3362, 3376, 3758, 3770, 3802, 3805, 3853
Residential segregation   3162, 3204, 3729, 3796, 3802, 3803
Resistance movements   4139
Resistance to change   790
Resource allocation   623, 761, 2180, 2330, 3086, 3502, 3975, 4034, 4210, 5463, 5487, 5824
Resource conservation   3443
Resource management   3439, 4375
Responsibility   140, 458, 656, 1490, 1694, 3534, 4857, 4891, 5258, 5573, 5786
see also: State responsibility
Retail trade   4106, 4131, 4163, 4180, 4184, 4573, 5174, 5447
Retired persons   67
Retirement   2037, 2045, 2064, 2067, 2074, 2559, 2850, 3304, 3376, 4255, 4344, 4411
see also: Early retirement
Return migration   3251, 3262, 3265, 3283, 3304, 3337, 3340, 3344, 3399, 3629

Subject index

Revenge 2692
Revolt 4886
Revolution 219, 1958, 1974, 3385, 5023
Revolutionary movements 4865, 5118
Rex, John 3158
Rhetoric 114, 481, 1102, 1402, 1419, 1420, 1466, 1546, 4857, 4989, 5009
Right 997, 2028, 3202
 see also: Extreme right
Right to culture 1401
Right to education 1709
Right to vote 3425
Right wing parties 4286, 4638
Rights 810, 1159, 1174, 2497, 2498, 2503, 2704, 2970, 3276, 3755, 4884, 5060, 5676
 see also: Basic rights, Children's rights, Civil rights, Economic rights, Human rights, Property rights, Social rights, Women's rights
Riots 3176, 5042, 5147, 5225
Risk 203, 206, 213, 524, 843, 1121, 1173, 1194, 2134, 2144, 2224, 2337, 3010, 3430, 3859, 4898, 5071, 5176, 5214, 5409, 5426
Risk management 863, 3479, 4421
Rites of passage 2923
Ritual 1124, 1272, 1328, 1547, 1590, 2621, 3529
 see also: Penitential rites
Ritual games 2040
Rivers 5015
Road safety 5037, 5117, 5360, 5379
Road traffic 3917
Road transport 3909
Roads 3916
Robots 4143
Rock music 1621, 1630, 1635, 2158
Role 454, 2903, 3360, 4858, 4924
Role conflicts 898, 901, 911
Role expectations 898
Role playing 897
Role prescriptions 908
Roman Antiquity 1300
Romanticism 1033
Rostow, Walt Whitman 4015
Rousseau, Jean-Jacques 128

Rule of law 5445
Ruling class 1356, 1565
Rumours 1410
Rural areas 1216, 1776, 1999, 2023, 2074, 2184, 2256, 2420, 2555, 3285, 3384, 3520, 3543, 3559, 3565, 3567, 3570, 3576, 3578, 3579, 3585, 3594, 3602, 3604, 3607, 3609, 3617, 3625, 3627, 3634, 4021, 4128, 4622, 4886, 5172, 5692, 5765
Rural communities 1217, 2404, 2530, 2563, 2662, 2910, 3515, 3542, 3551, 3563, 3573, 3591, 3595, 3598, 3620, 3643, 5837
Rural development 774, 2669, 3510, 3545, 3614, 3623, 3624, 3625, 3626, 3628, 3629, 3630, 3631, 3632, 3633, 3634, 3635, 3636, 3637, 3998, 4742
Rural economics 3559, 3995, 4128
Rural employment 4305
Rural life 3549, 3571, 3608, 3610
Rural planning 3539, 4737
Rural policy 3587, 3633, 3634
Rural population 2203, 3536, 3554, 3559, 3568, 3601, 3995
Rural poverty 3548, 3585, 3599, 4051, 5346
Rural society 1972, 3580, 3590, 3597, 3600, 3615, 3616, 3632
Rural sociology 3558, 3568, 3601, 3606
Rural transport 3597
Rural women 2827, 2842, 2864, 2939, 3553
Rural youth 3566
Rural-urban migration 1406, 2023, 3081, 3155, 3296, 3356, 3359, 3364, 3365, 3366, 3371, 3372, 3373, 3379, 3382, 3384, 3385, 3537, 3538, 3540, 3541, 3643, 3948, 4081, 4254, 4289
Rural-urban relations 1952, 3544, 3546
Rushdie, Salman 1315
Russian language 1563
Russian Orthodox Church 1288, 1304
Russians 3055, 3146
Sacred 114, 122, 1255, 1547
Sadness 691

Subject index

Safety 4440
see also: Occupational safety, Road safety
Sample surveys 457
Samples 335
Sampling 262, 4649
Sanctions 1195, 2652, 4382
see also: Penal sanctions
Sanitation services 3688
Sartre, Jean Paul 1028, 1548
Satanism 1251, 1272, 1328
Satisfaction 462, 952, 2307, 3595, 5395
see also: Job satisfaction, Life satisfaction, Marital satisfaction
Saver, Carl 3486
Savers 4208
Savings 4199, 4208
Savings banks 825
Scandals 5604
Scepticism 7
Schäffle, Albert 1363
Schisms 1300
Schizophrenia 2339
Scholarships 3042
School administration 1737, 1745
School failure 1767
School population 1660
Schooling 1670, 1682, 1683, 1695, 1726, 1732, 1769, 1782, 2263
Schools 357, 438, 708, 794, 1569, 1641, 1642, 1653, 1656, 1660, 1665, 1673, 1679, 1681, 1692, 1698, 1716, 1717, 1730, 1736, 1738, 1739, 1740, 1743, 1749, 1756, 1760, 1763, 1773, 1775, 2086, 3050, 3206, 4872, 5293, 5493, 5572
see also: Nursery schools, Primary schools, Private schools, Secondary schools, State schools
Schutz, Alfred 223
Schwarz, Norbert 359
Science 24, 26, 88, 99, 150, 426, 428, 752, 781, 1226, 1239, 1273, 1336, 1343, 1345, 1348, 1351, 1356, 1561, 1657, 1688, 2221, 4226, 4843, 4970, 5433, 5694

see also: Behavioural sciences, Communication sciences, History of science, Natural sciences, Philosophy of science
Science fiction 214, 1618
Science policy 251, 1350
Scientific and technical progress 1337, 1349
Scientific communities 1337, 1342, 4540
Scientific discoveries 43, 98, 1350
Scientific progress 1342, 1355
Scientific research 1337, 1342, 5794, 5828
Scientists 589, 1337, 1342, 1350, 3368
see also: Social scientists
Sea transport 4061
Seasonal workers 4254
Seasonality 5093, 5155, 5442
Sebeok, Thomas A. 1424, 1425
Secession 4921
Secondary analysis 51, 60, 64, 67, 71, 76, 4515
Secondary education 1729, 1757, 1772, 1774, 1775, 1777
Secondary schools 965, 1771, 1773, 1776, 1778, 2529, 4324, 4541, 5404
Secrecy 2239, 4983
Secret police 4835
Secret societies 763, 4835
Sects 1252, 1300
Secularism 1283
Secularization 482, 1252, 1270
Securities issues 4200
Sedentarization 3472, 3530
Segregation 2815, 3192, 3806, 3807, 3808, 4443, 5465, 5779
see also: Occupational segregation, Racial segregation, Residential segregation
Self 96, 104, 438, 463, 481, 500, 514, 528, 537, 586, 597, 603, 1016, 1069, 1606, 2082, 2095, 2699, 3086, 4761, 5786
Self-concept 532, 574, 575, 576, 577, 578, 580, 581, 587, 588, 590, 592, 593, 595, 596, 598, 599, 643, 750,

Subject index

902, 1249, 1616, 2082, 2561, 2569, 3329, 4016, 4816, 5306
Self-determination   4775
Self-employed workers   1970, 4282, 4293, 4294, 4324, 4359, 4503
Self-esteem   458, 464, 473, 483, 490, 543, 563, 581, 582, 583, 589, 591, 594, 596, 600, 670, 726, 1249, 2079, 5238, 5320, 5837
Self-evaluation   470, 482, 485, 579, 582, 613, 649
Self-expression   2106
Self-government   1760, 4713
Self-help   499, 3635, 4366, 5544
Self-management   3522, 4717
Self-perception   436, 442, 469, 470, 484, 493, 495, 520, 540, 573, 575, 585, 592, 599, 619, 652, 2546, 4408
Self-reliance   5469
Semantics   696, 1192, 1462, 1493, 1494, 1497
Seminars   895
Semiology   1594
Semiotics   26, 97, 116, 997, 1068, 1425, 3202, 4774, 5445
Sensory organs   2945
Separatist movements   4921
Service industry   1970, 3203, 3333, 3590, 4115, 4462
Service industry workers   4619
Sex   1038, 1868, 2181, 2190, 2380, 2785, 2849, 2907, 3000
Sex customs   2666
Sex differentiation   434, 570, 664, 1714, 1914, 1964, 2379, 2462, 2586, 2651, 2695, 2698, 2791, 2826, 4443
Sex discrimination   1714, 2173, 2330, 2740, 2932, 2934, 2936, 2937, 2938, 2939, 2940, 2942, 2943, 2944, 4311, 4321, 4326, 4333, 4346, 4347, 4350, 4509, 4648, 5136
Sex distribution   2190, 2536
Sex equality   2679, 2785, 2794, 2931, 2941, 4324, 4487
Sex inequality   2726, 2786, 2813, 2815, 2924, 2935, 4238
Sex roles   128, 410, 633, 1119, 1161, 2651, 2666, 2668, 2694, 2698, 2751,
2772, 2862, 2868, 2879, 2885, 2911, 2912, 2952, 2953
Sexism   951, 1652, 2812, 2933, 2941
Sexology   2996
Sexual assault   594, 735, 1432, 1557, 2123, 2461, 2692, 2771, 5044, 5069, 5076, 5078, 5079, 5086, 5088, 5094, 5130, 5157, 5200, 5221, 5230, 5292, 5445, 5561, 5586
Sexual behaviour   240, 353, 641, 673, 937, 2156, 2162, 2212, 2233, 2240, 2254, 2296, 2313, 2316, 2325, 2345, 2346, 2731, 2778, 2923, 2945, 2947, 2949, 2952, 2953, 2955, 2957, 2958, 2961, 2963, 2965, 2966, 2972, 2976, 2977, 2978, 2981, 2982, 2986, 2996, 2997, 3000, 3001, 3002, 3004, 3005, 3006, 3007, 3008, 3009, 3010, 3011, 3013, 3014, 3015, 3017, 3021, 3022, 5070, 5085, 5089, 5182, 5301, 5355, 5367, 5403, 5590
Sexual harassment   358, 544, 2967, 2993, 3012, 4332, 4348
Sexual intercourse   2325, 3001
Sexual perversions   2975, 2987, 3018, 5445
Sexual reproduction   2221, 2224, 2242, 2247, 2254, 2468, 2655, 2972
Sexual taboo   2963, 2975
Sexuality   707, 937, 1889, 2080, 2313, 2345, 2597, 2614, 2651, 2655, 2657, 2664, 2865, 2878, 2907, 2908, 2911, 2947, 2951, 2953, 2959, 2966, 2969, 2987, 2988, 2995, 2996, 2998, 2999, 3001, 3002, 3003, 3004, 3007, 3016, 3020, 3483, 4495, 5002
Sexually transmitted diseases   2324
Sheep   3078
Shevchenko, Taras   4774
Shipbuilding   3509
Shoe industry   4097
Shortage
  see: Housing shortage
Siblings   552, 2381, 2386, 2399, 2412, 2452, 2958, 5571, 5847
Signs   1377, 1425, 1462
Silk   2813

Subject index

Simmel, Georg   114, 122, 171, 172, 173, 198, 205, 212, 1070, 1094, 1122, 4756
Simulation   392, 718, 824, 4997
Simulation techniques   5476
Singhalese   4979
Single European market   5509
Sisters   3009
Siting decisions   3450
Size of enterprise   4483
Skilled workers   3403, 4264, 4501
Skills   432, 665, 1027, 1133, 2618, 3384, 4153, 4489, 4490, 4492, 4564, 4565, 4566, 4568
Slang   1368
Slavery   890
Sleep   66
Small and medium sized enterprises   2448, 2674, 4071, 4081, 4085, 4091, 4100, 4120, 4123, 4127, 4128, 4129, 4130, 4198, 4207, 4474, 4485, 4569
Small groups   723, 736, 740, 766, 767
Small states   1120
Small towns   2039, 3565, 3663, 3686, 3846, 3874
Small-scale farming   3584
Small-scale industry   4133
Smith, Adam   3967
Smith, Dorothy   168
Smoking   290, 1121, 2151, 2349, 2355, 5365
Sociability   1122, 1458
Social accounting   291
Social accounts   688, 4600
Social action   32, 143, 182, 406, 1174, 1929, 1931, 3531, 3615, 3970, 4920, 5308
Social adaptation   3058
Social anthropology   605, 1025, 1051, 2131
Social assimilation   3327
Social behaviour   373, 393, 767, 2337, 2808
Social change   35, 94, 220, 406, 701, 774, 974, 976, 1000, 1008, 1047, 1049, 1076, 1092, 1211, 1217, 1236, 1313, 1317, 1478, 1602, 1618, 1640, 1680, 1695, 1719, 1922, 1925, 1927, 1928, 1929, 1930, 1931, 1932, 1933, 1934, 1936, 1937, 1939, 1940, 1941, 1942, 1944, 1945, 1947, 1948, 1949, 1950, 1952, 1953, 1954, 1955, 1956, 1957, 1958, 1960, 1961, 1962, 1965, 1967, 1968, 1969, 1970, 1972, 1975, 1976, 1978, 2050, 2079, 2130, 2136, 2150, 2171, 2176, 2273, 2444, 2493, 2506, 2514, 2530, 2610, 2676, 2710, 2810, 2888, 2903, 2914, 3064, 3142, 3187, 3367, 3544, 3575, 3600, 3609, 3611, 3620, 3643, 3646, 3702, 3728, 3779, 3863, 3955, 4005, 4056, 4292, 4311, 4350, 4403, 4477, 4680, 4748, 4760, 4785, 4829, 4834, 4874, 4917, 4918, 4920, 4925, 4928, 5032, 5161, 5229, 5340, 5435
Social co-operation   711, 758
Social cognition   102, 109, 506, 659, 662, 667, 766, 917
Social conditions   302, 378, 640, 757, 970, 978, 988, 990, 1046, 1088, 1096, 1113, 1283, 1506, 1643, 1823, 1831, 1895, 1919, 1920, 1923, 1924, 1934, 1938, 1950, 1955, 1956, 1959, 1961, 1963, 1964, 1970, 1977, 1979, 2066, 2077, 2139, 2178, 2186, 2218, 2417, 2445, 2514, 2640, 2683, 2700, 2709, 2716, 2729, 2745, 2773, 2871, 2879, 2894, 2950, 3035, 3038, 3059, 3115, 3164, 3192, 3215, 3234, 3330, 3336, 3381, 3407, 3473, 3603, 3671, 3724, 3725, 3738, 3778, 3921, 3923, 3939, 3992, 4020, 4054, 4057, 4058, 4062, 4142, 4233, 4373, 4404, 4799, 4833, 4957, 5036, 5053, 5054, 5060, 5062, 5276, 5282, 5316, 5321, 5326, 5354, 5412, 5507, 5732
Social conflicts   259, 682, 683, 686, 805, 1089, 1883, 3176, 3187, 3713, 4308, 4627, 4915, 4942, 5007, 5059, 5300, 5439
Social consciousness   1841, 2160
Social contract   647, 2706, 3701
Social control   157, 166, 216, 485, 894, 1076, 1082, 1083, 1086, 1087, 1088, 1089, 1091, 1448, 2614, 3213,

Subject index

4047, 4469, 4923, 5043, 5114, 5163, 5205, 5222, 5295, 5307, 5310, 5386
Social democracy 4672, 4922
Social democratic parties 2931
Social desirability 1176
Social development 84, 153, 389, 1854, 1935, 1966, 3547, 5052, 5548
Social differentiation 212, 663, 1839, 1855, 1863, 2060, 3807, 3809
Social distance 2832
Social dynamics 404
Social economics 3973, 4375
Social environment 1122, 1127
Social equality 571, 2714, 3172, 4065
Social equilibrium 234
Social exchange 654, 1050, 1242, 2561
Social forces 1519, 3980
Social group work 5545, 5619
Social history 992, 1115, 1117, 1389, 1848, 1889, 1897, 1901, 1923, 1971, 1979, 2099, 2983, 3103, 3144, 3192, 3196, 3267, 3320, 3341, 3509, 3925, 4862, 5482
Social housing 3761, 3763, 3769, 3861, 3901, 5452, 5454, 5469, 5480, 5488, 5490, 5491, 5495, 5497, 5498, 5518
Social identity 1652, 1846
Social indicators 315, 321, 1699, 2357, 2383, 4000, 5308, 5760
Social inequality 922, 929, 1652, 1682, 1746, 1834, 1836, 1840, 1842, 1844, 1881, 1906, 1912, 1913, 1914, 2020, 2048, 2060, 2173, 2679, 2839, 3137, 3373, 4013, 4036, 4042, 4206, 5312, 5315, 5326, 5343, 5627, 5778
Social influence 834, 918, 1206, 1941, 2162, 2436, 5392
Social integration 910, 1041, 1122, 1640, 1749, 1992, 3164, 3217, 3272, 3516, 3674, 3826
Social interaction 45, 148, 611, 652, 665, 669, 671, 723, 764, 1015, 1363, 1427, 3956, 4398, 4424, 4745
Social isolation 1916, 3011, 3034, 3215, 5047, 5321, 5348
Social judgement 573, 2046, 2094

Social justice 128, 167, 401, 942, 948, 971, 1455, 1913, 2993, 3470, 4394, 4600, 5053, 5215, 5511
Social life 631, 801, 990, 1080, 1109, 1113, 1918, 3646, 4404
Social medicine 2347, 2816, 5633, 5696, 5698
Social mobility 303, 1291, 1851, 1852, 1853, 1858, 1860, 1865, 1870, 1878, 2413, 2413, 2841, 2844, 3770, 3802, 3805, 4049, 4498, 4962, 4975, 5341
Social mobilization 4911, 4969
Social movements 220, 816, 1005, 1048, 1282, 1917, 1959, 1969, 1973, 2086, 2736, 3232, 3450, 3616, 4792, 4862, 4864, 4867, 4868, 4871, 4872, 4873, 4875, 4877, 4878, 4879, 4884, 4885, 4887, 4894, 4895, 4897, 4898, 4899, 4901, 4904, 4905, 4906, 4907, 4908, 4912, 4917, 4918, 4923, 4924, 4925, 4926, 4928, 4930, 4931, 4933, 4935, 4936, 4939, 4941, 5126, 5508
Social networks 218, 260, 261, 265, 298, 666, 672, 711, 715, 719, 752, 842, 2463, 2861, 2954, 3351, 4372, 5503
Social norms 1029, 1090, 1463, 1479, 2145, 5022
Social order 91, 132, 157, 174, 182, 404, 1081, 1640, 1833, 1868, 2445, 2849, 5508
Social participation 1048, 2174, 3084, 3513, 3652, 4894, 4918, 4920, 4935
Social pathology 5049
Social perception 408, 547, 612, 620, 624, 630, 643, 662, 663, 670, 691, 922, 962, 1353
Social philosophy 1199, 1205, 5472
Social planning 3826
Social pluralism 1935
Social policy 32, 982, 1088, 2031, 2074, 2201, 2319, 2498, 2504, 2624, 2715, 2886, 3192, 3580, 3611, 3767, 4259, 4296, 4300, 4486, 4590, 4708, 5042, 5050, 5054, 5151, 5229, 5268, 5342, 5348, 5456, 5476, 5480, 5499, 5500, 5501, 5504, 5509, 5510, 5515,

Subject index

Social problems 5524, 5531, 5532, 5606, 5707, 5723, 5742, 5766, 5768, 5831
Social problems   407, 522, 963, 1265, 1550, 1740, 1832, 1947, 1964, 2129, 2144, 2152, 2974, 3440, 3585, 3728, 3900, 4920, 5039, 5041, 5042, 5045, 5047, 5048, 5049, 5050, 5051, 5052, 5053, 5054, 5055, 5056, 5057, 5058, 5060, 5065, 5071, 5080, 5089, 5092, 5093, 5095, 5097, 5106, 5107, 5110, 5118, 5126, 5127, 5130, 5143, 5171, 5172, 5180, 5181, 5199, 5206, 5210, 5214, 5224, 5238, 5242, 5247, 5248, 5257, 5260, 5271, 5277, 5282, 5286, 5290, 5308, 5309, 5317, 5332, 5337, 5339, 5362, 5372, 5386, 5387, 5392, 5393, 5395, 5398, 5405, 5406, 5409, 5412, 5416, 5422, 5426, 5581, 5725
Social protest   220, 4897, 4918, 4936
Social psychiatry   413, 5850
Social psychology   361, 362, 363, 368, 369, 373, 391, 394, 404, 406, 407, 408, 413, 414, 415, 416, 417, 418, 419, 422, 426, 428, 429, 551, 624, 663, 733, 928, 1084, 1102, 1966, 1978, 3966, 5162
Social reform   1863, 2502, 4987, 5338, 5505
Social rehabilitation   4722
Social relations   352, 605, 647, 722, 757, 793, 896, 983, 1479, 2095, 2766, 3180, 4873, 4970, 4982
Social representations   428, 2387, 3569
Social research   43, 49, 59, 60, 75, 250, 264, 328, 2069, 2426, 2995, 3248, 4355, 5570, 5594, 5618
Social rights   1897, 2803, 3580, 4827
Social roles   570, 896, 1353, 5497
Social science research   1, 3, 38, 70, 209, 231, 248, 251, 252, 283, 289, 306, 386, 2764
Social sciences   5, 11, 13, 14, 16, 26, 27, 34, 40, 41, 42, 46, 48, 52, 63, 74, 75, 80, 103, 110, 117, 119, 138, 158, 193, 214, 227, 232, 238, 246, 256, 297, 338, 455, 458, 875, 1199, 1318, 1346, 1396, 1554, 1919, 2696, 3468, 3962, 5035, 5510
Social scientists   3368
Social security   2803, 3023, 3425, 3575, 4309, 4382, 4384, 5318, 5453, 5464, 5465, 5485, 5486, 5496, 5503, 5505, 5506, 5510, 5512, 5513, 5516, 5520, 5521, 5783
Social security funds   4391
Social services   1730, 2329, 3023, 3594, 4210, 4459, 5082, 5312, 5455, 5457, 5466, 5468, 5476, 5477, 5487, 5489, 5493, 5499, 5500, 5514, 5557, 5562, 5585, 5602, 5605, 5616, 5625, 5647, 5684, 5697, 5703, 5709, 5716, 5725, 5729, 5739, 5746
Social space   3483
Social status   222, 1684, 1836, 1851, 1857, 1867, 1872, 1904, 2046, 2081, 2082, 2083, 2134, 2254, 2332, 2366, 2576, 2698, 3056, 3185, 3897, 4557
Social stereotypes   753, 928, 3045
Social stratification   303, 910, 1684, 1707, 1837, 1841, 1843, 1847, 1850, 1858, 1859, 1861, 1865, 1866, 1878, 1882, 1886, 1888, 1890, 1893, 1894, 1895, 1898, 1902, 1907, 1912, 1914, 1917, 2832, 2841, 3095, 3802, 4032, 4352, 4978
Social structure   187, 218, 222, 268, 618, 827, 987, 1018, 1076, 1084, 1113, 1434, 1746, 1822, 1825, 1834, 1836, 1842, 1862, 1863, 1864, 1872, 1873, 1882, 1904, 1915, 1919, 1927, 1976, 2082, 2429, 2504, 2532, 2835, 3081, 3529, 3533, 3597, 3660, 3897, 3987, 4175, 4190, 4498, 4511, 4828
Social surveys   112, 258, 273, 328, 333, 335, 338, 344, 345, 356, 3361
Social systems   432, 774, 1072, 1090, 1208, 1819, 1821, 1824, 1829, 1832, 1839, 1957, 2672, 3972, 4148, 4967, 5050
Social theory   94, 126, 127, 136, 154, 158, 162, 163, 165, 173, 185, 192, 196, 206, 207, 212, 214, 215, 216, 221, 297, 427, 510, 768, 1033, 1059, 1066, 1148, 1354, 1875, 1886, 2706,

Subject index

2995, 4196, 4762, 4776, 4801, 5445, 5621, 5781, 5853
Social values   467, 516, 726, 1077, 1085, 1139, 1178, 1767, 2423, 4050, 5091, 5284, 5487
Social welfare   248, 5458, 5464, 5472, 5472, 5500, 5507, 5525
Social work   2075, 2170, 3024, 5047, 5052, 5359, 5460, 5536, 5541, 5542, 5543, 5546, 5547, 5548, 5549, 5551, 5552, 5553, 5554, 5555, 5560, 5562, 5563, 5565, 5567, 5569, 5573, 5575, 5576, 5578, 5579, 5583, 5584, 5585, 5586, 5587, 5591, 5596, 5601, 5603, 5604, 5605, 5606, 5607, 5608, 5609, 5610, 5611, 5612, 5613, 5616, 5620, 5623, 5625, 5626, 5628, 5629
Social workers   3321, 4351, 5247, 5514, 5540, 5546, 5557, 5564, 5574, 5583, 5594, 5614, 5615, 5617, 5622, 5628, 5630
Socialism   1205, 1921, 1975, 3977, 3991, 4464, 4771, 4784, 4785, 5517, 5760
see also: Market socialism, State socialism
Socialist development   1902, 3764
Socialist economies   4243
Socialist parties   4830
Socialist societies   4832
Socialist states   1299, 2672, 2858, 3821, 4760, 4799, 4829
Socialization   576, 690, 1098, 1731, 1767, 1770, 2125, 2163, 2172, 2688, 2883, 2926, 4259, 4275, 4542
see also: Political socialization
Society   212, 321, 1052, 1651, 1815, 1820, 1824, 1830, 3438, 3694, 3973, 4766, 4791, 4820, 4864, 4921, 4987, 5011, 5290, 5434
see also: Agrarian society, Capitalist society, Civil society, Class society, Consumer society, Industrial society, Information society, Mass society, Post-communist societies, Post-industrial society, Rural society, Secret societies, Socialist societies, Traditional society, Urban society

Socio-economic development   155, 1542, 1751, 2191, 2258, 2444, 2458, 2762, 3557, 3633, 3686, 3751, 3966, 4023, 4030, 4227, 4298, 4362, 4685, 5780
Sociobiology   1248, 1914, 5087, 5254
Sociolinguistics   386, 671, 1103, 1464, 1465, 1466, 1467, 1468, 1474, 1478, 1482, 1489, 1495, 1496
Sociological analysis   285, 422, 1970, 1992, 4161, 4205
Sociological methodology   10, 53, 106, 113, 193, 228, 229, 235, 241, 244, 245, 249, 253, 254, 260, 311, 324, 329, 344, 347, 350, 882, 898
Sociological research   44, 47, 54, 57, 61, 62, 66, 112, 233, 237, 244, 245, 295, 330, 347, 359, 406, 454, 1553, 1597, 2941, 3704, 4196, 5308
Sociological theory   4, 17, 18, 111, 150, 151, 152, 155, 157, 159, 161, 167, 169, 170, 176, 178, 179, 181, 184, 187, 188, 189, 191, 193, 194, 195, 197, 198, 201, 203, 204, 209, 210, 213, 217, 220, 224, 225, 312, 436, 456, 639, 692, 1090, 1175, 1256, 1355, 1498, 1687, 1828, 1830, 1839, 3090, 3134, 3474, 3665, 4653
Sociologists   36, 86, 243, 244, 1839, 4556, 5324, 5348
Sociology   10, 15, 22, 25, 28, 30, 31, 32, 33, 35, 45, 63, 69, 73, 79, 101, 160, 186, 199, 243, 967, 1039, 1040, 1058, 1062, 1066, 1070, 1098, 1356, 1824, 1966, 1969, 2164, 3074, 3158, 4240, 4556, 4760, 5258
see also: Applied sociology, Criminal sociology, Economic sociology, Educational sociology, Electoral sociology, History of sociology, Medical sociology, Occupational sociology, Political sociology, Rural sociology, Teaching of sociology, Urban sociology
Sociology of art   142, 1624
Sociology of knowledge   98, 108, 467, 1239, 1345, 1353, 1358, 1551, 1826

Subject index

Sociology of law 1088, 1119, 1189, 1196, 1197, 1198, 4561, 4802, 5198, 5228
Sociology of organizations 805, 806, 827, 879, 886, 889
Sociology of religion 150, 1213, 1219, 1221, 1226, 1234, 1246, 1252, 1255, 1257, 1258, 1261, 1285, 1289, 1305, 1327
Sociology of science 24, 1347, 1359
Sociology of sport 4742
Sociology of the family 65
Sociology of work 4241
Sociometry 4931
Software 1136, 4229, 4730
Soil erosion 3560
Soil fertility 3564
Solidarity 1081, 4710, 4713, 4922, 4980, 5030
Solvent abuse 5404
Songs
  see: Folk songs, Religious songs
Sons 1329, 2241
Sorokin, Pitirim A. 4778
South Amerindians 1494, 3115, 3902
Sovereignty 5025
Spanish language 420, 1404, 1435
Spatial dimension 387, 1000, 1068, 2818, 3437, 3482, 3483, 3484, 3524, 3735, 3759, 3807, 3812, 3814, 3854, 4180, 4228, 5029, 5754
Spatial distribution 2020, 2364, 3804, 4220
Spatial models 314, 3454, 3800, 3810, 3811
Special education 1668
Species 1430
Speech 137, 1360, 1392, 1421, 1432, 1485, 2707
Speech analysis 2631
Spencer, Herbert 5033
Spiritualism 1272, 1328
Sport 576, 583, 908, 1547, 1790, 2148, 2149, 2789, 2882, 2938, 3055, 4133, 4615, 4720, 4724, 4727, 4728, 4729, 4736, 4741, 4743, 4744, 4746, 5285
  see also: Sociology of sport

Springsteen, Bruce 1635
Squatters 3751, 3755, 3762, 3780, 3781, 3905, 4911
Stabilization policy 4210
Staff 5622
Stages 2621, 2631
Stalin, Josef 562
Standard of living 910, 1877, 2342, 2498, 4024, 4027, 4031, 4045, 4210, 5314, 5635
Standardization 1042, 1729, 1777
State 6, 183, 1297, 1696, 1783, 3047, 3089, 3090, 3188, 3232, 4101, 4209, 4464, 4540, 4646, 4808, 4831, 4928, 5005, 5025, 5471, 5510
  see also: Nation state, Small states, Socialist states
State aid 3828
State formation 3076, 3094, 4771, 4924
State government 5761
State intervention 3768, 3893, 3920, 4229, 5473
State responsibility 4214
State schools 1674
State socialism 2858, 4825, 4839
Stateless 3276
Statistical analysis 76, 1922, 3025
Statistical decision 4267
Statistical methods 64, 264, 288, 289, 291, 306, 307, 308, 319, 421
Statistical models 260, 277
Statistics 232, 1549, 1705, 1964, 2066, 2218, 5399, 5558
  see also: Industrial statistics, Population statistics
Step-parents 2455
Stereotypes 544, 724, 754, 894, 917, 938, 1614, 1636, 2787, 2846, 3205, 3240, 4731
  see also: National stereotypes, Social stereotypes
Stimuli 465, 1366
Stochastic processes 262, 296, 4032
Stock exchange 4200, 4204, 4709
Stockholders 4202
Stoetzel, Jean 404
Stories 214

Subject index

see also: Life stories
Story telling   1438, 2075, 4448
Strategic planning   831, 845, 5073
Strikes   2773, 4621, 4622, 4624, 4626, 4628, 4629, 4634, 4676
Structural adjustment   2669, 2786, 3927, 3931, 4056, 4210, 4224, 5006, 5350, 5780
Structural analysis   261, 1018
Structural change   3331, 3708, 3834, 4136, 5097, 5777
Structural unemployment   4369, 4387
Structuralism   97, 163, 979, 1628
Student behaviour   660, 681, 1649
Student movements   4860, 4928
Students   363, 452, 460, 482, 538, 598, 918, 930, 965, 969, 1029, 1146, 1654, 1711, 1739, 1741, 1790, 1815, 2562, 2976, 3042, 3109, 4324, 5136
Subcontracting   4117, 4122
Subculture   307, 1097, 2165, 2788, 5090, 5154, 5516
Subjectivity   174
Subsidies   2376
see also: Employment subsidies
Substance abuse   2314, 5041, 5109, 5194, 5197, 5362, 5366, 5369, 5371, 5374, 5376, 5385, 5389, 5395, 5401, 5406, 5414, 5424, 5428
see also: Dependency rehabilitation
Suburban areas   2320, 2746, 3162, 3652, 3663, 3667, 3685, 3690, 3710, 3711, 3786, 3795, 4299, 4352
Succession   787
Sugar   1971
Suicide   122, 143, 317, 2574, 2617, 2974, 3038, 3440, 5047, 5371, 5409, 5414, 5422, 5423, 5424, 5425, 5426, 5427, 5428, 5429, 5430, 5431, 5432, 5804
Supermarkets   4161
Supervisors   644, 4409, 4441
Supply   4273
see also: Food supply, Labour supply, Power supply
Supply and demand   2299
Surgery   2229

Surrogate motherhood   2209, 2242, 5552
Survey data   290, 2350
Surveys   240, 274, 309, 325, 327, 330, 334, 340, 343, 349, 351, 936, 946, 950, 959, 969, 1295, 1515, 1762, 2322, 2632, 2976, 2992, 3001, 3774, 4273, 4393, 5134, 5655
see also: Mail surveys, Panel surveys, Pilot surveys, Sample surveys, Social surveys
Survival strategy   444, 3070, 3102
Sustainable development   3448, 3452, 3490, 3555, 3878, 3908, 4210
Swedes   1566
Symbolic interaction   1064
Symbolism   424, 1231, 1402, 1423, 1593, 1836, 3501, 3578, 3721
see also: Body symbolism
Symbols   114, 1321, 1363, 1425, 1493
Symposia   5059
Systems analysis   768
Systems theory   477, 1927, 2464
Taboo
see: Incest taboo, Sexual taboo
Tactics   2602
Tagalog   3159
Take-overs   4290
Tales
see: Fairy tales
Tamils   1319, 3037, 4298
Tanaka, J.S.   573
Tanala   2879
Taoism   495, 1253
Tatar   3140
Tattooing   2987
Tax revenue   4842
Taxation   4209, 4251
see also: Double taxation
Taxes   5467
Taxonomy   3710
Tea   4717
Teachers   58, 708, 997, 1394, 1641, 1643, 1677, 1708, 1736, 2846, 3202, 3206, 4541, 4542, 4550, 4552, 4558, 4602, 4667, 4872, 5388
Teaching   390, 1357, 1417, 1688, 1693, 1763, 1807, 5826

529

Subject index

Teaching methods 1815
Teaching of sociology 23
Teamwork 783, 844, 4413
Technicians 1099
Technological change 1349, 3884, 4145, 4151, 4152, 4153, 4155, 4270, 4302, 4430, 4451, 4506, 4712
Technology 203, 752, 824, 828, 891, 1027, 1336, 1352, 1460, 1561, 1599, 2662, 2934, 3596, 3686, 4115, 4146, 4147, 4150, 4217, 4229, 4369, 4405, 4531, 4605, 4997, 5045, 5671, 5773
see also: Agricultural technology, Biotechnology, High technology, Information technology, New technology, Reproductive technology
Technology transfer 3558, 4154
Telecommunications 1449, 1456, 1518, 4079, 4430, 4452
Telematics 1457, 4680
Telephone 346, 1458, 1459, 4169, 4430
Television 1310, 1442, 1443, 1444, 1472, 1517, 1545, 1570, 1571, 1572, 1573, 1574, 1575, 1576, 1577, 1578, 1579, 1580, 1581, 1582, 1583, 1584, 1585, 1586, 1587, 1588, 1589, 1590, 1591, 1592, 1593, 2433, 2891, 3200, 5855
Telework 4452, 4453
Temples 1231
Temporal dimension 92, 436, 4560, 4745, 5029
Temporary employment 4469
Terminology 74, 1368, 1880
Territoriality 3233, 3518, 3809
Territory 3141, 3438, 4790, 5025
see also: Overseas territories
Terrorism 1530, 4888, 4937, 5090, 5445
Tertiary education 1804, 4069, 4564
Textile industry 1892, 2817, 2883, 4108, 4338, 4694
Texts 1255
Thanatology 173, 1124
Thatcher, Margaret 4257
Thatcherism 3785, 4257

Theft 5115, 5124, 5131, 5176, 5302, 5436
Theology 4989
see also: Christian theology
Theory of culture 57, 1045, 1225
Theory of education 1661, 1669, 1679
Therapeutic groups 5618, 5619
Therapeutics 3496, 5837
Therapy 396, 411, 3350, 5538, 5539, 5556, 5590, 5597, 5624, 5634
see also: Family therapy
Thieves 5155, 5160, 5442
Threat 582, 600, 1089, 2652
Thucydides 5028
Thünen, Johann Heinrich von 1441
Time budgets 4745
Tobacco 2151, 2348, 5365
Tolerance 922, 968, 1241, 4772
Tools 1108
Top management 900, 2798, 4519
Torture 5854
Totalitarianism 4838
Totemism 2526
Tourism 3442, 3590, 3691, 4186, 4719, 4723, 4731, 4738, 4748, 4750, 4752
Tourist trade 4747, 4749
Towns 2199, 2367, 3471, 3543, 3642, 3661, 3702, 3709, 3717, 3753, 3764, 3923, 3927, 3929, 3931, 3954, 4298, 4805, 4904, 5131, 5436
see also: New towns, Small towns
Toxicity 5344
Toys 1444
Trade 4137, 4673
see also: Agricultural trade, Free trade, International trade, Retail trade, Tourist trade
Trade union action 4680
Trade union members 1853, 4067, 4651, 4659, 4660
Trade union membership 4649, 4655, 4658, 4663, 4675, 4688, 4689, 4694, 4700
Trade unionism 4010, 4678, 4691
Trade unions 775, 1892, 2794, 3418, 4066, 4286, 4357, 4358, 4439, 4483, 4544, 4600, 4602, 4605, 4606, 4611,

Subject index

4650, 4652, 4653, 4654, 4657, 4658, 4661, 4662, 4664, 4665, 4666, 4667, 4668, 4669, 4670, 4671, 4673, 4674, 4676, 4677, 4679, 4682, 4683, 4684, 4685, 4686, 4687, 4690, 4692, 4693, 4695, 4696, 4697, 4698, 4699, 4700, 4701, 4702, 4703, 4704, 4705, 4706, 4707, 4708, 4712, 4872
Trademarks   1184
Tradition   1024, 1027, 1331, 1354, 1629, 1833, 1941, 2610, 3563, 3611, 3902, 4939
 see also: Cultural tradition, Oral tradition
Traditional medicine   5643
Traditional society   1079, 1095, 2275
Traffic   3894, 3914, 3917
 see also: Road traffic
Traffic accidents   395, 5037
Training   483, 583, 1386, 2089, 2809, 4146, 4262, 4563, 4566, 4568, 4571, 4572, 4573, 4574, 4576, 4592, 4997, 5212, 5481, 5531, 5540, 5574, 5595
 see also: In-service training, Vocational training
Training courses   4418
Training methods   4567
Transaction costs   717, 2581
Transactional analysis   617
Transfer   3561
 see also: Population transfers, Technology transfer
Transition from school to work   3050, 4574
Translation   997, 3202
Transport   3591, 3812, 3911, 3912, 3917, 3919
 see also: Air transport, Public transport, Road transport, Rural transport, Sea transport, Urban transport
Transport policy   3893, 3920
Travel   3597, 4751
Trees   2196
Triad   912, 5595
Tribal development   1689
Tribes   1782, 2935
Trusts   115, 815, 4134, 4151

Tuberculosis   2320
Turks   2154, 3082, 3234, 3340, 5623
Twins   548, 553, 2353
Typology   3312, 4739
Uncertainty   330, 863, 4148, 5679
Underclass   1074, 1099, 1897, 1908, 1916, 3050, 5261, 5320, 5321, 5324, 5334, 5348, 5406
Underdevelopment   1891
Underemployment   3096
Unemployed   2127, 4210, 4312, 4365, 4366, 4373, 4378, 4395
Unemployment   449, 2137, 3238, 3377, 4040, 4247, 4259, 4275, 4336, 4364, 4367, 4369, 4370, 4371, 4372, 4376, 4377, 4379, 4381, 4382, 4383, 4384, 4386, 4388, 4389, 4390, 4391, 4392, 4393, 4394, 5091, 5315, 5364
 see also: Frictional unemployment, Structural unemployment, Urban unemployment, Youth unemployment
Unemployment duration   3651, 4374, 4378
Unemployment levels   5096
UNESCO   1948
Uneven development   4228
Universality of culture   996
Universities   50, 252, 527, 681, 852, 918, 1730, 1742, 1779, 1780, 1781, 1785, 1791, 1793, 1797, 1798, 1803, 1807, 1808, 1812, 1813, 1815, 1816, 1817, 1818, 2942, 2983, 3027, 3042, 5130, 5493
University management   864, 1810
Unmarried mothers   2161, 2610, 5332
Unmarried persons   2388, 2784, 2915, 5272
Unskilled workers   4412
Upward mobility   892, 3054, 4049, 5341
Urban anthropology   3721, 3735, 3762, 4073
Urban architecture   3650
Urban areas   1567, 1710, 2199, 2223, 2256, 2270, 2320, 2522, 2592, 2917, 3285, 3537, 3543, 3644, 3660, 3662, 3668, 3678, 3687, 3689, 3691, 3697, 3700, 3708, 3714, 3715, 3720, 3722,

Subject index

3732, 3750, 3765, 3775, 3797, 3798, 3838, 3858, 3895, 3927, 3938, 4130, 4236, 4393, 4805, 4855, 5148, 5171, 5172, 5353, 5433, 5446
Urban communities   1949, 3176, 3379, 3502, 3504, 3517, 3533, 3542, 3649, 3656, 3678, 3703, 3713, 3720, 3728, 3730, 3764, 3848, 3856, 4201, 4862
Urban concentration   3759, 3854
Urban decline   3839
Urban design   3867, 3880
Urban development   3741, 3817, 3820, 3821, 3828, 3830, 3831, 3832, 3833, 3836, 3837, 3839, 3843, 3866, 3869, 3874, 3876, 3878, 3881, 3882, 3884, 3885, 3894, 3925, 3938, 4103
Urban economics   3666, 3671, 3754, 3839, 3878, 3933, 4033
Urban employment   3835, 4264, 4371
Urban environment   3657, 3664, 3675, 3695, 3701, 3872, 3880, 3909, 5103, 5411
Urban geography   11, 3457, 3639, 3727, 3735, 5020
Urban growth   3663, 3667, 3672, 3693, 3739, 3819, 3835, 3840, 3842, 3936
Urban history   2065, 3926
Urban housing   3729, 3731, 3735, 3739, 3746, 3747, 3766, 3768, 3776, 3780, 3783, 3788, 3789, 3882, 3903, 3905, 3906, 5779
Urban life   1086, 1368, 1899, 3034, 3052, 3058, 3081, 3643, 3646, 3649, 3656, 3659, 3674, 3695, 3702, 3723, 3921, 4269, 5047, 5726
Urban management   862, 3849, 3917, 3945
Urban movements   4862
Urban planning   2309, 2828, 3225, 3539, 3743, 3758, 3759, 3763, 3790, 3808, 3809, 3813, 3815, 3816, 3818, 3822, 3824, 3826, 3827, 3834, 3838, 3841, 3844, 3845, 3848, 3849, 3852, 3853, 3854, 3855, 3859, 3860, 3861, 3864, 3865, 3872, 3873, 3877, 3878, 3879, 3880, 3882, 3883, 3885, 3886,
3887, 3888, 3889, 3890, 3892, 3893, 3899, 3912, 3920, 3939, 4223, 5491
Urban policy   3648, 3683, 3725, 3793, 3814, 3818, 3823, 3832, 3837, 3848, 3850, 3860, 3863, 3870, 3871, 3874, 3875, 3921, 3922, 3943, 3946, 3948, 4385, 4859, 5052, 5587
Urban politics   3726, 3804, 3852, 3899, 4941
Urban population   3376, 3536, 3749
Urban poverty   1600, 3382, 3741, 3776, 3777, 3780, 3783, 3843, 3852, 3895, 3897, 3898, 3899, 3900, 3902, 3903, 3904, 3905, 3906, 3908, 4068, 5274, 5312, 5329, 5334, 5337, 5344, 5446, 5603
Urban renewal   1710, 1899, 3666, 3788, 3793, 3825, 3829, 3846, 3847, 3850, 3851, 3856, 3857, 3864, 3868, 3871
Urban society   1491, 3665, 5640
Urban sociology   1844, 3653, 3655, 3657, 3660, 3666, 3684, 3694, 3701, 3705, 3711, 3712, 3713, 3714, 3718, 3719, 3721, 3744, 3749, 3764, 3781, 3786, 3796, 3811, 3907, 3919, 3941, 5103, 5171, 5353
Urban space   862, 3709, 3774, 3867
Urban structure   3666, 3673, 3690, 3726, 3814, 3839, 4202
Urban transport   3910, 3913, 3918
Urban unemployment   3651, 4375, 4385
Urban women   2917, 3705
Urban-rural migration   3652
Urbanism   3950, 5168
Urbanization   2002, 2168, 2202, 2258, 2382, 3155, 3250, 3352, 3374, 3377, 3379, 3544, 3546, 3790, 3791, 3815, 3848, 3852, 3882, 3885, 3890, 3892, 3896, 3899, 3921, 3922, 3923, 3924, 3925, 3927, 3928, 3929, 3930, 3931, 3932, 3933, 3934, 3935, 3937, 3938, 3939, 3940, 3941, 3942, 3943, 3944, 3945, 3946, 3947, 3948, 3949, 3950, 3951, 3952, 3953, 3954, 3955, 3956
Utilitarianism   5797
Utz, Arthur   1177

Subject index

Validity 88, 2120, 5565
Value 95, 690, 809, 4194, 4319
Value judgement 924
Value systems 1077, 1078
Values 132, 175, 310, 770, 839, 1020, 1056, 1071, 1149, 1150, 1167, 1220, 1289, 1644, 1884, 2670, 2918, 3153, 3329, 3528, 4024, 4093, 4248, 4327, 4464, 4950, 4983, 5272
Vehicles 5670
Velarde Fuertes, Juan 999
Velázquez, Diego 1594
Verbal behaviour 1367, 1430
Verbal communication 476, 496, 669, 1472, 1576
Verbs 505
Vico, G. 90
Victims 628, 3223, 5078, 5120, 5131, 5201, 5238, 5250, 5257, 5265, 5436
Victims of crime 5099, 5135, 5140, 5170, 5172, 5173, 5199, 5255, 5299, 5437
Victims of rape 1432, 1544, 5044
Victims of violence 2534, 2659, 5092, 5167, 5237, 5239, 5245, 5249, 5377, 5443, 5573, 5586, 5618
Videos 1555, 4732
Vietnamese 3335, 3345
Villages 1217, 1322, 1457, 2185, 2367, 2563, 2790, 2864, 3441, 3471, 3557, 3571, 3572, 3590, 3598, 3603, 3610, 3611, 3618, 3626, 3629, 3632, 3846, 3944, 5643, 5837
Villey, Michel 150
Violence 684, 693, 1374, 1587, 2660, 2692, 2786, 2917, 2985, 3187, 3188, 3194, 3218, 3229, 3722, 4773, 4818, 4868, 4905, 4989, 5089, 5125, 5131, 5135, 5154, 5155, 5160, 5169, 5174, 5177, 5226, 5242, 5256, 5304, 5305, 5433, 5434, 5435, 5436, 5437, 5438, 5439, 5441, 5442, 5444, 5445, 5446, 5447, 5448, 5449, 5622
  see also: Communal violence, Domestic violence, Political violence
Visual arts 1594, 1850
Visual communication 1437
Viticulture 4607

Vocabulary 1377
Vocational education 1811, 4523, 4563, 4564
Vocational guidance 4501
Vocational training 1730, 1738, 3324, 4528, 4565, 4569, 4570, 4576, 5493
Voluntary organizations 798, 831, 836, 3637, 4883, 5320, 5526, 5527
Voluntary work 429, 836, 2102, 3309, 3637, 4324, 4460
Voters 4991
Voting 200, 3425
Voting behaviour 1842, 1900, 2853, 4948, 4961, 4971, 4973, 4975, 4991
Voting turnout 4960, 4973
Vygotsky, L.S. 90
Wage bargaining 4592, 4597
Wage determination 4002
Wage differentials 910, 2793, 2795, 2809, 3211, 3231, 4001, 4003, 4010, 4016, 4018, 4037, 4067, 4282, 4319, 4323, 4345, 4609
Wage discrimination 4263, 4321, 4350
Wage structure 1672
Wages 2277, 2465, 3326, 3390, 4003, 4019, 4044, 4064, 4246, 4287, 4288, 4326, 4329, 4663
  see also: Minimum wages, Relative wages
Wagner, Richard 147
Waldheim, Kurt 3220
War 403, 565, 923, 943, 1602, 2097, 2112, 2742, 2933, 5021, 5033, 5417
Waste
  see: Hazardous waste
Water 3688
Water distribution 4584
Water resources 5015
Way of life 1847, 2356, 2481, 2964, 3429, 3541, 5678
Wealth 1151, 3617, 4032, 4059
Wealth distribution 4065
Weapons 2692, 4885
  see also: Nuclear weapons
Weber, Max 14, 25, 133, 134, 139, 142, 146, 147, 150, 159, 180, 182,

533

Subject index

183, 184, 186, 202, 203, 205, 1033, 1160, 1175, 1213, 1219, 1305, 3134
Welfare 1177, 1178, 2003, 2087, 2091, 2092, 2093, 2458, 2672, 2924, 3455, 3777, 3904, 4017, 4021, 4313, 4411, 4566, 5072, 5270, 5274, 5312, 5313, 5315, 5354, 5356, 5465, 5481, 5486, 5494, 5499, 5502, 5508, 5521, 5523, 5529, 5530, 5535, 5552
see also: Social welfare
Welfare economics 5501
Welfare policy 3983, 5270, 5480, 5497, 5505
Welfare state 286, 926, 1887, 1888, 2502, 2803, 3330, 3580, 3907, 4832, 4840, 5271, 5456, 5461, 5463, 5473, 5475, 5482, 5489, 5492, 5496, 5501, 5509, 5510, 5513, 5515, 5517, 5520, 5613, 5684
Well-being 292, 460, 493, 561, 585, 765, 2055, 2059, 2078, 2082, 2407, 2498, 2569, 2574, 2589, 3139, 3443, 4052, 4060, 4063, 4167, 4468, 5030, 5656, 5796
Welsh language 1568
West Indians 78, 3043, 3055, 3059, 3068
Western civilization 1239, 1345, 2422, 2775, 5011
Western countries 1047, 1841, 3196, 3936, 5032, 5142, 5429, 5453, 5506, 5559
Whales 4943
White collar workers 1905, 4419, 4668
Whites 475, 578, 719, 2331, 2354, 2405, 2485, 2586, 2605, 2680, 2867, 2920, 3028, 3031, 3147, 3149, 3162, 3184, 3190, 3198, 3203, 3231, 3233, 3241, 3796, 4003, 4032, 4402, 4789, 5281
Widows 2059
Williams, Raymond 1634
Witchcraft 5445
Wittgenstein, Ludwig 90, 137, 148, 149, 1425
Wives 536, 2554, 2584, 2595, 2694, 2823, 2850, 3328, 4324, 5257, 5573

Women 82, 144, 410, 499, 527, 578, 615, 656, 678, 685, 1021, 1131, 1143, 1161, 1351, 1387, 1391, 1524, 1609, 1637, 1690, 1723, 1782, 1858, 1860, 1917, 2085, 2126, 2162, 2218, 2242, 2262, 2273, 2311, 2317, 2397, 2405, 2420, 2425, 2432, 2444, 2467, 2494, 2495, 2504, 2534, 2556, 2576, 2577, 2578, 2597, 2599, 2607, 2614, 2650, 2655, 2659, 2664, 2665, 2668, 2675, 2676, 2677, 2681, 2682, 2685, 2689, 2690, 2692, 2694, 2695, 2696, 2699, 2700, 2701, 2703, 2704, 2708, 2709, 2710, 2711, 2712, 2713, 2714, 2729, 2744, 2752, 2759, 2763, 2769, 2773, 2775, 2777, 2778, 2786, 2787, 2789, 2800, 2804, 2818, 2829, 2832, 2837, 2840, 2841, 2844, 2848, 2855, 2859, 2861, 2862, 2863, 2868, 2874, 2875, 2876, 2877, 2879, 2882, 2891, 2898, 2900, 2902, 2903, 2905, 2909, 2915, 2919, 2920, 2923, 2924, 2925, 2929, 2933, 2936, 2949, 2951, 2953, 2957, 2969, 3001, 3002, 3006, 3022, 3055, 3064, 3124, 3203, 3260, 3262, 3268, 3273, 3348, 3359, 3397, 3398, 3499, 3500, 3562, 3628, 3688, 4021, 4023, 4192, 4318, 4320, 4332, 4333, 4336, 4344, 4346, 4356, 4651, 4720, 4726, 4728, 4752, 4902, 4905, 4928, 4971, 4994, 5094, 5121, 5130, 5136, 5160, 5167, 5173, 5177, 5178, 5210, 5238, 5239, 5242, 5245, 5248, 5249, 5250, 5253, 5255, 5256, 5257, 5265, 5266, 5273, 5276, 5365, 5377, 5391, 5418, 5419, 5443, 5449, 5586, 5618, 5649, 5659, 5825
see also: Married women, Rural women, Urban women
Women and politics 2502, 2705, 2736, 2760, 2787, 2799, 2831, 2833, 2853, 2855, 2858
Women workers 2267, 2271, 2277, 2479, 2569, 2661, 2670, 2680, 2687, 2767, 2790, 2792, 2794, 2797, 2801, 2812, 2813, 2816, 2817, 2824, 2830, 2833, 2836, 2838, 2842, 2851, 2854, 2856, 2868, 2901, 2910, 2921, 2932,

Subject index

2940, 2942, 3203, 3562, 3590, 3596, 4141, 4171, 4234, 4312, 4313, 4315, 4318, 4323, 4323, 4324, 4327, 4331, 4334, 4337, 4339, 4340, 4341, 4342, 4351, 4352, 4353, 4354, 4356, 4357, 4358, 4359, 4361, 4362, 4363, 4401, 4419, 4458, 4491, 4493, 4512, 4519, 4524, 4537, 4550, 4556, 4619, 4641, 4648, 5178, 5615, 5630
Women's education   1692, 2543, 2557, 2811, 2935, 5704
Women's emancipation   2792
Women's employment   2211, 2252, 2490, 2793, 2811, 2819, 2820, 2857, 2867, 2893, 2935, 4249, 4310, 4311, 4322, 4324, 4335, 4360, 4384, 4636
Women's health   2187, 2222, 2229, 2336, 2346, 2662, 2677, 2678, 2774, 5355, 5576, 5654, 5657, 5666, 5681, 5704, 5761, 5773
Women's movements   1282, 2724, 2743, 2745, 2747, 2749, 2762, 2765, 2779, 2780, 2781, 2782, 4867, 4909, 4938
Women's organizations   816, 2684, 4359
Women's participation   1309
Women's promotion   2767, 2798, 2929, 2936, 4493, 4555
Women's rights   2697, 2702, 2714, 2715, 2722, 2730, 2735, 2745, 2761, 2776, 2852, 2899, 2928, 3012, 4359
Women's role   914, 1125, 2706, 2867, 2891, 2903, 2921, 2923, 2927, 3628, 4361
Women's status   1188, 1970, 2273, 2678, 2679, 2693, 2790, 2845, 2847, 2855, 2858, 2860, 2875, 2892, 2893, 2914, 4316
Women's studies   68, 2663, 2691, 2716, 2741, 2744, 2748, 2950
Women's work   2669, 2822, 2918, 2919, 3628
Woodland   3606
Words   1492
Work accidents   4415, 4442, 4444
Work at home   2434, 2889

Work environment   4407, 4428, 4509, 5362
Work ethic   557, 1010, 4248, 4408, 4464
Work incentives   4426, 4437
Work motivation   907, 4397, 4408, 4449, 4460, 4463
Work organization   4099, 4136, 4405, 4410, 4432
Work place   54, 774, 810, 901, 1154, 1474, 3801, 3919, 4399, 4400, 4423, 4424, 4428, 4443, 4459, 4625, 4645, 4970, 5000
Work standards   4398
Work study   4745
Workers   625, 1853, 4082, 4113, 4298, 4303, 4308, 4580, 4659, 4682, 4713
see also: Agricultural workers, Commercial workers, Disabled workers, Domestic workers, Foreign workers, Industrial workers, Manual workers, Migrant workers, Office workers, Older workers, Professional workers, Seasonal workers, Self-employed workers, Service industry workers, Skilled workers, Social workers, Unskilled workers, White collar workers, Women workers, Young workers
Workers' movements   4612, 4674, 4680
Workers' participation   4413, 4426, 4446, 4709, 4710, 4711, 4712, 4713, 4714, 4715, 4716, 4718
Workers' representation   4640
Workers' rights   4641
Workers' stock ownership   4586, 4588, 4709
Working class   81, 1477, 1838, 1884, 1889, 2902, 2950, 3070, 3792, 4270, 4396, 4612, 4620, 4674, 4832, 4913
Working class culture   1108, 1892, 1905, 1918, 3040, 3670
Working conditions   1523, 4008, 4332, 4412, 4418, 4427, 4429, 4431, 4433, 4450, 4457, 4471, 4472, 4486, 4525
Working groups   649

535

Subject index

Working life   1932, 2403, 2554, 4396
Working mothers   914, 961, 2271, 2468, 2680, 2839, 2890, 2901, 2922, 4314, 4320, 4325, 4339, 4349, 4447, 5389
Working time   4402, 4439, 4451, 4458, 4745
Working time arrangements   2883, 4447, 4454
Works councils   4707
Works of art   1626
Workshops   4400
World Bank   4210
World economy   3051, 3404, 3934, 3973, 4109
World order   1074, 1270, 1310, 1388, 1927, 3982, 5010, 5017, 5018, 5020, 5023
World politics   5008
World population   2394
World religions   1318
  see also: Christianity, Hinduism, Islam, Judaism
World view   3441
World War One   3978
Wright, John K.   3464
Writers   1637
Writing   1378, 1395, 1403, 1419
Xenophobia   3196, 3218, 5438
Yezierska, Anzia   3055
Yoruba   2030
Young workers   4002, 4307
Youth   583, 749, 925, 970, 1122, 1234, 1325, 1522, 1536, 1680, 1695, 1719, 1970, 2040, 2125, 2127, 2129, 2130, 2132, 2136, 2137, 2138, 2139, 2140, 2141, 2142, 2143, 2144, 2146, 2148, 2149, 2150, 2151, 2154, 2160, 2163, 2164, 2165, 2166, 2167, 2169, 2170, 2171, 2172, 2173, 2174, 2175, 2176, 2177, 2178, 2421, 2451, 2552, 2690, 3082, 3194, 3197, 3218, 3278, 3329, 3540, 3541, 3724, 3728, 3825, 4053, 4127, 4307, 4365, 4372, 4739, 4992, 5064, 5213, 5226, 5261, 5287, 5298, 5304, 5435, 5438, 5536, 5601, 5626, 5841
  see also: Rural youth

Youth and politics   1650, 4882, 4886
Youth culture   1647, 1918, 2131, 2133, 2155, 2159, 2169
Youth employment   4259, 4279
Youth policy   2174
Youth unemployment   4368
Zapotec   684, 3132, 4939
Zoning   3872, 4859
Zulu   2425

INDEX DES MATIÈRES

Abandon d'enfant 5072, 5077, 5082, 5296
Abandon d'études 1773
Aborigènes 1859, 1980, 1984, 3239
Absentéisme 4420
Absorptions 4290
Abus de drogues 1196, 1549, 1964, 2145, 4465, 5041, 5224, 5235, 5266, 5282, 5368, 5370, 5372, 5375, 5381, 5382, 5384, 5386, 5387, 5390, 5391, 5393, 5394, 5396, 5397, 5399, 5400, 5401, 5403, 5405, 5407, 5412, 5413, 5416, 5418, 5420, 5421
Abus des âgés 5046, 5236
Accès à l'éducation 1691, 1781
Accès à l'emploi 4253, 4376
Accès à l'information 430, 1452, 2308, 3023
Accès au marché 4176
Accidents
 see: Accidents de circulation, Accidents du travail, Accidents nucléaires
Accidents de circulation 395, 5037
Accidents du travail 4415, 4442, 4444
Accidents nucléaires 3257, 3460
Accomplissement scolaire 997, 1010, 1638, 1653, 1655, 1657, 1677, 1681, 1741, 1775, 1780, 1911, 2412, 3202, 4498, 4520
Accords de paiement 2469
Acculturation 1046, 3055, 3100
Accumulation de capital 3884
Acquisition de connaissances 148, 507, 508, 529, 697, 735, 742, 766, 793, 822, 1377, 1475, 1666, 1789, 2067, 2752, 3979, 4089, 4151, 4997, 5133, 5581
Acquisition du langage 148, 505, 507, 1461, 1463, 1470, 1475, 1486, 1561, 1566

Actif 793
Action collective 200, 301, 715, 730, 3555, 4324, 4862, 4898, 4923, 4945, 5126
Action politique 124, 832, 2705, 4883
Action sociale 32, 143, 182, 406, 1174, 1929, 1931, 3531, 3615, 3970, 4920, 5308
Action syndicale 4680
Actionnaires 4202
Actionnariat ouvrier 4586, 4588, 4709
Activistes 1853
Activité bancaire 4115
Activité de construction 4593
Activité e´conomique 3429, 3995
Activité politique 2853, 4863, 4913, 4935
Adaptation au changement 518, 3073
Adaptation culturelle 420
Adaptation des immigrants 2138, 3180, 3317, 3318, 3319, 3321, 3329, 3332, 3336, 3337, 3338, 3340, 3341, 3343, 3344, 3349, 3350, 3620
Adaptation sociale 3058
Adhérents au parti 4951
Adhésion syndicale 4649, 4655, 4658, 4663, 4675, 4688, 4689, 4694, 4700
Administration 891, 1375, 1741, 4849, 4858, 5720, 5840
 see also: Administration de l'enseignement, Administration de la santé, Administration du développement, Administration financière, Administration publique, Administration scolaire
Administration centrale 2657, 3767
Administration de la santé 5709
Administration de l'enseignement 1714, 1717, 1736
Administration du développement 2669

Index des matières

Administration financière 4203
Administration locale 327, 1930, 3648, 3764, 3819, 3820, 3830, 3876, 3893, 3920, 4575, 4595, 4845, 4848, 4849, 4855, 4856, 4862, 5270, 5287, 5485, 5528
Administration publique 4214, 4564, 4806, 4842, 4843, 4845, 4846, 4850, 4851, 4852, 4853, 4854, 4857
Administration scolaire 1737, 1745
Adolescence 755, 2094, 2125, 2158, 2232, 5414, 5428
Adolescents 280, 579, 629, 705, 1612, 1639, 2041, 2097, 2107, 2126, 2128, 2134, 2135, 2145, 2147, 2152, 2153, 2156, 2157, 2161, 2162, 2163, 2166, 2168, 2207, 2296, 2411, 2421, 2518, 2616, 2617, 2618, 2912, 2986, 3009, 3010, 3109, 3724, 4173, 4465, 4882, 5080, 5094, 5279, 5291, 5310, 5389, 5539, 5620
Adoption d'enfant 2496, 2503, 2614, 2646, 3024, 5594
Adorno, Theodor 977
Adultes 469, 666, 735, 1417, 2041, 2356, 2378, 2399, 2488, 2497, 2546, 2643, 4025, 4721, 5556
Affectation des ressources 623, 761, 2180, 2330, 3086, 3502, 3975, 4034, 4210, 5463, 5487, 5824
Affiliation 565, 1303, 3252
see also: Affiliation religieuse
Affiliation religieuse 1303
Africains 3042, 3320
Âge 930, 1412, 1632, 1802, 1814, 2044, 2045, 2046, 2050, 2051, 2053, 2054, 2055, 2056, 2058, 2059, 2063, 2066, 2067, 2068, 2069, 2070, 2071, 2072, 2073, 2077, 2078, 2079, 2081, 2082, 2083, 2085, 2354, 2394, 2395, 2401, 2410, 2432, 2465, 2508, 2570, 2612, 2635, 3291, 3376, 3399, 3517, 3728, 3918, 4054, 4306, 4733, 4745, 4973, 5468, 5470, 5474, 5478, 5483, 5519, 5554, 5708, 5721, 5723, 5726, 5730, 5731, 5732, 5736, 5740, 5742, 5743, 5744, 5748, 5800
see also: Abus des âgés, Aide aux gens âgés
Âge
see: Vieillesse
Âge au mariage 2542, 2543, 2551, 2557, 2599, 2875
Agression personnelle 544, 684, 693, 705, 706, 1771, 1778, 2895, 3014, 4982, 5433
Agression sexuelle 594, 735, 1432, 1557, 2123, 2461, 2692, 2771, 5044, 5069, 5076, 5078, 5079, 5086, 5088, 5094, 5130, 5157, 5200, 5221, 5230, 5292, 5445, 5561, 5586
Agriculteurs 1099, 3385, 3561, 3562, 3581, 3592
Agriculture 1334, 3491, 3558, 3568, 3569, 3580, 3606, 3715, 4310
Agriculture à temps partiel 4341
Agriexploitation 3078, 3560, 3607, 4323
see also: Agriculture à temps partiel, Agriexploitation collective, Petite exploitation agricole
Agriexploitation collective 3607
Agroindustrie 4087, 4603
Aide 2805, 3828, 3945
see also: Aide à l'étranger, Aide au développement, Aide de l'État
Aide à l'enfance 1957, 2089, 2091, 2113, 2114, 2124, 2143, 2403, 2478, 2491, 2521, 2609, 2645, 2647, 2862, 2890, 4339, 4343, 4459, 4486, 4494, 4609, 5072, 5521, 5522, 5523, 5524, 5525, 5526, 5527, 5528, 5529, 5531, 5532, 5533, 5534, 5535, 5536, 5537, 5552, 5558, 5569, 5582, 5588, 5600, 5601, 5604, 5620, 5666
Aide à l'étranger 4211
Aide au développement 3945
Aide aux gens âgés 2040, 2043, 2047, 2050, 2062, 2065, 2074, 2084, 2401, 2415, 2432, 2612, 2863, 4494, 5145, 5236, 5450, 5460, 5462, 5470, 5474, 5478, 5479, 5484, 5519, 5718, 5728, 5733, 5734, 5735, 5737, 5738, 5739, 5741, 5761
Aide de l'État 3828

Index des matières

Aires métropolitaines 2599, 3648, 3653, 3684, 3690, 3725, 3759, 3799, 3819, 3831, 3835, 3850, 3854, 3881, 3915
Ajustement industriel 4126
Ajustement structurel 2669, 2786, 3927, 3931, 4056, 4210, 4224, 5006, 5350, 5780
Alcool 1029, 2348, 2349, 2355, 2534, 2634, 5117, 5182, 5360, 5365, 5367, 5379, 5380, 5396, 5423, 5425
Alcoolisme 632, 1137, 4364, 5239, 5266, 5280, 5359, 5361, 5362, 5364, 5366, 5368, 5371, 5373, 5377, 5388, 5391, 5392, 5395, 5402, 5408, 5409, 5419, 5424, 5426, 5541, 5560, 5568
Algèbre 261
Algorithme 318, 729
Aliénation 1094, 1096, 1097, 1253
Alimentation 584, 595, 1110, 1115
Aliments 2376, 4162, 4187, 5597
Alliances 826, 1091
Allocations de maternité 5666
Almond, Marc 2992
Alphabétisation 1385, 1395, 1405, 1461, 1640, 1645, 1647, 1663, 1666, 1728, 2191, 4275, 5735
Altruisme 603, 604, 627, 815, 1132, 1206, 5773
Aménagement de l'espace 3786
Aménagement d'habitation 1938, 2004, 2100, 2443, 2446, 2513, 2583, 2616, 3512, 3744, 4021
Aménagement du temps de travail 2883, 4447, 4454
Aménagement urbain 2309, 2828, 3225, 3539, 3743, 3758, 3759, 3763, 3790, 3808, 3809, 3813, 3815, 3816, 3818, 3822, 3824, 3826, 3827, 3834, 3838, 3841, 3844, 3845, 3848, 3849, 3852, 3853, 3854, 3855, 3859, 3860, 3861, 3864, 3865, 3872, 3873, 3877, 3878, 3879, 3880, 3882, 3883, 3885, 3886, 3887, 3888, 3889, 3890, 3892, 3893, 3899, 3912, 3920, 3939, 4223, 5491
Amérindiens 1859, 3102, 3115, 4303, 5371, 5424, 5432, 5563

see also: Amérindiens du Nord, Amérindiens du Sud
Amérindiens du Nord 1097, 1110, 3032, 3038, 3085
Amérindiens du Sud 1494, 3115, 3902
Amitié 621, 631, 678, 2135, 2145, 2447, 2624
Analyse causale 2008
Analyse comparative 25, 237, 272, 911, 1753, 1927, 1973, 2377, 2536, 2672, 2803, 3234, 3538, 4018, 4432, 4740, 4901, 4948, 5001, 5142
Analyse conjoncturelle 781
Analyse de discours 162, 276, 975, 997, 1365, 1374, 1385, 1403, 1434, 1466, 1472, 1490, 1537, 1576, 2756, 2904, 3202, 5009
Analyse de régression 278, 299, 308, 319, 320, 1982, 3997, 5568, 5635
Analyse de réseau 260, 298, 316, 713, 760, 773, 813, 909, 1493, 4079, 4117, 4372
Analyse de systèmes 768
Analyse des données 56, 263, 264, 266, 267, 268, 271, 273, 274, 275, 279, 282, 283, 287, 289, 293, 294, 295, 300, 301, 304, 305, 306, 310, 312, 314, 318, 320, 322, 323, 326, 744, 2276, 3248, 5462
Analyse des politiques gouvernementales 5050
Analyse du discours 2631
Analyse économique 291, 2260, 4324
Analyse factorielle 283
Analyse fonctionnelle 3874
Analyse historique 25
Analyse marxiste 126, 153, 204, 1893, 2756
Analyse mathématique 2009, 5104
Analyse multidimensionnelle 2033
Analyse multivariée 294, 748, 2059, 2213
Analyse organisationnelle 260, 775, 780, 782, 795, 885, 1222, 1277, 4548
Analyse par agrégats 785
Analyse par grappe 313

Index des matières

Analyse qualitative   256, 306, 313, 1780
Analyse quantitative   256, 294, 408, 4377
Analyse régionale   2027, 2324, 3894, 4068, 4068, 4617
Analyse secondaire   51, 60, 64, 67, 71, 76, 4515
Analyse sociologique   285, 422, 1970, 1992, 4161, 4205
Analyse statistique   76, 1922, 3025
Analyse structurale   261, 1018
Analyse transactionnelle   617
Analyse transculturelle   302, 338, 416, 1009, 1120, 1176, 1203, 1615, 2698, 2873, 2900, 4436, 5386
Analyse transnationale   338, 3201
Anarchie   988
Anarchisme   4778, 5100
Angoisse   581, 641, 2307, 3299
Animaux   370, 636, 1118, 4559, 4884, 5060, 5796, 5820
  see also: Animaux domestiques, Moutons
Animaux domestiques   2526
Anonymat   71
Anorexie   2153, 2664, 2718
Anthropogéographie   2733, 3292, 3463, 3475, 3476, 3504
Anthropologie   5, 210, 1061, 2428, 5112
  see also: Anthropologie culturelle, Anthropologie économique, Anthropologie linguistique, Anthropologie médicale, Anthropologie philosophique, Anthropologie sociale, Anthropologie urbaine
Anthropologie biologique   2049
Anthropologie culturelle   986
Anthropologie économique   4073
Anthropologie linguistique   1490
Anthropologie médicale   1110, 1335, 2313, 2345, 3007, 5373, 5411
Anthropologie philosophique   2885, 5028
Anthropologie sociale   605, 1025, 1051, 2131

Anthropologie urbaine   3721, 3735, 3762, 4073
Anticipations de rôle   898
Antillais   78, 3043, 3055, 3059, 3068
Antiquité
  see: Antiquité romaine
Antiquité romaine   1300
Antisémitisme   309, 941, 997, 3044, 3193, 3195, 3202, 3220, 3221, 3240
Apartheid   1330, 1930, 3057, 3189, 3214, 4818
Apatrides   3276
Apparence physique   606, 608, 613, 630, 1857, 2648, 2973, 2977, 4016
Appartenance au groupe   714, 725, 734, 753
Appartenance ecclésiale   1274
Appel   5213, 5298
Apprentissage   4148
Aptitude   375, 543
Arabes   643, 2411, 3865, 3944
Arbitrage   688, 718, 4577, 4629, 4646, 4647
  see also: Arbitrage forcé
Arbitrage forcé   4646
Arbres   2196
Architecture   998, 1594, 1598, 1633, 2671, 3576, 3680, 3891, 3955
  see also: Architecture domestique, Architecture urbaine
Architecture domestique   1117, 3773
Architecture urbaine   3650
Arendt, Hannah   2739
Argent   836, 1391, 4035
Argot   1368
Armée de terre   4994
Armes   2692, 4885
  see also: Armes nucléaires
Armes á feu   1203, 4811
Armes nucléaires   4945
Art contemporain   2040
Art décoratif   1605
Art dramatique   1594
Artisans   4324
Artist   1629, 1850
Arts   439, 993, 1038, 1111, 1256, 1604, 1607, 1609, 1615, 1627, 1629, 1632, 1636, 1943

Index des matières

see also: Art contemporain, Art dramatique, Arts visuels, Histoire de l'art, Oeuvres d'art, Sociologie de l'art
  1034, 1480, 1595, 1603
Arts visuels   1594, 1850
ASEAN   4594
Asiatiques   578, 660, 3025, 3031, 3033, 3036, 3041, 3043, 3073, 3085, 3101, 3109, 3114, 3216, 3246, 3322, 3336, 3393, 4318, 4512, 4789
Asile   3055, 3427
Aspects juridiques   371, 444, 810, 1168, 1190, 1193, 1201, 1212, 4639, 4647, 4814, 4902, 5213, 5298, 5394, 5458, 5787, 5794
Assimilation culturelle   1483, 1871, 3036, 3160
Assimilation des immigrants   3055, 3060, 3270, 3323, 3325, 3330, 3332, 3334, 3335, 3338, 3346, 3347, 3348, 5851
Assimilation ethnique   3160
Assimilation sociale   3327
Assistance   3945, 5480
Assistance socio-psychologique   409, 642, 700, 2421, 5206, 5559, 5560, 5561, 5567, 5572, 5577, 5590
Associations   775, 798, 3374, 3581, 3951, 4653
Associations de quartier   3704, 4941
Assurance maladie   2326, 5755, 5761, 5771, 5773, 5783, 5844
Assurances
  see: Assurance maladie
Astrologie   2527
Ateliers   4400
Atlas   3778, 5507
Attitude envers le travail   956, 1523, 4407, 4409, 4414, 4455, 4478, 4586, 4701
Attitude moraliste envers le travail   557, 1010, 4248, 4408, 4464
Attitudes   47, 102, 109, 240, 281, 304, 310, 341, 345, 374, 486, 506, 653, 659, 749, 917, 918, 919, 920, 921, 922, 923, 927, 929, 930, 931, 932, 933, 935, 936, 937, 942, 943, 944, 949, 951, 953, 954, 957, 958, 960, 961, 965, 968, 970, 971, 1133, 1136, 1223, 1243, 1366, 1382, 1383, 1846, 2065, 2127, 2156, 2160, 2178, 2235, 2430, 2476, 2559, 2562, 2572, 2619, 2765, 2846, 2866, 2998, 3001, 3002, 3149, 3218, 3240, 3294, 3434, 3449, 3459, 3489, 3986, 4113, 4171, 4365, 4461, 4610, 4789, 4950, 5094, 5284, 5363, 5438, 5450, 5540, 5551
  see also: Attitudes patronales, Attitudes politiques, Attitudes raciales, Attitudes religieuses
Attitudes patronales   758, 866, 3979, 4410
Attitudes politiques   200, 925, 939, 1263, 1650, 1835, 1900, 2039, 4986
Attitudes raciales   3040, 3147, 3153, 3165, 3166, 3191, 3194, 3198, 3199, 3206
Attitudes religieuses   482, 1262, 2971
Attraction interpersonnelle   653, 2542
Auditeurs   409
Augustine [Saint]   148
Autoassistance   499, 3635, 4366, 5544
Autobiographies   228, 257, 259, 528, 540, 2960
Autobus   3918
Autodétermination   4775
Autodéveloppement   5469
Autogestion   3522, 4717
Automobile   1100, 4074, 4185, 5037, 5302, 5360
Autonomie   1760, 4713
Autoritarisme   544, 545, 977, 1034, 5445
Autorité   54, 184, 778, 1236, 2658, 2785, 2806, 4159, 5777
  see also: Autorité politique, Autorités religieuses
Autorité politique   4808
Autorités religieuses   1222
Avortement   563, 603, 935, 1266, 2181, 2205, 2206, 2208, 2210, 2215, 2221, 2225, 2226, 2229, 2233, 2234, 2235, 2243, 2715, 2853, 4902, 4988, 5044, 5060, 5784, 5785, 5786, 5819, 5823

Index des matières

Bahamón Dussán, Augusto 5398
Baisse de la fécondité 2280, 2287, 2294, 2299
Baisse de la mortalité 2481
Bakhtin, M.M. 90, 165
Baleines 4943
Bandes 749, 5090, 5154, 5378
Bandes dessinées 1361
Banque mondiale 4210
Banques 4198, 4207
 see also: Banque mondiale, Caisses d'épargne
Banti, Anna 2693
Bases de données 74, 76, 4553
Basques 2131
Bateson, Gregory 454, 1256, 2409
Bâtiment 505, 1231, 1598, 2309, 3576, 3844, 3880
Baudrillard, Jean 10, 118
Beaux-parents 2455
Beck, Frank 5582
Becker, Gary 200
Bédouin 3530
Benjamin, Walter 131
Besoins de logement 354, 4911, 5272, 5470
Besoins d'éducation 1709
Besoins fondamentaux 3898, 4061, 5329
 see also: Besoins de logement
Bible 2876
Bibliographies 74, 82, 1501, 1502, 1923, 2341, 3088, 4042, 4293, 4810, 5359, 5736, 5800
Bibliothèques 1817
Biculturalisme 1031
Bien-être 292, 460, 493, 561, 585, 765, 2055, 2059, 2078, 2082, 2407, 2498, 2569, 2574, 2589, 3139, 3443, 4052, 4060, 4063, 4167, 4468, 5030, 5656, 5796
 1177, 1178, 2003, 2087, 2091, 2092, 2093, 2458, 2672, 2924, 3455, 3777, 3904, 4017, 4021, 4313, 4411, 4566, 5072, 5270, 5274, 5312, 5313, 5315, 5354, 5356, 5465, 5481, 5486, 5494, 5499, 5502, 5508, 5521, 5523, 5529, 5530, 5535, 5552
 see also: Bien-être social
Bien-être social 248, 5458, 5464, 5472, 5472, 5500, 5507, 5525
Biens durables 4185
Biens publics 3972, 3975, 4859, 4944
Bière 4072
Bilinguisme 1561, 1562, 1564, 1565, 1566, 1568
Binet, Alfred 404
Biographies 81, 228, 259, 1394, 1838, 2076, 4774
Biologie
 see: Biologie humaine
Biologie humaine 2247
Biotechnologie 1334, 3432, 5801
Blancs 475, 578, 719, 2331, 2354, 2405, 2485, 2586, 2605, 2680, 2867, 2920, 3028, 3031, 3147, 3149, 3162, 3184, 3190, 3198, 3203, 3231, 3233, 3241, 3796, 4003, 4032, 4402, 4789, 5281
Bodin, Jean 150
Bogdanov, Alexander 151
Bohémiens 3113, 3120, 3121, 3130, 3215, 3235, 3803
Boissons
 see: Boissons alcoolisées
Boissons alcoolisées 2175, 5344
 see also: Bière
Bonheur 474, 2544
Bouddhisme 495, 1130, 1218, 1257, 1317
Bouddhistes 1308
Bourdieu, Pierre 1028, 1676
Bourgeoisie 1849
Bourse 4200, 4204, 4709
Bourses d'étude 3042
Brasserie 4072
Braudel, Fernand 150
Britanniques 3055
Brodolini, Giacomo 5482
Browne, Robert S. 3244, 3507
Buber, Martin 2409
Budgets 270
 see also: Budgets temps
Budgets temps 4745
Buffon, G.L.L. 2

Index des matières

Bureaucratie 779, 796, 800, 811, 842, 913, 4073, 4243, 5697
Burt, Cyril 1500
Bush, George 403, 5021
Buveurs 3233, 5380
Cadres 787, 858, 2840, 2929, 2936, 4252, 4290, 4434, 4436, 4449, 4527, 4529, 4532, 4533, 4534, 4610, 5630, 5646
  3198, 4092, 4397, 4502, 4509, 4519, 4526, 4858
Cadres supérieurs 900, 2798, 4519
Café 4076, 4077, 4083
Caisses de sécurité sociale 4391
Caisses d'épargne 825
Campagne 4076
Campagne électorale 2804, 4946, 4947, 4960, 4964, 4980, 4985
Camps de concentration 5188
Camus, Albert 459
Cancer 932, 2317, 2382, 2774, 3430, 3940, 5773
Candidats 2787, 2804
Capital 2809, 3727, 3791, 3884, 5005
  see also: Capitaux étrangers
Capitalisme 1074, 1151, 1275, 1305, 1864, 1881, 1888, 1891, 1975, 2999, 3226, 3719, 3967, 3977, 3978, 3981, 3983, 3987, 3990, 4080, 4104, 4270, 4308, 4464, 4765, 4784, 5036, 5760
Capitaux étrangers 4229
Caractère 95
  see also: Caractère national
Caractère national 378, 1020, 1080, 5024
Carnavals 1613
Cartes géographiques 534
Cartographie 238, 3484
Castes 1782, 1843, 1861, 1869, 1884, 2935, 5639
Catastrophes naturelles 672, 3458, 5038
Cather, Willa 3055
Catholicisme 1266, 1284, 1287, 2540, 2541, 5829
Catholiques 1264, 1275, 1278, 1285, 1289, 2579
Causalité 8, 102, 109

Causes de décès 2365, 2366, 2385, 2387
Cécité 2328
Célibataires 2388, 2784, 2915, 5272
Censure 1034, 1439, 2719, 2750
Centralisation 4848
Centre villes 4075
Centres de recherche 70, 252
Cerveau 517, 1369, 5791
Chances d'éducation 1746, 1834
Chances d'obtenir un emploi 3379, 4336, 4376, 4379, 5531
Changement culturel 1077, 1217, 1391, 1616, 3132, 5229
Changement d'alimentation 1104, 1114
Changement d'attitude 766, 920, 921, 2476, 4399
Changement démographique 1698, 1986, 1990, 1991, 1992, 1996, 2001, 2006, 2015, 2018, 2021, 2026, 2029, 2031, 2033, 2179, 2184, 2186, 2191, 2192, 2193, 2196, 2198, 2203, 2205, 2276, 2291, 2389, 2453, 3286, 3357, 3413, 3565, 3641, 3666
Changement d'organisation 774, 779, 790, 804, 809, 819, 820, 821, 825, 828, 829, 833, 838, 840, 848, 860, 868, 871, 900, 955, 2898, 4155, 4452, 5648, 5677
Changement économique 1008, 1856, 1916, 1939, 1967, 3977, 4043, 4055, 4064, 4102, 4120, 4140, 4308, 4627, 4771, 5096
Changement linguistique 1384
Changement politique 976, 1478, 1933, 1936, 1939, 1970, 1975, 2150, 2656, 2657, 3057, 3992, 4005, 4102, 4388, 4595, 4638, 4656, 4818, 4826, 4829, 4834, 4839, 5059
Changement religieux 1220, 1232, 1263, 1270, 1277, 1286
Changement social 35, 94, 220, 406, 701, 774, 974, 976, 1000, 1008, 1047, 1049, 1076, 1092, 1211, 1217, 1236, 1313, 1317, 1478, 1602, 1618, 1640, 1680, 1695, 1719, 1922, 1925, 1927, 1928, 1929, 1930, 1931, 1932,

Index des matières

1933, 1934, 1936, 1937, 1939, 1940, 1941, 1942, 1944, 1945, 1947, 1948, 1949, 1950, 1952, 1953, 1954, 1955, 1956, 1957, 1958, 1960, 1961, 1962, 1965, 1967, 1968, 1969, 1970, 1972, 1975, 1976, 1978, 2050, 2079, 2130, 2136, 2150, 2171, 2176, 2273, 2444, 2493, 2506, 2514, 2530, 2610, 2676, 2710, 2810, 2888, 2903, 2914, 3064, 3142, 3187, 3367, 3544, 3575, 3600, 3609, 3611, 3620, 3643, 3646, 3702, 3728, 3779, 3863, 3955, 4005, 4056, 4292, 4311, 4350, 4403, 4477, 4680, 4748, 4760, 4785, 4829, 4834, 4874, 4917, 4918, 4920, 4925, 4928, 5032, 5161, 5229, 5340, 5435
Changement structurel   3331, 3708, 3834, 4136, 5097, 5777
Changement technologique   1349, 3884, 4145, 4151, 4152, 4153, 4155, 4270, 4302, 4430, 4451, 4506, 4712
Chansons populaires   1616
Chants
  see: Chansons populaires, Chants religieux
Chants religieux   1287
Charisme   902, 1275, 4984
Châtiment   654, 960, 1182, 1269, 5095, 5101, 5111, 5180, 5187, 5190, 5193, 5196, 5205, 5215, 5220, 5235, 5300, 5420
Chauffage mondial   3450
Chefs d'entreprise   2797, 4102, 4103, 4110, 4120, 4135, 4141, 4185, 4567
Chemins de fer   3915
Cherchant revenus d'investissement   3782
Chin, Yao-chi   29
Chinois   411, 475, 2527, 3295, 3347, 4011, 4305, 5116
Chirurgie   2229
Chodorow, Nancy   2509
Choix collectif   640, 1173, 4780
Choix du conjoint   608, 2421, 2522, 2561, 2600, 2796, 2807, 2869, 2945, 2977, 2981, 3003
Choix d'une profession   4550, 5553

Choix rationnel   200, 234, 441, 1081, 1245, 4963, 5119
Chômage   449, 2137, 3238, 3377, 4040, 4247, 4259, 4275, 4336, 4364, 4367, 4369, 4370, 4371, 4372, 4376, 4377, 4379, 4381, 4382, 4383, 4384, 4386, 4388, 4389, 4390, 4391, 4392, 4393, 4394, 5091, 5315, 5364
  see also: Chômage des jeunes, Chômage frictionnel, Chômage structurel, Chômage urbain
Chômage des jeunes   4368
Chômage frictionnel   4387
Chômage partiel   3096
Chômage structurel   4369, 4387
Chômage urbain   3651, 4375, 4385
Chômeurs   2127, 4210, 4312, 4365, 4366, 4373, 4378, 4395
Chrétiens   971, 1302
Christaller, Walter   1441
Christianisme   28, 1214, 1262, 1267, 1268, 1270, 1272, 1273, 1279, 1281, 1294, 1303, 1316, 1326, 1328, 1332, 1674, 5819
  see also: Catholicisme, Pentecôtisme
Cinéma   1608, 2956, 2996
Circoncision   2324
Circonscriptions administratives   5777
Circulation   3894, 3914, 3917
  see also: Circulation routière
Circulation routière   3917
Citoyenneté   1021, 1812, 2665, 2672, 2803, 2993, 3139, 3260, 3271, 3722, 4471, 4762, 4809, 4949, 4952, 4980, 5456
Citoyens   327, 444, 3461, 3649, 4869, 4870, 4933
Civilisation   302, 1003, 1023, 1037, 1054, 1120, 1145, 1229, 1323, 1535, 1966, 2741, 4080, 4958
  see also: Civilisation contemporaine, Civilisation islamique, Civilisation occidentale
Civilisation contemporaine   1051, 1057, 1145, 1826
Civilisation islamique   55, 1310
Civilisation occidentale   1239, 1345, 2422, 2775, 5011

Index des matières

Clans 3610
Classe 54, 133, 144, 440, 939, 1022, 1111, 1635, 1643, 1746, 1764, 1834, 1835, 1841, 1861, 1864, 1877, 1878, 1879, 1880, 1881, 1882, 1889, 1890, 1894, 1896, 1898, 1902, 1906, 1909, 1910, 1911, 1913, 1914, 1915, 1917, 1918, 1940, 2119, 2173, 2323, 2342, 2672, 2763, 2826, 2839, 2890, 2909, 2918, 3085, 3170, 3198, 3222, 3226, 3509, 3529, 3873, 4037, 4047, 4051, 4057, 4066, 4653, 4727, 4732, 4773, 4784, 4826, 4895, 4906, 4913, 4922, 5105, 5406, 5690, 5754
see also: Bourgeoisie, Classe dirigeante, Classe inférieure, Classe moyenne, Classe ouvrière, Sous-classe
Classe dirigeante 1356, 1565
Classe inférieure 1122
Classe moyenne 947, 1117, 1707, 1870, 1889, 1891, 1899, 1901, 1904, 2167, 2918, 3788, 4104, 5175, 5406
Classe ouvrière 81, 1477, 1838, 1884, 1889, 2902, 2950, 3070, 3792, 4270, 4396, 4612, 4620, 4674, 4832, 4913
Classification 312, 882, 2196, 3028, 3797, 3798
Clergé 1299
Clientélisme 842, 3615, 4473
Climat 2366, 5093
Clubs 763
Coalition 1958
Cocaïne 5109, 5370, 5374, 5415
Code civil 1122
Code déontologique médical 1118, 2239, 5736, 5789, 5791, 5793, 5795, 5798, 5800, 5802, 5803, 5804, 5806, 5808, 5809, 5810, 5813, 5815, 5816, 5820, 5821, 5822, 5825, 5829
Code pénal 1201, 3656
Cognition 105, 366, 370, 424, 502, 510, 511, 513, 515, 516, 535, 680, 750, 782, 828, 873, 1134, 1639, 4162, 5008
see also: Cognition sociale
Cognition sociale 102, 109, 506, 659, 662, 667, 766, 917

Cohabitation 2525, 2547, 2567, 2575, 2610, 4337
Cohésion du groupe 728
Cohortes 2249, 2293
Coleman, James 127
Collectivisme 455, 3603
Collectivité 244, 335, 369, 406, 717, 811, 1075, 1138, 1540, 1582, 1689, 1703, 1713, 1752, 1844, 1850, 1978, 2162, 3186, 3342, 3370, 3506, 3513, 3516, 3519, 3520, 3521, 3522, 3524, 3529, 3532, 3534, 3589, 3626, 3632, 3681, 3682, 3764, 4082, 4212, 4761, 4836, 4859, 4949, 4970, 5041, 5043, 5097, 5185, 5237, 5239, 5377, 5458, 5555, 5578, 5707, 5712, 5831
see also: Collectivités locales, Collectivités rurales, Collectivités urbaines, Communauté scientifique, Communautés ethniques, Communautés religieuses
Collectivités locales 3533, 3535, 3572, 3670, 3825, 4453
Collectivités rurales 1217, 2404, 2530, 2563, 2662, 2910, 3515, 3542, 3551, 3563, 3573, 3591, 3595, 3598, 3620, 3643, 5837
Collectivités urbaines 1949, 3176, 3379, 3502, 3504, 3517, 3533, 3542, 3649, 3656, 3678, 3703, 3713, 3720, 3728, 3730, 3764, 3848, 3856, 4201, 4862
Collège électoral 5112
Colonialisme 378, 1837, 1891
Colonies 1022
Colonisation 3954
Colonisation rurale 3530, 3751
Cols blancs 1905, 4419, 4668
Columbus, Christopher 1622
Comédie 1433
Comités d'entreprise 4707
Commerce 1659
  4137, 4673
  see also: Commerce agricole, Commerce de détail, Commerce international, Libre échange, Tourisme international
Commerce agricole 3575

Index des matières

Commerce de détail 4106, 4131, 4163, 4180, 4184, 4573, 5174, 5447
Commerce international 4074
see also: Importations
Commercialisation 1134, 1167, 1667, 3868, 4170, 4186
see also: Commercialisation des aliments, Publicité
Commercialisation des aliments 3575
Communalisme 3542
Communauté scientifique 1337, 1342, 4540
Communautés ethniques 3047, 3057, 3125, 3191, 4512
Communautés européennes 1195, 1209, 2765, 3191, 3407, 3418, 3561, 3588, 4524, 4547, 4712, 4716, 4940, 5510
see also: Marché unique européen
Communautés religieuses 1235, 1302, 1304, 3146
Communes 3512
Communication 386, 676, 689, 696, 701, 723, 762, 803, 861, 1043, 1310, 1363, 1369, 1375, 1378, 1393, 1402, 1403, 1410, 1412, 1413, 1414, 1417, 1420, 1424, 1427, 1430, 1436, 1438, 1446, 1449, 1458, 1459, 1460, 1472, 1504, 1505, 1506, 1508, 1514, 1518, 1521, 1525, 1576, 1926, 2421, 2829, 2976, 3823, 3824, 4079, 4453, 4477, 4963, 4977
see also: Communication de masse, Communication interculturelle, Communication interpersonnelle, Communication non-verbale, Communication orale, Communication politique, Communication verbale, Communication visuelle
Communication confidentielle 4814
Communication de masse 896, 1501, 1502, 1508, 1509, 1558
Communication interculturelle 416, 1009, 1026, 1054, 1474, 5011, 5030
Communication interpersonnelle 601, 607, 637, 638, 661, 674, 1398, 1417, 1465, 1476, 1495

Communication non-verbale 393, 687, 1377, 1487
Communication orale 671, 1364, 1365, 1466, 1490
Communication politique 1409, 1519, 4946, 4947
Communication verbale 476, 496, 669, 1472, 1576
Communication visuelle 1437
Communisme 1881, 2858, 4760, 4769, 4822, 4832
Compagnies d'assurance 4358
Compensation 3975, 4415, 4580, 4705, 5201
Compétences 432, 665, 1027, 1133, 2618, 3384, 4153, 4489, 4490, 4492, 4564, 4565, 4566, 4568
Compétitivité 1751
Complexe militaro-industriel 4082
Comportement antisocial 2168, 5285
Comportement collectif 609, 784, 1929, 4915
Comportement culturel 380
Comportement de classe 1900
Comportement de l'étudiant 660, 681, 1649
Comportement de l'organisation 37, 758, 788, 791, 799, 803, 815, 818, 820, 832, 834, 835, 838, 855, 857, 858, 861, 867, 2812, 3296, 4095, 4176, 4471, 4828
Comportement du consommateur 2602, 4158, 4159, 4160, 4162, 4163, 4164, 4171, 4173, 4174, 4177, 4182, 4183, 4187, 4189, 4191, 4196
Comportement du groupe 545, 664, 702, 716, 733, 756, 1029, 2586, 2587, 3104
Comportement économique 3959, 4046, 4093, 4199
Comportement électoral 1842, 1900, 2853, 4948, 4961, 4971, 4973, 4975, 4991
Comportement en groupe 746
Comportement individuel 432, 441, 511, 906, 1496, 2125, 3250, 4094
Comportement judiciaire 1210
Comportement politique 4976, 4986

Index des matières

Comportement rationnel 4963
Comportement religieux 1245, 1248, 1325
Comportement sexuel 240, 353, 641, 673, 937, 2156, 2162, 2212, 2233, 2240, 2254, 2296, 2313, 2316, 2325, 2345, 2346, 2731, 2778, 2923, 2945, 2947, 2949, 2952, 2953, 2955, 2957, 2958, 2961, 2963, 2965, 2966, 2972, 2976, 2977, 2978, 2981, 2982, 2986, 2996, 2997, 3000, 3001, 3002, 3004, 3005, 3006, 3007, 3008, 3009, 3010, 3011, 3013, 3014, 3015, 3017, 3021, 3022, 5070, 5085, 5089, 5182, 5301, 5355, 5367, 5403, 5590
Comportement social 373, 393, 767, 2337, 2808
Comportement verbal 1367, 1430
Composition de la population 2200
Composition du groupe 714, 744
Comptabilité 850
  see also: Comptabilité sociale
Comptabilité sociale 291
Comptables 1133, 4535, 4536
Comptes sociaux 688, 4600
Comte, Auguste 404
Comtés 2936
Concentration urbaine 3759, 3854
Conception de soi 532, 574, 575, 576, 577, 578, 580, 581, 587, 588, 590, 592, 593, 595, 596, 598, 599, 643, 750, 902, 1249, 1616, 2082, 2561, 2569, 3329, 4016, 4816, 5306
Conciliation 4623
Concurrence 305, 844, 1049, 4032
  see also: Concurrence interpersonnelle, Concurrence parfaite
Concurrence interpersonnelle 758
Concurrence parfaite 4273
Condamnation pénale 3169, 5182, 5196, 5207, 5367
Conditions de travail 1523, 4008, 4332, 4412, 4418, 4427, 4429, 4431, 4433, 4450, 4457, 4471, 4472, 4486, 4525
Conditions de vie 2108, 2139, 3115, 3330, 3647, 4007, 4008, 4036, 4274, 5339

Conditions d'emploi 4262, 4268
Conditions économiques 978, 999, 1046, 1870, 1895, 1924, 1938, 1961, 1963, 2045, 2066, 2077, 2127, 2186, 2555, 2709, 2871, 3059, 3164, 3179, 3226, 3508, 3612, 3662, 3671, 3857, 3894, 3923, 3934, 3985, 3994, 4020, 4035, 4037, 4054, 4059, 4062, 4080, 4142, 4206, 4233, 4365, 4373, 4388, 4397, 5036, 5282, 5354, 5412
Conditions politiques 978, 1603, 1920, 1923, 3994, 4822, 4825
Conditions sociales 302, 378, 640, 757, 970, 978, 988, 990, 1046, 1088, 1096, 1113, 1283, 1506, 1643, 1823, 1831, 1895, 1919, 1920, 1923, 1924, 1934, 1938, 1950, 1955, 1956, 1959, 1961, 1963, 1964, 1970, 1977, 1979, 2066, 2077, 2139, 2178, 2186, 2218, 2417, 2445, 2514, 2640, 2683, 2700, 2709, 2716, 2729, 2745, 2773, 2871, 2879, 2894, 2950, 3035, 3038, 3059, 3115, 3164, 3192, 3215, 3234, 3330, 3336, 3381, 3407, 3473, 3603, 3671, 3724, 3725, 3738, 3778, 3921, 3923, 3939, 3992, 4020, 4054, 4057, 4058, 4062, 4142, 4233, 4373, 4404, 4799, 4833, 4957, 5036, 5053, 5054, 5060, 5062, 5276, 5282, 5316, 5321, 5326, 5354, 5412, 5507, 5732
Conflit 676, 687, 689, 1856, 2554, 3126, 4872, 5702
  see also: Conflit conjugal, Conflits culturels, Conflits de classe, Conflits de rôles, Conflits interethniques, Conflits internationaux, Conflits interpersonnels, Conflits politiques, Conflits raciaux, Conflits religieux
Conflit conjugal 2578, 2617
Conflits culturels 1010, 1013, 1310, 2138, 2952, 3052, 3081, 3150, 3329, 3343, 5605
Conflits de classe 3987, 4765
Conflits de rôles 898, 901, 911
Conflits du travail 4126, 4623, 4625, 4626, 4627, 4628, 4629
Conflits interethniques 3117, 3148, 3159, 3168, 3177, 3500

Conflits internationaux 5003, 5016
Conflits interpersonnels 679, 680, 689
Conflits politiques 1933, 5819
Conflits raciaux 3086
Conflits religieux 1324
Conflits sociaux 259, 682, 683, 686, 805, 1089, 1883, 3176, 3187, 3713, 4308, 4627, 4915, 4942, 5007, 5059, 5300, 5439
Confréries 1288
Confucianisme 495
Congé de maternité 4338
Congrégations 1290
Conjoncture démographique 251, 2014, 2197, 2202, 3080, 3357, 3379, 3415
Connaissance 24, 55, 99, 103, 105, 106, 113, 132, 253, 439, 607, 674, 716, 809, 853, 874, 1073, 1102, 1341, 1343, 1346, 1350, 1354, 1357, 1464, 1663, 1679, 1692, 1693, 1803, 2658, 2662, 3884, 4150, 4400, 4551, 4857, 4928, 5357, 5363, 5540, 5575, 5668
  see also: Sociologie de la connaissance
Conscience de classe 1883, 1884, 1885, 1902, 2654
Conscience politique 2160
Conscience sociale 1841, 2160
Conseil municipal 4845
Conseillers 5573, 5595
Conservateurs 4910
Conservation de la nature 3442, 3575
Conservation des ressources 3443
Conservatisme 925, 939, 3615, 4286, 4768, 4781
Consommateurs 1444, 4115, 4156, 4192, 4195, 5745
Consommation 884, 3881, 4159, 4165, 4166, 4175, 4180, 4192, 4193, 4197, 5314
  see also: Consommation alimentaire, Consommation de masse, Consommation des ménages
Consommation alimentaire 1105
Consommation de masse 1122
Consommation des ménages 4039

Constitution 1920, 4771
Construction de l'état 3076, 3094, 4771, 4924
Construction de logement 3627, 3741, 3843
Construction nationale 3144
Construction navale 3509
Consumérisme 1637, 1724, 4184, 4193, 4195, 5727
Contact linguistique 757, 1468
Contes
  see: Contes de fées
Contes de fées 5586
Contestation de groupe 4920
Contestation politique 1077, 1282, 2705, 4878, 4882, 4903, 4916
Contestation sociale 220, 4897, 4918, 4936
Contraception 673, 2211, 2212, 2216, 2219, 2233, 2240, 2263, 2722, 2955, 2976, 3008
Contrat de travail 4583
Contrat social 647, 2706, 3701
Contre-culture 3519
Contremaîtres 644, 4409, 4441
Conventions collectives 4601
Conversion religieuse 1276
Coopération économique 4134
Coopération sociale 711, 758
Coopératives 798, 1902, 3503, 3730, 4717
  see also: Coopératives agricoles, Coopératives de logement, Coopératives de production, Coopératives industrielles
Coopératives agricoles 2825, 4077
Coopératives de logement 3734
Coopératives de production 4247
Coopératives industrielles 4710
Coran 1322
Corps humain 72, 149, 154, 1106, 2095, 2217, 2865, 5641
Corps législatif 4837
Corrélation 785
Corruption 5132, 5186
  see also: Corruption politique
Corruption politique 1499, 4959
Cosmologie 103

548

Index des matières

Costume   1106, 1107, 3113
  1119, 1126, 4728
Côtes   3357, 3492
Coup d'état   1537
Cour de justice des Communautés
  européennes   4788
Cours de formation   4418
Cours d'eau   5015
Courses de chevaux   2938
Courtisement   614, 629, 641, 2551,
  2579, 2624
Courtoisie   1370
Coût   3911, 3914, 4138, 5558
  see also: Coût de l'enfant
Coût de l'enfant   2292
Coûts de la vie   2098, 5314
Coûts de transaction   717, 2581
Coutume mortuaire
  see: Rites funéraires
Coutumes   1080, 1083, 1122, 2515,
  2964
  see also: Coutumes familiales,
  Coutumes sexuelles
Coutumes familiales   2406
Coutumes sexuelles   2666
Covariance   266, 271, 472, 2364
Création d'emplois   4251, 4599
Créativité   439, 480, 3823
Crêches   4314, 4494, 5528
Crédit   4196, 4251
  see also: Crédit à la consommation
Crédit à la consommation   4172
Cree   1110
Créole   3126
Crime commerciale   4101
Crime organisée   5116, 5118, 5127,
  5139, 5142, 5151, 5158
Crimes internationaux   5123
Criminalité   2157, 3895, 5128, 5143,
  5152, 5165, 5178
  see also: Criminalité économique
  5536, 5601
  see also: Délinquance juvénile
Criminalité économique   4200, 5186
Criminologie   5069, 5077, 5091, 5098,
  5101, 5108, 5111, 5112, 5123, 5125,
  5131, 5140, 5144, 5146, 5149, 5150,
  5162, 5163, 5182, 5187, 5193, 5194,
  5220, 5231, 5296, 5299, 5300, 5306,
  5308, 5367, 5376, 5436
Crise du logement   3741, 3843
Crise économique   1987, 2539, 3976,
  3994, 4058, 4064, 5058
Crise financière   4204, 4210
Crise morale   3976, 5808
Crise politique   3976, 4757
Crises culturelles   1026
Critique   159, 439, 979, 988, 995,
  1036
  see also: Critique littéraire
Critique littéraire   97, 1012
Croissance démographique   2002,
  2188, 3480, 3499, 3666, 4027, 4081
Croissance économique   1945, 3565,
  3934, 4026, 4220, 4273, 4796, 5345
Croissance urbaine   3663, 3667, 3672,
  3693, 3739, 3819, 3835, 3840, 3842,
  3936
Croix Rouge   5851
Croyance   374, 942, 948, 1020, 1237,
  1318, 3578, 3959, 4835
  see also: Croyances ethnomédicales,
  Croyances populaires, Croyances
  religieuses
Croyances ethnomédicales   2313,
  2345, 3007, 5373, 5411
Croyances populaires   374
Croyances religieuses   1216, 1217,
  1248, 1249, 1250, 1314, 2449, 2497,
  3052
Cubains   3115, 3395, 3414, 4135
Cultes   2910
Culture   29, 167, 186, 204, 225, 230,
  372, 404, 423, 461, 514, 578, 676,
  690, 696, 772, 791, 823, 890, 973,
  974, 975, 976, 979, 982, 987, 988,
  989, 990, 991, 993, 999, 1000, 1001,
  1006, 1011, 1013, 1015, 1020, 1022,
  1030, 1033, 1036, 1040, 1043, 1049,
  1052, 1053, 1055, 1056, 1060, 1073,
  1076, 1077, 1086, 1102, 1111, 1184,
  1212, 1408, 1449, 1510, 1518, 1538,
  1596, 1604, 1607, 1634, 1647, 1663,
  1836, 2411, 2448, 2515, 2650, 2779,
  2791, 2903, 3035, 3072, 3091, 3115,
  3139, 3228, 3471, 3556, 3568, 3620,

Index des matières

3679, 3701, 3786, 4003, 4009, 4080, 4165, 4219, 4248, 4953, 4958, 4974, 4979, 5183, 5371, 5373, 5401, 5424
see also: Culture bourgeoise, Culture d'entreprise, Culture de jeunes, Culture de masse, Culture matérielle, Culture musicale, Culture nationale, Culture ouvrière, Culture politique, Diversité des cultures, Droit à la culture, Subculture, Théorie de la culture, Universalité de la culture
Culture bourgeoise   1022
Culture de jeunes   1647, 1918, 2131, 2133, 2155, 2159, 2169
Culture de masse   1005, 1014
Culture de pauvreté   5320
Culture d'entreprise   791, 792, 820, 877, 890, 4096, 4104, 4112, 4114, 4168, 4179, 4448, 4483
Culture et développement   1008
Culture matérielle   983, 1117, 1127, 1871, 4074
Culture musicale   1631
Culture nationale   1125, 2165, 3960
Culture ouvrière   1108, 1892, 1905, 1918, 3040, 3670
Culture politique   338, 986, 1035, 1282, 1928, 1944, 3596, 4767, 4926, 4949, 4952, 4957, 4970, 4988
Culture populaire   445, 1079
979, 992, 1001, 1002, 1004, 1012, 1019, 1035, 1038, 1103, 1120, 1368, 1505, 1535, 1536, 1555, 1575, 1584, 1592, 1600, 1609, 1618, 1636, 1637, 1675, 2146, 2630, 3027, 4724
Cultures agricoles
see: Cultures fruitières
Cultures fruitières   4607
Curriculum   1666, 1723, 1757, 1770, 1772, 1774
Cycle de vie   489, 2057, 2468, 2481, 2489, 2643, 2892, 3351, 3745
Cycles économiques   3286, 3759, 3854, 5211
Danse   1619, 2791
Darwin, Charles   2406
Datation   536, 614, 638, 5130
Débilité mentale   4721

Déboisement   4210
Décentralisation   1735, 1737, 3731, 4215, 4597, 4618, 4680, 4840, 4841, 4967
Déchets
see: Déchets dangereux
Déchets dangereux   3460
Décision   759, 4318, 4416, 4433
see also: Décisions d'implantation
Décision statistique   4267
Décisions d'implantation   3450
Déclin économique   5036
Déclin urbain   3839
Déconstruction   160, 1061
Découvertes scientifiques   43, 98, 1350
Déesse   2655
Dégâts   2147
Dégradation de l'environnement   998, 2382, 3450, 3480, 3492, 3896, 3909, 3930, 3940, 4861
Délinquance juvénile   599, 749, 755, 4805, 5077, 5085, 5140, 5181, 5189, 5200, 5202, 5208, 5213, 5226, 5285, 5286, 5287, 5288, 5289, 5290, 5291, 5292, 5293, 5294, 5295, 5296, 5297, 5298, 5299, 5300, 5301, 5302, 5303, 5304, 5305, 5306, 5307, 5308, 5309, 5310, 5589, 5599
Délinquantes   5121, 5220
Délinquants   371, 388, 599, 960, 1202, 1207, 1209, 2965, 5069, 5077, 5091, 5094, 5107, 5108, 5111, 5119, 5125, 5133, 5140, 5144, 5156, 5160, 5163, 5164, 5172, 5182, 5191, 5192, 5193, 5194, 5196, 5197, 5199, 5201, 5212, 5213, 5214, 5215, 5221, 5224, 5226, 5228, 5231, 5232, 5233, 5245, 5288, 5295, 5296, 5298, 5299, 5300, 5304, 5306, 5309, 5367, 5376, 5385, 5405, 5410, 5599
see also: Délinquantes
Délits   656, 957, 960, 1081, 1517, 1557, 2652, 2985, 3038, 3223, 3229, 3236, 3650, 3656, 3657, 3895, 4888, 5090, 5091, 5093, 5094, 5095, 5096, 5097, 5100, 5101, 5102, 5103, 5104, 5105, 5108, 5109, 5110, 5114, 5120,

Index des matières

5122, 5123, 5124, 5127, 5128, 5129, 5131, 5133, 5134, 5136, 5138, 5141, 5143, 5144, 5145, 5146, 5147, 5148, 5150, 5151, 5153, 5155, 5156, 5159, 5161, 5163, 5166, 5168, 5169, 5171, 5172, 5173, 5175, 5176, 5180, 5187, 5189, 5208, 5225, 5227, 5255, 5265, 5285, 5287, 5289, 5297, 5300, 5302, 5303, 5307, 5308, 5309, 5374, 5386, 5410, 5436, 5442, 5444
see also: Crime commerciale, Crime organisée, Crimes internationaux, Victimes de crime
Demande   3771, 4472, 4497, 4874, 5474
Demande de main-d'oeuvre   3894, 4497
Démocratie   4, 29, 210, 723, 988, 1455, 1579, 1703, 1812, 1842, 1933, 1961, 3057, 3116, 3148, 4026, 4685, 4767, 4771, 4775, 4780, 4783, 4820, 4822, 4840, 4894, 4953, 4970, 5778
see also: Démocratie chrétienne, Démocratie libérale, Social-démocratie
Démocratie chrétienne   4892, 4893
Démocratie libérale   4819
Démocratisation   122, 1731, 1938, 1945, 2656, 4210, 4791, 4796, 4839, 4941, 4949, 4993, 5511
Démographie   1988, 1993, 1994, 2001, 2002, 2007, 2008, 2011, 2017, 2019, 2020, 2028, 2032, 2036, 2122, 2185, 2189, 2199, 2215, 2219, 2244, 2247, 2282, 2283, 2300, 2325, 2348, 2349, 2414, 2492, 2507, 3110, 3190, 3268, 3300, 3583, 3933, 4170, 4344, 4554, 4954, 5340
see also: Démographie ethnique, Démographie historique
Démographie ethnique   3190
Démographie historique   1997, 2013
Densité de population   2003, 2972, 3743, 3744, 3845
Dentisterie   5644
Déontologie   1171, 4798, 5817
Départements et territoires d'Outre-Mer   1996, 2020, 3304

Dépenses
see: Dépenses de santé, Dépenses publiques
Dépenses de mènage   4157, 4178
Dépenses de santé   2389, 5748, 5749, 5750, 5753, 5767
Dépenses du secteur éducatif   1648
Dépenses publiques   3810, 4188, 4210, 5473
Dépeuplement   2014, 2016, 4231
Dérèglementation   1200, 1726, 3767, 4840
Déroulement de carrière   3031, 4317, 4473, 4493, 4501, 4516, 4534, 4537, 4541, 4554, 4566, 5004
Des gens d'un certain âge   2035
Désastres   830, 897, 1512, 1530, 3460, 3703, 3910, 5038, 5344, 5585, 5835
see also: Catastrophes naturelles
Déségrégation   1749
Désertification   3429, 3438, 3439, 3472, 3480, 3485, 3499
Désintégration de la famille   2413, 2491, 5395
Désirabilité sociale   1176
Dessin   1594
Dessins humoristiques   707
Détermination du revenu   4611
Déterminisme   125
Dette   4172, 4203, 5315
see also: Dette extérieure
Dette extérieure   3619, 5006, 5012
Développement
see: Développement économique, Développement rural, Développement socio-économique, Développement soutenable, Développement urbain
Développement agricole   3584, 3634
see also: Révolution verte
Développement capitaliste   1972, 4126, 5211
Développement cognitif   367, 389, 501, 503, 504, 508, 509, 512, 514, 517
Développement culturel   212, 998
Développement de l'éducation   1751
Développement de l'enfant   404, 498, 503, 1377, 1486, 1587, 2090, 2095,

Index des matières

2099, 2106, 2107, 2110, 2111, 2114, 2631, 2639, 2645, 2688
Développement des collectivités 245, 3505, 3507, 3508, 3510, 3521, 3525, 3526, 3531, 3611, 3681, 3825, 3877, 3970, 4201
Développement du curriculum 1647, 1736
Développement économique 1093, 1451, 1768, 1864, 1990, 2708, 3211, 3216, 3440, 3507, 3820, 3839, 3931, 3968, 4015, 4046, 4074, 4211, 4212, 4213, 4224, 4230, 4231, 4232, 4416, 4773, 5354
Développement forestier 3568
Développement industriel 3525, 3832, 3980, 4102, 4217, 4229
Développement inégal 4228
Développement moral 1143, 1648
Développement national 1561, 4004, 4277
Développement politique 1650
Développement régional 1967, 3369, 3591, 3855, 3894, 4117, 4220, 4222, 4224, 4226
Développement rural 774, 2669, 3510, 3545, 3614, 3623, 3624, 3625, 3626, 3628, 3629, 3630, 3631, 3632, 3633, 3634, 3635, 3636, 3637, 3998, 4742
Développement social 84, 153, 389, 1854, 1935, 1966, 3547, 5052, 5548
Développement socialiste 1902, 3764
Développement socio-économique 155, 1542, 1751, 2191, 2258, 2444, 2458, 2762, 3557, 3633, 3686, 3751, 3966, 4023, 4030, 4227, 4298, 4362, 4685, 5780
Développement soutenable 3448, 3452, 3490, 3555, 3878, 3908, 4210
Développement tribal 1689
Développement urbain 3741, 3817, 3820, 3821, 3828, 3830, 3831, 3832, 3833, 3836, 3837, 3839, 3843, 3866, 3869, 3874, 3876, 3878, 3881, 3882, 3884, 3885, 3894, 3925, 3938, 4103
Déviance 1968, 2974, 5113, 5114, 5137, 5150
Dévolution 5758

Dewey, John 123, 891
Dialectes 1467, 4876
Dialectes créoles 1470
Dialectique 93
Dialogue entre les cultures 5030
Diaspora 3059, 3098, 3408
Dictionnaires 73, 1838
Différences de generations 1262, 1900, 2039, 2531, 4320
Différenciation culturelle 1385
Différenciation économique 3798
Différenciation raciale 2331, 2375, 2589, 2590, 2591, 3170, 3770, 3805, 4003, 4246, 4263, 5779
Différenciation résidentielle 3809
Différenciation sexuelle 434, 570, 664, 1714, 1914, 1964, 2379, 2462, 2586, 2651, 2695, 2698, 2791, 2826, 4443
593, 678, 680, 696, 1188, 1654, 1858, 1868, 2055, 2181, 2182, 2187, 2380, 2410, 2548, 2624, 2652, 2669, 2670, 2702, 2703, 2742, 2758, 2783, 2785, 2793, 2795, 2796, 2804, 2805, 2806, 2807, 2808, 2809, 2810, 2814, 2815, 2817, 2818, 2821, 2826, 2829, 2834, 2837, 2838, 2841, 2846, 2848, 2849, 2851, 2852, 2853, 2859, 2872, 2939, 2944, 2957, 2966, 4001, 4010, 4263, 4319, 4326, 4327, 4330, 4331, 4340, 4355, 4417, 4428, 4537, 4555, 4560, 4562, 4592, 4787, 5406, 5419, 5422, 5465
Différenciation sociale 212, 663, 1839, 1855, 1863, 2060, 3807, 3809
Difficulté de langue
see: Dyslexie
Diffusion de la culture 1026, 1047, 3072, 5032
Diffusion des innovations 3558, 4147
Diffusionisme 179, 314
Dilemme du prisonnier 711, 762
Dimension de la famille 2244
Dimension de l'entreprise 4483
Dimension de l'organisation 825, 4100
Dimension spatiale 387, 1000, 1068, 2818, 3437, 3482, 3483, 3484, 3524,

Index des matières

3735, 3759, 3807, 3812, 3814, 3854, 4180, 4228, 5029, 5754
Dimension temporelle   92, 436, 4560, 4745, 5029
Diplômés d'université   1846, 4564
Direction de crise   400
Direction de l'entreprise   2813, 3545, 3836, 4078, 4080, 4088, 4091, 4093, 4118, 4121, 4123
Dirigeant politique   491, 904, 2884, 4984, 5481
Discours politique   5009
Discrimination   726, 966, 1279, 1565, 1641, 1646, 1786, 2932, 2942, 3079, 3185, 3242, 3475, 4645, 5645, 5705
see also: Discrimination dans l'emploi, Discrimination raciale, Discrimination salariale, Discrimination sexuelle
Discrimination dans l'emploi   936, 1474, 3324, 4253, 4281, 4311
Discrimination raciale   3139, 3156, 3181, 3192, 3210, 3211, 3212, 3215, 3217, 3223, 3224, 3230, 3233, 3235, 3238, 3241, 3243, 3385, 4381, 5688
Discrimination salariale   4263, 4321, 4350
Discrimination sexuelle   1714, 2173, 2330, 2740, 2932, 2934, 2936, 2937, 2938, 2939, 2940, 2942, 2943, 2944, 4311, 4321, 4326, 4333, 4346, 4347, 4350, 4509, 4648, 5136
Disparités régionales   2020, 2301, 2507, 3179, 4000, 4036, 4051, 4060, 4224, 4230, 4232
Disponibilités alimentaires   4022
Disponibilités énergétiques   4670
Dissidents   4877
Dissuasion   5189, 5196, 5289
Distance sociale   2832
Distribution   440, 740, 2249, 2310, 4026, 4040
Distribution de l'eau   4584
Diversification   795, 825, 4111, 4266
Diversité des cultures   254, 693, 1020, 1646, 1920, 2002, 2740, 3693
Divigeant   404, 439, 894, 900, 902, 903, 906, 1534, 2884, 3047, 3069, 4410, 4426, 4504, 4527, 4740, 5471

see also: Dirigeant politique
Division du travail   1863, 1868, 2457, 2553, 2570, 2593, 2816, 2821, 2822, 2838, 2849, 2859, 2889, 2930, 4089, 4236, 4292, 4324
Divorce   2183, 2405, 2424, 2469, 2470, 2471, 2472, 2473, 2474, 2475, 2477, 2478, 2479, 2481, 2482, 2483, 2484, 2485, 2486, 2487, 2489, 2490, 2492, 2493, 2494, 2495, 2501, 2584, 2704, 5579
Divorcés   2481
Domination   545, 3232, 4875
Dominicains   3030, 3395
Don   1128
Donagan, Alan   121, 486
Données d'enquête   290, 2350
Double imposition   3698
Droit   150, 935, 1122, 1180, 1183, 1190, 1194, 1200, 1206, 1207, 2096, 2499, 2704, 2760, 2845, 2928, 3214, 3575, 3698, 4227, 4258, 4633, 4643, 4801, 4949, 5157, 5230, 5458, 5543, 5793
see also: Droit communautaire, Droit coutumier, Droit criminel, Droit de la famille, Droit du travail, Droit international, Droit naturel, Droit public, Histoire du droit, Loi islamique, Philosophie du droit, Sociologie du droit
Droit à la culture   1401
Droit à l'éducation   1709
Droit communautaire   2970
Droit coutumier   1188
Droit criminel   371, 1179, 1182, 5153, 5182, 5188, 5227, 5367
Droit d'auteur   1184, 3971
Droit de la famille   1190, 2424, 2472, 2473, 2501, 2611, 2704
Droit de l'air   395
Droit de vote   3425
Droit des affaires   4268, 4639
Droit du travail   2794, 3575, 4605, 4631, 4632, 4633, 4634, 4635, 4636, 4637, 4638, 4639, 4641, 4642, 4643, 4644, 4645, 4646, 4648, 4659, 4686
Droit international   3124, 5023

Index des matières

Droit naturel   1155, 1158, 3470
Droit public   3071
Droite   997, 2028, 3202
 see also: Extrême droite
Droits   810, 1159, 1174, 2497, 2498, 2503, 2704, 2970, 3276, 3755, 4884, 5060, 5676
 see also: Droits de l'enfant, Droits de l'homme, Droits de la femme, Droits de propriété, Droits du citoyen, Droits économiques, Droits fondamentaux, Droits sociaux
Droits de la femme   2697, 2702, 2714, 2715, 2722, 2730, 2735, 2745, 2761, 2776, 2852, 2899, 2928, 3012, 4359
Droits de l'enfant   2096, 2100, 2101, 2496, 2500, 3276, 5061, 5070, 5542
Droits de l'homme   5, 150, 455, 969, 1744, 2197, 2740, 2899, 3189, 3415, 3470, 4788, 4799, 4809, 4823, 4828, 5241, 5464, 5612
Droits de propriété   2410, 3974, 4771
Droits des travailleurs   4641
Droits du citoyen   944, 1034, 4625
 see also: Droit à l'éducation, Droit de vote
Droits économiques   4615
Droits fondamentaux   5745
Droits sociaux   1897, 2803, 3580, 4827
Dummer, Ethel Sturges   36
Durée du chômage   3651, 4374, 4378
Durkheim, Emile   86, 87, 114, 122, 143, 160, 164, 201, 211, 1839, 1863, 1868, 2849, 4015, 5429
Dynamique   796, 867, 1091, 2411, 3536, 3884, 4230, 5004
Dynamique culturelle   4906
Dynamique de groupe   618, 623, 721
Dynamique de la population   1484, 2020, 2026, 2184, 2250, 2297, 2302, 2396, 3338
Dynamique sociale   404
Dyslexie   498
Eau   3688
Écclésiastiques   2655
Échange   265, 650, 906, 1363, 2520, 2531, 3546
 see also: Échange social
Échange d'information   364, 1452
Échange social   654, 1050, 1242, 2561
Échantillon   335
Échantillonnage   262, 4649
Échec   997, 2808, 3202
 see also: Échec scolaire
Échec scolaire   1767
Ecole   1674
École de Chicago   36, 50
Écoles   357, 438, 708, 794, 1569, 1641, 1642, 1653, 1656, 1660, 1665, 1673, 1679, 1681, 1692, 1698, 1716, 1717, 1730, 1736, 1738, 1739, 1740, 1743, 1749, 1756, 1760, 1763, 1773, 1775, 2086, 3050, 3206, 4872, 5293, 5493, 5572
 see also: Ecole, Écoles maternelles, Écoles primaires, Écoles privées, Écoles secondaires
Écoles maternelles   1664
Écoles primaires   1767, 2846
Écoles privées   1901
Écoles secondaires   965, 1771, 1773, 1776, 1778, 2529, 4324, 4541, 5404
Écologie   107, 1141, 1336, 3434, 3442, 3443, 3444, 3453, 3455, 3465, 3470, 3473, 3495, 4072, 4670
 see also: Écologie humaine
Écologie humaine   3443, 3458, 3462, 3467, 3479, 3491, 3498, 3612
Écologisme   165, 2762, 4891
Économie centralement planifiée   4635
Économie de bien-être   5501
Économie de la communication   1449, 1518
Économie de la santé   5747, 5751
Économie de l'éducation   1667, 1794, 1803, 4275
Économie de marché   3986, 3990, 4043, 4227, 4635, 4771
Économie d'énergie   4177
Économie du travail   4482
Économie et politique   3338, 4229, 4855
Économie islamique   4416
Économie mixte   3983

Index des matières

Économie mondiale   3051, 3404, 3934, 3973, 4109
Économie politique   1897, 2668, 3384, 3532, 3718, 3913, 4785
Économie régionale   4226, 5058
Économie rurale   3559, 3995, 4128
Économie sociale   3973, 4375
Économie socialiste   4243
Économie urbaine   3666, 3671, 3754, 3839, 3878, 3933, 4033
Écosystèmes   998
Écriture   1378, 1395, 1403, 1419
Écrivains   1637
Édition   1422
Éducation   40, 41, 123, 390, 439, 1027, 1056, 1378, 1638, 1640, 1641, 1643, 1644, 1647, 1650, 1651, 1652, 1655, 1658, 1659, 1665, 1666, 1667, 1671, 1672, 1673, 1675, 1678, 1680, 1682, 1683, 1685, 1688, 1689, 1690, 1700, 1706, 1710, 1721, 1724, 1731, 1735, 1738, 1740, 1741, 1745, 1762, 1782, 1791, 1814, 1815, 1840, 1864, 1932, 1933, 2086, 2136, 2169, 2171, 2176, 2232, 2405, 2412, 2645, 2784, 2983, 3054, 3421, 3566, 4019, 4041, 4280, 4370, 4500, 4544, 4563, 5038, 5264, 5279, 5323, 5510, 5547, 5576
   see also: Accès à l'éducation, Économie de l'éducation, Éducation de base, Éducation des adultes, Éducation des femmes, Éducation des minorités, Éducation des parents, Éducation du consommateur, Éducation en matière de population, Éducation familiale, Éducation interculturelle, Éducation préscolaire, Éducation religieuse, Éducation spéciale, Enseignement bilingue, Enseignement industriel, Enseignement post-scolaire, Enseignement post-secondaire, Enseignement primaire, Enseignement privé, Enseignement professionnel, Enseignement public, Enseignement secondaire, Enseignement supérieur, Histoire de l'éducation, Hygiène, Relations parents-enseignants, Théorie de l'éducation
Éducation de base   1713, 4490
Éducation des adultes   1696, 1783, 1784, 1785, 1789, 1802, 1811, 1814, 4490, 4571
Éducation des femmes   1692, 2543, 2557, 2811, 2935, 5704
Éducation des minorités   5623
Éducation des parents   1725
Éducation du consommateur   4159
Éducation en matière de population   2018
Éducation familiale   1226
Éducation interculturelle   1474, 1645, 1646, 3054, 3174
Éducation préscolaire   1664, 1702, 2121
Éducation religieuse   1321, 1322, 1648, 1674, 1712, 1792, 3616
Éducation spéciale   1668
Effectifs en ouvriers   2026, 2396, 2420, 2842, 3937, 4271, 4289, 4302, 4318, 4333, 4362, 4490
Effet   641, 680, 955, 1442, 1556, 2955, 3540, 4016, 5389
   see also: Effets psychologiques, Effets sur l'environnement
Effets psychologiques   395, 665, 4290
Effets sur l'environnement   3449
Efficacité administrative   859
Efficacité organisationnelle   784, 844, 851, 851, 858, 871, 907, 5845
Égalitarisme   140, 1840
Égalité   123, 128, 140, 988, 1896, 2268, 2928, 4350, 5467, 5650
   see also: Égalité des sexes, Égalité économique, Égalité sociale
Égalité de chances   1742, 1800, 1813, 4242, 4258, 4346, 4803
Égalité de rémunération   2794, 4319, 4321, 4326, 4333
Égalité des sexes   2679, 2785, 2794, 2931, 2941, 4324, 4487
Égalité économique   4065
Égalité sociale   571, 2714, 3172, 4065
Église catholique   1265, 1282, 1283, 1291, 1297, 1299, 5511

Index des matières

Église et État 1296, 1297
Église orthodox grecque 2998, 3122
Église orthodox russe 1288, 1304
Église orthodoxe 1298, 1301, 5829
Églises 778, 1231, 3091
Églises Chrétiennes 245, 899, 1280, 1282, 1290, 1300
 see also: Église catholique, Église orthodox grecque, Église orthodox russe, Église orthodoxe, Églises protestantes, Hutterite, Mennonites, Mormonisme, Presbytérianisme
Églises protestantes 1271, 1286, 1293, 1295, 1297
Ego 549, 600
Élaboration d'une politique 1712, 1730, 1792, 3862, 4807, 5048, 5476, 5493, 5703
Électeurs 4991
Election à la Deuxième Chambre 4960
Élections 3325, 4954, 4971, 4977
 see also: Élections des gouverneurs, Élections locales, Élections parlementaires, Élections présidentielles
Élections des gouverneurs 4965
Élections locales 3636, 4972
Élections parlementaires 284, 3308, 4964
Élections présidentielles 4947, 4985, 4991
Électricité 4664
Électronique 166, 1448, 1457
Élèves 245, 332, 1677, 1720, 1960, 2327, 3340, 5404
Élite 331, 1122, 1565, 1816, 1845, 1895, 3042, 4102, 4104, 4928, 4978, 5034, 5036
 see also: Élite politique
Élite politique 4978
Émancipation 2858, 4764, 4925
 see also: Émancipation de la femme
Émancipation de la femme 2792
Émeutes 3176, 5042, 5147, 5225
Émigrants 3256, 3310
Émigration 1950, 3253, 3289, 3297, 3327, 3344, 3400, 3401

Émissions de valeurs mobiliéres 4200
Émotion 167, 228, 436, 447, 453, 454, 467, 506, 530, 534, 550, 569, 570, 572, 581, 590, 646, 691, 692, 694, 696, 697, 699, 701, 702, 703, 704, 708, 709, 799, 1436, 1998, 2152, 2407, 2428, 2585, 2593, 2629, 2953, 3133, 4380, 4462, 5078
Empirisme 117, 769, 1095, 1142, 2766
Emploi 936, 1811, 1876, 1907, 2020, 2089, 2137, 2252, 2396, 2479, 2553, 2584, 2817, 2921, 3145, 3239, 3249, 3326, 3912, 4028, 4057, 4224, 4237, 4242, 4255, 4256, 4263, 4282, 4287, 4288, 4291, 4299, 4303, 4306, 4307, 4309, 4316, 4320, 4346, 4352, 4355, 4356, 4411, 4412, 4435, 4439, 4444, 4490, 4510, 4514, 4565, 4566, 4578, 4673, 4686, 4692
 see also: Accès à l'emploi, Conditions d'emploi, Emploi à temps partiel, Emploi à temps plein, Emploi des femmes, Emploi des jeunes, Emploi rural, Emploi temporaire, Emploi urbain, Plein emploi
Emploi à temps partiel 2397, 2792, 4284, 4343
Emploi à temps plein 2792
Emploi des femmes 2211, 2252, 2490, 2793, 2811, 2819, 2820, 2857, 2867, 2893, 2935, 4249, 4310, 4311, 4322, 4324, 4335, 4360, 4384, 4636
Emploi des jeunes 4259, 4279
Emploi rural 4305
Emploi temporaire 4469
Emploi urbain 3835, 4264, 4371
Employés 644, 829, 834, 956, 4124, 4340, 4358, 4407, 4410, 4438, 4440, 4466, 4474, 4475, 4571, 4573, 4586, 4588, 4640, 4655, 4677
Employés de bureau 3203, 3711, 4352, 4431, 4470, 4489, 4491
Employés de commerce 4501
Employés des services publics 4496, 4575
Employeurs 4011, 4438, 4440, 4475, 4609, 4666

Index des matières

Emprunt   4208, 5006
Énergie
   see: Énergie géothermique, Énergie nucléaire
Énergie géothermique   3555
Énergie nucléaire   3445, 4897
Enfance   537, 568, 2040, 2094, 2104, 2120, 2419, 2458, 3112, 5078, 5080
   see also: Prime enfance
Enfants   148, 390, 391, 438, 498, 502, 505, 535, 560, 583, 611, 616, 708, 943, 1377, 1444, 1463, 1475, 1522, 1564, 1702, 1725, 1730, 1771, 1778, 2086, 2087, 2088, 2097, 2098, 2099, 2101, 2103, 2105, 2108, 2112, 2117, 2121, 2149, 2263, 2335, 2338, 2404, 2405, 2443, 2452, 2456, 2462, 2470, 2472, 2488, 2498, 2510, 2511, 2513, 2525, 2544, 2638, 2644, 2646, 2783, 2906, 3112, 3206, 3259, 3264, 3313, 3343, 3434, 3647, 4053, 4199, 4739, 5006, 5071, 5076, 5184, 5262, 5264, 5268, 5283, 5318, 5320, 5322, 5323, 5343, 5388, 5395, 5435, 5493, 5494, 5521, 5530, 5538, 5542, 5552, 5555, 5558, 5571, 5582, 5597, 5598, 5600, 5602, 5604, 5613, 5674, 5724
   see also: Enfants des migrants, Enfants doués, Enfants handicapés
Enfants à la garde de l'État   2088, 2100, 2143, 5536, 5550, 5601, 5613
Enfants des migrants   3317, 3340, 3343
Enfants doués   2109, 2166, 2402, 2637, 2912
Enfants handicapés   502, 2631, 2645, 5525
Enfants martyrs   568, 2116, 2123, 2398, 2461, 2636, 2641, 2771, 2965, 3019, 5061, 5062, 5063, 5064, 5065, 5066, 5067, 5068, 5069, 5070, 5071, 5073, 5074, 5075, 5076, 5077, 5078, 5079, 5080, 5081, 5082, 5083, 5084, 5085, 5086, 5087, 5088, 5254, 5296, 5301, 5316, 5317, 5445, 5549, 5555, 5561, 5582, 5584, 5596, 5842
En-groupe   725, 743, 745, 750, 754, 767, 771, 3086

Ennui   4463
Enquêtes   240, 274, 309, 325, 327, 330, 334, 340, 343, 349, 351, 936, 946, 950, 959, 969, 1295, 1515, 1762, 2322, 2632, 2976, 2992, 3001, 3774, 4273, 4393, 5134, 5655
   see also: Enquêtes par correspondance, Enquêtes par panel, Enquêtes sociales, Pré-enquêtes, Sondages
Enquêtes par correspondance   4649
Enquêtes par panel   275, 355
Enquêtes sociales   112, 258, 273, 328, 333, 335, 338, 344, 345, 356, 3361
Enquêteurs   342, 346
Enregistrement   1599
Enseignants   58, 708, 997, 1394, 1641, 1643, 1677, 1708, 1736, 2846, 3202, 3206, 4541, 4542, 4550, 4552, 4558, 4602, 4667, 4872, 5388
Enseignement   390, 1357, 1417, 1688, 1693, 1763, 1807, 5826
Enseignement bilingue   1561
Enseignement de la sociologie   23
Enseignement industriel   1707
Enseignement post-scolaire   1804, 4069, 4564
Enseignement post-secondaire   1804, 4069
Enseignement primaire   1732, 1766, 1768, 1769, 1770
Enseignement privé   1748, 1765
Enseignement professionnel   1811, 4523, 4563, 4564
Enseignement public   1648, 1674, 1748, 1756, 1765
Enseignement secondaire   1729, 1757, 1772, 1774, 1775, 1777
Enseignement supérieur   204, 1651, 1712, 1781, 1785, 1786, 1787, 1788, 1790, 1792, 1793, 1794, 1795, 1796, 1799, 1800, 1805, 1806, 1809, 1810, 1818, 4654
Enterrement   1327
Entreprise agricole   2910, 3551, 3561, 3607, 4323
   see also: Fermes familiales
Entreprises   713, 877, 1756, 3216, 4073, 4078, 4084, 4086, 4092, 4119,

4124, 4138, 4205, 4237, 4251, 4260, 4416, 4475, 4569, 5141
see also: Entreprise agricole, Entreprises capitalistes, Entreprises étrangères, Entreprises familiales, Entreprises industrielles, Entreprises multinationales, Entreprises privées, Entreprises publiques, Localisation d'entreprise
Entreprises capitalistes   1888
Entreprises conjointes   3979, 4582
Entreprises étrangères   4098
Entreprises familiales   4073, 4088, 4131
Entreprises industrielles   4113, 4449
Entreprises multinationales   847, 857, 861, 1166, 4109, 4114, 4480, 4481
Entreprises privées   800, 4140, 4527
Entreprises publiques   789, 4527
Entretiens   51, 286, 325, 328, 329, 331, 333, 336, 348, 359, 360, 420, 837, 1386, 4396, 4456, 4815, 4816, 5260
Entretiens en profondeur   339, 352, 358
Environnement   203, 1147, 1526, 1542, 1998, 2024, 2065, 2188, 2854, 3447, 3448, 3452, 3459, 3461, 3462, 3474, 3477, 3490, 3495, 3799, 3911, 4185, 4562, 5060
see also: Milieu culturel, Milieu de travail, Milieu familial, Milieu professionnel, Milieu social, Milieu urbain
Envois de fonds   3371, 3999
Épargnants   4208
Épargne   4199, 4208
Épidémiologie   260, 2303, 2320, 2324, 2339, 2344, 5361, 5693
Epilepsie   531
Épistémologie   27, 100, 101, 103, 104, 110, 112, 113, 114, 115, 116, 626, 1339, 1679, 4779, 5039
Épouse   536, 2554, 2584, 2595, 2694, 2823, 2850, 3328, 4324, 5257, 5573
Époux   608, 677, 2064, 2163, 2214, 2524, 2536, 2545, 2560, 2564, 2578, 2583, 2602, 2838, 2856, 3000, 4178, 4278, 4541, 5256, 5593
Équilibre
see: Équilibre social
Équilibre social   234
Équipement des ménages   4177
Équité   1455, 1741, 1800, 3972, 4210, 4256, 5650, 5769
Érosion du sol   3560
Erotisme   2732, 2878, 2959
Esclavage   890
Espace social   3483
Espace urbain   862, 3709, 3774, 3867
Espacement des naissances   2244, 2264, 2267, 2278, 2381, 2412
Espèce   1430
Espérance de vie   2052, 2357, 2378, 4038
Esprit de parti   4966
Esthétique   7, 1055, 1443, 1628
Esthétique urbaine   3867, 3880
Estime de soi   458, 464, 473, 483, 490, 543, 563, 581, 582, 583, 589, 591, 594, 596, 600, 670, 726, 1249, 2079, 5238, 5320, 5837
Établissements d'enseignement   1716
Établissements humains   351, 3894
État   6, 183, 1297, 1696, 1783, 3047, 3089, 3090, 3188, 3232, 4101, 4209, 4464, 4540, 4646, 4808, 4831, 4928, 5005, 5025, 5471, 5510
see also: État socialiste, État-nation, Petits États
État fédéral   3187, 4954
État providence   286, 926, 1887, 1888, 2502, 2803, 3330, 3580, 3907, 4832, 4840, 5271, 5456, 5461, 5463, 5473, 5475, 5482, 5489, 5492, 5496, 5501, 5509, 5510, 5513, 5515, 5517, 5520, 5613, 5684
État socialiste   1299, 2672, 2858, 3821, 4760, 4799, 4829
État-nation   1407, 1819, 2657, 3074, 3164, 4776
Éthique   121, 122, 137, 142, 150, 210, 228, 398, 486, 880, 916, 986, 1122, 1131, 1133, 1135, 1136, 1137, 1138, 1140, 1143, 1144, 1145, 1147, 1148,

Index des matières

1151, 1152, 1153, 1154, 1155, 1156, 1157, 1158, 1160, 1162, 1163, 1164, 1165, 1167, 1169, 1170, 1175, 1176, 1177, 1263, 1275, 1520, 1639, 1712, 1792, 2337, 2701, 2752, 2885, 2943, 2988, 3452, 3455, 3462, 3521, 3967, 4528, 5026, 5028, 5755, 5761, 5788, 5801, 5805, 5823
see also: Attitude moraliste envers le travail, Code déontologique médical, Déontologie, Éthique protestante
Éthique protestante   147, 1305
Ethnicité   423, 938, 1084, 1313, 1380, 1407, 1415, 1488, 1541, 1647, 1782, 1856, 1992, 2043, 2131, 2415, 2592, 2650, 3002, 3027, 3034, 3040, 3048, 3052, 3055, 3061, 3070, 3079, 3085, 3089, 3090, 3091, 3093, 3094, 3100, 3101, 3102, 3103, 3104, 3105, 3106, 3107, 3109, 3110, 3111, 3112, 3113, 3114, 3116, 3117, 3118, 3119, 3120, 3121, 3123, 3124, 3125, 3127, 3128, 3129, 3131, 3132, 3133, 3134, 3135, 3137, 3138, 3140, 3141, 3142, 3143, 3149, 3151, 3152, 3153, 3177, 3178, 3185, 3188, 3205, 3268, 3270, 3308, 3570, 3796, 3907, 4303, 4725, 5010
Ethnocentrisme   119, 728, 3151, 3166, 3191, 3196, 3221
Ethnographie   85, 1061, 1394, 1447, 3066, 3135, 4545, 4713
Ethnolinguistique   1488
Ethnologie   3947
Ethnométhodologie   1434, 1466, 3095
Ethnomusicologie   1616
Ethnopsychiatrie   3343
Ethnopsychologie   3144
Ethologie   5087, 5254
Étiologie   2718, 5075
Étiquetage   508
Étiquette   1148, 1370
Étrangers   997, 1429, 2952, 3040, 3152, 3185, 3199, 3202, 3246, 3271, 3294, 3309, 3317
Étude du travail   4745
Études asiatiques   1659

Études culturelles   57, 984, 985, 986, 995, 1012, 1078, 1519, 1602, 1675, 2699, 3665
Études de marché   4175
Études des femmes   68, 2663, 2691, 2716, 2741, 2744, 2748, 2950
Études littéraires   2655
Études sur le développement   209, 4221
Études sur les effets mésologiques   4210
Étudiants   363, 452, 460, 482, 538, 598, 918, 930, 965, 969, 1029, 1146, 1654, 1711, 1739, 1741, 1790, 1815, 2562, 2976, 3042, 3109, 4324, 5136
Etzioni, Amitai   886
Eugénisme   3175, 5812
Euthanasie   2226, 5787, 5792, 5793, 5804, 5805, 5808, 5814, 5827
Évaluation   281, 375, 437, 526, 656, 771, 1780, 1807, 2858, 4267, 5335, 5476, 5567, 5568, 5632, 5720, 5840
see also: Évaluation de programme, Évaluation des emplois
Évaluation de programme   4267
Évaluation de soi   470, 482, 485, 579, 582, 613, 649
Évaluation des emplois   4425, 4478
Évangélisme   1268, 1282, 1326
Éventail des salaires   910, 2793, 2795, 2809, 3211, 3231, 4001, 4003, 4010, 4016, 4018, 4037, 4067, 4282, 4319, 4323, 4345, 4609
Évitement   3097, 5564
Évolution   3258
  see also: Évolution humaine
Évolution des emplois   4417
Évolution humaine   2254, 5637
Exil politique   2576
Exilé
  see: Exil politique
Exode des compétences   5612
Expectation   639, 1677, 4414, 5132
  see also: Anticipations de rôle
Expérience religieuse   772, 1224
Expériences   94, 1338
Expérimentation   2923, 5802
  see also: Expérimentation d'animal

559

Index des matières

Expérimentation d'animal   1118, 5788, 5794
Experts   860, 4816
Explication   8, 83, 688, 1890, 4764
Expositions   1604
Expression de soi   2106
Expression faciale   675
Extrême droite   4932, 4982, 5435
Extrêmisme   4982
Fabrication industrielle   343, 3687, 4130, 4136, 4143, 4144, 4146, 4277, 4479, 4488, 4489, 4513, 4588, 4676, 4687
Façon d'élever les enfants   5291
Facteurs culturels   3486, 4316
Facteurs psychologiques   438, 448, 562, 616, 2048
Faible revenu   2212, 2861, 3746, 3766, 3776, 3825, 3903, 4394, 5330
Faillite   2469
Faim   1104
Famille   616, 914, 1021, 1575, 1605, 1620, 1684, 1691, 1767, 1997, 2087, 2125, 2180, 2201, 2213, 2222, 2237, 2269, 2315, 2352, 2386, 2400, 2401, 2404, 2408, 2409, 2410, 2411, 2414, 2415, 2416, 2419, 2422, 2423, 2425, 2426, 2430, 2431, 2432, 2437, 2438, 2440, 2442, 2444, 2447, 2448, 2452, 2453, 2456, 2459, 2464, 2466, 2468, 2476, 2489, 2496, 2499, 2504, 2505, 2506, 2508, 2514, 2523, 2524, 2528, 2530, 2532, 2543, 2568, 2585, 2593, 2611, 2612, 2617, 2622, 2635, 2647, 2648, 2674, 2680, 2866, 2868, 2892, 2919, 2924, 2986, 3038, 3327, 3328, 3350, 3566, 3744, 4315, 4322, 4331, 4349, 4404, 4905, 4983, 5055, 5143, 5184, 5237, 5261, 5269, 5272, 5328, 5339, 5343, 5395, 5469, 5479, 5581, 5594, 5595, 5603
   see also: Famille monoparentale, Sociologie de la famille
Famille monoparentale   2407, 2427, 2443, 2458, 2459, 2480, 2485, 2498, 2504, 2510, 2511, 2513, 2582, 2615, 2633, 2927, 5065, 5317, 5332, 5356, 5522, 5524

Farrell, James T.   50
Fascisme   1644, 4915, 4932
Fécondité   330, 440, 1989, 2001, 2008, 2019, 2030, 2038, 2191, 2192, 2199, 2205, 2211, 2214, 2216, 2223, 2231, 2233, 2244, 2249, 2250, 2252, 2253, 2254, 2256, 2257, 2258, 2260, 2261, 2262, 2265, 2266, 2268, 2269, 2270, 2271, 2272, 2273, 2274, 2275, 2276, 2277, 2279, 2282, 2283, 2284, 2285, 2286, 2288, 2289, 2290, 2291, 2295, 2296, 2297, 2298, 2301, 2418, 2444, 2453, 2875, 3366, 4317, 4342, 4349, 4356, 5808
   see also: Fertilité du sol
Fédéralisme   4790, 5470, 5761
Fémininité   589, 1087, 1608, 2159, 2651, 2870, 2872, 2880, 2881, 2882, 2887, 2904, 2905, 2908, 2967, 2982
Féminisme   85, 104, 124, 228, 379, 410, 632, 700, 1021, 1161, 1449, 1518, 1690, 2228, 2502, 2655, 2656, 2663, 2669, 2682, 2683, 2691, 2694, 2696, 2700, 2705, 2706, 2717, 2718, 2719, 2720, 2723, 2724, 2725, 2726, 2727, 2728, 2729, 2730, 2732, 2733, 2734, 2735, 2736, 2737, 2738, 2739, 2741, 2742, 2743, 2744, 2745, 2747, 2749, 2750, 2751, 2752, 2755, 2758, 2760, 2761, 2763, 2764, 2765, 2768, 2769, 2770, 2771, 2773, 2776, 2778, 2779, 2780, 2791, 2853, 2865, 2878, 2908, 2928, 2931, 2959, 2979, 3453, 3487, 4777, 4905, 5510, 5659
Femmes   82, 144, 410, 499, 527, 578, 615, 656, 678, 685, 1021, 1131, 1143, 1161, 1351, 1387, 1391, 1524, 1609, 1637, 1690, 1723, 1782, 1858, 1860, 1917, 2085, 2126, 2162, 2218, 2242, 2262, 2273, 2311, 2317, 2397, 2405, 2420, 2425, 2432, 2444, 2467, 2494, 2495, 2504, 2534, 2556, 2576, 2577, 2578, 2597, 2599, 2607, 2614, 2650, 2655, 2659, 2664, 2665, 2668, 2675, 2676, 2677, 2681, 2682, 2685, 2689, 2690, 2692, 2694, 2695, 2696, 2699, 2700, 2701, 2703, 2704, 2708, 2709, 2710, 2711, 2712, 2713, 2714,

Index des matières

2729, 2744, 2752, 2759, 2763, 2769, 2773, 2775, 2777, 2778, 2786, 2787, 2789, 2800, 2804, 2818, 2829, 2832, 2837, 2840, 2841, 2844, 2848, 2855, 2859, 2861, 2862, 2863, 2868, 2874, 2875, 2876, 2877, 2879, 2882, 2891, 2898, 2900, 2902, 2903, 2905, 2909, 2915, 2919, 2920, 2923, 2924, 2925, 2929, 2933, 2936, 2949, 2951, 2953, 2957, 2969, 3001, 3002, 3006, 3022, 3055, 3064, 3124, 3203, 3260, 3262, 3268, 3273, 3348, 3359, 3397, 3398, 3499, 3500, 3562, 3628, 3688, 4021, 4023, 4192, 4318, 4320, 4332, 4333, 4336, 4344, 4346, 4356, 4651, 4720, 4726, 4728, 4752, 4902, 4905, 4928, 4971, 4994, 5094, 5121, 5130, 5136, 5160, 5167, 5173, 5177, 5178, 5210, 5238, 5239, 5242, 5245, 5248, 5249, 5250, 5253, 5255, 5256, 5257, 5265, 5266, 5273, 5276, 5365, 5377, 5391, 5418, 5419, 5443, 5449, 5586, 5618, 5649, 5659, 5825
see also: Femmes mariées, Femmes rurales, Femmes urbaine
Femmes et politique   2502, 2705, 2736, 2760, 2787, 2799, 2831, 2833, 2853, 2855, 2858
Femmes mariées   2311, 2553, 2572, 4318, 4363
Femmes rurales   2827, 2842, 2864, 2939, 3553
Femmes urbaine   2917, 3705
Féodalisme   3987
Fermes familiales   2910, 3556, 3561, 3580, 3596
Fermeture d'usine   4139
Fertilité du sol   3564
Fêtes   1125, 1309, 3052, 4928
Fétichisme   1225, 2987
Feu   2433
Fiabilité   341, 760, 773, 859, 2619
Fiancée   1857
Fibres végétales   4108
Fille   689, 1329, 2630, 2760, 2870, 5089
Films   1573, 1574, 1578, 1596, 1600, 1602, 1612, 1614, 1617, 1618, 5445

Fils   1329, 2241
Finance   836, 1578, 3737, 5716, 5746
 see also: Finances locales
Finances locales   3364, 4859
Finkielkraut, Alain   1056
Fiscalité   4209, 4251
 see also: Double imposition
Fixation du prix   3916, 4190
Fixation du salaire   4002
FMI   4210
Foi   1273
Folklore   1438
Fonction publique   4330
Fonctionnaires   4484
Fonctionnalisme   197, 1411
Fondamentalisme religieux   1226, 1279, 1282, 1307, 1310, 1312, 1315, 1317
Force armée   403, 763, 4993, 4995, 4996, 4997, 5000, 5021
Force du marché   1718, 3980
Forces politiques
 see: Groupes de pression
Forces sociales   1519, 3980
Forêts   4266
Formalisation   1497
Formation   483, 583, 1386, 2089, 2809, 4146, 4262, 4563, 4566, 4568, 4571, 4572, 4573, 4574, 4576, 4592, 4997, 5212, 5481, 5531, 5540, 5574, 5595
 see also: Formation en cours d'emploi, Formation professionnelle
Formation à la gestion   856, 4569
Formation de classe   1874, 1891
Formation des attitudes   3147, 4657
Formation en cours d'emploi   4575, 5514
Formation professionnelle   1730, 1738, 3324, 4528, 4565, 4569, 4570, 4576, 5493
Foster, Peter   58
Foucault, Michel   89, 124, 162, 166, 190, 885, 1676, 2771, 2772, 2865, 2975
Foulbe   3142
Foule   404, 4915
Franc-maçonnerie   1235

Index des matières

Fraternité 744, 763
Fratrie 552, 2381, 2386, 2399, 2412, 2452, 2958, 5571, 5847
Fraude 5110, 5129, 5139, 5141, 5186, 5516
Freidson, Eliot 4546, 5700
Freud, Sigmund 377
Frontière 3488
Fulani 3575
Funèbres 1130
Fusions d'entreprises 4290
Gains 54, 3268, 4019, 4037, 4041, 4047, 4066, 4282, 4513
Gains de capital 3733
Garçons 5261, 5293
Gauche 997, 3202, 4901, 4916
Gaz 4665
Généralisation 996
Génération 440, 2040, 2609, 3114
Générations politiques 4916
Gènes 5799, 5810, 5812
Génétique 548, 553, 729, 2289
 see also: Génétique humaine
Génétique humaine 255, 554, 1335, 2224, 2289, 5799, 5809, 5812
Génocide 941
Genre 12, 339, 342, 379, 527, 593, 594, 621, 631, 697, 1021, 1084, 1107, 1351, 1465, 1609, 1635, 1657, 1692, 1714, 1741, 1858, 1885, 1972, 2004, 2103, 2189, 2246, 2278, 2311, 2323, 2330, 2363, 2504, 2509, 2519, 2536, 2561, 2570, 2654, 2655, 2658, 2661, 2664, 2666, 2667, 2668, 2672, 2673, 2686, 2690, 2694, 2696, 2699, 2707, 2724, 2732, 2763, 2770, 2784, 2787, 2788, 2799, 2801, 2802, 2803, 2807, 2809, 2813, 2816, 2824, 2833, 2835, 2841, 2854, 2867, 2881, 2882, 2884, 2907, 2909, 2911, 2934, 2935, 2965, 2966, 3000, 3085, 3245, 3262, 3450, 3562, 3628, 4091, 4238, 4328, 4329, 4345, 4350, 4352, 4550, 4556, 4732, 4913, 4922, 4971, 5083, 5117, 5130, 5238, 5243, 5365, 5379, 5532, 5690, 5828
Genre de vie 1847, 2356, 2481, 2964, 3429, 3541, 5678

Genre humain 2
Gens de maison 2859, 4401, 4522
Gentileschi, Artemisia 2693
Géographie 111, 194, 1068, 1110, 2733, 2766, 3211, 3261, 3333, 3389, 3431, 3432, 3433, 3435, 3441, 3447, 3464, 3468, 3471, 3481, 3484, 3487, 3493, 5068, 5393
 see also: Anthropogéographie, Géographie de la population, Géographie économique, Géographie historique, Géographie politique, Géographie urbaine
Géographie de la population 2194
Géographie économique 3639
Géographie historique 1032
Géographie politique 5020
Géographie urbaine 11, 3457, 3639, 3727, 3735, 5020
Géométrie 3493
Géopolitique 752, 1187, 3476, 3985, 4763, 5018, 5020
Gériatrie 5733, 5734
Gérontologie 2040, 2044, 2045, 2046, 2056, 2061, 2063, 2076, 2083, 2612
Gestion 439, 851, 852, 853, 854, 855, 858, 860, 865, 867, 868, 869, 870, 871, 886, 1113, 1708, 1735, 2707, 2901, 4044, 4105, 4114, 4357, 4427, 4436, 4461, 4507, 4528, 4530, 4582, 4585, 4600, 4607, 4715, 4718, 4787, 5617, 5770
 see also: Cadres supérieurs, Direction de crise, Gestion administrative, Gestion d'entreprise agricole, Gestion de l'environnement, Gestion de la production, Gestion de risque, Gestion des ressources, Gestion des universités, Gestion du personnel, Gestion financière, Gestion industrielle, Gestion urbaine
Gestion administrative 4484, 5481
Gestion de commerce 861, 872, 4086, 4116, 4260, 4716
Gestion de la dette 4203
Gestion de la production 4598
Gestion de l'environnement 1243, 3578, 3638

Index des matières

Gestion de risque   863, 3479, 4421
Gestion d'entreprise agricole   2854
Gestion des ressources   3439, 4375
Gestion des sociétés
  see: Gestion de commerce
Gestion des universités   864, 1810
Gestion du personnel   4311, 4474, 4475, 4476, 4477, 4478, 4479, 4480, 4481, 4482, 4483, 4484, 4485, 4486, 4508, 4616, 5000
Gestion financière   4178, 5118
Gestion industrielle   4090, 4104, 4155, 4239, 4504
Gestion urbaine   862, 3849, 3917, 3945
Giddens, Anthony   174, 222, 1055, 1875, 4776
Glueck, Sheldon   5288
Goffman, Erving   45, 1148
Goldman, Emma   2730
Gorbachev, Mikhail   448
Gouvernement   1756, 4806
  see also: Administration centrale, Administration locale, Gouvernement des États
Gouvernement des États   5761
Gramsci, Antonio   13
Grandes villes   1844, 2482, 2909, 3058, 3093, 3097, 3132, 3267, 3296, 3385, 3504, 3542, 3545, 3638, 3640, 3641, 3645, 3647, 3648, 3649, 3650, 3651, 3652, 3654, 3656, 3658, 3659, 3660, 3664, 3665, 3666, 3669, 3671, 3676, 3677, 3678, 3681, 3682, 3688, 3694, 3696, 3700, 3706, 3713, 3721, 3723, 3725, 3726, 3744, 3753, 3758, 3769, 3790, 3796, 3797, 3817, 3823, 3828, 3831, 3839, 3847, 3848, 3852, 3853, 3856, 3868, 3879, 3882, 3890, 3891, 3892, 3897, 3899, 3900, 3908, 3912, 3917, 3925, 3932, 3933, 3934, 3935, 3938, 3941, 3943, 3946, 3955, 3956, 4076, 4084, 4269, 5020, 5107, 5124, 5144, 5274, 5337, 5387, 5495
  see also: Villes capitales
Grands-parents   2521
Grecs   1003
Green, Thomas Hill   5517

Grèves   2773, 4621, 4622, 4624, 4626, 4628, 4629, 4634, 4676
Grossesse   2134, 2161, 2217, 2232, 2264, 2281, 2533, 2575, 2675, 2836, 5637, 5683, 5691, 5764, 5766, 5825, 5828
Groupements professionnels   4018
Groupes de pression   1439, 4861
Groupes de travail   649
Groupes d'égaux   649, 755, 2104, 2163, 5143
Groupes d'intérêt   3782, 4914, 4928
Groupes ethniques   307, 933, 1048, 1270, 2605, 3023, 3025, 3026, 3033, 3036, 3041, 3045, 3046, 3048, 3061, 3075, 3095, 3097, 3105, 3110, 3113, 3115, 3118, 3122, 3154, 3187, 3201, 3204, 3209, 3215, 3219, 3240, 3242, 3333, 3518, 3770, 3805, 3806, 4263, 4967, 5031, 5152, 5705
Groupes linguistiques   757
Groupes majoritaires   738
Groupes minoritaires   968, 1375, 3803, 4372
Groupes religieux   1218, 1302, 1892, 2579, 5606
Groupes restreints   723, 736, 740, 766, 767
Groupes thérapeutiques   5618, 5619
Guérillas   5118
Guérison   2313, 2345, 3007, 5373, 5411, 5851
Guerre   403, 565, 923, 943, 1602, 2097, 2112, 2742, 2933, 5021, 5033, 5417
Guerre dans la Golfe   403, 425, 433, 1169, 1541, 3415, 4927, 5021, 5617
Guerre des Malouines   5034
Gurvitch, Georges   208
Gustafson, James   5829
Habermas, Jürgen   21, 137, 189, 1005, 1055, 1157, 1197, 1514
Habitudes   1122
  see also: Habitudes alimentaires, Habitudes de lecture
Habitudes alimentaires   1113, 1115, 4158

Index des matières

Habitudes de lecture 1492, 1597, 1725
Hall, John A. 4776
Handicapés 670, 936, 1092, 1095, 1811, 2308, 2309, 2319, 2329, 2552, 2729, 2750, 4253, 5566, 5607, 5645, 5717, 5719, 5773
Handicapés mentaux 5191, 5707, 5831, 5839
Handicapés physiques 5678
Harcélement sexuel 358, 544, 2967, 2993, 3012, 4332, 4348
Harré, R. 90
Hassidisme 3053
Hauerwas, Stanley 5829
Hayek, Friedrich A. von 91, 132
Hegel, Georg Friedrich W. 136, 2558
Hégémonie 380, 1231, 1505, 2661, 2909, 3973
Heidegger, Martin 605
Hérésies 1283
Héritage 2406, 2500, 3532, 3561
Herméneutique 8, 96, 286, 1357, 1420, 1592, 1693
Herod 1327
Heroïné 5403, 5415
Héros 4774
Hétérosexualité 2968, 3000
Heures de travail 4193, 4454
  see also: Horaire variable de travail
Hiérarchie 807, 892, 913, 1842, 2658, 2785, 4735
Hindouisme 1259, 1307, 1319, 1843
Hindous 1324, 1843, 1861, 1869, 3114, 3264
Hirsch, Jr., E.D. 1647
Hispaniques 2509, 2532, 2591, 2680, 3051, 3084, 3085, 3100, 3115, 3200, 4003, 4372, 4845, 5281, 5563
Histoire 12, 15, 34, 164, 1067, 1503, 1666, 2693, 3063, 3213, 3226, 3527, 3542, 4096, 4218
  see also: Histoire agricole, Histoire coloniale, Histoire culturelle, Histoire de l'Église, Histoire de l'entreprise, Histoire de langues, Histoire du travail, Histoire industrielle, Histoire locale, Histoire orale, Histoire politique, Histoire religieuse, Histoire sociale, Histoire urbaine 214
  see also: Histoires de vies
Histoire agricole 1971, 4083
Histoire coloniale 1464, 2920, 3755
Histoire culturelle 3066, 3401
Histoire de la médicine 5664, 5699
Histoire de la sociologie 7, 17, 19, 21, 29, 50, 61, 210
Histoire de langues 1468
Histoire de l'art 1594
Histoire de l'éducation 1670, 1688, 1715, 1793, 1816
Histoire de l'Église 1006, 1293
Histoire de l'entreprise 4096
Histoire des idées politiques 4777
Histoire des science sociales 1, 20
Histoire des sciences 1335, 1340
Histoire du droit 1197
Histoire du travail 1862, 4396, 4544, 4665, 4667, 4672, 4674
Histoire industrielle 3936
Histoire locale 1848
Histoire naturelle 2
Histoire orale 4396, 5672
Histoire politique 1034, 4822, 4979
Histoire religieuse 28, 1006, 1300
Histoire sociale 992, 1115, 1117, 1389, 1848, 1889, 1897, 1901, 1923, 1971, 1979, 2099, 2983, 3103, 3144, 3192, 3196, 3267, 3320, 3341, 3509, 3925, 4862, 5482
Histoire urbaine 2065, 3926
Histoires de vies 540, 2992, 3557
Historiens 14
Historiographie 404, 1006, 2666, 2777
HIV 810, 933, 2313, 2314, 2315, 2316, 2320, 2341, 2343, 2344, 2346, 2978, 3001, 3008, 3010, 3011, 5267, 5355, 5400, 5567, 5575, 5770, 5774
Hmong 3332
Hobbes, Thomas 5028
Hobson, John Atkinson 20
Holisme 2717
Holocauste 560, 941, 1627, 3107

Index des matières

Homicide   698, 3440, 5125, 5148, 5155, 5164, 5243, 5442
see also: Meutre
Hommes   339, 656, 678, 700, 763, 1415, 1602, 1860, 2078, 2151, 2259, 2349, 2378, 2385, 2405, 2413, 2432, 2495, 2534, 2577, 2578, 2604, 2647, 2804, 2822, 2829, 2832, 2840, 2866, 2873, 2888, 2895, 2896, 2897, 2899, 2907, 2916, 2953, 2957, 2961, 2965, 2978, 2992, 2997, 3011, 3014, 3016, 3020, 3268, 4002, 4316, 4339, 4381, 4419, 4537, 4971, 5092, 5156, 5247, 5251, 5256, 5261, 5410
Hommes de loi   561, 1204, 1544, 2807, 2856, 2940, 3214, 4345, 4553, 4561
Homogamie   2568
Homosexualité   353, 659, 917, 1614, 1617, 2327, 2545, 2567, 2624, 2728, 2878, 2896, 2946, 2947, 2950, 2959, 2961, 2962, 2963, 2964, 2969, 2970, 2971, 2973, 2974, 2978, 2980, 2983, 2984, 2989, 2992, 3001, 3011, 3013, 3456, 4495, 4645, 4863, 4995, 4996, 5244, 5445
Hôpitaux   5206, 5671, 5673, 5686, 5689, 5743, 5751, 5759, 5765, 5806, 5845
see also: Hôpitaux psychiatriques
Hôpitaux psychiatriques   5125, 5849
Horaire variable de travail   2397
Hormones   705, 2187, 2604
Hors-groupe   712, 725, 743, 750, 754, 767, 771, 1375, 3045, 3086
Huile   3440
Humanisme   4766, 4785
Humanités   1, 238
Humour   451, 454, 471, 668, 690, 704, 1052, 1433, 2629
see also: Plaisanteries
Hutcheson, Francis   1164
Hutterite   2279
Hygiène   2357, 2976, 3482
Hypothèques   3243, 4174, 4201
Hypothèse   364, 3147
Idéalisme   126, 297, 812

Idées politiques   602
see also: Histoire des idées politiques
Identification   262, 283, 1366, 3032, 3128, 5624
see also: Identification à une classe sociale
Identification à une classe sociale   4962
Identité   154, 258, 443, 450, 452, 464, 500, 584, 586, 643, 754, 770, 1010, 1016, 1043, 1316, 1332, 1397, 1398, 1573, 1658, 2095, 2133, 2185, 2596, 2651, 2728, 2870, 2946, 2951, 3048, 3094, 3105, 3106, 3107, 3113, 3120, 3122, 3136, 3139, 3152, 3180, 3185, 3252, 3276, 3282, 3284, 3329, 3332, 3475, 3482, 3493, 3502, 3524, 5810
see also: Identité culturelle, Identité de groupe, Identité nationale, Identité professionnelle, Identité régionale, Identité sociale
Identité culturelle   980, 998, 1008, 1015, 1047, 1407, 1527, 1573, 1658, 2155, 2964, 3058, 3087, 3093, 3113, 3124, 3267, 3296, 3570, 3659, 4408, 4955, 5027, 5032
Identité de groupe   745, 753, 770, 1107, 1119, 1675, 1935, 3135
Identité nationale   1003, 1006, 1020, 1021, 1022, 1287, 1585, 1675, 2131, 2202, 2755, 3134, 3140, 3271, 3518, 4731, 4743, 4950
Identité professionnelle   5574
Identité régionale   34, 980, 998, 3113, 3526, 3527, 3528
Identité sociale   1652, 1846
Idéologie   120, 122, 162, 168, 178, 682, 700, 939, 945, 980, 1137, 1139, 1231, 1269, 1287, 1375, 1547, 1584, 1837, 1886, 1894, 1941, 2505, 2677, 2823, 2908, 3165, 3459, 3977, 4286, 4595, 4783, 4808, 4915, 4966, 4988, 5009, 5659
see also: Idéologies politiques
Idéologies politiques   3106, 4760
Îles   2563, 3097, 3555, 3557, 4723
Illégitimité   2507

Index des matières

Images 114, 521, 1074, 1391, 1437, 1543, 1614, 1898, 1945, 2358, 2865, 2872, 2876, 2891, 2905, 2906, 3033, 3152, 3569, 3668, 3868, 4824, 4889, 5027
Imagination 94, 114, 480, 1466
Imitation 1615
Immigrant clandestins 3274, 3277, 3288, 4677
Immigrants 236, 245, 560, 1017, 2020, 2269, 2900, 3030, 3039, 3050, 3054, 3055, 3056, 3068, 3069, 3077, 3101, 3103, 3112, 3114, 3125, 3146, 3180, 3234, 3254, 3257, 3266, 3267, 3270, 3272, 3298, 3302, 3306, 3309, 3318, 3320, 3325, 3326, 3329, 3345, 3346, 3348, 3350, 3395, 3406, 3425, 4135, 4244, 4309, 4318, 4539, 4813, 4961, 5127
see also: Immigrant clandestins
Immigration 1950, 2740, 3041, 3055, 3253, 3267, 3268, 3269, 3271, 3277, 3289, 3293, 3308, 3309, 3327, 3333, 3339, 3394, 3402, 3407, 3416, 3963, 4371, 5128
see also: Immigration clandestine
Immigration clandestine 915
Impérialisme 981, 1013
Importations 4074
Impôts 5467
Impression 1184
Incertitude 330, 863, 4148, 5679
Inceste 2958, 2975, 5040, 5044, 5066, 5082, 5087, 5089, 5254
Indépendance 2559, 4644, 4924
see also: Indépendance économique
Indépendance économique 4224
Indicateur 668, 4030, 4436
see also: Indicateurs démographiques, Indicateurs économiques, Indicateurs sociaux
Indicateurs démographiques 557
Indicateurs économiques 315, 3577, 4055
Indicateurs sociaux 315, 321, 1699, 2357, 2383, 4000, 5308, 5760
Indiens 1468, 3056, 3057, 3114, 3156

Individu et société 316, 446, 458, 461, 466, 477, 494, 715, 3592, 4779
Individualisme 455, 800, 1206, 3513, 4761, 4767, 4780, 4950
Individualité 173, 212, 466, 577, 819, 1033, 1605, 2626
Individus 96, 114, 388, 435, 443, 444, 457, 458, 461, 486, 487, 488, 516, 523, 544, 547, 549, 550, 556, 563, 565, 570, 574, 575, 592, 597, 643, 650, 653, 739, 785, 818, 1430, 1431, 1853, 2317, 2628, 3474, 3770, 3805, 4047, 4067, 4179, 4421, 4508, 5119, 5564, 5823
Indonésiens 3408
Induction 152
Industrialisation 1907, 2514, 3630, 3632, 3982, 4031, 4076, 4125, 4238
Industrie 825, 888, 1943, 2514, 3355, 3440, 4151, 4217, 4298, 4523
see also: Agroindustrie, Construction navale, Fabrication industrielle, Industrie agro-alimentaire, Industrie automobile, Industrie cinématographique, Industrie culturelle, Industrie d'armement, Industrie de la chaussure, Industrie de la construction, Industrie de la viande, Industrie du disque, Industrie du meuble, Industrie du vêtement, Industrie électrique, Industrie électronique, Industrie exportatrice, Industrie informatique, Industrie métallurgique, Industrie pétrochimique, Industrie pharmaceutique, Industrie textile, Localisation industrielle, Petite industrie, Secteur tertiaire
Industrie agro-alimentaire 4329
Industrie automobile 2788, 4074, 4446, 4525, 4715
Industrie cinématographique 1601
Industrie culturelle 1623
Industrie d'armement 4082
Industrie de la chaussure 4097
Industrie de la construction 4244, 4591
Industrie de la viande 4126

Index des matières

Industrie du disque   1599
Industrie du meuble   4677
Industrie du vêtement   2883, 4070, 4298
Industrie électrique   4429
Industrie électronique   2661, 4697
Industrie exportatrice   4488, 4687
Industrie informatique   4412
Industrie métallurgique   4679
Industrie minière   3280, 3492, 3602, 3640, 4210
Industrie pétrochimique   4514
Industrie pharmaceutique   1282
Industrie sidérurgique   4139, 4236, 4518
Industrie textile   1892, 2817, 2883, 4108, 4338, 4694
Inégalité de revenu   3598, 4012, 4013, 4028, 4029, 4032, 4037, 4053, 4059, 4066, 4263, 4340
Inégalité de sexes   2726, 2786, 2813, 2815, 2924, 2935, 4238
Inégalité économique   929, 1840, 1914, 2048, 4042, 4045, 4206, 5258
Inégalité raciale   3145, 3201, 3231, 3244, 4012, 4242, 4514
Inégalité sociale   922, 929, 1652, 1682, 1746, 1834, 1836, 1840, 1842, 1844, 1881, 1906, 1912, 1913, 1914, 2020, 2048, 2060, 2173, 2679, 2839, 3137, 3373, 4013, 4036, 4042, 4206, 5312, 5315, 5326, 5343, 5627, 5778
Infanticide   2181
Infirmières   911, 1412, 4629, 5698, 5713, 5834
Inflation   4206
Influence culturelle   1037, 1113, 2255, 4083
Influence interpersonnelle   280, 546
Influence sociale   834, 918, 1206, 1941, 2162, 2436, 5392
Influences politiques   1644, 4695
Influences religieuses   1127
Information   77, 341, 353, 824, 953, 1392, 1449, 1460, 1517, 1518, 3676, 4168, 4187, 4267, 4529, 4814, 5048
   see also: Accès à l'information, Information politique

Information financière   4204
Information politique   1499
Informatisation   4229, 4324, 4649
Ingénierie   4432, 4666
Ingénierie génétique   5810
Ingénieurs   1654, 3031, 4704
Initiation   4200
Injures   395
Inkatha   2425
Innovation agricole   3558
Innovations   819, 821, 1629, 1721, 3883, 4148, 4170, 4452, 5578
   see also: Innovation agricole
Inondations   2197
Insémination
   see: Insémination artificielle
Insémination artificielle   5807
Institutionnalisation   1343, 5564
Institutionnalisme   883
Institutions   63, 200, 802, 805, 870, 1375, 1941, 2088, 2143, 3615, 4536, 4604, 4801, 5582, 5588, 5600, 5717, 5744
   see also: Établissements d'enseignement, Institutions financières
Institutions financières   4290, 4480
Insurrection   5118
Intégration culturelle   994, 3256, 3324
Intégration économique   3333
Intégration européenne   1384, 1521, 3075
Intégration internationale   3421
Intégration régionale   4840
Intégration sociale   910, 1041, 1122, 1640, 1749, 1992, 3164, 3217, 3272, 3516, 3674, 3826
Intellectuels   46, 452, 1028, 1034, 1036, 1284, 1925, 3027, 3029
Intelligence   116, 370, 388, 440, 475, 497, 547
   see also: Intelligence artificielle
Intelligence artificielle   1344
Interaction conjugale   696, 2259, 2538, 2550, 2555, 2559, 2571, 2586, 2602
Interaction en groupe   720, 731, 742, 762

Index des matières

Interaction sociale   45, 148, 611, 652, 665, 669, 671, 723, 764, 1015, 1363, 1427, 3956, 4398, 4424, 4745
Interaction symbolique   1064
Interdépendance   2436, 3973
Intérêt   2562
Intérêt de classe   1887
Intérêt public   3086
Intermariage   2540, 2563, 2579, 2592, 2605
Internationalisation   1270, 1563, 3295, 5005, 5030
Internationalisme   5098
Intervalles génésiques   2255, 2265, 2287, 2352, 2608
Intervention de l'État   3768, 3893, 3920, 4229, 5473
Intimité   2596, 2958, 5243
Intoxiqué
   see: Toxicomanes
Inuit   1110, 1399
Invalidité   670, 2318
Invasions   4911
Inventions   4096
Inventoire   567
Investissements   2376, 4205
   see also: Investissements de l'entreprise, Investissements étrangers
Investissements de l'entreprise   4205
Investissements étrangers   4074, 4098, 4142
Iraniens   3125
Irrigation   2197, 3575
Islam   103, 239, 1021, 1180, 1307, 1308, 1309, 1311, 1312, 1314, 1315, 1316, 1318, 1319, 1320, 1321, 1332, 1453, 2845, 2925, 3062, 5559, 5790
   see also: Coran
Islam et politique   1310, 1317, 1934
Isolement social   1916, 3011, 3034, 3215, 5047, 5321, 5348
Italiens   3047, 3069, 3103, 3253, 3258, 5403
Itinérants   3130
Jalousie   694, 697, 702
Japonais   2477, 4194, 4480
Jaspers, Karl   129
Jazz   1611, 1631

Jeu   1055, 2040
Jeu de rôle   897
Jeûne   1309
Jeunes et politique   1650, 4882, 4886
Jeunes filles   2153, 2653, 2683, 5085, 5301
Jeunes travailleurs   4002, 4307
Jeunesse   583, 749, 925, 970, 1122, 1234, 1325, 1522, 1536, 1680, 1695, 1719, 1970, 2040, 2125, 2127, 2129, 2130, 2132, 2136, 2137, 2138, 2139, 2140, 2141, 2142, 2143, 2144, 2146, 2148, 2149, 2150, 2151, 2154, 2160, 2163, 2164, 2165, 2166, 2167, 2169, 2170, 2171, 2172, 2173, 2174, 2175, 2176, 2177, 2178, 2421, 2451, 2552, 2690, 3082, 3194, 3197, 3218, 3278, 3329, 3540, 3541, 3724, 3728, 3825, 4053, 4127, 4307, 4365, 4372, 4739, 4992, 5064, 5213, 5226, 5261, 5287, 5298, 5304, 5435, 5438, 5536, 5601, 5626, 5841
   see also: Jeunesse rurale
Jeunesse rurale   3566
Jeux   265, 305, 317, 4732, 5057
   see: Jeux rituels
Jeux d'argent   4739
Jeux de balle   4615
Jeux rituels   2040
Jones, Grace   1060
Jouets   1444
Journalisme   1504, 1519, 1520, 1523, 1552, 1558
Journalistes   1524, 1559, 4405
Judaïsme   1155, 1268, 1272, 1316, 1326, 1328, 1330, 1331, 1332, 1333, 2971, 5829
   see also: Hassidisme
Jugement   526, 612, 620, 716, 754, 1167, 1187, 4422, 4788, 4965, 5206
   see also: Jugement de valeur, Jugement social
Jugement de valeur   924
Jugement social   573, 2046, 2094
Juges   4554
Juifs   431, 643, 841, 931, 941, 1325, 1327, 1333, 1627, 2034, 2058, 2075,

Index des matières

2415, 3044, 3049, 3053, 3055, 3060, 3061, 3063, 3064, 3065, 3068, 3088, 3107, 3113, 3125, 3128, 3134, 3141, 3146, 3209, 3220, 3240, 3349, 3865, 4520
see also: Lubavitch
Jumeaux 548, 553, 2353
Jung, Carl 377, 492, 2834
Juridiction
see: Juridiction criminelle
Juridiction criminelle 5095, 5153, 5180, 5227
Jurisprudence 4632
Jury 741, 751, 1409, 2123, 3224
Justice 123, 444, 539, 654, 657, 738, 751, 810, 1156, 1173, 1191, 1212, 3450, 3785, 4382, 4600, 4846, 5028, 5101, 5187, 5212, 5213, 5224, 5226, 5298, 5304, 5405
see also: Justice criminelle, Justice distributive, Justice économique, Justice sociale
Justice criminelle 539, 1181, 1207, 2991, 4797, 4970, 5105, 5157, 5186, 5188, 5190, 5191, 5192, 5197, 5200, 5201, 5202, 5208, 5210, 5211, 5213, 5216, 5222, 5228, 5230, 5245, 5248, 5287, 5292, 5294, 5297, 5298, 5385
Justice distributive 761, 948, 4423, 5755
Justice économique 971
Justice sociale 128, 167, 401, 942, 948, 971, 1455, 1913, 2993, 3470, 4394, 4600, 5053, 5215, 5511
Kant, Immanuel 121, 129, 1158, 2558
Kelabit 3352
Kibboutz 2268
King, Rodney 3176
Kitzinger, Sheila 2675
Kohlberg, L. 880
Krupskaya, N.K. 1715
Laïcisme 1283
Langage 137, 164, 445, 1108, 1192, 1214, 1351, 1362, 1367, 1373, 1377, 1379, 1386, 1390, 1395, 1397, 1398, 1399, 1406, 1408, 1411, 1416, 1417, 1421, 1426, 1429, 1430, 1436, 1463, 1473, 1475, 1476, 1479, 1481, 1485, 1541, 1570, 1628, 1880, 2707, 2805, 2829, 3349, 3680, 4790, 4876, 5057
see also: Langues officielles
Langue allemande 679, 1376, 1564
Langue anglaise 679, 1368, 1370, 1381, 1382, 1405, 1468, 1469, 1488, 1492, 1561, 1563, 1568
Langue catalane 1383
Langue espagnole 420, 1404, 1435
Langue française 229, 1362, 1483, 1484
Langue galloise 1568
Langue italienne 1471
Langue maternelle 1380, 1399, 1482
Langue occitan 4876
Langue russe 1563
Langues officielles 1429, 1435, 1562, 1565
Leaders 899, 912
see also: Leaders politiques
Leaders politiques 4985
Lecteurs 97, 1441, 1725
Lee, Ivy 1169
Législation 2836, 3459, 4210, 4257, 4311, 4641
Légitimation 1676, 4037
Légitimité 184, 443, 821
Leite, Gabriela Silva 2960
Lenin, V.I. 448
Lesbiennes 1617, 2545, 2728, 2754, 2779, 2949, 2950, 2951, 2954, 2962, 2969, 2970, 2973, 2974, 2979, 2980, 2984, 3000, 3456, 4495, 4863, 4995, 5445
Lewin, Kurt 404
Li, Zehou 1925
Libéralisation 974, 4902
Libéralisme 939, 1035, 1056, 1138, 1896, 3062, 4102, 4761, 4770, 4771, 4772, 4783, 4785, 4981
see also: Néolibéralisme
Libération 4994
Libertarisme 1670
Liberté 125, 800, 891, 944, 1039, 1598, 2242, 2715, 2833, 4822
see also: Liberté de l'enseignement
Liberté de conscience 1296
Liberté de la presse 1439

Index des matières

Liberté de l'enseignement 159, 1744, 1779, 1799
Liberté d'expression 2732, 4894
Liberté religieuse 1250
Liberté surveillée 4101, 5204, 5212, 5221
Libre échange 3426
Licenciements 4295, 4630, 4659, 4660
Lieu de travail 54, 774, 810, 901, 1154, 1474, 3801, 3919, 4399, 4400, 4423, 4424, 4428, 4443, 4459, 4625, 4645, 4970, 5000
Ligne aérienne 395
Limitation des armements 4885
Linguistique 743, 1022, 1462, 1463, 1472, 1473, 1475, 1476, 1479, 1481, 1483, 1484, 1487, 1491, 1493, 1576, 3349
see also: Sociolinguistique
Littérature 26, 50, 97, 993, 1013, 1028, 1480, 1481, 1596, 1603, 1607, 1634, 1637, 2693, 3055
see also: Littérature populaire, Poésie, Romans
Littérature populaire 1622
Livres 1597, 1623
Localisation d'entreprise 3759, 3854
Localisation géographique 5653
Localisation industrielle 3355, 3687
Locke, John 4770
Lockouts 4235, 4604
Logement 1099, 1112, 1998, 2168, 2334, 3372, 3567, 3729, 3730, 3731, 3732, 3734, 3736, 3737, 3738, 3739, 3740, 3749, 3750, 3751, 3752, 3753, 3756, 3759, 3760, 3761, 3762, 3763, 3764, 3765, 3766, 3767, 3768, 3770, 3771, 3773, 3774, 3775, 3778, 3779, 3781, 3784, 3785, 3786, 3787, 3789, 3790, 3791, 3792, 3801, 3805, 3825, 3854, 3861, 3890, 3901, 4188, 4589, 5315, 5452, 5469, 5470, 5480, 5483, 5488, 5490, 5491, 5497, 5518, 5744
see also: Logement urbain, Logements sociaux
Logement urbain 3729, 3731, 3735, 3739, 3746, 3747, 3766, 3768, 3776, 3780, 3783, 3788, 3789, 3882, 3903, 3905, 3906, 5779
Logements sociaux 3761, 3763, 3769, 3861, 3901, 5452, 5454, 5469, 5480, 5488, 5490, 5491, 5495, 5497, 5498, 5518
Logiciel 1136, 4229, 4730
Logique 43, 382, 405, 439
Loi islamique 221, 1190, 2501
Loisir 1633, 2132, 2172, 2868, 4193, 4720, 4721, 4722, 4725, 4726, 4729, 4731, 4733, 4735, 4739, 4740, 4745, 4751
Loyauté 645, 4163
Loyer 3757
Lubavitch 1333
Luhmann, Niklas 169, 216, 477, 1197
Lukes, Stephen 216
Machiavélisme 1109
MacIntyre, Alasdair 972
Macroéconomie 291
Mafia 5158
Magie 1239, 1345
Main-d'oeuvre féminine 2840, 4328, 4342, 4349, 4550
Maintien de l'ordre 4787, 4798, 4803, 4804, 4805, 4816, 4836, 5047, 5133, 5134, 5203, 5217, 5246
Maintien du revenu 4247
Malades 411, 2497, 3322, 5409, 5426, 5564, 5634, 5642, 5658, 5662, 5675, 5676, 5795, 5805, 5822
Maladie diététique 2153
Maladie mentale 267, 326, 396, 468, 568, 656, 667, 1224, 1436, 2105, 2314, 2339, 2549, 3345, 4442, 5084, 5217, 5281, 5414, 5428, 5586, 5838, 5847, 5849, 5850
Maladie sexuellement transmissible 2324
Maladies 481, 932, 2304, 2305, 2306, 2310, 2313, 2317, 2320, 2321, 2328, 2335, 2341, 2343, 2345, 2347, 2350, 2356, 2419, 2667, 2774, 3007, 3409, 5373, 5411, 5634, 5695, 5701, 5753
see also: Anorexie, Epilepsie, Maladie sexuellement transmissible, Maladies professionnelles, SIDA, Tuberculose

570

Index des matières

Maladies professionnelles 4442, 5762
Malnutrition 4034, 5335
Mann, Michael 4776
Mannheim, Karl 130, 144, 1662
Maori 997, 3202
Marché 811, 1285, 1803, 2842, 3285, 4162, 4175, 4181, 4185, 4350, 4540, 5118, 5463, 5532, 5747
see also: Marché du logement, Marché du travail, Marché foncier, Marché noir
Marché du logement 3733, 3736, 3742, 3745, 3754, 3757, 3772, 3791
Marché du travail 203, 1991, 2025, 2670, 2801, 2824, 2901, 2932, 3030, 3238, 3285, 3286, 3314, 3319, 3324, 3335, 3372, 3389, 3420, 3541, 3894, 4023, 4178, 4249, 4252, 4258, 4261, 4263, 4272, 4273, 4278, 4279, 4281, 4283, 4284, 4285, 4291, 4296, 4301, 4313, 4316, 4317, 4320, 4322, 4327, 4328, 4336, 4347, 4354, 4369, 4379, 4382, 4385, 4387, 4390, 4487, 4488, 4514, 4533, 4538, 4587, 4591, 4637, 4639, 4641
Marché foncier 3732, 3754, 3838
Marché noir 5186
Marché unique européen 5509
Marcuse, Herbert 120, 136
Marginalité 2158
Marginaux 3749
Mari 536, 2554, 2607, 5253
Mariage 333, 702, 2286, 2296, 2362, 2405, 2420, 2421, 2453, 2454, 2476, 2501, 2523, 2533, 2535, 2536, 2539, 2541, 2542, 2544, 2547, 2548, 2552, 2558, 2560, 2561, 2562, 2564, 2567, 2575, 2576, 2579, 2580, 2581, 2583, 2584, 2590, 2591, 2592, 2598, 2599, 2600, 2601, 2604, 2605, 2608, 2704, 2850, 2862, 3287
see also: Âge au mariage, Intermariage, Mariages interraciaux, Remariage
Mariages interraciaux 2351, 3127
Marine de guerre 5004
Marques commerciales 1184

Marx, Karl 93, 162, 1193, 1225, 1902, 1903, 4015, 4773
Marxisme 141, 1864, 1902, 3983, 3987, 4221, 4759, 4764, 5445
Masculinité 589, 1087, 2624, 2660, 2873, 2878, 2881, 2882, 2887, 2888, 2894, 2896, 2897, 2898, 2908, 2916, 2959, 2967, 2982, 3020, 4105, 4509, 5092, 5102, 5433
Matérialisme 374, 812, 1128, 4966
Maternité 616, 2252, 2255, 2425, 2467, 2502, 2525, 2557, 2610, 2615, 2618, 2632, 2684, 2734
see also: Maternité de substitution
Maternité de substitution 2209, 2242, 5552
Maternité précoce 2122, 2260, 2292, 2296, 2458, 2517, 2618, 3009
Mathématiques 4324
Maya 3926
Mead, George 223
Médecament social 2347, 2816, 5633, 5696, 5698
Médecament traditionnelle 5643
Médecine 2359, 3016, 3447, 5275, 5641, 5675
see also: Chirurgie, Histoire de la médicine, Médecament sociale, Médecament traditionnelle
Médecins 4547, 4549, 5641, 5646, 5648, 5649, 5658, 5668, 5669, 5679, 5686, 5701, 5747, 5795, 5817
Médiation 642, 676, 676, 686, 718, 728, 2424, 2486, 3813, 5007, 5043, 5199
Médicaments 1196, 2571, 5197, 5224, 5372, 5385, 5393, 5400, 5405, 5407
see also: Cocaïne, Heroïné, Trafic de la drogue
Mémoire 528, 529, 530, 531, 532, 533, 534, 535, 536, 537, 538, 539, 540, 541, 542, 569, 674, 725, 1024, 1421, 5081, 5842
Mémoires 259
Menace 582, 600, 1089, 2652
Ménagères 2902, 2917, 2921, 2922, 4317, 5467

571

Index des matières

Ménages   1111, 1460, 1999, 2000, 2011, 2025, 2098, 2180, 2437, 2463, 2508, 2513, 2520, 2532, 2570, 2635, 2746, 2822, 2838, 2842, 2861, 2901, 2921, 2924, 2972, 3273, 3512, 3532, 3597, 3742, 3744, 3745, 3771, 3964, 4021, 4034, 4046, 4057, 4238, 4384, 5038, 5240, 5261, 5330, 5474, 5480
Mennonites   3135, 3532
Ménopause   2042, 2750
Menstruation   2187
Mentalité   381, 802, 3040
Mère   689, 914, 961, 1720, 2238, 2335, 2443, 2485, 2504, 2523, 2582, 2614, 2630, 2631, 2633, 2634, 2644, 2675, 2870, 2879, 2901, 4317, 4343, 5084, 5320, 5356, 5532, 5586, 5654, 5704
see also: Maternité précoce, Mères célibataires, Mères travailleuses
Mères célibataires   2161, 2610, 5332
Mères travailleuses   914, 961, 2271, 2468, 2680, 2839, 2890, 2901, 2922, 4314, 4320, 4325, 4339, 4349, 4447, 5389
Messages   384
Mesure   279, 281, 292, 309, 383, 1165, 1483, 2005, 2227, 5319, 5565, 5673
Mesure de la personnalité   2094
Mesure du revenu   4030, 4068
Métaphore   927, 1378, 3435
Méthode de production   3987
Méthode des moindres carrés   299, 746
Méthodes contraceptives   2162
Méthodes de formation   4567
Méthodes de planification   830
Méthodes de recherche   59, 226, 231, 233, 240, 246, 256, 259, 273, 282, 293, 318, 328, 353, 360, 363, 551, 1378, 2426, 4614
see also: Travail sur le terrain
Méthodes pédagogiques   1815
Méthodes statistiques   64, 264, 288, 289, 291, 306, 307, 308, 319, 421
Méthodologie   8, 58, 138, 152, 189, 221, 226, 227, 229, 239, 240, 247, 287, 338, 856, 1066, 1388, 1394, 2007, 2013, 2028, 2518, 2672, 2844, 3539, 4425, 4572, 5057, 5214
see also: Méthodologie anthropologique, Méthodologie économique, Méthodologie sociologique
Méthodologie anthropologique   336
see also: Observation participante
Méthodologie économique   3962
Méthodologie sociologique   10, 53, 106, 113, 193, 228, 229, 235, 241, 244, 245, 249, 253, 254, 260, 311, 324, 329, 344, 347, 350, 882, 898
Métis   3132
Métissage   3197
Meutre   3038, 5136
Mexicains   2609, 3054, 3115, 3127, 3324, 3346, 3390, 3426, 4902
Michelangelo   2992
Microordinateurs   4564
Microsociologie   1929
Migrateurs   1541, 2163, 3058, 3078, 3081, 3093, 3098, 3155, 3242, 3251, 3259, 3284, 3285, 3295, 3296, 3319, 3321, 3322, 3338, 3342, 3343, 3351, 3354, 3366, 3398, 3412, 3417, 3538, 3642, 3659, 3667, 3693, 3734, 5623, 5705
Migration   1270, 1851, 1970, 1989, 2000, 2005, 2014, 2022, 2023, 2026, 2321, 2439, 2892, 3061, 3113, 3122, 3186, 3248, 3250, 3252, 3255, 3256, 3258, 3262, 3263, 3273, 3275, 3281, 3282, 3286, 3287, 3288, 3290, 3291, 3292, 3294, 3299, 3303, 3305, 3312, 3314, 3316, 3358, 3359, 3378, 3384, 3385, 3393, 3395, 3420, 3421, 3423, 3426, 3428, 3540, 3579, 3620, 3693, 4222, 4374, 5403
see also: Migration de retour, Migration de travail, Migration externe, Migration forcée, Migration internationale, Migration interne, Migration intrarégionale, Migration rurale-urbaine, Migration urbaine-rurale

Index des matières

Migration de retour   3251, 3262, 3265, 3283, 3304, 3337, 3340, 3344, 3399, 3629
Migration de travail   3382, 3390, 3403, 3544, 3629, 4303
Migration externe   3353
Migration forcée   2197
Migration internationale   2018, 2026, 2038, 2192, 3286, 3305, 3311, 3392, 3395, 3396, 3397, 3399, 3402, 3403, 3404, 3405, 3408, 3409, 3410, 3411, 3412, 3413, 3415, 3416, 3419, 3422, 3424, 3426, 3427, 3428, 4289
Migration interne   351, 2000, 2022, 2192, 3032, 3286, 3352, 3353, 3354, 3355, 3358, 3360, 3361, 3362, 3363, 3367, 3368, 3369, 3370, 3372, 3374, 3375, 3376, 3377, 3378, 3380, 3381, 3383, 3386, 3387, 3388, 3389, 3391, 3502, 3537, 3653, 3659, 3762, 4254
Migration intrarégionale   3286
Migration rurale-urbaine   1406, 2023, 3081, 3155, 3296, 3356, 3359, 3364, 3365, 3366, 3371, 3372, 3373, 3379, 3382, 3384, 3385, 3537, 3538, 3540, 3541, 3643, 3948, 4081, 4254, 4289
Migration urbaine-rurale   3652
Migrations alternantes   2320, 3280, 3315, 3356, 3910, 4352
Milieu culturel   1127
Milieu de travail   4407, 4428, 4509, 5362
Milieu familial   2433, 4019
Milieu professionnel   4459, 4472
Milieu social   1122, 1127
Milieu urbain   3657, 3664, 3675, 3695, 3701, 3872, 3880, 3909, 5103, 5411
Militaires   1171, 2823, 4996 2933, 5000, 5001, 5002, 5003, 5004
Militaires et politique   4997
Militants   176
Militarisme   2933, 4776, 4999, 5033
Mines
 see: Mines d'or, Mines de houille
Mines de houille   3525
Mines d'or   4295, 4589

Minorités   464, 738, 1375, 1616, 1709, 1782, 1786, 3023, 3060, 3070, 3074, 3076, 3096, 3144, 3172, 3179, 3216, 3217, 3229, 3239, 3327, 3685, 4435, 4845, 5215, 5456, 5546
 see also: Minorités ethniques, Minorités linguistiques, Minorités religieuses
Minorités ethniques   78, 816, 922, 1031, 1616, 1740, 1992, 2154, 2420, 2619, 3043, 3044, 3047, 3051, 3056, 3066, 3067, 3071, 3074, 3076, 3079, 3082, 3092, 3096, 3097, 3150, 3153, 3156, 3161, 3162, 3163, 3166, 3167, 3181, 3199, 3224, 3254, 3264, 3320, 3336, 3374, 3419, 3530, 3808, 4071, 4085, 4091, 4107, 4123, 4128, 4198, 4207, 4700, 4789, 4828, 5623, 5631
Minorités linguistiques   1376, 1383, 1400, 1406, 1407, 1418, 1474, 1564, 3046, 3270
Minorités religieuses   3105
Mise en oeuvre d'une politique   1727
Missions religieuses   1236
Mobilisation politique   4886, 4896, 4917, 4938
Mobilisation sociale   4911, 4969
Mobilité ascendante   892, 3054, 4049, 5341
Mobilité de la main d'oeuvre   3286, 3355, 4269, 4281, 4282, 4297, 4438, 4539
Mobilité professionnelle   2643, 4028, 4269, 4330, 4417, 4491, 4497, 4515, 4547, 4679
Mobilité résidentielle   351, 1484, 1851, 3275, 3362, 3376, 3758, 3770, 3802, 3805, 3853
Mobilité sociale   303, 1291, 1851, 1852, 1853, 1858, 1860, 1865, 1870, 1878, 2413, 2413, 2841, 2844, 3770, 3802, 3805, 4049, 4498, 4962, 4975, 5341
Mode   1106, 1107, 1126, 1129, 4106, 4173
Mode de production asiatique   3969, 3991

573

Index des matières

Modèles   262, 269, 270, 278, 279, 280, 283, 297, 299, 446, 472, 485, 510, 522, 677, 730, 747, 768, 781, 832, 1049, 1104, 1207, 1660, 1814, 1890, 1981, 2128, 2364, 2483, 2486, 2580, 2639, 3014, 3071, 3919, 3928, 4146, 4147, 4466, 4513, 4586, 4733, 5251, 5532, 5595, 5774
see also: Modèles de décision, Modèles dynamiques, Modèles économiques, Modèles linéaires, Modèles mathématiques, Modèles non linéaires, Modèles statistiques
Modèles culturels   4249
Modèles de décision   296, 317, 767
Modèles dynamiques   284
Modèles économiques   2262, 2437, 4017
Modèles linéaires   574
Modèles mathématiques   261, 268, 793, 1091
Modèles non linéaires   284, 311
Modèles spatiales   314, 3454, 3800, 3810, 3811
Modèles statistiques   260, 277
Modélisation   748, 4183
Modernisation   29, 35, 180, 209, 813, 1618, 1680, 1700, 1719, 1921, 1935, 1945, 1946, 1963, 1975, 1977, 2490, 2708, 2835, 3600, 3621, 3717, 4031, 4076, 4108, 4206, 4741, 4851, 4852, 4853
Modernisme   118, 480, 1033, 1059, 1943, 1951, 4807
Modernité   172, 972, 991, 1016, 1023, 1032, 1039, 1270, 1331, 1926, 1973, 2910, 3029, 3193, 3481, 3652, 3719, 4221
Modes de production
see: Mode de production asiatique
Modes de vie   1122, 1127, 1899, 1970, 2172, 2423, 2521, 2992, 3512, 3541, 3647, 4163, 5655, 5667
Moines   1242
Monarchie   1543
Montagnes   3557, 3568
Montesquieu, Charles de Secondat   86
Morale   127, 132, 3964, 5818

Morales   122, 225, 404, 1127, 1135, 1141, 1144, 1150, 1163, 1172, 2337, 2991, 3444, 5095, 5180, 5786, 5817, 5819, 5820
Moralité   135, 137, 645, 1138, 1140, 1144, 1145, 1153, 1159, 1162, 1178, 1282, 4830, 5026, 5137, 5785, 5786, 5797
see also: Moralité politique
Moralité politique   1499
Morbidité   2203, 2322, 2333, 2340, 2361
Mormonisme   2157, 3383
Mort   147, 257, 927, 1016, 1124, 1234, 1327, 1409, 2182, 2194, 2358, 2370, 2377, 2387, 2421, 2526, 5409, 5426, 5759, 5791, 5793, 5821
see also: Causes de décès
Mortalité   1168, 1964, 1986, 1989, 2192, 2348, 2349, 2354, 2355, 2356, 2358, 2360, 2361, 2362, 2365, 2367, 2368, 2369, 2370, 2371, 2372, 2373, 2374, 2375, 2377, 2379, 2380, 2381, 2382, 2383, 2384, 2385, 2388, 2418, 3940, 4013, 5315, 5821
see also: Mortalité des enfants, Mortalité infantile
Mortalité des enfants   2108, 2276, 2351, 2352, 2353, 2363, 2386
Mortalité infantile   2350, 2357, 2359, 2366, 2373, 2375, 2376, 2381, 5666
Mosquées   1231
Motivation   330, 437, 565, 590, 733, 737, 3469, 4380, 4414, 4437, 4997, 5773
see also: Motivation d'accomplissement
Motivation au travail   907, 4397, 4408, 4449, 4460, 4463
Motivation d'accomplissement   565, 907
see also: Accomplissement scolaire
Mots   1492
Moutons   3078
Mouvement anticuléaire   4897, 4909
Mouvementes féministes   1282, 2724, 2743, 2745, 2747, 2749, 2762, 2765,

Index des matières

2779, 2780, 2781, 2782, 4867, 4909, 4938
Mouvements contestataires   4866, 4874, 4875, 4877, 4919, 4927
Mouvements de résistance   4139
Mouvements d'indépendance   1516
Mouvements écologiques   4861, 4879, 4880, 4881, 4889, 4940, 4943
Mouvements étudiants   4860, 4928
Mouvements nationalistes   2780, 2833
Mouvements ouvriers   1264, 4308, 4624, 4662, 4672, 4681, 4691, 4938 4612, 4674, 4680
Mouvements pacifistes   4885, 4909, 4927, 4938, 4945
Mouvements paysans   3500
Mouvements politiques   4861, 4902, 4903
see also: Mouvement anticuléaire, Mouvements révolutionnaires
Mouvements religieux   398, 1238, 1240, 1241, 1254, 1260, 1282, 1288, 1973, 2923
Mouvements révolutionnaires   4865, 5118
Mouvements séparatistes   4921
Mouvements sociaux   220, 816, 1005, 1048, 1282, 1917, 1959, 1969, 1973, 2086, 2736, 3232, 3450, 3616, 4792, 4862, 4864, 4867, 4868, 4871, 4872, 4873, 4875, 4877, 4878, 4879, 4884, 4885, 4887, 4894, 4895, 4897, 4898, 4899, 4901, 4904, 4905, 4906, 4907, 4908, 4912, 4917, 4918, 4923, 4924, 4925, 4926, 4928, 4930, 4931, 4933, 4935, 4936, 4939, 4941, 5126, 5508
Mouvements urbains   4862
Moyen Âge   5313
Moyens de communication   403, 896, 989, 1030, 1043, 1074, 1103, 1169, 1310, 1441, 1445, 1448, 1449, 1498, 1499, 1500, 1501, 1502, 1505, 1506, 1507, 1508, 1509, 1510, 1512, 1513, 1514, 1515, 1517, 1518, 1519, 1520, 1521, 1523, 1524, 1525, 1526, 1527, 1528, 1529, 1530, 1531, 1532, 1533, 1534, 1535, 1536, 1537, 1538, 1540, 1541, 1544, 1545, 1546, 1548, 1549, 1550, 1551, 1552, 1553, 1554, 1555, 1556, 1557, 1558, 1559, 1570, 1574, 1579, 1609, 1675, 1704, 2146, 2891, 4194, 4204, 4743, 4900, 4947, 4960, 4970, 4974, 4985, 5021, 5048, 5435
see also: Presse
Multiculturalisme   236, 994, 1010, 1015, 1017, 1030, 1044, 1648, 1675, 1992, 3027, 3039, 3083, 3085, 3089, 3094, 3180, 3643, 3652, 3659, 3693, 4772
Multilinguisme   1560, 1563, 1567, 1569
Musées   236
see also: Musées historiques
Musées historiques   4747
Musique   1596, 1611, 1616, 1625, 5295
see also: Ethnomusicologie, Musique pop, Musique rock
Musique pop   1613, 2163
Musique populaire   1276, 1599, 1621, 1630, 5295
Musique rock   1621, 1630, 1635, 2158
Musulman   1308, 1310, 1311, 1313, 1318, 1319, 1320, 1323, 1324, 1861, 2650, 2685, 2845, 2864, 2875, 3062, 3125, 3139
Mutilations corporelles   2987
Mythes   2, 1237, 1666, 2305, 2655, 4014
Mythologie   1237
Naissance   2181, 2218, 2245, 2246, 2248, 2264, 2288, 2331, 2403, 2533, 2675, 5637, 5683, 5691, 5764, 5766, 5825
Narcissisme   560
Narration d'histoires   1438, 2075, 4448
Nation   1022, 1380, 3090, 3094, 3099, 3150, 4913, 4921, 5005
Nationalisme   991, 1006, 1015, 1021, 1022, 1260, 1308, 1415, 1585, 1871, 2425, 2686, 2735, 2744, 2800, 2831, 3037, 3074, 3089, 3099, 3104, 3108, 3111, 3118, 3119, 3129, 3161, 3178, 3210, 3230, 4763, 4774, 4775, 4776, 4905, 4950, 4979, 5010, 5025

see also: Nationalisme culturel
Nationalisme culturel   3036
Nationalité   3144, 5181, 5286
Naturalisation   3113
Nature   931, 3437, 3443, 3453, 3462, 3465, 3578, 5373
Nature humaine   370, 1164, 3464
Nazisme   1523, 3175
Négociants
see: Trafiquants de drogue
Négociation   651, 657, 2259, 2437, 4243, 4619
see also: Négociation collective, Négociations salariales
Négociation collective   4357, 4581, 4584, 4585, 4590, 4599, 4604, 4638, 4676
Négociations salariales   4592, 4597
Négociations de paix   728
Néoconservatisme   4905
Néolibéralisme   4883, 4903
Nietzsche, Friedrich   186, 4777
Niveau de vie   910, 1877, 2342, 2498, 4024, 4027, 4031, 4045, 4210, 5314, 5635
Niveau du chômage   5096
Niveaux d'enseignement   1912, 2542, 4324, 4342, 5380
Noël   1128, 1593, 2868
Noirs   78, 719, 970, 1215, 1249, 1276, 1631, 1636, 1731, 1904, 2129, 2135, 2331, 2354, 2427, 2485, 2522, 2528, 2544, 2586, 2588, 2590, 2591, 2605, 2680, 2700, 2723, 2769, 2867, 2895, 2906, 2976, 3027, 3028, 3029, 3035, 3043, 3055, 3060, 3068, 3070, 3085, 3087, 3147, 3148, 3160, 3165, 3169, 3173, 3184, 3192, 3198, 3208, 3226, 3227, 3231, 3233, 3238, 3245, 3423, 3501, 3507, 3770, 3795, 3796, 3805, 4032, 4071, 4123, 4372, 4379, 4402, 4491, 4514, 4652, 4679, 4720, 4789, 4845, 4855, 4989, 5118, 5134, 5147, 5148, 5225, 5281, 5406, 5563, 5631, 5638, 5688, 5779
Nomades   3130, 3164
Nomadisme   3472

Noms   538, 1122, 2572, 3332, 3466, 4774
Normalisation   1042, 1729, 1777
Normes de qualité   2227, 4712
Normes de travail   4398
Normes sociales   1029, 1090, 1463, 1479, 2145, 5022
Nostalgie   1575
Nouvel ordre économique international   5011
Nouvelles   814, 1410, 1449, 1518, 1537, 1539, 1558
Novghorodtsev, P.I.   177
Nuptialité   2286, 2539
Nutrition   1105, 1114, 1115, 2093, 4025, 5335
Obesité   490, 584, 1104, 1110
Objectivité   113, 1520
Obligation   458
Observation   106, 4438, 5048
Observation participante   1048
OCDE   1991
Oeuvre dramatique   1582, 1583, 1593, 1791
Oeuvres d'art   1626
Offre   4273
see also: Disponibilités alimentaires, Disponibilités énergétiques, Offre de main d'oeuvre
Offre de main d'oeuvre   3328, 3377, 3771, 3894, 4081, 4245, 4275, 4281, 4284, 4323, 4337, 4498, 5537
Offre et demande   2299
Ontologie   104, 1591
Opérations des initiés   557, 5186
Opinion   934, 954, 1534
see also: Opinion politique, Opinion publique
Opinion politique   29, 4962
Opinion publique   344, 345, 915, 926, 938, 946, 960, 962, 963, 964, 967, 1037, 1278, 1519, 1534, 1557, 1938, 2210, 2217, 2235, 2237, 2243, 2327, 3205, 3209, 3227, 4118, 4671, 4824, 4988, 4990, 5014, 5347, 5417, 5768
Opposition politique   3636, 4873
Optimisme   561, 597, 2317

Index des matières

Ordinateurs   116, 166, 340, 720, 1136, 1446, 1447, 1743, 3596, 4271, 4403, 4551, 4564, 4730
see also: Microordinateurs
Ordre mondial   1074, 1270, 1310, 1388, 1927, 3982, 5010, 5017, 5018, 5020, 5023
Ordre public   957, 1079, 1196, 5107, 5108, 5144
Ordre social   91, 132, 157, 174, 182, 404, 1081, 1640, 1833, 1868, 2445, 2849, 5508
Ordres religieux   1242
Organes sensoriels   2945
Organisation   773, 777, 781, 784, 789, 797, 800, 811, 816, 823, 827, 839, 842, 843, 846, 847, 850, 859, 862, 865, 881, 897, 2684, 4067, 4148, 4203, 4283, 4433, 4578, 4670, 4871, 4912, 4924, 5118, 5673
see also: Organisation administrative, Organisation communautaire, Organisation de l'entreprise, Organisation du travail, Organisation économique, Organisation industrielle, Sociologie des organisations
Organisation administrative   776
Organisation bénévole   798, 1265
Organisation communautaire   3503, 3508, 3509, 3511, 3515, 3531, 3730, 5757
Organisation de l'entreprise   525, 819, 845, 872, 4448, 4532
Organisation du travail   4099, 4136, 4405, 4410, 4432
Organisation économique   4124, 4138
Organisation industrielle   3834, 4236, 4620
Organisations   340, 469, 668, 717, 721, 778, 783, 785, 787, 792, 793, 794, 796, 808, 810, 813, 814, 826, 828, 830, 849, 851, 853, 854, 863, 876, 880, 952, 1042, 4101, 4151, 4168, 4181, 4331, 4398, 4456, 4908
see also: Organisations agricoles, Organisations bénévoles, Organisations de masse,
Organisations féminines, Organisations internationales, Organisations non-gouvernementales, Organisations non-profit, Organisations professionnelles
Organisations agricoles   3636, 4912
Organisations bénévoles   798, 831, 836, 3637, 4883, 5320, 5526, 5527
Organisations de masse   4914
Organisations féminines   816, 2684, 4359
Organisations internationales   807, 847, 5008, 5035
Organisations non-gouvernementales   774, 846, 1935, 4912
Organisations non-profit   841, 899, 3503, 4132, 5471, 5489
Organisations professionnelles   4538, 4548
Orientation professionnelle   4501
Orphelinats   2653
Ortega y Gasset, José   223
Outils   1108
Ouvriers industriels   1853, 4108, 4449, 4488, 4489, 4510, 4518
Ouvriers non-qualifiés   4412
Ouvriers qualifiés   3403, 4264, 4501
Paganisme   1260
Paiement   4263, 4434, 4451, 4618
see also: Égalité de rémunération
Paiements   2493
Paix   923, 943, 4989, 5019, 5035
Palestiniennes   2689, 2780, 2933, 3145, 3297, 3518
Panafricanisme   3027
Paradigmes   18, 249, 529, 780, 889, 2974
Parenté   2429, 2441, 2442, 2445, 2448, 3104, 3388, 3950, 4117, 5503
Parents   473, 684, 719, 1673, 1702, 1725, 2503, 2518, 2519, 2546, 2613, 2616, 2637, 2643, 2644, 2646, 2890, 5143, 5309, 5388, 5581, 5591, 5592, 5602, 5620
see also: Beaux-parents
Pareto, Vilfredo   150, 189, 210, 453
Park, Robert   14

Index des matières

Parole 137, 1360, 1392, 1421, 1432, 1485, 2707
Parsons, Talcott 189, 192, 1812
Parti socio-democrate 2931
Participation au groupe 807, 3529
Participation de la citoyenneté 3534, 3813, 5455, 5514, 5662
Participation de la collectivité 717, 3505, 3510, 3517, 4792, 5680
Participation des femmes 1309
Participation des travailleurs 4413, 4426, 4446, 4709, 4710, 4711, 4712, 4713, 4714, 4715, 4716, 4718
Participation électorale 4960, 4973
Participation politique 1949, 3325, 4869, 4870, 4882, 4907, 4917, 4933, 4952, 4969, 4981
Participation religieuse 1274, 1285
Participation sociale 1048, 2174, 3084, 3513, 3652, 4894, 4918, 4920, 4935
Partis communistes 4830, 4951
Partis conservateurs 4686, 5723, 5742
Partis de droite 4286, 4638
Partis politiques 849, 4783, 4869, 4870, 4890, 4910, 4914, 4933, 4934, 4964, 4972, 4980, 5492
 see also: Parti socio-democrate, Partis communistes, Partis conservateurs, Partis de droite, Partis socialistes
Partis socialistes 4830
Passage à la vie active 3050, 4574
Passé 40, 1024, 2690
Pastoralisme 2903, 3472
Paternalisme 648, 4105, 4589, 4607
Paternité 2648
Paternité-maternité 2440, 2471, 2476, 2486, 2497, 2546, 2566, 2621, 2626, 2638, 2639, 2640, 2908
Pathologie 3673
Pathologie sociale 5049
Patriarcat 2406, 2835, 3483, 5808
Patrimoine culturel
 see: Préservation du patrimoine culturel
Patrimoine des ménages 4065
Patriotisme 753
Paupérisation 5484

Pauvres 2223, 2270, 3761, 3777, 3901, 3904, 3984, 4006, 4053, 4366, 5137, 5278, 5321, 5333, 5335, 5348, 5351, 5464, 5490, 5494, 5723, 5742
Pauvreté 1916, 1982, 2073, 2119, 2346, 2354, 3242, 3540, 3543, 3769, 3896, 3897, 3907, 3930, 3996, 3997, 3998, 4006, 4030, 4034, 4040, 4042, 4048, 4049, 4059, 4210, 4233, 4372, 5062, 5065, 5226, 5273, 5281, 5283, 5304, 5311, 5313, 5314, 5315, 5316, 5317, 5318, 5319, 5324, 5325, 5326, 5327, 5330, 5331, 5332, 5335, 5336, 5338, 5339, 5340, 5341, 5342, 5343, 5345, 5347, 5349, 5350, 5351, 5352, 5353, 5354, 5355, 5356, 5357, 5401, 5486, 5495, 5705, 5723, 5742, 5779
 see also: Culture de pauvreté, Pauvreté rurale, Pauvreté urbaine
Pauvreté rurale 3548, 3585, 3599, 4051, 5346
Pauvreté urbaine 1600, 3382, 3741, 3776, 3777, 3780, 3783, 3843, 3852, 3895, 3897, 3898, 3899, 3900, 3902, 3903, 3904, 3905, 3906, 3908, 4068, 5274, 5312, 5329, 5334, 5337, 5344, 5446, 5603
Pays
 see: Pays arabes
Pays arabes 1050, 1707, 1867, 2198, 3289, 3669, 3817
Pays capitalistes 4594
Pays d'accueil 4528
Pays en développement 209, 402, 1013, 1166, 1282, 1507, 1705, 1727, 1907, 1935, 1987, 2007, 2022, 2103, 2223, 2270, 2288, 2341, 2350, 2357, 2859, 2871, 3373, 3375, 3399, 3407, 3420, 3439, 3510, 3571, 3604, 3638, 3664, 3707, 3716, 3721, 3776, 3816, 3849, 3887, 3903, 3937, 3943, 3949, 3982, 4013, 4034, 4229, 4691, 4750, 4844, 4907, 5006, 5019, 5504, 5636, 5643, 5665, 5675, 5830
 see also: Pays moins développés
Pays industrialisés 4321
Pays islamiques 1318, 1323, 1707, 2750

Index des matières

Pays moins développés   2299, 2353, 4154
Pays multiethniques   3039, 3212, 3829
Pays occidentaux   1047, 1841, 3196, 3936, 5032, 5142, 5429, 5453, 5506, 5559
Paysage   1416, 3463, 3466, 3467, 3494
Paysannerie   3613, 3614, 3623, 3985, 4088
Paysans   3081, 3385, 3612, 3615, 3616, 3617, 3618, 3619, 3620, 3621, 3622, 4083
Peinture   1594, 1605, 1624, 5445
Peirce, Charles Sanders   1372, 1425
Penchant   1121, 5358
 see also: Toxicomanie
Penrose, Roger   1344
Pensée économique   157, 3958, 3959, 3994, 4009
Pensée philosophique   148, 1027, 1135, 1144, 1661, 1678
Pensée politique   1033, 4770, 4778
Pension   2045, 3580, 4411, 5492
Pentecôtisme   1276
Pénurie
 see: Crise du logement
Perception   12, 107, 465, 476, 525, 674, 754, 834, 1029, 1249, 1379, 1399, 1412, 1825, 2942, 3456, 3668, 4045, 4179, 4285, 4977, 5001, 5247, 5450, 5539, 5595
 see also: Perception interpersonnelle, Perception sociale
Perception d'autrui   533, 606, 620, 622, 634, 643, 649, 724, 743, 1069, 1325, 4422
Perception de soi   436, 442, 469, 470, 484, 493, 495, 520, 540, 573, 575, 585, 592, 599, 619, 652, 2546, 4408
Perception interpersonnelle   573, 616, 680, 2094
Perception sociale   408, 547, 612, 620, 624, 630, 643, 662, 663, 670, 691, 922, 962, 1353
Père   685, 1329, 2238, 2435, 2500, 2611, 2623, 2625, 2760, 5785

Perestroika   963, 1552, 1956, 4833, 4987
Performance du groupe   488, 618, 732
Performance économique   3960, 4115, 4124, 4449
Périodiques   1393, 1440
Persécution religieuse   1300
Personnalité   393, 544, 545, 547, 549, 550, 552, 554, 555, 557, 558, 559, 560, 561, 562, 563, 564, 565, 566, 567, 568, 569, 570, 572, 573, 576, 586, 587, 592, 597, 643, 650, 755, 977, 1184, 2317, 2628, 3966, 4436, 4456, 4984, 5516
Personnel   5622
Personnel médical   2816, 4459, 4545, 4557, 5081, 5668, 5672, 5706, 5715, 5735, 5762, 5813, 5826, 5842
Personnes mariées   333, 625, 2257, 2362, 2388, 2537, 2552, 2569, 2597, 4278, 4337, 4505
Perspective mondiale   3441
Perspectives économiques   1936, 4272
Persuasion   919, 1366, 2436, 5679
Perte   5545, 5634
Perte d'emploi   449, 4380, 4386
Perversions sexuelles   2975, 2987, 3018, 5445
Pessimisme   597, 691
Pesticides   4421
Petite enfance   2118, 2209, 5062, 5316, 5681
Petite exploitation agricole   3584
Petite industrie   4133
Petites et moyennes entreprises   2448, 2674, 4071, 4081, 4085, 4091, 4100, 4120, 4123, 4127, 4128, 4129, 4130, 4198, 4207, 4474, 4485, 4569
Petites villes   2039, 3565, 3663, 3686, 3846, 3874
Petits États   1120
Peur   394, 932, 940, 957, 1612, 3697, 4835, 5120, 5265, 5445
Pharmacologie   5401
Phénoménologie   201, 605, 3694
Philippins   2281
Philosophes   127

579

Index des matières

Philosophie   8, 16, 43, 117, 124, 125, 129, 131, 132, 135, 136, 138, 143, 250, 367, 513, 987, 1039, 1058, 1145, 1182, 1197, 1244, 1246, 1348, 1351, 1615, 1644, 1688, 2733, 2757, 4760
see also: Morale, Philosophie de l'éducation, Philosophie politique, Philosophie sociale
Philosophie de la science   1065, 1338, 1346
Philosophie de l'éducation   1357, 1693
Philosophie du droit   1173, 1179, 1191, 1192, 1199, 1205
Philosophie politique   127, 132, 157, 1191, 1842, 3228
Philosophie sociale   1199, 1205, 5472
Phonologie   1492
Photographie   230, 598, 1620
Piaget, Jean   880
Placement familial   676, 2646, 2648, 5569, 5841
Plaisanteries   479, 2040
Planification de la famille   2207, 2214, 2216, 2220, 2223, 2227, 2230, 2236, 2239, 2241, 2263, 2269, 2270, 2272, 2278, 2527, 3499
Planification de la santé   5824, 5826
Planification de l'éducation   1660, 1699, 1701
Planification de l'entreprise   4105, 4406
Planification de l'environnement   2027, 3764, 3894
Planification du développement   1937, 2852
Planification économique   4215
Planification énergétique   3604
Planification linguistique   1371
Planification régionale   3857, 3879, 3894, 4215, 4218, 4223, 4225
Planification rurale   3539, 4737
Planification sociale   3826
Planification stratégique   831, 845, 5073
Plantation   4603, 4717
Plein emploi   4247

Pluralisme   1138, 1282, 1646, 3054, 3060, 3090, 3174, 3407, 4772
see also: Pluralisme religieux, Pluralisme social
Pluralisme religieux   1285
Pluralisme social   1935
Poésie   1480, 1622, 5446
Police   412, 957, 1517, 3163, 3181, 3298, 3570, 4409, 4495, 4786, 4789, 4792, 4795, 4797, 4800, 4802, 4810, 4811, 4812, 4813, 4814, 4817, 4818, 4824, 4836, 5147, 5161, 5181, 5190, 5206, 5225, 5286
see also: Police secrète
Police secrète   4835
Politiciens   491, 1579, 2990, 3820, 4837, 4959
Politique   885, 1558, 1931, 2225, 2830, 3077, 4045, 4801, 4820
Politique agricole   3548, 3564, 3575, 3583, 3587, 3588, 3619, 4210
Politique budgétaire   4210
Politique comparée   338
Politique culturelle   1026, 1034, 1045, 1049, 1535, 1597, 3864
Politique de bien-être   3983, 5270, 5480, 5497, 5505
Politique de développement   3634, 3636
Politique de la jeunesse   2174
Politique de l'éducation   1513, 1644, 1663, 1696, 1697, 1698, 1700, 1703, 1704, 1705, 1706, 1708, 1710, 1711, 1712, 1713, 1714, 1716, 1717, 1718, 1719, 1720, 1721, 1722, 1723, 1727, 1728, 1729, 1731, 1732, 1733, 1734, 1736, 1738, 1755, 1759, 1769, 1773, 1777, 1781, 1783, 1792, 1794, 1804, 1805, 2256, 3324, 4264, 4654
Politique de l'emploi   4245, 4247, 4251, 4257, 4261, 4267, 4279, 4286, 4375, 4388, 4486, 4693
Politique de l'environnement   3430, 3443, 3473, 3498, 3877
Politique de stabilisation   4210
Politique démographique   2031, 2195, 2201, 2220, 2241, 2287, 2334, 2390, 2394, 2761, 2941

Index des matières

Politique des arts 1610
Politique des media 1533, 1586
Politique des prix
  see: Politique des prix alimentaires
Politique des prix alimentaires 2376
Politique des revenus 5465
Politique des transports 3893, 3920
Politique d'immigration 3274, 3290, 3294, 3311, 3417
Politique d'innovation 1350
Politique d'intégration active 1166, 3165, 3184, 3224, 4242, 4311, 4435
Politique du logement 3172, 3423, 3729, 3743, 3747, 3748, 3758, 3777, 3793, 3794, 3845, 3853, 3904, 5498
Politique du travail 4251, 4257, 4267, 4355, 4629
Politique économique 1870, 1991, 3508, 3855, 4214, 4215, 4217, 4228, 4233, 4300, 4639, 4781
  see also: Politique industrielle
Politique ethnique 3201
Politique étrangère 562, 5024
Politique familiale 2087, 2101, 2124, 2408, 2418, 2440, 2465, 2496
Politique fiscale 4771, 4842
Politique foncière 3554, 3882
Politique frontalière 5031
Politique gouvernementale 2096, 2502, 3210, 3234, 3272, 3375, 4253, 4569, 5259, 5372, 5421
Politique industrielle 4127, 4673
Politique internationale 5680
Politique linguistique 1390, 1400, 1401, 1418, 1428, 1435, 1464, 1561, 1562, 1565, 1567, 1801, 3046, 3270, 4946
Politique locale 3534, 3881, 4941
Politique mondiale 5008
Politique pénale 1207, 2991, 5153, 5189, 5192, 5215, 5222, 5227, 5235, 5289, 5420
Politique publique 1449, 1518, 1730, 2318, 2714, 3050, 3505, 3722, 3767, 4124, 4169, 4821, 4842, 4929, 4981, 5226, 5304, 5493, 5598, 5777, 5818
Politique régionale 4219
Politique rurale 3587, 3633, 3634

Politique sanitaire 2205, 4970, 5755, 5757, 5762, 5763, 5768, 5769, 5770, 5771, 5773, 5774, 5775, 5776, 5778, 5780, 5782, 5783
Politique scientifique 251, 1350
Politique sociale 32, 982, 1088, 2031, 2074, 2201, 2319, 2498, 2504, 2624, 2715, 2886, 3192, 3580, 3611, 3767, 4259, 4296, 4300, 4486, 4590, 4708, 5042, 5050, 5054, 5151, 5229, 5268, 5342, 5348, 5456, 5476, 5480, 5499, 5500, 5501, 5504, 5509, 5510, 5515, 5524, 5531, 5532, 5606, 5707, 5723, 5742, 5766, 5768, 5831
Politique urbaine 3648, 3683, 3725, 3793, 3814, 3818, 3823, 3832, 3837, 3848, 3850, 3860, 3863, 3870, 3871, 3874, 3875, 3921, 3922, 3943, 3946, 3948, 4385, 4859, 5052, 5587 3726, 3804, 3852, 3899, 4941
Politisation 3132, 4992
Pollution 2382, 3500, 3664, 3859, 3940, 5693
  see also: Pollution de l'air
Pollution de l'air 2366
Polygamie 2418
Polygynie 2990
Popper, Karl Raimund 100, 101, 1346
Popularité 4960
Population 1950, 1981, 1995, 1997, 2007, 2010, 2013, 2017, 2019, 2020, 2021, 2023, 2024, 2034, 2036, 2186, 2198, 2225, 2272, 3289, 3386, 3428, 3536, 4035, 4046, 4356, 5340
  see also: Population indigène, Population mondiale, Population rurale, Population scolaire, Population urbaine
Population indigène 2197, 3034, 3058, 3079, 3093, 3124, 3155, 3643, 3667, 4303, 4371, 4828, 5127, 5837
Population mondiale 2394
Population rurale 2203, 3536, 3554, 3559, 3568, 3601, 3995
Population scolaire 1660
Population urbaine 3376, 3536, 3749
Populisme 997, 3202

Index des matières

Pornographie 2679, 2719, 2750, 2865, 2949, 2956, 2994, 3004, 4169, 5445
Porter, Cole 2992
Portoricains 3115, 4023
Ports 3762
Positivisme 114, 201, 217, 889, 924
Post-fordisme 2880, 3708, 4126
Postmodernisme 10, 110, 111, 118, 119, 120, 122, 126, 156, 178, 194, 195, 492, 833, 865, 889, 1055, 1056, 1057, 1058, 1059, 1060, 1061, 1062, 1063, 1064, 1065, 1066, 1067, 1068, 1069, 1070, 1071, 1072, 1073, 1074, 1122, 1197, 1310, 1358, 1394, 1443, 1667, 1669, 1678, 1944, 1951, 2736, 3481, 3497, 3521, 3844, 4807
Post-structuralisme 88, 97, 4779
Pouvoir 565, 651, 654, 696, 740, 810, 834, 886, 893, 894, 895, 905, 906, 909, 913, 967, 989, 1082, 1510, 1565, 1598, 1663, 1692, 1751, 1827, 1928, 1978, 2662, 2687, 2771, 2772, 2894, 2916, 3021, 3069, 3117, 3865, 4047, 4535, 4694, 4780, 4821, 4873, 4928, 4944, 5659
Pouvoir de la collectivité 3514, 4944
Pouvoir de négociation 623
Pouvoir local 1571, 3608
Pouvoir politique 1343, 1508, 1529, 3047, 3423
Pragmatique 140, 945, 1414
Pragmatisme 196, 958, 4286
Prairies 3114
Pratique de la pêche 3124
Pratique religieuse 1271, 1302, 1314
Pratiques culturelles 1597
Pré-enquêtes 2612
Préjugé 417, 917, 997, 1646, 3201, 3202, 3219, 3220
  see also: Préjugé racial
Préjugé racial 3206, 3221
Première guerre mondiale 3978
Presbytérianisme 1271
Prescription de rôle 908
Préservation 365, 3576, 3891
  see also: Conservation de la nature, Conservation des ressources

Préservation du patrimoine culturel 3844, 3864, 4747
Presse 940, 1441, 1445, 1498, 1503, 1512, 1516, 1520, 1522, 1523, 1525, 1542, 1543, 1546, 1547, 1549, 1557, 4405, 4905, 4985
Prestige 3618
  see also: Prestige professionnel
Prestige professionnel 1872
Prêtres 1299, 1301, 2998
Prêts 825, 4174
  see also: Prêts bancaires
Prêts bancaires 4201
Prévention de la délinquance 3658, 5101, 5106, 5107, 5144, 5163, 5169, 5174, 5177, 5187, 5415, 5444, 5447, 5449, 5555
Prévisions 2026, 2302, 5402
  see also: Prévisions démographiques
Prévisions démographiques 1980, 1985, 1988, 1989, 2012, 2025, 2027, 2028, 2368, 3894
Prière 1214
Primates 1377, 2698, 2869
Prime enfance 530, 2118
Prise de décision 260, 268, 392, 400, 401, 518, 519, 520, 521, 522, 523, 524, 525, 526, 527, 714, 738, 739, 741, 756, 784, 831, 850, 863, 866, 879, 895, 1121, 1150, 2204, 2437, 2602, 2603, 2713, 2827, 2854, 3461, 3965, 4090, 4116, 4416, 4434, 4821, 4857, 5071, 5476, 5662, 5679, 5703, 5817, 5822
  see also: Prise de décision en groupe
Prise de décision en groupe 523, 723, 737, 739, 759, 767
Prison 166, 396, 2450, 4499, 4517, 5122, 5179, 5183, 5184, 5185, 5188, 5195, 5198, 5214, 5216, 5218, 5219, 5220, 5223, 5229, 5231, 5232, 5233, 5234, 5610
Prisonniers 442, 2450, 3169, 5179, 5184, 5231
Privation 4061, 5073
Privation relative 5319

582

Index des matières

Privatisation   1026, 1529, 3607, 3767, 3772, 3867, 3977, 3988, 3993, 4118, 4121, 4216, 4584, 4595, 5451, 5535
Prix   3756, 4187, 4729
   see also: Prix du logement, Prix relatifs
Prix du logement   3759, 3777, 3854, 3904
Prix relatifs   200
Probabilité   290, 323, 371, 5462
Problèmes sociaux   407, 522, 963, 1265, 1550, 1740, 1832, 1947, 1964, 2129, 2144, 2152, 2974, 3440, 3585, 3728, 3900, 4920, 5039, 5041, 5042, 5045, 5047, 5048, 5049, 5050, 5051, 5052, 5053, 5054, 5055, 5056, 5057, 5058, 5060, 5065, 5071, 5080, 5089, 5092, 5093, 5095, 5097, 5106, 5107, 5110, 5118, 5126, 5127, 5130, 5143, 5171, 5172, 5180, 5181, 5199, 5206, 5210, 5214, 5224, 5238, 5242, 5247, 5248, 5257, 5260, 5271, 5277, 5282, 5286, 5290, 5308, 5309, 5317, 5332, 5337, 5339, 5362, 5372, 5386, 5387, 5392, 5393, 5395, 5398, 5405, 5406, 5409, 5412, 5416, 5422, 5426, 5581, 5725
Procès civil   810, 1173
Processus législatif   2237, 2237
Processus stochastiques   262, 296, 4032
Procréation   2218
Producteurs   4122
Production   2661, 4089, 4146, 4150, 4341, 4510
   see also: Modes de production, Production agricole, Production industrielle
Production agricole   2188, 3560, 3575, 3593, 4083
Production alimentaire   3584, 4087
Production animale   4087
Production d'énergie   4664
Production industrielle   4090, 4277
Productivité   4413, 4437, 4555, 4587, 4588, 4619, 5673
   see also: Productivité agricole, Productivité industrielle

Productivité agricole   3564, 3584
Productivité industrielle   1010
Produit intérieur brut   4004
Produits de base   1443
Professeurs   1136, 1515, 1815
Profession legale   2937, 4324, 4553
Professionnalisation   4551
Professionnalisme   1036, 4545, 4994, 5686
Professions   2189, 2913, 3897, 4037, 4111, 4240, 4446, 4493, 4516, 4534, 4541, 4542, 4559, 4562, 5263, 5628, 5659
   see also: Profession legale, Professions médicales, Professorat
Professions médicales   4543
Professorat   452, 1515, 1786, 1867, 2829, 2942, 2944, 4537, 4544, 4555, 4556, 4560, 4654, 4663
Profit   4035
Programmation
   see: Programmation linéaire
Programmation linéaire   287
Programmes de développement   5348
Programmes de recherche   1948
Programmes d'ordinateur   181
Progrès scientifique   1342, 1355
Progrès scientifique et technique   1337, 1349
Prohibition de l'inceste   3019
Prohibition sexuelle   2963, 2975
Projections démographiques   1981, 1983
Projets de développement   3555
Prolétariat   1137
Prolétarisation   1907
Promotion de la femme   2767, 2798, 2929, 2936, 4493, 4555
Propagande   1169
Propriétaires   3760, 4124
Propriétaires fonciers   3574, 3582, 3606, 3617
Propriété   2410, 2709, 3672, 3847, 3993
   see also: Propriété foncière, Propriété intellectuelle, Propriété privée
Propriété du domicile   3026

583

Index des matières

Propriété foncière 1440, 3708, 3759, 3854
3582, 3589
Propriété intellectuelle 1184
Propriété privée 3589
Propriété publique 3582
Prospérité 4048
Prostitution 2316, 2948, 2960, 2991
Protection de l'enfance 2091, 2092, 2096, 2113, 2116, 2124, 2620, 5064, 5070, 5551, 5583, 5596, 5603
Protection de l'environnement 365, 3436, 3469, 3489, 4869, 4870, 4891, 4943
Protection des animaux 3443
Protection des données 71, 77
Protection légale 2697, 3276, 4332, 4823
Protestantisme 1137, 1269, 1281, 1295
Protestants 1263, 1289, 1292, 1293, 1294, 1296, 1303, 1306, 2579
Proust, Marcel 2992
Prudhommes 4644
Psychanalyse 404, 473, 5445
Psychiatre 371, 396, 398, 411, 420, 421, 427, 2048, 2154, 3082, 3322, 4459, 5047, 5586, 5713, 5834, 5836
see also: Psychiatrie sociale
Psychiatrie sociale 413, 5850
Psychologie 246, 366, 367, 372, 374, 377, 378, 382, 385, 389, 399, 400, 401, 402, 405, 406, 409, 410, 412, 418, 499, 515, 545, 667, 755, 873, 1052, 1143, 1473, 1500, 1683, 1909, 2154, 2699, 2713, 2727, 2759, 2873, 2953, 2968, 3082, 4196, 4455, 4643, 5146, 5223
see also: Psychologie clinique, Psychologie de l'éducation, Psychologie de l'enfant, Psychologie de l'environnement, Psychologie économique, Psychologie évolutionniste, Psychologie expérimentale, Psychologie génétique, Psychologie industrielle, Psychologie politique, Psychologie sociale
Psychologie clinique 379

Psychologie de l'éducation 390
Psychologie de l'enfant 2095, 2111, 4199
Psychologie de l'environnement 387, 3431
Psychologie économique 3957, 3966, 4172
Psychologie évolutionniste 5087, 5254
Psychologie expérimentale 362, 392
Psychologie génétique 548, 553
Psychologie industrielle 835, 4235
Psychologie politique 1402, 4753, 4754, 5008
Psychologie sociale 361, 362, 363, 368, 369, 373, 391, 394, 404, 406, 407, 408, 413, 414, 415, 416, 417, 418, 419, 422, 426, 428, 429, 551, 624, 663, 733, 928, 1084, 1102, 1966, 1978, 3966, 5162
Psychologues 2491, 4235
Psychométrie 550, 567
Psychopathologie 129, 373, 574
Psychosociologie 959, 3259, 4386
Psychothérapie 390, 425, 431, 539, 2759, 3350, 5586
see also: Psychothérapie de groupe
Psychothérapie de groupe 735, 736
Public 1517, 1531, 1592, 1612
Publicité 1439, 1440, 1441, 1442, 1443, 1444, 1445, 2796, 2880, 4156, 4169, 4186, 4189, 4192, 4194, 5642
Puériculture 1664, 2431, 2467, 2638, 2645, 5524
Punjabi 3127
Qualification professionnelle 3266, 4324, 4539
Qualification requise pour l'emploi 4262, 4489
Qualité de la vie 474, 1790, 2108, 2394, 2488, 3567, 3707, 4007, 4020, 4026, 4034, 4036, 4038, 4050, 4063, 4068, 5045, 5183, 5635, 5667, 5811
Qualité des produits 4190
Quartier 2074, 2986, 3522, 3816, 3857, 3951, 5138, 5331
Quechua 3078, 3093
Questionnaires 51, 324, 328, 329, 344, 347, 349, 350, 351, 359

Index des matières

Quiché 1415
Quinn, Warren 1170
Race 361, 423, 961, 1084, 1910, 2323, 2589, 2785, 2885, 3024, 3026, 3028, 3055, 3085, 3094, 3101, 3108, 3136, 3137, 3160, 3169, 3170, 3172, 3182, 3197, 3213, 3222, 3230, 3241, 3483, 3770, 3805, 3873, 4032, 4161, 4491, 5226, 5304, 5334, 5406, 5596, 5638
Races humaines 1369
Racisme 58, 417, 941, 951, 997, 1187, 1646, 1910, 2170, 2700, 2782, 3085, 3171, 3175, 3178, 3183, 3187, 3194, 3196, 3197, 3202, 3207, 3208, 3210, 3213, 3216, 3219, 3222, 3225, 3226, 3227, 3228, 3229, 3230, 3232, 3233, 3236, 3237, 3242, 3245, 3288, 3808, 4545, 5090, 5147, 5149, 5225, 5433, 5546, 5626, 5690, 5705
Radicalisme 1970, 2754, 3174
Radio 409, 1511, 1539, 1570, 1589
Radiodiffusion 409, 1184, 1511, 1525, 1558, 1570, 1586, 1589
Raisonnement 199, 382, 510, 874, 1150, 3015
Rang de naissance 2180, 2189
Rassemblement des données 267, 326, 331, 332, 334, 337, 339, 340, 346, 353, 354, 355, 357, 773
Rastifarianisme 1276
Rationalisation 1113, 4239, 4429
Rationalisme 142, 1252
Rationalité 134, 169, 203, 210, 866, 1033, 1116, 1629, 3965, 4847, 4956
Rationnement 5750, 5767, 5824
Rawls, John 123, 150
Read, Grantley Dick 2675
Réadaptation des délinquants 960
Réadaptation sociale 4722
Reagan, Ronald 4985, 5009
Réalisme 91, 201, 1466, 5028, 5134
Rébellion 380, 1075, 4773
Reboisement 3568
Recensements 1483, 3173, 3389
 see also: Recensements de population
Recensements de population 67, 536, 1980, 1982, 2005, 2261, 3025, 3997

Récession 1172, 4376
Recettes fiscales 4842
Recherche 37, 40, 41, 58, 232, 237, 244, 337, 339, 403, 856, 1441, 1808, 2315, 3460, 3539, 3677, 3961, 4425, 4690, 5021, 5181, 5286, 5691, 5703
 see also: Recherche action, Recherche démographique, Recherche empirique, Recherche en sciences sociales, Recherche interdisciplinaire, Recherche médicale, Recherche organisationnelle, Recherche pédagogique, Recherche scientifique, Recherche sociale, Recherche sociologique, Recherche sur l'opinion publique, Recherche sur la communication, Recherche sur la gestion, Reserche opérationnelle
Recherche action 774, 1048
Recherche démographique 2030
Recherche d'emploi 483, 4382, 4390, 4391
Recherche empirique 303, 1220
Recherche en sciences sociales 1, 3, 38, 70, 209, 231, 248, 251, 252, 283, 289, 306, 386, 2764
Recherche et développement 1805, 1808, 1818
Recherche interdisciplinaire 3, 9
Recherche médicale 947, 5753, 5788
Recherche organisationnelle 340, 782, 812, 817, 837
Recherche pédagogique 43, 1394, 1643, 1681, 1686, 1694, 1787, 1788
Recherche scientifique 1337, 1342, 5794, 5828
Recherche sociale 43, 49, 59, 60, 75, 250, 264, 328, 2069, 2426, 2995, 3248, 4355, 5570, 5594, 5618
Recherche sociologique 44, 47, 54, 57, 61, 62, 66, 112, 233, 237, 244, 245, 295, 330, 347, 359, 406, 454, 1553, 1597, 2941, 3704, 4196, 5308
Recherche sur la communication 1456, 1515, 1519
Recherche sur la gestion 4531, 4616
Recherche sur l'opinion publique 959
Récidivisme 599, 5185

Réciprocité   601, 650, 690, 3523
Récits   104, 242, 243, 257, 481, 540, 588, 658, 1385, 1606, 2588, 5034
Récolte   3566
Récréation   4720, 4725, 4729, 4734, 4737
Recrutement   837, 1825, 4438, 4935
Recyclage   3489
Redistribution du revenu   3580, 3804, 3972, 4065, 4214
Réforme   1263, 3212, 3819, 3838, 3869, 4670, 4968, 5218, 5229, 5755, 5761, 5768, 5783
see also: Réforme agraire, Réforme de l'enseignement, Réforme de logement, Réforme économique, Réforme foncière, Réforme légale, Réforme sociale, Réformes constitutionnelles, Réformes politiques
Réforme agraire   3547, 3550, 3586, 3621
Réforme de l'enseignement   1676, 1697, 1701, 1715, 1730, 1733, 1734, 1738, 1752, 1754, 1756, 1761, 1762, 1795, 4970, 5493
Réforme de logement   3666, 3748
Réforme économique   1953, 1963, 2000, 3986, 3989, 4056, 4216, 4227, 5051
Réforme foncière   3554, 3583
Réforme légale   1207, 1211
Réforme sociale   1863, 2502, 4987, 5338, 5505
Réformes constitutionnelles   1297
Réformes politiques   1960, 3922, 4791, 4987, 5338
Réfugiés   2142, 2269, 3055, 3261, 3276, 3278, 3288, 3297, 3301, 3302, 3306, 3310, 3320, 3322, 3335, 3336, 3410, 3411, 3427, 3985, 4244, 5851
see also: Réfugiés politiques
Réfugiés politiques   2576, 3247
Reggae   1276
Régimes démocratiques   4796
Régimes fonciers   2854, 3554, 3556, 3574, 3582, 3589, 3605, 3606, 3626, 3754, 4828

Index des matières

Régimes militaires   5445
Régimes politiques   4765, 4769, 5022
see also: Régimes militaires
Régionalisation   3404, 4617
Régionalisme   111, 194, 1429, 4782
Régions   1072, 2015, 2343, 3137, 3437
Règlement de conflits   676, 679, 681, 682, 683, 684, 685, 686, 688, 718, 872, 895, 1050, 1935, 4448, 4469, 4621, 4625, 4647, 5007
Réglementation   485, 1086, 1200, 2214, 2237, 3701, 3732, 3754, 4273, 4291, 4440, 4549, 4587, 4613, 4856, 5151, 5533, 5598
Régulation des naissances   2220, 2231, 2232, 2273, 2722, 2761, 2996, 5665
Régulation sociale   157, 166, 216, 485, 894, 1076, 1082, 1083, 1086, 1087, 1088, 1089, 1091, 1448, 2614, 3213, 4047, 4469, 4923, 5043, 5114, 5163, 5205, 5222, 5295, 5307, 5310, 5386
Réhabilitation de l'état de dépendance   632, 5194, 5376
Relation rurale-urbaine   1952, 3544, 3546
Relations centre-peripherie   1022, 3714, 3830
Relations civils-militaires   4993, 4998
Relations culturelles   1120, 3284
Relations de dépendance   579, 2057
Relations de voisinage   3523, 3703, 5099
Relations des sexes   641, 700, 2238, 2482, 2548, 2650, 2655, 2656, 2671, 2726, 2746, 2766, 2786, 2800, 2827, 2850, 2887, 2888, 2916, 2930, 2933, 2967, 2985, 3016, 3021, 3493, 4178, 4324, 4389
Relations du travail   4235, 4262, 4329, 4429, 4430, 4449, 4458, 4474, 4577, 4578, 4579, 4582, 4583, 4585, 4587, 4588, 4592, 4594, 4595, 4596, 4598, 4600, 4601, 4602, 4603, 4605, 4606, 4607, 4608, 4611, 4613, 4614, 4615, 4616, 4617, 4619, 4620, 4621, 4623, 4626, 4628, 4629, 4630, 4638, 4640,

Index des matières

4641, 4644, 4646, 4647, 4653, 4654, 4663, 4671, 4673, 4682, 4692, 4693, 4695, 4696, 4702, 4706, 4707
Relations économiques
  see: Relations économiques internationales
Relations économiques internationales 861, 999, 4109, 5030
Relations entre générations 2031, 2040, 2288, 2525, 2635, 5435
Relations Est-Ouest 5009, 5017
Relations extérieures 1047, 1362, 5013, 5017, 5032
Relations familiales 403, 1720, 2086, 2402, 2421, 2426, 2436, 2439, 2450, 2451, 2454, 2460, 2464, 2465, 2512, 2516, 2531, 2619, 2620, 2637, 2641, 2645, 2649, 2746, 2922, 4982, 5021, 5569
Relations gouvernement central-local 4858
Relations hommes-femmes 393, 606, 614, 629, 633, 638, 641, 655, 2535, 2547, 2593, 2606, 2624, 2778, 2869, 2871, 2981, 2985, 3017, 5251
  see also: Époux
Relations humaines 605, 4448
Relations interethniques 1046, 2592, 3046, 3055, 3060, 3068, 3088, 3099, 3144, 3145, 3146, 3150, 3155, 3157, 3161, 3163, 3167, 3171, 3176, 3179, 3242, 3317, 3327, 3421, 5705
Relations intergroupes 712, 721, 726, 727, 728, 745, 747, 767, 768
Relations internationales 403, 1942, 1945, 1959, 3415, 5003, 5008, 5009, 5013, 5014, 5021, 5022, 5023, 5025, 5026, 5028, 5030
Relations interpersonnelles 337, 457, 488, 560, 577, 590, 602, 610, 611, 617, 619, 620, 626, 628, 635, 639, 640, 642, 644, 645, 648, 650, 651, 652, 657, 658, 660, 664, 665, 671, 673, 675, 677, 678, 690, 694, 695, 696, 701, 702, 708, 709, 710, 716, 734, 756, 759, 905, 906, 1029, 1122, 1412, 1436, 1479, 2169, 2355, 2586, 2587, 3001, 4935, 5852
Relations médecin-malade 5702
Relations parents-enfants 685, 1289, 1329, 2102, 2115, 2163, 2471, 2486, 2493, 2611, 2611, 2612, 2617, 2619, 2621, 2622, 2623, 2624, 2625, 2626, 2627, 2628, 2629, 2630, 2631, 2632, 2636, 2640, 2642, 2644, 2645, 2649, 2941, 5065, 5317, 5343, 5579, 5637
Relations parents-enseignants 1673
Relations publique 1169, 1445, 1523, 1545, 4786
Relations raciales 867, 1675, 1930, 2592, 2605, 3068, 3115, 3143, 3147, 3153, 3158, 3171, 3173, 3174, 3175, 3176, 3182, 3183, 3184, 3185, 3189, 3190, 3192, 3208, 3218, 3219, 3226, 3327, 3407, 3770, 3805, 3857, 3922, 5438
Relations sexuelles 2325, 3001
Relations sociales 352, 605, 647, 722, 757, 793, 896, 983, 1479, 2095, 2766, 3180, 4873, 4970, 4982
Relativisme 982
Religion 122, 142, 397, 1215, 1220, 1223, 1228, 1229, 1230, 1233, 1239, 1243, 1244, 1246, 1247, 1256, 1261, 1264, 1268, 1269, 1280, 1283, 1289, 1326, 1345, 1348, 1856, 1921, 2594, 2762, 2837, 2905, 3529, 4132, 5517
  see also: Religion civile, Religion mondiale, Religion primitive, Sociologie de la religion
Religion civile 1297
Religion et politique 1281, 1282, 1287, 1297, 1299, 5819
Religion mondiale 1318
  see also: Christianisme, Hindouisme, Islam, Judaïsme
Religion primitive 1239, 1345
Religiosité 1267, 1279, 1282, 1316, 1332, 2156, 2157, 2415, 5152
Remariage 2455, 2580
Rendement de l'éducation 1815
Rénovation urbaine 1710, 1899, 3666, 3788, 3793, 3825, 3829, 3846, 3847, 3850, 3851, 3856, 3857, 3864, 3868, 3871
Répartition de la population 4230

Index des matières

Répartition du revenu 3170, 4014, 4032, 4034, 4048, 4206
Répartition en zones 3872, 4859
Répartition géographique 5747
Répartition par âge 4487
Répartition par sexe 2190, 2536
Répartition spatiale 2020, 2364, 3804, 4220
Répertoires 75, 78, 2308, 3043, 3511
Représentation des travailleurs 4640
Représentation politique 4830
Représentations sociales 428, 2387, 3569
Répression 569, 1086, 1201, 3701, 4026, 4923
Reproduction artificielle 5790
Reproduction culturelle 1028
Reproduction sexuelle 2221, 2224, 2242, 2247, 2254, 2468, 2655, 2972
Réseaux de communication 1582
Réseaux d'information 1341
Réseaux sociaux 218, 260, 261, 265, 298, 666, 672, 711, 715, 719, 752, 842, 2463, 2861, 2954, 3351, 4372, 5503
Reserche opérationnelle 5636
Résidence 5172
Résistance au changement 790
Résolution de problème 382, 442, 476, 766, 895, 1679, 5050
Responsabilité 140, 458, 656, 1490, 1694, 3534, 4857, 4891, 5258, 5573, 5786
 see also: Responsabilité de l'État 4535, 4786, 5647, 5662
Responsabilité civile 1173, 1202
Responsabilité de l'État 4214
Ressources de la mer 3450
Ressources en eau 5015
Ressources forestières 3605
Ressources humaines 437, 439, 2014, 2277, 3286, 3566, 3685, 4023, 4246, 4252, 4264, 4265, 4305, 4375, 4377, 4416, 4456, 4480, 4500, 4506, 4530, 4568, 4616, 5578, 5687
Ressources naturelles 3439, 3491, 4266
Résultats électoraux 4664, 4965

Retard intellectuel 404, 502, 1475, 2452, 5191, 5363, 5592, 5731, 5848
Retraite 2037, 2045, 2064, 2067, 2074, 2559, 2850, 3304, 3376, 4255, 4344, 4411
 see also: Retraite anticipée
Retraite anticipée 4439
Retraités 67
Réussite dans les études 1655, 1767, 2826
Réussite professionnelle 2405, 2607, 4498
Réveil religieux 1317
Revenu 1970, 2074, 2435, 3799, 3996, 4026, 4035, 4045, 4052, 4161, 4167, 5524
 see also: Faible revenu, Revenu des ménages, Revenu familial
Revenu des ménages 3598, 4025, 4157
Revenu familial 2480, 4053
Revenus d'investissement
 see: Loyer
Révolte 4886
Révolution 219, 1958, 1974, 3385, 5023
Révolution verte 3564
Rex, John 3158
Rhétorique 114, 481, 1102, 1402, 1419, 1420, 1466, 1546, 4857, 4989, 5009
Richesse 1151, 3617, 4032, 4059
Rire 459
Risque 203, 206, 213, 524, 843, 1121, 1173, 1194, 2134, 2144, 2224, 2337, 3010, 3430, 3859, 4898, 5071, 5176, 5214, 5409, 5426
Rites de passage 2923
Rites funéraires
 see: Enterrement, Funèbres
Rites pénitentiels 1300
Rituelle 1124, 1272, 1328, 1547, 1590, 2621, 3529
 see also: Rites pénitentiels
Robots 4143
Rôle 454, 2903, 3360, 4858, 4924
Rôle de sexes 589, 638, 754, 2059, 2548, 2554, 2559, 2624, 2674, 2688,

588

Index des matières

2783, 2789, 2790, 2810, 2822, 2840, 2863, 2866, 2869, 2877, 2883, 2886, 2889, 2890, 2895, 2896, 2900, 2906, 2908, 2912, 2913, 2917, 2918, 2926, 4316, 4353, 4428
Rôle des femmes   914, 1125, 2706, 2867, 2891, 2903, 2921, 2923, 2927, 3628, 4361
Rôles conjugaux   1122, 2563, 2565, 2603
Rôles professionnels   911
Rôles sexuels   128, 410, 633, 1119, 1161, 2651, 2666, 2668, 2694, 2698, 2751, 2772, 2862, 2868, 2879, 2885, 2911, 2912, 2952, 2953
Rôles sociaux   570, 896, 1353, 5497
Romans   26, 997, 1606, 3202
Romantisme   1033
Rostow, Walt Whitman   4015
Rotation de la main-d'oeuvre   4467
Rousseau, Jean-Jacques   128
Routes   3916
Rumeur   1410
Rushdie, Salman   1315
Russes   3055, 3146
Sacré   114, 122, 1255, 1547
Sage-femmes   5637, 5659, 5672, 5764
Saissonalité   5093, 5155, 5442
Salaire minimum   4566
Salaires   2277, 2465, 3326, 3390, 4003, 4019, 4044, 4064, 4246, 4287, 4288, 4326, 4329, 4663
  see also: Salaire minimum, Salaires relatifs
Salaires relatifs   3266
Sanctions   1195, 2652, 4382
  see also: Sanctions pénales
Sanctions pénales   5111, 5193
Sang   3008
Sans-abri   267, 326, 5259, 5260, 5262, 5263, 5264, 5265, 5266, 5269, 5271, 5272, 5277, 5278, 5279, 5280, 5282, 5284, 5322, 5323, 5328, 5333, 5391, 5408, 5412, 5459, 5695, 5761
  267, 326, 354, 1097, 5047, 5259, 5260, 5261, 5267, 5268, 5270, 5273, 5274, 5275, 5276, 5277, 5283
Santanisme   1251, 1272, 1328

Santé   134, 248, 357, 384, 391, 415, 457, 474, 511, 955, 1088, 1110, 1121, 2074, 2078, 2304, 2305, 2311, 2313, 2321, 2322, 2342, 2347, 2355, 2367, 2375, 2432, 2857, 3007, 3447, 3477, 3647, 3654, 3675, 3716, 3799, 4330, 4353, 4406, 4440, 4548, 4722, 4740, 5315, 5373, 5392, 5400, 5411, 5636, 5655, 5656, 5664, 5696, 5732, 5754, 5763, 5769, 5777, 5851
  see also: Santé d'enfants, Santé de femmes, Santé mentale, Santé publique
Santé de femmes   2187, 2222, 2229, 2336, 2346, 2662, 2677, 2678, 2774, 5355, 5576, 5654, 5657, 5666, 5681, 5704, 5761, 5773
Santé d'enfants   420, 719, 2093, 2108, 2115, 2119, 2122, 2330, 2331, 2333, 2350, 2381, 2634, 5343, 5534, 5653, 5674, 5681, 5693, 5752, 5756, 5846
Santé mentale   363, 431, 449, 484, 569, 577, 579, 593, 616, 635, 786, 2048, 2082, 2153, 2307, 2334, 2338, 2398, 2491, 2625, 2634, 2919, 3242, 3414, 3749, 5041, 5081, 5343, 5586, 5621, 5655, 5705, 5720, 5752, 5781, 5832, 5833, 5836, 5837, 5840, 5841, 5842, 5843, 5844, 5845, 5846, 5850, 5851, 5852, 5853, 5854, 5855
Santé publique   2229, 2320, 2337, 2345, 3008, 3482, 5441, 5640, 5663, 5682, 5753, 5771
Sartre, Jean Paul   1028, 1548
Satisfaction   462, 952, 2307, 3595, 5395
  see also: Satisfaction au travail, Satisfaction conjugale, Satisfaction de l'existence
Satisfaction au travail   955, 4008, 4115, 4331, 4461, 4463, 4464, 4465, 4466, 4467, 4468, 4470, 4471, 4472, 4473, 4477, 4510, 4533, 4701
Satisfaction conjugale   2539, 2544, 2546, 2549, 2565, 2573, 2585, 2588, 2589, 2596, 2606, 2624

Index des matières

Satisfaction de l'existence   355, 438, 460, 474, 478, 493, 2045, 2071, 2108, 3595, 4024, 4031
Saver, Carl   3486
Scandales   5604
Scène   2621, 2631
Scepticisme   7
Schäffle, Albert   1363
Schismes   1300
Schizophrénie   2339
Schutz, Alfred   223
Schwarz, Norbert   359
Science   24, 26, 88, 99, 150, 426, 428, 752, 781, 1226, 1239, 1273, 1336, 1343, 1345, 1348, 1351, 1356, 1561, 1657, 1688, 2221, 4226, 4843, 4970, 5433, 5694
  see also: Histoire des sciences, Philosophie de la science, Sciences de la communication, Sciences du comportement, Sciences naturelles
Science du folklore   1528
Science politique   30, 368, 404, 5463
Science-ficition   214, 1618
Sciences administrative   429, 783, 4095, 4176, 4844
Sciences de la communication   1387, 1396, 1454
Sciences du comportement   239, 472, 883, 2104, 3431, 3436, 3457
Sciences juridiques   9
Sciences naturelles   3, 1346
Sciences sociales   5, 11, 13, 14, 16, 26, 27, 34, 40, 41, 42, 46, 48, 52, 63, 74, 75, 80, 103, 110, 117, 119, 138, 158, 193, 214, 227, 232, 238, 246, 256, 297, 338, 455, 458, 875, 1199, 1318, 1346, 1396, 1554, 1919, 2696, 3468, 3962, 5035, 5510
Scientifiques   589, 1337, 1342, 1350, 3368
  see also: Spécialistes en sciences sociales
Scolarité   1670, 1682, 1683, 1695, 1726, 1732, 1769, 1782, 2263
Scrutin
  see: Sondages d'opinion publique
Sebeok, Thomas A.   1424, 1425

Sécession   4921
Secours aux sinistrés   1512
Secret   2239, 4983
Sectes   1252, 1300
Secteur agricole   3577, 4324
Secteur informel   2797, 3984, 4033, 4070, 4081, 4130, 4137, 4210, 4662
Secteur privé   2798, 3774, 5198
Secteur public   819, 3286, 4018, 4420, 4439, 4585, 4618, 4655, 4692, 4729, 5526, 5647, 5687, 5727
Secteur tertiaire   1970, 3203, 3333, 3590, 4115, 4462
Sécularisation   482, 1252, 1270
Sécurité   4440
  see also: Sécurité du travail, Sécurité routière
Sécurité alimentaire   2188, 5349
Sécurité de l'emploi   4268
Sécurité du travail   4406, 4418, 4421, 4440, 4445, 4696, 5396
Sécurité routière   5037, 5117, 5360, 5379
Sécurité sociale   2803, 3023, 3425, 3575, 4309, 4382, 4384, 5318, 5453, 5464, 5465, 5485, 5486, 5496, 5503, 5505, 5506, 5510, 5512, 5513, 5516, 5520, 5521, 5783
Sédentarisation   3472, 3530
Ségrégation   2815, 3192, 3806, 3807, 3808, 4443, 5465, 5779
  see also: Ségrégation professionnelle, Ségrégation raciale, Ségrégation résidentielle
Ségrégation professionnelle   2806, 4028, 4292, 4347, 4353, 4355
Ségrégation raciale   3162, 3214, 3729, 3796, 5148, 5689
Ségrégation résidentielle   3162, 3204, 3729, 3796, 3802, 3803
Sémantique   696, 1192, 1462, 1493, 1494, 1497
Séminaires   895
Sémiologie   1594
Sémiotique   26, 97, 116, 997, 1068, 1425, 3202, 4774, 5445
Sentiments   435, 3299

Index des matières

Séparation maritale   2482, 2483, 2486, 2488, 2535, 2556, 2566, 2587
Service charge de faire respecter la loi   412, 4792, 5137, 5393, 5417
Service des pompiers   1829, 4460
Service financières   4105
Service postal   334, 4714
Services collectifs   3594, 4795, 5259, 5459, 5460, 5462, 5606, 5708, 5730
Services de santé   457, 2227, 5387, 5632, 5635, 5639, 5644, 5646, 5663, 5680, 5706, 5722, 5743, 5751, 5752, 5757, 5758, 5761, 5771, 5772, 5777, 5833, 5836, 5839, 5843, 5844, 5846
Services de voirie   3688
Services d'emploi   4262, 5481
Services d'information   78, 1452, 2308, 2319, 2329, 3023, 5477, 5554
Services publics   787, 1533, 3684, 3785, 3988, 4755, 4990
Services sociaux   1730, 2329, 3023, 3594, 4210, 4459, 5082, 5312, 5455, 5457, 5466, 5468, 5476, 5477, 5487, 5489, 5493, 5499, 5500, 5514, 5557, 5562, 5585, 5602, 5605, 5616, 5625, 5647, 5684, 5697, 5703, 5709, 5716, 5725, 5729, 5739, 5746
Sexe   1038, 1868, 2181, 2190, 2380, 2785, 2849, 2907, 3000
Sexisme   951, 1652, 2812, 2933, 2941
Sexologie   2996
Sexualité   707, 937, 1889, 2080, 2313, 2345, 2597, 2614, 2651, 2655, 2657, 2664, 2865, 2878, 2907, 2908, 2911, 2947, 2951, 2953, 2959, 2966, 2969, 2987, 2988, 2995, 2996, 2998, 2999, 3001, 3002, 3003, 3004, 3007, 3016, 3020, 3483, 4495, 5002
Shevchenko, Taras   4774
SIDA   810, 933, 1409, 2303, 2304, 2305, 2312, 2315, 2320, 2323, 2324, 2325, 2327, 2341, 2344, 2345, 2346, 2731, 2946, 2961, 2978, 2997, 3001, 3002, 3005, 3007, 3008, 3010, 3013, 3015, 3021, 3500, 4633, 5267, 5355, 5384, 5400, 5407, 5411, 5540, 5567, 5575, 5634, 5668, 5669, 5714, 5753, 5770, 5782

Signes   1377, 1425, 1462
Simmel, Georg   114, 122, 171, 172, 173, 198, 205, 212, 1070, 1094, 1122, 4756
Simulation   392, 718, 824, 4997
Singhalese   4979
Sites historiques   4747
Situation de famille   765, 2004, 2557, 2574, 2598, 4389, 5425
Situation de l'emploi   4615
Smith, Adam   3967
Smith, Dorothy   168
Sociabilité   1122, 1458
Social-démocratie   4672, 4922
Socialisation   576, 690, 1098, 1731, 1767, 1770, 2125, 2163, 2172, 2688, 2883, 2926, 4259, 4275, 4542
see also: Socialisation politique
Socialisation politique   4806, 4983
Socialisme   1205, 1921, 1975, 3977, 3991, 4464, 4771, 4784, 4785, 5517, 5760
see also: Socialisme d'État, Socialisme du marché
Socialisme d'État   2858, 4825, 4839
Socialisme du marché   4825
Société   212, 321, 1052, 1651, 1815, 1820, 1824, 1830, 3438, 3694, 3973, 4766, 4791, 4820, 4864, 4921, 4987, 5011, 5290, 5434
see also: Société agraire, Société capitaliste, Société civile, Société de classe, Société de consommation, Société de l'information, Société de masse, Société industrielle, Société post-industrielle, Société rurale, Sociéte´s socialistes, Société traditionnelle, Société urbaine, Sociétés post-communistes, Sociétés secrètes
Société agraire   1874, 2275, 3614, 3623, 4323
Société capitaliste   3232, 4856
Société civile   1078, 1954, 1979, 4771, 4775, 4790, 4793, 4794, 4799
Société de classe   1854, 1871, 3969
Société de consommation   1129
Société de l'information   1014, 1451

Index des matières

Société de masse 1505
Société industrielle 1230, 1828, 2254, 3973
Société post-industrielle 253, 1893, 1906, 1975, 4745, 4928
Société rurale 1972, 3580, 3590, 3597, 3600, 3615, 3616, 3632
Société́s socialistes 4832
Société traditionnelle 1079, 1095, 2275
Société urbaine 1491, 3665, 5640
Sociétés post-communistes 976, 1751, 1761, 1864, 1975, 2073, 2150, 3140, 3586, 3603, 3992, 4064, 4224, 4248, 4507, 4612, 4681, 4769, 4771, 4781, 4793, 4819, 4825, 4826, 4829, 4834, 4865, 4937
Sociétés secrètes 763, 4835
Sociobiologie 1248, 1914, 5087, 5254
Sociolinguistique 386, 671, 1103, 1464, 1465, 1466, 1467, 1468, 1474, 1478, 1482, 1489, 1495, 1496
Sociologie 10, 15, 22, 25, 28, 30, 31, 32, 33, 35, 45, 63, 69, 73, 79, 101, 160, 186, 199, 243, 967, 1039, 1040, 1058, 1062, 1066, 1070, 1098, 1356, 1824, 1966, 1969, 2164, 3074, 3158, 4240, 4556, 4760, 5258
see also: Enseignement de la sociologie, Histoire de la sociologie, Sociologie appliquée, Sociologie criminelle, Sociologie de l'éducation, Sociologie de la profession, Sociologie économique, Sociologie électorale, Sociologie médicale, Sociologie politique, Sociologie rurale, Sociologie urbaine
Sociologie appliquée 32, 5502
Sociologie criminelle 5119, 5160
Sociologie de la connaissance 98, 108, 467, 1239, 1345, 1353, 1358, 1551, 1826
Sociologie de la famille 65
Sociologie de la profession 4542, 4546
Sociologie de la religion 150, 1213, 1219, 1221, 1226, 1234, 1246, 1252, 1255, 1257, 1258, 1261, 1285, 1289, 1305, 1327
Sociologie de la science 24, 1347, 1359
Sociologie de l'art 142, 1624
Sociologie de l'éducation 1103, 1662, 1684, 1686, 1687, 1691, 1692, 4498
Sociologie des organisations 805, 806, 827, 879, 886, 889
Sociologie du droit 1088, 1119, 1189, 1196, 1197, 1198, 4561, 4802, 5198, 5228
Sociologie du milieu 6, 3446, 3451, 4421
Sociologie du sport 4742
Sociologie du travail 4241
Sociologie économique 1931, 3958, 3961, 3963
Sociologie électorale 4956, 4972
Sociologie industrielle 835, 1643, 4234, 4237, 4239
Sociologie médicale 3242, 5700, 5705, 5850
Sociologie politique 610, 1538, 4756, 4757, 4758, 4831, 4972, 4974
Sociologie rurale 3558, 3568, 3601, 3606
Sociologie urbaine 1844, 3653, 3655, 3657, 3660, 3666, 3684, 3694, 3701, 3705, 3711, 3712, 3713, 3714, 3718, 3719, 3721, 3744, 3749, 3764, 3781, 3786, 3796, 3811, 3907, 3919, 3941, 5103, 5171, 5353
Sociologues 36, 86, 243, 244, 1839, 4556, 5324, 5348
Sociométrie 4931
Soeur 3009
Soi 96, 104, 438, 463, 481, 500, 514, 528, 537, 586, 597, 603, 1016, 1069, 1606, 2082, 2095, 2699, 3086, 4761, 5786
Soie 2813
Soin dans la communauté 2074, 3703, 5270, 5274, 5457, 5466, 5468, 5554, 5586, 5603, 5708, 5709, 5710, 5711, 5712, 5713, 5714, 5715, 5716, 5717, 5718, 5719, 5720, 5721, 5722, 5723, 5724, 5725, 5726, 5727, 5728, 5729,

Index des matières

5730, 5731, 5738, 5740, 5742, 5746, 5834, 5840
Soins   615, 628, 1161, 2102, 2441, 2465, 2538, 2548, 2552, 2612, 2635, 2667, 2843, 2863, 4494, 5630, 5724, 5847
Soins médicaux   2497, 2816, 5271, 5631, 5637, 5638, 5642, 5670, 5670, 5677, 5686, 5692, 5736, 5759, 5763, 5771, 5775, 5799, 5800, 5812, 5817, 5843
Soins médicaux généraux   786, 949, 2125, 2236, 2389, 2394, 2662, 2853, 3425, 3496, 4459, 5366, 5478, 5568, 5627, 5631, 5632, 5635, 5638, 5643, 5648, 5649, 5650, 5651, 5660, 5662, 5665, 5667, 5669, 5671, 5673, 5674, 5675, 5676, 5682, 5683, 5687, 5688, 5689, 5690, 5691, 5692, 5694, 5698, 5701, 5704, 5706, 5707, 5713, 5717, 5718, 5720, 5727, 5732, 5734, 5735, 5738, 5743, 5744, 5745, 5747, 5748, 5753, 5755, 5756, 5760, 5765, 5766, 5768, 5769, 5773, 5783, 5805, 5809, 5813, 5829, 5831, 5834, 5837, 5840, 5845, 5849, 5855
see also: Soins médicaux, Soins médicaux primaires, Soins médicaux privée
Soins médicaux primaires   5639, 5652, 5653, 5661, 5670, 5670, 5680, 5775
Soins médicaux privée   5685, 5687
Solidarité   1081, 4710, 4713, 4922, 4980, 5030
Solitude   462, 695, 1122, 2105, 5047
Sommeil   66
Sondages   457
Sondages d'opinion publique   274, 327, 950, 952
Sorcellerie   5445
Sorokin, Pitirim A.   4778
Sous-classe   1074, 1099, 1897, 1908, 1916, 3050, 5261, 5320, 5321, 5324, 5334, 5348, 5406
Sous-développement   1891
Sous-traitance   4117, 4122
Souveraineté   5025
Spécialisation flexible   4087

Spécialistes en sciences sociales   3368
Spencer, Herbert   5033
Spiritisme   1272, 1328
Sport   576, 583, 908, 1547, 1790, 2148, 2149, 2789, 2882, 2938, 3055, 4133, 4615, 4720, 4724, 4727, 4728, 4729, 4736, 4741, 4743, 4744, 4746, 5285
see also: Sociologie du sport
Springsteen, Bruce   1635
Squatters   3751, 3755, 3762, 3780, 3781, 3905, 4911
Stabilité conjugale   2008, 2594
Stalin, Josef   562
Statistique   232, 1549, 1705, 1964, 2066, 2218, 5399, 5558
see also: Statistiques de population, Statistiques industrielles
Statistiques de population   3396
Statistiques industrielles   343
Statut de la femme   1188, 1970, 2273, 2678, 2679, 2693, 2790, 2845, 2847, 2855, 2858, 2860, 2875, 2892, 2893, 2914, 4316
Statut économique   2083, 2332, 2354, 2366, 2504, 4011, 4316
Statut juridique   2709, 5542
Statut professionnel   1851, 2559, 2784, 2851, 4278, 4505, 4520, 4521
Statut social   222, 1684, 1836, 1851, 1857, 1867, 1872, 1904, 2046, 2081, 2082, 2083, 2134, 2254, 2332, 2366, 2576, 2698, 3056, 3185, 3897, 4557
Stéréotypes   544, 724, 754, 894, 917, 938, 1614, 1636, 2787, 2846, 3205, 3240, 4731
see also: Stéréotypes nationaux, Stéréotypes sociaux
Stéréotypes nationaux   1945
Stéréotypes sociaux   753, 928, 3045
Stérilité   2251, 2259, 5577, 5699, 5807
Stimulants du travail   4426, 4437
Stimulus   465, 1366
Stoetzel, Jean   404
Stratégie de développement   4074
Stratégie de survie   444, 3070, 3102
Stratification professionnelle   4316

593

Index des matières

Stratification sociale   303, 910, 1684, 1707, 1837, 1841, 1843, 1847, 1850, 1858, 1859, 1861, 1865, 1866, 1878, 1882, 1886, 1888, 1890, 1893, 1894, 1895, 1898, 1902, 1907, 1912, 1914, 1917, 2832, 2841, 3095, 3802, 4032, 4352, 4978
Structuralisme   97, 163, 979, 1628
Structure agraire   3985
Structure de classe   1684, 1843, 1873, 1875, 1876, 1886, 1888, 1893, 1895, 1897, 1907, 1916
Structure de la famille   278, 2180, 2412, 2420, 2507, 2509, 2515, 2517, 2529, 2892, 3950, 3973
Structure de l'organisation   776, 786, 807, 816, 824, 903, 916, 4090, 4499, 4513, 4585
Structure des salaires   1672
Structure du marché du travail   4246, 4280, 5004
Structure économique   3125, 3666, 3964
Structure politique   1888, 4828
Structure professionnelle   4487, 4511, 4514
Structure sociale   187, 218, 222, 268, 618, 827, 987, 1018, 1076, 1084, 1113, 1434, 1746, 1822, 1825, 1834, 1836, 1842, 1862, 1863, 1864, 1872, 1873, 1882, 1904, 1915, 1919, 1927, 1976, 2082, 2429, 2504, 2532, 2835, 3081, 3529, 3533, 3597, 3660, 3897, 3987, 4175, 4190, 4498, 4511, 4828
Structure urbaine   3666, 3673, 3690, 3726, 3814, 3839, 4202
Stupéfiants   5156, 5410
Subculture   307, 1097, 2165, 2788, 5090, 5154, 5516
Subjectivité   174
Subventions   2376
  see also: Subventions à l'emploi
Subventions à l'emploi   4251
Succession   787
Sucre   1971
Suédois   1566
Suicide   122, 143, 317, 2574, 2617, 2974, 3038, 3440, 5047, 5371, 5409, 5414, 5422, 5423, 5424, 5425, 5426, 5427, 5428, 5429, 5430, 5431, 5432, 5804
Supermarchés   4161
Suprématie du droit   5445
Surabondance de main d'oeuvre   4295
Surdité   2631
Surpeuplement   2014, 3768
Symboles   114, 1321, 1363, 1425, 1493
Symbolisme   424, 1231, 1402, 1423, 1593, 1836, 3501, 3578, 3721
  see also: Symbolisme du corps
Symbolisme du corps   2664
Symposia   5059
Syndicalisme   4010, 4678, 4691
Syndicats   775, 1892, 2794, 3418, 4066, 4286, 4357, 4358, 4439, 4483, 4544, 4600, 4602, 4605, 4606, 4611, 4650, 4652, 4653, 4654, 4657, 4658, 4661, 4662, 4664, 4665, 4666, 4667, 4668, 4669, 4670, 4671, 4673, 4674, 4676, 4677, 4679, 4682, 4683, 4684, 4685, 4686, 4687, 4690, 4692, 4693, 4695, 4696, 4697, 4698, 4699, 4700, 4701, 4702, 4703, 4704, 4705, 4706, 4707, 4708, 4712, 4872
Syndiqués   1853, 4067, 4651, 4659, 4660
Systèmes de communication   1519
Systèmes de parenté   2456
Systèmes de planification   3478, 4188
Systèmes de production   376, 4090, 4136, 4143, 4149
Systèmes de valeur   1077, 1078
Systèmes d'enseignement   1686, 1697, 1747, 1750, 1751, 1752, 1753, 1754, 1755, 1757, 1759, 1760, 1761, 1764, 1765, 1774, 1789, 4324
Systèmes d'information   852, 1014, 1393, 1457, 4079
Systèmes d'information géographique   3454, 4079
Systèmes économiques   798, 3974
Systèmes juridiques   1183, 1208
Systèmes politiques   380, 1819, 4829, 4838, 4901, 4902

Index des matières

Systèmes sociales 432, 774, 1072, 1090, 1208, 1819, 1821, 1824, 1829, 1832, 1839, 1957, 2672, 3972, 4148, 4967, 5050
Tabac 2151, 2348, 5365
Tabou
  see: Prohibition de l'inceste, Prohibition sexuelle
Tactique 2602
Tagalog 3159
Tamouls 1319, 3037, 4298
Tanaka, J.S. 573
Tanala 2879
Taoïsme 495, 1253
Tatar 3140
Tatouage 2987
Taux de fécondité 2002
Taux de natalité 1986, 2192, 2250, 2280, 2300, 2302
Taxonomie 3710
Tchèques 3144
Techniciens 1099
Techniques de gestion 851, 4094, 4508, 4532, 4714
Techniques de simulation 5476
Techniques du corps
  see: Tatouage
Technologie 203, 752, 824, 828, 891, 1027, 1336, 1352, 1460, 1561, 1599, 2662, 2934, 3596, 3686, 4115, 4146, 4147, 4150, 4217, 4229, 4369, 4405, 4531, 4605, 4997, 5045, 5671, 5773
  see also: Biotechnologie, Technologie agricole, Technologie de l'information, Technologie de pointe, Technologie reproductive, Technologies nouvelles
Technologie agricole 3564
Technologie de l'information 918, 1184, 1450, 1451, 1453, 1454, 1455, 1456, 4144, 4155, 4403, 4419, 4453, 4836
Technologie de pointe 4226
Technologie reproductive 2209, 2224, 2228, 2237, 2237, 2238, 2259, 2734, 5699, 5773, 5790, 5803, 5818
Technologies nouvelles 918, 2235, 4403, 4430, 4565, 4605, 5830

Télécommunications 1449, 1456, 1518, 4079, 4430, 4452
Télématique 1457, 4680
Téléphone 346, 1458, 1459, 4169, 4430
Télétravail 4452, 4453
Télévision 1310, 1442, 1443, 1444, 1472, 1517, 1545, 1570, 1571, 1572, 1573, 1574, 1575, 1576, 1577, 1578, 1579, 1580, 1581, 1582, 1583, 1584, 1585, 1586, 1587, 1588, 1589, 1590, 1591, 1592, 1593, 2433, 2891, 3200, 5855
Témoinage 1181, 1204, 1490, 2123, 2266, 2322
Temples 1231
Temps de travail 4402, 4439, 4451, 4458, 4745
Tension mentale 395, 403, 412, 421, 433, 447, 487, 491, 568, 574, 585, 625, 628, 650, 669, 672, 911, 2115, 2120, 2317, 2419, 2550, 2554, 2635, 2644, 2802, 2919, 2974, 3100, 3318, 3460, 3707, 4386, 4427, 4433, 4450, 4459, 4472, 4517, 4521, 4558, 4740, 4800, 5021, 5038, 5371, 5395, 5424, 5545, 5586, 5617, 5835
Terminologie 74, 1368, 1880
Territoire 3141, 3438, 4790, 5025
  see also: Départements et territoires d'Outre-Mer
Territorialité 3233, 3518, 3809
Terrorisme 1530, 4888, 4937, 5090, 5445
Tests empiriques 804, 3170
Textes 1255
Thanatologie 173, 1124
Thatcher, Margaret 4257
Thatcherisme 3785, 4257
Thé 4717
Théologie 4989
  see also: Théologie chrétienne
Théologie chrétienne 1131, 2655, 2701, 2752, 2876
Théorie critique 120, 131, 977, 979, 1057, 1063, 1514, 4925, 4963, 5445
Théorie de chaos 3, 38, 155, 157, 3494

Index des matières

Théorie de contrôle   1122, 1173, 1185, 2242, 4329, 5489
   see also: Contrat de travail, Contrat social
Théorie de la consommation   4167
Théorie de la culture   57, 1045, 1225
Théorie de la décision   4981
Théorie de la dépendance   4229
Théorie de la planification   3497
Théorie de l'action   218
Théorie de l'éducation   1661, 1669, 1679
Théorie de l'organisation   429, 866, 873, 874, 875, 876, 877, 878, 879, 880, 881, 882, 883, 884, 885, 886, 887, 888, 889, 890, 891, 892, 4096, 4114, 4136, 4138, 4611, 4653, 4844
Théorie de systèmes   477, 1927, 2464
Théorie des catastrophes   3924
Théorie des jeux   268, 429, 1563, 4963
Théorie du change   883
Théorie du groupe   769, 818
Théorie économique   886, 2721, 3244, 5108
Théorie feministe   633, 879, 1063, 1143, 1339, 1714, 1723, 2651, 2658, 2675, 2699, 2703, 2717, 2721, 2731, 2738, 2739, 2740, 2746, 2748, 2753, 2754, 2756, 2757, 2759, 2766, 2769, 2770, 2772, 2775, 2777, 2843, 2853, 2878, 2896, 2928, 2941, 2959, 2968, 2975, 3493, 4726, 5445
Théorie générale   3711, 5117, 5166, 5379
Théorie juridique   1187
Théorie politique   1032, 2706, 4777, 4783, 4807
Théorie sociale   94, 126, 127, 136, 154, 158, 162, 163, 165, 173, 185, 192, 196, 206, 207, 212, 214, 215, 216, 221, 297, 427, 510, 768, 1033, 1059, 1066, 1148, 1354, 1875, 1886, 2706, 2995, 4196, 4762, 4776, 4801, 5445, 5621, 5781, 5853
Théorie sociologique   4, 17, 18, 111, 150, 151, 152, 155, 157, 159, 161, 167, 169, 170, 176, 178, 179, 181, 184, 187, 188, 189, 191, 193, 194, 195, 197, 198, 201, 203, 204, 209, 210, 213, 217, 220, 224, 225, 312, 436, 456, 639, 692, 1090, 1175, 1256, 1355, 1498, 1687, 1828, 1830, 1839, 3090, 3134, 3474, 3665, 4653
Thérapeutique   3496, 5837
Thérapie   396, 411, 3350, 5538, 5539, 5556, 5590, 5597, 5624, 5634
   see also: Thérapie familiale
Thérapie familiale   2421, 5545, 5586
Thucydides   5028
Thünen, Johann Heinrich von   1441
Tolérance   922, 968, 1241, 4772
Torture   5854
Totalitarisme   4838
Totémisme   2526
Tourisme   3442, 3590, 3691, 4186, 4719, 4723, 4731, 4738, 4748, 4750, 4752
Tourisme international   4747, 4749
Toxicité   5344
Toxicomanes   5156, 5282, 5410, 5411, 5412
Toxicomanie   56, 5370, 5375, 5387, 5399, 5416
Tradition   1024, 1027, 1331, 1354, 1629, 1833, 1941, 2610, 3563, 3611, 3902, 4939
   see also: Tradition culturelle, Tradition orale
Tradition culturelle   495, 1933, 3034, 3103
Tradition orale   3484
Traduction   997, 3202
Trafic de la drogue   5129, 5375, 5383, 5386, 5397, 5398, 5415, 5417
Trafiquants de drogue   5378
Traité de Maastricht   4296, 4590
Traitement de l'information   385, 516, 725, 4156
Traitement des données   306, 918, 4271
Traitement hospitalier   5621, 5695, 5781, 5853
Traits de personnalité   556, 634, 641

Index des matières

Tranche d'âge   1581, 2035, 2038, 2040, 2200, 2536, 2622, 3305, 4255, 4533, 5422
Transfert   3561
   see also: Transfert de technologie, Transferts de population
Transfert de technologie   3558, 4154
Transferts de population   3248
Transition de régime   3977, 3990, 3992, 4791, 4796, 4834
Transport   3591, 3812, 3911, 3912, 3917, 3919
   see also: Transport aérienne, Transport maritime, Transport public, Transport routier, Transport rural, Transport urbain
Transport aérienne   1530, 4450
Transport maritime   4061
Transport public   3214
Transport routier   3909
Transport rural   3597
Transport urbain   3910, 3913, 3918
Travail   293, 1426, 1838, 1868, 1907, 2019, 2038, 2584, 2822, 2849, 2890, 3239, 3384, 4099, 4285, 4300, 4304, 4305, 4352, 4384, 4406, 4452, 4486, 4497, 4613, 4687, 5686
   see also: Division du travail, Main-d'oeuvre féminine, Travail agricole, Travail des enfants
Travail à domicile   2434, 2889
Travail agricole   3562, 4276, 4622, 4656
Travail bénévole   429, 836, 2102, 3309, 3637, 4324, 4460
Travail de nuit   5047
Travail d'équipe   783, 844, 4413
Travail des enfants   2103, 4250, 4298
Travail des femmes   2669, 2822, 2918, 2919, 3628
Travail ménager   1122, 2434, 2457, 2553, 2570, 2671, 2822, 2823, 2838, 2889, 4057, 4324
Travail social   2075, 2170, 3024, 5047, 5052, 5359, 5460, 5536, 5541, 5542, 5543, 5546, 5547, 5548, 5549, 5551, 5552, 5553, 5554, 5555, 5560, 5562, 5563, 5565, 5567, 5569, 5573, 5575, 5576, 5578, 5579, 5583, 5584, 5585, 5586, 5587, 5591, 5596, 5601, 5603, 5604, 5605, 5606, 5607, 5608, 5609, 5610, 5611, 5612, 5613, 5616, 5620, 5623, 5625, 5626, 5628, 5629
Travail social des groupes   5545, 5619
Travail sur le terrain   336, 337, 358
Travailleurs   625, 1853, 4082, 4113, 4298, 4303, 4308, 4580, 4659, 4682, 4713
   see also: Cols blancs, Employés de bureau, Employés de commerce, Gens de maison, Jeunes travailleurs, Ouvriers industriels, Ouvriers non-qualifiés, Ouvriers qualifiés, Travailleurs âgés, Travailleurs agricoles, Travailleurs du secteur tertiaire, Travailleurs étrangers, Travailleurs handicapés, Travailleurs indépendants, Travailleurs manuels, Travailleurs migrants, Travailleurs professionnels, Travailleurs saisonniers, Travailleurs sociaux, Travailleuses
Travailleurs âgés   4422
Travailleurs agricoles   3274, 4254, 4421, 4603
Travailleurs du secteur tertiaire   4619
Travailleurs étrangers   3242, 3256, 3289, 3375, 3417, 3418, 3425, 3921, 4274, 4281, 4401, 5512, 5705
Travailleurs handicapés   4441
Travailleurs indépendants   1970, 4282, 4293, 4294, 4324, 4359, 4503
Travailleurs manuels   4515
Travailleurs migrants   2665, 3249, 3260, 3274, 3279, 3307, 3353, 3354, 3417, 3999, 4254, 4277, 4404, 5512
Travailleurs professionnels   1588, 1730, 2814, 4534, 4538, 4539, 4546, 4549, 4551, 4559, 5493
Travailleurs saisonniers   4254
Travailleurs sociaux   3321, 4351, 5247, 5514, 5540, 5546, 5557, 5564, 5574, 5583, 5594, 5614, 5615, 5617, 5622, 5628, 5630
Travailleuses   2267, 2271, 2277, 2479, 2569, 2661, 2670, 2680, 2687, 2767,

Index des matières

2790, 2792, 2794, 2797, 2801, 2812, 2813, 2816, 2817, 2824, 2830, 2833, 2836, 2838, 2842, 2851, 2854, 2856, 2868, 2901, 2910, 2921, 2932, 2940, 2942, 3203, 3562, 3590, 3596, 4141, 4171, 4234, 4312, 4313, 4315, 4318, 4323, 4323, 4324, 4327, 4331, 4334, 4337, 4339, 4340, 4341, 4342, 4351, 4352, 4353, 4354, 4356, 4357, 4358, 4359, 4361, 4362, 4363, 4401, 4419, 4458, 4491, 4493, 4512, 4519, 4524, 4537, 4550, 4556, 4619, 4641, 4648, 5178, 5615, 5630
Tremblements de terre   3910
Triade   912, 5595
Tribunaux   2469, 5157, 5230
   see also: Prudhommes, Tribunaux pénaux, Tribunaux pour enfants
Tribunaux pénaux   1204
Tribunaux pour enfants   5209
Tribus   1782, 2935
Tristesse   691
Troubles de la personnalité   571
Trusts   115, 815, 4134, 4151
Tuberculose   2320
Turcs   2154, 3082, 3234, 3340, 5623
Types de consommation   4249
Typologie   3312, 4739
UNESCO   1948
Unification d'Allemagne   849, 1388, 1920, 1963, 1970, 2139, 2192, 2416, 2819, 3661, 3679, 4024, 4065, 4336, 4336, 4635, 4639, 5029, 5314
Union européenne   3311, 3839, 3946, 4296, 4361, 4590
Universalité de la culture   996
Universités   50, 252, 527, 681, 852, 918, 1730, 1742, 1779, 1780, 1781, 1785, 1791, 1793, 1797, 1798, 1803, 1807, 1808, 1812, 1813, 1815, 1816, 1817, 1818, 2942, 2983, 3027, 3042, 5130, 5493
Urbanisation   2002, 2168, 2202, 2258, 2382, 3155, 3250, 3352, 3374, 3377, 3379, 3544, 3546, 3790, 3791, 3815, 3848, 3852, 3882, 3885, 3890, 3892, 3896, 3899, 3921, 3922, 3923, 3924, 3925, 3927, 3928, 3929, 3930, 3931, 3932, 3933, 3934, 3935, 3937, 3938, 3939, 3940, 3941, 3942, 3943, 3944, 3945, 3946, 3947, 3948, 3949, 3950, 3951, 3952, 3953, 3954, 3955, 3956
Urbanisme   3950, 5168
Usage de solvants   5404
Usage des stupéfiants   2314, 5041, 5109, 5194, 5197, 5362, 5366, 5369, 5371, 5374, 5376, 5385, 5389, 5395, 5401, 5406, 5414, 5424, 5428
   see also: Réhabilitation de l'état de dépendance
Usage du tabac   290, 1121, 2151, 2349, 2355, 5365
Usines   4099
Utilisation de la main-d'oeuvre   4260
Utilisation des terres   2023, 3552, 3560, 3564, 3584, 3606, 3644, 3708, 3756, 3780, 3813, 3814, 3848, 3865, 3867, 3869, 3872, 3883, 3905, 4737, 4859
Utilitarisme   5797
Utz, Arthur   1177
Vacances d'emploi   4513
Valeur   95, 690, 809, 4194, 4319
Valeurs   132, 175, 310, 770, 839, 1020, 1056, 1071, 1149, 1150, 1167, 1220, 1289, 1644, 1884, 2670, 2918, 3153, 3329, 3528, 4024, 4093, 4248, 4327, 4464, 4950, 4983, 5272
Valeurs culturelles   3045
Valeurs sociales   467, 516, 726, 1077, 1085, 1139, 1178, 1767, 2423, 4050, 5091, 5284, 5487
Validité   88, 2120, 5565
Variation régionale   307, 1105
Véhicules   5670
Velarde Fuertes, Juan   999
Velázquez, Diego   1594
Vengeance   2692
Verbes   505
Vêtements   1108, 2167
Veuve   2059
Vico, G.   90
Victime de viol   1432, 1544, 5044
Victime de violence   2534, 2659, 5092, 5167, 5237, 5239, 5245, 5249, 5377, 5443, 5573, 5586, 5618

Index des matières

Victimes   628, 3223, 5078, 5120, 5131, 5201, 5238, 5250, 5257, 5265, 5436
Victimes de crime   5099, 5135, 5140, 5170, 5172, 5173, 5199, 5255, 5299, 5437
Vidéo   1555, 4732
Vie active   1932, 2403, 2554, 4396
Vie communautaire   3056, 3511, 3513, 4247
Vie conjugale   2481, 2543, 2565, 2568, 2573, 2603
Vie économique   3244
Vie familiale   1460, 1970, 2397, 2403, 2417, 2421, 2447, 2460, 2461, 2463, 2526, 4537
Vie privée   77, 946, 1197, 3735
Vie quotidienne   1095, 1101, 1102, 1109, 1116, 1123, 1127, 1590, 2120, 3199, 3456, 3958, 4745, 4928
Vie religieuse   1278, 1309
Vie rurale   3549, 3571, 3608, 3610
Vie sociale   631, 801, 990, 1080, 1109, 1113, 1918, 3646, 4404
Vie urbaine   1086, 1368, 1899, 3034, 3052, 3058, 3081, 3643, 3646, 3649, 3656, 3659, 3674, 3695, 3702, 3723, 3921, 4269, 5047, 5726
Vieillesse   631, 2040, 2045, 2048, 2052, 2060, 2065, 2069, 2080, 2393, 3996, 4683
Vieillissement   228, 399, 2018, 2040, 2044, 2048, 2049, 2056, 2057, 2060, 2061, 2064, 2065, 2071, 2074, 2075, 2084, 2272, 2390, 2396, 2643, 2677, 3760, 3996, 4157
Vieillissement de la population   1802, 2036, 2294, 2389, 2391, 2392, 2393, 2394, 2395, 2396, 4284, 5649, 5721, 5726, 5740
Vietnamiens   3335, 3345
Villages   1217, 1322, 1457, 2185, 2367, 2563, 2790, 2864, 3441, 3471, 3557, 3571, 3572, 3590, 3598, 3603, 3610, 3611, 3618, 3626, 3629, 3632, 3846, 3944, 5643, 5837
Villes   2199, 2367, 3471, 3543, 3642, 3661, 3702, 3709, 3717, 3753, 3764, 3923, 3927, 3929, 3931, 3954, 4298, 4805, 4904, 5131, 5436
see also: Petites villes, Villes nouvelles
Villes capitales   3727, 3833
Villes nouvelles   3692, 3826
Villey, Michel   150
Viol   544, 594, 2715, 2956, 3017, 3697, 5087, 5093, 5094, 5126, 5157, 5173, 5182, 5206, 5230, 5254, 5255, 5367, 5445
Violence   684, 693, 1374, 1587, 2660, 2692, 2786, 2917, 2985, 3187, 3188, 3194, 3218, 3229, 3722, 4773, 4818, 4868, 4905, 4989, 5089, 5125, 5131, 5135, 5154, 5155, 5160, 5169, 5174, 5177, 5226, 5242, 5256, 5304, 5305, 5433, 5434, 5435, 5436, 5437, 5438, 5439, 5441, 5442, 5444, 5445, 5446, 5447, 5448, 5449, 5622
see also: Violence communale, Violence domestique, Violence politique
Violence communale   3187
Violence domestique   684, 700, 2461, 2534, 2577, 2578, 2595, 2597, 2620, 2636, 2641, 2659, 2763, 5087, 5173, 5203, 5210, 5236, 5238, 5239, 5240, 5241, 5242, 5243, 5244, 5245, 5246, 5247, 5248, 5250, 5251, 5252, 5253, 5254, 5255, 5257, 5377, 5573
Violence politique   4888, 5440
Viticulture   4607
Vocabulaire   1377
Vol   5115, 5124, 5131, 5176, 5302, 5436
Voleurs   5155, 5160, 5442
Vote   200, 3425
Voyages   3597, 4751
Vulgarisation agricole   3596
Vygotsky, L.S.   90
Wagner, Richard   147
Waldheim, Kurt   3220
Weber, Max   14, 25, 133, 134, 139, 142, 146, 147, 150, 159, 180, 182, 183, 184, 186, 202, 203, 205, 1033, 1160, 1175, 1213, 1219, 1305, 3134
Williams, Raymond   1634

Index des matières

Wittgenstein, Ludwig   90, 137, 148, 149, 1425
Woodland   3606
Wright, John K.   3464
Xénophobie   3196, 3218, 5438
Yezierska, Anzia   3055
Yoruba   2030
Zapotèque   684, 3132, 4939
Zone aride   3439
Zones industrielles   3640, 3868, 3933
Zones résidentielles   3663, 3666, 3735, 3742, 3755, 3774
Zones rurales   1216, 1776, 1999, 2023, 2074, 2184, 2256, 2420, 2555, 3285, 3384, 3520, 3543, 3559, 3565, 3567, 3570, 3576, 3578, 3579, 3585, 3594, 3602, 3604, 3607, 3609, 3617, 3625, 3627, 3634, 4021, 4128, 4622, 4886, 5172, 5692, 5765
Zones suburbaines   2320, 2746, 3162, 3652, 3663, 3667, 3685, 3690, 3710, 3711, 3786, 3795, 4299, 4352
Zones urbaines   1567, 1710, 2199, 2223, 2256, 2270, 2320, 2522, 2592, 2917, 3285, 3537, 3543, 3644, 3660, 3662, 3668, 3678, 3687, 3689, 3691, 3697, 3700, 3708, 3714, 3715, 3720, 3722, 3732, 3750, 3765, 3775, 3797, 3798, 3838, 3858, 3895, 3927, 3938, 4130, 4236, 4393, 4805, 4855, 5148, 5171, 5172, 5353, 5433, 5446
Zulou   2425